The Guidance of
Learning Activities

WILLIAM H. BURTON

Retired, Harvard University

The Guidance of

Learning Activities

A Summary of the Principles of Teaching
Based on the Growth of the Learner

APPLETON-CENTURY-CROFTS
EDUCATIONAL DIVISION
New York   MEREDITH CORPORATION

TO

Virginia Nottingham Burton

Preface

Two paragraphs of great significance for teacher education occur in the Preface to Stephens, *Educational Psychology,* both first and second editions.[1] Teacher education has been in the past too narrowly concerned with the so-called practical aspects of classroom operation, to the neglect of the one thing which enables one to distinguish between good and poor practical techniques, namely basic theory.

The text is addressed to two prospective teachers within the same individual. It is addressed to the teacher-practitioner and to the teacher-theorist. The emphasis on the teacher-practitioner, of course, is in no way surprising. The emphasis on the teacher as a theorist, on the other hand, may be somewhat unusual and may call for an explanation.

Throughout the book, the theoretical needs of the teacher are shown to be very real. The teacher cannot contemplate such a complex process as education without forming opinions. He is bound to generalize and to seek to introduce some order into the separate facts of education. These opinions and generalizations formulated by the teacher may have far-reaching practical consequences, especially if they come to be widely held. The future of education, in fact, may depend more on the careful and accurate forming of views than on any ordinary increase in pedagogical skill. Conversely, inept theorizing may be just as disastrous as lack of practical competence.

Two tragic cases are cited below to illustrate the prevalence of incredible ignorance among teachers. Later it will be shown that the picture is not all black. The first case is that of a group of science teachers in one of the current science training courses who revolted against discussion of modern methods of teaching. "These methods are not applicable to high schools. We could not use them with high school classes." And then the blubbery old cliché, "May be good theory, but not practicable." The science teachers, many with years of experience, were unaware that the methods described had actually originated in a high school, are now in use in innumerable high schools. Half a dozen textbooks, including two in the teaching of high school science, present these methods with supporting evidence for their success. But the particular group of science teachers, carefully selected for this course, were wholly innocent of any facts. *Worse, they were quite ignorant of any basic concepts or theory dealing with either the teaching or the learning process!* Nevertheless they expressed themselves with vigor. They made no check of the literature in the field. No one suggested looking into the matter before condemning the methods. What price scientific attitude and method?

The second case illustrates ignorance of, or indifference to, not theory but the

[1] J. M. Stephens, *Educational Psychology* (New York, Holt, Rinehart & Winston, 1951 and 1956), Preface.

simple "practical" operations in the classroom. The late Dr. W. S. Gray[2] made a detailed study of methods of teaching reading in 100 typical classrooms. His findings are important.

Thirty per cent of the teachers in 1948 were using methods based on principles and practices of 1900.

Forty per cent in 1948 were doing a very little with silent reading, despite the fact that the decade 1910-1920 saw the great development of aims and methods in this area. *Twenty per cent* only of the forty per cent were giving children reading experience in the content fields.

Twenty-five per cent, however, were working for objectives which had been recognized as valuable as early as 1937: meaning; development of independence and self-reliance in evaluating content; expanding free reading; developing taste; better oral reading (oral reading as an objective, not as a method of teaching).

Five per cent only were teaching with recognition of the fact that purpose and type of reading materials used must be related to the types of outcomes desired.

The fifty-year lag in methods of teaching in reading is no worse than the lag in other fields and until quite recently was definitely shorter than the lag in teaching science and mathematics. The point is not one of comparison of fields but is of vital importance for *all* teaching and learning.

The picture is, of course, not as black as indicated. New practices, experimentation and inquiry are well established in many areas, especially the elementary school. The secondary school is in the throes of an educational revolution. The inevitably rising tide of modern thinking is lapping even at the doors of the conservative liberal arts college. Many colleges pride themselves on their indifference to the "passing whims of the moment." A new day is dawning, however, in many of these colleges. Startling new organizations of materials, interdisciplinary approaches, provocative new methods of teaching are appearing. Several teachers colleges refuse to deal with traditional or outmoded methods of teaching, with the curriculum of our grandfathers. Students are introduced to validated new theory and practice.

But let no one be deceived. The battle for the improvement of education is not won. Powerful interests, in fact, oppose certain incontestably better materials and methods. We are, in this book, concerned with both aspects: principles and methods, theory and practice. The protests against modern methods appear quite often. Illustrative lessons are rejected as show pieces from selected schools, even though some come from schools in seriously underprivileged areas. The naïveté and ignorance displayed in these statements is less tragic than is the insight they afford into some portions of teacher education. Descriptions of new materials and methods and valid data supporting them are available in quantity in texts and in professional periodicals.

The point is well stated by Petersen and Hayden:[3]

Historians of the future might well refer to the present educational era as the "age of contradiction." We have, on the one hand, a growing mound of reputable theory and valid research which points the way to effective teaching in the elementary school.

[2] William S. Gray, "Changing Conceptions of Basic Instruction in Reading," *Basic Instruction in Reading in Elementary and High Schools,* Supplementary Educational Monographs, no. 65 (Chicago, Univ. of Chicago Press, 1948), pp. 1-6.

[3] Dorothy G. Petersen and Velma D. Hayden, *Teaching the Elementary School Curriculum* (New York, Appleton-Century-Crofts, 1961), Preface.

On the other hand, we have a substantial amount of classroom practice which is rooted in tradition, habit, lack of experience, or lack of knowledge, which is not supportive of the high quality of education demanded by our modern democratic culture.

Teaching is not a routine or rule-of-thumb process; it is a genuine intellectual adventure. Teaching demands the ability to adapt boldly, to invent, to create procedures to meet the ever-changing demands of a learning situation. Continuous, imaginative anticipation of the mental processes of the learner is necessary. The ability to keep subtle and intricate learning processes moving toward desirable outcomes without domination or coercion does not result from training in devices and tricks of the trade.

The effort to prepare teachers by giving them mastery of devices, "how to's," or techniques is futile; it is detrimental to both teacher and teaching. The operator of devices usually can *manage* a classroom rather well but, paradoxically, in many cases does not stimulate learning. A teacher fundamentally ignorant of moral values, who has never developed any values or appreciations of his own, cannot stimulate the growth of character no matter what devices he has been given. To give devices for the development of "citizenship" to a teacher ignorant of the structure and process of democratic society is absurd. Devices will not improve the questioning technique of a teacher ignorant of the aim of education and of the processes of learning. When we say a teacher does not guide discussion well, does not adjust to individual differences, does not evaluate outcomes properly, we are really saying that his information and skill in thinking are inadequate. Notebooks full of devices will not cure this. The education of the teacher is at fault. The basic fact is that a teacher must be an educated person, both generally and professionally.

The modern professional teacher must possess a system of principles and habits of thinking which guide the operational process. We need not at this point be concerned because the public flatly refuses to pay for adequately trained teachers. We need not be disturbed because untold thousands of teachers have developed what some call the "civil service" point of view—complacent operation of relatively meaningless routines in the comfortable security of classrooms where no one challenges or evaluates. We may take courage because of the growing number of teachers who refused the comfort of a status quo, who are alert and eager to grow and improve. We must keep our eyes on what might be possible, what will in fact be necessary if democracy is to survive.

The principles of teaching will have both philosophic and scientific bases. The philosophic base, it goes without saying, in the United States and all democratic countries is democracy. The principles and values of democracy have never been more important as guides to life. Attacks from both right and left make it essential that the teachers of future citizens are guided in all their processes by the principles of democracy. The application to education of scientific method for the solution of problems is further advanced with us than in any other country. The findings and principles based thereon are easily available.

A tragic facet of the current scene is that neither democratic principles nor scientific findings are widely used in school administration, supervision, or teaching. Stubborn opposition to democratic process and scientific fact is often manifested by influential school leaders. Professional opposition is usually based on (a) honest ignorance of the facts, or (b) selfish desire to preserve a comfortable status quo. Opposition to democratic process and to known facts about learning which originates outside the profession is practically always of sinister import. Educational workers must be informed and on guard against efforts to impair the schools as instruments of democracy.

Progress toward democratic methods is, however, steady if slow. A majority of dynamic, younger leaders are committed to modern methods in all areas, particularly teaching, curriculum development, and guiding learners. The literature on formal or traditional principles and processes is now practically non-existent. A number of teachers colleges no longer give training in the traditional procedures. The current uproar over "modern," "informal," "progressive," "democratic," methods, over the "three R's," "discipline," "fads and frills," should deceive no one. A part of this attack is based on honest ignorance of the facts. A part of it is simply a brazen effort to cut costs, to cheat the children. A part of it, unhappily, is a definite effort to undermine our American democracy.

Efforts to improve the teaching of our children will undoubtedly suffer setbacks here and there. But the facts derived from experimental comparisons of classroom methods, from studies of results achieved by the learners, are extensive, conclusive, and mounting all the time. The methods of democracy are superior so far as we now know. The present volume therefore presents a sincere analysis of those principles which should guide a modern professional teacher. Traditional principles and methods, although minimized, are included, since many teachers will, perforce, use them for some time to come. A good deal of the historical and scientific material included in the first edition has been omitted. The author does not believe it any longer necessary. It is easily available in any of a dozen references.

The author is often asked whether his book is for elementary or secondary teachers. Here we have another serious misunderstanding growing out of inadequate understanding of education. The basic principles, the necessary habits of thinking, are the same for all teachers from nursery school through college. The variations are in the techniques and will be made by competent teachers as they adjust to differing levels of maturity, backgrounds of experience, and aims and interests of the learners.

The plan and organization of this volume illustrate, it is hoped, the principles presented within it. The student's experience, present knowledge, and interests constitute the starting-point. Examination of one's own naïve and incomplete knowledge raises questions. The organized knowledge in the field, including scientific research and democratic philosophy, is introduced in answer to problems raised. A few critics insist that students be introduced directly to, and trained by means of, the systematic organized body of material in the field. The writer believes this to be futile with young, immature, inexperienced students. The scientific and philosophic background, sadly lacking in so many practical teachers, must certainly be introduced, but it is best introduced when needed. An orderly and systematic view of the field must be eventually the possession of any teacher who wishes to be competent. The mature, systematic organization will be achieved and understood better if developed by the student than if imposed upon him. Older students possessing adequate background of experience and study may proceed more directly to study of the systematized information.

The style of writing is directed to students, not to mature scholars in the field. Simple, practical exposition has been the aim, but, it is hoped, with no sacrifice of standards of taste and style.

The term *learning process* refers always to the outward, observable, and describable activities through which pupils go when engaged in learning. The term does not refer to the inner learning processes which are the object of study by psychologists. The term *learning activity* has been used in place of *process* wherever possible.

The first and second editions of this volume were used widely in this and other countries. Critical evaluations have been made by large numbers of students, public school teachers and supervisors, teachers college instructors and directors of training. Stimulating analyses were received from instructors in Holland, Belgium, Finland, and Japan. Extensive rearrangement and revision has resulted from such comments. Specific contributions of many students and teachers are acknowledged in footnotes. Special acknowledgment is due Dr. Vincent J. Glennon of Syracuse University, and Professor J. Edward Casey of the University of Rhode Island, each of whom reported in detail concerning their use of the book over some years. Dr. B. Othanel Smith of the University of Illinois read the chapter on the definition of units and generously made a meticulous analysis.

Those who aided materially with the third edition include Dr. Robert Reichart and Dr. Denis Baron of Oregon State University; Dr. Chester C. Frisbie, Director, Department of Public Education, Lewis and Clark College, Portland, Oregon, and his colleague Dr. C. Douglas Babcock. These men not only made detailed analyses and criticism of the previous edition but secured from their students about eighteen written critiques of the volume. All four men made specific suggestions of considerable value, most of which were used in this revision. Much material on college teaching was supplied by Dr. Delmar Goode of Oregon State University. The author is sincerely grateful for the help of all those who contributed.

W. H. B.

Foreword to Instructors

An instructor who teaches this volume as subject-matter-to-be-learned, to be mastered in and for itself, as subject matter unrelated to real situations, might as well not teach. Subject matter is necessary but useful only to the extent that it is taught in connection with its function.

A course in principles of learning and teaching, or method of teaching, as the older courses were called, may be taught in any of several ways:

1. A typical, traditional course giving principles which will be applied somewhere at a later time, either in student teaching or as part of an in-service program. This program will have some value with capable and experienced teachers, but little or none for pre-service trainees.

2. Part of a combination of observation-participation-teaching paralleling the text. Teaching in some sequences occurs from the very beginning. This usually confuses student teachers and usually prevents the development of clearly understood systematic principles. Some students are antagonized by this procedure.

3. Part of a combination sequence as in (2) but with actual teaching delayed until students have built sufficient background concerning children and their behavior through observation and through helping the teacher in various ways and have sufficient understanding of principles and practices through combined observation and study of the text.

4. Study of the research investigations in learning and teaching on which principles are based. This is rare and is usually at the insistence of research experts who have not much familiarity with classroom procedures. (The writer has observed this only twice. In each instance students began student teaching with complete ignorance of the myriad details. Both teachers and pupils were hopelessly confused. In one case the schools receiving student teachers revolted and refused teaching privileges until the next year's class had been trained in more practical ways.)

Instructors using this volume as a text will make changes and adaptations in the order of the chapters, in the emphasis put upon certain topics, in the use of readings, questions, and exercises. Classes made up of experienced teachers may omit certain chapters which would need detailed study in classes made up of inexperienced beginners. Certain exercises could not be done by beginners; some others would be a waste of time with experienced teachers. Teacher-training schools with short terms will need to select carefully the material to be used. Background may sometimes need to be sacrificed to practical necessity. The material, in short, will be adapted to many situations, to differing levels of maturity and experience. An outsider cannot tell a given instructor how to organize his course, nor should anyone attempt to do so. The following suggestions are general and for the guidance of all, regardless of local adaptations and changes.

1. A competent course in principles of teaching (or in anything else) cannot ever be taught solely from a book. This volume and any volume will be unsuccessful unless supplemented in certain definite ways.

a. An observation school or observation privileges in nearby co-operating schools is an inescapable necessity.

b. Large collections of specific materials must be provided for scrutiny, analysis, and guidance.

(1) Source units, courses of study, proposed teaching units; logs of completed units; numerous charts, working plans, overt results of all kinds produced by a group while organizing and carrying on a unit.

(2) Daily lesson plans of traditional type, but improved as suggested in the text.

(3) Typical traditional daily or short-term assignments ranging all the way from thoroughly bad to excellent. A good collection is noted in Chapter 11. Instructors should build local collections.

(4) Tests of all kinds: intelligence, achievement, diagnostic, improved essay examinations, problem situations, inventory, etc. The instructor in tests and measurements usually has a collection which may be used.

(5) New type report cards; descriptive marking systems; cumulative record cards; any and all types of blanks used in administering a large school; school registers for rural and small schools; daily plan books; and all types of instruments for securing background material about the learning situation.

These materials are not to be used as models for imitation. A profusion of them will prevent this. Their proper use is to illustrate, to prevent verbalism, and to prepare for participation. Audio-visual aids probably cannot be made available in one local collection because of the enormous extent and variety of these materials. A local collection of samples from various areas and levels is valuable. Visits to nearby schools and school museums or audio-visual departments should be provided.

2. Observation, increasing participation, and eventually apprentice teaching must accompany study of the text by inexperienced students. The course might, in fact, start with observation and analysis; but in any event participation and study of principles are inseparable phases of one problem. Experienced teachers need to make careful analyses of their own and of observed teaching, to participate on an advanced level, even perhaps to demonstrate.

3. Bibliographies in the volume are deliberately confined to a selection of immediately useful references. Samplings of both primary and secondary materials are included. Instructors and students will of necessity keep the bibliographies up to date through class reports of current books and articles. *The periodical literature is so extensive and appearing so continuously that a listing beyond that already included in footnotes is a waste of time.* A regular exercise with each chapter or problem may well be a report upon related articles, monographs, or other treatments.

Comments on the size of the volume and upon the difficulty of introducing students to all areas within a semester were frequently received. The author agrees that this is an "out-size" effort but emphasizes that dire necessity dictated the content. Significantly, no instructor suggested any material for exclusion and every topic received unstinted commendation from various commentators. New materials were, in fact, freely suggested.

Adjustment of the volume to given situations is expected. With classes of inadequate background, there is little that can be done other than consider all areas as best one can. However, classes with good backgrounds in psychology of learning, and/or child study, and/or psychology of adolescence, and/or dynamics of personality development can take the first eleven chapters with speed and ease. One class took these over from the writer and supplemented them with reports on pertinent research and with discussions based on their observations. (Experienced teachers used their own experience.) Chapters 7, 8, 9, 10 can safely be skimmed or omitted with well-prepared students. Chapters 3 and 4 may be treated similarly under the same conditions but usually merit some study. Chapters 1, 5, 6, 11 should probably be studied carefully by all regardless of background. Third, the application of the very methods advocated in the volume, particularly in Chapter 9, make it quite possible to analyze adequately far more than can be "covered" by formal methods. The author has no difficulty giving his classes, excepting those of no background at all, adequate contact with the content in an ordinary semester or summer session. The best help will be received, probably, through the use of group attack and group methods on certain topics or problems.

Contents

Part I

THE PRINCIPLES OF LEARNING

What is learning, either process or product?
What does one do in order to learn?
What are the results of learning?
How does one know he has learned?
How does one know that what he has learned is worth learning?

What is teaching?
How does one get pupils to learn?

Teaching is for the purpose of aiding pupils to learn. Learning results from the activities of the learner, which may or may not be in line with the activities of the teacher.

What then are the details of teaching? Why that's easy! One assigns lessons in a textbook, a chapter, or topic, or some problems. The students recite on this at the next sessions, having studied the material in between. One may show a film, or lecture, or take the class somewhere to observe. One gives quizzes and examinations from time to time to see if the pupil has learned. Students who pass the examinations have learned, those who fail have not. If many pupils fail it is because they are lazy, indifferent, or even stupid. If many pass it is because the teaching was successful. All this is nothing but common sense.

What are the details of learning? That too is easy! Learning is what you do in school. Learning consists in studying books, answering questions, asking questions, reciting, writing papers, and so forth. What you learn is subject matter from a book, or sometimes what you have observed in or out of school. The material must be worth learning or it would not be in the book. Bringing learning about is easy. Lessons are assigned and pupils must learn them in order to pass. Again all this is nothing but common sense. *But common sense—as it usually is in technical matters—is quite mistaken.*

There is more to teaching and learning than appears on the surface. You may be surprised to hear that none of the activities cited above constitute teaching or learning, though many of them are involved from time to time. Astonishing as it may seem, passing examinations does not necessarily prove that anything of importance has been learned. A number of things learned in school are of no value to anyone anywhere. Paradoxically, *forcing* pupils to learn may effectively *prevent* learning. There is indeed

1

more to learning and teaching than appears on the surface.

Everyday common-sense observation and knowledge are not to be disregarded, for analysis of them will contribute to an organized understanding of learning. The most important aspects of learning can never be uncovered, however, through common-sense observation or by experience alone; knowledge of critical, systematic research investigations of learning is necessary. Moreover, there must be understanding of the philosophy and purposes of education as a whole before principles of learning and teaching can be selected properly. This volume approaches the selection of principles through analysis of the student's common-sense knowledge and own direct experience, a fragmentary and inadequate basis which will be supplemented throughout the book by study of essential scientific investigations and by analysis of the purposes of education.

The illustrations in Chapter 1 will focus attention upon the limited information and background of the student, will start organizing it, and will raise questions that require further study to settle. This preliminary analysis deals with common-sense illustrations and with beliefs already familiar to the student. Scientific studies of learning, of the nature of the learner, and of the effect of specific factors upon learning appear later. The concepts of learning developed in this first chapter will be incomplete, but they are likely to differ so sharply from the naïve conceptions possessed by most students that the ensuing systematic presentation will be vitalized. The incompleteness of this first presentation must be emphasized. Instructors and students will raise innumerable questions, especially as to details and implications. This is as it should be. The writer has deliberately sacrificed a logical, systematic, complete-from-the-beginning treatment for the sake of more vital student purpose. The first attack upon learning is through the student's own present ideas, contacts, and purposes. A systematic theory of learning will be built into and will correct the student's existing system of ideas.

A PRELIMINARY GENERAL READING ASSIGNMENT

The following reading assignment should be completed within the first six or eight days of the course. It will introduce both experienced and inexperienced teachers quickly to the broad outlines of the pedagogical revolution of the past quarter century. The books refer largely to elementary and junior high-school levels, but the problems discussed are rapidly becoming acute in the secondary schools.

The reading is neither extensive nor difficult and can be covered easily within the time allowed. A quiz or a one-day discussion may well be held at the conclusion of the reading. Do not be disturbed by startling statements. Withhold vigorous agreement or disagreement, particularly the latter, until later in the course. Do not be misled by an early copyright date; the material is still important.

The books should be read in the order listed if library facilities permit. Where the supply of books is insufficient, students may follow the order as closely as possible.

The following five books are for students and for teachers with very little training. Experienced teachers can profit greatly by reading them if not already familiar with the content.

HOPKINS, L. Thomas, *Interaction* (Boston, Heath, 1941), pp. 41-49, 80-92, 207-209, 344-347, 172-205.

PEDDIWELL, J. Abner (Harold Benjamin), *The Saber-tooth Curriculum* (New York: McGraw, 1939), Ch. 2. Students need not stop with this chapter if they desire to read further.

LEONARD, J. Paul, and EURICH, Alvin, *An Evaluation of Modern Education* (New York, Appleton, 1942), Preface; Ch. 2; Summary of Evidence and Conclusions at ends of Chs. 3, 4, 5, 8; Chs. 7, 9.

CHAMBERLIN, D., CHAMBERLIN, E., DROUGHT, N. E., and SCOTT, Wm. E., *Did They Succeed in College?* (New York, Harper, 1942). Note the Table of Contents; thumb through the book to get the general line of development; read any one chapter, depending upon individual interests.

CALDWELL, Otis W., and COURTIS, Stuart A.,

Then and Now in Education: 1845-1923 (Yonkers, N. Y., World Book, 1924).

The last three books listed above deal with criticisms of American education and answers thereto, but are to be skimmed here for insight into procedures in modern schools.

Students who wish to go into the criticism extensively (probably later in this course or in some other course) should consult:

Scott, C. W., and Hill, Clyde W., *Public Education Under Criticism* (Englewood Cliffs, N. J., Prentice-Hall, 1954). An extensive discussion, quoting impartially from both sides.

The books by Arthur Bestor, Mortimer Smith, and Albert Lynd and the bulletins of the Council for Basic Education should be introduced when students have sufficient background, together with the answers to these critics. This will come better, perhaps, in more advanced courses.

The following references are somewhat more advanced than the foregoing. Students may select one or two for quick skimming. Class reports would be of value here.

Ambrose, Edna, and Miel, Alice, *Children's Social Learning* (Washington, D. C., Association for Supervision and Curriculum Development, 1958). An excellent, readable summary of relation between personality and education with particular reference to our democratic society. Excellent footnotes and bibliography for extended reading.

Bryson, Lyman, *The Drive Toward Reason* (New York, Harper, 1954).

Brameld, Theodore, *Ends and Means: A Mid-Century Appraisal* (New York, Harper, 1950), Chs. 2 and 4.

Hopkins, L. Thomas, *The Emerging Self in Home and School* (New York, Harper, 1954).

Jersild, Arthur T., *When Teachers Face Themselves* (New York, Teachers College, Bureau of Publications, Columbia Univ., 1955). A valuable reference on some little understood factors.

Lawrence, K. Frank, *The School as Agent for Cultural Renewal*, 1958 Burton Lecture, Harvard Graduate School of Education (Cambridge, Mass., Harvard Univ. Press, 1959).

Miel, Alice, *Changing the Curriculum: A Social Process* (New York, Appleton-Century-Crofts, 1946). Provocative, forward-looking treatment.

Sayers, E. V., and Madden, Ward, *Education and the Democratic Faith* (New York, Appleton-Century-Crofts, 1959). A bold treatment, challenging many stereotypes. Readable.

Ulich, Robert, *Crisis and Hope in American Education* (Boston, Beacon, 1951). One of the very best brief summaries on our problems and challenges.

———, *Philosophy of Education* (New York, American Book, 1961). One of the best brief treatments of major problems. An impartial and balanced view is given on controversial points. Good reading.

A few advanced students may wish to read further, even though this is a beginning course. They might try two other books by Robert Ulich:

Conditions of Civilized Living (New York, Dutton, 1946).

The Human Career (New York, Harper, 1955).

See also:

Spindler, George Dearborn, *The Transmission of American Culture*, 1957 Burton Lecture, Harvard Graduate School of Education (Cambridge, Mass., Harvard Univ. Press, 1959).

Many other advanced books could be cited.

CHAPTER 1: Illustrations of Learning as It Occurs In and Out of School

Learning, as has been indicated earlier, is not a simple business. Section 1, below, is devoted to typical illustrations of learning within the school situation. They show the complexity and the ramifications of learning within everyday school projects.

Technical terms are avoided in favor of everyday language. Piecemeal analysis and the development of the more remote implications are deliberately omitted so that an uncomplicated story may be presented. The immediate aim is to outline the whole situation, free from distracting details, thus presenting a reasonably clear picture of a total learning situation as it develops.

Once the general outline is established, succeeding chapters will bring out details which have meaning only when seen in relation to the whole situation of which they are a part. Technical terms and systematic critical analysis will be introduced as the student achieves insight and meaning. Some understanding of a total, sequential activity and its setting is necessary before one can understand various factors within the activity.

Other illustrations, both simple and complex, will be given from time to time.

1: A SOMEWHAT COMPLEX ILLUSTRATION, CUTTING ACROSS SUBJECT-MATTER LINES IN ORDER TO MEET STUDENT INTERESTS AND NEEDS.

An English class in an industrial arts high school [1] had undertaken the showing with marionettes of *The Emperor Jones,* all eight scenes. An excellent stage had been constructed, complete with necessary lighting effects; machines for sound effects devised; scenery designed, constructed, and painted; eight-inch marionettes made, complete with costumes and accessories. The apparatus for manipulating the figures had been prepared by the boys, following the best professional models. At the same time lines had been learned and characters discussed. All this took some weeks, but at last everything was ready. So far the boys had used familiar tool skills learned at any industrial arts school. Any new skills of this kind that were necessary had been quickly mastered.

[1] Industrial Arts High School, Lynn, Mass. Miss Esther V. Ambrose (Mrs. Benjamin Daye), teacher.

Rehearsals started. Four students were selected as the off-stage voices to accompany the action of the marionettes. The stage, the marionettes, all the apparatus for light, sound, and manipulation worked perfectly. But something was wrong. Everyone knew something was wrong. The boys said, "It doesn't click"; the play was not real, it was not convincing. The off-stage voices came from boys who were saying words, speaking pieces. Performance was conscientious but unreal and unconvincing. The teacher worked to get over the idea that the "voices" must bring the feeling, the emotion, the mood of the actors. The boys tried hard to manage their voices, to get the proper inflection and emphasis. The play remained wooden, lifeless, unreal.

Then one evening, with frustration just around the corner, one of the voices electrified the teacher and students! The swaggering braggadoccio of Emperor Jones, changing shortly to cringing fear, became real! The Emperor was no longer a jiggling marionette, the voice was no longer speaking a piece. The Emperor was living and everyone knew that he was angry and afraid, cloaking this with blustering defiance, that he was trembling with fear. The audience was carried into identification with a real person, the Emperor. Listeners felt his fear and anger. They shivered as the Emperor blustered at Smithers. They walked boldly with him into the forest and started with him when he saw the imaginary ghost of a man he thought he killed; they trembled at the scene with the Witch God!

Into the silence which followed, came the voice of the boy who had been the Emperor, speaking with a mixture of astonishment, wonder, and bad grammar! "Why—if you want to sound like these guys—you gotta feel like they do." The boy had just learned a profound principle. Actors call it "being in character." We say he just learned it, but the learning had been developing for some time, affected by quite a number of factors.

What had the boy learned? Stated in over-all terms, he had achieved a new perception of the total situation, of its details, and most important of all, a new perception of himself and of his part. Put in simple language, the boy had learned:

An actor must be the person he portrays.
An actor cannot just say the words the script puts in his mouth—he must feel the hopes, fears, ambitions, frustrations, which lie behind the words.
An actor must identify himself, achieve empathy, with the character he is portraying.

Psychologists differ in the terminology they use, calling these learnings: perceptions, meanings, understandings, or principles. Others call them insights. These differences do not matter for the moment.

How had the boy learned? The answer is of profound importance for all teaching and learning. The boy had learned by experiencing the things learned. A combination of circumstances brought this about. Previous readings and discussion, exhortation and demonstration by the teacher, more and more familiarity with the play, produced a moment in which the boy "got the point." He not only got it but could convey it to others. The determination of the class to make a go of the project, the desire of each to make his part contribute, was a factor, too.

The more the boy spoke with understanding and feeling, the more adept he became. This is the best meaning of practice. No amount of formal drill without insight can perfect learning. No amount of subject matter learned (memorized) [2] under assignment

[2] The emphasis on "stuff-em-with-subject matter," drill and more drill, hours of homework, which emerged out of national guilt complexes following Sputnik, is happily receding. Subject matter properly acquired is a necessary component of learning. Mere learning of subject matter *as such* does not guarantee use of it, nor even understanding. Ample, valid, experimental evidence on this point will be presented in later pages.

will produce the desired learnings. The learner must experience or undergo the desired learning outcome; he must distill the essence and be able to recreate the experience so that others also understand and feel.

Practice with insight after meaning has been achieved and subject matter learned functionally, that is, in meaningful situations, are both useful and necessary for learning. We will have more to say about practice and about subject matter later.

After this incident, the off-stage voices stopped trying to manipulate tones and volumes. Their attention now was on trying to reproduce the feelings of the characters, to fear with them, to rejoice, to be angry, to be grieved. They had learned that mere techniques would not do it. Reality and feeling are the keys. The spoken words came as the voice succeeded in "getting into character." (In a similar instance a girl burst into tears as she portrayed a particularly heartbreaking scene. The task here was to tone down her feelings.)

What did the group learn? The previous illustration focused chiefly on one boy, although all the others learned with him. One related constellation of learning outcomes was featured. Many more learning activities and outcomes also appeared as the project developed. Before summarizing these, let us outline the major activities out of which learning developed.

What did the class do? Through both individual and group work they achieved the following things:

A miniature theater suited to marionettes was built. (Originally they planned a circular platform with a revolving stage, but this had to be abandoned.)

A lighting system was devised, complete with footlights, spotlights, headlights, a dimmer, with a switchboard controlling the system. (Some original ideas suggested by individuals were tested and incorporated.)

A set of sound machines was created, in particular a very successful wind machine.

A set of eight-inch marionettes were made, with duplicates for many: the Emperor, Smithers, The Witch God, Old Native Woman, chain-gang members, and others.

The apparatus for manipulating the marionettes—wires, bars, and so on—was designed and executed.

The necessary stage properties—throne, signet, guns—were constructed.

The costumes for the marionettes were designed and made. The boys balked at first. Sewing was sissy stuff and for girls. As outsiders took over, the boys became interested and enthusiastic. They made costumes with pleasure. (Perhaps being "costumers" instead of mere seamstresses helped.)

The necessary materials—a long list: lumber, cardboard, nails, bolts and screws, wire, lightbulbs, switches, cloth, and many others—were planned, budgeted, purchased, and checked, as in any shop.

Free materials were sought and brought in.

Scenery was designed, constructed, and painted.

A photographic record of the entire operation from start to finish was kept. This necessitated trying out several types of camera, various methods of lighting, posing, arranging effects, and so on.

Invitations were written and sent to parents, friends, and to teachers in another high school.

Tea, coffee, and cake were served to the audience after the performance. This was planned and handled entirely by the boys. The teacher was a guest at the showing.

Rehearsals brought many problems and changes. Many things had to be replanned and reconstructed. Ideas and attitudes were changed as well as the material constructions.

The students received guidance and stimulation from several persons:

    Class teacher
    Shop teacher
    Drawing teacher
    Former W.P.A. teacher
    Man from the Federal Arts Project
    Families of teacher and students

What learning activities or processes occurred? The chief learning at all times was doing the thing to be learned. The foregoing list of major activities are all learning processes in their own right and contain within them innumerable subsidiary learning activities.

The boys, obviously *used many tools and machines,* and thus skills which they had learned in their industrial arts courses. They *planned* the several construction projects, *replanned* when necessary, consulted *books* extensively, *consulted experts* from other areas. For instance, no one in the class knew how to make marionettes. The onetime W.P.A. teacher met with the group, since she had had considerable experience with marionettes and puppets. The students *listened,* read *booklets, remembered, asked questions, made suggestions.* They *studied diagrams, watched demonstrations, analyzed* diagrams and demonstrations as well as what they read.

They analyzed particularly their own constructions which did not work. This called for *identifying and stating mistakes or difficulties, thinking* up new ways to do things, *checking their ideas* against books, others' opinions, and experience.

All the crucial processes of *reflective thinking* were involved in the project. To *take time to think* is one of the most valuable learning activities. This includes *recognizing and defining problems; arriving at possible answers; developing these answers through further observation, seeking information, reasoning, and guessing what might happen; trying out tentative conclusions; and checking to see what happens.*

The experiencing of, and reacting to, *attitudes* is a subtle and complex aspect of learning activity. The class was definitely *affected* by success, failure, praise, negative criticism, by their own enthusiasms and frustrations. Rivalry with the classical high school across town was a strong influence on learning. The *attitudes* of confidence or the lack of it, of optimism or pessimism, definitely affected the learning process.

This highly abbreviated summary indicates that learning is something far different from the common lay conception, which is also held by far too many teachers. Theirs is a limited and futile conception of the learning process: read and listen, recite; read and listen, recite; with occasional brief and formal excursions among the learners' own ideas. The modern teacher, of course, attempts to provide instead, a rich and varied experience with dozens of mental, emotional, and physical reactions. Learning is not a simple, single process, but rather, a complex of numerous and various procedures. Modern teachers should know this, but full understanding will come as a severe shock to many teachers from first grade through college.

What learning products were achieved?

Listing of specific learnings would take two pages or more. The account here will be limited to classes of learning, with illustrations here and there. (Students will find Exercises 1 and 2, rewarding since they call for the derivation of the specific learnings indicated in the illustration.)

First and obviously, many *tool skills* were improved, old *motor skills* were improved, and new ones achieved. A list of *mental skills* was hinted at in preceding paragraphs. Students achieved some *abilities* in planning, defining problems, suspending judgment, trying to foresee results, checking, and many others.

Many *principles* and *generalizations* about materials, methods, and persons were achieved. Many modern texts call these *understandings.*

Large numbers of *facts* about materials, methods, persons, and social processes, were learned. Let us digress a moment to mention the vigorous controversy which rages over the teaching of facts in school. The school long ago fell into the error of substituting knowledge of facts for other necessary types of learning. Much teaching consists of pounding in facts from a textbook. Factual knowledge is accepted as the chief, and in many cases, the only outcome of learning; memorization is the process of learning.

Other extremists have attempted to throw all facts out of school and to deny memorization a place. The confusion results from a historical development explained later. In our illustration above, the facts the boys learned were not ends in themselves; they were valuable solely because they contributed to principles and eventually to the major outcomes of the project. The facts had meaning only because of this relationship. Facts as ends in themselves, as all too commonly taught, have no meaning. [3] They do not constitute learning responses which are useful in the world. Facts are legitimate objects of study when they are themselves immediately useful, or, what is more common, contribute materially to understandings, attitudes, and values.

Certain *attitudes* important for life activities were learned. The boys, for instance, learned that *persistence through difficult and unpleasant tasks is necessary and quite bearable in order to achieve a desired end.* Let us again digress to analyze another common controversy. Many parents and teachers think that children and adolescents are best taught to do the difficult and disagreeable things in life by being forced to do them. It is even said that the training is better if the pupil actively and consciously dislikes the task he is forced to perform. The direct opposite is true, as shown by ample evidence. Children and adults learn to do unpleasant, distasteful things while pursuing purposes which they deem worthwhile. Granted acceptance of a desirable end in view, people will undergo the harshest experiences to achieve that end. Forcing people to do unpleasant, harsh, and distasteful things, far from "preparing them for the realities of life," teaches them to avoid difficulties, to sidestep, and in many cases, to lie and to cheat. [4]

Important *attitudes* of co-operation, willingness to listen to others, to arrive at group agreement, to accept criticism, to abide by agreements, to submerge self for the sake of the group effort were learned or improved. These are well stated in the students' own words when they summarized the project.

I used to think that puppet shows were baby stuff . . . . I know how to make a puppet from head to toe—and how to manipulate one—I also learned the necessity of co-operation in such an undertaking—I will appreciate any theatrical performance better hereafter—I know the work that goes into every detail having had to do some myself and watched my friends doing it—the manipulation of the puppets has taught me patience.

I learned how to work with different materials—I was fascinated by the various objects used to get sound effects—I have learned to follow directions—to be patient when everything seems to go wrong.

From this project I had a lesson in discovering what I could really do if I had to.

The thing that struck me the most was how necessary it was for many people to do hundreds of little jobs well in order to put on even as simple a production as a marionette show.

I didn't like the idea of working on a marionette show but was talked into it by a classmate—if I had my chance all over again I'd jump at it—I found that it was not only enjoyable but educational as well. I learned to read so as to portray a character—learned to read ahead and watch my marionette—to get more feeling into my words—learned voice control and expression. This show was the first thing in my high school days which showed the importance of English to the students.

Learned to try things with a paint brush—got satisfaction in effects I created with light and color—got real pleasure in doing odds and ends, seeing them completed, knowing that

[3] For a recent, extensive discussion of facts and learning, see *Education for Effective Thinking,* by William H. Burton, Roland L. Kimball, and Richard L. Wing (New York, Appleton-Century-Crofts, 1960), Ch. 6. An extensive bibliography is also given.

[4] See Ch. 4, pp. 63-69 for details on this important point.

each small task brought the whole job nearer to completion.

This was my first experience in learning how to work with older people—taught me to study them and discover the smoothest way to get along with them—artistic people are temperamental—I learned to be patient, something new to me—learned to study all moves before going ahead.

Among other things I learned not to waste other people's time by asking foolish questions—discovered I didn't have to ask so many after trying to figure out answers before asking.

I learned that with a little ingenuity almost anything can be done even though it may seem impossible at first.

I was surprised to find out what I could really do. I learned to put my mind to a thing and stick with it until it was finished—also learned how to act when greeting and serving people—how to answer questions they might ask—was glad of the chance to watch the guests at the tea—particularly the men, to see how they would act at a tea and how they would speak.

These statements and many others made by students give some idea of the numerous and diverse learnings achieved. The statements also illustrate a factor in the learning process which has not been stressed so far in order to keep the account simple. Students here were clearly gaining *perceptions* of themselves, of their fellows, of the necessities of the situation, of the nature of the goal and the operations necessary for its achievement. The whole learning process and product is affected by the learner's *perceptions* of himself, others, and the elements in the project. This will be developed in some detail in Chapter 6, and briefly elsewhere.

A few student comments afford keen but tragic insights into some school procedures.

Vivid, purposeful learning is possible within formal subjects. A beginning student may doubt that school learning situations in the formal subjects can be as natural, interesting, and vivid as putting on a marionette show. It may be said that any class would work hard "to get the show on the road." Achievement of this is regarded as worthwhile and rewarding by the boys. But what do they care about studying the War of 1812? Of course boys will persist through difficulties, unpleasantness, and hard work because the end-in-view, the marionette show, is worth it. But will he ever persist thus in learning correct language usage, or attitudes of co-operation, or skill in solving quadratic equations, unless he is forced to. Let us not be too sure! It is granted of course that all of school life cannot be maintained at a high level of interest and enthusiasm, but it has been demonstrated that competent teachers can keep so much of it at desirable levels that the whole is thereby vitally affected.

Many traditional teachers and beginning students also ask other questions. What is the behavior pattern resulting from study of the voyage of the Mayflower? From a study of Japan? From a study of the Emancipation Proclamation? From a study of honesty in advertising? Of propaganda in the news? What behavior patterns result from study of Tennyson's *Idylls of the King*? What effects in everyday behavior can result from studying the heroic deeds of long dead heroes—Richard the Lion Heart, King Arthur, Nathan Hale, Washington at Valley Forge (not to mention Davy Crockett).

These questions are due to lack of knowledge about learning. Many intellectual and emotional patterns of response are indicated in these activities. When a student reacts to propaganda by looking for facts and their sources, by studying motive and setting, he is displaying a behavior pattern and a very important one. The bulk of it is subjective, although overt aspects will quickly arise if he discusses the matter with a newspaper publisher.

Again we may note the tragic implications for teacher training contained in the foregoing questions.

2: A SOMEWHAT SIMPLE ILLUSTRATION IN WHICH REQUIRED, FORMAL SUBJECT MATTER IS SKILLFULLY RELATED TO PUPIL'S LIFE INTERESTS AND NEEDS.

We may now analyze a learning situation which differs notably in complexity and in relation to subject matter from the opening illustration. [5]

An eleventh-grade class studies the Civil War in relation to current problems in their lives. [6] A non-college-preparatory group studying United States History had arrived at the textbook discussion of the Reconstruction Period. Newspapers at the moment were chronicling the end of the Russo-Finnish war with headlines: RUSSO-FINNISH PEACE. The teacher had planned to discuss this, but before he could, a boy of Finnish parentage asked if the teacher had seen the headline. Yes, but what did the headline mean? The class said that it meant that the soldiers would quit fighting and go home. Is that what peace means? Why, yes, of course! The class was quite content to let it go at that; anybody knows that peace means that fighting stops. The teacher kept the student-initiated discussion alive with some seemingly innocent, casual questions, and in short order, the group was wrangling vigorously over what peace really did mean. Pretty soon

[5] The Appendix will present a number of illustrations taken from everyday teaching situations. Great numbers of such illustrations are available in the periodical literature, in yearbooks, and textbooks. The following are samples of recent publications. Many others are available.
Creating a Good Environment for Learning, 1954 Yearbook of the Association for Supervision and Curriculum Development (Washington, D. C., National Education Association, 1954). Excellent.
Learning and the Teacher, 1959 Yearbook of the Association for Supervision and Curriculum Development (Washington, D. C., N. E. A., 1959).
W. R. Rucker, *Curriculum Development in the Elementary School* (New York, Harper, 1960). Chapters 7-15 contain a wealth of illustration.
[6] Senior high school, Salem, Mass. Lawrence B. Fennell, teacher.

there emerged some major questions which the teacher seized upon and wrote on the board. How can all the discharged soldiers be put to work again? What will they do if there is no work for them? How will the cost of caring for the wounded be met? What is to be done with all those whose homes were destroyed? Will charity care for these or will extra taxes be necessary? What can be done about the violent hatreds and fears which must have arisen out of the fighting and destruction? The students were astounded at the complex and far-reaching meaning of the simple word *peace*. Merely stopping the fighting is a very small item in securing peace. Peace, they discovered, means a period of most difficult problem-solving for both victor and vanquished. How can these dangerous problems be solved? One boy asked how we had done it after our own wars. This set off arguments about the experiences of their own fathers in getting adjusted after World War I. Another student actually proposed that we study our wars to see what we did do, not merely to see what problems the Russians and Finns might have, but because we might be in World War II before we knew it! Several students agreed that it would be a good thing to know in case we ever did have a large army to care for after a war. Other boys said that they themselves might actually be in this war if we entered it. Whereupon an electric current seemed to run through the class— *they themselves* would be an actual part of this "problem-after-peace" situation. Attention sharpened vigorously. The teacher then exercised leadership and induced the students to put their questions into some sort of organization. Throughout the period, the pupils engaged in lively interchange, making suggestions, selecting and rejecting, manifesting the same interested participation which they give to their own affairs outside of school. The teacher began to give references to build up an assignment, and among others was the required text. This despised book was attacked with enthusiasm? So far was the class carried from the typical classroom situation that as the period ended, one boy, sensing what the teacher had done, exclaimed, "Oh boy, did you put that one over on us!" This procedure was not mere trickery in any sense. It exemplifies admirable teaching skill, operating to make meaningless subject matter useful. Interest persisted because the class saw clearly the relationship between material in the text and a possible life situation in which might be found their elder brothers and, in the not-too-distant future, themselves.

Note again the changing perceptions of the students and the apparent effect on their interest and effort.

Two basic over-all characteristics of learning are, (a) integration and (b) the effect of the learner's perceptions. The two most important characteristics have been merely hinted at so far. The account has been simple and confined to terms and aspects of learning readily recognizable by beginning students. Detailed presentation will appear in later chapters, but a brief account is necessary here.

The integrating nature of the learning situations. First, all the learning activities of the students in the two illustrations were *unified around one central purpose:* to present a marionette show, to discover how we had handled post-war problems in this country. All the reading, listening, thinking, practicing, constructing, all their emotional drives and attitudes were aimed at the over-all purpose. *Second,* these activities were *continuous* and *simultaneous,* which means that they were related to one another in a useful way. The reading and listening was not done for the purpose of memorizing facts or principles which might be useful to the project at a future time. They were done for the sake of some immediate question, problem, or construction. The application of what was read to real problems in turn gave more meaning to the reading. The students did not read or listen to explanations in a separate period and study them for their own sake. They did not "study" references to acquire a theoretical knowledge apart from the project. Instead, all these learning activities went on in what is called an "experiential continuum." Each experience which was undergone by the learners was based on experiences which had preceded, and each experience as it eventuated definitely affected each succeeding experience.

A *third* important characteristic of an *integrating* learning process is that it is vividly and functionally *interactive* with the environment. The discussion of learning so far has stressed the inner, or psychological, aspect. Equally important is the fact that the learners were moved by influences completely outside themselves, by their total social and physical environments and their perceptions thereof. The members of the class had accepted the aim and purpose, which in turn affected each individual. Other persons affected the learning of all. Students in turn affected other persons and other students by accepting, rejecting, or modifying suggestions made by the others. Each student affected the environment in so far as he could select or change any part of it. Other environmental factors, the school administration, the books available, the marking system, the course of study, the teachers, and their methods all affected and were affected by the group activities.

A learning experience *unified* around a purpose real to the learners and which is *continuous, simultaneous,* and *interactive* with the environment is called an *integrating* experience. The things learned are integrated into the dynamic personalities of the learners. *They are truly a part of the person and not something memorized for the sake of repetition on demand.* They will not remain dormant but will enter into subsequent behavior. *Integration* means that the learner identifies himself with the learning experiences; that the learning outcomes become a part of his personality; that the skills and abilities, attitudes, and principles are woven into the already existing fabric of his knowledge and abilities.

One can learn verbally, through study of subject matter, understandings, facts, attitudes, and values. Descriptions of skills may be read. There is no guarantee nor evidence anywhere that this alone will affect behavior. More will be said in later chapters. What we seek is a "behavior pattern" or personality adaptation into which the learning factors are integrated.

The learner's perceptions affect learning. Alert parents and teachers have long noted that individuals from young children to adults do better on tasks deemed worthwhile. Learners who set up goals, or willingly accept them from others, learn more rapidly and with eventual integration. Learners do not do well when they do not see the value of the goals. This is true also if learners are antagonized by persons or conditions. Worst of all, learners coerced toward goals and activities they do not accept, that is, perceive as worthwhile, do not learn what is desired but learn many undesirable things. Learners often are pursuing goals quite different from those the teacher thinks they are! Learning depends upon how the learner *perceives* the goal, the other persons, and all factors in the situation.

Most important of all are his *perceptions* of himself. Children or adults possessing *self-concepts* of confidence and security attack problems without hesitation and usually achieve whatever success their abilities permit. Children or adults whose *self-concept* is that of a fearful person, of a person not quite sure what he can do or how to do it, is usually in difficulty.

This is sufficient explanation for the moment. This factor will be developed in some detail in Chapter 6.

The term *behavior pattern* includes both inner subjective responses and overt motor reactions. The illustrations given contain quite a number of behavior patterns, i.e., constellations of meanings, facts, abilities, skills, and attitudes all integrated into a response which operates as a unit. Construction projects were prominent in one, emphasizing *overt motor skills and abilities,* but each of these patterns included *many intellectual and emotional responses.*

Habits of thinking, for instance, are among the most important behavior patterns one may learn. The uncritical observer may be misled because the greater part of the pattern consists of mental skills of analysis, comparison, use of criteria, drawing inferences, logical development of consequences. Overt manifestations may be delayed and may give no hint of the extensive subjective operations involved.

Emotional and appreciational patterns of behavior are learned by everyone and are no less behavior, even though much of the response is internal.

Patterns of behavior may be intellectual, emotional, motor, social, or moral in major emphasis. The integration of inner and outer reactions will differ greatly from pattern to pattern and from person to person.

An over-all definition of learning. We have so far discussed learning as process (experiencing) and as product (various types). Most psychologists offer an inclusive definition of learning, [7] some of which have the added advantage of indicating the purpose and result of learning.

Learning may be regarded as the total changes (both the gross aspects of behavior and the physiological changes assumed to be taking place) which occur in an individual as a result of his responses to representative stimuli, present or past.

Learning may be defined as a change in behavior which results from experience.

[7] Louis P. Thorpe and Allen M. Schmuller, *Contemporary Theories of Learning* (New York, Ronald, 1954), p. 8.

G. Lester Andersen and Arthur I. Gates, "The General Nature of Learning," in *Learning and Instruction,* Forty-ninth Yearbook of the National Society for the Study of Education (Chicago, Univ. of Chicago Press, 1950), p. 34.

Karl C. Garrison and J. Stanley Gray, *Educational Psychology* (New York, Appleton-Century-Crofts, 1955), p. 228.

Learning may be defined as the process whereby, as a result of experience, some changes or modifications in patterns of adjustment occur.

The writer's definition is:

Learning is a change in the individual, due to interaction of that individual and his environment, which fills a need and makes him more capable of dealing adequately with his environment.

In the chapter following this, we will compare these non-technical definitions with those of the systematic theorists in psychology. So far summaries and definitions have been based on two illustrations. No matter how vivid they are, isolated instances prove nothing—though they may well illustrate something proved elsewhere.

Modern methods possible with all types of schools, all levels of students. The foregoing analysis of two learning situations, brief as it was, must have aroused a suspicion that many school learning situations are not all that they should be. It is clear, even to beginners, that many school learning situations occur in drab environments—limited, inadequate, uninspiring; some in detrimental environments which definitely interfere with or prevent learning. Often the purposes are not real to the learners; they lack life and power; they have no connection with the real life of the learner. The pupil learns not because he desires what he learns, but in order to avoid unpleasant consequences, to please his parents or a teacher whom he likes, or to get into a college to which the neighbors' children go. He learns because it is more comfortable than not to learn. He cannot use anywhere else many of the things he learns in school.

Instead of vivid and diverse learning experiences, the child is often provided only with some dull reading, listening, memorizing, and repeating. Instead of abilities and skills, vital principles and attitudes clearly necessary and useful in everyday life, the pupil often gains only memorized verbalisms which are not understood even when repeated letter perfect. Instead of being continuous, many school experiences seem almost designed to interrupt the natural continuity of the learning process. Interaction is always present in any situation, but it may be interaction with but a few limited aspects of the environment. Only a few of the more intellectual reactions of the total organism may be exercised.

The picture, however, is not so black as the foregoing paragraphs might imply. Learning experiences which utilize all the natural biological and psychological principles of learning have been appearing in schools for a long time now. Many schools now provide vivid and dynamic learning opportunities which are in response to purposes recognized by the pupils as important in their lives. The types of learning activities engaged in by pupils in good schools are as wide as life itself. The results are behavior patterns of motor, intellectual, aesthetic, and moral types, plus knowledges, attitudes, appreciations, abilities, and skills which are widely varied; and all are clearly useful in the immediate world of the learner. In well-organized schools the outcomes at each level, useful for themselves, will develop progressively into outcomes useful in the wider adult life of the pupil.

Improved practices do not just come about. They are the result of continued, painstaking, systematic, critical thinking and effort on the part of enlightened teachers. The revolution of the last forty years in teaching and learning has not come easily. What occurs in modern schools is often incomprehensible to the unthinking traditional teacher. Basic changes have been necessary in the curriculum, in textbooks, in the administration of the schools, in the organization of the school day—in fact, in every aspect of school life. Back of these changes in technique were more important changes in the basic aim and philosophy of education. The whole relation of education to the society in which it exists had to be re-examined. This fundamental upheaval is still going on and will doubtless continue for generations. Knowledge of the total educative process is essential before the details of technique can be intelligently considered. It is assumed that this background has been developed in other courses. The present volume must of necessity be confined to analysis of the teaching-learning situations as it is hoped they will develop in classrooms.

Critics of improved methods are fond of saying, as has been noted, that these methods work only with "selected" classes, small groups, bright children, and in schools equipped with all kinds of materials. This is pure nonsense. The ability and ingenuity of the teacher are the crucial factors—as they are with good traditional methods also. Many critics are sincere, though uninformed. Others can be rightfully suspected of using criticisms as defense mechanisms.

The marionette-show unit involved a group of distinctly average boys, non-college bound. The history class was definitely well below college-preparatory level. The industrial arts students did have much material, designed and made more, bought a good deal. The U.S. history class had no materials whatever, being limited to magazines and a few books. The Appendix will present a unit dealing with the American flag, carried on with elementary grade pupils too retarded to be included in typical class groups. A first-grade unit was carried on by middle-class children, while the health study involved representative students from a better than average community. The students studying stage design were the only group which included advanced students majoring in a special field. The stage design unit and the one on health were the only ones for which ample materials were available.

Organic connection between life and education, between experience and learning, possible and necessary. Scientific evidence and systematic logical arguments are delayed until later chapters. At this stage we

rely chiefly upon analysis of everyday knowledge already possessed by the student. Is there, then, any warrant in common-sense knowledge for the theory of learning presented? Let us examine the stream-of-life experience within which we all live and learn.

The life of any normal adult consists of carrying on a series of organized activities for ends and purposes which the individual believes are worthwhile. Individuals engage in earning their livings, in rearing families, in participating in local and national political affairs, in securing pleasure and relaxation, in maintaining health, in educating themselves, in religious activities, and so forth. These major social activities necessitate scores and hundreds of subsidiary activities. Parents plan the education of their children, they budget their incomes, they plan for and buy homes, they study nutrition, they learn to play games, they read magazines, they serve on committees, they plan vacations, they plan the buying of clothes, they plan a picnic for tomorrow. These adult activities may vary in extent and importance from planning marriage and a career to planning the arrangement of flowers in a small garden.

These activities are life. The adult learns from them hundreds of facts and principles, attitudes, mechanisms of social co-operation, abilities, skills, and patterns of behavior. He perfects these acquisitions through further experiences. The adolescent is similarly engaged. He seeks training for various vocations and professions. He engages in activities for pleasure. He seeks information concerning problems of courtship, marriage, and getting along with people. Investigations show that adolescents have many real questions dealing with life and engage willingly in extensive study to obtain answers. The adolescent, like the adult, carries on many and varied life activities, usually directed toward some purpose which he believes worthwhile. Little children are not ordinarily concerned with securing "food, clothing, and shelter," with problems of courtship and marriage. Their purposes and activities are more immediate and simple, but nonetheless real to the children. They play games, they keep pets, they play with toys and even construct some, they build huts, they carry on feuds with other children, they form associations, they assist parents in the home, altogether carrying on a long list of activities.

In short, if we observe any individual who is, as we say, "going about his business," we shall see that he is engaging in a series of activities which may not all be related to each other, but each of which is (a) directed toward a goal or purpose recognized by the individual and accepted by him as worthwhile at the time, (b) continuous with other life activities, (c) interactive with other persons and with factors in the environment, and (d) integrative for the individual in that it restores or maintains his equilibrium or successful adjustment within his environment. In fact, the testimony of biologists, sociologists, and psychiatrists indicates clearly that frustrated, unhappy lives result from activities which are (a) purposeless, (b) disjunctive, that is, unrelated to worthwhile life activities, (c) in disunity and conflict with the environment. In extreme cases there results social rebellion or neurotic personality.

Vital, real-life activity is actually a series of natural experiences, each unit more or less organized as circumstances demand. This is true of all living organisms from the amoeba upward. Life is a continuum of experiences. Not all life experience results in desirable learnings. Even the desirable learnings may not be learned economically through natural experiencing. The school exists as an institution to guide and improve natural experiencing.

DISCUSSION QUESTIONS FOR CHAPTER 1 AND APPENDIX

Note. The lists of study and discussion questions, and of things to do, are very extensive for all chapters. Each student is not expected to be prepared to contribute to class discussion on all questions. Each student may select several of interest to him, and the instructor may at times assign specified questions for all. This will usually ensure that all or a majority of questions are considered. Instructors will decide which questions suit the needs of a particular class. They will often develop questions of their own. Committee assignments on some questions are desirable.

1. Prepare a written account of a learning process, preferably an out-of-school illustration. Give an adequate and detailed description without being verbose. The case may be one actually experienced by you, or one you observed. The description of a learning process in this section is useful as a guide but should not be followed slavishly. Different types of learning experiences will call for different types of description.

Be sure to show (a) how various types of learning activity entered and (b) what learning products, general and specific, eventuated.

2. For the second illustration in this section or any one in the appendix, work out for oral report the probable learning activities.

3. Report in similar manner the possible learning products. State some of both general and specific outcomes. Be careful to state these in terms of the level of maturity indicated by the illustration.

4. Observe several lessons in the campus school or in nearby co-operating schools, preferably a sequence covering several days. On the basis of the *actual procedure,* express and support your judgment that the teacher was or was not relating the learning experiences to the real-life needs of the pupils. Give detailed illustrations and arguments.

5. Recall, if you can, from your own school experience cases in which (a) the teacher did skillfully and successfully relate formal school materials to life and (b) cases in which you now believe the teacher missed opportunities to do this.

6. Students with teaching experience may present here a brief, preliminary list of any differences between traditional methods and those hinted at in this chapter.

7. Take any formal assignment observed, or select a typical assignment yourself in your major subject. Make a vital connection between it and typical life interests and needs of pupils for whom the assignment would be designed.

Here you need make only a simple beginning. The purpose is not to secure a finished assignment but to sensitize you to the problem. Later, after studying the principles in detail, you will construct sample good assignments.

8. Many uninformed critics of modern education assert that subject matter and books are discarded, "thrown out of the window." You will know more about this later, but what would you say on the basis of the brief introduction you have had in this chapter?

9. Critics similarly say that modern education does away with authority and "lets the pupils do what they please," lets them determine the curriculum and "study what they please." You will need further study, of course, for a complete answer to this criticism, but what would you say on the basis of your present knowledge?

10. Someone has said that the desks and the traditional arrangements of a schoolroom were designed chiefly for listening purposes. What are some changes which would have to be made in typical elementary or secondary schoolrooms if modern methods (so far as you can understand them at this point) were introduced? Make several points. Have you seen any changes already under way?

11. Students without teaching experience and without much work in educational psychology may attempt here an analysis of value.

    a. List factors of any nature whatever in or out of school which you think might aid, encourage, or facilitate the pupil's learning procedures.

    b. List factors which you think may discourage, interfere with, or inhibit the learning process.

    c. Which of the factors listed might be more under the control of the teacher; which less?

12. Describe a behavior pattern which might plausibly result from study of the Mayflower Compact and other similar documents. Outline as best you can at this beginning stage what meanings, facts, and attitudes would probably be integrated within the pattern.

13. Do the same for a pattern which might result from study of a number of pieces of literature so selected that a useful pattern could result.

14. Do the same for patterns which might result from a study of The Immigrant in America; of The Rise of Labor Unions; of The Rise of the Corporation.

15. Can you see at this stage of the game why the great bulk of teaching in secondary schools does not result in behavior patterns?

Why it does not even produce any great number of meanings and attitudes of use to the student? (This point will be developed a great deal more in succeeding chapters.)

16. Give such evidence as you can from experience and observation that pupils finishing secondary schools do not possess a great many of the behavior patterns which obviously would be useful in practically all everyday activities.

17. What types of outcomes do the students secure from typical everyday schooling?

READINGS

It is suggested that this chapter be handled without supplementary reading. The aim is to utilize student experience, to arouse questions, and to avoid the acquisition of verbalisms by the student. The data of experience, though usually inadequate and biased, are convincing and carry meaning. It is better to begin with some inadequate, even incorrect, meanings and develop from there, than to introduce memorization of verbalisms which may result from too early contact with text material.

THE USE OF FILMS

Excellent films are now available to illustrate practically every major phase of teacher education. One or two texts have listed from one to three good films at the close of certain chapters. The writer had planned to make exhaustive listing for each chapter in this volume but the amount of material found made this impossible.

Catalogues and handbooks are now available, produced by city or state departments, departments of education, by colleges, by industry, and by committees of various sorts. These publications do what no individual can do, namely, give exhaustive listings with annotations.

College libraries will usually contain from one to half a dozen of these catalogues. Lacking this, inquiry will easily discover several within easy reach.

Teachers are urged to make extensive use of films in connection with this text (or any text in the field). The body of the text gives, later, a brief outline of preparation for viewing the film, a method of directing students' attention, and a method of using the viewing as a basis for analysis and inference.

CHAPTER 2: The General Principles of Learning

Differences among learning theorists. The effort to summarize principles of learning which underlie desirable teaching situations is seriously complicated by the fact that there are approximately a dozen learning theories available. No one has yet formulated a systematic theory satisfactory in all respects. But many facts about learning are known and accepted. There is also agreement that experimental procedures should be used to validate facts and principles. Serious differences, however, remain between the various theories regarding the nature of certain facts, the primacy of other facts, and the interpretation of facts. These differences must, of course, affect any statement of basic theory and derived principles.

Beginning students need not, the writer believes, make a detailed study of learning theory. Advanced students, majors in psychology, and instructors will need to do so. Beginners should know what is meant by systematic learning theory, know some of the major characteristics and differences. Summary readings are available:

HILGARD, Ernest R., *Theories of Learning*, rev. ed. (New York, Appleton-Century-Crofts, 1955).

McCONNEL, T. R., "Reconciliation of Learning Theories," Chapter 7 in *The Psychology of Learning*, Forty-first Yearbook of the National Society for the Study of Education, Part II (Bloomington, Ill., Public School Publishing Co., 1942).

MOWRER, O. Hobart, *Learning Theory and Behavior* (New York, Wiley, 1960).

———, *Learning Theory and the Symbolic Process* (New York, Wiley, 1960).

THORPE, Louis P., and SCHMULLER, Allen M., *Contemporary Theories of Learning* (New York, Ronald, 1945).

The volumes by McConnel and by Thorpe and Schmuller are the easiest to read and best suited to beginners. The two by Mowrer are very scholarly treatments for psychologists and advanced students. Hilgard, the author believes, is the best all-around summary for general reading. A useful summary will be found in Chapter 9 of J. M. Stephens, *Educational Psychology*, rev. ed. (New York, Holt, Rinehart & Winston, 1956).

The differences between theorists are due in part to differences in basic viewpoint and accepted premises. Sometimes two or more theories deal with different types of learning problems, different motivations, or other factors without sufficient attention to, or development of, a systematic theory to cover more ground. Sometimes, even, disagreements will cut across the groupings of theorists so that some in one camp are in agreement with some in the rival camp and in disagreement with their colleagues. These differences cannot, in the present state of knowledge, be shrugged off when we are dealing with efforts at systematic theory.

Hilgard has reduced the confusion considerably by classifying the ten or a dozen theories into two basic groups which he labels, *stimulus-response* (connectionism, conditioning, behaviorism), and *cognitive* (Gestalt, organismic, sign-significate). Some theories do not fit clearly within either group. The learning process is, therefore, described and explained somewhat differently by the various schools. All the statements, furthermore, are subject to change as research develops.

There is no single, systematic, inclusive theory as yet available, no final set of "laws" of learning. The situation is, however, not nearly as bad as it seems. Hilgard properly points out that we do know a great deal about learning and can set up a reasonably consistent statement of principles which are useful in everyday teaching. He avoids premature systematization on the one hand and naïve eclecticism on the other, showing that something can be learned from the serious efforts of each group of theorists. In any practical situation, as contrasted with efforts to build a systematic theory, his is a sensible view. Pure theory, an absolute necessity for full understanding, is not available. Therefore, we accept facts and principles regardless of theoretic origin, provided only that they have been demonstrated, that they promise to be useful in everyday practice. This is not random eclecticism; effort is made to maintain internal consistency in the summary of principles.

Educational workers need not take seriously statements by certain psychologists interested in systems rather than applications, that the connectionist theory and "laws" are wholly correct—or hopelessly out of date. The field theory and its "laws" may be labeled absurd, or Gestalt may be said to be the only correct view. Earnest teachers given to critical analysis of their own experience and problems have long since discovered that suggestions from all schools make sense on given problems. Theoretical differences,

basically important as they are, may be left to competent psychologists. School workers may do what the psychologists themselves actually do on occasions, attempt to use those principles which best serve their needs —always with due regard for consistency. [1]

Agreement among learning theorists. Textbooks on learning and teaching carry, among them, a considerable list of principles of learning believed to be basic to good teaching. The so-called practical schoolman may be jarred a bit to discover that learning theorists agree on only a limited number of these principles, namely, about fifteen. These are not listed separately here since they appear within the various summaries in this and later chapters.

General principles of learning. Principles of learning are worded differently by various psychologists. Readers may substitute any wording or order of listing they prefer in place of the composite list here. Many supporting details and explanations will appear from time to time in this and later chapters. Wording here leans toward traditional terminology in order to avoid too much confusion among students. The new ideas, particularly those centering around the place of the self-concept and self-acceptance of goals and outcomes, are, however, clearly indicated.

Learning Process

1. The *learning process is experiencing, doing, reacting, undergoing.* The actual pattern to be learned is the chief aim, but a multitude of varied learning activities and outcomes also occur.

Active participation and acceptance by the learner is necessary and is superior to the type of seeming passive reception often accompanying a lecture or motion picture.

[1] Four paragraphs here and several principles in the following list are repeated from an article by the author, "Basic Principles in a Good Teaching-Learning Situation," *Phi Delta Kappan*, Vol. 39 (March 1958), pp. 242-248.

2. *The learning process occurs through a wide variety of experiences* and subject matters which are *unified around a core of accepted purpose.*

3. The individual's responses during learning are *modified* by their consequences.

The learner responds as a whole: body, mind, and emotions. First responses to a new situation are usually a vague, somewhat undifferentiated whole. Further responses brings further analysis and differentiation of details. Increasing familiarity and insight improve the responses. (Note Chapter 7 on the learner.)

4. The learning situation is dominated by a purpose or goal *set or accepted by the learner* and leading to socially desirable results. The purposes and goals arise in the life of the learner and are perceived as having value for him.

Learners *carry on other purposes, both related and unrelated* to the dominant or accepted purpose.

5. The learning process, *initiated by need and purpose,* is likely to be *motivated by its own incompleteness,* though extrinsic motives may sometimes be necessary. (See discussion of motivation in a later chapter.)

6. The learning situation, to be of maximum value, must be *perceived by the learner as realistic, meaningful, and useful.*

7. The learning process proceeds most effectively when the experiences, materials, and desired results are *adjusted to the maturity and experiential background* of the learner. (See summary on readiness in Chapter 7.)

8. The learning process proceeds best when the learner *can see results, has knowledge of his status and progress, when he achieves insight and understanding—personal meaning.* That is, the learner is aided by information about successful performances, knowledge about his own mistakes, knowledge about his improvement. All this contributes to the development of a desirable self-concept, which in turn affects how and what he learns.

9. The learning process and achievement are materially affected by the *level of aspiration* set by the learner.

Individuals need practice in setting realistic goals for themselves; goals neither so low as to elicit little effort, nor so high as to foreordain failure. Realistic goal-setting leads to more satisfactory improvement than does unrealistic goal setting.

10. The learner will *persist through difficulties,* over obstacles, and through unpleasant situations to the extent that he perceives the objectives to be worthwhile.

11. The learning process and achievement is *materially related to individual differences* among learners. The capacity of the learner is a critical factor in deciding what is to be learned, and by whom.

12. The *personal history of the learner*—for example, his reaction to authority (many other factors could be cited)—may hamper or enhance his ability to learn given materials, or learn from a given teacher.

13. *Tolerance for failure* is best developed through providing a backlog of success that compensates for experienced failure. Again the learner's perception of himself is affected and in turn affects effort.

14. The learning process proceeds best under the type of *instructional guidance* which stimulates without dominating or coercing; which provides for successes rather than too many failures; which encourages rather than discourages.

Instructional guidance will usually be received from *several persons* within the environment.

15. The learning process in operation is a *functioning unity* of several procedures which may be separated arbitrarily for discussion.

16. The learning process is stimulated to best effort when it operates *within a rich and varied environment.*

(This discussion of process is elaborated in some respects in Chapter 7 on the learner.)

Learning Product

17. The *learning products are socially useful* patterns of action, values, meanings, attitudes, appreciations, abilities, skills. The products are interrelated functionally but may be discussed separately.

18. The *learning products achieved* by the learner are those which *satisfy a need,* are useful and meaningful to the learner, and are so *perceived by him.*

19. The *learning achievements are incorporated into the learner's personality* slowly and gradually in some instances and with relative rapidity in others. The realness of the conditions under which learning takes place and the readiness of the learner contribute to integration.

20. When properly achieved and integrated, the learning products are *complex and adaptable,* not simple and static.

21. *Transfer to new tasks* will be better if, in learning, the learner can discover relationships for himself and if he has experience during learning of applying the principles within a variety of tasks.

22. *Repetitive practice is inescapable* in the over-learning of skills, or in the memorization of unrelated facts that must be automatized. *But note that mere repetition* not only will not perfect learning but *may be accompanied by seriously detrimental learnings.* Repetition must be motivated, the learner must see meaning in the use of the practiced item. Above all the thing to be practiced should be first met in a meaningful situation. (This is a controversial subject among untrained teachers and the lay public. It should be summarized adequately from the experimental literature. See also Chapter 19).

23. *Spaced or distributed practice* or recall is more advantageous than long practice periods.

SUPPLEMENTARY READING ON PRINCIPLES OF LEARNING

Material on the principles appears throughout the book, but some reading at this point is desirable. Textbooks in educational psychology are more bitterly attacked by students than are books in almost any other area. Scrutiny of available volumes fully justifies the criticisms. It is difficult to see how some of the texts achieved publication. A few cases justify the suspicion that the writers themselves had not read any texts in the field. The following list does not contain all the good ones but it is most carefully selected. The incompetent texts have at least been omitted.

CRONBACH, Lee J., *Educational Psychology* (New York, Harcourt, Brace & World, 1954). Chapter 3, excellent. Use index for types of learning. One of the best reference books.

GARRISON, Karl C., and GRAY, J. Stanley, *Educational Psychology* (New York, Appleton-Century-Crofts, 1955). Chapters 11-20, good all-round discussion.

LEE, J. Murray, and LEE, Dorris M., *The Child and His Curriculum*, rev. ed. (New York, Appleton-Century-Crofts, 1960), Ch. 4.

————, *The Child and His Development* (New York, Appleton-Century-Crofts, 1958). Chapter 11 and other references in the index.

RUSSELL, David H., *Children's Thinking* (Boston, Ginn, 1956). Use index. Many valuable discussions.

SAWREY, James M., and TELFORD, Charles W., *Educational Psychology* (Boston, Allyn and Bacon, 1958), Ch. 2.

SNYGG, Donald, and COMBS, Arthur W., *Individual Behavior* (New York, Harper, 1949). Summarizes a new frame of reference, that of the individual himself in contrast to the outside or "objective" field as frame. A bit difficult for beginners but should be attempted. Better understanding will emerge as the basic concept is developed in later pages. Chapters 1, 5, and 11 are best to begin with. Phenomenology

STEPHENS, J. M., *Educational Psychology*, rev. ed. (New York, Holt, Rinehart & Winston, 1956), Chs. 8-15. Valuable and useful account.

THOMPSON, George G., GARDNER, Eric R., and DI VESTA, Francis J., *Educational Psychology* (New York, Appleton-Century-Crofts, 1959), Chs. 3 and 11.

At this point a student may make a five-minute report based on the partial list of principles of learning set forth by Snygg and Combs on pages 239-240. Note also the principles applied to conditioning on page 357. Differences in wording of the discussions of the phenomenal field and the relation of principles so stated to selected principles from the list of twenty-three set forth on pages 18-20 above should be brought out for class benefit.

Preserving the learner's security as he meets new experiences. One most important aspect of learning was not illustrated openly in the two illustrations in this chapter. When a child comes to school for the first time, he enters a new world. Things are not as they were in the warm familiar world at home. Being a little afraid is normal, and so also is the need for security. The abandonment of old and trusted knowledges and values and the acceptance of new values and behavior patterns is a serious matter for learners at all levels. The older the learner the more he has identified with his knowledges and values and the more necessary it is to conduct learning enterprises so that security and mental health are preserved.

Distrust, fear, and insecurity are quite normal reactions to change. The need for security is equally normal and must be respected by adults and not sneered at, as it sometimes unhappily is. The general strategy is to begin with the known and to proceed with challenges likely to beget success, to proceed slowly enough so that the learner may develop insight and understanding and may achieve appropriate skills for operating new knowledge and values.

1. Begin with problems real to the learners involved, but which contain challenge. Dealing with the familiar and with a challenge which is not overwhelming reduces tension.

2. Begin with problems which will likely yield success. Failure on a self-selected problem is not so devastating as is failure on an imposed task.

3. Allow time for development of understanding and for achievement of new skills and behaviors.

4. Develop a strong group feeling, but with full respect for the individuals within the group. (See Ch. 9 for discussion of group process.)

5. Provide an atmosphere of freedom and spontaneity. An emotional climate free from tensions contributes to confidence and security.

6. Provide support in the form of recognition for contributions, praise for results.

7. Provide assurance that individual learners may contribute freely, may differ with the majority, may suggest new leads. Creative activities when accepted not only aid the learner in achieving results, but contribute to security.

8. Recognize and build upon differences in interests and special abilities within the group. A favorable effect results from aid given to learners in understanding themselves, both their capabilities and limitations, and in understanding their relationship with others and with the group.

9. Adjust the pace carefully to the individuals and the group. Slow acceptance and development are natural.

The learner's security is complicated when relearning is necessary, doubly so when undesirable values and patterns of behavior

must be eliminated. A few principles may be noted. [2]

1. The process and principles governing the acquisition of socially acceptable learning and of learning detrimental to society are basically alike.

2. Re-education is the achievement of changes in the learner's knowledge, belief, and values.

3. Re-education affects the cognitive structure of the individual, his perception of the physical and social worlds, that is, it changes his knowledge, beliefs, and expectations.

4. Re-education modifies the learner's personal values with respect to group and interpersonal relations.

5. Re-education influences the learner's behavior in social situations.

6. First-hand experience does not guarantee correct concepts; the total learning situation must be conducive to a change in cognition.

7. An individual's perception of the facts and values of a situation affects his behavior.

8. The possession of correct facts in the face of false perceptions does not assure change in inadequate social stereotypes.

9. Inadequate stereotypes are as difficult to obliterate as are incorrect concepts stemming from ignorance and misinformation.

10. Changes in emotional reaction do not necessarily follow acquisition of correct factual information.

11. A change in the "culture of the individual" is equivalent to a change in values, a change in the perception of social relationships, a change in "action-ideology."

    a. Hostility to re-education may stem from loyalty to old values.

    b. The new set of values must be freely chosen and accepted if re-education is to be successful.

12. Emotional acceptance of the new set of values must be a gradual process.

13. The new set of values necessary to change behavior is acquired frequently with

[2] Kurt Lewin and Paul Grabbe, "Conduct, Knowledge, and Acceptance of New Values," *The Journal of Social Issues* (August, 1954), pp. 56-64. Available also in Kenneth Benne and Bozidar Muntyan, *Human Relations in Curriculum Change* (New York, Holt, Rinehart & Winston, 1951), pp. 24-33. See also Kurt Lewin, "Field Theory and Learning," in *The Psychology of Learning*, Forty-first Yearbook of the National Society for the Study of Education, Part II (1940), pp. 215-242. The principles here are reworded and rearranged from the original statement.

belongingness to the group subscribing to the new values. A strong "we feeling" aids in changing values.

(At this point a few other principles might be listed, but they would be repetitions of, or obvious inferences from, general principles of learning.)

The vital distinction between general and special education affects the application of principles. A truly enormous amount of useless argument, waste of time and energy, can be eliminated if the distinction between general and special education, between lower and higher levels of maturity, is kept clearly in mind.

General education consists of all experiences, materials, and outcomes needed by all citizens for the general purpose of living, as persons and members of a society. Special education consists of professional, technical, or other vocational training. The differences between the two are basic.

General education can be concerned only with the learner and must be based on his needs and purposes. The needs and purposes of immature learners are, at the moment, more important than the cultural heritage formulated by adults, though both are important. General education can be carried on *only* in terms of the developing maturity, the expanding insights of the learner. General education, its content, procedures, and standards, must be tailored to the learner with due regard for his potential contribution to society. The whole purpose of general education is to develop the powers and abilities of the individual and to *introduce* him to the cultural heritage. The purpose of general education is not served by forcing the cultural heritage upon learners without regard for the level of maturity, or for the great and numerous individual differences among learners.

General education, however, is not the whole story. Success in earning a living demands scores of specialized learnings. Innumerable values, understandings, attitudes and appreciations, abilities and skills must be acquired not for the general activities of life but for the specialized processes of a trade or of a technical or professional pursuit. The process of acquiring these specialized learnings may and does differ in important respects from that of acquiring the more general learning outcomes.

In the *first* place, the learner ready to specialize has arrived at the higher levels of maturity, his experience is broader, his insights readier and keener. He can now learn through reading and can study independently. He has progressed through and beyond the stage of motivation based on simple and more immediate purposes. He can conceive or accept purposes, the realization of which is delayed, the training for which is long. Most important, his achievement is now measured in terms of the requirements of the special field, not in terms of his personal growth and development. In the *second* place he has, through repeated differentiation and individuation, recognized that items may be abstracted from functional wholes and treated separately. More important, he can recognize the necessity and use of logically organized abstracted materials. These two achievements mean that the learner is now capable of learning through vicarious, particularly verbal, experience. He can generalize and transfer understandings, skills, and other learnings to new situations. He is quite capable of learning now through logically organized subject matter abstracted from the original and real situation. In fact, one of the surest marks of mental maturity is the ability to learn through verbal generalizations and to transfer this learning. Only the mentally immature remain in the stage of learning through direct experience. Direct experience, the functional organization of subject matter around purposes, is necessary with beginning learners but becomes cumbersome with those of greater maturity. The unification of subject matter without regard for subject lines is a necessary organization with little children, but might confuse and certainly would delay mature learners who can grasp meanings abstracted from the original setting.

Special subjects, organized as separate entities, are therefore natural and expected upon the upper levels. Their legitimacy in graduate and technical schools is unquestioned. The junior college and the high school need at present a mixture of general unified courses and special subjects. The increasing inclusion in high school of all the children of all the people also necessitates methods adapted to different levels of maturity. Better organization within the special subjects and better teaching in them are also emerging. A few authorities believe that the secondary program may eventually be wholly unified as the elementary program is in many places. This does not seem necessary or desirable, even if possible.

1. The principle that learning is best organized around simple and rather immediate needs and purposes, that subject lines be abandoned for a unified curriculum for immature learners, does not preclude the organization of special subjects in logical form for use by mature learners pursuing more remote life purposes.

2. The unified curriculum of the elementary school, the secondary core curriculum organized around life problems, orientation and survey courses are best suited to earlier maturity levels and for first contacts with broad general fields of human knowledge.

3. The specialized courses organized in terms of their own logic and designed to serve adult life purposes are justifiable and useful on upper maturity levels.

4. The logically formulated subject-matter fields of the adult are outcomes rather than tools or means. As learners progress from lower to higher maturity levels, they are likely to invent similar organizations of their own. Forcing adult formulations on learners in advance of maturity prevents the acquisition not merely of the facts and principles, but prevents insight into the logical organization itself. Forcing also inevitably ensures the acquisition of detrimental attitudes toward the subject, the school, and toward intellectual endeavor.

The most spectacular blunder, made usually by untrained teachers of long experience, is to enforce in the area of general education the impersonal standards of achievement which can operate only in special education. Insistence in general education on rates of learning, types of study, and organizations of material suited to special education is equally disastrous. The companion error made by superficially trained young teachers is to retain the methods suited to immature learners and useful in general education, when teaching specialized courses. This distinction will appear again and again in this course, and failure to keep it clear will result in senseless argument and wasted time.

QUESTIONS, REPORTS, AND PROJECTS

1. We will now make a more detailed analysis of the illustrations in Chapter 1 or in the Appendix or any observed lesson or any recalled from your own school days.

Analyze orally and in running discourse the selected illustration, showing clearly how several of the listed principles of learning were exemplified or violated. It is not expected that all principles will appear in any one illustration. Several reports should be made.

This exercise refers chiefly to the first list containing twenty-three principles, but a student may choose to illustrate principles from any of the lists.

2. If the answer to Question 1 does not bring it out, state here what purposes pupils are usually, or likely to be, following when the teacher thinks that his imposed purposes are being followed?

3. It is not so necessary to connect certain subjects in secondary school and college with the everyday interests, or "felt needs," of the learner. It is not necessary at all in graduate school. Why not?

A complete answer will be derived after further study, but preliminary understanding may prevent confusion which otherwise seems to arise in early discussions. Note later discussions of differences between general and special education as they appear.

4. The following exercise may be unrewarding unless students are urged to make very detailed answers. But when well done, with class discussion of two or more contrasting answers, the exercise usually has good results. The instructor may select reports from a student who has gone all his life to traditional secondary

schools and colleges and from one who has had experience with good modern teaching. An outline on the board aids class analysis.

    a. Prepare a detailed, step-by-step account of your procedure in studying (learning) in a given field such as history, literature, music, a science, or mechanical drawing.

    b. Derive from the account (or make the account in this form) a list of activities which you think are learning *processes;* a similar list of which you think are learning *outcomes.*

(Students usually gain much from the revelation that (*a*) their study and learning processes are so meager, formal, and verbalistic, and that (*b*) learning processes and products are often confused in their minds.)

5. Mention briefly differences in your study procedures which depend upon different instructors, different methods of assigning, teaching, and testing.

    a. List some differences in activity and outcome which depend upon sharp differences in the factors mentioned.

    b. Do any processes and outcomes dependent upon differences in factors mentioned seem superior to others? Justify your answers.

6. What have Questions 4 and 5 to do with the points under discussion here?

7. What have you learned, if anything, up to this point concerning the processes, outcomes, and principles of learning?

Note. Some ideas have doubtless been clarified, some desirable confusion has probably been induced in your mind, and even more desirable, some doubts have emerged concerning ideas which you have always heretofore accepted. The confusion and doubt need not discourage you; they are essential conditions for learning. Ask any questions you wish at this point.

8. Be on the alert constantly to note skillful avoidance of confusion between the principles, processes, and standards of general and special education.

Note errors in classroom procedure or in discussion, based on failure to distinguish clearly between the nature and process of the two areas of education.

A group of liberal arts graduates without experience or previous courses in education suggested that formal exercises be minimized somewhat in favor of discussions interpreting their classroom observations in relation to the text. Experienced teachers have suggested short papers giving evidence of their recognition and use of principles from the text. These work well and may be of use to instructors.

READINGS

The desirable sources for reading are included in the body of the chapter or in footnotes. Students wishing to follow up the individual research studies on any point will find them in the bibliography or footnotes of the references included in this chapter.

It might be well to have one or two brief summary reports on selected groups of research studies so that students may be introduced early to the nature and place of research in determining facts, to the difference between fact and opinion. Concerning fact and opinion students might wish to glance through Chapter 6 of *Education for Effective Thinking,* by William H. Burton, Roland B. Kimball, and Richard L. Wing (New York, Appleton-Century-Crofts, 1960).

CHAPTER 3: Learning Is Experiencing

(Every) school worker . . . from superintendent to cadet teacher . . . , both theorist and practitioner, has one basic responsibility—*fashioning learning opportunities.*

It would be difficult to improve on Dr. Alice Miel's [1] statement above. We will not gild the lily. We will add a statement by Dr. Arthur W. Combs: [2]

It is partly true that people do behave in terms of the forces which are exerted upon them . . . [A] new conception of human behavior substitutes for the idea of behavior as a function of stimulus, the idea that *behavior* is the result of how things seem to the behaver. . . .

Learning, modern psychology tells us, is a problem of *the discovery of personal meaning.*

A few short sentences, but they present the essence of a revolutionary change in our beliefs about learning, which has been developing for some years. Emphasis shifts from manipulation of the environment, though that is still important, to working for growth in the learner. Education has long been carried on as if the pupil passively absorbed knowledge, values, and attitudes put before him, as if he *received* his education. We cannot *give* anyone an education; he must *get* it. The products of learning are

achieved by the learner through his own activity. Another assumption was that the materials learned passively would remain in cold storage and function when needed. This is flatly contradicted by evidence.

Learning opportunities are arranged for one sole purpose—to facilitate experience through which learning takes place. Everything the learner does is affected by all aspects of the environment, persons, materials, circumstances. They are affected not necessarily by these things as they are, but by these things as the learner sees and values them, and as he sees himself.

1: EXPERIENCE AS THE SOURCE OF KNOWLEDGE, VALUES, AND SKILLS.

Evidence and inference which support belief that experience is the method of learning. So far all this sounds sensible and plausible, but the definition rests upon illustration and not upon evidence or upon reasoned conclusions. How do we really know that experiencing is actually a process of learning? If experiencing is one of several valid learning procedures, how do we know that it is the most desirable? What evidence exists? What inferences are justifiable?

The relation between experience and learning is so obvious to the average citizen that many are disposed to regard explanation and analysis as pedantic redundancy. School

---

[1] "Learning More About Learning," a pamphlet (Washington, D. C., N. E. A., 1959), p. 1.

[2] *Ibid.,* pp. 7 and 11. The entire pamphlet, particularly the chapter on Anthropology and Learning is well worth reading.

leaders and teachers are, however, some-times caught talking nonsense because their general education did not include at least semitechnical explanations of the origin of knowledge, the nature of society, and the processes of democratic societies—all of which arose from experience. Technical study would carry us far into the fields of philosophy, epistemology, biology, social theory, anthropology, the newer psychologies, and the methods of judging the conduct of human beings. The beginning student need not be dismayed. Sound explanations simple enough for quick understanding are available, and they will serve in the absence of more basic study.

Teaching is not, as is thought by the uninformed, the mere training of individuals in the simple skills of reading, writing, and arithmetic, and possibly some elementary facts about citizenship. Learning is far more than the mastery of the so-called "fundamentals." Teachers cannot possibly understand, let alone participate successfully in, teaching and learning unless they have some insight into the way knowledge originates, into the way individuals learn, into the nature of the type of individual and of society which should result from learning or educational growth, into the relation between personality and organized society, and into the methods of determining whether desirable learning has taken place.

Principles of learning which are offered as a basis for teaching must meet the following qualifications. They must:

1. Rest upon a valid theory of the origin of knowledge.
2. Rest upon facts concerning the nature of the learning activity.
3. Rest upon facts concerning the nature, development, and behavior of individuals.
4. Square with the aims of our democratic society.
5. Square with valid evidence of successful learning.

This means that there is, or should be, an organic connection between life and education, between experience and learning. Let us examine that connection and the five points listed above. In the following paragraphs we shall endeavor to discuss the points as they are functionally related, thus avoiding mechanical separation. Some separation is necessary in order to avoid complex discourse. Succeeding chapters will carry the presentation further.

Where does knowledge come from in the first place? How do we know what we know? How did we come by the things we now know? How did there come into being originally all the facts, understandings, meanings, beliefs, attitudes, and skills which we use every day? As we say, "Who made them up in the first place?"

The average citizen and the average teacher have a ready and simple answer: knowledge comes out of books or from lectures; one gets knowledge from reading or listening. This is partly true, although the error in it is a grave one which has handicapped, perverted, and inhibited teaching and learning for generations.

But, we may ask, *Where did the knowledge now compiled in books come from in the first place?* This question leads us into the field of epistemology. Many students will shy away from this word. So-called practical teachers will dismiss it contemptuously as "more theory." There is, however, a very simple explanation for the word, and the explanation is of basic importance for teachers. *Literally thousands of teachers are today talking pure nonsense about their own teaching procedures because they know nothing of the simple facts in the field of epistemology, which is nothing more than the study of the origin of knowledge.* Let us examine later the epistemological basis for individual learning and for the accumulated learnings of the group.

Social and moral conventions and behavior patterns are also taken for granted by the average citizen. Where do the accepted patterns of behavior which we use every day come from? The reply is usually, "Oh, you just learn them"; sometimes, "Why, we always had them." We must ask, as about the facts in the books, *where did these things come from in the first place?* The history of the evolution of our conventions and processes of group life is essential to the teacher. These things too came from experience.

Relation between the individual's learning achievements and his experience. The illustrations used in Chapter 1 demonstrated that experience was the method of learning and determined the results. These are, however, single anecdotes or illustrations. Is there any organized, systematic evidence derived from many cases under controlled conditions? Fortunately there is. A very large number of inventory studies have been made of children's behavior, concepts, facts, interests, values, and attitudes. These show a close and inescapable relation between experience and the type of meanings, facts, values, and behaviors possessed. The many studies of juvenile delinquency now available show the effect of environmental and experiential factors on the attitudes and values of the individuals. Social anthropologists, through study of many cultures, have shown that the behavior of children is imposed by the culture. [3] The culture determines the experiences through which the children go; these experiences in turn mold the children's behavior. A combination of outside stimulus and learners' acceptance or rejection is to be seen.

A monumental summary of the scores of studies dealing with concept development by children and youth will be noted below. Detailed listing is therefore omitted here. Two studies only are mentioned because of their findings and historical interest.

The first and most famous inventory of children's information made in the United States was directed by G. Stanley Hall in 1883. Trained assistants investigated the information possessed by children in a very poor Boston tenement district. For the first time there was revealed to teachers and educators generally the astounding gaps in information and the even more astonishing misinformation possessed by many little children. The connections with life experience was clear. Much material in primers and beginning readers was quite incomprehensible. [4] Children easily learn the trick of repeating from memory things they do not understand, which in the absence of enlightened checking, passes for learning. The writer observed an incident in 1950, sixty-seven years after Hall's study, which shows that its lesson has not yet been learned by all—though we hope the case represented a tiny minority. Before a large conference of teachers, a professor of education defended a first-reader story about a collie dog, "Why —every little child anywhere knows a collie dog!!" But a teacher from a tenement district challenged him with this experience. He said he had shown the children an incomplete picture of a collie and asked what was the matter with it. After long scrutiny and some answers indicating no familiarity at all, one boy capped the problem with an answer which the other children accepted as probably good, "Maybe its feathers is dirty"!!

An extensive inventory study was made from 1924 to 1935 by Burton [5] and his students, inquiring into the political, economic, and social information and attitudes possessed by children from grades five to nine.

[3] Studies by Mead, Benedict, Metraux, Boas, Carpenter, Bunzel, Yee, and many others are available. See the chapter on Anthropology and Learning in the pamphlet "Learning More about Learning," referred to in footnote 1.

[4] G. Stanley Hall, "The Contents of Children's Minds on Entering School," *Princeton Review* (May, 1883), pp. 249-272. This study is reviewed and cited in many early textbooks in education. It is as important today as when it was derived. An account of the study is also available in Hall's *Aspects of Child Life and Education,* edited by Theodate L. Smith (Boston, Ginn, 1907).

[5] William H. Burton, *Children's Civic Information, 1924-1935,* Southern California Education Monographs, No. 7 (Los Angeles, Univ. of Southern California Press, 1936).

Approximately 9000 children were examined. The study included four economic and social levels, several national and one racial group, and several parts of the country. Ample evidence was discovered showing not only the relation between experience and learning, but also the effect on learning of half a dozen factors which limit experience. One important finding was the differences that existed in knowledge and attitudes between social classes and economic levels. These differences have been confirmed and many details uncovered by the extensive inquiries into communities in the United States since approximately 1935.

Investigations into concept development by children and its relation of language, as summarized by Russell. [6] Chapter 5 of Russell's volume notes 163 studies of concept development and of the relation of language thereto. A few of these references cite still other summaries. A six-page summary and critical analysis of Piaget's work in this field is well worth reading. The 163 references

[6] David H. Russell, *Children's Thinking* (Boston, Ginn, 1956). In addition to Chapter 5, Chapter 8 may be examined, for it contains an account of the general process of concept development.

Other brief, useful accounts of concept development are found in:

Lee J. Cronbach, *Educational Psychology* (New York, Harcourt, Brace & World, 1954), pp. 287-309, 254-255, 607-612. Excellent.

Karl C. Garrison and J. Stanley Gray, *Educational Psychology* (New York, Appleton-Century-Crofts, 1955), pp. 109 ff.

J. M. Stephens, *Educational Psychology,* rev. ed. (New York, Holt, Rinehart & Winston, 1956), pp. 366-372. Excellent brief treatment. There is a very good bibliography on page 543.

George G. Thompson, Eric F. Gardner, Francis J. Di Vesta, *Educational Psychology* (New York, Appleton-Century-Crofts, 1959), pp. 238-239 and Ch. 15. Excellent.

Two references present concept formation and also the relation of the self-concept to learning:

J. Murray Lee and Dorris M. Lee, *The Child and His Development* (New York, Appleton-Century-Crofts, 1958), pp. 408-414. Pages 379-405 include the reference to self-concept. This may be delayed until we come to Chapter 7.

———, *The Child and His Curriculum,* 3rd ed. (New York, Appleton-Century-Crofts, 1960), pp. 81-85. Chapter 2 deals with the self-concept and learning. This may be delayed until Chapter 7.

cover eight categories of concepts: mathematical, scientific, time, social, aesthetic, of the self, of humor, and miscellaneous concepts. The social concept category is broken down into nine subgroups. This is possible with the other categories also. The coverage is practically complete for this type of learning. This chapter is the best single reference available. Summaries of investigations into other types of learning are few, but original studies are easily found in the literature. All show the inescapable relation between experience and learning.

A simplified and generalized illustration. The following exposition is based upon actual incidents revealed in several studies of children's experience and learning. Little children reared in large cities often say, when questioned, that milk comes from bottles. Pressed further as to the real source of milk, they will say that the bottles come from the store. Their knowledge and belief that milk comes from bottles is *wholly correct as far as their experience goes!* The naïve parent or teacher then says that we easily remedy that by *telling* the child that milk comes from cows or by having him read a book with pictures. The child may *agree* and may *repeat* the statement, but he does not then *know* that milk comes from cows. The statement, glibly repeated, may actually have no meaning at all for the child. It is a verbalism. Scientific analyses of the ideas of children show that many from both the slums and the best residential districts in large cities do not know what a cow looks like. They have no idea how milk is secured from a cow. Many children imagine a cow to be about the size of a dog or a tiger; one child said it was the size of a mouse. These children acquired their curious ideas through seeing pictures in books; the pictures not being carefully scaled throughout the volume, cows on one page were the same size as dogs or mice on another. Again, the children's ideas are *wholly correct as far as their experience has carried them.* The child will *know* what a cow looks like and how milk is secured only by experiencing: in this case by seeing a cow being milked. Several psychological experiments have involved just that—taking the child to the farm. After *experiencing* the situation many children refused for some time to drink milk at all! The experience changed both their *knowledge* and their *behavior!* Being *told* that milk comes from cows did not affect behavior because the children did not *know* what that meant. They merely *agreed* or *accepted* the verbal statement. The futility of verbalism will be presented in detail in Chapter 5. Knowledge, attitudes, appreciations, special abilities, and skills all come from experience.

The principle that learning comes through experiencing is recognized not only by psychologists and educationists but by insightful and intuitive individuals everywhere. Poets and novelists often express the point admirably. Thomas Wolfe put it thus: [7]

Again, the world is full of people who think they know what they really do not know—other people have had their convictions and beliefs and feelings for them. With Mrs. Jack, it was at once obvious that she knew what she knew. When she spoke of the little tailors sitting crosslegged on their tables, and of the delicate and beautiful movements of their hands, or when she described the beauty and dignity of the great bolts of cloth, or when she spoke with love and reverence of the materials and instruments she worked with, one saw at once that she spoke in this manner because she had used and known all these things, she had worked and wrought with them, and her knowledge was part of her life, her flesh, her love, her marrow, her tissue, and was melted and mixed indissolubly with the conduits of her blood. This is what knowledge really is. It is finding out something for oneself with pain, with joy, with exultancy, with labor, and with all the little ticking, breathing movements of our lives, until it is ours as that only is ours which is rooted in the structure of our lives. Knowledge is a potent and subtle distillation, a rare liquor, and it belongs to the person who has the power to see, think, feel, taste, smell, and observe for himself, and who has a hunger for it.

[7] *The Web and the Rock* (New York, Harper, 1930), p. 380.

Parents and teachers who think that knowledge comes generally from books and lectures are at the stage of the children who think that milk comes from bottles. They are right as far as their experience (previous teaching and learning) has carried them. We may repeat a question asked earlier: Where does the material compiled in books come from in the first place? Before answering that question, we recall the hint given previously that would aid the average citizen to understand the relation of experience to knowledge—except that he overlooks the clue! Ask the ordinary individual where knowledge or facts may be gained, and he is very likely to reply that they are to be found in books, dictionaries, cyclopedias, and libraries. Some will list experience as a source also, but many will not. Now ask these same persons where the ability to skate, to dance, to write shorthand, or to operate for appendicitis comes from, and all will reply, "Why, from doing it, of course." Some will add that the study of books and pictures is necessary, but that the main thing is to practice the thing to be learned. With this distinction in mind, let us examine experience in relation to both academic and non-academic learnings.

Experience seen more easily as a source in non-academic learnings. The average citizen and the majority of teachers fail to see the significance of the answer concerning skill learnings. *All* learning comes from experience. The repeated and refined experience of mankind has been compiled in written form, but the original source is concealed. Schools use written accounts of experience instead of experience itself, which has led to serious malpractice in the so-called content subjects. Much more will be said of this serious blunder later on.

Let us compare non-academic learning and academic learning in four important respects, beginning with the former. *First,* teachers who aid pupils in learning how to swim, to type, to draw, to cook, or to dress tastefully can see without argument that pupils learn by experiencing and in no other way. The shop teacher is under no delusions; he knows that both *skill in* and *understandings about* the use of tools will come only through experience with those tools. [8] The music teacher also knows that her pupils will learn only through doing. *Second,* the shop teacher, the art teacher, and the track coach know that skills are not achieved at once or even rapidly. Learning by incantation, common in academic subjects, has no standing in the practical arts. *Third,* these teachers look for the appearance of the skill itself as proof that learning has taken place. They would not dream of accepting a verbal description or definition of the skill in place of the skill itself. *Fourth,* these teachers know that skill learnings will never be achieved equally well even by pupils of the same age or capacity. These teachers take continued practice and adaptation to individual differences as a matter of course.

The four points may now be considered in relation to academic learnings. *First,* the teacher charged with aiding pupils to develop values, meanings, attitudes, or even to absorb facts, cannot see so easily that these learnings rest equally upon experience. He is handicapped by what is actually one of the most useful of human inventions, namely, language! Understandings, values, and attitudes can be described in words, which can be repeated by anyone who can read or who will listen and remember. The teacher, unfortunately, has been trained and habituated all his life to accept words in place of meaning; pious statements in place of values.

[8] Incredible as it may seem, there were instances where groups of women who were to take over motor-pool duties to free men were trained in the operation and maintenance of motor vehicles from books and diagrams. Examinations were also conducted without the vehicles. The results would ordinarily have been regarded as uproariously funny but in the tense war situation they were anything but funny. This type of prodigious blunder occurs every day with academic learnings in school and college—and goes largely unnoticed except by the well-trained psychologist.

The pupil has been similarly habituated by much secondary school teaching to present this spurious coinage. [9]

The writer observed a high school teacher dictating a long description packed with definitions and generalizations, which the students painfully copied. When he had finished, the teacher was bombarded with questions about the meaning of the material. The teacher replied in exasperation, "You know that as well as I do; I just dictated it to you!" He had dictated the *words.* The *meanings* could come only through experience.

[9] Instructors and students may wish to make a brief excursion into semantics. Interesting and easily understood materials are available.

J. B. Carroll, *The Study of Language* (Cambridge, Mass., Harvard Univ. Press, 1953).

Stuart Chase, *The Power of Words* (New York, Harcourt, Brace & World, 1954). Used to be called *The Tyranny of Words.* Popular and easily read.

Committee on the Function of English in General Education, *Language in General Education,* Report of the Commission on Secondary School Curriculum of the Progressive Education Association (New York, Appleton, 1940).

Henry A. Gleason, *An Introduction to Descriptive Linguistics* (New York, Holt, Rinehart & Winston, 1955). Good introductory treatment.

S. I. Hayakawa, *Language in Thought and Action,* rev. ed. (New York, Holt, Rinehart & Winston, 1949). Extensive bibliography.

H. R. Huse, *The Illiteracy of the Literate* (New York, Appleton, 1933). Out of print but well worth reading if in college library.

Alfred Korzybski, *Science and Sanity: An Introduction to Non-Aristotelian Systems and General Semantics* (Lancaster, Pa., Science Press, 1933; 2nd ed., 1941). One of the first treatments in this field. Less popular today.

C. K. Ogden, *Jeremy Bentham's Theory of Fictions* (New York, Harcourt, Brace, 1932). See also Bentham's original writing if available.

C. K. Ogden and I. A. Richards, *The Meaning of Meaning* (New York, Harcourt, Brace & World, 1946). Not too easy to follow.

Hugh Walpole, *Semantics* (New York, Norton, 1941). Easy reading, although not very tightly organized.

Two quick one-chapter summaries are available:

William H. Burton, *Readings in Child Development* (Indianapolis, Ind., 1956), Ch. 2. Chapters 8 and 9 also of interest.

———, Roland B. Kimball, and Richard L. Wing, *Education for Effective Thinking* (New York, Appleton-Century-Crofts, 1960), Chs. 9 and 10. Many exercises which can be used here. Brief selective bibliography.

Second, the ease with which words can be memorized and repeated leads teachers into another basic error: failure to realize the amount of time actually necessary for the achievement of a genuine understanding or attitude. The descriptive words are all clear to the teacher; meanings and illustrations are in his mind. He forgets almost entirely the long slow process by which adults have achieved their beliefs and attitudes. Teachers seem to believe that if pupils can list arguments in favor of co-operation and describe the processes, they are thereby able to co-operate in many different and intricate situations. A boy is told to act as chairman of a committee, and the procedure is described to him. He is then expected to operate as a chairman, without benefit of observation, participation, or critical analysis. Realization of the values of the democratic process, the meanings of its mechanisms, and the far-reaching effects of its use are absolutely necessary for co-operative group action or leadership. These things are not acquired by talking about them.

If learning actually took place, as these teachers evidently believe it does, we could master almost anything overnight. French could be mastered in ten days by dividing the language into ten parts and learning one part each day. (Well, maybe thirty days!) The ills of our complex society could be understood (sic) by memorizing a list of the causes of our troubles. Comparable learning in physical skills would produce world champions overnight. All we would need to do would be to tell a boy to go out and jump 10 feet high or run 100 yards in nine seconds. He could do this, or lift himself by his boot straps, as well as he can achieve difficult and intricate meanings by listening to words. If this sounds fantastic and overdrawn, the student can step into a high school and find these errors in most classrooms. He should take an open mind with him, however. Meanings are conveyed through words under certain recognizable conditions, which will be discussed in Chapter 5.

Third, the teacher is handicapped because the functioning of understandings, values, and attitudes in behavior is not as easily observable as are skills. Verbalisms are too often accepted, as indicated above. Students are, in fact, often irritated when by chance they fall into the hands of a competent teacher who asks that values and understandings be demonstrated in action instead of described in words. A college class made serious protest when they were given problems to solve, asserting that their detailed description of how problems were solved should have been called for.

Fourth, since all pupils can memorize and parrot words about equally well, the huge individual differences in learning are obscured. The difference in understanding among pupils, *all of whom can say the same words,* is often literally enormous. It may range from no understanding at all to adequate, functioning meaning.

A seventh-grade history class was asked: "What is meant by the parallel of thirty-six thirty?" in the textbook sentence. None gave a meaningful answer. Some repeated or paraphrased the sentence, a sad commentary on formal teaching which requires recitation of the text, or mastery (?) of the subject matter. Answers included: [10]

The latitude and place. The two lines of the year thirty-six. Well they kept it even—same amount of territory for the slave and free states. A certain place on the globe which is 36 degrees west longitude, 30 degrees north latitude. Around 36 and 30. The year 336. Even numbers. About this many slaves in all north, south, and west and east. It means they established (put in homes) that many people. One answer had the merit of honesty—I haven't the slightest idea.

Children were asked what the word *primitive* meant to them in the following sentence:

Since there were no matches in 1763, the most primitive way of starting a fire had to be

[10] The three quotations here are taken, with permission, from *The Psychology of Learning,* Forty-first Yearbook of the National Society for the Study of Education, Part II (1940), pp. 40 ff. Experienced teachers can supply many more.

used. A piece of very hard stone called flint was struck against a bit of steel. This produced a spark which was caught in tinder or in soft, dry cloth.

Meanings used by the children to interpret *primitive* included: "the only way," "the easiest way," "the most important way," "the best way they could think of," "the most used method," "the most dangerous way," "a new way." Incidentally, the writer annually finds graduate students who have no meaning at all for *tinder, trencher,* and *primitive*.

A fifth-grade history book contains the sentence:

Daniel Webster said of Hamilton, "He smote the rock of national resources, and abundant streams of revenue burst forth. He touched the dead corpse of public credit and it sprang upon its feet."

Children got the following meanings:

Daniel Webster said that Hamilton a plenty of government has burst forward. He put his hand on dead people and free to everybody and it grew to its feet. When he touched the dead they would spring to their feet.

Daniel Webster said of Hamilton, "He stopped mother nature and fake rivers came instead. He stopped public credit and it was returned to him."

The figurative language is a complicating factor here, but the real point is that the understanding presented is complicated. Pupils cannot possibly achieve it, even in simple language, without a background of much reading and learning. Understanding grows out of repeated experiences, and does not "spring to its feet" when the teacher lays her assigning hand upon it.

Much of the popular complaint about the teaching of American history would be silenced if educators were allowed to write history in terms of children's understandings and to teach it realistically. Incidentally, such exhibits as that cited above and others available should cause many typical history teachers to lose much sleep while they ponder the intelligibility of the texts they use.

Concepts, principles, attitudes, or complex special abilities are the products of long, slow growth processes involving many experiences. They cannot develop overnight out of "assignments." The academic teacher will be aided by keeping in mind the easily observable development in non-academic learnings. Pupils do not develop motor skills immediately. So also with mental skills, social skills, and concepts. Time, varied experiences, contacts, and illustrations are necessary. [11]

There must be not only many experiences illustrating the understandings and attitudes to be achieved but a great variety of these experiences. Different minds are illuminated by different experiences. The modern school is committed to the belief that a rich and varied series of experiences is necessary to learning.

Because of the gap between life and the school, because of the wider use of books (invaluable instruments though they are), the vital connection between experience and learning is often obscured for many academic teachers. The correction of this error is one of the pressing problems of the current period. The modern elementary school is well on its way to basing learning on experience. The high school is about to come under terrific pressure to do likewise. If our verbal and unrealistic high school fails to make this adjustment with some speed, it may be reduced to a small formal institution outside the vigorous educational life of the country. Words and books are among the most important aids to learning, as will be shown later, but they may also effectually prevent genuine learning.

The accumulated culture of the race is derived from experience. Culture did not exist *a priori* nor did it spring into existence by fiat. Human knowledge and patterns of

[11] Several good studies are available which make critical analyses of textbook content and wording in relation to the maturity and background of learners.

social and ethical behavior arose out of man's efforts to solve his problems. As early man tried to secure enough to eat, clothing with which to cover himself, and shelter from the elements, he discovered, evolved, and invented many facts, meanings, attitudes, and ways of behaving. He developed behaviors which enabled him to get along with other people, to act within a group; eventually, he attacked the problems of intergroup relations. He evolved methods of manufacturing goods, mechanisms of barter and exchange. Eventually, he developed ideas and ways of behaving in relation to the unknown or supernatural. Whole volumes have been devoted to this, so we need not labor the point.

Early man gained another important idea from his experiences: that knowledge and behavior patterns change, improve, become more accurate and more useful as experience is extended and refined. All learners acquire their knowledge, values, attitudes, and behaviors through experience, and then refine and reorganize these after further experience.

The average citizen, however, is greatly impressed by the printed word. "What the book says" is the final authority. The responsibility rests in part upon our inadequate teaching of reading on the upper levels, our verbalistic education divorced from reality, and our emphasis on memorization of subject matter. The teacher whose aim is to "cover the text" and little else is doubtless miseducating children and youth. Primacy is attributed to printed accounts, while the experience behind them is overlooked and unknown. Just as with the milk in the bottles, so also with knowledge in books and in other repositories: we must go back to the original source.

Experience must not be regarded too narrowly. The emphasis to this point has been upon the so-called pragmatic, more properly the empirical, origin of knowledge and behavior. The first knowledge derived by anyone clearly comes empirically from direct experience. The vast bulk of human knowledge and behavior for dealing with everyday affairs is equally empirical in origin. The conduct of teaching, therefore, in the common schools and in general education, will be based upon this conception of knowledge.

Mature minds, however, produce mental constructs which are not derived directly from experience and which cannot be observed directly in the practical world. Capable individuals go beyond experience to produce [12] abstract generalizations, values, ideals, hopes, and aspirations. They go beyond experience, however, by means of rational and describable processes of reasoning, contemplation, and speculation. The roots of these processes are in experience. "Going beyond experience" does not mean doing so in a capricious, irrational, or mysterious way. One may not legitimately "transcend" experience through an obscurantist disregard for facts and logic, the known principles and controls of thinking.

The discussion of this vital problem here is brief to the point of superficiality; first, so that certain points may stand out starkly, and second, because students should have met extended discussion in other courses.

Instructors who wish to present a different interpretation, or who wish to show students various accounts, may do so through excellent, easily available, modern summaries.

Moral values, "absolute" values, "eternal" truths. Many persons first meeting the empirical theory of knowledge think that it has no place for moral values, for standards of truth, love, and beauty; no place for the so-

[12] Good discussions of abstractions and abstract words can be found in all of the better texts in educational psychology and in many texts on the teaching of reading.
Advanced students may be interested in looking at more difficult presentations in:
Carl G. Hempel, *Fundamentals of Concept Formation in Empirical Science* (Chicago, Univ. of Chicago Press, 1952).
C. K. Ogden, *Bentham's Theory of Fictions* (New York, Harcourt, Brace, 1932). Contains Bentham's original statement preceded by a 150-page introductory analysis by Ogden.

called higher things which transcend earth-bound experience. The public schools are often accused of being "godless," of failing to teach moral or religious truths and values. This is pure nonsense. We should note first that the parochial schools supported by four or five church groups do not themselves teach religion; each teaches the doctrines and values accepted by the denomination or sect in question. Second, the public school, like the parochial school, is much exercised about moral and spiritual teaching. Many earnest efforts are being made to discover better ways to aid children in achieving moral values.

Liberal empiricism has ample place for religious ideals,[13] truths, and values; for

[13] Selected chapters or parts of chapters may be used:

Theodore Brameld, *End and Means in Education; A Midcentury Appraisal* (New York, Harper, 1942). See also other books by this author.

Frederick S. Breed, *Education and the New Realism* (New York, Macmillan, 1939). An older book but presents a view which differs from the others.

Thomas H. Briggs, *Pragmatism and Pedagogy* (New York, Macmillan, 1940). Another older book still valuable.

John S. Brubacher, ed., *The Public School and Spiritual Values* (New York, Harper, 1944). See also other books by this author.

R. Freeman Butts, *The American Tradition in Religion and Education* (Boston, Beacon, 1950). Other books also.

Everett W. Hall, *Modern Science and Human Values* (Princeton, N. J., Van Nostrand, 1956).

L. Thomas Hopkins, *Interaction* (Boston, Heath 1941), pp. 44-49; 80-92. Excellent brief summary.

John A. Hutchinson, *Faith, Reason, and Existence* (New York, Oxford, 1956).

Charles H. Judd, *Education as the Cultivation of the Higher Mental Processes* (New York, Macmillan, 1936).

E. V. Sayers and Ward Madden, *Education and the Democratic Faith* (New York, Appleton-Century-Crofts, 1959). An unusual and provocative book. Excellent bibliography.

Lewis Mumford, *Values for Survival* (New York, Harcourt, Brace, & World, 1946). Others by same author.

Robert Ulich, *Conditions of Civilized Living* (New York, Dutton, 1946).

——, *Fundamentals of Democratic Education*, rev. ed. (New York, American Book, 1961).

——, *The Human Career* (New York, Harper, 1955). An unusual and sensitive treatment.

aesthetic values; for hopes, dreams, and aspirations toward better men and better worlds. These hopes and aspirations, these values, are rooted in the facts of experience, and not in fantasy which mysteriously "transcends," by defying, facts.

Religious leaders who are disturbed by pragmatic or empirical thinking might recall that the tremendous power of the ideals and teachings of Jesus resulted, in part, from the fact that these teachings sprang straight from the everyday experiences of common people, dealt with everyday experiential problems, and were in everyday language. If these ideals have lost power in the modern world, as religious leaders tell us, it may be in part because formalized religion has made verbalisms of these teachings, often flatly refusing to adapt the original teachings to current problems—that is, to relate religious beliefs to experience.

Argument over eternal and absolute can be avoided without loss. We may leave the eternal and the absolute properly to the metaphysicians. On the one hand, to call certain principles eternal or absolute will not make them so if they are not. Many utterly absurd and thoroughly detrimental principles and creeds in religion, economics, politics, racial and social relations, and in education are now preserved because of the false sanctity involved in the label *eternal* or *absolute*. We must, of course, be sharply on guard against the opposite of absolutes: fleeting creeds and principles based on expediency, opportunism, a seeming need of the times. It is necessary to avoid the extremes of relativism as well as of absolutism and authoritarianism.

On the other hand, to deny certain principles the label *eternal* or *absolute* will not impair them if they should turn out to be absolute—if we could ever find out!

Calling principles eternal or absolute will not make them any better guides for self-reliant, secure, and courageous minds. To refuse to call them eternal or absolute will not impair in the slightest their power to guide the conduct of intelligent individuals, provided the principles are clearly justified not by arbitrary edict, but by their contribution to the betterment of living.

Confusion due partly to nature of language. Individuals who are naïvely unaware of the part language plays in shaping thinking can be honestly mistaken in believing that there are eternal truths not based on experience. Our common words, particularly those dealing with truth, moral values, religion, and God, descend from an ancient world in which primitive man cowered in fear before an evil universe. Unable to understand or manage the elemental forces which sometimes killed him, sometimes made life possible and pleasant, primitive man developed explanations which today we call myths. But these myths were truth to early man. Because of his experience in living, he attributed absolute power to unseen gods, some beneficent, some evil. The edicts of these gods, as understood by man, were to be defied only under severe penalty. Methods of placating or winning the favor of powers, spirits, or gods were developed. These rituals and formulas became sacred, became fixed, were regarded as eternal truths. The penalty for tampering with or doubting these was ostracism or death. Many persons today overlook the fact that these "fixed and eternal truths" were developed by primitive man out of his experience with a world he could not possibly understand. His explanations were the very best he could devise.

The language and attitudes of the ancient world have persisted into the modern universe. The physicist, the biologist, the mathematician, the philosopher of today have discovered huge amounts of information at which ancient man could not even guess. Modern man finds the universe not *fixed* and *eternal,* but *dynamic* and *emergent.* Facts and truths have changed, even in the realms of physics and mathematics. Changes are even greater in other fields. The language of the ancient world persists, however, to confuse men's minds. Much honest confusion results from attempting to portray the dynamic, emerging world of modern man by using words whose meanings were established in the ancient static world.

Discovering and teaching persistent truths to children and youth may be more important than quibbling over eternal absolutes. Many principles and values, particularly in philosophy, ethics, religion, and aesthetics, with particular application to the problems of group living and individual morality, have been derived from real-life situations so often and over so long a period of time that we may safely call them *persistent* truths.[14] These persistent truths are incorporated into the cultural tradition of any given society or civilization. Such principles seem to be subject to slow change over long periods of time; but for any given society and time, they are the accepted basic principles, truths, and values in ethics, morals, government, family life, and even in more mundane affairs of economics, health, and the like.

The important thing for the citizen, the parent, the teacher, is to see clearly those principles which form the core of cultural unity and to introduce children and youth to them. The principles which persist are basic and fruitful for better living as defined by the society in which we live. The routines of everyday living, the mechanisms and processes through which life goes on, cannot be properly selected without reference to a core of values and principles. The impor-

[14] Little is gained by asking beginning students to struggle with the question as to whether "persistent" truths are revelations of some absolute truth, the *Ding an sich,* a noumenon.

An excellent discussion by Aldous Huxley (*Ends and Means,* Harper, 1937) points out that while ethical judgments are variable as between regions and nations, the judgments do tend to approximate as knowledge grows and non-attachment increases. Ethical doctrines pronounced by Confucius, Buddha, Jesus, and others illustrate a *consensus gentium.* The consensus is greater with higher levels of civilization and with the conquering of social prejudice.

tance of this will be stressed again in a later chapter discussing the aims of education.

The important point will bear repeating. Each civilization has values, truths, meanings by which it lives. These are *basic* and *fundamental* truths. They are, unquestionably, truths which are *persistent*. It is not necessary to raise the issues of *eternal* or *absolute* truth. It is always necessary to raise the issue of *functional validity* or *functional truth*. Education must see that succeeding generations are introduced to these persistent truths which function in determining the unity, continuity, and betterment of the ongoing life of the community. Education must also make clear how these functioning truths are derived and improved. [15]

Failure to understand the experiential basis of academic learning is the tragic error of education. Some instructors and students may think that the past few pages were a digression. The basic theme of this chapter is at the center of every paragraph: experience is the basis of learning. The fact that the immediately preceding pages strike some as a digression indicates how far teaching has strayed from basic principles. The result is the formal, verbal, unrealistic secondary school and general college. A completely symbolic education is offered as a preparation for a completely real world. A great deal more will be said on this subject in Chapter 5.

DISCUSSION QUESTIONS FOR SECTION 1

This extensive chapter contains much material new to students, who lack introductory courses.

[15] The empirical account of the origin of knowledge, despite the liberal interpretation given in the foregoing pages, will be unacceptable to fundamentalists among the Protestants and to Catholics because of the omission of "revelation" as a source of knowledge. Instructors in Catholic colleges will have cared for this as a matter of course. Fundamentalists and instructors in other colleges who have many Catholic students, and individual Catholic students anywhere, will find ample reference material.

The sections may need to be taken separately, with supplementary reading in some cases. The writer has found it very beneficial to devote a class hour to free discussion, based on student questions as a starter.

1. Illustrate naïve errors on the part of children and adults traceable to lack of experience. Do likewise for errors or for differences of opinion owing to experience in differing environments.

2. Illustrate with specific cases the difference between opinion based on personal experience and conclusions based on technological data. Any field may be used: health, housekeeping, child-rearing, government, business. Note particularly newspaper and magazine articles dealing with popular errors in these fields.

3. Illustrate from experience or observation the curious misunderstandings of children and adults when they encounter in printed materials words beyond their experience.

4. The text refers to factors which might limit the experience of an individual, hence limit his learning and information. What might some of these be?

5. Many writers, general as well as professional, refer to the origin of the liberal curriculum as "largely vocational." Most, if not all, so-called "liberal education" had its origin in useful pursuits. What has this to do with our problem here?

6. Prepare a detailed summary showing the bearing upon classroom teaching of your answers to the preceding questions.

7. Individual students or small committees may report on any new materials similar to those in the footnotes throughout the section.

8. Why is it not possible to teach effectively (as stated in the section) without some knowledge of (*a*) the nature of organized society, (*b*) the nature of human personality, (*c*) the relationship between institutions and individuals, and the relation of education to both. This is a basic and far-reaching question. It should be analyzed at some length by students. Several major points can be made.

9. Read carefully the discussion of skill learning and academic learning. Make a number of significant points, with illustrations, for the guidance of teachers.

Note during observations (*a*) skillful avoidance by academic teachers of the errors implied, and (*b*) cases of serious error.

2: VICARIOUS EXPERIENCE SUPPLEMENTS DIRECT EXPERIENCE; CRITICAL ANALYSIS SUPPLEMENTS BOTH

So far we have emphasized direct, first-hand experience. Books and lectures, as well as teaching methods based on them, have been minimized as sources of knowledge. The average person knows very well, however, that much valuable learning is derived from books, lectures, pictures, maps, posters, museum exhibits, and from abstract symbolic presentations.

Direct experience, omitting details for the moment, is the best method of learning. Some things can be learned only through experience. Some persons, usually the slower or duller, seem to learn most of what they do learn through direct experience. But most persons do not learn solely by direct experience, nor do they learn some of the most important things which they know by that route. Even the dull learn many simple but important items by vicarious experience. Persons of mental maturity, possessed of good reading skills and a high degree of ability to handle abstractions, possessed of a wealth of direct experience, can and should learn many fairly complex things through vicarious experience. One of the surest indices of mental maturity is, in fact, the ability to read critically, to use abstractions, and to learn by means of them. For this type of learner, direct experience can become boring, wasteful of time and energy.

The learning of many things for many persons takes place through *vicariously* experiencing the *direct* experience of others. In many instances the long, laborious processes of discovery can be short-circuited. Learners can appropriate ideas, understandings, and attitudes by reading, pondering, and analyzing the experiences of others. It is even possible to reduce materially the time and labor necessary to acquire a motor skill if one observes demonstrations, reads

directions, and analyzes one's own attempts at direct experience.

Few of us will be fortunate enough to "experience" directly the delta of the Nile, the geography of India, the contents of the world's art galleries, the life of the nomads of Asia Minor. Furthermore, no one can experience four thousand years of history, nor the actual life of Shakespeare, nor the crossing of the Rubicon. A vivid and reasonably complete vicarious experience with Caesar may contribute, however, to the ability to cross one's own Rubicons as they appear in life.

One can experience the first meeting of the Continental Congress, the storming of the Bastille, the westward march of the pioneers *vicariously* by reading, reflecting, dramatizing, seeing motion pictures, and constructing implements. The *vicarious experience* must be a truly *active* process; the learner must relive the events as far as that is possible. He must *hear* the tramp of the rabble on the cobblestones of Paris, he must *see* the light in the old North Church, must *hear* the shot heard 'round the world, must *thrill* with Lewis and Clark at sight of the Pacific. "I do not like it," said the little Scotch girl, with flashing eyes, "when the book says, 'The Picts and Scots were driven back.'" Is it real to her? Is she experiencing and learning? We have all seen learners on all levels so absorbed in vicarious experiences as to be oblivious to interruptions. Persons who faint at plays or motion pictures, who shudder and weep genuine tears and not those of sentimentalism, whose heartbeat and breathing are affected, are all having vicarious experiences which simulate the direct. Chemical analyses show that vicarious experience brings about changes in blood composition and in body secretions which approximate the changes in persons undergoing the real experience. Untold numbers of high-school and college students have organized their later lives on the basis of vivid and compelling *vicarious* experiences. It goes without saying that merely to read passively, to view without reaction, to be able to repeat from memory is no guarantee that the hearer has appropriated understandings or attitudes from the experience. Merely to go through the motions is not to have vicarious experience. The failure to profit from vicarious experience because of its lack of any degree of reality is to be seen in much teaching of literature and history in secondary schools and colleges.

The adjustment of vicarious experience to level of maturity is beautifully portrayed in Browning's poem, "Development."

My Father was a scholar and knew Greek.
When I was five years old, I asked him once
"What do you read about?"
    "The siege of Troy."
"What is a siege and what is Troy?"
    Whereat
He piled up chairs and tables for a town,
Set me a-top for Priam, called our cat
    Helen, enticed away from home (he said)
By wicked Paris, who crouched somewhere
    close
Under the footstool, being cowardly,
But whom—since she was worth the pains,
    poor puss—
Towzer and Tray, our dogs, the Atreidai,—
    sought
By taking Troy to get possession of.
————Always when great Achilles ceased to
    sulk,
(My pony in the stable)—forth would prance
And put to flight Hector—our page-boy's self.

This taught me who was who and what was
    what;
So far as I rightly understood the case
At five years old; a huge delight it proved
And still proves—thanks to that instructor sage
My Father, who knew better than turn straight
Learning's full glare on weak-eyed ignorance,
Or, worse yet, leave weak eyes to grow sand-
    blind;
Content with darkness and vacuity.

The levels of direct and vicarious experience. Since the directness of experience has a fundamental effect upon learning, it is of value to know the approximate levels of remoteness from direct experience repre-

sented by types of vicarious experience. The following scheme is illustrative: [16]

I. DIRECT EXPERIENCE—*actual participation, doing, undergoing (including dramatizing)*
II. VICARIOUS EXPERIENCE
  A. *Through direct observation.*
    1. Seeing actual events take place; handling concrete objects and materials.
    2. Seeing the events acted out as in drama or pantomime, by persons who represent the original characters and who use authentic costumes and settings.
  B. *Through pictorial means.*
    1. Seeing motion-picture portrayal of events, of persons, of processes.
    2. Seeing photographs of persons, places, objects.
  C. *Through graphic means.*
    1. Using maps, diagrams, graphs, blue prints, and similar representations of objects, facts, and relationships.
  D. *Through verbal means.*
    1. Reading narrations and descriptions of persons, places, events, and things.
    2. Listening to narrations, descriptions of persons, places, events, and things.
  E. *Through symbolic representation.*
    1. Use of technical symbols, terminology, formulae, indices, coefficients, or other special recondite signs.

Both direct and vicarious experience must be subjected to critical analysis to be fruitful. We come now to an even more fateful aspect of the problem. The very primacy and vividness of experience which is the thesis of this chapter leads a certain type of thinker into serious error. The primacy and vividness of personal experience is peculiarly convincing. It is accepted as automatically self-validating. Naïve individuals are actually unable to see the grave error in so accepting personal experience as final. Naturally sensitive and logical persons see the point immediately. Most of us have to learn

[16] The modern school makes increasingly extensive use of many varied instructional aids through which to supply a diversity of vicarious experiences. These materials are usually discussed in connection with each subject in the special-method courses. See Chapter 17 later.

it—by experiencing the difficulties which ensue from the error!

Everyday conversation bears witness to this compelling power and self-validation of experience. "My experience shows. . . ," "In my experience. . . ," "I saw this with my own eyes. . . ." The average citizen uses these terms with finality. There is no further appeal; his experience settles the matter. Naïve individuals even become quite angry when the validity of their experience is challenged. More intelligent persons are often genuinely confused. School superintendents (principals and teachers) who solve their problems by reference to "my experience" betray their ignorance not only of experience but of superintendence as well.

Nearly everyone trusts "opinion," "experience," rarely knowing that facts exist going far beyond the fragmentary and meager experience of one person. The untrained mind of the average citizen rejects facts even when these are obvious. The average man, if sharply pinned down about the basis of his opinions based on experience would, if honest, be forced to say, "My experience has been the few haphazard observations I made, which I do not remember too well, which I interpreted with considerable bias."

Parents and teachers often repress young people by saying, "When you have had as much experience as I have had. . . ." These adults are, as often as not, in gross error. There is no guarantee whatever that mere years of experience are years of fruitful educative experience, no guarantee that they beget superior wisdom. In fact "years-of-experience" is actually often a serious barrier to wisdom. The crucial point is the *kind* of experience with which the years have been filled. The *reactions* of the experiencer are vital. The *analysis* of experience is far more significant than any amount of simple *repetitive* experience. Many persons who claim "twenty years of experience" have often in truth had but one year of experience—repeated twenty times! Their experience may be the repetition of narrow, limited activities

unenlightened by reading, observing, comparing; unleavened by doubting, thinking, analysis, let alone by experimental checking.

The catch lies here: Personal experience by itself and for one person standing alone is inevitably *limited, fragmentary, hopelessly biased by prejudice and rationalization, limited by ignorance of the canons of logic, and subject to direct and primary error because of the absence of instruments of precise measurement.* Personal experience, to be valid, must be subjected to critical, logical analysis; checked against the collective experience of thousands of persons; subjected to check through controlled experimentation and by instruments of precision. The ordinary individual is wholly unaware of these pitfalls which are common knowledge to trained thinkers. [17] *Even worse, the individual is often unaware that what he calls his experience is actually not his experience at all!* It is his opinion as to what he thinks his experience is. It is his idea about his experience, and not his experience actually.

Personal experience in simple, non-complicated, repetitive everyday affairs, experienced over and over by all individuals, is a reasonably reliable basis for knowledge. In complex and technological matters, it is a common source of gross errors in knowledge and belief. It is perhaps significant that highly trained scholars and technicians rarely are heard to say, "In my experience. . . ." Often such men remain quietly outside social-group discussions which are based on "my personal experience." Often these scholars and technicians are regarded as poor mixers or odd. Perhaps they are merely bored with exchanges of uninformed opinion, no matter how vivacious the exchange!

[17] It is not within the scope of this volume to enter into a detailed analysis of pitfalls in everyday thinking about experience; however, short, easily read summaries are available, for example:
William H. Burton, Roland B. Kimball, and Richard L. Wing, *Education for Effective Thinking* (New York, Appleton-Century-Crofts, 1960). See particularly Section 2 of Chapter 6, though whole chapter is useful. Note Preliminary Exercises, pp. 114-115; Exercises 6-19, pp. 117-120; 1-8, p. 121.

Important implications for teacher education. The whole point is vitally important for beginning teachers. They will often hear from certain older teachers of the great value of methods based on "experience." Methods based on psychology and research are often decried as "theoretical." Many older teachers claim that methods "based on experience" get results. This is dangerous nonsense. Any and all methods, no matter how atrocious psychologically, will get results. What these teachers really mean is that they get certain results which they can see, can describe, and which they accept. A difficulty is that these are not all the results they get. They are often the least valuable results; and valuable or not, they are achieved at far greater cost than by reputable methods. The really serious aspect is that many wholly honest teachers do not know at all what results they are actually getting over and above the simple and trivial ones they accept. Methods based on unanalyzed experience do not carry proof with them. Pestalozzi, unquestionably a great teacher, made some momentous contributions to method based on raw personal experience. He also made some historic blunders. On the basis of personal experience and self-validated results he could not distinguish the sound from the unsound.

Uncritical experience in teaching is almost more detrimental than beneficial. Literally thousands of teachers are, by their own experience, actually prevented from learning how to teach well! They are prevented even from discovering that they are doing poor teaching. Unaccompanied by critical analysis and study of researches, teaching experience is likely to be distinctly detrimental. Twenty years of experience in teaching is too often twenty years of experiencing the wrong way to teach the wrong things. Many of the older teachers persist in going through teaching motions which have a purely capricious basis and which cannot achieve reputable learning. Teachers who rather aggressively rely upon "their experience" and reject "theoretical" methods seem to condemn as theoretical any methods (*a*) which they do not understand, (*b*) which they are unable to operate successfully, and (*c*) which necessitate the abandonment of long-used routines.

Modern teachers are aware of the limitations of personal experience. Fortunately, with many alert teachers, experience, instead of bringing smug satisfaction with supposedly "successful methods," spurs them to analysis, criticism, and experimentation in a search for the correction of errors and the improvement of techniques. Instead of seeing perfection in the mediocre devices, the crudely constructed "practical" methods, they see rather the pitiful inadequacy of these things. Some pupils do not learn; that assignment did not go; interest suddenly died in a project; why does this error persist? Why do the pupils not know things which seem impossible not to know? What is meant by functional unit? How can you let pupils participate in setting up learning situations? What are professors of methods talking about, anyway, when they say pupils should help organize the curriculum? The older uncritical teacher has an answer for all these. If pupils do not learn and lessons do not go, it is because the pupils are dull and lacking in background! Professors are theoretical!

With the mentally alert teacher the difficulties listed above cause questioning, the trial of new methods, the reading of new books, and the critical analysis of one's own procedures. Critically analyzed experience is extremely valuable and is often productive of worthwhile improvements in method; utilized in conjunction with experimental data, the results of analyzed experience will be sound.

The foregoing discussion of the necessity for analyzing experience applies to any human activity: rearing children, training animals, succeeding in a vocation or profession, getting along with the neighbors, raising flowers or vegetables, maintaining one's physical or mental health, and so forth. The teacher is by no means the only person to be led into stupid and absurd practices by reliance upon "experience." The businessmen and "statesmen" who pride themselves on being practical, and who are so contemptuous of political and economic "theorists," have nearly wrecked the world. They make two blunders. *First,* they base their action on narrow, fragmentary, misinterpreted practical experience, completely unaware of the powerful forces and influences which silently operate beneath the surface of the easily observed, practical, overt world. The governor of a Southern state interviewed on television during one of the school segregation riots, displayed an ignorance of the civilization in which he lives so incredible that it would disgrace a college sophomore in any first-class institution. *Second,* they do not know that a *pure* theorist is very rare and serves very special research purposes. The *so-called* theorists are for the most part scholars who take into account the hidden forces and influences which "practical" men [18] neither know about nor understand when told about them. "Practical" men, like their stone-age ancestors, blame undesirable conditions upon maleficent spirits, "theorists," "radicals," "unfair business practices," "there have always been depressions and there always will be," "enemies of our economic system," "that man in the White House," "too much government interference," "not enough government intervention," "labor racketeering." The "practical" labor leader replies with his own assortment of whipping boys: "conspiracy of the money powers," "capitalist profiteering." These men have never engaged in the difficult, arduous, subtle activity of analyzing experience.

Alert teachers are increasingly avoiding the blunder of basing technique on limited practical experience, unaware of the inescap-

[18] Frank Pakit, "Let's Stop Being So Practical," *Saturday Evening Post,* Vol. 233, No. 19 (November 5, 1960), pp. 64 ff. An excellent hard-hitting discussion. Remarkable as appearing in a popular magazine, but more may be looked for.

able facts and principles of psychology, sociology, anthropology, epistemology, and philosophy which do not show on the surface but which *ultimately* determine results. It is to be hoped that some day teachers will never say "our experience" without meaning their critically analyzed experience. Methods based on unanalyzed experience are often flatly contradicted by valid data.

Two important cautions concerning the balance between direct and vicarious experience. Extremists among the moderns, the "ultra" progressives, very often speak and practice as if learning could come only through direct experience, as if everyone had to learn everything by direct experience. This is nonsense. First, highly intelligent learners, as has been said, do not have to learn everything that way. Even persons of reasonably simple intellect can do much valid learning without complete, direct experience. Second, to carry on all learning situations with real materials in actual lifelike situations is flatly impossible even if it were psychologically sound, which it is not. To the extent, however, that the extremists, especially in the early days of modern teaching, forced attention to the necessity of direct, lifelike experience, they served an important purpose.

Extremists among the conservatives, particularly in high schools and colleges, make the opposite error. They often preach and usually practice as if all learners could learn practically everything worthwhile through vicarious experiences, particularly those of reading and listening. This too is nonsense. Scores of teachers, some of them "famous" and in well-known colleges, do a thoroughly incompetent job because of this misconception of the nature of learning. Certain types of learners, oddly enough, do learn much this way; others learn very, very little. Some learnings cannot be acquired this way at all. The evil of extreme emphasis on verbal learning will be elaborated further in Chapters 4 and 5.

DISCUSSION QUESTIONS FOR SECTION 2

1. After a series of observations in co-operating schools, describe the use of types of vicarious experience which seemed vivid and educative. How did the teacher manage them?

2. Report similarly cases in which the use of vicarious experience was dull or routine. Try to suggest how the situation might have been improved.

3. Report skillful adjustment of levels of vicarious experience to the types of learners involved. Report errors in such adjustment.

4. With examples from school cases of learning through vicarious experience, illustrate:
   a. the appropriation of understandings or attitudes from others.
   b. the short-circuiting of discovery.
   c. the speed-up of time needed for acquiring a motor skill.

5. Let us see how well we and other teachers analyze our own experience. Present any one or two of the lettered statements to friends and ask for expression of opinion (do not explain in detail what you are doing).

After expression of opinion, particularly if it is emphatic, gently press such questions as; "How do you know?" "What makes you think so?" "How do you know it works out that way?"

Report your experiences for class discussion, showing clearly whether the individuals had ever really analyzed their experience, or had just accepted statements or jumped to conclusions without any data or analysis.
   a. Do you think that students should be *required* to study Latin or algebra?
   b. Is six years of age the best time to start to school? Could it possibly be five, or even four, or delayed until seven or nine?
   c. Was teaching better or poorer, as a rule, when you went to school than now?
   d. Who is probably the best judge of a child's mental prowess: his mother, who has reared four children; a well-trained school teacher who has taught him for six months; a child psychologist who has examined him twice for two hours?
   e. Are our schools better than, poorer than, or about on a par with European schools?
   f. Are boys or girls as a rule the brighter in school?
   g. In an ordinary group of thirty children, say high-school freshmen, about how much faster do you think the fastest could read than the slowest?
   h. Do you think that nearly all children could be taught to draw acceptably if taken young enough and taught correctly?

6. Experienced teachers may list a number of educational beliefs which rest upon experience and/or authority which the informed teacher knows to be absurd in the light of data. Explain how you came to give them up.

7. Explain in organized manner, in considerable detail, and with illustrations why "personal experience—observation—what I saw with my own eyes—what I have done for twenty years," is so often wrong. (There are about eleven possible reasons; students should try to get six or seven.)

8. Watch for naïve self-validation of results by teachers. Report cases in which you caught this. (In all such questions as these protect the persons involved by omitting names and locations.)

9. Explain further the statement that: "Teachers do not always know what results they are getting: Any and all methods will get results: Results are often achieved at far greater cost than by reputable methods."

10. Watch for instances in which individuals in everyday affairs, or teachers in discussing classroom problems, report as experience what is actually not their experience at all, even though the reporter is wholly honest in thinking that it is. Show analytically that the report is really an opinion about, or an interpretation of, the experience and not the experience itself.

11. Watch particularly for the opposite situation, namely, teachers who discuss their experience in keenly analytic, objective manner; who refer to valid technical data; who indicate that constant analysis is the key to growth. Report observations and conversations in detail as these are important illustrations.

12. Important! Summarize the methods you have used or may use to aid the pupils to learn how to analyze their own experience.

3: THE RELATION OF IMPOSING OF KNOWLEDGE IN ADVANCE OF EXPERIENCE TO LEARNING BY EXPERIENCE AS THE KNOWLEDGE IS NEEDED

Many parents and teachers are sincerely afraid of the proposition that children should learn by real experience suited to their needs and by as-real-as-possible vicarious experience. They express the fear that certain "necessary" learnings will be left out unless imposed by adults who know better in advance what the child really needs. Let us look into this interesting and very real problem.

Caution concerning the practice of imposing knowledge and habits in advance of experience and understanding. The aim of education is commonly stated as "preparation for life." The reference by both lay and professional workers is usually to adult life. The method of preparing for adult life has commonly been through inflicting upon the child "what was good for him." Adult views of life were forced upon children through adult-selected and adult-organized subject matter. Children for generations have been made to study various materials because "these will be useful when you grow up." Critical observers of this type of education have been aware of its tragic failure. *Modern students have supplied ample evidence to show that the memorization of adult-organized, static subject matter does not produce functioning learning.* Discussion here will not be interrupted by a summary of this research. See Chapter 5, Section 2.

Critics of the modern school often express the fear that "necessary materials will be left out if the curriculum is based on pupil purpose," that "things pupils will surely need when they grow up will be omitted." This fear is based upon definitely erroneous beliefs about (*a*) the process of learning, (*b*) the nature of the learning individuals, and (*c*) the meaning of "preparation for life."

Critics both from the right and left often miss the real point. Mursell gives the clue in asking: [19] "What to do with subject mat-

[19] Advanced students and curriculum makers can profit by reading at this point Mursell's admirable summary, pp. 5-27, in his *Developmental Teaching* (New York, McGraw, 1949). Similar material with some excellent illustrations will be found in an earlier book by Mursell, pp. 4-11, in *Successful Teaching* (New York, McGraw, 1946).

ter?" *It may be used within, but not imposed upon, the learner's experience.* The relation between pupil need or purpose and systematically organized subject matter will be analyzed in Chapter 5 and in Chapter 13.

Preparation for life is a process of growth and cannot be imposed. We should not arbitrarily impose upon the learner a curriculum based on "what he will need to know when he grows up." Rather, we must develop those understandings, attitudes, and abilities which the pupil needs *now* in the solution of his *current* problems. These turn out to be similar to those which he will need *later* in solving *adult* problems. *Pupils will progress through levels of maturity, participating at each level in a variety of learning experiences.* The patterns, understandings, attitudes, and abilities needed in adult life begin their growth in the nursery. They will grow and expand through continuing experiences until the learner emerges into adult life. Pupils will pursue problems and projects of value to them at their particular maturity level. To do this they will need to work together, to plan procedures, to make decisions, to understand differing personalities, to be tolerant of differences of opinion, and so on. But all of these abilities are equally necessary in adult life. The learner progresses toward adulthood by developing through experience at each maturity level better insights, better attitudes, better abilities.

One of the most important factors in developing in the learner acceptance of deferred values is continuing experience in planning and executing projects of immediate, current, and personal value to him. He thus learns through direct experience the necessity of looking ahead for consequences, of taking actual reality into account, and of searching the experience of other persons for guidance. He learns to be cautious, to defer decisions until he has "prepared" sufficiently, and then to translate them into action. He learns the necessity of persistence and hard work *now* to develop skills and understanding necessary to the *future* completion of a project. This was shown clearly in *The Emperor Jones* project. When the learner himself sees the necessity for study in advance, the psychological setting is favorable. The learner is prepared for adulthood by the operation of natural growth processes, instead of having a vague and meaningless "preparation" forced upon him. Modern teachers' guides and outlines of scope and sequence in curriculums are increasingly illustrating this view. Recent texts on teaching do the same.

The same procedure holds for the more complex learnings necessary to adult adjustment to the political, social, and economic order of the day. The traditional school includes in upper grades abstract descriptions of community organization, services, and processes. There is much meaningless gibberish about the executive, the judicial, and the legislative branches of the government; about how to amend the Constitution; about Robert's rules of order. The modern school knows that studying *about* institutions and processes is of little value. Direct observation and, wherever possible, participation are provided under the new methods. Even little children in the primary school are being introduced directly to the organized community in which they live by experiences appropriate to their ages. [20]

Natural limits to preparation by imposing learning in advance of need. Further insight into the problem may be acquired by challenging the whole conception. Is it even possible that pupils can "prepare in advance"? An examination of the activities of individuals at different levels of maturity supplies a clue. Does a four-year-old child "prepare" in advance for Christmas? Can he plan ahead something to be fulfilled at a much later date? He may talk about Christ-

[20] Note units in the Appendix dealing with the community. Modern texts, particularly in the teaching of social studies, contain many such units.

mas, express joy at prospective presents, tell what he expects to give mama and papa—and tomorrow have completely forgotten. Small children will hide a toy or treasured object in order to preserve it for use in activities "planned" for next week. Next week they have completely forgotten the use "planned in advance." They may even come on the hidden toy and wonder how it got there. Candy, cake, and other tidbits are hidden because they are to be saved for "tomorrow." These things often spoil before they are remembered again. A six-year-old boy, or a first-grade group may, however, plan quite adequately for tomorrow's continuation of today's problems. Periodic reviewing of plans and accomplishments, with periodic revision of plans for the future, are necessary as the project goes forward. Such planning periods are found in all modern schools. Through them pupils learn to plan for ever more remote futures.

A ten-year-old boy will save money over a period of weeks for a knife and for fishing equipment to use on a future vacation trip. Farm children in their 'teens plan very well a year in advance for agricultural projects of value to themselves. A boy entering high school may look ahead to a given type of employment upon graduation. He then willingly "prepares in advance" four years of high-school work. Still others, looking to advanced medical or legal training, may willingly subordinate present desires to a long-time program of preparation in advance. The first point then is: *The ability to understand the necessity for learning in advance is conditioned in part by maturity.*

A second aspect of the situation is even more important. *The individual planning a program in advance of use is doing so in terms of present needs, problems, and decisions.* The students referred to in the preceding paragraph were not preparing in advance for a distant and uncertain future through blind mastery of materials which were meaningless at the moment. They were preparing in advance for a definite *future,* as definite as it can be, in response to a *present* decision. In order to follow a *present* choice and interest they will learn many things for use in the foreseen *future*. They will even search through materials from ancient history to zoology if they *now* think these may aid them in the *future*. This is a totally different psychological situation from that of wading through ancient history and algebra under forced assignments and on the vague promise that the materials may be of use "some day." One cannot prepare for a future which is unclear and uncertain. Instead of *being prepared in advance,* the pupils will *learn to prepare in advance.*

The point has been made so expertly by Hopkins that his paragraph is reproduced in full.

This projection of present experience into the future does not represent deferred values. It is a comprehensive and thoroughgoing search for all pertinent information on which to make better decisions in the present. From the standpoint of the learner facing his own situation there are no deferred values. Anticipating the future is merely raw material which he can use for a more thoughtful consideration of a present problem. This ability to project the future into the present varies with individuals. Beyond the normal limit of such ability there is nothing to work with except a great void. Forcing a pupil into this void to do things recognized by others but not by him has little desirable effect. While resource leaders should constantly bring their richer experience before unit-learning groups, it must be filtered through the child's ability to make it a real asset in the study of his immediate problem. Adults offer the concept of deferred values to rationalize forcing a child to learn the facts and develop the skills which they demand but which he cannot intelligently integrate within his immediate experience. [21]

The provisional imposing of necessary learnings on young children. The discussion so far has emphasized the difficulties, if not the impossibility, of imposing knowledge and habits in advance of experience

[21] L. Thomas Hopkins, *Interaction* (Boston, Heath, 1941), p. 345.

and understanding. This emphasis is necessary to correct the gross errors in the opposite direction which characterize too much current education. It is perfectly clear to any honest observer, however, that there are certain good and necessary meanings and habits which must be imposed on young children before they can possibly understand why. Convenience and even the safety of life may demand this. The crucial aspects are (*a*) the learnings imposed, and (*b*) the method of imposing them. The learnings imposed should be

1. Those the genuine necessity of which is apparent to competent observers.
2. Those with which the maturing learner will eventually agree.
3. Kept to an absolute minimum.
4. Regarded as not final but as tentative and provisional.
5. Unlearnable at that time by any other methods.

Parents and teachers should be very sure also that the desired ends cannot be achieved by any other means than by imposing them.

Parents and teachers are prone to force any and all kinds of beliefs and habits on children. Too often, this is clearly done to save the adult inconvenience, not to educate the child. Impatience, egotism, desire for dominance, and ordinary ignorance account for much of this. Hence, that which is imposed lacks validity, a fact soon discovered by the growing child; and the natural result is distrust of anything proposed by an adult. Parents and teacher may be assured that in the majority of instances the behavior of children can be properly controlled without resort to arbitrary prescription.

The way in which learnings are imposed is even more important than their content. Desirable methods will:

1. Be those of social conditioning instead of those of dogmatic and abitrary demand.
2. Permit constant critical examination by the learner as he grows up.

3. Lead the learner as rapidly as possible to see that the belief or habit imposed is sensible and desirable.

Too many persons impose even desirable learnings dogmatically, closing the child's mind to that later critical examination which leads to rational acceptance. The child at each level of maturity should study within his limits the origin of individual and social requirements, the reasons for them, and how they evolved. Questions should be freely permitted and patiently answered. This keeps the learner's mind open so that later he may himself modify beliefs and procedures. Too often questions are ignored or arbitrarily silenced, explanations refused.

The error in much school learning, home training, and religious teaching lies just here. The child grows up and discovers that some of what he was told earlier is not true; that the convenience of others rather than his own good was being served; that vested interests were looking out for their welfare, not his. Parents and religious leaders are prone to blame "loss of faith" on higher education. They might well look to the early teaching of religion and ideals.

The development of many virtues so earnestly desired by teachers and parents, such as honesty, taking responsibility, persistence through difficult tasks, and truthfulness is actually prevented by the arbitrary methods used in attempting to demand or force acceptance of the virtues. Development of these desirable qualities is far more sure by giving children an opportunity to exercise them in real experiences. Parents and teachers may be very sure that they are on the wrong tack if they often find it necessary to insist on conformity and if they constantly say in response to questions, "You do this because I say so . . . ," ". . . because it is good for you," or "you'll see why when you grow up."

Occasional imposition on older learners. Many parents and teachers who agree with modern principles of learning through purposeful experience will still raise a question about some pupils and some learnings. They ask: Is it not possible to *force* a pupil to keep on with a thing which he does not like and for which he sees no reason, until he does develop not only liking but understanding and skill? It is unquestionably true that this does happen. Nearly everyone has had the experience or has seen it happen with pupils. Many pupils who "hated" art, or mathematics, or poetry writing, have become adept in those fields because they were *forced* by some teacher to stay with it until interest and ability developed. Teachers who believe in this method of forcing, however, overlook two very important points. First, for each pupil who actually does develop interest and ability as a result of arbitrary forcing, there are scores who develop instead a dislike, even a bitter hatred, for school, its methods, and learning. Many pupils have been driven from our high schools by these harsh methods. The evidence on this is clear-cut and voluminous. Teachers who believe in forcing interest must do so in the face of this serious detrimental result.

Second, the pupils who do develop interest and ability thereby prove that they had a latent ability for the field and a reason for doing the work. *The teacher who believes in forcing may be supplying excellent evidence of his own inability to teach such pupils.* Continued inability of the teacher to tap the reservoir of pupil ability and to connect the material with the life interests of the pupil may be the real reason for the arbitrary and harmful method of "making him like it."

The present writer hesitates even to suggest that forced attention is ever safe, because scores of lazy, incompetent, uninspired, unprofessional teachers use this as an excuse to force anything and everything on pupils. It is also an excuse for grossly incompetent procedures in the classroom, for continued refusal of teachers to apply intelligence and ingenuity to their problems, for continued refusal to study their pupils and to investigate causes of learning difficulty. To be fair, however, it is doubtless true that sometimes pupils will appear whom a competent teacher cannot reach under ordinary conditions. These will be rare. If the teacher is reasonably sure on the basis of tests or other evidences that the ability is present, is reasonably sure that interest will eventually develop, and most important, is sure that the developed interest is worthwhile for everyday living, he may risk the methods of forced attention.

We must beware particularly of the frequent testimony: "My! How I hated the piano lessons (or violin, or dancing, or cooking, or what not)! But my parents made me stick to it—and now I am very glad!!" Many of these cases are easily explained under the principles discussed above. Often, moreover, circumstances of adult life make renewal of skills sensible. In many, many instances, however, the testimony simply isn't true. Analysis of cases reveals any of several reasons for the false statement.

Summary on imposed learning. There will, then, be some imposition of knowledge and behavior patterns at various levels and in advance of experience and understanding. Parents and teachers must be sure, however, that the learning is necessary, and that the method of imposing it is reasonable. No damage is done if the learner can look back when he is older and agree that what was done was sensible and right. Damage comes from an uncompromising demand for conformity in things that do not matter.

Brief note on preparation in advance in the adult world itself. Incidentally, we may note that the adult world, which demands so vigorously that the school force preparation for the future upon children, does a notoriously bad job in preparing for its own future. Thousands of adults financially able to purchase life insurance, that is, to prepare for the future, do not voluntarily buy it. It must be sold to them. Scores die without having made a will—failing, ironically, to provide for the future of their children whom they insist the school must be sure to prepare! The structure of installment buying rests in part upon the inability of the adult to forego immediate pleasures and save for outright purchase. Adult society completely failed to plan for future urban developments, though the mounting problems were clear to experts, many of them even to the average citizen. City planning emerged when forced by the seriousness of some of the problems. Adult society has been utterly uninterested in planning to handle in advance the problems which were inevitable as we changed from an agrarian to an industrial order. Adult society has been criminally negligent in failing to plan for the future use of natural resources, for the population explosion, or preventing political and industrial breakdowns, for military protection. The German nation prepared far in advance for World War II. That nation held to that preparation for the *future* because of a—to them—burning purpose growing out of *present* conditions. The Allied Nations neglected preparation because they did not see the reasons—though competent observers did—and later were forced to prepare under serious handicap as a result.

Functional learning through experience is the method of democracy. Principles of learning, to be valid, not only must be based on a sound theory of knowledge and of the learning process, but must also square with the aims of the society which is to use them. An authoritarian society uses authoritarian methods of imposition and indoctrination, since a docile, loyal type of individual and an obedient society are desired. Many religious bodies utilize principles of learning designed to secure individuals who accept uncritically and unswervingly the desired creeds and attitudes. Many of the early Greek and Latin city-states used methods designed to produce critical and creative individuals. The very term *Socratic method* persists today. Some modern religious bodies use methods designed to produce individuals whose religious faith rests upon informed understanding rather than upon blind acceptance.

A democratic society is dynamic, experimental, emergent. The principles of democratic life have been presented often and ably in educational literature. The student should have had adequate detailed discussion in introductory courses preceding this one; an extended summary will not be repeated here. Democracy requires individuals worthy of respect, willing to take initiative and responsibility in co-operative group living. Respect for the individual will be accorded those who earn it through worthwhile contributions to common group activities. Democratic individuals need to plan and carry on projects co-operatively, to make decisions, to be tolerant of differing opinions. Individuals will avoid frustration and gain acceptance in the group by contributing each in terms of his interests, abilities, and maturity.

The method of functional learning through experience would seem clearly superior to study of the same assigned materials by all levels and types of individuals—superior to working toward standards imposed without regard to levels of growth or maturation.

DISCUSSION QUESTIONS FOR SECTION 3

1. Recall the analysis made by the class of the lettered statements about requiring Latin or Algebra (Page 42). Is there anything to add or subtract from what was said then?

2. Illustrate safe and desirable instances of learning imposed on young children; on adolescents; on adults. (Students often confuse imposition with legal requirements or restrictions on adults—stopping for traffic lights, signaling turns, penalties for stealing, for libel, and many others. If this comes up, have the group reason out why these are not impositions).

3. If you can observe or inquire when an adult says, "I-hated-the-lessons-but-am-glad-my-parents-forced-me-to-continue," try to determine whether the statement is made because "it is the thing to say," whether it is a truthful statement, or what factor in adult life changed his view.

4. Explain your understanding of the phrase "directional-process goal" used by Hopkins; the "lines of growth" as used by Mursell. Use specific illustrations. Ask for explanations if not clear, as this concept is basic.

5. Rugg and Shumaker say, on page 102: "The new school organizes itself around the child's intention to learn; the old school organized itself around the teacher's intention to teach him."

And on page 118: "The school must not only explore (the child's) interests, his capacities, his needs at any stage of his development; it must also focus its mind constantly upon the stages to come—indeed in the last analysis, upon the very end point in adult civilization."

   a. Show wherein these statements are in agreement with this section? In disagreement? In agreement or disagreement with Mursell?

   b. Make an organized list of implications for teaching. (As would be expected, the lists will differ depending upon the amount of experience in teaching.)

   c. What changes would need to be made in the administration of schools, in curriculum and method, or in any other aspect of the teaching-learning situation, if the ideas summarized here could be put in effect?

6. List several implications for the teacher derived from the discussion of deferred values. What differences might these implications make in your teaching?

4: THE IMPLICATIONS FOR TEACHING

Hopkins [22] cites the case of a college professor who was pleased because his son, though only in the primary grades, was already learning to spell. Some of his colleagues in the field of education pointed out that the boy was learning to spell words in fixed lists, predetermined and handed out for mastery. The professor replied that he was not concerned with the methods, the "fool theories" of educators. He wanted "results," and his

[22] L. Thomas Hopkins, *op. cit.,* p. 6.

son's perfect spelling papers showed that this school was getting them. Two years later the boy was failing about half the time in spelling and very heartily disliked spelling. Worse, he was failing also in reading, geography, and arithmetic. It took some time for the professor-father to see that the *methods* by which his son learned to spell had much to do with whether he would *continue to learn to spell*—and in fact whether he would *continue to learn other things as well.* The boy had been taught by methods which do not approximate the way in which correct spelling is acquired and used in real life. The words learned served no purpose other than to lead the learner on to another meaningless and useless list. Children taught spelling, reading, and arithmetic in situations where the knowledge or skill is necessary to meet some purpose of the learner, to solve some problem confronting him—that is, through a lifelike experience—will keep on learning and liking to learn. The value and use of the material is immediately apparent to the child. In the illustration above, the learning experience was not lifelike.

Parents are much disturbed these days because modern schools seem not to be teaching reading, writing, and arithmetic in the primary grades as adequately as "when I went to school." These same parents did not learn those things in the primary grades either—but they do not realize that! It is quite true that modern schools are delaying much formal arithmetic until later grades. Younger learners not only lack sufficient maturity (more of this in Chapter 7), but do not have a large enough *background of experience* to understand arithmetical abstractions. The modern school gives a large amount of experience with informal, functional arithmetic, the use of numbers in situations which are real to the child and understandable by him. It is quite true that primary pupils in modern schools do not make as high scores on standard tests in arithmetic as do pupils in traditional schools. But the tests are misleading. The high-scoring pupils often cannot apply the isolated skills they have mastered. Many inimical attitudes and incorrect habits of calculation are not revealed by the tests. Finally, and most important, learning memorized in isolation from real situations soon fades away. This latter fact is true on all levels. A study at Dartmouth [23] showed that many students who passed the college entrance board examinations successfully later proved quite unable to remain in college. These students had gone to famous preparatory schools which pride themselves in "getting their students through the college entrance examinations." Crammed for these examinations beyond their true learning capacity and ability, the students could "pass" the tests, but later indicated that functional learning had not taken place.

Children who learn arithmetic later, when mature enough and possessed of adequate experience, and who learn through lifelike experiences, soon surpass pupils in traditional schools. Even the skill of reading, thought by many parents and teachers to be the prime vehicle of much learning, cannot be acquired until there is a sufficient background of *experience!* Many parents and and teachers are fooled because primary children can say words, can "read" through a piece in the reader. Tests for comprehension show that the children do not understand the meaning of the words—hence they have not truly read. The parents of a small boy well below school entrance age said they had "taught" him to read. He could read from any book, the *Atlantic Monthly,* or the newspaper. The writer handed the boy a book printed in Spanish and one printed in French. The boy read these as easily as he did the English—and with the same degree

[23] E. T. Chamberlain, Jr., Report of a Four-Year Study of the Accomplishments at Dartmouth College of Students in the Class of 1940 from Public and Private Schools (mimeograph material, 1942). See also *Did They Succeed in College?* Vol. IV, *Adventure in American Education* (New York, Harper, 1943). Similar studies have appeared more recently in several colleges.

of comprehension! The parents learned the difference between reading and saying words. A supervisor once convinced a teacher that the glib "reading" of her first graders was not reading at all, by cutting the page in half and turning over the top half only. The pupils then read the story which went with the picture on the top half of the page. The words were not even in sight. The pupils had memorized the appropriate rigmarole to go with each picture and reproduced it on cue. Before reading can be meaningful, there must be a great deal of experience with things and processes. Again learning rests upon experience. From this experience the child acquires a store of meanings. He now learns easily the labels for these, namely, words. He can then translate words into meanings—he can read. *Reading, the very technique which so many think is a substitute for experience, is itself not possible until sufficient experience has been lived through.*

There is very much more to be said about the implications for teaching in the fact that learning rests upon experience. All the chapters in this volume are devoted to this. For the moment we will emphasize that a teacher's methods will be determined in part by his conception of the origin of knowledge— by his epistemology. His methods will be determined in part by his conception of learning and of the learner. Finally, his understanding of the nature and process of democracy will affect this practice of teaching.

Teachers who believe that knowledge is static, is predetermined, and is safely filed away in written sources, will assign segments of this organized knowledge to be learned, that is, to be memorized. These teachers will then quiz the pupils in oral recitation, and have them write papers from day to day to see if the material is well remembered. At the end of given segments, they will quiz on a grander scale in final examinations. These teachers overlook the fact, or do not know that this material assigned to immature

learners was compiled and organized by mature adult minds. [24]

Teachers who believe that knowledge arises from experience in the course of pursuing vital purposes will regard the older assign-study-recite-test procedure when used indiscriminately as a form of mumbo-jumbo. Teaching-learning situations for these teachers will be as much like real-life, purposeful activities as possible. Their pupils will participate in setting up situations, the answers to which the pupils will need and want. The goals recognized by the teachers will be growth in desirable understandings, attitudes, and abilities and not memorization of subject matter. The teacher knows these goals cannot be achieved quickly or in final form. He regards them as directional-process goals (see Chapter 6), which in simple language means goals which direct the process of learning and which are achieved at successive levels of maturity through the continued process of experiencing. These teachers will sometimes test and examine, to be sure, but they will chiefly be concerned with the appearance of the desired learnings in the behavior of the learners. They will make much use of behavior records, observation outlines, interviews, interest inventories, and so on. Even skills will be tested by applications rather than by standard tests, although standard and other tests may serve a diagnostic purpose.

Each group of teachers will be talking nonsense as far as the other group is concerned. Which group is right depends upon the validity of the epistemological, biological, and psychological research by scholars in those fields. Put simply, this means that those teaching procedures will be the sounder which more nearly approximate the procedures through which knowledge, ability, and

[24] In this connection, an interesting sentence occurs in Vera Sanford's *A Short History of Mathematics* (Boston, Houghton, 1930): "Euclid's work was more formal than are the elementary geometries of today. He was writing for mature thinkers who needed no introductory work to convince them of the value of the subject."

attitude actually come into being. Currently, knowledge is believed to emerge out of experience and the analysis of experience.

Each group also may fail to see that there are important outcomes to be gained from organized subject matter itself, on the proper level of maturity. The continuity and increasing complexity of methods of thinking, and of meanings within any specialized area, are vital outcomes. All experience cannot be direct. What are the implications of teaching in the fact that vicarious experience of different degrees is necessary? In general, pupils can learn adequately through vicarious experience (a) if they possess a wide background of direct experience related to the vicarious material, (b) if they possess a degree of mental maturity sufficient to handle abstractions, to apply generalizations, and to learn thereby, and (c) if the teaching techniques are based on awareness of the shortcomings of vicarious experience. The teacher, in framing these techniques, must take into account the necessity of pretesting or otherwise becoming aware of the learners' previous background, and must have wide knowledge of the general environment, the social and economic level from which the learners come. The teacher and the school will endeavor to supply as much realia as possible, to supplement gaps in background as rapidly as possible.

The more direct the experience, the greater number of pupils will profit, particularly in heterogeneous groups; the less direct the experience, the fewer will profit and the greater will be the diversity of levels of understanding. More direct methods need to be used with young children, dull children, less well-educated and less sophisticated persons; less direct methods may be used as maturity increases, with the brighter pupils, and with better educated individuals. In some instances, on upper levels and with certain types of learning, it may be that the more abstract methods are more valuable. The greater diversity of reaction will not merely reveal the individual differences among the learners, but will bring out many different contributions and original suggestions, many individual slants on the problem.

Many schools are still using traditional subject matter and following a theory of learning which advocates memorization of that subject matter. However, even in such situations learning will be improved by the effort to use the processes of experiential teaching and learning within the framework of the subject matter. Suggestions on this will be found in Chapter 13, after the implications of the two types of teaching have been more fully developed.

DISCUSSION QUESTIONS FOR SECTION 4

1. Report in detail any observed illustrations of functional teaching.
2. Report illustrations of experience techniques used with traditional subject matter.
3. Report in detail observed cases of "learning" without understanding.

GENERAL DISCUSSION QUESTIONS FOR THE CHAPTER

1. Dewey and his students have made wide use of the phrase, "Learning is the reorganization of experience."
   a. If you have met the phrase before, explain its meaning and relate it to the definition of learning in this chapter.
   b. If you have not met the phrase before, attempt to interpret it in common-sense terms and relate it to this chapter.
2. Psychologists agree that learning is a social process. What are the implications of this statement? Many college students disagree with the statement. Can you see why?
3. An advanced and interested student, preferably one majoring in English, may present a review and comment upon Ch. 11, "Language and Meaning," of the Forty-first Yearbook, Part II, of the National Society for the Study of Education. In small, well-prepared classes this chapter may be read as a basis for a class analysis.
4. Work out a small observation outline based on the content of this chapter. Observe a number of teachers and note the extent to which they use:
   a. Direct and vicarious experience by levels.

b. Vicarious methods when direct methods would be possible.

c. Techniques designed to make verbal methods safe.

5. What major ideas in this chapter (new to you or clarified for you) seem to you to be of major importance in aiding you to guide learning?

READINGS

The only extensive discussion is that of Hopkins. One or two others have good brief summaries. Many books contain only passing references. This is regrettable since the topic is basic.

CRONBACH, Lee J., *Educational Psychology* (New York, Harcourt, Brace & World, 1954), pp. 8-13, 56, 300-302, 348, 47-49.

DEWEY, John, *Experience and Education* (New York, Macmillan, 1938), Ch. 1 and pp. 44-52. (Valuable with following chapter also.)

HILDRETH, Gertrude, *Child Growth Through Education* (New York, Ronald, 1948), Chs. 2, 5, 6.

HOPKINS, L. Thomas, *Interaction* (Boston, Heath, 1941). An older book but still the best treatment.

Pages 41-49, 80-82. Excellent on differentiating the subject from the experience curriculum, plus historical background for each.

Pages 207-209. Simple definition and explanation of experience.

Pages 344-347. Excellent statement on preparation in advance of understanding; on deferred values.

Pages 172-205; Ch. 5, "How Does Philosophy Affect the Curriculum?" Vivid, concrete statement.

Index. Use for references on flexibility of curriculum and beliefs.

LEE, J. Murray, and LEE, Dorris M., *The Child and his Curriculum* (New York, Appleton-Century-Crofts, 1960). Use Index.

———, *The Child and His Development* (New York, Appleton-Century-Crofts, 1958). Use Index.

MACOMBER, G. G., *Principles of Teaching in the Elementary School* (New York, American Book, 1954). Use Index.

MOSSMAN, Lois C., *The Activity Concept* (New York, Macmillan, 1938), Ch. 9, pp. 157-175, and the Appendix, pp. 177-184. An older book but the only one with a first-class account of the development of the activity concept, hence of extension of range of experiencing in learning.

MURSELL, James L., *Developmental Teaching* (New York, McGraw, 1949), Ch. 1.

RUGG, Harold O., and SHUMAKER, Ann, *The Child-Centered School* (Yonkers, N. Y., World Book, 1928), pp. 5, 40-49, 58-59, 62, 96, 102-103, 118, 256, 310, 313.

WHEELER, Raymond H., and PERKINS, Francis T., *Principles of Mental Development* (New York, Crowell, 1932). The original statement of the organismic position in relation to learning. Interesting but subject to misinterpretation by the superficial reader.

CHAPTER 4: The Characteristics of Educative Experience

The illustrations of learning in the first chapter and in the appendix reveal certain desirable characteristics. They were (*a*) unified around a purpose real to the learners, (*b*) continuous with the on-going life of the learners, (*c*) interactive with the environment of the learners, and (*d*) contributory to the integration of the learner.

The class which dramatized *The Emperor Jones* was influenced toward the project by various factors. The high school class studying United States history differs in that the purpose did not emerge naturally out of everyday activities of the learners' since the stage was set by the teacher. The teacher ingeniously related the subject matter to everyday interests and problems. When pupils see such connections and accept the purpose, then continuity, interaction, and integration are possible and very probable. This is wholly legitimate, and the ability to make such connections is a marked asset of competent teachers.

The purpose in these and other cases was real to the learner. The projects or assignments were clearly continuous with their everyday experience, and conducive to desirable learnings. Extensive interaction with the environment was necessary. Functional learnings were being achieved and integrated.

The evidence supporting these characteristics of educative experience. How do we know that these are in fact the characteristics of learning experiences? First, the similarity between these and natural-life activities was briefly summarized in the latter part of Chapter 1. Second, further evidence will be presented in Chapter 7 where we discuss the nature of the learner. Third, various chapters will contain reference to individual studies and to summaries of research which supply evidence that the type of learning experience here described is superior to the more formal, imposed, assigned, discontinuous experiences involving limited, formal interaction with a limited, academic environment.

The development of this chapter will not be interrupted to summarize the evidences available as indicated above. One very important point, however, does need to be clarified before proceeding: namely, the difference between educative and miseducative experiences. Obviously, purposeful, continuous, interactive, and integrating experiences can have detrimental as well as beneficial results.

The outcomes of learning experiences must be socially desirable. Everything one does is experiencing. All living is experiencing. Everything one does produces learning willy-nilly. But not all learnings may be desirable. Learning experiences may be educative or miseducative. Specifically, purposeful, continuous, interactive, and integrating experiences can produce better burglars as well as better bishops. More ardent totalitarians can be produced as easily as more devoted believers in democracy. How then do we discriminate between experiences which are likely to be educative and those likely to be miseducative?

We tend to say immediately that making better burglars, more skillful looters of the public treasury, and more adept exploiters of the public represents an undesirable type of learning, growth, education. Why? This query leads directly to the ultimate aim of education, hence to the end point of learning experiences. Each civilization has a cultural tradition. Each civilization sets up an ideal individual and an ideal society as its goals. We have accepted the democratic individual in a democratic society as the goal toward which education will contribute. The democratic individual is one worthy of respect, who realizes his unique personality within a co-operative society which holds the common good to be paramount. The worth of an individual is determined in part by his contribution to the common co-operative effort toward a better society. Desirable learning experiences are those which in the long run tend to encourage growth toward accepted democratic understandings, attitudes, and abilities. (More on this in Chapter 6 on Goals.)

1: EDUCATIVE EXPERIENCE IS UNIFIED AROUND THE PURPOSE OF THE LEARNER.

Critics of modern education have long said that modern or progressive education "lets the pupil do what he wants to do." This unfounded criticism represents not merely a popular error but indicates also fundamental ignorance or misunderstanding of a basic principle of life and learning. Activity does not take place without some need. Learning does not take place without interest of some sort in the process and outcome. Many older teachers argue about pupil interest. Some say they will not cater to the interests of

pupils. Such teachers completely miss the point. The problem is not whether children are to learn with interest or without it. They *never* learn without it. The real problem is to determine what kind of interest it shall be and from what it shall be derived. *No competent and responsible educational leader has ever said anywhere at any time that the pupil is to do what he wants to do.* It has been said, however, that the pupil should "want what he does," if he is to learn.

Purpose is not to be confused with impulse. The critics quoted above have fallen into their error through failure to distinguish among impulse, desire, wish, and a purpose. The first three are often fleeting, capricious, superficial. Even when they are not, they are but the initial phases in the development of a purpose. *A purpose, in contrast, is a consciously selected goal.* A purpose is selected with knowledge of the possibility of fulfilling it, with knowledge of the requirements for fulfilling it, and with knowledge of the probable consequences of failure. Postponement of overt action until judgment of possibilities and consequences has been made is necessary to transform an impulse into a purpose.

The pursuit of fleeting, capricious impulses is not only not educative; it is likely to be definitely miseducative. *To go through the careful process of defining a purpose, of observing the conditions which will affect fulfillment, of weighing consequences, not only leads to educative activity but is in itself one of the most important series of educative activities.*

Purposes emerge out of activity initiated by need for adjustment. Purpose does not initiate experience, nor does purpose necessarily emerge early in an activity. The initiating and sustaining cause of experience, according to biologists and psychologists, is some sort of strain, stress, or tension in the organism. Something is amiss or awry. A balanced, comfortable, complacent situation is disturbed either through a change in existing relationships, an interruption or interference from outside, or the emergence of a new factor. The terms *strain, stress,* or *tension* should not dismay the beginning student. These words are used technically here. In common-sense terms they merely mean that individuals need to take action of some sort in order to restore the normal, desired state of comfortable equilibrium.

The concepts here are difficult for students meeting them for the first time; hence further explanation is given. On the *physical* level, the tension or stress may be called a loss of physical equilibrium. Consider for a moment a stone resting on a hillside. It is in equilibrium. No action takes place. Rain eventually washes away enough dirt so that the stone becomes physically unbalanced; it is out of equilibrium. It then rolls downhill to a new base. Equilibrium has been reestablished. Now, the stone, being an inanimate object, does not have needs or purposes and does not take action consciously. Figurative language, however, and some admitted oversimplification will greatly aid the student in seeing the fundamental point here. We may say the stone was "uncomfortable"; it "needed" to roll downhill; hence, it "took action," "had the experience" of rolling downhill for the "purpose" of restoring equilibrium. This metaphorical and oversimplified statement is as clear a statement of the initiation of purposeful activity as is possible. Naturally the situation on the human level is much more complex, as we shall see shortly. We may get ahead of the story, however, to point out that ideal learning situations arise when the pupil is placed in a situation where *he* needs to take action of some sort to find out something *he* needs to know or to acquire some skill *he* needs and *sees* that he needs. The traditional school too often demands that the pupil take action for purposes *someone else* sees, but not the pupil. This is rolling uphill!

On the *animal* level, tension results from some need for adjustment, physical or biological. The animal needs something to maintain life. Activity results. He does something about it. He may seek food, grow a heavier coat, migrate, hibernate, or fight. He has experiences resulting from adjustment, need, or tension. Through these he learns many things useful to him then and later.

On the *human* level, tension results from loss of mental as well as physical equilibrium. Situations arise in which the comfortable state of the organism is disturbed. The individual may or may not know what is the matter. He is vaguely disturbed, is uneasy, wishes he knew what to do. He really needs to find out something, to achieve some attitude, to acquire some skill; but he does not know this yet.

The individual may or may not develop a purpose out of a given tension. He may ignore the stress and dismiss it. He may meet it through routine activity and accept an inadequate solution. He may take action guided by uncritically accepted wishes, desires, and impulses. But he may be dissatisfied with incomplete disposal of the tension. The routine or uncritical activities designed to meet it may be deflected or obstructed. The experience and the activities now become matters of conscious concern. The individual, like the stone, needs to take further action. He needs further experience. [1]

The individual "determines to do something about this." When he arrives at the stage of consciously determining to do something about it, a purpose is emerging out of the initial confusion of feeling and activity.

[1] The writer is greatly indebted to Dr. John P. Wynne, who contributed to the paragraphs here through conferences, letters, and through his pamphlet, *The Educative Experience* (Farmville, Va., Farmville Herald Press, 1940), which is probably the best available statement in print. Wynne coined the term *principle of experience need* to designate the beginnings of learning experience on the human level.

Considerable fruitless argument has developed over the pupil purpose, need, or needs approach which we will analyze in Chapter 6 on Aim. We are here concerned with pupil need or purpose as an inescapable factor in a dynamic learning situation. The development of a total curriculum needs more than immediate needs, as we have already hinted on page 54.

It requires further definition, analysis, and evaluation. The preliminary impulses must be criticized, reviewed in imagination, and the consequences must be judged. A desirable line of action must be deliberately selected from several choices. Further planning then continues. *All educational activities, whether they be called units, enterprises, undertakings, assignments, or what not, should be such that the individual finds a purpose in them.* The purpose selected then is the motive drive for continued action. A purpose can come only from the individual himself; however, activities in which he may find purposes may be suggested and initiated by any factor in his environment. The teacher very often, perhaps typically, proposes activities out of which the pupil under guidance may construct purposes. The details of initiating learning activities are treated in the chapters on the unit and the assignment.

Again we turn to the illustrations in Chapter 1 and the Appendix. In all cases the students came to school in a comfortable frame of mind. They were at peace with the world. The school environment set up or suggested new goals, offered prestige for certain achievements. The students could have gone about their business undisturbed by these factors. They were, however, dissatisfied, out of equilibrium, under mild tension. A need to do something about the situation was present. Students thought about the situation. Some perhaps (as testimony in *The Emperor Jones* project showed) tried various activities to avoid the project and restore security. Some were induced by classmates to try the activity. Eventually the classes chose to go ahead. A purpose had emerged, leading to a series of continuous, interactive activities.

The Appendix contains several lessons which further illustrate these points. The children who learned about health protection were interrupted by various happenings —vaccinations, health examinations, and the like. These differed from the normal routine activities. The tension here was probably a pleasant one. They asked questions: Why does the doctor do this? How does vaccination keep us from getting sick? Out of these random inquiries, the teacher skillfully brought forth a purpose which the children seized upon and accepted. In the class which designed the scenery and costumes for the musical comedy, the purpose arose almost immediately out of the normal activities of initiating a course in design. The first-graders, who studied community helpers, were first attracted by puzzlement over who could have cared for their plants during the vacation. To them this was an odd variation of normal routines with which they were familiar. Their mental equilibrium was thoroughly disturbed, as is the case with little children. Again the tension here was probably a pleasant and interesting one. A welter of questions and suggestions arose. The teacher skillfully seized those which led to a purpose acceptable to the children, and they made plans that resulted in learning experiences.

To repeat, learning experiences are best initiated by seizing upon purposes which all pupils have, or by setting the stage so that desirable purposes emerge.

The elements in purpose. Purposes, as has been said, may be suggested by any aspect of the environment: teacher, physical facilities, social or intellectual relationships, or what not. The purpose can come only from the learner, however. In order to learn he must set up or wholly accept a purpose, plan for its accomplishment, and later decide whether or not his efforts to satisfy the purpose have been successful. This is very different from the all-too-common school situation wherein the teacher sets (assigns) the purpose and demands that the pupil fulfill it. Not only may the purpose be meaningless to the student but, what is much worse, in some cases he can see no relationship between the purpose and the activities demanded for its fulfillment. Finally, the pupil often cannot judge whether he has succeeded or not until he receives the arbitrary decision of the one who set the task and now sits in judgment on the results. *The pupil is thus robbed of nearly all the important benefits of a learning situation.*

The setting and achievement of educative purposes would seem to demand the following:

1. A careful analysis of the situation in which the purpose is to be fulfilled.
   a. Observation of the persons and materials with which interaction will take place.
   b. Recall of any previous experiences which might bear on the present one.
   c. Judgment as to the possible consequences of any contemplated action within the given situation.
2. A plan of action through which the purpose is to be achieved. (This is tentative and provisional. Planning continues as the experience develops.)
3. A series of evaluations constantly underway.
   a. To determine, as the plan develops, whether the activities and materials are well chosen.
   b. To determine to what extent the purpose has been successfully achieved.

Observation is necessary, because putting a purpose into effect necessitates interaction with persons and things in the environment. It is only common sense to take stock of the assets and liabilities within the situation before embarking upon an activity. Search of one's own store of knowledge is again only common sense. Clues and other aids will arise through recall of earlier experiences, direct or vicarious. Many errors and false starts can thus be avoided. Judgment of consequences is equally a matter of ordinary intelligence.

Given the foregoing, one may then plan intelligently what to do to achieve the purpose, thus dissipating the tension out of which the purpose arose. Self-evaluation of one's own purposes and procedures is an inescapable part of setting and achieving purposes. Otherwise the individual will not learn how to adjust purpose to material and to personal strengths or weaknesses. The ability to judge one's undertakings is an important ability for life. The modern school, far from being unorganized, is far superior to the traditional school in giving pupils experience in defining purposes, in organizing experiences for their satisfaction, and in evaluating their success. All this is a far cry from "allowing pupils to do as they please." These factors are matters of conscious concern (see Chapters 12 and 14) to teachers who wish to guide pupils into desirable learning situations.

The relation between purpose and "motivation." One question asked by all teachers in training (and by many with experience) is "How do you motivate pupils to study, to work, to *learn?*" Experienced teachers often ask "How can you get lazy and indifferent or defiant pupils to study and learn?" Motivating is a real problem to all who guide children and youth, to all who presume to leadership among adults. The basic general answer should be apparent from the preceding pages. Children ordinarily are not motivated to *learn anything;* they are, rather, motivated to relieve tension, to remove any disturbing condition or problem, to restore the pleasantness and security of equilibrium. *In doing this they learn many things.*

When asking about motivation, many earnest but naïve teachers seem to be seeking a technique, a stunt, a bag of tricks which will motivate. We can give teachers considerable help with motivation, but first we must emphasize that there is no known formula, or bag of tricks, or set of devices which will motivate pupils.

Individuals are motivated by purposes and goals which make sense to those individuals; which restore the natural equilibrium of the individual. Motivating then becomes the subtle task of seizing upon natural purposes already existing within the on-going activities of the learners, or of setting the stage, manipulating the environment so that purposes meaningful to the learners are brought to light. Many school subjects, assignments, and settings for learning do not motivate because they do not disturb the equilibrium or security of the learner. They contain nothing he wants to know, nothing he can see use for, hence he does not care and will not work. Subjects and assignments can be made meaningful by skillful teaching.

To provide motivation the teacher must study and know his individual pupils and the groups as such. [2] Effective motivation is geared to the interests, activities, and maturities of the learners. Ease of motivation by the teacher is directly related to his knowledge of the learner's characteristics and to his ingenuity in making connection between them and the desired learning experiences.

Intrinsic and extrinsic motivation. Intrinsic motivation has just been discussed, but we will illustrate briefly. Intrinsic motivations are inherent in the learning situation and meet pupil needs and purposes. The desire to achieve certain skills useful in solving life problems; to acquire information and understanding; to develop attitudes making for successful, enjoyable life; to secure recognition of our contribution to group effort; to secure acceptance by others of one's willingness—all these are real and sound motivations. Recognition of one's own progress, increasing insight into the problem being solved, into the skill being mastered, affect effort favorably.

The pupil's growing ability to understand his fellows, to contribute to discussion, increasingly to recognize merit in art or music, and literally thousands of similar learning outcomes are recognized as motives by pupils living in a functional learning situation. These pupils do not need extrinsic motivation. Here learning and the reward are the same. As Emerson said, "The reward of a thing well done is to have done it." Skeptics

[2] Chapter 10 summarizes techniques for studying individuals.

may say that pupils will not work for these rewards. On the contrary, no rewards are as effective, provided the teacher and pupils have developed a learning situation that will contribute directly to solution of problems which are real to the learner.

Extrinsic motivation necessary as schools are now constituted. Extrinsic motivation resides in some factor outside the learning situation. The commonest forms are marks, credits, diplomas, degrees, prizes, medals, and membership in honor societies. Rivalry and competition are used. The teacher's personality, desire for his approval, and liking for the teacher will be found. Negative extrinsic motives are sarcasm, ridicule, and punishment each of which is ineffective and detrimental.

Teachers may be seen standing with grade book in hand, marking every recitation, every lapse from attention, every piece of disorder. It is difficult to imagine a practice more inimical to education or to the mental hygiene of all concerned. The teachers have on their hands groups of pupils who have undergone years of conditioning in school systems operating with archaic curriculums under incompetent teaching procedures. Pupils have to be policed and bullied because (a) previous schooling has reduced them to that status in relation to learning, and (b) required subjects have been forced upon learners who have no interest, aptitude, or use for those subjects. Parents are often to blame for the latter, but teachers should not condone the practice without protest. The improvement of curriculums and of methods is a school-wide responsibility, and the teacher should speak up or seek employment in better systems.

The general principles of motivation. Scores of experimental investigations are available, dealing with one or another aspect of motivation. The number of studies is so large that a sampling is useless. Summaries are available, furthermore, to which the student is referred. These were noted in Chapter 2: Hilgard; Thorpe and Schmuller; McConnel; Mowrer.

1. A motivated learner learns more readily than one who is not motivated. Motives may be general or specific, intrinsic or extrinsic.

2. Motivations which are too intense (especially pain, fear, anxiety) may be accompanied by distracting emotional states and by undesirable learning products.

3. Excessive motivation may be less effective than moderate motivation, especially for certain kinds of tasks.

4. Learning under intrinsic motivation is preferable to learning under extrinsic motivation.

5. Purposes and goals which make sense to a learner, which meet a need, which restore the natural equilibrium of the learner, are effective.

6. Purposes and goals should be geared to the interests, activities, and maturities of the learners.

7. Adjustment by the learner of his levels of aspiration to possible achievements or goals is a valuable stimulus to further learning.

8. Extrinsic motivations operate as follows. [3]
   a. Motivation by reward is generally preferable to motivation by punishment; motivation by success, preferable to motivation by failure. Marks, rewards, punishments operate as follows:
      (1) Marks, rewards, and punishments not functionally related to the learning situation will beget learning, but it is learning soon lost and accompanied by detrimental concomitant learnings.
      (2) The more closely the mark, reward, or punishment used as motive is a natural outcome of the learning process, the better effect it has. Learning is stimulated and undesirable concomitants are at a minimum.
      (3) The more clearly the learner sees that the mark, reward, or punishment is an inherent aspect of the learning situation, not artificial

and imposed, the better the learning which results.
   b. Social motives of competition and rivalry operate as follows:
      (1) Routine skills and factual information are readily acquired under these motives without immediate detrimental results.
      (2) Certain conversational skills and more general types of thinking may be encouraged but may have detrimental concomitants.
      (3) Creative work—imaginative work generally—is not affected favorably.
      (4) Individual mental hygiene and social welfare generally can suffer severely under motives of rivalry and competition. Unhappiness, frustration, and cheating may result with the individual; exploitation, social injustice, and waste may result with the group.
   c. The newer social motives of co-operation, recognition by one's fellows, opportunity for participation in planning and decision-making, seem to have very beneficial effects upon immediate and later learning. (A considerable revolution in human thinking concerning competition and co-operation, both in world affairs and in individual concerns, is underway. Data are appearing from time to time which should be noted.)
   d. Commendation and praise for work well done are excellent incentives. Indiscriminate or undeserved praise has a detrimental effect. Praise is better than condemnation, but the latter is preferable to ignoring the learner's efforts.
   e. Goals and levels of aspiration set by the learner's family or social class may be effective, but may also have serious ill effects.
   f. Liking for the teacher seems to be a safe incentive with very young learners. With older learners liking must be combined with respect. The teacher's personality should be used sparingly as an incentive, since this type of motivation can invite detrimental concomitants.
   g. Sarcasm and ridicule secure only the most undesirable and detrimental learning outcomes. (Continued use of sar-

[3] Learning theorists differ considerably among themselves on these points. The summary here is an effort to give such guidance as is possible lacking a final systematic theory.

casm can only result from stupidity on the part of the teacher, or as an outlet for a frustrated personality.)

9. Learning without purpose and learning to do difficult, unpleasant, distasteful tasks under compulsion and coercion does not train the learner to persist with unpleasant learnings in real life. This does not mean that difficulty is to be eliminated from learning experience. Learners will persist through serious difficulties if the objective is deemed worthwhile. That is, learning under purpose is the best guarantee of persistence in learning to overcome difficulties.

10. The maintenance of interest (or motivation) is important in learning. This can be done by several means, of which the following are illustrations:

 a. Use a variety of learning activities or experiences.
 b. Adapt closely to individual differences, especially in group work.
 c. Make use of success and recognition by the group.
 d. Adapt to levels of maturity and experimental background.
 e. As the teacher, manifest sincere enthusiasm.
 f. Take stock and replan from time to time.

Discussions of specific classroom techniques under principle are useful. As noted earlier there are no stunts or tricks which will motivate. Accounts of actual procedures in class are, however, very useful, particularly to beginning students. One or more of the following references, or other similar ones, may be read here.

CRONBACH, Lee J., *Educational Psychology* (New York, Harcourt, Brace & World, 1954). Good statements. Use Index.

LEE, J. Murray, and LEE, Dorris M. *The Child and His Development* (New York, Appleton-Century-Crofts, 1958). Chapter 12, unusually good.

STEPHENS, J. M., *Educational Psychology*, rev. ed. (New York, Holt, Rinehart & Winston, 1956). Good. Use Index.

THOMPSON, George G., GARDNER, Eric F., and DI VESTA, Francis J., *Educational Psychology* (New York, Appleton-Century-Crofts, 1959). Many very good discussions. Use Index.

Other similar volumes can be found.

Further commentary on selected principles. Widespread interest on some points, together with misunderstanding and error on others warrants some explanation.

1. *Reward and punishment.* Both of these were prominent in the early writings of Thorndike, though later they fell into disrepute, particularly punishment. Modern research indicates that punishment under certain circumstances and administered with due regard to all elements in the situation has some value. Indiscriminate use is accompanied by bad results. The untrained, practical teacher is particularly likely to make mistakes here. He sees that marks and punishment "get results." He does not see that these results are often ephemeral and eventually useless. Worse, he does not see certain results which do not come out in the open at the time.

2. *Competition, rivalry, co-operation, as motives.* Competition and rivalry have been used for centuries as motives in school and elsewhere. Effort unquestionably results. Some learnings, which are for individual rather than co-operative use—for example, arithmetic or spelling—seem to be acquired with few or no detrimental concomitants. Competition with one's own record seems to be desirable. In recent years, however, two very grave questions have arisen. Is individual mental hygiene promoted by emphasis upon rivalry and competition? Is social welfare promoted by these motives?

Many persons are convinced that competition is the rule of life: the survival of the fittest. This may have been true under simpler biological conditions in the animal world and under a condition of scarcity of economic goods. A co-operative world is just as natural and feasible under humane ideals, civilized conceptions of biological factors, and an economy of abundance. Competition is no more inherent and inevitable than co-operation. It is significant that in the business world, with its ancient slogan "competition is the life of trade," the chief aim of some powerful business leaders is to eliminate competition and achieve monopoly.

We may digress briefly to note the profound revolution now taking place in human thinking concerning competition and co-operation. The concept of a ruthlessly competitive world developed during the first part of the nineteenth century, based on the writings of Malthus, Darwin, and Thomas Huxley. Phrases from these men were eagerly seized upon: "struggle for existence," "survival of the fittest by natural selection," "the strong survive, the weak go to the wall." Here was a biological, hence a natural, law as basis for competition between men, communities, and nations, for ruthless exploitation of inferior, "weaker" classes and races. Political chauvinism and the newly born industrialism blossomed into systems with no scruples against the wasteful exploitation of natural resources or the cruel exploitation of children and adults.

Competition as the law of life became firmly established as a belief and a practice, justified as a biologic law of nature. We now know that this was an inadequate, incorrect interpretation both of the writings of early biologists and of the facts themselves. Huxley, who first supported the ruthless competitive view, later spoke strongly for the balanced view that co-operation is as natural as competition. He saw the necessity for ethical restraint of unbridled competition. Kropotkin lectured vigorously in opposition to Huxley's first views. Darwin himself repudiated the narrow interpretation of his biological findings and wrote *The Descent of Man* as a corrective to the one-sided interpretations of his *Origin of Species*. English and American sociologists, and later biologists, joined the effort to correct the misconception. Co-operation, mutual assistance, and ethical restraint are not only as "natural" as competition but are necessary if the

fanatical type of individualism is not to destroy civilization. The benefits of competition, properly operated, are apparent to everyone. The benefits and absolute necessity of co-operation must be realized and quickly if we are to avoid serious evil. The proponents of the ruggedly individualistic competitive life make a serious error in harping constantly on the achievements and benefits of this system while neglecting the serious evils which also attend it. This is more than a matter of application to the classroom or to community affairs; it is a cosmic matter and might involve survival. The totalitarian enemies of our system pay no attention to and refuse to discuss its benefits and achievements. Their appeal is based squarely on our weaknesses and abuses. The correction of these is one of our most important tasks.

All this may seem a far cry from the use of competition as a motive in the second grade. Not at all. Basic concepts and patterns of behavior which are to operate all through life are involved. The old slogan and practice, "every man for himself and devil take the hindmost," may be replaced by the firm belief, "co-operate or die."

Psychologists and psychiatrists are deriving increasingly important bodies of data showing the definitely detrimental effects of competition. Genuine unhappiness, frustration, cheating, and worse seem inevitable. Sociologists and political scientists, and some economists, are increasingly of the opinion that many social problems in the community and in international relations are seriously aggravated by the competitive point of view. Co-operative and common group effort are as necessary in the world as competition, particularly if we are to have reasonable peace and stability. Both serve useful purposes, each in its place. Again we have a vital relationship between classroom teaching and the larger affairs of public policy.

The time is not long past when anyone who even whispered that competition might not be the basis of all good in the universe would be labeled un-American or subversive, if not in fact contumacious toward God's Holy Ordinance. Today only a minority of industrialists and politicians are unaware of the shaping events and fateful changes in our social order. The literature on competition-co-operation is so large that one is at a loss to suggest a minimum list. Excellent books are available by anthropologists, economists, political scientists, sociologists, and others. Students at this stage probably do not need extensive reading. The situation does, however, point up the importance of including anthropology in teacher education.

Here are a few older references before and at the time of Darwin's first book:

DARWIN, Charles, *The Origin of Species; The Descent of Man* (any of several editions).

DRUMMOND, Henry, *The Ascent of Man*. Published in 1894 in opposition to the extreme individualistic view.

HUXLEY, Thomas H., "The Struggle for Existence and Its Bearing on Man," *Nineteenth Century* (February, 1888).

KROPOTKIN, Petr, *Mutual Aid as a Factor in Evolution*. Published as a book in 1902, containing the lectures in answer to Huxley's first position and delivered from 1890 to 1896.

———, *Ethics* (New York, Dial, 1924). Ashley Montague believes this book marked the turning point leading to the present emphasis on co-operation.

MALTHUS, Thomas R., *Essay on Population* (any edition).

The more recent books go far beyond the early ones based on biology and anthropology, to include political, economic, and social problems.

HAYS, H. R., *From Ape to Angel* (New York, Knopf, 1960), pp. 298-301 (religious emphasis), 364-367, 397.

MEAD, Margaret, ed., *Co-operation and Competition among Primitive Peoples* (New York, McGraw, 1937).

MONTAGUE, Ashley, *On Being Human* (New York, Henry Schuman, 1950). A tiny but powerful and moving book. Instructors and students may read at one sitting for quick summary of the present status of the analysis of co-operation and competition.

SAYERS, E. V., and MADDEN, Ward, *Education and the Democratic Faith* (New York, Appleton-Century-Crofts, 1959). The most extensive current summary. Gives the individualistic position in detail as well as the co-operative.

Extensive bibliographies are included in Hays and in Sayers and Madden. Volumes by Allport, Boas, Linton, Parsons, Kluckhohn, Burkheim, and others are of interest and value.

The chief meddlers here are those parents and some teachers who say that children must be subjected to severe competition in school, particularly in marking, because competition is the law of life and children must get used to it. This group overlooks the fact that in life competition is not between individuals and groups of utterly unlike abilities, interests, and goals. The evil effects of enforced competition where it does not belong are attested by unlimited data gathered by psychologists, psychiatrists, counselors of various types. There is ample room for proper competition without making it universal. It is not so in life.

3. *Maintenance of interest is an important factor.* Initial impetus is given to units or to assignments of respectable size by purposes originated or accepted by the pupil. Everyone knows, however, that interest flags, enthusiasm fluctuates, and periods of effort alternate with periods of indifference. A boy's purpose to become an engineer will motivate him to persist in high school and to persist through a series of mathematics courses. This will not motivate him, however, for all individual lessons, nor for all parts of these courses. Teachers know that it is necessary to keep remotivating to renew interest from time to time. The traditional school too often did this by threats, punishments, and sarcasm at worst; by marks, rewards, and honors at best. These latter must sometimes be used, but it is better to seek

positive, intrinsic, subsidiary motives, as indicated in No. 10 above.

A direct challenge to the teacher. The clear implications are that the requirements for teacher training should be progressively and seriously stiffened. Good teachers should be employed and charged with the responsibility for securing functioning learning outcomes. The following quotation develops admirably some of the more specific teaching implications: [4]

Instead of requiring the pupils to take a course such as English or mathematics, it would seem much more reasonable to employ good teachers and to put the requirement upon the teacher. Suppose, for example, that an English teacher were employed and informed that every student in the school, or at least a very large percentage of the students, was expected to show definite improvement in English during the course of a school year, but that no pupil would be required to register in an organized English course. Under these conditions the teacher would be very much concerned with discovering and using those purposeful activities of high school students that require good usage of English for their attainment. If a good teacher were expected to follow such a program and if good usage of English is important, one should expect good results, and at the same time many of the undesirable features of required courses in English would be avoided. Such a program would inevitably lead to rather drastic revision of the course of study in all of the required subjects. It would quickly become apparent that some things now included in courses have no real function in promoting satisfactory living while other things are very important. If a school should adopt a plan in which requirements, grades, honor societies, and the like, were either dispensed with entirely or minimized, it would become necessary for teachers and administrators to be much more concerned about the real values of school subjects. It would probably be impossible to induce students to learn some of the things now included in a course of study, and rather drastic revision of the entire curriculum would take place. Such revision would, however, be in the direction of eliminating really useless material and adding material that has functional value.

Learning without purpose: Learning to do difficult, disagreeable, distasteful tasks in life. A fantasy of the human mind, the persistence of which is equaled only by its absurdity, holds that children must be forced to perform difficult, disagreeable tasks whether they like it or not, as preparation for similar situations in real life. This belief is contrary to simple logic and is flatly contradicted by large amounts of factual data in various fields. Nevertheless, few fallacies in the fields of child-rearing and teaching are as persistent as this.

The following statement and question were made in a teachers' discussion group:

It is necessary in life to do, from time to time, disagreeable and distasteful tasks. Furthermore, the individual has to do them whether he likes it or not. As a preparation for life, pupils in schools should be made to do many things which are difficult, distasteful, and unpleasant. If the pupils do not like it, they should be made to do these things anyway, because only thus can they be prepared for the doing of what must be done when earning one's living and meeting the harsh realities of life. The modern school which allows the pupil to do what he pleases does not prepare for life. Is this not true?

Other statements often heard are:

I make my pupils learn what is good for them whether they like it or not.
Pupils in school better make up their minds to learn—and like it.
I will not tolerate any nonsense. If you don't like doing these things, all the better. It will prepare you for life.
Out in the world individuals aren't asked what they will do. They are told. They take orders and like it or they get fired.

Widely accepted as these beliefs are, they are silly. Unfortunately, these beliefs are often used by lazy and indifferent teachers to cover up their own inability to teach without coercion. Even worse, the beliefs are

[4] Robert W. Frederick, Clarence E. Ragsdale, and Rachel Salisbury, *Directing Learning* (New York, Appleton, 1938), p. 65.

used by some frustrated and insecure individuals as an excuse for the bullying and domineering which salves their own feeling of inferiority.

They are often held, however, in all honesty and sincerity because of ignorance of the nature of the individual, of the nature of learning, of the nature of purpose. This can be remedied.

Discussion will be extended here somewhat because of the widespread misconceptions and for the sake of disseminating information.

Certain misconceptions support the error. The ancient misconception that individuals are by nature weak, perverse, or actually evil, persists. This is one of the less desirable legacies of our Puritan tradition. Harsh discipline and coercion are believed necessary to transform bad children into good children with sufficient moral fiber to do difficult and distasteful things. Actually, there is ample evidence from child study, from analyses of juvenile delinquency, from analyses of elimination of pupils from school, to show that most of the bad conduct, delinquency, poor learning, and refusal to stay in school resulted not from the nature of childhood but directly from the coercive education. The huge body of data available can be found by anyone who knows how to use a library.

The nature of learning and of purpose has already been presented in this and the preceding chapter. Utilizing pupil purpose in no sense means "letting pupils do what they please." It does not mean that pupils will miss or avoid socially necessary learnings; nor that they will escape doing hard and difficult things. Far from it. Utilizing pupil purpose means making things sensible and meaningful to the learner. The modern school has no lack of hard, difficult, even distasteful things to be done, but it makes them sensible to the learner by showing that they are necessary for the accomplishment of a desirable goal. More will be said of this later.

A smugly held cultural assumption also affects this matter. It is assumed that certain forced learnings will somehow automatically carry over into life. This is contradicted by all the known facts on transfer.

Evidence from out-of-school situations. Let us examine the implications of the matter which are broader than those of the classroom. "Out in the world a person must do difficult, unpleasant tasks whether he likes it or not. He will not be asked if he wants to." This statement is flatly contradicted by both logic and evidence. "Out-in-the-world," purpose is still the drive to action. No one does anything without a purpose unless he is a prisoner or a slave. Plato long ago defined a slave as one who accepts his purposes from another. No one washes dishes, cleans sewers, collects garbage, tends a monotonous machine process, persists in difficult research fifteen hours a day for the sake of doing difficult, distasteful things. Most certainly no one does these things because he was trained to do distasteful things in school. These things are all done in the course of accomplishing a purpose—usually that of earning a living. In many cases the purpose is to create, to discover, or to invent. These lead to earning a living, to be sure, but this is subordinate. Many creative artists and advanced scholars persist through most arduous difficulties for the sake of intellectual purposes.

When individuals secure positions "out in the world," *they either choose or knowingly accept the purposes connected with the work for which they are paid.* Individuals who do not act under chosen or accepted purposes lead mediocre, unhappy, discontented, rebellious lives. They become neurotic, antisocial; and in some cases, they turn out to be social rebels. It is flatly untrue that persons "out in the world" do what they do not want to do *and live successful lives.*

1. *The evidence gathered from business management is enlightening.* Those who run things "out in the world" have let down badly those who assert that employment forces individuals to do unpleasant things

whether they like it or not, that purposes of the employees are never consulted. Industry is actually spending *millions of dollars* to avoid this very error! Highly paid, technically trained personnel experts make every effort to place employees in work for which they are fitted, which they wish to do. Exactly the same principle is followed as in modern education—make effort meaningful, sensible, by making it purposeful to the worker.

One of the most remarkable studies of all time bearing upon this problem was carried on for twelve years by the Western Electric Company, and finally published under the title *Management and the Worker*. [5] The research started out to discover those factors which would enable employees to increase production. Attention was given to physical factors of light and eyestrain, rest pauses, change of work, relation of wages to output, and many others. But puzzlingly enough, a factor beyond these kept upsetting conclusions. Persistent research over years proved conclusively that the vital factor in improvement was a human and social one, namely, morale. The factors which enhanced morale and hence employee efficiency were just what modern psychology and education have contended. *Morale improves as employees may participate in planning their own work and conditions; when direction by foremen and others is friendly and democratic rather than autocratic; when suggestions from employees are accepted. Efficiency in employment is directly affected by the degree to which the worker finds purpose in it.* "Out in the world" big business is abandoning the "do-it-and-like-it" policy for one of purpose. As distinguished an industrialist as Edward R. Stettinius, Jr., Chairman of the Finance Committee of the United States Steel Corporation (1938), wrote a pamphlet on the

selection, placement, and motivation of executives. It reveals systematic consideration on the part of a great corporation to this whole problem of motivation and morale. The Western Electric study is analyzed in an interpretive article with educational implications by Goodwin Watson in *Progressive Education* for January, 1942. [6] This is excellent reading for teachers.

A popular article well worth reading, which discusses the efforts of 200 firms to test employees' temperaments and to fit them to proper positions, appears in *The Reader's Digest* [7] for January, 1942. This article, "Fitting the Worker to the Job," concludes with the statement, "Anybody might be a troublemaker on the wrong job. Fit him to the right job and he is usually a good worker. It is no favor to a man to hire him for a job that doesn't fit him. Find out what he can do; then find the right niche for him."

Articles and books on the human factors in business and industry are now so numerous that it is useless to make a listing. Any library can supply a wealth of material. Contrary to common belief, higher pay ranks well down in all studies of workers' views. The eleven factors listed first in most studies and many in the first quarter of the list deal with making the work more intelligent and successful. Anyone who believes that "out-in-the-world," individuals will be forced to do unpleasant, disagreeable tasks whether they like it or not is inexcusably ignorant of the facts.

2. *Evidence corroborating modern views appears in the "hard-boiled" management of fighting men.* Of all places where normal individuals would seem to have to accept difficult, distasteful tasks without recourse,

[5] F. J. Roethlisberger and others, *Management and the Worker* (Cambridge, Mass., Harvard Univ. Press, 1939). An account of the monumental research conducted by the Western Electric Company, Hawthorne Works, Chicago, Ill. Began in 1927. An epoch-making study.

[6] Goodwin Watson, "The Surprising Discovery of Morale," *Progressive Education*, Vol. XIX (January, 1942), pp. 33-41. An interpretive description of the Western Electric study with copious applications to education.

[7] Frank J. Taylor, "Fitting the Worker to the Job," *Reader's Digest*, Vol. 40 (January, 1942), pp. 12-16. Condensed from *Future* (January, 1942).

the army would seem to be the best illustration. The contrary is true in so far as desperate necessity permits. The army has one of the best-trained staffs of personnel technicians in existence. Men are tested and analyzed as carefully as possible in order to fit them to the proper type of service.[8] The "brass hat" type of officer holds all this in contempt—and in consequence has made some atrocious and costly blunders. Modern officers know the value of fitting soldiers to appropriate tasks. An excellent popular article appeared in *The Reader's Digest* for March, 1942, entitled "The New Army's Discipline." Descriptions of the army personnel work in sorting the men have appeared in newspapers and magazines in great numbers. Other related articles are available.

(Scores of returned soldiers from World War II advised the writer to omit the foregoing paragraphs, saying that they never met anywhere at anytime such procedure on the part of the army. They asserted that, on the contrary, it seemed that individuals were constantly assigned to tasks for which they were not fitted even though their own specialty was immediately available. The army slogan, "never volunteer," is a reflection of this situation. These were not passing "gripes" but sincere statements made again and again to the writer. The reports, if correct, in no way vitiate the principle involved, but merely show that army leadership was not taking advantage of known facts.

The very few students with commando experience also made significant reports. Commando groups evidently talked over every raid, its operation and time table, in groups with officers and men on a man-to-man basis. This, they reported, was not only so that each would know exactly what was to be done, and when, but because it had been found that full understanding of purpose, and the feeling that one could speak up, were essential to the tricky, close-knit operations of such groups.)

The remote purposes of the war were explained to drafted men by experts employed by the government. The more intelligent and educated an army is, the greater the necessity that it be imbued with purposes meaningful to the individuals. Mercenary armies are notoriously unreliable; they have no genuine purpose for which to fight. History shows again and again that men with a purpose in which they believe fight to the death. Again and again soldiers who have lost faith in their purposes will quit even though they risk being fired upon by their own officers.

Tragic facts emerging from the Korean War indicate again that developing purpose, moral values, and loyalties thereto is not an easy or quick job. It must be the result of long growth in understanding, not the memorization of documents or the repeating of patriotic statements which, having no meaning, are not really patriotic. There is no particular reason to explore brainwashing[9] to which a number of our men succumbed but if interested students wish, there are good references available.

3. *The evidence from critical observation and from psychiatry is clear-cut and voluminous.* The evidence from ordinary everyday observation is so easily available and so little understood. Here is another instance of complete failure to analyze one's own experience critically.

[9] Samples are:

Edward Hunter, *Brainwashing* (New York, Farrar, Straus, & Cudahy, 1956).

William E. Mayer, *Communist Brainwashing and Christian Values* (Provo, Utah, Brigham Young Univ. Extension Publications, 1960).

J. A. M. Meerloo, *The Rape of the Mind—The Psychology of Thought Control, Menticide, and Brainwashing* (New York, World Publishing, 1956).

Ministry of Defense, *Treatment of British Prisoners of War in Korea* (London, H. M. Stationery Office, 1955).

William Sargent, *Battle for the Mind* (Garden City, N. Y., Doubleday, 1957)

E. H. Schein, "The Chinese Indoctrination Programme for Prisoners of War," *Psychiatry,* Vol. 19, No. 149 (1956).

Secretary of Defense Advisory Committee on Prisoners of War, "The Fight Continues after the Battle," a report (Washington, D. C., U.S. Government Printing Office, 1955).

[8] Walter V. Bingham, "How the Army Sorts Its Manpower," *Harper's Magazine* (September, 1942), pp. 432-440.

Pierre van Paassen, in his *Days of Our Years,* [10] describes the authoritarian schools he attended in Holland. His descriptions of harsh masters, forcing children to learn, and his pictures of the insecure, neurotic children, should be read. Dickens' novels abound in keen, insightful accounts of the evils of forced learning. His writings on this subject have been summarized in two volumes: *Charles Dickens: Social Reformer* [11] and *Dickens as an Educator.* [12] The harshness of Hitler's totalitarian armies to subject peoples obscures the fact that Hitler's technique with the German youth was to give them purpose, to make them feel important, and to make them feel that they "belonged," since they were carrying out the high purposes of their nation. Significantly, and in point here, Hitler's policy of coercion of conquered peoples, no matter how ferocious, failed because it was contrary to fundamental natural laws.

Maslow and Mittelman [13] show clearly that harsh, coercive education destroys self-reliance and self-esteem in pupils. The remarkable experiment on "social climates" by Lewin, Lippitt, and White [14] shows clearly the disintegration of personality under "doing things whether you like it or not" in contrast to the extensive, integrative learning taking place under purpose. Frank and Ludvigh [15] have even shown that the presence of very unpleasant and disagreeable

odors materially reduces the efficiency of learning. Frank has a number of interesting studies on the relation between level of aspiration, difficulty of task, and achievement. Dollard [16] shows that when aggressiveness is built up without normal outlet in purposeful activity, the inevitable results are frustration and revolt. Wexburg [17] in his book, *Your Nervous Child,* states that when we educate for obedience we produce adult employees whose security disappears when they lose a position. Educated to obey, they do not know what to do next. They become the victims of demagogues and rabble rousers. This type of evidence from psychologists and psychiatrists and social workers can be duplicated in great volume. [18] Persons who persist in forcing difficult, distasteful tasks without purpose upon children are deliberately defying an enormous body of data; are deliberately risking the creation of unhappy, frustrated, neurotic, rebellious children and adults.

4. *Evidence from more limited school situations.* Evidence showing the evil effects

[10] Pierre van Paassen, *Days of Our Years* (New York, Hillman-Curl, 1939).

[11] W. Walter Crotch, *Charles Dickens: Social Reformer* (London, Chapman, 1913).

[12] James L. Hughes, *Dickens as an Educator* (New York, Appleton, 1902).

[13] A. H. Maslow and B. Mittelman, *Principles of Abnormal Psychology* (New York, Harper, 1941).

[14] Kurt Lewin, Ronald Lippitt, and R. K. White, "Patterns of Aggressive Behavior in Experimentally Created Social Climates," *Journal of Social Psychology,* Vol. 10 (May, 1939), pp. 271-299.

[15] J. D. Frank and E. J. Ludvigh, "The Retroactive Effect of Pleasant and Unpleasant Odors on Learning." *American Journal of Psychology,* Vol. 43 (January, 1931), pp. 102-108. See psychological abstracts for other references to Frank.

[16] John Dollard and others, *Frustration and Aggression* (New Haven, Yale Univ. Press; London, Oxford, 1940).

N. E. Miller and others, "The Frustration Aggression Hypothesis," *The Psychological Review,* Vol. 48 (1941), pp. 337-342.

Gardner Murphy, Lois B. Murphy, and Theodore M. Newcomb, *Experimental Social Psychology,* rev. ed. (New York, Harper, 1937). This is an exceptionally good reference.

[17] Erwin Wexburg, *Your Nervous Child* (New York, Boni, 1927).

[18] Stansfeld Sargent, "Effects of Difficulty Level upon the Thinking Process," *Psychological Bulletin,* Vol. 37 (October, 1940), p. 568.

———, "Thinking Processes at Various Levels of Difficulty; A Quantitative and Qualitative Study of Individual Difficulties," *Archives of Psychology,* No. 249 (1940).

Pauline Snedden Sears, "Levels of Aspiration in Academically Successful and Unsuccessful School Children," *Journal of Abnormal and Social Psychology,* Vol. 35 (1940), pp. 498-536.

A little indirect evidence will be found in William H. Burton, Roland B. Kimball, and Richard L. Wing, *Education for Effective Thinking* (New York, Appleton-Century-Crofts, 1960), Ch. 12. Also in David Russell, *Children's Thinking* (Boston, Ginn, 1956). Use index.

of coercive practices upon learning and school attitudes is so enormous that any sampling of illustrations or references is a mere drop in the bucket.

A boy in a high school known to the writer was caught during a class period engraving a head of Lincoln, using a pin on a piece of chalk. The teacher gave him an unmerciful and sarcastic tongue-lashing, advising him to put his attention on the school assignments which would be "good for him." The boy was, however, completely bored with regular school work. Another teacher, hearing of the incident, encouraged the boy to take courses in art. It was not long before the boy attracted attention in that work and in his other classes, since he saw the necessity of other learnings if he was to succeed as an artist. Previously, he had been on the verge of a revolt and demanding to leave school. He finally did leave the school—a beautiful bronze plaque which stands in the hall. He is now a distinguished artist. He could have been forced out of school by enforced education. This is only a story; it can be corroborated by massed data.

High school authorities were slow to see the implications of pupil interest in social and extracurricular activities. These activities are purposeful. Their educative value is now realized and they are being increasingly regarded as curricular. The high school was also threatened by educational activities organized within the CCC, the NYA, and the WPA. These educational programs were, until curtailed by the war, inviting increasing numbers of pupils because they served life purposes which the formal school did not. As stated elsewhere, the traditional high school will eventually have to make its curriculum purposeful or be superseded by an institution that will. Much that is now offered in high school is disagreeable and miseducative only because it is forced upon the pupil. The work is not related to life purposes. Recall in this regard the class studying the Reconstruction Period. By itself, this material must of necessity be uninteresting to a high school class, its mastery difficult and distasteful. Connected with a life interest and purpose, it does not become easy but it becomes intelligible, hence interesting and learnable.

The educational implications of difficulty. If there is any real merit in an aspect of learning which is in and for itself difficult, distasteful, and disagreeable, we should then, by the same reasoning, turn off the heating plant on cold days. We should arbitrarily make children go without lunch on some school days. Corporal punishment should be used on those who learn slowly or not at all. This is, of course, *reductio ad absurdum*. More sensible summaries may be made.

Acting because of purpose—which is exactly the same in school or "out in the world"—does not mean that one does only easy, pleasant things. It does not mean that the pupil may quit when "the going gets tough." It does not mean that the pupil may avoid hard or difficult learning situations which are socially necessary. The direct opposite is true. Purpose will motivate children and adults alike to persist through any number of difficult, distasteful situations for the sake of achievement. The chosen purpose makes the doing of distasteful things sensible. Furthermore, the difficult and the interesting are not at all antithetical. Difficulties met in the pursuit of purpose may be intensely interesting.

The only way any human being learns persistence is by following chosen or accepted purposes. It is actually true that, fundamentally, no person can force another free person to do anything. Children who lack purposes in school go through the motions, *but they do not do what it is thought they do.* There is definite precise evidence on this. Feelings and attitudes affect the total organism. *Pupils do not accept, seek, recall, or repeat what upsets their digestions, their emotions, their security and poise. Pupils do not learn what humiliates them. There is no emotional or intellectual allegiance to things learned under unhappiness.*

Forcing children or adults through difficult, distasteful tasks does not beget persistence or discipline. It ensures the direct opposite: avoidance of responsibility, sidestepping, "passing the buck" to others, antagonism, and finally either a broken spirit or rebellion. The learner profits from a learning experience to the extent that it serves a purpose of his. He willingly tackles and persists through unpleasant situations if he can see through them to a desired end. He does not persist through distasteful learnings because he has to, or because he has been trained to, but because they serve a purpose which is sensible to him. *Pupils learn what they accept. They do not learn what they reject.*

Long before scientific evidence was available, competent thinkers recognized the futility of learning under duress. Scores of statements are available in all kinds of writing, prose and poetry, fiction and non-fiction, biographies, essays, and polemics. One may be quoted because of its source and age. Freely translating from St. Augustine's *Confessions:* [19]

Time was also (as an infant) I knew no Latin; but this I learned without fear of suffering, by mere observation, amid the caresses of my nursery and jests of my friends, smiling and sportively encouraging me. This I learned without pressure of punishment to urge me on, for my heart urged me to give birth to its conceptions, which I could only do by learning words not of those who taught, but of those who talked with me; in whose ears also I gave birth to the thoughts, whatever I conceived. Hereby it clearly appears that a *free curiosity hath more force in our learning these things than a frightful enforcement.* [Author's italics.]

He then contrasts his experiences in learning Latin with learning Greek.

But why then did I hate the Greek literature that chants of such things (high adventures in war and love and mystery)? . . . For Homer

[19] Any translation or edition, Book I, Ch. 14.

himself was skillful in contriving such fictions, and is most delightfully wanton; but yet very harsh to me being a schoolboy. I believe that Virgil is no less to Grecian children when they are compelled to learn him, as I was to learn Homer; for to say truth, the difficulty of learning a strange language, did sprinkle as it were with gall all the pleasures of those fabulous narrations. *For I understood not a word of it, yet they vehemently pressed me with most cruel threatenings and punishments, to make me understand it.* [Author's italics.]

DISCUSSION QUESTIONS FOR SECTION 1

1. Illustrate with simple common-sense cases from your own experience, or as observed, the equilibrium-tension-restoration sequence. (Out-of-school reference here.)

2. Illustrate how the three points in purposing on page 57 operate in everyday affairs, simple or complex. Give an account in some detail from your own experience.

3. Apply the points to any one of the illustrations in Chapter 1 or Appendix. Show how you imagine each operated.

4. Observe a planning period or report one from your own teaching, showing how the purpose was developed.

5. What else besides purpose makes men carry on activities?

6. Why should pupils participate in setting up purposes? in planning for their execution? What is the part of the teacher here?

7. What is the relation of interest, of effort, of difficulty, of unpleasantness, to one another and to learning? Prepare a popular common-sense statement such as you might present to a P.T.A.

8. Illustrate with recalled or observed cases the errors of the traditional school.

9. What normal purposes of college students do many instructors usually neglect? Usually utilize?

10. What is meant by the expression, common in educational literature, "felt need"? What is the value of competent criticism of the common use of the term?

11. The text stated that a pupil's purpose to succeed in a vocation would ordinarily motivate him to persist in high school and in given sequences of courses, but would not necessarily motivate daily lessons or isolated sequences within courses. A teacher was heard to tell his college physics class that if they could not learn the material now studied they would not be able to do the third-year work when reached.

Is this good or poor technique? (Pay careful attention to the wording before answering.)

12. Pupils at certain levels are continually asking questions. They suggest many purposes. This may be an excellent indication of intelligence and desire to learn, or it may be merely a display of egotism, delight in gaining attention and being listened to.

 a. How can the teacher tell into which category a given pupil might fall?

 b. Give a number of specific illustrations from your observation.

13. Pupils in mechanical drawing are often asked to letter or decorate dance invitations, programs for parties, school posters. A requirement of the drawing department is that all plates must be neat and clean. This condition is more often missing than present in regular class-made plates, but is almost never lacking in the invitations, programs, and posters.

A boy taking piano lessons made little progress and after four years dropped the work. Several years later in college he took up piano on his own volition. In a short time he had made more progress than in the four years earlier and far more than could be accounted for by any carry-over.

Duplicate cases from your experience and observation showing the same situation and give analysis.

14. Observe and evaluate the extrinsic motivations used in a number of classrooms.

15. Watch for illustrations of the "difficult," "distasteful," forced-learning fallacy. They may be found in conversation with individuals or noted in observing teaching. If possible, secure through tactful conversation the reasons given by individuals who support the fallacy. Try to discover the specific background (more often lack of background) of experience, supposed fact, and so forth, and, if present, the personal frustrations or emotional immaturities which lead the individual into the error.

16. Cite from experience or observation, as adequately as can be determined, the actual results of imposition of difficult, distasteful things arbitrarily assigned.

17. Supplement from current periodicals, from observation, or other sources the evidence from the business world, or other out-of-school areas, cited in this chapter.

READINGS

The footnotes contain the material for supplementary reading. Other similar references are appearing from time to time and should be included.

2: EDUCATIVE EXPERIENCE IS CONTINUOUS AND INTERACTIVE

Experience is continuous. The learning experiences so far discussed in this volume were clearly connected with the past experience of the learner. They, as do all experiences, grew out of other experiences, past or passing. Any current experience uses meanings, insights, and skills learned in and carried over from past experiences. This is self-evident. It is also self-evident that all learning experiences are designed to affect and do affect experiences which follow.

Educative experiences are those through which the learner learns to do better the things he needs to do in order to become a competent member of his society. For instance, he will learn to read, to like to read, to choose better and better materials to read. Most important, he will learn to evaluate what he reads, to discriminate critically, to determine the reliability of what he reads. Many of the older schools provided experiences which were not continuous and interactive with real life, resulting in poor reading habits, dislike for reading, and a gullible belief in anything printed.

Arithmetical skills and the ability to judge when to use certain skills are developed by school experiences which are continuous with real-life problems. Other school experiences may teach the children the multiplication tables but not how or when to multiply—paradoxical as that may sound! Future growth is curtailed before it starts! Skills may be taught in one school so that in the future the learner can not only use them but also is in some measure inventive in using and improving them. Skills may be taught in another school in such fashion that the pupil is quite unable to apply them to new problems. This inability is widespread in adult life.

Speaking in general terms, we find that many typical school experiences expressly set up for the purpose of furthering learning are praised in one school, but condemned in another. The key lies in the degree of continuity and interaction. Many of the typical procedures of the older school are discontinuous with the pupils' normal life activities and provide but meagre limited interaction. Illustrations are memorizing the text; "covering" the text; limiting of experience to reading, writing, listening, reciting; insistence on the acquisition of isolated facts or skills; providing interaction with but a limited, academic environment; imposition; and working for marks. Conversely, many procedures are appearing in both old and new schools which provide excellent continuity and lifelike interaction. These are natural activities growing out of normal life processes, not imposed, providing for many and varied learning processes, and demanding interaction with a wide and varied environment.

Experience is interactive. All experience in and out of school involves interaction with persons and things. It is a commonplace that we consult persons, refer to books, use materials, visit places, observe processes, and participate. Learning is directly affected by the availability and accessibility of persons and materials, and by the use made of those which are accessible.

It is not so clear to the ordinary observer that we in turn affect the persons and things in the environment. That is, interaction should be *mutually contingent*. This means in simple terms that neither the individual nor the environment is *the* most important factor in an educative experience. Suffice it to say that the interactive relationship should be mutual to be educationally beneficial. The "individual cannot impose on his environment and his environment cannot impinge upon him." [20]

[20] L. Thomas Hopkins, *Interaction* (Boston, Heath, 1941), p. 208.

This principle is discussed at some length by Dewey,[21] by Hopkins,[22] and by Wynne,[23] particularly the last two. While all agree on the principle, there are minor differences in exposition and interpretation among these authors. The following paragraphs will again differ slightly from those of the other writers. The emphasis here is on making the basic point simple and clear for beginning students and teachers. Hopkins and Wynne both present a much more advanced statement, with implications extremely valuable for instructors and advanced students of method.

We do not merely *use* the environment; we *mutually interact* with it. We do not live *in* an environment; we live *with* it. We could not live without it. The individual is not *in* his environment as stones are *in* a wall, not as apples are *in* a box, not as pennies are *in* a pocket. He is in his environment as a plant is *in* the sunlight, and as sunlight is *in* the plant. The plant sits in the sunlight, to be sure, but the sunlight is just as surely in the plant. Furthermore, the plant is more than just sitting passively in the sunlight. The sunlight is not in the plant in the form in which it played upon the plant. It has been made over into something useful to the growth of the plant. The plant absorbs carbon dioxide, decomposing it, assimilating the carbon in conjunction with the sunlight, and returning much of the oxygen to the environment. Interaction has taken place. Both plant and environment have been changed. This is what is meant by living *in* the environment. In traditional schools the subject matter does not bring much sunlight into the lives of the human plants! The modern

[21] John Dewey, *Experience and Education* (New York, Macmillan, 1938), pp. 41-47.
[22] L. Thomas Hopkins, *op. cit.*, pp. 207-210.
[23] John P. Wynne, *The Educative Experience*. A pamphlet of 107 pages. Probably the most competent analysis now in print.
The writer gratefully acknowledges his indebtedness for guidance in preparing these paragraphs to the excellent discussions by Hopkins and Wynne. Correspondence and conversations with Wynne were also particularly helpful.

The Characteristics of Educative Experience   71

school, which incidentally uses far more subject matter than the traditional, attempts to have subject matter and learner interact as do sunlight and plant. Something is taken by the learner and made over into controls of conduct. The subject matter is changed in that it assumes a different place and value in the mind of the learner.

The ordinary interpretation of environment is also misleading. In common discussion, it *usually* means everything within immediate and not-too-distant range. This is the potential but not the actual environment. Another difficulty arises from the distinction sometimes made between a person's environment (immediate) and his background (remote). The actual environment includes those things, persons, and materials with which the individual interacts at a given time in pursuing current purposes. The actual environment may not include many immediate items in plain sight because these do not affect the activity under way. The actual environment may include many persons and materials remote in space and time; it may include items in Tibet or Utopia. Dewey facetiously says that when a person is building castles in the air, he is interacting with objects constructed in fancy. [24] The actual environment includes accounts in books written long, long ago, or books about things even further back. Again it may be pointed out that, contrary to many superficial criticisms, the modern school utilizes far more subject matter than the traditional school, and uses it more effectively. The modern school utilizes any and all of the cultural heritage which serves any useful purpose. It does not, however, impose arbitrary segments of ancient material because of vague and shadowy claims of value.

Internal and external factors in interactive experience are sometimes out of balance.
The inner and subjective factor in interactive experience is constituted of the learner's

needs, purposes, attitudes, interests, beliefs, habits, prejudices, aptitudes, disabilities, and so forth. The outer and objective factor includes the physical setting with its objective facts and controls, the social order with its conventions and institutions, the economic system, the religious systems with creeds and commandments, the educational system itself in all its ramifications, plus many other institutions, educative and miseducative.

Emphasis may be placed too heavily on the inner or subjective factors of need, purpose, attitudes. Continuity may then easily depend too much upon casual and accidental connections. The interaction may be so wide and so varied as to bewilder rather than educate. Here we have the error of the "ultra" progressives or moderns. The emphasis upon the "child-centered" school was eminently desirable when it emerged some years ago. It corrected the vicious overemphasis upon formal subject-center, adult-organized schools. There was considerable overcorrection among many superficial rank-and-file teachers. We are now well into a period of intelligent balance between the learner and the cultural heritage. It is significant that Rugg, who was co-author of *The Child Centered School,* [25] is also the author of several of the most influential texts on community influence upon schools, upon the background and heritage of our civilization.

The emphasis may be—and in the past all too clearly has been—placed too heavily on the external and objective factors. Continuity then depends upon adult aims and upon the internal logic of the subject matter. This continuity is not a continuity with the life of the learner. It is significant that in many instances the normal learning curve of young children slows or drops back as they enter school. They come from real-life situations in which they have been learning

[24] John Dewey, *op. cit.,* p. 42.

[25] Harold Rugg and Ann Shumaker (Yonkers, N. Y., World Book, 1928). (Incidentally, this is still one of the most effective volumes to give as initial reading to traditional teachers who are entering upon study of modern methods.)

many things by normal experience. They are now asked to forget this and enter upon a series of activities which are strange, and which, as far as the child can see, seem to have no use. There are scores of stories about children who fail in arithmetic miserably in the lower grades but who are found making change and doing errands involving computation quite well in real life. The interaction in schools, too heavily biased toward adult aims and subject matter, is narrow, limited, and formal. It is usually confined to but a few environmental factors —books, references, maps, teachers. Here we have the error of the "ultra" conservative. It is found in many colleges and high schools, and particularly in schools specializing in "college-preparatory" courses. The Dartmouth study referred to in the previous chapter shows that learning with this over-emphasis is not useful learning. As also indicated in Chapter 3, learning from books and through logically organized subject matter is legitimate and necessary upon certain levels of pupil maturity.

Both factors are essential. The needs and purposes of the pupil and the demands of the environment usually compiled into subject matter are equally important in the learning situation. The good teacher strives for balance. Teaching activities to this end are presented in Chapters 12 and 14. Meanwhile we may turn to an analysis of some of the broad general violations of the principles of continuity and interaction. Following that will be a summary of efforts being made to provide for proper continuity and interaction.

School experiences often violate the principles of continuity and interaction. Many everyday, accepted, even somewhat sacred practices in typical schools are in fact interferences with natural, continuous, interactive learning. Some procedures mentioned in the following paragraphs will shock many school workers. Recovery from shock should be followed by calm analysis.

The *course of study* made up of separate unrelated subjects is a case in point, particularly in elementary schools. The subjects are taught for the learnings supposed to reside within the material, and for use in later life. Little or no attempt is made to relate the learnings to the current life of the learner. In fact, little attempt is made to relate the subject-matter learnings even from subject to subject. Some subjects in the secondary school can hardly be related at all to the life of certain groups of pupils. Pupils regard these irrelevant materials as necessary evils required by the odd persons who manage the school. Continuity is obscure and in some cases must be non-existent. Interaction can only be restricted and narrowing. Even in the admittedly formal college-preparatory sequence there has developed a considerable lack of continuity toward the limited goal of college entrance. The college-preparatory sequence could profit enormously from the life interests which it callously and blindly ignores or actively represses. The typical course of study too often divides and fragments the dynamic world of children, to the confusion and distrust of the pupils. The attitudinal learnings accompanying many subjects, especially in the field of skills, are seriously inimical to education.

The *sequence* still found in many schools from ancient history to medieval or modern history, to English or American history, illustrates perfectly a continuity which is no continuity at all for the learner. In fact, even the subject-matter continuity does not exist in schools where each segment is taught as a separate whole. Relationships, trends, and sequences are not brought out. Relation to the life of the learner is usually ignored. Chronological history begins at *its* beginning, not at the *pupil's* beginning. A comprehension of chronology in history is an end point, a learning achievement, not a scheme to be imposed upon immature learners. [26] To deal with elements within any

[26] Research on children's time concepts are summarized in David Russell, *op. cit.* Use index.

unity as if those elements were themselves wholes, units, and end points is to destory the very unity with which we are dealing.

The sequence within a single subject may also be a false one. Spelling, for instance, would seem to be internally continuous, but it is not. The daily spelling lists are not, as a rule, continuous in any sense.

The sequence in the sciences, and the failure to relate meanings from science to science, is similar to that in history. Relation to life is also neglected. A class of city children faithfully learn five causes of forest fires as listed in the textbook. Years later some of them learned through direct experience that these were not the causes of forest fires.

In English the practice of mixing formal grammar and composition, appreciation of literature, and sometimes creative writing in the same course definitely prevents educative continuity. To insist on placing two or three of these elements not merely in the same course but in the same daily period is an absurdity of astounding magnitude. [27] Each of the three kinds of learning involved is definitely entitled to its own continuity, especially on upper levels where specialization is legitimate. In the lower grades, functional grammar should appear in connection with other aspects of English. The utter failure of the formal approach indicated is seen in the prevalence of quack courses—"learn to speak correctly in fifteen minutes a day." The school did not do the job, and the disillusioned adult turns to substitutes for functional study.

In many Latin classes, individual students stumble through two lines of translation and sink back into their seats. After some minutes the teacher may arbitrarily jump to grammatical analysis, and still later to oral or written drill on grammatical forms. Some schools take one day a week for "grammar day." Sometimes prose composition is included. To say that such procedure is educative is to approach imbecility. There is ample experimental evidence to show that pupils learn neither Latin nor to improve their English. One study shows clearly that high-school students in the United States do not learn to *read* Latin at all; they *decipher* it. There is no relation to current events, no attempt to give meaning. [28] And yet both Cicero's orations against Catiline and Caesar's discussions of conditions in Rome are directly applicable to the interpretation of certain conditions in many large American municipalities. The study of Caesar's Commentaries becomes an idiotic game of identifying constructions and guessing at gerundives. The profound effects of Caesar's wars upon the present civilization of Western Europe are not even mentioned, let alone understood. Continuity with life and interaction with life, hence desirable educative results, can be secured in Latin as in any other subject *with pupils capable of learning on that intellectual level and with teachers who are competently informed regarding the nature of learning and teaching.*

Assignments are often imposed by teachers without regard for possible contribution

[27] An excellent teacher with years of experience who read this book in manuscript suggested that this paragraph be eliminated since it was "fantastic"; no teacher would be guilty of such malpractice. Directed to visit half a dozen nearby high schools at random she was astounded to find the "malpractice" to be practically universal! Administrative impositions account for a part of this but much of it is based on simple unawareness of the nature of learning. Many excellent teachers are unaware how grotesque are the techniques of truly poor teachers, hence are often indifferent to efforts to raise professional standards.

Teaching techniques which are "fantastic" are evidently of long standing, as witness St. Augustine again: *At enim vela pendent liminibus grammaticarium scholarum, sed non illa magis honorem secreti quam tegimentum erroris significant.* (True it is, that there are curtains at the entrance to grammar schools; but they signify not so much the cloth of state to privacy, as serve for a blind to the follies committed behind them.) (To be strictly honest, we note that St. Augustine's original intent was not that of the present interpretation.)

[28] Charles H. Judd and Guy T. Buswell, *Silent Reading*, Supplementary Education Monographs, No. 23 (Chicago, Univ. of Chicago, November, 1922). Chapter 5 on Reading Foreign Languages contains astounding exhibits.

to the pupil's experiential continuum. The present is often completely ignored. *Recitation* procedures often ignore or actively repress questions and contributions growing out of the pupil's continuous and interactive experience outside school. Formal question-and-answer recitations rule out the normal interaction of social discussion. The use of one text or meager references and the insistence on "facts" or other measurable results force attention to items which are lifted out of a normal learning process. Cramming results instead of learning. *Testing methods* further violate continuity and interaction by measuring memorized facts, formulas, or teachers' statements. Worst violation of all is the attitude that tests and final examinations close and settle the learning. A pupil passes English but cannot use good English. He may pass first-year algebra but does not recognize equation problems in physics and chemistry. The "cram schools" which flourish in the vicinity of certain colleges, and even high schools, are material monuments to the incompetence of the regular instructors. *Marks* become the end point of learning, instead of knowledges and powers which are acquired through experience and are usable in continued life experience.

The *graded system,* each level an entity with materials assigned for mastery within given grade levels, completely ignores individual differences in ability and experience. The grade-a-year progress is likewise an interference with normal continuous learning. Within any given grade group there will be a range of several years in chronological age, in ability, hence in level of experience. The rate of learning differs so greatly from individual to individual that all arbitrary divisions and processes inevitably violate continuity. Worse, the *imposition* of failure upon children who have not met a set of arbitrary, unadjustable grade standards is not merely an interruption of normal continuity as determined by the pupils' ability, maturity, and natural rate of learning, but is conducive to serious detrimental effects upon mental hygiene. Here is one school practice which illustrates *par excellence* inimical and miseducative effects upon future growth. (See following pages for discussion of failure which is not detrimental.)

The typical *antisocial atmosphere* of many schoolrooms, regimentation, and teacher-imposed discipline definitely prevent social intercourse and co-operation. *Whispering, the natural and inevitable communication between normal individuals, is punished.* Interaction is specifically prohibited! The modern school takes advantage of natural tendencies to communicate; it forms pupil committees and lets them talk and discuss freely. Their findings are then contributed to the group project.

The very physical set-up of traditional schoolrooms confines experience to meager forms of interaction.

The values of extracurricular activities are not realized. Obvious clues in this field are often overlooked. Many boys who are competent, confident participators, even leaders outside school, have nothing to say in school. The school makes the blunder of labeling them stupid when there is ample proof that they are anything but stupid. The irrelevant and useless activities of the school do not invite participation. Similarly, the home environment is often overlooked as a source of worthwhile learning activities.

Going further afield, we may note interferences with continuity and interaction resulting from the failure of the *school personnel* to co-operate among themselves. The compartmentalization of the curriculum, departmental jealousies, and the like contribute to this. The stage-design project referred to earlier was made possible through the unselfish co-operation of several high school departments. It was handicapped somewhat by the refusal of one department to have anything to do with it. This department was concerned with prerogatives and not with the education of high school pupils. Interference from school board members often prevents continuity and interaction in the experience of the children. Insistence on certain texts and certain methods, refusal to listen to technical advice, the appointment of incompetent but politically connected teachers—all are cases in point. One school board prohibits any kind of excursions outside the school grounds. The children are to learn about the world, but they are to hang their clothes in the cloakroom and under no circumstances to go near the world.

The *political nature* of many school positions results in personnel so untrained and incompetent that educative experience for the children cannot result from the teaching procedures used.

Finally, many *teacher-training institutions* affect this matter by giving their trainees devices and techniques instead of principles and understandings basic in the learning process.

All of the foregoing represents interference with continuity and interaction, two inescapable aspects of learning. The total picture, however, is not all black; many school systems have made definite, in some cases extensive, efforts to avoid the violations just noted and to provide for highly desirable learning experiences.

Improvements designed to provide continuity and interaction. The whole range of improvements cannot be covered; the following represent samplings.

The elementary schools are substituting for the separate subject course of study the *unified program,* organized in functional units. The core for organization is not the logic of adult-organized subject matter, but the needs and purposes of the learner. Learnings valuable in later life are recognized to be the same as those now necessary. Continued experience in and out of school matures present understandings and abilities into adult form and use. Strict grade and subject divisions have long since been abolished in many good elementary schools. The administrative "period" of twenty or forty minutes has disappeared. An educative ex-

perience which is developing cannot be carried on in twenty-minute sections. It should not be interrupted by arbitrary requirements. (This should not be misinterpreted to apply to more mature study of special subjects on upper levels.)

Children should be, and in a few places increasingly are, taken to *visit school,* kindergarten, or preschool as the case may be. The preschool child should be taken to visit the first grade. The teacher should become acquainted with the prospective pupil's home and environment. A few enlightened nursery school teachers are visiting homes and working with mothers of very small children. The best type of continuity and interaction may result from this.

The secondary school is increasingly using various forms of correlation, fusion, or coordination of subject matter. Organization of related subjects into *broad fields* appears in many schools. A few are experimenting with even more total unification, after the elementary school pattern. The new *core curriculum* may be organized around subject-matter learnings or around the pupil's life problems. The *special subjects* themselves on the upper levels are being internally reorganized into more functional form. There is increasing effort everywhere to relate courses to life purposes. The college-preparatory division in a few advanced high schools shares effectively in this movement. *Work experience* is widely advocated as a prime means of providing continuity and interaction in the learning experiences of secondary school pupils. There is increasing recognition of the value of *extracurricular* activities. Their vitality for the learner is being utilized. *Individual differences* are being increasingly recognized as the secondary school faces the problem met by the elementary school from 1900 on, namely, providing education for all levels and types of intelligence, interest, aptitude, background, and probable destiny. The problem is being met not only with provision for different rates of learning, but with recognition of different levels of achievement.

Most important of all, it is being met through provision of different materials and activities within a lesson or unit. *Guidance* is an increasingly important improvement within the modern school.

The new processes of *team teaching* which are emerging in the country should be a definite aid to providing continuity, interaction, and integration.

The appearance of new courses is one of the most significant developments in this field. A fragmentary sampling includes Problems of American Democracy, Community Organization, Propaganda Analysis, Consumer Science, Household Chemistry, The Family, Comparative Economic Systems, Economic Geography, Nature of Personality, and Psychology for Life. Forerunners of these were earlier additions such as Community Civics, General Shop, General Language, Home Economics, and many others. One course in chemistry was made by a teacher who had faithfully kept track for some years of all the questions asked by pupils about chemical phenomena in everyday life. Another course in chemistry took up such things as the analysis of soaps, tooth pastes, baking powders, antifreeze mixtures, cosmetics, lubricating oils, and so forth. The results were not merely chemical knowledges useful every day, but such social results as a tendency to read advertising more carefully, a skepticism toward the typical extravagant advertising claims, and an increasing ability to prove that much advertising is deliberate falsification. There are die-hards who say that this is not chemistry. That is not the question. The obvious usefulness of the material to hundreds of thousands of citizens who will never need more formal chemistry, nor pass courses in it, makes argument absurd. Systematically organized courses in chemistry must be available also for those who can and will use them. The patterns of thinking involved as well as the information are important parts of special education. The more popular courses set up for the average student may well uncover interest

and ability, thus leading capable students into the organized discipline.

Curriculum reorganization, in the interests of continuity and interaction within and without the subject curriculum, is one of the most important tasks in education today.

Libraries announced during the depression years that adult reading of serious non-fiction books in the fields of economics, sociology, and government theory, especially those containing specialized discussions of capitalism, socialism, and democracy, increased enormously. The depression itself revealed the gross ignorance of so-called successful citizens concerning the social order in which they lived. The library report indicated the failure of the schools to prepare citizens for understanding of the world in which they live. The modern school, despite vicious criticism from vested interests, is trying with earnest sincerity to provide continuous, interactive contact with the problems of everyday living.

Criticism of the modern school also arises within the academic walls. Many, including professors of the liberal arts colleges, accuse the modern school of ignoring the *cultural tradition* of our civilization and of denying children contact with that civilization. This criticism is based on 100 per cent ignorance of what the modern school is doing and of the information and theory behind its efforts. The modern school possesses irrefutable data showing that hundreds of thousands of children now coming to high school cannot ever utilize the cultural materials provided for the more highly selected pupil population of bygone years. The modern school, far from denying these children cultural contacts, is making a tremendous effort to develop subject matter and methods which will bring these materials within the understanding of these children, to give them interactive experience with it in line with their purposes and within their interests and understandings. The modern school, contrary to the critics, is bringing cultural background to thousands of pupils who could get it under no other conceivable conditions. In some areas the modern school is doing a better job with this than did the traditional school with its more favorably selected population. [29]

Assignments, if made as such, are made increasingly within units organized around pupil purposes. Pupils are encouraged to *participate* in determining and carrying out learning situations. *Outside stimuli* to learning will be constantly introduced into classrooms: newspapers, magazines, radio presentations, moving pictures, and speakers. Definite efforts are made to produce a *social atmosphere.* Discussion, committee work, interchange of fact and opinion, and free movement are necessary in learning to work together in a lifelike manner. The introduction of movable furniture into elementary schools is a formal but important factor. Pupils are encouraged to ask questions and to contribute from their own experience. The urge to whisper is legitimized into committee discussion and socialized recitations.

The *sociality* of experience is neglected and even denied in many ultraconservative schools which quiz individuals on memorized, assigned materials. Here learning is a solitary process, and it is not educative learning! Personality and learning are social products. The value of any learning experience is greatly affected by the number, variety, and complexity of the associations and connections which accompany it. Even in systems of individualized instruction, the individual aspect is primarily in the practice of skills. The learning products thus acquired were socially produced in the first place and are learned for use in social situations.

Sociality of experience, however, involves more than this simple and obvious connotation. Social learning experiences should also constantly widen the individual's social interests, sympathies, understandings, and concerns. This is of basic importance in a world which is increasingly co-operative and interdependent.

More important, pupils will *go out to meet experiences.* The community will become one of the chief sources of learning situations and materials. Pupils will not merely visit community agencies, jails, courts, welfare organizations, museums, and libraries, but will participate in many community enterprises. The work experience mentioned above may become in the near future actual participation in the construction of public works, part-time employment in industry, agriculture, or military service. [30]

The formal *recitation* is giving way to *work periods* involving from twenty to eighty different learning activities. Emphasis is increasingly upon the achievement of behavior patterns, understandings, abilities, and attitudes instead of upon memorization of isolated facts or acquisition of isolated skills. Limited formal testing is giving way to continuous *evaluation* based upon observation of behavior. *Changed behavior* due to understandings and attitudes is the only true test of achievement. Percentage or letter marks have been for some time giving way to descriptive *records of behavior.* Examination and marking systems designed to punish, or reward, or to "finish" a subject are being replaced by diagnostic techniques designed to aid further progress.

Systems of *continuous progress* are slowly supplanting rigid graded systems. [31] Flexible

[29] An interesting and illuminating note on this problem which may be read at this point will be found on pages 420-423 of Raymond H. Wheeler, and Francis T. Perkins, *op. cit.*

[30] Part of one chapter is devoted later to interaction with the community. Meanwhile this discussion can be made concrete through reference to Morris R. Mitchell's article, "Youth Has a Part to Play" in *Progressive Education,* Vol. 19 (February, 1942), pp. 88-109. One-hundred-sixty-eight illustrations of participation are described. See also Stuart Chase, "Bring Our Youngsters into the Community," *Reader's Digest,* Vol. 40 (January, 1942), pp. 5-8. Many state and city bulletins and texts are available on this problem.

[31] John I. Goodlad and Robert H. Anderson, *The Nongraded Elementary School* (New York, Harcourt, Brace & World, 1959).
A Look at Continuity in the School Program, The 1958 Yearbook of the Association for Supervision and Curriculum Development (Washington, D. C., N. E. A., 1958). Deals with articulation.

grouping based on social maturity is a definite aid to continuity and interaction. Arbitrary *failure* imposed on pupils because of conditions beyond their control is increasingly being eliminated. Failure owing to faulty definition of problems, to faulty planning, to neglect of observable conditions—failure brought on by the learners themselves—is a definitely educative experience and has no detrimental effects upon mental hygiene. In fact, it is likely to contribute to good mental hygiene and to interaction by showing young people through their own practices how to meet and correct failure.

The appointment of trained, non-politically controlled, *competent personnel* is a definite aid in improving learning situations. Teachers should be parts of the community and live within its activities and problems. *Non-interference* by school boards with the technical and professional processes of education is well established in certain parts of the country. Finally, teacher-training institutions are increasingly sensitive to the need for training teachers in modern psychology and principles of teaching.

DISCUSSION QUESTIONS FOR SECTION 2

1. This section contains several pages listing general school procedures which violate the principles of continuity and interaction.
   a. Add to the general listings, if possible, from your experience or observation.
   b. Give specific illustrations of any two or three of the general categories. Take these illustrations from experience or observation only.
2. Proceed as in Question 1 above for the lists of general procedures designed in accord with the two principles.
3. Give from experience or observation specific illustrations of lack of balance between internal and external factors in interaction; illustrations of efforts by a school or a teacher to bring about a balance.
4. Illustrate with both in-school and out-of-school examples the fact that interaction changes both the individual and the environment.
5. What are some of the actual difficulties in the way of desirable interaction with the

environment during the period of schooling? Define and illustrate. What can you do as a teacher to get around these obstacles?

6. Suppose that the educators managing the elementary and secondary schools you attended had wished to use all that we now know about continuity and interaction. List some changes you think could have been made in general policy, administration, curriculum, methods of teaching, grouping, promotion, examining and marking, or any other factor. Be specific. Go beyond the items listed in this chapter.

7. Make a series of observations in classrooms. List and comment upon specific incidents, practices, or comments which are clear-cut violations of continuity and interaction. Which are equally clear-cut efforts to improve continuity and interaction?

READINGS

Readings are indicated in the footnotes. Other similar references should be noted as they appear.

3: EDUCATIVE EXPERIENCE CONTRIBUTES TO THE NATURAL INTEGRATION OF THE LEARNER

The concept *integration* is an important one in education. Emphasis differs depending upon the chief interest of the speaker or writer. The focus may be in individual personal integration or upon social integration; on the process; on the continuing result; or upon any of the factors involved in securing integration of the individual, curriculum, administrative organization and process, instructional procedure, integrative thread, instructional episodes, and others.

First, we may have reference to the process of integration in the person. In this process, the desired learning outcomes are achieved in such a way as to be woven into an already existing system of behaviors, understandings, attitudes, and abilities. The things learned become a part of the learner's personality. They have not merely been "added" to the "sum of knowledge possessed," to lie dormant until resurrected upon demand. They operate as dynamic factors in the continuous determination of human behavior. They truly constitute changes within the organism. Integration is continuous. There is no end point, in the sense of a status achieved. As the individual interacts with an ever wider environment, he selects and incorporates learnings into his personality.

Integration may also refer, if we define carefully, to the relationships of the individual to other individuals and to society. The learner "integrates" himself with other persons, with the values, conventions, and institutions of his society. This means that he comes to understand, influence, and get along with other persons; to understand, get along with, and improve the institutions within which he lives. These abilities are separated here only for purposes of discussion. All integrating takes place within a simultaneous, functional, learning experience.

Integration results from learning things which are truly useful and meaningful to the learner at the time and which will continue to be useful in everyday behavior, so far as we can see ahead. An integrating person is better able to maintain his physical and mental health, better able to attack and analyze new situations. The product of integration is an integrated person; or speaking more precisely, the product of integrating is an integrating person. The emphasis is on *integrating,* not *integrated.* An integrating personality is one which possesses a unified view of its world and of the place of that personality therein. An integrating personality is one in which knowledges, desires, and abilities are in essential agreement; one into which new controls are unified after being individuated. Integration in an intelligent, purposing individual means sanity, or wholesomeness of mind, body, and emotions.

It is important to know that integration is a primary characteristic of living organisms. Human beings are born physiologically integrated and continue to grow in an integrating fashion physically and mentally until par-

ents, teachers, and other factors interfere. The point is, particularly with young children, that the school should maintain and promote the normal, primary integration of living organisms by providing learning experiences which are purposeful, continuous, and interactive.

A few satirical paragraphs from Huxley's *Brave New World* [32] are used here to illustrate in humorous and exaggerated manner a learning process which is not integrative.

(A small boy asleep on his right side, the right arm stuck out, the right hand hanging limply over the edge of the bed. Through a round grating in the side of a box a voice speaks softly.

"The Nile is the longest river in Africa and the second in length of all the rivers of the globe. Although falling short of the length of the Mississippi-Missouri, the Nile is at the head of all rivers as regards the length of its basin, which extends through 35 degrees of latitude. . . . "

At breakfast the next morning, "Tommy," someone asks, "do you know which is the longest river in Africa?" A shaking of the head. "But don't you remember something that begins: The Nile is the . . . . "

"The-Nile-is-the-longest-river-in-Africa-and-the-second-in-length-of-all-the-rivers-of-the-globe . . . . " The words come tumbling out. "Although-falling-short-of . . . . "

"Well now, which is the longest river in Africa?"

The eyes are blank. "I don't know."

"But the Nile, Tommy."

"The-Nile-is-the-longest-river-in-Africa-and-second . . . . "

"Then which river is the longest, Tommy?" Tommy bursts into tears. "I don't know," he howls.)

That howl, the Director made it plain, discouraged the earliest investigators. The experiments were abandoned. No further attempt was made to teach children the length of the Nile in their sleep. Quite rightly. You can't learn a science unless you know what it's all about.

The last statement will come as something of a shock to certain high school and college

[32] Aldous Huxley, *Brave New World* (London, Chatto and Windus, 1958; first published in 1932), pp. 19-20.

teachers of science. Also, we might add, that the effort to teach students in their sleep has evidently not been abandoned in many modern college classes.

Factors which facilitate integration. The chief factor is establishing organic connection between life and learning. Pedagogical devices are important and useful, especially for beginning teachers but the fundamental requirement is that learning experiences be functionally connected with the life of the learner. The organic connection established, the devices become useful in carrying out details. Hopkins [33] has a useful statement:

Integrating behavior in any situation, then, is that in which the individual begins with, continues with, ends with, and carries on with a unified internal wholeness. To raise the level of action from physiological to thoughtful purposes with their more intelligent means of attaining and maintaining normal unitary behavior is the integrating goal and process.

Hopkins' volume published in 1937 was for twenty years the only summary statement. The National Society for the Study of Education brought things up to date in 1958 with an extensive summary, complete with illustrative and descriptive materials. [34] All major factors are covered: curriculum, administrative programs and processes, general classroom procedures, instructional episodes, integrating threads, and others. Three short summaries selected from the wealth available are given here.

Five approaches which have implications for integating learning experiences on the elementary level are suggested:

1. Organized effort on the part of teachers to agree on operational values for guiding the various enterprises in their schools;

[33] L. Thomas Hopkins, *Integration* (New York, Appleton, 1937), p. 6.
[34] *The Integration of Educational Experiences,* Fifty-seventh Yearbook of the National Society for the Study of Education, Part III (Chicago, Ill., 5835 Kimbark Ave., 1958).

2. Organized effort to understand the learner within whom integration must take place;
3. Analysis of and agreement upon certain bases for curriculum organization in elementary schools;
4. Analysis of the teaching-learning act as it actually takes place in elementary school classrooms;
5. Reorganization of the traditional patterns of elementary school patterns.

Regarding objectives, a factor of basic importance, the Yearbook Commission suggests:

1. Objectives which are appropriate to several courses, several departments, or to an entire college have more integrative implications than objectives specific to a single course.
2. Objectives which require the relating of specific facts to broad principles and generalizations have more integrative implications than knowing the facts.
3. Objectives which require relating knowledge and theory to problems and life experiences have more integrative implications than those which simply specify knowledge and understanding of fact and theory.
4. Objectives which involve feelings, beliefs, and values as well as the intellect tend to be more integrative than those which involve the intellect alone.

These have been discussed by psychologists and others for years and are widely accepted. It is well, however, to set them off like this for recall and emphasis.

Principles are suggested for teacher guidance in aiding the students:

1. He should strengthen the student's background so that the concepts to be grasped are well understood before integration is attempted.
2. He should guide the student's attention to the points of similarity which form the basis of the integrative framework.
3. He should make sure that the integrative framework is at a conceptual level appropriate to his students' ability and maturity.
4. If the exercise is likely to be threatening, either because of its context or the setting in which it takes place, efforts should be made to minimize the threat by establishing as permissive an atmosphere as possible.
5. Students are more likely to do what is required if they know what is expected of them.

The students should understand from the outset that integration of the material under consideration is a goal of the learning experience.

6. The teacher should take advantage of the students' various backgrounds to involve them in his presentation.

7. Since the teacher ultimately seeks to have the students display integrating behavior on their own, he must present the framework in such a way that the student can accept it and make it his own but not feel bound by it—not feel that his capacity for independent thinking is being crushed.

8. The teacher should "model" integrative behavior for his students. (That is, help them see how he himself arrives at new concepts). [35]

Again these are well known in one form or another in discussions of learning and teaching. The fifth principle could be misinterpreted very easily to indicate imposition, although the seventh principle takes care of this in part.

Factors which interfere with normal integration. This entire volume is, in fact, devoted to a discussion of integrative and nonintegrative educational factors. The preceding sections of this chapter on purposeful, continuous, and interactive learning lists a number of specific factors which facilitate or hinder integration. These are apparent on inspection and will not be repeated here. In addition to educational factors, there are a number of individual and social factors which interfere with integration. These have been well summarized by Lindeman: [36]

1. *Morphological:* Bodily structure and form may be so far asymmetrical as to cause the individual to consider himself to be incapable of complete identification with his fellows.

2. *Physiological:* The functions of the organism may make it difficult for an individual to keep pace with his fellows in a similar environment.

3. *Psychofunctional:* The operations of the mind may be so far disordered and illogical as to separate the individual from his fellows.

[35] *Ibid.,* pp. 173; 80; 62-63.
[36] E. C. Lindeman, in Hopkins, *op. cit.,* Ch. 2, p. 25.

(*Note:* The above-listed causes of disintegrativeness may be thought of as being "inner" conditions belonging to the individual, arising from accident, sickness, or heredity.)

4. *Technico-cultural:* The part which the individual is asked to play in society may be so highly specialized because of technical considerations that he is unable, in his occupational experience, to function in conscious relation to wholes.

5. *Sociocultural:* The social setting within which the individual is obliged to live may bring dissatisfactions because:

   a. He will be rejected by certain persons.

   b. He will be rejected by certain groups.

   c. He will not concur with the goals, ends, or values set by the group.

   d. He will not agree with the methods or means utilized by his fellows in pursuing their ends.

   e. He will resist attempts to enforce conformity upon him through dominance.

   (*Note:* Whereas the first three causes of disintegrativeness listed tend to set limits of creativeness for the individual because of the non-integrative quality of his person, the last two causes set similar limits in an external manner, that is, because of conditions existing outside the individual. Separations of this sort are, of course, arbitrary and artificial and may be used merely for purposes of simplicity.)

Illustrative evidence of integrative and disintegrative behavior. It is possible to observe children in and out of school and adults in everyday activity and to note certain ways of acting which are presumptive evidence of integration or lack of it. A brief sampling of such evidence and of the categories within which it falls (see page 83).

DISCUSSION QUESTIONS FOR SECTION 3

1. State clearly and wholly in your own words what you understand integration to be, both the process of integration and the continuing product. Use illustrations from school and from other social situations. Answers using the words of the book are particularly unacceptable here.

2. What is the use or importance of knowing about integration, quite apart from its use in educational procedure?

Integrating Personality	Non-Integrating, Sometimes Disintegrating, Personality
1. Active, curious about his surroundings; makes many and wide contacts.	Inactive, not interested in new experiences; prefers narrow, familiar environment.
2. Makes friends, talks, laughs (may whisper, create disturbance in school).	Shy, avoids contacts with others, "bashful," often called a "good" child by teachers and parents.
3. Shows sense of humor, can "take" a joke on himself; is a "good sport."	Over-serious, over-sensitive, afraid of being laughed at, resents "kidding."
4. Meets problems, "tensions," with confidence, even with pleasure.	Avoids, escapes, or refuses to face problems or difficulties of any sort; when escape is impossible, meets problems with "can't do it," obstinacy, tantrums, cheating, etc.
5. Defines problems, asks questions, tries to see "what it is all about"; willingly undertakes work of planning for solutions, work of carrying out plans.	Does not see what to do; "what is the assignment?"; grumbles that what is wanted "isn't clear"; "is this what you want?"
a. Plans and uses imagination in terms of reality.	*a.* Plans in terms of wishful thinking, in terms of materials and abilities not present or obtainable.
b. Uses past experience in solving difficulties.	*b.* Insists on fantastic solutions out of line with experience.
c. Gathers materials and organizes with discrimination.	*c.* Gathers materials at random; cannot produce usable outlines or classifications.
6. Willing to submit his suggestions and beliefs to criticism and test.	Refuses to submit to test or experiment; petulant under criticism.
7. Willing at same time to "stand up" for his contributions until convinced they are incorrect.	Unsure, backs down easily, constantly asks others, "Is this the answer you got? Do you think this is right?"
8. Willing to accept the consequences of his conclusions, to accept results of errors as well as fruits of correct decisions.	Denies liability for consequences of errors, "the other fellow's fault," "passes the buck"; claims credit for any successes, or for large share of group success.
9. Accepts responsibility commensurate with ability and level of maturity.	Avoids leadership; does not "come through" with his part promised or implied.
10. Distributes credit; takes modest pride in own contributions; is not over-bearing; does not bully; does not find it necessary to cheat.	Belittles others, over-asserts his own ability and contributions; bullies; cheats.
11. Expresses emotion but is not controlled by it; increases control over undesirable emotional expression; controls temper; does not insist on own way; does not cry, sulk, refuse arbitrarily to participate.	Undue failure to control undesirable emotional expression; cries, screams, "won't play," must have own way.
12. Works and plays with others; participates easily and naturally in co-operative activities; helps others as a matter of course.	Refuses to share; is overcompetitive, must always be at "top" of class, clamors for "A" grades; undermines others if possible.

13. Likely to have hobbies, pets, and special interests; uses books as sources of information or for pleasure.

Narrow and limited interests outside necessary activities; uses books as escapes from reality in some instances.

14. Habitually happy and confident (without being a Pollyanna); free from worry, doesn't whine for what cannot be achieved; confident of place with and respect from parents, teachers, and mates; in short, enjoys good mental hygiene.

Habitually gloomy and fearful, worries; always "stewing around," unhappy because of inability to avoid the inevitable; exhibits fear of parents, teachers, and mates; poor mental hygiene.

15. Generally in reasonably good health;

"Enjoys poor health"; ill-defined, non-localized pains and aches;

(This is not always given as an index of integration, but it is a reasonable inference from the organismic concept. Evidence is beginning to appear showing that certain illnesses are closely correlated with factors contributing to disintegration. A college student had innumerable colds which were found to be correlated with continued, serious failure in college courses.)

Attends to his normal physical needs without undue difficulty.

Nail-biting, nose-picking, etc.; nervous habits in regard to eating, elimination, etc.

3. Use Questions 6 and 7 for Section 1, applying them here to integration.

4. Illustrate any of the five approaches on page 81 that you have observed in action, indicating how integration may have been facilitated. Illustrate violations of these.

5. If you have met any of the five in previous courses or elsewhere state the setting and use.

6. Do the same for the objectives listed on page 81.

7. You have doubtless met the eight principles in other courses. Describe how they were stated and used there, making connection with the use here.

8. Describe as specifically as you can, and in detail, everyday classroom evidences which would aid you in distinguishing between integrating and non-integrating personalities. That is, give specific illustrations for any of the fifteen points listed on pages 83-84. Watch for cases during your observations. Do likewise for these points, but using out-of-school situations.

9. Illustrate any of the five general causes of disintegration listed on page 82, by describing specific instances. In-school or out-of-school material may be used. Note cases in psychiatric literature.

The following questions are based upon reading in Hopkins, *Integration*, Chapters 1 and 2, and are for advanced students.

6. Note the good list of criticisms on page 27 relating to so-called attempts at integration in

education as listed on page 26. The criticism of progressive education in number 6 is being corrected as rapidly as possible by the progressives themselves. How?

7. Illustrate and develop the far-reaching implications of the statement on page 28: "Contemporary educators have been conditioned in the direction of the mechanics of education."

8. Develop a series of educational implications for the two affirmations suggested, the first on page 29 and the second on page 31.

9. In everyday terms, what is the meaning of page 33?

10. Develop as concretely as possible the educational implications of the three points on page 34.

READINGS

The useful readings are all indicated in the footnotes. See also the good bibliography in the N.S.S.E. Yearbook. Students should make note of any new periodical articles which appear from time to time.

GENERAL DISCUSSION QUESTIONS FOR WHOLE CHAPTER

1. Re-examine Questions 8, 9, and 10 at the end of the first chapter. You are now in position to amplify greatly the simple answers made earlier. Answer each question again in a

more extended and organized statement. Make it in the form of a popular explanation to the lay public if desired.

2. What in general makes an experience miseducative—that is, prevents its having a favorable influence on later growth? Prepare a statement covering several major points, using concrete illustrations from your own experience or as observed in teaching.

3. *Written.* Two days may be allowed for preparation if desired. Proceed as directed in the middle paragraph, Billet, page 91. [37] These summaries are for your own benefit and not to be handed in. Then prepare to hand in a summary of principles as indicated in the last paragraph on page 97. A committee might well do this and report to the class. (This exercise will be found to be genuinely difficult but equally enlightening. It will at the moment extend and clarify the student's insight into the nature of principles of learning.)

4. *Oral or written.* Read carefully the discussion of levels of co-operation on pages 214-215 in Hopkins' *Interaction.* Note for a period of several days the level of co-operation operative in classrooms observed. Prepare a summary statement of critically analyzed illustrations.

[37] Roy Billett, *Fundamentals of Secondary Teaching* (Boston, Houghton, 1940).

(Protect teachers using poorer methods by not using names.) (Levels: compulsion; compromise, exploitation; bargaining; leadership; democratic co-operation.)

5. The principles of teaching and learning in the preceding chapters have been illustrated or exemplified frequently through quotations from poets, novelists, philosophers and other nontechnical writers: St. Augustine, Shakespeare, Charles Dickens, Robert Browning, Henry Adams, Thomas Wolfe, Pierre van Paassen.

   a. Analyze very briefly any one of the quotations indicated, showing in some detail what principles are being upheld.

   b. Report other similar passages from your general reading. (Be on the lookout for materials of this type during the remainder of the course.)

WRITTEN

Prepare a brief, compact paper showing what changes have taken place in your teaching, or changes that you are trying to make, because of what you have learned from Chapters 1, 2, 3, 4, and discussion thereon. (Students without teaching experience may confine their presentation to changes in their ideas about teaching and learning and to procedures they would hope to use.)

CHAPTER 5: Widespread Misconceptions Concerning Learning

The hardiest perennials among educational opinions are those which are not true. Certain erroneous ideas about learning and teaching have been subjected to a century of logically correct criticism. They persist. These ideas have been flatly disproved by conclusive amounts of valid statistical and experimental data. They persist. On what meat do these, our weird sisters, feed? They feed on an ancient blunder by uncritical teachers and laymen. Children are "taught" the multiplication tables. They are then tested by being asked to "say" the multiplication tables. Sounds sensible but is nonsensical. Tested by problems requiring application of the tables, a considerable percentage of the children cannot use the tables. Many do not even recognize situations calling for multiplication. What causes this? The formal school taught the skill (saying the tables) detached from real situations. Multiplication facts (or any other facts or skills) have, however, no meaning apart from real and sensible events within which they occur together.

Children learn the rules of grammar in and for themselves with no understanding of the function of the rules in aiding clear expression. Rules can be recited letter perfect by children who cannot construct a proper sentence, who would not know a conjunction from an injunction. They learned the rules and then were tested by more of the same— repeating the rules on request. Sometimes formal examples are identified. Testing in the formal school is rarely by continuous use in real situations.

Words are presented in formal lists. The test is to spell the words on a list dictated to them. The test is passed but the same words are misspelled regularly in compositions by many children.

Compositions are written to conform to rules with little attention to the content, for the sake of which the rules exist.

Dates in history are learned with no understanding of the social, economic, or political factors which made the date important. Geographical terms, the capitals of the states, lists of principal products are memorized, with no understanding of the relationship of any of these to geographical features of life. Testing is by *repeating* what was learned, not by *using* it.

These and many other absurdities *result from regarding various learning outcomes as independent factors which may be learned in isolation from use and meaning.* A real-life learning situation is a unified and whole event as the learner meets it. He achieves, for instance, a meaning or attitude, together with the facts related to the meaning, plus skills for carrying the meaning into action in later similar situations. The formal school has detached the fragments from the real situation and stresses them without relation to any real and whole situation. (Note that with adult learners this practice may be useful.) Skills are widely drilled upon in school but separated from any sensible use of the skills.

General commentary on misconceptions of learning and teaching. The misconceptions are a serious matter because of widespread acceptance among laymen and by a percentage of teachers. What are some of the chief misconceptions in circulation. All of them, we may note again, are contradicted by fact. Some are worded as to be very plausible.

A sampling. The following are general ideas.

1. Pure repetitive drill without meaning or insight is educative.
2. Homework of the traditional type is an aid to learning. (Note reference to "traditional" homework. Evidence is against this. Certain new types of homework or out-of-class work are useful.)
3. Children could do the work if they would only try.
4. Readiness and maturation are fool theories by professors.
5. We must force children to do what they are assigned.
6. Children must be disciplined, forced to respect authority. Then you can teach them.
7. One textbook thoroughly "covered" or mastered is sufficient in any course.
8. Mastery of the subject matter insures ability to use it in real situations. *Or do not* bother about subject matter, learn the attitudes and abilities governing research and study.
9. Homogeneous grouping is an aid to learning (or heterogeneous). *Or* homogeneous grouping (or heterogeneous) is a detriment to learning.

(The statements on subject matter and on grouping need to be sorted out and applied where they belong. The nonsense of these statements is enormous.)
10. Difficult, unpleasant problems are good for learning.

Nature of learning and of teaching easily misunderstood. The general public, many college professors, and a percentage of public school teachers believe that teaching is easily done. Most of them know little or nothing about learning. Learning is a subtle, intricate, and complex process. Teaching is one of the most difficult intellectual operations one can undertake. The fact that many teachers of mediocre intellect are seen operating easy routines; that many pupils seem to be learning with little effort should deceive no one.

The various groups of laymen, out to "save our schools," or to enforce "essential" or "basic" education, to force the schools to return to the practices of a half century ago when "education was effective" are incredibly ignorant of the processes of learning. They are equally ignorant about the old days and about the self-same criticisms that were widespread then—but that is another story. Some of these groups are entirely honest even though misinformed. Others are clearly dishonest, defiantly rejecting valid evidence derived under objective controls. The latter group may be ignored. You cannot argue with uninformed minds. The other groups should not be ignored, even though some pronouncements are weird to the point of unconscious humor. There are legitimate criticisms of education, and, though professional groups are far better informed on these and are trying to remedy them, lay groups often come up with serious points that should be recognized.

Serious misconceptions about learning are not confined to laymen. Schoolmen, we unhappily add, are sometimes as uninformed as laymen. Students will enjoy and profit from two articles by schoolmen which reveal unbelievable ignorance. Replies were made by other school workers.

McDOWELL, Bruce, "A Bill of Rights for Classroom Teachers," *Phi Delta Kappan*, Vol. xxxx, No. 8. (May, 1959), pp. 330-332. Replies are in *Phi Delta Kappan* for October, 1959, by James W. Merritt, Nancy Gayer, Virginia Bollotte.

RAFFERTY, Max, "The Seven Grim Fairy Tales," *Phi Delta Kappan*, Vol. xlii, No. 3. (December, 1960), pp. 114-120. Reply by Earl H. Hanson is in parallel columns with Rafferty's.

The two articles are written with sincerity but are, in the main, devoid of fact and logic. Some of the misconceptions border on the ludicrous. The articles are further marred by sarcastic distortion, name-calling and abuse, by rationalizations which are childish. Both writers, and others in similar vein, ridicule education courses. It is clear that they either (*a*) had no education courses, (*b*) had very poor ones, or (*c*) good ones they could not handle. Every professor of education knows that teacher education is a weak spot and is a severe critic of some things now going on in teachers colleges. Their criticisms are, however, deadly serious, based on detailed study and, most important of all, aimed at improving the situation. Progress will not be achieved through shoddy name-calling, brazen misrepresentation, nor through "everyone-is-wrong-except-me" arguments. Critics of learning and teaching would do well to heed the words of Sydney Hook [1] with reference to criticism which is "rude and contemptuous."

One is tempted to ignore Mr. . . . . or to retort in kind. But he speaks for many who feel and believe as he does, and if we are interested in the truth we must reply to his arguments, not his abuse. The trouble is that it is difficult to find a coherent argument.

[1] Sydney Hook, "Modern Education and Its Critics," Seventh Yearbook of the American Association of Colleges for Teacher Education (1954). Found also in Israel Scheffler, *Philosophy and Education* (Boston, Allyn & Bacon, 1958), p. 275.

Hanson, in his reply to Rafferty, has a cogent statement and implied rebuke.

I am all for writing about educational issues clearly and warmly, but honesty counts too. We have to be fair, not merely showy. I also think that in our business, which is primarily the development of intelligence in a base of sound character, communications ought to emphasize truth and logic, not name-calling, caricature, and distortion.

The various misconceptions overlap so widely that a deliberate attempt to discuss them separately is not wholly successful. The wholeness and integrity of learning situations is thus indirectly indicated.

The general state of affairs, with a hint at the more serious results, is found in the scathing indictment of the formal, traditional school by a physician:

A child begins many years of a kind of training that has this unique quality: that it is more or less divorced from any immediate usefulness, indeed from any immediate possibility of application. He learns things out of their context, about people who are dead, about . . . places he never expects to see. . . . He is initiated into the cabalistic mysteries of the symbolic arts. . . . Under social pressure of classroom and home he builds up a background, mostly verbal and pictorial, for his adult life in the community. Through childhood and adolescent years he slowly acquires vast, conglomerate systems of substituted behavior in these terms. If, as an adult, he develops a behavior disorder these symbolic systems are sure to enter into and complicate its symptomology, and sometimes to influence its course and outcome. [2]

The demand for drill on grammar rules illustrates two of the worst fallacies. One does not wish to labor the point. The issue, however, is of basic importance. Discussion will, therefore, be extended with an excellent illustration of a persistent blunder. There is insistent, near-violent demand that *grammar* be taught in all grades—and *drilled* in! On few points are facts more valid and volumi-

[2] Norman Cameron, *The Psychology of Behavior Disorders* (Boston, Houghton, 1947), p. 45.

nous; children may learn the rules of grammar but with no understanding of the application of these rules in aiding correct and clear expression. (The situation is different with adult learners.) Compounding the error, there is the further claim that studying grammar will teach one to think logically. The claims persist in the face of criticisms of grammar teaching over the past hundred years. The "good old days" were evidently not so good. Modern scientific evidence backs up the continuing criticisms.

A professor of English [3] has the following to say:

Within the subject of English—as in all other subjects, I would suppose—certain illusions have persisted for nearly half a century despite a great body of reputable research to disprove them. One of these illusions is the supposed efficacy of grammar for improving oral and written composition and in preparing pupils for college. In visiting English classrooms and talking with teachers of English, one is impressed with the persistence of their faith in a knowledge of formal grammar and in the drill-book exercise by which formal rules are supposedly applied automatically to the self-expression of the pupils. One is impressed, too, by the extent to which this formal learning and formal exercise still dominate the classroom activity, and still supplant the true exercise of the self-expression to which they are supposed to contribute. In my own frequent visits to English classrooms I am amazed at the extent to which pupils are engaged with the workbook and with the infrequency with which I find them actually practicing self-expression (writing, speaking, conversing, listening to each other, and replying). When I protest mildly my lack of faith in the formal drill, the teacher is likely to express surprise, or to remark that surely this is what the colleges want; correct usage and a knowledge of what is right and wrong. My reflection is: Yes, that is what the colleges want all right, but all our research on the subject proves that these are not the means for securing that kind of ability.

In all fairness it must be said that many of the teachers simply do not know the facts.

[3] Fred G. Walcott, "The Limitations of Grammar," *University of Michigan School of Education Bulletin*, Vol. 19, No. 4 (Ann Arbor, January, 1948), p. 49.

They know the subject matter but have no idea of proper methods for teaching it. Many teachers are, however, knowingly operating easy repeated routines which take no thought or preparation. The teaching machines can do this better and at less expense.

Still another aspect of the illusion about grammar (other subjects as well) is noted by another professor: [4]

Today many English teachers, on the assumption that teaching grammar teaches ordered thinking, erroneously reason that in their teaching of the parts of speech and Latin grammatical terminology they are teaching grammar, therefore ordered thinking and meanings . . . . Unfortunately these misunderstandings are the things which have taken us further away from our main goal which is to help the student grow in ability to think rationally.

It is odd that their teaching of grammar to develop ordered thinking does not affect the teachers' own thinking.

The evidence on the effects of teaching grammar (and on many of the other misconceptions) is to be found scattered through periodicals over the past half century. Excellent summaries are available in the Cyclopedia of Educational Research. Students wishing a scholarly and definitive summary on grammar will find it in:

POOLEY, Robert C., *Teaching English Grammar* (New York, Appleton-Century-Crofts, 1957).

This volume not only summarizes the evidence, it goes into method in detail. Historical and philosophic background are included.

Summary on grammar. The facts can be stated bluntly. A "thorough study of grammar" as an aid to usage has not an iota of evidence to support it. To most students the study of formal grammar has no closer connection with the writing of compositions than does any other school subject! Brighter pupils (and as we have hinted, adults) do gen-

[4] Richard M. Bassone, "Let's Talk Sense about English," *English Journal*, Vol. XLII, No. 7 (October, 1954), pp. 371-373.

eralize and apply rules from one field to another—when they remember to do so. [5]

One study may be cited as typical. Two high schools were matched, one given formal grammar for four years, the other instruction in expression and language usage. The first group of students improved steadily in defining and picking out grammatical terms, in parsing and in analyzing sentences, but did not improve at all in oral and written usage. The second group knew a respectable minimum of grammar but improved steadily in oral and written expression.

1: THE PROCESS OF LEARNING IS CONFINED TO MEMORIZING. THE ACCEPTED OUTCOMES ARE ISOLATED FACTS, SKILLS LEARNED IN ISOLATION, VERBALISMS.

Illustration of absurd emphasis on facts. The following brief composition about the Washington Monument was submitted by a twelve-year-old boy:

The Washington Monument is built of stone contributed by all the nations of the earth to honor the founder of this republic. From Arlington, across the river, where sleep the men who died for freedom, it looks like a giant spike which God might have driven into this earth, saying, "Here I stake a claim for the home of Liberty."

The teacher rejected this because certain "facts" were omitted: the height of the monument, the number of steps in the stairway within the shaft, the cost and time of construction, and the number of annual visitors. "But," said the boy, "I was trying to tell what the monument means and why it is

[5] We are not here primarily concerned with grammar, but interested students might wish to investigate for their own ends the development known as "structural grammar." Books are available by Paul Roberts, Charles Fries, D. J. Lloyd, and H. R. Warfel. Articles in periodicals are also easily available.

there." He was reacting to it as a whole possessing meaning; the isolated facts were not important.

This teacher illustrates one of the commonest and most serious misconceptions of learning. Learning is regarded as the memorization of facts: memorization, the process; facts, the outcome. Memorization and facts are legitimate concerns of learning, but not to the exclusion of other aspects. The boy in this particular case revealed a number of fine emotional reactions of appreciation, plus intellectual processes of understanding, and a number of mental skills. His pattern of reaction was an integrated one. The outcomes were several, here chiefly an understanding and an emotional attitude of appreciation.

Traditional school practice has been to treat the content of books and of courses as the learning to be mastered. Small pieces of this content, "lessons," were studied, that is, memorized to be recited to the teacher. This misconception of learning process and outcome has dominated the theory and practice of untold thousands of teachers of the "text-coverer" type. Laymen have accepted the view as correct and as based on centuries of practice. The interesting and significant thing is that this accepted view is not only incorrect, but represents a degeneration over a period of centuries from a far better concept. In fact, many so-called "modern," "new," "progressive" methods of teaching are not at all radical except when compared with current formal methods. Many are not radical experiments at all, but are closer in some respects to learning and teaching practices which greatly antedate the memorization-of-facts concept. Newer methods are, of course, based upon recent research into the psychological and biological nature of the learner and in that sense are definitely new.

The evolution of the separation between facts and meanings. The history of the progressive divorcement of facts from their proper relation to learning, and of their rise as end points in learning, is a long and interesting one. There seems to be a cycle in the history of education which repeats itself from time to time. At a given period, learning and life are closely interrelated: learning takes place in lifelike settings and for life purposes; the things learned are useful. Education and life are, as we say, functionally interrelated. Time passes. Formalism develops. Education becomes more remote from life—bookish and verbal, abstract and academic. Pupils learn *about* life, but they do not learn life. They repeat formulas and verbalisms, instead of grappling with real problems to achieve results usable in life. They engage in the limited learning processes of reading, listening, and repeating, to the exclusion of other processes which must enter into any realistic learning situation. [6]

The period during and following the Renaissance illustrates this process. The rediscovery of the classical literatures with accounts of the magnificent, democratic, and creative civilizations which once existed in the world, showed scholars that these free and advanced civilizations had been created by men like themselves, and could be recreated in the world. Schools sprang up everywhere to educate young men for leadership in a new world; the curriculum included Latin and Greek literatures, since they contained the value systems, understandings, attitudes, ideals, and appreciations upon which to build the new mode of life. Note carefully that these languages were not studied for "mental discipline," for the sake of memorizing the conjugations and the declensions, or for the ability to recognize ablative absolutes and datives of possession and to parse. The purpose of learning and teaching Latin and Greek was the *derivation*

from the subject matter of the basic and controlling understandings, meanings, and attitudes! The students *did not learn the subject matter;* they derived valuable learnings from it. The things learned were learned for use. But a change came. Time passed. The first flush of the new humanism cooled. The old master teachers passed on and their places were filled by less able men. More and more pupils came to school. Soon so much time and energy were spent on learning the form of the languages that pupils never did arrive at the understandings and meanings inherent in the content of those languages! Learning became the conjugating of verbs, the distinguishing between gerunds and gerundives, the finding of proper verb forms to use in indirect discourse. What the discourse *said* became of less moment! The cycle had been completed: learning forms and facts had replaced critical evaluation and derivation of meanings as the purpose of study. The vigorous, provocative fulminations of Cicero against Catiline in the Roman Senate became dull, dreary materials for grammatical analysis and translation. That these orations were vivid and enlightening avenues through which to understand life and conditions, through which to understand political machination and intrigue, was lost to sight. Today in our own secondary schools, materials such as these are still taught for language form, and not for the light they might shed on some aspects of our own national life.

Subject specialists as well as psychologists and educators recognize the weaknesses in this method of learning. This statement by Sumner is but one sample of many available: [7] "Pupils are not taught how to study mathematics—they are drilled on formulas. The result is overdeveloped memory and underdeveloped reasoning power."

Elementary school geography has been taught for generations not merely as facts divorced from reality, but, ironically, from a

---

[6] The cycle so briefly and superficially outlined here may be studied in greater detail in many sources, chiefly histories of education or histories of civilization. For a very brief, readable account, see Stephen Duggan, *A Student's History of Education,* 3rd ed. (New York, Appleton, 1948), Chs. 8 ff.

[7] S. C. Sumner, *Supervised Study in Mathematics and Science* (New York, Macmillan, 1922), p. 4.

reality which had nothing to do with elementary education in the first place. For most of us, geography was a matter of oceans, gulfs, bays, continents, capes, islands, isthmuses, latitude and longitude, zones—places—places—*places*. This geography came into being toward the end of the fifteenth and during the sixteenth century, the era of Columbus, Magellan, Drake, and other discoverers and navigators who found new worlds and circumnavigated the globe. The geography of places, prominent landmarks, latitude and longitude, distance—of prime importance in navigating and making landfalls—was organized by mature adults for use in the world. This became the subject matter for little children—a game of memorizing all sorts of isolated facts dealing with location, direction, and distance. The apotheosis of this type of geography was that ultimate absurdity of all elementary education, "saying the capitals of the states." The passing of time ameliorated this method, of course, and today elementary geography is well established in modern schools as something different. Places and locations are learned functionally—that is, in meaningful situations; the emphasis is on how man lives in his environment and the effect of environment upon all habits, customs, philosophies, and religions, as well as upon the elementary activities of securing food, clothing, and shelter. It involves more than this brief paragraph can indicate. Note, incidentally, the learning of places and locations by the public of the United States during the war in the Pacific, in North Africa, in Korea. This is as different from traditional "place" geography as day is from night.

The confusion induced in childish minds by this memorizing of fragmentary facts in isolation from their setting and meaning has been aptly satirized by Dickens in *Dombey and Son*. Incidentally, Dickens' novels are replete with protests against traditional nineteenth-century education and full of excellent pleas for the type of modern education which we are today developing.

When he had spelled out number two, he found he had no idea of number one, fragments whereof afterward obtruded themselves into number three, which slided into number four, which grafted itself onto number two. So that whether twenty Romuluses made a Remus, or *hic haec hoc* was troy weight, or a verb always agreed with an ancient Briton, or three times four was Taurus a bull were open questions with him.

The attention of the author was called recently to a modern illustration of Dickens' fictional satire. A girl, showing a visitor certain exhibits based on study of Egypt, said, among other things, "The Pyramids are a kind of mountain in Egypt. The Spinks was a lady that got stuck in the sand." Here again facts (*sic*) are wholly removed from setting and meaning. Evidently no effort had been made to show the relation of the Pyramids to the religion and superstition of the Egyptians. The tremendous drama involved in the forced labor of thousand of slaves working upon the Pyramids, giving significant insight into the social order, the understandings, and attitudes of the day, was apparently omitted. The place of the ruling classes, the pageantry of burials in the Pyramids, the recent explorations and exhumations were evidently ignored. The text was covered, however, facts learned, "results" achieved. Fortunately, scores of illustrations to the contrary can also be cited from modern schools.

Separation between facts and meanings furthered by administrative procedures. As more and more children came to school, more and more tasks were shifted to the school, and certain routines had to be established in order to get anything done. There evolved—unfortunately, we know now—the system of forty- or fifty-minute periods which so many take for granted. This was not the only system that might have evolved, and we now know better ways to manage the school day. The effect of the period system was that learning was chopped up into forty-minute segments. The emphasis inevitably was upon subject matter learnable in forty minutes or within a few such periods—namely, simple, isolated, fragmentary facts. The true learning outcomes—understandings, attitudes, appreciations, and abilities—are cumulative and develop best under reasonably continuous learning activities. How this can be accomplished is explained throughout this volume. The insistence that learning activities cease with the bell every forty minutes or so has been aptly satirized as "the ridiculous imperative." [8]

Skills may be learned in complete isolation from use. Skills can be abstracted from the total situation in which they naturally occur. This separation is even more absurd than that between meanings and facts. No one would dream of teaching swimming without putting the pupils in the water, or of skating without using skates on the ice. Schools, however, quite blandly teach the skills of addition and subtraction without any reference to situations requiring addition or subtraction. Composition is taught even though there is no reason to write, nor anything to write about. This nonsense is widely distributed throughout schools. Correction, we are happy to say, is well under way. Excellent teaching of skills within functional situations is growing rapidly, especially in the lower elementary grades.

Verbalism the most disastrous outcome. Learning words seems to possess an evil magic. Verbalism, clichés, empty words, old saws, bromides, clap-trap, come to have standing of their own without reference to meanings. The unrealistic, symbolic world created by and within the school accepts verbalisms as valid and meaningful.

High-sounding nonsense about literature or art or music is accepted as indicating understanding and/or appreciation. The simple, homely, interpretations given a poem

by a backward high school class were harshly rejected by a teacher who demanded that they see "truth, wisdom, and beauty" in the poem. The children do not know what this means, but they will quickly learn to say it. A junior high school class which asked a simple question about a piece of music was told: Harmonic tempo of music is usually in inverse ratio to the melodic tempo. The children have no idea what this means, but even though it is difficult to remember, they will have it ready for the examination papers.

The school is not alone in this. Verbalisms are heard in the form of pompous nonsense from prominent pulpits; specious pleading and legal sophistry from respectable (*sic*) lawyers; the lovely words of public officials denying responsibility for graft, corruption, and disaster clearly owing to their own incompetence and dishonesty; the twitterings of socially prominent but intellectually incompetent persons. Verbalisms are substituted for facts and meanings, and worse, they prevent meanings from emerging at all. [9] The substitution of meaningless words for facts, meanings, and even for processes, leads to many ludicrous blunders in life and in school. This simple summary can be supplemented by anyone from his own observation: "The wisdom of the lips is only wise when it is the habit of life."

The dilemma in the school situation is that despite the obvious dangers of *verbalism,* the use of *verbal methods* and of learning through words is legitimate and necessary in school. Education could not be achieved without use of verbal vehicles of vicarious experience. Common-sense definitions have been assumed to this point. The non-technical definitions given below will organize thought further.

[8] Robert W. Frederick, Clarence E. Ragsdale, and Rachel Salisbury, *Directing Learning* (New York, Appleton, 1938), pp. 219 f.

[9] Genuinely entertaining as well as enlightening reading on this general problem will be found in:
H. R. Huse, *The Illiteracy of the Literate* (New York, Appleton, 1933). Out of print but available in practically all college libraries.
Joseph Jastrow, *The Betrayal of Intelligence* (New York, Greenberg, 1938). Also out of print, harder to find, but in most college libraries.

A verbalism is a statement which is empty of meaning. It is an empty sequence of words. Words are substituted for meanings and facts. The statements sound good; they are socially acceptable; they ease one past a situation; but they have no reference to facts or to action based on the words. *Vox et praeterea nihil*—a voice and nothing more. The average citizen recognizes the situation as well as the psychologist. He uses the terms, *lip service, clap-trap, empty words.*

Verbal methods of teaching are methods which use words, oral or written, through which to convey meanings. Verbal methods are necessary. Verbalism can be avoided if verbal methods are based on (*a*) experience known to be possessed by the learner, (*b*) a level of maturity sufficient to handle abstractions, and (*c*) teaching methods designed to avoid the pitfalls of vicarious experiencing.

The end result of any type of experience can be either a verbalism or a genuine meaning. Genuine meanings should result from reputable verbal methods as noted above and elaborated below. Verbalisms usually result because of (*a*) violations of those methods, or (*b*) imposition of the verbalism in advance of, with disregard for, or in defiance of experience, or (*c*) the teacher's naïve, uncritical acceptance of verbalisms which confirms the habit of verbalizing.

Excellent supplementary material which should be read at this point will be found in *The Measurement of Understanding,* Forty-fifth Yearbook of the National Society for the Study of Education, Part I, pages 7-17.

Emphasis upon a limited concept of learning may effectually prevent the acquisition of many desirable learnings. The ability to reproduce memorized facts, to reproduce what has been read, the ability to outline lectures and readings, the ability to work exercises according to pattern are all legitimate outcomes of learning, under given circumstances. To limit learning, however, to these processes and outcomes is not merely to circumscribe the learner and to give him a meager, narrow education, but is actually likely to preclude the acquisition of numerous important and varied outcomes. Testing

such learning is obviously done by giving the pupil "more of the same." We ask him to reproduce facts in the book or in the professor's lecture instead of asking him to use these facts in solving a new problem. We ask for outlines of readings or lectures instead of critical reaction to the content. Glib reproduction is accepted. The learner soon succumbs to routine, and acquiescence takes the place of understanding, performance, and learning. It is just here that the error lies when the teacher says smugly and uncritically, "I get results, regardless of highfalutin theories of teaching." Certainly he gets results. He can prove he gets results. The difficulty is that the results are not worth anything. Worse, such results often preclude useful and meaningful results. Of course, an occasional pupil, bent on learning in spite of the method of teaching used, does react critically or attempt to apply in real situations some of the facts retained, and the results often prove embarrassing to both pupil and instructor.

Efforts to counteract this misconception go on continuously. Lazy and untrained teachers automatically oppose any suggested improvements in teaching; however, many earnest, sincere, and practical teachers also oppose them. They are no less uninformed than their unprofessional colleagues, but their opposition is honest. For the benefit of these honest, and doubtless educable, teachers, reference should be made to the history of civilization and of education. The particular errors which beset the practice of many experienced teachers and which exemplify the misconception here have been under attack since the beginning. A clay tablet several thousand years old contains the complaints of a merchant that his son, then in the store, had not learned in school to keep money straight, to compute accurately, to write legibly. The boy was careless and undisciplined. (Progressive education must be much older than we thought!) Long before Columbus discovered America, complaints were heard in Western Europe. Listen to Peter of Blois (*circa* 1200): [10]

Quid enim prodest illis expendere dies suos in his quae nec domi, nec militiae, nec in foro, nec in claustro, nec in curia, nec in ecclesia, nec alcui prosint alicubi, nisis dumtaxat in scholis?

The following protest was made in early colonial times by William Penn:

We press their memory too soon, and puzzle, strain and load them with words and rules; to know grammar and rhetoric, and a strange tongue or two, that it is ten to one may never be useful to them; leaving their natural genius to mechanical and physical or natural knowledge uncultivated and neglected; which would be of exceeding use and pleasure to them through the whole course of their life. To be sure languages are not to be despised or neglected. But things are still to be preferred.

Current efforts to improve teaching are not the caprice of theoretical psychologists and professors of education. They are merely the inevitable continuance of the effort to improve teaching in the light of more and more knowledge. The movement is welcomed by honest teachers even though it means discarding beloved routines; it will always embarrass and annoy the lazy and incompetent teacher.

The present reform, in its broad fundamentals, began in the Western world approximately 150 years ago, and began to affect practice noticeably about thirty years ago. In the United States, it became acute about fifty years ago; changed practices appeared in isolated instances, with more widespread effects from 1920 on.

During the early nineties, the normal schools of the United States introduced the Herbartian "five formal steps" as a lesson formula designed to get away from the conning of isolated facts in a series of "lessons." The learner utilized facts, to be sure, as well as narrative or descriptive materials, or any other necessary subject matter, but was led to derive from these a generalization, a rule, a principle, or an understanding which would be effective in meeting new situations and in controlling conduct. The Herbartian steps became seriously formalized, but they represented a worthy pioneer effort to rescue learning from the routine memorization of facts and to focus attention upon broader outcomes such as understandings, meanings, and principles.

Toward the turn of the century McMurry popularized the phrase "cold storage" education, in reference to the storage in the mind of great masses of fact which might possibly some day prove useful. Whitehead said: "But facts, like fish, will spoil if kept too long." Adams [11] matches this with: "Nothing in education is so astounding as the amount of ignorance it accumulates in the form of inert facts." More recently, Morrison dubbed as "lesson learning" the mastery of subject matter, the covering of textbooks, without deriving from them the understandings, meaning, attitudes, appreciations, or abilities which are true learning products. Morrison coined a neat aphorism when he said, referring to much current school practice, "the pupil learns his lessons but he does not learn." The pupil should, indeed, not learn subject matter but should learn from subject matter or from experience with subject matter.

Still later there appeared the socialized recitation, supervised study, direct method of teaching languages, emphasis upon language habits instead of upon grammar rules, problem-solving, the project, the subject-matter unit, and the functional or experience unit. All of these modern movements tend to

[10] For what does it profit them to spend their days in these things which neither at home, nor in the army, nor in business, nor in the cloister, nor in political affairs, nor in the church, nor anywhere else are any good to any one—except only in schools?

[11] Henry Adams, *The Education of Henry Adams* (Cambridge, Mass., The Riverside Press, 1918), p. 379.

focus attention upon the necessity of a wide variety of learning activities instead of memorization alone, and upon a wide variety of usable learning outcomes in place of the mastery of facts, the learning of textbooks, the covering of courses. Merely shifting from formal procedures to what seem to be modern methods is not sufficient. Projects, problems, and units appear in many places, but the end is still the same—mastery of isolated bits of information.

This account is necessarily brief to the point of superficiality; nonetheless, it illustrates the fundamental issue. Many other instances can be cited. The revolt begun in the schools of the United States about 1888 with the addresses of Eliot, Harper, and Dewey is a more recent illustration. During the nineties, education in the United States was at the peak of formalism and verbalism, remoteness from the real life of the nation. At the present writing we are again well into the period of realigning education with life, with consequent disturbance of old ideas about learning. In this account, we are for the moment chiefly concerned with explaining and destroying the misconception that learning consists of memorizing and repeating facts or empty verbalisms.

The implications for teaching. As the full meaning of the foregoing discussion develops, students begin asking what can be done about it. How may one teach so as to avoid these errors? More important, how does one get pupils to engage in genuine learning processes and to achieve useful outcomes? Questions often call for illustration of specific classroom devices or methods. This is especially true of those students who have themselves come through a traditional school and who have never met, until this moment, any conception of learning other than the formal memorize-the-text procedure. These students are often thoroughly bewildered. At this stage of the course, it is wholly impossible to give an adequate answer. Their own lack of background precludes it, not to mention the complexity of the total answer. This entire volume is designed to develop progressively detailed answers to this and other problems. Nevertheless, enough must be said here to indicate to the student that the problem can in fact be met, and to show him some of the simpler devices. It is also necessary to take advantage of the line of thought which is indicated by the student questions and which will be continuously stimulated and, it is hoped, satisfied as the course develops.

Major lines of attack to avoid this fallacy. *First,* the teacher must know the pupil's background of experience, his interests and ambitions, and his capabilities so far as they can be determined. Pressures from parents, from the social class, from the peer society must be known. Learning activities and objectives can then be geared to the child's level of maturity, his interests, present store of meanings, and attitudes. The unnatural pressures which drive to verbalisms, to inability to apply skills and facts, may thus be avoided. Pretests of information and understanding; inventories of interests, problems, questions, and ambitions; vocabulary tests; problem situation tests; improved essay examinations; biographies and sociometric analysis: all will yield information. Techniques for this are summarized in Chapter 10.

Second, the teacher should consciously break away from the "mastery-of-the-text" concept and give explicit attention to the total range of learning outcomes. Teachers should define explicitly the actual behavior patterns, meanings, attitudes, facts, and skills toward which learning may be guided. Teachers far too often do not know any objectives other than "cover the text" or "follow the course of study."

The nine types of outcome (illustrated very briefly below) are not separate and distinct, though any type of specific outcome may be the object of attention at a given time.

1. A *behavior pattern* is a characteristic way of reacting. It is an integrated collection of meanings, appreciations, and specific skills. A behavior pattern is the way an individual carries over into action what he has been learning.

2. A *value* is the worth, goodness, beauty, or desirability of any person, object, process, or belief. It is determined by the way in which it satisfies our purposes, desires, aspirations, or ideals. (Children are confused by abstract statements and do not use them, but they do have values which they state in their own words.)

3. *Functional knowledge* is any adaptive control of conduct which functions to make the results of one experience freely available in (transferred to) other experiences.

4. An *understanding is a general concept* that results from organizing and interpreting the meanings of various aspects of a given situation; from organizing and interpreting many specific illustrations; from generalizing experience. Understandings are in the form of generalizations, concepts, principles, theories, abstractions, universals, or generic statements. They are general, but they are not "generalities." They are distinctly not the vague, incoherent "general understandings" of the average citizen. They are definite meanings clearly stated in declarative sentences. They vary from broad, general understandings in courses of study to the more limited generalizations derived from given units or lesson series. The characteristics of valid understandings and, more important, the distinction between levels of understanding are clearly presented in the Forty-fifth Yearbook, Part I, referred to earlier, pages 27 to 43. This should be read at this point.

Here, by way of illustration, are some understandings:

Geographic environment vitally conditions the activities of people.

The growing complexity of modern life makes co-operation not only desirable but imperatively necessary.

The architecture for any region, the way men build their homes, churches, or other buildings, depends upon the materials at hand, the climate, the purpose for which the building is intended, and the conception of beauty possessed by the builders.

The development of culture is an evolving process.

Newspapers play a huge part in molding public opinion.

Newspapers carry propaganda as often as they carry news.

Absence of a large middle class in any country predisposes that country to autocratic government and to revolution.

The difficulties in deriving and stating understandings will be specially analyzed in Chapter 14. Literally thousands of illustrations are available and any sampling is hopelessly inadequate, but those listed above will suffice for preliminary contact.

5. An *appreciation is a liking for and tendency to choose*. It is a satisfying emotional response. These, too, are numerous, but much easier to state than understandings. Several different forms are acceptable. A few illustrations would include:

An appreciation of good poetry.

An appreciation of the ballet.

An appreciation of beauty in nature (or in sculpture, or in music, and so forth).

The desire to live an orderly and decent life and the tendency to choose things which contribute to that type of life. (This could be regarded as an attitude as well.)

The appreciation of the contributions of various nations, races, and individuals to the masterpieces of literature (or art, or scientific invention, and so forth). Appreciation of these things is distinctly different from understanding of the same things.

The enjoyment of unusual photographic shots and directional devices. (From a unit on moving pictures.)

The desire to make one's home beautiful and tasteful.

Wonder and joy at the evidences of the unseen power of God as manifested in the coming of new life in the world of nature. (This could be regarded as an attitude and also as an understanding.)

6. An *attitude is a relatively constant tendency to act* in certain directions and in accord with certain mental patterns. Attitudes may be primarily intellectual (based on knowledge and understanding) or emotional (based on appreciation). Attitudes are sometimes called mind sets, patterns of conduct, and so forth. Many of the appreciations cited above could be considered as attitudes also. Further illustrations:

An attitude of consideration and respect for other people when attending the theater. (This is manifested by observing such common courtesies as cheerfully taking one's turn in line, not entering late, not standing in front of people who wish to see, not eating candy, not crushing paper, and maintaining silence.)

Tolerance and respect for other person's opinions, together with the maintenance of independence of standards and opinions during discussion.

Respect for technical skills and contributions different from one's own. (This could be an appreciation as well.)

Attitude of willingness to co-operate. (There are definite understandings underlying co-operation and also appreciations regarding it; the attitude is still another thing.)

Attitude that school rules and regulations should be obeyed. (An accompanying understanding here would be: School rules are necessary and useful in getting things done, avoiding disorder and waste of time.) Here we may comment upon the part played by useless and arbitrary rules in developing antagonistic attitudes on the part of pupils.

Insistence upon reform of legislative machinery which will make it more simple, effective, and democratic.

Active tendency to participate in the civic responsibilities of a citizen.

Inquisitiveness toward natural and artificial phenomena; in learning how and why natural processes take place.

Perseverance in any task which has been accepted.

7. An *ability is a generalized power to carry on an integrated complex of related activities.* (An ability is difficult to define except in terms of itself. Illustrations will carry the point.)

Ability to read.

Ability to spell.
Ability to write.

These common but highly generalized abilities may be broken up into several dozen subsidiary abilities, each of which is a desired outcome of learning. Abilities, for instance:

To read with acceptable speed and comprehension.
To grasp at one glance an ever longer group of words.
To skim.
To find new materials in the solution of problems.
To read more rapidly silently than orally.
To evaluate what is read.

Before proceeding, it should be noted that many of the abilities listed above either can be classified as skills or can be broken down into more specific skills, as we shall presently. The fragmentary list does, however, indicate the complexity of outcomes in one supposedly simple subject. An even simpler subject—spelling—contains a diversity of outcomes undreamed of by the average citizen. Understandings, attitudes, abilities, and skills appear as follows:

Increasing sensitivity to one's own misspelling.
Awareness of society's attitude toward misspelling.
The attitude of desiring to spell correctly.
The development of systematic methods of studying spelling.
The attitude and habit of systematically attempting to determine causes for one's own misspelling.

Other general abilities often mentioned in courses and units are:

To co-operate with others in given undertakings.
To use newspaper and magazine reviews and criticisms in guiding one's selection of motion pictures to see or books to read or plays to attend.
To use logarithms and other mathematical formulas.
To conduct group discussion in orderly fashion.

To be able to check newspaper reports against standards, references, and sources of fact.

8. A *skill is facility in performance* of any given response; it is a relatively fixed, relatively automatic response to similar and recurring situations. Skills may be either mental or motor. The special abilities referred to above include within them scores and scores of skills. In the general ability to compute, for instance, there are found such minute skills as counting, using tables, adding odd and even numbers, adding two-place numbers, adding columns of more than four, five, or six numbers, measuring, weighing, estimating. What we commonly call addition, subtraction, multiplication, and division have within them a number of specific skills, most of which have to be learned.

Reading involves such subsidiary skills as skill in recognizing new words, skill in pronunciation, skill in combining contextual clues in order to interpret unfamiliar words. Other related skills are the skills in using a table of contents, an index, topic headings, footnotes, bibliography. Library skills include the use of the card catalogue, the *Reader's Guide,* the dictionary, book reviews, and similar tools. Skills useful both in securing content from reading material and in organizing outlines are skills in selecting a topic sentence, a summary sentence, and key word. Skills in punctuation, also, are necessary here. The reading of a map in general is an ability, but there are certain specific skills within it such as the reading of symbols for various elevations, types of vegetation, natural resources, cities, and rivers. In the field of mechanic arts, there are any number of subsidiary skills in using certain tools.

9. A *fact is any act, event, circumstance, or existence which comes to pass.* It is determined by measuring, counting, identifying, or by describing through consistent use of agreed-upon definitions of terms.

The listing of outcomes could be continued for many pages to include the many varied outcomes derived from individual courses, units, or other teaching-learning experiences. Supplementation may take place through class reports as indicated at the end of this section. Further discussion and illustration are in the later chapter on the construction of units.

Third, a wide variety of learning activities should be available. Teachers should deliberately break away from the read-question-recite-from-memory groove and use instead a wide variety of question types, readings, excursions, viewing of objects and processes and exhibits, group discussions, committee work, and other methods. The modern school uses these as a matter of course. The traditional school can greatly enrich learning experiences by using a variety of activities. Some idea of the diversity of learning experiences can be obtained from Mossman's [12] list:

1. Adventuring, exploring, trying, finding out, experimenting, investigating, searching, reaching, inquiring, extending, contemplating, collecting, examining, questioning, proving, asking, studying.
2. Creating, contriving, devising, proposing, constructing, imagining, planning, organizing, thinking, initiating.
3. Co-operating, pooling, suggesting, helping, contributing, outgiving, discussing, refuting, talking, reporting, proposing, sharing, participating, communicating.
4. Judging, evaluating, deciding, considering, concluding, forming an opinion, summarizing, formulating.
5. Consuming, enjoying, receiving, accepting, intaking, being affected, depending upon, listening.
6. Recreating, resting, renewing, playing, singing, dancing, relaxing.
7. Recording, drawing, writing, expressing, painting, sculpturing.
8. Repeating, reciting, practicing, drilling.
9. Obeying, accepting, following, conforming, submitting.
10. Dictating, controlling, ordering, forcing.

[12] Lois C. Mossman, *The Activity Concept* (New York, Macmillan, 1938), pp. 54-55. By permission of the publishers.

This list of eighty general types of activities indicates the possibilities. Students may wish to glance over Diederich's [13] list which groups 177 activities with some overlap into eight classes. The more specific use of these activities will be outlined in Chapter 14, on the development of units. A preliminary view of possibilities only is necessary here.

The implications are simple and important. Babies should be free to wriggle, to squirm, to reach, to kick, to crawl around. Growing children should be free to move about, to examine things, to talk to one another, to engage in co-operative projects. In nursery school, kindergarten, preprimary, and early primary grades children should be provided with a variety of realistic things to look at, to play with, to use. They should be engaged with a multitude of things which they can handle, thrown down, stand on, try to take apart, bite. Things likely to be dangerous or hurtful or that should not be destroyed may be kept out of the way. The importance of a rich and varied environment and of varied activity within that environment cannot be overestimated. A basis of reality is built as a defense against verbalism. The social environment should not be neglected, activities involving persons and social processes should be included.

Older children and adults will extend experience through taking trips and excursions, seeing new places, dealing with other types of persons, visiting museums, listening to lectures, observing still and motion pictures, witnessing radio and television programs, and finally reading a great variety of printed materials.

The extensive and interesting literature on readiness in various fields and on various levels is of interest here. Reports may be made by interested students.

Fourth, the teacher must consciously refuse to accept meaningless repetition of what

[13] Paul B. Diederich, *A Master List of Types of Pupil Activities,* Educational Research Bulletin, College of Education, Ohio State Univ., Vol. 15 (1936).

has been read, the glib use of words. It is staggering to see in some rooms, elementary pupils copying word for word from encyclopedias and other reference books. These materials are then read as class reports and many teachers seem utterly unaware that the pupil might as well be reading Chinese as far as any meaning goes. In a report on the cocoa industry, a child read glibly that "oil is expressed from the bean under pressure." Neither teacher nor pupils fluttered an eyelash. Later questioning developed that the boy had not the slightest glimmer of meaning for the sentence. He could not even guess what it might mean. He had copied from the encyclopedia. This might be said to be "education impressed on the bean under pressure." The teacher in question was quite dumbfounded that anyone should question the procedure used. Later, under sympathetic supervision, she corrected this difficulty with enthusiasm.

Fifth, skillful teachers will ask pupils to state their meanings in words which they use every day. This is a simple direct test of understanding or meaning. A verbalist cannot meet it.

A *sixth* effective method is to ask pupils to illustrate meanings with concrete cases from their own personal experience or observation. A verbalist ordinarily cannot do this. *Seventh,* particularly on upper levels, pupils may be directed to read several accounts, preferably some which differ somewhat or are in part contradictory, and to derive a meaning or understanding which can defended. *Eighth,* pupils may be asked to evaluate critically their own statements, to list evidence, or otherwise support their understanding against opposite views and against criticisms of assumptions underlying their understanding. All these devices direct pupils to those learning processes by means of which understandings instead of verbalisms may be derived. Analysis, critical, logical, and factual support are substituted for uncritical acceptance, naïve unawareness of assumptions, and lack of logic and fact.

DISCUSSION QUESTIONS FOR SECTION 1

The first three questions are simple ones of value to inexperienced teachers, or to teachers with very little training. Advanced students need not answer them but may be given the opportunity, if they wish it, to raise any questions about the implications.

1. A girl about to take the state teachers' examinations in various subjects discovered the night before the examination that she must take a quiz in agriculture. She had overlooked this in the announcement of the examination. She hurried out, bought the state-adopted text, and sat up most of the night to read it through. Next day she took the examination in agriculture and received a grade of 96.
Did she learn agriculture?
What did she learn?
What erroneous ideas of learning lie back of such a situation?
What detrimental beliefs about learning are encouraged by this common procedure?

2. A father complained about his son's education, saying he was shocked to find that the boy did not know where either Yucatan or Trinidad was, what hemp was, nor how to work problems by proportion.
Was the father partially, wholly, or not at all right in his criticism?
What definite questions might you ask this father in order to stimulate his thinking about education?
Could you use any of the facts the father referred to and construct a question which would truly test the boy's learning, or at least be aimed at testing it?

3. Another father complained that his son's education had not trained him to think, to do, or to attack ordinary problems, on his own initiative. The boy had unusually high grades, but according to the father, always came to the latter for planning and decisions which he should have been making for himself. When the boy asked to go to scout camp for a month, the father told him he could if he would make all the plans himself, putting in writing the equipment, clothes, money, and so forth, he would need. Immediately upon arrival at camp, the boy had to write home for money and practically every day he wrote for some items of equipment that all the other boys had brought with them.
Was the father partially, wholly, or, not at all right in criticizing what his son had been learning?
How do you account for the boy's high grades in the face of inability to act intelligently?

What, in general, is the matter with the type of education given to this boy?

4. Instead of answering any or all of the three foregoing questions students may bring in illustrations of the same things from their own experience and observation.

5. When teachers really understand the objectives of their teaching in the terms set forth in this section, the whole process of teaching takes on a very different aspect. How will it be different?

6. What is the meaning and significance of the statement that we should not learn subject matter but should learn from subject matter?

7. The desirable learning products briefly introduced in this section may appear in textbooks, but far more often they do not. Why not?

8. One author says that mathematics and the various physical and biological sciences are all primarily methods of thinking and that only in a secondary sense are they bodies of informational content. (*a*) What relation does this bear to the discussion in this section? (*b*) What guidance is there for teaching?

9. In a certain large city, a teacher was discovered teaching "community civics" who did not know where the city hall was, whether the city had council or commission form of government, who the local political leaders were, and was unaware of a burning issue which at the moment had the city so divided in factions that a special election was necessary. Yet this teacher was an honor graduate of a well-known university, had majored in history, and possessed the requisite hours in education.
   a. What obviously are the outcomes of learning for which she is working?
   b. Explain as well as you can how such a situation could possibly come about?
   c. What questions arise in your mind?
   d. Be on the lookout for similar observed situations in this or other fields.

(*Note.* In answering the next two questions, *reference should be constantly to the outcomes of general education only.* That is, answer with reference to those learnings needed by all citizens for the general purposes of living, other than vocational. There are scores of specialized learnings desirable for technical and professional pursuits which will be acquired through special courses on upper levels. We are not concerned with these learnings at the moment. Keeping this distinction sharply in mind will eliminate much useless argument, save much time and energy, but more important, will greatly clarify thinking.)

10. Show that useful facts, understandings, or attitudes applicable to the ordinary affairs of life do or do not result from learning:

    a. The capitals of all the states.

    b. The list of products grown in subtropical regions.

    c. How to compute cube root.

    d. Why the United States returned the Boxer indemnity money.

    e. How the Gettysburg Address is regarded and why.

    f. To recite from memory the Constitution of the United States; pages from *Hamlet, Lady of the Lake.*

    g. The argument in Burke's speech.

    h. How to dance a quadrille, a fox trot, a rhumba, any current dance form.

    i. How to recognize words in print.

    j. How to remain cool even under provocation to anger.

    k. That the square on the hypotenuse of a right-angle triangle equals the sum of the squares on the other two sides.

11. Illustrate the different levels of understanding, generalization, or principle which may be adequate for learners of different levels of maturity and experience. Several students should give illustrations so that several subject-matter areas are included.

12. Should any learning be required in school which shows no outcome in usable response?

    a. Give illustrations from current curriculums and school practice of materials and learned outcomes which are of no use anywhere in life.

    b. Give illustrations of materials and outcomes which could be acquired and which are clearly useful to all citizens constantly but which are not commonly included in current school curriculums.

13. Should there be any placing of knowledge in "cold storage" at all?

    a. If the answer is *yes,* how are we to know what things to learn which will be useful later? Could they not be learned and used at present and not reserved for the future?

    b. If the answer is *no,* what changes would need to be made in curriculums, materials, and teaching practices as at present operated?

CLASS REPORTS

1. Observe a number of teachers, or one teacher for several successive days. Prepare a brief summary report to be presented to the class, citing specific evidences of awareness or lack of it concerning the misconception of learning discussed in this section. Note the teacher's analytic and interpretive questions or the lack of them; his use of pupil experience; his use or neglect of real materials; his direction of class discussions; and his methods of supplementation.

2. Supplement the report with a listing of the various types of learning activities utilized by the children. Make a critical comment upon their appropriateness as used.

3. Modern courses of study are increasingly including statements of objectives; general for a course, subject, center of interest or unit; and specific for actual sample teaching outlines. These objectives when achieved are learning outcomes. Lists of learning activities are also suggested. Examine a few selected modern courses of study and report:

    a. The kind and form of statement of objectives, general, subject or unit, or other.

    b. The kind and form of statement of learning activities suggested for the teacher's use.

    c. One report should compare modern and traditional courses in these respects.

4. Treat in like manner any printed or mimeographed unit outlines available, and preferably the log of a unit which has been taught.

WRITTEN REPORTS

1. Verbalisms are decried as learning outcomes. At the same time, it is clear that verbal methods and verbal learning must be widely used. Verbal learning is, as pointed out above, quite satisfactory under certain circumstances.

    a. List and analyze one or two crucial major *educational* problems raised by this situation.

    b. List and analyze three or four important *teaching* problems confronting the classroom teacher in this connection.

SPECIAL READING

The writer has found that students are almost universally aided in understanding misconceptions of learning if they read the following reference. Students should be advised to avoid confusion and argument over Morrison's ideas on "permanence" and "mastery." We are here directly concerned only with the nature of learning outcomes.

MORRISON, Henry C., *The Practice of Teaching in the Secondary School*, rev. ed. (Chicago, Univ. of Chicago Press, 1931), Chs. 2, 3, 4, pp. 16-62. Chapter 2 is of particular value for this first misconception.

GENERAL READING

Beginning

BURTON, William H., *Reading in Child Development* (Indianapolis, Ind., Bobbs-Merrill, 1956), Ch. 2.
———, KIMBALL, Roland B., and WING, Richard L., *Education for Effective Thinking* (New York, Appleton-Century-Crofts, 1960), Chs. 9 and 10.
CANTOR, Nathaniel, *The Teaching-Learning Process* (New York, Holt, Rinehart & Winston, 1953), Chs. 2 and 3.
CURTIS, Margaret W., "Child Development: Concept," *Encyclopedia of Educational Research*, rev. ed. (New York, Macmillan, 1950), pp. 175-177.
DEWEY, John, *How We Think*, rev. ed. (Boston, Heath, 1933), Ch. 10, "Understanding: Conception and Definition," pp. 149-164, may be skimmed for quick introduction; Ch. 12, "Systematic Method: Control of Reasoning and Concepts," pp. 179-189.
KRAUSS, Ruth, *A Hole Is to Dig* (New York, Harper, 1952).
Learning and Instruction, Forty-ninth Yearbook of the National Society for the Study of Education, Part I (Chicago, Univ. of Chicago Press, 1950), Ch. IV, "How Children Learn Information, Concepts, and Generalizations," by W. A. Brownell and Gordon Hendrickson.
The Measurement of Understanding, Forty-fifth Yearbook of the National Society for the Study of Education, Part I (Chicago, Univ. of Chicago Press, 1946).
The Psychology of Learning, Forty-first Yearbook of the National Society for the Study of Education, Part II (Chicago, Univ. of Chicago Press, 1942), Ch. XI, "Language and Meaning," by Ernest Horn.

Words, Meanings, Verbalisms

BLACK, Max, *Critical Thinking: An Introduction of Logic and Scientific Thinking* (Engle-wood Cliffs, N. J., Prentice-Hall, 1949), Chs. 9-11.
———, *Language and Philosophy* (Ithaca, N. Y., Cornell Univ. Press, 1933).
CHASE, Stuart, *The Power of Words* (New York, Harcourt, Brace & World, 1954). An enlightening popular treatment.
HAYAKAWA, S. I., *Language in Thought and Action*, rev. ed. (New York, Holt, Rinehart & Winston, 1949). Extensive bibliography.
LARRABEE, Harold A., *Reliable Knowledge* (Boston, Houghton, 1945), Chs. 7 and 8. Good footnote bibliography. Excellent exercises.
OGDEN, C. K., *Bentham's Theory of Fictions* (New York, Harcourt, Brace & World, 1932).
WALPOLE, Hugh, *Semantics* (New York, Norton, 1941). A simplified account.

Advanced

COHEN, Morris R., and NAGEL, Ernest, *An Introduction to Logic and Scientific Method* (New York, Harcourt, Brace, 1934), Ch. 2.
HEIDBREDER, Edna, "The Attainment of Concepts: III The Process," *Journal of Psychology*, Vol. 24 (1947), pp. 93-138.
HEMPEL, Carl G., "Fundamentals of Concept Formation in Empirical Science," *International Encyclopedia of Unified Science*, Vol. II, No. 7. (Chicago, Univ. of Chicago Press, 1952).
HUMPHREY, George, "Abstraction and Generalization," in *Thinking: An Introduction to Its Experimental Psychology* (New York, Wiley, 1951), Ch. 9, pp. 265-307.

SAMPLE INVESTIGATIONS

BURTON, William H., and others, *Children's Civic Information, 1924-1935*, University of Southern California Educational Monographs, No. 7 (1936). Early European studies are listed in Chapter 3.
DEUTSCHE, Jean M., *The Development of Children's Concepts of Causal Relations* (Minneapolis, Univ. of Minnesota Press, 1937).
HEIDBREDER, Edna, "The Attainment of Concepts: VI, Exploratory Experiments on Conceptualization and Perceptual Levels," *Journal of Psychology*, Vol. 26 (1948), pp. 193-216.
MELTZER, Hyman, *Children's Social Concepts, A Study of their Nature and Development* (New York, Teachers College, Bureau of

Publications, Columbia Univ., 1925). An early and valuable study.

PIAGET, Jean, Several volumes by this author bear on concept formation.

SMOKE, Kenneth L., "The Experimental Approach to Concept Learning," *Psychological Review,* Vol. 42 (1935), pp. 274-279.

VINACKE, W. Edgar, "The Investigation of Concept Formation," *Psychological Bulletin,* Vol. 48 (1951), pp. 1-31.

HALL, G. Stanley, "The Content of Children's Minds on Entering School," *Princeton Review* (May, 1883), pp. 249-262. This is the great classic in the field. It dealt with information, but inferences are easily made concerning concepts. Many early textbooks in education cite this study and it is still of value.

Hall's study was duplicated in Kansas City in 1883. An account is found in *Aspects of Child Life and Education* by Theodate L. Smith (Boston, Ginn, 1907).

2: DESIRABLE OUTCOMES OF LEARNING ARE RECOGNIZED, BUT THE TYPE OF LEARNING STRESSED IS INADEQUATE TO PRODUCE THEM.

The material in this section is so closely related to that in the preceding one that overlap is inevitable. The error of accepting as satisfactory outcomes isolated facts and skills, and particularly verbalisms, leads to an even more serious error. Widespread confusion exists regarding the power of certain learning products to control conduct in the world. Many citizens and teachers sincerely believe that memorizing the Constitution will produce good citizens; that compulsory flag saluting produces patriotism; that learning much formal grammar aids one in writing and speaking good English; that the accumulation of great masses of fact will insure good thinking; that "hard" subjects train attention and concentration; that Latin and algebra train one to think. These are perfect illustrations of "substitutive" behavior. Not an iota of evidence exists anywhere to support these widespread beliefs.

Memorizing the Constitution produces the ability to repeat the Constitution, and has very little to do with producing the understandings, attitudes, and abilities necessary to citizenship. Good citizenship and patriotism alike are integrated patterns of action. To learn to be good citizens, pupils must perform the various activities making up good community living. The learning products must be not memorized formulas, but definite attitudes and habits of co-operation, tolerance, working together in groups, participation in give-and-take discussion, willingness to accept group decisions, ability to face and analyze change, and many others. Citizenship involves far more than the nominating of class officers, voting, and holding formal meetings under rules of order. Ability to patter glibly that "the government is made up of three departments, legislative, judicial, and executive," and the ability to run through the formula for amending the Constitution have practically nothing at all to do with understanding our government. A study of pressure groups, of factors coming between the citizen and his government, of factors affecting public opinion; studies of the reliability of newspapers, of local governmental problems, crime, police corruption, of the rise of new forms of municipal government such as the city manager and cabinet, of civil service reform, of deficiencies in our own democracy as well as of its splendid achievements, of community health and disease control; an analysis of local governmental organizations and problems at first hand—all these are far more likely to produce functioning learning.

Too great reliance on intellectual verbalism to control conduct. The school has traditionally relied upon intellectual understandings or meanings as the proper learning products with which one may meet life problems successfully. We may repeat, this is substitutive behavior at its worst. The school has traditionally neglected other types of learning, particularly integrated patterns of action, not to mention attitudes, appreciations, and values. [14]

An illustration: verbalism substituted for patterns of action.   Before taking up scientific evidence, we may cite one incident showing how disastrous this particular blunder concerning learning can be. In competition for a substantial prize offered by civic bodies, a high-school student submitted a remarkably fine "Civic Code" setting forth the ideals, duties, and functions of the good citizen. This code was widely distributed. The student was duly acclaimed as having learned remarkably well the basic things necessary to good citizenship. His teachers of civics and history were given credit for having produced desirable learning products. A few months after graduation from high school, this boy was caught red-handed planting a bomb in the office of the leading newspaper. At the police station, it was discovered that he had for some time been associating with and participating in the escapades of a gang of young hoodlums and bootleggers. He had been selling narcotics to high school students at the time he wrote the splendid code of the good citizen! The first reaction is to say that the boy had not really learned anything about citizenship. Not quite. *He had unquestionably learned— but not the appropriate learnings.* He had learned the proper *words* to say in response to given situations. He had learned *verbalisms about* citizenship. He had *not* learned the *understanding, attitudes, abilities, and patterns of behavior which really constitute citizenship.* To know what is right is one thing. To wish to do right and to possess the habits of right conduct are two quite different things. Transfer, of course, does exist, as will be shown a few pages further on. The trouble was not that he had not learned, but

[14] An interesting and provocative book by a layman discusses this general point and in fact the theme of this chapter. See Gove Hambidge, *New Aims in Education* (New York, Whittlesey House, 1940).

that he had learned the wrong kind of response for use in his own life.

But, says the naïve citizen, how can one possibly use these fine-sounding statements and still have no meanings to go with them? How can one act one way and make excellent statements upholding quite different behavior? We need not at this stage go into intricate psychological explanations. The fact is plain; we do this thing regularly and extensively. The social, political, and religious discussions of the average citizen around the dinner table, around the fireplace, in commuters' trains, in clubs, wherever groups meet, are largely made up of meaningless verbalism. As a further and ironic illustration, we may note that the average citizen recognizes this clearly even as he engages in the practice. He criticizes "lip service," "clap-trap," and "empty words." Unfortunately, these faults are present only in his friends and neighbors, in the opposite political party, in the other church, sometimes in his wife, but never in himself.

Psychologically, it is simple and easy to say one thing and to act otherwise. The practice is even socially acceptable, sometimes demanded; however, besides perpetuating ignorance and non-thinking, it is destructive of social and moral values—though this is not so easy to see. Verbalisms are used to cover up and gloss over reprehensible conditions in social intercourse, in the industrial world, in the church, and elsewhere. It is by no means far-fetched to say that this intellectual characteristic is one of the basic evils underlying the present ills of Western society.

What has all this widespread discussion to do with our original topic, learning? The formal traditional school which accepts verbalisms as end results, which imposes verbalisms on pupils, actually educates for this falseness of life. Pupil reports copied bodily and containing words which could not possibly have meaning for those pupils are accepted without question. Oral statements which are obviously divorced from any meaningful content are accepted without question or analysis. Untold numbers of teachers and curriculums are perpetuating this intellectual blunder. Fortunately, modern curriculums and increasing numbers of modern teachers are vigorously correcting the situation.

Skills learned in isolation do not always function in real situations. Commonplace illustrations of this are found in the pupils who spell words correctly in columns in the spelling lessons but misspell the same words in compositions. Good handwriting in the exercise books becomes illegible in everyday papers. Many pupils can add, subtract, multiply, and divide almost any given set of numbers, but they still fail miserably in problem-solving. Skill in addition is one type of learning. Ability to judge when to add is a wholly different one. Both must be learned, preferably in functional situations. A pupil has not "learned to add" until he has acquired both types of learning product.

The splitting of learnings and misconception of the power of certain learnings to control conduct can be extreme, as illustrated by the following case. A child was found who could add, multiply, subtract, or divide accurately when told what to do. Since she passed "standard tests," teachers and parents were satisfied. But she was unable to use these skills in life. Left to herself, she was likely to subtract numbers meant to be multiplied or divided, or vice versa. Oral diagnosis elicited the following statement:

I know what to do by looking at the examples. If there are only two numbers in the reading, I subtract. If there are lots of numbers, I add. But if there are just two numbers and one is littler than the other, then it is a hard problem. I divide to see if they come out even, but if they don't, I multiply.

This is an extreme case, to be sure, but there do appear many children who say, "If I only knew what kind of problem this was,

I could work it." They have acquired some learnings but not the necessary ones.

Many parents and teachers are proud that their children can "say the multiplication tables." Very often, however, some of these children cannot multiply well in real situations. It is much better to teach children to multiply in functional situations than to "say the multiplication tables." Later the children will probably construct the tables for themselves. That is the way the tables were made in the first place by bright, mature adults. Again we have an illustration of forcing subject-matter forms constructed by mature adults on immature children.

Scientific evidence that one learning product does not guarantee another. Can these incidents and common-sense generalizations be confirmed by scientific data? Yes, a very large number of investigations may be found in the literature. An extremely brief illustrative sampling follows.

Knowledge of subject matter does not guarantee either use of the material in functional situations or discriminatory judgments about it. Widely heard during the present period of criticism of the schools is a demand for "more subject matter, more subject matter. . . ." Lay critics and a certain percentage of liberal arts professors repeat this demand endlessly. The lay critics cannot be expected to know the facts. Teacher-training institutions, furthermore, are repeatedly charged with neglecting, subordinating, even eliminating subject matter (as if that were possible!). The charge against competent teacher training institutions can best be handled in one lone unacademic word—bosh.

Let us look at the facts, but first one or two summary statements bluntly stated:

1. Subject matter, the organization of principles and facts in any field, is *inescapably* necessary for thinking, for problem-solving, for discriminatory judgments in that field, and for everyday affairs.

2. No reputable educator anywhere, at any time, has ever neglected, deprecated, or in any way advocated the ignoring of subject matter.

But the matter is not that simple. Naïve advocates of "mastery of subject matter" as the aim and end of education would be severely shocked if they would look at the facts. The facts, experimentally derived and validated show:

3. Subject-matter mastery in a particular field *in no way assures* that the subject matter will be properly applied in any situation where it should be.

Subject matter is a *necessary* but not *sufficient* factor in thinking.

Knowing principles, facts, understandings is one thing, *applying* them is quite another.

The confusion over *learning* subject matter and *using* it is probably the most tragic illustration showing that one learning product does not guarantee another. To repeat, knowing and applying are not the same thing. Two different types of learning are involved.

The method of learning subject matter so that it be usable and the effect of type of organization within the subject matter will be presented in Chapter 13 on The Unit. Meanwhile we will examine, exclusively, objective data on the problem, together with statements from competent theorists.

Investigations of relation between subject matter and its use. Because of persistent misstatements to the contrary, we advisedly repeat the statement: subject matter is necessary and no one has ever denied it. We are concerned with another point: the use made of subject matter once it is possessed by a student. A number of excellent studies are available:

BLOOM, B. S., and BRODER, L. J., *Problem-Solving Processes of College Students* (Chicago, Univ. of Chicago Press, 1950).
BURACK, B., "The Nature and Efficacy of Methods of Attack on Reasoning Problems," *Psychological Monographs*, Vol. 64, No. 7 (1950).
————, and MOOS, D., "Effect of Knowing a Principle Basic to Solution of a Problem," *Journal of Educational Research*, Vol. 50 (1956), pp. 203-208.
DUNCKER, K., "On Problem Solving," trans. by L. S. Lees, *Psychological Monographs*, Vol. 58, No. 270 (1945).
HORROCKS, J. E., "The Relationship Between Knowledge of Human Development and Ability to Use Such Knowledge," *Journal of Applied Psychology*, Vol. 30 (1946), pp. 501-508.
MAIER, N. R. F., "Reasoning in Humans, I: On Direction," *Journal of Comparative Psychology*, Vol. 10 (1930), pp. 115-143.
————, "Reasoning in Humans, III: The Mechanisms of Equivalent Stimuli and Reasoning," *Journal of Experimental Psychology*, Vol. 35 (1945), pp. 349-360.
MALTZMAN, I., and others, "Some Relationships Between Methods of Instruction, Personality Variables, and Problem-Solving Behavior," *Journal of Educational Psychology*, Vol. 47 (1956), pp. 71-78.

These studies show, we repeat, that knowledge within a field in no way assures that it will be applied effectively in functional situations, nor that discriminatory judgments concerning it will be made. Mastery of subject matter without insight or understanding is not education.

Theoretical scholars have upheld the same point for over a century. An odd and interesting point is that academicians who so stoutly plead for "more subject matter" are unaware that the fallacy in this has been discussed by their own colleagues for a long time.

A century ago, in the midst of the Darwinian controversy, T. H. Huxley thundered at British audiences, "Sit down and learn *from* the facts." The facts, the subject matter, were there for all to see. *Everyone knew the subject matter.* The question was—*What did it mean?* What was to be learned *from* the subject matter?

As far back as 1849, Professor Thomas Dick in his Mental Improvement and Moral Improvement of Mankind, published in Philadelphia, discussed subject matter and method in terms quite acceptable to modern scholars:

Let no passages in any book be committed to memory before the leading ideas they contain are fully understood. If this principle were universally introduced into education, it would overturn almost every system of instruction which has hitherto prevailed, both in secular and religious tuition. An opposite principle has almost uniformly been acted upon; (catechisms . . . The Bible . . . speeches in the Roman senate . . .) have been prescribed as memorial tasks, before any of the ideas contained could be appreciated. . . . Of what use to stock and overburden the memories of childhood with a medley of words to which no correct ideas are attached?

Dick then goes on in both humorous and deadly serious vein to illustrate the absurdity of the "stuff-them-with-subject-matter" view of education.

Nearly a century ago the issue was up in American education, though the statement is on another angle of the same problem. Dr. J. R. Buchanan [15] of Kentucky, addressing the National Education Association in 1875, said:

I take it for granted that no intelligent teacher doubts the proper function of education to be the complete development of the man. The methods of that complete development are not yet understood, and its practicability in our schools and colleges is not clearly seen by many—but the old traditional notion that education is nothing more than a cultivation of the intellect by textbooks, or by any other means is not worthy of mention in this enlightened assembly.

Evidently the question of educating the whole child and the necessity of a method as well as subject matter was on the docket long before Dewey and the modern barbarians in the schools of education!

In modern times H. C. Morrison said in his monumental book which initiated a reform in secondary school teaching, "You do not learn subject matter, you learn from sub-

ject matter." Alfred North Whitehead upheld the same idea: "Education is what is left when all the facts have been forgotten." The same point was evidently in Henry Adams' mind when he said, "It is astonishing what a mass of inert fact can be piled up in the name of education."

No one would accuse Arthur Bestor of being a modern "educationist"! But he makes very interesting statements: "The learning of facts is not intellectual training, unless those facts are seen as conclusions of systematic inquiry and as a facet of larger knowledge." The same point was made long ago by René Descartes and Jean Jacques Rousseau. Again Bestor says: "The liberal disciplines are not chunks of frozen facts. They are not facts at all. They are powerful tools and engines by which a man discovers and handles facts. Without the scientific and scholarly discipline he is helpless in the presence of 'facts.'" Here Bestor is in agreement with Aristotle with his *Organon* (instrument), with Francis Bacon and his *Novum Organum* (new instrument), and with Jeremy Bentham who referred to his analysis of *Fictions* as an instrument for attacking problems and learning what things meant. These men never intended that their summations were to be learned—memorized and recited—but were to be *used,* in the derivation of meanings, new facts, and the like.

The late professor of history at the University of Madrid and distinguished scholar, Ortega y Gassett [16] said in this connection:

What has been the great historic advance in pedagogy? Beyond doubt, the turn it has taken under the inspiration of Rousseau, Pestalozzi, Froebel, and German idealism, amounting to a revolutionary avowal of the obvious. In education there are three elemental factors; what is taught (knowledge, wisdom), and the teacher, and the learner. Yet with peculiar blindness, education has centered about knowledge and the teacher. The learner was no factor in

[15] *National Education Association Proceedings* (1875), p. 42.

[16] José Ortega y Gassett, *Mission of the University,* trans. by H. L. Nostrand (Princeton, N. J., Princeton Univ. Press, 1944).

pedagogy. The innovation of Rousseau and his successors was simply to shift the center of gravity of the science from knowledge and the teacher to the learner, recognizing that it is the learner and his characteristics which alone can guide us in our efforts to make something organic of education.

A distinguished American, Ordway Tead,[17] former chairman of the New York City Board of Education and presently an editor with Harper & Brothers, says it thus:

A generalization is an intellectual package in which is wrapped up together the upshot of a body of evidence. It is a shorthand to the discussion of truths. But until the student beyond his mental grasp of a generalization finds it come to life in terms of *his* particulars, the learning is verbalistic and relatively ineffectual. This final reference back to the corroborative experience in specific cases has to be made by the student before he has learned.

Many others, including Robert Maynard Hutchins and President Griswold of Yale, might be quoted. A certain percentage of college teachers and the lay public in general would do well to know what the many scholars have to say about "subject matter."

We will, however, quote the remarks of a well-known fictional character, Sherlock Holmes. A client, astonished at Holmes deductions from the facts, said, "You see everything, don't you?" Holmes replied, "No, I see the same things you do, but I have trained myself to understand and interpret what I see"! The subject matter was the the same for both—but Holmes was able to *learn from the subject matter.*

In a summary article on the subject-matter learning controversy, Woodring shows that no competent scholar or subject-matter specialist upholds the view that mere mastery of subject matter is sensible.[18] He urges that we drop this stale controversy and concentrate on development of the best organizations of subject matter to facilitate teaching for functional aims.

Woodring might well have added that many rank-and-file professors and subject-matter specialists do uphold the incompetent view that subject matter is to be learned as is, and for itself, despite statements to the contrary by leading scholars in their own groups. We blush to admit that a few professors of education also defy the evidence and stand for the outmoded view. In a few teacher-training institutions there are faculty members who teach that subject matter is the end and make no reference to methods of learning subject matter which might affect later use of that subject matter. Clyde Russell, secretary of a state (Maine) teachers association, no less, reviewed a book dedicated to the importance of subject matter and its functional use.[19] In defiance of evidence and the best thinking of subject-matter specialists, Russell upheld the subject-matter-to-be-mastered view. He then went on to ridicule functional learning. Fortunately superficial views on subject-matter learning are being corrected by statements from such leaders as Morrison, Bestor, Whitehead, Ortega y Gassett, Tead, Hutchins, Griswold, and a host of others.

Any reader who may think the point has been unduly labored has simply not had the experience of arguing with the lay public and certain academicians who hold firm convictions in defiance of facts.

Another aspect of the same confusion is found in the claim that "learning" huge masses of fact first is a necessary foundation for thinking. This statement comes not only from the "text-covering" teacher who crams his pupils and from the teacher who is rationalizing his inability to do anything else but from many who should know better. Facts are necessary to thinking, but the necessary facts will be learned better during thinking or problem-solving. Facts and

[17] Ordway Tead, *College Teaching and College Learning* (New Haven, Conn., Yale Univ. Press, 1949), pp. 32-33.

[18] Paul Woodring, "Subject Matter and Goals in Education," *Educational Forum,* Vol. XXIV, No. 4 (May 1960).

[19] Clyde Russell, "Education for Effective Thinking" *New Hampshire Educator,* Vol. XL, No. 4 (September-October, 1960).

thinking are learned functionally and in part simultaneously. It is further claimed that pupils who know great masses of facts will be able to think well about and with these facts. A number of important scientific investigations flatly contradict these ideas. Tyler[20] found the correlation between information and ability to infer to be only .29. Judd[21] has shown the necessity of teaching directly for the various abilities and skills in thinking if they are to be achieved. Tyler,[22] Eurich,[23] Brueckner,[24] and others have demonstrated the necessity of testing for all of the major desired outcomes. Testing which shows the presence of some outcomes does not guarantee that others are also present. Each must be taught directly and tested for itself. The acquisition of facts or knowledge does not guarantee understandings, meanings, or abilities to use the facts. The acquisition of skills and processes does not necessarily bring with it desirable understandings and meanings which often need to be correlated with the processes. Many investigations show that pupils on both upper- and lower-school levels do not acquire the abilities of scientific procedure merely by taking science courses as taught at present.[25] Some teachers of science do not possess a scientific attitude nor do they use scientific procedures. This may account for some short-comings in the students.

Transfer between learning products. The foregoing might seem to imply that all learning is specific and that certain learnings alone will control given life situations. Nothing could be further from the truth. *First,* common sense shows that there is an overlapping of many everyday learnings in their ability to function in real situations. It is well known that facts and information do actually control behavior very well for certain types of intelligence and in certain types of situations. Emotional controls will, however, often direct behavior in direct defiance of the facts. *Second,* there are reliable scientific evidences that some transfer does take place under given conditions; that is, that various learning outcomes overlap in ability to control life situations.

For instance, returning to the grammar-language issue, it has been proved that a study of Latin will increase the bright pupil's English vocabulary, especially his knowledge of words derived from Latin, *but only when the methods of instruction are designed to secure this transfer.*[26] Dull pupils do not profit. In another study,[27] not only was no transfer secured, but the greatest vocabulary gains were made by the pupils who studied no foreign language at all! Even graduate students will fail to transfer simple principles. In one experiment[28] only 6 per cent failed to square $x + y$ correctly, but 28 per cent failed to carry the principle over to the squaring of $b_1 + b_2$. It has been shown that if one is to learn to define accurately and to use definitions properly, there must be definite critical analysis of the features of a definition. Mere drill in defining has little effect.

The flexibility and adaptability, that is,

[20] Ralph Tyler, *Measuring the Ability to Infer,* Educational Research Bulletin, College of Education, Ohio State Univ., Vol. 9 (1930), pp. 475-480.

[21] Charles H. Judd and others, *Education as the Cultivation of the Higher Mental Processes* (New York, Macmillan, 1936).

[22] Ralph Tyler, *Constructing Achievement Tests* (Columbus, Ohio, Ohio State Univ. Press, 1934), pp. 6-7.

[23] A. E. Eurich, in *Studies in College Examinations* (Minneapolis, Minn., Univ. of Minnesota Press, 1936), pp. 51-66.

[24] Leo J. Brueckner, "Intercorrelations of Arithmetic Abilities," *Journal of Experimental Education,* Vol. 3 (September, 1934), pp. 42-44.

[25] Francis D. Curtis, *Third Digest of Investigations in the Teaching of Science* (Philadelphia, Blakiston, 1939), p. 279.

[26] S. L. Pressey, *Psychology and the New Education* (New York, Harper, 1933), pp. 500-501.

[27] Clifford Woody, "The influence of the Teaching of First-Year French on the Acquisition of English Vocabulary," *Studies in Modern Language Teaching,* Vol. 17 (New York, Macmillan, 1930), pp. 149-184.

[28] E. L. Thorndike, "The Effect of Changed Data upon Reasoning," *Journal of Experimental Psychology,* Vol. 5 (1922), pp. 33-38.

the wider use of given learning products is decidedly enhanced by (*a*) deliberately teaching for transfer or generalizing, [29] (*b*) using lifelike situations in teaching, (*c*) providing for much application.

Transfer is also greatly affected by (*d*) the intelligence level of the learner. One important study showed that pupils of low IQ tend to improve in English more adequately if they do *not* study a foreign language; pupils of average IQ do about as well with or without foreign language study; and the pupils with high intelligence show improvement in English as a result of transfer from the study of foreign language. [30] Many other experiments, which need not be cited here, show clearly the relation of intelligence to transfer. Still others indicate that similarity between the situations—original learning and transfer situation—is a factor. [31]

Variations among pupils in transfer. Morrison described in interesting fashion certain significant differences among students in their reactions to traditional curriculums. If pupils are first traditionally tested on assigned material and then again genuinely tested for functional learning in handling new materials or situations, three types of pupils are discovered. [32] The first, which Morrison calls the *lesson learner,* makes excellent grades on prepared material; that is, a good daily showing on the assignment. These pupils, however, show no independent power with new material. They can read prepared assignments in French, but they cannot read French otherwise; they can work assigned exercises in mathematics, but they cannot recognize real situations which call for the application of the mathematical principles involved. These are the pupils who say, "What do I do next?" When pressed for interpretation or implication, they retreat behind the statement, "That is what the book said." These pupils have learned their lessons, but they have not learned. The second group is designated as the *transfer type,* since there is evidently some transfer from the daily preparation activities to real situations. In preparing the assignments, in doing the exercises, in studying the lessons, these pupils do actually acquire the desired learning product, whatever it may be. As indicated in preceding paragraphs, good teaching will aid this type. Transfer-type pupils do turn up under even the poorest kind of teaching. Under ordinary conditions the number is small. The third group Morrison calls the *direct learners.* Their processes are not easily explained. These pupils make a poor showing on the traditional school tasks; they do assignments badly; their recitations are distinctly unacceptable. Oddly enough, they do acquire genuine learning products and can demonstrate them. When tested in real situations, on new materials, and in lifelike cases, they manifest real power. They have achieved functional learning by direct processes of their own. Many of them are ill-adapted to traditional school conditions, some so much so that they become "problem cases." Often the fault lies with the school instead of the pupil. It is from this group that come many of the individuals who were conspicuous school failures but who are equally conspicuous for genuine success in life.

[29] G. P. Meredith, "Consciousness of Method as a Means of Transfer of Training," *Forum of Education,* Vol. 5 (1927), pp. 37-45.

[30] O. H. Werner, "The Influence of the Study of Modern Foreign Languages on the Development of Desirable Abilities in English," *Studies in Modern Language Teaching,* Vol. 17 (New York, Macmillan, 1930), pp. 97-145. Also, M. N. Woodring, *A Study of the Quality of English in Latin Translations,* Teachers College Contributions to Education, No. 187 (New York, Teachers College, Bureau of Publications, Columbia Univ., 1925).

[31] Students wishing further study of the problem of transfer will find an excellent summary in the *Cyclopedia of Educational Research* under "Transfer of Training" and "Formal Discipline." Pedro T. Orata, "Recent Research Studies of Transfer of Training with Implications," *Harvard Educational Review,* Vol. XI (1941), pp. 359-378. See other summaries by Orata.

[32] Henry C. Morrison, *The Practice of Teaching in the Secondary Schools,* rev. ed. (Chicago, Univ. of Chicago Press, 1931), pp. 57 ff.

The implications for teaching. It is clear that the only way to be sure that the numerous and diverse learning products we seek are achieved is to teach for them. There is increasingly among teachers a tendency to set down explicitly the desired learnings. We have too long simply taught and hoped that certain outcomes would eventuate. There is increasing understanding of the nature and power of different types of outcomes. We need not repeat what was said above about teaching for transfer. This involves giving practice in generalizing, in applying generalizations to new situations. Compartmentalized subject matter will be minimized and lifelike situations increasingly used in teaching. Pupils will be made conscious of the interrelations of knowledge. Attitudes and ideals likewise will be made objective. Finally, it will be recognized that transfer is never complete nor automatic.

DISCUSSION QUESTIONS FOR SECTION 2

1. Scores of pupils have no idea what they are saying when repeating the flag salute. Asked to write it out, there appear such expressions: I pejur legens; I plaig alegins; I pledge a legion; to the Republicans; one nation invisable; one nation inavisable; with liberty and jesters.
Show how this illustrates a number of misconceptions of learning.
How could this be corrected, granting that we should retain the constant compulsory repetition of the salute?
Suggest a number of more effective ways of developing reverence and love for the flag.
2. At a college gathering a professor of literature stated that vaccination was nonsense. A medical professor outlined in simple terms evidence to the contrary, but he was told courteously that nonetheless vaccination was foolish and ineffective.
Is this man likely to be wholly, partially, or not at all a competent professor of literature?
3. A candidate for teaching completes the required courses in education with a major in science. He is certificated to teach science. He is wholly ignorant, however, of what it means to be scientific.

What does it mean to be scientific?
Does it make any difference for his teaching whether he understands the "scientific attitude" or not?
Should his training in science affect in any way his views in art, religion, ethics, economics, and politics? Why, or why not?
How could he major in science and yet be "unscientific"?
4. A school superintendent referred to a certain high school teacher of science as very "unscientific" in attitude and method. A professor of chemistry, overhearing this, expressed doubt that such a thing was possible.

The incident with names suppressed was later repeated by the superintendent in an advanced class, whereupon the instructor blandly asked if the students had ever met science teachers who were unscientific. The class burst out laughing and pointed to a building across the quadrangle—"many over there." It was the chemistry building in which the chemistry professor operated!

Make several commentaries on both aspects of this incident.
5. Some years ago, the application of a student for a well-paid fellowship was refused because his grades were far below the required level. Personal reports indicated generally low-level attention, lack of methods of attack, and lack of persistence. Learning of this, the student came and pleaded to be accepted. He admitted frankly that his grades were low because he had gone out for campus activities, had enjoyed college life, and had put his attention on gaining benefits from college other than those derived from the classroom.

He said that he knew he could do the work if given the fellowship; he was settling down now and would dig in; he would study because it was easy for him; he would get his work done and on time; he would faithfully turn in the required reports. He was told, as kindly as possible, that in reality he would not dig in; he would not be able to do the work; he would not be able to organize and compile the detailed reports, even though he was given full credit for sincerity in saying and believing that he would do these things.

The instructor explained that he had had four years of excellent training in not digging in, in not studying, in not finishing on time, in not attacking problems that were difficult and complex. "But," said the student, "that doesn't make any difference now. I know I can do the work."

Explain the instructor's apparently hard-hearted attitude in terms of the accepted definition of learning.

Construct a brief statement setting forth what you think the student believed about the nature of learning, of the ability to do, to organize.

6. Tell another story similar to the story of the boy and the civic code, illustrating the error of misconceiving the use and power of certain learning products.

7. Observe a teacher or a number of teachers for evidence of awareness or ignorance of this misconception. It is very easy to fall into the error outlined in this section. Effort to recognize it as it occurs will sensitize students to the error. Prepare a report to be made in class. Look for the use of words beyond comprehension of pupils; for the acceptance of reports from pupils which obviously have no meaning for the pupil; for careful checking to see that pupils do understand the teacher's explanations and their classmates' reports; for skills drilled in isolation with no reason in use. Watch for careful definition by the teacher of her objectives in contrast with vague, hopeful, general statements as to desired outcomes. Watch for use of life situations and discussion of real problems. Watch for evidences of transfer and teaching for transfer.

8. The direct-learner type of pupil achieves functional learnings in a lesson-learning school. How do you account for this?

READINGS

FREDERICK, Robert W., RAGSDALE, Clarence E., and SALISBURY, Rachel, *Directing Learning* (New York, Appleton, 1938). Chapter 6, pp. 110-128, is an excellent supplement for this section. Probably only similar discussion available. Pages 459-492 of Chapter 24 deal with problem-solving and for that type discuss admirably the implications of this section. The book is unfortunately out of print.

Other current readings are indicated in footnotes and in the body of the chapter.

CLASS REPORTS ON TRANSFER OF TRAINING

Students who need further acquaintance with the facts of transfer will find that reports on investigations within their own major subject field will be interesting and particularly en-lightening. For instance, there have been scores of studies of transfer in the field of mathematics. Many have been done with Latin as a base; others use modern foreign languages. Studies on grammar and transfer would fill a small book.

Individual students or small committees may select a subject area and summarize a number of selected experiments. Various compiled summaries of references are available. These should be supplemented by current references from psychological and educational journals.

3: THE OUTCOMES OF LEARNING ARE THOUGHT TO BE SIMPLE INSTEAD OF COMPLEX, SINGLE INSTEAD OF NUMEROUS AND VARIED.

(thought of as purely intellectual, as compartmentalized, as definite and concrete instead of as adaptable responses)

Learning outcomes are actually numerous, varied, and complex. Traditional teachers tend to think of products of learning in rather specific and limited terms. The child is to learn a set of dates, the facts about the Declaration of Independence, the multiplication tables, the countries of South America —and that's that. Even when they try to develop attitudes and appreciations, as many good traditional teachers do, these are regarded as limited direct outcomes.

We have indicated earlier that such outcomes as behavior patterns contain many learnings integrated into a functioning whole. Meanings, understandings, attitudes, and special abilities are themselves not single and simple. Any given mental, emotional, or motor construct achieved by a learner on any level is made up of several learnings.

New points may be added here: The several learnings which emerge from any experience are achieved simultaneously. The complex of learnings may contain detrimental outcomes as well as the desired beneficial ones. The various learnings concomitant to the major objective are acquired whether the teacher has them in mind or not; sometimes even over opposition by the teacher.

Illustrations of varied outcomes. A young teacher assigned to a school in a remote oil field region of the Southwest arrived to find her school to be a dirty, ramshackle building set in a bare, sun-baked yard. Paint had long since peeled off. The inside was indescribably dirty. Floors, walls, and windows had evidently not been washed for a long time. There were no curtains, pictures, or decorations of any type. Her pupils were to be the difficult-looking children of poor laborers brought in to do the very rough work of the oil field. Truly a dreary prospect! Rising to the challenge, the teacher, in the few days remaining before school opened, scrubbed and cleaned. After using much soap and water, she bought and hung some bright, inexpensive curtains. She cut attractive pictures from old magazines and placed them about the room. With a few bright-colored decorations of various sorts, a potted plant or two requisitioned from one of the better homes, and some new paint, she gave life and color to the room. Long before the opening hour, the first of her pupils came to school: a bedraggled girl from a squalid cabin stood silently in the doorway and then entered shyly. She gazed around for some minutes, ignoring the teacher, and then spoke. "Hmm, a pretty house what you got here! I think mebbe I likes to live here better than by my house." Happily, expectantly, she entered this beautiful place. This youngster came to school to learn to read and write. Before the first lessons, she had begun to learn other important things— standards of cleanliness, neatness, and beauty. She had begun to respond to several aspects of the total environment. Her learning responses were numerous, varied, and eventually complex. They were stimulated by factors seemingly not directly connected with the obvious business of the school—reading, writing, and arithmetic.

Who can doubt that she worked harder and learned better even these more direct and obvious outcomes than she would have in the formerly dirty, shabby schoolroom?

At the other end of the educational system may be cited the instance of the college student majoring in chemistry. He was constantly at work in the laboratory on problems of his own which grew out of the class work. His fellows scoffed at him, urging him to drop all this extra work for the more worthwhile pursuits of the campus. Their chief argument was, "What do you get out of it? You can't get a grade or extra credit for it. *There is nothing in it for you.*" But there was. This student was acquiring an immense amount of information in his field, increasing his laboratory skills, and more important, was developing a genuine and aggressive intellectual interest in the field of industrial chemistry. He was learning much more than did his classmates and far more than the instructor set out to teach.

Responses may be positive or negative. The foregoing stories illustrate a fundamental fact about learning: Pupil responses to a given situation are numerous and not single, likely to be complex instead of simple. The additional responses may be negative or positive. A boy may learn to read, but he may also learn to detest reading, to avoid reading as a source of pleasure or information in solving life problems. These results are all secured by the teacher whether he wills it or not. Many adults acquired in school their present dislike for literature, art, and music. Part of this, in some cases, is owing to the nature of the individual, but much of it is unquestionably owing to the analytic methods used in school. Literature, which should be taught for enjoyment, has been taught as if literary production or critical evaluation were the desired outcomes. These aims are obviously pointless in all general classes in the fields mentioned. In addition, so-called "good literature" has been forced in adult form on immature secondary school pupils. Advanced literary forms have been forced on many high school pupils with the reading abilities and interests of sixth- or eighth-grade pupils. The inevitable result has been to bury the attraction beneath a tangle of analysis and criticism. The methods of teaching literature used in many high schools and colleges are so different from the method a normal mind would apply in reading for enjoyment that ennui, disgust, and antagonism result—in fact, are learned.

On the positive side, note that pupils may learn the ordinary content of history and at the same time learn to apply historical generalizations to current problems. The study of the stories of Nathan Hale and Benedict Arnold may develop several valuable understandings and appreciations quite apart from the historical facts. On the other hand, this natural process of making numerous and varied learning responses to a situation may be inhibited by poor teaching. Pupils may go through courses in civics and government but fail to acquire the ideals, attitudes, and habits of good citizenship. Many high school classes (and women's clubs) discuss "current events" vigorously, but do not care whether the local community is well governed or not. It is quite possible to study grammar and get good grades for repeating the rules but be unable to write a letter which will convey thought.

This characteristic of learning—that responses are diverse and are made simultaneously to more than one factor in the learning situation, and may be negative as well as positive—has never had the prominence it deserves until very recently. It now seems to be permeating the work of alert elementary teachers and more slowly gaining recognition on higher levels. The student, be he kindergartner or collegian, learns more than the text, the assignment, or what the teacher sets out to offer. The key is the teacher's method and manipulation of the total learning situation. Everyone has noted with the passing years a distinct change in the attitude of children, particularly in the lower

grades, toward school.[33] Today, eager youngsters, hating to miss any part of the school program, replace the

. . . Whining school-boy, with his satchel
And shining morning face, creeping like snail
Unwillingly to school.

Modern methods teach children more than "the three R's." They teach liking for school; pride in accomplishment; standards of conduct; ability to evaluate and use what is learned; willingness to persist in the face of difficulty; the more complex intellectual and emotional learnings such as generalized attitudes and ideals; neatness and accuracy; attitudes toward one's work, one's classmates and teachers; likes and dislikes for persons, processes, and ideas. True, carryover is not automatic, but it can be enhanced by proper teaching.

The implications for teaching. Again, as with the first misconception, only a few general suggestions can be given to satisfy the student's inquiries at this point. The general principle is that methods of teaching must take into account far, far more than do the simple procedures commonly associated with school-keeping. In fact, it seems that the bare routine facts which the school has insisted upon for generations can be "taught" and "learned" under almost any method. Certainly normal children seem to acquire eventually enough of reading, writing, and arithmetic in any and all schools to get along. To be sure, the time of acquisition will differ greatly from method to method, and in many cases pupils get little else. In order to achieve more subtle learning outcomes and to avoid undesirable ones, the

[33] Claire T. Zyve and others, *Willingly to School* (New York, Round Table Press, 1934). An interesting photographic record of activities in the new school.
Albion H. Horrall and others, *Let's Go to School* (New York, McGraw, 1938).
Were We Guinea Pigs? Ohio State University High School, Class of 1938 (New York, Holt, 1938).

teacher must take into account *all* the factors in the learning situation. The very appearance of the classroom, the decorations, the kind and amount of instructional materials, the teacher's attitude and temperament, his appearance and dress, the state of health of the pupil, the type of home from which he comes, the security and peace of that home or the lack of it, the type of rewards offered by the school, the provision for successes by pupils—all these and scores of others need to be taken into account by the teacher. This is all the more important when it is remembered that while some of the learnings desired will be *incidental to the chief purpose motivating the learner, they must be matters of conscious consideration by the teacher.*

The good teacher will utilize and encourage all spontaneous and self-motivated learning. He will be sympathetic with difficulties, with errors, and with slow progress. He will encourage and accept questions from pupils. He will know that when pupils are working purposefully on problems of value to themselves, various types of learning outcomes are sure to develop. He will make the numerous and varied learning outcomes matters of conscious concern and planning.

DISCUSSION QUESTIONS FOR SECTION 3

Analysis and oral discussion of the following questions should be completed before the reading is begun:

1. In one of Kipling's tales there is recounted the struggles of a little boy learning to read. He and his tutor wrestle with the problem long and valiantly, but progress is slow and halting. The process is an unhappy one for both participants. At last the day comes when the tutor says, "You have learned to read." The boy throws down his book, saying, "Now I can read—I shall never read again!"
List several learnings which undoubtedly took place here.
Which of these were consciously sought by the tutor? Which were not?

In advance of more technical knowledge on your part, attempt to explain psychologically the total outcome of this incident.

2. In an English class there arose vigorous discussion about aviation. Pupils were asking questions right and left. Finally, one asked the teacher if she could tell him how many times an airplane propeller turned per minute (revolutions per minute, or "RPM"). The teacher silenced the whole discussion, saying, "This is an English class, not one in aviation."
List as well as you can what learnings might have taken place (in English, personality, etc.) if the discussion had been encouraged.
List some that may have emerged under the given circumstances.
What would you have done, being ignorant of the answer to this question and on the basis of your present amateur understanding of teaching and learning?

3. A lower-grade geography class became involved in a warm argument as to the specific conditions which brought on rain in their locality. The teacher suggested that they write to the local weather bureau to find out.
List as well as you can several learnings which might emerge from this situation.
Should not the teacher have given the information needed at once? If so, tell why; if not, support that view.

4. Present in some detail illustrations from your own school experience (on any level) showing how learning outcomes emerged which were not within the probable purpose of the teacher. Attempt to show clearly the conditions which accounted for this.

5. Present a similar account showing that certain desirable and consciously desired learnings were inhibited or mutilated by given conditions.

6. Attempt on the basis of present understanding to explain why the principle which seems to be emerging in discussion of these questions is so important.

CLASS REPORTS

This particular misconception of learning and its correction are problems almost too difficult for the beginning student to report upon. It is necessary to have wider acquaintance with teaching-learning situations than is probably possessed at this point. Nevertheless, preliminary observations may be made.

Observe a number of teachers or one teacher for some days. Prepare a brief summary report citing specific evidences of the teacher's awareness or lack of it concerning this misconception. Note teacher-manipulation of the total environment; his sensitivity to pupil-personality and reaction; his attitude toward success, failure, effort, and the like; his reaction to irregularities or disturbances; his knowledge, so far as it can be seen, of the home conditions and out-of-school life of his pupils. An astonishing number of these can be observed during the ordinary course of a lesson or activity period.

Experienced teachers will be able to make important comments on this problem.

READINGS

HOPKINS, L. Thomas, *Interaction* (Boston, Heath, 1941), pp. 348-359. These pages contain the best available reading on this problem to date. The chapter containing them deals with evaluation, but this emphasis may be omitted by the student until evaluation is taken up later in this volume. For the moment, read for understanding of the complexity of outcomes. This reading should be done by every student, but it will be found difficult by those of less ability and background.

KILPATRICK, William H., *Foundations of Method* (New York, Macmillan, 1925), Chs. 1, 8, and 9. An older reference but very valuable. Written in conversational style which antagonizes some and attracts other students. Much can be skimmed. Easier for less able students.

DEWEY, John, *Experience and Education* (New York, Macmillan, 1938), pp. 12-17. Brief analysis of general principles involved here.

4: THE SYMBOLS OF LEARNING ARE OFTEN CONFUSED WITH AND MISTAKEN FOR THE OUTCOMES OF LEARNING.

Evils resulting from confusion between learning and the mark received. The school which sees learning—both process and product—as the memorization of facts and the acquisition of simple routine skills in isolation from use naturally tests learn-

ing by asking for repetition. A number of investigations [34] have been made showing that the kind of test given has a definite effect upon the kind of learning. Teachers and pupils work for whatever will satisfy the test. Tests of memory or of performance are easily marked. The pupil comes to attach very great importance to the mark, since the school itself values it so highly. Pupils work for marks; any and all methods are utilized, if only the mark may be won. Functional learning is lost to sight—if in fact it was ever present—in some schools where marks dominate, and certain definite evils result.

First, teachers, pupils, and the public fall into the error of thinking of the mark as a representation or symbol for some actual, valuable, functioning learning product. Recently a petition bearing several thousand signatures was presented in Boston against a modernized marking system in one of the high schools and demanding the return of the former percentage system, which, said

[34] F. S. Betten, "Morality of Our Grade Giving," *Catholic School Journal,* Vol. 38 (November, 1938), p. 264.

E. C. Class, "The Effect of the Kind of Test Announcement on Students' Preparation," *Journal of Educational Research,* Vol. 28 (January, 1935), pp. 358-362.

H. R. Douglass and M. Tallmadge, "How University Students Prepare for New Type Examinations," *School and Society,* Vol. 39 (March 10, 1934), pp. 318-320.

L. A. Kirkendall, "Teaching for Marks," *School and Society,* Vol. 49 (May 20, 1939), pp. 642-644.

R. W. Edminton, "Effects of Emphasizing How to Learn upon Course Content and School Marks," *Journal of Educational Psychology,* Vol. 28 (May, 1937), pp. 371-381.

Leonard Carmichael, "Relationship between the Psychology of Learning and the Psychology of Testing," *School and Society,* Vol. 31 (May 24, 1930), pp. 687-693.

Harry C. McKown, *How to Pass a Written Examination* (New York, McGraw, 1943).

Paul W. Terry, "How Students Study for Three Types of Tests," *Journal of Educational Research,* Vol. 27 (January, 1934), pp. 333-343; "How Students Review for Objective and Essay Tests," *Elementary School Journal,* Vol. 33 (April, 1933), pp. 592-603.

the petitioners, "is better because the percentage marks given really mean something" in terms of pupil achievement. On the contrary, this of all the possible systems is the most absurd. It is practically impossible to make it mean anything sensible, as will be shown later in the chapter on marking. A percentage mark represents no quantity of anything, but is an average of numbers used to stand for the teacher's guesses or estimates. All traditional systems of marking are arbitrary and unrelated to functional learning; marks often represent only the teacher's estimate or guess as to how well the pupil has done certain things. Research studies show that the estimate is sometimes very inaccurate.

Second, making the symbol the important thing inevitably results in a narrow conception of education and learning. Simple, limited outcomes are easily marked. Complex, subtle, and far more important learning achievements do not lend themselves readily to marking. The mark stands for facts memorized, for the pupil's ability to follow directions, to do as he is told, to perform certain routine skills in isolation from real use.

Third, definitely undesirable learning products result. The ideals of cramming and cribbing are not the worst of these. Cheating is an inevitable result of confusing symbol with learning. Catering to the personal views and the temperamental whims of teachers, and even resorting to open flattery, are methods of obtaining marks without any reference to learning achievements. Cramming and cheating are rendered quite impossible when functional learning achievements are evaluated in real situations and "marked" by means of descriptions.

Fourth, and especially with young learners, the resulting confusion, frustration, and mistrust are serious.

Special evils of the "passing grade." Emphasis upon this arbitrary hurdle has its own evils. The passing-grade concept is contrary to all the known facts about growth, which is continuous. [35] It is contrary to all we know about desirable learning achievement. It must inevitably be based on subject-matter standards instead of upon functional learning.

The resultant evils are serious. The "get by" complex is inevitable. Even good pupils come to work just enough to get a passing grade. The result is definite training in habits of half-effort and half-attention, in bluffing, and in acceptance of mediocre standards. Pupils working for passing grades never get the training which attends a vigorous and sustained attack upon problems of their own choosing, the outcomes of which are intrinsically valuable to the pupil. At the other end of the scale, the slow or dull pupil is discouraged and antagonized in attempting to make a passing grade which is quite beyond his capacity or rate of learning—even though he is doing eminently satisfactory learning for his ability and rate. Untold numbers of earnest, sincere, hardworking but slow or dull pupils have been driven out of school and denied an education because of an arbitrary and fanciful thing—the passing grade. But, says the (so-called) practical teacher, how could we operate schools without passing grades? Happily, many places are doing it.

Marks as indications of success. The question may be asked: Are not marks, after all, indications of valuable learning? If a pupil works for high marks, does he not learn? Not necessarily so, as schools are at present constituted. It is true that statistical studies show that except for some commercial pursuits—and contrary to public opinion—the high scholarship man in college is in fact the man who succeeds best in life. This is not the same thing as saying that working for high marks so trained him that he succeeded; that marks, without further explanation, represent valuable learnings. The student with high marks, as a rule and excluding the "grade hound" type, has learned and is on the way to success not

[35] See Chapter 22.

because he worked for high marks, but because the kind of work he did incidentally entitled him to high marks. His calibre of work resulted in desirable outcomes which naturally received high marks; he has developed habits of sustained attack, habits of study, ability to gather data, ability to discriminate, and so forth. Unfortunately, it is also quite possible in many schools and under many methods of teaching to receive high marks which do not represent real learnings.

Morrison [36] presents an exhibit showing the contradictions and confusions that result from testing memorization of facts and definitions and then attempting to interpret the results as evidence of functional learning. The theoretical records of two students in grammar are presented. They could be actual records from any number of schools.

For ease of discussion we may assume that each pupil during the course has one hundred chances to respond to questions involving the topics listed. Both receive identical average grades, which being "passing grades" are accepted as evidence of satisfactory proficiency in the given items of formal grammar—evidence that learning has taken place. But specifically, what learning?

[36] Henry C. Morrison, *op. cit.*, p. 44.

One pupil passed in all fourteen topics, the other failed five of them, but both received the same average grade. Is the learning similar in both cases? One pupil has no grade higher than 79, none lower than 70; the other pupil, two grades 90 or over, five lower than 70, and, in fact, one of 42. Both get the same passing grade. Can excess learning in understanding simple sentences compensate for failure to understand the relative clause? Obviously the appropriate learning outcomes are not involved at all. The teacher and the pupils are not concerned with them. The mark is the significant thing; and being accepted as evidence of learning, it actually obscures not only the appropriate learnings but also the fact that inappropriate, non-functional learning has taken place. The teacher, in all probability, failed to define clearly just what understandings and abilities were to be derived from reading, discussing, using, and writing about the fourteen points. *Without clear recognition of what is to be learned, certainly learning cannot be tested.* The tests given in this instance would assuredly have dealt with facts, details, drilled responses, faithful preparation of daily recitations, and not with the appropriate, functioning learning outcomes.

A graduate student in the writer's class, asked to give concrete illustrations of real-

Topic	Pupil A Per Cent		Pupil B Per Cent	
1. Parts of speech	81	Passed	72	Passed
2. Elements of the simple sentence	90	"	78	"
3. Adjective and adverbial modifiers	50	Failed	71	"
4. Phrase modifiers	74	Passed	73	"
5. Gender	85	"	70	"
6. Number	82	"	79	"
7. Person	94	"	76	"
8. Case	89	"	75	"
9. Tense	75	"	70	"
10. Relative clause	63	Failed	71	"
11. Compound sentence	58	"	70	"
12. Participle	77	Passed	71	"
13. Infinitive	42	Failed	72	"
14. Transitive and intransitive verbs	56	"	70	"
Average	73	Passed	73	Passed

life confusion between learning and the symbols of learning, turned in the following remarkable character sketch of a man he knows who is an honor graduate of a great university:

He can quote all the Shakespeare that he was ever told to memorize, yet he will not go to any play, let alone one by Shakespeare himself. He regularly gets a score of 90 on *Time's* "Current Events Test," yet he refuses to read any critical non-fiction books and he has not the slightest conviction concerning either the value or the worthlessness of the New Deal. Nor does he see why anyone in the United States should be concerned that the Loyalists lost in Spain. He wears a Phi Beta Kappa pin, yet he has never registered to vote. He knows where John Hancock's house stood on Beacon Hill, yet he walks through Boston Common on May Day oblivious to the speakers and to the drama of the events around him.

At college we all borrowed his notes because they were almost verbatim reports of the lectures, but we know he has had three jobs in four years. He can become as enthusiastic about the Bible as living literature as did Professor —— and he can give a clear intellectual account of Spinoza's ethics, yet he can and does regularly deal from the bottom of the deck when playing poker. He has all the symbols of learning—even a gold one—but the practice is a curious thing.

Prizes and other awards open to similar criticism. What has been said of marks applies also to any other type of intrinsic reward for learning. When a prize or medal or honor of any kind comes to have large value for itself, when as a symbol it becomes more important than the achievement for which it stands, it is distinctly detrimental to education.

These pages should not mislead students into sweeping rejection of marks. Shocking as it may seem to the uncritical, the common systems of marking are in serious need of overhauling. The whole system of awarding cups, medals, athletic letters, pins, even the present use of honor societies is inimical to learning and is in serious need of scrutiny. Fortunately, much real progress has been made in recent years. In many school systems, traditional marking has been radically improved; wholly new methods which utilize descriptive accounts of actual learning have been invented. The behavior record is another new development. Improved marking systems and modern substitutions therefor will be presented in detail in Chapter 22. The relation of marks and rewards to motivation was treated briefly in the section on purposeful learning in Chapter 3.

Credits, courses passed, as symbols of learning. A student may "pass courses" in English—hence have "learned"—but he cannot write intelligent discourse in other circumstances. The discussion of learning so far given in this book, introductory as it is, indicates that it is quite possible to pass courses and not to have learned anything usable in real life. The confusion here discussed has been satirized in a witty manner by Learned, of the Carnegie Foundation for the Advancement of Teaching.[36]

What is a "credit"? A school credit is a semester's installment-certificate toward promotion. It rests on the two-fold factor of time-spent-in-class and a passing mark awarded by a school or teacher. Its most objectionable, not to say irrational, characteristic, however, is not that it is awarded by a teacher or that it permits promotion, but resides in the fact that, once granted at the end of a half-year's study in any subject, it becomes inviolable and reacts to disintegrate the pupil's knowledge of the content of that subject much as strong acid corrupts living tissue.

By means of an outward formula we here suddenly convert a value which, if sincerely handled, might prove a useful increment in a child's process of *becoming,* into an executive product henceforth detached from its maker; the pupil views it altogether as something done and "done with." Since it is henceforth inviolable, it can freely be left behind and forgotten.

No vault on earth is so safe for all time as our school records; no security so immune to varying markets and worldwide depressions as

[36] William S. Learned, *"Credits" versus Education,* a pamphlet (New York, The Carnegie Foundation for the Advancement of Teaching, 1933), p. 3.

these coupons. Talk of "frozen credits"! Not in all the world in these hard times are there such masses of paper on which it is impossible to realize as in the offices of our school and college registrars. Fluid enough, mind you, for purposes of institutional exchange, and that always at par, but flat as Wall Street in 1931, from the point of view of demonstrable education.

The indictment against school credits holds that the use of such a currency serves to create and perpetuate what tends to become mere empty illusion. It completely deceives the pupil as to the meaning of education; it misleads the administrator as to the value of his carefully planned organization; and it misrepresents the achievement of the school to the public.

Learned then develops the deception practiced on the learner in the same terms as the misconceptions of learning are developed in this chapter. The entire discussion is well worth reading since it is replete with humorous, but at the same time devastating, illustrations of confusing *credits* with *education*.

Confusion between symbol and essence not uncommon in life. The blunder of confusing between true and false objectives and the substitution of the symbol for the reality is by no means confined to the so-called "impractical" schoolmaster. The so-called "hard-headed" businessman and other laymen generally make it constantly and make it in important affairs.

Certain business leaders hold up "rugged individualism" and "the American way" as symbols of the essentially good life. In many cases these symbols are euphemisms to cover thoroughly vicious practices. The true meanings of and relationships between individual enterprise and collective effort are deliberately beclouded. One type of labor leader offers the "down-trodden working man" as a symbol for a total class and thereby prevents true meanings from emerging. Fortunately, enlightened industrial and labor leaders are seeing ever more clearly that safety and happiness lie in getting at essential facts, in avoiding discussion limited to meaningless slogans and symbols.

Certain businessmen and politicians use the symbols *socialism* or *communism* to obscure the true meaning of anything which threatens their vested interests. Often the individuals thus using symbols to befuddle meaning actively perpetuate the conditions which bring on the honest discontent and revolt. Dealing with facts and meanings instead of symbols would aid in preventing this.

In the church there are uncounted thousands who say the creeds, attend services, perform the various rituals, and participate in sacraments, but whose lives are clearly governed by principles diametrically opposed to those promulgated in church. The repetition of creeds, participation in rituals, membership on church committees are accepted as evidences (passing marks!) of piety and right living when, as a matter of fact, they are cloaks for the opposite. The symbols are clearly substituted for the essence.

The implications for teaching. What has all this to do with learning and teaching? Again as in the preceding section of this chapter, we have an illustration of the vital relationship between education and society. Erroneous conceptions of education result in training individuals to accept separation of symbol from essence. In mature form, this is hypocrisy and dishonesty of a grave type. Competent education strives steadily toward valid meanings and the control of conduct by such meanings.

When the mark, the "passing grade," "the course credit," "passing the college boards," "passing the Regents," are the real aims for teachers and pupils, the tendency then is for the teacher to fail to make clear the desirable outcomes of learning. He may in fact be, and often is, ignorant of them himself; he uses compulsion and fear as motives, instead of pupil purpose and pupil recognition of need. Even when the teacher is aware of the discouraging state of affairs, he may find it very difficult to provide teaching-learning situations from which functional learning will emerge. He is likely to resort to external rewards.

This unhappy practice, being administrative and system-wide, is usually beyond the control of the teacher. This does not mean that nothing can be done. Quite apart from constantly participating in discussions of the problem and serving on committees engaged in reconstructing marking systems or report cards, the teacher should work to secure valuable learning outcomes in spite of the serious handicaps.

DISCUSSION QUESTIONS FOR SECTION 4

This particular misconception (the confusion between symbol and essence) is difficult to discuss at this stage of the course. Students may be encouraged, however, to search their own school experience for illustrations and to look for illustrations outside of school.

1. Morrison relates that a student called into conference because of unusually bad English in his written papers answered the criticisms by saying, "But I have always had good marks in English in both high school and college." When he was shown specific illustrations of incompetent sentences and absurd grammatical constructions, he tried to settle the matter by saying, "I will get my English grades from the registrar's office and bring them to you."

If this student had been asked to define learning and had honestly tried to construct a definition, what would he probably have said? Confine your answer sharply to the facts revealed in the adjoining paragraph.

How do you account for "good grades in English" coupled wtih poor performance in writing and speaking the language?

The instructor and the student were not speaking the same language. Show wherein they were not.

2. What is meant by a "gentleman's grade" as the phrase is commonly used in many colleges? (If you have never heard this expression, what do you think it means?)

What do those who seek gentlemen's grades believe learning to be?

What do they see as the purpose of the school?

What do they miss or fail to acquire?

What responsibility does the school have for this attitude and for curing it?

3. A curious paradox is to be noted in the attitudes of many people in general toward education. They sneer at "book learning" but spend money for it nevertheless. They sneer at the educated man but insist that their children get an education. Other similar illustrations could be given. These various contradictory attitudes are manifested at different times by one and the same group.

How do you explain this odd and paradoxical situation?

Can you analyze the situation and differentiate some elements justifying the criticism and distrust of education?

What, really, is the fundamental criticism and cause for this distrust.

4. In all country towns there are certain individuals whose erudition is respected. They are referred to as "well posted." Sometimes these people are intelligent and successful members of the community. In many instances they are distinctly neither successful financially nor leaders in the community—but they are "well posted."

What is the matter in the latter case—in terms of our present discussion?

Can you describe instances from your own observation which illustrate the type mentioned?

5. It has been said that, "The teacher should endeavor to distinguish between the attainment of knowledge (or other legitimate learning outcome) and the acquisition of the symbols of knowledge."

  a. Cite any illustrations you can recall of failure or success in this as noted in your own school experience on any level.

  b. Cite illustrations from outside school affairs of the real point involved, namely, confusion between symbol and essence. First seek illustrations involving learning.

  c. Cite specific evidences from conversations showing that a teacher is clearly, even if honestly, ignorant of the objectives of her own teaching.

6. Report upon any organized attempt, recalled or currently observed, on the part of a school system to meet the problem outlined in this section of the chapter. (Organized study of the reform of marking systems will be taken up in a later chapter.)

7. What is your critical reaction to the table of comparative marks quoted in this chapter from Morrison?

8. What are some of the desirable learning objectives constantly referred to in this chapter which are lost through symbol substitution? Generalized answers are acceptable at this stage of the course.

READINGS

FREDERICK, Robert W., RAGSDALE, Clarence E., and SALISBURY, Rachel, *Directing Learning* (New York, Appleton, 1938), selected paragraphs from Chs. 4 and 22. Excellent bibliographies in each chapter.

LEARNED, William S., *"Credits" versus Education*, a pamphlet (New York, The Carnegie Foundation for the Advancement of Teaching, 1933).

MORRISON, Henry C., *The Practice of Teaching in the Secondary School*, rev. ed. (Chicago, Univ. of Chicago Press, 1931), Chs. 3 and 4. Has been assigned previously in this chapter. Reread only if necessary.

WHEELER, Raymond H., and PERKINS, Francis T., *Principles of Mental Development* (New York, Crowell, 1932), pp. 306-309, 417-419.

SUMMARY EXERCISES AND REPORTS ON WHOLE CHAPTER

1. The chapter has listed four major misconceptions or erroneous ideas concerning learning activities and products. There are some twelve to twenty erroneous ideas of a minor nature which are widely believed. Some of these can be inferred from the discussion so far, others can be derived from one's own past experience, still others will not appear without further study.

   a. Make a list of minor erroneous concepts regarding the process and products of learning.

   b. List several desirable implications for teaching derivable from each of the four major misconceptions.

2. Confusion between symbol and essence or desired result is common outside school.

   a. Describe specific instances of this confusion observed or experienced in any area of human experience; business, politics, religion, or social life.

   b. Show definitely how the error in real life begets undesirable results ultimately just as it does in school.

CHAPTER 6: The Goals or Outcomes of Learning

We have outlined *how* the learner learns, indicating some factors which facilitate or hinder learning. The next questions are naturally: *What* should be learned? *Why* should it be learned?

The interrelationship between values and goals. In an earlier chapter, we pointed out that learning experiences may be educative or miseducative. We say that making better burglars, better exploiters of the public treasury, better looters of the public domain, more deceptive writers of editorials and advertisements, is undesirable education. We say that making better bishops, more devoted nurses and physicians, more devoted believers in democracy, is desirable education. Why? This leads us directly to a consideration of the ultimate aim of education, hence to the goals of learning. Each civilization has a cultural tradition. Each civilization sets up an ideal individual and an ideal society as its goals. Educational processes must be selected and managed with a view toward leading learners to these goals. The objectives of our classroom assignment or unit must be in line with our ultimate aims.

Current revival of interest in aims of learning. The world situation has focused attention sharply on schools and on education. Education can be diverted from its ultimate goal of preserving and improving the cul-

tural values thought to best serve all people. Narrower goals may be imposed, namely, the aims of state as defined by a group in power. This is no new thing in history, but developments in Hitler's Germany and elsewhere startled many Americans. The attempts to capture the schools of the United States by both subversive and loyal groups, by both open and undercover methods, has caused our citizens to study as never before not only the ultimate aims of education but also the immediate classroom goals of learning.

All education takes place within a culture containing its own values and processes. *Education serves the culture* by preserving it and providing some of the conditions for improving it. *Education serves the individual* by providing him with opportunity for the best development of his capacities. *Education serves both* when it develops moral beings with purposes and loyalties which are valuable both to the individual and to his society.

Serving the two ultimate ends is no easy task. Ulich writes: [1]

No country, so far, has been able to reconcile the two goals of modern education, that is, to supply on the one hand some degree of cultural unity within the nation and, on the other hand, the full development of individual talent. Nor has any country solved the dilemma

[1] Robert Ulich, *Conditions of Civilized Living* (New York, Dutton, 1946), pp. 11-12. Copyright, 1946, by E. P. Dutton & Co., Inc.

which stems from the two-fold obligation of education: namely, to serve specific interests such as preparation for a vocation and for loyal citizenship within an individual nation and to represent the universal values of humanity as a whole. Much of our present futile discussion about the contrasts between practical and liberal education stems from lack of insight into these deeper issues of education.

But the deepest reason for our present feeling of dissatisfaction with public education lies in the present lack of a generally recognized hierarchy of values which tells us what to put first and what to put last, and what, if deeply understood, can go together; and as, at least in such complex fields as education, there can be no good structural planning without a clear philosophy behind it, we have not yet built up a type of school which could show to the nation that there can be unity in a variety of educational goals, learning in connection with real experience, and responsibility and harmony between practical and liberal education. So far we have nothing but bad compromises.

The values specified for development will differ between cultures as each tries to define those ends thought to be the best human values as they conceive them. The cultural aim in the United States is to preserve and develop the democratic values. We believe these to serve best the ultimate goal of our society.

Clarification and definition of levels of objectives aids all educational workers. The utmost confusion exists, regrettably, in the statement of aims. Remote general aims and immediate limited aims are indiscriminately mixed. Organized, comprehensive statements are rare. The immediate pupil goals, "felt needs," are often accepted as a basis for education, to the neglect of long-time lines of growth; or remote, adult-conceived goals are listed while learner's goals are neglected or repressed. Another common error is to state objectives on one level which are in fact useful only on another level. The latter blunder is found all the way from (supposedly) basic statements from leaders to teachers' daily lesson plans. This will be illustrated a few pages further on.

1. *The broad social purposes or objectives of society (in so far as society can be thought of as having objectives) and hence the remote, general aims or purposes of education.* The aim of every society is to secure the good life for its members. This aim has been stated variously by different men for different societies and at different times: morality, character, preservation and transmission of the culture, citizenship, democracy, collectivism. Many printed courses of study have a page or a small chapter giving a statement of remote aims developed and worded by the local group. These remote, abstract categories are satisfactory for designating the all-inclusive end point, and for use among advanced scholars for whom such terms have meaning. As day-to-day teacher objectives, they are not immediately achievable.

2. *The more specific social purposes or objectives of given social groups.* If we are to come to closer grips with educating members of society, we must know the more specific social needs and purposes to be fulfilled. Lists have been appearing since early times, and with increasing definiteness since about 1860. In 1859 Spencer stated that the definite objectives of education were to prepare individuals for (1) self-preservation, (2) securing the necessities of life, (3) rearing a family, (4) maintaining proper social and political relationships, and (5) enjoying leisure time. [2] In 1918 the United States Office of Education presented its now famous Seven Cardinal Principles: training for (1) health, (2) command of the fundamental processes, (3) worthy home membership, (4) vocational efficiency, (5) citizenship, (6) worthy use of leisure, and (7) satisfaction of religious needs. [3] Various cultural-anthropological lists may be com-

[2] Herbert Spencer, *Education* (New York, Appleton, 1874).
[3] U.S. Bureau of Education, Bulletin No. 35 (1918). A similar bulletin published in 1929 by the University of the State of New York, entitled "Cardinal Principles in Elementary Education," is of interest.

bined into a list of definite social objectives of education as follows:

1. Physical adequacy—health and vigor.
2. Satisfying home and family life.
3. Gainful employment—satisfying to the person and adequate for support.
4. Participation with others in community activities—social and political.
5. Participation with others in religious activities—satisfaction of desire for some relation with the universe at large.
6. Participation with others in desirable recreational activities.
7. Ability to communicate thought to others and to understand their expression.

Recently, lists of definite social objectives with a socioeconomic emphasis have been sharing attention with the cultural-anthropological statements. The major functions of social life become the categories. Those used in the Virginia Curriculum, which have been widely used and modified, are as follows:

1. Protection and Conservation of Life, Property, and Natural Resources.
2. Production of Goods and Services and Distribution of the Returns of Production.
3. Consumption of Goods and Services.
4. Communication and Transportation of Goods and People.
5. Recreation.
6. Expression of Aesthetic Impulses.
7. Expression of Religious Impulses.
8. Education.
9. Extension of Freedom.
10. Integration of the Individual.
11. Exploration.

In 1938 the Educational Policies Commission of the National Education Association [4] undertook to restate the objectives of education in terms of individual behavior. Four major objectives were given with from eight to twelve subpoints. A sampling only of subpoints is given below.

1. *The objectives of self-realization.*

| The inquiring mind | Sight and hearing |
| Speech | Health knowledge |

[4] *The Purpose of Education in American Democracy* (Washington, D. C., N. E. A., 1938).

Reading	Health habits
Writing	Public health
Number	

2. *The objectives of human relationships.*

Respect for humanity	Courtesy
Friendships	Appreciation of the
Co-operation	home

3. *The objectives of economic efficiency.*

Work	Occupational choice
Occupational information	Personal economics
	Consumer judgment

4. *The objectives of civic responsibility.*

Social justice	Devotion to democracy
Social activity	
Tolerance	Social application of
Law observance	science

This statement has been widely quoted in textbooks and is accepted by many. It is, nevertheless, a naïve statement lacking discrimination and adequacy of organization.

This level of objective is usually summarized in printed courses in the form and wording satisfactory to the local group. Source volumes often contain discussions and diagrams showing the relation of objectives on this level to the materials and experiences for the learners. Objectives stated in the terms given above are out of place and detrimental in a teacher's unit.

3. *The teacher's purposes or objectives.* These are, as stated and illustrated several times in preceding chapters, the typical results the teacher desires for his pupils. Objectives here are stated in the form of definite understandings, attitudes, values, behavior patterns, skills, and so forth. Those which the given unit may develop in the pupil should be stated in the teacher's unit. He may then plan materials and experiences to bring about pupil activity toward these goals.

Uncounted thousands of teachers proceed every day without objectives, without anything remotely approximating an objective. They attempt only to cover the text, to follow the course of study, to go through the motions of teaching. This is one of the most tragic commentaries on teacher training and intelligence. It undoubtedly contributes to the low esteem in which teachers and teaching are held by certain sections of the public. Teachers without clear objectives cannot be other than incompetent.

4. *The pupils' purposes or objectives.* These are always the immediate things the learner wishes to accomplish. Illustrations are scattered through following pages, hence a brief summary statement only is given here. The questions asked, the problems raised for discussion, and free discussions among children and youth reveal many of their real objectives.

What keeps airplanes from falling?
What kind of tree should we plant in the school yard?
Could we repair this radio in the school shop?
Could we make dresses in the sewing class for the school party?
Why do the baseball teams generally train in Florida and the Southwest?
What does the Driscoll School have that we haven't which got them in the Sunday paper?
Why is our town named ———?
Why is the bay entrance called the Golden Gate?
What are Forty-Niners?
How can we tell a good cold cure from a poor one?
Why did people come to live here in the first place?
Can we write a play and act it out?
Can I get a book on how to be popular?
Can I learn to get along with girls (boys) at parties?
Where can I find out about courtship, marriage, sex, rearing children?
Am I too young to "go out with a boy," to go to dances, to use lipstick?
When is "old enough" to be seriously interested in a boy (or girl)?

Hundreds are available in the many studies of children's problems and the dilemmas of youth.

Some of these are major purposes as stated, around which units or assignments can be organized. Others are fragments which hint at larger objectives, which can be developed by the individual or by the group and the teacher.

Illustration of the levels. Let us examine specific classroom projects and note how the various levels of objective enter. The *broad social objective* of a fifth-grade reading lesson is literacy for the nation. Literacy of the population is a measure of a civilization and is necessary to the development of the best life therein. This objective is not an immediate concern of either teacher or pupil. To state it as a lesson objective would be ludicrous. A *definite social objective* of this lesson would be the development of reading skill in order to facilitate the continuous activities of communication. Social processes are immensely improved through easy communication of information. Again, this objective is not stated as a lesson aim. The *teacher's objectives* in the fifth-grade lesson might be to increase speed and comprehension, to improve vocabulary, to develop better taste in reading. The *learner's objectives* may be to enjoy a good story, to find out something, or to see what happens next.

A lesson in general science, or one using scientific materials in core units, illustrates the levels in a field quite different from reading. The *broad social objective* would be an understanding of the technological civilization in which the learner lives, and certain skills in getting along in that world. For instance, we educate toward the substitution of scientific fact for lore, superstition, and neighborhood beliefs. We educate for the belief that certain discomforts, shortages, and physical ills are not necessary in modern scientific society. We educate for the use of the scientific method in place of the method of uncontrolled, biased, fragmentary personal experience. These do not appear as objectives for units or lessons. A *definite social objective* might be certain scientific understandings and abilities in choosing a vocation and succeeding in it; another, scientific interests as recreational pursuits. *Teacher's objectives* here would be some definite scientific understandings, laboratory skills, recreational interests, and attitudes toward the world of science, its methods and achievements. *Pupil's objectives* might be to find out what makes firecrackers explode, how to remove a stain, how to prepare the soil for growing flowers in the school garden, or how to make an electric buzzer.

Caution concerning "felt needs." The pupil goals just mentioned are typical of "felt needs," of goals which arise naturally in the course of everyday living. A serious error has arisen just here, namely, basing the whole curriculum and instructional process on the immediate interests and problems of learners. The interests and problems, the felt needs of the learner, are inescapable necessities in any learning situation, especially on lower levels. (This was outlined in Chapter 3). Failure to go beyond immediate needs, however, is to remain on an immature level. Courses in Household Chemistry, Practical Arts, Camp Cookery, and Biology for Life are unquestionably valuable, but chemistry, mechanics, dietetics, health, and biology are all systematic fields, each with a structure and modes of thinking. Out of the practical courses dealing with odds and ends of information there should be developed interests in more systematic information, in the methods of thinking involved. This is necessary if learners are to go on from limited immediate concerns to dealing systematically with important life problems. The maturity and capacities of pupils have a bearing here. All goals must meet the level of maturity of the learner and also meet the level of maturity of the civilization in which the school exists.

A chief task of all teachers is to aid pupils to formulate goals which meet pupil needs, but which are capable of developing into socially necessary goals. [5]

[5] J. Murray Lee and Dorris M. Lee, *The Child and His Development* (New York, Appleton-Century-Crofts, 1958). Chapter 12 has a useful discussion of this point.

Relation of processes to ends often overlooked. The use of educational processes, including classroom techniques, without thought of ends involved in pseudo-education of the worst type. The end results are far-reaching and can be truly dangerous. The teacher whose aim for the pupils is "to cover the text" or "to follow the course of study" is far more common than we think. "Why are you teaching this lesson? What is the aim or purpose just here?" is too often answered by "It's the next lesson in the text (or course)."

Many teachers give as lesson aims vague abstractions such as beauty, citizenship, good use of leisure, and the good old standby, "learning to think." At the other extreme are teachers who are quite satisfied with narrow aims: learning the tables of 4's; mastering the spelling list; reading ten books.

Teachers should not feel hurt over these blunt statements of fact. Teachers are no worse than their leaders; in fact, confusion on the teaching level usually stems from ignorance on upper levels.

The selection and statement of objectives for courses of study, for assignments, for units, or for any type of educational material, is as a rule very badly done. The lack of organization, the naïve confusion between levels, the poor wording, the uncritical acceptance, constitute grave defects in materials and a serious criticism of educational workers on all levels, from professors of education to beginners writing their first lesson plans.

Failure to distinguish between remote, general objectives of education, and the immediate objectives of units or assignments. Many teachers and some leaders, when stating objectives for teaching situations, indicate hopeless confusion between certain *levels* of purpose or objective.

One group lists remote, general, often abstract, long-term objectives of education as immediate, quickly achievable objectives for limited learning situations covered by a unit or an assignment. In fact, these are often given as objectives for a single lesson. For instance, objectives for these limited units or assignments are often stated as the appreciation of beauty; the ability to think; good character; co-operation; understanding of democracy; citizenship. The use of this type of objective for single units or assignments is absurd for several reasons:

1. These objectives are achieved only through a continuing program over a period of time. They are properly the remote objectives to be achieved through many series of units in general education, through whole courses or groups of courses in specialized education.

2. These objectives give no help whatever in determining the immediate materials and procedures to be used for teaching processes.

3. These objectives are not dynamic. They do not stir to action.

Teachers and leaders enamored of this type of statement for objectives—who list "beauty," "culture," "ability to think," "democracy" as outcomes for limited learning situations—usually proceed in a vague, unorganized, pointless manner. They neither define nor specify. Materials and learning experiences are casual and random. Evidences of achievement cannot be produced, because the vagueness of the objective makes achievement difficult to measure. Demands for evidence bring the defense that "analysis kills the spirit." (The presence of the "spirit" seems to be accepted without evidence.) There is much lovely language about "higher things," but little attention to the workaday details necessary to achieve the valuable higher things which are hidden behind the flowery language. The euphemistic language, combined with the lack of forcefulness in the statements, actually lulls to inaction.

A natural error regarding methods of teaching and of learning follows. This group tends to sneer at the necessary tasks of preparation, of gathering and organizing materials and experiences, of studying and knowing children; it tends also to sneer at the daily routines, at practice, at the necessity for evaluating and producing evidence of effect.

Another group reverses the error above and states as objectives, not merely for limited lessons but for education in general, a series of narrow, limited, bread-and-butter aims. These are the *ad hoc* aims of the limited utilitarian; the aims of those who interpret literally and narrowly the principle that learning must be based upon the felt needs of the learner. The ability to pass college-entrance board examinations is a prime example of the narrow, non-educational objective. This group very often teaches pupils to read, but not how to discriminate news from propaganda; to read, but not to see the relation between a critically literate populace and the stability of the social order.

This group fails to see the fundamental, long-time objectives which, as such, may properly be stated in general, abstract terms. This group is likely to be mildly contemptuous toward "culture," "beauty," "appreciation of poetry." There is likely to be much hard-boiled language about the "practical," about "facts," with derogatory references to the "theoretical."

The natural error here regarding methods of teaching and learning is that much use is made of daily assignments, recitation of facts, drilling upon isolated skills, daily marking of performance. This group is impatient with the subtle developmental methods designed to develop understandings, to cause appreciations to emerge, to stimulate creative effort.

The exclusive use of this type of objective is detrimental because:

1. These objectives exclusively employed may very well prevent the teacher from seeing the fundamental, long-term objectives and thus prevent pupil progress toward them.

2. These objectives might be achieved without making any contribution toward the

achievement by the pupil of desirable generalized controls of conduct and behavior patterns.

The same confusion between levels is found among the lay public and certain academic critics. One group insists that the aim of education is "intellectual," the "training of the mind" and that alone. This is a remote long-time objective and only one of several. At the other extreme are the lay critics who insist that the aim is "to teach the fundamentals," "to teach the 3 r's." This is a narrow and limited aim, however necessary and desirable.

Failure to distinguish between teacher's objectives and pupil's objectives. In the traditional school, typical teacher objectives are memorization of facts by the pupil; achievement of designated skills in reading, arithmetic, language art, manual art; certain vocational skills; and many others. The teacher who is moving toward modern methods adds to these objectives others in the form of study habits, psychological traits, attitudes, and understandings which he hopes will develop in the learner. The modern teacher usually states his objectives in terms of understandings, attitudes and appreciations, general abilities, skills, and general behavior patterns which he hopes will develop in the learner. He may add fact and other subject-matter learnings if he wishes.

The pupils' objectives are, typically, things which they wish to do. They may wish to read a story to see what happens next, or for enjoyment of the exciting adventures narrated, or to secure definite information. They may wish to find out what keeps an airplane from falling or how a thermometer works. They may wish to make a model airplane or a thermometer which works. They may wish to know how newspapers are published; whether one can rely on news statements; whether advertisements are truthful or not.

The teacher's objectives and the pupil's objectives in any learning situation are not similar in form, but they are intimately related. The teacher's objectives are the desirable educational outcomes in the forms stated above which he hopes the pupil will achieve. The pupil's objectives are the immediate results which he sees and desires and which will result from his activity in solving the question in which he is interested. The teacher hopes so to guide the learning experience that desirable educational results (the teacher's objectives) will be achieved while the pupil is achieving his objectives. Failure to realize the difference and relation between teacher's and learner's objectives has caused not only much ineffective and useless teaching but has developed detrimental attitudes and practices and much pupil antagonism toward education. In many schools the pupil does not know or care what the teacher's objectives are. Worse, the teacher too often does not know or care what the pupil's objectives are. Because of this, teachers often cover the ground, go through the motions, and think that they have achieved their objectives when, in fact, they have achieved no educative results. The pupil has realized neither objectives of his own, nor those of the teacher.

Current variations of statement of aims. Two very provocative methods of stating aims represent a break away from the traditional forms. They are affecting practice and their influence is likely to increase.

The directional-process goal.[6] The ultimate objective of education is to develop those patterns of conduct, values, meanings, and attitudes necessary for effective living on the adult level within an evolving democratic society. The immediate objectives are

[6] This term was originated by L. Thomas Hopkins and elaborated in his volume, *Interaction* (Boston, Heath, 1941). Another similar discussion which does not use this terminology is found in James L. Mursell, *Developmental Teaching* (New York, McGraw, 1949), pp. 17-21, 22-27, and Ch. 2.

less mature forms of the remote goals—the directional-process goals toward which the pupil grows by achieving increasing levels of maturity, insight, skill, and understanding. The learner, progressing through a series of directional-process goals, will eventually see for himself the necessity for achieving socially desirable goals. All teaching or learning situations bear upon the remote aims. The learners do not know this, and to tell them would merely confuse them or, as often happens in traditional schools, antagonize them. The teacher, as the better-informed and more mature adult, exercises leadership and guidance so that the less obvious needs are not neglected. Thus a balance between immediate purposes (felt needs) and remote purposes is achieved functionally.

Students may find it helpful to examine certain modern courses of study, for instance, the New York State Curriculum Guide for Mathematics; the San Francisco Teaching Guide in the same subject; the Cincinnati Try-out Course in Science, Kindergarten—Grade Eight. Each course shows the progressive development within the field. Mathematics progresses from the simplest experiences children have with numbers up to the formal arithmetic which can be handled by eighth-grade learners. The pupil progresses along the line of development as his capacity and maturity permit.

Modern curriculums and guides list flexible social objectives for various age groups, thus enabling teachers to state immediate objectives for units or assignments.

The nature of the directional-process (or directional-progress) goals may be clarified through comparison with traditional grade-level or grade-progress goals. The formal school divides subject matter into segments and arbitrarily assigns certain segments to successive grade levels. Children who do not achieve the grade level are failed, even though they may have made all the progress possible for them. The directional-process

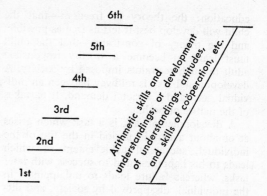

goal is represented not by grade steps but by a continuous line. The line represents any given subject area or area of personality growth. The child progresses along that line as his capacities and rate of learning permit. Many children who learn equally well, learn at quite different rates. The line represents a sequence through which learners grow as each individual's pattern permits. This type of goal is obviously based on the way pupils learn. The grade-level system often interferes with learning.

The learner progresses from his earliest contacts as a baby with number experiences, to such levels of mathematics as his capacity allows. The same is true with language expression, getting along with others, or any other given ability.

Developmental tasks as goals. The Committee on Human Development at the University of Chicago has contributed the concept of the "developmental task," [7] which is useful in considering the goals of education. The statement by the Committee aids in reconciling the "felt needs" of the learner with the more remote social ends.

The developmental-task concept occupies middle ground between opposed theories of

[7] Robert J. Havighurst, *Developmental Tasks and Education* (Chicago, Univ. of Chicago Press, 1948), pp. 4, 5, 6. Used with permission of the author.

An excellent elaboration is found in *Fostering Mental Health in our Schools*, The 1950 Yearbook of the Association for Supervision and Curriculum Development, Chs. 6 and 7.

education: the theory of freedom—that the child will develop best if left as free as possible; and the theory of constraint—that the child must learn to become a worthy responsible adult through restraints imposed by society. A developmental task is midway between an individual need and a societal demand. It partakes of the nature of both.

A developmental task is a task which arises at or about a certain period in the life of the individual, successful achievement of which leads to his happiness and to success with later tasks, whereas failure leads to unhappiness in the individual, disapproval by society, and difficulty with later tasks. . . .

Living is learning, and growing is learning. One learns to walk, talk, and throw a ball; to read, bake a cake, and get along with age-mates of the opposite sex; to hold down a job, to raise children; to retire gracefully when too old to work effectively, and to get along without a husband or wife who has been at one's side for forty years. These are all learning tasks. To understand human development, one must understand learning. The human individual learns his way through life.

The original source lists the appearance and growth of the developmental tasks from early infancy to adulthood. The concept is closely similar to that of the directional-process goal mentioned earlier.

A later volume by Havighurst [8] develops the concept in great detail. Educational implications are specifically outlined. The case studies are unusually valuable. The entire volume is excellent reading for students and instructors. The Epilogue: Case History of a Concept outlines the development of the idea and gives generous credit to the men and women who contributed over a period of some twenty-five years.

The aim of education in the United States. The general aim has been indicated several times in this chapter. We wish to develop moral personalities of worth and dignity; to preserve and improve our democratic society. The details have been admirably stated

[8] Robert J. Havighurst, *Human Development and Education* (New York, Longmans, 1953).

in many texts in Philosophy of Education, Principles of Education, History of Education. Duplication of these details is beyond the scope of this volume.

DISCUSSION QUESTIONS

1. Which ideas that you may have had about the aim of education are clarified by this chapter? Which contradicted? Which of the contradicted ideas persists in your mind, and which are you willing now to give up?

2. Ignorance of the remote aims of education is responsible for much error and bad practice in educational policy and in classroom procedure.

   a. Explain as well as you can at this stage why there is, among educational workers, widespread ignorance of the general aims, and of the hierarchy of aims.

   b. Note, during your classroom observations, two or three specific errors on the part of the classroom teacher due to unawareness of aims. Also note illustrations of good understanding of aims and relationship between aims, of relation of means to aims.

   c. Explain in general terms, with illustrations, the types of error into which educational workers other than teachers will fall because of unfamiliarity with the aims of education.

3. The form in which educational objectives on any level are stated varies widely and often contributes to confusion.

   a. Explain in some detail why these variations occur.

   b. Indicate in some detail how the unnecessary and confusing variations (as distinguished from natural and legitimate variations) may be corrected and eliminated.

4. Ask a number of teachers for the objectives of lessons you have just observed. Do not indicate surprise if none can be stated; accept without comment any formal or absurd aims; accept with commendation any competently expressed objectives. Bring the lists and any comments in for class discussion.

5. Review a number of current articles on the aim of education. Be sure to include one or more articles which include attacks and criticisms by laymen.

6. Examine a number of courses of study.

a. Note the broad general aim of education, if stated, and evaluate.

b. If no general aim is stated, examine the statement of specific objectives and also the objectives by subjects or units, to see if you can infer the general aim.

7. Examine the content of several kindergarten or primary courses of study.

a. Note how the far-away general aim of education is being approached even with these young children.

b. Contrast, if available, older courses or teachers' guides with fairly recent ones.

8. Examine books and articles on curriculum construction and find the list of criteria for the aims of education and their statement. Use these criteria in an analysis of the present chapter (or any other statements of aim you may find).

9. Find a collection of "aims of education" in general texts on principles or history of education. Analyze three or four of the aims in the light of this chapter.

10. Examine the annual reports of school systems and evaluate critically any statements made about aims. Examine any booklets which may be available, such as those published by individual schools, both public and private, setting forth the aim, program, and other interesting views on education. Critically evaluate statements dealing with aims of education.

11. *a.* What educational content and procedures commonly found in the schools now seem to you to be out of line with the modern aim of education?

b. What fundamental changes shall be necessary in typical schools in order to bring content and procedure more into line with the modern aim?

12. State what seem to be the two most striking principles developed in this chapter.

READINGS

American Educational Research Association, *Social Framework of Education* (Washington, D. C., N.E.A., 1955).

BLOOM, Benjamin S., and others, *Taxonomy of Educational Objectives* (New York, Longmans, 1956). Excellent basic analysis.

BRUBACHER, John S., *Modern Philosophies of Education*, rev. ed. (New York, McGraw, 1950), Ch. 4.

BRYSON, Lyman, and others, *Goals for American Education* (New York, Harper, 1950).

COUNTS, George S., *Education and American Civilization* (New York, Bureau of Publications, Teachers College, Columbia Univ., 1952).

CREMIN, L., and BORROWMAN, M., *Public Schools in Our Democracy* (New York, Macmillan, 1956).

CRONBACH, Lee J., *Educational Psychology* (New York, Harcourt, Brace & World, 1954). Chapter 2, very good.

Educational Policies Commission, *Education for All American Youth: A Further Look* (Washington, D. C., N.E.A., 1954).

HAVIGHURST, Robert J., and NEUGARTEN, Bernice L., *Society and Education* (New York, Allyn & Bacon, 1957).

HERRICK, Virgil, and TYLER, Ralph W., *Toward Improved Curriculum Theory* (Chicago, Univ. of Chicago Press, 1950). Supplementary Education Monograph, No. 71 (March, 1950).

IMHOFF, Myrtle M., *Early Education Theory* (New York, Appleton-Century-Crofts, 1959), Ch. 4.

KEARNEY, Nolan C., ed., *Elementary School Objectives* (New York, Russell Sage Foundation, 1953).

MURSELL, James L., *Principles of Democratic Education* (New York, Norton, 1955).

SMITH, B. Othanel, STANLEY, W. O., and SHORES, J. H., *Fundamentals of Curriculum Development*, rev. ed. (New York, Harcourt, Brace & World, 1957). Chapter 5, excellent.

The foregoing list is but a sampling; many more references are available. Footnote references have not been repeated here.

Part II

THE
LEARNER
AND
THE
TEACHER

The learner is no longer regarded as a passive agent but as an active participant in his own education. Children and youth are not the simple, uncomplicated beings the traditional school believed them to be. Each brings a personality to school with him, along with many other influences from his home, neighborhood, and social level. Some of these interfere with learning and teaching; others are important aids.

The teacher is emerging from his ancient role as task-setter and drill-master. He is more and more becoming a participating member of the learning group. *Eventually, it is to be hoped that the teacher will become the resource person in and for a group of learners.*

CHAPTER 7: The Learner and How He Learns

1: THE ORGANISMIC CONCEPT OF THE LEARNER.

The child comes to school, it is popularly supposed, to have his mind trained. To the great annoyance of many teachers, the child insists on bringing his body and his emotions with him. This semi-flippant statement introduces us directly to the modern concept of "the whole child." The whole child comes to school. More than that, he learns as a whole child: he learns all over and not by sections. Body or emotions cannot be educated without affecting each other and the intellect as well. Mind or intellect, body and emotions, are arbitrary designations; they are not separable entities but functioning aspects of a unified whole. The living child reacts as a unified, integrating whole. He cannot be divided up for teaching purposes. It is true that mature learners are capable of more differentiation than young children; hence they can subordinate one aspect to another more successfully. This makes possible specialized learning on upper levels.

The boy in Kipling's story learned to read (a perceptual and eventually conceptual affair), but he also learned to dislike reading (an emotional acquisition) and to avoid reading (an attitude). The little girl in the oil-field school came to secure the simple skills of reading, writing, and arithmetic, but the surroundings in which these were taught

stimulated emotional learnings. These children interacted in a unified manner with a whole learning situation. They could not be dissected to react piecemeal, nor could the learning experience be so controlled that only selected learnings would affect the child.

Any characteristic of the child may be considered separately for more explicit description or for diagnosis. [1] Analytic methods will give us more minute data about given aspects of the living whole. It must never be forgotten, however, that the living whole is primary: it determines the nature of the parts, and is more important than any of the parts. Interpretation of artificially isolated parts can be made only in terms of the nature of the living organism as a whole.

The biological origin of the organismic concept. This term *organismic concept* is borrowed from biology, where it is used to

[1] This chapter is particularly important in that it will supply an introduction to and overview of the large body of scientific experimentation and data which validates the principles developed in preceding chapters on a common-sense basis only. The deliberately oversimplified presentation here is amply safeguarded by footnote references to extensive original sources.

N.B. Classes which are well informed from previous courses in educational psychology may omit this chapter, or read it for quick summary. The majority of students will be found not too well prepared on this subject.

designate a total living organism. All living organisms are at birth integrated and integrating unities, and are possessed of functions, powers, or controls, called *gradients,* which tend to guarantee continued unity unless interfered with.

A gradient is, in simple terms, a rate and direction of living, or of metabolism, or of growth, or of rate of maturing, or of susceptibility to outside stimuli. To illustrate: In simple cells the greatest susceptibility to heat, pressure, and other stimuli occurs on the cell surface, and there is a steadily decreasing sensitivity toward the center. These gradients are the result of dynamic relationship with the environment; but, developing very early, they are primary and in turn determine local growth processes. Their operation in determining growth will be illustrated and summarized presently. The nature and function of these physiological gradients has been well established by extensive research in biology. The lifelong work of Child is a case in point, though many others have also contributed. [2]

Growth is affected both by gradients and by external influences. The growth of organisms seems to be (ordinarily) an orderly

[2] C. M. Child, *The Origin and Development of the Nervous System* (Chicago, Univ. of Chicago Press, 1921).
———, *Physiological Foundations of Behavior* (New York, Holt, 1924), Chs. 2, 11-15. The authoritative pronouncement.
———, "The Beginnings of Unity and Order in Living Things," *The Unconscious, A Symposium* (New York, Knopf, 1928), pp. 11-42.
R. S. Lillie, *Protoplasmic Activity and Nervous Activity* (Chicago, Univ. of Chicago Press, 1923).
G. E. Coghill, *Anatomy and the Problem of Behavior* (New York, Macmillan, 1929).
H. S. Jennings, *The Behavior of Lower Organisms* (New York, Macmillan, 1906).
A. A. Schaeffer, *Amoeboid Movement* (Princeton, N. J., Princeton Univ. Press, 1929).
References here and in the next footnote were selected from the original studies in the field, hence the early dates. Later studies have extended and refined several ideas but major concepts remain. Reports on later studies may be made if desired.
Recent summaries are listed at the end of this section.

and progressive differentiation of parts and functions out of an originally simpler and more homogeneous physiological pattern. Tissues become more specialized and organs of the body come into being, as will be illustrated below. This growth, which is the life and learning of the organism, is determined in part by the individual, inherited, organismic pattern. The gradients determine in part the possibilities, the rate, the range, the directions, and the complexities of adjustments, hence of life and of some learnings. The influence of the gradients is, however, neither deterministic nor absolutistic. The gradients may be altered and new gradients may be set up through outside influence. In fact, Child believes the primary gradients to be themselves an expression of a dynamic relationship between living organisms and environment. We may repeat that mutual interaction is fundamental.

An illustration of controlled physical growth. It is difficult to make concrete the foregoing abstract exposition. Illustrations are from biology and are rather technical. Protoplasm, as we know, is extremely plastic; hence structure and function are capable of considerable development. The body cells are structures through which the processes of life and growth express themselves. Natural growth in early stages is greatly affected by the primary physiological gradients.

Living organisms soon develop, for instance, an anterior-posterior gradient, a ventral-dorsal gradient, and another having its highest rate of sensitivity and metabolism in the middle and tapering off toward either end. Recall that gradients are rates and directions of sensitivity, in rate of metabolism, in direction of growth, and so on. The layer of cells in an embryo showing the marked head-to-tail gradient develops into the nervous system, the sense organs, and the skin. The layers of cells possessing the third gradient noted above become the inner lining of the digestive tract, the highest activity being in the stomach and upper intestine. Activity tapers off in both directions in terms of the gradient. Even more interesting proof of control of growth by the gradient is seen in experiments in which undeveloped nerve tissue from head and tail regions is interchanged.[3] The tissue which would have grown into a head now grows into the structures of the tail, and vice versa. The growth process is determined not by the nature of the tissue itself, but by the placement of the tissue within a gradient.

Primary unity in the nervous system. Franz, Child, Herrick, and more recently, Lashley have piled up evidence showing that the nervous system, so important to learning, functions as a unit, as a whole, and all over.[4] Misled by early work on specialized functions seemingly localized in the cortex, many neurologists and psychologists believed that the entire nervous system was highly specialized. Stress was placed on reflexes and the combination of reflexes into large units, on the conditioning of responses, and on specific learnings. The famous S-R bond theory of Thorndike was based on this. Later evidence has forced abandonment of these concepts. The brain and nervous system develop in accord with organismic laws. There is specialization and localization, but these develop out of an originally unitary system. Furthermore, the original unity and control are never entirely relinquished. The brain is a dynamic field of potentials in bal-

ance. An upset to equilibrium initiates action. This action involves the whole organism as a unit. The whole is not a sum of parts, reflexes, and the like, but is a unit which determines the functions of the parts.

In Lashley's experiments, various amounts of the cerebral cortex were extirpated in rats and other animals. According to the older theory of the functioning of the nervous system, there should have been much loss of specific habits which had been previously learned, that is, much loss of memory. The loss, however, was not nearly so great as had been expected; in some cases it was negligible. Furthermore, the habits and skills lost were quickly relearned and soon performed as well as before. This demonstrates conclusively that the learning of specific things is not simply the property of specialized neurones, but is a general function of the whole nervous system. In one striking instance, a rat which had been operated on lost the power to make right-hand turns in running a maze learned before the operation. Instead of relearning the right turn, the rat turned to the left, completing a 270-degree turn in order to go right. This is an astonishing demonstration of the flexibility of the nervous system. There is a general integrative, adaptive power or function which affects the whole system. The original learning of the habits now partly lost through extirpation of cortical tissue had evidently affected the whole nervous system in such way as to facilitate relearning. Patterns of learning instead of highly specialized localizations are indicated.

Naturally, there are differing degrees of integration and unity. Minor conflicts and inconsistencies do appear. There is, however, a fundamental tendency toward primary unity, all-over functioning, and organismic developments in the nervous system.

Lashley's work is the more important since it goes beyond animal experimentation and includes observation of human patients suffering from injuries to or disease within the brain and nervous system. Lashley and

[3] S. R. Detwiler, "Experiments in the Reversal of the Spinal Cord in Amblystoma Embryos at the Level of the Anterior Limb," *Journal of Experimental Zoology*, Vol. 38 (October, 1932), pp. 293 ff. Many other experiments are reported.

[4] S. I. Franz, "On the Functions of the Cerebrum," *Archives of Psychology*, No. 2 (March, 1907) and many other later papers and monographs.

C. M. Child, *The Origin and Development of the Nervous System*. Other later research papers and books.

C. I. Herrick, *Neurological Foundations of Animal Behavior* (New York, Holt, 1924).

K. S. Lashley, "Basic Neural Mechanisms in Behavior," *Psychological Review*, Vol. 37 (January, 1930), pp. 1-24; *Brain Mechanisms and Intelligence* (Chicago, Univ. of Chicago Press, 1929).

other neurologists report astonishingly little chaotic behavior or disorder in function, even when large and irregular lesions are found in the brain. There is often considerable loss of sensory or motor capacities; there may be actual amnesia, emotional deterioration, even dementia; but the general pattern of orderly behavior is evident even to the untrained observer. This is particularly true in amnesia.

A small number of very difficult investigations have been carried on, from which attempts are being made to derive some facts concerning neural activity in the cortex. The brain is described as a field of fluid dynamic energy potentials in balance. Activity results from disturbance of this equilibrium. Wheeler[5] and his students believe that the experiments show that gradients exist within the energy fields in the brain and that the gradients take different patterns in the case of different types of activity. This concept is similar to the one already presented for the physical organism: growth and activity controlled by interaction between gradients within the organism and the influence of the environment.

The facts are certainly not clear as yet. The foregoing paragraphs mean, in common-sense terms, that the mental activities of problem-solving, remembering, imagining, and the like are not separate types of activity involving discrete parts of the brain, but are each of them activities of the brain as a whole. This corroborates the general theory of learning and teaching so far developed.

Behavior follows the organismic pattern. The first reaction of living things, even in prenatal behavior, are reactions of the total organism. First movements are undifferentiated mass movements. The organism reacts all over. For proof one need not turn to the numerous animal experiments, but has merely to observe a baby crying. Instead of merely exercising the vocal cords to secure relief from a given discomfort, the baby cries all over. It cannot cry, as a matter of fact, without waving arms and legs, clenching and unclenching its fists, tossing its body around, and changing its rate of breathing.

Babies not only cry all over; they perform any act all over at first. A baby reaches for a rattle not merely with its hands and fingers but with its arms, legs, and body. In fact, a young baby cannot reach with its hands and fingers alone. It has neither matured the proper nerves and muscles, nor had the experience of differentiating the smaller movements. Eventually, arm or leg or head movements are differentiated out of the total movement. Finally, delicate movements of fingers or eyes may be made. Babies at first grasp objects with the whole hand, clumsily and without due adaptation to the shape of the thing grasped. The thumb cannot be opposed to the fingers. With maturation and experience, precise and specialized behavior is achieved. [6]

[6] C. M. Child, *Physiological Foundations of Behavior.*

G. E. Coghill, *Anatomy and the Problem of Behavior.* See also papers in periodicals.

C. I. Herrick, *op. cit.*

O. Irwin, *The Amount and Nature of Activities of New-Born Infants under Constant External Stimulating Conditions the First Ten Days of Life,* Genetic Psychology Monographs, Vol. 8 (July, 1930), pp. 1-92.

K. Koffka, *The Growth of the Mind,* rev. ed. (New York, Harcourt, 1928).

J. B. Watson, *Psychology from the Standpoint of a Behaviorist,* 2nd ed. (Philadelphia, Lippincott, 1924). See also many papers by Watson and his students.

George G. Thompson, Eric F. Gardner, and Francis J. Di Vesta, *Educational Psychology* (New York, Appleton-Century-Crofts, 1959). Chapters 1, 2, 3, are excellent reading to accompany the present chapter.

See also Cronbach and Stephens in Bibliography at the end of this section.

[5] Raymond H. Wheeler and Francis T. Perkins, *Principles of Mental Development* (New York, Crowell, 1932). Ch. 4, particularly pp. 70-71, reports a number of unpublished studies on this.

George W. Hartmann, *Gestalt Psychology* (New York, Ronald, 1935). The theoretical support for the views expressed here which preceded the physiological experimentation is largely in the German literature. It is well summarized in Ch. 13, particularly pp. 202-209.

The first attempts of children at handwriting, skating, or any other skill are undifferentiated mass movements. When first using a pencil, children write all over; the whole body seems involved. Maturation and experience, which bring contacts with many directive influences, eventually lead to a co-ordinated series of movements, a skill, which meets the need of the organism. So also, it should be emphasized, with adults learning to swim, to swing a golf club, to display certain social graces. Awkwardness, the colloquial designation of the learning period for skills, is not confined to adolescence.

Clearly, it is wasteful to try to secure given reactions from children in advance of maturation and experience. Realization of the facts revealed by long-continued research has accounted for important changes in schoolroom procedure. Small children are not held to small, precise handwriting as they were a few years ago. Activities which require many small, precise manipulations have been eliminated from kindergarten and primary school. Large objects and large movements are the rule. Natural activities fitted to the level of maturation have been substituted for precision drills in lower-grade physical education.

DISCUSSION QUESTIONS FOR SECTION 1

The majority of teacher-education institutions give students practically no biological background; hence material in this section will be new to most students and teachers. The writer has found it very valuable to devote an hour to free discussion. Students will usually have more than enough questions of their own, which may be supplemented by the following:

1. List any new concepts or beliefs which have come to you from this section and supplementary readings, and which you readily accept. Clarified and amplified ideas may be listed as well as new ones.

2. Recall any incidents from your own life or schooling, or incidents observed in the lives of others, which were perhaps puzzling or even inexplicable at the time, but for which you now have some explanation derived from the readings.

3. List any concepts or principles advanced by the reading which you cannot accept at the moment, or about which you are in doubt. State explicitly why you cannot accept them. This is an extremely important exercise, since it directs student and instructor to important points of emphasis or misunderstanding.

4. What accepted principles of education, what prevalent practices in education would have to be abandoned if the facts and principles in this section were accepted?

READINGS

The footnotes, as indicated on pages 137-139, contain the original and older studies: Child, Coghill, Herrick, Franz, Lashley, Lillie, and others. Modern studies will be found summarized in several of the following references. See particularly Kuhlen & Thompson below.

BARKER, Roger G., and WRIGHT, Herbert F., *One Boy's Day: A Specimen Record of Behavior* (New York, Harper, 1951).

BALDWIN, Alfred L., *Behavior and Development in Childhood* (New York, Holt, Rinehart & Winston, 1955).

BRECKENRIDGE, Marian E., and VINCENT, E. Lee, *Child Development*, 3rd ed. (Philadelphia, Saunders, 1955).

CANNON, W. B., *The Wisdom of the Body* (New York, Norton, 1939). The classic in the field.

FOREST, Ilse, *Child Development* (New York, McGraw, 1954).

GOLDSTEIN, Kurt, *The Organism* (New York, American Book, 1939). Excellent statement from physicians' viewpoint.

HILGARD, Ernest R., *Theories of Learning*, 2nd ed. (New York, Appleton-Century-Crofts, 1956). One of the best all around references available on history and development of learning theories. Bibliography of 59 pages, best available.

How Children Develop, a pamphlet, rev. ed. (Columbus, Ohio, Staff of Ohio State Univ. School). Especially good for beginners and parents. Good bibliography.

HURLOCK, Elizabeth B., *Adolescent Development*, 2nd ed. (New York, McGraw, 1955).

———, *Child Development*, rev. ed. (New York, McGraw, 1956).

JERSILD, Arthur T., *Child Psychology*, 4th ed. (Englewood Cliffs, N. J., Prentice-Hall, 1954).

JONES, Harold E., *Development in Adolescence.* (New York, Appleton-Century-Crofts, 1943). A detailed case study.

KUHLEN, Raymond G., and THOMPSON, George G., *Psychological Studies of Human Development* (New York, Appleton-Century-Crofts, 1952). An excellent collection of readings, old and new.

LEE, J. Murray, and LEE, Dorris M., *The Child and His Development* (New York, Appleton-Century-Crofts, 1958). Whole volume but particularly Chapters 2, 3, 4, 5, 6, 7, 10.

MARTIN, W. E., and STENDLER, Celia B., *Child Development: The Process of Growing Up in Society* (New York, Harcourt, Brace & World, 1953). This is one of the several modern anthropological studies of summaries available.

——, eds., *Reading in Child Development* (New York, Harcourt, Brace & World, 1954).

MILLARD, Cecil V., *School and Child: A Case History* (East Lansing, Mich., Michigan State College Press, 1954). An excellent case study.

MILLARD, Cecil V., and ROTHNEY, John M. W., *The Elementary School Child: A Book of Cases* (New York, Holt, Rinehart & Winston, 1957).

MUNN, Norman L., *The Evolution and Growth of Human Behavior* (Boston, Houghton, 1955).

OLSON, W. C., *Child Development* (Boston, Heath, 1949). Chapters 3, 4, 5 particularly. Selected bibliography. Comprehensive treatment to date of publication.

PRESSEY, Sidney L., and KUHLEN, Raymond G., *Psychological Development Through the Life Span* (New York, Harper, 1957).

RASEY, Marie I., and MENGE, J. W., *What We Learn From Children* (New York, Harper, 1956). Case histories.

REMMERS, H. H., RIVLIN, Harry N., RYANS, David G., and RYDEN, Einar R., *Growth, Teaching and Learning: A Book of Readings* (New York, Harper, 1957).

ROTHNEY, John M., *The High School Student* (New York, Holt, Rinehart & Winston, 1954). Case studies of typical adolescents.

TYLER, Leona E., *The Psychology of Human Differences,* 2nd ed. (New York, Appleton-Century-Crofts, 1956).

WHEELER, Raymond H., and PERKINS, Francis T., *Principles of Mental Development* (New York, Crowell, 1932). An older reference but with many useful summaries.

VALUABLE SOURCES OF NEW MATERIALS

Institute of Child Welfare, University of California, Berkeley
The Society for Research in Child Development
The Child Study Association of America
The White House Conference on Child Welfare
The University of Iowa Child Welfare Station
The Yale Clinic of Child Development
The Harvard Graduate School of Education Clinic
The University of Chicago Committee on Human Development
The University of Michigan Research in Child Development

Several universities and school systems publish from time to time summaries of studies made. The quarterly Review of Educational Research carries periodically a summary of studies in this field.

For further explanation with emphasis upon application for all sections of this chapter, the following are excellent:

CRONBACH, Lee J., *Educational Psychology* (New York, Harcourt, Brace, & World, 1954).

STEPHENS, J. M., *Educational Psychology,* rev. ed. (New York, Holt, Rinehart & Winston, 1956).

THOMPSON, George G., GARDNER, Eric F., and DI VESTA, Francis J., *Educational Psychology* (New York, Appleton-Century-Crofts, 1959).

Readers will be guided in each volume by chapter heads and the index.

2: MATURATION.

The term *maturation* refers to the natural process of growing, developing, or ripening. It has long been used by physiologists, anatomists, and neurologists to refer to observable changes in cells, nerves, muscles, bones, and organs. The progress of physiological maturation can be observed through laboratory dissection and X-ray photography. For instance, it was discovered long ago that the progressive myelination or sheathing of certain portions of the nervous system coincided with the ability of those nerve fibers to function. The progressive ossification of wrist bones in children has been photographed to provide another scale of progressive maturation. Various physical maturities are recognized, based on measurements of different parts of the body. The term is also widely used to refer to forms of growth other than the physical, for instance, mental maturity, social maturity, or emotional maturity.

Students in this field have borrowed the basic concept of development, namely, "age," and distinguish several "ages," each an index of growth in its field. Commonly used in education are:

1. Chronological Age
2. Mental Age
3. Educational Age (sometimes called Subject Age or Grade Level)
4. Anatomical Age (sometimes Dental or Carpal Ages)
5. Physiological Age
6. Social Age
7. Moral Age
8. Emotional Age

These are commonly designated by their initials, C.A., M.A., E.A., and so forth. Each has its own methods and units of measurement, and norms. Chronological age, the commonest in everyday discussion, is obviously the number of years and months since birth—one's age in the ordinary sense. Mental age represents the stage of mental development irrespective of chronological age. Educational age represents the grade reached in school as indicated by scores on standard tests. Anatomical age is based on measurement of certain anatomical features, for instance, ossification of wrist bones, eruption of teeth, and the like. Physiological age usually refers to the maturing of the sex organs and functions, though it may refer to any bodily organ. The social, moral, and religious ages are determined by inventories of habits and attitudes. Descriptive standards could be set up for emotional age, aesthetic age, or sports-and-games age.

If typical behaviors can be determined for average ages, the inventory for a given child can be translated into an age designation. The caution must be expressed that averages, norms, and ages of this type are often sadly misleading when applied to individual cases. The fundamental principle that growth is individual and patterned is more important than identification by age levels.

There is reasonable consistency and correlation between the ages in a given individual, though the growth studies show that variations are frequent enough to be important. A boy may be thirteen years old chronologically, eight mentally, seven educationally, and ten anatomically or physiologically. Another may be eleven chronologically but have a mental age of fourteen with correspondingly accelerated educational age.

Maturation is affected by heredity and by general environmental influences. The individual possesses a growth potential; he will develop no matter what. This process is called maturation. The physical organism and the simple behaviors develop thus. However, outside influences can and do affect maturation at any stage, and become particularly important in later development. This is particularly true of mental and social maturities.

Arguments raged years ago over "heredity *versus* environment." Competently informed individuals today do not wrangle over relative importance. The two factors are reciprocal, not rival, elements in a dynamic, unitary process of interaction. The individual contributes his organismic pattern of growth potentials and of capacities. The environment supplies situations in which growth potentials are expressed. Interaction results in growth and learning.

The human animal is born *with* a physical inheritance, born *into* a social heritage. The latter is but one part of the environment. His inherited potentials are not automatic nor specific in function. They are general, and capable of development into thousands of actualities through interaction with the environment. Heredity sets some limits as to what an individual *can* do and be; environment determines in some measure what he *will* do and be.

Students studying this text should have met long ago modern discussions of heredity and environment in the biological sciences, in psychology, in anthropology, in survey courses, or elsewhere. If they have not, they should not be in a course in principles of teaching. It simply is not safe to enter upon teaching without knowledge of the enormous amount of material available on this ancient topic.

Heredity and learning. Individuals obviously inherit certain anatomical traits common to the species, such as skeletal structure, neuro-muscular system, and bodily organs. Certain physiological functions are present from birth: digestion, elimination, breathing, oxygenation of the blood, and so on. The individual inherits a functioning organismic pattern plus the capacity and tendency to maintain integration and physical and mental health. Susceptibility to disease and to mental disturbances is present in potential. We are chary of going further. Reflexes and instincts once thought to be wholly inherited are now known to be largely if not wholly genetic. Some research indicates the primacy of certain limited instinctive reactions of fear, rage, and pleasure.

For our purposes we may concentrate upon the fact that we inherit an unbelievably plastic nervous system capable of almost any organization (learning). Plasticity is far more important than any possible fixed inherited tendencies. All human beings are born with some capacity to learn. The capacity differs from individual to individual. When parents or teachers say that a given child cannot learn, they mean they have been unable to stimulate that child to learn. It simply cannot be true that a child cannot learn. The fault lies with other persons or with the environment. All of the faults of

improper pacing, of the violations of readiness, are cases in point here. In properly organized teaching-learning settings, all normal persons learn. They cannot help it. Individuals sometimes *will* not learn, and it is then said they cannot learn. The two situations are not the same.

Certain misconceptions about heredity with special reference to education. Everyone has heard the cliché which so often beclouds human thinking and befuddles education and child-rearing: "You can't change human nature," or "Human nature doesn't change." The truth is that, properly understood, the only unchangeable thing about human nature is its changeability! Human nature is *acquired* nature. It changes constantly. If this were not so, cultural progress would be impossible, institutions could not evolve, behavior could not be controlled, and education would be a waste of time. Untold misery has been caused by stupid beliefs that greed and selfishness are ineradicable because part of "human nature." Generosity, altruism, and co-operation are just as much inherited. Human nature is unchangeable only in the sense that the primitive drives of self-preservation, relief of hunger and thirst, reproduction of the race, and one or two others are always present. The specific ways in which these operate and the personal-social-moral traits which develop are changeable from civilization to civilization, and widely within given civilizations. The central problem of education is the changing of *original, animal* nature into *human, civilized* nature.

The cliché referred to is used to excuse certain deplorable conditions existing in the world, not merely in education and child-rearing but in the areas of juvenile delinquency, crime, political malfeasance, economics, and many others. The verbalism obscures the facts and prevents intelligent effort to bring about better conditions.

The school and the home often blame heredity for undesirable attitudes and behaviors manifested by children. Parents and teacher are thus actually advertising their ignorance of the facts and demonstrating their own inability to cope with children. There are admittedly some extremely difficult problems, demanding diagnosis and remedial work by expertly informed individuals, but so long as we blame the matter on heredity we effectually prevent intelligent analysis and cure. We now believe that:

1. A child is not born with a tendency to be troublesome at home or in school; nor with a tendency to adjust with docility to the requirements of home or school. [7]
2. A child is not born with a tendency to be lazy in school; nor with a tendency to work persistently and continuously.
3. A child is not born with a tendency to be interested or uninterested in certain subjects.

Inheritance can have nothing to do with these tendencies. Each is learned as a product of interaction with conditions surrounding the child. The attitude the learner builds up as he grows is particularly important as a cause of the behaviors listed. To be sure, the inherited reaction time, that is, degree of sensitivity of the nervous system, the presence of certain congenital variations from normal physical structure, and the like may be predisposing causes; but in the main, and certainly with normal persons, learning is the significant factor in behavior.

Troublesome, lazy, uninterested pupils are products of homes, general cultural environments, and systems of education which do not satisfy the purposes of those pupils, which place pupils in situations maladjusted to their levels of maturity and to their aptitudes. Co-operative, persistent, interested pupils are products of educational opportunities adjusted to the purposes and growth of those pupils.

[7] The writer gratefully acknowledges his indebtedness for the general summary in these paragraphs to a clever discussion by L. Thomas Hopkins in *Interaction* (Boston, Heath, 1941), pp. 147-152. The ideas briefly noted here will be considered again in more detail in Chapter 23 on Classroom Management.

4. A child is not born with a tendency to be morally or socially good or bad; nor with a tendency toward either a good or a bad character.

Moral standards are not transmitted through the chromosomes! They are learned. Goodness and morality differ from culture to culture and even within a culture. Our society is no exception to the latter rule. It is a particularly difficult task to teach for good moral behavior in home and school within a civilization which contains so many powerful influences contrary to that moral teaching. [8] The correction of undesirable social or moral behavior which is already established is actually far too difficult for most parents and teachers at present levels of insight and training. Society acknowledges its incompetence by locking up offenders. The school blames its difficulties on heredity. This obscures the facts and again prevents intelligent attack on the actual causes.

5. A child is not born with a tendency toward a particular life occupation.

We hear of born teachers, born orators, born ministers of the Gospel. These "born" practitioners are usually adept without training. It is significant that none of us would submit to an operation by a "born" (untrained) surgeon. We do not hear of born engineers, born architects, born boilermakers, or born research psychologists. The fields in which "born" experts appear are usually those in which verbalism and personality will carry the person along and in which results are not immediate and objective. The truth is that even in these fields the "born" practitioner is a nuisance and a blocker of progress. In fields where expertly trained skill is obviously necessary, we hear no nonsense about "born" experts.

Inheritance conditions in a very general

[8] Recall in this connection, however, the discussion of "persistent" truths and standards in Chapter 3.

way one's choice of a given vocation. The actual decision is preponderantly affected by immediate conditions at the time of selection and by continuing conditions previous to selection.

Limited learning capacity does, of course, prevent certain individuals entering upon occupations demanding subtle insights or certain mental skills. But within the level open to such individuals, heredity does not dictate the specific choice made. Various levels of stability in the nervous system, various differences in the endocrine glands may influence individuals toward or away from certain general types of life work. Choice within the levels or types is made on other grounds.

The foregoing five points are often overlooked in excuses advanced by parents and teachers who are incapable of handling children. Fortunately, many competent teachers and educational leaders are engaged in basic, far-reaching reorganizations of the curriculum and of instructional methods designed to meet the problems involved.

Environment and learning. The system of education, the methods of teaching, the type of curriculum, the training and personalities of the teachers, the attitude of the parents, the security within the home, the placement of a given child within the family sequence, the size of the child in relation to other children in the neighborhood, the type of neighborhood, the socioeconomic status of the family, the type of housing, nutrition, climate, illness, play, and thousands of other factors all affect growth for good or ill.

Formal education is itself the process of stimulating, guiding, and directing development. Education does not cause growth, but stimulates and directs it. Teaching is an effort to see that the behavior resulting inevitably from maturation is socially desirable. It must be done with due regard to the maturation pattern and the conditioning power of outside factors. Schools, particu-larly the traditional type, have often been guilty of interfering with the growth of learners, particularly the brighter ones. On the other hand, many schools and parents have caused individuals to rise far beyond what might have been expected.

Development is in part natural, in part guided from outside. The development and learning of individuals are *in part* an inevitable and natural process and *in part* are stimulated and directed by outside influences of many and varied types. The first factor is often obscured when we speak of "learning" to walk or "learning" to think. Individuals will walk, think, imagine, develop ideas in any event. The second factor is often obscured when we speak of or explain certain acts, beliefs, and attitudes as "instinctive" or "inherited." Very few abilities are pure inheritances; very few, pure acquisitions. Growth, development, and learning result from the interaction of the growth potential, or maturation, and outside influences.

Caution concerning balance between the two factors. Disregard for or ignorance of the weight of either of the factors has resulted in some curious educational perversions. The older educational theorists, influenced by erroneous beliefs concerning the nature of the individual and his growth, spoke and acted as if desirable learning could come only through control, domination, even harsh repression of natural growth. The entire emphasis was placed upon outside influences, often of a repressive or coercive nature. This defiance of the natural maturation of individuals has been one important cause of many absurdities in traditional education, not to mention the stultification and unhappiness of the learners. It is wholly impossible to stimulate and guide growth and learning without proper regard for the unique organismic pattern of each individual. Many teaching procedures now widely used by experienced teachers must and actually do fail (even though the teacher is wholly unaware of his failure) because these procedures operate in direct defiance of the nature of the organism. Many classroom methods produce results which would astound the teacher if he only knew what was happening within the organism he is teaching! The results the teacher sees and accepts are often but a small and misleading part of the total reaction of the learning organism.

Extremists among modern educators, impressed by the revelations of research into the nature of growth, organismic patterns, and the like, fled to the opposite extreme. Many spoke and acted as if natural inevitable growth was, automatically, desirable growth. Environmental factors were regarded as artificial, often arbitrary, interferences with an otherwise wholesome process. Remove controls and interferences, they said, and learning will take place. The entire emphasis is here placed upon innate growth processes and patterns. It is, however, wholly impossible to stimulate and guide growth without taking into account the important effects of scores of environmental factors. Again, as pointed out in the preceding paragraph, teachers would be astounded if they but knew the results of their neglect of sound use of outside factors. Disregard of the necessities of guidance and outside influence was responsible for many of the nonsensical perversions of the otherwise sound early "activity" programs, and for the early ridicule of progressive education. This was the era when it was said by the lay public that modern education "let the children do what they pleased" and that drill had been abandoned. These misconceptions grew out of the work of misguided individuals and were never held by responsible leaders.

The trained educator of today avoids these extremes. The modern progressive school is organized, so far as is humanly possible, to bring the natural, unique pattern of individual growth into functioning interaction with a rich, varied, dynamic, and stimulating environment. To repeat, modern teaching is the encouragement and guidance of natural growth in accordance with socially desirable ends as determined by the given society. Neither of these two factors can be safely subordinated to the other.

Illustrations of the effect of physiological maturation upon behavior, with outside influence relatively ineffectual. The relationship between maturation of the nervous system and the development of correlative behavior is shown in one of Coghill's experiments. [9] Embryos of frogs and salamanders were placed in an anesthetic solution long before any signs of behavior were noted. The drug prevented movement but not natural growth or maturation. When these drugged and hence inactive animals had grown to the stage at which naturally developed animals were able to swim and move about they were placed in water. When the drug wore off, these animals swam and moved about practically as well as the others. The uncritical observer might say that the normal animals had "learned" to swim, but the experiment shows clearly that animals with no chance to learn or to move at all were able to swim when put into the water. Maturation was the dominant factor. Coghill shows that the growth of about .01 millimeter in the axones and dendrites changed salamanders from helpless, passive organisms into active, exploring animals.

A number of experiments have been made in which chicks were kept from pecking for some days after hatching. It was shown clearly that the pecking action resulted partly from maturation, partly from practice. Chicks which had been kept hooded for several days pecked imperfectly but better than newly hatched chicks, and they reached more quickly the same level of ability achieved by those which had had several

[9] G. E. Coghill, "The Early Development of Behavior in Amblystoma and Man," *Archives of Neurology and Psychiatry,* Vol. 21 (1929), pp. 989-1009.

days' practice. Many similar experiments are available. [10]

The physical growth curves of human beings during adolescence supply another excellent illustration. Modern growth studies show that there is a distinct spurt in growth at adolescence, preceded by a period of slower growth and followed by a similar period of decelerating growth. Although individuals differ in the onset and close of these periods and in the amount of growth, the pattern is unmistakable and is reported in all recent studies. Here we have a clear case of maturation.

Incidentally, we may note that G. Stanley Hall long ago discussed the adolescent spurt and its relation to education. Then the early statistical studies seemed to prove that there was no such periodic increase. These studies were cross-sectional, and the statistical treatment smoothed the growth curves to conceal the facts. Modern growth studies are longitudinal and show the spurt clearly.

Individual differences in the time of appearance of early physical behaviors persist whether or not special teaching, coaching, commendation, or condemnation is given. Just as man cannot add a cubit to his height

by taking thought, neither can he affect other physical or certain behavioral aspects in advance of sufficient maturation. These facts were noted but imperfectly understood from the very earliest days of child study. Modern studies supply reliable and valid data. [11] The monumental work of Gesell and his students at the Yale Clinic of Child Development should be made available to all students of teaching. [12]

[10] F. S. Breed and J. F. Shepherd, "Maturation and Use in the Development of an Instinct," *Journal of Animal Behavior*, Vol. 3 (1913), pp. 274-285.

Charles Bird, "The Relative Importance of Maturation and Habit in Development of an Instinct," *Pedagogical Seminary*, Vol. 32 (March, 1925), pp. 68-91; Vol. 33 (June, 1926), pp. 212-234.

Leonard Carmichael, "The Development of Behavior in Vertebrates Experimentally Removed from the Influence of External Stimulation," *Psychological Review*, Vol. 33 (January, 1926), pp. 51-58. Also see Vol. 34 (January, 1927), pp. 34-47; Vol. 35 (May, 1928), pp. 253-260.

W. E. Ritter, *The Natural History of Our Conduct* (New York, Harcourt, 1927).

H. C. Tracy, "The Development of Motility and Behavior Reactions in the Toadfish," *Journal of Comparative Neurology*, Vol. 40 (April, 1926), pp. 253-357.

G. E. Coghill, *Anatomy and the Problem of Behavior*.

———, "Integration and Motivation of Behavior," *Journal of Genetic Psychology*, Vol. 48 (1936), pp. 3-19.

[11] Wayne Dennis, "The Effect of Restricted Practice upon Reaching, Sitting, and Standing of Two Infants," *Journal of Genetic Psychology*, Vol. 47 (1935), pp. 17-32.

———, "Infant Development under Conditions of Restricted Practice and of Minimum Social Stimulation: A Preliminary Report," *Journal of Genetic Psychology*, Vol. 53 (September, 1938), pp. 149-157.

Orvis C. Irwin, *The Amount and Nature of Activities of New-Born Infants under External Stimulating Conditions the First Ten Days of Life*, Genetic Psychology Monographs, No. 8 (1930), pp. 1-92.

[12] Arnold Gesell and others, *The First Five Years of Life: A Guide in the Study of the Pre-School Child* (New York, Harper, 1940). This is a new edition of the volume, *The Mental Growth of the Pre-School Child* (New York, Macmillan, 1925). The 1940 edition is one of the most interesting and stimulating volumes for the average student. Definite readings should be assigned (see end of this chapter). There are illustrated in addition many methods for examining and evaluating behavior. On pp. 369-376 there is a most valuable bibliography of 142 selected titles.

———, *The Guidance of Mental Growth in Infant and Child* (New York, Macmillan, 1930).

———, and others, *An Atlas of Infant Behavior: A Systematic Delineation of the Forms and Early Growth of Human Behavior Patterns*, 2 vols. (New Haven, Yale Univ. Press, 1934). Illustrated by 3,200 action photographs.

——— and Helen Thompson, *The Psychology of Early Growth* (New York, Macmillan, 1938).

———, Catherine S. Amatruda, Burton M. Castner, and Helen Thompson, *Biographies of Child Development. The Mental Growth Careers of Eighty-four Infants and Children* (New York, Hoeber, Medical Book Dept. of Harper, 1939). 1939).

A. T. Jersild, *Training and Growth in the Development of Children: A Study of the Relative Influence of Learning and Maturation*, Child Development Monograph No. 10 (1932), pp. 16 ff. Contains excellent summary of studies.

M. M. Shirley, *The First Two Years* (Minneapolis, Univ. of Minnesota Press, 1933).

John B. Watson, *Psychological Care of Infant and Child* (New York, Norton, 1928). (*Continued*)

Illustrations of the effect of physiological maturation upon behavior, with outside influence relatively important. Criticism has been attached to some psychologists because of their reliance on animal experimentation in the interpretation of human behavior. Some inferences are possible, since, as Aristotle hinted long ago, there are some striking biological similarities between frogs and philosophers. However, because of differences in the circumstances under which evidence is derived, there is danger of error, particularly with reference to complex behavior.

Experimentation and dissection naturally cannot be used on living human subjects. However, much has been learned from the study of human subjects suffering from brain lesions, injuries, influence of drugs, and so forth. Much random evidence was collected in early days concerning maturation in the human foetus and in the post-natal periods, and concerning the relation between maturation and behavior.[13] In modern times embryologists have achieved a large body of valid data. Even some controlled studies have been made.[14] Observational and experimental evidence from these studies points to considerable similarity between animal and human maturation in the early physical stages of growth.

Controlled studies and common-sense observations both reveal further evidence about later stages of growth. Babies who have been kept off their feet by parents or physicians for various reasons until well past the age when babies usually "learn" to walk can very often stand up and walk nearly as well as those who have been "learning" for some time. The true learning period in those cases is distinctly shorter than for those who were free to walk earlier. Learning is clearly present, but maturation has played the dominant part. The power of maturation is further illustrated when we consult averages. Babies learn to walk on the average at about fourteen months, though there are wide variations in selected individual cases. Parents or other adults cannot accelerate the initiation of walking prior to proper maturation by any teaching, exhortation, punishment, or continued opportunity. In one study of twins, one child was given every opportunity to crawl, to creep, to climb, even to swim.[15] The other twin was deliberately neglected and was definitely unpracticed in these activities. The trained twin did not walk any earlier than his unpracticed brother.

Carrying the analysis further, it is to be noted that not only does walking appear when proper maturation has taken place, but that there is a fairly well-fixed series of preliminary abilities which must appear first and in sequence. The influence of maturation is indicated in that this sequence occurs without important variations. In this same connection, however, we may see more clearly the effect of environmental factors. The developmental sequence is clearly speeded or retarded by the type of surroundings in which the baby grows—the furniture and other objects, the amount of handling by adults, and the freedom or restriction of movement. The baby's own activities in attempting to crawl, to stand, to walk, all contribute to the skill achieved.

Another illustration may be seen in the behavior reactions which accompany the maturing of the sex organs. Maturation of the organs and the physiological manifestations are delayed until puberty. The typical acts of courtship, the ceremonies of marriage, indication of attraction to the opposite sex, interest in love stories are also delayed;

John B. Watson, Behaviorism, rev. ed. (New York, Norton, 1930).

Other summaries, both older and current, will be found in the Bibliography for Section 1 preceding, particularly Hilgard, Lee and Lee, Kuhlen and Thompson.

[13] Leonard Carmichael, "A Re-evaluation of the Concepts of Maturation and Learning," *Psychological Review,* Vol. 43 (September, 1936), p. 463.

[14] W. S. Ray, "A Preliminary Report on a Study of Foetal Conditioning," *Child Development,* Vol. 3 (June, 1932), pp. 175-177.

[15] Myrtle B. McGraw, *Growth: A Study of Johnny and Jimmy* (New York, Appleton, 1935).

but when they do appear are determined very largely by local influences. Sex behavior differs very widely between races and between regions even within one nation.

Mental and social maturity and learning. *Mental maturity.* Mental growth is not so easy to measure, since it must be measured indirectly through tests or observations. Measurement of mental growth or intelligence is further complicated because social stimulation, educational opportunity, and the like, strongly affect growth. The units of measurement are borrowed from chronological growth; namely, years and months. Tests of this type give us one measure of mental maturity, the M.A., or mental age. Another measure is the I.Q., or intelligence quotient, which is the relation between chronological and mental age.

The means of measurement in all these tests are subject to much controversy. The units of measurement are particularly unsatisfactory to the advanced students in the field. Doubtless newer instruments and units will be available to the teacher in the classroom. [16]

Intelligence and mental-age tests are of various forms, some calling for mechanical manipulation, some for verbal response, some for non-verbal response, and some for paper-and-pencil reaction. There are also scales and checklists for controlled observation of behavior. We need not go into details. Suffice it to say that the measures do have considerable reliability, each for its own type of material. The different tests seem to measure different abilities only in part, thus making more than one test necessary. Mental growth, like the physical, seems to be gradual and constant and seems to continue longer than physical growth. There are variations between children: each child seems to have a unique individual pattern, rhythm, and style of his own. There is consistency, but more variation than is found in natural physical growth. The separation of physical and mental here is arbitrary and for discussion only, since both are within one organismic pattern. The general laws and processes of growth should apply to body and mind, for each is a function of a unified organism. Just as the neurologist and embryologist study the growth of bodily structure, so the genetic psychologist seeks to discover how mental life and behavior develop. [17]

We do not know as much as we should like to about mental maturity, but some manageable principles are available, the application of which is even more important to education than are the principles of physical growth. It is futile to present curriculum material before the child has an adequate background of experience and mental maturity to understand it: for instance, formal arithmetic in the primary grades. Typical primers and first readers, until well after the turn of the century, were absurdly out of line with the mental maturity of the children. Another error is to expect results from children which satisfy adult standards. Children always draw things as they *are* instead of as they *see* them. Not until this period has been outgrown, that is, greater mental maturity achieved, will they stop drawing houses with the furniture showing through the walls, or men on horseback with both legs showing. In fact, at early levels of maturity the children may in fact *see* things this way. While visiting a school recently, the writer was presented by a proud primary child with a drawing of "Daddy Coming Home." Daddy was as tall as the house and was smoking a huge black pipe which, if in proportion, would have had a bowl the size of a bushel basket. Meeting "Daddy" and the pipe later, it was clear that the child probably did identify daddy-coming-home by the outsize pipe! The obvious failure to

[16] All recent growth studies and mental measurement investigations discuss this and make various suggestions.

[17] See again previous references to Gesell, Watson, and others. Also Jane Warters, *Achieving Maturity* (New York, McGraw, 1950).

develop the degree of skill in drawing which is easily possible for practically everyone is in part due to ridicule which inhibits natural growth. Some children are "dull" or serious problem cases not because they are inherently dull or bad, but because their normal mental and social growth was interfered with. Many an average or bright pupil has stopped learning and gives every evidence of backwardness, that is, low or retarded mental maturity, because of the injudicious remarks of parents, teachers, or playmates. Convince a child that he is stupid and he will often become so.

Training given in advance of maturity usually results in pseudo-learning which disappears shortly. Any number of experiments show that children who are coached for intelligence tests or given extra drill for passing subject-matter achievement tests will "learn," but only temporarily. The same thing occurs with scores of students who cram for college-entrance examinations. Crammed beyond their native ability to understand, or their experiential background, they will pass the examinations but shortly will flunk out of college. More will be said of this in Chapter 19 on practice. The natural development of mental maturity, far more than physical maturation, is affected by innumerable environmental factors.

Social maturity. This term has had wide circulation recently and refers to a vitally important aspect of development in the learner. Tests, scales, and checklists are available. [18] Social maturity is usually stated in terms of described levels of social behavior. Various aspects of conduct are used. Development of maturity may be noted, for instance, in recognition of the rights and responsibilities of self and of others, getting along with others, making friends, exercising leadership, manifesting co-operation with

a leader or a group, participating in common activities, acting in accordance with the social mores, customs, and institutions of the given social group, making moral judgments, and taking initiative. The Vineland Social Maturity Scale, for example, outlines the development of maturity in eating and dressing without help. [19] The same scale indicates that a normal six-year-old child can go to school alone; that a ten-year-old gets about his home town freely; that an eighteen-year-old can arrange fairly complicated trips to distant points. Another sequence indicates that a five- or six-year-old is socially mature enough to be sent with small sums of money to make specific purchases; that a nine-year-old can make small purchases for himself, exercising some choice and discretion; that a twelve-year-old can begin to buy some of his own articles of use; that a fifteen-year-old is able to have an allowance to spend and will have reasonable discretion in the use of it, and so on. Also studied as indicative of social maturity are interests, hobbies, attitudes, and fears.

Again, as with other maturities, outside influences play a tremendous part: parents, playmates, teachers, socioeconomic status, and many others are vital. [20]

Summary: principles dealing with growth processes of the learner. The foregoing

[18] Extensive lists of instruments dealing with personality traits, integration, social maturity, and so forth can be found in textbooks dealing with tests, measures, and evaluative techniques; in bibliographies and yearbooks (for instance those by Buros); in local collections.

[19] Edgar A. Doll, *The Vineland Social Maturity Scale* (Vineland, N. J., The Training School, 1936).

[20] It seems futile to cite studies at this point, since so many are becoming available. The following are representative.

Harold H. Anderson, *Domination and Integration in the Social Behavior of Young Children in an Experimental Play Situation,* Genetic Psychology Monographs, Vol. 19, No. 3 (1937).

———, "The Measurement of Domination and of Socially Integrative Behavior in Teachers' Contacts with Children," *Child Development,* Vol. 10 (June, 1939), pp. 73-89. See also numerous other studies by Harold A. Anderson.

Arnold Gesell. His various volumes are mines of information.

Clark Murchison, ed., *Handbook of Child Psychology,* rev. ed. (Worcester, Mass., Clark Univ. Press, 1933). Reference to many studies.

materials and other related statements may be summarized for quick reference.

1. The growth of living organisms is controlled in part by heredity, in part by environment.

2. Growth, in general, is an orderly, progressive differentiation out of the original organismic pattern. Growth in general is regular and even instead of saltatory and irregular, except as noted in No. 4 below.

3. Growth in individuals, in general, maintains the pace at which it starts. Exceptions are noted in No. 4 below.

4. Growth shows oscillations in rate at various ages and levels, between the sexes, and for various aspects of growth.

5. Growth oscillations in rate and amount are more rapid and intense the earlier the physiological changes of adolescence appear.

6. Growth in a given individual may vary greatly from the average, but will be in accordance with the general laws.

7. Growth of various items proceeds at differential rates; maturity is achieved at different times; but these differentials are subordinate to the general laws.

8. Growth irregularities, in the sense of variations from expectancy, do occur and may be either positive or negative.

The various growth studies disagree on the causation of these variations. It is not known positively whether certain types of irregularity are primarily owing to innate factors and certain others to environmental influences. In many given individual cases the immediate causes are only too obvious. Various congenital factors clearly affect the individual's mental and emotional growth and stability. In others, any of several environmental factors are clearly involved. In given individual cases, especially with school children, efforts to diagnose causative factors may yield very helpful data for the further guidance of the child. Further research is needed on causes.

9. Growth, in general, is rounded rather than uneven.

The factors are correlated positively with each other and do not ordinarily follow a pattern of compensation. Again, the growth studies are not conclusive. The correlations which exist are positive but low. Predictions concerning one element based on growth in another are uncertain. Some studies indicate an appreciable correlation between mental and physical growth; others do not. One study does show that boys and girls with early maximum-growth ages, and hence a more intense period of growth, do tend to be brighter than boys and girls whose maximum-growth ages are later and whose intensity of growth is not so great.[21] It also shows that there is no mental lag or inertia during the adolescent spurt or period of intense physical growth. Children do just as well in scholastic achievement and in mental tests during these periods as during periods of less intense physical growth. Scholastic slumps cannot be laughed off because "the child is growing so fast."

While the facts are not all in, it will probably be wise not to accept poor work in spelling and arithmetic from students who do quite well in history and geography. The former must be taught more effectively. It is rarely true that a pupil can do well in everything but "just cannot do arithmetic." It is more likely that arithmetic was poorly taught or was introduced in advance of maturation and readiness. The marked variations in performance of many specialists, expert in one field and poor in others, are usually owing to training.

Special Note on the Periods of Growth

The periods or levels of growth—infancy, early childhood, preadolescence, and adolescence—have been well summarized in many compact summaries and in whole volumes. Detailed discussion is omitted here; first, because the materials are readily accessible, and second, because many students will have studied the growth periods in other courses. Students without this

[21] W. F. Dearborn and John W. M. Rothney, *Predicting the Child's Development* (Cambridge, Mass., Sci-Art Publishers, 1941). Use index and table of contents. See also Willard C. Olson, *Child Development* (Boston, Heath, 1949), Ch. 3.

background should do outside reading, with perhaps class report summaries.

The phrase "periods or levels of growth" should not be misinterpreted to mean that there are sharply disjunctive periods or levels, clearly distinguishable from each other. Growth in the main is even, regular, and continuous. Levels can be discerned, however, within the growth continuum. The physical, mental, and social characteristics of children of three are quite different from those of youths of thirteen, or young people of twenty-three. The information possessed by children of three and thirteen obviously differs greatly. Similarly with interests and attitudes. Things which enthrall and motivate children of five are looked upon with condescension by those of fifteen. The implications for education are fundamental.

DISCUSSION QUESTIONS FOR SECTION 2

Use here again the four questions at end of Section 1. Students are encouraged to raise questions of their own.

Two questions on heredity and environment may be of interest but time should not be spent on them if students are already well informed on this subject.

1. Common opinion concerning heredity and environment contains many astounding misconceptions, downright errors, old wives' superstitions, and so on. List the general reason why opinion is so at variance with the facts. This is important for your own thinking.

2. Give illustrations from everyday observation, conversation, or current public discussions, of the "you-can't-change-human-nature" fallacy. Attempt the difficult task of seeing through the superficial thinking and giving illustrations in opposition.

READINGS

Ample material on maturation and on heredity and environment is available in volumes already cited in this chapter and in many others.

See also references at close of Section 1, particularly Kuhlen and Thompson and the bibliographies in Lee and Lee, *The Child and His Development*.

Children in Focus, 1954 Yearbook of the American Association for Health, Education and Recreation (Washington, D. C., N.E.A., 1954).

DEARBORN, Walter, and ROTHNEY, J. W. M., *Predicting the Child's Development* (Cambridge, Mass., Sci-Art Publishers, 1941).

GESELL, Arnold, *The Embryology of Behavior* (New York, Harper, 1945). Advanced discussion, difficult reading.

HAVIGHURST, Robert J., *Human Development and Education* (New York, Longmans, 1953).

JONES, Harold E., *Motor Performance and Growth* (Berkeley, Cal., Univ. of California Press, 1949).

JONES, Mary C., and BAYLEY, Nancy, "Physical Maturing Among Boys as Related to Behavior," *Journal of Educational Psychology*, Vol. 41 (March, 1950), pp. 129-148.

OLSON, Willard, *Child Development* (Boston, Heath, 1949).

RUSSELL, David H., *Children's Thinking* (Boston, Ginn, 1956).

SIMMONS, Katherine, *The Brush Foundation Study of Child Growth and Development II: Physical Growth and Development*, Monographs of the Society for Research in Child Development, Vol. 9, No. 1 (Washington, D. C., National Research Council, 1944).

3: MENTAL LIFE AND LEARNING.

Mental life of the individual not easily described. Descriptions of the biological nature of the individual and the development of his overt behavior are generally agreed upon by biologists, neurologists, psychologists, and anthropologists. Efforts to describe the origin, nature, and development of mental life and learning precipitate marked differences of opinion.

The development of various schools within a comparatively new field is inevitable. Each of the so-called schools represents one method of approach to, one partial explanation of, an area which is still being reduced to order and system through research and interpretation. Each is an honest effort to explain mental life. An earlier chapter summarized Hilgard's division of the schools into two groups: connectionist and field theory. [22]

Chief differences between the two most prominent views: connectionism and field theory. *First,* the connectionists generally explain behavior as learning which results from the effect of the environment acting upon the individual. The field theory holds that in the interaction between individual and environment (resulting in behavior), the native endowment of the individual is most important. The phenomenological version [23] of field theory holds that the field is that which is perceived by the individual. *Second,* it follows from the foregoing that the connectionist leans toward a mechanical explanation of behavior and of motivation, whereas the field-theory men believe the

individual to be in a state of dynamic equilibrium. The first group believe that behavior is touched off by stimuli much as a machine starts. The second group believe that disturbances to equilibrium motivate behavior. *Third,* the connectionists minimize certain central processes in knowing and thinking; the field theory makes much of insight. *Fourth,* connectionists stress past experience in explaining behavior, whereas the field theory places much emphasis on the present and current situation, the "field" within which the individual finds himself. *Fifth,* the connectionists regard whole situations as being built of parts. The field theory holds that wholes are primary and that parts have meaning only because of the field within which they fall.

The critical reader can see from the brief summary, and particularly if he reads outside material, that some of these differences are merely different angles on the same thing. A good deal of overlap will be found. The differences appear more acute in problems of motivation and in explanation of "trial-and-error" learning, as we will see later. Concrete materials in the following pages will supplement the foregoing abbreviated, abstract account.

Connectionist theories on mental life and laws of learning. What happens first in consciousness? No one can ever know just what does appear first in the mental life of a baby. The original "buzzing, booming confusion" does, however, eventually differentiate into recognizable phenomena.

The associationists hold that the individual first recognizes simple sensations, images, and effects. These elements are associated and connected as they occur in time and space. Learning takes place depending on the frequency, recency, vividness, similarity, and duration of the associative incidents and elements. Later, logical connections are recognized and constructed.

---

[22] In his 1956 revision Hilgard omits mention of Wheeler's version of field theory, namely, the organismic. The 1948 edition devoted Chapter 9 to this theory. The view was not developed further by Wheeler or his students, hence receded in importance. Hilgard points out that many of the terms and principles are valuable and survive in other accounts.

Since Hilgard's listing, another field theory view has emerged, namely, the phenomenological or personal field, outlined by Snygg and Combs. This has been mentioned in earlier chapters and will come up again in the chapter on the pupil as learner. Previous field theories are based on the physical or objective world. The phenomenological is based on the person's perception of that world and of himself. The field is the one as perceived by the learner. Behavior is not the result of stimuli in the world but the result of how the person perceives the world.

Snygg and Combs give the only detailed report, generously giving credit to the many men who contributed to the development of the new view. Modern educational psychologies, however, are increasingly giving analyses of the new view. For illustration see Chapter 19 in Thompson, Gardner, and Di Vesta which gives a good account and also an excellent bibliography. See also books by Arthur T. Jersild.

[23] For a quick summary of the phenomenal field and its educational implications, see:

Arthur W. Combs, "Personality Theory and its Implications for Curriculum Development," in *Learning More about Learning* (Washington, D. C., Association for Supervision and Curriculum Development, N. E. A., 1959).

The central doctrine of the connectionists is that of connection between stimulus and response. Associations are made between sense impressions and impulses to action. Bonds or connections are made which are strengthened or weakened according to the amount of use and the effects of the use. The most influential statement was Thorndike's *S-R* bond theory, with the laws of learning originally stated as follows:

The *Law of Exercise,* or of use and disuse. The more often a connection is exercised, the more firmly it becomes fixed.

The *Law of Effect.* Connections are strengthened or weakened in terms of the satisfaction or annoyance which accompanies their use.

The *Law of Readiness.* When a bond is ready to act, the action gives satisfaction; not to act, annoyance. A bond made to act when not ready will result in annoyance.

Thorndike and his students, and others, have made extensive modifications in these "laws." Emphasis on the law of exercise was greatly reduced because mere repetition without attention or interest is not educative. This resulted in added importance for the law of effect, especially in terms of satisfactions, rewards, and success. The theory of the weakening effects of annoyance was practically abandoned. The law of readiness as originally stated in terms of bonds had to be abandoned. However, the effects of satisfaction or of frustration resulting from the ability or the current desire of the learner to do what is to be done are obviously important. The term *readiness* as used today is not the same as Thorndike's law, as will be shown in later pages.

A number of subsidiary theories were added to the original system. *First,* the learner must be capable of making *multiple responses* to a stimulus. Otherwise, appropriate behavior could not appear to be rewarded, hence learned. *Second,* learning is guided to an important degree by the *"set"* or *"attitude"* of the learner. *Third,* a response well learned can be attached to stimuli other than the original one. This Thorndike called *associative shifting,* and gave it considerable importance. The familiar conditioning experiments illustrate this. *Fourth,* responses to novel situations can be made when the learner sees any *analogy* with previous situations. *Fifth,* the learner can react selectively to essential factors in the situation. Thorndike called this reacting to *prepotent elements.* This is closely allied to analysis and insight as developed by the field-theory exponents.

The connectionist views and laws have had far-reaching effect upon classroom procedures. Modifications and improvements are constantly under way. The theory is not static, as many of its practitioners seem to believe.

Field-theory explanations of mental life and laws of learning. According to the field-theory group, the earliest mental states are general, non-localized experiences of hunger, warmth, and pain. Mental life and learning begins with these primary undifferentiated wholes out of which specialized forms are differentiated.

The first recognizable experiences are possibly those of general lightness and darkness, followed eventually by recognition of fuzzy fields of differing degrees of brightness—window areas, for instance, differentiated from wall space. Naturally, the baby has no meanings to go with these early ones. Later, large objects begin to be separated from the general undifferentiated field, but animate and inanimate objects are not for some time differentiated from each other. Eventually, the baby has actually to differentiate himself from the total field within which he lives. [24] Whole persons, objects, events, and processes are perceived. These wholes are primary; that is, they are not composed or built up out of simple elements, but exist in their own right. With experience, and as he matures, the learner differentiates the

[24] Koffka, *op. cit.,* pp. 131 ff. This concept has also appeared for many years in all schools of psychology.

details (parts). These parts become wholes in their own right; and as learning proceeds, the learner becomes able to transpose these wholes into new situations. Transfer is possible, as indicated in a previous chapter, if learning has been truly integrative. The function and meaning of parts is determined at any given time by the whole within which they appear. This somewhat abstract summary will be clarified presently by illustrations from experimental studies and from common-sense observation. The increasing use in education of terms such as *frame of reference, pattern, structure, configuration,* and *gestalt* stem from the concepts just developed.

Field-theory principles of learning. The technical language in which field-theory concepts of mental life and learning were first stated was borrowed from technical studies in biology and physics. The words were new and confusing to students of education. The aim of the present volume has been to develop in the students understandings based upon their own very limited experience, before introducing the technical statements. It is significant that the recent presentations, particularly of gestalt psychology, make less use of the strictly technical language. Young and immature students will doubtless do better with such treatment. The technical language should, however, be known to the student. Previous chapters will have prepared the student, it is hoped, for simple understandings.

The *Law of Field Genesis* states that wholes evolve as wholes and are primary.

The *Law of Derived Properties* and the *Law of Determined Action* hold that the meanings and the behavior of the parts are determined by the wholes within which they occur.

The *Law of Field Properties* holds that the whole is more than the sum of the parts and that the properties of the field are not the same as the sum of the properties of the parts.

The *Law of Individuation* holds that parts come to have existence through the process of individuation, or differentiation, or structurization.

The *Law of Configuration* holds that a system of energy always functions as a unit and is able to adjust itself to a number of disturbing factors.

The *Law of Least Action* states that the organism or energy system will take the most direct route to the relief of tension or the restoration of equilibrium.

The *Law of Maximum Work* states that the organism or energy system will exert maximum effort to relieve tension or restore equilibrium. [25]

Field-theory psychologists make much use of the terms *initial delay, insight,* and *pacing.* Explanations are given a few paragraphs below. The interpretation of the terms *readiness* and *trial-and-error learning* differs from that of the older schools. All groups agree in the main on the use of such terms as *goal, purpose,* or *motive; learning by wholes* or *modified wholes; rhythm* or *distribution of work periods;* and *transfer.*

The whole is primary. Field-theory psychologists differ with the connectionists in holding that learning is not additive. Understandings, concepts, beliefs, attitudes, and skills are not achieved by adding fact to fact to fact, item to item to item, until a rational whole has been built up. Skills, whether in writing, in swimming, or in getting along with persons, are not achieved by drilling upon isolated parts which will later be put together to constitute a perfected ability. On the contrary, learning proceeds first through perceiving a living whole, even though imperfectly, which is important to the learner's purposes. Progressive differentiation of the components not only gives

[25] Raymond H. Wheeler and Francis T. Perkins, *Principles of Mental Development* (New York, Crowell, 1932). Chapter 2 contains an excellent detailed summary of the laws. Pages 370-383 contain interpretation of these laws in terms of learning. Latter discussion is somewhat too abstract to be of immediate use to teachers.

George W. Hartmann, *Educational Psychology* (New York, American Book, 1941). A comprehensive attempt to develop a volume on educational psychology from the gestalt point of view. Practical and useful.

Ernest Hilgard, *Theories of Learning,* 2nd ed. (New York, Appleton-Century-Crofts, 1956).

smaller wholes but contributes to understanding of the larger whole. Instead of proceeding from simple to complex, as has been said for centuries, learning begins with a complex unit which becomes simpler as better understood. The primary patterns are progressively differentiated into all manner of knowledges and skills.

The field-theory psychologist believes it to be absurd to teach facts out of relation to the situation in which they occur, or skills in isolation from use. No learning should be considered without reference to the total situation. A natural corollary is the increasing emphasis in teaching upon "wholes," that is, upon unitary organizations of subject matter and learning experiences, with decreasing emphasis upon fragmentary assign-study-recite sequences. This movement is of particular importance in the elementary schools, where it will likely dominate before long. The secondary school will utilize it in the rapidly expanding "core" curriculum. Specialized study of isolated knowledge abstracted from a field of specialization can be done by mature learners under definite assignment and study.

Illustrations from actual school practice are scattered through this volume, particularly in Chapter 4. All the violations of continuity and interaction, and the improvements in using those principles, are cases in point. One or two more may be cited here. The modern practice of teaching vernacular language skills which begins by encouraging children to express themselves, no matter how crudely, is sound. Out of the efforts to make something clear in circumstances important to the child, need will arise for better skills, grammatical rules, rhetorical forms. The pupil sees this for himself, instead of meeting it as a demand from outside which he cannot understand. These learnings emerge (are differentiated) from a sensible whole. To begin with grammar is to reverse the order and to violate all we know about learning. (In learning a foreign language, interested, mature adults do not necessarily follow the pattern used by young children learning their vernacular.) Studying literary works, whether Shakespeare's plays, Shelley's poetry, or Dickens' novels, through piecemeal analysis without reference to the wholeness of the work and the setting from which it grew is not merely a waste of time; undesirable learning outcomes are inevitable.

In teaching reading, we have long since abandoned the method of beginning with the a-b-c's and letter-combination charts. Whole thoughts interesting to and understandable by the learner are now used. The details of the total structure emerge with experience and teaching. The story of the progressive revolution in the teaching of reading over the past quarter century is one of the most vivid and enlightening accounts of the application of modern psychology to education. Once the child has a store of meanings which he can and does use to differentiate parts, these parts can in turn be used as aids in understanding new wholes. After the child has met in functional situations a number of words with the same root or the same prefix or suffix, the structure of the word can be called to his attention.

The same general shift in emphasis, from so-called elements from which wholes are to be built to wholes from which elements are to be differentiated, is to be seen in the teaching of arithmetic, writing, and art. The older practice in art, and in music as well, of insisting on young children's precise copying of models or pictures is one of the most reprehensible still to be found in the classroom.

The field gives meaning to the parts. The gestalt adherents point out that colors are definitely affected by the field within which they occur. Gray appears bluish on a yellow field. The apparent intensity of red or of green will be changed if either one is surrounded by a field of the other. We recognize melodies, places, persons, but are often unable to specify details, even the color of the eyes of a close friend. The parts must be specifically attended to, differentiated out of the field, to become known. Details are not necessary for recognition of the whole. Note, for instance, the difficulty witnesses have in describing to the police a burglar or hold-up man whom they can recognize immediately in a police line-up. The personality is a totality and is not recognized piece by piece.

An even simpler illustration is to ask what the word *bay* means. Meaning cannot be attributed until we have the total field in which the symbol occurs: a bay tree; a bay horse; a bay window (architectural); a bay window (anatomical), a bay in the hills; the bomb bay; gun bay, or sick bay; the hound's bay; a bay of the ocean; a bay in the woods (a meadow); bay rum; to bring to bay, or fight at bay. The symbol "O" on the typewriter looks identical in 1801, O! LOOK; but the meaning differs because of the field within which each appears.

Meaning is given the parts (events, persons, processes) by the field within which they occur. Relativity is hence an important principle. Parts may be differentiated out of wholes, and become smaller wholes with meanings of their own. These are transposable, that is, there is transfer of learning. Reading must be done to supplement this presentation if students are not already familiar with the details.

Individuation or differentiation of parts from the whole. A few research studies [26] and many common-sense illustrations may be cited. Andrews shows that a small child soon learns to recognize the face of his mother and the faces of other members of the family. [27] He soon learns to recognize the picture of a face. He can point, on request, to the eyes, the ears, the nose, the mouth. If the child is shown a picture of an eye by itself, or of a nose, or of an ear, however, there is no recognition. The eye is called a bird's nest, an egg, or other similar item. The ear becomes a coil of rope; the mouth, a stairway; the nose, a tent or a mountain. It is a year or two later before the child has learned to recognize these features when they are shown separately, that is, out of relation to the functioning whole of which they are parts. Still later, children learn to differentiate kind, harsh, tired, young, old, pretty, and ugly faces. Many similar studies are available. Individuals untrained in music recognize a melody without being able to identify a single one of the notes. Training enables us to differentiate out of a functioning whole the various parts. Similarly, melodies are not made up by building one note upon another, but usually appear as incomplete and inadequate wholes. The composer then develops the parts in terms of the original whole. (See the discussion of insight in the paragraphs below.)

This basic principle of modern psychology has long been used as the basis of a parlor game. A member of the group stands behind a screen and through a small hole displays some one feature such as an eye, an ear, the mouth, two inches of cheek or brow. Intimate friends usually cannot identify the individual. Married couples are usually completely unable to identify each other's hands thrust through the screen. The whole can be identified easily, but not the parts.

The discussion may be further clarified by a more typical everyday illustration. A very small boy visiting his grandparents who lived far to the north of his home, woke up one morning to find the ground covered with snow, with large wet flakes still falling thickly. This new and startling view of an otherwise familiar landscape was greeted with much excitement and a torrent of questions. "Well," said his grandfather, "you are

[26] The studies of early mental life should have come to the attention of students in a course preceding this one. In case this is not true, instructors and students may wish to make a brief excursion into that field at this point. Note special references in bibliography.

[27] Elizabeth A. Andrews, "The Development of Imagination in the Pre-School Child," *University of Iowa Studies*, Vol. 3, No. 4 (1930).

seeing your first snowstorm!" More excitement and questions! So far "snowstorm" is everything in sight, and to the child is one undifferentiated whole. He does not define nor confine snowstorm, its parts or internal organization do not concern him. But soon details come to his attention, in this case through contrast with the usual scene. "Look, how funny the bushes are—all covered with snow. They look like humps. Two are bent way over—won't they break?" "When will the snow stop?" "You can't see down the road—you can't see the house down there. It looks all white and you can't see through." He is beginning to differentiate details within the whole.

Later experience with more storms, with reading and pictures, and with his own maturation, and he will discover the relation of snowstorms to agriculture, to the water table, to irrigation, to winter sports, and many others. Still later he will distinguish between wet and dry snow, slippery and slushy snow, snow drifts. Extending the field as he grows up he will discover the relation to interference with traffic, accidents, delay of trains and grounding of planes, and others.

This phase of learning consists of differentiating the details, discovering complexity within what was originally seen as a simple unitary whole.

Insight. The technical meaning of *insight* is not too far removed from the common-sense meaning of seeing into, understanding, or apprehending a problem, process, or situation. Foresight is insight at its very best. Even hindsight is a form of insight, though a belated form. The feminine intuition and the masculine hunch actually refer to insight, though the ordinary user of those terms does not understand what has happened in his own mind. The elements of mystery or of "sudden" revelation bulk large with the average citizen. Insight, to the psychologist, is not mysterious or occult; it means a better grasp or understanding of the problem

or situation, gained, however, before complete experience with that problem or situation. As insight into the situation is gained, new responses appear which carry the learner further toward his goal. Furthermore, learnings are transposed from other situations, because insight enables the learner to recognize the applicability of older learning to the new situation. Using terms already developed in this chapter, insight means achieving a better understanding of the total pattern, the whole problem to be solved, the total skill to be acquired. Insight enables the learner to adapt, to discover, or to invent appropriate responses more easily. Insight is seeing what is to be done and how to do it. The field-theory psychologists have developed a considerable research background which, they believe, supports their definition of insight. [28]

The field-theory psychologists hold that understandings, attitudes, and meanings are first achieved through insight and later clarified through experience and application. Skills first learned through insight are then perfected through practice or drill. Referring again to walking, we note that the baby walks, that is, operates, however imperfectly, in an integrated pattern. Practice develops skill in the thing already functioning as a whole. Swimming is perhaps a better illustration. The learner flounders around in the first stages. He knows what he wants to do, but he does not know it clearly. The pattern is vague and general. As insight develops, there comes a point at which the individual can swim. Clumsy and uneconomical as it may be, it is swimming. The learner has dis-

[28] William F. Bruce and Frank S. Freeman, *Development and Learning* (Boston, Houghton, 1942), Ch. 15; also Index.
George W. Hartmann, *Gestalt Psychology* (New York, Ronald, 1935), Ch. 12. An excellent summary of experiments.
———, *Educational Psychology* (New York, American Book, 1941). Use the Index.
Each of these three references summarizes a large number of individual research studies. These are fully footnoted, hence individual references are not repeated here.

covered the characteristic structure and can perform the necessary movements. Skill is then achieved through practice. Rapid learning in the later stages of achieving a skill is often owing to the fact that excellent insight has been obtained earlier. Any adult who has learned golf will recognize very easily the place of insight in achieving the necessary complex motor co-ordinations. One amateur golfer of the writer's acquaintance took nearly one stroke per hole off his score (he had plenty of room) after overhearing a chance remark by a golf professional. The remark opened up a whole new insight into the nature of the pattern he was trying to achieve. Incidentally, this little incident illustrates clearly the function of the teacher in aiding the pupils to achieve insight.

Initial delay. Field-theory psychology recognizes a period of partial or seemingly complete inaction at the beginning of and at important points within any prolonged activity. We often hear children and adults say, when they are trying to do something, that they must first "get the hang of the thing," "get the feel of it." Reversing this, we often hear persons say that they are "not getting anywhere." This means that they cannot see what to do or how to do it. Parents and teachers often mistake this for dullness or inattention, and sometimes it is. Field-theory psychologists recognize a period of initial delay and attribute it to the necessity for first developing some insight into the problem. Teachers should expect and patiently allow for this period of seeming non-learning.

Pacing. If the level of difficulty of the new learning could be *perfectly matched* with the maturity level of the learner, then learning would take place on the first effort, say the gestalt psychologists. Since this theoretically perfect condition will not likely be achieved in many instances, particularly with heterogeneous groups of learners, the teacher will

endeavor to adjust learning situations as closely as possible to maturation and background. This is called *pacing*. The more closely the tasks of the school approximate the readiness of the learner, the faster learning through insight will take place. Pacing, properly done, aids the steady, regular development of intelligence and learning.

Learning situations which are beyond the maturation and experience level of the child, that is, which are "too hard," antagonize and discourage the learner. Since he can have no insight and since he cannot actually learn in such situations, he resorts at first to blind fumbling. Eventually, he will resort to cheating and lying. The habit of failure is built up, together with very undesirable attitudes and habits of work. The pupil eventually refuses to try and reverts to simpler methods of response which he knows but which will not meet the situation. Parents and teachers who believe that children should be "forced to do hard and difficult things whether they like it or not" are not merely talking innocent nonsense; they are actually stultifying the intelligence of the learner and building up serious personality and character problems for the future. The problems and skills to be achieved must often be reduced to the learner's level of maturity; otherwise they are "too hard." The pupil actually cannot learn. He is not stupid or obtuse, as many teachers think. Of course, care must be taken to see that lazy or indifferent learners are not avoiding tasks which they actually are capable of performing.

Learning situations which are below the maturation level of the learner likewise antagonize pupils. Bright children are especially bored and contemptuous of the teacher and of the school. They acquire habits of loafing, half trying, and being satisfied with mediocre results. Sometimes, individual children of brilliance are so antagonized by the drivel in some beginning readers that they refuse to react. They are then classified as poor readers, in a few cases actually as non-readers, in school, but are found to be reading quite difficult material outside of school. Hence, the problems and skills to be learned must often be raised to the level of pupil maturity.

Pacing, to repeat, is the effort to give learners opportunities to attack problems which increase in complexity as the learners' experience increases. Learning situations must be difficult enough seriously to challenge the learner, but at the same time be susceptible to solution. They must not be so easy that they do not challenge.

Insight and learning do not result, as a matter of course, merely from adjusting the learning situation to the learner's maturity level. The teacher plays an important role, as is illustrated throughout the volume.

Readiness. [29] A pedagogical principle, based on the foregoing psychological facts, which has had much discussion is that of *readiness*. It is the pedagogical counterpart, so to speak, of maturation but includes social and intellectual maturity as well. For example, we say that at a certain time a child is ready to read, ready for formal arithmetic, ready for the development of time sense in history, ready to participate in group activity, and so forth. His physical and neurological maturity and his experiential background are such that he could read, could do abstract arithmetic, could get along with other children co-operatively— if circumstances demanded these things.

This important principle is easily misinter-

[29] The general current use of the term *readiness* is not to be confused with the special use made by the connectionists, which refers to the readiness of neurological bonds to act.

Gertrude Hildreth, *Readiness for School Beginners* (New York, Harcourt, Brace & World, 1950). Many similar treatments available in general texts.

Lee J. Cronbach, *Educational Psychology* (New York, Harcourt, Brace & World, 1954). Chapters 4-7 summarize the psychological background for readiness.

Many accounts available in texts in teaching of reading, arithmetic, and other subjects.

preted. We are led to think of "readiness" as a definite locus or condition. This leads to three subsidiary errors: (*a*) neglect of the genetic development of any power, skill, or understanding; (*b*) waiting for the given condition of readiness to appear of itself; (*c*) assuming without investigation that readiness must be present.

In regard to (*a*) we know that growth is a steady, on-going process. The designation of any given point in the developmental sequence as readiness for the given learning must be largely arbitrary. The (*b*) type of error may cause teachers to overlook the value of stimulation, opportunity, and tryout, thus unduly delaying a given learning. The (*c*) error may result in too early stimulation and forcing because readiness is deemed to have been attained. This results in frustration and in formal attempts to bring on or induce readiness.

An analysis in terms of learning to read will illustrate these errors. Traditional primary teachers usually think of reading in but one way, namely, the interpretation of printed materials. Readiness, then, is the stage at which children are able to do this. Formal standard tests of reading encourage this view, as do the naïve conceptions of reading held by parents and public generally. Such a view causes parents and teachers to overlook the importance of a long series of preliminary developments which are all a part of developing reading attitudes and abilities. These are the opening and handling of books, looking at pictures (often upside down in the case of babies!), turning pages, identifying known objects in pictures by pointing, by using syllables, parts of words, or single words to indicate recognition or enjoyment. Later, the child says "tell me what it says," and "what is this picture about." He identifies pictures with appropriate stories; he recognizes and identifies letters and words. High school teachers often make the same error as primary teachers, failing to recognize that reading includes critical thinking and evaluation of what is read, discovering relationships, detecting illogical statements, anachronisms, and the like, drawing inferences, locating materials, deriving summaries from various sources, and many other abilities. Secondary school and college teachers who blame elementary teachers for failure to teach children to read often betray their own ignorance of what constitutes reading. The teaching of reading is rapidly becoming a standard part of the high school and college curriculum, and properly so.[30] Thus we see that it may be better to speak of a *succession of readinesses* than simply of *readiness*. Some writers advocate that the term be abandoned. These authorities would direct attention to the genetic sequence or continuous growth.

Simply waiting for readiness to appear may quite seriously delay ability to read, to compute, or to get along with other children. Opportunity and encouragement are important. On the other hand, assuming that readiness must be present because a certain age has been reached often results in attempt₇ to force learning in advance of maturation. Failing to secure results at an arbitrarily assumed point of readiness, teachers often resort to formal programs designed to bring about readiness.

The foregoing analysis applies equally to arithmetic; to language skills; to participation in group discussion; to learning to write legibly, swim, or take girls to parties.

The principle of readiness has profoundly affected education in recent years. Important changes have taken place in the teaching of reading, in the placement and teaching of arithmetic and language skills and grammar, to mention but a few of the prominent illustrations. Parents are often dis-

turbed because modern schools delay formal arithmetic until third grade or later. Children in these schools do make lower scores on standard tests than those in traditional schools. Parents, and many teachers, do not know that "passing standard tests" often indicates pseudo-learning which does not function in real life. Given a rich program of functional experience with number in primary grades, these same children will later equal or surpass the children in traditional schools, both in skills and application. This is not only demonstrated by evidence but is to be expected from the facts of growth.

Regardless of differences of interpretation, a very important point is involved: namely, *when* to introduce certain learning experiences. The problem is one of balance or pacing. The only way we can tell whether a state of readiness has been achieved is to give learners the opportunity to learn and then watch what happens. The concept of a series of readinesses is probably safer than the concept of a fixed locus for readiness. Guided by the learners' reactions, we can adjust to readiness or—if it is preferred—to growth.

Again we see the necessity of constant pretesting, of knowing intimately the pupil's previous experience, his interests and hobbies, his attitudes, the attitudes of the home, his aptitudes, his physical health, and his mental hygiene. Without adequate knowledge about learners, teachers will often frustrate and antagonize learners by misjudging readiness.

Trial and error versus retrial. The connectionists and associationists held that new responses appeared as elements in a "trial-and-error" process. The general sequence was something like this: The learner (*a*) has a goal, set, or purpose, but (*b*) does not see clearly how to achieve it. He (*c*) explores the situation, (*d*) somehow finding various ways to reach his goal. He may discover these by blind trial or by analysis.

[30] For an amusing and very stimulating discussion of this see H. R. Huse, *The Illiteracy of the Literate* (New York, Appleton, 1933); see also Joseph Jastrow, *The Betrayal of Intelligence* (New York, Greenberg, 1938). Also note the increasing number of research studies and textbooks for high school and college reading.

There is (e) the trial of these leads, and (f) the elimination of those which do not work, the acceptance of those which do, until (g) a successful response leads to the goal. The process is not sequential, as has been made clear before. Correct responses, it is held, arise out of blind, fumbling trials. Insight and understanding are not precluded, since they could occur in (d) above. Correct responses are seized and retained through the operation of the laws of exercise and effect.

The field-theory group maintains that *responses* are never repeated exactly. They believe also that blind trial and error could continue forever in some instances without producing a correct response. They believe the *stimulus-situation* is repeated and that thereafter each effort of the learner is a retrial of a pattern discerned more or less clearly. The learner does not fumble or try blindly; he tries consciously to achieve a result he can perceive or understand. Incorrect responses then become not errors in the trial-and-error sense but incorrect responses due to imperfect insight. Initial delay allows for study and analysis; guidance comes from outside aids; the repeated trials themselves are valuable instruments of further insight. The learner deliberately evolves and tries new procedures as he gains insight, or transposes and adapts known methods. Thought and judgment about the trials determine what is learned, not the trial-and-error procedure.

A reasonable summary would seem to be about as follows. True trial and error will undoubtedly occur when tasks are too far beyond the maturity and experience of the learner. The greater the adjustment between task and learner, the greater the reduction of waste in time and energy. Where tasks are well adjusted to maturity and experience but still challenging, insight with intelligent trials may substitute for trial and error. Certain writers contrast "blind" trial and error with "seeing" retrial.

The educational implications are important. The traditional curriculum and methods of teaching continually place learners in situations where they do not know what to do, where to turn, or why. Blind trial and error is natural and inevitable. This can be observed constantly in high school and college learning. Occasionally adults in industry must develop a special skill without sufficient background of experience. Trial and error is the only way open to these learners at first. But the teacher who sets up situations which demand trial-and-error learning and then condemns children for stupidity is seriously wrong. Trial and error must in these circumstances be accepted as natural. The enlightened teacher's efforts will be directed at sympathetic explanations, guidance, and the use of devices which may not at first be understood by the learner. The teacher's goal is the increasing ability of the learner to understand the task and take over self-analysis and self-guidance. Where adjustment between learner and task is very poor, this result is not possible; unthinking performance of the skill or operation of given formulas is all that can be attained.

The modern teacher attempts to adjust task to learner, but to retain enough of the unknown and the difficult to challenge the learner. Initial delay, preliminary observation and discussion, tentative trial, self-guidance, and participatory guidance by the teacher are all then accepted as natural. Guidance here will be within the learner's own processes and in terms of his level of insight.

Trial and error of the traditional type may also occur because of inattention, obtuseness, or poor physical condition resulting in lack of effort. This would also be true of failure to attain insight. Teachers should not jump to the conclusion that inattention is the cause, but should attempt to diagnose the trouble. Appropriate guidance and redirection should then follow.

Influence of field theory increasing. Field-theory psychology is rapidly achieving influence among modern teachers, even though it is not always clearly understood by them. Despite criticisms by some psychologists, field theory explains classroom situations and makes more sense to experienced teachers than do the other views.

Field theory is not new, having appeared in rudimentary form in scientific and literary writing for centuries. It is supported by certain philosophic views, by the quantum and relativity theories in physics and mathematics, by semantics in language, and by logic and scientific method. The central notion is that of a field within which events occur and which gives meaning to the items or parts included within it. We are already more or less familiar with this concept in physics and astronomy. No one would attempt to explain gravitation or the tides by studying these phenomena alone. These phenomena can be explained only by considering the total field or organization within which they occur. They can have no meaning whatever by themselves—in fact, cannot occur by themselves. They are phenomena of a field. The existence of certain planets was known long before they were actually discovered. Disturbances within the field of the solar system could be explained only by inferring extension of the field to include planets later discovered to exist. The problem of juvenile delinquency can never be understood by looking at the delinquent alone. The circumstances within which the behavior takes place is the key. In biology the field is the living organism, as indicated in the earlier pages of this chapter.

In psychology the field has, currently, three interpretations: organismic, gestalt, and topological. The organismic interpretation finds its basis and derived laws, as would be expected, in the biological concept of the living organism and its growth. Gestalt originates in and is based upon the analysis of perceptions which are regarded as primary wholes. The topological finds its wholes in child and group behavior. There is a definite tendency toward unity among the three interpretations, all of which are doubtless approaching the same central problem from different angles. The general laws of the field-theory process are exemplified in all three.

Competent scholars are applying the field-theory concept to world affairs. Wars, standards of living, tariffs, peace, stability, safety, divorce, transportation, and exchange of goods—these can never be understood until treated on the basis of a world field. Blind nationalism is not merely outmoded; it is an absurd contradiction of known facts.

DISCUSSION QUESTIONS FOR SECTION 3

The class may use the four questions at the end of Section 1 on page 140. Students are encouraged to raise questions of their own.

SUPPLEMENTARY REPORTS

The section covers so much ground, and for some students will introduce so much new material, that instructors may wish to supplement the abbreviated account with readings and reports. Reports might include:

Field theory
Connectionism
Principles or "laws" of learning
Maturation
Insight
Pacing
Readiness
Heredity and environment

Ample material is easily available in texts, handbooks, and periodical literature.

READINGS

The best source with which to start is the 1956 revision of Hilgard's *Theories of Learning*. The extensive bibliography will furnish unlimited leads.

Read also in advanced books about psychology—not textbooks in the field but critical summaries and questioning of psychology itself. Several are available.

4: THE LEARNER'S GOALS AND THOSE OF SOCIETY.

Learning, it is clear, is based on achieving goals or purposes set by the learner, satisfying needs of the learner. Learning is initiated with little children by simple, direct, felt needs. As stated several times elsewhere in this volume, a curriculum cannot be built on "felt" needs. There are many needs which a child will not feel but which must be fulfilled before the child becomes an adult. One error of the ultramodern school has been to confine attention to immediate felt needs. The corresponding error of the traditional school has been to force adult needs on immature children in advance of understanding. Children and adults do not learn what they do not need. The teacher is to aid and guide learners as maturity develops to see many needs which are not immediately felt but which are necessary for individual and societal well-being. Teachers must know the needs of immature learners and those of society, if they are to work successfully with learners. Even more important, teachers and parents should know that thwarting or frustrating the achievement of needs results in antagonisms, personality difficulties, and indifference to achievement in the future.

The maturity of the learner and his level of aspiration are crucial factors. Needs differ with levels of maturity, brightness, and aspiration. Needs differ significantly with social class origins, as do means of achieving needs.

Many classifications or listings of needs have been made. However, it must be remembered that although general lists are necessary, each child is a unique individual. His pattern of needs will not be the same as that of another. The general classifications by different authors will differ a bit in headings used and in organization, but all usually cover the major needs.

One inclusive list is that by Maslow: [31]

Self-actualization	Secondary
Prestige importance	
Peer and adult approval	
Self-esteem	
Independence	
Affection	
Physical security	
Physiological needs	Primary

In Maslow's "hierarchy of needs" those at the top become proportionately more important as those at the bottom are satisfied.

The physiological needs are easily listed and there is little argument about them: sleep, food, air, physical activity, and, later, sexual activity. General good health is a need and a goal.

Physical security is based on the child's recognition of a stable world that stays put. An even more important basis for both physical and emotional security is trust in adults, parents and teachers, who are fair and consistent.

Emotional needs is probably a better heading than *affection* which is itself a chief emotional need. Others are recognition and appreciation from others, both adults and peers. These in turn satisfy other emotional-intellectual needs such as self-respect, dignity of the person. Self-confidence and independence are basic needs and necessary for achievement of a balanced personality.

Intellectual needs are the desire to know, to understand, to find causes for effects, to master the methods of knowing such as manipulating, reading, listening, problem-solving, and others. The fact that some individuals seem to have lost the curiosity which

[31] A. H. Maslow, "A Theory of Human Motivation," *Psychological Review*, Vol. 50 (1943), pp. 370-396.

is satisfied by these really means that somewhere along the line the learner endured frustrating or thwarting experiences which developed indifference or antagonism. This is a challenge to the school.

Social needs include: secure relations with other persons, socially acceptable skills, self-reliance, self-control, responsibility, integrity, a system of values, respectful attitudes toward social institutions and conventions but always with the attitude that these might be improved, courteous attitudes toward differing races, nationalities, and religions. All these are especially with reference to our democratic society. Critics of education have made snide comments about the emphasis on "togetherness," "belonging," "groupiness," and the like in schools today. This is usually due to simple ignorance of the nature of human personality and of democratic society. Persons are social beings and without contact and groups would not become human. The conventions of our democratic society are designed, we hope, to serve the needs of unique individuals living together in groups and belonging to groups. Some of the criticisms are due to stupidity, and a few are sinister or devious attacks on enlightenment of the people.

Basic drive toward self-realization. Back of all needs and activities there is a constant and basic striving toward ever better realization of the self. Both history and individual case studies seem to confirm this. Observers are sometimes misled on seeing individuals who seem indifferent to improvement, respect, or anything else. Some have, as stated above, been antagonized into refusal to act. Others, it must not be overlooked, may be realizing quite well the self they wish to be. The self-concept is the determining item. Very low level intelligence may be the cause in other cases.

Many classifications available. The foregoing brief summary should suffice. Other classifications including up to forty or more specific needs may be found. Statements of developmental tasks and of directional progress goals, given elsewhere in this volume, are still other methods of stating needs.

QUESTIONS FOR SECTION 4

1. Examine the lesson descriptions in Chapter 1 and in the Appendix. What needs were probably being met? Which neglected? Which might the teacher need to sidetrack for the moment?

2. Observe one or more lessons and answer the same questions.

3. Observe lessons with special reference to needs which can be satisfied easily and quickly; those needing long-term development; those likely in conflict with each other?

4. Note in observed or described lessons whether goals were set co-operatively; set by teacher and accepted; set by teacher and imposed?

5. Describe the skillful meeting of needs by a given teacher? Describe failure to meet needs? How would you suggest dealing with those ignored, or partially met?

6. Converse with a child, a youth, an adult as to spare-time activities, reading, listening to radio, viewing TV, playing games, working at hobbies, and so on. What needs seem most prominent? Get accounts from two or more persons.

7. Note in school or in life the thwarting or obstructing of reputable needs. Give evidences of frustration or other reaction. Note cases where self-respect or dignity is threatened.

8. Note or recall an occasion in which your own needs were not met. Give your reactions.

9. List the needs you think this text or course will meet. Are there any so far not met by the materials given?

READINGS

Ample material is available in several of the texts already listed in this and other chapters. The periodical literature should also be checked, as new material appears constantly.

CHAPTER SUMMARY

A brief summary [32] here may make clearer the relation of the learner to the situations in which he learns best, or well. Students may wish to ask questions or to extend the brief statements.

[32] This outline also appears in the volume *Group Process in Physical Education* (New York, Harper, 1951) to which the writer was a contributing author and editor.

The Learner	The Setting for Learning
1. The learner, like all living organisms, is a unitary, integrating whole. The whole person comes to school, bringing mind, body, and emotions.	1. The desirable setting for learning with functional learning experiences will provide for natural integration of feeling-doing-thinking.
2. The learner, like any other living organism, seeks always to maintain equilibrium or balance.	2. Desirable learning experiences will provide opportunity for success in meeting needs and solving problems, but will also provide constant challenge to go beyond the immediate situation.
3. The learner is a goal-seeking organism, pursuing purposes in order to satisfy needs, thus to maintain equilibrium.	3. The desirable setting for learning will be dominated by purpose and goal set up by the learner or group of learners, either by themselves or with appropriate guidance from the total group including the teacher.
4. The learner is an active, behaving, exploratory individual.	4. The process of learning is doing, reacting, undergoing. The setting must provide freedom to explore, to construct, to question, to differ, to make mistakes: freedom to develop creative contributions. The limits of freedom are democratic controls, rights of others, and good taste.
5. The learner has a pattern and rhythm of growth peculiar to the individual. Notable differences exist between individuals, in speed of learning, energy output, depth of feeling, facility of insight.	5. Widely different, varied types of learning experiences should be provided, adaptable to levels of maturity, to different rates, interests, abilities, and so forth.
6. The learner comes to school with a personality, a set of aims and values, social habits.	6. The purposes and experiences used should arise out of and be continuous with the life of the learner. The family background and social-class pressures, as well as the individuality of the learner, must be taken into account. The experiences must possess maximum lifelikeness for the learner, must be socially desirable.

7. The learner is immature in relation to adult standards, though he may be quite mature within his peer group.

7. Learners need sympathetic guidance while building intelligence and personality within their own experiences. They need protection from experiences in which they could not yet act intelligently; protection from fears and anxieties; protection suffcient to ensure security and status with both adults and peers; plus challenge to grow, to conquer problems, to develop self-reliance. The learner needs guidance from adults who know and understand the problems of a growing personality; who see learning as a developmental process.

The adult guide will stimulate and guide without dominating or coercing.

8. The learner is a social animal, if normal, and naturally seeks activities involving other persons.

8. The setting must provide many varied opportunities to work in the "we" relationship, developing eventually into self-directed group activity.

The whole range of interactive human relationships, the co-operative group process, is essential to the development of mature socialized personality.

A primary child jostled and knocked down by another child jumps up to counterattack with enthusiastic violence. A second child in similar circumstances runs crying to the teacher for sympathy and protection. Still a third child neither fights nor runs to adults; he stands off and calls the attacker by bad names. A fourth child may pick himself up and quietly walk away. The uninformed observer will likely attribute the different behaviors to the "nature" of the children. Some children, they say, are "naturally" aggressive, some timid, and so on. This simple explanation is no longer safe. The type of inherited nervous system and physical build does play a part, but a very large proportion of the behaviors are learned. The children's reactions are in part responses to cultural pressures of various sorts.

Three high school boys stand before the principal, suffering reprimand for a disturb-

[1] This chapter may be omitted with classes which are well informed from previous courses in sociology, guidance, and so on. The majority of students will not be well informed. For extensions and additions to references cited in footnotes of this chapter, see Readings on pages 183-184.

ance in which they have been caught. One boy is ashamed and truly embarrassed. A second is sullen and unresponsive. The third is cockily defiant. The first boy knows his family will strongly disapprove his participation in the misdemeanor. The social-class influence will be embodied in the attitude of the home; people like us do not do things like that. The second and third boys have no such concern for family reaction. Their families are indifferent to certain types of misbehavior, are mildly antagonistic to school and to authority. The sullen and the defiant boys endure the reprimand without embarrassment. They know, furthermore, that as soon as they can escape and join their fellows out behind the gymnasium, their misbehavior and defiance will be heartily approved by a jury of their peers.

The behavior of children and youth is affected by many complex cultural factors. Each child brings to school a collection of values, beliefs, and attitudes, plus behavior patterns through which the values and meanings are expressed. Cultural factors over which he has no control play an important part in making him what he is. These factors affect and are affected by the biological process of growth, or maturation, and individual differences; by the interests, purposes, and needs which the individual develops.

The constellation of influences playing upon the child is complex; the effect of single components difficult to trace. Influence is often subtle and hidden from casual observation. Anyone who rears or teaches children must possess such facts as are available to him. Equally, one must be extremely cautious in drawing generalizations, in attributing certain results to one or another factor without reference to the whole picture. There is no such thing as "the child"; each one is "a child" with his unique collection of beliefs and behaviors.

The general effects of cultural impositions. The culture in general and the particular segment of the culture within which individuals grow up influence learning and behavior in a fundamental manner. Teacher education, until recently, has neglected this vital factor in learning and teaching.

Social anthropologists early supplied valuable clues through their study of primitive cultures. [2] Mead points out, for instance, that the Samoan child shows no period of rebelliousness while growing up. These children from early ages perform tasks which assist the adults of the community. Socialization comes about through association in age

[2] Margaret Mead, *From the South Seas* (New York, Morrow, 1939) containing "Coming of Age in Samoa," "Growing up in New Guinea," and "Sex and Temperament in Primitive Societies."

———, "The Primitive Child," in Carl Murchison, ed., *A Handbook of Child Psychology* (Worcester, Mass., Clark Univ. Press, 1939).

———, "Research on Primitive Children," in Leonard Carmichael, ed., *Manual of Child Psychology* (New York, Wiley, 1946).

Ruth Benedict, "The Educative Process—A Comparative Note," Thirteenth Yearbook of the Department of Supervisors and Directors of Instruction (Washington, D. C., 1940), Ch. 8.

———, *Patterns of Culture* (New York, Penguin, 1934).

groups, ties with parents being rather loose. Boys' and girls' play groups are entirely segregated (sex differentiation coming as a result of the difference in tasks assigned boys and girls). Gang antagonism is the only relation between the sexes until puberty. Samoan children are never called upon to make choices that conflict with group or parental choices. Submission to or defiance of the parent does not become an issue. The child owes no emotional allegiance to father or mother because there is a large household of fostering adults. Samoan children, from early childhood, have association with and access to the facts of sex, birth, and death. Kaffir children, on the contrary, manifest violent antagonism to all adult superiors. Kaffir children are given all the dirty tasks to do and are told fanciful lies about the "facts of life." By preadolescence, the Kaffir children have developed a small outlaw state with a secret language and spy system of their own.

The Manus children, while undergoing no period of rebellion against adult authority, develop very differently from the Samoan. Age groups are not distinct, various ages and both sexes playing together. The mixed groups are dominated by older bullies, but otherwise childhood is highly unrestrained. No one is taught to work. The result of years of non-cultural participation (quite the opposite of the Samoan situation) is that overbearing, undisciplined children become quarrelsome, overbearing adults.

Other illustrations could be given, but these are sufficient to show that the social attitudes and behavior of individuals are not a matter of natural growth or individual choice, but are results of cultural participation.

Benedict believes the chief difference between education in primitive societies and our own is that the primitive child does not go through a long period of "preparation for life." Activities and behavior are the same or very similar for child and adult. Important factors in child-rearing and education in our society are (1) the long period of dependency, (2) control by women during early years, (3) the small amount of responsibility given children (particularly in urban areas), (4) the role of the father in child training, and (5) the great variety of cultural patterns confronting and confusing the child.

Some indication of the difficulty children have in adjusting is seen in the succession of attitudes, often conflicting, manifested by adults toward the children. Murphy, Murphy, and Newcomb[3] present an interesting series of changing attitudes to which the child must adjust:

1. Adoration, admiration as a baby to the age of approximately two years.
2. Prohibitions, irritation, restraint, physical punishment as he begins to "get in the way" to the age of five or six.
3. Mothering, entertainment from the kindergarten and primary teachers, to the age of nine.
4. Scolding from the principal for cutting up in school, rebukes from policemen for hitching on to cars and sneaking rides in subways (from nine till puberty).
5. Ridicule as an awkward adolescent.
6. Last-minute gestures toward control from parents, teachers, and police as in later adolescence he begins to drive a car and lead his own life.
7. Pride of home and school when he gets on the college football team.

Another interesting sequence, for the purposes of this study, is the series of demands from the group on the boy at different periods:

1. He is expected to be cute and beautiful, the idol of the family from birth to two or three.
2. He is expected to keep out from underfoot and give the adults the chance to take care of the new baby (from two until six in most families).

3. He is expected to sit still in school and learn to read and do numbers (beginning elementary school).
4. *By his own age-group he is expected to prove that he is male and is independent of grown-ups* (later elementary school).
5. The girls expect him to learn to dance and look nice and drive a car (early adolescence).
6. The school expects him to throw all his energy into winning for the ———— high school.

Cultures impose upon their participants a basic set of social habits for controlling everyday life activities. Certain general roles are expected of all children as they grow up. These include a sex role, an age role, in developed cultures a social-class role, and sometimes a caste role based on race, color, or creed. The social classes in modern society differ considerably in approving or stigmatizing certain beliefs, values, and behaviors. We will examine the class structure in some detail, as it is an important determiner of learning and behavior.

The general nature of social-class structure in the United States. A class-structured society, with classes based on arbitrary distinction and with no mobility from class to class, is contrary to our democratic beliefs in the dignity of the individual and our beliefs about the nature of society. A society as complex as that of the United States is bound to contain many different kinds of groups, each with its influence upon individuals: urban, rural, geographic, religious, ethnic, economic, occupational, and social. Flexibility and mobility characterize our groupings, though rigidity already appears in the older parts of our country. The distinctions between classes are far less arbitrary than in older societies. The term *class* as applied to society in the United States has nothing in common with Marxist concept of class.

The social class is the most influential factor in our lives, and we now know a good

[3] Gardner Murphy, Lois B. Murphy, and Theodore M. Newcomb, *Experimental Social Psychology* (New York, Harper, 1937), pp. 325-327.

deal about its structure and effects. [4] During the last twenty years sociologists have been studying intensively several American communities. *Yankee City,* a study by Warner and Lunt, [5] describes a typical New England community; *Deep South,* by Davis, Gardner, and Gardner, [6] deals with the Southern states; and *Hometown,* by Warner, Havighurst, and Loeb [7] deals with the Middle West. Many other available studies are listed in the bibliography.

These investigators have begun to reveal an accurate picture of the social-class system of American communities. Their results are of interest to educators who seek a more adequate understanding of the environment and its relation to human learning. The social-class theory proposed and supported by these investigators has implications for the socialization and formal education of all youth.

The investigators of the social life of Yankee City assumed at the beginning of their study that the economic order was of the greatest importance in the lives of the people. This hypothesis was soon dropped because of the force of the collected evidence. A social-class hypothesis was substituted. The members of this community were greatly influenced by a social-class order in which they looked upon people as being higher or lower on the rungs of a social ladder. The evidence from the other communities studied also supported this view.

[4] The next twelve to fifteen pages are taken with a few changes from *Growth and Development of the Preadolescent,* by Arthur W. Blair and William H. Burton, for which the pages were originally prepared by Burton.

[5] W. Lloyd Warner and Paul S. Lunt, *The Social Life of a Modern Community and The Status System of a Modern Community,* Vols. I and II, Yankee City Series (New Haven, Yale Univ. Press, 1941).

[6] Allison Davis, Burleigh B. Gardner, and Mary R. Gardner, *Deep South* (Chicago, Univ. of Chicago Press, 1941).

[7] M. Lloyd Warner, Robert J. Havighurst, and Marton B. Loeb, *Who Shall be Educated?* (New York, Harper, 1944). Contains reference to *Hometown* and other similar investigations.

By use of the test of participation—that is, determining who goes around with whom— and by the study of those who possess the highly evaluated characteristics in terms of acceptance, namely, type of house, education, and a large number of other symbols, they were able to place the people in three social strata. Each of these strata, Upper, Middle, and Lower class, had two divisions; thus there were six classes which, they believed, existed in the social hierarchy in Yankee City. Marriage ordinarily occurred between persons of the same social level. An individual could rise or fall, that is to say, be socially mobile, in the social hierarchy. A short description of each of these groups is provided by the authors; it may be supplemented through further reading.

A casual analysis of the interview material from which these sketches have been drawn clearly indicates that there is a recognized rank order where people are striving for social recognition. Their values differ in the several strata and within the same social levels. Certain simple generalizations are possible, however, which tell us something of how these people evaluate themselves and others in the world around them. It is clear that the upper-Upper class believes in the efficacy of birth and breeding, and the individuals in that class possess each in varying degrees and with proportionate feelings of security. Money is important, but its chief importance is to allow one to live properly.

The lower-Upper class also believes in birth and breeding. They cannot use their money to buy birth, but they can spend it to acquire the proper Upper class secular rituals which they hope will secure them the high rank they seek. Money is very important to them, but they are willing to spend large portions of it to secure proper recognition for themselves or their children and to marry their children into the class above them.

The upper-Middle class believes in money, but many of them also believe in what they call comfort. Some of them know that money is not enough to be at the top. Nevertheless, most try to get more money to gain higher status. More money is always important. Many of them want money for its own sake and because its mere accumulation has value.

The lower-Middle class also wants more money and more comfort. They believe that money and morals are the keys to all of their problems. They are more secure, however, than the two lower classes, and most of them have greater psychological security than the people of the upper-Middle class.

The individuals in the upper-Lower class tend to be ambitious. They want money, but they are trying to acquire the symbols of higher status such as "nice furniture," "pretty yards," and "a good education." Such things differentiate them from the class below and make them more like the people just above them. They are much nearer the bare struggle for existence than the lower-Middle class, but they utilize their money for neat looking clothes, good magazines, and to "give our children a better education than we had."

The lower-Lower class cares little for education. Money is important because it shuts the door on the ever present wolf of want, but it is not of such importance that a parent would force his children to go to school that they might acquire an education in order to get a better job. Money is to be spent, not saved.

These oversimplified summaries are manifestly inadequate. Our social structure is too complex to be described in such simple generalities. Too many people in each of the several classes do not fit into these categories. [8]

Although intensive studies have been made in only a few widely separated places, the investigators, Warner and others, find considerable support for the conclusion that this social-class system holds for the entire country with the following modifications: the younger the community, the less marked are the distinctions between social classes and the greater is opportunity for mobility; the larger cities are not as clearly differentiated in class structure as are the smaller cities.

Differences between group values and behaviors of vital importance for individual children. The social classes differ materially, as can be gathered from the foregoing paragraphs, in approving or stigmatizing certain beliefs, values, and behaviors. The middle and upper classes particularly stigmatize,

[8] W. Lloyd Warner and Paul S. Lunt, *The Social Life of a Modern Community* and *The Status System of a Modern Community.*

in the lower classes, what the upper classes call laziness, shiftlessness, irresponsibility, ignorance, immorality. Within the lower classes, however, some of these are accepted ways of behavior, possessing background and rationale. The lower classes are likely to resent in the upper classes what lower-class individuals call "snootiness" or snobbery, good manners, proper language, lack of aggressiveness, or unwillingness to fight.

Children in the middle class largely resist strongly the class values and habits imposed upon them. Children in the lower classes quite generally accept their class values and behaviors. The reasons for this and its real significance for understanding children will be developed a few paragraphs further on.

The efforts of parents and teachers to socialize children precipitate constant conflict between the psychological drives of the children on the one hand, and the pressures of the culture on the other. The child's need for physical activity, for sensory enjoyment, for self-direction, and for prestige with agemates fights hard against restraints, controls, and demands for conformance.

Many of the conflicts between parents and children or teachers and children result from grave lack of insight into the nature and effects of constant pressure, open or subtle, to conform to social values and roles. Parents and teachers regard the procedures they use in socializing children as natural and desirable. *The adults* are often not even aware that there is any pressure. *The children* are keenly aware of it. The emotional cost to both may be very high. Parents are irritated and angry. Children become destructive, antagonistic, or sullen, or retreat into periods of negativism. These are defenses against the constant "cultural bombardment." The more social the requirement, the more arbitrary and unjust it seems to the "natural" child.

The schoolroom brings all this into sharp focus, with serious difficulties resulting. The school, in general, attempts to impose middle-class values upon huge numbers of lower-class children. Worse, the school is not set up to cope with the non-verbal types of intelligence often found among children who have not had access to or constant contacts with books. Problems set by the school are, therefore, not the same problems at all when tackled simultaneously by upper- and lower-class children. The motivations are not at all alike. Many lower-class children simply do not value the objectives and processes of the school; hence, they do not try. The school immediately dubs them "unintelligent," "unco-operative," or "stubborn." The old class clichés may enter again; these children are "lazy," "shiftless," "irresponsible." The fact often is that the school simply does not meet their needs or ambitions, does not operate within their framework of motivations and values. The specific results of this will be summarized briefly later on.

Difficulties of child-rearing and of schooling might be alleviated. The detailed implications of the foregoing for socialization and education cannot be developed in this volume except in summaries. We may digress for a paragraph or two here, however, because of the grave importance of the immediate discussion. The method of cultural training has basic effects upon children's acceptance *inwardly* of the cultural objectives. This is basically different from outward conformance. The effects upon morality, mental hygiene, and personality generally, are far too important to be neglected.

Ample evidence is available in general psychology and in clinical analyses to indicate that arranging circumstances in home and school so that the child can identify himself with the total social group, including adults, may be far more effective than imposition and pressure. Allowing the child to share and participate in the common life and to aid in making decisions for the total group, in contrast to having decisions arbitrarily made for him, might alleviate many of the conflicts. The child will feel secure

and respected and will receive guidance from adults, thus getting experience in considering evidence and making decisions. Allowing the child full membership in the social groups of which he actually is a part (though often denied participation) might reduce the cleavage between the adult society and the peer culture of teen-agers.

The specific effects of social-class structure on growth and schooling. Two particular studies may be noted which have brought together the application of research findings on social class to child training and schooling. Davis and Dollard [9] studied the life histories of over 100 Negro children in the South, seeking answers to these questions: (*a*) What do his parents want to teach him? (*b*) What methods do they use to teach him? (*c*) What do they actually succeed in teaching him? The answers derived varied, as with white populations, depending upon the social class of the child's family.

Warner [10] and others have collected from the various investigations the findings which are most applicable to education. Evidence supports the hypothesis that social class is a significant determinant of personality in our culture.

The studies show that the general effect of social-class status is, with one or two notable exceptions, similar for Negro and white populations. The lower class differs markedly from middle and upper classes with respect to certain behaviors such as aggression, sexual expression, and school learning. The methods of training or of permission, the end results, the very aims of the training differ. This is particularly true in the years following infancy. In the very earliest years, lower-class Negro children meet the same set of standards regarding feeding, elimination, and masturbation as do upper-class children. The children vary

[9] Allison Davis and John Dollard, *Children of Bondage* (Washington, D. C., American Council on Education, 1940).
[10] Warner, Havighurst, and Loeb, *op. cit.*

as much in one class as in another in the amount of emotional strain and kinds of emotional patterning derived from this training.

Lower-class parents punish their children frequently and severely, and provide them with few rewards. Middle- and upper-class parents use physical punishment much less frequently, but reward their children either materially or through status. Lower-class parents cannot afford either type of reward.

One contrast will highlight the significant differences between the classes. Middle- and upper-class parents are quite shocked at the severity of punishment, the thrashings and beatings meted out to lower-class children. Lower-class parents are equally astounded at a middle-class punishment—which is possibly not so widespread nowadays, but is still common—namely, sending the child to bed without his supper, or denying him the tasty dessert. Food is too important with the lower classes, deprivation too serious a matter, to be thus used.

Punishment does not seem to force the lower-class child into better behavior, does not move him toward middle-class patterns of respectability.

The school, it is shown, often actually interferes with social mobility because of its middle-class teachers and standards. The school may serve as a sorting or selecting agency which affects the efforts of individuals to move upward in the social structure. Here we have a startling denial of the American dream that education is a factor in "bettering one's self." The school possessed of greater knowledge, insight, and sympathy can be the road to improvement for all.

The lower-class child learns in the very early grades that it is not only his parents and their friends who do not expect him to "go far" in school. His teacher shares the same belief. She brings to the classroom her middle-class standards and procedures. Children in school are drawn from the social classes in approximately these percentages:

3 per cent from the upper class, 38 per cent from the middle, 58 per cent from the lower class. The teaching body, in contrast, is drawn almost entirely from the middle class. Many teachers simply cannot communicate with lower-class children. The teachers do not know that many children have never sat down to a meal. One child staying for a period in a good home said, "Do you always eat like in the movies?" Asked to explain she said, "Well, you always set the table and sit down together to eat." Teachers do not know what it means always to wear hand-me-downs, always to have to fight for what one wants or needs. Children are affected basically by these conditions. Children also are unaware that many words and language forms they use every day are not acceptable in a different social strata. The teacher's reproval and obvious displeasure over the ordinary language of these children merely antagonizes them. Consciously or unconsciously, the teacher denies lower-class children the satisfactions necessary for their wholehearted participation. The basic motivation of parents and teachers in the upper-lower and the lower-middle classes is the desire for upward mobility. These groups believe education is one chief means of improving status. They therefore support the school and its program, and in so doing impose their values, goals, and habits on the larger group within the school, the lower-class children.

The middle-class school régime does not socialize lower-class children. Evidence shows that many children at about nine years of age begin to show hostility toward adult standards of cleanliness, orderliness, promptness, and other widely accepted social habits, as well as to show some physical symptoms of regressive behavior. Davis suggests that children from the lower-class families remain "unsocialized" and "unmotivated" from the viewpoint of middle-class culture because (*a*) they are humiliated and punished too severely in school for having the lower-class culture which their own mothers and fathers and siblings approve, and (b) because the most powerful reinforcements in learning, namely, those of emotional and social rewards, are systematically denied to the lower-class child by the systems of privilege existing in the school and in larger society. In other words, children from the lower classes may have shown some early conformity to the school and social demands, but during the years of later childhood they come to realize that being "good" is not going to "pay off" at school, at home, or in the community. This may possibly account for the failure of the children of the lowest classes to accept middle- and upper-class standards of conduct.

Deferred rewards create tensions for middle- and upper-class children. The studies and observations made do not limit this "hostility toward adult standards" to a lower class or a low socioeconomic group. In fact a study by Long[11] of parent reports of undesirable behavior showed their children from eight through eleven tended to be irritable, willful, easily discouraged, and to have many fears. Within the population represented by this group very few differences of behavior tendencies could be associated with factors other than age; there was no relation to the education of parents, to the socioeconomic pattern, or to other behavior tendencies.

Is it not possible that the culturally desirable behavior of the middle- and upper-class child "breaks down" during these years because of the remoteness of the rewards for such behavior, and as a release for some of the anxiety resulting from fear or failure to achieve the symbols of status his family regards so highly? The learning of complex social habits always takes place under certain emotionally toned conditions. In general, we learn to avoid or inhibit that which produces pain or unpleasantness and to follow that course which brings satisfaction, pleasure, or, at worst, the least un-

pleasantness. Davis and Dollard[12] stress this point and also show as a result of their study that "as the child grows older the effective learning rewards are those of status, those associated with middle- and upper-class privileges and dominance." In the class setting, the reinforcements to learning are of long range and the learning drive is intense anxiety. It is also pointed out that considerable anxiety is built up in the middle- and upper-class child due to constant restraint of aggressive and sexual behavior. These children are actually undergoing "a long period of renunciation which middle-class socialization demands" without any immediate rewards. Physically, they are capable of much more freedom than they are given; intellectually, they are seeking reality. These factors make it easier to understand why these children reject some of the standards of adults and choose to imitate the behavior of some of their fellows who do not have these restraints or anxieties. There is, at least, some clue here to this particular reaction of most preadolescents.

School achievement affected by class origins of children. As a part of this apparent reaction to adult standards, it may be profitable to consider the relation of this social-class picture to the actual work of the school, for instance in the fourth, fifth, and sixth grades. The rewards for school work become increasingly those of status as the child moves from the primary grades into the intermediate grades, especially in the typical school where physical restraint and academic pursuits are stressed. In these grades the great bulk of remedial problems in reading and in the other intellectual skills appear. Some of the reactions of these children to the work of the school is explainable on the basis of the hypothesis presented in the preceding paragraph. Habits of speech, reading, recreation, and attitudes toward the arts are not successfully taught the lower classes in school because these habits and attitudes

[11] Alma Long, "Parents' Reports of Undesirable Behavior," *Child Development* (1941), pp. 43-62.

[12] Davis and Dollard, *op. cit.*

have no value in the family, clique, or associations of the lower-class family. Miller and Dollard [13] approached this problem in this way:

Part of the seemingly mental inferiority of lower-class children at school may be traced to lack of reward. In the first place, teachers are not so likely to pay attention to them, praise them, and confer little signs of status, such as special tasks, as they are to reward middle-class children in these ways. In the second place, these children never have experienced, or seen close at hand in the lives of relatives, those advantages of better jobs which are the rewards for educational merit, and they consequently see less promise of attaining such positions. The teacher is less likely to reward them, and their training has invested the types of event which the teacher controls with less acquired reward value.

In the middle-class family and environment the teachers meet support for their methods and goals in child training. It can be seen then that the school and its program may mean very different things to the child, depending upon the values his social class places on education. Some children must adjust to groups whose standards of behavior and social controls are different and often contradictory; other children live in a world where all groups have the same code and pattern of conduct. During later childhood many lower-class pupils become retarded or often drop out of school because of this conflict; middle-class pupils exhibit some resistance to these adult values, and often seek other values from their small groups of age-sex mates.

The intelligence quotient and social-class origins of children. The I.Q. score is so widely used in so many ways within the school and so widely affects popular thinking that we digress for a brief summary here.

Three statements may be made for emphasis and to set the stage:

[13] Neal E. Miller and John Dollard, *Social Learning and Imitation* (New Haven, Yale Univ. Press, 1941), p. 33.

The school is not set up to capitalize upon the non-verbal types of intelligence often found among children who have not had access to or constant contacts with books.

The lower-class child learns in the very early grades that it is not only his parents and their friends who do not expect him to "go far" in school. His teacher shares the same belief.

Bright children show no unique or fixed personality pattern which differentiates them from the less bright (in the age-sex groups or gangs which do not follow class lines).

The early days of the intelligence-testing movement produced a number of generalizations which we have had difficulty living down. The most vulnerable one for the current discussion was to the effect that high intelligence is correlated with high socio-economic status. Intelligence was said not to be found widely among children of the "lower classes." Voices raised against these and other superficial clichés were feeble and unheeded at first. Today we have ample evidence that intelligence tests are heavily weighted toward facility in verbal abilities, arithmetic skills, and handling of abstractions. The tests reflect the narrow verbal nature of typical schooling. They do measure capacity to do school work as at present organized. They do not measure a wide range of intellectual skills which are of vital importance in real-life problem-solving, but which are not called for by the present verbalized educational process. The tests do not touch at all upon other aspects of intelligence which involve judgment and insight in social situations, in dealing with persons, or inventiveness in mechanical matters. Creative intelligence of all kinds is ignored by typical intelligence tests. [14]

[14] The classic summaries on this are in the Twenty-seventh Yearbook of the National Society for the Study of Education and in the many studies by Beth L. Wellman and her associates. See also Forty-third Yearbook.

Beth L. Wellman, "Growth in Intelligence under Differing School Environments," *Journal of Experimental Education* (December, 1934), pp. 59-83.

Alice M. Leahy, *Nature-Nurture and Intelligence*, Genetic Psychology Monographs, Vol. 17, No. 4 (1935), pp. 235-306.

Evidence currently appearing indicates that, as hinted in earlier studies, the tests are also strongly weighted in favor of upper-class experience and content. The public generally and school authorities have quite widely accepted the belief that children of the less favored social classes are less intelligent than those from the privileged classes. The lower-class children have become aware of this and accepted the dictum that they are "dumb." The school has kept on with its obviously narrow, highly verbalized form of education. It is odd that the evidence of everyday common sense did not have more effect than it did, prior to the appearance of current research studies. Scores of pupils "dull" in school were obviously highly intelligent and bright outside of school. Uncritical school authorities and the public dismissed this as "one of those things," thereby overlooking a clue of vital importance.

Extensive research still under way has shown clearly that when the questions or problems of the intelligence tests were changed so that content and wording were equally familiar to all levels of children, wide differences in intelligence scores were

reduced or disappeared. Children from the lower social classes did as well as those from the upper groups. Check tests were devised in which the procedure was reversed; questions were phrased in very literary or "high-brow" terms. The lower-class scores fell far below those of the upper classes. The children, however, had previously made comparable scores on simply worded problems which tested the same thing as the "high-brow" question.

Tests devised by Davis and Hess [15] attempt to measure reasoning, memory, observation, critical objectivity, and creativeness. Syllogisms, problems of logical classification, inductive reasoning, arithmetical reasoning, and of imaginative insight are included. Language and content are free from social-class bias. Individual differences were found as always, but there were no differences between socioeconomic groups.

All this is vital in understanding the effect of the social-class structure on schooling and on the personality of children. We may say safely that:

The typical intelligence test favors upper-class children and discriminates against the lower-class group in its language and content.

The typical intelligence test is limited to a narrow range of verbal skills and does not test an adequate range of intellectual skills.

The school offers a narrow verbalized education with success to children who are also successful in the verbal intelligence tests.

The school erroneously classifies as dull many children whose abilities, interests, and ambitions are neither tested by intelligence tests nor stimulated by the curriculum.

Social-class origin, therefore, has marked effect on the school attitude toward the child's "intelligence" and achievement. Worse, it has a serious detrimental effect upon the child's attitude. He accepts the belief that he is "dumb"; he fails to try, is

Marie Skodak and Harold M. Skeels, "A Follow-up Study of Children in Adoptive Homes," *Journal of Genetic Psychology* (March, 1945), pp. 21-85.

Walter F. Dearborn and John W. M. Rothney, *Predicting the Child's Development* (Cambridge, Mass., Sci-Art Publishing Co., 1941).

Bernardine Schmidt, *Changes in Personal, Social, and Intellectual Behavior of Children Originally Classified as Feeble-Minded,* Psychological Monograph, Vol. 60, No. 5. (Reported also in *School and Society,* December 29, 1945, pp. 409-412.)

Samuel A. Kirk, "An Evaluation of the Study by Bernardine Schmidt Entitled Changes in Personal, Social, and Intellectual Behavior of Children Originally Classified as Feeble-Minded." *Psychological Bulletin* (July, 1948), pp. 321-333. A criticism with reply immediately following, pp. 331-343.

J. Murray Lee and Dorris M. Lee. *The Child and His Curriculum,* rev. ed. (New York, Appleton-Century-Crofts, 1950), pp. 38-44. An excellent non-technical summary. (This material is omitted in the 1960 revision, but appears on pages 105-106 of *The Child and His Development,* 1958, same author and publisher.)

[15] Allison Davis, "Education for the Conservation of Human Resources," *Progressive Education* (May, 1950), pp. 221-226. Preliminary report.

convinced that the school will do him little good.

The school is in serious need of extensive reorganization of curriculum and method of teaching. The writer has been struck constantly by the fact that teachers using modern group methods on common projects or units often exclaim over the "unusual" performance of children hitherto classified as "dull." The wider range of activities in modern curriculums and methods, the diversified problems met, actually do appeal to wider ranges of intellectual endeavor. There will always be children who are less able than others, but these and the bright ones will appear anywhere regardless of class lines.

Social-class lines disregarded by children in formation of their own gangs and cliques. The formation of the "gangs" of children of the same age and sex, the typical behavior of these gangs, and the resistance of adults to this gang life can also be better understood if seen within the framework of the social-class pattern. Children at early levels of development appear to choose their special groups, regardless of social-class membership. Warner[16] points out that social-class structure does not begin to affect clique or group formation until junior and senior high school. The play groups, in school at least, during the elementary age period show no relation to social class. The case studies of Davis and Dollard[17] also reveal that social status does not begin to be recognized or felt by individuals until the beginning of junior high school. The study of Long[18] previously cited, emphasized that behavior tendencies at this level show a greater correlation with age than with education of parents, socioeconomic pattern, or other factors. Davidson[19] has some very interesting evidence in this connection. In a study of highly intelligent children from nine to twelve years old with varying economic and social backgrounds, her purpose was to determine the relationship of that background to personality development. She found no high relationship between family income or status and specific traits of personality, and because this disagrees with a large number of studies which have found such a relationship, she suggests that the developmental trends of this age group are so overwhelming and significant to the children themselves as to obscure or to place temporarily in the background the effect on the personality of economic circumstance or social status. Children at this age do not sense the great differences in income, nor do they sense the distinctions between classes of people, she concludes. Significant also is her evidence to show that bright children show no unique or fixed personality pattern that differentiates them from the less bright.

Although their gangs may not be structured along class lines during the elementary school years, children become aware of the symbols of the social classes as a part of their general learning process. Studies show a slight disagreement as to just when children first become aware of class differences. Hollingshead[20] found that first-graders in Elmtown knew that some people are rich and some poor. Stendler[21] in her Brasstown study believed the evidence showed that first-graders used *rich* and *poor* as halo terms. *Rich* meant generally good, clean, and what they would like to have. *Poor* referred to generally less favorable characteristics.

Stendler says that children go through four stages of awareness in relation to class symbols: preawareness, beginnings of awareness, acceptance of adult stereotypes, and recognition of individual differences among children regardless of their social-class member-

---

[16] Warner and Lunt, *op. cit.*

[17] Davis and Dollard, *op. cit.*

[18] Alma Long, *op. cit.*

[19] Helen H. Davidson, *Personality and Economic Background* (New York, King's Crown, 1943).

[20] A. B. Hollingshead, *Elmtown's Youth* (New York, Wiley, 1949).

[21] Celia B. Stendler, *Children of Brasstown* (Urbana, Ill., Bureau of Research and Service, College of Education, Univ. of Illinois, 1949).

ship. The first two levels are natural to immature children; the third we would like to short-circuit, though it is unlikely that we can; the fourth is a desirable democratic view. Stendler found that many children had not reached the fourth level by the eighth grade, which is in partial contradiction to studies quoted in preceding paragraphs. Some children reach the fourth stage as early as the fourth grade.

Stendler makes the provocative suggestion that lower-class values and behaviors have some positive aspects which are overlooked in the school emphasis on middle-class values. Studies of personality development and adjustment among lower-class children are, in her estimation, very much needed. This seems both reasonable and important.

Upper-class children choose the less controlled behavior of lower classes. The following hypothesis is therefore proposed as an explanation of the motivation toward the unique group life of the preadolescent. Children of the upward-mobile classes, because of the remoteness of the rewards for socially approved behavior and in an effort to release some of the anxiety associated with the fear of failure to achieve status, choose to imitate the behavior of the children from the lower classes, who are allowed more freedom, more aggression, and who receive more immediate satisfactions. Miller and Dollard [22] have shown that most of our socialization takes place through imitation. They describe four types of persons imitated in such learning: superiors in (1) age and grade, (2) social status, (3) intelligence, or (4) technical skill. In what ways do children of the lower class appear superior to middle- and upper-class children? It is apparently not age, grade, intelligence, or technical skill, but it is the symbols of superior social status which lower-class children appear to have. The case studies of Davis and Dollard show that whereas the lower-lower-class child has

considerable freedom to explore the society around him, the middle-class child is systematically prevented from doing this; the lower-class child may experience many forms of aggression, but the middle-class child's aggression is chronically suppressed; the lower-class child has early instruction in sexual matters, whereas such information is forbidden the middle-class child. In short, it appears that the middle-class child "has the status of a much younger child; his free movement is controlled until he is late in adolescence." So whether the later childhood group actually contains a member who has lower social status or not, the children in such a group can find around them in the pattern of the lower-class child's life a kind of behavior that to them seems much more desirable than the constantly restrictive standards of parents and teachers.

It should also be remembered that one of the constantly recurring characteristics of the upward-mobile social classes is their insistence that their children do not associate with children of inferior social status. Even when this is enforced, it is apparent that during these particular years of childhood the child imitates the behavior of the lower class to some extent. In this social-class context, the conflict between adults and these older children takes on greater significance. The observation by some students of childhood that preadolescents appear to be rejected by parents and teachers and that understanding and trust between children and parents is lost at this period is substantiated to some extent by the analysis of social-class structure.

The family influence: broad generalizations. The family is the primary socializing unit. Children begin to transform their uncontrolled expression, their uninhibited exploratory behavior into those modes of behavior approved and rewarded by the family. Children accept the beliefs held by the loved adults around them and value the things approved by the family. The socializing

[22] *Op. cit.*

process is neither simple nor easy. It runs counter to the normal impulses and desires of children. Resistance to the "cultural bombardment" develops at many points. The family is the instrument through which the values, meanings, and behavior of the particular social class involved are passed on.

Trained teachers and supervisors have known for long that the behavior of a child in school is some indication of the kind of home from which he comes. Children who are unduly aggressive toward other children, who are hostile to the teacher, who are tense and on edge, usually come from homes in which there is tension, hostility, and antagonism between the adults, and between adults and children. It is a commonplace that children who have good language and speech habits come from homes where good English is spoken. Exceptions to all similar generalizations do appear, however. Children from happy, adjusted homes sometimes become maladjusted when they meet reality. They have taken the happiness of the home for granted, failing to see the effort and planning which made it possible.

The informed, competent teacher tries to gather all possible information about his children and their backgrounds. He is thus able to diagnose or account for given behaviors in school and to map programs for improvement which will be in accord with the facts. The untrained teacher, no matter how long his experience, and unless he has unusual insight, makes his worst blunders here. The motives of the children are completely misread; efforts at improvement are based on foolish misconceptions of the dynamics of behavior.

Children in any classroom will vary widely in their conceptions of what constitute desirable goals and of what constitutes success in achieving the goals. Children's ideas of goals and of success do not always coincide with the teacher's beliefs concerning these things. The children should not be condemned; they should be studied and aided. Families of the upper social classes generally wish their children to do well in school, to learn what the school offers. Children from the lower classes generally bring to school the family attitude that school is not too important and has little to do with what goes on outside. Startling exceptions to these generalizations appear constantly. More will be said of these and related facts in later paragraphs on the influence of social-class membership.

The social climate is just as important in the home as Lewin showed it to be in school clubs and classes (reported in Chapter 9). Children from democratically managed homes, in which children shared family discussion and decision and were treated with respect and consideration, manifest friendly, co-operative behavior in school. They are more honest than children from autocratically managed homes, take responsibility as a matter of course, and are reliable. Children from autocratic, domineering families are tense and on edge. They quarrel freely with other children, fight among themselves, are disobedient and generally troublesome. They do not take responsibility and cannot be counted upon to fulfill obligations. [23]

Children well adjusted as early as nursery school age [24] were found to come from

[23] J. P. Anderson, *A Study of the Relationships between Certain Aspects of Parental Behavior and Attitudes and the Behavior of Junior High School Pupils* (New York, Teachers College, Bureau of Publications, Columbia Univ., 1940).

W. Brown, Joan Morrison, and Gertrude B. Couch, "Influence of Affectional Family Relationships on Character Development," *Journal of Abnormal and Social Psychology*, Vol. 42 (1947), pp. 422-428.

Horace Champney, "The Variables of Parent Behavior," *Journal of Abnormal Psychology*, Vol. 36 (1941), pp. 525-542.

M. J. Radke, *The Relation of Parental Authority of Children's Behavior and Attitudes*, Univ. of Minnesota Child Welfare Monographs, No. 22 (Minneapolis, Univ. of Minnesota Press, 1946).

Many similar studies are available; these are but samples.

[24] Dorothy W. Baruch, "A Study of Reported Tension in Interparental Relationships as Co-Existent with Behavior Adjustment in Young Children," *Journal of Experimental Education*, Vol. 6 (1937), pp. 187-204.

homes in which there was little or no hostility between parents, few conflicts over work, friends, relatives, or sex. The parents were in substantial agreement on the rearing of children and could discuss problems quietly.

Children from some homes get along with other children immediately and as a matter of course. Other homes send out children who are suspicious of others, slow to co-operate with others, and inclined to quarrel as a matter of course. Some children are conditioned to an overcompetitive point of view and are not happy unless beating or dominating another child. Other children participate quite happily in play and school work in which winning over someone does not enter.

A good summary is found in the 1950 Yearbook of the Association for Supervision and Curriculum Development: [25]

The ways in which children's social learnings vary regardless of group membership are innumerable. A child learns to be aggressive or submissive; to be competitive or co-operative; to expect acceptance and approval from adults, or criticism and rejection; that to be "good" is to keep quiet and comply, or to act independent and resourceful; to respond to rebuffs with hostility, or to keep feelings concealed. He learns to expect certain things of parents and other adults and himself; to value certain roles, and to reject others. Each of these represents a more or less adequate technique of handling the situations he encounters.

Students are urged at this point to supplement the very brief summary by reading some concrete materials. [26]

[25] *Fostering Mental Health in Our Schools* (Washington, D. C., The Association for Supervision and Curriculum Development, 1950), pp. 23-24.

[26] Elementary teachers will find excellent concrete illustrations in the 1950 Yearbook mentioned above, Ch. 2. A first-class summary of research studies is in Willard C. Olson, *Child Development* (Boston, Heath, 1949), Ch. 9.

Secondary teachers will find similar material in:

Peter Blos, *The Adolescent Personality* (New York, Appleton, 1941).

Luella Cole and John J. B. Morgan, *Psychology of Childhood and Adolescence* (New York, Rinehart, 1947).

The peer society. As soon as they outgrow the egoistic and individualistic period of early childhood, children begin to form friendships, one and one, several, eventually in small cliques or gangs. [27] The children's society in our culture is far removed from the truly outlaw state of the Kaffir children, but is based in part on rejection of adults and of their standards. A basic change in our society has been the shift of population from rural to urban areas. Children and youth today have none of the tasks and responsibilities that were theirs a generation ago. Denied participation in everyday affairs, they lack the warm relationship with adults, and particularly feel that they are being kept out of things that matter. The inevitable result is the formation of a peer society which provides warmth and security. Society gives children no worthwhile occupations, manual or intellectual, and then condemns children when energy plus leisure lead into mischief, misbehavior, eventually delinquency. Some authorities on juvenile delinquency believe that strong persistence of gangs well past the

Urban H. Fleege, *Self-Revelation of the Adolescent Boy* (Milwaukee, Wis., Bruce Pub., 1945).

C. M. Fleming, *Adolescence* (New York, International Universities Press, 1949).

Karl C. Garrison, *The Psychology of Adolescence,* rev. ed. (Englewood Cliffs, N. J., Prentice-Hall, 1951).

Robert Havighurst and Hilda Taba, *Adolescent Character and Personality* (New York, Wiley, 1949).

Harold E. Jones, *Development in Adolescence* (New York, Appleton, 1943).

Paul H. Landis, *Adolescence and Youth* (New York, McGraw, 1945).

[27] Early studies may be of interest:

Paul H. Furfey, *The Gang Age* (New York, Macmillan, 1926).

F. M. Thrasher, *The Gang,* rev. ed. (Chicago, Univ. of Chicago Press, 1937).

Charlotte Buhler, "Social Behavior of Children," in Carl Murchison, ed., *A Handbook of Child Psychology* (Worcester, Mass., Clark Univ. Press, 1933).

F. J. Brown, *The Sociology of Childhood* (New York, Prentice-Hall, 1939).

Ernest J. Chave, *Personality Development in Children* (Chicago, Univ. of Chicago Press, 1937).

Numerous periodical articles report research studies.

age of puberty is evidence that worthwhile activities are not being provided. Ordinarily, the association of children with their own society begins in childhood, is well advanced in preadolescence, and begins to wane as the adolescent achieves status in adult society.

The structure and processes of the children's society is often tragically overlooked by adults. The children's society, however, gives the child approval and security; it advances his independence; it give him opportunity for vital democratic experiences. The face-to-face-relations, the participation in group discussion and group decisions are all essential parts of growing up, of socialization, and most important, of learning the ways of democracy.

The peer society, like any other society, has its values, codes, organization, and modes of behavior. These are always different from those of adults, and often in opposition. The children, however, are loyal to and guided by their codes, not those of parents and teachers. To ignore this is bad enough; to attempt to overrule by coercion is merely asking for real trouble. We will be fooled if we go along expecting children to accept our goals, manners, and values. We need to understand the peer society and its workings. Adults need not abdicate their roles and responsibilities. Parents and teachers can play important parts in guiding children by indirect influence. Home and school can offer experiences through which children can achieve independence. Children and youth must have experience in making decisions and in abiding by the consequences, in making mistakes and in correcting them. Parents and teachers cannot keep children in submissive obedience to authority and then all of a sudden expect them to take their places in society, exercising independence, making decisions and so on. Many authorities believe that the persistence of infantile fixations and immature reactions to responsibility in adulthood result in part from the authoritarian regime of the school and home. Positive and permissive attitudes in parents

and teachers, sympathetic insight into the difficulties attending first exercises of independent judgment, sympathetic assistance in diagnosing failures, are all methods of aiding children within their own affairs. Confidence and self-reliance and the acceptance of responsibility result. [28]

A child may be confused by inconsistency and contradiction between cultural pressures. The family, the neighborhood, the peer society, the social class, and caste if any, not only contribute to the individual as indicated above; they set goals. Each of these institutions defines for children the things that are "good," "desirable," "proper" from the point of view of the given institution. Children universally will try to reproduce and give allegiance to any value, belief, or behavior approved by the group in question, if it is within their powers at the given level of maturity.

Some children come to school with ideas of what behavior is "nice," the thing mother will approve. Other children come to school with no such ideas, behaving as they wish to with little regard for anyone. Children come to school believing that they are "good," that their beliefs and ways are the proper ones. They learn with astonishment during the primary grades that other children regard them and their ways with contempt. The latter children find that they in turn are looked down upon.

The school complicates the matter by presenting still other values, patterns of behavior, and motivations. Children from different

[28] Interesting supplementary reading will be found in:
Arthur W. Blair and William H. Burton, *Growth and Development of the Preadolescent* (New York, Appleton-Century-Crofts, 1951). Use the index.
Fostering Mental Health in Our Schools, The 1950 Yearbook of the Association for Supervision and Curriculum Development (Washington, D. C., The Association, 1950), Chs. 3, 9, 10.
Mary Jane Loomis, *The Preadolescent* (New York, Appleton-Century-Crofts, 1959). Excellent, Part I particularly.

types of homes adjust to the school with greater or lesser ease.

The child becomes increasingly conscious that behavior approved by the home may be disapproved by the school. Also, he finds that actions which are punished by home and school are well rewarded by hearty approval from one's peers.

DISCUSSIONS, OBSERVATIONS, AND REPORTS

1. Make observations, if possible, in two or three schools serving very different socioeconomic classes. Note contrasting behaviors. Note especially incidents which seem to reverse expectancy.

What efforts are being made to reach the children in these schools on their own level, as contrasted with "talking to them" or attempting to impose other behavior upon them?

2. One or more committees might develop a list of the characteristics of the various social classes in our society. Three or more of the many references available on the American social structure could be used. Several committees could cover a considerable part of the literature.

3. Similar reports could be made developing the general effect of this social structure and its demands upon children.

4. A report might be made here, if time permits, on the general processes of socialization in our culture. This report might be delayed until later chapters on knowing the child, aim of education, evaluation, and others have been studied. The point to bring out is the possibility of using processes of socialization that do not depend upon imposition and pressure, even though these processes may be necessary. Consult the literature on general psychology, mental hygiene, principles of teaching, sociology, and so forth.

5. A summary of the findings from studies of primitive societies may be made, if there is time and the class is interested.

6. Describe and evaluate any efforts you have observed or read about which endeavor to capitalize on the non-verbal types of intelligence.

7. A report summarizing and noting implications might be made of Hall's famous study, *Content of Children's Minds on Entering First Grade,* and Burton's study, *Children's Civic Information, 1924-1935.*

8. Experienced teachers may report on the serious gaps existing between children's information (on various levels and in various residence areas) and the content of given school books. The beginning readers are particularly prone to ignore the content of the minds of children from severely underprivileged areas.

9. A report similar to No. 7 might be made on children's attitudes. A number of studies are available in monographs and in periodical literature.

10. The implications of the material in this chapter with reference to classroom teaching, types of texts, and curriculum organization are very great and very important. Individuals or small committees may select any principle or set of principles, or any bodies of fact herein and attempt to develop some of the implications. Pay particular attention to the types of motivation and appeal made to the class with relation to the standards and motives of the particular class of children.

This question can well be discussed for one or two class sessions.

READINGS

Social Class Structure as Reinforcing the Attitude of Adults and Behavior of Children during Later Childhood

BLUMENTHAL, Albert, *Small Town Stuff* (Chicago, Univ. of Chicago Press, 1932).

DAVIS, Allison, "Child Training and Social Class," in Barker and others, eds., *Child Behavior and Development* (New York, McGraw, 1943).

———, *Social Class Influences Upon Learning* (Cambridge, Mass., Harvard Univ. Press, 1948).

———, and DOLLARD, John, *Children of Bondage* (Washington, D. C., American Council of Education, 1940).

———, GARDNER, Burleigh B., and GARDNER, Mary R., *Deep South* (Chicago, Univ. of Chicago Press, 1941).

———, and HAVIGHURST, R. J., *Father of the Man* (Boston, Houghton, 1947).

DOLLARD, John, *Class and Caste in a Southern Town* (New Haven, Yale Univ. Press, 1937).

HOLLINGSHEAD, A. B., *Elmtown's Youth* (New York, Wiley, 1949).

LONG, Alma, "Parents' Reports of Undesirable Behavior," *Child Development,* Vol. XII (1941), pp. 43-62.

LYND, Robert S. and Helen M., *Middletown* (New York, Harcourt, 1929).

———, *Middletown in Transition* (New York, Harcourt, 1937).

MOE, Edward O., and TAYLOR, Carl G., *Culture of a Contemporary Rural Community: Irwin, Iowa,* Rural Life Studies No. 5 (Washington, D. C., Bureau of Agricultural Economics, 1942).
Other Rural Life Studies:
No. 2, *Sublette, Kansas*
No. 3, *Landoff, New Hampshire*
No. 6, *Harmony, Georgia*

STENDLER, Celia B., *Children of Brasstown,* University of Illinois Bulletin.

———, "Social Class and the Curriculum," *Educational Leadership,* Vol. VII, No. 6 (March, 1950), pp. 371-375.

WARNER, W. Lloyd, "Educative Effects of Social Status," Section II in Burgess and others, *Environment and Education,* Supplementary Educational Monographs (Chicago, Univ. of Chicago Press, 1942).

———, and LUNT, Paul S., *The Social Life of a Modern Community* and *The Status System of a Modern Community,* Yankee City Series, Vols. I and II (New Haven, Yale Univ. Press, 1941).

———, and others, *Democracy in Jonesville* (New York, Harper, 1949).

WARNER, William L., and others, *Social Class in America: A Manual of Procedures for the Measuremeint of Social Status* (Chicago, Science-Research Associates, 1949).

WEST, James, *Plainville, USA* (New York, Columbia Univ. Press, 1945).

WHYTE, William Foote, *Street Corner Society* (Chicago, Univ. of Chicago Press, 1943).

General References

BARKER, R. G., KOUNIN, J. S., and WRIGHT, H. F., *Child Behavior and Development* (New York, McGraw, 1943).

DAVIDSON, Helen H., *Personality and Economic Background* (New York, King's Crown, 1943).

DAVIS, Allison, "American Status Systems and the Socialization of the Child," *American*

Sociological Review, Vol. VI (1941), pp. 345-354.

FROMM, Erich, *Escape from Freedom* (New York, Farrar and Rinehart, 1941).

GORER, Geoffrey, *The American People: A Study in National Character* (New York, Norton, 1948).

HAVIGHURST, Robert J., and TABA, Hilda, *Adolescent Character and Personality* (New York, Wiley, 1949).

HORNEY, Karen, *The Neurotic Personality of Our Time* (New York, Norton, 1937).

KLUCKHOHN, Clyde, *Mirror for Man* (New York, Whittlesey House, 1949), Chs. 8, 9, 10.

———, *The American Culture: Generalized Orientation and Class Pattern. Seventh Symposium: Conflicts of Power and Modern Culture* (New York, Harper, 1947).

———, "The Way of Life," *The Kenyon Review* (Spring, 1941).

———, and MURRAY, Henry, eds., *Personality in Nature, Society, and Culture* (New York, Knopf, 1948). As a source book.

MEAD, Margaret, *And Keep Your Powder Dry* (New York, Morrow, 1942).

MILLER, Neal E., and DOLLARD, John, *Social Learning and Imitation* (New Haven, Conn., Yale Univ. Press, 1941).

MORENO, J. L., *Who Shall Survive?* (New York, Beacon House, 1945).

MYRDAL, Gunnar, *An American Dilemma* (New York, Harper, 1944), particularly Ch. 1.

OLSON, Willard C., *Child Development* (Boston, Heath, 1949), Ch. 9 and other scattered materials.

PARSONS, Talcott, *Essays in Sociological Theory* (Glencoe, Ill., The Free Press, 1949), particularly Part I; Ch. III; Part II; Chs. VIII, X, XI, XII.

PERRY, Ralph Barton, *Characteristically American* (New York, Knopf, 1949).

SCHLESINGER, Arthur M., *Paths to the Present* (New York, Macmillan, 1949).

WARNER, W. Lloyd, HAVIGHURST, Robert J., and LOEB, Martin B., *Who Shall Be Educated?* (New York, Harper, 1944).

The bibliographies and footnotes in this chapter have been carried over with very few changes from the previous edition. These references include most of the original studies and cover the upsurge of interest in the areas treated. Studies are now less frequent but should be found and reported. More detail is available, and some cautions have been developed, concerning the original major ideas.

HAVIGHURST, Robt. J., *Human Development and Education* (New York, Longmans, 1953).

KUHLEN, Raymond G., and THOMPSON, George G., *Psychological Studies of Human Development* (New York, Appleton-Century-Crofts, 1952). Chapters 4, 8, 9, 10, 11, especially good.

MEAD, Margaret, and MACGREGOR, Frances G., *Growth and Culture* (New York, Putnam, 1951).

METRAUX, Rhoda, "Anthropology and Learning," in *Learning More About Learning* (Washington, D. C., Association for Supervision and Curriculum Development, N. E. A., 1959).

Current texts on educational psychology carry good summaries, varying in length. For illustration use the index in Cronbach; Lee and Lee; Stephens; Thompson, Gardner, and Di Vesta; and similar volumes.

In addition note current studies on social class; on family influence; on peer society.

CHAPTER 9: The Individual Lives in a Group

Two contrasting views of group process or group dynamics are available. Group process and related concepts are denounced and abused in the current jeremiad against the schools. Sarcastic remarks are made about "groupiness," "togetherness," and there are more serious criticisms holding that individuality will be lost in groups, "rugged individualism" will be destroyed, conformity will be enforced to the detriment of individual and creative thought. The bulk of this comes from critics ignorant of group dynamics, those who have never read the principles, and from those quite ignorant of the organization of any society. Some criticism comes from individuals who have seen or heard about bad practice in specific instances and have then overgeneralized. There are dangers and misuses of group dynamics as will be shown later, but these are largely unknown to the average critic.

However, responsible scholars who know the field and who, moreover, see group process in relation to life as a whole, have a very different view. Let us quote a leader [1] in the field:

No other problem in human affairs today seems to be so crucial and so fateful as that of

[1] Muzafer Sherif, "A Glance at Group Relations at the Crossroads: Introduction," Ch. 1 in *Group Relations at the Crossroads,* Muzafer Sherif and M. O. Wilson, eds. (New York, Harper, 1953). An excellent symposium on basic principles and issues. Good bibliographies.

References on more immediate and detailed operation of group processes will be given later.

group relations. Concern over group relations is not primarily the result of long-standing academic development in the area of universities and other scientific establishments. The problem, both in its intra- and intergroup aspects has forced itself to the foreground in the course of momentous events of recent decades. The developments in technology, in mass media of communication and transportation, socioeconomic developments, have brought human groups, with their diverse or conflicting interests, goals and cultures, into closer and closer functional relationship. Even within groups, such developments have brought changes in the mode of living and outlook, in the accustomed pattern of interpersonal relations. This state of flux, instability, unrest and conflict, culminating in catastrophic clashes of global proportions, creates urgent problems which cannot simply be put aside or considered at leisure.

Group dynamics is concerned, on the one hand, with the importance of human relations, of working and getting along together in groups. This applies to all types of groups, family, local community, intracommunity groups, industrial and labor organizations, national groups. On the international scene the most obvious danger lies in the ability of groups, raised to the national level, to get along. The mechanisms of co-operation, of interaction, of interchange, and of common decision do not exist on that level.

Group dynamics is concerned, on the other hand, with the importance of poised, mature, socialized personality. Evidence shows clearly the prevalence and increase of emotional instability and of more serious types of personality maladjustment. Over 75 per cent of persons dismissed from positions in trade, industry, and technical occupations are dismissed for personality difficulties, not for technical inefficiency. (And there are some who are violently opposed to "life-adjustment education"!)

The use of group process in the classroom is not a gimmick, not the invention of some professorial theorist. It is the deadly serious business of training future citizens in the skills of democratic life: the deadly serious effort to make democracy work. Democracy lives and can survive only through freely operated decision-making by the members of that democracy. Democracy is, in fact, people deciding things together.

Democracy depends for its existence on group thinking. The democratic method of solving problems and reaching decisions is one of free discussion wherein all are at liberty to express their views. Common agreement is reached through the interaction of individuals of all types and of all levels of insight within the group. Decisions are then understood and invite belief and loyalty. The method encourages another democratic principle—respect for the individual. Security for the individual and solidarity for the group are secured.

The democratic method, furthermore, frees creative power in astonishing ways as no other method can. A group engaged in solving a problem which is real to them will find need for many kinds of ability, many types of skill and insight. Contributions to the common problem may come from any and all members of the group. Leadership is actually exercised by any member as the activity proceeds.

The development and extension of insight is fundamental. The significant thing is that remarkable changes in attitude and behavior take place in activities where all may contribute, where all suggestions are received courteously and adopted or rejected after group consideration. The authoritarian situation, with teacher-imposed acceptance or rejection often not understood by the pupils and sometimes accompanied by emphasis on failure, inhibits the free flow of ideas. Security is lost, antagonism develops. Above all, democratic attitudes and behaviors are not learned. Many current threats to democracy are based on our failure to prepare citizens versed in the democratic method. The school, historically, has been authoritarian in its administration and classroom procedures.

The school is involved. One of the major jobs of any curriculum is to change attitudes and behavior. We are here concerned with the behavior making up co-operative, participatory group living—the behavior of democracy. All behavior has a cause. What are the determiners of desirable behavior? Of undesirable behavior? How can classroom living be utilized to develop better human relations, better ways of working and playing together?

Cunningham [2] and her associates, who have done the most complete piece of work on this problem, point up the teacher's problem and the significance of the group with a list of questions:

Have you ever wondered why things go well with one group, but less well with another although there may be fewer individual "problem" children in the group which has the most trouble?

Have you ever found that certain classroom procedures are successful with one group but not with another, or at some times but not at others even within the same group?

Do you sometimes feel baffled and wonder what to do next when a group seems to go "wild" for no apparent reason? Or when the group fails to respond to what you thought was a "sure-fire" suggestion? Or when the group laughs at Tom's clowning but says it's "silly" if David does the same thing?

[2] Ruth Cunningham and associates, *Understanding Group Behavior of Boys and Girls* (New York, Teachers College, Bureau of Publications, Columbia Univ., 1951), p. 1.

Are you curious about why certain boys and girls are more popular in the group, even though others seem to you equally attractive? Or why certain youngsters are chosen as captains of teams, or chairmen of committees, although you think others are obviously better qualified?

Hasn't it amazed you to find the group showing great tenderness and sympathy toward unfortunate group members, interspersed with outbursts of equally great cruelty of group members to one another?

Have you ever wished you could do more to help Betty make friends and become better accepted by the group?

Why is it that on occasion the group is capable of unusual depth of insight and is willing to give time and energy to the solution of a problem, and then, soon after, reverts to immature, superficial behavior?

Haven't you often thought that if you knew how to find answers to these questions, you might be able to provide better learning and living for pupils in your group?

Every teacher is involved. Each day he meets with a group or several groups and becomes a participant in the activities of the group. He is a status leader, but may play any of several roles. He can dominate because of his status power; he can dominate no less through personal appeals, emotional or otherwise. He can withdraw into extreme passivity, sometimes mistaken for permissiveness. He can be truly permissive and at the same time be a responsible participant in group life, serving in various ways. The real question is: How may he best stimulate and aid the growth of the group and the individuals in it? The teacher is one of the major determinants of behavior. He may utilize any of scores of minor specific determinants or any of several larger over-all patterns.

Cunningham [3] identified five patterns in the groups studied, the names of which are self-explanatory.

1. Adult rule, pupil obedience.
2. Planless catch-as-catch-can control.

[3] *Ibid.,* pp. 25-45. Excellent detailed discussion.

3. Teacher planning with individuals.
4. Adult-directed group planning.
5. Group self-management through group planning.

The social climate of the classroom is crucial. The pattern of interaction in a classroom is a major determinant of group morale and of group reaction. Cunningham discovered, however, that in some instances a poor pattern operated by a kind teacher produced a good climate; a good pattern could fail to produce a good situation.

What are some of the factors affecting social climate? Responsibility rests upon all group members. Many roles may be played by each, many types of leadership exercised. The roles and the nature of leadership will be elaborated a few pages below. Meanwhile we are establishing general factors contributing to the necessary social climate. Some of the major determinants of desirable, cooperative, participatory behavior, the behavior of democracy include:

A permissive atmosphere. This is the responsibility of all members as well as of the status leader.

Control imposed by the problem, by the available facts, by the considerations of coherent discourse. This control is the balance to permissiveness.

An accepted universe of discourse. This promotes communication.

An accepted value system and conceptual scheme. This also promotes, control, communication, and coherence of discourse.

Permissiveness can become lack of responsibility, with group activity degenerating into random discourse. This is the misunderstanding of permissiveness held by uninformed critics. The accepted problem and related facts are controls, and any member of the group may feel free to ask that discussion be on the point. *Permissiveness is not absence of control,* it is a pervading atmosphere which encourages any and all to contribute—to the point. Control is thus in the situation and not exercised by some person over other persons as in a police situation. Other factors are illustrated:

A common problem or goal which is an actual problem to the class group.

The goals, teachers', learners', societal, set by the group, and changed from time to time as the study develops, must be clearly achievable, with the results useful in the real situation.

The experience of working together, reaching decisions, and carrying group thinking over into action.

Flexibility in setting up goals, in changing goals as necessity indicates, in processes and materials.

Group solidarity (eventually) which gives security through belonging and contributing, and also a feeling of belonging to the larger whole, the school.

Aid given to isolates in improving their human relations.

Minimum of conflict between the code of the teacher, and the code, symbols, language, prestige-giving factors of the peer culture.

Ease of communication both as to language and channels.

Realization by the pupils, eventually, of the processes and benefits of group life.

Certain other factors less under the control of the teacher are:

The curriculum and school program generally.
The living conditions within the school.
The health and well-being of the learners.
The scale of values possessed by the children.
The home and community mores, customs, conventions.

Objective evidence is emerging supporting superiority of democratic methods. The question often arises: Do we know that democratic methods are superior? Its slowness, susceptibility to error, on the part of the learners are often mentioned in discussions of democratic methods; the lack of competent teacher leadership is also brought up. Not all those who oppose democratic methods are lazy authoritarians seeking an easy method of classroom control in the interests of comfort and avoidance of effort. Some sincerely believe that non-democratic methods of authority and imposition are better; some believe these methods necessary and inescapable. It is held that immature learners, even in college, may not be entrusted with democratic participation in classroom control and the development of the learning situations. Their beliefs are honest, but based, unfortunately, on beliefs inherited from predemocratic social thinking. Lack of information about the nature and abilities of learners also enters. The firm faith in the possibilities of human nature, the conviction that persons working on their own problems can supply answers, is not yet developed.

Evidence so far is not extensive, but it is increasing and so far is consistently on the side of democratic methods. Some experiments have been made with school learners, others with adults both in industry and in school work. In addition a good number of logical analyses are available. The classic study, "Patterns of Aggressive Behavior in Experimentally Created Social Climates," by Lewin, Lippitt, and White [4] should be known

[4] Kurt Lewin, Ronald Lippitt, and R. K. White, "Patterns of Aggressive Behavior in Experimentally Created Social Climates," *Journal of Social Psychology,* Vol. 10 (May, 1939), pp. 271-299.
This study is also reported in some detail with photographs in Goodwin Watson, "What Are the Effects of a Democratic Atmosphere on Children," *Progressive Education,* Vol. 18 (May, 1940), pp. 336-342. A good brief account with excellent photographs appears in *The New York Times Magazine* (December 15, 1940).
See also studies by Bingham, Embree, Hopkins, Mowrer, and others between 1939 and 1945.
For current studies on many aspects see:
William C. Morse, "Diagnosing and Guiding Relationships Between Group and Individual Class Members," Ch. XI in *The Dynamics of Instructional Groups,* Fifty-ninth Yearbook of the National Society for the Study of Education (Chicago, Univ. of Chicago Press, 1960). About 60 studies in footnote references. See other chapters.
Muzafer Sherif, "The Concept of Reference Groups in Human Relations," Ch. 9 in *Group Relations at the Crossroads.* Bibliography of 48 titles. Other chapters in this volume have excellent bibliographies.
J. M. Stephens, *Educational Psychology,* rev. ed. (New York, Holt, Rinehart & Winston, 1956). Chapter 18 contains excellent discussion, bibliog-

by all prospective teachers. A few related studies are available in the periodical literature of the early 1940's and may be reported by students if desired. Modern studies, several score of them, are on many of the different aspects of group process: changing attitudes and behavior, decision-making, effects of pressure, role-playing, and others. Class reports may be made in connection with topics in this chapter.

In the Lewin, Lippitt, and White study, a number of school clubs and learning activities were led in turn by three different teachers. One conducted affairs with as thoroughly democratic methods as possible, another with autocratic methods, whereas the third proceeded with laissez-faire attitudes and lack of controls. The groups of pupils were rotated between the three teachers for periods of time but were not informed of the experiment. Disinterested observers kept stenographic and photographic records of each meeting and of the individual members of the learning group. Analysis of these records plus analysis of reports made by the pupils themselves were the basis for conclusions drawn. In the autocratic set-up the leader was forced to assume more and more responsibility as time passed, whereas in the democratic situation the pupils gradually undertook more and more responsibility and carried it successfully. The democratic atmosphere caused pupils to be friendly, cooperative, talkative, more constructive in suggestions, and more appreciative in their comments. In the autocratic situation the pupils showed more tension, were either subdued or defiant, and were aggressive toward each other, expressing more hostility, resentment, and competition. They did much less smiling, joking, and moving about. Under democratic conditions, individuality within group efforts developed well, whereas group work disintegrated under autocracy. Under laissez-faire conditions, aggressiveness, squabbling, and hostility increased. The product and achievement in the democratic situations were distinctly superior to the other two. Questioned as to which teachers they preferred, over 95 per cent of the pupils chose the one who used democratic methods.

Unsocial behavior a serious matter. We may return for a moment to the opening discussion: Mental hygienists and students of personality generally, indicate that an unsocial attitude and behavior is probably the most serious problem of personality development. The growth of the democratic life is blocked. The inference is clear: The school must provide opportunities for children and youth to work and play together in groups. The denial and bafflement of communication and co-operation resulting from outmoded concepts of classroom control and process is detrimental to the life of the individual and of the school. Instead of banning and punishing whispering or other undercover communications, it is better to plan projects which necessitate talking to each other. Instead of banning movement and exchange of materials, again it is better to plan projects which necessitate sharing procedure and results, division of labor, and group evaluation. Social skills and competencies can be achieved only in social situations. Each individual, if not warped by previous treatment, desires to be an independent, respected, and self-respecting person, and at the same time to have satisfying reciprocal relationships with other personalities. Given any opportunity, human relations will grow and improve. Evidence in support of this view is constantly increasing.

---

raphy of 70 titles, and list of eight other sources of studies.

The two great classics from the field of industry are still among the best despite early copyright dates. Less extensive current studies may be reported by students.

Elton Mayo, *Human Problems of an Industrial Civilization* (New York, Macmillan, 1933).

F. J. Roethlisberger and others, *Management and the Worker* (Cambridge, Mass., Harvard Univ. Press, 1939). Account of a monumental research carried on at Western Electric Company, Hawthorne Works, Chicago, begun in 1927.

A general definition of a group and of group process. A mere collection, or aggregation of persons is not a group.

A group is a small social system. It consists of persons influencing and being influenced by one another and attracted to the same or similar concerns, goals, and values. [5]

All working groups, including, of course, the classroom group, have certain characteristics in common. All groups, for example, have a *goal* they seek to achieve; they have *participants* who are joined together for the purpose of achieving the goal; the activities of the group are founded in some type of control or *leadership;* the group has explicit or implicit *relationships to other groups* or institutions. [6]

Group process is the way in which individuals function in relation to one another while working toward a common goal. The relationships within a democratic group are participatory and co-operative. Modern educational psychology shows that not only are the typical outcomes of the school learned as well or better through group process, but that basic attitudes and interactive behavior are probably learned only in this way.

Group process, from simple discussion group to elaborate sociodrama, is not mere conversation, idle gossip, or play-acting. A group of uninformed persons pooling their ignorance will achieve nothing. The exchange of ignorant opinion, no matter how vivacious, serves no useful purpose. Six times zero is still zero. The group itself is not a random collection of persons.

Group process, as indicated several times, is problem-centered. The problem must be of concern to the group, understandable by members, dynamic enough to beget action, and realistic enough to be solvable. Reality motivates group members to search for information, to utilize all resources within themselves and the environment. The degree to which the problem is shared determines the degree of "groupness." Above all, *the problem must be one susceptible to development through a "meeting of minds" and not one for which a precise, demonstrable answer is available.*

Group process is not merely another "method" of teaching or learning. Participation and interaction do far more than develop typical outcomes of learning; they affect profoundly the individuals themselves. Each person in contributing not only affects the problem and its setting, not only affects other persons; he affects himself as no other experience can. He develops the personal-social-moral traits of the socialized individual.

A general book such as this cannot give space to detailed definition and background theory. The brief statement above can be supplemented through reading any of the following references.

AMBROSE, Edna, and MIEL, Alice, *Children's Social Learning: Implications of Research and Expert Study* (Washington, D. C., Association for Supervision and Curriculum Development, 1958). Far the best summary of the objectives and outcomes of social learning processes, together with excellent discussion of certain factors affecting social learning.

BAXTER, Bernice, and CASSIDY, Rosalind, *Group Experience: The Democratic Way* (New York, Harper, 1943), Chs. 1 and 3.

BENNE, Kenneth, and MUNTYAN, Bozidar, *Human Relations in Curriculum Change* (New York, Holt, Rinehart & Winston, 1951). Extensive materials in Part III. Use Index.

DE HUSZAR, George B., *Practical Applications of Democracy* (New York, Harper, 1945), Chs. 1-3, 10, 11, especially, but whole volume is an excellent reference.

The Dynamics of Instructional Groups, Fifty-ninth Yearbook of the National Society for the Study of Education (Chicago, Univ. of Chicago Press, 1960). Excellent chapters on basic theory.

[5] Max R. Goodson, "The 'Person' and the 'Group' in American Culture and Education," Ch. 2 in *Group Relations at the Crossroads,* p. 14.

[6] Jacob W. Getzels and Herbert A. Thelen, "The Classroom Group as a Unique Social System," Ch. 4 in *The Dynamics of Instructional Groups,* p. 53.

KOZMAN, Hilda C., ed., *Group Process in Physical Education* (New York, Harper, 1951), Ch. 5.

SHERIF, Muzafer, and WILSON, M. O., *Group Relations at the Crossroads* (New York, Harper, 1953). An excellent symposium.

STILES, Lindley J., and DORSEY, Mattie F., *Democratic Teaching in Secondary Schools* (Chicago, Lippincott, 1950), Chs. 12 and 13.

TRECKER, Harleigh B., *Social Group Work: Principles and Practices* (New York, Woman's Press, 1948).

WILES, Kimball, *Supervision for Better Schools* (Englewood Cliffs, N. J., Prentice-Hall, 1950). Not on supervision but actually a good summary of principles of group process.

WILSON, Gertrude, and RYLAND, Gladys, *Social Group Work Practice: The Creative Use of Social Process* (Boston, Houghton, 1949).

The volumes by Ambrose and Miel, Sherif and Wilson, and the one published by the National Society for the Study of Education each contain excellent bibliographies. Many pamphlets and handbooks are available from various sources and are usually available in college libraries. References on the actual details of procedure will be given later.

The birth and growth of a group. When first introduced, group work gets off to a slow start. A defensive attitude is often noted at first, as individuals consider what is acceptable behavior and look around to see who's who. Some time may elapse with younger groups before group process begins to function, though more mature groups may get under way more rapidly. Even with adults there will be some reluctance, uncertainty, and even open opposition. It is well to spend some time getting acquainted.

Sociometric analyses from time to time will give the teacher insight into the texture of the group, indicating relationships, groupings, and the like. These relationships change from time to time.

The situation is further complicated because each pupil brings with him certain values, conventions, social patterns of his own. Worse, older students may bring several verbalizations and stereotypes to which previous classroom experience, or life experience, have conditioned them. The stereotypes will almost certainly be authoritarian and not democratic.

The school must recognize child society, the processes of which are real to children, whereas the imposed processes and values of adult society are not. The teacher or a number of interested persons cannot make, or form, or call a group into being. All a teacher can do is provide the permissive conditions and atmosphere in which democratic group processes can emerge. The teacher, however, is not passive, nor does he adopt a laissez-faire attitude. Above all he cannot be authoritarian. He takes certain actions as we shall see later. The extent and nature of participation by a status leader will depend upon the level of growth and insight present in the group itself.

A good analysis of the growth of a group has been given by Thelen and Dickerman [7] in reporting the operation of the 1948 session of the National Training Laboratory on Group Development. The phases set forth are not necessarily sequential, nor are they always found just as described. *First,* the stereotypes derived from past experience drive individuals to attempt to place themselves in those positions within the authoritarian structure to which they have been accustomed. Each sees the others as individuals and not as group members; the leader will want to run things so that "we get things done"; and other similar ideas dominate. *Second,* if the leader truly believes in democratic process and will stand fast against the effort to establish authoritarian protocol, he will precipitate a period of hostility, conflict, and frustration. Group development will "make or break" at this point. Wrangling

[7] Report of the Second Summer Session, National Training Laboratory in Group Development (Washington, D. C., Division of Adult Education Services, N. E. A.). Available also in *Educational Leadership* (February, 1949), pp. 309-316, and sumarized in Benne and Muntyan, *op. cit.,* pp. 105-114.

over problems which are really carry-overs from older accustomed beliefs and procedures may destroy the group, or more accurately, cause it to be stillborn. The utmost skill is necessary so that the group may see the differences in goals, processes, and decisions between authoritarian and democratic life.

Third, if the hazards of the second phase are conquered, an important characteristic develops, namely, cohesiveness among members. This, however, is cohesiveness based on a beginning realization of the nature of a group but not yet on realization of the purpose of a group. A good deal is learned at this point, however, about the attitudes, processes, and positions within the group. *Fourth,* a group finally sees that it is the purpose and real problem-solving that is crucial. The arguing of side issues disappears as important problems capable of solution and of affecting the life of the group come to the fore. The group is then eager to go about its proper business.

Major types of group processes. A general volume such as this cannot possibly discuss all phases of the democratic process. The following short descriptions will give teachers guidance in getting started. Any amount of supplementary reading is available.

Group work on a project or problem
  A problem arises and is defined.
  A plan for attack and solution emerges and
    is revised constantly as the project develops.
  A tentative summary or conclusion emerges.

*Group processes valuable in defining, attacking,
    and solving problems*
  Group planning
  Committee work
  Sharing findings and results
  Research for the group

Group discussion (useful at any stage)
  The buzz group

Group roles with special responsibilities
  Leader   Observer
  Recorder   Resource person

General member roles
  (Listed later in discussion)

Role-playing
  Psychodrama
  Sociodrama

Group work on a project or problem. The chapter on developing units (Chapter 14) will present the method of group attack on problems. Details are more appropriate there, since they can be placed within an orderly sequence. The following summary will emphasize the salient points.

a. A problem arises. [8] Problems will be found in the everyday conversation of students, in questions asked, in current events, through inventories of pupil interest, through a problem census, and in course of study materials. The problem may be discovered or suggested by any member of the group.

b. The problem is defined. The teacher and the course of study in traditional schools usually define the problem and give directions for study. The modern school regards definition and clarification of the problem as an important learning experience. The whole group engages in discussion so that all see the problem clearly, hence can begin suggesting lines of attack, sources of materials, and learning experiences. Sometimes a small committee is appointed to make preliminary clarification in order to save time which would otherwise be expended by the total group. The teacher may define in order to start discussion for clarification and attack. Redefinition from time to time is characteristic of all real group discussions.

c. The problem, its implications, possibilities, and varied solutions, is considered by the group. Orderly, sensible procedures of thought are desirable as an ideal for which to aim. Orderly thought is an outcome to be achieved through much experience with thought-in-process. Teachers must expect and accept that actual problem-solving will differ greatly from the smooth and sequential development which sometimes appears in discussions of "how to think." Actual problem-solving in real situations includes innumerable errors and corrections, digressions, discussions ending in blind

[8] W. H. Burton, R. B. Kimball, and R. L. Wing, *Education for Effective Thinking* (New York, Appleton-Century-Crofts, 1960). Chapters 1, 2, 4, and 8 outline the problem-solving process.

alleys, the laborious trial and checking of guesses, the tedious process of validating and evaluating. Terms must be defined and redefined; schemes for classifying one's ideas must be made and often scrapped. Analysis, selection, and discrimination of ideas and processes is continuous. Many, many errors and successes appear before the problem is solved. These and many others are the essence of dynamic thought-in-process. The individual learns the best methods of proceeding, of avoiding errors, by discovering them within his own problem-solving processes.

All this seems, to some teachers, to be both a waste of time, and training in bad habits. The direct opposite is true. No one can learn to think, to solve problems, without thinking and solving problems. No one can achieve the many desirable personal abilities and skills, desirable social and moral traits, without undergoing experiences which demonstrate the value of these outcomes.

We may make or break the democratic process at just this point. All persons in the group will have unique contributions to make, odd as that may sound in some groups. All have both right and responsibility to contribute. Creative suggestions may come from any member. The atmosphere must be fully permissive, all contributions being received with courteous attention and disposed of after group insight into their merits and defects. Leadership shifts from child to child as contributed knowledge or creative suggestion is tossed into the discussion.

d. *The group seeks knowledge and experience beyond its own resources.* A group cannot chat itself to truth. The right to contribute carries the obligation to search for new materials and experiences beyond the present resources of the group. References will be consulted, various types of resource persons interviewed, excursions of many types made.

The group will learn under guidance to distinguish between data which are not affected by discussion and accepted beliefs or ideas which are determined by consensus.

The untrained individual makes no distinction at first between reputable group discussion and ordinary conversation. He uses the expression "I agree," or "I disagree," "in my opinion," or "my experience shows." This is utter nonsense when dealing with factual material. Scientific materials may be attacked, disagreed with, only through critical analysis of their origins and not through expressing "opinions." Opinions, agreements, or disagreements when backed by new facts or by logical analysis are

valuable in dealing with interpretation or application of facts.

e. *The machinery for co-operative process develops out of the situation, is not set up in advance.* The committees and study groups among the students, the various projects will be set up as needed. Channels of communication must be provided which work both ways.

Co-ordination of the work of many persons and subsidiary groups must be provided. Responsibilities, rights, and authorities must be defined.

f. *Tentative summaries and conclusions are made.* Consequent action is based on the tentative conclusions which, in turn, lead to further discussion, modification, and to continuous growth.

The necessity for a problem as the focus of all group effort cannot be overemphasized. Group work does not deal with assigned text material or informational background. These factors enter in their proper place, as will be shown in the following pages.

The major operating principles of group living with reference to the classroom. A number of listings of the principles of group living in the classroom have been made by different authors. The one prepared by Burr, Harding, and Jacobs [9] covers the problem so adequately that it is reproduced here in full:

1. *Good group work originates with purposes, plans, and problems as the children see them.* One of the best ways to develop genuine group work is to start where the children are, with statements of purposes, plans, and problems in their own language. The teacher may be able so to guide children that they broaden their horizons as to purposes and procedures for accomplishing these purposes, extend their concepts of planning, and see more in their problems than they originally were able to see. But as a starting point for good group work, the teacher must genuinely accept as significant the objectives and plans of the group. As has been said so many times, the development level

[9] James B. Burr, L. W. Harding, and L. B. Jacobs, *Student Teaching in the Elementary School*, 2nd ed. (New York, Appleton-Century-Crofts, 1958), pp. 151-153.

of the children indicates to the teacher what is suitable for a given group.

2. *Good group work begins by pooling the contributions of all the members of the group.* From the beginning, it is desirable that every member of the group should feel that he has an important part to play in group decision-making and group action. One very effective way for the teacher to begin group work is to lead the children to pool their contributions—to look at and think together about the whole job before attempting to attack the parts. Such a period of orientation is not wasted time. Without this, intelligent group planning is impossible. Furthermore, from this the teacher gets his clues for guiding further group work.

3. *Good group work provides appropriate responsibilities for committees and individuals.* Good group work depends on personnel as well as on purposes and procedures. When the purposes and procedures are clearly defined, the next question inevitably is "Who is to do what?" There are many responsibilities in group work which must be assumed by the group as a whole. In these instances, use of personnel resources calls for freeing and helping every child to do critical thinking. In other instances it is both efficient and democratic to allocate to committees of children or individuals well-defined responsibilities where their particular aptitudes and expertness will contribute significantly. While important matters in decision-making are never put into the hands of the few, certain phases of the work may be better done by the few than the many. Herein committees and individuals gain significance through such participation for the good of the group. Moreover, individual drives and interests are synchronized with the group's purposes and efforts.

4. *Good group work teaches the individual how to participate effectively in co-operation with others.* Since all effective group work grows out of the co-ordinated efforts of individuals, each child must learn how to become a good group member. He must have opportunities to learn more about how to discuss, how to release tensions, how to pool his thinking with that of the members of the group. The child can be helped to know when he has responsibilities for assuming leadership and when he properly accepts the leadership of others. He can be taught, through the processes of group work, that co-operation is something which people work to get and to keep through the democratic concern which each individual has for the good of his group.

5. *Good group work depends upon democratic procedures for unlocking resources, resolving conflicts, and reaching decisions.* Democratic procedures are in operation when individual differences are constructively prized and utilized, when agreements are reached by at least majority consent, and when conflicts are resolved by working for better mutual understanding. If group work is to be democratic, outcomes with which children can effectually deal should not be arbitrarily teacher-planned in advance. External authority should not be autocratically employed in making decisions. "Right" and "wrong" in conflict situations cannot be handed down as law or regulation by one dominant person. Rather, every child must be guaranteed the opportunity to make his best contributions. He must have a voice in setting up the rules by which the group will operate. He must have the right, when in a minority, to continue to work constructively for the adoption of the minority's plans. He must be assured an objective, dispassionate hearing in conflict situations. These are the ideals toward which the teacher works with a group. The teacher always remembers, however, that the school should provide opportunity to experiment with democratic procedures of operation rather than demonstrate a finished performance. Through years of guided experience in group work, children grow both in their faith in this way of working together and in their efficiency and effectiveness with group processes.

6. *Good group work develops leaders who create conditions in which every member wants to bring his best thinking and work to the co-operative undertaking.* In democratic groups, leadership is shared in terms of the abilities which are needed in specific situations. No one in the group—not even the teacher—monopolizes the leadership role. In fact, much of the teacher's leadership talents are directed to the development of children's potentialities for assuming executive functions. As the teacher works to develop child leaders, he teaches his group members to be wary of any form of dictatorship. In group products that demand the distinctive talents of every member, he demonstrates the worth of every individual to the group rather than reliance upon the favored few. Through group processes, he makes clear that good leaders free and encourage other members to make their best contributions to the group. Good group leaders avoid favoritism, mechanical reliance on orderliness, docility, blind allegiance, and "bossism." Good group leaders place their responsibility for the group welfare above personal prestige, power, or gain. When children are given opportunities for lead-

ership, they gain stature and have a tendency to rise to the demands of such responsibility.

7. *Good group work demands continuous appraisal of group accomplishment.* As group work progresses, evaluation is as necessary as planning and decision-making, for out of critical evaluation further purposing and planning grow. Evaluation not only appraises the present status of group work; it serves also as an impetus to feelings of group accomplishment and group pride. Consideration of "What have we done?" and "How well have we done it?" in relation to "What did we set out to do?" keeps children realistic in terms of success and failure. Evaluation also is a major means of fostering "groupness" in co-operative undertakings. In devoting time to appraisal of work done and consideration of the processes by which the accomplishments have been achieved, the teacher is giving the children not only important learnings as they relate to subject matter but also valuable, practical citizenship experiences in democratic group living.

8. *Good group work eventuates in broad participation, co-operatively efficient group action, and constructive changes in individual behavior.* In the continuous evaluation of group processes and products, these three interrelated goals are of major import. Wider and more mature participation on the part of each member is one evidence of success with group work. A second is that increasingly less time is wasted in getting jobs done, that pooled intelligence and effort are used both effectively and efficiently. A third evidence is that the individual is developing in his abilities to synchronize his purposes and plans with those of the group; that he is participating in such ways that his talents and abilities are resourcefully used in pushing ahead the group undertakings; and that he is holding himself accountable to the group for meeting his responsibilities as efficiently and well as he can. When successive experiences in co-operative endeavors show evidences of a group's progress in these respects, group work has been successful.

9. *Good group work calls for appropriate recognition for the group.* As children have successful group experiences, they need prestige and recognition for their group. They need to feel, individually, pride in group accomplishment. They need, collectively, to get satisfaction from a co-operative undertaking well done. They need individually to get desirable approval for their contributions to the group. They need to enjoy the "we-ness" of products. Thus, children will want to pursue further those types of experiences which give them satisfac-

tion, security, and status. When group work provides such worthwhile rewards, children are encouraged to want to know more about and do better with co-operative procedures in group situations. In this way both the individual and the group as a whole profit from experiences of working together democratically.

Subsidiary group processes valuable in problem-solving. The brief summary here should be supplemented through reading, demonstration, and practice.

Group planning. The general nature of this is indicated in the foregoing discussions. Planning will be developed in some detail in Chapters 13 and 14 on the development of units where it is an integral part of the process. In addition see:

BURR, James B., HARDING, L. W., and JACOBS, L. B., *Student Teaching in the Elementary School,* 2nd ed. (New York, Appleton-Century-Crofts, 1958), Ch. 7.

CUNNINGHAM, Ruth, and associates, *Understanding Group Behavior of Boys and Girls* (New York, Teachers College, Bureau of Publications, Columbia Univ., 1951). Extensive and detailed analysis.

LANE, Howard, and BEAUCHAMP, Mary, *Human Relations in Teaching* (Englewood Cliffs, N. J., Prentice-Hall, 1955), Ch. 17.

LEE, J. Murray, and LEE, Dorris M., *The Child and His Curriculum,* 3rd ed. (New York, Appleton-Century-Crofts, 1960), pp. 77-81, 123-133, 159, 179-181, 197-198. Good bibliography.

LINDBERG, Lucile, *The Democratic Classroom: A Guide for Teachers* (New York, Teachers College, Bureau of Publications, Columbia Univ., 1954). Discussion and illustrations.

MIEL, Alice, and associates, *Co-operative Procedures in Learning* (New York, Teachers College, Bureau of Publications, Columbia Univ., 1952).

MOUSTAKAS, Clark, *The Teacher and the Child* (New York, McGraw, 1956). See particularly Chapters 4-8.

PARRISH, Louise, and WASKIN, Yvonne, *Teacher-Pupil Planning* (New York, Harper, 1958).

Meanwhile we may list a number of general points:

The general initial technique, as indicated above, is group discussion in defining and exploring some purpose or objective relevant to the curriculum and the life of the pupils. The teacher and class talk over what may be done, list things which must be done, provide for division of work and for sharing findings.

Lists of subproblems, questions, and tasks are formulated. These include anything that has to be done; developing bibliographies, study in the library, making card indexes, working models, designing experiments, and particularly making summaries from time to time.

Charts or running outlines of what to do are developed. Work is laid out by the group for long- and short-term projects. Charts may vary all the way from listings of very general questions, problems, or tasks with very general directions or guidance, to the listing of minute questions and tasks together with specific suggestions for procedure. The charts supply guidance for action and later a basis for evaluation during the process and at the end.

Lists should be made of resources of all types, personal and material; sources of information, tools, and construction materials.

Division of work is provided.

Provision is made for unification through sharing and through discussion looking toward integration of all efforts into the original plan.

(See Chapters 14 and 15 for some illustrations of the above.)

Committee work. Work on any unit or project is co-operatively distributed among individual students and groups. Committees may be large or small, organized around any phase of the unit, and set up at any time. This way far more work is done (and later shared), many more resources utilized than could be handled by a teacher and class working as a whole. Individual talents and interests may be utilized for the good of the group.

The most frequent type of committee is the work committee, through which the bulk of a unit is carried on, although there often are planning committees and evaluation committees as well. Committees may be used in working out aspects of group life not connected with the unit. All exemplify group living leading to understanding and skill in democratic life.

A class may nominate chairmen and members, or chairmen may select their committee members. Sometimes the teacher will appoint some or all. Children usually choose to work on areas for which they have some background and skill; they usually choose congenial companions. Sometimes children may be assigned in order to broaden their views and skills. Committees change anyway as the unit develops and may be changed sometimes by the group. Children thus learn to work with many types of persons, have opportunity to study new areas. The development of cliques is minimized. Committees have a chairman and a recorder, plus any special officers as needed.

Committees should not go to work until plans have been so clearly developed that all members know what to do as a starter. Plans change as work develops.

Sharing experiences, findings, and summaries is a regular feature of unit development. All working committees are, in fact, obligated to place all findings before the whole group. Sharing is not confined to organized units. Little children in kindergarten and early primary grades will relate, quite spontaneously, tales about the baby at home, about the new kittens, about a trip to the beach—and if the teacher is not careful, will relate family affairs! Children bring in toys, books, or pets to show the others. They tell of things seen on the way to school, of new buildings, of street work, or of neighborhood events. The range of materials and experiences would take a page to list. Older children bring in not only books, but also models, machines, exhibits from trips in this and foreign countries.

Skillful teachers capitalize on this excellent form of group work. First, it brings to the group a huge amount of information and experience. Second, it prepares the children for the more organized reporting and sharing to come. Third, some of the best creative expression emerges in language, graphic and plastic art, construction, problem-solving thinking. The child learns to be sensitive to his audience and in turn to be a good listener himself. Most important of all, children see every day the fact that different kinds of children, different kinds of skills and abilities are all useful to the group. Children learn how to make their own unique contributions to the group. Responsibility to one's peers is learned under the best possible conditions. The group is able to profit from individual contributions, to balance group and individual goals, and to develop pride in the group, its members, and its accomplishments.

The teacher's role is to encourage sharing when readiness is present and to manage without dominating, seeing that contributions keep coming along and that discussion ensues. The teacher also protects children from undue and unkind criticism. Children will be on different levels of maturity, some attempting to share with the group things which the others have outgrown. The teacher aids the group in working out criteria for determining what is interesting and worthwhile.

Supplementary discussion of sharing will be found in most of the references given just above on planning.

Group discussion is useful at all stages. Some groups starting group discussion try to use Robert's Rules of Order. This is natural in view of past experience. The preceding pages should make clear that "rules of order" are a definite handicap to free democratic discussion. There must be order but the chairman and the group will be responsible for keeping it subordinate to the free discussion. Free give-and-take motivated by purpose and engaged in by sincere individuals will not require rules of order.

A little fear and insecurity inevitably accompany first attempts at democratic discussion. Teachers and students long conditioned to authoritarian domination have difficulty learning the new skills of leadership and of participation. The actual details can be learned only by engaging in group discussion. Time and experience will refine understanding and skill.

Group discussion may be aimed at clarifying a goal or policy or setting these up in the first place. It may be devoted to exploring implications, resources available, at developing an orderly method of attack, at forecasting consequences of certain procedures or decisions. Consensus within the whole group rather than a majority agreement is the desired outcome. More will be said of this later.

Conclusions developed may or may not agree with given views already in print. Even when the group arrives at a conclusion already well known in the field, the supporting arguments have been developed by the group. The children have identified themselves with the problem, the process, and the conclusion. This is very different from acquiescing to something they have read or been given in lecture. The decision, reasons for it, and consequences are clearly known to the individuals and hence beget loyalty. This is important, since individuals and groups must be committed to action based on their thinking. The group is also interested in the processes of arriving at conclusions whether by consensus or by majority vote.

Initiating discussion. Anyone can start a discussion, although it may be some time before group members can conquer their fears and stereotypes left over from authoritarian procedures. A real problem cannot fail to start individuals thinking and talking. A statement may be made or a question asked by a teacher, whereupon a pupil may suggest a modification. The teachers and students will support or deny the original statement. A resource person may inject a wholly new interpretation of the problem or of the immediate phase. Vigorous give-and-take may result, with small groups sometimes becoming absorbed in their circle of discussion. The whole group will eventually receive and use the thoughts of the small groups. The teacher provides conditions for free and easy argument and is aided by emergent leaders and by increasing participation. Each alert person, probably within an hour, has exercised leadership by a contribution of special knowledge, by asking a question, by making a creative suggestion. An individual may emerge as a leader for a considerable period if he becomes the center of a definite interchange. Each group member may be a leader or a participator at any time. This may go on for an hour or for a series of lessons covering some time.

The difference between formal logic and thought-in-progress. Orderly, sequential procedures in thinking are highly desirable as an ideal for which to aim. The actual processes of thought in the solution of actual problems, however, follow no such orderly and smooth sequences as formal outlines of problem-solving or of logic would imply. Formal logic, in simple terms, represents a summary of correct thought after the thought has taken place. Logic is the process of proof of thinking rather than thinking itself. The summary is smooth and sequential. The actual process of thought-in-progress is something very different. The logic of inquiry or process is distinguished from the logic of proof or of post-procedural summary. A better term is *thought-in-progress*.

Actual problem-solving in process includes innumerable errors and corrections, digressions, discussions ending in blind alleys, the laborious trial and checking of guesses, the tedious process of validating and evaluating. Terms must be defined and redefined; schemes for classifying one's ideas must be made and often scrapped. Analysis, selection, and discrimination of ideas and processes are continuous. Many, many errors and successes appear before a difficult problem is solved. These and many others are the essence of thought-in-progress but are never seen in the summaries of formal logic. The individual learns the best methods of proceeding, of avoiding errors, by discovering flaws within his own problem-solving processes. Experience with problem-solving

will enable him to achieve the understandings and skills of orderly thought without having them thrust upon him through the formulas of formal logic.

Thought-in-progress has its own order and controls. [10] The values of democratic interchange must not obscure the necessity for order, control, and reasoned conclusion.

Controls in dynamic thought reside in the problem, in known facts, in "reasonableness" of process, and finally in the democratic obligation to stay on the point and to accept responsibility for what one says. Any member of the group may demand that contributors "stay on the point," give sources of facts, support statements by more than assertion, and accept all inferences fairly drawn from their statements. A participant may not wander aimlessly as in ordinary conversation, may not skip from item to item without connection, may not escape responsibility for random, inconsistent, or even contradictory statements. He may not "agree" or "disagree" with demonstrable factual materials. He cannot hide behind such expressions as "my experience shows" or even worse, "one opinion is as good as another." He must cite facts and sources. No one has a right to an opinion when contrary competent, sufficient, and valid facts are available. Anyone has the right, of course, to question the facts, to examine the methods and controls under which the facts were derived, to suggest further investigation or experiment. To hold opinions in defiance of all the facts we have is not independence, it is infantilism. Attempting to establish something through pooling of opinion where there exists in reality a basis in measurement and experimentation is absurd. This not only befuddles discussion but sets

[10] John Dewey, *Logic: The Theory of Inquiry* (New York, Holt, 1938). Advanced students may wish to examine this excellent but difficult treatment.

Burton, Kimball, and Wing, *op. cit.* Chapters 1 and 2 give the general outline. Details are supplied in Chapters 4, 5, 6, 7 and 8.

up false ideas about validity and proof. Conversely, the attempt to reduce to figures materials which can rest only on verbal description, while less frequent, equally confuses thinking.

A group cannot chat itself to truth. The enthusiastic exchange of ignorant opinion is not democratic discussion. The democratic right to participate carries the democratic obligation to stay on the point, to base one's contribution on facts or carefully critical analysis of experience, to accept responsibility.

Difference of opinion is inevitable and desirable. When all persons participate in planning policies, in organizing plans of action, and in making decisions, will there not be endless argument, disagreement, even dissension? The preceding paragraphs do not mean that everyone must think alike, that all must agree in every detail. This would be impossible even if desirable. There will always be diversity within agreement, differences within unity. A few persons are genuinely annoyed, others are discouraged by the variety and diversity of human opinion and thought.

Difference of opinion and exchange of ideas so annoying to some are, in fact, a wholesome sign. The situation has vitality and the individuals are growing. New research, creative contributions, will always stir discussion between conservatives and liberals. Persons of different levels of ability, training, and experience inevitably will differ. The resultant discussion and study among honest persons under a competent chairman is the road to growth. Even objectors of a somewhat temperamental type, extremists perhaps, are valuable members of the group. They not merely prevent complacency but often contribute new ideas of real worth. Unorthodox thinkers, "heretics," should not be excluded or ignored. They may be a nuisance at times, but they do serve the group well upon occasion.

Endless argument, quarreling, and quibbling dispute do go on in many groups. The cure is not a return to imposed authority but earnest effort to rise to the level of mature democracy. Group discussion will be effective in so far as (1) we have faith in individuals, (2) the group possesses sincere convictions on the value of democratic actions, and (3) the chairmen are competent leaders of discussion.

The continuous discussion of differences of opinion, of the implications of facts, will develop a core of group-accepted principles and processes. Attention to the remaining periphery of diversity is important both for securing new ideas and for guaranteeing democracy.

Consensus and majority vote. The most sensitive phase in group discussion is that of decision-making. Writers on the subject are unanimous that group consensus and not simply majority vote is the more desirable outcome. However, situations arise which demand immediate action but in which general consensus cannot be quickly arrived at. Impatient individuals then blame group process—when, in fact, the difficulty lies in the situation. When under such pressure, it is sensible to act on majority vote, or on a consensus less inclusive than originally hoped for, but, as always to listen to minority views then and as the situation develops. Fully understood, however, the idea of consensus should be acceptable to all. The "either-or" reaction is never fruitful.

Students of the field have made very pertinent statements which should be examined at this point. Thelen [11] says:

The description of the goal should represent group consensus, not majority vote. It is the description of the goal that makes individual action meaningful because the proper relation-

[11] Herbert A. Thelen, "Engineering Research in Curriculum Building," *Journal of Educational Research* (April, 1948), pp. 579-596. (Available also in Benne and Muntyan, *op. cit.,* pp. 84-98. Excellent statement. See also footnotes there.)

L. P. Bradford and Ronald Lippitt, "Employee Success in Work Groups," *Personnel Administration* (December, 1945), pp. 6-10.

ships in time and among the group of individual actions can be understood only in the light of the group's purposes. If all members do not feel commitment to the same goal, then there will be continuous friction in working, the capacities of some members will be only partially utilized, there will be ambiguity in the evaluation of contributions (and hence lack of security), and there will be minorities that may induce disintegrative forces. For consensus, the alternatives must be discussed or studied or practiced with until only one emerges as being clearly advantageous (i.e., with more positive valence than the others).

The level of aspiration must be selected realistically with an eye to expectancy of the group in its particular situation. . . . The selection of the level of aspiration represents the action of two conflicting tendencies: to avoid the hurt of failure by keeping the level below probable achievement and to gain the highest social approval by pushing the level above probable achievement. The level of aspiration should make probable (actual) success (possible) as distinguished . . . from "success without success," "spurious success," and failure. The continual clarification of goals, of group recognition of the extent to which barriers are too high or too low for the individual members, and of provision for evaluation of group and individual progress helps in making group participation a success experience.

The level of aspiration must be continually revamped in response to changing perception of the changing realities in the situation. The higher the level of aspiration, the more change is required for success, and *therefore the more threat to the group.* As long as a group deals with the problem at the "irreal" level of academic debate and speculation, the level can be quite high with a minimum of threat; one can *discuss* possible desirability of making over the entire social order. But when the discussion becomes a consideration of desirable immediate behavior which is visualizable, the level of aspiration will have to drop considerably if the threat to the group is to remain at the same level. Much of the disappointment and complaint of group members stems from failure to understand and accept this fact.

A similar statement is made by Benne, Bradford, and Lippitt: [12]

[12] K. D. Benne, L. P. Bradford, and Ronald Lippitt, "Stages in the Process of Group Thinking and Discussion," in Benne and Muntyan, *op. cit.,* pp. 68-84.

Where persistent difference occurs, it is usually better to ask the group to find what it can agree on and where it differs and to commit itself as a group only insofar as it has reached common agreement. Where a group is not committing itself to group action but to personal action by members of the group, a variety of commitments may be invited over and above the common commitment of all members. It is healthy for members to commit themselves publicly to do something about the problem discussed, even if personal commitments differ. However, the expectation which the group is building as to successful group discussion is toward consensus as the only adequate basis for common action.

A clear statement is presented by Miel: [13]

Give full opportunity for every member of the group to contribute every suggestion that occurs to him.

Keep the gathering of suggestions as a phase of the discussion separate from the evaluation of the suggestions. This usually insures a more impersonal discussion of suggested solutions.

Allow plenty of time for pooling of facts and harmonizing of conflicting values.

Before final votes are taken use straw votes to uncover minority opinion early in the process. In this step allow each voter to register as many choices as he wishes.

Seek for a consensus by allowing full discussion of the minority view before entertaining final motions.

If after adequate discussion the group is still fairly evenly divided as to the proper course of action on a given matter, consider whether or not a decision really must be made at the time. Often it is better to postpone making a decision until further study can be made by all parties.

If a decision of some sort must be made, have it understood that the decision is a trial one whose results will be carefully reviewed in order that the large minority will co-operate as wholeheartedly as possible.

The key lies in the level of aspiration. If consensus on one level cannot be achieved, we may try for it on another. Emphasis upon

[13] Alice Miel, *Changing the Curriculum: A Social Process* (New York, Appleton-Century-Crofts, 1946), pp. 139-140.

See also Fred N. Kerlinger, "Authoritarianism of Group Dynamics," *Progressive Education,* Vol. 31 (April, 1954), pp. 169-173.

the trial or tentative nature of a decision also encourages consensus. Delaying decision for further study is often necessary.

Nevertheless, decision by majority vote will continue to be used for a long time and will often be used where it is not necessary. Understanding of the mechanism is therefore of real importance. We quote Benne, Bradford, and Lippitt again:

The group rightly aims then at consensus in action as the goal of discussion. Can it always be achieved? The answer is obviously "No." At times majority opinion is the best that can be attained. This is usually adequate in procedural matters, *e.g.*, when and where we shall meet, whether we shall break up into smaller groups for certain phases of discussion, whether we shall invite in a certain consultant, etc.

The writers, accepting fully the aim of consensus, venture to say that majority vote will be used often in more important matters than indicated by the paragraph quoted. Endless differences between individuals, between individuals and groups, would paralyze action if there were no such mechanism for reaching decision. When all levels of insight and background are represented in policy-making and action-planning there are bound to be differences, sometimes of considerable degree. There is no way to proceed other than majority vote if we are faithful to the method of democracy. [14]

Mankind long ago evolved the concept of majority vote to meet the need for action. Majority rule can be a tyranny, however, as well as an instrument of democracy. To avoid this several steps may be taken. First, no one should ever be *coerced* by or into following a majority decision. Second, a majority decision should be reached only after the freest discussion among all members, after all have been heard, after all objections have been elaborated, after all minorities have presented their arguments. Every participant has thus had the opportunity to help form the decision. More important, all mi-

norities have had full opportunity to win the group to their views. Third, the majority decision should be accepted as "tentative, with results to be carefully reviewed." Fourth, and most important, the decision should be open to re-examination upon request if any individual is able to present new evidence or point out a blunder in the reasoning or if results are not in line with expectancy. Re-examination of decisions is the safety valve.

A decision reached under these conditions represents a freely achieved agreement among a considerable number of the group. It is the best thought of the group to that moment. We must be sure that the decision actually was freely determined and is not a hasty or superficial or imposed conclusion. Faith in the group is a democratic principle. Are we not justified in having faith that "a large minority will co-operate as wholeheartedly as possible" under the conditions indicated? A group truly endowed with a democratic conscience should recognize an obligation to "go along" with the best group decision at the moment, to avoid "continuous friction," to see that "capacities of all members are utilized," and to control "disintegrative forces." The rights of the minority are fully protected by the democratic process itself.

Some Suggestions for Participating in Co-operative Thinking Through Group Discussion

Prepared for the
Michigan Study of Secondary School
Curriculum by

J. Cecil Parker [15]

1. Each person should do his own thinking. Don't try "to save time" by telling the group the right answer. The leader is not a group instructor, but a social engineer, trying to arrange conditions so that each will do creative thinking.
2. Group discussion is not a debating society. We do not argue for the fun of it. The

---

[14] Thelen, *op. cit.*

[15] Adapted from Goodwin Watson, William H. Kilpatrick, H. S. Elliott, S. A. Courtis, and others.

issues are of great importance; wise men disagree in their views; our task is to find more truth than we bring to any group meeting. We are in a co-operative quest. Our thinking is creative rather than combative.

3. Ask yourself which ideas, experiences, and differences are basic, fundamental and most worth discussing.

4. When discussion wanders, restate the question and get a new start. Sometimes, if the side line is especially important, put it up to the group, "Shall we follow this interesting issue that has come up, or shall we return to the plan of discussion originally adopted?"

5. Make short statements, not speeches.

6. Do not pass any important matter that is not clear to you. Sometimes individuals hear unfamiliar terms and assume that everyone else must understand; hence they fear it would be humiliating to ask for explanations or illustrations. This is untrue. Have you not often been glad when someone else asked for clarification on a point on which you had been none too clear? Others may profit too, but you are in the group to learn, and you must not hesitate to ask.

7. If you find yourself talking more than other members of the group, train yourself to pass over minor points and to speak on only a few carefully chosen issues.

8. Use special care to be fair to positions represented by a minority or not represented at all in the group. If you are aware of a position not being adequately represented, present it as its adherents would like to hear it stated, then explain your disagreement.

9. Challenge contributions you cannot fully accept. Do not keep your disagreements quiet in the mistaken notion that it is better manners to pretend to agree when you do not. Make inquiry concerning the assumptions involved in the contribution.

10. The "either-or" attitude is on the whole not fruitful. Search rather for new means which enable both sets of values to be pursued without clash. Our concern in co-operative thinking is not simply to choose between two ways we now know, but if possible to find a way of integrating the values of both, thereby creating an improved solution. However, avoid smoothing over differences. Differences should be probed with questions to make them clear and sharp.

11. When there is some confusion over a diversity of opinions expressed, a minute of silence can do much to help members rise to a clearer perspective of what has been said. In suggesting this pause, the chairman should restate the precise issue under discussion. After the pause the members may be more able to co-operate in detecting the root of the disagreements. This may be in the partial nature of the experience and evidence used, or in a difference in the sense of values. Try to keep in mind some ends everyone wants.

12. Be on the lookout for different uses of the same word. Call for illustrations whenever this difference becomes confusing. Do not wrangle over a verbal definition.

13. Trust the group. There is no person in it who is not superior to the rest in at least one respect. The experience of all is richer than the experience of any. The group as a whole can see further and more truly than its best member. Remember that every member of the group is an individual just as you are.

14. For every discussion there is available a limited amount of time. Each individual should help make it possible to utilize the time more effectively. To attempt too much in too short a time fosters a habit of slipshod and superficial thinking.

15. Summarize (1) whenever a major point is finished before going on to the next; (2) whenever the discussion has been fairly long drawn out or confused; (3) shortly before the close of the period. Try to use the words of members of the group, rather than your translation.

The list just below is reproduced from the previous edition, since the references are still valuable. One or two are out of print but usually found in college libraries.

AUER, J. Jeffery, and EWBANK, Henry, *Handbook for Discussion Leaders* (New York, Harper, 1947).

BENNE, Kenneth D., BRADFORD, Leland P., FENNER, Mildred, and LIPPITT, Ronald, *Role-Playing and Discussion Method* (Washington, N.E.A., 1950).

DENNY, George V., Jr., *A Handbook for Discussion Leaders* (Town Hall, 123 West 43rd Street, New York).

EWBANK, Henry, and AUER, J. Jeffery, *Discussion and Debate*, 2nd ed. (New York, Appleton-Century-Crofts, 1951).

FANSLER, Thomas, *Discussion Methods for Adult Groups*. A pamphlet which with others may be obtained from the Service Bureau for Adult Education, Division of General Education, New York Univ.

Group Discussion and Its Technique, Bureau of Agricultural Economics (Washington, D. C., Government Printing Office).

HALL, D. M., *The Dynamics of Group Discussion* (Danville, Ill., Interstate Printers and Publishers, 1950).

A Handbook for Discussion Leaders (Carnegie Endowment for International Peace, 405 West 117th Street, New York). Topic No. 9 contains excellent specific discussions of mechanics and arrangement of groups.

EVANS, Hubert M., "The Social Character of Problem Solving," *Progressive Education* (April, 1949), pp. 161-165.

It Pays to Talk It Over (Washington, D. C., National Institute of Social Relations).

Learning Through Group Discussion (Junior Town Meeting League, 400 South Front Street, Columbus 15, Ohio).

SLAVSON, S. R., *Creative Group Education* (New York, Association Press, 1948).

Suggestions for Discussion Group Members (Washington, D. C., Department of Agriculture).

Talking It Through, A Manual for Discussion Groups (Washington, D. C., National Department of Secondary School Principals, N.E.A., 1938).

UTTERBACK, William E., *Decision Through Discussion* (Columbus, Department of Speech, Ohio State Univ.)

Additional more recently published volumes include:

BRADEN, W. W., and BRANDENBERG, E., *Oral Decision Making* (New York, Harper, 1955).

BONNER, Hubert, *Group Dynamics: Principles and Applications* (New York, Ronald, 1959).

CORTWRIGHT, R. L., and HINDS, G. L., *Creative Discussion* (New York, Macmillan, 1959).

GORDON, Thomas, *Group Centered Leadership* (Boston, Houghton, 1955).

KELLNER, J. W., *Group Discussion Processes* (New York, Longmans, 1956).

LASKER, Bruno, *Democracy Through Discussion* (New York, Wilson, 1949).

MILES, M. B., *Learning to Work in Groups* (New York, Teachers College Bureau of Publications, Columbia Univ., 1959).

Several references included in earlier lists in this chapter are also useful here.

Periodical literature is a rich source of materials on all phases of group process, too numerous to list. Instructors and students should note new materials constantly.

The buzz group. An effective supplementary device for large group discussion is the buzz group, sometimes called the "six-six" procedure. Groups of approximately six persons consult for about six minutes for various purposes.

A large group often inhibits individuals from expressing themselves, especially in a close argument. The problem often is not sharply clarified. Differences of opinion are not easily handled in the large open discussions. The extent of agreement or disagreement is not always clearly assessed. Small groups which consult or "buzz" for from five to thirty minutes carry group thinking forward rapidly. Each group reports quickly to the reassembled groups. The small groups can be formed on a moment's notice, or they can be set up a day or more ahead, depending on the nature of the problem or impasse. Often the six or so persons sitting next each other can simply draw together without dispersing the large group into separate rooms. Sometimes a longer period and dispersal is necessary. Groups may be formed at random or by choice of given aspects of the immediate problem. The "buzzing" can be completely informal, without even a chairman, or it can be carefully structured with an outline, chairman, recorder, observer, and even resource person. The teacher is often the resource person.

Buzz groups must know exactly what is to be done before going into session.

Clarify the problem, topic, or issue, either the major one or any subproblem as it arises.

List the specified agreements and disagreements within the groups.

List a series of questions to which the large group should adhere in place of random discursive discussion.

Advantages of the buzz group are:

Explanations of any topic or process can be given more effectively in small groups.

Getting acquainted more rapidly can be achieved.

Wider participation is encouraged.

(Any number of very specific points may be used as a basis for buzzing, depending upon the given problem or topic under discussion by the total group.)

Reporting to the main group can be oral, with a master list kept on the blackboard to prevent repetition and loss of time. A combined report may be prepared by the reporters from the several groups. Reports are often effectively dramatized through sociodrama, skits, or pantomimes.

Teachers can develop with children excellent understanding and use of this device, which is also a real-life procedure.

Caution: group process is not always satisfactory. The account of group process here is deliberately simplified to make major characteristics stand out. The process will, it is hoped, be usable and generally successful in everyday situations suitable for group attack. Critical analysis has been omitted except for this paragraph. Critical studies are becoming increasingly available and reveal certain dangers in group process. These studies are not concerned with misapplication and misuse but with dangers appearing in situations where group process is legitimate. Certain individuals for instance, simply do not respond to group dynamics, even after some experience. Tensions, frustrations, antagonisms, and disintegrative conflict result. The unintentional pressure of the group situation causes some individuals to desert opinions and standards which would be of real value if maintained during discussion. Others, sensing this background pressure, resent the situation and may resort to stubborn opposition. Pressure distorts judgment even when no pressure is intended. A serious difficulty arises when individuals hold private opinions and conclusions which are quite different from their expressed opinions and conclusions. This gives a "hidden agenda" which is a block to honest group decision.

One often hears the criticism that group process makes for conformity. It can do so, but as often it makes for non-conformity. Most important is the fact that individuals belong not to one but to several groups. Different standards and values, different ends and processes are met regularly. The individual sees these differences and is in some measure freed from blind conformity. It is to be noted also that some degree of conformity is necessary for the preservation and functioning of any group. Primitive tribal groups enforced conformity as a matter of survival. More sophisticated groups in dynamic, fast-moving modern civilization are as likely to be saved by bold, creative breakthrough of individuals or small groups which defy conformity. Democratic process could not proceed without conformity to stated norms of discourse, agreement on facts, goals, and some others. Democratic group process, on the other hand, could not contribute vitally to the group without acceptance of difference and divergence within the group.

Other illustrations of difficulty can be given. Some difficulties are remedied through study and practice of group techniques; others do not respond to this.

Critical summaries are available:

CARTWRIGHT, Dorwin, and ZANDER, Alvin, *Group Dynamics* (Evanston, Ill., Rowe, 1953). Comprehensive critical summary of research to date of publication. Specific difficulties revealed and discussed. Some accounts are in the difficult language of a certain school of research and will need to be translated for the average school worker.

National Training Laboratory of Group Development, *Human Relations: An Assessment of Experience, 1947-1953* (Washington, D. C., N.E.A., 1953). Good readable account. Pages 67-77 refer to selected studies of a critical nature.

National Society for the Study of Education, *The Dynamics of Instructional Groups,* Fifty-ninth Yearbook (Chicago, Univ. of Chicago Press, 1960), Chs. 2, 4, 5, 6.

SHERIF, Mustafer, and WILSON, M. O., eds., *Group Relations at the Crossroads* (New York, Harper, 1953), Chs. 2, 3, 8, 10.

Dangers in the misuse of group process.
Group process is not a passing fad; it is the method of democracy in action. Training in the method is inescapable in a democracy. Like any procedure, however, it is subject to misuse and to inept use as it is learned. Many critics have been antagonized by examples of thoroughly shoddy thinking which is passed off as group process. Individuals who do not know the principles and have not yet understood the skills sometimes proceed as if any random flubdub conversation is group process. Time-wasting, disorderly, ignorant-of-facts procedures in planning or in a sociodrama are accepted as group attack. This is nonsense.

The dangers which precipitate the incompetent procedures are, some of them:

1. The procedure is not problem-centered at all but deals with the study of an area or topic, that is, of systematic subject matter. This is gross misapplication of the method.

2. The problem may be a fictitious one, not real or compelling to the group. This results in forced and unreal discussion or no discussion at all.

3. The problem may be one susceptible to precise answer on the basis of available data. Problems for group attack must be those which are to be solved through consensus, the meeting of minds. Nothing is more time-wasting or infuriating to informed persons than to see a group wrangle (however earnestly) for an hour or more over a point that could be settled through looking in the *Encyclopedia of Educational Research,* the *World Almanac,* or any standard reference work.

4. The problem may be too difficult for the group. The lack may be in information, in skill in group attack, or in general maturity of outlook in the field. A senseless waste of time ensues, not to mention the development of false ideas of group work. To repeat an earlier statement, the exchange of uninformed opinion will not develop valid conclusions.

5. Inept leadership, whether authoritarian or laissez faire (mistaken for permissiveness), can effectually distort or destroy group process.

6. Irresponsible demands for participation by groups who have heard that this is the method of democracy but who have no knowledge of the process and who (as yet) feel no responsibility to study the method and develop skill.

These are the individuals who cite "my experience" or "my opinion" and who do not know the difference between this and evidence or reasoned conclusions.

Deliberate sabotage by subversives and other trouble-makers may be mentioned here.

The physical setting for group process.
This is far more important than is thought at first. A pleasant room with comfortable furniture is essential. Chairs and tables should be arranged so that all group members can see each other. Ample blackboard space is necessary for keeping summaries or developing charts. Facilities for showing motion pictures or filmstrips are desirable. Tape recorders can be used effectively. Quiet and protection from interruptions should be secured. The simple device of serving tea or coffee with cakes is important. The chief purpose of all these arrangements is to secure as normal and pleasant a social situation as possible. Discussion can still go on without some of the desirable facilities if the group is sincerely interested, but improved physical arrangements are very helpful.

Group roles with special responsibilities to the group. Democratic group process permits any member to play at one time or another any role which may properly appear. Group process, as has been stated, is not mere unorganized conversation or play. Responsibilities are delegated by the group in order that progress may be made. The major specialized roles are those of Leader, Recorder, Observer, and Resource person.

Leadership in democratic process. Distinction must be made between "status" leadership and "shared" or "emergent" leadership. A status leader is one who occupies a position of leadership through appointment, election, ownership, or force. A superintendent of schools, a classroom teacher, a chief of police, a factory owner, a gang leader are all status leaders. Until modern times, status leaders exercised their leadership in authoritarian manner. Under democratic conditions the status leader can perform important functions. He should endeavor (a) to set a permissive tone for all affairs under his jurisdiction. This in turn encourages (b) free discussion, contribution, difference of opinion, and (c) leadership on the part of others as is necessary during the discussion or construction. The status leader, in addition to being primarily concerned with the improvement of human relations as indicated, may also (d) serve as resource person for certain phases of the work, and finally (e) aid in co-ordinating the efforts of all in the group.

Status leadership which operates democratically substitutes leadership for authority. Free expression is encouraged. Any member may at a given moment exercise leadership through a suggestion or an argument. Suggestions influence the trend of discussion, objections are raised, compromises are suggested. Each of these is a case of "shared" or emergent leadership. The study by Lewin, Lippitt, and White showed clearly the great superiority of democratic or shared leadership over both the authoritarian and the laissez-faire types.

A permissive climate is not easily achieved. The leader must abandon the traditional concepts of power and dominance and place his faith in the willingness, sincerity, and ability of persons to solve problems which are real to those persons. The traditional urge to dominate is displaced by the more civilized urges to aid, encourage, and inspire. The success of others, which means their growth, is the reward of the status leader.

The teacher will receive all problems (even "gripes"), all suggestions with courteous attention. Negative reaction inhibits children, whereas recognition of the simplest sort frees and encourages them. The teacher will build a free, permissive, and creative atmosphere by being consistent and honest. A friendly, informal manner eases tension and encourages expression. Occasionally time must be taken with trivial questions if the children are to be convinced that they may really bring up their problems. The teacher may need to protect a child or small group from more sophisticated classmates who would ridicule simple questions and suggestions. Adequate detailed knowledge about the group and the individuals in it aids the teacher in adjusting process to individual interests, strengths, and weaknesses.

The teacher's manner, personality, and type of leadership are among the most significant factors affecting human growth and socialization in the classroom. Teachers' attitudes toward children make significant differences not only in traditional subject-matter learnings but in the development of personality traits.

The status leader and the appointed leader have responsibility for starting discussion, keeping it going, and indicating the need for summary. Any responsibility of a status leader may be assumed at any time by a member of the group.

1. Start the discussion (if it does not start itself) by asking a question or a series of them, by making comments on the selected topic, by asking someone to express an opinion, by referring to a newspaper or magazine article, a cartoon or picture, or by any other of many devices.

2. Guide discussion by calling for comments upon any contribution, by asking for evidence for statements, by asking questions, by calling for transitional summaries: "How far have we progressed?" "What comes next?" "What points of disagreement remain?"

3. Ask questions or call upon persons to ensure that all shades of opinion are brought out.

4. Endeavor to make discussion general by refraining from answering questions from the platform; by throwing questions back to the group; by encouraging answers and contributions from all parts of the group.

5. Call ceaselessly for facts to back up statements. This is a most effective means of keeping out senseless remarks and encouraging the sincere group members.

6. Summarize or call for summary, raise direct questions, call for further pointed comment at any point where the discussion bogs down, then openly move on to the next point.

7. Remain, so far as responsibilities permit, in the background, but do not neglect the duty of guidance and stimulation.

The recorder. The recorder is like a secretary, but he has the further responsibility of sorting out pertinent comments. He records the major issues and selects contributions that bear on the issues. Careful listing must be kept of those topics or problems raised but referred for later discussion. The recorder ordinarily makes his report at the close of the session but may break in if too many issues get before the group without being disposed of systematically.

The observer. The observer, unlike the recorder, pays little attention to the content but focuses sharply on the method or process of the discussion. An outsider, or outgroup observer, is usually more effective at first until the role is understood, whereupon in-group members may act as observers. Observers must preserve and demonstrate honesty and objectivity, must avoid any appearance of superiority to the group, or the report and advice will be ineffective. Groups are always a little afraid of observers at first, but skillful observers and leaders plus helpful objective analyses of group activity, will overcome this. The observer's comments and interpretations may be rejected by the group. The observer, as hinted, may confine reports to descriptions of what took place or may include interpretations. This depends upon the maturity and willingness of the group and upon the demonstrated ability of the observer.

The feedback of comment from the observer aids all members to become aware of their own characteristics; aggressiveness, defense, escape, earnestness, sincerity, courtesy and tact, or too great bluntness.

The observer will be greatly aided by using some criteria or guides to keep the observations pertinent and objective. Jen-

kins [16] has suggested three levels through these illustrations:

Group Discussion Observation

Name of Group.............. Date........

A. *Direction and Orientation*
   1. How far did we get? (Was agenda covered? Time spent on details?)
   2. To what extent did we understand what we are trying to do?
   3. To what extent did we understand how we are trying to do it?
   4. To what extent were we stymied by lack of information?

B. *Motivation and Unity*
   1. Were all of us equally interested in what we are trying to do?
   2. Was interest maintained or did it lag?
   3. To what extent did the group feel united by a common purpose?
   4. To what extent were we able to subordinate individual interests to the common goal?

C. *Atmosphere*
   1. What was the general atmosphere of the group?
      a. Formal or informal?
      b. Permissive or inhibited?
      c. Co-operative or competitive?
      d. Friendly or hostile?

MEMBER CONTRIBUTION OBSERVATION

A. *Contributions of members*
   1. Was participation general or lopsided?
   2. Were contributions on the beam or off tangent?
   3. Did contributions indicate that those who made them were listening carefully to what others in the group had to say?
   4. Were contributions factual and problem-centered, or were the contributors unable to rise above their preconceived notions and emotionally held points of view?

B. *Contributions of special members of the group*
   1. How well did special members serve the group?

[16] Reprinted from "Feedback and Group Self-Evaluation," by David H. Jenkins, *Journal of Social Issues* (Spring, 1948), pp. 54-55, by permission of *Journal of Social Issues*.

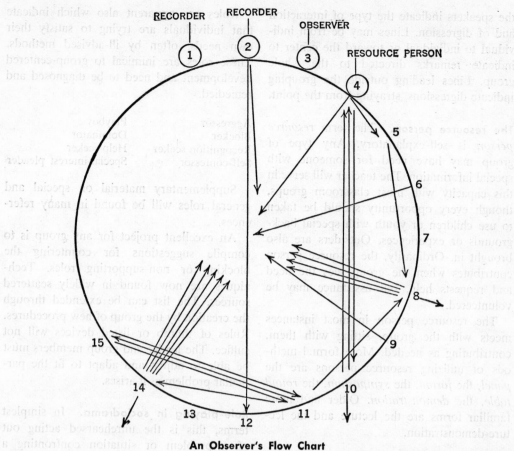

An Observer's Flow Chart

This represents the third quarter-hour of a one-hour discussion. The sample is given because the lines for an hour become too congested. This group had no chairman. Two recorders were necessary to catch all action. The resource person entered the discussion, twice to comment to individuals, once to the group as a whole, and was twice called upon. The resource person was not called on during the first half hour. The recorder gave one student information, evidently voluntarily and once threw in advice for the group. Two students said nothing, and only three were off the point. The majority of contributions were to the whole group, showing good interaction. Interchanges between two persons are also shown.

a. Leader?
b. Recorder? (may ask for clarification at times which in turn helps the group)
c. Resource person?

End-of-Meeting Suggestion Slip[17]

What did you think of this meeting? Please be frank. Your comments can contribute a great deal to the success of our meetings.

[17] *Ibid.*, p. 56.

1. How did you feel about this meeting? (check)
   No good ( ) Mediocre ( )
   All right ( ) Good ( ) Excellent ( )
2. What were the weaknesses?
3. What were the strong points?
4. What improvements would you suggest?

The illustration above is called a "flow chart," since it shows the flow and direction of discussion. Lines drawn from the speakers indicate the type of interaction and of digression. Lines may be from individual to individual or toward the center to indicate remarks directed to the whole group. Lines leading outside the grouping indicate digressions, straying from the point.

The resource person. The term *resource person* is self-explanatory. Any type of group may have need for someone with special information. The teacher will serve in this capacity with most classroom groups, though every opportunity should be taken to use children or youth with special backgrounds or experiences. Outsiders are also brought in. Ordinarily, the resource person contributes when the group sees the need and requests help, but assistance may be volunteered.

The resource person in most instances meets with the group, sitting with them, contributing as needed. More formal methods of utilizing resource persons are the *panel,* the *forum,* the *symposium,* the *round table,* the *demonstration.* Older and more familiar forms are the lecture and the lecture-demonstration.

General roles played by members. From time to time all members of a group play brief roles as they contribute, ask questions, or object. Several writers in the field have identified groupings of these roles which cannot be elaborated in detail here. The titles are mostly self-explanatory.

Roles which facilitate and co-ordinate group activities are:

Initiator-contributor	Elaborator
Information seeker	Co-ordinator
Opinion seeker	Orienter
Information giver	Evaluator-critic
Opinion giver	Energizer
Procedural technician	

Roles which build up group attitudes and encourage group morale include:

Encourager	Expediter
Harmonizer	Standard setter
Compromiser	Follower

Roles are apparent also which indicate that individuals are trying to satisfy their own needs, often by ill-advised methods. These roles are inimical to group-centered development and need to be diagnosed and remedied.

Aggressor	Playboy
Blocker	Dominator
Recognition seeker	Help-seeker
Self-confessor	Special-interest pleader

Supplementary material on special and general roles will be found in many references.

An excellent project for any group is to compile suggestions for countering the blocking or non-supporting roles. Techniques are now found in widely scattered sources. The list can be extended through the creation by the group of new procedures. Rules of thumb or listed devices will not suffice. The leader and group members must be able to adjust and adapt to fit the particular problem as it arises.

Role-playing in sociodrama. In simplest terms, this is the unrehearsed acting out of a problem or situation confronting a group. Spontaneous drama and discussion are natural outlets for tension, natural methods of disseminating views and of informing one's self.

The sociodrama can be used by teachers at all levels. Several members of the group enact a scene in the presence of the whole group. The scene may deal with real problems of human relation within the class or with any materials being studied which permit different interpretations. Social studies, history, and literature provide many opportunities, as does unit teaching on any level.

By virtue of the sociodrama, skill in the democratic process is improved. Communication is speeded. More important, however, individuals gain greater insights into their own beliefs, tensions, honest convictions, and prejudices. Greater understanding of other persons results. Real attitudes and values are revealed. The analysis of difficulties in group thinking is enhanced. Roles may be reversed for a second playing. The audience is invited to participate and make suggestions both during the scene and after.

Spontaneity is the essence; hence there should be no rehearsal. The actors should have a brief period together for planning the general setting, line of development, and views to be expressed. The discussion following the scene is thought by many to be the most valuable part of this technique. (The typical dramatization of plays is still valuable in school but for other reasons. A planned sequence, a script, and rehearsal are in order with dramatization.)

The general procedure [18] is as follows:

A. *Demonstrating a sociodrama for a new group*
   1. Select a simple, illustrative situation that will be fun and meaningful.
   2. Select a volunteer cast.
   3. Arrange the scene, using a few simple props if necessary.
   4. Inform the cast about the scene and what is to be done.
   5. Develop and enact the scene. As it progresses, the director may secretly suggest to one of the cast a problem which will encourage argument or discussion.
   6. Encourage audience participation by stopping the scene from time to time to get new ideas.
   7. Try out new ideas. The actors may be asked to try out suggested ideas of members of the audience. Members of the audience may be asked to replace members of the cast for that purpose.
   8. Reverse roles. Members of the cast may be asked to exchange roles to increase opportunity and variety of participation.
   9. Discuss the scene after it is concluded. The director asks questions regarding the subject of the scene, the

problems presented, and the solutions suggested.
   10. Limit the demonstration to ten or fifteen minutes.

B. *Performing a real-life situation*
   1. Select a scene which is related more directly to the kinds of problem situations this group has encountered.
   2. Decide roles. The director may ask the audience to help in selecting the roles and indicating how they should be played.

Extensive materials on the sociodrama are available in many sources. Volumes already cited in this chapter contain discussions. Additional references are:

HAAS, Robert B., ed., *Psychodrama and Sociodrama in American Education* (New York, Beacon House, 1949).
MORENO, J. L., *Who Shall Survive?* (New York, Beacon House, 1934). The early classic in the field; covers many aspects of sociometry.
——, *Psychodrama*, Vol. I (New York, Beacon House, 1946). Descriptions of typical life situations, reactions of role players, instructions to players, etc.
SHOOBS, Nahum E., *Psychodrama in the Schools*, Psychodrama Monographs, No. 10 (New York, Beacon House, 1944).
Note other Psychodrama Monographs, also the magazines *Sociometry*, *Sociatry*, and any others dealing with human relations or personnel problems whether in school or in industry.

Psychotherapy in the classroom. Discussions of therapy through everyday teaching and of relationships between therapy and teaching are increasing in the literature for teachers. A number of the principles of teaching stressed throughout this volume are equally valuable as principles of therapy. Teachers can greatly aid learners of all ages to live normal, happy, adjusted lives, and to overcome fears, frustrations, and tensions as they arise. The preventive and remedial effects of these sample principles are obvious:

1. Teachers understand and accept the concept of the whole child. The child's mind, body,

[18] Hilda Kozman, ed., *Group Process in Physical Education* (New York, Harper, 1951), pp. 206-207.

and emotions and the relationships between them are a normal concern of the teacher.

2. Teachers accept and treat all children and youth as individuals with unique potentialities for development, who are capable of eventually and progressively taking over direction of their own lives.

3. Teachers accept each individual as he is, alert or dull, bright or stupid, clean or dirty, co-operative or resistive, energetic or lazy, orderly and workmanlike, or disorderly and slovenly.

4. Teachers treat individuals with respect, sympathy, and with sensitivity to the inner life and feelings as expressed by the child.

5. Teachers are properly permissive and properly firm, and always kindly, warm, and outgoing.

All the facts are not yet in, but it seems clear that normal, happy, integrating individuals are those whose inner drives and basic desires are not in conflict with reality and with the necessity for purposeful, controlled behavior. The person with inner frustrations and tensions may be mildly disturbed or seriously neurotic. Disturbed human relations, feelings of isolation and insecurity, belief in the hostility of others result in defensive behavior, aggression, withdrawal, or some substitutive reaction.

Organized therapeutic treatment by trained personnel is not our concern here. The classroom teacher in his everyday teaching can have, however, marked effects for good or ill on the life of the learner.

The use of group methods just outlined provides excellent opportunity for therapy. Co-operation, free discussion, mutual aid and affection, the opportunity to make personal contribution to group effort with accompanying recognition, all give security, "belongingness," and confidence. Feelings may be expressed; obstacles resulting in tension and frustration may be openly expressed and examined. The individual gains insight and courage to attack his own personal difficulties positively. The defense mechanisms once used no longer are necessary.

All the methods for arriving at a knowledge of the individual, outlined in the following chapter (particularly the projective techniques), aid in individualizing teaching; hence aid in therapy. The whole structure of unit teaching, presented later, gives opportunity for all types of children and all levels of ability to make their contribution to group effort. The permissive attitude of teachers will encourage self-direction and assumption of initiative and responsibility. The sympathetic guidance of the teacher will protect the child from too early assumption of too great responsibilities, from humiliating and destructive experiences.

The individual devices of autobiography writing, the guess-who test, everyday play, doll or puppet play, expression of fantasy, and many others are all valuable therapeutic as well as pedagogical devices.

The freedom to choose one's companions (sociometric grouping), to change membership or be reassigned, to choose one's free reading material, one's project, or part in a group project, are all aids to tranquillity. Children often seek through reading answers to problems which worry them and on which little adult guidance is given. Sex development and bodily changes, where babies come from, personal problems of grooming and of dating, are illustrations.

This topic, vital as it is, cannot be treated at greater length in a general volume. Students will doubtless have further contact with it in courses in child study and in adolescent psychology. The periodical literature is packed with current materials. Supplementary readings are found in these references and particularly in the bibliographies they contain:

AXLINE, Virginia M., *Play Therapy* (Boston, Houghton, 1947).

FOREST, Ilse, *Early Years at School* (New York, McGraw, 1949). Use Index.

KOZMAN, Hilda C., ed., *Group Process in Physical Education* (New York, Harper, 1951), pp. 182-186.

OLSON, Willard C., *Child Development* (Boston, Heath, 1949), Ch. 11. Excellent bibliography.

ROGERS, Carl H., *Counseling and Psycho-therapy* (Boston, Houghton, 1942).

SYMONDS, Percival M., *The Dynamics of Human Adjustment* (New York, Appleton-Century-Crofts, 1946). Use Index.

WERNER, Wolff, *The Personality of the Pre-School Child: The Child's Search for His Self* (New York, Grune and Stratton, 1946).

DISCUSSION QUESTIONS

The class is assumed to be reasonably well informed from the readings about:

The general nature of group process, its philosophy, psychology, and purposes.

The appropriate occasions and problems on which it may be used.

The typical procedures and how structured.

The kinds of groups which may be formed: by purpose; by level of maturity and background; others.

The major roles with responsibilities, the supporting member roles, the nonsupporting roles.

The general principles governing the operation of group processes.

The methods of arriving at decisions, of keeping discussion and thinking moving along, of avoiding impasses, of carrying decisions into action.

The necessary and desirable physical arrangements.

The values and limitations, facilitating factors and obstacles, advantages and disadvantages.

The author has found that it is absolutely essential that class members do have preliminary understanding, even if limited, of the foregoing. To proceed without understanding is to invite pointless, rambling discussion, annoyance, and eventually antagonism to group process.

Instructors may make direct inquiry to determine background. Another device is to use here, in a preliminary way, Exercise No. 3 on page 214. Still another approach is, after reading the chapter, to consider the discussions through which the preceding seven chapters have been analyzed. Alert classes can recognize and comment upon much of group process in their own experience.

Two other things are also essential. Students must have clear understanding of (1) the differences between an area, a topic, a question, a problem; and (2) the difference between the solution of a problem through group attack and the study of an area or topic—the acquisition

of subject-matter background through systematic instruction.

Students should ask questions before proceeding if any of the above is not reasonably clear.

1. The following questions, in addition, have been raised by many class groups:

How is group process initiated?

Is group process worth the time it takes? Might this differ with the types of problem, level of maturity, and background of experience of the group?

What should a group do with "unreconstructed rebels," that is, individuals who flatly refuse to participate?

Does group process in school administration, supervision, and curriculum development indicate lay participation?

What are the rights and duties of minorities in group discussion, in arriving at decisions, and after decisions have been accepted?

How do we preserve the security of the individual as he moves over into new and strange processes; that is, eliminate fear of the new or of personal discomfiture?

Will groups (children or adults) learn best by participating in group processes; by a preview and discussion of principles and techniques; or by demonstrations?

Is a group decision *always* the best decision? Why or why not? What is meant by *best* decision?

Can group process be forced upon the group?

2. Another good method of introduction is afforded by oral reports from any students in the class who might have had previous experience with group process in any of its forms.

3. A third method of introduction is through demonstration of certain procedures:

Sociodrama   Symposium
Panel   Round table
Forum   Group discussion

EXERCISES

The questions accompanying the chapters in this volume are, with a very few exceptions, problematic in nature. Interpretations or applications to hypothetical situations are required. Group discussion is therefore the desired method. Real problems are often brought in as discussion proceeds, particularly by experienced teachers.

The hypothetical and real problems often lead to more elaborate treatment, thus involving other group methods from planning to sociodrama.

(The text is not designed to be handled by typical recitation methods [repetition of content] and should not be so handled. Classes lacking sufficient background may need to acquire content, but if so, the situation should then be handled as systematic instruction for this purpose. Group attack on problems must then wait until sufficient background and experience in the field have been achieved.)

1. The class discussions may be used, when facility has developed, to illustrate the making of flow charts, to give practice for observers, recorders, leaders, resource persons.

2. The class may be divided, one half acting as observers, to note and report upon the ways the responsible roles were played and the number and effectiveness of member roles which appeared. Critical analyses should be participated in by the whole group.

3. A valuable exercise for all levels of students is to list the actions which should characterize the procedures of the leaders, recorders, observers, and resource persons. Textbooks and articles give good lists in general terms, but few give the actual processes, for instance, of keeping the discussion on the point, of avoiding or overcoming an impasse, of controlling trouble-makers, of moving toward a partial summary.

4. A group of experienced teachers who bring in a real problem from the field which warrants extended treatment may manage it as a group project. All the phases of group planning, discussion, committee work, sharing information and experience will enter. Use can be made as justified of the sociodrama, the panel, the forum, the symposium, the round table, the demonstration.

The instructor may be assigned the role of observer or resource person. With inexperienced groups attempting a project, the instructor may well act as leader for one or two meetings, though it is better if group members can assume leadership from the beginning. (A few advanced classes have, on occasion, taken over part of the course and managed it on their own.)

5. Students observing experienced teachers may report upon the social climate of the classroom, giving key characteristics and reasons for desirable and undesirable climate, high or low morale. Make similar report on any aspects of group process observed. (Protect teachers at all times by refraining from the use of names.) Experienced teachers may report their own problems, difficulties, or successes, for discussion and analysis.

6. Report any periodical articles dealing with experimental studies of social climate, extending the list in this chapter.

7. The instructor will need to judge how far a general course can go into the matter of therapy in the classroom. Other courses will, in many institutions, give further detail. Reports may be selected, if time permits, from such areas as:

The dominative or integrative behaviors of children.

The effect of the teacher's personality on classroom behavior.

The carry-over effect on classroom behavior from the home.

Causes of frustration and aggression; methods of alleviating the conditions; the same for fears and fantasies.

Summary of conditions making for desirable social behavior.

Summary of some studies of personality patterns.

The rejected child; the popular child; the aggressive child; the recessive child; others.

The use of any of the projective techniques (next chapter) for therapeutic purposes.

A report may be made on psychiatry and the classroom teacher if there is interest.

(The list could be extended indefinitely. Students and teachers will find enormous amounts of material. If interest develops in advanced discussion of psychotherapy, students may review and make quick summaries from such sources as Frank, Lewin, Myrdal, Freud, Adler, Jung, Horney, and from writers on mental hygiene generally.)

8. The class should make extensive study and set up detailed lists of the characteristics of the socialized personality. The same thing may be done for behaviors characteristic of the unsocial, or antisocial individual.

READINGS

The extensive bibliography on this general subject would be unduly cumbersome if given in one list; hence it has been distributed by major topics through the chapter.

WRITTEN

Read and analyze discussions of the three levels of democracy (talk-democracy; consent-democracy; do-democracy) until you are reasonably familiar with the meaning, characteristics, and particularly with the consequences of each.

Report orally or make written summary of the appearance of each in your everyday life. Look at social gatherings, local governmental affairs, church management, club management, or any other group to which you belong or can observe. Note also assumptions concerning this which lie behind editorials, commentators' columns, speeches, sermons, and so on.

Write a brief, compact paper based on a series of classroom observations showing the prevalence of any or all of the levels of democracy listed above. Experienced teachers may write their contacts and conclusions since ordinarily they will not be in a position to observe.

Note. The situation indicated in Question 4, a real problem brought in and developed in some detail by group process, may occur with any of the areas treated in this textbook. Group process may be used at any time during the course when such a problem emerges and is of sufficient reality to the group.

CHAPTER 10: Knowing the Pupil as an Individual and as a Group Member

1: SECURING INFORMATION.

Competent teachers know that to teach anyone, in other words, to stimulate him to learn, one must know and understand him. One must understand him, furthermore, as he sees himself, as he sees his social and physical world. As we said earlier, learners learn what they need and can use. One does not stop, however, with the learner's naïve limited needs but aids him to see needs beyond the immediate situation. Adequate data can be compiled on all students, if funds and staff are available, although it may not always be possible to use the data if the classes are very large and the teachers overworked.

Goals cannot be set nor teaching procedures organized without accurate knowledge of pupil needs, abilities, ambitions, interests, rates of maturation, previous school and life experience, health, general home and cultural background, and many other phases of the pupils' lives. Learning difficulties, behavior problems, and personality maladjustments cannot be diagnosed and remedied without accurate information about the past experiences of the pupils involved, their abilities,

and their temperaments. Evaluations of achievement cannot be attempted without the guidance which comes from analysis of background information. Educational and vocational guidance must be mere guesswork in the absence of comprehensive data about the individual. All these types of data are necessary for normal and average children as well as for the subnormal, the problem cases, and other special cases.

The traditional school often naïvely ignored all this. A few dishonest or lazy teachers still defiantly refuse to base their teaching upon the nature of the learner, thus effectually sabotaging learning. Even many recently trained teachers are often unaware of important facts concerning their pupils. One study showed that one-fourth of the teachers queried knew approximately one-fourth of the information deemed necessary. In some instances teachers are far too overworked to make adequate studies of their pupils. In the absence of central cumulative records these teachers can do little.

A large number of instruments and techniques have evolved for securing continuous and voluminous information about the learner.

Permanent cumulative-record systems.

School systems are increasingly using cumulative-record systems which include many varied types of information. The systems vary from simple 3 x 5 cards with as few as eight items to extensive folders (10 x 16) with several cards which include many items. One card lists 117 types of information. The average number is between forty and forty-five. The total number of subpoints runs well into the hundreds. An analysis of several cards reveals that certain major categories occur rather consistently.

Personal data, name, birth date, race or nationality, sex, address, name of parent or guardian, date of original entrance to school.
Scholarship (school marks), achievement-test scores, intelligence rating, social and character-trait ratings, emotional stability, social maturity, health, special abilities and disabilities, aptitudes, extracurricular interests and activities, scholastic honors or prizes, punishments.
School progress.
Attendance, entrance, and withdrawals with changes of residence.
Home conditions and family history.
Vocational and educational plans.
College or vocation entered upon leaving school.
Out-of-school employment.
Photograph.
Space for notes.

Scores of cumulative-record systems are in use and available for inspection. Many state and city school systems have developed cards of their own. Commercial publishing houses issue others. Various teachers' associations have contributed cards. The majority naturally reflect the traditional school but with clear evidence of modern developments.

Diederich [1] proposed a number of other categories which should be included. The years which have passed have increased the importance of his categories. Details are omitted here.

[1] Paul B. Diederich, "Evaluation Records," *Educational Method,* Vol. 15 (May, 1936), pp. 432-440.

1. *Personal pattern of goals.* These are to be written and evaluated from time to time by the learner.
2. *Records of significant experiences.*
3. *Reading records.* Free reading, to be interpreted in terms of maturity of learner, type and quantity of materials.
4. *Records of cultural experiences.*
5. *Records of creative expression.* This has become of great importance today—long after Diederich's first listing.
6. *Anecdotal records of pupils.*
7. *Records of conferences.*
8. *Records of excuses and explanations.*
9. *Records of tests and examinations,* with an interpretation by the teacher.
10. *Health and family history.*
11. *Oral English diagnosis.* A diagnosis of the pupil's pronunciation, enunciation, quality of voice, diction, usage, force, etc., without knowledge of pupil; to be used in subsequent work.
12. *Minutes of student affairs.*
13. *Personality ratings and descriptions.*
14. *Questionnaires.* These include all interest and personal questionnaires pupils are asked to fill in. They should be interpreted and filed in the pupil's folder.
15. *Records of courses and activities.*
16. *Administrative records.*

The nature of the information recorded.

Many of the categories in the cards used by various school systems are self-explanatory, whereas in others interpretations differ from system to system. *School marks* may be recorded by subjects, by divisions within subjects, by broad fields, or in terms of understandings, appreciations, and the like derived from the subject. They may be entered quarterly, semestrally, annually, or at irregular periods; in percentages, by letters, descriptive terms, paragraph descriptions, or statistical indexes. *Achievement-test-information* usually includes, in addition to the score, the name of the test, the form, and the date on which the score was made. Some records include extensive data giving norms for ages and grades, percentile ranks, and the like. Many record the relation of achievement score to intelligence rating. A few include profile or graphic representation.

Social and character-trait ratings are usually in the form of judgments expressed in terms of a rating scale or check list which is either included in the card or used separately with only the result noted. One hundred different traits, approximately, appear once or more in the widely used cards, though a single card rarely includes more than eight or ten. The average is four or five. There is little uniformity or agreement among cards on this item. The trait names are often misleading because of overlap between synonymous terms and confusion between traits and symptoms. Investigations show, however, that trained raters using clearly defined terms will agree sufficiently to produce ratings of value in diagnosis and guidance. Ratings of emotional stability and social maturity are not yet common but are clearly increasing.

The health records contain similar items from card to card though the amount of information and the method of recording vary greatly. Teachers should be trained to recognize the common symptoms of everyday illnesses and to detect physical abnormalities. Rogers recommends that the following be included on the record: [2]

[2] J. F. Rogers, *What Every Teacher Should Know about the Physical Condition of Her Pupils,* U.S. Office of Education Pamphlet, No. 68.
Other references of value include:
Health in Schools, Twentieth Yearbook of American Association of School Administrators, rev. ed. (Washington, D. C., N. E. A., 1951).
Ben W. Miller, "A Critical Evaluation of the Effectiveness of the Teacher in the Physical Inspection of Public School Children," *Research Quarterly,* Vol. 14 (May, 1943), pp. 131-143. Watch for similar summaries currently.
D. B. Nyswander, *Solving School Health Problems* (New York, The Commonwealth Fund, 1942).
Delbert Oberteuffer, *School Health Education* (New York, Harper, 1949).
George M. Wheatley, *What Teachers See* (New York, Metropolitan Life Insurance Co., 1948).
———— and Grace T. Hallock, *Health Observation of School Children* (New York, McGraw, 1951).
In addition watch publications of various committees, the periodicals dealing with health, and particularly the more general periodical literature.
The very large literature on vision and hearing testing is not sampled, but interested students can find it easily.

Has had: Measles; scarlatina; diphtheria; whooping cough; mumps; frequent sore throat; rheumatism; earache; running ear; frequent colds; dyspepsia; epilepsy.

Has now: Chronic cough; headache; blurred vision; impaired hearing; bad breath.

Habits: Sleeps 6—7—8—9—10 hours; windows closed. Uses coffee; tea; tobacco; candy between meals. Bowels irregular. Plays in open air 1—2—3—4 hours. Works 1—2—3—4 hours after school. Does not wear overshoes in wet weather.

Home conditions: Poor; bad. Food inadequate. No breakfast.

Physical defects:
General appearance: Thin; obese; poor color; listless; drooping.
Height . . . . Weight . . . .
Nervous symptoms: Speech defect; tic; excitable; dull.
Face: Unclean; pallor; cyanosis; skin disease; other.
Hair: Pediculosis; ringworm; favus; unclean.
Eyes: Headache; errors in reading; book too close; congested lids; crusted lids; stye; inflamed; letter test RE—LE; with glasses RE—LE.
Ears: Discharge; audiometer, voice, or watch test: right ear; left ear.
Nose: Discharge; obstruction.
Throat: Inflamed; tonsils diseased; obstructive.
Teeth: Decayed permanent; need adjustment; diseased gums; unclean.
Neck: Lymph glands visible; easily palpable; goiter.
Chest: Asymmetrical; expansion poor; expansion unequal.
Heart: Enlarged; irregular; rapid; shortness of breath on exertion.
Abdomen: Hernia.
Back: Scoliosis; rotation of spine; stoop; hunchback.
Upper extremities: Unvaccinated; hands cold; cyanotic; skin disease (scabies, ringworm, other).
Lower extremities: Clubbed; shoe deformities; turned inward.
Clothing: Insufficient; too much; ill-kept.
Shoes: Ill-fitting.

Summary of correctible conditions . . . .

. . . .

Recommendations of physician: . . . .

Parents informed: ....

Treatment: ....

Results of treatment: ....

Schools are increasingly employing nurses wherever units are large enough. The teacher in these cases needs to refer cases rather than to act on her own. In any event teachers should note such things as:

Continued sneezing, coughing, sniffling.
Undue flushing or undue pallor.
Red, watery eyes.
Running nose and/or sore throat.
Fever.
Nausea, diarrhea.
Unusual rash or skin eruptions.
Dizziness.
Others could be listed.

Special abilities, disabilities, or aptitudes are recorded in the form of scores, exhibits of work done, or teacher comments based upon observation. Extracurricular interests are usually indicated by records of participation, office held, honors won. Distinction is often made among intellectual, social, athletic, cultural, and hobby activities. Students' accounts of their own special interests are sometimes included. These may be answers to questionnaires or original paragraphs composed by the pupil. School progress is shown by age-grade progress records, regular or irregular promotions, grades repeated.

Home conditions and family history usually include:

1. Occupation of (*a*) father and (*b*) mother.
2. Number of brothers and sisters.
3. Nationality of parents.
4. Education of (*a*) father and (*b*) mother.
5. Place of residence: with mother, father, uncle, aunt, grandparents, brother, sister, guardian, alone, married, or in institution.
6. Marital status of parents: (*a*) divorced, (*b*) separated, (*c*) remarried—father, (*b*) remarried—mother.
7. Citizenship of parents.
8. Ability of parents to read or write English.
9. Race of (*a*) father and (*b*) mother.
10. Religion of (*a*) father and (*b*) mother.

11. Health of (*a*) father and (*b*) mother.
12. Home surroundings, rating of.
13. Home atmosphere, rating of.
14. Neighborhood, rating of.
15. Associates, rating of.
16. Amusements.
17. Use of leisure hours.

Home and neighborhood ratings involve the use of fairly complicated social-rating cards which enquire into all manner of material and cultural factors which are significant for health and learning. An earlier chapter noted the influence of home, neighborhood, and social class on life and learning. A number of cards are available which rate total home background and selected items within the home or within the neighborhood. These can be located in some texts on measurements, in yearbooks, in catalogues of measuring instruments.

All formal and informal instruments of evaluation, diagnosis, and marking supply data. The score or more of instruments and techniques described here and in Chapters 20 and 21 all supply data for the cumulative record or may be used by the teacher to secure the data. Tests, formal and informal, examinations, check lists, scales, codes, diaries and logs, behavior records, diagnostic instruments, interviews, inventories, time samples, exhibits, and marks are all useful.

Direct inquiry may be made by teachers. Specific and more detailed information must often be secured by individual teachers direct from the pupils. A large number of methods are available.

Projective techniques. Projective techniques cause the pupil to express or "project" his interests, desires, attitudes, or views. Certain of the devices are innocent-appearing but are devised to bring to light personal data. Attitudes and overt actions on the part of some pupils may often be understood in the light of the highly subjective data obtained by these devices. Attitudes, interests, and views unknown to teachers and to pupils themselves are often brought to light.

Pupil autobiographies are widely used and are often very significant. With little children, guidance can be given without interpreting the resulting story. [3]

Everybody has a story. When you look at a person, you learn part of his story.

Look at the people at the top of this page. The pictures tell you part of their story. If they could talk, they would tell you much more.

Everybody has a story. We like to tell our stories to other people.

Perhaps you have heard your father say, "When I was little. . . ." Then he tells his story.

Your Own Story

You have a story too. Your friends are in your story. Your good times are a part of it. Even your pets may be a part of your story. You can write your own story in words and pictures. Other people will want to read it. You will have fun writing it.

Then a number of paragraphs are given containing general hints and guides, but allowing freedom of expression to the child:

How to begin your story
These are my friends
My favorite sports
These are my hobbies
This is my favorite animal
Other things I like best
Things I like to read
My trips and travels
More about me
The time I had the most fun in my life

A direct approach may be made with older children.

Free compositions on topics chosen by the children are excellent devices for securing insight into the experiences and nature of the learner. Often compositions may be suggested which give *reasons for liking* books read, movies seen, games chosen, and the

[3] *Young America Readers* (October 13, 1949). Used with permission of Young America Magazines, Silver Spring, Md.

like. *Requests to tell what studies* should be added to the curriculum, which dropped, or *plans for future study* are useful. *Drawing, painting, finger-painting, making things,* and the *choice of voluntary projects* all aid in revealing the personality.

A *story or poem may be read* to the class, which is then asked to *explain, interpret,* or *otherwise comment.* A story may be read but not completed, and the students asked to *write out their ideas of a suitable ending. Pictures may be used in the same way:* complete ones to be interpreted, incomplete representations to be filled out.

Doll play, especially with younger children, is very revealing. Feelings and attitudes appear which the child would never dare express openly.

Fantasy serves much the same purpose. Imaginative stories made up by children should be carefully regarded as imaginative by both teacher and children. Important revelations usually appear.

Dramatic play has been used for a long time. *Role-playing* is a comparatively recent addition to the list.

Two technical procedures, the *Rorschach Technique* [4] and the *Thematic Apperception Test,* demand special acquaintance and are not often used by classroom teachers. A number of research studies concerning them are available.

The seven or eight projective techniques noted, exclusive of the Rorschach Technique and the Thematic Apperception Test, are simple and suited to everyday use. These are a tiny sampling of the large range available, both simple and highly specialized. Instructors and students especially interested in projective techniques may consult the 700-page volume by Harold H. Anderson and

[4] Bruno Klopfer, Douglas M. Kelley, and Nolan D. C. Lewis, *The Rorschach Technique: A Manual for a Projective Method of Personality Diagnosis* (Yonkers, N. Y., World Book, 1944). Advanced technical discussion for professional workers in personality problems. Teachers can examine briefly for general information concerning a technical procedure.

Gladys L. Anderson, *An Introduction to Projective Techniques,* published by Prentice-Hall in 1951.

Inventories and questionnaires. *Pupil interests, problems, fears, and ambitions* may be discovered through direct listing by the child or through a prepared questionnaire. Sometimes needs and problems are included in the same questionnaire, or they may be listed separately. Schorling suggests the following compact list for preliminary inquiry.[5]

Questionnaire on Interests and Needs of Pupils in Junior and Senior High Schools

Directions: In order to be of more help to boys and girls, we are trying to find out some of the things that interest them, some of the things that trouble them, and some of the things that they want to know more about.

Will you assist us by thinking very seriously about a few questions and by answering them carefully?

You need not sign your name, so do not be afraid to write whatever is in your mind.

School ....

Grade .... Age .... Sex ....

Senior high school course ....

Part I

1. What are some of the things that you like about school? (Underline the one thing that you like best.)
2. What are some of the things that you dislike about school? (Underline the one thing that you dislike most.)
3. Which subjects in school do you think will do you the most good?
4. Which subjects do you think will do you the least good?
5. What would you like to have taught in your grade (or school) that is not taught now?
6. What other help or information which you are not now receiving would you like to receive in school?
7. In what ways do you think that your classwork could be made more interesting?

[5] Raleigh Schorling, *Student Teaching,* rev. ed. (New York, McGraw, 1949), pp. 406-407.

8. Think about the teachers you have had in school and name some things about teachers that you have liked. (Do not name teachers.)
9. Think about the teachers you have had in school and name some things about them that you have not liked. (Do not name teachers.)
10. How much time do you spend in study each day outside of school?
11. To what clubs or organizations do you now belong? in school? outside of school?
12. Do you attend church? Sunday school?
13. What club, social, or leisure-time activities do you wish your school would provide?
14. What social activities do you wish the community would provide?
15. What other opportunities do you wish the community would provide?

Part II

(Give Part I and Part II on different days.)

School ....

Grade .... Age .... Sex ....

Senior high school course ....

1. In what particular thing are you most interested?
2. What things do you most enjoy during your spare time?
3. What magazines do you read?
4. What kinds of books do you like best?
5. What kinds of news do you read in the the daily newspaper?
6. How often do you attend movies?
7. What is your favorite radio program?
8. What means of recreation do you have: at home? in your neighborhood?
9. Write down some of the things that trouble and worry you about:
   a. school?
   b. home?
   c. your health and appearance?
   d. personal traits, habits, feelings?
   e. boy-and-girl relationships?
   f. getting along with others?
   g. your vocation (your future work)?
   h. money matters?
   i. religion, death?
   j. other things?

   (Go back and underline the one thing that worries you most.)

10. Do you have a regular allowance? What kinds of things do you buy with it?
11. When you have a personal problem, to whom do you go most often?
12. What do you consider your strong points to be?
13. What do you consider your weak points to be?
14. Are you having an opportunity to develop your talents? (If not, why are you not?)
15. What work besides school work do you do outside of school?

Other well-known inventories will illustrate the type and range available:

Kuder Preference Record, Science Research Associates, 57 West Grand Avenue, Chicago 10, Ill., 1956.
Vocational Interest Blank for Men, revised (Strong), Stanford Univ. Press, Stanford, Cal., 1938. (Others by Strong available.)
Haggerty-Olson-Wickman Behavior Rating Scales, Harcourt, Brace & World, 750 Third Avenue, New York 17, N. Y., 1930.
Mooney Problem Check List, Psychological Corporation, 522 Fifth Avenue, New York, 1950.
Manual for SRA Junior Inventory, Form S, 2nd ed., Science Research Associates, 1957.

Personality, character, and attitude tests are numerous though there is considerable argument about their validity. The good ones are nevertheless very useful. A very brief sampling:

Adjustment Inventory (Bell), Stanford Univ. Press.
California Test of Personality, forms for kindergarten to adult level, California Test Bureau, Hollywood, Cal.
School Inventory (Bell), Stanford Univ. Press.
Guilford-Zimmerman Temperament Survey, Sheridan Supply Co., Beverly Hills, Cal.
Life Adjustment Inventory (Wrightstone-Doll), Acorn Publishing Co., 9-13 Front Street, Rockville Centre, N. Y.
Minnesota Multiphasic Personality Inventory, Psychological Corporation.
Personality Inventory (Bernreuter), Stanford Univ. Press.

Many more can be found in the appropriate listings in any of Buros Yearbooks.

The individual as a member of a social group. The reaction against the traditional lockstep school inaugurated a period of great emphasis upon the individual child. This was highly desirable as a corrective to early mass education. Emphasis upon the unique nature of the individual and upon individual differences must not blind us, however, to the importance of knowing about the pupil as a social being, as a member of a group. Many problems cannot be solved by data, no matter how extensive, about the individual as an individual. Information about reactions within different types of groups is needed.

Social climate is important in the setting for learning. The younger, better-trained teachers and older ones who have kept up realize the vital importance of the social and emotional climate in the classroom. A large number of teachers still, however, make two serious errors when they say that (*a*) social climate is no concern of theirs, and (*b*) social climate is the same for all children within a given room. The statements are more than wrong; they are absurd.

The importance of group-behavior factors has been clearly suggested in the chapters on evaluation and diagnosis, particularly the latter. Many a peculiar piece of conduct, many a success or failure, many problem cases are explained not by strictly individual data but by data about the individual-in-a-group. Huge amounts of data will be secured when the instruments already discussed under the headings of evaluation and diagnosis are used. Still other types of information will be obtained by using the devices suggested in this chapter. The teacher will be chiefly concerned, usually, with social behavior within the classroom. English and Raimy, [6] who have provided one of the best discussions of social development, suggest the following questions:

1. *Is he accepted by other children?* By all

[6] Horace B. English and Victor Raimy, *Studying the Individual School Child* (New York, Holt, 1941), p. 65.

of his classmates or just a few? How warmly do you think he is accepted or liked? Does he have a few particularly good friends? Does he have a few or many "enemies"? If rejected, is he rejected by both sexes or just by one? On what do you base your answer?

2. *How much does he participate: (a)* in recitation or other formal schoolroom activities? *(b)* in the more social activities such as playing games or talking to a neighbor? Does he seem to participate more than the average child in both *(a)* and *(b)* or less? Your evidence? If he withdraws, is it from particular children or from all? from some activities or all? from the teacher?

3. *Does he come into conflict with the rules of the class?* With the habits and customs of the other children? occasionally? frequently?

4. *Does he seem to have a feeling of responsibility to the group?* to certain children or to the whole class? When things go wrong with another child, does he try to help? Does he defend class standards or does he defend wrongdoers? Does he defend wrongdoers if they are particular friends?

5. *Does he usually seem to be co-operating in social activities or competing?*

6. *What is his relationship to the teacher?* Does he seem to like her and does she seem to like him? Is he docile and compliant? take her for granted? seem to be stimulated by her? Is he made ill at ease and self-conscious when she pays attention to him? Is he encouraged by her praise? How does he take rebukes she administers to him?

These general questions can be asked about every child. Many other aspects of social behavior may be important in describing the social adjustment of the particular child you are studying. The kind of clothes worn may have marked influence, for instance. You are specifically cautioned, therefore, not to limit your statements to these questions.

Social growth and social behavior, like all other aspects of growth and behavior, are relative to the situations in which they develop. Some children conduct themselves when with older and larger children in a manner which they never use when with younger and smaller children. Some boys are intelligent, competent leaders on the playground but are shy and retiring, even unco-operative, in the classroom. The place of a child in the family (youngest, oldest, in the middle) and his size in relation to the children of the neighborhood affect his behavior. The presence in a given classroom of a football hero or of the most beautiful girl in school has a definite effect upon the patterns of behavior which develop in that room. The removal of either of these individuals changes the behavior of all other pupils. The same thing is true of the presence or absence of a known brilliant student, of an unusually slow or stupid individual, or of certain minority groups.

How does a child act with his brothers and sisters, with parents, with other adults, with teachers, with older or younger groups of children, with children in the classroom and on the school grounds, at a picnic, in the neighborhood? How do children react to the separation of parents? How do they react to and with wealthier or poorer adults or children; to and with children of different color, race or nationality, religion?

We may ask, finally, why pupils act one way with one teacher, but quite differently with another? Do teachers treat all children alike? How does the social climate differ for the child who is "teacher's pet" and for the one he nags and scolds constantly? Does the social climate differ between the pupil who gets the highest grades but is not a leader and the one who is a recognized social leader whether or not his academic standing is high? Questions could be multiplied endlessly. An extended discussion of the individual as a member of a group was given in Chapter 9, the bearing of which is apparent here.

The sociogram. The sociogram is a diagram which shows personal relationships existing within a group of persons. The extent of the likes and dislikes, tensions, and cliques existing within a class are often unknown to the teacher, even though he has some general knowledge. Information revealed by sociograms is useful in directing the grouping of children for various types of activity. More important, it aids the teacher in bringing opportunity to rejected or ignored children. Opportunities for leadership may be arranged to better effect.

Children may be asked to write down for the teacher's eye alone:

With whom would you most like to _____

(fill in with one below)

Work—upon a class committee in planning our next unit; in gathering material for the unit; in arranging an interview. (Make three or four choices.)

Play —with on the playground; at class picnic (or ride with on bus or car to the picnic; go with to movies). (Make four choices.)

Live —sit with at the cafeteria lunch tables each day for the next month. (Make four choices.)

With whom would you prefer not to _____

Questions sometimes used as a basis for making a sociogram but rejected by most authorities include:

Guess who is the most popular boy (or girl) in the room?
What two persons do you most admire?
Who are your two best friends in the group?
Who are the best sports?

These questions call for mere choice by recognition and do not indicate any dynamic relationship between the persons involved.

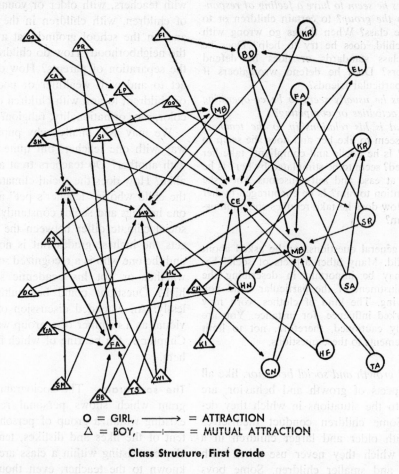

O = GIRL, ——→ = ATTRACTION
△ = BOY, ——⊢—— = MUTUAL ATTRACTION

Class Structure, First Grade

Class of 21 boys and 14 girls. Unchosen, 18; pairs, 3; stars, 5; chains, 0; triangles, 0; intersexual attractions, 22. From Henry J. Otto, *Elementary School Organization and Administration*, after Moreno, *Who Shall Survive?*, p. 35.

The children must know that their choices and rejections will not be made public. They must know also that the teacher will make honest effort to use the results in carrying on class organization. Rapport and confidence between teacher and pupils must be absolute. Sociometric inquiry cannot be attempted until the children have been together long enough to know each other and thus make intelligent choices. Under no circumstances will this type of inquiry be successful with newly formed or otherwise unacquainted groups.

The teacher then tabulates the choices each pupil has made as well as the names of those who have chosen him. The class list used should separate the boys and girls in columns. The diagram is made from the tabulation. Simplification results from putting boys on one side of the diagram, girls on the other. Any symbols may be used: squares for boys, circles for girls, or triangles, each with identifying initials. The symbols for those pupils who are most chosen should be placed nearest the center of the diagram; others should be placed progressively outward until those not chosen at all are on the edges. Lines are then drawn to represent the choices, the arrow showing direction of choice. Mutual choices can be indicated by two arrows or a double line. Study of the completed diagram reveals a number of

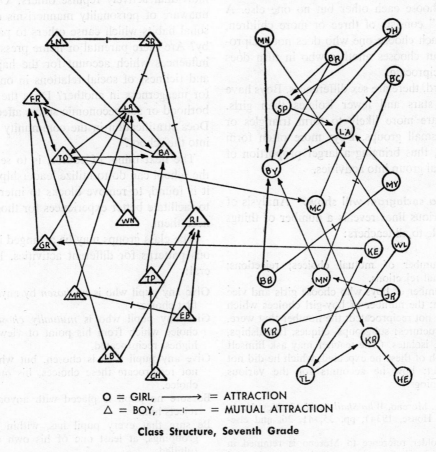

O = GIRL, ———→ = ATTRACTION
△ = BOY, ——⊢—— = MUTUAL ATTRACTION

Class Structure, Seventh Grade

Class of 14 boys and 18 girls. Unchosen, 5; pairs, 15; stars, 5; chains, 2; triangles, 0; intersexual attractions, 2. From Henry J. Otto, *Elementary School Organization and Administration*, after Moreno, *Who Shall Survive?*, p. 41.

things, some of which are new to the teacher who has been dealing with the children daily. First, note the large number of boy-girl choices in the first grade, with but two in the seventh grade. Moreno [7] shows approximately 19 per cent intersexual choices in the first grade, dropping to 1 per cent in the fifth, rising to four by the eighth. This is in keeping with the facts about sex latency.

Second, consider the isolates or unchosen children. In general, about 35 per cent are isolates in kindergarten, 15 per cent in fifth grade, and progressively fewer thereafter. Mutual pairings show steady increase from kindergarten upward. The leaders, or often-chosen children, are referred to as "stars." Another relationship is the "triangle": three who choose each other but no one else. A "chain" consists of three or more children, who each choose one who does not reciprocate but chooses another who in turn does not reciprocate.

Third, there are sex differences. Boys have fewer stars and fewer isolates than girls. Girls are more likely to form triangles or other small groups. Boys more often form chains, thus bringing a larger proportion of the total group into activities.

What a sociogram will show. Analysis of the various lines reveals a number of things valuable to all teachers:

The number of mutual choices; rejections; mutual rejections.

The number of boys who choose girls and vice versa; the number of boy-girl choices which were not reciprocated; the number that were.

The structures: subgroups, cliques, friendships, stars, isolates. (The teacher may ask himself which of these he expected; which he did not expect; how he accounts for the various groupings.)

[7] J. L. Moreno, *Who Shall Survive?* (New York, Beacon House, 1934), pp. 35, 41, 26, and elsewhere.
The older reference to Moreno is retained in this revision because it was a pioneer study, and because it shows more clearly than some current studies the salient points. Many good recent studies are available.

The cleavages, that is, absence of choices between subgroups within the total group which might be due to such factors as:

boy-girl division	academic ability
economic background	after-school work
nationality	prestige factors
religion	others

From the sociogram, the teacher receives information of value in directing learning. The pupils are sensitized to and given practice in making a wise choice of co-workers in a variety of life situations.

We can see in part the richness or poverty of human relations and social experience for various individuals. We attempt to find out causes, especially for rejection and for meagerness of social contacts. Does a given individual actively repulse others? Or is he unaware of personality mannerisms or personal habits which cause others to pass him by? Are there parental or home pressures or influences which account for the happiness and richness of social relations in one case, for meagerness in another? Does the neighborhood or socioeconomic status affect this? Does stratification in the community extend into the school?

The next thing, of course, is to see what the school can do to utilize leadership where it is found, to remove blocks to interaction, to facilitate better experiences for those who need them.

The class groups may be arranged in various patterns for different activities. In general:

Give any pupil who is *unchosen* by anyone his first choice.

Give any pupil who is *mutually chosen,* the choice which from his point of view is the highest reciprocated.

Give any pupil who is chosen, but who does not reciprocate these choices, his *own* first choice.

Be sure no pupil is placed with anyone who rejects him.

Be sure that every pupil has, within all the groupings, at least one of his own choices fulfilled.

It must be remembered that choices will practically always show changes over a period of time, whereupon new groupings should be arranged.

The most-often chosen children are intellectually and emotionally the most able to give help to the least chosen, and in careful groupings usually do give this help. The less popular child gains in security and is able to make more realistic choices, and is thus likely to be chosen more often himself. The teacher in both groupings and in the guidance of learning activity will try to develop means for aiding all toward better human relationships. Close watch is kept to note changes, so that beneficial regroupings may be made.

Interpretations must be made with caution. The sociogram is not an end, to be made and filed away. It should stimulate attention and further observations of individuals and groups. When making interpretations, teachers should remember that the validity of the pupils' choices are dependent upon the degree or rapport and morale established in the class. No effort should be made to press for answers if there is any antagonism or suspicion present.

The structure within groups is a changeable thing and must be restudied from time to time. Fluidity is considerable with younger children, tending to stabilize somewhat with age.

The requirement that several choices be made is important. Individuals may thus be forced to go beyond their own little clique or triangle and reveal more than would be shown by limited responses. The Horace Mann-Lincoln Institute of School Experimentation suggests, because of the fact just mentioned, that sociograms be supplemented through application of a Social Distance Scale.

An admirable summary of the little we do know has been made by Lee and Lee [8]

[8] J. Murray Lee and Dorris M. Lee, *The Child and His Curriculum,* 2nd ed. (New York, Appleton, 1950), pp. 102-103. See Chapter 5 in 3rd ed., 1960.

under the heading, *What have we learned about children's relationships from sociometric measurements?* [9]

There is so much more to be learned about children's relationships that really the surface has only been scratched so far. However there are a few things we do know. We know that the children in the top eighth of the class in popularity when compared with the bottom one-eighth "proved definitely to be more extroverted, to have a higher sense of personal worth, a stronger feeling of belonging, to express more acceptable social standards, to possess superior school relations, and to be more

[9] Jean Criswell, "Social Structure as Revealed in a Sociometric Retest," *Sociometry,* Vol. 2 (October, 1939), pp. 69-75.

Many studies are available, a few samples only are given here:

D. P. Asubel, H. M. Schiff, and E. B. Gasser, "A Preliminary Study of Developmental Trends in Socioempathy: Accuracy of Perception of Own and Others Sociometric Status," *Child Development,* Vol. 23 (1952), pp. 111-128.

M. E. Bonney, "Sociometric Study of Agreement Between Teacher Judgment and Student Choices," *Sociometry,* Vol. 10 (1947), pp. 133-146.

————, and Seth A. Fessenden, *Bonney-Fessenden Sociograph* (Los Angeles, California Test Bureau, 1955).

Rodney A. Clark and Carson McGuire, "Sociographic Analysis of Sociometric Variations," *Child Development,* Vol. 23 (June, 1952), pp. 129-140.

H. Otto Dahlke, "Determinants of Sociometric Relations among Children in Elementary School," *Sociometry,* Vol. 16 (Nov., 1953), pp. 327-338.

E. F. Gardner and G. G. Thompson, *Syracuse Scales of Social Relations* (New York, Harcourt, Brace & World, 1959).

N. E. Gronlund, *The Accuracy of Teachers' Judgments Concerning the Sociometric Status of Sixth-Grade Pupils* (New York, Beacon House, 1951).

Helen H. Jennings, *Sociometry in Group Relations: A Work Guide for Teachers* (Washington, D. C., American Council on Education, 1948).

Onas C. Scandrette, "Classroom Choice Status Related to Scores on Components of the California Test of Personality," *Journal of Educational Research,* Vol. 47 (December, 1953), pp. 291-296.

Arthur Singer, "Certain Aspects of Personality and Their Relation to Certain Group Modes and Constancy of Friendship Choices," *Journal of Educational Research,* Vol. 45 (September, 1951), pp. 33-42.

Walter D. Smith, *Manual of Sociometry for Teachers* (Ann Arbor, Child Development Laboratory, Univ. of Michigan, 1951).

attractive in facial appearance." Whether popularity caused these various factors or was caused by them, there is no objective evidence. Even attractive facial appearance is greatly influenced by the child's attitudes and feelings. A sullen, rebellious face is never as attractive as a happy eager one. It is most probable that popularity and these other factors all develop along together, each influencing the others.

In studying the social acceptance of children they have found that neither race, color, high social position, intelligence, nor achievement necessarily determine acceptability. There is a positive relationship between social acceptance and personal ability in intelligence and achievement, but it is not high. There is a desire on the part of most children for friendship with leaders. This was shown in the sociogram on page 98, where the isolates chose "stars" or near stars.

Pupils choose different children for different purposes. When they were asked to designate the one they had most fun with and a workmate there was little relation between these two choices. High IQ and scholastic proficiency by themselves have not proved to be sufficient qualities for acceptance as workmates.

Children recognize ability to do things and tend to enter into social relationships with the child who possesses and demonstrates such ability.

In general, the more social relationships a child has the happier he is. There is some indication that in general the brighter the child, the more social relationships he has, although other factors are more important.

A very important fact is that the earlier the attempt is made to improve relationships the

better are the chances for satisfying and lasting results. In fact, if such relationships haven't been pretty well established by the end of the sixth grade, the chances are very much less that they will be. It is also quite certain that the child will not be able to do it without specific, direct, and understanding help.

A very useful "Sociometric Analysis Schedule" in the form of fourteen questions appears in Jennings' volume on pages 28 and 29. It is also available in Lee & Lee, *The Child and His Development,* pages 284 and 285.

The Social Distance Scale. This instrument enables us to determine to what degree a given individual is accepted or rejected by the group and to what degree he accepts or rejects the group. The device was originally developed by Professor E. S. Bogardus [10] at the University of Southern California. Succeeding workers have produced various other similar scales. Using a scale developed at Horace Mann-Lincoln Institute of School Experimentation, Cunningham [11] gives the following fragmentary illustration:

[10] E. S. Bogardus, "A Social Distance Scale," *Sociology and Social Research,* Vol. 17 (1933), pp. 265-271.
[11] Ruth Cunningham and associates, *Understanding Group Behavior of Boys and Girls* (New York, Teachers College, Bureau of Publications, Columbia Univ., 1951) p. 172.

Range of Social Acceptance of Two Pupils
(In a Group of 32)

Item on Scale	Checks for Child 1 (Most Accepted)	Checks for Child 2 (Least Accepted)
1. Would like to have him as one of my best friends	20	2
2. Would like to have him in my group but not as a close friend	7	15
3. Would like to be with him once in a while but not often or for a long time	3	4
4. Don't mind his being in our room but I don't want to have anything to do with him	1	3
5. Wish he weren't in our room	1	8

In the entire group of 32 children, only four did not have their names checked on the entire range of five items of the scale (two were not checked on item 5, nor two on item 4).

Other instruments available. A number of valuable techniques for studying children's reactions are available. Space prohibits reproduction here, but many of these instruments should be presented to the class through exhibits and reports. The following list follows the organization in the volume by Cunningham and associates, [12] but many other discussions are available, particularly in the periodical literature.

The Social Distance Scale
Check Sheet for Opportunities in Human Relations
Check Sheet for Describing People
"Things to Improve about Myself"
"Complaint Box," and "Letters to the Teacher"
Springfield Interest Finder
Social Analysis in the Classroom
California Personality Test
The Wishing Well
Guide for Group Observation (Several teacher-devised)

Sociometric analysis based on one personality trait. Children not only are affected by the group in which they live and learn. Each affects the group, thus changing the social environment for himself and the others. Children play very, very different roles within a group, with accompanying differences in the effect of the group on the child. An interesting study has been made by Murphy based on the one reaction of sympathy expressed or received by given children in distress situations—falling down, bumping head, cutting finger, and so forth. The diagram[13] on page 230 shows the astonishing differences in sympathy as given and shown between two children.

The "Guess Who" test. The "Guess Who" test is also sometimes known as the Reputa-tion, Identification, or Opinion Test.[14] More information can be obtained by this means than is usually revealed by the other techniques. The reasons for the "reputations" children have among their peers is valuable information. Prestige factors, things valued or rejected are made clear. Sometimes, startling and enlightening discrepancies between the teacher's opinion of a given student and the opinion of his peers come to light.

The usual form is to arrange a number of one-sentence descriptions, usually paired sentences such as:

Here is someone who is always ready to take a chance at things which are new and unusual, is never worried or frightened.
Here is someone who is always worried or scared, won't take a chance when something unexpected or unusual happens.

Any number of traits can be used: talkative-silent, restless-quiet, leader-follower, tidy-unkempt, enthusiastic-listless, and so on for many others. Teachers may devise any number of paired statements to serve local purposes.

Each student writes down the name of the fellow student who best fits the statement made. Some tests allow the student to write "self" if desired.

The children must have been together long enough to be well acquainted. Rapport with and confidence in the teacher must be absolute, as with other types of personal inquiry. Names may or may not be signed, but in no instance may the teacher allow the choices to become public.

Making information available to teachers. Teachers have argued among themselves for years as to the value and the ethics of pass-

---

[12] The instruments are all discussed and illustrated in Cunningham and associates, *op. cit.*, Ch. 11 and appendix. The chapter also contains an interesting detailed case study in which the various instruments were applied and the results summarized.

[13] L. B. Murphy, *loc. cit.* (New York, Columbia University Press, 1937).

[14] See the monograph by Caroline Tryon. Also several references to work of Stuart Stoke. Also texts in clinical psychology, and in diagnosis of personality.

Ohio Recognition Scale, published by the Ohio Scholarship Tests (Columbus, Ohio, State Department of Education), is a sample instrument, though many others are available.

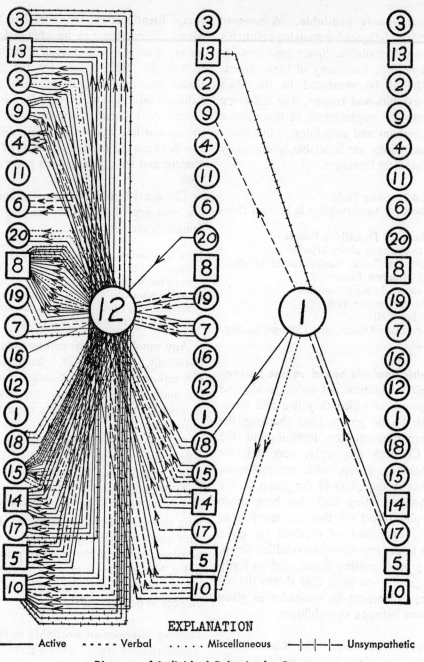

EXPLANATION

———— Active   - - - - Verbal   . . . . . Miscellaneous   —|—|— Unsympathetic

Diagram of Individual Roles in the Group:
Julius (12), 49 Months, and Alex (1), 51 Months

Although close to the same age and developmental level, this markedly extroverted boy and extremely introverted boy have strongly contrasting roles in the group. (Girls are numbered in squares, boys in circles, from the youngest at the top to the oldest at the bottom.) From Henry J. Otto, *Elementary School Organization and Administration,* after L. B. Murphy, *Social Behavior and Child Personality.*

ing on information about individual pupils from teacher to teacher, either by word of mouth or by statements in school registers. It is said that such information may very seriously handicap a student in the eyes of the next teacher or give a student marked advantage. All types of prejudice and bias, favoritisms, partiality, and the like are feared. The whole argument indicates a serious deficiency in professional information and attitude. The competent teacher knows, first, that a given individual's behavior is determined in part by the surrounding circumstances and that changes do take place with changed situations. She knows, second, that good teaching is quite impossible without adequate detailed information. All information available may be freely exchanged by trained teachers of mature mentality. The total picture gathered by the school concerning any and all pupils should be open to any teacher. A high school which has recently installed an extensive and expensive "guidance" department soon develops a truly huge amount of valuable data about all students. If teachers who ask for information to help them diagnose difficulties and aid pupils are told that all the data must remain "confidential," and will not be given out, the central purpose which directed the collection of the data is defeated.

EXERCISES: CUMULATIVE RECORDS

An extensive exhibit of cumulative-record forms should be in possession of the instructor or in the school library.

About all that can be done here is to familiarize students with the types of cards available through seeing and handling them.

1. An interested student may, if desired, supplement the local exhibit through reference to texts which contain recent cards, through securing new ones from local schools, or from publishers.

2. A representative of one or more cooperating school systems may be invited to exhibit and explain the cards used locally, together with some sample interpretations of actual data.

3. Experienced teachers or representatives from local systems may exhibit and explain cards for evaluating socioeconomic status.

The strengths and weaknesses of the instruments exhibited in Questions 2 and 3 should be brought out in the reports or through questions from the class.

Master List of All Types of Instruments

The single best reference here is:

BUROS, Oscar K., *Mental Measurements Yearbook* (Highland Park, N. J., The Gryphon Press). Each is labeled by number, First, Fourth, etc. The current one as this is written is the Fifth, 1957. There is a section on Cumulative Records, in addition to the lists of instruments of inquiry.

Readings

ALLEN, Wendell C., *Cumulative Pupil Records* (New York, Teachers College, Bureau of Publications, Columbia Univ., 1943).

AYER, Fred C., *Practical Child Accounting* (Austin, Tex., The Steck Co., 1949). Probably the most comprehensive volume available.

RUCH, Giles M., and SEGEL, David, *Minimum Essentials of the Individual Inventory in Guidance,* Vocational Division Bulletin 202, Occupational Information and Guidance Series 2 (Washington, D. C., U. S. Office of Education, 1940).

SEGEL, David, chairman, *Handbook of Cumulative Records,* Bulletin No. 5 (Washington, D. C., U. S. Office of Education, 1944).

EXERCISES: METHODS OF STUDYING CHILDREN

1. Experienced teachers should report, with exhibits for the benefit of the group, their use of any of the devices which they may have used or observed in their schools:

Projective techniques (any of those listed).
Inventories and questionnaires.
Acceptance-rejection scales (or others similar).
Sociograms.
Social Distance Scales.
Guess who (Identification, Reputation, Opinion).
Any of the others listed on page 229.

2. With classes made up of inexperienced students, an experienced teacher or other officer from a nearby school system may be invited to

make a report as above. (Several persons if necessary.)

3. A number of short reports should be made by individuals or small committees based on immediately current periodical literature dealing with any one of the techniques listed above.

4. Arrange if possible to see use of any of these devices demonstrated preferably with participation by students in administration and interpretation of them.

5. Secure data from any of the instruments applied in nearby schools and ask class to summarize and interpret.

6. Experienced teachers may report a case study, without identifying names. (Inexperienced students may report on case studies found in the literature, of which many are available.)

7. Show as explicitly as you can, on the basis of present level of training, what value there might be to you as a teacher in knowing:
   a. Economic status and general neighborhood from which a given pupil comes.
   b. Nature of home and family life.
   c. Place of child among siblings (note contradictory evidence on this in recent studies).
   d. Size of the child in relation to others in neighborhood.
   e. One thing child most dislikes doing (most likes).
   f. Psychiatric facts about aggression-domination characteristics, frustrations, daydreaming, or any other item.

8. Brief book reviews may be made on any general volume in the bibliography below, or any volume in the categories noted at top of list but not illustrated.

READINGS FOR SECTION 1

Valuable material dealing with the problems of this section are to be found in classes of volumes which are omitted from the bibliography in the interests of saving space. These are books on such subjects as:

Clinical psychology   Educational psychology
Child study   Personality diagnosis
Adolescent psychology Guidance

American Council on Education, *Personality Rating Scale* (Washington, D. C.).

American Council on Education, Commission on Teacher Education, *Helping Teachers Understand Children* (Washington, D. C., 1946).

BAKER, H. J., and TRAPHAGEN, Virginia, *The Diagnosis and Treatment of Behavior-Problem Children* (New York, Macmillan, 1935). An older reference of value. The Detroit Behavior Scale is discussed in detail. Case studies.

BUROS, Oscar K., Yearbooks on mental measurements, referred to on previous page. Published periodically. Exhaustive.

BONNEY, Merle E., *Popular and Unpopular Children, A Sociometric Study*, Sociometry Monographs No. 9 (New York, Beacon House, 1947).

CRISWELL, Joan H., *A Sociometric Study of Race Cleavages in the Classroom*, Archives of Psychology, No. 235 (New York, Columbia Univ. Press, 1939).

CUNNINGHAM, Ruth, and associates, *Understanding Group Behavior of Boys and Girls* (New York, Teachers College, Bureau of Publications, Columbia Univ., 1951). Chapters 4 and 9 should be read by everyone.

D'EVELYN, Katherine E., *Individual Parent-Teacher Conferences: Practical Suggestions for Teaching*, No. 9 (New York, Teachers College, Bureau of Publications, Columbia Univ., 1945).

DRISCOLL, Gertrude, *How to Study the Behavior of Children: Practical Suggestions for Teaching*. No. 2 (New York, Teachers College, Bureau of Publications, Columbia Univ., 1941).

EDWARDS, A. L., *Techniques of Attitude Scale Construction* (New York, Appleton-Century-Crofts, 1957).

ENGLISH, Horace B., and RAIMY, Victor, *Studying the Individual School Child* (New York, Holt, 1941). Another older reference containing an excellent simple discussion of value to all teachers.

How Children Develop, University School Series No. 3, rev. ed. (Columbus, Ohio State Univ.), 1949. A brief but valuable picture of the developmental needs of children.

How to Construct a Sociogram, Horace Mann-Lincoln Institute of School Experimentation (New York, Teachers College, Bureau of Publications, Columbia Univ., 1947). A practical manual of instructions containing many aids and shortcuts.

HYMES, James L., Jr., *A Pound of Prevention: How Teachers Can Meet the Needs of Young Children* (Caroline Zachry Institute, 17 East 96 Street, New York 28, 1941). A very practical treatment valuable to all teachers.

JENKINS, Gladys Gardner, SCHACTER, Helen, and BAUER, William W., *These Are Your Children* (Chicago, Scott, 1949). A new kind of book on child development, fascinating, scientific, profusely illustrated and easily understood. Equally valuable for parents.

JENNINGS, Helen Hall, *Leadership and Isolation* (New York, Longmans, 1943). An analysis of the choice process within the individual which underlies his acceptance and rejection of others. A contribution to the sociometric method.

———, *Sociometry in Group Relations, A Work Guide for Teachers* (Washington, D. C., American Council on Education, 1948). Step-by-step techniques for diagnosing relationships in school groups, with discussion of psychological principles involved and suggested remedial action.

JERSILD, A. T., and HOLMES, F. B., *Children's Fears*. Child Development Monographs, No. 20 (New York, Teachers College, Bureau of Publications, Columbia Univ., 1935).

———, MARKEY, Frances V., and JERSILD, Catherine L., *Children's Fears, Dreams, Wishes, Daydreams, Likes, etc.* (New York, Teachers College, Bureau of Publications, Columbia Univ., 1933). Gives intimate glimpses into the minds of children from five to twelve.

Juvenile Delinquency and the Schools, Forty-seventh Yearbook of the National Society for the Study of Education, Part I (Chicago, Univ. of Chicago Press, 1948). "Emphasizes importance of teachers' understanding of children's needs and problems, and skill in human relationship."

LEE, Edwin A., and THORPE, L. P., *Occupational Interest Inventory* (Los Angeles, California Test Bureau, 1956).

LIPPITT, Ronald, and WHITE, R. K., "Social Climate of Children's Groups," in R. A. Barker, ed., *Child Behavior and Development* (New York, McGraw, 1943), pp. 458-508.

LUNDBERG, George, *Social Research* (New York, Longmans, 1942).

MORENO, J. L., *Who Shall Survive? A New Approach to the Problems of Human Interrelations* (New York, Beacon House, 1934).

RASEY, Marie I., *Toward Maturity* (New York, Hinds, 1947). A very "different" sort of book, very much worth reading. It gives hundreds of "thumb-nail" sketches illustrating points being made. Written from the child-study point of view.

REMMERS, H. H., *Introduction to Opinion and Attitude Measurement* (New York, Harper, 1954).

———, and GAGE, N. L., *Educational Measurement and Evaluation*, rev. ed. (New York, Harper, 1955).

THORPE, L. P., MEYERS, C. E., and SEA, Marcella, *What I Like to Do* (Chicago, Science Research Associates, 1954).

WARNER, W. Lloyd, HAVIGHURST, Robert J., and LOEB, Martin B., *Who Shall Be Educated?* (New York, Harper, 1944).

WOOD, Ben D., and HAEFNER, Ralph, *Measuring and Guiding Individual Growth* (Morristown, N. J., Silver Burdett, 1948). A very readable presentation of individualized education, based on careful study and cumulative records, which results in the careful guidance of students toward their own unique goals.

ZACHRY, Caroline B., *Personality Adjustments of School Children* (New York, Scribner, 1929). Readable case studies of various types of personality problems with a chapter on adjustment and the school.

2: ADJUSTING TO INDIVIDUAL DIFFERENCES.

Probably a very early generalization on the part of every child is that one parent is more easily handled than the other. It is soon learned that some people are good-natured, others not; some are quick, some slow; and so on. The fact of individual variation is obvious and may be observed everywhere. The veriest beginner in teaching will note that pupils differ materially in many ways. Although children of any age group have certain fundamental characteristics in common, thus making group instruction possible, they do differ greatly in many details, thus making individual attention necessary. No two children in any class will have exactly the same inherited tendencies. Each will have been influenced by all the myriad factors in differing home, school, and street environment.

Sex differences. Differences owing to sex are neither so great nor so important for learning as once thought. Boys as a rule are more active and aggressive, less neat, and less exact than girls. Boys possess funds of information from reading and from outside contacts that girls do not have, and vice versa. Differences in informational background, however, are becoming less under modern conditions of life. The sexes seem to differ also in certain social reactions, boys being more pugnacious and impatient of restraint; girls, more docile and sympathetic.

The social order is only now freeing itself from centuries of belief in the inferiority of women. The sexes do differ greatly in certain interests and special abilities, but these are usually the result of training or social pressure. Certain attitudes have developed toward women which in turn determine many of the interests and occupations open to women. Furthermore, the part to be played by each in the world has further accentuated the differences in interests, tastes, and skills. Girls are not given mechanical toys and are not expected to study the physical and mechanical sciences, whereas boys are directed to these fields. Girls are more often guided to esthetic fields and to those connected with homemaking. However, the wars of this century have broken down many of the barriers which have kept girls and women out of certain occupations.

The sexes do differ in rate of development, girls always being a year or so more mature than boys of the same chronological age. The difference at the preadolescent period is considerable. Girls even in the primary grades are sufficiently ahead of boys so that they tire less easily and can use their accessory muscles earlier. Boys, unable to compete in certain school tasks, unable to sit still as long, seek relaxation by bodily movements. This in turn is branded as bad behavior and increases the teacher's unfavorable opinion. Insult is added to injury when the girls' behavior and achievement is held up to the boys. A great deal of adjustment needs to be made to the growth differences between the sexes.

Differences in intelligence. The so-called intelligence test actually tests but one aspect of general ability—namely, the ability to learn, through visual-verbal means, facility with language and to handle abstractions. This type of intelligence is admirably fitted to the formal verbal curriculum. Other types of learning and of ability are equally important and will be noted later. The next few paragraphs deal with intelligence in the limited academic sense.

There is no real difference between the sexes in this type of intelligence. Social pressure and training, mentioned above, account for seeming differences.

Bright or dull children tend usually to be well or poorly developed in all traits except when environmental influences, chiefly special education, interfere.

The differences among imbeciles, morons, ordinary children, and very bright children are obvious, and no one denies that they need differing treatment and do differing amounts of work. But in the ordinary schoolroom the differences are much less marked than those just mentioned and are more difficult to detect. Even when the class is divided roughly into three groups—slow, average, and fast—these groups shade off imperceptibly into one another. With a normal distribution of intelligence, the lowest 10 per cent of the class is not capable of doing anything like the amount of academic work covered by the highest 10 per cent, nor even as much as the middle 10 per cent. Sometimes the distribution will be such as to place the majority of the class toward the lower end of the curve; sometimes, well toward the upper end.

Recent research on the nature of intelligence and its measurement seems to indicate that though limits for individual development are set, the limits for most normal people are relatively wide. It is also indicated that original differences in intelligence, though modifiable, tend to persist: that is, the bright child tends to remain bright; the dull one, dull. Furthermore, contrary to popular belief, the bright child is also likely to be physically active, socially developed, and interested in a variety of things. He will usually play more games than the duller classmates, enter into more activities, display leadership in various ways. He is not an anemic bookworm, but is, paradoxically, more normal than the normal child.

The following generalized characteristics for gifted and dull children are recognizable and of assistance to the teacher.[15]

For the bright pupils:

1. Ease of assimilation and, as a rule, quick reaction time—ability to absorb the same amount of material in a fraction of the time required by an average group. Power to learn is a distinctive characteristic of gifted children. They show marked ability to "absorb" knowledge much more quickly than average children. They read more rapidly, remember more, and with greater vividness. Superior students have a greater degree of concentration, waste less time, and grasp an idea at its first presentation.

2. Voluntary power of sustained attention, mental endurance, and tenacity of purpose—gifted pupils have unusual power of focusing their attention upon a task; and they are able to stay by a thing without fatigue longer than the average.

3. Intellectual curiosity, originality, and initiative—the superior student is comparatively self-directing.

4. Power of generalization—they quickly see underlying principles, relate similarities, and foresee results.

5. Ability to work with abstractions—the gifted student not only learns facts, but he also delves into the principles underlying the facts

[15] *Vitalizing the High-School Curriculum*, Research Bulletin, Vol. 7, National Education Association (September, 1929).
An interesting and valuable body of material concerning the nature and development of intelligence and concerning the characteristics of different levels is to be found in the series of studies by Wellman and Stoddard and the critiques thereof. *Intelligence: Its Nature and Nurture*, Thirty-ninth Yearbook of the National Society for the Study of Education, Part II (Bloomington, Ill., Public School Publishing Co., 1940), Ch. 26. *Ibid.*, Part I, Ch. 11.
See other articles by Beth L. Wellman and George D. Stoddard, by Florence L. Goodenough, and by various others who debate the findings.

and into the inferences to be derived from them. Generally speaking, the gifted pupil is superior in quickness of observation, in wealth of associated ideas, in power of discrimination, and in reasoning ability.

6. Ability "to know when they do not know"—many gifted children seem particularly competent in self-criticism.

7. Versatility and vitality of interest—this is closely allied to their wide range of interests in the degree of special talent found among gifted children.

For dull pupils:

1. Slow in reaction time—it takes them longer to think things through than the average pupil. They are slow in getting under way and weak in transfer and use a thing in the situation in which they learn it. They cannot transfer it out of its original setting. Hence the dull child must acquire through direct teaching much knowledge that the bright child acquires quite incidentally.

2. Short in span of attention—they lack ability to carry a sequence of ideas long enough to reach a point off in the distance.

3. Illogical—this is partly owing to their limited number of ideas. The amount of material assimilated and used in a given situation is limited. The dull pupil usually becomes a pattern-reaction individual, for, lacking the ability to organize things for himself, he tries to live by rule-of-thumb. Dull pupils have little initiative. They are better able to execute than to plan. The dull pupil understands and learns general processes through situations in which specific habits and automatic responses are formed. Dull pupils are dependent upon constant guidance and sympathetic encouragement of the teacher.

4. Inability to take a body of material and out of it to draw facts which are pertinent to the problem in a given situation.

5. Inability to work with abstractions—dull pupils think most often in terms of immediate objectives, and they deal largely in things concrete. With dull pupils, we must put emphasis upon details, not upon broad general ideas. The dull pupil generalizes and applies processes only to problems well within his training and experience.

6. Lacking in power to evaluate their efforts, and consequently often unable to correct their failures.

7. Narrow range of interests.

8. More emotional in attitude than the superior pupil.

Special educational programs for the gifted and for the retarded. A general volume does not have space for specialized issues despite their basic importance. An excellent and ample literature exists dealing with programs for special groups. Interested students may read widely. Class reports may be made if interest is sufficient. Specialized training programs for teachers of special types are increasing.

Differences in special capacities and abilities. If any group of children is given a set of simple arithmetic problems well within their grasp, one or two pupils will do from three to six times as many problems as one or two other pupils, the rest of the class falling in between. In one class a pupil did three problems while a classmate was doing twenty. In another class one pupil did five while his seatmate did forty-four. The median student in one of these classes was four times faster than the slowest student. In a spelling class, one boy got twenty words right while a classmate got ninety-six, the median pupil getting seventy. Differences in speed of reading between the fastest and the slowest pupil may be as much as nine to one. Knowing this becomes highly important in high school and college when it is realized that one pupil may actually read fifty pages of print while a classmate is reading six to eight pages. Differences in comprehension are also great. Wide differences can be noted in ability to express one's thoughts orally and in writing. Similar differences are noted in motor skills, in taste, in appreciation, and in other items.

These special abilities rest in part upon inherited capacity, in part upon training. Early research indicated that the ordinary capacities needed in daily life are rather evenly distributed. That is, an individual is likely to be reasonably good, or rather mediocre, or quite poor in all fields rather than strikingly good in one or some, and mediocre or poor in others. Current research shows that there may be some exceptions to this

rule. The whole matter needs scrutiny and careful interpretation by teachers. It is probably safe to be suspicious of poor performance in one field coupled with obviously good results in most others. Poor performance in such instances may be due to lack of interest, lack of energy, or personal whims rather than to being "born short." Pupils who perform well in some subjects can be expected to perform about as well in most others and vice versa. The few striking exceptions to this general rule should be treated sympathetically.

Differences in social intelligence, mechanical ability, and emotional stability are often overlooked by the academic school. Many children who do not learn easily under formal school conditions have potentialities of value to them and to society. Many who do not learn easily by visual-verbal means do possess abilities to judge and manage other persons. They learn in social situations. Others possess valuable mechanical abilities.

Students on all levels differ widely in personal and social qualities, and the school should do its utmost to develop capacity for leadership in those who show aptitude to develop ability, to understand other people, and to manage social situations. In some instances, the teacher may have to redirect or repress a wrong type of leadership if it appears.

The quick bright pupil usually has better comprehension and better learning than the slow pupil. However, some children are quick but superficial, tending to shift attention rapidly and to be satisfied with mediocre results. Such children often even maintain that these results are good. These learners need to be controlled carefully for best results and to be led to improve their own judgment or results. Still other children are quick to resent control or differences of opinion. These children are usually positive in likes and dislikes and have poor judgment when excited. Fortunately, many of this type usually cool off quickly and may be very good thinkers when not excited. They need guidance in self-control through social means and in the suspension of judgment. Other pupils will be slow, and their interest hard to arouse. Some slow pupils are good thinkers when interested; others, not.

Some first-rate thinkers of delicate temperamental balance go to pieces easily under fire of rapid questioning or examination. Still other children, especially older students who are overly emotional, are prone to take things too seriously. They need a little fun injected into the proceedings. They usually do better when handled quietly rather than by rebuke. Some students have "single-track" minds and tend to go to pieces temperamentally when the teacher tries to stimulate class discussion.

Racial and national differences. Teachers in the United States are concerned with this type of difference as are few other teachers in the Western world. For many years our large cities, and even some rural areas, have had whole schools filled with children of foreign-born parents: Irish, Scandinavians, Italians, Bohemians, Poles, Greeks, and so forth. Today Mexican children fill many schools in the Southwest, as do Japanese and Chinese on the Pacific coast, Puerto Ricans, Cubans, and other Spanish-speaking people in some Eastern cities. In addition, the American Negroes constitute a native group differing from other native American groups. There is a very large literature on the physical and mental characteristics of various racial and national groups and upon their differences from one another.

The first and most important statement to make is that nearly all common opinions on racial differences are incorrect. National and racial prejudices are potent factors in producing seeming inferiority in attitudes, in learning in school, and in other performances. In this country, we see usually the poorest type of foreign peoples, since commonly only the underprivileged emigrate. We think of Italians as short and swart, as slow learners but esthetically sensitive; of the Japanese as short and strong, as excellent memorizers, as proud and warlike; of the Chinese as strong, as good memorizers, as patient, docile, and non-pugnacious. This is because we see only one type, namely, that which emigrates. Our limited observation and literary practice cause us to think of the French as dark and highly excitable, rational and artistic; of the Germans as blond and phlegmatic, efficient in science and industry. The truth is that many physical and mental types are found in all races.

Early interpretations of intelligence-test scores held that there were marked racial differences in intelligence and that many children of foreign-born parents had lower I.Q.s than children of native-born parents. This corroborated ordinary observation. But as in the case of physical traits, common-sense views and early interpretations were wrong. *First,* it was recognized that the language factor was vitally important since intelligence tests depend almost entirely upon oral and written language and reading. *Second,* further research brought to light the effect of environment, particularly schooling, and of social and cultural surroundings upon the intelligence-test scores of native-born American children. *Third,* immigrant children made appreciably higher scores on tests for illiterates, which avoid the language difficulty, than they did on typical intelligence tests. *Fourth,* it was noted that immigrant children and adults rated borderline or even lower by our intelligence tests were normally effective in familiar, necessary, and everyday activities. Types of stability, foresight, and planning were present which were wholly incompatible with the test results.

Historical evidence indicates that exceptionally high-grade intelligence must have been operative in the ancient Greek, Chinese, and Egyptian civilizations. In the case of the Chinese, a legitimate interpretation is that the dominance of certain religious beliefs progressively stifled this intelligence. Primitive tribes from time to time produce remarkable leaders. Among the American Indians, Chiefs Joseph and Geronimo were highly intelligent men by all ordinary and practical means of estimating intelligence.

What then becomes of "Nordic superiority"? There isn't any! It is, of course, perfectly true that certain nationalities seem to produce numbers of outstanding leaders and to produce masses characterized by higher intelligence and skills than others. All the evidence points clearly to the conclusion that this is owing less to race and nationality than to climate, natural resources of the country, food supply, and to dominant religious or political faiths. The extent of free educational opportunity is known to be vitally important. This is but further illustration of the laws of growth as previously set forth. These laws hold for all races and nationalities.

As with physical differences, it was seen that the differences were not primarily racial but owing to environmental causes, sometimes so long continued as to produce differences which cannot be overcome in a short time.

Environmental factors are the key. Upperclass Italians are tall and intelligent. In fact, a typical Roman business executive, entrepreneur, or professor looks much like his colleague in London or New York. The favored classes in Japan are nearly as tall and quite as intelligent as similar classes in any European country. After measuring nearly one million children in 1909, Dr. Tadasu Misawa stated he believed that the Japanese are improving structurally. [16] Economic, social, and other environmental factors are more important than race. Japanese children born and reared in California are well above Japanese averages for height and weight. American children in the same state are above the norm for the United States. In China, children eat food of about one-half the caloric value of that of American chil-

dren. Their *average* height and weight, heart beat, and vital index are lower; but the growth *curve* is entirely normal.

At age twelve, American children are 2 inches taller and 6 pounds heavier than English children. American boys of today between six and eighteen are significantly taller than those of fifty years ago. This is attributed to our higher standard of living, less child labor, better food, more leisure, better health knowledge, and similar factors. Studies of European nations show that wars regularly reduce the average height of the nation significantly and that a generation is necessary for recovery.

The modern scientific view. There are, then, no basic and permanent differences between races. There will be large, serious, and measurable differences, however, between given groups in a given situation.

Some years ago the schools of the United States enrolled large numbers of foreign-born children and children of recent immigrants. The fathers were usually unskilled or semiskilled workmen. The cultural level in the homes was low. Language difficulties were common. Poor nutrition produced differences in height, weight, and energy, all affecting achievement in school. Centuries of underprivileged living had had their effect. These groups differed not only among themselves, but markedly from American children. What was overlooked for some time was that these children did not differ greatly from American children of the same social and economic levels. History has shown also that as these groups of immigrants achieved better economic levels and moved to better homes with accompanying better nutrition and health, they were gradually assimilated.

Special reports should be made on studies dealing with locally prominent races and nationalities. Students must be exceptionally careful, however, in interpretation. The studies vary in reliability, in extent, and in recency. The utmost care will often be necessary to determine just what a study does

---

[16] "A Few Statistical Facts from Japan," *The Pedagogical Seminary*, Vol. 16 (March, 1909), pp. 104-112.

show. Simple local investigations may be made if facilities permit.

Summary statements may be of value:

1. Common opinions regarding racial and national differences are usually incorrect.
2. These opinions are incorrect because based upon limited observation of non-typical cross-sections.
3. Comparisons between similar social and economic classes within two groups are safer than comparisons of averages for the whole group.
4. Mental and physical characteristics of all types and levels are found in all races and nationalities alike.
5. Some races and nationalities seem to have a larger proportion of desirable mental and physical traits.
6. The superiority of certain groups results less from race than from a large number of environmental factors and to combinations thereof.

Obviously, the task of education and of the school system and those operating it is to eliminate in so far as humanly possible the unfavorable differences. This is done by compensating for poor home background and environmental factors, by combating racial prejudices. The school must make up when it can for deficiencies in social and cultural contacts, in nutrition, and in health knowledge.

Teachers' adjustment to the fact of variation among learners.   There are ordinarily three errors made by teachers in reacting to variation among learners. *One* is ruthlessly to disregard the fact of variation and to teach as one wishes to teach, or as the plan books says to teach, regardless of intelligence level, special ability, temperament, or other items of variability. This teacher usually teaches to the middle group in the class. The *second* error is to overstress either extreme. The dull group gets far more than its share of time in patient coaching in and after school. A few very bright and unusually gifted children are exploited at the expense of the majority. The *third* type of

error is a common one with naïve thinkers, namely, thinking of other people in terms of one's self. This teacher understands only those pupils in the class who approximate his own speed or slowness of thought, his temperament, his breadth or narrowness of view. They fare well; but the wrath of the ruling god is visited upon those whose minds, temperaments, and reactions differ from his. However, the vast majority of teachers with modern training and view are keenly aware of the problem and sincere in their desires to adapt instruction within reasonable limits to meet the situation. Many teaching and administrative devices have been worked out to aid teachers.

The recent anthropological studies of American communities have focused attention on another factor in teacher adjustment to individual and group differences. Teachers in general come from the lower-middle class and are committed to the values and conventions of that class. The values, conventions, and modes of behavior of other classes, particularly those lower than that of the teacher, are very different from those held by the teacher. [17] Less often noted are striking differences between the values of the teacher and those of the upper-upper class. Teachers today are becoming increasingly aware of class differences and of being on guard against judging one group by the standards of another.

Instructional provisions for individual differences.   Teachers make a number of direct and immediate adjustments to the individual differences in ability and interest found in their classrooms.

The *traditional school* carefully adjusts assignments and questions asked during recitation to the individual differences present in the group. The whole supervised-study

[17] "Subcultures and Threat to Learning," *Learning More About Learning* (Washington, D. C., Association for Supervision and Curriculum Development, 1959), pp. 81-82. A very enlightening brief statement.

procedure was a major effort to make such adjustments. Individual instruction is the logical outcome of adjusting completely to individual differences and is illustrated by the Winnetka and Dalton plans, though each of these provides also for social or group-learning situations.

The *modern school* makes excellent provision for individual differences to the extent that modern unit teaching is used. The working period, with its great diversity of learning activities and experiences, can provide for far more types of pupil interest and ability than any other procedure now in use. The modern school also makes use of flexible subgrouping within a class, with constant reorganization of groups, in the skill learnings.

Administrative provisions for individual differences. A number of methods for adjusting to individual differences go beyond the teacher's immediate control and require administrative provision. The systems of individual instruction mentioned above are both administrative and instructional in nature.

The *traditional elementary school* uses effectively such devices as:

Grouping of various kinds and on various bases.
Curriculum organization into two- and three-track systems.
Special classes, opportunity rooms, skip sections, coaching classes.
Irregular promotions.
Case studies resulting in special provision.

The *modern elementary school* relies on social-maturity grouping, frequent reorganizations of the groups, and continuous progress. These dovetail with the instructional provision of many varied activities.

The *high school* has been seriously backward in providing for individual differences, although currently there are a number of important developments. For years the chief provision for individual differences was retardation and elimination from school. The next step was to vary the rate of progress, which was a polite way of saying that dull children took longer and brighter ones less time. This was all based on the ancient (and badly outgrown) academic tradition of the high school.

Realization of the real task confronting the modern high school has brought considerable extension of subjects and organized sequences. Several routes through the school are now provided, except in small schools and in the backward areas. Diversification of offerings is the next big development which must occur in the secondary school.

The developing core curriculum, with its use of modern unit teaching, is extending the superior methods of the elementary school upward.

Billett's [18] summary of provision for individual differences in secondary schools made in 1932-33 still stands. Berthold's [19] extensive study in 1951 not only listed the provisions but secured figures on differences between policies and practices, as well as value judgments, from 105 administrators. The major provisions in Billett's survey were still prominent, due probably to the persistence of the academic tradition. Berthold's list of 160 items is too long to reproduce, but certain encouraging points may be noted. Increases are to be seen in:

Socialized procedures: discussion groups, forums, excursions, visits, displays.
Planned assignments, syllabi, outlines, sequential units of work.
Curriculum adjustment: differentiated curricula, optional units, flexible courses, common assignments differentiated in rate in various ways, enriched offerings, provisions within classes.
Use of specialists of many sorts.

[18] Roy O. Billett, *Provisions for Individual Differences, Marking and Promotion,* Bulletin No. 17, U.S. Office of Education (1932). Monograph No. 13, National Survey of Secondary Education (1933).
[19] Charles A. Berthold, *Administrative Concern for Individual Differences* (New York, Teachers College, Bureau of Publications, Columbia Univ., 1951).

Frequencies with which Various Provisions for Individual Differences were Reported in Use, or in Use with Unusual Success, by 8,594 Secondary Schools*

PROVISION	USE		USE WITH ESTIMATED UNUSUAL SUCCESS		COLUMN 4 DIVIDED BY COLUMN 2
	Number	Per Cent	Number	Per Cent	
1	2	3	4	5	6
1. Variation in number of subjects a pupil may carry	6,428	75	795	9	0.12
2. Special coaching of slow pupils	5,099	59	781	9	.15
3. Problem method	4,216	49	444	5	.10
4. Differentiated assignments	4,047	47	788	9	.20
5. Advisory program for pupil guidance	3,604	42	540	6	.15
6. Out-of-school projects or studies	3,451	40	439	5	.13
7. Homogeneous or ability grouping	2,740	32	721	8	.26
8. Special classes for pupils who have failed	2,612	30	350	4	.13
9. Laboratory plan of instruction	2,611	30	323	4	.12
10. Long-unit assignments	2,312	27	349	4	.15
11. Project curriculum	2,293	27	365	4	.16
12. Contract plan	2,293	27	465	5	.20
13. Individualized instruction	2,145	25	309	4	.14
14. Vocational guidance through exploratory courses	1,911	22	186	2	.10
15. Educational guidance through exploratory courses	1,900	22	193	2	.10
16. Scientific study of problem cases	1,343	16	146	2	.11
17. Psychological studies	1,077	12	70	1	.06
18. Opportunity rooms for slow pupils	946	11	172	2	.18
19. Morrison plan	737	9	175	2	.24
20. Special coaching to enable capable pupils to "skip" a grade or half grade	726	8	114	1	.16
21. Promotions more frequently than each semester	686	8	103	1	.15
22. Remedial classes or rooms	593	7	90	1	.15
23. Adjustment classes or rooms	544	6	55	1	.10
24. Modified Dalton plan	486	6	52	1	.11
25. Opportunity rooms for gifted pupils	322	4	69	1	.21
26. Restoration classes	191	2	24	0	.13
27. Dalton plan	162	2	15	0	.09
28. Winnetka technique	119	1	14	0	.12
29. Other	101	1	...	..	...

* Roy O. Billett, *Provisions for Individual Differences, Marking and Promotion*, Bulletin No. 17, U.S. Office of Education (1932). Monograph No. 13, National Survey of Secondary Education (1933).

Constant curriculum revision, differentiation based on needs revealed by research.

Cumulative records, complete personality records, case studies as basis for guidance.

Home-school relationships, encouragement of contacts, exchange of information.

The emphasis upon major curricular changes is very encouraging, as is that on socialized procedures and on the use of more precise data. The opinion survey showed that interest and attention to the problem have increased greatly. Some differences exist between announced policies and actual practices here and there. A minimum of callous indifference to the problem still exists.

Independent individual experience. The schools of yesteryear (and too many this year) utilized "busy work" to keep children busy and out of the way while the teacher worked with still other children. Busy work sometimes gave practice in desirable school skills but very often was unrelated to learning. "Seat work" replaced this in most schools. Children were given sensible drill materials, free reading material, things to do which related to the work of the class. The workbook grew out of this procedure. The current emphasis upon independent work experiences is excellent, replacing the earlier formal items.

Morrison long ago advocated the "voluntary project" as a supplement to the class unit. Today, a large number of kinds of truly educative experiences are available.

An excellent list of such independent projects is given by Burr, Harding, and Jacobs:[20]

1. *Recreational reading.* Children can profitably devote time to the reading of fiction, biography, poetry, and information. They can also read picture books or children's magazines and newspapers that are available.

2. *Research reading.* The individual may do reading either on topics or problems for which he has assumed responsibility to the group or in which he has a personal, special interest.

3. *Creative writing.* Children can be encouraged to create original stories, poems, descriptions, book reviews, news items for the school paper, informal essays, letters, riddles, diaries, and so on. In some cases, children may make personal copies of group-dictated materials.

4. *Creative art work.* Children may profitably work in various art media: painting, modeling, carving, crayoning, weaving, sewing, knitting, making block and spatter prints, and the like. This period may also be utilized for making holiday favors and gifts; for room decorations; for costume-making.

5. *Manipulatory experimentation.* Individuals may work with concrete materials that help to build concepts in mathematics, science, and the social studies; with puzzles that develop perception of likenesses and differences; with games that purposefully develop skills.

[20] *Student Teaching in the Elementary School,* 2nd ed. (New York, Appleton-Century-Crofts, 1958), pp. 180-181; 183.

6. *Practice on skills.* Children may work with practice materials on specific skills in which they recognize their individual need for improvement. The individual might be working with one of the following, for example: handwriting, multiplication combinations, practical spelling lists, editing written work.

7. *Room and school duties.* In carrying out room responsibilities, children may: catalog or straighten the room library; care for plants or pets; tidy the housekeeping corner or supply cupboard; get midmorning lunch supplies or rest equipment ready for the group; mount pictures for the room materials bureau.

In carrying out school responsibilities, children may: pump up soccer balls; act as school librarians; serve as school receptionists; care for school grounds; arrange hall bulletin boards; participate in all-school committee responsibilities.

8. *Activities related to room enterprises.* Sometimes there are jobs related to the unit of work or other room enterprises that individuals indicate a willingness to take on during independent work periods. Examples are: assembling an exhibit; arranging a bulletin-board display; making labels for a collection; planning a report or oral reading; arranging a bibliography of reading materials; making charts, graphs, slides, models; organizing the produce for the room grocery store.

9. *Work involving small groups.* Sometimes a small group of children may need to work together: two working together in practice on a specific skill; three or more planning a dramatization, or organized games for the play period; a committee group checking on research reading, dividing responsibilities for individual work, rehearsing group reports.

10. *Evaluation activities.* Individuals may be given opportunities to evaluate materials that are to be used in some way by the group. Examples include: selecting the pictures for a roller movie; locating pictures to be used in the opaque projector; making choices of original stories and poems for the room newspaper; self-checking one's own work on skills; scanning book lists for recommendations for the room library; rereading charts or stories previously read in directed reading periods; writing biographical sketches; writing summary reports of achievements for the parents.

11. *Special-occasions activities.* At times, when something very special is imminent, the independent work period time may be devoted to activities appropriate to the occasion: making invitations to a program for parents; mak-

ing Halloween masks; preparing "parent permission" blanks for a room trip; preparing original greeting cards for a child who is out of school ill; making a copy of a dictated "thank you" note; working on gifts for children in another country.

Early busy work and some seat work was not designed to adapt school to individual differences, except incidentally. The emphasis, furthermore, was on formal fact and skill learnings. Modern independent work is an excellent method of adapting to individual differences, since there is opportunity for practically all types of individual interest and ability.

The activities can be used, as indicated, as a regular part of school work or individually. They can be used for special occasions, holidays, and the like. The home as well as the school can participate.

One inheritance from ancient schools, monitorial duties, is now being used for adaptation to individual differences and for educative purposes.

Burr, Harding, and Jacobs suggest a simple set of standards in question form which the teacher may use: [21]

1. Does the child plan his job sufficiently before beginning the work?
2. Does he efficiently get his materials ready for work?
3. Does he avoid interfering with the work of others?
4. Is he developing self-reliance?
5. Is he able to concentrate on the job at hand?
6. Does he manage his time economically?
7. Does he care for equipment properly?
8. Does he conserve supplies considerately?
9. Does he see his job through to satisfactory completion?
10. Are his products worthy of his best efforts?
11. Is he efficient in cleaning up and putting materials away at the end of the work period?
12. Does he satisfactorily follow through on his plans and live up to his agreements?
13. Is he developing further insight into what constitutes good work habits?

[21] *Ibid.*

DISCUSSION QUESTIONS

A Simple Informative Set which May Be Omitted by Advanced Students and Experienced Teachers

1. The instructor should obtain in advance enough practice sheets for one of the well-known arithmetic tests. Select easy problems in the fundamentals which can be worked with great speed. Give each student a sheet and allow ten or fifteen minutes for working. Place scores on board.
   a. Note the lowest and highest score made.
   b. How many times is the lowest score contained in the highest?
   c. How many individuals approximated the lowest score? The highest score?
   d. What is the most frequent score made, that is, the mode?
   e. How many times is the mode contained in the highest score? The lowest score?
   f. How many were surprised at the range of difference even in a college class? Why were you?

Differences in a college class should be smaller than in high school or elementary group. Let us examine one of the latter groups.

2. Answer the question under (1) above for each of the following. In each table use the lowest score mentioned and the highest.

If instruction is adapted to the mode or middle of the class, how much time will the brightest pupils have to waste? How many times too fast for the slowest?

3. The class should mark with a (1) the occupation in the list below which they like the best, with a (2) the next best, and with a (3) the third best. The instructor will prepare a table on the board as students read off their choices.
   a. Note the disagreement.
   b. Wherein are these differences quite unlike those illustrated in questions 1 and 2?
   c. How do you account for these?
   d. Are such differences of any importance in teaching?

List of Occupations to Choose From

Touring leisurely in your own car.
Reading detective stories, adventure, and romance.

SPEED OF READING IN 3B GRADE		ADDITION PROBLEMS CORRECT, 6TH GRADE		SPEED OF READING IN HIGH SCHOOL	
No. of Pupils	Words per Minute	Correct Answers	No. of Pupils	No. of Pupils	Words per Minute
1	76-100	5- 6	1	2	76-100
8	101-125	7- 8	1	1	101-125
4	126-150	9-10	4	20	126-150
3	151-175	11-12	4	27	151-175
2	176-200	13-14	2	49	176-200
1	201-225	15-16	4	29	201-225
		17-18	9	15	226-250
		19-20	13	17	251-275
		21-22	21	7	276-300
		23-24	13	0	301-325
		25-26	9	2	326-350
		27-28	12	2	351-375
		29-30	4		
		31-32	4		
		33-34	1		
		35-36	1		
		37-38	1		
		39-40	2		
		41-42	1		
		43-44	0		

Reading travelogues, the *National Geographic*, Scientific discoveries, etc.
Sitting on the beach, lying in a hammock.
Seeing moving pictures.
Hearing the symphony.
Playing bridge or other card games.
Playing tennis, golf, or other outdoor games.
Eating an excellent dinner.
Fishing.
Caring for a garden, growing flowers, etc.

4. Parents and teachers have a great store of erroneous ideas concerning the way in which children differ, particularly concerning very bright or very dull pupils. Can you recall any of these? Discuss them briefly and list them for further discussion after study of the text.

5. Is the emphasis of most teachers upon students as groups of learners or as individual learners? Why? From your own observation illustrate particularly good and particularly bad practice.

6. Disregarding purely personal attraction, do you expect to find your most interesting students among the boys or the girls? Why?

7. A mother complains that the school and teacher are not giving her little boy a square deal. He is not being put through school as fast as his older brother was, or as fast as his play-

mate who lives next door. Organize a five-minute talk to make to this parent.

8. A student, judged by the teacher to be of good average ability, is absent three months because of illness. Upon recovery, he studies with a tutor for a very short time and rejoins his class, keeping up without difficulty.

List three or four questions that this incident suggests to you, supplying tentative answers to your own questions.

9. Is it true that "the more we study, the more we know"?

A Few Trial Applications

10. A high school history class is made up about as follows: Two boys and eight girls are of the docile type who will "get" any assignment given. They do not *understand* what they study and have neither interest in it, nor ability to apply it. Three boys and two girls are intensely interested in history, reading independently both high-class historical novels and some original sources. They find the text and the class a bit slow and have probably more knowledge of historical thinking than the teacher. Six boys and five girls vary from good to poor. The boys aren't interested, but understand it without great difficulty. The girls have no inter-

est; it is "all Greek" to them. This latter group, not being docile, make little effort.

You cannot, of course, solve this problem at this stage of the course, but what would you as a teacher suggest doing as far as you can see now?

11. How do you think you would proceed (give simple suggestions) to adapt instruction to:

    a. A girl of emotional type, superior ability in working with ideas, impulsive and suggestible.

    b. A boy who is "a man of action," a realist, preferring to deal with things and to deal quickly.

    c. A boy who is a good thinker, but oversanguine as to his abilities and results, and who has poor mental balance.

12. Why is the matter of adapting instruction to variation so seriously neglected on the high school and college level?

13. Billet, who has worked on individual differences intensively, says that far more is known about adapting to individual differences than is utilized. The actual practice of teachers and administrators does not use much that is well known. Why do you suppose this is true?

14. Experienced teachers may explain to the class the devices of all types, which are used in the school systems represented, through which individual differences are met.

15. Reports may be made based on current periodical literature which describes the procedures used by given teachers or school systems.

Independent Experiences

16. To what degree should teachers permit pupils to concentrate on a special capacity? Analyze the several angles necessary in answering this question, and present a supported argument.

17. Experienced teachers may report what independent experiences are commonly used in their classes. Present descriptions, motivation, and results.

18. Students in training may answer the above question on the basis of observation.

19. Experienced teachers may tell how they plan to increase and extend the use of independent experiences.

20. Reports may be made of current periodical articles dealing with any and all phases of adapting to individual differences. Pay particular attention to curricular adaptations.

READINGS

Any standard text in Principles of Teaching may be consulted, though the typical treatments are less extensive than in this chapter.

Standard texts in child study and in adolescence usually contain material on individual differences.

Periodical literature is the best current source.

CHAPTER 11: The Teacher Is a Member of a Group of Learners

Teaching is primarily and always the stimulation of the learner.

Teaching is not inculcating subject matter, nor conveying information, nor "passing on the cultural heritage of the race." It is all of these and more. Learners awakened and inspired by good teaching will do far more than *absorb* the cultural tradition of their society; they will *understand* it. The learner once awakened to the inviting and adventurous nature of learning will not stop exploring, evaluating, and deciding. He will continue his own growth and development, increase his respect for the values of his society, and endeavor to contribute to that society.

A teacher who is to inspire respect for the basic values of the society in which the learner is to live must know and believe in the long cultural history of that society. A teacher who is to aid learners to develop a courageous attitude toward our changing, emerging, often frightening world, must know how human beings live and grow, must know their motivations and frustrations, must know that each individual is unique, that creative expression may appear on any and all levels.

A teacher, it should go without saying, must have intimate and facile knowledge of

any subject matters he must use. But he must have equally intimate knowledge of the way persons learn, of the ways of inviting and encouraging learning. The comment often heard among college teachers, "if you know your subject matter you can teach it," is not mere nonsense; it is detrimental and vicious nonsense. However, devotion to "methods" with neglect of scholarly preparation in subject matter, for which teachers colleges have been widely criticized, is equally detrimental. Excessive emphasis either upon subject matter or upon the processes of teaching, to the neglect of aims, is pathetic superficiality.

A teacher fundamentally ignorant of the structure of his society and equally ignorant concerning the growth of human personality cannot aid individuals to become citizens of their world. A teacher fundamentally ignorant of ethical values and of persistent truths, a teacher who has never developed any values or appreciations of his own, cannot contribute to the growth of moral character.

Subject matter, methods, evaluation, diagnostic procedures—all are important; but the final essence is the teacher who stimulates and inspires the learner.

"The Undying Fire." The fundamental, far-reaching effects of education upon civilization must be achieved through more immediate effects upon the individual. The individual results will be in the form of meanings and understandings about the world and life; of attitudes toward life and one's part in it; of behavior patterns embodying the meanings and values. These things and the teacher's part in securing them are indicated in part by the stirring words which H. G. Wells puts in the mouth of his schoolmaster: [1]

What is the task of the Teacher in the world? It is the greatest of all human tasks. It is to ensure that Man, the Divine grows in the souls of men. . . . We can release him into a wider circle of ideas beyond himself in which he can at length forget himself and his meager personal ends altogether. We can open his eyes to the past and to the future and to the undying life of Mankind. So through us and through us alone he escapes from death and futility.

For five and twenty years I have been giving sight to the blind: I have given understanding to some thousands of boys. My boys have learned the history of mankind so it has become their own adventure; they have learned geography so that the world is their own possession. I have taught languages to make the past live again, and to be windows upon the souls of alien peoples. Science has played its proper part; it has taken my boys into the secret places of matter and out among the nebulae . . . [I have kept] the utilities in their due subordination.

Some of my boys have already made good businessmen—because they were more than businessmen. . . . But I have never sought to make businessmen and I never will. My boys have gone into the professions, into the services, into the great world and have done well. I have had dull boys and intractable boys but all have gone into the world gentlemen, broadminded, good mannered, and understanding, unselfish, masters of self, and servants of man, because the whole scheme of their education has been to release them from base and narrow things.

The duties of the classroom are difficult and exacting, sometimes even exasperating. The trivial accidents and incidents of the

[1] H. G. Wells, *The Undying Fire*, pp. 60-61. Copyright, 1919, by H. G. Wells. Quoted by special permission of The Macmillan Company.

daily round alternately exalt and depress us, inspire and annoy us, so that it is not always easy to remain "faithful to the Heavenly vision." But no matter what the effect of unstable, shifting daily trivia, these basic truths remain: "Teaching is the greatest of all human tasks"—"Civilization is a race between education and catastrophe." Aristotle stated it: "The destiny of empire depends upon the education of youth."

The ivory tower and the workaday world. Does the foregoing sound like the unattainable idealism of the ivory tower? The huge number of unprepared—actually uneducated —teachers to be seen everywhere, the great amount of gross incompetence observable in classrooms everywhere, may convince some that insuperable obstacles exist between ivory tower and workaday world. The public at present certainly does not pay for the type of teaching we describe. The encouraging fact is that, despite the truly serious obstacles and weaknesses, the leadership works unceasingly toward the ideal goal.

The demands of teaching. Teaching demands wide knowledge, subtle insights, complicated skills, dynamic personality. This is no ivory tower statement. Failure to secure the best teaching could be disastrous—in fact may be an element in the current moral and spiritual breakdown in Western society.

Effective teaching is a complex affair, depending upon the integration of several factors. What are the knowledges, the classroom procedures, the personal characteristics of the effective teacher? We do not actually know precisely what makes a teacher effective. The analyses made so far have all been fragmentary, but the profession is attempting to develop some answers.

Studies have been made of *desirable traits;* of *classroom techniques* used by teachers judged to be effective or ineffective. These have been determined both by *student judgment* and *analysis by experts.* The effect of the *teacher's personality type* upon the learner has been investigated. *Achievement by pupils* was naturally one of the first means used to evaluate the teacher. Types of *training* and even *specific courses,* types of *experiences* have been analyzed. The *critical incident technique* has been applied recently. The *competencies* necessary for good teaching have been listed.

The research worker, whose aims, procedures, and setting are different from those of the practical operator of the schools, points out, correctly, that none of the investigations has yielded valid and conclusive answers. The practical worker should not be confused or blocked by this. To keep the schools running he must go ahead and subjectively set up definitions and characteristics of the effective teacher as best he can. The many studies, fragmentary though they be, will contribute valuable guidance.

Sources of knowledge and skill. Educational leaders in the workaday school world must of necessity come to tentative agreements upon the knowledges, experiences, social and professional skills, and elements of desirable personality in what we believe to be effective teachers.

Limited space prohibits more than an outline, but the inferences are easily drawn, the implications very far-reaching.

1. *The cultural history and tradition of the society within which one teaches. The way society lives and grows.*

   Knowledge of the ethical and spiritual values which serve as an integrating core for the society, but which also transcend the society by leading on toward ever better values and practices; of societal organizations, mores, customs, institutions, accepted everyday taboos and conventions; of the origin and evaluation of both values and institutions; of the effects upon both individuals and institutions of interaction between the factors.

   Skill acquired through varied life experience; travel in, and observation of, different parts of the country, different modes of life, different socioeconomic groups; participatory observation, preferably actual field work with social agencies; participation in

the work of ordinary community organizations; work experience.

2. *The way human beings live and grow and learn.*

   Knowledge of the biologic organism, the neural system, the psychological processes, the methods of personality development, psychiatric analysis of personality disorders.

   Skill acquired through study of one's own personal problems of living (maintenance of health, methods of solving problems, eliminating personality defects, and many others); observation of one's fellows and their methods of handling their problems; observation of children at different maturity levels and of different socioeconomic status; participation in caring for children; observation of analysis of problem-cases at guidance clinics or by psychiatrists.

3. *The way individuals and environments interact and affect each other.*

   Knowledge of behavior—its dynamics, development, consequences; of the effect of social and physical environments on personality.

   Skill acquired through participation in community organizations; observation, perhaps some elementary participation in work of behavior clinics, juvenile courts, charitable institutions, social-welfare agencies, playgrounds, settlement houses, community centers of all kinds; observation of adult economic and political organizations, participation in their activities when possible; attendance upon public forums; attendance upon legislative agencies in session; participation in work of school-guidance clinics and in counseling; notation and attempted explanation of individual differences; work experience.

4. *The way democracy operates as a total social theory.*

   Knowledge of the emergence of political democracy; the problems of currently emerging economic and social democracy; racial and religious tolerance; freedom of speech and utterance; pressure groups and vested interests; relation between fact and power in the management of public affairs, and so on.

   Skill acquired through participation in all community organizations available; attendance, participatory observation, and actual participation where possible as in 2 and 3 listed above.

5. *The way subject matter and all other educational materials and learning activities further the development of personality in a democratic society.*

Knowledge of the principles and processes of democracy; of the principles and processes of personality development; of the processes of interaction; of subject matter; of the inner processes of learning as far as they can be known; of the outer manifestations of learning; of the effect of all environmental factors on learning; of subject matter not merely in a major field but over several fields necessary to the points already enumerated above.

Skill acquired through critical analysis of one's own problem-solving processes; through observation, participation, and finally through teaching under guidance; operating diagnostic techniques; planning remedial measures; planning over-all teaching procedures; participating in curriculum organization.

6. *The way valid experimental investigations of the process of learning, the nature of the learner, the transfer of training, of the evaluation of results, of many other factors, affect teaching.*

Knowledge of the vast technological background built up by the application of scientific methods to educational problems.

Skill acquired through analysis of certain of these investigations; through reading critical accounts of studies; through carrying on a few simple experimental studies during preservice training and later as a regular teacher.

7. *The way valid philosophical criticisms of results and processes, of ultimate ends, in the light of values, affect teaching.*

Knowledge of the ethical or moral or spiritual values and ends accepted by the society in question; of the processes of analytic criticism; of the processes of speculative philosophy as well as of the pragmatic.

Skill acquired through study of some of the philosophic analyses available; participation in elementary analysis of accepted materials and practices in the light of accepted values.

Certain basic understandings are necessary. Teachers must know and sincerely believe that:

1. Learning can be done only by the learner.

No amount of teacher activity or effort is of any value unless learning activities result.
2. The needs, interests, abilities, problems, and purposes of learner, whether sensible or not, are the only fruitful starting point and continuing motivation for learning activity.
3. The less sensible interests, purposes, and activities of the learner—that is, the socially wasteful or useless, the selfishly individualistic—are to be made over through the sympathetic guidance of the teacher.
4. Subject matter is useful and meaningful only as it serves some worthwhile need or purpose of the learner.
5. The teacher can help students to learn, can aid them in overcoming difficulties, in overcoming undesirable habits and attitudes, only as she understands the mental and emotional processes of the individual.
6. Democracy can be successful only in so far as individuals are prepared for understanding of and intelligent participation in it; are given a genuine faith in it and an ardent desire to make it work.

One profoundly important general professional attitude is so necessary that its presence or absence may spell the difference between competence and incompetence.

Competence in teaching is not possible at all without an ardent desire to grow and to improve both personally and in professional knowledge and skill; willingness to give up easy, well-known routines; willingness to study the new and go through the arduous and difficult process of learning new ways.

An interesting chart, originally presented by Lee and Lee in *The Child and His Curriculum,* showing the knowledges and skills an elementary teacher must have appears on page 250.

Hopkins cleverly characterizes the widespread unwillingness to change, to study, to improve as "the professional disease of teachers." [2] Unfortunately, many powerful influences work against improvement among teachers, not the least of which is poor preliminary training. Another important obstacle to progress is the natural inertia of

[2] L. Thomas Hopkins, *Interaction* (Boston, Heath, 1941), p. 435.

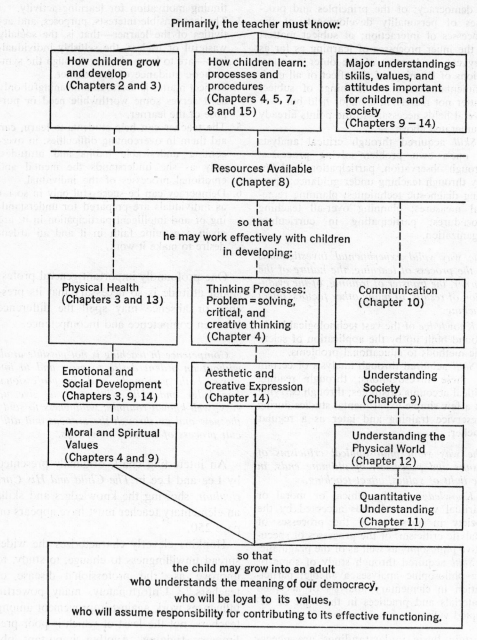

Primarily, the teacher must know:

| How children grow and develop (Chapters 2 and 3) | How children learn: processes and procedures (Chapters 4, 5, 7, 8 and 15) | Major understandings skills, values, and attitudes important for children and society (Chapters 9 – 14) |

Resources Available
(Chapter 8)

so that
he may work effectively with children
in developing:

Physical Health (Chapters 3 and 13)	Thinking Processes: Problem = solving, critical, and creative thinking (Chapter 4)	Communication (Chapter 10)
Emotional and Social Development (Chapters 3, 9, 14)	Aesthetic and Creative Expression (Chapter 14)	Understanding Society (Chapter 9)
Moral and Spiritual Values (Chapters 4 and 9)		Understanding the Physical World (Chapter 12)
		Quantitative Understanding (Chapter 11)

so that
the child may grow into an adult
who understands the meaning of our democracy,
who will be loyal to its values,
who will assume responsibility for contributing to its effective functioning.

The Work of the Elementary Schoolteacher

From J. Murray Lee and Dorris M. Lee, *The Child and His Curriculum* (New York, Appleton-Century-Crofts, 1960).

those individuals who dislike being disturbed by new ideas and new methods with their attendant effort. The administration sometimes seems to reward those who do not disturb the peace. Tenure and salary increments are granted on the basis of mere length of service or college credits acquired rather than upon demonstrated growth in professional insights and skills. The successful teacher must have the force of personality to overcome these, to pursue professional study continuously, to experiment with new methods under controlled conditions, and to be "divinely discontented." Studies show older teachers to be much less well informed than younger ones.

Fundamental importance of basic knowledges and skills. Is all this really necessary? After all, teaching must be simpler than that—hasn't it been done by less extensively trained individuals for a long time? It has been so done and therein may lie one of the tragedies of civilization. The individual who truly wishes to understand the nature of education must acquire adequate understandings from anthropology, biology, sociology, psychology, and psychiatry; should have read thoughtfully a history of civilization; should have studied, if only briefly, the evolution of one or more human institutions such as marriage, government, language, money, the alphabet, or the number system. A course in comparative religion would be highly desirable. [3] A teacher's aims and procedures are inevitably determined in part by the theory he holds regarding human nature and its motivations, the nature of society, the nature of knowledge, the kinds and operation of behavior controls. A whole series of

[3] It is significant that a philosophy of education written by church leaders who naturally place first, knowledge of the spiritual nature of the learner and of the spiritual values accepted by mankind, insists strongly that there must be knowledge also of societal organization, anthropology, and similar items. See J. D. Redden and F. A. Ryan, *A Catholic Philosophy of Education* (Milwaukee, Wis., Bruce Publishing Co., 1942), pp. 44-48.

new interpretations has appeared in the fields mentioned above, plus certain areas in medicine and therapy, demography, group dynamics, and semantics. Classroom teaching can never be other than mechanical tinkering if the teacher does not possess understandings of society and its institutions, knowledge concerning human personality and its development, knowledge of the relations between society and the individual. Above all, the teacher must see the relation of education to both factors: the evolutionary, emergent society, and the growing, developing individual.

Education is not, as is thought by the uninformed, the simple business of training individuals in the simple skills of reading, writing, and arithmetic. Education is one of the fundamental institutions and social forces through which society and civilization are perpetuated and improved; through which each individual realizes his unique possibilities. Education is not confined to the school; but, for the moment, we are concerned with teaching within the school which has been set up as the instrument of organized society.

The basic materials more widely affect elementary education and the more alert teacher-education institutions. The secondary schools are far behind in basing curriculums and teaching on valid principles now available. Folklore and old wives' tales about the nature of children and youth, about human motivation and learning, about control of behavior, and about society still supply the basic theory for many teachers.

Discouraging effect of the narrow view upon earnest teachers, whether beginners or experienced. A distinguished school superintendent recently stated at a national convention, "Ninety per cent of a new teacher's ambitions, aspirations, enthusiasms, dreams for a career are spiked during his first year of teaching." Signs of a better day are appearing, as shall be seen, but this superintendent comments upon a serious state of affairs in education. The young teacher going into the field should be forewarned to resist the disillusion which may result as he comes into competition with experienced teachers who hold the narrower view. Good teaching is artistic and creative, requiring fine personality and skill; but it is true that far too many untrained, indifferent, in some cases lazy, dishonest individuals are teaching. At least, they draw pay as teachers. Their work is distinctly unsatisfactory. They sneer at training and decry the subtleties of teaching skill.

Teachers of this type appear in schools for different reasons. A large group will always be found in school systems where political or religious affiliations are more important than professional training and standards. These teachers are secure and defiant toward any demand for even rudimentary evidence of competence. In fact, in school systems dominated by politics, whether civil or religious, it is the earnest, competent teacher eager for professional improvement who is in disfavor with colleagues and administration. It is a genuine menace to education and to democracy to have operating in the classrooms stupid, incompetent, blandly dishonest individuals secure in their tenure and defiant of any demands for professional improvement or for reputable results with the children. The immediate effect is discouragement to both young enthusiastic beginner and conscientious older teacher. Each year, a number of competent persons either are driven out of the profession or give up and fit into the groove of least resistance.

Another group of incompetents get into the profession because of the refusal of teacher-training institutions and of employing officers to establish and maintain standards of selection. Persons of obviously unsuitable personality are accepted for training, certificated, and employed. Under pressure, these persons break. Defense mechanisms appear: chiefly a retreat to simple beliefs and simple skills. There is refusal to co-operate, to study, to try new methods. Children's needs are ignored; order is secured by force; sound principles are defied. Everything new is decried as "theoretical." The glaring demonstration of intellectual and emotional immaturity, not to mention instability, manifested by some experienced teachers is again a disheartening exhibit. These persons are just as dangerous to teaching as are the politically secure incompetents.

The young teacher must realize that these discouraging examples are not truly representative of the profession. They are dangerous, very noticeable, and get publicity. The great majority of teachers are going quietly and competently about their business, eagerly studying new developments, spending time and money freely for training which will improve their professional skill.

We should note also that this difficulty is common to the professions, the ministry being, if anything, worse afflicted than teaching. In medicine, law, and engineering, there are quack doctors, shyster lawyers, and incompetent technicians. Few of them, however, could maintain a high degree of security in these professions by operating on the level at which a fair number of teachers live and work.

The *basic* reason for the ease with which wholly inadequate school superintendents and classroom teachers can continue to operate is that the general public has never understood the nature of education as a social force, nor the nature of the teaching process. It has never, therefore, demanded the requisite standards of training and evidences of continued competence. Low salaries are a natural result which in turn operate further to preclude extended training. A *secondary* reason is that we have had no reasonably valid methods of determining teaching competence which would convince the layman. The public often accepts and defends teaching procedures which are clearly inefficient. A *third* contributing cause, which grows out of the basic one, is that students come to the technical work of teacher-training with a hopelessly inadequate and unbalanced background in the general liberal arts and basic sciences. Fortunately, co-operation between divisions of liberal arts and schools of education is beginning to be seen. The general education of the public is a necessary part of educational leadership. The young teacher may take part in this in numerous ways and should resist the inertia which comes from realization that the same salary—and sometimes even greater prestige —is going to a few mountebanks and charlatans in the profession who have neither training nor personality—and do not care.

A better situation is emerging. Prospective teachers who have been given well-organized education and training are themselves recognizing the necessity and value of that training. Groups of younger and more recently educated parents increasingly ask for materials on modern education and child-rearing. Publications for teachers and parents who wish information are increasing in number.

Recognition of the value of modern teacher education, together with the teacher shortage, has emboldened many teacher candidates. Their reactions are evidence of the value of the training. A few years ago, a superintendent, after interviewing candidates for positions, reported indignantly that the teachers insisted on asking him questions after he had quizzed them and before they would discuss contracts. The questions were significant:

1. Will I be permitted to use in your schools some of the improved modern methods of teaching which I have studied and which are demonstrably better than the older methods?
2. Will I be given supervisory assistance by supervisors or principals in using and improving my work?
3. Will I be protected from certain old-timers on the staff who will sneer at modern methods and bring pressure on me to revert to outmoded routines?

This questioning is now quite commonplace. Well-educated teachers are refusing to work in systems which do not value well-trained staff members. The alert, forward-looking superintendent welcomes this change with hope and enthusiasm. The writer unhesitatingly advises students (unless driven by severe economic pressure) to refuse to waste their time where their training and education will not be utilized.

Another evidence of progress is that an increasing number of teachers colleges are refusing to give training in the methods of yesteryear.

The personal characteristics of the effective teacher. Teachers lacking adequate philosophic and technical background are foredoomed to failure or to mediocrity. Personality is, however, an important asset in any social science or occupation involving personal relations. Two teachers of equal intelligence, training, and grasp of subject matter may differ considerably in influence and in the results they achieve. Part of the difference is clearly accounted for by the effect of personality on the learners.

Many of the foregoing pages testify to the importance of personal leadership on the part of the teacher and to the necessity of possessing certain personality traits effective in meeting pupils and parents, in diagnosing learning difficulties, in remedying emotional difficulties in pupils, and in many phases of teaching. Superintendents and boards of education are increasingly interested in desirable personality as well as in background of training and of experience. Statistics show that the vast majority of individuals dismissed from positions in industry are dismissed because of personality defects—for inability to get along with persons—and not for technical incompetence. No figures are available concerning teachers, but everyone can testify to the evil effect, within a group, of one or two inadequate or warped personalities and to the almost miraculous effect of a few serene, poised personalities.

A great number of studies have been made to determine the desirable characteristics of teacher personality. The opinions of superintendents and other school officers, of psychologists, psychiatrists, and personnel workers have been sought. Fellow teachers and the pupils themselves have all figured in the research.

A sample from one of the most interesting of the investigations is given below.[4] It is based upon the opinions of 3,725 high

[4] Frank W. Hart, *Teachers and Teaching* (New York, Macmillan, 1934), pp. 131-132, 250-251.

Reasons for Liking "Teacher A" Best, Arranged in Order of Frequency of Mention, as Reported by 3,725 High School Seniors	Frequency of Mention
Is helpful with schoolwork, explains lessons and assignments clearly and thoroughly, and uses examples in teaching	1,950
Cheerful, happy, good-natured, jolly, has a sense of humor, and can take a joke	1,429
Human, friendly, companionable, "one of us"	1,024
Interested in and understands pupils	937
Makes work interesting, creates a desire to work, makes classwork a pleasure	805
Strict, has control of class, commands respect	753
Impartial, shows no favoritism, has no "pets"	695
Not cross, crabby, grouchy, nagging, or sarcastic	613
"We learned the subject"	538
A pleasing personality	504
Patient, kindly, sympathetic	485
Fair in marking and grading, fair in giving examinations and tests	475
Fair and square in dealing with pupils, has good discipline	366
Requires that work be done properly and promptly, makes you work	364
Considerate of pupils' feelings in the presence of the class, courteous, makes you feel at ease	362
Knows the subject and knows how to put it over	357
Respects pupils' opinions, invites discussion in class	267
Not superior, aloof, "high hat," does not pretend to know everything	216
Assignments reasonable	199
Is reasonable, not too strict or "hard-boiled"	191
Helpful with students' personal problems, including matters outside of classwork	191
Dresses attractively, appropriately, neatly, and in good taste	146
Young	121
Work well planned; knows what class is to do	110
Enthusiastically interested in teaching	108
Gives students a fair chance to make up work	97
Homework assignments reasonable	96
Recognizes individual differences in ability	86
Frank, "straight from the shoulder," a straight shooter	78
Personally attractive, good looking	78
Teaches more than the subject	74
Interested in school activities	68
Sticks to the subject	53
Modern	52
Sweet and gentle	50
Pleasing voice	50
Intelligent	42
Prompt and businesslike	41
Sincere	36
Knows more than the subject	32
Has pep	31
Uses good judgment	22
Cultured and refined	20

Too cross, crabby, grouchy, never smiles, nagging, sarcastic, loses temper, "flies off the handle"	1,708
Not helpful with schoolwork, does not explain lessons and assignments, not clear, work not planned	1,025
Partial, has "pets" or favored students, and "picks on certain pupils"	859
Superior, aloof, haughty, "snooty," overbearing, does not know you out of class	775
Mean, unreasonable, "hard-boiled," intolerant, ill-mannered, too strict, makes life miserable	652
Unfair in marking and grading, unfair in tests and examinations	614
Inconsiderate of pupils' feelings, bawls out pupils in the presence of classmates; pupils are afraid and ill at ease and dread class	551
Not interested in pupils and does not understand them	442
Unreasonable assignments and homework	350
Too loose in discipline, no control of class; does not command respect	313
Does not stick to the subject, brings in too many irrelevant personal matters, talks too much	301
"We did not learn what we were supposed to"	275
Dull, stupid, and uninteresting	275
Too old-fashioned, too old to be teaching	224
Not "fair and square" in dealing with pupils	203
Knows the subject but "can't put it over"	193
Does not hold to standards, is careless and slipshod in her work	190
Too exacting, too hard; gives no chance to make up work	183
Does not know the subject	170
Does not respect pupils' judgments and opinions	133
Too changeable, inconsistent, unreliable	122
Lazy, not interested in teaching	115
Not friendly, not companionable	98
Shows boy or girl favoritism	95
Dresses unattractively or in bad taste	92
Weak personality	85
Insincere	75
Personally unattractive	65
Does not recognize individual differences in pupils	64
Voice not pleasant	63

school seniors concerning the best-liked and least-liked teachers.

These lists are significant. Note that personality traits monopolize the top rankings after the first item which deals with teaching technique as it immediately affects pupils. Note also that the comments made by the students are specific descriptions. No one can misunderstand them. Incidentally, it is interesting to note the least specific characteristic, "cultured and refined," a typical verbalism, is last, with only twenty mentions. High school students do not mince words. Mastery of subject matter, which is vital but

badly overemphasized by specialists, ranks sixteenth in both lists.

Hart's general findings have been corroborated many times by later studies. Witty,[5] in connection with the "Quiz Kids" program, received 12,000 letters on the theme, "The Teacher Who Helped Me Most." Analysis revealed that the twelve top ranking traits were:

Co-operative, democratic attitudes; kindliness and consideration for the individual; patience;

[5] Paul Witty, "An Analysis of the Personality Traits of the Effective Teacher," *Journal of Educational Research* (May, 1947), pp. 662-671.

wide interests; personal appearance and pleasing manner; fairness and impartiality; sense of humor; good disposition and consistent behavior; interest in pupil's problems; flexibility; use of recognition and praise; unusual proficiency in teaching a particular subject.

The best current discussion of discipline [6] selects one of the traits mentioned for special comment:

A sense of humor is obviously the most essential characteristic of skillful handlers of discipline problems. One personality trait most injurious to successful discipline is false dignity. We know of no other single personality trait which would cause so much confusion, uproar, and mismanagement as this one.

We may stress also "consistent behavior." Few things confuse children more, or produce undesirable behavior more quickly than inconsistent treatment from adults. Consistent fairness and fulfillment of promises from adults give the child a sense of security. This in turn begets confidence and effort. Baxter's [7] earlier detailed studies of teacher-pupil relationships gave conclusive evidence that the behavior of teachers has great effect upon the pupil's sense of security, freedom from tension, courtesy, resourcefulness, and

seeking of social recognition. Repeated some years later the analyses corroborated the early findings. [8]

One study [9] reversed the usual form of question and asked, "From what did you suffer most in school?" The answers are revealing and should be taken to heart by teachers. "Sarcasm, excessive demands, contempt, and corporal punishment." Sarcasm, as stated earlier, can result only from genuine stupidity or from a frustrated personality. Excessive demands, as will be shown in a later chapter, result in much unnecessary failure by pupils, with accompanying antagonism and bad behavior.

Many other studies [10] dealing with elementary and secondary teaching are available. Studies are also available on the college level [11] which show that the more mature students still rank first the professor's interest in his students and their problems and his willingness to give attention to them.

The general attitude of the teacher. An older study by a psychiatrist supplies excellent guidance in this problem. Anderson, [12] after listing such general traits as

[6] George V. Sheviakov and Fritz Redl, *Discipline for Today's Children and Youth*, Department of Supervision and Curriculum Development (Washington, D. C., National Education Association, 1944), p. 59.

[7] Bernice Baxter, *Teacher-Pupil Relationships* (New York, Macmillan, 1941).

[8] William U. Snyder, *Recent Investigations in Mental Hygiene in the Schools*, Educational Research Bulletin (November, 1945), pp. 222-224.

[9] Willi Schohaus, *The Dark Places in Education*, trans. by Mary Chadwick (New York, Holt, 1932).

Paul Witty, "Some Characteristics of the Effective Teacher," *Educational Administration and Supervision* (April, 1950), pp. 193-208.

David Jenkins and Ronald Lippitt, *Interpersonal Perceptions of Teachers, Students, and Parents: An Action Research Project for the In-Service Training of Teachers* (Washington, D. C., N. E. A., 1951).

F. M. Calabria, "Characteristics of Effective Teachers," *Education Research Bulletin*, Vol. 39 (April, 1960), pp. 92-102. Reply to this by E. G. Guba, *Education Research Bulletin*, Vol. 39 (September, 1960), pp. 157-159.

W. J. Popham and R. R. Trimble, "Minnesota Teachers Attitude Inventory as an Index of General Teaching Competence," *Educational and Psychological Measurement*, No. 3 (Autumn, 1960), pp. 509-512.

Teacher Competence, Its Nature and Scope (San Francisco, California Teachers Association, 1957).

[10] Wilbur B. Brookover, "Person-Person Interaction Between Teachers and Pupils and Teaching Effectiveness," *Journal of Educational Research* (December, 1940), pp. 272-287.

Robert N. Bush, "A Study of Student-Teacher Relationships," *Journal of Educational Research* (May, 1942), pp. 645-656.

R. H. Ojeman and F. R. Wilkinson, "The Effect on Pupil Growth of an Increase in Teacher Understanding of Pupil Behavior," *Journal of Experimental Education* (December, 1939), p. 143.

[11] Weston A. Bousfield, "Student's Rating on Qualities Considered Desirable in College Professors," *School and Society* (February 24, 1940), pp. 253-256.

[12] V. V. Anderson, *Psychiatry in Education* (New York, Harper, 1932), p. 300.

insight, sense of reality, adaptability, interest, integration, social adjustment, sense of responsibility, resourcefulness, and good work habits, makes an enlightening comment upon the teacher's total attitude:

The mental attitude . . . of an individual probably constitutes the most important element in the atmosphere of the classroom. The disgruntled, sour, sarcastic, sharp and bitter teacher has a general attitude of mind that is most dangerous to the shy, timid, oversensitive child. The suspicious, doubting, supercilious teacher does untold damage to the pupil whose daily life is filled with one long series of threats against his own security. The overanxious, demonstrative, worried teacher has built up an attitude of mind that commonly develops in the classroom regression tendencies in pupils, is responsible for baby ways of behaving, and halts the maturing process so essential to the mental health and growth of children. And so it is, in their effect on the personalities of each and every pupil in the classroom, those influences emanating from the teacher's attitude of mind are fraught with the greatest possibilities for good or evil.

The studies by Lewin and his associates, quoted earlier in Chapters 3 and 9, testify to the positive side of this same problem. Learners preferred the democratic teacher to the autocratic or laissez-faire leaders. *Mere preference* is not the point. Learners *accomplished more* with the help of co-operative, democratic teachers, both in subject-matter learning and in the development of personal-social-moral traits. The superiority of settings for learning under the guidance of democratic personalities was overwhelming.

Tiedeman [13] discovered the significant fact that dislike for and antagonism toward the autocratic, domineering type of teacher personality increases with the age of the pupils, at least through junior high school. Added experience and maturity evidently increased insight into the evils of poor personality, and increased respect for the co-operative teacher.

Two other studies, referred to later [14] in this chapter, show the same to be true for high school and college students.

An extensive series [15] of recent studies supplies even more specific evidence. Differences between dominating and socially integrative teachers were studied in second-grade rooms. Four degrees of domination were listed ranging from domination in conflict to domination while working together with no conflict. Integration was described on two levels: (1) teacher and pupils not working together, but the class feeling secure in consulting the teacher and (2) to full co-operative participation by the teacher. The most extreme differences were found, as would be expected, between the teacher who dominated in conflict and the completely integrative teacher. All previous results were conclusively corroborated. Children's reactions, attitudes, and personalities were most favorably affected by the integrative teacher. The dominating teacher stimulated increased resistance from the children with detrimental results on mental hygiene and behavior. The study revealed also that the bad behavior learned under the dominative teacher did not persist when the children encountered a new teacher in the third grade. This is another practical illustration of the effect of the immediate social situation on human beings. The domineering teacher

[13] Stuart C. Tiedeman, "A Study of Pupil-Teachers Relationships," *Journal of Educational Research* (May, 1942), pp. 657-664.

[14] Note later references to studies by Harold P. Fawcett and Herbert A. Thelen.

[15] Harold H. Anderson and Joseph E. Brewer, *Studies of Teachers' Classroom Personalities II,* "Effects of Teachers' Dominative and Integrative Contacts on Children's Classroom Behavior," Applied Psychology Monograph No. 8, American Psychological Association (Stanford Univ., Cal., Stanford Univ. Press, June, 1946).

Harold H. Anderson, Joseph E. Brewer, and Mary F. Reed, *Studies in Teachers Classroom Personalities III,* "Follow-up Studies of the Dominative and Integrative Contacts in Child Behavior," Applied Psychology Monograph No. 11, American Psychological Association (Stanford Univ., Cal., Stanford Univ. Press, December, 1946).

continued to be domineering with her new second grade; the integrative teacher also proceeded as before. The dominating teacher persisted in techniques that clearly contributed to conflict and turmoil in her room, and which repressed initiative and spontaneity. Very significant was the finding that the integrative teacher materially reduced the resistance of the few children who were in conflict with her; the dominating teacher did not.

The mental hygiene of the teacher. We cannot in this volume present an extended treatment of the mental hygiene of the teacher, which belongs elsewhere. A brief note does seem necessary, since it is obvious that many unfortunate influences on children and learning flow from frustrated, maladjusted teacher personalities. Maladjusted teachers clearly produce maladjustment in children.

A number of studies of teachers attending summer schools [16] shows them to be a little less well adjusted than other women students. Studies of teachers in service reveal serious maladjustment in many cases. The study of New York City teachers [17] made some years ago showed, in the opinion of the examiner, that 1,500 of the 37,000 teachers were mental cases, some of them severe. Psychiatric examination would have benefited about 4,500 more. The examiner in this case, however, believed the percentage of psychotics among teachers to be no higher than in the general population. Even then, approximately 40,000 children would be exposed to a psychotic teacher each year. The

same study cited the figures from a New Jersey investigation showing that a child had a 7 to 1 chance to have at least two emotionally maladjusted teachers somewhere during elementary and secondary schools.

These studies, and those made in fields other than teaching, all stress the necessity for normal, balanced living, for attention to health, and particularly for recreation. [18] One study [19] showed that former teachers confined in an institution for mental cases had none of them ever had a hobby or avocational interest. Fair and honest administration and supervision, alleviation of too heavy loads, pensions, congenial associates, and community approval all make for emotional normality.

Summaries above are incomplete. A total list of characteristics of the effective teacher would go far beyond the personal. Reference is usually made to skills in classroom management, skills in instructional processes, efforts made toward improvement and professional growth, participation in community affairs, and skills in co-operating with others. Students may examine other sources for supplementary material on this score (see Exercise No. 1).

It must be kept sharply in mind that the personal traits listed are abstractions. They are derived through analysis of behavior; for

[16] Leigh Peck, "A Study of the Adjustment Difficulties of a Group of Women Teachers," *Journal of Educational Psychology,* Vol. 27 (September, 1936), pp. 401-416.

[17] Leo J. Alilunas, "Needed Research in Teacher Mental Hygiene," *Journal of Educational Research* (May, 1945), pp. 653-665.

Joseph T. Shipley, *The Mentally Disturbed Teacher* (Philadelphia, Chilton, 1961). Specific case studies and excellent general discussion. A shocking revelation.

[18] Dorothy Baruch, "Let the Teachers Have Their Vices," *Educational Method* (February, 1942), pp. 230-235.

John A. Bronson, "Problem Teachers," *Educational Administration and Supervision* (March, 1943), pp. 177-182.

Fit to Teach, Ninth Yearbook of the Department of Classroom Teachers (Washington, D. C., N. E. A., 1938).

Paul C. Palmantier, "Why Teachers Go Crazy," *Journal of Education* (December, 1947), pp. 290-291.

Leigh Peck, *op. cit.,* pp. 401-416.

J. B. Stroud, "The School Administrator and Problems of Teacher Adjustment," *Elementary School Journal* (April, 1945), pp. 451-454.

Many others are available.

[19] Frances Mason, "A Study of 700 Maladjusted School Teachers," *Mental Hygiene* (July, 1931), pp. 576 ff.

behavior must be observed to determine presence of traits. Many school systems have developed lists of sample behaviors illustrative of the traits. Training in observing is also necessary.

Adding personality traits together will not produce a desirable personality. The integrated personality is far more important than the abstracted parts. Various combinations produce differing but desirable personalities. The lists of traits are useful chiefly as a basis for discussion and guidance.

Experimental studies of teaching procedures. It is very difficult to secure reliable and valid data concerning the efficiency of a given teaching method or general pattern of instruction. The experimental factor is extremely complex, and therefore difficult to control. *First,* teaching is a highly variable performance. There are wide limits within which a teacher may vary his activities and yet be reasonably successful. This is natural and desirable but makes it almost impossible to isolate any given characteristics which will always appear in the work of good teachers, others which will always appear in the work of poor teachers. *Second,* teaching procedures not only vary greatly, but the factor of appropriateness further complicates analysis. A given activity may be quite appropriate at one time and not at another. The appropriateness of any given method or device depends upon the field within which it operates, that is, the total teaching-learning situation. The teacher's purpose, the maturity and purposes of the learners, the materials available, the policy of the school, and many other factors enter. The import of all this is that given processes may appear in the work of both good and poor teachers and be reasonably satisfactory evidences of good teaching in one situation and not in another. A *third* factor which makes comparative studies practically impossible is that different general patterns of instruction serve, in part, different purposes. It is not fruitful to compare experimentally "problem-

project" methods with "recitation" methods, since different purposes are served by the two types. A more productive method of determining the worth of general patterns is to analyze them in terms of valid psychological principles and to scrutinize the demonstrable results.

Some differences in individual abilities among teachers can be determined. An investigation of teaching efficiency by Lancelot shows that the effect of the instructional procedures of designated teachers upon the efficiency of the pupils' later learning can be measured with some precision. Pupils who had preliminary mathematics courses with some instructors did consistently better in advanced courses than those trained by other instructors. One instructor, who was a hopeless failure teaching freshmen, was accidentally discovered to be the most efficient of all the group in teaching seniors. [20]

Another set of studies, directed at determining the effect of class size on learning, yielded incidentally some important facts concerning teaching ability. *First,* it was clear that classroom methods and techniques necessarily differ between large and small classes, even though the general principles are the same. *Second,* some individuals developed and utilized methods fitted to large classes, achieving as good results as did other individuals with small classes and methods applicable thereto. *Third,* and very interesting, some teachers were unable to acquire control of the methods suitable to large classes even when those methods were available. This would seem to show that there are important differences between persons in their ability to do given describable types of teaching. Some persons do suitable work with small classes but not with large; others do just as well with much larger classes. The data did not show whether those expert with

[20] William H. Lancelot, "A Study of Teaching Efficiency as Indicated by Certain Permanent Outcomes," first essay in *The Measurement of Teaching Efficiency* (New York, Macmillan, 1935).

large classes could teach small groups as well. [21]

Probably the most extensive investigation of teaching ability is Barr's effort to determine characteristic differences between good and poor teachers. [22] Forty-seven teachers of social studies in high school deemed to be superior and forty-seven deemed well below average in teaching skill were studied over a long period and by means of several techniques. Detailed stenographic records were made; trained observers studied the teachers at work; various time charts were made; the teachers analyzed their own work. Practically every conceivable act and every expression of teacher and pupil were considered, about thirty-seven factors in all. The following fragmentary samples are illustrative: [23]

Characteristic comments made by poor teachers but not by good teachers. Are you working hard? . . . Aren't you ever going to learn that word? . . . Anything wrong? . . . Don't get too noisy . . . Don't let this go over your heads . . . Go on . . . Everyone sit up straight, please . . . I'm afraid you are confused . . . I shouldn't agree with you . . . Indeed . . . Speak up . . . Next topic . . . No, that's wrong . . . Yes, that's right . . . Oh, dear, don't you know that . . . Oh, sit down . . . Say something . . . and so on, through nearly one hundred expressions.

Characteristic comments made by good teachers but not used by poor teachers. Aha, there's a new idea . . . Are you going to accept that answer? I should like more proof . . . Ask the class . . . But there is another point . . . Can you prove your statement? . . . Can you supply a better word? . . . Does that answer the question? . . . Don't you really think you could? . . . Give a concrete example . . . I am not quite clear on that, think a moment . . . I'm afraid that question cannot be settled . . . Let's stick to the question . . . Now be careful . . . Now where did you find that? . . . Probably my question was not a good one . . . and so on, through a long list.

Poor teachers, almost without exception, make some form of textbook assignment; twenty-one of them merely made a page-to-page assignment; ten supplemented the textbook with questions and special topics. The majority of good teachers used some form of assignment other than the textbook assignment; seven used the problem-project assignment; and two used the unit assignment. Where good teachers did use the textbook assignment it was always supplemented by topics, questions, or references; ten, for example, used a form of running comment upon the chief topics. No good teacher made merely a page-to-page assignment.

Poor teachers made, according to the early data, far more assignments than did the good teachers, but took much less time in the making. The good teachers were evidently making fewer assignments, each one covering a topic or unit of respectable size and taking some time to develop.

Poor teachers asked more fact and fewer thought questions than did the good teachers and answered more questions for individual pupils. Good teachers referred more questions to the group and used pupil questions as the basis for discussion.

Naturally, there was much overlap between the activities of poor and of good teachers. Final results showed that there were no *critical* factors, that is, factors which appear exclusively with either poor or good teachers. Nevertheless, there were characteristics which did appear more consistently with one group. The good teachers were superior in:

1. Ability to stimulate interest.
2. Wealth of commentarial statements.
3. Attention to pupil's recitation.

[21] Earl Hudelson, *Class Size at the College Level* (Minneapolis, Univ. of Minnesota Press, 1928). This study contains a summary of similar studies prior to 1928.

Dora V. Smith, *Class Size in High School English* (Minneapolis, Univ. of Minnesota Press, 1931).

Margaret McGuire, *Experimental Adaptations of Teaching Procedures to Large Geometry Classes.* Unpublished material, Univ. of Minnesota. Referred to in Hudelson's monograph, also in bulletin of the National Association of Secondary School Principals.

[22] A. S. Barr, *Characteristic Differences in the Teaching Performance of Good and Poor Teachers of the Social Studies* (Bloomington, Ill., Public School Publishing Co., 1929).

[23] *Ibid.*, pp. 39-48.

4. Topical or problem-project organization of subject-matter.
5. Well-developed assignments.
6. Frequent use of illustrative materials.
7. A well-established examination procedure.
8. Effective methods of appraising pupils' work.
9. Freedom from disciplinary difficulties.
10. Knowledge of subject matter.
11. Conversational manner in teaching.
12. Frequent use of pupils' experiences.
13. An appreciative attitude (as evidenced by nods, comments, and smiles).
14. Skill in asking questions.
15. Definite study helps.
16. Socialized class procedures.
17. Willingness to experiment.

Even though no critical factors were found, the small contributing differences are significant. Teaching is a complex, variable performance, success in which is attained through the skillful combination of many subsidiary items as indicated above.

Recent studies show superiority of democratic methods. Older studies on the effectiveness of democratic methods in teaching are summarized in two volumes referred to earlier: Leonard and Eurich, *An Evaluation of Modern Education;* and Chamberlin and others, *Did They Succeed in College?* Graham [24] has produced evidence showing significant growth in democratic attitudes and behavior patterns in children taught by teachers using participatory democratic methods. Fawcett [25] has shown that a high school class in geometry taught by participatory sharing methods instead or by the usual method knows as much subject matter as fellow students who "covered the text." The students taught by democratic methods were definitely superior in achievement and use of habits of thinking and in transfer of these

[24] Alva W. Graham, "Do Teachers Who Use Democratic Methods Develop Democratic Attitudes?" *Elementary School Journal* (September, 1946), pp. 24-27.
[25] Harold P. Fawcett, *The Nature of Proof,* Thirteenth Yearbook of the National Council of Teachers of Mathematics (New York, Teachers College, Bureau of Publications, Columbia Univ., 1938).

skills to other situations. Thelen [26] tried the democratic, sharing methods with a freshman chemistry class on the college level. Students in the experimental section knew more subject matter than those who went through the textbook and manual method and were quite superior in thinking skills, particularly critical analysis. The extensive study by Giles [27] some years ago is widely known. A very recent study [28] describes the use of democratic methods not only with students but with parents and teachers in attacking a community problem. Other samples may be found in Alberty's volume [29] on the curriculum and in Stiles and Dorsey, [30] *Democratic Teaching in Secondary Schools.*

The preparation of college teachers at long last beginning to receive attention. The bulk of available material on the preparation of teachers deals with teachers in the elementary and secondary schools. Special preparation for college teachers has, for definite reasons, been neglected in the past. Today the absolute necessity for exploring this area is recognized.

Some harsh criticisms will be made below but the picture is by no means all black. Illustrations of excellent efforts at training college teachers and descriptions of procedures will finally be given.

The *first* obstacle to the consideration of college teaching methods is the ancient cliché, "if you know your subject you can

[26] Herbert A. Thelen, "A Methodological Study of the Learning of Chemical Concepts and Certain Abilities to Think Critically in Freshman Chemistry," *Journal of Experimental Education* (September, 1944), pp. 53-75.
[27] H. H. Giles, *Teacher Pupil Planning* (New York, Harper, 1941).
[28] Louis M. Klein, "A Different Kind of High School P.T.A.," *School Board Journal,* Vol. 118 (April, 1949), p. 37.
[29] Harold Alberty, *Reorganizing the High School Curriculum* (New York, Macmillan, 1947), pp. 352-374.
[30] Lindley J. Stiles and Mattie F. Dorsey, *Democratic Teaching in Secondary Schools* (Philadelphia, Lippincott, 1951).

teach it." This is repeated even in the face of incontrovertible evidence to the contrary. Delmer Goode, editor of the quarterly journal *Improving College and University Teaching*, says on this point: [31]

This notion not only tends to discourage special preparation for teaching in college or university but also causes any question of a professor's teaching quality to seem like an attack upon the soundness of his scholarship. Hence the rarity of programs designed to prepare graduate students for college and university teaching, or for the in-service improvement of teaching faculties. Where programs exist they are generally neglected or even despised.

The *second* piece of folklore based upon simple ignorance and upon an erroneous concept of learning is "Teachers are born, not made." The acclaim which greeted Barzun's *Teacher in America* indicates how widely this simple error is accepted. The intricate, intensely personal processes of stimulating learners can no more be achieved by uninformed "born" practitioners than can surgery, diagnostic medicine, or engineering. No one claims that training alone can make a teacher nor denies the necessity for certain spiritual, clearly personal attributes.

A *third,* and serious obstacle, is the naïve ignorance and/or the mulish antagonism toward schools of education manifested by many rank-and-file professors in arts, letters, and science. Schools of education are obviously badly organized in many instances. Course sequences are messy and unsystematic. Some very superficial material is to be found. Many schools of education are, due to their newness, about where the respectable sciences such as astronomy and chemistry were in their beginnings. Academicians should look to the beginnings of their own disciplines before condemning education courses in blanket terms.

Certain schools of education are, how-ever, developing rapidly. Bold experimentation is going on both in course materials and sequences and in the introduction of students to teaching and internship. One or two of these schools are definitely in advance of the other divisions within their universities. A large amount of wholly valid material on learning and teaching is available within the literature of professional education. Some of the books on teaching have appeared in several revisions over the years, are used in this and other countries. One or two have achieved gross sales records of close to one million dollars. To ignore this is silly.

A *fourth* obstacle is the feeling, natural enough to some extent, on the part of professors that any discussion of "methodology" is a criticism of themselves and their classroom procedures. This is just personal immaturity and will disappear as better understandings are achieved.

A few illustrations of progress and truly noteworthy achievements will later balance the indictments above.

Some beginnings. The feeblest and most incompetent effort at preparation of college teachers is based on the assumption that any well-educated liberal arts graduate can be given a few verbal descriptions, materials, and processes and thus be fitted to teach. This assumption is based on an incredible ignorance of the educative process. A number of colleges give a few "counseling conferences," or a series of one-hour lectures toward the end of undergraduate or graduate study. One series, probably the only one in print is found in Cronkhite's *A Handbook for College Teachers.* [32] This consists of a random collection of desultory pronouncements. The lectures are related only by temporal sequence and in that they were delivered from the same rostrum. No attention at all is given to central planning in terms of needs and actualities of classroom procedure. There is no central core around which the lectures

[31] "Report of the Pacific Northwest Conference on Higher Education, 1960," *Improving College and University Teaching* (Corvallis, Oregon State Univ.), p. 33.

[32] Bernice B. Cronkhite, ed. (Cambridge, Mass., Harvard Univ. Press, 1950).

can be integrated. Internal contradictions are to be noted. A few of the lectures constitute prima facie evidence that teachers cannot be prepared this way—certain of the persons giving the lectures indicated complete innocence of any knowledge concerning the educative process. One or two of the lectures contained good practical advice, but with no guiding concepts.

A far better effort along similar lines is found in Dobbins' *Expanding Resources for College Teaching*.[33] This is a good collection of articles presenting discussion of advantages and disadvantages of college teaching. It contains very general but good material.

Three [34] summaries show that such makeshift practices are slowly disappearing, with more adequate programs emerging. It is particularly gratifying to note that not only are formal courses being tried, but apprenticeship teaching or internship is being given serious consideration. The personal characteristics of teachers are coming in for attention.

Still better are recent books by single writers, with an occasional symposium. The following are representative:

BUXTON, Claude E., *College Teaching: A Psychologist's View* (New York, Harcourt, Brace & World, 1956). Well written but on very formal aspects of teaching. Written by a psychologist, the volume oddly ignores the

[33] Charles G. Dobbins, ed. (Washington, D. C., American Council on Education, 1956).
[34] Fred J. Kelley, *Toward Better College Teaching* (Washington, D. C., Federal Security Agency, Office of Education, 1950).
Fred J. Kelley, ed., *Improving College Instruction* (Washington, D. C., American Council on Education, 1951).
College Teaching as a Career (Washington, D. C., American Council on Education, 1958).
The first of Kelley's reports contains good summaries of new developments, as of that date. The second contains lectures and discussions at the Chicago Conference, December, 1950. Good general ideas but not so good as the first report. The third reference is a collection of essays on the advantages and disadvantages. Very good on general statements.

huge body of psychological research on learning and teaching.
COOPER, Russell M., ed., *Two Ends of the Log: Learning and Teaching in Today's College* (Minneapolis, Univ. of Minnesota Press, 1958). Several excellent articles included.
DIEKHOFF, John S., *The Domain of the Faculty* (New York, Harper, 1956). Well written and stimulating. Covers much ground, reader should make selection.
DOUGLASS, Paul, *Teaching for Self-Education* (New York, Harper, 1960). Very well-written advanced discussion. Not too clearly on teaching but very useful.
MARSHALL, Max S., *Two Sides of a Teacher's Desk* (New York, Macmillan, 1953). Contains good bibliography.
JUSTMAN, Joseph, and MAIS, Walter, *College Teaching: Its Practice and Its Potential* (New York, Harper, 1956). Much very good material, divided between principles and practices. Somewhat formal view of teaching, not too critical in discussing specifics.

A significant comment is that no one of these books makes any reference to the literally huge and very useful literature to be found in widely used textbooks in principles of teaching or general methods.

A new day is dawning. College teachers themselves have traditionally ignored or disregarded with contempt proposals for either analysis of teaching or preparation for it. A few history professors can be heard making remarks about the educative process and its improvement which are flatly contradicted by considerable historical fact. A chemistry professor loudly demands "more subject matter and less methodology" but is quite unaware that the college of education on his own campus gives no courses in general methodology! This fact could have been ascertained by an elementary application of scientific method. Another chemistry professor repeats endlessly that all education professors say and believe that "We teach children, not subjects." This statement has not been heard in competent educational circles for over a quarter of a century. We might gently call attention to Whitehead's remark about college teachers, "The ancients taught wisdom; we teach courses." [35] A professor of English recently commented over television on grammar textbooks as now used in elementary and secondary schools. His remark indicated that he had not seen any of the books which have been published within ten years.

In contrast, we may note that many professors have written excellent inspirational books about teaching. Currently a significant change of attitude seems to be appearing. Many professors are speaking of "methods of teaching" or "methodology" without the connotation that this is a naughty word. Several isolated requests for attention to improvement of college teaching have come from departments other than the school of education: from departments of philosophy, of business administration, of law, and from several liberal arts departments. One major institution planned to inaugurate a new division in the graduate school, the Department of College Teaching. Plans were excellent but were dropped when the school could not secure the one man it wanted to head this.

Gilbert Highet has given us in *The Art of Teaching* [36] a superb piece of writing and an example of scholarship in the very best sense of that word. His chapter on "Great Teachers and Their Pupils" should be read by every teacher from nursery school to the graduate level. Highet's discussion of actual teaching methods applies best to an extremely limited area in which able students deal with systematic materials and could not be applied generally. The entire volume, however, is replete with discussions, both wise and charming, of the subtle emotional and personal aspects of teaching which do apply everywhere. Robert Ulich has presented a balanced and scholarly chapter "On the Education of Teachers" in his volume *Crisis and Hope in American Education.* [37] The skillfully written summary is one of the best over-all general statements available. Reference is largely to teachers below college level, but the application to college level is explicit in places and implicit everywhere. Marie Rasey presents, in *This is Teaching,* [38] an account of classroom methods which lies at the pole opposite those presented by Dr. Highet. The actual conversations are reported almost verbatim. Certain readers dislike the conversational style and express annoyance at the slow development of ideas and at the changes of attitude. But that is exactly what happens in real learning. The college teacher has been the most naïve of all in believing that his students learned the substance contained in his lectures and at the rate of his procedure. Difficult reading or not, Rasey's book presents a type of teaching which will inevitably pervade more and more classrooms. The teacher is a member of the learning group, often only a consultant. The content of the course develops in terms of the interests and backgrounds of the students, but with due regard for the systematic organization of materials and modes of thinking within the area being studied. Harold Taylor's *Essays in Teaching* [39] is a vigorous and forthright treatment of college teaching as conceived by the moderns, breaking sharply with traditional concepts.

One of the best pieces of argumentation concerning college teaching to appear anywhere is that by Father Thomas L. O'Brien, S.J., [40] which deals with the lecture "method." He makes a deadly indictment, based on systematically organized fact and logic. His whole paper is superb.

Two other vigorous and provocative presentations are by Ordway Tead, and while they do not deal minutely with teaching they are stimulating discussions of conditions. The subtitle of the first document is significant.

[35] *The Aims of Education.*
[36] (New York, Knopf, 1950).
[37] (Boston, Beacon, 1951).

[38] (New York, Harper, 1950).
[39] (New York, Harper, 1950).
[40] *Proceedings of Pacific Northwest Conference on Higher Education* (Corvallis, Oregon State Univ., 1960). Father O'Brien's paper appeared in a panel discussion. Pp. 19-30.

The Climate of Learning; A Constructive Attack on Complacency in American Colleges (New York, Harper, 1958).

College Teaching and College Learning (New Haven, Conn., Yale Univ. Press, 1949). Vigorous and provocative. Excellent references.

The one book in the field which does discuss in detail most of the major classroom procedures is:

McKeachie, Wilbert, *Teaching Tips: A Guide-Book for the Beginning College Teacher* (Ann Arbor, Mich., George Wahr, 1951; 4th ed., 1960).

The author frankly states in both Foreword and opening chapter that his book is not an outline of a course in college teaching. It is just what the title implies, a handbook for beginners. There is no systematic organization in the volume, nor is one needed under the circumstances. McKeachie has done more research in this field than any other man in the field and hence leans heavily on his findings. His bibliography covers fourteen pages and constitutes a mine of information. Like the other authors he fails to list the systematic treatments of principles of teaching or learning. He does, however, get down to brass tacks on practically all classroom techniques.

Two professional groups have issued volumes of some size on their particular problems:

Blauch, Lloyd, and others, *Teaching in College and University* (American Association of Dental Schools, 1945). An older reference but one of the very few that presents learning and teaching in detail and accurately, with reference to the body of research available.

The Accounting Teachers Guide (American Accounting Association, 1953). Mostly on accounting. References to teaching are meager and formal. Not comparable to dental reference above but commendable as a first attempt.

Two other references, one very old, should be noted:

Eells, Walter C., comp., *College Teacher and College Teaching: An Annotated Bibliography* (Atlanta, Ga., Southern Regional Board, N.E.A., 1957). An enormous listing but with notable lack of strictly educational listings.

Pressey, S. L., *Research Adventures in University Teaching* (Bloomington, Ill., Public School Publishing, 1927). The pioneer study. Excellent accounts of research studies on factors affecting teaching. Still valuable despite date. Could well be followed up with current research inquiries which have been lacking for some time.

A recent book on philosophy of education, a field which should certainly have relation to teaching, has some excellent brief summaries concerning teaching which are applicable to any level:

Ulich, Robert, *Philosophy of Education* (New York, American Book, 1961), pp. 200-206, 207-224.

Teacher domination versus pupil freedom.
The rise of modern or progressive education precipitated a long-continued argument about domination and freedom in the classroom. Learning the fundamentals, discipline, and obedience to authority were stressed by one group; the child-centered school, freedom, and creative activity by the other. There is, as we shall see, no real opposition between these sets of terms.

Oversimplifying and exaggerating for the sake of emphasis, we may say that one group seems to believe that learning takes place only under the thumb of the teacher. Learning for them is dominated and directed by the teacher. The teacher, as the wise adult, plans the route and, with varying degrees of domination or compulsion, sees to it that the pupil follows that route. The cultural inheritance, organized into subjects, is the core and system of organization.

The other group seems to believe that learning will take place only if the learner is free. Remove stimulation, guidance, and teacher participation; let the natural impulses of children find expression, and learning will result. This group "views with alarm" any type of teacher participation. The needs and purposes of the learners, refined little if at all by teacher participation, are the core and system of organization.

A balanced view. The foregoing extremes are found today usually in the writings of lay critics. The professional teacher has long since achieved a view on teacher participation and pupil freedom which is practical and technically sound. This view has been stated several times in different connections in preceding chapters. Spontaneous and vivid learning purposes are to be seized. The teacher is also to set the stage and stimulate learning. The teacher is not to be at the mercy of immature purposes but will guide learning in terms of pupil maturity and socially desirable results. As Dewey said, there is no sense in having an experienced, mature adult around if he is not to aid the less experienced, immature learner to progress. [41]

The real danger is not in adult participation, but in too much of it, or the wrong kind, in the undue interruption of on-going learning activities. It is very easy to interrupt and to dominate. Often so much teaching goes on that no learning can take place. It is unquestionable, however, that wise stimulation and guidance are necessary to learning. Teacher activity is to stimulate learning activity. The nature of learning activity will then determine teacher activity.

The crux: Guidance without domination. As indicated many times in previous pages, the good teacher stimulates, encourages, participates in, and guides the learning activity of the pupil. In order to guide without dominating or coercing, the teacher needs two basic bodies of knowledge with the principles and techniques derivable therefrom. In addition, he must possess a poised, integrating personality himself, and he must sincerely believe in democracy.

First, a teacher must have keen, reasonably accurate insight into what is taking place *within the learner.* Just what is happening within the mind and emotional nature of the students? Teachers (and parents) cannot ever be successful without a considerable degree of ability to see just what understandings, attitudes, and habitual tendencies are actually being acquired by the learner. Just what happens when a pupil reads a given paragraph, sees a picture, observes at first hand slum living conditions, listens to arguments on social justice, is "picked on" in the kindergarten playroom, is reprimanded, is praised, listens to a lecture, participates in groups containing dominant and recessive children, and so on through ten thousand specific incidents? The adult is prone to interpret what happens within the pupil in terms of what the adult wishes, hopes, or demands will happen. *The adult constantly interprets the inner processes of the learner in terms of his own adult reactions.* The astounding unawareness manifested by some teachers of what actually happens within pupils under certain teaching conditions is unbelievable to one who has not observed it. The subtle, delicate, almost uncanny insight into the minds and emotions of learners, whether children or adults, manifested by other teachers is also almost unbelievable. It is an entrancing experience to see this type of teacher adjust his procedures to the nuances of feeling and understanding within the learner. That is the subjective side.

Second, a teacher must have equally keen insight into the part played by the objective world of things and persons in bringing about these results within the learner and into the effect the learner has upon the environment. The teacher who sees how various types of experience, various types of surroundings, various specific aspects of the outside environment affect learning, can then manipulate that environment to secure natural effects without domination. We need not repeat the details which were set forth in Chapter 4 concerning the process and the results of interaction with the environment.

The *third* requisite is as important as the

[41] John Dewey, *Experience and Education* (New York, Macmillan, 1938), pp. 33 ff.

required knowledge noted above. A balanced, integrating personality can achieve satisfactions in many ways without resorting to dominance over others. Insistence on domination nearly always results from lack of security, lack of good mental hygiene, and feelings of inferiority.

The *fourth* necessity is a sincere belief in democracy. This means that the teacher will accept the uniqueness of each individual and aid each to develop his capacities, whatever they may be, in accord with socially desirable ends and values.

More immediate principles of guidance derivable from the foregoing are listed below. The list is not exhaustive and may be amplified.

1. Begin with pupils' own questions, problems, arguments, real-life activities; aid them in formulating their own purposes.

2. Help them to adopt the accepted purposes of their own group, eventually the desirable purposes of their own society.

3. Allow for democratic procedure in planning, developing ways and means, choosing and carrying on activities, so that each individual can suggest plans, contribute ideas, materials, and so forth. The teacher as a part of the group also contributes ideas and lets pupils participate in judging her suggestions. Because of her longer view and more mature experience, she guides their purposing, planning, and activity beyond the immediate and the trivial.

4. Welcome suggestions and build up a mutuality of purpose, aim, and morale.

5. Make the experience so vivid and so much a part of the learners' lives that the experience itself suggests further purposes to be explored.

6. Recognize the need for re-evaluating goals and for changing them as they are approached, so that valuable guidance and growth can result.

7. Provide opportunity for decisions to be made, allowing (within safe limits) the individual to make his own; refrain from making decisions for learners. Accept mistakes as normal.

8. Help each individual to recognize his assets and liabilities in terms of his possible contributions to group activities, to develop accordingly, and to accept satisfaction suitable to his own level of ability. [42]

[42] An excellent discussion similar to this one and expanding it somewhat will be found in Stiles and Dorsey, *op. cit.*, pp. 256-259.

Teaching is not a routine process: It is original, inventive, creative. Teaching is not a routine or rule-of-thumb process; it is a genuine intellectual adventure. The mechanical use of formulas and devices, slavish dependence upon methods and techniques recommended by training institutions or by fellow teachers will not beget learning. Teaching demands instead the ability to adapt boldly, to invent, to create procedures to meet the ever changing demands of a given learning situation. Teaching demands continuous, imaginative anticipation of the mental processes of others, the ability to think quickly, to phrase questions and answers so as to stimulate thinking, the ability to keep intricate and subtle learning activities organized and moving toward a desirable outcome without at the same time dominating or coercing. Teaching necessitates a broad background of technological information.

Teaching cannot possibly be done on the basis of common sense or experience alone. A surgeon could not possibly learn how to operate for appendicitis on the basis of common sense and raw experience. Engineers do not build tunnels from two sides of a mountain to meet squarely in the middle on the basis of common sense or raw trial and error. To do either of these things on the basis of common sense or experience alone would result in many deaths and in huge waste of money. These things are done successfully on the basis of lengthy, difficult professional training which includes a period of experience under guidance. Naturally, later experience and critical analysis of that experience play a large part in improving skill, but this experience and analysis are enlightened by the preparatory training in basic technology. Furthermore, there is demanded in addition the ability to make courageous adaptations of known procedures to unexpected conditions and unusual variations, and the ability to invent new procedures. So it is with teaching. A teacher can no more teach little children to read on the basis of her common sense or uncritical experience than can the surgeon operate or the engineer carry out projects. An even closer parallel can be drawn between the diagnosis of illness by the physician and the diagnosis of learning difficulty by the teacher.

How then will the actual necessary skills be developed? Largely through the resolute critical analysis of one's own experience. This analysis is possible only with teachers who see clearly that teaching is in fact dynamic instead of static, an exciting intellectual enterprise, and whose self-analysis is illuminated by adequate general and technological background. Teaching, more than most human activities, demands the use of judgment, imagination, initiative, and enthusiasm. Particularly does it demand the use of freely working, creative imagination.

Teacher education lags but is undergoing improvement. A genuine tragedy of education—and it could be a very real tragedy for democracy—is that teacher education is still in crude, primitive form. Students preparing to be physicians and surgeons take a series of necessary background courses in physiology, chemistry, biology, and anatomy; and they include a wide range of experiences during their internship. Similarly, students preparing for engineering or architecture cannot be accepted without adequate preliminary work in various branches of physics and mathematics. There is also a period of work experience accompanying the theory, plus apprenticeship in the field. This training cannot be waived. The difficult work of these professions simply cannot be carried on, or even learned, without adequate background and without experiences to develop skills. Teaching is far more intricate than most professional operations. It is in fact one of the most difficult of all human activities if carried on successfully. The necessary background is enormous—and largely missing. Training in the skills is trivial in its insufficiency. Fortunately, this situation is keenly felt by leaders. The current upsurge of activity in the improvement of teacher training is

one result. The extension of the older "practice teaching" into an internship of respectable duration and responsibility is under way. [43] The slow but steady upgrading of standards for teacher certification (except for emergency pressures resulting from depression and war) is another result. Teacher-training institutions are only slowly emerging from the competitive and political stage. Their long isolation from the life of the nation will disappear as they attempt to give their students experience with work and with life. There is a slowly growing insistence that admission standards be sharply scrutinized. A few schools are exercising guidance during high school. A few actually reject applicants who are clearly unfitted for teaching through mental inability, emotional instability, or some other personality defect. [44] (Low salaries and low public regard for teachers are serious obstacles to getting desirable candidates into teacher-training schools; hence retard the improvement of teacher training.)

The schoolmen should contradict at every opportunity the assertion that the legal requirements for teachers' certificates are too high, are a "racket" [45] by means of which

[43] W. R. Rucker, *An Analysis of Trends in Student Teaching.* Unpublished Doctoral Dissertation, 1951, Harvard Graduate School of Education.

[44] See the many publications and activities of the Commission on Teacher Education of the American Council on Education; the work and publications of the National Association of Supervisors of Student Teaching; of the American Association of Teachers Colleges; of the National Society of College Teachers of Education; bulletins containing the National Survey of the Education of Teachers; of the Research Division of the N. E. A., and of many regional associations.

See particularly the activities and reports of the National Commission on Teacher Education and Professional Standards (TEPS).

N. D. Cory, "Incentives Used in Motivating Professional Growth of Teachers," *North Central Association Quarterly,* Vol. 27 (1953), pp. 387-409.

J. D. McAulay, "Qualifications of a Good Teacher," *Peabody Journal of Education,* Vol. 32 (1954), pp. 22-25.

[45] W. H. Burton, "The Influence of Educationists Upon the Requirements for Teachers' Certificates," *Journal of Teacher Education,* Vol. VI (June, 1955), pp. 100-104. A survey of the certifi-

professional educators have protected their courses. First, the requirements in the most strict states are still pitifully inadequate. Second, there is no known instance of legislative campaigns by teacher-education institutions being directed at the inclusion of given courses or requirements. The constantly rising requirements (and they will go far higher) result from enlightened public opinion. Occasions have arisen, in fact, in which certain teacher-education institutions, far from protecting an existing racket, were hard put to it to develop materials to meet new legal requirements.

The foregoing criticism is sometimes voiced by superintendents interested in securing teachers at low cost, often by an uninformed lay group, and quite often by liberal arts professors. Conflict with the latter group is lessening, however, as the advantages of interaction are realized. No less a leader than President Conant of Harvard has suggested that professional educators and liberal arts faculties cease fighting over their differences and get together on the many points of agreement. Competent professors of education are thoroughly respectful of scholarship in the arts and sciences. Many references in this volume and throughout the literature indicate the very great use made by schools of education of the new advances in anthropology, biology, sociology, medicine, literary interpretation, his-

torical interpretation, and in many other fields. Schools of education can make important contributions to any departments in the colleges which have achieved an intellectual maturity sufficient to understand the importance of the study of education for their own survival.

DISCUSSION QUESTIONS

The first five questions are designed to stimulate discussion among beginning students without teaching experience; experienced students may read these for general effect without stopping to answer in detail.

1. A teacher complains that her pupils are dumb. They answer in monosyllables, fail to prepare or do outside reading, turn in belated and slovenly papers. The teacher is earnest, works hard, prepares carefully, asks many questions, tries to arouse interest and enthusiasm in the pupils.
It may be, of course, that she actually has a dull group; however, what other explanations might be possible?

2. A professor describing one of his own class periods stated that a point in the lecture aroused immediate questions from the class. The students asked for information, began citing illustrations pro and con, arguing enthusiastically among themselves. "But I soon put a stop to that," said the professor. "I told them that if they wanted to talk, to talk to me . . . that I would not tolerate such discussions among members of the class."
Organize arguments showing that the professor was wholly, partially, or not at all right.

3. A high school student handed in voluminous and carefully outlined book reviews. The work took a long time and was carefully done. The teacher asked the student if he had gained from the books any new ideas which he might use in his everyday affairs. He asked, in a friendly way, just what was the benefit to be derived from the lengthy outlines. The boy stared blankly and was quite disappointed in not receiving a top grade.
What made the boy feel that such reports were the proper thing?
Wherein did his present teacher probably differ from previous teachers?
What is the significance of this little story for learning and teaching?

4. Certain professors decry courses in "principles of teaching" by asking, "How can you train teachers in general?" They contend that

<hr/>

cating agencies of the forty-eight (then) states. Four other references are footnoted.

Marshall D. Wattles and Henry Osibov, "The Content of Teacher Education," *Journal of Teacher Education*, Vol. XI (December, 1960), pp. 464-469.

Morris L. Cogan, "Professional Requirements in Programs for the Preparation of High School Teachers," *Journal of Teacher Education*, Vol. IX (September, 1958), pp. 271 ff.

The Journal of Teacher Education should be followed for current articles on this and other problems of teacher education, personality, and proficiency.

T. M. Stinnett, "The Co-operative T.E.P.S. Conferences in Retrospect," *Phi Delta Kappan*, Vol. XLII (November, 1960), pp. 61-66. Interesting and dramatic story of interchanges between liberal arts professors and those in professional education.

we must train them specifically to teach English, to teach arithmetic, or to teach in the kindergarten. They profess not to believe that there are any general principles applying to such diverse things as teaching analytic geometry and teaching first-grade reading.

On the basis of your own limited observation, what do you think about it?

Are there principles of learning and teaching which might be important at any age and in any subject? If you think not, tell why. If you think so, then describe or define or illustrate in your own words.

5. Consider two teachers, one teaching a dog to jump through a hoop and the other teaching a boy how to multiply. Grant that in each case the teaching is soundly and expertly done.

Wherein might principles and procedures be alike? Wherein widely different? (Complete answers are impossible at this stage. Valuable and preliminary analysis, however, can be made by the student.)

The following group of seven questions calls for further analysis than that demanded by the foregoing. Experienced teachers may start discussion with these.

6. A certain proportion of college professors is often heard to say, "if you know your subject you can teach it." They usually add that courses in education or in principles of teaching are useless.

Cite evidences from your own experience as a student showing the truth or error of this view.

List the probable reasons why this statement is made by those who do make it.

7. It is often said of some professors, "He is a notable scholar; he certainly knows his subject, but he cannot teach." Students phrase it, "He can't put it over."

Explain in some detail what is meant by these statements.

How do you explain such a situation?

What suggestions can you make for remedying it?

8. The graduates of a certain college possess an excellent mastery of the subject matter within their major and minor fields of study. They seem to have unlimited familiarity with and grasp of the content, both of the texts and of the lectures. These students, however, did unusually poor practice teaching. They manifested little imagination, little ingenuity, and no creativity. They were quite unable to stimulate or guide learning. Two who had taken honors in history failed miserably in teaching history in their practice period.

What explanations may be advanced? Make several points.

9. School superintendents often complain that the teachers of, say, mathematics or history whom they employ know the subject matter from A to Z, but they know little about the learners and care less. Why should superintendents complain about this?

10. A man directing athletic teams is called a "coach" instead of a "teacher." What is the difference between teaching and coaching? the likeness?

11. Why do some excellent athletes, expert performers in baseball or football, make poor coaches? Why do some mediocre players make excellent coaches?

12. Would it be best for an inexperienced teacher to begin by analyzing and/or imitating an expert teacher; by studying the nature of the learning process and method principles based thereon; or by beginning to teach, thus learning by experience?

The final group of nine questions carries the discussion toward some general conclusions.

13. A pupil says he does not want to learn. Another says he will not learn. The teacher is the guide and director of learning, but is she concerned if there is no learning process going on to direct?

14. Make a list of the chief difficulties or weaknesses of teaching as you saw it in high school or college.

15. Make a similar list of the chief merits and strengths of teaching as you saw it in high school or college.

16. Everyone entering teaching expects to engage in the preparation of lessons. Not everyone realizes that he will have to engage also in a large number of other activities in addition to the preparation of lessons. Make a list of important activities in which you think you may have to engage, directly or indirectly connected with teaching.

17. Someone has said, "The best teacher is she who teaches least." What does this mean? Do you agree or disagree?

18. If a teacher is concerned not with getting a student to memorize but to respond variously, what are some of the traditional teacher activities that should disappear? Some new ones that might be given a larger place, particularly in high school and in college?

19. What significance, if any, do you attach to the generally accepted view that teaching in the elementary grades, particularly in the primary, is done better than in the secondary school, and that college teaching is more poorly done than either? Make several points.

20. Courses using this text are often entitled "Principles of Teaching." In many schools they are called "Methods of Teaching." What might the difference be? Why do you suppose some schools use one emphasis; some, the other?

21. There are many genuinely excellent teachers and a large number of good average ones. Their techniques are, however, susceptible to great improvement. In addition, there are scores of genuinely poor and incompetent teachers. Why is teaching, in general, not too expertly done? Outline several methods of attack upon the problem.

EXERCISES AND REPORTS

1. A small committee should analyze a collection of studies dealing with desirable personality qualities for teachers. Construct a composite list which is compact but adequate.

2. An individual or small committee should construct a check list or rating card covering the teacher and her technique. (Students are advised that the rating of teachers in terms of a formal check list is not good practice today. Check lists are used as diagnostic instruments and as bases for discussion. Experienced teachers co-operate with supervisors in setting up standards and lists. The construction of such a list is, therefore, a good exercise.)

3. Make a series of observations in a classroom or classrooms and report upon the specific devices used by skillful teachers for exercising leadership without dominance. Report similarly on those who dominate where it is not at all necessary. (Protect all concerned by avoiding the use of names.)

Experienced teachers can report upon their own difficulties and growing skill here.

Reports and Discussion on Some More Aspects of the Teacher's Role

Advanced students may be able to omit all the foregoing questions and devote attention to the following and others similar which they may raise.

1. List arguments showing that the teacher should understand the cultural history and traditions of his society. List arguments showing the dangers when he does not. List observed practices or statements showing that a given teacher or group do not know these things? That they do.

2. Answer the same questions relating them here to knowledge of the relationship of persons to the institutions and conventions of society.

3. Relate briefly any historical accounts of these two items.

4. Report in detail any current discussions of the "subject matter versus method" wrangle, which is by no means over.

5. Describe and critically evaluate any new advances in teaching. (Reports may be made here of team teaching and of the use of teaching machines, or they may be made at the conclusion of Section III.

6. Report briefly on any observational studies made of everyday teaching and teachers. (For instance: *Learning and the Teacher*, 1959 Yearbook of the Association for Supervision and Curriculum Development.)

7. Individuals or small committees may make reports reviewing *The Teacher's Role in American Society*, Lindley J. Stiles, ed. (New York, Harpers, 1957). Each part might be the subject of a separate review.

8. Do the same for *The Teacher of Teachers*, Harold Rugg (New York, Harpers, 1952).

9. A report may be made on *Improving Instruction in Professional Education*, 1958 Yearbook of the Association for Student Teaching.

10. Reports may be made on several recruiting pamphlets directed to prospective teachers. These are published by state departments of education, by colleges and universities, by teachers associations, and by some of the foundations.

11. A report may be made on *The Teacher and Professional Organizations*, T. M. Stinnett (Washington, D. C., National Education Association, 1953).

READINGS

References in footnotes and in exercises are not repeated here in order to save space.

ADAMS, Fay, *Educating America's Children* (New York, Ronald, 1946). Ch. 2 is excellent.

BAXTER, Bernice, *Teacher-Pupil Relationship* (New York, Macmillan, 1941). Contains much concrete material.

BRUCE, Wm. F., and HOLDEN, A. J., Jr., *The Teacher's Personal Development* (New York, Holt, Rinehart & Winston, 1957).

BURR, James B., HARDING, L. W., and JACOBS, L. B., *Student Teaching in the Elementary School*, 2nd ed. (New York, Appleton-

Century-Crofts, 1958). Whole book very valuable. Use the index for special topics.

GLENNON, Vincent J., *The Road Ahead in Teacher Education* (Syracuse, N. Y., Syracuse Univ. Press, 1957).

LANE, Howard, and BEAUCHAMP, Mary, *Human Relations in Teaching* (New York, Prentice-Hall, 1955). First class general reading for all teachers.

OLSON, Willard C., *Child Development* (Boston, Heath, 1949). Chapter 11 is an extremely valuable treatment and a good deal of other information can be picked up in Chs. 8, 9, 10, and elsewhere in the book.

REDL, Fritz, and WATTENBERG, W. W., *Mental Hygiene in Teaching* (New York, Harcourt, Brace & World, 1951).

RUGG, Harold, and BROOKS, B. Marian, *The Teacher in School and Society* (New York, Harcourt, Brace & World, 1950).

SCHORLING, Raleigh, *Student Teaching*, rev. ed. (New York, McGraw, 1949). The whole volume is of value.

——, and WINGO, G. Max, *Elementary School Student-Teaching* (New York, McGraw, 1950). Contains much material which duplicates Schorling's book on the secondary level, plus much material especially adapted to the elementary school.

STILES, Lindley J., and DORSEY, Mattie F., *Democratic Teaching in Secondary Schools* (Chicago, Lippincott, 1951). This whole volume is packed full of unusually good material. Use the index and chapter headings.

WOODRUFF, Asaheld, *The Psychology of Teaching*, rev. ed. (New York, Longmans, 1951). This is an interesting and valuable book with much valuable information for the teacher. The treatment is a mixture of the psychology of learning and of teaching. Use the index for special topics.

Literary, Inspirational, and Other General Discussions of Teachers and of Teaching

Vivid inspirational discussions of teaching and of its importance are appropriate in an introductory text to be used in a first course with students who are seeking vocational guidance. The present text is concerned with principles and techniques of teaching and with students who have presumably chosen their vocation. Training rather than guidance is the general aim. Nevertheless, general non-technical presentations about teaching, its joys and sorrows, its rewards, tangible and intangible, its moments of dull monotony, its moments of thrilling adventure, are of interest to many students on any level. The following titles are samplings of a much wider list that is available. Students may add others to the list as they discover them in their general reading.

BENSON, E. F., *David Blaize* (New York, Doran, 1916).

HIGHET, Gilbert, *The Art of Teaching* (New York, Knopf, 1950). Methods recommended are formal but chapter on great teachers and their methods is excellent.

PALMER, G. H., *The Ideal Teacher* (New York, Houghton, 1910).

PERRY, Bliss, *And Gladly Teach* (New York, Houghton, 1935).

PHELPS, W. L., *Teaching in School and College* (New York, Macmillan, 1912).

WELLS, H. G., *The Story of a Great School Master* (London, Chatto, 1924).

——, *The Undying Fire* (London, Cassell, 1919).

WOODLEY, O. I., and WOODLEY, M. V., *The Profession of Teaching* (New York, Houghton, 1917).

EXTENSION OF DISCUSSION

Instructors will determine how far to extend discussion based on this chapter. On advanced graduate levels, a course will doubtless be given dealing with teachers and their education. Reading material is widely available on:

New departures in teaching
  Teacher aids of various types
  Team teaching
  Teaching machines
  Television

New departures in teacher education
  Internships
  Learning on the job
  Various proposals to curtail or extend professional education
  Various proposals concerning educational psychology, psychology of learning, principles of teaching, etc.

Recruitment practices
Certification
Tenure
Teachers unions

RECRUITMENT

Many colleges, state departments of education, and corporations issue booklets about teaching. They vary greatly in size and even more in worth. Students may wish to look over some which are usually found in college libraries. The list here is a very small sample.

BURTON, W. H., *Vocational and Professional Monographs; Teaching*, 3rd ed. (Cambridge, Mass., Bellman, 1962).

KEARNEY, Nola C., *A Teachers' Professional Guide* (Englewood Cliffs, N. J., Prentice-Hall, 1958).

TICHEY, Robert W., *Planning for Teaching* (New York, McGraw, 1958).

SHARP, D. Louise, *Why Teach?* (New York, Holt, Rinehart & Winston, 1957).

VAN DELLEN, Deabold B., and BRITELL, R. W., *Looking Ahead to Teaching* (Boston, Allyn & Bacon, 1959).

WHITELAW, John B., *Teaching Opportunities*, U. S. Office of Education, Circular No. 589 (1959).

SUMMARY EXERCISES AND REPORTS RELATING GENERALLY TO SECTIONS I AND II

1. Suppose that the educators managing the elementary and secondary schools you attended had been able to utilize all that we now know about the characteristics of the learner and of the desirable setting for learning. Organize a report showing changes which might have been made in: general policy, administration, curriculum, methods of teaching, grouping, promotion, examining and marking, or any other factor. Be specific.

2. Make a series of observations in classrooms. List and comment upon any specific incidents and practices which seem to be clearcut efforts to proceed *in accordance* with the facts about the learner and the setting for learning. Do the same for illustration of *violations* of the facts.

3. Proceed as in 1 and 2, now using the "laws" of learning as the factors on which to base changes, to observe in the classroom. Select any law or set of two or three from either school. Pay particular attention to *maturation, insight, readiness*.

4. Attempt a forecast into the future. What probable future developments can you see resulting from better understanding of: the *organismic concept*, the *principles of learning* (any selected one or related group of several), the *desirable setting for learning?*

5. Students who have not had courses in child psychology, psychology of adolescence, or equivalents will profit greatly from the following exercise. Those with adequate background may omit it.

Compile for class distribution lists of characteristics of early childhood, of the preadolescent period, of adolescence, or of any designated level of growth. The characteristics will usually be in terms of behaviors (individual and social) and/or interests and/or achievements. The literature is extensive and easily available. Lists may be constructed by individuals or by small committees.

The educational implications may be developed in class discussion.

Part III

THE ORGANIZATION OF THE SETTING FOR LEARNING

Utilizing either traditional or modern principles

A teacher must have some idea of the course of events likely to occur when he steps before a class to participate in and to guide learning activities. This is true whether the teacher plans in advance or plans co-operatively with the learning group. What guidance exists for a teacher who is about to organize a teaching-learning situation?

Two general organizations of teaching materials appear in our schools. The general organizations for teaching are (*a*) the assign-study-recite-test procedure and (*b*) the unit. A serious mistake is made if the theories and organizations are placed in opposition to each other. Each has a use. The tendency to regard "traditional" and "assign-study-recite-test" as equivalent, to regard "modern" and the "unit" as equivalent, are quite natural errors. First, the older theory and practice have been continued when better methods were available, and contrasts derogatory to the older methods were inevitable. Hence, the older methods came quite naturally to be identified as "traditional" or "formal" or "outdated." Second, the older organization based on assignments has deteriorated in many secondary schools and colleges into a grotesque caricature of teaching. Again notable improvements were available and were ignored. Third, the miraculous success of functional units based on new knowledge about learning, properly developed by competent teachers, has contributed to the "either-or" error.

The facts are quite clear. The assign-study-recite-test procedure can be thoroughly modernized and used where it is appropriate. The unit, on the other hand, in the hands of superficial individuals, can be just as cut-and-dried as the most "traditional" methods.

The real necessities are, first, to rid each theory and practice of errors of misinterpretation and, second, to use each in its appropriate place.

Brief summary of reasons and principles basic to each theory. The older theory and practice were inherited from the days when elementary education consisted of the bare rudiments of the three R's given to the children of the masses, when the liberal subjects followed by professional training were available only to the selected few from the socially favored classes. Education was naïvely "preparation for life." Adult thinking dominated the aim, the course of study, and the teaching process. The learner, his nature, interests, needs, the differences between individual learners, were ruthlessly subjugated to the adult-centered and adult-enforced education.

The new theory and practice developed out of the great extension of the concept of democracy and the great body of new knowledge about living organisms and their growth produced by research in biology, psychology, medicine, and psychiatry. Cultural anthropologists gave new impetus to modern views by revelations regarding group life and development. The profound change in our social order produced by the rise of the masses and the extension of technology also contributed. The current philosophic emphasis on less speed, on time to learn, on time to meditate and contemplate are factors. Many details have been included in previous chapters. The effects will be demonstrated in immediately following chapters.

The proper placement and use of each theory and practice. A summary statement of the use of each theory and practice may be given here before proceeding to more detailed analysis.

The education of little children, of beginners on almost any level, and in the area of general education, will proceed best as the most effective types of units are utilized by teachers.

The education of students who can learn through reading, who are mature enough to learn through abstractions, and who are entering upon areas of specialization, will proceed properly through the modern and improved version of assign-study-recite-test.

Even in the special subjects, units can be organized with effect, particularly on the early levels. The assignment procedure becomes more effective and economical on the upper levels. Overlap of various types exists, as will be seen later.

One error made by uninformed administrators and teachers is the naïve effort to deny validity either to the old or to the new procedure. Lack of information plus immature wishful thinking is responsible. Many resort, particularly with respect to the new, to that last refuge of the incompetent thinker: "It's all theory; it won't work in practice." They fail to realize that "it" is working already in countless hundreds of elementary classrooms, in many core curriculums in secondary schools.

A *second* and more serious blunder is to brush the problem aside with the assertion that no real difference exists and that the same results can be achieved by either method. The difference is basic and irreconcilable; no mere difference between formulas is involved, no mere difference in classroom devices. The results achieved are of different orders and belong to different levels of education. Denial of the difference results in the arbitrary application of one or the other theory and practice to the whole range of education without regard for either the needs of the learner, the nature of the subject matter, or the needs of society.

Administrators and teachers who apply the traditional form of assign-study-recite to *all* levels betray their beliefs, conscious or unconscious, that

1. Society and education are static and authoritarian.
2. The learner is passive and receptive.
3. The learning process is associative or additive (the terms *atomistic* and *mechanistic* are often used).
4. The teacher is a task-setter and drill-master.

Those who would apply the functional unit useful with beginners to the upper levels of education are evidently unaware that:

1. The ability to handle systematically organized materials is a mark of maturity.
2. The ability to learn through vicarious experience, notably verbal abstractions, is a mark of maturity.
3. The ability to make application from logically organized materials to specific instances and problems (to transfer) is a mark of maturity.
4. The mature learner need not waste time on learning processes which are inescapable for the beginning learner.

Those who believe in the modern unit for beginning learners and for general education, who use the improved or modernized assignment procedure with mature learners and in areas of specialization, believe that:

1. Society and education are dynamic and democratic.
2. The learner is a behaving organism, an active participant in his own education.
3. The learning process is continuous, interactive, purposeful experiencing.
4. The teacher is a participating guide.

The two procedures indiscriminately applied cannot possibly produce the same results. The application of the traditional assignment method can result only in molding, indoctrinating, or coercing individuals into conformity with accepted beliefs and values through unrelieved imposition of selected segments of the cultural heritage. The proper use of modern assignments and of units aims at developing responsible, creative individuals who will realize their unique possibilities within a flexible, co-operatively determined society. The cultural heritage will be discovered, but not thrust upon the learners. Learners will discover how the cultural heritage was produced, and hence what it means.

Contrasts between the truly traditional and the modern pointed up through use of extremes. Only the striking differences between traditional and modern practice can be emphasized here. The older procedure is not so stereotyped, nor the new so perfect,

as may appear here. Many variations of each procedure and mixtures of the two are found in practice. The following chapters in this section will supply ample detail for supplementing these abbreviated summaries.

Condensed summary of principles underlying traditional practice. An admirable summary prepared by Wrightstone [1] reveals the immediate implications of the older principles when they are applied to the classroom.

1. The classroom is a restricted form of social life, and children's experiences are limited therein to academic lessons.
2. The quickest and most thorough method of learning lessons is to allot a certain portion of the school day to instruction in separate subjects, such as reading, phonics, word drill, language, arithmetic, history, geography, health, and stories.
3. Children's interests which do not conform to the set curriculum should be disregarded.
4. The real objectives of classroom instruction consist to a major degree in the acquisition of the content matter of each subject.
5. Teaching the conventional subjects is the wisest method of achieving social progress.

Condensed summary of principles underlying the newer practices. The same author [2] has stated the implications of modern principles as follows:

1. The classroom is a form of democratic social life and the children reconstruct their experience therein.
2. These experiences grow from the children's social activities, and various parts of the newer type of curriculum are integrated around a central problem suggested by the children's social activities.
3. The organization of the curriculum for integration of pupil personality is paramount to traditional and formal organization of subject matter.
4. A dynamic organismal-environmental concept of learning is preferable to a mechanistic stimulus-response concept.

[1] J. Wayne Wrightstone, *Appraisal of Newer Practices in Selected Public Schools* (New York, Teachers College, Bureau of Publications, Columbia Univ., 1935), p. 9.
[2] *Ibid.,* p. 10.

5. A pupil's interests are viewed as signs and symptoms of growing powers and abilities.

6. Interests and powers are developed by activities, and not alone by passive assimilation of knowledge.

7. A mastery of principles and practices of intelligent living is more important than memory of specific facts.

8. Each pupil personality is inherently social in origin and character.

9. The true unit of educative experience is a realistic study of a problem and a cooperative creative solution.

10. Education is the foundation upon which social progress and refinement are based, and consequently education must concern itself with vital problems in the world of both child and adult.

The outline [3] below summarizes in sharply contrasting form the chief differences between the older and the newer practices. The points listed under the older practices are roughly in order of progression from the badly stereotyped to the more sound. The modernization of the older practices is set forth at length in Chapter 12.

[3] See at this point the diagram on page 338-339 which presents this material from a different angle.

Traditional Instructional Practice	Modern Instructional Practice
I. OUTCOMES	
Memorization of subject matter. Repetition of formulas and recipes. Ability to follow recipes. Achievement of adult-designated levels of skill through drill in isolation from use.	An integrated and integrating individual. Controls of conduct such as: understandings, appreciations and attitudes, special abilities. Achievement of levels of skill suited to level of maturity through practice related to use and purpose.
II. TESTING THE OUTCOMES	
Essay tests containing arbitrarily selected questions. Standardized objective tests. Homemade objective tests.	Balanced and tested essay questions with explicit methods of marking. Inventories, interviews, case studies. Problem-situation tests. Observation of behavior. Various techniques for observing and recording behavior. Anecdotal records.
III. MARKING AND REPORTING OUTCOMES	
Arbitrary per cents, numbers, or letters based on arbitrary sampling of subject matter—or based on uncontrolled subjective judgment of teacher. Use of very general descriptive terms such as *Excellent, Good, Poor,* etc. Formal report card giving fragmentary account of subject-matter achievement and practically no account of other learnings.	Paragraphs descriptive of actual types of behavior, levels of skill, etc., prepared by teacher. Printed statements, sentences or short paragraphs descriptive of actual types of behavior, levels of skill, etc., printed and arranged for checking by teacher; a behavior scale. New type report cards giving as adequate as possible reports on various types of learning.
IV. IMPROVING LEARNING	
Repetition after school; more drill. Exhortation. Scolding or other punishment.	Diagnostic tests and analyses. Remedial teaching. (Theoretically, under expert teaching diagnostic and remedial procedures would become less and less necessary.)

V. Curriculum Improvement

Determined by textbooks used or constructed by specialists. Correlation of subject matter, fusion, new subjects, centers of interest. Broad field organization. Better organization within special subjects; subject-matter units.	Determined by co-operative planning. In the elementary school a unified program: in the secondary school, extension of unified program in the core curriculum; fusion, new subjects. Broad field organization. Functional units within the special subjects.

VI. Individual Differences Cared for

Irregular promotions. Special sections. Homogeneous grouping on limited basis; no change in materials or methods. Opportunity rooms. Special organizations touching administration, curriculum, and instructional practice: Gary (or platoon), Winnetka, Dalton.	Grouping on basis of social maturity with frequent rearrangement due to flexibility in shifting individuals: accompanying changes in material and method. Disappearance of fixed, arbitrary, grade (or other) levels of achievement. Normal levels of achievement indicative of adjustment to demands of the world must eventually be achieved but at rate consistent with individual's capacity and rate of work. (This is all sometimes called the "no failure" plan, which is a very misleading term. "Continuous progress" plan is a better designation.) New types of furniture, rooms, buildings.

VII. The Teacher

A task-setter and drill-master. (Often kindly and sympathetic but none the less a task-master.)	A participating guide and stimulator; a consultant.

VIII. The Pupil

A docile performer of tasks, a follower of recipes. A failing pupil is stupid or perverse.	An active, free participator in determining, organizing, and carrying out learning situations. A failing pupil needs diagnosis to discover factors interfering with normal growth.

The Assignment-Study-Recite-Test Organization	*The Functional Organization Utilizing Pupil Purpose and Socially Significant Material*

I. Assignment

I. Initiating a Unit

Arbitrary assignment of pages, exercises, topics, or chapters. Intellectual preparation through recall of related information (Herbartian). Differentiated assignments—minimum essentials for all plus enrichment—two- and three-track systems. Problems and projects with varied assignment.	Co-operative selection and definition of a purpose or purposes (pupil- or teacher-initiated). Pupil acceptance the important thing. Co-operative organization of plan of attack. Co-operative distribution of work and contributions.

The Assignment-Study-Recite-Test Organization	The Functional Organization Utilizing Pupil Purpose and Socially Significant Material

II. STUDY
 	
Unsupervised individual study of assigned text.
Supervised study of assigned text.
Unsupervised or supervised study of supplementary references.
Study coach for individuals and small groups.
Homerooms.
Formal teaching of study procedures.
 	
III. RECITATION
 	
Individual answers to fact questions.
Individual and group reports.
Socialized recitation.
 	
IV. TESTING
 	
Essay tests containing arbitrarily selected questions.
Standardized objective tests.
Homemade objective tests.
	II and III. WORKING PERIOD OF A UNIT
	
	Individuals and small committees carry on various activities: consult many printed sources, interview persons, listen to lectures, make excursions, perform experiments, hold group discussions, hear committee reports, and make analyses thereof, make original and creative contributions, gather exhibits of real materials, construct apparatus and illustrations, paint, draw, etc.
	
	IV. DEMONSTRATION OF LEARNING
	
	Balanced and tested essay questions with explicit methods of marking.
	Inventories, interviews, case studies.
	Problem-situation tests.
	Observation of behavior.
	    Various techniques for observing and recording behavior.
	    Anecdotal records.

School experiencing can be aligned with life experiencing. One of the chief merits of modern teaching procedure, set forth in earlier chapters, is that it follows the natural process of learning in real life, improved by organization and guidance from a trained and sympathetic teacher. The close relation between learning in real life and in school is shown in the outline below.

The Processes of Natural Experiencing	The Corresponding Processes in School Experiencing
On-going behavior is in process. Behavior is interrupted, something interferes; a new need or want arises, a new venture appears. Equilibrium is disturbed. Purposes emerge. "I must do something about this." Purposes are clarified and defined both by analysis and by experience in trying to achieve. Efforts to satisfy needs and purposes arise. Procedures emerge and are refined.	On-going behavior is in process. Behavior is interrupted. Pupils ask questions about their own problems, about things they do not understand or which confuse them. Pupils respond to motivations by teacher or environment. Problems, projects, things to do or to find out are proposed by pupils or stimulated by the teacher. Purposes are defined as the initiation of a unit and clarified continuously as the unit develops. Procedures are planned and executed for carrying on the unit.

The Processes of Natural Experiencing	The Corresponding Processes in School Experiencing

Increasingly intelligent behavior results. Controls emerge for further use in new situations.	Procedures are refined as used. Outcomes of the unit appear as controls of conduct.
	    Understandings
	    Attitudes and appreciations
	    Special abilities
	    Skills

Learning does not take place at once or through one or a few experiences.

Further experience is necessary.	More units, study, and practice follow.
Controls are individuated and integrated continuously through experience: facility developed subject to change. Behavior is changed; control over life situations is improved.	Controls become a part of the personality; the organism has been changed; learning has taken place subject to change. Behavior is changed; control over school situations and increasingly over life situations is improved.
Proof of learning is its appearance in the modification of behavior. New needs arise and the process continues.	Proof of learning is its appearance in the modification of behavior. New units arise out of old ones or out of new needs, problems, questions; the process continues.

A somewhat more detailed expression of the same general conception of life and learning is found in the chart prepared by Paul Hanna, page 282. Other similar charts are available in textbooks and in recently published courses of study (teachers' guides).

The teacher's choice of procedures. The teacher does not always have free choice of methods. The factors which should determine his classroom procedures are:

1. The maturity and experience of the learners and of the group involved; the range and type of individual differences.
2. The immediate "felt" needs of the learners; the more remote goals of the learners; the socially desirable goals for learners.

A number of factors beyond the control of the teacher often dictate the choice of both materials and methods. Tragic misuses of methods can result. The factors [4] are:

[4] See Exercises No. 4 and 5 for elaboration of these.

1. The philosophy and aim of the school system.
2. The administrative policy of the leadership.
3. The dominant community opinion.
4. The nature of the curriculum.
5. The adequacy of instructional materials, the teacher's load, length of school day, the teacher's administrative and extracurricular assignments.
6. The training, capacity, and personality of the teacher.

The improvement of the teacher's use of instructional organizations. Well-trained, earnest teachers will be found using either of the basic schemes skillfully. Good teachers may improve within the general method which they are using, or they may, under favorable conditions, change from one basic scheme to another deemed to be better. The stimulation of teacher growth in the classroom, for both good teachers and the great numbers of mediocre and poor teachers, is an inescapable responsibility of the entire staff.

A Flow Chart of a Complete Educational Experience*

Individual with past experience → faces a new situation, novel to him, resulting in → a disturbance, disequilibrium

out of which emerges a *purpose* → *To Do Something,* → i.e., share a thought or feeling, acquire object or information, express a mood, etc.

Each type of behavior suggested has its own medium or expression: → constructing, dramatizing, reading, asking questions, writing, speaking, figuring, drawing, etc., → and each medium has its own appropriate skills, techniques, facts, attitudes, appreciations, etc.

which have to be acquired in the normal process of achieving the purpose set, → and when these skills, facts, attitudes are thus built into the learner in normal goal-seeking. → they give satisfaction in restoring the equilibrium of the personality and leave him ready to face the next novel situation with increased power to live and learn.

* Or of a complete living experience, to be more exact. Chart prepared by Paul R. Hanna, Stanford University, in connection with a speech entitled "Living and Learning in Our Modern World" delivered before the Public Education Society of San Francisco.

Improvement will be stimulated regardless of which type of organization is favored if supervisors and teachers will keep certain questions in mind as they develop instructional situations:

1. Are the problems to be attacked of basic importance?
2. Are the problems of immediate value or need to pupils? Are they of such a nature that pupils will readily see values and needs and make the problems their own?
3. Are the problems within the range of pupil maturity and experience, thus having some probability of successful attack? Are they of sufficient challenge to stimulate further growth?
4. Are there sufficient and varied sources to which pupils can turn, such as books, references, audio-visual materials of all sorts, community resources of many types, both personal and material?
5. Are the learning experiences and activities which are planned for accomplishing the desired results the best that can be provided in the given circumstances?

In improving any kind of teaching or learning, problems and purposes are central; materials and experiences are the means.

Efforts to aid teacher growth of whatever kind must be carried on with proper regard for the experience and convictions of those teachers. Teachers should not be asked, except for sound reasons, to abandon or to modify principles and practices in which they have confidence. Great changes are not expected overnight. First steps forward are short. Improvement at first will be concerned with whatever scheme and type of device the teacher is now using.

The growth of teaching personnel will come about slowly and naturally through experience. Growth is not fostered by authoritative order nor by the absence of competent and friendly guidance. Individual differences are as important in dealing with teachers as in dealing with children. Growth within any staff will progress unevenly with respect to the individuals in the group, and this must be accepted.

Co-operative effort in the stimulation of improvement can usually be secured if careful attention is given to building the teachers' feeling of security with the new practices as they develop. The entire personnel will participate. The idea that teachers may take part in the constructive programs designed to improve the total setting for learning is relatively new. A professional attitude in education is, however, growing. Evidence derived throughout the country indicates that a very effective aspect in improving educational programs is participation by the staff in their planning and execution. Changing one's teaching for the better is neither complex, difficult, nor frightening if one starts with the known and the familiar.

A number of manageable methods may be listed for initial attack, no matter whether we are undertaking to improve the assign-study-recite procedure or the unit organizations. In each case we wish to bring about:

1. Better connection and relationship between the needs, continuing interests, and maturity levels of the pupils and the materials and learning experiences of the school.
2. Increased use of desirable purposes as the core around which learning situations are organized. Purposes will be found both in curriculum areas and in the personal and community experiences of the pupils.
3. Greater pupil participation in planning and carrying on learning situations of whatever type.
4. More adequate provision for individual differences through greater diversity and variety of learning experiences and of materials, particularly the provision of reading materials on levels appropriate to the students' reading ability.
5. Greater emphasis upon interaction with other persons, with the community, and with life; greater use of community resources, both personal and material.
6. Better evaluation of all types of outcomes, which in turn brings better statements of objectives; increased pupil participation in evaluation.

Two dangers to be aware of are (a) formalism, which may overtake the most dynamic practices; and (b) superficial, half-baked treatment of crucial principles under any of the plans. [5]

Change and improvement in teaching processes inevitable. The teacher in the modern school must be a vastly better educated person than was found formerly. He must know much more about subject matter and method, about the learner and his growth, about the setting for and environment of learning, about interaction between learner and environment.

Teachers should not be confused or discouraged by the fact that instructional practices change from time to time. They do not change capriciously or at random. They change continuously in an orderly, systematic, and progressive manner as new facts come to light. The successive "waves" of emphasis on new teaching procedures are not mere passing frills or new devices. New procedures are not disconnected interjections into the educational process. The various changes are built one upon another. The long succession from assignments, to problems, to projects, to activities, to units is an orderly development. Each improvement is based upon and grows out of preceding organizations. A certain index of ignorance and lack of training are the comments occasionally heard, such as: "they are always changing things in education," "there is no sense to all this changing of methods," "I go right on teaching the old way and sooner or later they shift back and I'm in style again." The trained and intelligent teacher will scrutinize new suggestions carefully and demand evidence of their value but will gladly use improved methods, just as he uses improved transportation, lighting, housing, plumbing, methods of communication, methods of food

preparation, medicine, surgery, government, manufacturing and distribution and packaging of goods, and ten thousand other improvements. Individuals who assert that school curriculums and methods, alone of all human enterprises, must not progress and change may be suspected of intellectual and emotional immaturity.

Caution concerning introduction of new methods. Superintendents and teachers who realize the superiority of modern methods often attempt to change practice too rapidly. Teaching practices, like all other complex social techniques, cannot be changed quickly and easily. Beliefs, attitudes, and particularly the habits of years do not change overnight. Many communities have been antagonized by the confusion resulting from the introduction of new practices before proper preparation has been made. Progress cannot be achieved in advance of public understanding and support. This is a supervisory problem, but it needs to be noted here.

A program of at least three years (preferably five) should be planned, during which time the teaching staff and the community will study the philosophy and the scientific background of old and new methods. The professional staff will evolve a philosophy and goals of their own, and eventually a new curriculum and teaching practice. Local study is the most effective, but this should be supplemented by special courses, summer workshop experience, eventually a local workshop, visits to other systems, and exhibits. An outside consultant is advisable. The pupils as well must be familiarized with the new procedures, since they, like the teachers, have been proceeding for years under quite different assumptions. Experiments show that it takes some time before pupils accustomed to teacher-dominated procedures and fixed assignments will fully believe that they may participate, make suggestions, express opinions, or work on things of value and interest. New administrative and supervisory policies are necessary. The commu-

[5] One state education department program of curriculum improvement has issued a separate bulletin of 121 pages devoted wholly to the problems involved in improving teaching through the stimulation of teacher growth on all levels. The bulletin contains a wealth of specific illustrations used by all levels of teachers, together with a brief compact summary of principles. *A Forward Step*, Curriculum Bulletin No. 7 (Augusta, Me., State Department of Education, 1948).

nity must be carried along with the program, since it is fundamental that parents be informed, understand the new, and believe that they are fully in the confidence of the school leadership. Finally, the new curriculum and methods should be introduced gradually through tryouts here and there, with replanning in the light of these tryouts. Final introduction of the new on a system-wide basis should come when all have had opportunity to inform themselves, to observe, to try out new methods under sympathetic supervision.

Criticisms of modern curriculums and teaching methods. Teaching practices and basic educational principles have been criticized from earliest known times. Criticism is always intensified in time of crisis or insecurity. During World War II (as with all other wars) the schools were criticized for failure to prepare children and youth for wartime duties, failure even to make them patriotic. Criticisms heard in peace time as well as in war claim that the schools (a) do not teach the "fundamentals," i.e., the three R's, (b) do not discipline the children and teach them respect for authority, (c) let the pupils do what they want to, (d) do not prepare for citizenship, (e) do not have standards, and (f) do not produce leaders. Currently, the charges are also raised that (a) the schools are teaching for socialism and/or communism and (b) modern methods produce delinquency. The criticisms come very close to being pure nonsense but are serious because of the number of persons who bandy them about. A literally huge amount of valid and conclusive evidence exists which contradicts

[6] *Important.* Instructors should determine how far to digress into study of the experimental evidence concerning the comparative merits of traditional and modern methods. The needs of the specific class should determine this. The topic is so significant in both in-service and preservice education of teachers that it should never be entirely omitted. The readings suggested at the opening of Part I may prove sufficient. The witty satire on the stubborn persistence of worthless methods contained in *The Saber-tooth Curriculum* may be discussed again here.

the charges. The evidence [6] can be found by any literate person who can use a library.

A widely disseminated argument against modern methods and against the improvement of education is: "Traditional education cannot be so bad since all our successful men of today were trained under it." This is nothing but a well-rotted cliché. Traditional education was the only kind the preceding generation could get! A five-pronged analysis will answer this naïve and uncritical statement. First, let us see if, in the management of our society, we have been so successful after all. Second, and this might have come first, let us define *successful* more critically and then examine the situation. Third, let us study the cases of men who were truly successful in the social and moral sense and note how many of them openly revolted against the traditional education they had to endure; how many flatly refused to stay in school and take it. Fourth, let us see how many men deemed socially and morally successful attained their fame through lifelong battles to improve the sorry type of education available. Fifth, how do we account for the huge numbers who were not notably successful, but who received the same education as the successful men?

Special Note on Team Teaching. The author suggests that students read this note at this point, and perhaps examine a few key references. Observations should be made, if team teaching is available in the neighborhood. Trying to demonstrate how a team might plan should probably be delayed until after Chapter 17. Knowledge of how classrooms are ordinarily organized and operated is necessary first.

Team teaching is a currently new method of organizing the setting for learning. Anderson, [7] the chief authority to date, points out

[7] Robert H. Anderson, *Team Teaching: A Bibliography* (Washington, D. C., Association for Supervision and Curriculum Development, 1960). This is a complete listing of references to date of publication. Indispensable for anyone dealing with this new development. Bibliography covers eight pages.

that the roots of the new procedure undoubtedly are to be found in many previous plans for grouping children and managing instruction. The non-graded elementary school also probably figures in the movement. Anderson strongly recommends that students have some familiarity with the early movements beginning with the ancient Lancastrian Plan, followed by the Dalton and Winnetka Plans, Wirt's Platoon System, Hosic's Co-operative Group Plan, concluding with the ungraded school.

The new development probably started in the Franklin School at Lexington, Massachusetts, in 1957, as part of the joint program of research and development sponsored by the Harvard Graduate School of Education and certain public school systems. The system has spread so rapidly that there is the danger, ever-present in education, of bandwagon acceptance of something not well understood. Both the theoretical basis and the practical operation is not simple. Several models are at present emerging.

A team usually consists of three or more teachers who will plan together the work for a large number of children, usually 25 to 30 children per teacher. The team plans a program of instruction, carries it out, and makes assessment of results. Elementary and secondary schools are both involved. Plans and organization can be vertically within a subject or group of subjects or cutting across subject lines, as is typical in the elementary school. Clerical assistance is strongly recommended.

The basic assumptions are: several teachers will have more competencies than one teacher; co-operative planning will therefore be profitable to all concerned; specialized knowledge can be brought to a very large group of learners at one time; the individual teacher will usually teach his own class as usual; there can be more flexibility in pupil grouping.

The weaknesses of departmentalized teaching are avoided and its advantages

realized. The same is true for the self-contained classroom procedure.

A film shown nationally in 1961 illustrated both good and bad points. The chief criticism, one in which the present writer strongly agrees, is that lecturing to a large group of students, particularly in the elementary school, violates all we know about learning. [8] Subsequent discussion in small groups alleviates but does not cure the difficulties resulting from lecture presentation.

Other methods of handling the large combined group are emerging. Three teachers in the Corvallis, Oregon, high school have been operating a type of freewheeling experimental approach in which anything can be tried once. The course in Problems of American Democracy is organized into typical areas. Several major areas were introduced to the students in lectures given by outside sources; fifteen sections of students were at the typical lecture meeting. Student reaction to lecturers ranged from enthusiasm, with many benefits cited, to indifference and bafflement. The latter response was usually to scholars who were unable to approximate the student level of language and meaning. However, other professors gave demonstrations with their lectures. For instance, the professor of textiles brought a number of suits, dresses, and other articles manufactured from textiles. He described and explained and at the same time took the garments apart, showing exactly how they were put together, where the difficulties came, the uses of different materials. The students accepted this with enthusiasm. Several businessmen who were invited—bankers, industrialists, agents —fared about as did the professors: some were able to reach the students, some were not. One professor took twenty-five students with him to the auditorium platform

[8] If available the devastating critique of the lecture method by Father Thomas L. O'Brien in the *Proceedings of the Pacific Northwest Conference on Higher Education* (Corvallis, Oregon State Univ., 1960), pp. 20-30, should be read.

and left the other 250 seated as an audience. He then taught a lesson which was broadcast over the public-address system. Thus everyone saw the emergence from the students' own responses to problems posed, the general outlines and characteristics of critical thinking. Questions from the class and from the audience indicated excellent understanding. In the future the teachers at Corvallis plan to try several other approaches together with an improved lecture presentation.

This new technique, so briefly described here, will almost surely become a standard method of organizing the setting for teaching and learning. Anderson's bibliography, noted in footnote 7, plus current developments should be studied without fail.

DISCUSSION QUESTIONS

1. Students without teaching experience may wish to raise questions directed at clarifying or extending any concepts indicated in these pages or in Chapter 1 of the Twelfth Yearbook referred to in the readings below.

2. Summaries of evidence concerning the success of modern methods may be presented here by interested students, if this was not done earlier in the course. A review of any of the two or three books assigned for general reading at the outset of the course may be given, if not done earlier.

3. Instructors and class groups who wish may summarize any number of current articles in lay magazines attacking or defending modern classroom practice. A valuable exercise is to list the positive statements made by attackers of American free public education and then summarize the evidence from reputable educational research.

4. Students without teaching experience should read pages 223 to 226 of the Yearbook, *Learning and Instruction*, raising such questions as they wish.

5. Experienced teachers may take any one of the factors affecting choice of teaching procedures and report for class information how the selected factor did operate in a given situation, how any detrimental factors were overcome. (Several reports may be made.)

6. Students without experience may find accounts of programs for the improvement of teaching procedures and report for class information. (Materials may be found in surveys, city, state, or county bulletins.) Distinguish between actual programs and outlines of suggested principles and activities.

7. Experienced teachers may report on actual programs of improvement in which they may have participated.

8. Students in training may report from their observations what they believe to be instances of skillful use (a) in appropriate areas of good modernization of older methods, (b) of modern methods, (c) of bad errors in either respect.

9. Students often ask for summary definitions, or for lists of characteristics differentiating between "traditional" and "modern" schools. Several such lists appear in the literature.

A small committee may prepare such a list for class discussion. Use existing lists, supplementing them from other general discussions.

READINGS

A large amount of historical background material which appeared in Chapter 8 of the first edition of this text has been omitted from this edition in order to save space. The author regrets this very keenly because of the widespread unawareness among educational workers of the background of current developments in education. There is great need at the present for better teaching of the history of education.

It is respectfully suggested that, if time permits, Chapter 1 in *Newer Instructional Practices of Promise* be read by all students.

Newer Instructional Practices of Promise, Twelfth Yearbook of the National Department of Supervisors and Directors of Instruction (Washington, D. C., N.E.A., 1940). Chapter 1 contains much the same material as was included in Chapter 8 referred to above. (This chapter may be read if older edition is available.)

ANDERSON, Robert H., *Team Teaching:* A Bibliography (Washington, D. C., Association for Supervision and Curriculum Development, 1960).

BURTON, William H., *Introduction to Education* (New York, Appleton, 1934). An older reference, but valuable for compact summary of many factors influencing modern practice. Chapter 23 contains much material supplementing the account just given. Note chart on p. 634. Chapter 9 covers many other items besides instructional practice, summarizing many influences which have affected our schools.

Rugg, Harold O., *American Life and the School Curriculum* (Boston, Ginn, 1936). Interesting historical summary.

Parker, Samuel C., *The History of Modern Elementary Education* (Boston, Ginn, 1912). Despite the date, this is still the best summary of historical background of elementary education.

Learning and Instruction, Forty-ninth Yearbook of the National Society for the Study of Education, Part I (Chicago, Univ. of Chicago Press, 1950).

Toward Better Teaching, 1949 Yearbook of the Association for Supervision and Curriculum Development (Washington, D. C., N.E.A., 1949). This book is typical of many current educational publications in that it is specifically descriptive of actual practices. Organization in terms of principles is much more loose than in the Twelfth Yearbook above. This anecdotal type material is very valuable for beginners provided they are not drowned in the descriptions and fail to see the necessary conceptual systems.

Learning and the Teacher, 1959 Yearbook of the Association for Supervision and Curriculum Development (Washington, D. C., N.E.A., 1959). This returns to the approach used in the Twelfth Yearbook, *i.e.,* in terms of general principles, but contains much excellent specific explanation.

CHAPTER 12: The Improvement of Assign-Study-Recite Procedures

The assign-study-recite-test organization of teaching carries its own definition within its descriptive title. The learning situation is organized around materials and experiences which are assigned by the teacher. The pupils then study in various ways. The results of their studying are presented and shared during a recitation period. Testing of results occurs at the conclusion of a series of assignments and may occur at stated times within the sequence. The procedure may range from deadly dull, rigid, and imposed to vivid and provocative, depending upon the ability of the teacher. Pupil participation may be ignored; there may be even harsh rejection of pupil interests and motives, not to mention suggestions. On the other hand, provision may be made by more enlightened teachers for pupil participation in developing assignments, to the limits set by pupil maturity and experience.

The assign-study-recite-test formula will be used for many years to come. Untold thousands of teachers are using and will continue to use it where it is not appropriate, some of them because they have no choice, others because they do not know they are wrong. Still other teachers will use it in its proper place, that is, in the special subjects, on upper levels, and with students with sufficient maturity and experience to be able to learn through reading and to manage verbal abstractions. In either event it is only simple common sense to take advantage of all improvements in the scheme which are available.

1: THE IMPROVEMENT OF ASSIGNMENTS.

The assignment is the key to teaching and to learning under this organization. The assignment largely determines what pupils do and how they do it; hence it determines the results achieved. The very meaning of *assignment* has been, as we shall see, definitely expanded to cover far more than reference to books. The improvement of this key factor, the assignment, is important and necessary.

Objective investigations indicate low-level assignments predominate. The results of a large number of investigations are available, covering such aspects of the assignment as type, number, placement, time used, and effectiveness. [1] Statistical and other ob-

---

[1] William Carr and John Waage, *The Lesson Assignment* (Stanford, Cal., Stanford Univ. Press, 1931); *The Encyclopedia of Educational Research;* Gerald A. Yoakam, *The Improvement of the Assignment* (New York, Macmillan, 1932); the last volume is devoted chiefly to pedagogical considerations but contains references to the objective findings; see also the *Review of Educational Research,* appropriate issues.

jective investigation of the assignment dropped off sharply after approximately 1930 to 1932, and the extensive current literature is chiefly descriptive of current practices.

Older statistical studies and the more recent surveys and samplings, one or two made or sponsored by the writer, reveal an astonishing state of affairs. The meager, vague, unanalyzed, wholly inadequate type of assignment predominates in the secondary school, practically to the exclusion of all other forms. One investigator reports that more than four-fifths of the procedures—in social studies, of all places—involved nothing more than page assignments to a single textbook! These were followed by a typical oral quiz, readily answered by memorizing or paraphrasing the text. That these formal methods are widespread at all levels can be verified by any competent observer who will visit any high school or elementary school for a few days. Despite fifty years of attack by competent critics armed with unlimited, valid evidence, there persists the wholly unexplained assignment aimed only at "covering the text." *It would be difficult to devise an educational practice so grossly ineffective, so certainly calculated to interfere with learning, as a page assignment to a single text followed by a formal verbal quiz.* Yet, this is the practice used by huge numbers of secondary-school teachers.

Evidence also shows that vague, indefinite assignments that lack the power to motivate are common causes of children's failure to learn. Teachers often comment on the record of pupil failures, usually contending that lack of effective study habits is the cause. Lack of adequate study habits is in truth a cause of failure, but the type of assignment which does not demand reputable study habits and does not give any help in developing these habits is equally to blame.

Pupil participation in developing assignments is negligible, although definite indications are to be found which show increasing attention to and adaptation to students' interests and abilities. There is a slight tendency for assignments to become more detailed and in some instances to be accompanied by study guides, problems, and more extensive projects.

The following paragraphs will present in historical sequence the improvements which have been made in the technique of assigning lessons. Many teachers limited by administrative policy, insufficient supplies, or inadequate training may improve their present techniques through knowledge of what has been done by other teachers under similar limitations.

A primitive form of assignment is the arbitrary designation of pages, exercises, topics, or chapters. The familiar type of assignment, criticized above, is usually made hurriedly as the bell rings: "Take the next ten pages." "Take the next chapter." "Work the next ten problems on page 92." This is an assignment in only one sense—the pupil knows what pages to cover. The teacher indicates where a real assignment may be found, though in some instances no real assignment may be there at all. He does not tell what the assignment is or how to handle it. No known purpose of teaching or of learning is served. The teacher's only objective must be to "cover the text," regardless of whether the "covered" material is of any use or meaning to the pupil! Study guides or aids and questions, even of the formal type, are not provided. A real purpose, objective, or outcome for the pupil is completely missing. He must have either no objective or a viciously false one, such as memorizing the material, pleasing the teacher, or getting a passing mark. No real evaluation of results is possible.

Some teachers may be using this kind of assignment because of an invalid curriculum policy, because of limitations of instructional supplies, or because of inadequate professional training. Existing conditions must be taken into account in judging them. Nevertheless, teachers should try to improve their techniques to the absolute limit within the conditions, participate in efforts to improve the local situation, or go elsewhere. Teachers *habitually* using the primitive type of assignment where limiting factors are not present are open to severe criticism. They either do not know about or deliberately ignore the known facts about the importance of pupil purpose, the limitations of a single text, and the wide range of difficulty in instructional materials and the range of abilities among pupils. Laziness on the part of the teacher may be a factor here and also varying degrees of stupidity.

Assignments of the somewhat limited type are *occasionally* legitimate when made within an on-going sequence with mature students. If an objective was properly established in the beginning and if the work has proceeded along fruitful lines, the need for supplementary material is easily seen by the pupils and quick reference may be made. The group will have appraised its progress and decided what to do next.

An early improvement embodied brief intellectual preparation for the assignment. The Herbartian methodology, introduced into this country just before the turn of the century, stressed the preparation of the pupil's mind for the assignment to come. Learning was believed to derive from books and other forms of presentation. The pupil was to be given some introduction, however, to the book assignment or other experiences. The teacher might discuss with the class some important current event, might refer to previous experiences in or out of school, or ask a series of leading questions. A background of information related to the assignment, named by the Herbartians the "apperceptive mass," was thus called to the forefront of consciousness. The assignment to books, references, and related experiences could then be connected with ideas and interests now in the child's mind.

The greater knowledge we now have concerning the variety of learning experiences makes this technique relatively superficial today. Adequately conducted, this step in the Herbartian procedure was in its day a marked improvement over earlier methods. It could be used to advantage today by many teachers who still use the primitive form of assigning.

The pretest and the assignment. The pretest introduced about 1925 by the neo-Herbartians, chiefly H. C. Morrison [2] and his followers, was a related technique, designed to furnish more adequate information concerning the pupil's background as a basis for assignments to come. The purposes are two: to give the teacher insight into the needs, abilities, interests, and individual differences within the class group; to lead pupils to see some connection between their present situation and what they are about to learn. Ideally, no assignments should ever be made without pretesting, but this is probably too much to ask under present working conditions. Many alert teachers, however, make astonishingly effective use of the technique. The average teacher, owing to faulty training and uncritical experience, is far too prone to organize courses and assignments in terms of the materials and with little or no reference to the needs, abilities, or even information of the pupils.

The form of the pretest may be a class discussion, an oral or written test of traditional type, a standard achievement or diagnostic test, an inventory of information, interests, needs, and attitudes, a check list of behavior traits, a problem-situation test, or any other instrument or technique which will supply pertinent data to the teacher.

This type of testing has nothing to do with evaluation of the pupils' achievement. Pupils must be told that it has nothing to do with marking, despite the familiar word *test*.

Many lesson-plan or unit-organization

[2] Henry C. Morrison, *The Practice of Teaching in the Secondary School*, rev. ed. (Chicago, Univ. of Chicago Press, 1931), p. 82 and elsewhere in volume. See also discussion of pretest in other recent books.

forms used in teacher-training institutions and many plan books used by teachers in service provide a place for summarizing data about the class group and individuals therein. Compiling these data from pretests and other sources, particularly for several classes, will take some time and energy just previous to the close of any semester. The benefits are well worth the work. Large numbers of teachers find that they are able to do this under practical conditions, and astonishingly good use is made of such data in many schools. [3]

Differentiated assignments employed: Minimum essentials for all, plus enrichment for average and bright pupils. The great body of fact revealed by modern research concerning individual differences in ability, in interests, and in rates of learning profoundly affected teaching and the settings for learning.

The materials deemed absolutely necessary were assigned as minimum essentials to be learned by all. Extended reading in other books or related sources was given to brighter pupils. Often the supplementary reading was more of the same kind covered by the minimum essentials. Reading could be extended, however, in terms of depth as well as breadth. Supplementary assignments, for instance, included reading of contradictory accounts or of several incomplete versions. Summary reports had to be made to the whole class, resulting in comparisons of arguments and conclusions. The use of processes other than reading and memorizing is important, as will be shown below.

Difficult reports were assigned to the brighter pupils, easier ones to the slower children. This often avoided the undesirable division in the group, since slower pupils are

not likely to recognize that their assignments are less difficult if they are similar in form to those of other class members. The slow pupil profited so far as his rate and ability would permit. He gathered data, evaluated various statements, formulated summaries, and participated in class discussion. He gained in self-confidence, his interests were expanded, and he got the satisfaction which comes from group membership.

The dominant conception still, however, was the mastery of facts and ideas and essential knowledge in the subject matter. The term *minimum essentials* is in bad repute today because of its established connotation of facts to be retained and of things to be learned by all pupils. Questions may be raised as to the nature and extent of minimum essentials. The beginnings of more varied learning experiences were, however, to be seen. The assignments at their best began more and more to reflect modern knowledge of learning as it appeared.

The organization of supplementary assignments of worth presents great opportunity for ingenuity and originality in the teacher. The objection is often raised, however, that no teacher has time to organize any efficient system of supplementary assignments under practical working conditions. This is true in part. It is not expected that every teacher will organize all his courses this way immediately. His system of assignments will be built up over a period of time. Since such assignments are based on subject matter and not on pupil needs, they can be used again with minor adjustments. Within a department, the staff can share the work of developing assignments. In addition, there is good material to be found in the periodical literature. The preparation of good supplementary assignments is a distinct step forward and can be done by competent teachers without undue strain on time and energy.

Assignments were expanded to include study guides, questions, and many diverse learning activities. The differentiated as-

[3] Good illustrations should be available in assignments and unit plans collected by the instructor. Some printed units contain such data. An illustration of partial summary of such data will be found on p. 510 of Roy O. Billett's *Fundamentals of Secondary School Teaching* (Boston, Houghton, 1940). Note the materials Billett says are omitted in this summary, since they are very important.

signments increasingly included study guides, questions, and job sheets. Many of these additions still emphasized memorization of extracted facts, but many also stressed comparison and evaluation, the organizing of arguments, and the drawing of conclusions. In some cases the study guides, questions, or job sheets called for the performance of routine tasks and chores. In their better form, the questions and guides were a distinct improvement over mere page assignments. The use of study guides may, however, divert teachers and pupils from the possibilities of co-operative planning. The setting up of precise and important questions or problems co-operatively with the class is a far superior practice, although one which did not appear for some time.

Eventually many diverse activities pertinent to the problem were suggested in assignments: interviewing persons, observing processes, visiting historic or otherwise important places, trying out things in little experiments, serving on committees, making exhibit materials, preparing dramatizations, and making various visual aids, charts, or diagrams.

Though still dominated by text-covering, by fact-memorizing, by teacher imposition, these procedures did begin to carry the student toward the exercise of powers of analysis, selection, judgment, and original organization. Even those who think of learning largely as the mastery of text material have recognized that the way in which that material is attacked is strongly influenced by the nature of the assignment. The mental processes required may be simple and few, analytic and numerous, straightforward or genuinely muddled; the outcomes may be superficial or basic, depending upon the assignment.

Superior teachers, in making assignments, include sufficient time to develop explicitly the objectives and the methods for achieving the objectives. An assignment may often include one or more periods of free class discussion for clarification of objectives and for preparing for difficulties to come. Not all sources, procedures, and difficulties can be handled in any one assignment, but over a period of time good assignments will progressively develop power on the part of the pupil, leading eventually to independent study and learning.

Hard words, idiomatic phrases, and other linquistic difficulties are explained. Lists of study questions are often mimeographed as aids to the pupil in finding, evaluating, and organizing material for presentation in class. Every assignment cannot be halted long enough to clear up all difficulties; we cannot even indicate all possible sources of information nor all learning activities. But properly made assignments will progressively bring the pupil to mastery of the use of dictionaries, encyclopedias, supplementary books, tables of contents, indexes, marginal headings, graphs, charts, pictures, and other sources of information. Intelligent use of such details facilitates learning. The pupil guided by proper assignments will also learn to outline properly, to take notes, and to discriminate materials for outlining. He will learn under guided assignments when to read rapidly and skip detail, when to read slowly and carefully. He will learn to find other sources and to make intelligent choices and comparisons. These procedures are all elements in the study process and will be discussed in the following section, but it is to be emphasized here that proper assignments must take them all into account.

Pupil participation in organizing the questions, problems, and projects is a recent development. A good index of teaching skill is the ability to make inviting connections between the required subject matter and the interests of the students. Setting up provocative questions which are designed to cause learners to react to text materials instead of merely to accept them is another desirable technique. These connections and questions are certain to provoke discussion, argument, or difference of opinion. The skillful teacher may then derive from the class discussion a series of supplementary study questions. A number of individual and group assignments may supplement the original over-all reference. The teacher may develop a fairly extensive conversation concerning a current event, a new book, an important moving picture, or a local occurrence. Again, argument and difference of opinion will arise, or group effort to derive understanding or to make applications will be initiated. Recall the connection made by the teacher between the text material on the Reconstruction Period and natural everyday interests and purposes of high school students.

After the principal problem has been stated, discussion may ensue regarding the data to be gathered and the sources thereof. A half dozen minor assignments, to an individual or to a small group, might be made. Here we have valuable pupil participation in finding worthwhile questions and in suggesting ways and means of studying.

The procedure indicated above represents a move away from teacher-imposed questions or assignments to teacher arousal of questions from the pupils. The pupil is participating. This procedure is still teacher-dominated and aimed at covering fixed text material, but is a huge step forward.

The sequence of assignments. Since the typical assignment procedure is based upon a textbook, or group of books, or printed course of study, the sequence is determined for the teacher. His skill will be utilized in attempting to relate this predetermined sequence to the normal interests and needs of his pupils. In some instances, he can within his own courses vary the fixed sequence to make it more teachable.

Wherever a liberal school gives good teachers an opportunity to develop their courses more independently, whether freely or within a loose framework, better sequences of assignments, that is, better materials and related experiences, are likely to result. In any event, teachers should not quietly ac-

cept nor themselves construct pointless, unorganized, unco-ordinated series of assignments. They should assume responsibility for establishing a defensible sequence.

The foregoing paragraphs briefly sketched some of the historical steps in improving the assignment and also introduced the student to some of the problems. Let us turn to a summary of the problems and difficulties, the principles, and the characteristics of desirable assignment technique.

Difficulties and problems confronting the teacher making assignments. Several studies have been made, but the summaries are poorly stated and very badly organized. The following paragraphs are based on an analysis of various summaries.

Two serious obstacles to good assignment technique seem to reside within the teacher and can be cured only by the teacher. These are unwillingness to take the necessary time and unwillingness to exert the very real effort demanded. The assignment, too often slighted, is an important part of teaching procedure. It requires time for pondering, for critical study, for written organization, for tryout, for discussion with others. It requires systematic and continuous effort. Good assignments simply cannot be "dashed off."

The other difficulties are inherent in the construction of assignments but can be overcome by competent teachers willing to spend time and effort. These are:

Finding provocative and convincing connections between subject and life needs or interests.

Producing clear and definite statement of objectives.

Providing appropriate and challenging study guides and aids.

Making sure all pupils understand objectives and methods of procedure (know what to do).

Providing adequate variations in requirements to fit range of differences in the group.

Gauging difficulty of requirements and time necessary for accomplishment by different levels of ability.

Avoiding extremes of too much or too little.

Providing continuity.

Ensuring correlation with other subjects and other activities.

Providing means of evaluating pupil progress and achievement.

The characteristics of good assignments. The broad general characteristics of good assignments are easily stated. Even in traditional schools the aims of mental discipline through memorization of subject matter, of knowledge for its own sake, are giving way to the aim of furthering the growth in the pupil of desirable understandings, attitudes and appreciations, and abilities useful in organized society. The assignment is aimed not so much at mastery of subject matter as at the use of subject matter in experiences which further growth. This is true even when the focus of attention is in the subject matter, and when subject matter is determined in advance. The alert teacher asks, how will this assignment bring to the pupils materials and experiences which will aid in developing useful personal qualities?

1. The objective, the thing to be done, should be stated in clear, simple language. The ability to do this is not immediate and automatic. Study and practice are necessary.

2. A provocative and convincing connection should be made between the subject matter of the assignment and the typical activities, interests, and needs of the pupils' current lives.

3. Assignments, while connected with and motivated by pupil need and interest, must also serve desirable social purposes of education, that is, lead to the development of outcomes useful in the organized society of democratic life.

Pupil interest does not here refer to the fleeting or transient interests which children may bring to school, though these can often be developed into continuing interests. Pupil interest here means the more or less permanent, learned interests. It is recognized that some interests which are not permanent operate over respectable lengths of time and are thus usable.

4. Study guides, questions, and other aids should be included. Commercial guides may be of some help to weak teachers, providing they focus on questions worthy of pupil atten-

tion. Many guides, however, abound in "busy work" and useless chores, so that there is real danger of formality and lack of attention to individual differences and to local needs. Cooperatively arranged questions and guides are of value.

5. Assignments must provide for different levels of achievement and for greatly varied learning activities, in accordance with the range of differences in ability, interest, and needs within the group. Of supreme importance is the supply of all kinds of instructional materials, including audio-visual aids, and particularly reading materials which vary in difficulty in accordance with variations in reading ability within the group. Supplementary materials and aids should be supplied as financial ability permits. Teachers and pupils can manufacture a great many at little cost, if this is necessary.

6. Assignments should be directed toward study which fulfils pupil and teacher needs, the needs being made apparent either by preliminary discussion or from information about the class which may be secured by the teacher from the cumulative records or other sources.

7. Assignments should initiate and motivate substantial units of work. Subsidiary planning for each day and week must be clear and explicit both for guidance and for determining progress. Day-by-day assignments of truly fragmentary type should be avoided rigorously, since, if these are used, the benefits of the large unit are lost and study degenerates into fragmentary memorization. Periodic summaries of progress with attendant reorganization of assignments is desirable. Several studies show that good teachers make far fewer assignments than poor teachers but devote much more time to assigning. A small number of assignments requiring greater time indicates the use of large units. The belief that the teacher must break up learning into thirty- or fifty-minute chunks, one to be assigned each day, is referred to by Frederick, Ragsdale, and Salisbury as the "ridiculous imperative"! [4]

8. Assignments should receive all the time necessary for explanations, for answering pupil questions, for developing an adequate plan of action, for arranging subsidiary individual and committee assignments, and for making sure that all know what is to be done. The time necessary may vary from a few minutes to two periods or more.

[4] Robert W. Frederick, Clarence E. Ragsdale, and Rachel Salisbury, *Directing Learning* (New York, Appleton, 1938), p. 219.

Extended planning of this type must be truly realistic and dynamic; it must not degenerate into a formal pattern. Lists of trivial questions are sometimes posed mechanically by the children, who realize that this subterfuge sometimes placates the teacher. The teacher should, over a period of time, guide the children toward the recognition of major and minor questions and toward forms of organization which are actually adapted to the immediate problem at hand. The teacher may suggest the major problem and some minor projects himself, both as a matter of getting important problems before the class and as a part of the guidance process.

9. Assignments may be made at any stage of the lesson in such way as to take advantage of or to develop need or interest and at the same time preserve continuity.

10. Assignments should be such that evidence of progress and achievement can be ascertained each day with reasonable ease. Many careless assignments are of such nature that neither teacher nor pupil can demonstrate that the assignment is being accomplished. The learning indicated by the assignment must be either measurable or observable in some objective manifestation.

11. Pupil participation in selecting and developing assignments and methods of procedure is definitely desirable.

12. The expenditure of considerable time and energy on the part of teacher and pupils and careful, detailed planning are fully justified by the importance of assignments.

Types of assignment. The total number of types of assignment listed by various authors actually runs into the scores! Distinctions without differences abound. All kinds of trivial and non-fundamental characteristics are used as bases of classification. It is futile to reproduce the lists. Probably the most sensible listing is Yoakam's, divided into two categories: "old-type" and "new-type" assignments.

His old-type list includes: page, paragraph, topical, chapter, question, exercise, experiment, and theme assignments. The new-type list contains: problem, project, unit, contract, job-sheet, term syllabus, guide sheet, the indeterminate, and the goal book.

The present writer is less interested in classifying assignments and more interested

in securing good assignments, of whatever type. There are certain desirable characteristics which should be common to all good assignments. These have been set forth—comprehensively, it is hoped—in the foregoing list of principles and characteristics.

It is impossible to include here adequate illustrative material; a whole volume would be necessary. The writer, with a collection of several hundred assignments before him, attempted to select a series for inclusion here which would illustrate the salient features. Since many modern assignments cover several pages, the amount of space necessary for a good series of illustrations is not available in the present book. Other volumes [5] of this type include one or two brief assignments or fragments thereof. These should be read quickly. This is helpful, but is not even the proverbial drop in the bucket. *Particular emphasis must be placed upon the necessity of having available an adequate collection of assignments good, bad, and indifferent, from all school levels and in all subjects, from units and projects.* This collection can be built up by instructors over a period of time. Meanwhile, collections in print must be utilized. It is quite impossible to guide students in developing an assignment technique without opportunity to analyze good and bad assignments.

The most adequate collection in print is in the volume by Yoakam, already referred to in this chapter. Chapters 2, 3, and 4 contain a truly astonishing array of assignments, illustrating practically every characteristic of all types. Lacking collections of their own,

[5] Older books by Billett, Morrison, Brink, Butler, Yoakam, Waples, and others writing during that period contain illustrations in varying amount and of varying excellence, but worth examining. Recent books often treat the assignment with a brief descriptive statement of little help to students. Part of this is doubtless due to the disrepute in which assignments are held, despite their wide use. It may also be due to the rise of co-operative planning. In this connection note particularly reference at the end of this section to the 1959 Yearbook of the Association for Supervision and Curriculum Development, *Learning and the Teacher,* and other titles there.

instructors are urged to make provision for definite, systematic study of Yoakam's materials. Exercises are provided at the end of this chapter, and instructors will devise many others to suit the needs of their own class groups.

DISCUSSION QUESTIONS FOR SECTION 1

This set of questions is for students without experience, and may be omitted with classes made up of experienced teachers.

1. A teacher tried the following experiment. She assigned a lesson and said that instead of waiting until they went home, the students could take the next fifteen minutes of the period for study. A few pupils were utterly unable to begin; others took the whole fifteen minutes to get started; some looked around helplessly and imitated others; some went to work immediately. But all these pupils had been coming to class each day with their home work completed with reasonable correctness.
What legitimate inferences may be drawn regarding the nature of the pupils' home study?
What kinds of training were probably taking place, so far as we can tell; what kinds not being accomplished?
What faults may have appeared in the assignments?
If given faults are present, what advice might be given?
What difficulties might appear which were not the fault of the teacher?
2. Under what conditions can lessons be assigned legitimately by pages, chapters, lists of problems?
3. In many schools assignments are written on the board and copied by the students. Critically evaluate this procedure.
4. When a pupil says, "I did not know where the lesson was," there may be several explanations. Suggest them.
5. Should a teacher ever permit digressions from the assignment during the recitation or discussion period? Ever permit abandonment of the assigned materials and activities?
6. Under what circumstances can a teacher properly assign without a pretest?
7. What would be your attitude and what would you do, if your classes presented an organized protest asserting that your assignments were too long?
8. Report for class discussion any good descriptions of assignments found in the current literature.

EXERCISES AND REPORTS

The only available collection in print of individual assignments is the volume by Yoakam. Instructors should build up collections for use by students here. Careful analysis of Yoakam's materials will be of real value to students.

1. Read Chapter 2 in Yoakam. This is a collection of assignments with comments by Yoakam. You will not always agree with his analysis, and you can develop many more points than space permitted in his book. Many of his points and illustrations are striking. Some of the assignments are grotesque caricatures of good procedure—but were actually used by some teacher. A number of good ones are also included.
   a. Does the general picture presented in this chapter agree with your personal experience as a student in elementary and secondary schools? Explain.
   b. What were two or three of the most striking things for you in this chapter?
   c. Select any one of the illustrations, good or bad, and develop a far more detailed analysis than that given in the text.
2. Note carefully the type of assignments you see in your classroom observations. Make notes as soon as you leave the observation room and then analyze in class in terms of the principles in this chapter.
3. Chapter 3 in Yoakam, "Types of Assignments and Assignment Materials," contains an unusually good collection of assignments illustrating the types which Yoakam distinguishes. Class members or small committees may select one or two to be analyzed in the light of the twelve principles in this volume. Show for each principle that the assignment does or does not exemplify it. Do not hesitate to disagree with or extend the analysis in Yoakam.
4. Chapter 4 in Yoakam, "The Characteristics of a Good Assignment," includes another good collection based on the characteristics of desirable assignments. Proceed as in Exercise 3.
5. Examine the excellent modern-unit assignments in Billett, Chapters 17 and 18. Analyze any one assignment in the light of the twelve principles.
6. Work out a different approach or introduction for any one of these assignments.
7. Billett gives on pages 540 to 544 and 576 four units without accompanying assignments. (One each on Growth of Language, Reading and Understanding of Graphs, Understanding and Prediction of Weather, Corrective Work in Physical Posture.)

Work out a detailed assignment to accompany the unit as there given.

Note. The assignments in Billett cannot be attempted by students not well prepared in the subject matter of the individual units. For prepared students these exercises will be most important.

8. A common-sense treatment of assignments of particular value to beginning students is found in *Successful Teaching*, by James L. Mursell (New York, McGraw, 1946), Chapter 8. Exercises at end of chapter will be stimulating to both beginners and experienced teachers.

9. *Final and most important. To be done by all students.* Prepare a detailed, modern-type assignment. You will have to have an actual class in mind or a theoretical set of data set up as a basis for the assignment. This may be for actual use if you are a teacher in service, for practice teaching if you are in training, or for class analysis if you are neither in service nor training. Take any aspect of your major subject or school level and prepare a workable assignment.

READINGS

Current discussions of the assignment are almost non-existent. Older references given in footnotes and in the exercises give much good material.

The attention of students is called, however, to the rise of discussions of planning. These appear chiefly in discussion of the unit, but general statements are beginning to appear. All students can read with profit the following:

Learning and the Teacher, 1959 Yearbook of the Association for Supervision and Curriculum Development (Washington, D. C., N.E.A., 1959), Chs. 3 and 4.
See also:
BROGAN, Peggy, and Fox, Lorene K., *Helping Children Learn* (New York, Harcourt, Brace & World, 1955). Good general treatment aiding planning.
BURR, J. H., HARDING, L. W., and JACOBS, Leland B., *Student Teaching in the Elementary School*, 2nd ed. (New York, Appleton-Century-Crofts, 1958), Ch. 5 and elsewhere.
LANE, Howard, and BEAUCHAMP, Mary, *Human Relations in Teaching* (Englewood Cliffs, N. J., Prentice-Hall, 1955). An excellent general discussion with many indirect bearings on planning. Good reading for all teachers.

SCHORLING, Raleigh, *Student Teaching,* rev. ed. (New York, McGraw, 1949), Chs. 6 and 7.
———, *Elementary School Student Teaching* (New York, McGraw, 1950), Chs. 6 and 7. Similar to previous reference.

2: THE DEVELOPMENT OF INDEPENDENT STUDY HABITS.

The questions and exercises which follow will introduce the student to some of the general problems of the section. Many other problems will appear. The questions may be discussed in class; but if not, a thoughtful reading will serve the purpose. Incidentally, these questions are illustrative, though in very simple ways, of the study questions or guides referred to in the previous section.

1. Analyze your own study processes and be ready to report:
   a. How your procedure differs from subject to subject.
   b. How your procedure differs from instructor to instructor.
   c. How the instructor's assignment and method of teaching influence your studying.
   d. How any other outside factors influence your studying.
2. If you have noticed the influence of your own attitude and understanding on study, report:
   a. How your like or dislike for a subject affects your actual studying.
   b. How your like or dislike for the instructor influences your studying.
   c. How your understanding of the value of the subject influences you.
   d. How knowing what to do and how to do it aids you. How failure to understand what to do handicaps you. Illustrate concretely.
3. What are some obvious evidences that many students (perhaps including yourself) do not know how to study?
4. Consider your own study activity and report on the:
   a. Influence of amount of time and time of day.
   b. Influence of immediate physical surroundings.

c. Influence of your present mental state, including the influence of immediately preceding mental activity.

d. Influence of your present physical well-being or lack of it.

e. Influence of yesterday's activities or of tomorrow's anticipated activities.

5. Do you study your hardest or your easiest subjects first?

When assignments consist of "take the next ten pages" and no further explanations are given, when recitations consist of oral quizzes to see how much of the "ten pages" has been remembered, then "study" can be only memorization and nothing else. This primitive conception still influences the practice of thousands of teachers, although psychological and sociological research has long since demonstrated its absurdity and has led to important improvements. Many of these studies have already been adequately discussed in earlier chapters. A brief summary here, however, will give emphasis to the special problem of this chapter.

First, it will be recalled that the learning process was discovered to be far more complex than had been thought. Second, it was increasingly realized that study, properly interpreted, is learning, and utilizes the numerous, various techniques of learning. Third, studies of pupil failure revealed that thousands of pupils had no conception whatever of study habits. Many did not even know how to read well enough to do the traditional type of study. Worse, thousands of teachers knew no more about learning and studying than did the pupils, hence could not help them. The studies of failure also revealed the influence of many factors far outside the schoolroom which affected study. Fourth, increasing knowledge of individual differences focused attention on the differences in rate and kind of study. Finally, it has been increasingly realized that the *direction of study is a function of the regular total teaching process and not a special set of devices or techniques.* The work period of the modern unit makes learning and study-ing synonymous. Supervised study gave way to "directed study," and that to "directed learning," and finally to "guidance in learning." This is not a mere change in terminology but reflects steadily increasing insight into the problem. [6] This is, however, a little ahead of the story. A brief historical summary will illuminate present problems.

Study was at first, and still is, unguided memorization. The foregoing paragraphs show that the formal assignment of pages or topics, with no aim other than that of covering the text, still dominates the schools. Study was, and still is, largely an effort to remember the text material. Study guides, even those of a most formal, busy-work type, did not appear for a long time. Some textbooks today contain guides ranging from formal, routine, memory questions and chores to fairly good suggestions for sensible learning experiences related to the material. Study guides, as noted earlier, are of value in some circumstances but can easily interfere with the development of better processes in which procedures are co-operatively developed. Limitation to single texts, inadequate supplies, and overloaded programs have helped to perpetuate the practice of unguided memorization. Part of the responsibility for conditions existing today, however, must be attributed to unawareness of the facts about learning, to inertia, or to flat refusal to do the work necessary for better procedures. Refusal to do the necessary, difficult work in developing reputable teaching method is far more widespread than is realized by conscientious teachers, or by

[6] It is significant that the two best books on study have the word *directing* in their titles: *Directing Study in the Secondary School,* by William G. Brink, and *Directing Learning* by Robert W. Frederick, Clarence E. Ragsdale, and Rachel Salisbury. The word *guiding* is appearing increasingly in the titles of books on teaching, learning, and study. References to "supervised study" have practically disappeared.

William A. Brownell, "What Has Happened to Supervised Study," *Educational Method,* Vol. 17 (May, 1938), pp. 373-377.

laymen. College and high school teachers, with brilliant exceptions, are the chief offenders.

Supervised study appears. The reaction to the proven inadequacy of unguided memorization and particularly to pupil failure through ignorance of study procedures was a direct attempt to improve pupil study habits. Increasing understanding of the nature of study, gained by analysis of the process, aided the effort. Supervised study programs sprang up everywhere. It was sincerely believed at the time that an important step forward was in the making. There were high hopes and glowing claims, but experience and research deflated the claims and dimmed the hopes. Here we have one more illustration of what happens when willing and enthusiastic persons undertake something for which they are not trained. Elaborate administrative plans were made, daily schedules rearranged, physical facilities and materials provided, much money spent. Teachers and administrators started supervising study with energy and eagerness. *The fact that practically no one knew how to supervise study did not disturb anyone—until later.* The careful, systematic training of teachers should have come first, although there were other causes of failure, as will be shown. Many earnest teachers did not know what or how to supervise.

The first reference to "supervised" study appears in the *Reader's Guide* during the period 1915-1917. The peak of popularity and practice was from 1917-1925. By 1935 the topic had practically disappeared from the literature. Emphasis had shifted to identifying study with learning and to developing study habits as natural outcomes of regular teaching-learning situations.

The older forms will persist, however, in many schools for years. Many teachers will have to operate within these schemes; hence, a brief analysis of typical supervised study procedures should be made here.

Study rules. The first effort to improve study could hardly be called supervised study. Sets of study rules and suggestions were presented to pupils in the pious hope that application would be automatic and fruitful.

The rules referred to physical conditions, time and place habits, and to a few of the more obvious general rules for reading, understanding, memorizing, and outlining. Suggestions were heavily weighted toward the more formal types of assign-study-recite procedure. Such rules are sound and useful with mature students. Elementary and secondary pupils, lacking explanation or assistance, merely pasted the rules in textbooks or desk covers and forgot them.

It should be noted that even in the very earliest and more formal period prophetic voices were raised, pointing to the identification of study with total learning. McMurry's volume on *How to Study and Teaching How to Study,* published in 1909, clearly identified study with learning as it was then understood and identified teaching how to study with the general teaching process. The child-study movement started even earlier, when G. Stanley Hall and his students focused attention on the importance of the pupils' learning processes and attitudes toward study.

Administrative schemes. Reeder says that the movement presaged by McMurry, Hall, and the child-study group was stunted and perverted by the American predilection for administrative machinery. [7] In the enthusiastic construction of administrative devices, schedules, and physical facilities for supervised study one important aspect was seriously neglected—the actual technique of supervising and helping pupils at study! The essential aspect of the movement was lost in its own furniture and machinery.

Reeder goes on to say that part of the difficulty was the error, natural enough under traditional conditions, of regarding study as

[7] Edwin H. Reeder, "Directing Children's Study of Geography," *Educational Method,* Vol. 17 (May, 1938), p. 387.

the individual, silent study procedure of individual pupils and regarding it further as a separate, discrete aspect of the total learning process. His diagnosis is undoubtedly correct.

The chief administrative provisions developed are listed below, since many teachers may have to work within one of them. Each of them is discussed at considerable length in texts on study and in the periodical literature. In areas where such plans are in operation and will be met in practice by students and teachers, detailed class reports may be made for further understanding.

1. Double periods, part discussion, part study.
2. Single periods divided between discussion and study.
3. Homogeneous ability grouping.
4. Special remedial classes in reading.
5. Special remedial classes in high school subjects.
6. Individualized instruction.
7. Case study of serious difficulties.
8. Study coach or study supervisor.
9. Library study plan.
10. Study-hall plan.
11. Homeroom supervision of study.
12. Daily extra period for supervised study.
13. Course in how to study.

Experimental data on the value of these devices. A very large number of controlled investigations, usually of the parallel group type, were made. The advantage on the side of supervised study was too slight to be significant. The truth of the matter was that the experiments really compared various administrative schemes for facilitating supervised study and did not compare supervised study techniques at all. In fact, supervised study itself had not yet been defined sufficiently to permit valid experimental research. No real process had as yet been developed. A good effect of this inconclusive experimentation, however, was to focus the growing attention on the actual process itself.

The processes of study and of the technique of supervision were neglected. The chief defect in all the schemes and the weakness of printed discussions was the absence of any systematic discussion of specific details of the actual procedure to be utilized by the teacher. Specific practices cannot be prescribed for so intricate and individual a matter as developing study habits, but certain general directions for teacher guidance can be offered. These will be indicated in later paragraphs.

Supervised study gives way to guided development of study habits. The general aim of modern guidance of study is identical with the general aim of teaching, namely, the development of independence in the use of certain understandings, attitudes, habits, skills, and patterns of behavior. The general process is that of providing opportunities for the exercise of these in learning experiences which are meaningful to the pupil.

What then are the desirable study habits and skills?

Study habits in better traditional schools. Nearly fifty books have been published dealing with study processes. Several score more general books devote a chapter to the subject. Forty or more study manuals have been prepared for use by elementary and secondary school students.

The best known of the older books on study are those by Bird, Brink, Brotemarkle, Crawford, Frederick-Ragsdale-Salisbury, Kitson, Parr, Pitkin, Salisbury, Sandwick, and Whipple. [8]

[8] Although many of these books are out of print, they should be available in a good library.
Charles Bird, *Effective Study Habits* (New York, Appleton, 1931).
William G. Brink, *Directing Study Activities in the Secondary Schools* (New York, Odyssey Press, 1937). Excellent and extensive bibliographies on all aspects.
R. A. Brotemarkle, *How to Study* (Philadelphia, Univ. of Pennsylvania Press, 1930).
C. C. Crawford, *Studying the Major Subjects* (Los Angeles, Univ. of Southern California, 1930).
———, *The Technique of Study* (Boston, Houghton, 1928). One of the first books.
Robert W. Frederick, Clarence E. Ragsdale, and Rachel Salisbury, *Directing Learning* (New York,

All are valuable, the two best being those by Brink and by Frederick-Ragsdale-Salisbury.

All of these volumes are based on traditional methods of teaching. The suggestions are based on the assign-study-recite-test process and the writers have made material contributions to the improvement of that process. They do not discuss study in terms of guiding learning activity, as it is coming to be discussed by the moderns. The two volumes singled out above, however, lean strongly that way. The six references on planning given at the close of Section I on page 298 carry the discussion far over toward modern assigning, which in turn affects study procedures. A list of more recent books on study is sampled here. Others are available.

ARMSTRONG, W. H., *Study is Hard Work* (New York, Harper, 1956).

COLEMAN, J. C., and LIBAW, Frieda B., *Successful Study* (Chicago, Scott, Foresman, 1960).

DUDYCHA, George J., *Learn More with Less Effort* (New York, Harper, 1957).

KALISH, Richard A., *Making the Most of College: Guide to Effective Study* (San Francisco, Wadsworth, 1959).

KITSON, H. D., *How to Use Your Mind*, rev. ed. (Chicago, Lippincott, 1951).

SHAW, Philip B., *Effective Reading and Learning* (New York, Crowell-Collier, 1956).

Appleton, 1938). Excellent and extensive bibliographies. Summary bibliography at back.

H. D. Kitson, *How to Use Your Mind* (Philadelphia, Lippincott, 1926). One of the earlier summaries.

Frank W. Parr, *How to Study Effectively* (New York, Prentice-Hall, 1938). Good.

W. B. Pitkin and others, *Learning How to Learn* (New York, McGraw, 1935).

Francis P. Robinson, *Diagnostic and Remedial Technique for Effective Study* (New York, Harper, 1941). College level.

Rachel Salisbury, *Better Work Habits* (Chicago, Scott, 1932).

R. L. Sandwick, *How to Study and What to Study* (Boston, Heath, 1915). One of the very first books of this type.

Guy M. Whipple, *How to Study Effectively* (Bloomington, Ill., Public School Publishing Co., 1929).

ROBINSON, Francis P., *Effective Study,* 3rd ed. (New York, Harper, 1960). Extensive. Contains also an excellent bibliography.

An interesting development currently is the appearance of books dealing with reading as an aid to study. Studies have shown that many study and learning difficulties were due to inability to read well in general or in the content of special subjects. Illustrations are:

BROOM, Leonard S., and SHELDON, W. D., *Developing Efficient Reading* (New York, Oxford, 1959).

CARTER, Homer L. J., *Effective Reading for College Students* (New York, Holt, Rinehart & Winston, 1957). (Another by same author deals with reading in junior high school.)

GUILER, Walter S., and RAETH, Claire J., *Developmental Reading* (Chicago, Lippincott, 1958).

LEWIS, Norman, *How to Read Better and Faster,* 3rd ed. (New York, Crowell-Collier, 1958).

MONSON, Samuel C., *Word Building* (New York, Crowell-Collier, 1958).

SPACHE, George D., and BERG, Paul C., *The Art of Efficient Reading* (New York, Macmillan, 1955).

STRANG, Ruth, *Study Type Reading Exercises* (New York, Teachers College, Bureau of Publications, Columbia Univ., 1951).

WEDEEN, Shirley U., *College Remedial Reader* (New York, Putnam, 1958).

Brink made a valuable analysis of sixteen general books to determine the study habits and aids most frequently mentioned. He classified them under four major heads with eighteen subdivisions. The wealth of detail can only be indicated here; for instance, there are 180 different suggestions on how to read more effectively. How to take examinations received the next highest number, indicating the far too great emphasis on examinations in teaching practice. Sixty different suggestions were made concerning outlining, memorizing, problem-solving, and making written reports. His general summary was: [9]

I. PHYSICAL CONDITIONS FOR STUDY
   A. *Environmental.* (Have a definite time and place for study; secure proper light, heat, ventilation, and furniture; seek a quiet place and freedom from distraction; have suitable materials available.)
   B. *Physiological.* (Be obedient to the laws of hygiene; seek bodily change and relaxation during long periods of study; stop short of physical fatigue.)
II. PSYCHOLOGICAL PREREQUISITES FOR STUDY
   A. *Attention.* (Form the habit of forced attention; concentrate on task to be performed; have confidence in yourself; avoid impossible tasks.)
   B. *Motivation.* (Have favorable attitudes, interests, and incentives; find definite aims; have definite goals in view; relate tasks to larger goals; avoid monotony in study activities.)
   C. *Development of habits.* (Practice accurate repetition; make positive attack; practice reactions which will be useful later.)
   D. *Planning.* (Distribute periods for study; analyze tasks; keep record of how you spend time.)
   E. *Self-evaluation.* (Test yourself for personal characteristics; note your methods and standards of work.)
III. STUDY HABITS RELATING TO PREPARATION OF ASSIGNMENTS
   A. *Reading.* (Have purpose; improve speed; improve accuracy; enlarge vocabulary; make mental summaries; formulate questions on reading; underline important points; adapt type of reading—e.g., rapid or intensive—to purpose; read assignments first as a whole and then reread more carefully; give attention to paragraph headings.)
   B. *Outlining and note-taking.* (Organize materials read or heard; make brief outlines; make detailed outlines; evaluate important points; take concise notes; use abbreviations; take notes on lectures and from books.)
   C. *Memorizing.* (Have purpose; comprehend material to be memorized; dis-

tribute practice periods in rote memory; be accurate in first reading; concentrate during repetitions; use mnemonic devices; adapt method— i.e., whole or part—to type of material; practice frequent recall; keep record of progress.)
   D. *Problem-solving.* (Get problem clearly in mind; collect all pertinent data; test hypotheses; evaluate conclusions.)
   E. *Reviewing.* (Space reviews properly; use notes; make brief outlines; ask questions.)
   F. *References.* (Use library and such reference aids as dictionary, bibliographies, footnotes, periodicals, record references efficiently; make careful bibliographies.)
   G. *Making written reports.* (Choose subject carefully; limit problem; select details; organize materials; make tentative outline; use varied vocabulary; use literary devices; write first draft rapidly; allow time to elapse before revision.)
IV. STUDY HABITS RELATING TO CLASSROOM ACTIVITIES
   A. *Recitation.* (Be a good listener; ask pointed questions; join in class discussions; take notes; plan oral reports; practice making the report aloud.)
   B. *Lecture.* (Listen for points of view, the plan, and the important points; take notes; evaluate; relate to your experience.)
   C. *Examinations.* Prepare by using summaries and notes; going over main points; making brief outlines; answering questions in text; concentrating on difficult parts; distributing study.)
   D. *Laboratory.* (Observe and analyze carefully; represent ideas graphically; take notes; write up reports clearly.)

Another valuable analysis was made of thirty-eight how-to-study manuals designed for use in the secondary schools. [10] A total of 3,743 specific references to 517 different study habits or skills were found. Many of them had important subdivisions. The 517 items, of which 313 were mentioned more

[9] William G. Brink, *Directing Study Activities in Secondary Schools* (New York, Odyssey Press, 1937), pp. 41-48. Used by permission of the publisher.

[10] Samuel R. Laycock and David H. Russell, "An Analysis of Thirty-eight How-to-Study Manuals," *School Review*, Vol. 49 (May, 1941), pp. 370-379.

than four times, were grouped under twenty-four main divisions or types of study activity. The list covers five-and-one-half pages of solid type. As with Brink's analysis, the largest number of references were to habits and skills in reading; the second largest number, to preparing for and taking examinations. Then followed general learning habits, outlining and note-taking, classroom activities, memorizing, and using the library. The physical and psychological conditions of studying came next.

The foregoing lists are of *general* study skills usable in nearly all types of work. In addition to these, there are a number of *specialized* study skills peculiar to various special subjects. For instance, study in mathematics requires skills in reading formulas, in making and reading graphs, and in using mathematical equipment such as slide rules, protractors, and squared paper. Both mathematics and science require skill in associating verbal statements with drawings, diagrams, and other schematic representations. Science requires skill in setting up apparatus and sometimes in making or repairing it, in gathering specimens, in interpreting technical vocabularies. Geography requires skill in reading maps, globes, and pictures. Brink has attempted the most complete listing of the special skills, but his lists are heavily loaded with general skills. [11] He includes one chapter on study in the modern integrated program which, while largely a description of integrated programs, is the best of all efforts to identify study with learning. Skills pertinent to various special subjects may be summarized in class reports by students who are interested.

Study habits in the modern school. As noted earlier, the foregoing lists are based upon the traditional assign-study-recite-test method. They are influenced by the conception of study as mastery of book materials, listening to lectures, preparing oral and written reports, preparing for and taking formal examinations, and so forth. They do represent, however, some of the genuine and important improvements in the older process.

The modern school identifies study with learning. All of the activities utilized in learning apply equally in developing study habits. All the traditional practices listed above are accepted, plus many others arising out of the co-operative, interactive experiencing of the learner. We need not repeat the total list here, since it has been included more than once in earlier chapters. Prominent activities will be the co-operative identifying, defining, and analyzing of problems and the co-operative planning of means of solution; judging materials and processes; aiding in group decisions and in carrying plans through; planning interviews and observational visits; conducting experiments, constructing apparatus; planning and constructing exhibits, and many, many others.

Guidance for the teacher in either type of school. Teaching in general should aim to develop independent study habits. The study procedures of the modern school will be clearly indicated in a later chapter on unit development. There will be, however, need and place for the more formal study skills in either type of school. There is need therefore for specialized individual and group help, plus special practice under guidance.

From the beginning there have been two methods of study supervision or guidance of the pupil. First, supervision of students studying at their desks, with individual or group aid; and second, training in study habits during regular class procedures by means of effective teaching. A later development of the second method has been the direct teaching of study habits in courses designed for that purpose. The first procedure developed in the traditional school; the second, in the modern.

A third development, the improvement of reading abilities essential to the use of books,

[11] Brink, *op. cit.*, Chs. 5, 6, and 8-14 inclusive.

has received only incidental attention as far as study is concerned. The improvement of instruction in silent reading is beneficial in the improvement of study, but it is not enough. A considerable number of investigations show that many pupils fail or have difficulty in some or all curriculum fields because they cannot read properly. Increasing attention is being devoted (1) to the improvement of reading ability, with special reference to various subjects in the curriculum, and also (2) to the writing of text materials with regard for pupil maturity and experience. The extension of reading instruction into high schools and colleges is slowly gaining ground, and it should be a major factor in improving study and learning. Our chief emphasis should probably continue to be on facilitating the development of essential study abilities through everyday class work.

1. *Teach in such a way as to utilize and give constant practice in numerous and varied study (learning) activities.* In the traditional school this necessitates attention to study aids and guides in the assignment, and the making of assignments which give practice in the varied study activities indicated in the previous pages. The traditional, formal, question-and-answer recitation will need to give way to more socialized forms and to working periods, as we shall show in the following section. In the modern school, good functional teaching will as a matter of course, include the beginnings of desirable study habits. Diagnosis of difficulty and special individual help will supplement this. In either the traditional or modern school there should be a sufficient variety of activity to suit individual differences in study interests, abilities, rates, levels of achievement, and the like.

2. *Be sensitive to and diagnose cases of inefficient study or actual ignorance of study procedures.* Ample evidence shows that difficulty with study is not at all confined to the dull, the lazy, and the uninterested. Many bright, willing, and interested pupils need much specific, detailed help with study skills. [12]

Teachers must constantly be on the alert to detect in class discussions, in papers, and in all contacts with the pupil, evidence of poor study habits, or of ignorance of how to study. Much can be learned from recitation procedures, remarks, and curious errors. In addition, a number of investigations have been made of pupil procedures from which we can derive methods of diagnosis. Chief among these are (*a*) questionnaires to the pupils about their study habits, (*b*) interviews with students, (*c*) observation, (*d*) test, and (*e*) analysis of students' schedules, outside activities, and so forth.

Diagnosis by means of interviews, observation, and analysis of scheduled activities and time distribution is self-explanatory in the main. Good teachers can devise means of their own and can secure guidance from periodical literature. Questionnaire analyses are also fairly simple. The teacher may make out a list of questions to be checked or answered briefly by pupils. Direct inquiry can reveal the presence or absence of certain study habits.

Analysis by direct testing is perhaps the most reliable. In a 1939 bibliography Hildreth [13] lists twenty-two instruments for testing study habits. Some of these cover a wide range; others are designed to test in detail one important skill with its subdivisions. Many instruments in her list are now out of print, but others can be found in Buros Yearbooks, in publishers' catalogues, and in the periodical literature. Tests may be on

[12] Raleigh Schorling, *Student Teaching*, rev. ed. (New York, McGraw, 1949). Pages 181-183 contain an excellent compact listing of numerous study activities gathered through observing pupils at work.

Leo J. Brueckner and Guy L. Bond, *The Diagnosis and Treatment of Learning Difficulties* (New York, Appleton-Century-Crofts, 1955). Good discussions. Use index.

See also books on educational psychology.

[13] Gertrude H. Hildreth, *A Bibliography of Mental Tests and Rating Scales*, 2nd ed. (New York, The Psychological Corporation, 1939), pp. 155-156.

use of books and libraries, dictionary or encyclopedia use, outlining, taking notes, study attitudes, studiousness, study habits, and the like.

Other tests are constantly appearing. Probably the most important addition is the *Iowa Every-Pupil Tests of Basic Skills,* which contains one section on *Work-Study Skills.* [14] There are two batteries, one for grades 3, 4, and 5; the other, for grades 6, 7, and 8. Detailed tests are presented for map-reading skills, use of references, use of the index, use of the dictionary, use of graphs, charts, and so on. Another new test by Edgar and Manuel includes, in addition to the more common skills mentioned above, a test for critical thinking in the use of printed materials. [15] A new test on the college level is the *Southeastern Aptitude Examination* which has a brief study-skill section. [16] It is to be noted also that many of the ordinary achievement battery tests include a section on work-study skills both for general range and for some specialized habits.

A large literature has developed around the use of these tests and the results secured. It can be sampled to advantage through class reports. One of the tests may be administered to the class.

3. *Give direct, specific help suited to individual or group needs as revealed by diagnostic methods.* The numerous investigations of direct methods of giving help justify the conclusions that (*a*) a combination of reading about and discussing study habits plus direction through definite assignments is superior to assignment-recitation procedure without definite study directions; (*b*) definite practice in study procedures is superior to reading about and discussing methods of study; (*c*) ability to carry on certain study procedures is specific as far as that study process is concerned, although there is transfer under certain methods of instruction; (*d*) bright, interested pupils profit rather easily from reading about and discussing study habits; but dull, backward, and uninterested pupils do not; (*e*) dull or uninterested pupils profit from definite, directed practice. All pupils benefit from practice, but it is necessary for the dull.

Reading about and discussing specific study difficulties. The teacher must have time to work with pupils in slow, painstaking discussions of difficulties and methods of improvement. He must be reasonably expert in discovering the mental processes of his pupils. This will yield sensible explanations of what often appear to be non-sensible statements made by pupils. As indicated in the chapter on teaching, our ideal is guidance without dominance. We aim to enable the pupil to find and correct his own difficulty and thus gain in power. Each pupil should be stimulated, by questions keyed to his level of maturity and insight, to display the highest level of analysis and self-dependence of which he is capable. Those who guide must never fall into the error of doing the work for the pupil.

The chief difficulty with the literature on supervised study is, as has been noted, the lack of detailed discussion of actual procedure in individual cases. Usable material would consist of stenographic accounts or teacher logs of hundreds of actual cases of pupil difficulty and teacher help. It would be a voluminous piece of writing and take many months to compile from accounts furnished by scores of teachers. The best that can be done here is to give some random illustrations and to discuss some general principles as definitely as is possible. The developing literature on planning, referred to earlier, has good materials.

Lack of interest. Many study difficulties with bright and dull students alike arise, not because the pupils are incapable nor the material too difficult, but because there is

[14] H. F. Spitzer, *Iowa Every-Pupil Tests of Basic Skills: Advanced Battery; Elementary Battery* (Boston, Houghton, 1940).

[15] J. W. Edgar and H. T. Manuel, *A Test of Study Skills* (Austin, Tex., The Steck Co., 1940).

[16] Published by Univ. of Georgia Press. No date given.

no incentive to do the work. The pupil may even think he is trying to work, but there is no real underlying drive. This is not uncommon and is quite natural in the traditional school, where the emphasis is on the subject rather than the pupil. The teacher's task is then to make some connection between the material and the pupil's real interests and purposes. Failing to make the intrinsic worth of the material clear, he will have to turn to secondary or extrinsic motives. The preparation of provocative and interesting questions and exercises is one device. An interesting activity once started has considerable momentum and power to generate interest. Tactfully suggesting to pupils their own deficiencies in reading and in ability to use libraries, research aids, and the like will often stimulate worthy effort. Resort to the use of socialized recitations, visual materials, or construction projects will stimulate many learners. Individual graphs of progress are another legitimate aid. Commendation for good work is effective with most children; hence provision for opportunity to succeed is important. Threats, personal appeals, individual rivalries, or marks should not be used as incentives. The most effective motive is realization by the pupil that the learning will serve one of his purposes. Hence the stress of the new school on pupil purpose. [17]

Occasionally disinclination to study is a disciplinary problem and must be dealt with accordingly. In any event, the pupil's attitude toward study is vital, and the ingenious teacher will examine it.

In some instances the teacher's help will be directed at correcting out-of-school conditions responsible for lack of interest. Nutritional deficiencies, too much outside work or social activity, indifference in the home, poor mental hygiene, emotional stresses, and scores of other factors are inimical to good study attitudes. Many seemingly dull pupils are made over by remedial measures applied

[17] There are literally hundreds of research studies on all aspects of motivation. This abbreviated summary is derived from them.

early enough. An extreme instance was that of a little girl who was regarded as permanently retarded because she could learn so little so slowly. Inquiry revealed that her father, having an emotional antagonism toward eating candy or sugar, had denied the child a normal sugar intake. With this remedied, the girl approached normal learning activity. This is an extreme case, but many outside factors seemingly far removed must be taken into account.

Inability to see the problem clearly. Many pupil difficulties in studying resolve themselves into a lack of understanding of what to do. Even when the assignment is definite and apparently clear to all, there will be a few individuals who do not know what to do and do not know exactly what their trouble is. This usually occurs in pupils who, having had everything done for them by their parents, have escaped responsibility and initiative. Long-term treatment will involve training in the range of study habits. For the moment, the teacher is justified in giving direct assistance. The problem and methods of procedure simply have to be explained in words of one syllable, illustrations given, and direct suggestions made as to sources and methods. Care must be taken, of course, to differentiate legitimate cases from lazy, inattentive pupils whose difficulties are not those of the type just discussed.

Cases are reported in which parents complained that too many problems were assigned and no suggestions given. One teacher, much amazed, outlined his explicit method of assignment, in turn amazing the parents. The child admitted hearing all this but did not see how it related to her problems. Here was a more than ordinarily serious inability to see problems, to connect directions with problems, and to analyze. It may even have involved lack of growth in good language habits, resulting in inability to understand anything except simple sentences. In such a case training must be specific and long-term.

Lack of knowledge of sources and how to

use them. Ignorance of sources and how to use them is far more common than is supposed, often appearing among beginning graduate students. Some students are unaware that more information is needed. Others, knowing that it is necessary, do not know where to get it. Still others know vaguely that dictionaries, encyclopedias, the atlas, periodical indexes, and other sources are available but do not know how to use them economically, if at all.

A graduate student prepared a bibliography of magazine references on a topic and then reported to the writer that not one of the references was in the library! Asked where he had looked for guidance in locating them, he replied, "In the card catalogue." Asked if he had not noted in the *Reader's Guide,* after each reference he had listed, such abbreviations as "Sch & Soc," "Sch Rev," "Ele Sch Jrnl," "Rev of Ed Res," he replied that he had, but not knowing what they meant, he had paid no attention to them!

Supplying definite references in an assignment is a beginning step. Later, specific training in finding sources may be given. Independence in finding a range of sources should ultimately result. Direct teaching is necessary in the use of dictionaries, cyclopedias, indexes, guides to periodical literature, standard volumes such as the *World Almanac, Who's Who,* and anthologies.

Finally, pupils must be trained to judge sources critically. During a study of United States-Mexican relations at the time of the border clashes during World War I, a girl contended that the best way to help Mexico would be to send an army to clean up the country. Asked why, she replied that her parents and others had said that Mexico was a small place about the size of Arizona and that we could put it in order quickly. Instead of rejecting this or arguing about it, the teacher apparently accepted it and asked the pupil to prepare for the class a series of statements comparing Mexico with other countries in regard to area, population,

transportation, topography, and so on. After a session with cylopedias, atlases, and other reference books, the pupil came back not only with more accurate information but with a wholly changed attitude toward sources. This incident points to a slogan which should be used not only in school but elsewhere: "Do not argue; look up the facts." So much discussion is nothing more than an irresponsible exchange of silly opinions.

Inability to judge the worth of facts. [18] Pupils (and adults) who say, "It says so in the book," or "I read it in the paper," are obviously not discriminating either sources or facts. Even worse are pupils who try to remember everything read upon a topic and who advance one fact as of equal value with any other. Sometimes a fact insisted upon by a pupil may be so inconsequential that it could be totally eliminated without loss to the lesson. Major and minor facts are listed co-ordinately or interchanged in outlines. This disability is extremely difficult to remedy. Probably the most useful approach is through questioning and conversation, not by argument or direct correction. The pupil should be asked to tell in his own words why he regards one fact as important as another. The "if that, then this" technique may be used with good students. The process is to reduce one of his statements to absurdity by showing that if he believes something he is insisting on, then he inevitably must believe this other direct implication. The direct implication should be one that is improbable, ridiculous, or impossible. Asking pupils to show the exact relationship between facts and the question under discussion often helps to indicate that not all facts are equal, although they may be related to the problem. Eventually, training in rapid reading, skimming, and outlining helps.

[18] For this and the next two points and any others dealing with thinking, many suggestions are found in:
William H. Burton, Roland B. Kimball, and Richard L. Wing, *Education for Effective Thinking* (New York, Appleton-Century-Crofts, 1960).

A sixth grade was given several sources and asked to select just those facts which bore on the lesson. One boy said, "How do you know what is wanted?" whereupon another answered immediately, "You can tell by looking at the set of questions we just put on the board." Later there was a discussion about selecting "main thoughts" from pages or paragraphs, whereupon the first boy said, "What gets me is how you know your main thought." Class and teacher suggested the following aids: "Do these facts relate to the problem?" "Do they aid in answering any of the study questions?" "Do they seem to contradict any other facts you have gathered?" "Do they raise further questions?"

Difficulties with analysis. The foregoing paragraph leads us to another common and serious difficulty. The procedure in modern schools, which is coming to be used in older ones, also, of having the pupils suggest subquestions to be answered in the course of solving the main problem, is extremely helpful. Class and teacher together work out a list of questions on the board and reorganize them into related groups. Often the difficulty is with language. Vast numbers of schoolboy "howlers" result from the natural interpretations placed by immature minds upon complex discourse. These remarks are clues to the alert teacher. One student reported that the Battle of Bunker Hill was the only victory the British had won during the Revolutionary War. Questioned by his schoolmates, he pointed to the text which said, "The British cared for no more victories at such a cost." Hasty and poor readers are regularly confused by negative statements and by indirect, metaphoric discourse of any kind. The need for training in the several kinds and levels of reading is indicated.

In mathematics (but not in beginning arithmetic) it is helpful to ask a pupil to state exactly what he is trying to find out, in what terms the answer is likely to be, and what processes will likely lead to the answer. Training in regularly checking processes and results is beneficial.

A college team playing field hockey found that they could secure the ball and work it down the field again and again only to fail in shooting goals. A conference for analysis was called. The forwards, who were doing the shooting, were unable to analyze the difficulty, but a halfback standing directly behind the line of play discovered that the forwards shot straight at the guards every time instead of at the open spaces between guards. A dub golfer of the writer's acquaintance was once asked how he kept out of sand traps so much better than did more expert players. He replied that he always aimed straight at traps, since he had discovered that his ball never went where he aimed it! He had been "studying" his golf.

Difficulties arising in drawing inferences or making generalizations. Closely related to the foregoing difficulties in using sources, evaluating materials, and analyzing problems are the difficulties attendant upon using all collected data in coming to a conclusion. Errors range from reasonable but incorrect inferences to wild guesses. Before he can help, the teacher must diagnose the causes of the error or impossible guess. Sometimes no sensible basis will seem possible, but skillful, sympathetic questioning by the teacher will usually reveal one. Failing to discover through analysis the pupil's thought process, he may ask the pupil to tell in his own words how the information he has gathered bears upon the conclusion he has reached. Part of the difficulty is the inability of young pupils to suspend judgment.

Pupils who make honest though highly illogical inferences must be distinguished from talkative, superficial bluffers, or those who were not paying attention and hence guess wildly. Holding the latter relentlessly to an analysis and explanation of their own statements is a good device.

It should be noted also that some dull or slow children make wild guesses simply because they cannot keep up with the thought of the class but nevertheless wish to be participating. Sympathetic assistance and the provision of opportunities for success on their level will eliminate this.

The discussion of the foregoing six difficulties is hopelessly brief and inadequate. It is for illustrative purposes only. An adequate discussion would fill volumes. Every teacher will profit by alert analysis and recording of his own experiences. The foregoing pages may assist in starting the process.

Special practice in specific habits. Numerous investigations show clearly that definite, systematic practice in meaningful situations will improve the study and learning of all pupils, particularly the slower ones.

As far back as 1923, Beauchamp[19] demonstrated that even the more complex skills could be improved under guidance. In a controlled experiment of considerable size, his experimental groups showed substantial gains over control groups in four significant and difficult skills. These were (1) studying a paragraph to determine its central idea and then picking out the outstanding ideas of the paragraph, (2) formulating questions one could answer thoroughly only if he understood a topic, (3) reading entirely through a unit to determine its general plan and then grouping the major facts presented around this plan, (4) giving the pupils a method for solving thought questions.

The value of practice in systematic outlining and in note taking, especially in covering extensive materials, has been demonstrated by several studies. Literally scores of studies have been made of the methods and results of improving reading skills of all kinds and on all levels. Classes for the improvement of reading skills as an aid to study are now found in many colleges.

A study by McKinnon and Burton[20] evaluated the effect of definite, detailed instruction in certain specific study processes in history at the eighth-grade level. Four processes were used: (1) comparison, (2) identifying and expressing cause-and-effect relationships, (3) outlining, and (4) selecting and organizing subject matter from several sources. Each of these processes was broken down into subprocesses. For instance, comparison included six: (*a*) ability to discover basis for comparison, if there be comparable facts; (*b*) ability to select the distinguishing characteristics present; (*c*) ability to classify the distinguishing characteristics present; (*d*) ability to list likenesses; (*e*) ability to list differences; and (*f*) ability to formulate a summarizing statement. All this may sound simple, but it is astonishing how many graduate students will list similarities when asked to contrast items or will list differences when asked to show similarity.

Each of the skills was made the object of definite instruction in conjunction with regular lessons in history. The results were:

Based on data similar to the foregoing and on all four techniques mentioned, the following conclusions seemed justified: (1) Definite, detailed instruction in the designated techniques of study in history definitely improved the pupils' ability to use those techniques, as well as their ability to use the subprocesses. (2) In the case of factors and subprocesses which are mechanical in nature, the effect of corrective exercises appears earlier and mastery is more complete than in the case of factors which involve thought content. (3) Instruction in three of the study techniques, namely, sensing cause-and-effect relationships, outlining, and selecting and organizing materials, had a beneficial effect on ability to make comparisons. The first three focus attention on subprocesses which are important in comparison. (4) Ability to outline varies in proportion to the number and kinds of mechanical aids which are supplied in the material, namely,

[19] Wilbur L. Beauchamp, *A Preliminary Experimental Study of Technique in the Mastery of Subject Matter in Elementary Physical Science,* Supplementary Educational Monograph No. 24, Studies in Secondary Education, I (Chicago, Univ. of Chicago Press, 1923).

[20] Nettie J. McKinnon and William H. Burton, "An Evaluation of Certain Study Procedures in History," Elementary School Journal, Vol. 40 (January, 1940), pp. 371-380.

paragraph and topical heads, marginal comments, table of contents, and so forth. (5) Children of eighth-grade level can approach mastery of the mechanics of outlining. (6) Increased ability in outlining in other subjects. (7) Selection and organization of material on a given problem presents greater difficulty (for eighth-grade pupils) than does the objective representation of an author's thought relationships, as, for instance, in outlining. (8) The trial-and-error method of procedure in the various types of mental activity required in study procedures is wasteful of the pupils' time. (9) Exercises requiring an evaluation of material, such as discrimination between major and minor points, offer difficulty to eighth-grade pupils. (10) The number of errors in a given exercise varies directly in proportion to the length and the complexity of the exercise.

The following problems are suggested for further investigation:

1. How close could mastery, or nearly perfect facility, be approached in given study procedures? What additional instruction and practice would be necessary?
2. What are the specific difficulties present in the inability of pupils to cope with problems of sentence structure?
3. How many items may be included within the span of attention of pupils of given levels? That is, how long and how complex may exercises be at given levels?
4. What factors, if any, other than inability to comprehend are present in the omission of major and minor points?
5. What further transfer might be expected with the improvement of still other study techniques?
6. How would the use of carefully weighted materials and exercises affect the findings on a given study technique?

Improvement by this route necessitates the organization by the teacher of systematic opportunities for practicing the skills selected for improvement. Preferably this should be in conjunction with the regular teaching of assigned lessons.

An unusually well prepared and provocative example of prepared opportunities for practicing study skills on the college level is to be found in Francis P. Robinson's *Diagnostic and Remedial Techniques for Effec-*

tive Study.[21] This is a new type of book which, it is to be hoped, will be the forerunner of many others like it. It is neither text nor workbook, though containing many features of both. It cannot be used by a student alone, but is designed as a working aid for student and study coach or counselor.

4. *Organize a definite course in how-to-study.* This fourth suggestion is not co-ordinate with the preceding three. Organized how-to-study courses are over and beyond the suggestions given above and will be organized in those situations which require them. They have appeared separately in many high schools and colleges and seem to be increasing. The material usually found in such a course is rapidly gaining a place as part of the core curriculum in secondary schools, and as part of "freshman week" or orientation courses on the college level.

The chief difficulty is that of co-ordinating the content of such a course with the pupils' regular subjects. No type of learning can be developed in isolation from the material to be studied. Ideally, all training in study skills should be carried on in regular courses. Many teachers, however, are not able to do this. Compromises are necessary. Several methods of managing the course have emerged.

First, the course may have its own content, the study techniques, which may be examined and operated in practice exercises. The assignments in the regular subject courses would be used as illustrations when and as desired. *Second,* the entire how-to-study course may be co-ordinated with the usual assignments in regular courses. The subject-matter courses constitute the core, and appropriate study skills are developed systematically by giving assistance with the regular assignments. *Third,* the how-to-study course may devote three days a week to developing study skills while assisting with regular assignments, and two days to direct

[21] 3rd ed. (New York, Harper, 1960).

The Improvement of Assign-Study-Recite Procedures   **311**

attack on its own material. Which organization is used depends upon the ability, insight, and attitude of the personnel concerned. On the one hand, some teachers are not able to co-ordinate their regular work with the study course because they lack skill in modern assignment-recitation procedures. On the other hand, it is very difficult for one person to give study helps to all pupils in all subjects.

Advantages of the how-to-study course. Combining the statements from several references, we find that the following advantages are claimed: [22]

1. It centralizes responsibility in one or at most a few individuals.
2. Different subjects have many common study techniques.
3. It places responsibility for improving study habits in the hands of a specialist who has had definite training for the work.
4. It makes possible the co-ordination of efforts toward improving study habits within the school.
5. It makes possible much needed research in the field.
6. It offers a new approach with accompanying enthusiasm.
7. It adds valuable material, useful in general life activities, to the general education of pupils.
8. It will have immediate as well as deferred value, hence will be attractive to the pupils.
9. It will aid in showing the child that the school is essentially friendly and disposed to aid him with difficult problems—that is, how to get his lessons.
10. It will reduce failures and improve mental hygiene.
11. It will save much time for pupils and teachers.
12. It invites public support, since parents are already suspicious of home assignments and pupil difficulties.
13. It will aid in showing pupils that study is not peculiar to the school but must be done effectively in all life activities.

Limitations and objections to the course.

Similarly, a list of limitations includes the following:

1. It is nearly impossible for one person to teach all pupils how to study.
2. It is almost impossible to tie up study suggestions with the specific study situations presented in each of the different subjects.
3. It may tend to cause subject teachers to shirk their responsibilities for directing the development of study habits.
4. It is difficult to obtain a teacher capable of offering such work effectively.
5. Smaller schools often cannot afford to offer such a course.

As distinguished from limitations, certain criticisms and objections appear:

1. Such a course is unnecessary, since each pupil will develop his own methods of study. (He will, and his methods will more than likely be wasteful and inefficient.)
2. A study specialist, introduced into a school, may cause friction. (He might, but ordinarily teachers will welcome any sensible help with their problems.)
3. The program is overcrowded and another course merely makes it that much worse. (Much dead and useless material could well be eliminated to make room.)
4. The course would not receive credit for college entrance. (This is merely one more instance of arbitrary requirements which stupidly interfere with education. The entrance requirements are progressively changing to become more rational.)

Experimental data on the value of the how-to-study course. Data from studies of the separate study courses are of interest. Mills [23] found that when a how-to-study class was taught as an academic subject, without relation to the courses being taken, or taught by someone not a member of the regular high-school staff, pupil achievement was not improved. Bird, [24] studying college-level courses, found that the courses were

[22] Brink, *op. cit.*, p. 56.
Frederick, Ragsdale, and Salisbury, *op. cit.*, pp. 281-282.

[23] H. C. Mills, "How-to-Study Courses and Academic Achievement," *Educational Administration and Supervision*, Vol. XXI (February, 1936), pp. 145-151.
[24] Charles Bird, *Effective Study Habits* (New York, Appleton, 1931), p. vi.

particularly beneficial to the more capable students. The latter point is the opposite of many findings on the elementary and secondary level and may be due to the greater maturity and clarity of purpose on the upper levels or to the superior quality of the courses which were given. Winter [25] found that among college freshmen the greatest benefits were realized by students in the lower decile and a half. This is in keeping with the general findings in the lower schools. Pressey [26] gave systematic training in study habits required in typical college courses to groups of students who were about to be dismissed from college because of low marks. Approximately 80 per cent of the students so aided did satisfactory work in college from then on. Although the how-to-study course has some value and is often used, current emphasis is more upon diagnosing the pupil's specific learning difficulties and helping him to overcome them. Teaching for the development of study habits in connection with regular subject courses is more frequent than the separate study course. For example, the principal abilities required in using books are being developed in the reading program, which includes not merely specific instruction in the reading period but also, increasingly, planning for integration of reading abilities with other curriculum fields.

Home study. The volume by Brink does not mention home study in the index. Frederick, Ragsdale, and Salisbury devote seven pages to listing the claimed advantages and disadvantages with reference to a few experi-

[25] John E. Winter, "An Experimental Study of the Effect on Learning of Supervised and Unsupervised Study among College Students," *Journal of Educational Psychology,* Vol. XXVII (February, 1936), pp. 111-118.

D. R. Entwistle, "Evaluation of Study Skills Courses: A Review," *Journal of Educational Research,* Vol. 53 (March, 1960), pp. 243-251.

[26] Luella C. Pressey, *Research Adventures in College Teaching* (Bloomington, Ill., Public School Publishing Co., 1927); "The Permanent Effects of Training in Methods of Study on College Success," *School and Society,* Vol. XXVIII (1928), pp. 403-404.

mental studies. These will not be summarized here, since the arguments seem clearly opposed to home study. The few statistical studies show that home study is not a significant factor in affecting the achievement of pupils. Results are about the same with or without home study.

There is, however, one aspect of this topic which must not be overlooked. Home study of the traditional formal sort may be dispensed with as far as the evidence now shows; however, as we move toward modern teaching which identifies study with learning and which utilizes not one or two but a large number of varied study activities, a different situation emerges. If we are to develop independence in attacking and studying problems and if learning is to occur in situations which approximate life, then there must be continuous interaction between the pupil and his total environment. There will be many things to be done outside of school, quite different, however, from the home study of the formal school.

The current uproar about schools and the improvement of learning has produced a flood of materials on home study. Much of it is nonsense written by laymen and uncritical educators who fall in with the current demand for more study—for what ends and how done is not critically examined. Excellent ideas are also being put forward. Students should read a sampling of current periodical literature and develop conclusions.

Initiating a program of guided study. Earlier supervised study and the newer guided learning and study have suffered, as have all new movements in education, from ill-advised introduction. Enthusiastic principals and superintendents come home from a summer-school course in modern methods and arbitrarily introduce a new departure into a system wholly unprepared for it. The story is told of a superintendent who announced to the teaching staff one Friday, "Beginning Monday, we will proceed on the supervised study basis." A school board of the writer's acquaintance called its superintendent in and said they wished the curriculum and methods brought up to date. They wished a complete new curriculum to replace the old formal one—"and have it done by the last of next month"!

All new departures must be studied systematically; teachers and staff and community must be given time to discuss and understand. Administrative adjustments and processes should come last.

In many places where supervised study was introduced hastily, teachers have actively opposed it, have refused to co-operate, or have hailed it as a relief from work. Pupils were turned loose to "study" while teachers read newspapers, marked papers, visited, or did their own work. Communities to whom the new movement was not explained condemned it without investigation as a fad or frill. Pupils to whom explanation and training were not given failed to participate and often did poorer work than before. Any new departure requires careful preparation before introduction. The following preparation should precede the introduction of supervised or guided study:

1. Systematic study of the item with special reference to the local situation:
    a. By administrative staff—of the nature of supervised or guided study, obstacles, difficulties, advantages, plans now in operation.
    b. By teaching staff—of the nature of learning, of study, of development of independence in study skills.
2. Explanation to community to ensure understanding and support.
3. Explanation to student body to ensure understanding and participation.
4. Provision of administrative mechanisms, materials, etc., in advance.
5. Provision of a systematic set of records of procedure and results.

DISCUSSION QUESTIONS FOR SECTION 2

This list may be omitted by classes made up of experienced teachers.
1. Explain the following situations:
    a. In a supervised study hour many hands were up; there was a continuous call for the teacher's guidance. Pupils did little until the teacher came to them, and soon needed help again.
    b. Parents welcomed supervised study as a modern procedure, but soon noticed that the children were not learning; in fact, their standard scores were lower than those of the children in neighboring cities.
    c. A superintendent refused to introduce supervised study, saying that it was a waste of time where he had observed it—that teachers merely used the time to correct papers, to prepare other lessons, to read books, and so on.
2. Recall and be ready to describe cases in your own study where you would have liked a little explanation or help from a teacher.
3. Recall and describe some cases where you were in a position to get help and did receive it.
4. Cite specific cases in which the instructor's assignment affected, for good or ill, your studying.
5. Do likewise for his handling of the recitation.

INDIVIDUAL EXERCISES AND REPORTS

The following list goes beyond the limited summary in this section. Students may choose individually and make oral reports to class.
1. Summarize a number of recent articles which present evidence that pupils do not know how to study, have inefficient study habits, and so on.
2. Collect and analyze several sets of study rules, especially recent ones. Make an oral report, with perhaps a mimeographed set derived from the analysis.
3. Interested individuals or small committees may summarize recent discussions of any of the administrative schemes listed on page 301.
4. Make an oral class summary of any current stenographic accounts or other detailed case studies of actual technique in aiding individuals or small groups with study difficulties.
5. Examine several listings of general study habits or skills. If necessary, suggest changes in the list given in this chapter. Present to class any new ideas or different forms of organization.
6. Interested individuals or small committees may organize lists of special study skills

peculiar to their major subjects. (A number of reports should be made covering important subjects. Reports should be extremely critical in distinguishing the special from the general skills.)

7. An individual may report recent articles describing provision for practice in given specific habits: outlining, memorizing, note-taking, map-reading, various forms of reading, and so on. This can be a very valuable report.

8. An individual may report recent literature on the how-to-study course.

9. An individual or small committee may report on the new reading courses appearing in high school and college. This is a very important new development.

10. An individual may summarize the arguments and the experimental studies (making careful distinction between them) on home study. This might be in the form of a talk before a parent-teacher association.

11. An individual may report any current accounts of the planned introduction of a study program into specified school systems.

12. An individual, or several, may organize the type of data which might be used in an assembly presentation designed to introduce a new study program to high school students. (This report permits of considerable originality of form and content.)

13. Work out a series of questions which you might ask a fourth-grade child, a high-school freshman, a college freshman, in order to focus his attention and stimulate his thinking about any one of the following.

The necessity and value of:
 a. Critical evaluation of what is read.
 b. Techniques for securing quickly the essential facts and ideas from a large mass of material.
 c. A diversity of sources.
 d. The possession of facts with which to support statements.
 e. Knowing what one is looking for in studying.
 f. Organization and system in studying.
 g. Any other study essentials as desired.

14. Where conditions permit, students may assist in diagnosing study difficulties of an elementary or secondary school pupil or of a class. Report procedures and results to class.

15. The instructor may administer to the class study-skill tests on the college level, compile results, and analyze in class discussion.

16. A small committee may report later on specific remedial measures applicable to any of the weaknesses revealed by diagnosis.

SPECIAL EXERCISE ON DEVELOPMENT OF STUDY HABITS

It is important for the teacher to know the procedures for developing good study habits in pupils.

The writer has found that the following exercise is of great value. A separate class period can be devoted to it with profit, allowing as many individual summaries as time permits.

1. Each student should find and report on a current article which describes either
 a. The procedures used by a classroom teacher to aid pupils in developing skill in certain specified study skills, or
 b. The account of a controlled research study on the same problem.

2. A student may choose to report on any recently published study manual for any level from elementary school through college.

3. Analytic reports may be made of observed lessons in which guidance for the development of study habits was particularly skillful; was neglected; was arbitrarily refused.

READINGS

General Books on the Study Processes

The twelve general books on study which were listed in the first and second editions of this book appear in the footnote on page 301. Many of them are now out of print. Samples of current books of this type were included in the text, page 302.

Specialized Treatments of One or More Items

The literature on this type of study training was for a time very large. A moderate number of books are still coming out. Aid is given on such items as outlining, note-taking, use of graphs, summarizing, use of library, use of reference sources, organization of study activities, spelling, handwriting, and many others.

Interested students will find ample material in the periodical literature.

Study Manuals

Laycock and Russell, in the study referred to on page 303, listed thirty-nine manuals. Many are out of print but new ones come along constantly. An exhaustive list is impossible. The following is a very brief sampling. Others may be found.

Cole, L., *Student Guide to Effective Study* (New York, Holt, Rinehart & Winston, 1960).

Garrison, Roger H., *The Adventure of Learning in College* (New York, Harper, 1959).

Nason, Leslie J., *You Can Get Better Grades* (Long Beach, Cal., Imperial Press, 1960).

Pettit, Lincoln, *How to Study and Take Exams* (New York, Rider, 1960).

Wilcox, Glen W., *Basic Study Skills* (Boston, Allyn & Bacon, 1958).

Morgan, Clifford F., and Deese, James, *How to Study* (New York, McGraw, 1957).

Weigand, George, and Blake, W. S., Jr., *College Orientation: A Study Skills Manual* (Englewood Cliffs, N. J., Prentice-Hall, 1955).

3: IMPROVEMENT OF THE RECITATION.

In 1897 there appeared a book entitled *The Method of the Recitation.*[27] In 1928 appeared *The Passing of the Recitation.*[28] The two volumes, published a third of a century apart, symbolize the revolution which has taken place in educational thinking. In 1897 the recitation was so important in teaching-learning as to warrant a volume of its own. In 1928 the recitation was recognized by the leadership as being not merely outmoded but a definite detriment to learning. In 1935 Bossing[29] wrote that "Among responsible writers in the field of secondary school methods the re-citation concept of the recitation has been *passé* for twenty years." The quotation refers only to writers and leaders. Vigorous, pointed criticism of the formal question-and-answer recitation for forty years has had little effect upon the so-called practical teacher. Precise surveys show that this type of recitation, based on memorized

[27] Charles A. McMurry and Frank M. McMurry (Bloomington, Ill., Public School Publishing Co., 1897).
[28] V. T. Thayer (Boston, Heath, 1928).
[29] Nelson L. Bossing, *Progressive Methods of Teaching in Secondary Schools* (Boston, Houghton, 1935), p. 405.

materials, still predominates in school. It is probably the most absurd of the vestigial remains from prehistoric practice. Recitation will for various reasons continue to be used in many schools. We must endeavor, therefore, to improve it as much as possible. Many devices to relieve its dullness and sterility are available.

The traditional recitation. The typical recitation period is one in which isolated, formal facts are called for. The study process is memorization of usually one text, unrelieved by explanations or other references. No power of any value to the learner can result.

The word *recitation* is one of the most common terms in the educational vocabulary. If we break the word into its parts: *re-citation,* we find that it is not an ill-chosen word as schools are all too commonly conducted. Class periods are given over to reciting knowledge which has been carried over bodily in memory from the original citation. Perhaps on rare occasions such a procedure may be necessary; but only when the materials justify themselves through use in a normal, functional learning procedure. We know, however, that facts are better learned, better remembered, and better used when derived from functional learning situations.

Defects of the traditional recitation procedure. The typical, traditional recitation, with exceptions so rare as to be almost nonexistent, can be condemned utterly. Just as the traditional assignment "take the next ten pages" indicates a teacher naïvely ignorant of the nature of teaching and of learning, or a very lazy teacher, so also does the continued use of traditional recitation procedures. What then are the evils of this process?

1. The underlying psychology is unacceptable. The atomistic-mechanistic concept of learning, adding fact upon fact upon fact (or skill, or concept), does not add up to useful learning outcomes.

2. The outcomes—fragmentary isolated facts, learning in non-functional situations—are not usable in real life. Some pupils do learn by this method and carry over the learning for use in life, but the mediocre and dull do not. It is uneconomical learning at best.

3. The functional learning outcomes—understandings, attitudes, appreciations, skills, and special abilities—are for most pupils actually precluded by the recitation procedure. The initiative, judgment, creativity, and personal development of the individual are stifled for the most part. The premium is upon rote memory and not upon developing power to cope with meaningful problems.

4. The teacher dominates. A number of scientific studies now available show the value of pupil participation.

5. The teacher is at best a hearer of lessons; at worst, a policeman or dispenser of punishment. To do better than this requires ingenuity, much hard work, and thorough insight into the processes of learning.

6. The impression made on pupils is undesirable. An attitude of antagonism, distrust, and suspicion is engendered. This is the direct opposite of the desired attitude and ability to do co-operative work.

7. The individualistic, competitive recitation is antagonistic to the democratic, co-operative philosophy of life and of education. The recitation situation is not lifelike.

8. The nervous tension created inevitably results in bad mental hygiene.

9. Individual differences among learners are often neglected, sometimes arbitrarily disregarded.

10. Time is wasted in large quantities.

It is recognized that many of these evils are alleviated and even avoided by alert, sympathetic teachers, traditional though they may be. This, however, does not alter the fact that the evils are inherent and, with most teachers, actively present.

Demands for improvement appeared long ago. The weaknesses of the recitation system were recognized almost before that system had crystallized. Early criticisms have been mentioned elsewhere in this volume and presented in detail in other sources; they need not be repeated here. Suffice it to say that by 1915 the best writers on teaching method were including definite and important suggestions for improvement. Demands were made that the recitation period become a "thinking" or even a working period. Fact questions were to give way to thought questions. It was suggested that many references be used and pupils be given opportunity to interpret, compare, and draw their own conclusions. It was pointed out that rapid-fire questioning must give way to a procedure which allowed time to think. Discussion, argument, and interchange of opinion were to be provided for. Some "radicals" even went so far as to suggest that pupils might define and plan attack on new problems during the recitation period. Still others suggested that the pupils themselves find and bring in some of the supplementary references. Application exercises were mentioned.

These writers were driving toward the modern conception of a working period but were still dominated by the textbook or printed material conception of study and learning. They did see the importance, however, of providing for reflective thought, co-operation, judgment, and even for creative expression. They realized also very keenly the necessity of developing favorable attitudes among the pupils toward the classroom and toward education.

In the hands of good teachers, the activities of a modern daily recitation period are widely different from those of the traditional school. It is no longer a quiz period, a period of marking time between study activities, but a period in which thought is carried forward and new work taken up. There is active and wide pupil participation. Latterly the term *laboratory period* has been borrowed from the science and practical-arts courses and denotes a varied working period. Even more recently the workshop name and procedure have been allied with the recitation. As has been said in previous chapters, if we carry the improvement of traditional techniques far enough we are led naturally to the modern methodology.

Specific improvements appear. *The discussion or conversational method.* Just before the turn of the century, the Herbartians introduced the *developmental method* into this country. During the recitation period the teacher developed the topic or subject or guided the solution of simple problems by means of questions in informal conversation. The pupil contributed from his past experience in answer to questions. Guided by the questions, pupils could rather accurately develop tales or accounts which they would later read in a book. Problems of considerable length could be solved by following the lead of the questions in a search for related past experience. That this is the original meaning of the term *developmental method* is quite clear from the original German sources. Throughout the German literature on pedagogy appear references to a procedure designated as *darstellend entwickelnder Unterricht*—an unwinding, unraveling, spinning out of a presentation. The available lesson plans or accounts of lessons taught which are found in German sources are of conversational, discussional lessons. In this country the term came to be used very carelessly, being applied to lessons in which pupils made formal reports and even to lessons in which the teacher "developed" the topic by lecturing. Because of this confusion, Parker in 1915 suggested that the term *conversational* method be used.[30] The term is a good one and is self-explanatory. The formal question and answer gives way to connected conversation in the development of some topic or theme. Pupil participation is extended. Desirable learning outcomes are possible when pupils argue, compare, judge data, search sources, and draw conclusions.

Group process or group discussion as developed in this country (recall Chapter 9) is the modern counterpart of the older "developmental" lesson.

The socialized recitation. The term *socialized recitation* had great vogue about 1920

[30] Samuel C. Parker, *Methods of Teaching in High Schools* (Boston, Ginn, 1915), Ch. 18.

when a considerable literature appeared. In addition to informal conversations, many more forms of pupil activity were admitted to the recitation period. Each child participated as he was able, or was given the opportunity to do so. A group of pupils engaged in varied activities together in pursuit of a common assignment approximates a true social situation as far as the formal school can achieve a social situation; hence the term *socialized recitation.*

There has been some useless wrangling over definitions. Some enthusiasts have insisted that the only recitation entitled to the designation *socialized* is that in which the teacher turns the period over to the class, which appoints a chairman and conducts the lesson independently. This formal procedure is still widely used. It has value but may become subordinated to its own machinery, as often happens. Considerable explanation of the technique will be found in books on method and in the periodical literature, but not of late. Obviously, elimination of the teacher is not fundamental in securing a social situation! Would one conclude that the teacher is not eligible to associate with his pupils? The teacher does not abdicate his position of leadership and guidance. He may play an important part and still have a socialized recitation. Minimizing teacher dominance is desirable and is probably one of the outcomes of the newer recitation developments. It is not correct, however, to limit the term to recitations of this type. Many other procedures are socialized recitations. The essential thing is that the class be stimulated to free discussion, to give-and-take argument, to searching for data, to evaluating and discriminating, to division of labor, to co-operative group activity. Teacher guidance, as in all types of procedure, is necessary.

A socialized procedure may appear at the very outset when a new topic is being taken up. The class can be stimulated to discuss ways and means of attacking the problem, even reasons for attacking it at all. Many pupils will have experiences to contribute.

The contribution recitation, or discussion based on assigned reports. The term has practically died out, but the procedure is still widely used. The recitation, or class discussion, is based on a report or series of reports (contributions) made by individuals or small committees. Training in the discovery, organization, and evaluation of data is secured, together with practice in drawing and verifying inferences. In reporting, the pupil must organize his material to be of interest to his audience. There is training in oral expression and self-confidence. Questions may be asked during the reports, and afterwards there should be free give-and-take discussion. There is stimulation to interest and to thinking; there is training in meeting argument.

Values of the socialized procedures. We may apply the term *socialized* to all these improvements. They are difficult for beginners; for poorly trained or lazy teachers; for earnest, sincere teachers who possess no flair for conversation, for the guidance of discussion, and for stimulation of the mental reactions of other people. In the hands of skilled traditional teachers, they are worthy teaching procedures. With them it is possible to avoid many of the real evils of traditional recitation and to achieve some of the desirable learning products. The general values seem to be as follows:

1. A valid learning process, interactive experiencing, is at least approached.
2. The learning outcomes desirable in a democracy are attainable in some degree. The best type of training results when pupils are stimulated to participate and to advance opinions, are held for evidence, are stimulated to organize and to defend beliefs. Reflective thought is stimulated; initiative and creative effort are encouraged. Pupils achieve social responsibility and social co-operation.
3. A premium is placed on pupil participation. The lesson is centered in learning activity and not in teacher or subject matter. In many places where new methods are intro-

duced pupils are openly suspicious! It is a sad commentary on teaching that it takes some little time for children, and often college students as well, to understand that they may express opinions, argue and debate, differ with text or teacher, or ask for further information. A graduate student told the writer recently that until he entered the course in principles of teaching in the first graduate year, he had not opened his mouth during four years of preparatory school and four years of college. Even if considerably exaggerated, this commentary is significant.

4. Pupils receive valuable training in oral expression, both in organized reports and in give-and-take argument.
5. Pupils get valuable training in leadership, in the conduct of meetings, and in the control of discussion more than when the formal types are used. Incidentally, the teacher profits in like manner.
6. Pupils develop wholesome attitudes toward the classroom, the school, and toward education in general.

Dangers in the socialized procedures. The new developments are not without their limitations and pitfalls. Chief among them are:

1. The form may be substituted for essence. In some cases the appointment of chairmen, the formal rigmarole of getting recognized by the chair, the necessity for adhering to rules of order completely prevent the essential thing: socialized activity. The novelty of procedures often attracts more attention than the process which the new procedures are to facilitate. Another substitution of form for essence occurs when pointless discussion is permitted under the misapprehension that it is connected discourse. *The aim is not just to have discussion and pupil argument but to have that discussion and argument headed for an objective.*
2. Time may be wasted on digressions, on wandering, pointless argument, or on pure quibbling. This is inherent in all social discourse. Anyone familiar with the popular "study groups" sponsored by women's clubs, by men's organizations, and even by many educational institutions knows just how witless free discussion can become. City councils, state legislatures, national committees are often prime illustrations of stupidly incoherent, muddled procedure; although in some of these groups, such a process is deliberate and carefully calculated. A few teachers openly permit

unorganized, wandering discussion under the delusion that discussion of any type is superior to formal recitations. Some of them insist that the pupil thus gets training in self-expression, thinking, and discussion. He is in fact getting first-class practice in not sticking to the point, in not organizing material, in not considering data systematically, and in developing irresponsibility in stating opinions.

3. Discussion techniques may be utilized with too simple material. It is a waste of time to develop concepts which can be grasped through simple exposition, oral or written.

4. The teacher may abdicate his position of leadership. This is not implied in any modern procedure.

5. The discussion may be monopolized by a few aggressive, bright, or superficial show-off pupils. This is not peculiar to improved recitation procedures nor even to fully modern methods. It happens in the most formal school. Teachers should develop discussional techniques for holding these people for facts, for calling in other quieter pupils to agree or disagree, for securing contributions from all.

6. Continuity may be lost. This is always a danger in discussion, conversation, and committee work, in real life as well as in school. As stated above, pointless digressions must be controlled; however, there will always be digressions which represent legitimate side excursions. Related questions, data, or circumstances need to be discussed at the time. If normal extensions are not permitted, then we regress to a formal, controlled recitation procedure. Hence there must be provision for periodic summary and reorientation. Even if continuity is not lost through the complexity of the discussion, periodic recapitulations are necessary, since the pace of truly socialized procedure cannot be planned. It becomes necessary from time to time to stop to restate the problem, to survey what has been accomplished, and then to replan subsequent activity.

Values achieved and dangers avoided by careful preparation and active guidance. No one can tell another person just how to conduct a free discussion or any other socialized procedure. The specific devices will be wrought out of experience, enlightened by such psychological principles as we can give. Native ability plays a very large part. As has been said before, a good teacher must possess some vivacity and some flair

for manipulating mental processes. A skillful conversationalist or competent chairman alone can guide conversation in desired directions. The extremes of domination and of pure anarchy must be avoided, which calls for systematic planning in addition to native ability. A few principles may be of assistance.

1. *The teacher is directly responsible for the establishment of favorable attitudes.* This is true in all teaching but more so in any recitation procedure, no matter how socialized, since that procedure is not a natural one. Pupils feel no urge toward it. The general principles and suggestions which have been made throughout this volume will not be repeated here, but a few may be recalled:

First, seek smooth connections between the material and the natural interests of the pupils. This provides as functional and meaningful a situation as can be achieved under the forced limitations of the recitation period. This will invite purposeful activity from most pupils, which is probably the best-known way of developing favorable attitudes.

Second, invite participation upon all possible occasions.

Third, use any contributions that are at all practicable and commend those pupils trying to contribute or participate.

Fourth, arrange opportunities to contribute and participate with regard for individual differences, thus ensuring opportunity for success.

Fifth, give sympathetic assistance to those who are having difficulty.

Sixth, maintain in yourself an attitude of sincere interest and alert participation.

2. *The teacher must discover the readiness of the group for socialized procedures.* This includes knowledge of past experience with such methods, summary of the informational background, and determination of level of maturity. Diagnostic and pretest techniques have been listed elsewhere and will not be repeated here.

3. *The teacher must make careful advance preparation.* Some think that since it is to be free discussion, no preparation is necessary. No other belief could be further from the truth. *An unplanned and uncon-*

trolled socialized period is fully as detrimental to learning as the formal question-and-answer recitation. What the teacher needs is not a formal plan but a general outline of the desired continuity; he should have illustrations ready. The skillful teacher learns to anticipate requests for explanation, digressions, or other difficulties. He controls the discussion by calling for periodic summaries and reorientation.

4. *The teacher must ensure participation by all and eventually secure pupil responsibility for participation.* At first, he will distribute questions, tasks, reports, committee memberships—any and all opportunities to participate. This distribution will be so done as to invite volunteering. He should encourage conversation and fairly vigorous argument. The modern teacher not only accepts but stimulates activities and discussions which would not take place in the formal atmosphere of the older school. Incipient disciplinary situations are bound to arise, but they are part of the problem of developing pupil responsibility and self-discipline. This does not mean that the teacher permits breaches of good manners or of necessary order, but that he controls them in such manner as to develop the desired self-discipline. In stimulating participation, he will need to meet the matter of monopoly by show-offs and by eager but yet unsocialized pupils.

5. *The teacher should seek pupil cooperation in planning and conducting the socialized procedures.* This is part of the two preceding points but is important enough for separate emphasis. If invited to participate and commended for it, pupils soon assume initiative and responsibility.

A note in defense of the teacher. The preceding discussion of the recitation has contained some harsh criticisms of teachers who habitually use the typical, unsound, traditional recitation procedures. These criticisms are correct, and they should not be minimized or disregarded. However, a recognition of certain practical circumstances with which teachers must contend will explain their difficulties in part. More important, it will direct the attack to a quarter not mentioned previously. In many high schools the teacher must deal with two hundred or more pupils per day. In some schools, he will have these pupils distributed over two, three, and sometimes four subjects. Often no free periods are provided for either relaxation or a glance at the coming lessons. It is difficult to blame teachers who select a good textbook, divide it into as many page assignments as there are school days, and then machine-gun the pupils with fact questions during the recitation period. At least they "cover the text," though that, unaccompanied by explanation, is a prime pedagogical sin. Even this sweatshop condition cannot be used to condone some of the recitation practices one sees on every hand. Pending the distant day when enough teachers can be employed to do the work properly, teachers should exert unceasing pressure, as vigorously as is safe, on principals and superintendents who could do much to provide facilities and opportunities for improved recitation procedures. Meanwhile, teachers will endeavor, as good ones everywhere are doing, to improve the recitation even under present conditions. The harsh criticisms are only for those teachers who do not do what could be done under given circumstances. In many schools the recitation procedure could be revolutionized almost overnight.

DISCUSSION QUESTIONS FOR SECTION 3

1. Did the material in this chapter sensitize you to, or explain for you, any of the understandings (generalizations) and attitudes toward teaching you held previous to entering this course?

2. Did any new ideas, new interpretations of old ideas, or questions arise in your mind? List them.

3. Show how some of the principles previously advocated for modern teaching apply in the improvement of the recitation.

4. Explain how a pupil could make a "good recitation" without any worthwhile learning having taken place.

5. Some teachers claim that the traditional recitation procedure is useful because it enables them to cover more ground than other methods. What is the fallacy in this point of view?

6. Toward which educational aims does the traditional recitation period actually contribute?

7. Illustrate concretely the formation of undesirable attitudes through use of typical recitation procedures. Do not merely list the attitudes; illustrate them from your experience or observation.

8. Show how the traditional recitation prevents the development of power in oral expression.

9. Examine the discussion questions on this topic in Bossing, pages 519-520; in Butler, page 181; in Frederick, Ragsdale, and Salisbury, pages 178-179. Critically evaluate them in the light of what has been said about study guides and recitation questions in this and in the preceding two chapters.

EXERCISES AND REPORTS

Individuals or small committees may make very brief reports showing the bearing on recitation procedures of some of the new principles of planning and group discussion. These can be very brief as the general topic will come up again in connection with the working period of the unit.

READINGS

The volumes by McMurry, Thayer, and Morrison contain historical background. Discussions will be found in texts on general methods up to approximately 1950. Since then little has appeared strictly on the recitation, but there is excellent material under headings of planning and group discussion. In this connection recall and study selected passages from books previously listed in this and in earlier chapters: Burr, Harding, and Jacobs; Fifty-ninth Yearbook of the National Society for the Study of Education; Lindberg; Miel; Moustakas; Parrish and Waskin; Schorling; Sherif and Wilson.

The heading "recitation" does not appear often in the guides to professional periodical literature.

4: THE DAILY LESSON PLAN IN THE ASSIGN-STUDY-RECITE PROCEDURE.

General textbooks on the principles of teaching have for many years included a chapter on lesson-planning. Arguments for planning, objections to planning, obstacles and dangers, together with the values, were set forth in some detail. New knowledge about learning and teaching has greatly changed our concepts about planning; hence a change is noted in textbooks over the years. The historical development (until 1924) was traced by Mossman. [31] Texts published prior to 1930 differ significantly from those coming later in that the later books omit the lengthy arguments for planning, the summary of uses and values. These are increasingly regarded as obvious and self-evident. Current treatments are clear-cut summaries of the technique of planning, with descriptions of schematic outlines.

Planning was concerned with the daily lesson until comparatively recently. This is natural in the assign-study-recite conception. Modern assignments cover far more than do the traditional, and planning therefore covers more than the daily segment. Units cover still more extended areas of time and material, necessitating still different types of planning, which are presented in Chapter 13.

Constructing daily plans and those for comparatively short periods of several days will be a feature of teacher-training for some time to come. The majority of school systems also require that teachers keep some type of plan, however brief. The procedure for daily planning may therefore be considered with profit, always realizing that daily plans should be in series and not isolated. Plans, moreover, are not rigid instruments to dominate teaching, but flexible guides. Any system of planning should be as brief and

[31] Lois C. Mossman, *Changing Conceptions Relative to the Planning of Lessons*, Teachers College Contributions to Education, No. 147 (New York, Teachers College, Bureau of Publications, Columbia Univ., 1924).

simple as the given circumstances permit. Cumbersome plans defeat the desired end.

The essential elements in a lesson plan. The purpose of lesson planning is to co-ordinate teaching, learning, and materials so that desired outcomes are achieved. Many different forms of organization are used in teacher-training institutions and in school systems. Some give a minimum of direction, allowing student or teacher to present his procedure as he sees fit. Others provide pre-pared blanks with definite space provided for introduction, aim, pivotal questions, sum-mary, and the like and require the student to indicate his procedure in the proper place. Many printed plan books are available com-mercially. Many systems provide for a two-column arrangement, subject matter on one side and method on the other. Still others insist on a somewhat formal division of the teaching period, and hence of the plan, into review, recitation, directed study, assignment, and so forth. It is probably better to avoid such arbitrary divisions or timetables and to plan the lesson in a more natural manner. The following outline, developed through several years of tryout, is suggested as a useful scheme. It may be modified to suit individual preferences.

Lesson-Plan Outline

1. *Objectives*
   Teacher's: What he hopes to accomplish during the class period or periods.
   Pupil's: A proposed or probable aim.
2. *Subject matter*
   Indicated either by (*a*) page references in text and supplementary books or (*b*) an outlined summary.
3. *Learning activities to be utilized* (whether the lesson is to be a traditional recitation, modern discussion period, working period, study period, drill, excursion, experiment, or whatever form).
   A written account showing in some detail how the teacher proposes to make a con-nection between subject matter and the life needs and interests of the pupils, to initiate the lesson and keep it moving toward the objectives.
   Items to include, though not necessarily in any one plan: pretesting, arousing inter-est and motivating; presenting and explain-ing or conducting class discussion of new material; providing for varied learning experiences, reports, excursions, inter-views; stimulating analysis and discrimi-nation; providing for possible digressions and wrong answers; handling disagree-ments and controversies; summarizing and connecting with previous experiences.
   This part of the plan, in short, indicates what the teacher expects to do and say while before the class.
   Samples of proposed questions and expected answers should constitute the bulk of this part of the plan. The size of the samples will differ with the experience and level of skill of the student or teacher.
4. *Summary* (if indicated in a particular lesson)
5. *Assignment*
6. *Bibliography*
   For both teacher and pupil if not sufficiently indicated already in (2) above.
7. *Instructional aids*
   If not sufficiently indicated already in (4) above.

Lesson plans are designed for specific situ-ations. A speech or a sermon is sometimes criticized as having been taken "out of the barrel," meaning that it has been resurrected from a store of previously used speeches. The implication is that the speech or sermon was dull and uninteresting. Dullness results from a number of causes: here, significantly, probably from lack of connection between the speech and the needs or interest of the audience. We have all had the experience of telling a joke or good story which was en-thusiastically received in one situation and not in another. Teachers often teach a very satisfactory lesson, but when they try to re-peat it next semester or year, it does not turn out well and may even fail. Teachers having two or more sections of the same subject have even found that a lesson proce-dure which was most effective with the nine o'clock section failed miserably with the eleven o'clock group, or vice versa. The implication for teaching is clear and unmistakable. Plans for teaching must be based on the characteristics of the group to be taught, upon the necessities of the materials available. Plans should be filed and used in revising succeeding plans, but rarely, if ever, used over again. Teachers who have developed teaching routines which they use over and over and over again (an all too common procedure) are, practically without exception, genuinely incompetent. A few such teachers are interesting and entertaining and do secure some results with pupils. Reputable and adequate results can never be obtained, however, where the pupil and his learning process are subordinated to the routine.

The analysis of typical lesson plans. The present discussions are confined to the general characteristics of planning. Not only does space prohibit the inclusion of illustrative units and plans, but detailed and specific treatment should be reserved for the special-methods course or for the supervisors of practice in any given school. However, if it is desired to give some training (and in some schools it must be given in the principles-of-teaching course), collections of sample plans are easily accessible. The exercises and references immediately following will care for this matter.

Some objection is raised to using collections of plans and units, because it is said that these exhibits are formal and crystallized and are not real plans. This is a quibble. Such exhibits are valuable and necessary for training purposes. It is true, of course, that teachers should not try to use cut-and-dried plans, developed by someone else for another situation. All teachers, particularly those in training, will have their thinking and planning stimulated through careful analysis and discussion of the plans made for others.

SOURCES OF LESSON PLANS FOR ANALYSIS

1. *The card catalogue*
   a. The texts in general method, in principles of teaching, and in the direction of prac-

tice teaching published prior to 1930 include, practically without exception, collections of sample plans. The plans are for formal traditional teaching, but many embody the best of the traditional procedures. The collections are, some of them, extensive and include various types of plan. The modern volumes are more likely to include sample unit outlines instead of daily plans, and to refer to the periodical literature for illustrative materials.
   b. The texts on the teaching of special subjects are also good sources of illustrative plans.
   c. The manuals which accompany series of texts in specific subjects often contain a few sample plans.

2. *The Education Index*
   Scores of articles are available dealing with the planning or teaching of specific lessons. These are more frequent in periodicals designed for use by classroom teachers than in the more general magazines.

3. *The local training school*
   The instructor or training-school staff should have built up a large collection of actual plans. This collection should contain good, bad, and indifferent plans, thus affording varied types of analysis by students.

DISCUSSION, EXERCISES, AND REPORTS FOR SECTION 4

1. Individuals or small committees may analyze for form only a selected number of traditional and modern daily plans. Compare forms with that given in this chapter. Develop a new form if desired.
2. Individuals or small committees may analyze a few very good older plans to determine the theory of learning and teaching which is implied. Compare critically point by point with the principles advanced in this volume.
3. Individuals or small committees may analyze and report upon plans found in the current periodical literature, noting form, content, and principles of teaching and learning implied.
4. Construct a lesson plan for one day's work or for a relatively short period of time. This daily plan must be selected from a total classroom sequence which is typical of everyday teaching. Teachers in service may submit their own on-going plans. Students should organize a plan to fit a sequence being observed

or may construct a plan based on a given piece of subject matter.

5. Following the type of discussion which will result from analysis of plans submitted in (4) above, a series of daily plans covering a sequence of some size may be constructed. In real situations this would be in outline form to allow for changes from day to day as the work developed. In very formal situations plans are made far in advance. Consult references on modern planning.

   a. Beginning students should make these plans in considerable detail in preparation for practice teaching, using preferably material they will actually teach in the near future.

   b. Teachers in service should use the actual materials and sequences appearing in their daily work.

Supplementary Exercises

The following exercises may precede those above with classes made up of young, beginning students who possess little background and as yet little observational contact with schools in operation.

1. The instructor may analyze critically and in some detail a lesson plan or series of plans, copies of which are accessible to the class. The development should be conversational, with free questioning from the class.

2. The instructor and class may construct a plan in class, working out details conversationally and with stress on class contributions to the development. This may take two class periods or more. A class preparing for elementary teaching may do this as a committee of the whole. Those preparing for secondary teaching will need to divide into committees in terms of subject field. One committee and the instructor may develop an illustrative plan.

Plan Books

A number of plan books for teachers are available commercially. Many school systems have organized their own books. Semester outlines, weekly organization, and questions for single lessons are usually required. An exhibit of these books should be available for examination by students. Students may collect a few from nearby school systems.

READINGS

Excellent detailed treatments of general principles, arguments, obstacles and pitfalls, and values are to be found in certain well-known textbooks in principles of teaching, notably those by Bossing, Butler, Umstattdt, and Wynne.

Current treatments of value are found in previous references on planning, sharing, and other forms of daily and long-term procedure.

CHAPTER 13: The Unit

1: DEFINITIONS AND DESCRIPTIONS.

The revolt against formal, stereotyped education produced more than improvements in the traditional assign-study-recite-test procedure. New and basically different organizations of teaching-learning situations arose. The first of these was the so-called "project"; later came the "activity." Each represented a step forward and contributed to the development of more complete and unified schemes of organization. The term *unit* is currently accepted as the name for the newer methods of organizing and is now widely used.

Three streams of thought contributed. *The first* appeared in 1926 when Morrison [1] pointed out that there *must be some external organization of subject matter and experiences which best correlates with the internal learning products we wish the learner to achieve.* The products of learning distinguished by Morrison were attitudes of understanding or of appreciation, numerous specified acquired abilities, a wide range of cultural interests, and an achieved ability to carry on self-dependent intellectual life. The achievement of any of these special or generalized outcomes constituted a change in the personality of the learner, or what Morrison called an "adaptation." (The term was borrowed from biology.)

[1] Henry C. Morrison, *The Practices of Teaching in the Secondary School,* rev. ed. (Chicago, Univ. of Chicago Press, 1931), Ch. 2.

Morrison condemned sharply the fragmentary factual knowledge, the memorized subject matter, the crass verbalisms which resulted from everyday teaching. The term *assignment* does not appear in his index, and in suggesting what he called the unit he was clearly moving far in advance of the typical assign-study-recite process, far in advance of subject matter organized without regard for its use. He goes so far as to point out that many textbooks contain "unteachable materials," material which is nothing but ground to be "covered" and which is of no service to the learner. In place of the typical subject-matter-to-be-covered-under-assignment, he proposes that a unit of learning be:

. . . a comprehensive and significant aspect of the environment, of an organized science, of an art, or of conduct, which being learned results in an adaptation in personality.

The potentialities of Morrison's then revolutionary proposition were unfortunately not realized. References to units of "conduct," *to change in the learner as constituting learning,* to changed behavior as proof of learning, were overlooked. The subject-matter minded teachers of the day seized upon his excellent findings concerning organized subject matter and the derivation of learning products from experiences with subject matter. They overlooked his distinction between learning products and the assimilative experiences through which the products could be achieved. To Morrison's chagrin, his scheme, with its remarkable possibilities, was turned into a glorified method for organizing and presenting subject matter to be learned as such—one of the very things he had set out to cure.

What Morrison saw as one of the important outcomes—namely, skill in reflective thought or problem-solving and the achieved ability to carry on self-dependent intellectual life—did not reappear strongly until Smith in 1950 presented the "process" unit, which stressed methods and patterns of thinking as outcomes.

The failure to realize the full implications of Morrison's work bound us to the "subject-matter unit" and delayed the development of more adequate theory and practice. In fairness to all concerned, it must be said that Morrison placed heavy emphasis upon properly organized subject matter as a prime factor in producing changes in the learner. While he clearly foreshadowed certain important developments in the processes of teaching and learning, he did place much of his trust in the proper organization and use of subject matter.

A second stream of thought contributing to the development of the unit concept came from those who were trying to fit education to the nature of the learner. They had already developed and used widely the "project" and the "activity curriculum."

The third influence did not appear until 1950, although it was clearly implied in Morrison's early statement. Smith [2] pointed out that the revolt against overemphasis on formal subject matter was affected as much by the rise of the theory of instrumental logic as by the new psychology of child behavior. His point is that patterns of thought and

[2] B. Othanel Smith, "The Normative Unit," *Teachers College Record,* Vol. 46 (January, 1945), pp. 219-228.
———, William O. Stanley, and J. Harlan Shores, *Fundamentals of Curriculum Development* (New York, Harcourt, Brace & World, 1950), Ch. 23.

The writer acknowledges with great pleasure the assistance given by Professor Smith, who read this chapter critically and supplied excellent guidance.

effective habits of thinking are basically important outcomes of learning.

A flood of new terms and schemes appeared. The subject-matter exponents produced the subject-matter unit, the unit of learning, the unit of understanding (and of appreciation), the unit of adaptation, and the topical, theme, and survey units. The phrase "center of interest" was used by some to mean a systematic organization of subject matter attached to an interest of the learner; by others, to mean an interest of the learner around which subject matter from various sources might be organized. Contrasting with the subject-centered organizations there appeared the unit of work, the unit of behavior, and finally the unit of experience.

Early efforts at systematic definition. Indifferent, untrained, or lazy teachers usually asserted that no one knew what a unit was or denounced it as a fad or another device; some, taking refuge in that final resort of the incompetent thinker, designated the new development as "theoretical." Careful thinkers, however, had recognized (*a*) that the widely varied terminology was typical of any new dynamic development and, far more important, (*b*) that there was a fundamental agreement underlying the superficial confusion. Every competent writer agreed that here was a movement seeking to replace the fragmentary, piecemeal, disjunctive methods of traditional education. All agreed that the term *unit* means simply oneness, wholeness, or unity. The argument began when a basis of unity was sought. The factor determining unity in a teaching-learning situation must lie in one of three places: the subject matter, the learner, or the particular process used in a given situation.

If we omit the long historical outline, suffice it to say that three types emerged during the formative period:

A *subject-matter unit* is a selection of subject-matter materials, and of educative experiences centering upon subject-matter materials, which are arranged around a central core found within the subject matter itself. The core may be a generalization, a topic, or a theme. The unit is to be studied by pupils for the purpose of achieving learning outcomes derivable from experiences with subject matter.

An *experience unit* is a series of educative experiences organized around a pupil purpose, problem, or need, utilizing socially useful subject matter and materials, and resulting in the achievement of the purpose (solution of the problem or satisfaction of the need) and in the achievement of learning outcomes inherent in the process.

A *process unit* is a series of educative experiences organized around basically important patterns or habits of thought. Socially useful subject matter and necessary learning activities are utilized in achieving the desired outcomes.

It must be noted here, and elaborated later, that these distinctions are arbitrary and if overemphasized will set up basically incorrect dichotomies. The distinctions may be of value to students and beginning teachers in enabling them to see different emphases and to see the hierarchy of outcomes. An over-all definition for *unit* will be given shortly.

Subject-matter units are aimed chiefly at substantive outcomes derived from the subject matter through typical study processes. Experience units are aimed chiefly at developing various learning skills and abilities. Both, of course, use subject matter and experiences. The process units (discovery and verification, normative, criticism) aim at ascertaining laws, generalizations, explanations, descriptive principles; at formulation of policies, making decisions under policy, determining or reconstructing goals; at development of skills of critical evaluation. Smith quotes research summaries showing that effectual intellectual habits can be achieved through study of subject matter only when they are made primary aims. An earlier chapter carried a summary on this point.

Before proceeding to the one over-all definition let us note the benefits of the early efforts to define units. Efforts at definition

have sensitized teachers as never before to aspects of teaching and learning which had been overlooked or forgotten. Teachers are far more conscious of the necessity for (*a*) stating outcomes for their teaching, (*b*) selecting subject matter and providing pupil experiences which bear on the stated outcomes, (*c*) adjusting all situations to the capacities of the learner, and (*d*) demonstrating real change in the learner and in his behavior as proof of learning. Correctives are being widely applied to the aimless "covering of the text" which itself often has little or no sensible organization and to the genuinely stupid practice of accepting repetition of material as proof of learning. Teaching has improved greatly wherever effort has been made to use modern unit organizations.

Continued emphasis upon sharp distinctions in terms of content and dominant aim might lead, however, to (*a*) formalized schemes and (*b*) to neglect of the very aim which originally stimulated the new developments, namely, the continuing integration of the learner.

A basic definition of the unit. The teacher who is conscious of the ultimate goal—integration within the learner—will therefore plan all units toward that end. All units will deal with subject matter and materials, with processes of study and thought, combined in educative experiences best suited to ultimate and immediate goals.

The important thing is to provide a combination of subject matter and processes which will have real meaning for the learner, which will aid him in continuously integrating his learning.

The differences between units which are basically alike will be in the emphasis put upon subject matter and substantive outcomes therefrom, upon learning experiences of all kinds, upon processes of problem-solving, critical evaluation, or other patterns of thought. Integration within the learner will sometimes be aided by emphasis upon one of these, sometimes by emphasis upon another. A proposed definition:

A unit is any combination of subject-matter content and outcomes and thought processes into learning experiences suited to the maturity and needs (personal and social) of the learners, all combined into a whole with internal integrity determined by immediate and ultimate goals.

Definitions of this type are only now appearing in the literature. One brief one may be quoted: [3]

A unit, or unit of work, can be defined as a purposeful learning experience focused upon some socially significant understanding which will modify the behavior of the learner and enable him to adjust to a life situation more effectively.

The key point in determining varying emphases between units lies in the level of maturity, the experiential background, the purposes, needs, and interests of the learner. These factors inescapably determine which experiences will be educative, that is, will enhance the integrating growth of the learner.

The education of *little children,* of *beginners* on almost any level, and of all classes *in the area of general education* will proceed best via units wherein the purposes, problems, interests, and "felt needs" of the learners largely determine the amount and complexity of subject matter to be included and the degree of attention to be given to the study or thought processes wherein direct experience predominates over the vicarious.

The education of students who have *adequate reading ability,* who have achieved sufficient maturity to be able *to learn through verbal abstractions,* and who are entering upon *areas of specialization* which involve a look to the future will proceed best via

units wherein ultimate social goals and more remote personal goals, with due regard for the necessity for challenge now, will largely determine the amount and complexity of subject matter and the degree of attention to the study of processes of learning and of thought; wherein greater use will be made of vicarious experiences.

The use of systematically organized subject matter and direct attention to processes of thought involved should increase naturally with the child's increasing maturity, experience, and realization of future needs. [4]

The thoroughly modern assign-study-recite procedure also meets conditions for mature learners, since it too aims at integration. Modern assignment teaching will doubtless play a large part on upper levels of specialization. Traditional assignments aim at covering text material. Sincere teachers trying to improve ordinary assignments will progress toward better assignments and units.

The characteristics and values of the unit. The following list is taken, with a few changes in wording and sequence and with a few additional commentaries, from the excellent volume by Hanna, Potter, and Hagaman: [5]

Possesses wholeness and coherence.
Based on the personal-social needs of the learners.
Provides well and easily for individual differences.
Promotes democratic group living.
Is life centered.
Cuts across subject lines, thus providing for the interrelatedness of subject matter. (This is particularly useful in lower grades, the core curriculum, and in any phase of general education. Units are also constructed within subjects or within broad fields.)
Based on the modern conception and principles of learning.
Provides for differing maturity levels.

[3] Lavone A. Hanna, Gladys L. Potter, and Neva Hagaman, *Unit Teaching in the Elementary School* (New York, Holt, Rinehart & Winston, 1955), p. 100. The authors state in a footnote that "understanding" includes a large range of outcomes.

[4] Smith, Stanley, and Shores, *op. cit.* Pages 572-574 contain an excellent statement somewhat similar to the development here.
[5] See complete bibliographic reference in Readings just below.

Provides for normal drives and motives.
Emphasizes problem-solving. (Note however that units may be informational surveys, fact finding, normative, and case study in form.)
Planned co-operatively.
Provides for functional use of skills.
Uses large blocks of time.

READING REFERENCES FOR THE UNIT

A general book such as this one cannot develop all details on the major topics included. One volume on the unit stands out and should be read carefully in connection with the three chapters here on the unit.

HANNA, Lavone A., POTTER, Gladys L., and HAGAMAN, Neva, *Unit Teaching in the Elementary School* (New York, Holt, Rinehart & Winston, 1955). This is a comprehensive treatment, not only of the nature and development of units and the subsidiary processes therein but also of the social, psychological, and democratic values of unit organization. For Section 1 of this chapter, students may read with profit Chapter 5.
Chapters 1, 2, 3, and 4 may be read at any time as excellent general background.

QUESTIONS

Some questions and reports listed in the next section may be approached here if desired.
Ample opportunity should be given for students to ask any and all questions they wish at this point.

2: DIFFERENCES IN EMPHASIS WITHIN UNITS.

The summary in Section I clearly indicated that units for little children and beginners, or in areas of general education, will emphasize materials, learning outcomes, and experiences which are of immediate value to the learner. Less attention is given to the substantive outcomes which may be derived from systematically organized subject matter. There is also less emphasis on the patterns of thought which are used by the learner. The dominating aim is to secure an answer to the learner's problem or question.

With increasing maturity in the learner, increasing attention may be devoted in units to the organization of the subject matter itself, to the type of outcomes derivable from experiences with subject matter; more conscious attention may be given to the patterns of thought which are used and which may be acquired as assets by the learner. The extension of the learner's system of ideas, the improvement of his habits of study and thought, are now the dominating aims.

The emphasis within a unit is implied but not guaranteed by the title. Textbooks all contain lists of unit titles illustrative of the several varieties of so-called "subject-matter" units and of "experience" units. A few very recent publications contain illustrative titles for "process" units. The same titling can be used, not to distinguish types of units but to indicate the probable emphasis within the unit.

A title can clearly imply the teacher's intentions as to emphasis on content and outcome. The implications can usually be fulfilled well enough in printed or written unit plans. The actual emphases for a given unit can be discovered only by observing the unit in progress. The genius of the teacher and the extent of pupil participation are the primary factors in determining the emphases within a unit as it develops.

Unit titles which imply emphasis upon the learner's problem and subject matter and outcomes from it, with patterns of thinking subordinated to the problem. The learner pursuing his problem meets organized subject matter in functional situations, builds up a good background of meaning and of fact, acquires practical, non-analytic familiarity with patterns of problem-solving, of critical evaluation, which become bases for more systematic learning as maturity increases.

Good illustrations of titles for units which purport to aid integration on this level include:

How Can We Keep from Being Misled by Advertisements?

How Can We Detect Propaganda in the News?

How Is Our Community Supplied with Milk?

Why Is Oakland, Where We Live, One of the Important Cities of California?

Why Do So Many People Live in the Bay Area?

How Can We Learn How to Learn?

Why Did People Come Across the Plains to Oregon in the First Place?

How Can We Understand Our Science-Centered World and Live Securely in It?

In What Ways Are Pressure Groups and Compulsions Affecting Us?

How to Get the Most for Our Money in Buying Clothing, Food, Medicine, Household Appliances?

How Can We Learn to Get Along with Other People?

How Can We Predict Tomorrow's Weather Accurately?

Is It True that Newspapers Slant the News?

How Can We Organize and Operate a School Library? (This grew out of a gift of a considerable collection of books.)

How Can We Start and Operate a School Newspaper?

One group which started off with the unit, "How Can We Detect Propaganda in the News?" changed the title as the unit developed to "What Can We Believe?" The original interest in everyday propaganda developed into interest in problems of belief in the claims of democracy in contrast to other forms of government, in the claims of ethical and religious teachings, the claims of scientific research, and so on through several major life interests.

The children in a third grade in Brockton, Mass., asked a number of questions which their teacher seized upon and developed into a unit on "What We Want to Know About Our City." In Lynn, Mass., the Tercentenary Celebration of 1929 naturally stirred great interest among students. Many units were developed out of children's questions which led directly into study of the immediate environment.

Incidentally, one important material outcome of the Brockton study was the production by the third-grade children of "Our Story of Brockton," which was published in mimeographed form and covered 120 pages. In Lynn, the fourth-, fifth-, and sixth-grade pupils of the city produced a series of "History Stories of Lynn," which the School Committee printed as a 252-page reader for youth in these grades. Similarly, an advanced group of students in a Middle-Western high school produced a vivid and interesting history of ancient times. This group, starting a course in Ancient History, complained constantly and bitterly about the dreary textbooks available. The teacher asked, partly in desperation and partly in hope that something might eventuate, why they did not write one that suited them if they did not like those available. The students accepted the suggestion with enthusiasm. In passing, let it be noted that the amount of subject matter covered in these units was several times that which could ordinarily be included under assignment.

Unit titles which illustrate the changing emphasis from learner's problems to organized subject matter and to problem-solving processes as such. A unit entitled "Our Fruit from Tree to Table" grew out of a vigorous discussion among children whose parents were wholly dependent upon fruit growing or labor in that type of agriculture. The questions and arguments, very real and immediate to the children, set off a train of events which was well organized by them and by the teacher. Search for and use of systematically organized materials was prominent. Many problem-solving decisions had to be made by the children. "So, You Want a Job" led high school seniors into a series of excursions into organized information on job opportunities and careers and into many real problem-solving situations. There was also critical evaluation of the policies of industries and of public bureaus. College students produced a unit based on their own experiences immediately following World War II: "Making the Transition from Veteran to Civilian." "Getting it the Hard

Way" was an interesting inquiry by children in an underprivileged city area into the effects of early escapades and delinquency on their own chances for employment. This called for much information, problem-solving, and evaluation, not to mention soul-searching concerning policies of behavior. "A Handbook for Our Junior High School" sounds like a faculty-imposed project dealing with routine compilation of routine information. Actually, the project started as a result of repeated questions and complaints from parents and new pupils. The handbook developed with very little direction from the faculty. "How to Get There in Our City," "Taking Care of the Furniture in Our Home," and "Meeting the Community Needs in ————" all grew out of everyday problems but led to the use of systematic materials, evaluation, and problem-solving. One of the most interesting units ever observed by the writer ended up with the title "Why Is There So Much Fighting in Our Suburb over the Veterans' Housing Project?" The whole community, in addition to the children in the junior high school, were concerned with an immediate, local, and very human problem which led them to examine policies, prejudices, and democratic values as never before.

Unit titles which imply emphasis upon more remote personal needs or problems, on social goals, with systematic subject matter and patterns of thinking becoming prominent both as content and as outcome. Learners eventually recognize the value of more remote goals and begin to meet and use systematically organized knowledge. They give more careful and direct attention to the methods of intellectual attack on their problems.

Illustrations of unit titles which might be expected to aid integration on the more mature level include:

The Development of Transportation and Its Effect on Our Civilization.

(Similar units based on Sanitation, Communication, Manufacturing, Distribution of Goods, etc.)
The Colonization of America.
The Winning of the West (Or The Westward Movement).
The Development of our Constitution.
The Geography of Central America.
The Properties of Gases.
The Age of Chivalry.

Some teachers prefer to use as the title a generalization which will be an outcome of the unit.

Newspapers Play a Large Part in Molding Public Opinion.
Tyranny Too Long Continued Breeds Revolt.
Abundant Supply Causes Prices to Fall and Thereby Stimulates Demand.
Short Supply Causes Prices to Rise and Thereby Stimulates Production.
Producers and Manufacturers Often Interfere with the Natural Working of the Law of Supply and Demand.
Civilization Began to Appear When People Learned to Specialize Because More Goods Could Be Made. In Primitive Times, Each Family Made All Its Own Goods But Could Not Make Much That Way. Each Craftsman, for Centuries Carried on His Specialty in His Own Home or Shop. The Invention of the Steam Engine, Nearly Two Hundred Years Ago, Made Possible the Use of Power-Driven Machinery.
Chemical and Physical Continuance of Life upon the Earth Is Dependent upon the Water Cycle.

Still other titles indicate very clearly that the major outcome is systematic knowledge on the part of the learners. Morrison suggested some sixteen units of this type within an over-all Survey of Civilization. Samples are:

How Civilized Man Lived.
The Brilliant Greeks and What They Did for Civilization.
The Great Road Builders and Lawmakers.
The Monastery and the Castle.
Europe Spreading over the Seas.
From Slave to Free Man in All Ages.
The Coming of Science.

Units suited to younger learners might include: "Indian Life," "The Cave Man," "Medieval Life," "Life in Holland," "Plantation Life in the Ante-Bellum South."

The following are a few studies in which the writer has observed or participated:

The History of the Development of Our Democratic Rights and Obligations.
Our Government in Action (any level, segment, or activity).
The United Nations: A Study in International Co-operation.
What Our Community Does.
    How the Community Protects Persons and Property.
    How to Get There in My Community (points of interest, cultural significance, suburban, and slum areas, segregation of ethnic and national groups, housing, transportation).
The Story Behind Greater Boston's Way of Living (can be applied to any city).
Crime Presents a Problem.
Crime and Punishment. (This turned into a study of punishment in human history covering many centuries.)
Marriage and the Family in Our Industrial Civilization.
Fluoridization of City Water Supply. (Despite the fact that volumes of evidence are available, public discussion has developed some incredibly absurd remarks and arguments. Pamphlets have been published and widely circulated which not only amuse students but raise the question of the authors' mental balance.)

The use of titles in question or problem form. Using questions or problems as titles is favored by many because problems usually do stimulate more interest and effort than general topics. Care must be exercised, however, to see that the questions and problems are real and not formal. Several titles already given in declarative or descriptive terms are often found in texts or courses of study in such form as:

How Did the American People Conquer the West? (The Westward Movement).
Why Did the European Nations Colonize North America? (The Colonization of America).
How Has Man Invented and Improved Methods of Communication? (Communication).

These are not true problems but are really questions; they are formal, adult-conceived questions. These call for no more problem-solving than would the same materials under declarative titles.

A unit dealing with the Bill of Rights could be thrown into a form requiring real problem-solving: "What Caused the Bill of Rights to Be Left Out of the Original Constitution?" Standard text references not only do not present this unit from the angle implied; they present conflicting statements and views. Students would have to discover materials, read and compare, analyze arguments, and draw conclusions.

A unit, mentioned in Chapter 1, which dealt with the reconstruction period in our history, ended up with the title "How Has the United States Solved Post-War Problems in the Past?" This requires some problem-solving, but of limited type, since good answers can be found in the subject matter. A somewhat better title might have been "Why Was the South So Resentful of the Reconstruction Period?" This would call for some scrutiny of accounts of policy and for evaluation of statements.

A teacher was presenting a typical unit on the geography of Africa at the very time of the invasion of North Africa in World War II. She adhered carefully to the typical formal outline for such units and attempted to use such pseudo-problems as "What Are the Surface Features of North Africa?" and "What Is the Climate of Africa?" She was arousing practically no interest. Meanwhile the pupils, following the invasion in the newspapers, kept breaking in with questions of their own: How can we be bogged down in the mud? It's all desert in North Africa and never rains. The paper says there was snow in the Atlas Mountains in Africa. How can that be? It's all Sahara Desert. I never knew there were swamps in North Africa. Why are the Arabs trying to make so much money out of our soldiers? Why couldn't the English catch up with Rommel when he retreated? The teacher finally "caught on" and seized upon the pupil questions. Hardly any of these questions coincided with the questions she had prepared or which the textbook covered. The pupils, following their own questions under teacher guidance, utilized far more subject matter than the teacher had planned or the textbook contained. Their enthusiasm also enhanced the outcomes.

Many projects or units are informational instead of problem-solving in nature. Such topics as the following will result in excellent study and great amounts of information:

How is (our town) supplied with pure milk?
How can we predict tomorrow's weather accurately?
Do newspapers slant the news?
How can we keep from being misled by advertisements?

Critical skills enter at many points in the above projects, but the chief activity is study. Now, then, if we change the titles a little, we get another order of lesson.

Did the (local newspaper) suppress or slant the news regarding the recent action of the city council in dealing with local gambling spots?
Do *Time, Life,* and *U. S. News and World Report* give objective accounts on a given topic, or is there a constant slant?
Did pressure groups force the school board to change the graduation requirements?

With these there will be some genuine problem-solving and critical thinking (if the authorities do not demand that the school stop dealing with such things!). The contrast can be shown further:

How can we detect propaganda in the news?
Does the (local or a selected national newspaper) mix propaganda in with the news?

The first can be answered reasonably well by typical study skills and through accessible sources. The second will necessitate the derivation of original data (if it can be gotten), the development of hypotheses, and the use of most careful inference.

Problems that cannot be answered. Objection is raised by many to the use of certain areas and to certain specific problems in social studies courses on the ground that the students cannot possibly solve them or act on the findings if they do get solutions. As for that, neither can their parents solve these problems, nor the state legislature, nor the courts, nor any other organization of adults. Constant study and effort over many years are necessary. The democratic nations were a long time in solving, and then only in part, the evils of unjust imprisonment and punishment by authoritarian rulers. Trial by jury and voting by the public on highly technical issues were solutions of early evils, but these solutions now need further study and new solutions. In the area of civil liberties solutions are still being sought. As this is written, the problem of school integration in the South is in process of solution; legal processes, social pressures, public discussion, police power, and mob violence have all been called in.

The important point is that individuals will never be able to solve this type of problem unless they get practice. People hardly ever solve difficult problems at the first approach. Solutions for some current social problems cannot be derived under present conditions and knowledge. Compromise and tentative working decisions are all that are possible by any group on any level. Another reason for studying these problems in school is that students get practice in gathering pertinent information from different sources, in critical evaluation, and in making conclusions. Oddly enough, some critics of the schools which use these problems assert that students discuss them in an informational and conceptual vacuum. They seem to ignore the fact that informational and conceptual vacuums can be filled only through this kind of practice in gathering information and in developing concepts.

The real danger in discussion of these problems is that unskillful teachers may lead students to believe that such problems can be solved on the basis of superficial examination or, worse, that they can be solved without long, expert analysis and continuing reorientation.

A very few samples of such problems are given here:

Is lobbying a justifiable practice in local and national legislatures?

What are the facts about our foreign policy? About foreign aid?

Is a sales tax desirable, either in itself or as an offset to income taxes?

What problems and tensions persist in our society because of our transition from an agricultural to an industrial economy?

What advantages and what evils have attended the great growth of the cities?

To what extent are moral standards changing in our society? What are the reasons for this? Are the changes all, not at all, or partially good or bad?

What effect has the industrial system had on family life?

What is going on in China? Should we recognize Red China?

Should there be a pooling of world resources?

What is the relation between population, food supply, and birth control?

What might be the effects of peacetime use of atomic energy?

What is the relation between churches, Sunday-school attendance, and delinquency in a given community?

What are the advantages of the free-enterprise system? Are there evils that need correction?

Should we study socialism or communism in the schools?

Are the current criticisms of the school justified, wholly, partially, not at all? (Failure to teach the 3 r's; inability to maintain discipline; progressive education as cause of the evils; homework lacking).

Is membership in the United Nations and NATO in the national interest?

Big government, big business, and big labor often interfere with the free working of the law of supply and demand. Take several specific instances, and try to determine the advantages or evils.

What are the facts about U. S. foreign policy in regard to Red China? With regard to travel in Red China by U. S. newspapermen? With regard to recognition and trade? With reference to Formosa?

What are the facts about U. S. policy with reference to Berlin? In regard to internal disorders in Latin America? Foreign aid? Aid versus trade? Foreign alliances? Farm subsidies and surplus products?

These problems are certainly not solvable by students at any level or, as has been said, by most adults. But they must be given attention, must be under constant study, or certain evils will never be corrected, certain important social benefits never realized. Students working on these problems get the best possible training for continued attention to them in adult life. Every known study skill and process of critical thinking will enter. Group discussion with all its benefits will become thoroughly familiar.

Without discussion of these problems in school and college, students are not only bound to be ignorant of many critical issues of the day, but, what is worse, they will grow up holding many erroneous beliefs. As was shown in an earlier chapter, the questioning of many beliefs taken for granted is a real necessity today. Dr. H. J. Muller in his *Uses of the Past* points out that the uncritical acceptance of the concept of original sin is responsible in part for a callous and unrealistic acceptance of many social evils, the easy acceptance of slavery, and many hideous religious astrocities. Belief that "you can't change human nature" has caused irresponsible and unrealistic thinking in tragic degree.

Controversial problems in the classroom. The same general principles hold here as were summarized just above for problems for which no final answer is immediately available. A good deal of thinking must deal with controversial problems, varying from simple everyday affairs up to matters of political policy, social programs, and economic decisions. Adults—from average citizens to national leaders who do not always do too well in managing major controversial problems—should conceivably have done much better had they had school discussion of such problems. Everything that has been said in previous chapters about the nature of thinking and learning to think applies here. Children come into contact with controversial problems as soon as they can understand the conversation of older children and adults. They meet them as soon as they can look at pictures and read. Even the comic strips often deal with current controversial problems, too often with a definite propaganda bias. Social, moral, economic, and political problems confront them at every turn. Children and youth will deal with controversial problems, and no one can prevent it; they will be conditioned by all manner of contacts and will form opinions in any event. They will do this, either on the basis of random and often biased contacts with street corner and neighborhood gossip or through honest and orderly discourse under the auspices of the school.

Illustrations of different emphases within units. Brief commentary upon the units mentioned in the first chapter and the appendix may clarify all this a little more.

The unit on "People Who Help Us in School" in the appendix utilized no formally organized subject matter whatever. None was available in the particular situation. The unit on the American flag arose as did the first one; again there was no formal material available for such a unit, but a good deal of material in organized form was eventually drawn from various sources. In many communities the course of study might contain organized materials for each of these units. Material on the American flag is increasingly included. Outlines on the community are appearing which contain material dealing with the co-operation of persons within the community.

The unit on "Protection of Health and Safety in Merced" arose out of spontaneous pupil questioning and utilized immediately a well-organized outline of materials available in the course of study. The pupils sought out this subject matter and achieved the desired outcomes by using it in functional situations. Modern courses which contain the source materials on the community supply good outlines on the Police Department, Fire Department, Health Department, and others. The children in Merced did not study these as formal outlines to be memorized but used them as guides in visiting the departments, interviewing officials, and observing the operation of the departments. Their learning outcomes were their own and phrased in their language. Such emphasis upon materials and outcomes is far different from units (or assignments) in which the systematic material is studied as an end in itself.

The units on stage design and the Reconstruction Period arose, one out of student questions, the other out of a stage setting by the teacher. There was active pupil participation in planning and carrying out the first unit, less so in the second one. In each the emphasis, however, was on the systematic subject matter available and on the principles which govern the organization of the materials.

A summary, in general terms, of the contrasting emphases within units prepared for different levels of maturity and purpose. (See pages 338-339.) Characteristic emphases within the assign-study-recite procedure are included here to show the development from traditional to modern organizations of teaching and learning. Good assignments made out by teachers who try to meet their students' needs will be closely related to the unit. Typical formal assignments represent the other extreme.

Two points in the following summary and in other similar summaries usually disturb certain teachers. First, the reference to "no fixed outcomes required of all" is widely misunderstood. Second, the attitude toward the nature and use of subject matter disturbs the more traditional teacher. Actually, these points are easily explained.

Outcomes of learning situations, either under assignment or the unit organization, are not fixed nor uniformly attained. This statement startles many teachers and students, especially if made out of context. Undesirable reactions which may follow are these: (*a*) many teachers are antagonized and refuse to analyze the statement; (*b*) superficial teachers use the statement as an excuse for haphazard, unplanned activities, for omission of all standards, for avoiding responsibility for results.

The facts are easily grasped. A good unit or a good modern assignment will bring pupils into contact with many learning outcomes: meanings, facts, attitudes, appreciations, skills, patterns of behavior, processes of study, and problem-solving. Different individuals will achieve similar outcomes in differing degree and will acquire different outcomes from any given experience because of differing needs, backgrounds, interests, and capacities. Outcomes will differ from group to group, due not only to individual differences among learners but also to differences in learning situations.

The very nature of learners, of the learning process, and of the settings within which learning takes place *actually prohibits the possibility of fixed outcomes required uniformly of all.* A series of units or assignments will, over a period of years, give all pupils opportunity to achieve those outcomes which are desirable for successful living. These outcomes will never be achieved in final and complete form; they become directional progress goals. [6]

Properly explained, the statement that there are not and cannot be fixed outcomes required uniformly of all learners is not startling. It is merely a recognition of facts which have existed since teaching began.

[6] L. Thomas Hopkins, *Interaction* (Boston, Heath, 1941). Excellent similar statements will be found on pp. 264-265; 5, 11, 13.

Teachers have been bamboozled by the fiction dominant in the traditional school that outcomes were fixed and achieved by all learners. It is highly unlikely that any teacher ever lived who secured uniform outcomes with her pupils. The fixed subject-matter goals of the old school were and have always been pure fiction. The facts given in the preceding paragraph show why uniform learning is impossible. Teachers attempting to secure uniform learning, testing for it, and failing students on this basis are proceeding in flat defiance of demonstrable facts.

The nature and use of subject matter. The important facts concerning the origin of subject matter were illustrated in Chapter 5, so summary statements only will be given here. Traditional subjects came into being when mature, adult scholars, well trained and informed in a given field, abstracted materials originally related functionally to life situations and organized these abstracted items into sequences determined by the static logic of the materials themselves, and not in terms of dynamic use. Traditional teachers who impose the subject curriculum on little children should be interested to note that not only was it formulated by adult experts but it was formulated for the purpose of *preserving* the culture, not *teaching* it (let alone *improving* it)! No wonder immature children have difficulty with the subject curriculum!

The teacher who insists that subject matter is something that must be "covered," that it be learned as an end and outcome, is giving *prima facie* evidence of specific, definable lack of information concerning:

1. The very nature of subject matter itself.
2. The origin and organization of subject matter.
3. The use of subject matter in learning, in scholarship, in anything.
4. The process of learning in school and in the world.
5. The nature of learners and the differences between them.

Comparison of Formal Assignment Procedure and Units on Two Levels

Assignments as typically used. (The extreme type of formal assignment is the basis here. Many assignments are far superior to those indicated here, but the formal type is still dominant. Improved assignments will be characterized by closer approach to the characteristics of units.)	*Units for little children, beginners, and for all levels within the area of general education; units which are dominated by the immediate purpose of the learner.*	*Units for more mature students and within areas of specialization; units which are dominated by more remote personal purposes and by social goals.*
1. Begin in the intention of adults to teach approved subject matter to pupils.	Begin in the intention of the learner to achieve some immediate purpose; to satisfy some felt need.	Begin in intention of learner to achieve more remote personal and social purposes, the values which he sees now. Can begin with acceptance of purpose from teacher. Learner accepts aid in either case from teacher in clarifying and stating purpose.
2. Are for the purpose of having pupils "cover" the material and acquire the logically arranged material as the learning outcome. (Good assignments are increasingly aiming at derivation of useful learnings from the subject matter.)	Are for the *immediate* purpose of satisfying a need of the learner, with the *ultimate* purpose of developing desirable meanings and facts, attitudes, skills, and patterns of thought.	For the purpose of deriving systematic knowledge in the form of principles or facts, attitudes, and patterns of thought, not as ends but as aids in the satisfaction of more remote goals.
3. Are organized logically around a core within the subject matter. (It must be noted that many assignments and the subject matter used have no organization of any sort.)	Are organized psychologically around purpose of the learner.	Increasingly organized around systematic materials with more attention to developing patterns of thought, but always with due regard for the purposes of the learners. (Again the materials and patterns are not isolated nor ends in themselves.)
4. Are prepared in advance, by the teacher, or by a course of study committee familiar with the materials and their logic. (Good assignments are increasingly using pupil participation.)	Are organized as they develop by a group facing a new situation for the first time, and not familiar with the materials and patterns of thought necessary to meet the situation.	Can be preplanned to considerable degree by teacher and accepted by pupil, but always planned with pupil goals in mind and with as much pupil participation as the given situation permits.
5. Are usually organized (when organized at all) logically in terms of the materials, usually from simple to complex, often chronologically.	Are usually organized functionally and in disregard of subject lines; from simple to complex but often from complex to simple.	Are organized far more in terms of the systems within materials and patterns of thought, but always with regard to maturing student purposes.

6. Are controlled by the teacher, by adult committee, by course of study.	Are controlled by a co-operating group of learners which includes the teacher as an active participant; uses course of study as needed.
7. Are usually centered in the past, in the "accumulated," not the accumulating" culture; little reference to present or future; reference to future usually theoretical.	Are usually centered in present and future; use accumulated materials from past freely in solving present problems.
8. Rely on formal methods, assignments, distinct lesson types, and printed materials as chief sources; learning experiences few and formal.	Utilizes co-operatively planned procedures suited to the situation, uses sources in great variety; learning experiences numerous and varied.
9. Give all pupils the same contact with the same materials; some provision for individual differences.	Gives contact with many materials and patterns of thought; individual differences cared for variously and almost automatically.
10. Have fixed outcomes known in advance, required uniformly for all learners.	Do not have fixed outcomes known in advance and required uniformly of all learners.
11. At conclusion, evaluate through the use of formal tests of subject-matter acquisition, usually of fact or skill.	Evaluate many complex outcomes continuously, with constant use of many instruments, formal and informal.
12. Close with a backward look, so-called "review," and are done with when finished.	Leads to new interests, problems, and purposes.

Controlled by the social purposes of the school and by systems of thought within the subject matter, but always with regard to pupil purpose and with pupil participation as warranted.

Usually concerned with future needs which are, however, recognized now by learner, and with social needs; uses current materials and accumulated materials (subject matter), the future value of which is sensible to the learner now.

Utilizes and increases facility in the use of meanings and patterns of thought which were derived earlier in the co-operative experiences; printed materials and more sophisticated patterns of thought prominent, supplemented by many references and aids.

Gives contact with many materials and patterns of thought, but with more conscious attention to their intrinsic value; individual differences cared for systematically.

Same in all units.

Same in all units.

Same in all units.

Logical arrangements of subject matter will aid the teacher, but not the beginning learner. Mature learners will eventually achieve insight into, and be able to use, systematic arrangements of materials.

Subject matter for little children must be selected from their own everyday life experience. No other subject matter can have meaning for them. The school then guides the growth of children from this first simple, naïve, and immediately functional organization of subject matter to the more complex, logical, and generalized organization of the special subjects which is appropriate for higher levels of maturity. The teacher not only has to know more subject matter than before, but she has to see and to be able to develop relationships between subject matters. She must be able to relate subject matter to the everyday activities of learners on different levels of maturity. Within the special subject areas on the upper levels, she must be able to organize material functionally.

In addition to being familiar with typical text and supplementary reference materials, the teacher must know where extensive bibliographies are available and be able to use them expeditiously. She must also be easily familiar with the museums, exhibits, and collections available in the school and community; familiar with the resources of the physical and social environment.

Logical versus psychological organization of subject matter. Rousseau [7] pointed out long ago that there are two arrangements of any set of facts or ideas. One chain of thought is developed logically in terms of underlying principles existing in the material. The other chain of thought is one in which each fact or idea calls up another fact or idea as association, curiosity, and individual interest dictate. The former is the organization of material *that has been learned and is already understood by the learner; the latter*

[7] Others who make the same point include Descartes, Comenius, Locke, Whitehead, Ortega y Gassett, Dewey to mention a few.

sequence is the organization of the material as the learner meets it. The former is subject matter organized in terms of itself; the latter, an organization in terms of purposes, desires, and likes and dislikes.

As an example, it seems rather logical to teach the geography of any country in the following order: location as determined by latitude and longitude and in relation to surrounding countries and waters; the climate, involving prevailing winds and topography; the vegetation and products which depend, in part, on the foregoing; industries; commerce and trade; transportation; cities; people; and government. But the ordinary youngster would probably be attracted to a study of Holland through pictures of windmills and dikes. A study of Brazil might be started by a discussion of the tremendous amount of coffee consumed in the United States. Adams suggests that the study of the feudal system in England and in France would be initiated with the perfectly natural question, "Why are there hedgerows in England and not in France?" To follow rigidly a logical scheme of organization would be to violate not only the laws of the material but the interest and experience of the learner.

History affords a good illustration of the difference between the so-called logical and the desired psychological organization. History seems to demand, by its very nature, a chronological sequence; but we know that small children have no grasp of long time intervals, or recognition of the fact that ancient social conditions are out of keeping with present-day conditions. This subject should begin, as it usually does, in a study of the social conditions with which the pupil comes in direct contact. The first step away from home might be, for city children, the study of a farm. This would involve construction on the sand table, stories, pictures, trips if possible, collection of pictures, making booklets, and the like. Tales of Indian life, of the Vikings, of the shepherds and other early people would lead the pupil to history as such. A further study of the local community in some detail would then be in order. This would give the class an insight into chronological sequence through concrete, understandable material. Many modern courses of study provide for intensive investigation of the local community by children of various levels from the third grade up. A number of these studies have been referred to in various places in this volume. Students may read with benefit any units or printed accounts which may be available.

Not long ago the subject matter in reading, drawing, and writing was selected and organized in terms of the elements of the processes involved, with little regard for the psychological processes of the learner. Children, and adults as well, grasp things as wholes, and analyze later if necessity demands. For that reason, writing and drawing courses based on a mastery of isolated curves and angles violate the learning processes and are even detrimental at times to quick, orderly learning. Writing and drawing should begin with crude efforts, and improvement should be sought by comparison with better models. Writing scales have been of great value in this situation.

In reading, it is perhaps best to begin with word or sentence wholes, to pick out simple words or groups of words, and from them to work out the phonograms that may be necessary. Such phonic work as is necessary should be based upon sight words that were first learned as wholes.

The current uproar over the use of phonics in reading is a case in point. Beginning with phonics and imposing scores of phonic combinations on the child stems from ignorance of the nature of reading. Reading is not sounding or saying words, it is dealing with meaningful symbols. Sight words or small sequences of words for which meaning is known must come first. Phonic unlocking of new words then follows with the necessary sound symbols derived from known words.

The shift from formal gymnastics to plays and games is in line with organizing subject matter to correspond with learner interests and activities. The muscular development and hygienic benefits supposed to be derived from gymnastics are much more efficiently obtained through whole-hearted, happy play.

The modern school has long since substituted functional number experiences for the formally organized arithmetic materials which discouraged so many children in the past, and which actually prevented the proper learning of arithmetic. Even in schools where formal subject matter is used in early grades, changes have taken place. Good teachers do not teach the multiplication tables and number combinations in the sequence dictated by logic. Experimental evidence shows that many tables and combinations coming late in the logical series are actually easier to learn than some of the earlier ones.

The logical organization of subject matter is that of the adult, of the informed person, of the mature mind. It is for the sake of the subject matter itself. Such organization fractionizes the world for the immature learner. The child lives in a concrete personal world in which his practical purposes, desires, and emotional reactions are the threads of organization. He is not and should not be concerned with subject matter as such. He uses material from any and all sources as he needs it to solve a problem or to satisfy some desire. Hence, he attacks and masters subject matter not as it is logically and systematically organized but as it happens to fit his pursuits and purposes. Consequently, the organization of material for early levels should be psychological and not logical. Many of the lesson-plan forms used about the country call for outlines of both types. A logical statement of subject-matter material is set forth either in outline form or by reference to appropriate textbooks. Then, in that part of the plan which is an account of classroom procedure, subject matter appears in psychological sequence. The logical statement of subject matter will, within reasonable limits, stay put; but the psychological arrangement will have to be changed for each group with which it is used. Learners will differ in desires and interests, in background, in various abilities—all of which will affect the psychological organization. The results of a pretest aid in determining the psychological organization in any given case.

Assignments and units differ in use of subject matter. The original meaning of "textbook" was: a source of brief compact statements in summary form which were to be amplified, extended, and clarified through reading, discussion, reflection, and other activities. When learning degenerated into covering the textbook and mastering the subject matter it contained, assignments naturally became fragmentary and disjunctive. Chapters within texts are too often discursive, descriptive, expository discussions of details loosely or not at all related. Assignments based on poorly organized chapters are even more fragmentary and arbitrary. Finally, assignments are often dictated by administrative necessities and not on principles of learning. Traditional assignments are usually arbitrary, fragmentary bits of material.

Teachers are likely to include everything in sight in assignments or units for fear that they will commit the cardinal sin of the traditional school and "leave out necessary subject matter." A survey of science [8] courses in a certain area contained a tabulation of the separate subject-matter items included under the topic "air." Over a range of several courses, individual units, and assignments, practically every known item in the field of physics eventually found itself within this topic. Conversely, "air" appeared as a subhead in practically every other topic in the field of physics. Such organizations are obviously mere conglomerations of information thrown together by individuals who

[8] Wilbur L. Beauchamp, *Instruction in Science,* Survey of Secondary Education, Bulletin No. 27 (Washington, D. C., U.S. Office of Education, 1932), p. 20. Wide observation in traditional high schools reveals little or no improvement since 1932.

know neither physics nor the process of learning nor the principles of organization. The desirable procedure is to include only that subject matter which explains, develops meaning, or gives facts through which understanding of the given topic comes.

Modern assignments have been greatly improved by thoughtful teachers. Whereas traditional assignments control class work for one day, or for two or three days at most, the modern assignment deals with larger and larger bodies of material and may control class work for several days or even a week or more. A series of modern assignments may be, and often is, unitary. Assignments of either type are, as a rule, shorter and take less time to complete than a unit, since the latter deals with larger bodies of subject matter and a greater diversity of learning experiences. The distinction, however, is not one of time or length; it is in form of organization and desired outcomes.

The unit, on the other hand, is a thoughtfully organized whole constructed around a recognizable core. The objective of many teachers who use units is still achievement by the pupil of subject-matter mastery; however, the number of teachers is steadily growing who use units, not for memorization of subject matter, but for the derivation of desirable understandings, appreciations, and other controls of conduct.

Relation of units to the course of study. A well-known story about the modern curriculum concerns the father who reported that his child had studied "Boats" from kindergarten through the third grade. He wondered if it would be possible in the fourth grade to get the child off the boat—perhaps onto a train or even a bus! Considerable confusion does result in school systems where the staff, without adequate background, undertake unit teaching. The unit is treated as merely another technique—a novelty, the latest fashion. Teachers and supervisors start making units with enthusiasm, but at random. There is often no consultation between grade groups. The situation is further complicated by those who interpret with narrow literalness the principle that all units must be based on pupil needs and purposes. This may cause the same unit to appear on various levels. The total result of unorganized effort is usually a collection of units covering a wide variety of topics and problems, with no unity. Senseless repetition occurs, with omission of materials and experiences that all would agree should be common to all learners. What is needed is an over-all plan.

Teachers, furthermore, are often puzzled as to where to find units and how to choose them. Heretofore they have relied for direction and for content upon the printed course of study or upon single textbooks. Under sympathetic training and supervision, they will now learn that units are not "found"; they have to be constructed. Even then, there is the question as to the relation of units to the course of study.

The use of units should be within the framework of a curriculum commonly agreed upon, preferably constructed co-operatively. We are not concerned in this volume with the details of determining scope and sequence of the curriculum. There are various methods of determining these which teachers will meet as they participate in reorganization programs. A good course of study should aid and not dominate a teaching situation.

A comprehensive program of curriculum reorganization and course-of-study development should precede the introduction of unit teaching or be simultaneous with it. This not only prevents confusion, overlap, and omission; it is one of the best programs for the improvement of the total teaching-learning situation and for the stimulation of professional growth in the participants.

A modern course of study differs widely from the traditional in several respects. It is not a mere outline of subject matter with a few suggestions to teachers. It is, instead, a mine of information on both subject matter and learning activities and includes lists of materials and teaching aids, diagnostic devices, and modern evaluation instruments. Modern courses often contain instructions for constructing units, outlines for units, and sometimes sample units. The most recent courses are produced not in one outlined volume but in a series of volumes, each with a unit title. The course of study is an orderly sequence of these volumes which are general sources of scores of specific units to be constructed by the teachers.

Source units. The volumes which make up modern courses are often called "source units" or "course-of-study units." The volumes are actually sources *of* units, sources *of* suggested approaches, materials, and learning experiences which may be organized by teachers and pupils into classroom units.

Source volumes are extensive collections of *possible* problems, materials, and experiences which may be organized by the teacher around either subject-matter cores or pupil purposes. The contents are so extensive and varied that a teacher cannot possibly use the material as the basis for day-to-day teaching. He will use it instead as a handbook of guidance and assistance, as a reservoir of ideas and suggestions, and as a source of many teaching plans for individual units. These source volumes are constructed usually by committees or other organizations within a curriculum program. They represent the pooled suggestions and contributions of many teachers, the results of many teaching try-outs. They should be in loose-leaf, mimeographed form and be revised constantly.

The scope of source units differs from system to system. Some are designed for use in one grade or at best two or three adjacent grades; others may cover four, six, or even eight grades. The latter type suggests units for different levels based on the same general theme. The illustrations in Chapter 1, "Who Helps Us in School," a first-grade unit, and "How Merced Protects My Health and Safety," a fifth-grade unit, could conceivably be drawn from the same source volume on "The Community and Its Organization." Source volumes on The Home, The Family, The Community, The Farm, Transportation, Communication, South America, Problems of Democracy, and so on, interminably, could quite well supply guidance for teaching situations suited to several levels of maturity. Biddick suggests: [9]

These problems should, however, be such as would concern pupils of different ages and be so stated as to indicate the need of progressive development from year to year. Thus, the unit on the care of young children might begin with the problem of caring for younger brothers and sisters. The same unit could well include consideration of child care as a part-time job for girls, and on the most mature level deal with the psychology of children as a means of understanding human beings and guiding their development. The teacher using such a unit (source suggestions) would be helped to see and to assist pupils in viewing each experience in relation to the process of growth rather than as an isolated unit of work. This should make possible continuous growth without the feeling of constantly dealing with "old stuff."

The beginning teacher will usually not be concerned with the construction of source materials, though she may be included on curriculum committees—an opportunity which would afford desirable in-service training. Experienced teachers in good systems are very likely not only to serve on committees but to find themselves chairmen of such committees and thus in position to exercise leadership in improving the course of study. Chiefly, however, teachers will be concerned with using and improving volumes of source materials.

Many school systems have worked out co-operative procedures and outlines for the construction of these volumes. Many examples will be found in the books on curriculum and on teaching. Every school faculty or curriculum committee can well afford to study several procedures, to study their own views and resources, and then to construct co-operatively an outline of their own.

It goes without saying that these source volumes must be of manageable size. They must also be written in simple, non-technical language easily understood not only by experienced teachers but by reasonably well-trained beginners.

The *log of a unit* is a written account or diary of the learning experience as it actually develops. It should be written as the unit proceeds, rather than after the unit has been completed. Analysis of logs contributes to the improvement of units yet to be developed; serves as a basis for evaluating the learning experience in the light of its purpose, its adjustment to individual differences, its actual demonstrable outcomes. Analysis of logs contributes significantly to needed changes in the curriculum pattern. A log may or may not follow the outline pattern used for planning the unit originally.

The *plan for a classroom unit* will be developed in detail in the next chapter.

DISCUSSION QUESTIONS, EXERCISES, AND REPORTS FOR SECTION 2

Examination of illustrative units imperative. Modern teacher training cannot be carried on successfully without (a) ample opportunity to observe teaching in process, either traditional or modern or both, and (b) ample opportunity to examine many assignments, unit sources, unit plans, and logs of units in printed, typed, or mimeographed form, and (c) ample opportunity to plan teaching procedures and attempt them in an apprenticeship period. These aspects go on simultaneously but may be separated for discussion. We are here primarily concerned with (b). Instructors and local workshops must build up a large collection of such materials and keep it up to date. These local collections should contain both material gathered from the field generally and that constructed by students and teachers-in-training. Various forms may be represented. A guidance form for constructing units should not be imposed on the group but determined co-operatively.

Students in training must supplement this

[9] Mildred L. Biddick, *The Preparation and Use of Source Units* (New York, Progressive Education Association, no date, probably 1940), pp. 15-16.
See also I. James Quillen, *Using a Resource Unit*, Bulletin in the Problems of American Life series, published by the National Association of Secondary School Principals and the National Council for the Social Studies, Departments of the National Education Association (1942).

chapter with continuous examination of units; otherwise study is a waste of time, resulting not in understanding of units but in verbalisms about units. Discussion based on questions resulting from preliminary examination of units should contribute to the desired understanding.

Sources of Units for Examination

The *"source units"* or *source volumes* are not easily available, since they are usually produced by local curriculum groups for local use. Ordinarily they are not distributed commercially and can be secured only from the school systems producing them.

1. *The local collection.* Instructors and local workshops must secure an adequate sampling of source volumes from representative school systems.

2. *State, city, and county school systems.* Teachers and students or curriculum committees may secure samples by direct purchase. Many school systems will supply a price list. Several systems do not distribute their materials.

3. *The Preparation and Use of Source Units* by Mildred L. Biddick (New York, Progressive Education Association, undated, probably 1940). Practically the only extensive discussion of the construction of source units. Contains excellent source unit as illustration.

4. The volume by Hanna, Potter, and Hagaman, listed as a reference to the preceding section of this chapter, contains outlines of four excellent source units in Chapter 16, pp. 393-531.

The various types of *classroom unit* are more easily accessible to students, teachers, and curriculum groups.

1. *The local collection.* An extensive, varied, and up-to-date body of material must be built up by local instructors and workshops.

2. *The card catalogue in the library.*
   a. Many individual units and logs are available in book form.
   b. A few collections of outlined units are available in book form.
   c. Many sample units appear in texts on teaching and on curriculum construction. (See illustrative list below.)
   d. Many illustrative units appear in bulletins published by teachers colleges, city and state systems, or individuals.

3. *The Education Index.* This is probably the best single source of current units. Use the heading "Units" and subheads thereof. Scores of references will be found to original sources, especially magazines, courses of study, bulletins, yearbooks, etc.

4. *Courses of study* issued by state, county, and city school systems.

5. *Textbooks* on teaching or on curriculum construction. Various types are available. (See bibliography at end of following chapter.)

6. *The commercial publishing houses.* Many companies publish units, materials, and outlines. These vary from excellent to completely incorrect.

7. *Yearbooks* of city, state, and national associations of teachers, principals, supervisors, curriculum groups.

8. Catalogues are available from various publishing houses, teachers colleges, and state school systems. These can be located through *The Education Index* or the *Cumulative Book Index.*

Bases for Class Discussion

1. Bring to class a list of questions on which you wish discussion and explanation. These will be based upon your:
   a. Examination of a number of source volumes to discover general structure and content.
   b. Examination of a number of modern city and state courses to note the type of sample teaching units and logs presented.

2. Describe and comment upon a source volume (bring to class if possible) which you believe to be a good one in aiding students to understand units and their use. (Or select one deemed to be poor.)

3. Describe and compare two source volumes which differ materially in any aspect of form or content. This will enable the class to observe quickly several forms.

4. Make preliminary examination of phases of units and present preliminary questions, if these are necessary for understanding of source volumes. Detailed discussion of the phases must wait until completion of the next chapter.

5. Select from the twelve-point outline on pp. 338-339 the three points which seem to you most clearly to indicate the important differences between teaching beginners and teaching more mature students. Support your choice with reasons.

Exhibit and Discussion by the Teacher

Groups of beginners or traditional teachers without background often profit from analysis of a given source volume, given slowly and informally by the instructor.

CHAPTER 14: Planning and Developing Units

The type of unit used by a given teacher should be determined by the factors noted in the preceding chapter: the maturity, experience, and needs of the learner in relation to desirable social goals. It will often be determined, however, by the administrative policy and course of study of the school system in which he teaches.

The teacher will have large choice, even freedom, within the local framework in the best school systems. Teacher freedom and responsibility will depend upon the vision of superintendents and principals in those formal systems which are beginning to move toward modern curriculums and methods. The teacher will have very little, often no, choice at all in the truly formal and traditional systems.

Choosing a unit for planning. A number of major and minor sources are available. Each source will operate, as indicated above, in terms of the course of study and administrative policy.

1. *Courses organized in source units.* Modern courses are increasingly organized in source volumes from which teachers gain suggestions for units, materials, and experiences. Early source units were sometimes haphazard in relationship to each other and to the total school program. Modern source volumes are systematically organized within a scope and sequence.

2. *Courses organized as outlines of subject matter to be covered.* These vary from limited statements to those containing much material, suggestions of processes, evaluation and diagnostic procedures.

Units derived from either of these two sources should be within some desirable sequence, whether based on immediate needs of learners, or upon more remote personal and social goals. The ingenuity of the teacher and the skill with which course materials were originally organized should tend to relate units to learners' maturity and needs or make them clearly acceptable to learners.

Preplanning by the teacher is essential and legitimate, but even with units of this type there should be increasing use of pupil participation. The pupil will learn to plan, to discriminate, to organize properly, only by doing these things.

3. *Courses organized around the on-going activities of the learning group.* Units may also arise from the conversations, arguments, or questions of the learners; from events in their lives or communities. Organized material may or may not be available in the course of study. Materials and processes will be drawn from many sources. Preplanning by the teacher is necessary, but will be far more general and tentative than with units based on the course of study. Planning will be far more participatory, with the very scheme of the unit being subject to development as the learning experience proceeds.

4. *Courses organized from the textbook.* The textbook is the course of study and the only source of units (or of assignments)

available to teachers in a tragically large number of systems. The simple ignorance which permits the one-text-to-be-covered procedure should have disappeared from schools generations ago. It has not.

The teacher who tries to rise above this sordid level of education will find that his own ingenuity is the real source of good units (or assignments). By examining the subject matter imaginatively, the teacher will see how much of it can be rearranged into teaching-learning organizations which will be far superior to the original scheme. Teachers in traditional schools who have any opportunity and encouragement at all toward improvement of teaching will have to discover their own units.

5. *Leads for later units emerge within units in progress.* Leads to other units often develop within a current unit. Pupils themselves usually suggest more than can be followed up. Suggested leads may be evaluated quickly at the time and noted for future reference. Good planning by teachers will provide for the appearance of these. The chief difficulties here are that some teachers may not recognize desirable suggestions, may override those offered by pupils and sometimes may drag in arbitrarily problems for future work.

Sources of aid for the teacher in choosing and developing units. Typical instruction in principles of teaching should be supplemented from the very beginning with all possible observation, participation, and eventually, direct experience. Understanding of the unit concept and first efforts to develop units will be aided by these activities:

Read and analyze in class any available printed, stencil-reproduced, or typed unit plans or logs of units. The instructor should have a large collection built up over the years. Other materials are available commercially.
Visit well-trained teachers to observe and discuss what is going on.
Visit demonstration schools.
Read descriptions and records of activities in given rooms in connection with visits.

Consult teachers who are experienced in modern teaching.
Analyze up-to-date course of study documents.
Consult supervisors.
Enroll in courses dealing with unit construction; in workshops.
Make guided studies of children's needs.
Study the facilities of the school and community.
Analyze one's own experience.
Attend exhibits of pupil work.
Attend lectures on child development.
Read discussions of the philosophy and psychology of the newer methods.

The values of these procedures are obvious. The danger to be avoided is the tendency to imitate too closely or to carry over teaching procedures bodily from one situation to another. The latter is a serious error and is a reversion to the traditional subject-matter-to-be-covered point of view.

Just what does a teacher do in preparing units? Two preliminary activities must precede the development of a unit or series of units.

First, the characteristics of the individual learners and of the group must be studied. The cumulative records of the school and various other sources will supply information concerning intellectual abilities, emotional status, social maturity, school achievements, special abilities and disabilities, special intellectual, emotional, and physical needs, socioeconomic status, type of home and neighborhood, social classes represented, and many other useful data.

Second, the course-of-study documents and all available aids in the school and in the community must be studied. The teacher must be intimately acquainted with all available resources.

In preparing units for all grades, the teacher should follow this general line of action:

a. An overview is presented.
b. Teachers' objectives as clearly recognized by the teachers are stated.

c. An approach, introduction, or orientation is developed.

d. The learners' objective appears, is recognized and stated.

e. A planning period is provided.

f. A working period is provided in which learning is carried forward. Replanning enters here from time to time.

g. The learners' objective is achieved together with some or all of the teacher's objectives.

In the paragraphs which follow, these procedures will be considered in some detail.

An overview is presented. The nature and scope of the unit is explained in any one of three forms. Details omitted, the three forms are: (1) a description in running discourse; (2) a series of "leads" in the form of themes, topics, or generalizations; (3) a series of "leads" in the form of actual or probable pupil problems, questions, or proposals.

Criteria for evaluating the overview. In examining an overview, the following questions may be asked:

1. Is consideration of each lead listed necessary to the solution or understanding of the problem?
2. Is there developmental relationship between the parts of the problem as listed?
3. Will each theme, topic, or problem contribute to meeting the needs of the pupils in school and out?
4. Does each offer opportunity to acquire socially desirable outcomes?
5. Is each of the listed activities within the range of understanding of the pupils for whom it is intended?
6. Does each offer specific opportunity for a diversity of pupil activity to meet the various levels likely to be found within the learning group?
7. Does the overview as a whole give the reader a good idea of the unit and its divisions?

Common weaknesses to be avoided in formulating the overview are:

1. Needless repetition of material which appears more properly elsewhere in the outline: objectives, planning, activities, or subject matter.

2. Vagueness and generality of the outline and of the leads individually.
3. Extensive, intricate, detailed outlining of any or of several phases, making for confusion and lack of balance.

The teacher's objectives. A brief summary will recall important points made in Chapter 6.

1. The teacher's objectives are the typical things that the teacher and the school wish to develop in the learners.
2. The pupils' objectives are typical things which they wish to do.
3. The objectives of the teacher and of the learner are not the same on beginning levels but tend to become similar, eventually identical, on upper levels.
4. The teacher's objectives are achieved in and by the learner while he is primarily concerned with the satisfaction of his own aims.
5. The teacher's objectives are achieved only through a continuing program over a period of time. They are the more remote objectives to be achieved through many units in general education, through whole courses or groups of courses in special education.

Danger of confusion between teacher's and pupil's objectives. Unlimited confusion results from an error inherited from the traditional school with its reliance upon imposition, that is, the assumption that the objectives of teacher and of pupil are one and the same. Nothing could be further from the truth in the primary school, though the two do merge on upper levels. Overlap exists a little on all levels. Elementary children often engage happily in activities performed by adults around them, notably reading, drawing, and computing. These children do seek, and are motivated by, many of the things the teacher seeks. Many older children, on the other hand, do not achieve the maturity necessary to see the value of remote personal or social goals. These individuals are still motivated by immediate personal goals.

Students and some experienced teachers often open their lessons with a statement to the learners of the objectives held by teacher or school. Student teachers and some with experience often ask whether they should not set their aims before the learners, to provide initial motivation and organization. The question indicates adherence, often not recognized explicitly, to the older theory of imposition of materials and outcomes upon the learner. Whose motivation is involved? Whose organization? Children are not motivated by typical social goals, no matter how true and necessary these are. Children are bored, often antagonized, by statement of and insistence upon typical adult objectives. These matters, ordinarily, have little or nothing to do with the lives and concerns of these children. They are not dynamic, as are the learners' own goals—namely, solutions of problems or answers to questions which are real to these learners.

The effective teacher instead develops or seizes upon a legitimate learner's aim. He then arranges the learning experiences, whether preplanned or developed with the children, so that the learner, in satisfying his own vivid and compelling motive, achieves many of the things the teacher had in mind as desirable objectives of learning. The units described in Chapter 1 and in the Appendix were organized around pupil problems or questions during the solution of which the pupils inevitably learned many facts and meanings, amplified certain attitudes and appreciations, achieved many motor and mental skills. The processes of problem-solving, of critical evaluation, of discrimination and decision all were employed. The pupil working on his goals inevitably achieved many of the teacher's goals. The teacher who sets-out-facts-to-be-learned, who focuses only on the ultimate meanings and attitudes, is not really aware of how learning takes place.

The teacher lists the objectives which are specific to the given unit. The teacher will list, following the overview, the facts, meanings, attitudes, appreciations, skills and abilities, and behavior patterns which may be *touched upon in the unit.* Illustrations of typical objectives of all classes were included in Chapter 5, hence will not be repeated here. Other illustrations of understandings (or meanings) will be found a few paragraphs below. The unit on "Colonial Life," reproduced in Chapter 15, illustrates how many outcomes can be correctly stated. Various schemes for listing objectives are acceptable. One will be illustrated in the unit outline at the close of this chapter.

The general objectives, which are the outcomes derived from many units or courses, are not listed in teaching outlines. General objectives are summarized in all good courses of study, source units, or other course documents. Source volumes often contain discussion and diagrams showing the relation of these objectives to the materials and experiences designed for the learners. The writer believes that restating general objectives in teaching units makes for confusion, sometimes for vagueness in operation. Many unit outlines, however, contain space for a sample of the remote general objectives. Instructors and students who are helped by these statements should include them. The writer is, ordinarily, opposed to such statements as:

To develop the ability to think.
To develop the ability to use reading (or arithmetic) as a tool.
To develop good language usage (to speak well; to write well).
To develop the ability to work in groups (to co-operate; to take responsibility).
To develop study skills (outlining; taking notes; skimming; summarizing).
To develop skills necessary to good learning.
To develop the type of individual best suited to life in a democracy.

These are all sound and good as remote, general objectives. They do not supply guidance in the selection of materials and experiences. Each of them may be broken down into two or a dozen specific aims which can be made the object of direct attack within given units.

Pseudo-objectives. Teachers often offer as objectives statements which look and sound like objectives but which are not. Illustrations are:

To provide vivid experiences for the children.
To enrich the child's environment and provide experiences which will develop his personality and show growth in traits that are socially desirable in a democratic environment.
To provide experiences that will enable the child to grow in ability to understand and evaluate certain social, ethical, economic, and political relationships among individuals in the community.
To provide opportunities for developing and improving skills.
To provide for individual differences.
To provide opportunities for sharing, assuming responsibility, planning, making decisions.
To provide opportunity for expression and creative work; for construction of things.

These statements are directives to the teacher, not objectives. The teacher as a matter of course will do all these things while pursuing the real objectives, which are learnings to be achieved by the students. The real objective, for instance, might be "the understanding that the statement issued from the City Hall in Toonerville may not be an accurate representation of the city's affairs." Many different types of experiences will be necessary, yet the objective is not the experiences but the meaning derived from the experiences. "The provision of vivid experiences for the children" is, as an objective, quite naïve Experiences for what purpose? The word *objective* implies that the teacher seeks some degree of pupil achievement.

The form and wording of objectives is very important. Teaching cannot be effective, learning will not be successful, if the objectives are vague, muddled, or ambiguously or incorrectly stated. Teachers have no trouble in describing skills or specialized abilities as objectives. Behavior patterns are also easily described. Appreciations are likewise defined easily enough, but there is considerable confusion in the use of *appreciation* and *understanding*. Straightforward, descriptive wording is essential.

Consistency in form of statement is as important as the wording. Statements may begin with an infinitive, a participle, or other grammatical form, but there should be uniformity throughout the list.

Consistent Form	Inconsistent Form
To give a better understanding. . . .	An understanding that. . . .
To aid in securing. . . .	To aid in securing. . . .
To help the child realize. . . .	Helping the child realize. . . .

1. *Appreciation and understanding should be distinguished.* The word *appreciation* is all too commonly used when *understanding* should have been used. "I *appreciate* what you mean" usually signifies "I *understand* what you mean." Appreciation is an emotional reaction; understanding, an intellectual one; though naturally they are interwoven in real situations. Appreciation indicates liking for and tendency to choose, whereas understanding indicates comprehension. "To appreciate what good health depends upon—" should probably be stated as an understanding, "Good health depends upon—." Many units contain such objectives as: to appreciate the work of the Weather Bureau (or the Health Department or the Fire Department); to appreciate the community; to appreciate the home; to appreciate the historical background of—; and so on. These may contain some elements of appreciation but should more accurately be broken down into several specific understandings.

2. *The understandings which are sought can be stated properly with a little care.* Stating understandings as objectives presents several difficulties. Students and teachers regularly fall into certain common errors. The chief difficulty lies in securing definite, precise wording. The worst possible method of stating understandings is that which uses the expressions: to understand *something of,* to understand *about,* to understand *how;* for instance, to understand *something of* our glorious institutions, to understand *how* in-

dustry has affected music, an understanding *of* the community, an understanding *of* the homes and industries *of* the people, and so forth. Such statements are wholly inadmissible. They tell *where* the understandings are but not *what* they are. These examples merely indicate vague and indefinite areas from which definite understandings could be derived and stated if one knew how. Statements of this type indicate that the teacher does not himself see the understandings, that he does not understand adequately the use of language, and very probably, that he does not think through clearly. The words *of* and *how* cannot be used in defining understandings. (In order to avoid confusion later, let it be noted here that in stating appreciations, the form using the word *of* is quite satisfactory.)

A somewhat better but still inadequate method of stating understandings is one from which the understanding is easily inferred, but the understanding itself is not explicit. This type is often further complicated by being stated in question form: "What effect has the shift in labor responsibility had on our homes and home life?" This is ridiculous as an objective. A better statement would be: "The understanding that the shift in labor responsibility has had a seriously detrimental effect upon the home, upon the home life, and upon the home training in the industrial centers of the world." The meaningless objective, "What the change in policy of the employer has been regarding the health and safety of the employee," can be translated into a workable one, namely, "The policy of employers of labor, at first, was to disregard utterly the health and safety of the employee. Agitation brought about legal restraints upon employers. In the more enlightened industries, the employer sees to it, even if only for his own good, that the health and safety of his employees is safeguarded."

The wording of the understandings sought in many courses of study and in many units is so inconsistent and inexact as to be almost semiliterate. Many of the incorrectly worded statements could be reworded easily and made into reputable understandings. Others need to be translated into understandings rather than to be reworded. What some teachers list as understandings are items of information and not understandings at all. Illustrations of *incorrect* wording:

An understanding of how the people of the Sahara region fit their ways of living to a land of little rainfall, restricted water supply, lack of vegetation, lack of fertile soil, never-ending heat.
The significance of the nearness to the Arctic Circle in determining the length of day and night, temperature, and seasons.
The influence of religion and festivals in the lives of these tribes.
The comparative size of the region.
An understanding of the family.
An understanding of markets.
Understanding of different methods of transportation.
An understanding of some of our problems.
Understanding of how people get along together.
Understanding of how our city protects our safety.

Illustrations of *correctly worded* understandings, both broad, general ones from courses of study and more definite ones from units, include:

Man is dependent upon the wise use of plants and animals for food, clothing, and shelter. (*General*)
Definite standards are necessary in the selection of actors and in the direction of actors if we are to produce a worthwhile, creative interpretation. (*More definite*)
It is possible to seek and find information needed to answer one's ordinary problems.
Much scientific knowledge yet remains to be discovered.
Experimentation and invention are stimulated by competition and in turn modify the growth of industry. (*General*)
Many industrial leaders suppress new inventions which would benefit the public but reduce profit. (*Definite*)
Civilization has not always existed as it is at present but has evolved out of continuous social change. (*General*)
Buildings reveal civilizations and living conditions of the times in which they were built.

The pyramids give insight into the absolute tyranny of the Pharaohs, the widespread slave labor, the stratification of society, the religious beliefs and pageantry of the times. The Medieval cathedrals reflected a very deep religious feeling prevalent at the time and also a suicidal disregard for certain economic principles. (*Definite*)

The basis of power in our form of government is popular opinion.

A family must work out a system for the management of its money, and adjustments will need to be made to ensure desirable relationships.

Vague and incompetent statements of objectives may be thrown into sharp contrast with carefully prepared statements. A unit on "The Earth and Its Relations to the Universe" was found to have as objectives the following incoherencies:

To understand the heavens as a whole.
To know the nature of the stars.
To identify stars and constellations.
To understand the force of gravity.
To know the nature of the solar system.
To know the planets.
To know the nature of comets.
To become familiar with the nature and the effect of the sun.
To know the nature of the moon.
To know how an astrolabe is constructed.
To know about geysers.

A competent teacher prepared an organized, detailed list of reputable objectives for the same unit. The following is a brief sample from the list of understandings:

The universe of which this earth is a part consists of millions of bodies with vast distances between them.

The earth is but one of a large number of bodies which affect one another in their physical conditions.

The movements of the various bodies which compose the universe are determined by the action of certain forces and as a result there is order.

The forces which act upon the bodies in the universe are known and as a result their movements can be predicted with great accuracy.

The conditions of life upon this earth are influenced by the relations of the earth to the other heavenly bodies.

The universe, and the earth as a part of it, has developed through a process of gradual change and this process is still going on.

Objectives must be subject to measurement or evaluation. Each legitimate objective, as it begins to be achieved by the learner, will affect his behavior. By testing we can easily measure achievement of simple fact or skill learnings. Evidence for the more complex learnings must be secured through observation, through collection of significant incidents or anecdotes, and through inventories and other devices.

Teachers will be aided very greatly in stating objectives if they will look ahead to try to determine the type of evidence which must be found to prove that learning did take place. Vague and indefinite objectives will be discredited at once, because no methods of evaluation could be devised nor evidence of learning identified. The demand for evidence is also a corrective to those teachers who have never thought about objectives and who do not know the objectives of their own teaching.

The teacher's objectives should be stated always in such form that evidence of achievement by learners can be derived.

Criteria for teacher's objectives. Making a statement of objectives, the teacher must bear in mind a number of criteria. The objectives should be:

1. *Socially desirable,* that is, recognizable directional progress goals leading toward the accepted general aim of education.
2. *Achievable,* by the level of maturity of the group, and permitted by the available resources.
3. *Developmental,* that is, leading to constantly higher levels of achievement.
4. *Varied* enough to appeal to varied interests and abilities (that is, to care for individual differences), to challenge all to further growth.

5. *Limited* enough in number to permit of definite organization without undue diffusion of effort.
6. *Susceptible to evaluation.* Evidence of actual progress by the learner may be secured.
7. *Co-operatively* set up whenever possible, particularly the pupil's objective.
8. *Worded clearly* and *consistent* in form.

The list may be extended or amended by students and instructors.

An approach or series of approaches is planned. Teachers for generations have planned how to "arouse interest," how to "motivate" pupils to effort. Good traditional teachers have never been satisfied with merely assigning lessons; they have attempted to arouse interest or otherwise prepare the students. Poor traditional teachers are so in part because they ignore, defy, or actively repress pupil interest. This not only handicaps learning but greatly increases the difficulty of the teacher's own work. The Herbartians called the first step of a lesson *preparation.* Kilpatrick used the term *purposing,* and Burton popularized the term *setting the stage.* Modern terms are the *approach,* the *initiation,* and the *orientation phase* of the unit.

The teacher's unit plan will show how he meets the challenge. He will plan to utilize interests, purposes, or other motives which may be present, or will plan how to manipulate the learning situation to cause these to arise. The general sources from which approaches may be developed are indicated below.

A. *Approaches may be derived from the natural on-going activities of the learners in and out of school; from events in or characteristics of the immediate environment.*

1. Seize upon any pupil discussion, argument, comment, or question out of which a unit may be developed readily. These opportunities may appear in and out of class, in formal or informal groups. The range of opportunity here is as wide as the life of the group.
2. Utilize any materials brought from home: curios, souvenirs, utensils, clothes, *objets d'art* from foreign countries or from other regions within our own country; pets; toys; flowers, seeds, fungi, minerals, and other material from the natural environment; apparatus from mechanical areas.

B. *Approaches may be developed through the arrangement of the environment.*

1. Arrange an attractive exhibit or display on the bulletin board, the wall, a table, or exhibit shelf.
   a. Pictures, posters, picture postcards, of historic or geographic places and events, of costumes, of customs, of festivals, of living conditions, of industrial or agricultural processes. These may be ancient or modern, or show contrasts between the two.
   b. Book covers, extracts from reviews, illustrations.
   c. Books opened to interesting pictures or exciting passages.
   d. Apparatus from science, from medicine, from industrial or agricultural processes; household appliances. These, too, may be ancient or modern.
2. Arrange a "beauty spot." This is a form of exhibit or display, but is listed separately because it usually has an aesthetic instead of a utilitarian emphasis.
   a. Artistic flower arrangement.
   b. Artistic productions of any type: graphic art, ceramic products, textiles, and so forth, from foreign countries or other regions of our own country.
3. Capitalize upon any important event which occurs. Deliberately ask questions or otherwise initiate a conversation upon:
   a. Any important current event reported in the papers or occurring locally.
   b. The presence of foreign visitors.
   c. A motion picture showing locally.
   d. A vacation or other trip taken by teacher or pupil.
   e. Any other interesting or remarkable experience undergone by any member of the group.
4. Make an excursion or visit to a famous place or person; to a factory, a farm, or some other place of special interest.
5. Read an extract from a book, a magazine article, a poem.

6. Show motion pictures, lantern slides, stereoscopes; play records.
7. Refer to experiences in a previous unit.
8. Undertake a local project suggested by school, or by some local organization, such as beautifying the school grounds, conducting a clean-up campaign, or holding a garden contest.

C. *Approaches on the upper levels and within the specialized subjects may be no more than the announcement of the next topic or problem. Any unit in a well-organized course on this level will usually lead on into the next one.*

These general sources of approaches differ in effectiveness with varying levels of maturity, varying backgrounds of experience, varying socioeconomic status of the home, and other factors.

Sources of assistance for the teacher in planning approaches. Initiating a unit is fundamentally different from giving out assignments. A stimulating, provocative approach is the product of a keen, vivid, creative imagination. Literal-minded persons, slow and stodgy individuals, no matter how earnest and conscientious, no matter how devoted to children, do not ever achieve greatness as teachers. The alert, imaginative teacher sees in many everyday happenings the opportunity to initiate series of learning activities. He is constantly seizing upon openings which many other teachers may not see—or seeing, may actively repress. Because approaches are unique and made to fit given situations, because they rest so clearly upon the individual genius of the teacher, it is very difficult to give teachers effective advice about planning them. Such advice would not be desirable even if it were possible. Adequate detailed guidance would require the listing, discussion, and analysis of hundreds of specific cases, an impossibility in a general volume or even in a limited, specialized one. Teachers must read widely in collections of units, in courses of study, and in specialized bulletins. Some general principles of planning an approach to a unit, however, can be listed.

First, adequate knowledge of typical interests likely to be found within given age and group levels is necessary.[1] There is overlap, to be sure, but certain interests are very likely to be present in given situations. The questions the teacher asks himself are: What things invite attention, provoke discussion, inevitably stimulate action? What things will persons seize upon and react to; what will they ignore and be indifferent to? The astounding ignorance of the answers to these questions among parents and untrained teachers results in wasted effort, antagonism, and undesirable outcomes. *Second,* intimate knowledge of the learner and of his learning processes is necessary. The first part of this volume is designed to help the teacher achieve this. *Third,* the teacher needs an easy grasp of the course of study, and wide general knowledge resulting from a first-class general education. *Fourth,* reading of many units and logs will supply hints and aids. Hundreds of illustrations are available. Materials should not be taken over from units developed under other conditions, but insight is undoubtedly gained through study of the successful work of other teachers. *Fifth,* visiting to observe good teachers at work gives similar assistance.

Pupil participation in initiating learning experiences is important. Securing the participation of pupils will motivate them to identify themselves with the undertaking. Traditional teachers often ask what is to be done when an approach does not motivate all pupils in the group. The retort is to ask what they themselves do when their assignments similarly fail to attract all pupils! An assignment by its very nature must always attract and motivate far fewer individuals than will an adequate approach with its varied types of opportunity for different types of pupils. Approaches are very easily adapted to the various elements within a class group, just as modern assignments are in some measure. The natural, on-going activity of

[1] Devices for discovering interests were summarized in Chapter 10.

the classroom, with the tacit assumption of necessity for *doing*, carries still other pupils along in either assignments or approaches. We may go further than these generalizations; various diagnostic steps may be taken if any considerable number of pupils do not respond. The teacher should

1. Critically scrutinize his approach to see whether
   a. He has provided a varied range of learning activities in prospect.
   b. He has provided a varied range of materials.
   c. He has not taken freedom and responsibility from the children to such degree that he has reduced their participation to following directions, carrying out assignments, doing as they are told.
2. Patiently observe the uninterested individuals and, as opportunity arises, aid them to find more vivid interests in the on-going process.
   a. Note typical choices of activities, materials, and associates in the schoolroom and on the playground.
   b. Give many opportunities to try new materials, tools, or processes.
   c. Talk over frankly the reasons for lack of interest in an effort to find one.
3. Tactfully and courteously exert pressure to get participation started to see if interest will develop. Drop pressure if not effective in a reasonable time.

As a last resort, work may be required, just as it is in the traditional school and with the safeguards set up in a previous chapter.

Continued motivation is necessary during development of the unit. Since the topic of interest is under discussion, it may be noted that traditional teachers often ask what is to be done if pupils lose interest in the unit at any time. The retort again is, What was done when pupils lost interest in assignments before completion? Interest fluctuates in all human undertakings. One of the general and constant tasks of all teachers is to maintain interest and attention. The normal range of activities and materials within a unit, the constant co-operative determination of what is to be done, the constant replanning, the

constant objective evidences of progress— all contribute to continued interest. When further stimulation is necessary, devices such as those indicated in Chapter 4 may have to be utilized.

Characteristics of a good approach. The approach serves to invite and stimulate learners to educative activity. The genius and creativity of the individual teacher is called upon here as in few other aspects of teaching. The approach will make or break the unit.

The approach must be developed in some detail in any written preplan. The teacher, particularly the student in training, should not say: I will develop an aim; I will stimulate conversation; I will lead the pupils to plan appropriate activities. Anyone can *say* this and be quite unable to *do* any of it. The teacher must show *explicitly* just how he will stimulate conversation, develop an aim, and lead the pupils. This usually necessitates the inclusion of some proposed conversation. Students often say that they cannot imagine what pupils will say, ask, or answer. Individuals for whom this is actually true should consider some other occupation, for they can never succeed as teachers. The truth is that nearly anyone can learn to do this with a little guided experience. The inclusion of this inescapably necessary detail ensures that the teacher has a realistic knowledge of pupil needs, interests, purposes, backgrounds, and general methods of thinking. The use of non-existent needs, interests, and thought sequences is prevented. Arriving at desired outcomes by magic is eliminated. Properly done, this detailed outline, especially during preliminary stages, will not make competent individuals dependent upon the written sequence. Rather, security and independence will be fostered. Needless to say, a plan is not to be followed slavishly.

A good approach to a unit will be:

1. *Dynamic*, indicative of action and likely to promote it with normal individuals.

2. *Stimulating,* leading the learners in the direction of planning so that they start suggesting what to do. (An odd error by some teachers is to prepare and actually use a good approach, and then drop it. The planning is omitted and the working experiences assigned by the teacher as though there had been no approach.)
3. *Based on natural interests,* fitted to levels of maturity.
4. *Diversified* enough to challenge many types of interest, ability, and ambition.
5. *Based on community* interests, needs, and resources.
6. *Adjusted to emotional tone or climate* within which the group is operating.
7. *Participatory* as fully as is possible in the given situation.
8. *Critical of the worth of suggestions.* (The teacher and the group should minimize and eliminate proposals for trivial or superficial units, trivial questions. The teacher and group should develop and enlarge the worthwhile and socially desirable units, projects, and questions.)

The pupils' objective. The pupils' aim in a teacher-dominated situation will be stated by the teacher. The teacher is often unaware of the degree of acceptance or non-acceptance by the learners. The pupils' aim in less formal situations may come from the pupils after guided conversation or skillful stage-setting by the teacher. The teacher may even state an aim which he believes will be immediately acceptable because of its relation to the learners' interests. In a truly participatory situation, the pupils' aim emerges in the course of activity. This is not to say that the teacher cannot anticipate it, nor to say that he can do no tentative preplanning. The teacher does not stand around and wait for the pupils to think of something to do. It is foolish not to think through the situation and attempt to foresee what purposes are likely to arise in the given situation. It is therefore sensible and no violation of modern principles to plan for the emergence and development of likely pupil purposes. Co-operative definition of the purpose as it emerges and co-operative planning for its development then follow.

The breakdown of a major aim into subsidiary questions and activities will be illustrated in the discussion of the planning period, given later.

The major aim will usually emerge during the approach period, and as soon as it begins to be clear, breakdown and planning will naturally follow. The writer therefore places the pupils' aim just after the approach in the planning outline. Instructors and students may wish to place it elsewhere.

Do not state activities as aims. An error similar to that made in stating teachers' aims may occur here. Teachers sometimes give the following as pupils' aims: to draw a map; to have a debate; to make a booklet; to draw a cartoon; to make models. These are activities which will occur as the learners pursue an aim. Sometimes an activity may coincide with an aim, as, for instance, to paint a mural. Ordinarily, this will be an activity within a unit; the mural is made to illustrate something within the unit. An advanced art class, however, could have this as a legitimate major project. The unit in stage design mentioned in the Appendix, falls in this category, in part.

Criteria for judging the pupil's aim. The pupil's objective is usually a *major* problem or question he wants answered; a major constructive project; a creative undertaking; a topic or theme to investigate; an area to be surveyed. Fulfillment of the following criteria should ensure that the aim is *dynamic,* actually motivating to activity.

The pupil's major objective should be *capable of breakdown* into manageable subsidiary questions, topics, or projects. These become centers for study and construction.

The pupil's *major objective and the list of subsidiary aims* should be enlarged or further refined through co-operative discussion and guidance from the teacher so that worthwhile, socially desirable aspects may be included; so that trivial and superficial aspects may be eliminated.

The pupil's major objective should preferably *emerge* from on-going life interests and activities, from discussion, or if necessary, from stage-setting by the teacher.

The pupil's major objective and subsidiary aims should be in the *language of the pupil*, not that of the adult.

The working period is planned and developed. A functional learning situation utilizes experiences, subject matter, and other materials when and as they are needed. Various activities within the total situation are interrelated and simultaneous. The major parts of a unit become separate only when they are abstracted from the unified whole for the purpose of description and analysis. The approach and the working period are not separated by a line or at a given moment. Pupils always begin suggesting what to do while the problem is still being identified and defined. Planning what to do and the doing of it go on continuously and simultaneously. Evaluation is also continuous and concomitant. The working period is the most thoroughly integrated part of the good unit. The following discussions of phases of the working period must not be interpreted to mean that there are separate, formal steps. The actual development of a unit is a continuum.

The planning period. A salient characteristic of a good unit is participatory planning and control by the group. The pupils, under guidance from the teacher, should have a large share in planning, deciding, and evaluating. Only thus can they learn to plan, to select, to judge, to participate in making group decisions.

Plans are made for the long period of the total unit. Sometimes pupils participate in setting up plans for the semester or year. Plans are made also in more definite form for shorter periods within the unit. Constant replanning is a desirable characteristic of unit development. Initial planning with upper-grade pupils may be reasonably detailed and extend over a period of time. Initial planning with little children is briefer and simpler, with much detailed planning developing continuously within the working period.

The children in the unit on stage design mentioned in the Appendix made a list of the things which had to be done during the progress of the whole unit, added others from time to time, and replanned continuously:

What we must know (in order of pupil suggestion):
1. Nature of all characters
2. All the action
3. Scenes
   a. Season
   b. Day or night
   c. Material for scenery
4. Source of money to be spent
5. Lights
6. Costume material
   a. Period
   b. Making
7. Properties
8. Color
9. Publicity
10. Direction

Other problems were added as the unit developed. These were regrouped and organized for attack in further planning. Five categories were set up: scenery, characters, publicity, costumes, direction. Each of these was in turn broken down, as for instance:

Scenery
1. Layout
2. Color schemes
3. Lights
4. Period or style

This was still further itemized as actual operations were planned by the pupils:

Scenery	What	How
1. Paint	powder, liquid, glue; old scenery flats	buy it; secure from art department
2. Wood		
3. Brushes	new materials, large and small, new and old	buy; find; secure from art department
4. Tools for construction	carpenter tools	bring from home; high school shop

Costumes	What	How
1. Material	amounts and kinds; accessories	old clothing from home; buy; rent wigs, etc.
2. Making	sewing; mixing, using dyes	home-economic dept. art and shop departments

Committees were organized, and the many varied activities proceeded apace with group conferences for progress reports, for the solution of difficulties, and for replanning.

In order to guide long- and short-term planning without dominating, the teacher must know—as has been indicated several times previously—the children, their abilities, their interests and backgrounds, their environment, and the influences affecting individuals and the group. The teacher must also be on the alert to see that objectives and activities are balanced. No one interest or activity should dominate; none should be neglected.

Planning with and by pupils in a formal situation is limited. Pupil participation will usually be confined to dividing the work of finding and analyzing sources, compiling material in answer to questions assigned, arranging for presentation of summaries to the whole group, or planning and conducting group discussions. Some teachers give pupils much opportunity to assist in making up quizzes or tests, and in creating better types of evaluation instruments.

Co-operative, participatory planning in the better situations is, in contrast, predominant, including all persons and all sorts of activity and material. This type of planning has been treated in the past, unfortunately, in meager, inadequate fashion in general textbooks. Some good discussions have always been available in the bulletins and course of study guides from advanced school systems. Published logs of unit and units themselves were very useful. Today, as indicated several times in preceding pages, a good literature is developing on modern planning. [2] The following summary was based chiefly on the experiences of the writer and many teachers in developing units. It is in line with currently developing materials.

General initiatory techniques in planning. The general initial technique in planning units is usually group discussion. Pupils and teacher talk over, accept, or reject suggestions, finally list the things that must be found out and the things which must be done, and provide for division of labor, what to do, and how to do it.

Planning-discussions usually start when pupils wish to know or find out something, to make something, to try out or experiment with something, or to go to see some famous person or place. A pupil or the group, for instance, may ask a question, or a question may be suggested by some event. Soon a list of questions develops which may be written on the board and later transferred to a chart. The type and scope of these initial questions differ naturally with level of maturity. A third grade, interested when a postman appeared with a registered letter, asked questions until twenty-four had been listed by the teacher. The following samples illustrate third-grade interests and insights.

How long does the postman have to work every day?
What time does he collect the mail from the box out front?
How does mail get to the airport?
What do the men do in the mail car on trains?
What does the post office look like behind the windows?
What happens to the letters back there?
Does our postman have to work behind the windows too?
Who pays the postman for bringing our letters?

These questions and others like them developed into an excellent unit on the post office, which was in turn one of a series called "The Community and Its Organization."

[2] See references in Chapter 13 and in Hanna, Potter, and Hagaman.

At the other extreme, we have the following questions sampled from a list asked by high school seniors.

Why is one brother or sister sometimes very unlike the other members of the family?

What do you think about cousins getting married?

If a woman listens to beautiful music and studies and plays music before her child is born, can she thus increase the musical ability of her child?

Is it hazardous to adopt children?

What are the main factors contributing to broken homes?

Should not some homes be broken up for the sake of the children?

This list developed not into a unit but into a major course in the senior year. Many important units were organized within the field opened up.

A highly successful course in sex education for young girls in a Corvallis, Oregon, school was organized almost entirely around questions asked by the pupils.

Before the class has exhausted its capacity for asking questions, some individuals will have started suggesting sources of information and methods of securing it. This initiates the working out of plans for some of the typical activities of the traditional school: finding and reading sources in the library or elsewhere; preparing summaries for an oral or written report; making and discussing the reports; summarizing. In a modern school, planning of other elements also occurs: dividing the work among individuals or committees; organizing the committees; providing for reports to the total group; planning group discussions which resolve conflicting statements, evaluate, and summarize. Planning will often include organizing excursions and visits, interviews, doing experiments, constructing things, or gathering exhibits. These latter call for planning how to actually do these things, how and where to secure tools and materials. Constant replanning and evaluation will be necessary. Throughout there will be planning for the giving and taking of responsibility, for exercising initiative and leadership.

The whole series of activities may start not with a series of questions but with a proposal to construct or create something. This soon leads to a need for information, for division of labor, for bringing the individual contributions to the group, and for getting the benefit of pooled thinking. The range of activities will be similar to that in the first illustration above, but in different order. Regardless of where and how planning starts, it will usually involve several typical procedures.

Typical procedures usually appearing during planning. These do not appear all in one planning sequence, nor do they appear in any fixed order. The range and sequence of planning activities depend upon the particular situation being planned.

1. *List questions on which information is wanted, or make plans for the construction of something.* This was illustrated in the immediately preceding pages. The questions or plans may refer to a major or minor aspect of the unit, depending upon its nature. In some instances the procedure will include planning bibliographies, planning so-called library research, the making of card indexes, making blueprints, making working models, and so forth.

2. *Make charts of what to do.* This is self-explanatory. Work is laid out by the group for both the long and the short term. Charts are kept before the group constantly for guidance in the future and for checking as various tasks are completed. Charts may vary all the way from listings of very general themes, topics, or problems, and very general direction or guidance, the listing of minute questions and parts of topics together with very specific directions as to how to proceed.

3. *Find and list sources of information, tools, or construction materials.* The most common sources of information and of plans for making things are printed materials, texts, supplementary books, periodicals, and

pamphlets. The modern school increasingly supplements this source with a wealth of others: photographs, motion pictures, real objects, charts, maps, diagrams, experiments, visits to museums, factories, or mills.

4. *Divide the work among committees.* A feature of the modern learning period is the diversity of learning activities. This necessitates co-operative distribution of work among individuals and groups. This in turn makes possible class contact with far more material and learning experiences than is ever possible under the assign-study-recite procedure. More important, it provides for individual differences in interest and ability in ways which the traditional schoolroom procedure cannot duplicate. Summaries and group discussions bring the group into contact with all of the diverse materials and activities utilized within the total project. Committees formed may be large or small; they may be organized around any aspect whatsoever of the unit. We may have committees to:

1. Find information
   a. In the library.
   b. In the community.
   c. In museums.
2. Gather materials and exhibits from the community.
3. Interview other persons and arrange for their appearance in the classroom.
4. Make things: houses, cages, models, murals, relief maps, furniture, costumes.
5. Summarize.

The pupil may:

1. Choose his committee.
2. Be suggested for membership by other pupils.
3. Be selected by the chairman.
4. Be assigned by the teacher.

The chief factor in pupil choice is interest. Ordinarily, pupils choose:

1. To work on things they can do well, can succeed with; to avoid the new and strange, the "too hard."

2. To work with friends, with those of the same socioeconomic status; to avoid pupils held to be inferior in socioeconomic status.
3. To work with others of similar general ability.

These are natural social tendencies. There are definite advantages to both group and individual in the first and third type of grouping. There are also definite limitations. Rounded development for the individual, continued progress in conquering the new and "too hard," respect for different types of personality and leadership are all important objectives of education. Pupils must acquire facility in several fields, must learn to give and take in heterogeneous groups, must learn to accept responsibility and exercise leadership over varied groups, must learn to accept ability and leadership no matter what its origin. Cliques, especially those based on socioeconomic or intellectual snobbishness, should be avoided.

The teacher, then, has certain responsibilities for adjusting committee memberships. He may assign given pupils to committees or otherwise rearrange memberships for the purpose either of aiding a child to develop some needed interest or ability, or to strengthen a committee. The pupil should always understand, in so far as he can, and agree to the change of assignment.

In the modern school with its diversified activities the pupils themselves soon learn the necessity of having various kinds of ability and personality on one committee. They soon learn to distribute responsibility and work in terms of available personnel. In fact, children often demand changes in committee membership for the same reasons that motivate teachers to make changes.

Pupil recognition of and adjustment to differences was clearly illustrated in the writer's experience with one of his sixth-grade groups. The class was almost entirely made up of "rough-and-ready," somewhat noisy, not too well-behaved extroverts. One boy alone came from a distinctly superior type of home and possessed excellent social training. He manifested an ability to speak to teachers and visitors without embarrassment, to think on his feet, and to carry off difficult situations which usually reduced the more boisterous children to stammering or silence. This boy was by no means a "sissy." He participated in sports and escapades with the others; but he was rarely, if ever, chosen for positions of leadership on the playground or in other pupil activities. One day, however, the whole group was caught red-handed in a serious misdemeanor which could not possibly be overlooked by the school. Word came that the principal would see a committee to talk things over, hear explanations, and decide what should be done. The class with one voice chose the suave young diplomat as a committee of one to meet with the principal! They knew that if anyone could save the situation, he could. This recognition by the pupils of types of leadership and ability has a definite moral for teacher guidance. Pupils may be made conscious of the problems involved and stimulated to care for their own rounded development.

Committee chairmen should ordinarily be elected by the pupil groups. Sometimes the teacher may have to appoint chairmen. In any event, children should develop through experience their own standards for choosing a chairman. One primary group decided that a good chairman was one who:

1. Is not too "bossy" but gets things done.
2. Does part of the work himself.
3. Is kind and friendly.
4. Is on time.
5. Comes early and gets things ready for work.

Upper-grade committees may have a secretary, a property clerk, and any other special officers they need.

Finally, just before committees are released to take up their work, the teacher goes over the plans with them so that each pupil may demonstrate that he knows clearly what his part is in the common undertaking.

5. *Provide for group discussion.* Plans will include provision for integrating group effort by discussion, evaluation, and re-planning. Ordinarily, the following activities will be included:

1. Reporting progress, checking up, and re-examining plans in the light of progress and difficulties to date.
2. Rearranging plans, things to do, questions to answer, assignments.
3. Regrouping of personnel.
4. Reporting important difficulties from any area which need group analysis and pooling suggestions.
5. Evaluating materials, processes, results.
6. Summarizing and culminating (this may utilize oral and written reports, pictures, drawings, murals, cartoons, graphs, diagrams); a dramatization (play, pantomime, dance); construction of models, exhibits of innumerable types. Some mature groups take motion pictures of the unit as it develops.
7. Keeping a list of leads to future work.

Criteria for judging planning procedures. Criteria here may apply either to the process itself, or to the teacher's participation in it.

The planning period should:

Be based upon, follow, and flow smoothly from the approach activities and move smoothly into the working period.

Be fully participatory, providing opportunity and encouragement for all members of the group to participate, utilize all kinds and levels of interest and ability, receive with consideration the contributions of all types of pupils.

Begin and continue on the basis of the readiness, maturity, and background of the pupils (not on the basis of the teacher's superior information and ability); stimulate all members to continue exploring all phases of the problem, all types of materials and sources of materials, all types of learning experiences, all methods of organizing the procedure.

Take into account the personal and material resources of the community and the accessibility of these resources. (That is, it must be realistic.)

Neither overwhelm the learner with a frightening amount of materials nor with the teacher's superior knowledge; nor, on the other hand, allow restriction to one text or a few references, to a few formal experiences.

Continue until suggestions begin to shift over toward the actual operations of the working period.

Lead, without coercion, to a suitable continuity of experience, that is, to order and structure for the project to come.

Provide for flexibility in itself and in the plans developing; provide for free interchange between individuals.

Provide for necessary reconsideration of plans and for replanning later during the working period.

Provide for evaluation en route and at the end of the project or problem.

Maintain a tempo of planning not so rapid that students do not really see what is being done and to be done, nor so slow that they become bored and lose interest.

Provide opportunity throughout for developing independence and self-direction, for achieving responsibility both to self and to the group.

Lead to better and better learning and productivity for individuals and groups.

The teacher should have thought through the materials, the possible problem, the probable responses to the group. A tentative planning sequence is thus developed. This aids the teacher in participating without imposing his own plan or driving toward it.

The teacher should:

Assume responsibility for preplanning, for encouraging group planning; arrange situations necessitating planning.

Give increasing independence to the group in planning.

Function as a group member, playing various roles—resource person, facilitator, evaluator—aiding pupils to see and define needs, to stay on the point, to foresee consequences both desirable and undesirable, to recognize the achievement of their goals.

Manifest sensitivity to changes in the attitudes and the attention of the group, to the climate of feeling and understanding, to pupil digressions.

Planning which is not participatory, which is guided without insight and sensitivity, will lead only to (*a*) uninterested acquiescence by the pupils or (*b*) old-fashioned assignment of materials and responsibilities.

Serious and common errors by teachers in developing units are (*a*) omission of any planning with pupils, and (*b*) describing the planning in general terms without mention of the actual procedures. The first leads to the imposition of assignments. The second leads also to the imposition of assignments and, moreover, to real confusion when the work gets under way.

Supplementary discussions of planning. Instructors and students in some numbers have written the author suggesting the inclusion here of an extensive collection of verbatim accounts of group planning. Space simply prohibits this, but the suggestion is excellent. Other instructors have written concerning the use of stenographic accounts of planning which they have collected. The author has stressed from the beginning that this and all general texts must be supplemented with specific materials and personal observations.

Today, as already indicated several times, there are good current discussions of modern planning. A few of the older discussions may be noted as useful:

Group Planning in Education, 1945 Yearbook of the Association for Supervision and Curriculum Development. Chapter 3 contains four short but excellent samples. Chapters 4-12 contain somewhat more general descriptions of cases. Chapters 13-20 contain excellent simple presentation of general theory.

Horace Mann-Lincoln School Institute of School Experimentation, *The Teacher's Role in Pupil-Teacher Planning* (New York, Teachers College, Bureau of Publications, Columbia Univ., 1947). Section I contains four detailed cases; Section II, general principles and guidance for teachers.

Samples from secondary schools:

GILES, H. H., Teacher-Pupil Planning (New York, Harper, 1941). This is the classic in the field. Excellent general theory plus about twenty illustrative accounts taken from classroom procedure.

STILES, Lindley, and DORSEY, Mattie F. (reference above). Pages 336-367 contain valuable specific descriptions.

Samples from physical education, camping, community experiences on several levels are:

BAXTER, Bernice, and CASSIDY, Rosalind, *Group Experience* (New York, Harper, 1943). Pages 22-54 contain good general accounts. Chapter 3, excellent general theory liberally illustrated with specific items (camping, community).

KOZMAN, Hilda C. and others, *Group Process in Physical Education* (New York, Harper, 1951), pp. 314-343, plus excellent bibliography containing at least eleven references to other specific accounts.

Do not overlook current revisions of texts in general and special methods and those for student teachers.

The working period. The working period begins when planning has been carried to the point that the group knows how to start doing the things it has planned. The working period in modern teaching differs from the traditional recitation period in almost every detail. Three characteristic differences indicate the completeness of the contrast. First, the sepulchral, morgue-like quiet, which parents and traditional teachers mistake for "order" and "discipline," is gone. In its place there are considerable movement and the subdued hum of activities in progress. There develops the discipline of self-control, which is far better than the discipline of imposed authority. Second, the limited, formal activities of the recitation have been replaced by a large number of varied activities. There are, of course, various types of socialized and improved recitation periods between these extremes. Third, modern learning experiences are not chopped into short, disjunctive fragments controlled by the length of the class period. The elementary school provides continuous periods of activity up to half a day. The core curriculum in the secondary school increasingly utilizes a two-hour working period. Even with the special subjects studied in short periods, the learning activities in a modern school are continuous over considerable periods of time.

The learning activities or experiences. A list of approximately eighty learning activities compiled by Mossman was quoted on page 99. Understanding of the nature and possible diversity of learning activities will be clarified by examining two other lists arranged on different bases. Diedrich [3] presents approximately 177 possible activities organized in eight groups. These groups, with a few samples from each, are as follows:

Visual activities (thirteen in all). Read; look at pictures, observe experiments, demonstrations, exhibits; observe other people at work or play.

Oral activities (forty-three in all). State a fact or principle; relate an event; ask a question; offer a suggestion; express (or relinquish) an opinion; take part in an interview; conduct a recitation or discussion; interrupt.

Listening activities (eleven in all). Listen to formal presentation of material; listen to conversation or group discussion; listen to a play; listen to the radio.

Writing activities (twenty-two in all). Write a story (or essay, poem, play, scenario); write a report; correct a badly written paper; copy material; make an outline (or summary, or list); take a test; fill a questionnaire.

Drawing activities (eight in all). Draw or paint a picture; draw a graph, chart, diagram; draw a map; draw a pattern.

Motor activities (forty-seven in all). Perform an experiment; select materials; hold an exhibit; construct a model (furniture, toys, cages); repair personal or school property; play a game; dance; care for pets; make a garden.

Mental activities (twenty-three in all). Imagine; memorize; detect a problem; analyze factors involved; see relationships; come to a decision.

Emotional activities (twenty in all). Interest; boredom or indifference; delight; snobbishness; courage; judicial calm; mirth.

[3] Paul B. Diedrich, *A Master List of Types of Pupil Activities*, Educational Research Bulletin, College of Education, Ohio State Univ., Vol. 15 (September 16, 1936).

Diedrich says that the last classification includes the emotional accompaniments of all the other activities. It is also obvious that all types overlap freely. The reading and listening activities are also mental, and so on through the list.

Whipple has prepared another list, based on a still different scheme of organization. [4] Although it was prepared many years ago, it is still one of the best lists available.

What Pupils Do in an Activity

I. *Work with Visual Materials*
  1. Collect pictures and other illustrative materials.
  2. Study pictures, stereographs, slides, and motion pictures for special purposes; listen to explanations, ask questions.
  3. Examine exhibits.
  4. List interesting questions while examining visual materials.
  5. Select visual materials for use when giving an oral report.
  6. Arrange exhibits; write labels and explanations.
  7. Organize and file materials for future use.

II. *Excursions and Trips*
  1. Visit museums, aquariums, zoos.
  2. Call on business firms for needed information and materials.
  3. See demonstrations of processes, e.g., soap manufacture, making of paper.

III. *Study of Problems*
  1. Search for information in answer to important questions.
  2. Consult encyclopedias and reference books for needed information.
  3. Bring books from home and from the public library to supplement the school collection.
  4. Write to business firms for needed information and materials.
  5. Carry out directions given on guide sheets prepared by the teacher.
  6. Take notes from several books in preparation for discussion or a report.
  7. Interpret maps; find locations.
  8. Perform experiments, such as making

⁴ Gertrude M. Whipple, *What Pupils Do in an Activity*, Course of Study Bulletin No. 162, Los Angeles City Schools.

soap, preparing dyes for monastic lettering, caring for bulbs.
  9. Evaluate information from different sources; determine the accuracy of conflicting statements.
  10. Organize material read in preparation for discussion or for an oral or written report.
  11. Prepare and give informing and interesting oral reports.
  12. Prepare brief, written reports for definite purposes, e.g., use in a class-book, explanation of an exhibit.
  13. Prepare a bibliography of books used in the study.
  14. Skim material to list interesting subjects for further study (also to locate material of value).

IV. *Appreciation of Literature*
  1. Read interesting stories for pleasure.
  2. Read poems for pleasure.
  3. Listen to reading for pleasure and information.

V. *Illustration and Construction*
  1. Prepare charts and diagrams.
  2. Make blueprints.
  3. Draw and construct maps: product maps, relief maps, pictorial maps.
  4. Prepare posters.
  5. Prepare illustrations, maps, and diagrams for a book.
  6. Prepare scenery for a play.
  7. Prepare a frieze.
  8. Make articles for an exhibit, such as cuneiform tablets, parchment, model of a feudal castle.
     (Accurate representation after careful study.)

VI. *Work Involved in Presenting Information*
  1. Suggest ways in which interesting information can best be presented.
  2. Censor and edit material for books.
  3. Keep an organized bulletin board up-to-date.
  4. Plan and give an assembly program.
  5. Write and give dramatizations.

VII. *Checks and Tests*
  1. Take informal and standardized tests.
  2. Prepare tests for other pupils.
  3. Keep growth graphs.

Criteria for learning activities and experiences. Each proposed activity should be scrutinized to see if it is:

1. Recognized by children as usable in achieving their purposes

2. Recognized by the teacher as leading to socially desirable ends.
3. Appropriate to the maturity of the group; challenging, achievable, leading to new learnings, providing for application of old learnings.
4. Varied enough to provide for balanced development of the learner; many types of individual and group activity.
5. Possible within the resources of school and community.
6. Varied enough to provide for individual differences within the group.

Teacher responsibility for best use of learning activities. When varied learning experiences first appeared, many teachers made two serious mistakes. The errors were natural but disastrous. They resulted from poor training, poor supervision, and the passive attitude carried over from the traditional school. First, activities were used indiscriminately and without relation either to the objective or to each other. Varied activity apparently was believed to be educative in itself. Activity for activity's sake is usually miseducative. Second, activities were introduced and allowed to proceed without guidance—each like the wind, which "bloweth where it listeth." This was a natural carryover from the traditional school where responsibility was limited to passing out assignments and hearing recitations. The teacher was relieved of responsibility by the fixed text, the fixed framework of the course, and the fixed, formal outcomes.

Teachers should try to provide opportunity for experiences which are of value to learner in achieving his purposes. An enlightening study has been reported by Cunningham [5] and her associates. Children in various grades were asked (1) to rank in value a total of forty learning experiences which would contribute to their goals; then (2) to rank the same experiences in order of opportunity to have them. The results were

[5] Ruth Cunningham and associates, *Understanding Group Behavior of Boys and Girls* (New York, Teachers College, Bureau of Publications, Columbia Univ., 1951), p. 265.

revealing and a bit shocking. Many experiences deemed of considerable value by the learners were not provided freely by the school. The following table is a sample from the total study and will make clear the necessity of providing opportunity for experiences over a wider range than is common.

The study also shows that many experiences valued highly by the pupils but not provided well by the school are the very ones which are aimed at broadening and extending learning beyond immediate school life. Very few things are as important as widening social experience. The school can, without great expense or inconvenience, very greatly increase the range of learning experiences it offers.

The modern teacher accepts definite responsibility not only for aiding pupils to choose appropriate activities but for directing the course of those activities in a sensible manner. This is not too difficult for trained teachers. It would take a small volume to illustrate in detail the educative use of many activities. One illustration of common misuse and of good use for an everyday technique will serve as illustration here. The oral report was one of the earliest departures from fixed recitation procedure. Hence it is commonly and widely used, in fact too commonly and too widely. Many other methods for gathering and reporting should be used; and far more important, the oral report when appropriate should be properly used. Too many teachers have pupils report and then drop the matter or ask (without much hope), "Are there any suggestions or criticisms?" One of two things usually results. First, there are no comments; the report is an isolated thing apart from any real interest to all, because no advance preparation for the reception of the report was made. No one really cares, and so no one says anything; a few faithfuls may make some desultory and formal suggestions. Second, pupils often develop the habit of analyzing and commenting upon every tiny detail, supplementing with useless detail, indulging in

Experience	Value Rank	Opportunity Rank	Difference in Rank
EIGHTH GRADE (group of 32)			
Take part in community affairs	9	32	23
Be a member of a club	9	28	19
Do work for the community without pay	16	35	19
Observe adults engaged in various types of work	7	20	13
Visit communities other than my own	13	24	11
FOURTH AND FIFTH GRADES (group of 34)			
Visit communities other than my own	2	37	35
Be a leader or a representative of a group of people my age	2	24	22
Work or play in groups in which adults are members (not including teachers or youth leaders)	21	37	16
Meet people who come from outside my community	15	31	16
Talk with adults engaged in various types of work	13	28	15
Take part in community affairs	8	22	14
Be a member of a group which makes its own rules	19	31	12

meaningless palaver—quibbling the report to death.

An oral report, to be educative, must be a natural, necessary part of a sequence of learning; must be in answer to definite questions to which the group actually needs the answers; must supply information which can be put to use. It must be preceded by questions and followed by discussion. To ask "Are there any suggestions or criticisms?" is formal and focuses attention on static elements of form and content. To ask questions aimed at clarifying understanding, applying to the common problem and using the content, directs attention to the dynamic functioning of the material. The pupils themselves will ordinarily have more than sufficient questions to ask after a report which is of use to them. The teacher should have many key questions ready. Reports are designed to serve purposes and must not be allowed to waste their sweetness on the desert air.

The same general principle holds for the use of each of the many learning activities which may appear in a learning situation.

The subject matter used in the working period. The general nature, organization, and use of subject matter was outlined in some detail in the preceding chapter. Certain critics libel the modern school by saying that subject matter is disregarded, even omitted. This is pure nonsense, based on ignorance of the history of education. The modern school uses far more subject matter than the traditional school and uses subject matter as it was originally intended to be used. Subject matter is a means to an end—the achievement of desirable learning outcomes. The traditional school makes subject matter an end in itself, something to be learned as it is. Morrison aptly said long ago: "The student does not learn subject matter; he learns from subject matter." Another of Morrison's succinct statements, referring to the traditional school in which subject matter is learned, is also to the point: "The student has learned his lesson but he has not learned."

The selection and use of subject matter of all kinds (not merely text material) and from all types of sources is an important part in the development of a good unit. The following criteria may be used:

1. Does the material selected indicate that the teacher has adequate mastery of the material available for the topic or problem?

2. Does the material selected indicate that the teacher has seen between materials important relationships which might not be apparent upon superficial examination?

3. Does the organization of the selected materials indicate that the teacher has articulated them both with the course of study governing his situation, and with the life activities and needs of the pupils?

4. Are the materials selected and the sources indicated authentic and reliable?

Other criteria could be listed, but the significant points have already been made over and over again:

Is the subject matter selected and used suited to maturity, interests, and abilities?
Does it lead to higher levels of achievement?
Does it lead to desirable outcomes?

Cautions concerning the working period. The following cautions point out errors which are easily made.

The working period is not sharply distinguished either from the approach or from the planning period. Planning moves smoothly into working out the emerging plans.

The working period should not be delayed or postponed in an effort to carry all individuals along at the same rate and level.

The working period should not be formal or imposed but fully participatory. The teacher should be on guard against taking over "to save time" and proceeding to assign tasks preconceived by himself.

The working period should not rigidly carry out the original plan; replanning and remotivation will occur at any time.

The working period should not stop short of co-ordination of the work of all. Sharing is by means of individual and committee reports and by group consideration of any general difficulties or conclusions.

The chief error in writing plans for the working period is to list merely the activities and subject matter which may be used. The teacher must show how each of these appears and is woven into the work in proc- *ess. A mere list of activities can be copied by anyone. The important thing is to show how these activities are actually utilized.*

Evaluation techniques are developed and used. Evaluation in the modern school is continuous, is participatory, and is exercised on all aspects of the unit from preliminary planning to final outcomes. Materials, processes, discussions, suggestions—all are evaluated as they appear. Pupils will develop many of the techniques co-operatively, since one important outcome of all units is increased ability to evaluate, that is, to discriminate, to judge, to support conclusions. Old-fashioned quizzes and examinations do not disappear but are greatly minimized since they test, usually, less important outcomes. Their nature is also greatly changed.

Attention today is upon such learning outcomes as behavior patterns and such controls of behavior as meanings, understanding, appreciation, and attitudes. The clue to these lies in the learner's behavior; hence constant observation in many different situations is far more important than paper-and-pencil testing. The pupil is learning, not so that he can be tested, but in order to be able to use in functional situations what he has learned.

Tests, measures, scales, and the many techniques for observing and recording behavior are usually the content of a separate course in the training of the teacher. A later chapter will contain a summary, but complete treatment of evaluation is out of place and impossible in a general volume such as this. Students and teachers may derive from the brief summary (but preferably from extended courses) knowledge to enable them to select or devise instruments designed to evaluate the stated outcomes of the unit. The outline at the end of this chapter will indicate what is wanted in the preplanning stage. The techniques are not applied indiscriminately but related to stated objectives.

Resources of the school system and of the community are listed. Each unit will use a multitude of instructional aids and community resources (see Chapter 17).

A bibliography is selected and listed. A bibliography for a unit will usually be in two parts, one indicating books for the teacher and the other, books for the pupil.

1. Are the books listed important and significant for the topic or problem? Balanced between older and current publications?

2. Are the bibliographies sub-classified, annotated; library classification numbers given when available?

3. Are authors' and publishers' names, copyright date, and prices included? (This latter is not always necessary but is very valuable in the new units and in sample units and should be included in source volumes without fail.)

Leads to other units may be listed. Leads to other units often grow out of a unit in progress. Pupils themselves usually suggest more than can be followed up.

Culminating activities. The term *culminating activities* stems from Morrison's book in which units were definitely terminated with appropriate activities. These should be natural parts of the unit, neither forced early nor unduly delayed by an arbitrary time limit. They should appear when the objectives of the unit have been achieved to a degree which indicates that the unit has served its purpose. Culminating activities are, naturally, summary accounts or exhibits or syntheses. They are for the benefit of the learning group and may be of value to adult (parent) audiences, although the latter is not their purpose. They commonly take the form of oral reports or "floor talks," written accounts which may sometimes be mimeographed or printed, assembly programs given before parents or other pupils, a play or dramatization, a dance program or exhibit, exhibits of creative products in fine arts, construction of exhibits ranging from the sand table in the lower grades to more pretentious life-habitat groups in high school, construction of models, demonstration of machine processes, products or skills, demonstration of mental or motor skills. Sometimes a unit may culminate in participation in or control over some community enterprise.

Errors to avoid:

Do not recapitulate the entire unit, dragging in all details. Skill in selecting and arranging significant exhibits is itself a culminating activity of importance.

Do not insist on culminating activities if they interrupt a natural moving on to another unit, if they bring a unit to an abrupt and empty ending.

Do not use tests and examinations under any circumstances; use a wide range of materials and methods of presentation.

Do not strive for a polished, finished performance; rather show the growth and development of the learners in several areas, and varied types of pupil ability, interest, and contribution.

Culminating activities are not discussed in detail in this volume, since units are not thought to terminate or culminate but to be continuous. This does not mean that summary reports and exhibits may not be made at any appropriate time. It is important, however, to maintain natural continuity of activity.

The relation of the unit to discipline, to drill, and to the introduction of participatory processes. The organization of materials and activities in the unit, the changed classroom situation, the encouragement of pupil participation are so different from procedure under the old-fashioned assignment that certain questions are constantly asked by students and teachers. Teachers who have been steadily improving the type of assignments used supply a part of the answer. The rest is clearly implied by the principles of learning as we now know them.

What is the relation of the unit to drill? Modern teaching stresses varied and diverse experiences through which the learner builds up meanings, attitudes, and behavior patterns. Skills, however, are perfected through practice or drill. Unit outlines deal chiefly with the non-skill learnings, thus giving rise to the belief that drill is neglected or even omitted. The issue is further complicated by the fact that extensive research upon the effect of drill on the learning of skills has flatly contradicted cherished beliefs held by traditional teachers. Largely unaware of the facts, many teachers jump to the conclusion that the moderns do not use drill. Still another factor is the traditional belief that skills can be learned in isolation and then applied. Schools for generations have had drill on skills which had no meaning for the child and which he could not apply despite letter-perfect "drill."

The whole problem is important enough to justify a separate chapter (Chapter 19). Suffice it to say here that under modern principles it is known that *skills should be met first under meaningful conditions,* that is, in functional situations. The pupil is then given practice after he sees the sense of the matter. Drill itself, as will be shown, is far from the simple procedure traditional teachers believe it to be.

Teachers who are planning units will note the skills which deserve perfecting through practice and provide that practice. Two schools of thought are found. One holds that practice should be provided naturally as the unit proceeds and that sufficient practice can be given this way to ensure skill. Research does not uphold this view, that incidental drill is sufficient. The second view is that separate practice periods be regularly provided in the school day wherein learnings are developed which were first met, and met often enough, in sensible situations so that the need for practice is apparent to the children. The majority of schools follow the second view. However, teachers should utilize all the natural or incidental practice which any unit provides.

How is order preserved during the diversity of activity and free movement of children which is necessary for successful learning? The question of order or "discipline" seriously disturbs students in training or teachers contemplating trial of modern methods. Abandonment of the enforced and repressive "discipline" of the older school does present a basic problem. The teacher is entitled to explicit advice sympathetically given. A separate chapter comes later, but for the moment a summary can be given.

Parents and traditional teachers visiting a modern school for the first time are often disturbed, even aghast. The quiet rows of pupils sitting patiently waiting to be called upon have disappeared. There is a room full of diverse action going on simultaneously. Some of the children may be at their desks, some at reading tables, some at a modeling table, some at the sink or tool bench. Some are even sitting on the floor. Others may be out in the hall painting on a fifteen-foot panel spread on the floor. Individuals and small committees may be talking together. In primary rooms some pupils may be watering flowers, feeding rabbits or chickens, or watching bees through a glass window in the hive. Properly understood and properly handled by a competent teacher, this variety of action is nothing to be disturbed over. Evidence shows this to be the most efficacious setting both for learning and for the development of democracy.

The most frequent question asked by both beginning and experienced teachers who wish to try modern methods is: How can we have a lot of different things going on at the same time without serious disorder? We cannot be everywhere at once; will not the children get out of hand? How can one teacher guide and direct several different activities at the same time? These questions are based in part on an erroneous conception of learning and are an outgrowth of ideas naturally held by those accustomed to the processes of the typical traditional school. These questions do point, however, to the necessity of highly trained teachers. The questions are real; and everyone will sympathize with the natural fear of embarking upon an unknown and complex process. Unquestionably, many good teachers hesitate to undertake modern methods for fear they cannot manage a number of diverse activities going on at once. The important thing is to venture in and try it! Ability to control an enthusiastic group engaged in various activities will come with experience. The experience must be preceded by and accompanied by education in the necessary principles. Teachers are entitled, however, to more than these generalizations; they deserve definite guidance. Observation of practice in good schools is a material aid.

First, let it be stated frankly that a modern working period can degenerate into a noisy, meaningless activity in the hands of a teacher who is a poor planner and organizer. This is as true of the traditional recitation as of the modern working period. The bad name which modern methods have had to live down comes from the early days when untrained enthusiasts attempted to use newer methods without first clearly understanding the difficulties. Disorder and near-bedlam resulted. This was all very funny and received much publicity. Publicity was *not* given to the excellent examples of orderly, enthusiastic groups carrying on diverse activities without confusion, nor to the violent disorder often found in traditional schools. The first requisite, then, is a teacher thoroughly informed and skilled. A teacher with an organized and an organizing mind, with knowledge of the psychology of learning, with knowledge of the principles of leadership, and possessed of some executive ability is necessary to the orderly management of the working period.

Second, it must be realized that under the impetus of a purpose real to them, children normally work along without disorder and without supervision. Much of the disorder in the classroom, particularly in the traditional school, results from the fact that the children do not really care about what is going on; it is irrelevant to their lives.

Granting the two foregoing basic premises, a number of specific suggestions may be listed. The teacher will:

1. Guide the group during the planning period to develop *plans which are so definite and so clear that all know what to do and how to do it.*
2. *Check with individuals and committees before they disperse* for work to see that the more detailed plans are definite and clear.
3. *Anticipate difficulties* in carrying out plans and be ready to call a group conference when the difficulty occurs and before discouragement and work stoppage can result in disorder.
4. Guide during the planning period so that *sufficient work is outlined to keep all individuals and groups busy* over a reasonably long period of time. Replanning will keep the sequence going so that lack of work does not cause disorder.
5. *Call for replanning conferences* as work develops unevenly. Workers may be reassigned and activities redistributed.
6. *Keep in touch with the varied activities* by moving from group to group, by participating, by asking questions, by making suggestions, thus exercising both guidance and control.
7. *Foresee certain common opportunities for disorder* and forestall them by *developing with the pupils regular routines:*
   a. For having all materials, tools, and supplies ready before need for them arises;
   b. For distributing materials, tools, supplies, books, papers, quickly and in an orderly manner;
   c. For using reference materials, particularly when many pupils wish to consult an inadequate number of references;
   d. For holding conferences with individual children who ask for help;
   e. For using as helpers any individuals who may for any reason be unoccupied for a time;
   f. For moving groups, for observing as groups, without crowding or jostling.
8. *Introduce new activities to small groups directly concerned so that tryout will be without the confusion* which might result from misunderstandings within a large group and from too many persons trying a new process without sufficient guidance.
9. Give constantly, *direct and indirect training in the conventions and routines of group work:* taking turns; not interrupting; turning to some other aspect of one's work instead of standing around waiting for tools or materials in use elsewhere; signing in and out for tools and materials; and so forth.

10. *Develop with the pupils flexible plans for their own activities:* budgeting time, scheduling group conferences, and announcing times for individual conferences.
11. Develop constantly, directly and indirectly, the understanding that *freedom carries responsibility, and that self-control and co-operation are advantageous* to the pupils themselves and are not merely something required by the school.

Finally, let it be noted that in schools where modern methods once get under way and are thoroughly understood by the pupils, the pupils themselves exert vigorous and open pressure upon those who would disturb the orderly procedure. This is true from kindergarten to college.

The introduction of participatory processes. Teachers willing to try modern methods are often uncertain about just how to begin. Teachers in many places, also, are forced by local policy to use formal assignment techniques and to place undue stress on subject matter as an end. The first thing to say is that in either situation change should be slow, with one thing introduced at a time. The second is that even in the most backward subject-matter school, participatory processes can be utilized to the great benefit of all concerned. The teacher in the latter circumstances will not only improve his children's learning but will himself progress steadily toward permanently better methods.

The chief principle is that pupil participation, suggestion, and judgment be invited at every possible time. The teacher may begin modestly with but a single step at a time, progressing patiently as the situation and his own increasing skill warrant. Valuable practices include the following:

1. Discovering pupil needs, purposes, and interests through observation of behavior, informal conversations, direct questioning, telling something about the organized materials which the teacher knows she must "cover."
2. Developing co-operatively with pupils:
   a. The center or centers of interest within the materials thus discovered.
   b. The leads, themes, topics, or problems into which the center of interest can be organized.
   c. The selection of materials and activities.
   d. The delegation of responsibility for various materials, activities, and contributions.
   e. The continuous evaluation of materials, learning experiences, suggestions, and conclusions.
3. Providing as much direct experience as possible: utilizing all the resources of school and community to supplement the necessarily vicarious experience of the subject-matter sequence.
4. Aiding different individuals to find opportunities within the general group activities for their unique abilities and ambitions.
5. Aiding the learners progressively to see the very nature of the processes by which they learn, thus aiding them toward independence and transfer.
6. Aiding and guiding the learners constantly toward the acquisition of functional learning outcomes, in so far as these are possible, from subject-matter organizations.
7. Aiding pupils to relate the functional learning outcomes they accept to the formal learnings set out by the course of study, to compare the two, to see the fundamental difference between the two, to note discrepancies between them and to decide whether the discrepancies need to be remedied.

Hopkins suggests that the last two points can be achieved better at the end of a year than at the end of individual units. [6] Three reasons are given: pupils will have seen the overlap from unit to unit for given learnings; will have had time to see and learn the process of planning and evaluating before being bound by too many prescribed learnings; will be less irritated by meaningless formal requirements once they have had time to develop enthusiasm for and insight into the modern processes and functional results.

Summary on planning. We may now summarize planning under three major heads:

[6] L. Thomas Hopkins, *Interaction* (Boston, Heath, 1941), p. 270.

general preliminary planning, planning a specific unit, and planning daily events.

General preliminary planning. The activities of the teacher in getting ready for a semester's work are in general as outlined below.

I. *Make a semester preview.* (Good source units supply this in large part.)

A. *Make a general plan for semester or other time division.* This will be based upon:

   1. A study of the course-of-study area suggested for the grade or group.

     a. List main divisions or phases of the total area. (This will appear in modern courses; but if not the teacher must make his own organization.)

     b. List subtopics or subproblems for each main division.

     c. Keep all this related in an organized outline. This should give a good overview of the area.

   2. A study of the maturity, interests, and abilities of the type of children generally found in the group under consideration.

     a. Translate the logical topics and outline resulting from (*a*), (*b*), and (*c*), listed above into a group of natural, human-interest, out-of-school topics or problems likely to interest the group. If more or less direct translation cannot be made, then

     b. Construct a list of naturally interesting topics or problems which should arise within the area designated and with the particular group.

On the basis of these studies the teacher will write a general plan for studying the materials, or for developing purposes likely to be found within the group. This will be general, since formality or rigidity at this stage would limit participatory planning and variation of procedure as actual units developed later.

B. *Make a study of class personnel.* This will be based upon:

   1. A study of the characteristics, needs, abilities, and interests of the specific group; an estimate of the probable nature and amount of previous experience.

   2. A study of the characteristics, needs, abilities, and interests of the individuals within the group through analysis of general-ability scores, achievement scores, interest inventories, and other data as shown in cumulative records. (In many instances these data are not kept and must be secured by the teacher himself directly from the pupils.)

   3. A study of the general community and of the immediate neighborhood environment from which the group comes.

II. *Make a tentative selection of definite units in sequence.*

This will be based upon and fitted to the information revealed by the two parts of the preview described above.

A. For units within a course outline: study analytically the source volumes available; become familiar with the range of materials, experiences, approaches, and references.

B. For units independent of an outline: study analytically the data revealed concerning the personnel and the community; become familiar with the possible sources of units and direct experiences within the physical and social environment; become familiar with extensive bodies of material in libraries, museums, and other sources.

C. For either type of unit: consult informally with principal and supervisors for assistance in further fitting groups and units together.

D. List a proposed series of units.

Planning specific units. The following is but one outline for guiding unit planning. Teachers should not be required to follow it. Others are available. Each school may set up similar outlines of its own. These outlines are merely guides to keep in mind, and they emphasize the chief points to be cared for.

Teacher's Outline for a Proposed Unit

The title should be as attractive as possible to teacher and pupils. The wording should be brief and unambiguous. Avoid both too narrow restriction and vague generality

I. The Overview

The overview is a brief statement of the nature and scope of the unit. Some writers include also a justification of the unit and an explanation of its place in the total course of study, but the majority of unit makers rely upon the complete titling and the statement of objectives to make these points clear. A few writers omit the overview. One of three forms is used by those who include it.

1. A description of the unit in running discourse.
2. An outline of "leads" in the form of topics, themes, or generalizations. This type of lead constitutes a table of contents.
3. An outline of "leads" in the form of actual or probable pupil questions, problems, and proposals. This type of lead is, at first, incomplete. The leads develop as the unit does.

II. The Teacher's Objectives

The objectives should be stated in complete declarative sentences, not in fragmentary phrases or single words.

Objectives specific to the unit should be listed, the general objectives having been noted in the course-of-study documents. (Teachers who wish may, of course, list some of the general objectives if it aids their thinking, but *these must not be confused with the specific objectives*.)

The following is but one sample form. Teachers may devise any form which makes the objectives clear, but must fill in the specifics.

1. Understandings, meanings, generalizations.
2. Attitudes.
3. Appreciations.
4. Special abilities.
5. *Skills.* (Some teachers prefer to separate these into (*a*) motor, (*b*) mental, (*c*) social.) (These are the items which will need practice or drill here or later.)
6. Behavior patterns.
7. Facts.

III. The Approach

A brief account of the most probable introduction or approach. Two or three may be indicated, since various levels of maturity, interest, and ability must be motivated. The account will show either how the teacher plans to utilize pupil activities and purposes likely to be present, or how he will set the stage to motivate the learners. The point is that the teacher will here make clear just how he plans to get the particular teaching-learning situation under way.

IV. The Pupil's Aim or Objective

The major objective which it is hoped the learners will develop or accept is stated here. (The writer places this here because the learner's aim usually emerges during or at the conclusion of the Approach. Some teachers prefer to insert this elsewhere in the outline, which is their privilege.)

V. The Planning and Working Period

The teacher will indicate here how he hopes to develop initial planning out of the approach. He will then indicate in some detail how he plans to keep the situation going once it is under way.

This involves planning (in advance or co-operatively) questions, exercises, readings, experiments, excursions, reports, interviews, group discussions, socialized, recitations, individual and group reports, development of study habits, setting up committees, exercises for organizing, summarizing, memorizing, practicing, encouraging creative effort.

Individual work and small or large group undertakings will be indicated as the situation demands.

Possible methods of diagnosis and of remedial measure for any difficulties or special disabilities uncovered in the preview or later will be discussed.

The term *desired outcomes* in the diagram below confuses some students until it is pointed out that these are the same as the teacher's objectives stated earlier. Their inclusion here as outcomes is for the sake of emphasizing that the problems, questions, and learning experiences *must* relate to outcomes and not just be listed hopefully and at random.

The form in which this part of the plan is presented may be either in (*a*) running discourse, or (*b*) columns as below. Either is satisfactory so long as the clear relationship between procedures, use of materials, and outcomes is shown.

Problems and Questions	Learning Experiences	Materials

Desired Outcomes	Bibliography

(Some outlines include a column relating evaluation techniques directly to outcomes.)

VI. *Evaluation Techniques*
The teacher will show with illustrations how he proposes to gather evidence showing that the objectives of the unit have been developed, and to what degree. Most important of all, he will show clearly how he develops continuous, participatory evaluation, leading to self-evaluation by learners. Any and all kinds of instruments may be used.

(Do not merely list tests, scales, descriptive methods, and so on, but show how each one used is related to the desired outcome. Do not list the items which will be evaluated, a common but inexplicable error in many teacher's plans.)

VII. *Bibliographies*
1. Books useful to the teacher in planing the unit. (Not all outlines require this.)
2. Books useful to the learners. This list must often be classified in two ways: by parts of the unit; by levels of maturity within the learning group.

VIII. *Audio-visual materials, and other instructional aids, with sources*
Films, filmstrips, still pictures; exhibits and models, tools, realia of any kind which are available in school or community, together with location of source.

Planning daily sequences within a unit.
The making of daily lesson plans, whether by teachers in training or in service, has been associated with the assign-study-recite procedure and was treated in connection with that procedure. Experienced teachers and supervisors, however, have noted for some time that many beginning teachers who possess a good general grasp of unit organization are lamentably weak in operating the day-by-day events. Experienced teachers constantly ask the writer for advice about "breaking down the unit" into the things which happen day by day. Textbook discussions of unit teaching are regrettably weak on this particular problem. The essence of unit planning is the flexible organization of long-time sequences, the absence of fixed fragments to be completed under deadline. Nevertheless, the development of the unit day by day cannot be neglected. The teacher, as the unit develops, notes what happens; notes what may need attention in the immediate future; notes uneven development either of the unit itself or of the learners; notes excellent or ineffective use of resources and persons; notes many other factors. He calls the group together for planning the more minute sequences within the unit, though not necessarily every day. In any event, subsidiary planning involves certain points.

1. Estimating group and individual progress, anticipating any possible inequalities in progress, anticipating difficulties and interruptions. Definite notes are made. This leads to the next point.
2. Calling the group together when necessary at the opening of the work period.
   a. To replan any major element in the unit which needs it; to rearrange responsibilities, committee memberships. This may be necessary because of unexpectedly good progress or of the opposite; of unforeseen events.
   b. To analyze any serious obstacle which developed the day before or over a few days; to evaluate critically suggestions for solution.
3. Calling the group together not for major replanning but periodically for the sake of coherence and maintenance of common understanding, to discuss:

a. What has been done.
b. What remains to be done.
c. What comes immediately next.
d. How all these are things related.
e. What new general suggestions may be offered.
4. Planning and making notes on how to meet difficulties which he can see will arise surely, but which the pupils cannot see until experience leads to insight.
5. Foreseeing and making notes on how to meet emergency group discussions in the midst of and interrupting the general activities.

The stage reached in the development of the unit must also be considered. The approach and planning period of the general unit plan can be so written as to indicate clearly the sequence of events. The working period is more complicated because a varied series of events is developed simultaneously. The writer believes, however, that the general account of the proposed working period given in the general plan can and should be so written as to indicate clearly a probable sequence of events. This can then be supplemented through attention to the points summarized above which deal with the day-by-day developments.

The tendency of some teachers to outline the working period around the logical series of subject-matter leads found in the overview gives little guidance for sequential daily experiences. Outlining the working period of a proposed unit around the question-and-problem leads derived from the pupils will give guidance for planning daily sequences.

Criteria for evaluating a unit. Literally scores of criteria are available in books, in course of study, and in the periodical literature. They differ widely in wording and in arrangement but all cover the same essential points. Students and teachers may adopt or construct a list for their own use. The writer believes that criteria calling for "yes-and-no" answers should be avoided, since this often encourages students unconsciously to omit careful, critical analysis. It is better to state criteria in a form which demands specific evidence.

Criteria for Evaluating Units

Cite evidence that the unit:
1. Is closely related to the typical interests and needs likely to be found in the on-going life of the learners.
2. Will bring learners into contact with aspects of life which are of both immediate and continuing social significance.
3. Is appropriate to the maturity levels within the group; is challenging without being too difficult; will be revealing to pupils of their own unique capacities and limitations.
4. Is possible within the available resources of the school, the immediate community, and the accessible environment (direct experience).
5. Will provide naturally for use of materials dealing with other places, other peoples, other times (vicarious experience).
6. Will provide naturally for a great variety of individual and co-operative group activities—physical, mental, emotional, and social; thinking-feeling-doing.
7. Will lead (as far as can ever be foretold) to socially desirable learning outcomes; understandings and insights, attitudes, appreciations, and values, skills, and behavior patterns which will very likely be used by citizens generally.
8. Will stimulate (as far as can ever be foretold) critical thinking and evaluation of the learner's own procedure in selecting purposes, in planning means of achieving them, in selecting materials and processes, in accepting outcomes.
9. Will lead to other desirable learning experiences.
10. Is of such length as to be comprehensible as a unit by the level of maturity involved; that is, is of such length that the pupil can have insight into it.
11. Is related to the general course of study goals and framework.

Many teachers and curriculum workers prefer sets of criteria which have more detail, either in the form of illustrative evidences or of questions under each heading. A very useful set of criteria using subquestions is presented by Caswell and Campbell.[7]

[7] Hollis L. Caswell and Doak S. Campbell, *Curriculum Development* (New York, American Book, 1935), pp. 388-389.

1. Do the pupils have a dominating purpose?
    a. Is the type of behavior required compatible with the aims of education?
    b. Is the plan of action to realize the purpose based on the past experience of the pupils?
    c. Do the pupils believe the purpose is worthwhile?
    d. Did the purpose arise from stimuli of a kind the pupils will meet in out-of-school experiences?
    e. Have the pupils mastery of the abilities needed to carry out the plan successfully or can they master them in reasonable time?
2. Have the pupils engaged in a series of activities planned by them and the teacher to realize their purpose?
    a. Do the children recognize the part the various activities in which they engage are to play in realization of the purpose?
    b. Do the various activities contribute to realization of the aims of education?
    c. Are the activities suited to the mental, physical, and emotional characteristics of the individuals who engage in them?
3. Have the children evaluated their activities in terms of the purpose they set out to achieve?
    a. Has the plan of action been continuously revised and improved as steps have been taken in its development?
    b. Have the children recognized the need for more adequate mastery of certain abilities and have steps been taken to achieve such mastery?
    c. Have the children considered the enterprise as a whole when completed to see what improvements could have been made?
    d. Have the children canvassed other related enterprises in which they would like to engage?
    e. Did the enterprise develop conduct of the desired type?

The foregoing criteria are for application to the total, over-all unit. Each phase of the unit has separate criteria, as shown earlier in this chapter.

DISCUSSION, EXERCISES, AND REPORTS

This chapter must be supplemented by reading and by detailed analysis of many unit plans and logs of units. The period of study should culminate in the making of a preplan for a unit. The exercises listed below have proved effective in several situations.

Each instructor will need, however, to determine his own sequence of events. The experience and background of his class group, his aim, and the time available will all aid in determining how detailed the study, analysis, and unit construction should be. In any event this major aspect of training cannot be slighted without genuine loss to the student.

The time necessary and the degree of detail in discussion will vary greatly between groups. Inexperienced students preparing for practice teaching will need three or four times as long as experienced teachers who are studying the new methods.

The writer has also found that one of the most effective devices is to present to the class two or three units in detail, ranging from primary to secondary. A detailed log must be available together with complete illustrations of question lists, charts, exhibits, articles constructed, models, illustrations, pictures, written work, practice material growing out of the unit, etc. The log should be read slowly with the actual exhibits as constructed by teacher and pupils presented at proper points; comments should be interpolated; class questions encouraged. This may go on for two or more days while students are studying the chapter and analyzing units. A skeletonized outline of this type of analysis will be found in the following chapter.

1. Individual students or small committees may examine several unit plans or logs available in the local collection or other source. The unit should be briefly described to open class discussion. *Each major phase* should then be analyzed in the light of the criteria in this chapter. (Criteria from other sources may be used whenever preferable. New criteria may be developed by class groups.)

The analysis should not merely list the weaknesses but should include correction in so far as the group is able to suggest improvements.

2. Individual students or small committees may attempt to outline a preplanned unit. This will require time and recurrent discussion. After a general outline is developed, each phase should be prepared in some detail until a reasonably complete unit preplan is produced. Each student eventually develops one or more units.

(This cannot be completed under two or more weeks. The class proceeds to other problems in the course while carrying this project forward.)

3. Report in class any other good accounts of the development of the learning experiences found in texts or periodical literature.

4. Report in class any accounts found (usually in periodical literature) of the development of specific items such as pupil interviews with interested adults, school excursions, planning organizations, construction, the handling of group discussion.

5. Report analytically on any teaching observed with particular reference to the development of learning experience.

SUGGESTED READINGS

The discussions of unit construction are still in emergent stage, which accounts for the unevenness of the reference materials available.

Course-of-study manuals and local bulletins often contain good materials. The *current periodical literature* contains unlimited amounts of valuable illustrative discussion.

References to elementary school practice outnumber those to secondary school practice very greatly. Secondary teachers, however, may read with great profit the discussions of elementary school situations. A few secondary references will be given in addition at the close of the list.

GENERAL REFERENCES ON SELECTION AND PREPLANNING

The majority of these follow the older division of units into subject-matter and experience types. Note especially those which do not, namely, Burr, Harding and Jacobs; Schorling; Schorling and Wingo.

BIDDICK, Mildred L., *The Preparation and Use of Source Units* (New York Progressive Education Association, no date, probably 1940).

BURR, James B., HARDING, Lowry W., and JACOBS, Leland B., *Student Teaching in the Elementary School*, 2nd ed. (New York, Appleton-Century-Crofts, 1958), Chs. 5, 6, 9, 10, 11. Some of very best discussions available. Good bibliography.

HANNA, Lavone A., POTTER, Gladys L., and HAGAMAN, Neva, *Unit Teaching in the Elementary School* (New York, Holt, Rinehart & Winston, 1955). The best all-around treatment.

LEE, Murray J., and LEE, Dorris M., *The Child and His Curriculum*, 3rd ed. (New York, Appleton-Century-Crofts, 1960), Ch. 7. One of the best brief discussions. Good bibliography.

MACOMBER, F. G., *Guiding Child Development in the Elementary School* (New York, American Book, 1941), Chs. 1-5. Very good for beginners and for experienced teachers wishing to change methods.

MELVIN, A. Gordon. Four books by this author published by the John Day Company, Inc., New York, are replete with excellent concrete illustration for elementary grades. *The Technique of Progressive Teaching* (1932), *The Activity Program* (1936), *The Activated Curriculum* (1939), *Method for New Schools* (1941).

MORRISON, Henry C., *The Practice of Teaching in the Secondary School*, rev. ed. (Chicago, Univ. of Chicago Press, 1931). The original and classic reference on early definition of subject-matter unit. Much material still of value.

RUCKER, W. R., *Curriculum Development in the Elementary School* (New York, Harper, 1960). Several good illustrations in various chapters.

RIVLIN, Harry N., *Teaching Adolescents in Secondary Schools*, 2nd ed. (New York, Appleton-Century-Crofts, 1961), Ch. 6. Good discussion for high school teachers.

SCHORLING, Raleigh, *Student Teaching*, rev. ed. (New York, McGraw, 1949). Excellent concrete discussions, pp. 141-146. Secondary level. Supports one unit view.

———, and WINGO, G. Max, *Elementary School Student Teaching* (New York, McGraw, 1950), pp. 174-183. Excellent concrete materials. Supports one unit.

SMITH, B. Othanel, STANLEY, Wm. O., and SHORES, J. Harlan, *Fundamentals of Curriculum Development* (New York, Harcourt, Brace & World, 1950). Chapter 23 only discussion of process units available and contains excellent bibliography of supporting references.

STRICKLAND, Ruth G., *How to Build a Unit of Work*, Bulletin, No. 5, U. S. Office of Education (Washington, D. C., 1946). Elementary level.

UMSTATTD, J. G., *Secondary School Teaching*, rev. ed. (Boston, Ginn, 1944), Ch. 9.

Texts on special methods of teaching in given subjects (science, literature, etc.) often contain excellent discussions with illustrations.

CHAPTER 15: The Analysis of an Illustrative Unit

FIFTH GRADE LEVEL. GENERAL AREA: COLONIAL LIFE.

(Pupils' General Aim and Its Development Are Indicated during the Analysis)

This unit [1] was chosen because, although developed on the fifth-grade level, it illustrates very clearly the general procedures that can be used from first grade through high school. Content and controls would differ, of course, with the different levels of maturity and experience.

The analysis is designed to show several important characteristics of unit development.

1. The use of a source unit in developing a teaching unit.
2. The stage setting out of which the unit grew. Stage setting is legitimate, even though it is more desirable to develop units out of natural experiences of children.
3. The natural on-going development of the unit with full pupil participation: the absence of preplanned details imposed on the children.
4. The detailed development of the pupils' plans from broad vague questions to eventual specific problems and tasks.
5. The co-operative nature of the pupil planning, the distribution of the work.
6. The replanning necessitated by difficulties, obstacles, failure, and by necessity for arrang-

[1] The unit was taught and the original log written by Miss Frances Phelan, then 5B teacher in the Miller School, Burbank, Cal. The analysis and comments were added by the present writer.

ing several pieces of work to go on simultaneously.

7. The teacher's skill in letting pupils discover their own difficulties and errors necessitating the replanning.
8. The modern use of subject matter as means, not end. The subject matter was not learned, but used in furthering learning.
9. The teacher's management of the total on-going situation.
10. The natural development of understandings, attitudes, appreciations, and skills.
11. The emergence out of natural settings of typical skill learnings. Oral and written language skills, reading, writing, and spelling, using libraries and references, and compiling materials all appeared as necessary to the completion of a pupil purpose.

How the unit started. The teacher planned to use one of the approaches suggested in the source unit, "Colonial Life," which was an area allocated to the fifth grade by the general course of study. She hoped to direct the interest of the children toward life in the early settlements in America.

Pictures of colonial and pioneer homes were secured from the County and City Visual Education departments. An array of books on colonial life was placed in the library. A bulletin board arrangement was made of bright book jackets illustrating the stories in the library. Particularly colorful books were stood up on the browsing table and opened to interesting pictures.

A beauty spot was arranged with a wooden bowl and gourds. Trenchers, a pewter bowl, a tinder box, wooden spoons, Indian corn, and other things suggestive of early American living were arranged in conspicuous places in the room.

Candle moulds, a spinning wheel, exhibits of skins, and other things were also available but were not displayed. The teacher wished to first direct the interest toward homes and living conditions and then to let the other materials be introduced as the children asked for them in carrying on their activity.

The teacher here preplans very tentatively but in no way imposes on the learners. She knows that the other materials and many other activities she has not provided, nor perhaps even thought of yet, will be requested by the children as they discover the need.

The actual initiation of the unit. The children trooped into their new room at the beginning of the term, the dominant question seeming to be, "What are we going to study?" They were eager to examine and to discuss the new and strange things in this new room; pleased to have new sets of books and materials.

The teacher passed out a set of books, "The Story of America," and said, "These books tell many interesting things about our grandfathers and grandmothers, about our great-grandfathers and great-grandmothers and even about their fathers and grandfathers, too. Look through them to see if you would like to have lived with them."

The children enjoyed looking at the pictures and reading bits to one another here and there. They made comments to one another and to the teacher. Of particular interest were the colored pictures showing men and women dressed in what the children called "funny clothes." Meetings of the colonists and Indians, life in the log cabins, and pictures of groups going to church protected by the men carrying heavy guns attracted much attention and comment.

Maxine said, "Are we going to study about Abraham Lincoln and George Washington?

My sister did when she was in your room last year." The teacher said, "That would make interesting study. Did you find a picture of either Lincoln or Washington in your book?" The little girl showed us the pictures she had found of Lincoln reading in front of a fireplace. "Gee, did he have to read like that? It's not very good light," was the comment of Allan. "It looks like he lived in a cabin way up in the mountains," remarked Pauline. "Oh we know a lot about Lincoln," interrupted Bobby, "let's study something new." "Did you find a picture that interested you?" the teacher asked Bobby. "Yes, I like the one on page 193, showing Pocahontas saving John Smith as he was about to be put to death." Bobby volunteered that he had read a part of this story and liked it very much. He then expressed the wish that they could make it into a play and act it out. "What part of the story did you think was especially good?" asked the teacher. "I liked the part telling about John Smith being captured and bound." (Comments follow freely from many children.) "I wonder if the Indians captured many of the white people?" "I wouldn't like to be them if they're captured by the Indians." "I don't think they captured very many because all the men in the pictures are carrying guns." "The Indians just have bows and arrows." "My father has a powder horn that belonged to his grandfather." "What's a powder horn?" Jack explained what a powder horn was and looked like, volunteering that perhaps he could bring it to school for all to see. Meanwhile the teacher found a picture of a powder horn hanging above the mantel in the picture of a colonial fireside on page 233. "My mother has a warming pan just like that one in the picture. Maybe I can bring it to show tomorrow."

"Maybe we could build a house like a colonial house. We could bring these things from home and make it look like a real one. We could act out things about life in those days. Some of us could be Indians and some could be white people." (This went on for some time, developing details but in unorganized fashion.)

"We had a big pueblo in Mrs. Brown's room when we were studying Indians. It was so big we could go in it and play. If we make a cabin, let's have it big enough to play in."

This type of spontaneous random discussion continues naturally, The general purpose to build a colonial house is accepted without any very serious definition. Discussion moves on to "things we want to do" in connection with this, so far vaguely defined, project. The teacher begins to write on the board some of the proposals which are being made. This results in a list. The total list does not emerge the first day, items being added from time to time.

Things We Want to Do

1. Find out more about our grandparents and great-grandparents who first settled our country.
2. Build a log cabin big enough to "keep house in."
3. Furnish our cabin.
4. Play stories of early days in America.
5. Make rifles, powder horns and shot pouches.
6. Make a collection of heirlooms, pictures, and clippings.
7. Go on an excursion to the Colonial Museum at Glendale.
8. Make a time line showing dates of important happenings in our country's early history.
9. Make a large map of our country showing the location of the early settlements.
10. Braid a rug.
11. Make a small quilt.
12. Design samplers.
13. Learn songs of the early days.
14. Learn dances of the early days.
15. Paint pictures.
16. Write stories.
17. Make book covers.
18. Make clothes worn by people in the early settlements.
19. Invite our parents to see our cabin on the afternoon of Open House in the school.
20. Get a program ready for our parents, explaining about our log house and about life in the early settlements.
21. Serve a colonial tea to the parents who visit our room.

The following day the children had a lively discussion as to the procedure to be followed in carrying out their plans.

"Their plans" are obviously still general and vague and not yet truly plans. The children do not as yet know this. The continuous refinement of the pupils' undertaking from its first vague questions to definite working plans and division of labor is a feature of the unit. Note in following pages how the general plans continually placed the children in difficulties. Meeting these difficulties as they arose resulted in ever closer defining and planning by the children. The problems were the children's own and recognized as such.

It soon became apparent that the children held various ideas concerning the appearance of colonial homes, concerning methods of construction and of the activities of the earliest settlers. Many ideas were hazy and inaccurate. Several children made statements which were immediately contradicted or challenged by others.

The teacher at this and similar points exercises guidance instead of answering questions, settling problems, which if continued, rob the pupils of the chance to find out the necessity of defining, securing correct information, and evaluating.

The teacher asked the children what they intended to do about these conflicting ideas and arguments about facts.

One child said she thought we should study the pictures on display more carefully and also look for more pictures. Correct ideas could then be secured.

Another child had noticed that there were evidently several kinds of homes among colonists and pioneers. She wondered if it was not a mistake to think them all alike, or that all lived in log cabins.

A third child asked if there was any place we could go to see colonial houses, furniture, and things. He recalled that while studying ranch life in early California the class had been taken to see Casa Adobe, an original Mexican dwelling dating from earliest times. The teacher told them that there was, in fact, a very good colonial museum in Glendale, the adjoining town. She said that she was sure arrangements could be made for a visit to this museum.

One of the more impetuous and active boys disapproved of the delay which would ensue while arrangements were being made to visit the museum and advocated more intensive search of the library and picture collection and more discussion so that the class could decide on types of houses and get to work. After discussion the class decided that both could be done. The pupils would exhaust the local library and pictures while the teacher made arrangements with the Glendale Colonial Museum for a visit.

Note that the children themselves bring in subject matter. They insist on reading widely, more widely than they would under assignment. Good teachers take responsibility for keeping activities going once they are started by the children.

The general questions are made more specific. The teacher then asked the pupils where they were going to get reading material beyond that furnished by school sources. What were they going to read about? How would they know when they had found something of value to the discussion? This led to the formulation of an astonishing list of questions by the group. Additions to the list from day to day brought the total to seventy-four questions. This list was printed on a chart and kept before the class. Questions answered satisfactorily were checked off as the group decided that they had secured a workable answer.

Our Problems

1. In what kinds of homes did the early settlers live?
2. Of what materials were they made?
3. Why were some homes so different from others?
4. Did they all have fireplaces?
5. How is cooking done over a fireplace?

7. Did they make their own rifles or did they buy them?
11. What is the difference between a musket and a rifle?
12. What is a puncheon floor?
13. How are the cracks filled in between the logs?
16. What was burned in the lamps?
17. How were the lamps made?
30. Did the pioneers ever buy and sell as we do?
31. Did the settlers have money?
32. How did they make friends with the Indians?
47. Where did they get their shoes?

The list continues up to a total of seventy-four, not all of which appeared the first few days. All aspects of colonial life were covered. The last question asked why early American furniture was so expensive today!

Though the children called these problems, they were more truly questions to be answered.

The following day a little girl brought a homespun quilt that had been made by her great-grandmother. Several boys had located pieces of wood from which to fashion models of rifles and muskets. All the children were now repeating comments made by their fathers and mothers about colonists and pioneers.

Pupils see need for order and system in their work. Although new ideas were being introduced, though interest and enthusiasm were high, the questions on the list were not being answered. The children themselves began to criticize their own procedure, saying that they had probably better get at those answers so that working plans could be made. It was recognized that the interesting discussion, though it had many values, was delaying some of their major purposes.

The teacher gave out some new sets of readers, "Long Ago," to Group II, which now read for background on some of the questions. Group I continued to work with "The Story of America" and with library material. The children started perusing this material. Soon they were locating interesting pictures and paragraphs. They insisted on reading paragraphs of interest whether they pertained to the questions or not. They were becoming genuinely confused through the very wealth of material, through the many diverse ideas being constantly offered. Again they criticized themselves, making it clear that they were wasting time and "not getting anywhere."

Here again is a situation calling for teacher guidance. The old-fashioned "practical" teacher would step in, take control and direct the learning activities toward the desired end without allowing the children the experience of seeing how and why. "Practical" teachers would be disturbed by the foregoing illustration of confusion among the children, not recognizing that this is an excellent learning situation.

The teacher then asked if the children would like to know how to use books more efficiently and how to search for information in more businesslike fashion the way older people do. She mentioned the use of the Table of Contents and the Index. The children had had previous experience with these devices.

Here is seen the necessity for several experiences with a given learning outcome. The class had had one previous experience in which they had learned to use the Table of Contents, the Index, and certain other study aids. These skills cannot be developed at once; the understanding accompanying them will not be recalled immediately. The mention by the teacher recalled the previous experience, and the pupils immediately began to utilize the Index. After a few real experiences such as this, the understanding and skill involved will function automatically.

The children themselves now began to suggest "topics" under which the questions could be grouped, thus making for more systematic search for information. Other pupils began grouping the questions almost before the list of topics had been settled upon. Topic headings agreed upon were: homes, houses, fireplaces, rifles, powder horns, weapons generally, colonial life, pio-

neer life, colonial homes. Others were added later.

The pupils now began to exclude certain questions from the current inquiry so that attention might be focused on those questions immediately necessary for starting the project. The food of the colonists, methods of barter, farming, and so forth, were reserved for later treatment. Attention was focused on the construction of the homes, the fashioning of weapons, and the furnishings of the homes.

The pupils themselves will attempt systematization when working upon problems of real interest to them. This is very different from going through exercises upon outlining or organizing under assignment and apart from any real material which needs organizing.

Preliminary planning emerges. One illustration of the technique worked out by the children is as follows:

To have furniture and utensils for our house, we must:
1. Read to find out what kind of furniture and utensils the early settlers used.
2. Plan the kinds we want in our house.
3. Make plans and drawings of them.
4. Make a list of the materials we need.
5. Collect the materials ourselves, ask the children to contribute, and ask the teacher for school supplies.
6. Make the articles.

It was soon recognized that the questions could not be answered quickly, that material would have to be saved up for some time and made into a report which would answer a question or questions. Furthermore, several different books would contain material upon one question. The children themselves suggested writing a question upon a sheet of paper and then listing each book and the page numbers where information could be found.

The children have here started a procedure which led them, without assistance from the teacher, to develop a card file. Cards were made for each of the major topics: books, dates, publishers, and page numbers being listed. After the children had developed this adequately, the teacher typed the cards and placed them in a cardboard file. The pupils developed a set of suggestions, which were pasted upon the top of the box.

To Use Reference Card File

Things to keep in mind when looking up a reference:
1. Know exactly for what you are looking.
2. Be sure to get the correct book.
3. Be sure to get the correct page.
4. Know where to start reading. (Decide where to start by scanning the page to find some word or phrase which has to do with what you are trying to find out.)
5. Know when to stop. (Do not read more than is necessary to answer the question.)

Research work on the questions continued for some time. Notes were kept from day to day. The teacher occasionally aided an individual or small group which had difficulty with the index, with organizing notes, or with other skills.

From time to time questions were answered either through brief statements or through more elaborate reports. Many questions began to be checked off the list. Plans for action based upon the findings began to appear. The reports varied, naturally, in adequacy and in clarity and in method of presentation. The class finally, after much discussion of given reports as they were made, decided that directions for making reports would materially improve the situation. The following set of simple rules was evolved by the group.

When we give our reports we should:
1. Have in mind what we are going to say.
2. Talk plainly.
3. Keep to the subject.
4. Show some pictures or other material.

This illustrated the natural emergence of a demand for good English, for clarity and logic. Experiences such as this will develop far better English, outlining, and methods of presentation than formal methods ever can.

An outline of the findings about pioneer homes was made on the board. This outline will be omitted here to save space. Its nature and content can be inferred directly from the later list of learning activities. The outline covered appearance of houses, materials and methods of construction; fireplaces and cooking methods; cooking utensils and dishes; tables, chairs, beds, and other furniture; rugs, samplers, and decorations; lighting, candles, and lamps.

An interesting problem arose at this point. The boys and girls who were looking up information about the muskets and flintlock guns were unable to determine from the reading material just how these guns looked and operated. They could get no guidance for constructing models. All available books including encyclopedias were consulted, but the children were disappointed and confused. The teacher said she would see what she could find for them. The method of meeting this difficulty appears a few paragraphs further on. This incident illustrates the necessity for aid from the teacher, sometimes from other adults, as the unit develops.

Planning for specific activities begins to appear. The next day attention focused upon the question: How shall we build our colonial home? Much discussion ensued with many references back and forth to the reading material and reports. Just how did the pioneers build their houses and out of what materials? What changes would we need to make in building a smaller model in the classroom? It was decided to make a simulated log house which would fit on one side of the classroom. The teacher volunteered that she could secure a number of refrigerator packing boxes and other similar things if the children thought they could use these. She gave the measurements of these boxes. Measurements were then made on the floors and walls to see if three or more of these boxes put together would make a house of sufficient size. The children then decided to use just three sides, leaving the fourth side open so that the home activities could extend into the room. One of the schoolroom windows was included within the limits of the house, thus providing light. The group decided to paint the sides with yellow-brown calcimine to represent logs, the chinking to be done in yellow-gray calcimine. Dimensions were easily agreed upon. All were eager to get to work with hammers and saws. The boys all started without further preliminaries. It was soon apparent that no headway could be made in this manner.

Further systematizing and division of labor are arranged. As confusion increased one boy called a halt saying, "If we all try to work at once and all try to work on putting up the walls, we just get in each other's way. Some of us ought to leave this and go to work on the rifles or the chairs or something." A girl immediately joined in, saying that she and her friends would like to make the fireplace and the "things" for it. Other similar suggestions were made, resulting in the beginnings of division of labor.

At the close of this period the teacher mentioned that soon we would need to decide what furniture and utensils to have and to be planning their construction.

During the reading period in the afternoon the two more advanced groups read a description of muskets and flintlock rifles which the teacher had written and mimeographed. This included descriptions of powder horns and shot pouches. The teacher had read the available materials and then constructed in a suitable vocabulary an essay which the children could read and understand. Teachers and pupils in modern school must often manufacture their own subject matter. The slow group does this also. The girls were as interested as the boys and made many excellent suggestions.

The slower reading group had this material read aloud to them by the teacher. These children then made a brief co-operative story incorporating their own understandings derived from the material. This was written on the board by the teacher as it was worked out by the pupils and then

reread by the group. Here we see the reduction of too difficult reading material, first to the level of the good readers and then to the level of the slowest in the group. The slow group placed copies of their own story in their notebooks to be used for reference as they too engaged in the construction work.

The following morning more wood for rifles and furniture was brought in together with some gourds, a warming pan, and other colonial utensils. The teacher had placed in a prominent place a picture of the interior of a log cabin so that other suggestions for furniture and decorations could be found. The little girl who had brought the warming pan was delighted to find a similar warming pan in the picture. All the children were interested to know that this object which they held in their hands was actually once a part of the furnishings of an early home.

Suggestions now came thick and fast for things to be made: chairs, tables, a bed, quilts, dishes. Suggestions for material accompanied this list, together with discussion of ways and means of securing them. Several children volunteered to bring some of the actual utensils from home.

A number of additions were made to the original list of "Things we want to do."

The class started with enthusiasm to carry out their own suggestions. This necessitated reading, making plans, securing materials, constructing things, arranging time and tools, and so on. The class very soon realized, as they had when starting the construction of the house itself, that organization and system were necessary if things were to be done, if time and energy were to be conserved. Omitting the detailed conversation, suffice it to say that the group organized itself into a series of committees to carry on specific parts of the total project.

1. Walls for the house	7. Samplers
2. Fireplace	8. Dishes (later
3. Tables and chairs	table utensils)
4. Cooking utensils	9. Bed
5. Quilt	10. Lamps
6. Rug	

As the work developed it was found that further reading and research was necessary. Each committee then was responsible for both construction and research. Reports were made from time to time, so that the entire group profited from the specialized reading of the committees.

Many formal teachers are afraid that the division of labor in modern unit teaching means that the children will not learn the same things, will not "cover" the same material. First, let it be said that all children do not and cannot learn the same things in the same way from any given body of material. There will always be individual differences. Second, all the really necessary and desirable learning outcomes will be achieved by all children in terms of their individual differences as they work through a series of units. The teacher is responsible for managing the learning activities so that all children have experience with all desirable learnings. Third, the group reports mentioned above do bring the information at least before the whole group.

Committees may be formed in any of several ways. In this case pupils generally volunteered, some were selected by their mates, and in a few instances the teacher suggested membership and changes from one committee to another. Committee lists and memberships are usually made into a chart and placed where all can see.

The children in group discussion decided that each committee should make a plan for work before actually beginning any construction. Children now went to work reading, conferring with each other, beginning the drawing of models, and drawing or painting pictures from which to work, which later would be presented to their own committee and sometimes to the whole group for discussion, suggestions, and final approval.

Through this reading and conferring many differences of opinion were cleared, hazy points clarified, materials reorganized, and working spaces arranged or changed as necessary.

The total unit was now well launched. The planning activities continued throughout as construction proceeded. Evaluation began to appear and was also constant as individuals and groups analyzed suggestions and working plans. Usually several suggestions were offered for the solution of each little problem, precipitating analysis and judgment. The availability and cost of materials, the skills necessary, and the personnel were constantly under discussion. Certain plans had to be actually tried out tentatively before launching a final effort.

The remainder of the log will not be reproduced, the foregoing illustration serving to outline the general procedure for getting a unit under way and organized. The following lists will serve to show the major learning activities engaged in, the typical modern outcomes, and some of the typical formal learnings. The evaluation techniques are missing from this account.

Major Learning Activities

1. Made a time line. Used cord 12-feet long and colored cards, dating it from the time of the first settlement in Jamestown until the winning of Independence from England. (This line was not intended for beauty, but the children greatly enjoyed placing a card with the name and date of the event on or by the correct knot.)
2. Made a map of the United States. The children transferred a map of the United States onto kraft paper by using the still film machine. The map showed the forty-eight states and the principal rivers. On it, by using different colors of calcimine, they showed the locations of the six successive frontiers in our country's settlement. Reference map in *Adventuring in Young America* by McGuire and Phillips, page 233.
3. Constructed a log cabin with necessary accessories for play purposes. Built a fireplace of apple boxes, painted to represent stones. Similarly, made a chimney over the fireplace.

   Constructed the following pieces of furniture:

   Table (Made from the top of the refrigerator box. It was found that colonists used old packing boxes for some of their furniture.)

A Turn-Up Bed (Made of branches and laced with brown cord instead of the hemp or rawhide.)

Cradle

Chair

Made the following articles that were usually found on or hanging by a pioneer's fireside:

a. Crane
b. Rifle
c. Powder horn
d. Shot pouch
e. Bullet mould
f. Candlestick
g. Betty lamp
h. Wooden bowl
i. Wooden spoon
j. Wooden griddle shovel
k. Gourd dipper
l. Gourd ladle
m. Warming pan
n. Broom (of branches)
o. Mortar and Pestle—A short log was partially hollowed out. A child brought in an oblong stone for the pestle.
p. Tinder box
q. Dutch Oven (An apple box was used as the basis for construction.)
r. Hour Glass
s. Griddle. We started to make our pans by covering metal pans with strips of newspaper and paste. This was easy to do but it was difficult to put on the legs and the handles.
t. (The children covered a large book with brown paper, labeled it "The Bible" and put it on the fireplace. They brought in quills for pens and some old pans that we used in playing. They also saved some old medicine bottles for the mantel, for they found that the pioneers often settled in low places by the rivers and because of the dampness sometimes suffered from rheumatism. Deer antlers were brought in to hang over the mantel and hold the rifle.)

Made trenchers and other table utensils. (The teacher had requisitioned blocks of soft pine for the work and the children hollowed them out with a brace and a bit and chisel. One little girl took a block home. Her father burned out a hollow for her, as the pioneers did. She scraped out the charred wood.)

Made a small braided rug. (For a while we had a skin on the floor of the cabin. We replaced it later with the rug.)

Made a small quilt. The girls had fun looking up and bringing in old quilt patterns. Our room mother, whose little girl was one of the quilt committee, was very fond of quilts and brought a lovely one to school to show the children. She told them something of the work entailed in making a beautiful quilt.

Worked on a hooked rug. The teacher had started one and so brought it to school for the children to see. Some of the girls experimented in working on it.

Made several samplers, to put in the house, conceiving own designs. The girls did not have time to actually make the samplers, but the designs for them were made on manila paper and colored with crayola.

Made flintlock rifles, powder horns, and shot pouches. The rifles were made of long pieces of wood. Molding was used for ramrods. One boy's father cut metal strip for the boys to nail on to represent the hammer. The teacher bought a sack of horns from a packing house. They were scraped and sanded and completed with pieces of soft wood and string. The pouches were made of burlap.

4. Children brought to school articles associated with early American life. Brought in skins and traps. (A friend of one of the boys allowed him to bring to school skins of a bob cat, a raccoon, and a rabbit. These skins were hung on the walls of our house "to keep out the cold drafts." The boys were much interested in the traps that were brought with the skins. They all had license numbers on them.)

Brought in exhibits of articles used in colonial and pioneer times. Quilt, sampler, warming pan, and spice grainer were among the best.

5. Learned songs of colonial days. (List in master unit.)

6. Learned dances of the pioneers:

Pop Goes the Weasel
John Brown
Uncle Steve's Quadrille
Sicilian Circle
The Minuet

Dances were learned during physical education periods. Needless to say the pioneer clothes were not worn during the Minuet. This stately dance served to emphasize the difference in the people living in different localities in our country at the same time.

7. Relived phases of colonial and pioneer life in a log cabin. Material for the playtime was gathered in various ways. Some of it developed from a desire to play certain stories read to the class by the teacher or stories read in reading groups.

Some of it was suggested from the background reading or discussion in connection with definite problems. Casual pleasure reading and imagination supplied many interesting play activities.

With help of the lively imaginations of the children, the cabin became a part of Plymouth, Penn's Woods, Boonesborough, or the Northern Woodlands.

The favorite location for the cabin, however, was Boonesborough. Possibly the fact that the motion picture "Daniel Boone" was current and the story of happenings in Boonesborough were of particular appeal to adventure-loving boys accounted for this preference.

8. Made clothing of the pioneers. Developing as a corollary to the interest in furnishing and playing in the log cabin was the desire of both boys and girls to dress up. Although temporarily satisfied with their rifles, shot pouches and powder horns, the boys soon were beginning to wonder what they could add to their costume to make it more complete.

Some of the girls wondered if they could bring long dresses from home to wear. The teacher asked if they would like to make clothes to wear in the log cabin. Of course the answer was an enthusiastic "yes." Pictures from the visual education department were studied and books were conned. Such a variety of types and styles of clothing were worn in early America!

The children had to decide whether they would be New Englanders in doubtlets and breeches, Virginians in silk, satin, and laces, or frontiersmen in skins and homespun. To the boys, Daniel Boone was a "real fellow" and they aspired to wear the deerskin shirts and coonskin hats as he did.

The girls agreed to make sunbonnets and scarfs that were part of the apparel of the women of the frontier. More reading was done first, illustrations drawn, and patterns made.

The boys made the following articles of clothing: "deerskin shirts," belts, and "coonskin caps." (Burlap sacks were used.)

The girls made: sunbonnets and scarfs. Some of the girls supplied their own material. Others used unbleached muslin. Many brought full skirts from home to complete their costume.

9. Made a spinning wheel for play purposes. This activity was not foreseen by the teacher. However, one morning a boy arrived in school with an old bicycle wheel and stated that he was going to get "Bert" to help him make a spinning wheel for the cabin. The teacher had difficulty in imagining what the outcome would be. However, with the aid of books on clothing from our school library, the boys worked with enthusiasm and determination. They succeeded in making a rather respectable spinning wheel and in explaining how to use it to the class. Although it didn't work very well in really spinning yarn, it was clear that the principle of its use was understood by the constructors. The girls enjoyed using it during play time.

10. Made imitation horn-hooks.

11. Tanned a rabbit skin. (Directions Bonser and Mossman.)

12. Washed, carded, spun, and wove wool. The art supervisor brought some raw wool to our room and showed the children how to wash it, card it and spin it. She left with them raw wool, carders, a spindle and a colonial box loom. During work period and at play time the children experimented with some of the processes.

13. Made candles. Candle-making was shared by all. Some made the candles, using a candle mould, which was an exact reproduction of the colonial type, secured from the art department. Others dipped theirs. Two of the boys had made a candle rack of branches on which the dipped candles were hung. The story from *Candlelight Tales* by Margaret Phelan was enjoyed at this time.

14. Made soap. Recipe was secured from Teachers' Guide to Child Development— Intermediate Grades, page 170.

15. Gave oral reports to solve class and committee problems and contributed findings and ideas to the class enterprise.

16. Painted pictures of early settlers engaged in home activities or depicting an episode in an early settler's life.

17. Wrote stories of people of the early settlements, their activities, and their homes in which individual children were particularly interested.

18. Made a book with a child-designed cover to compile the stories, reports, and poems written by the group members during the study.

19. Prepared a short program for the parents to be given on the day of Open House. It was decided to serve "tea" to the parents and to divide the class into committees to guide the visitors and explain everything they wished to know.

It was necessary to refer back to our questions and reorganize our learnings so that we might most effectively present the most important things we had learned about early settlers and living in early settlements. See chart "Outline of Our Study."

The children decided upon general topics about which our questions asked. These were written on the board, and suggestions were made for the rearrangement of their order. Important subtopics were listed under each topic. Each child volunteered to prepare a report on one of the subtopics so that the class might review their learnings. After the reports each committee felt quite prepared to explain to the visitors what they wished to know. The Outline was as follows:

I. *Where the Early Settlers Lived*
   A. The Virginia Settlement
   B. The Plymouth Settlement
   C. The Massachusetts Bay and Connecticut Settlements
   D. The New York Settlement
   E. The Carolina and Maryland Settlements
   F. The Pennsylvania Settlement
   G. The Georgia Settlement
   H. The Kentucky Settlement

II. *How the Early Settlers Lived*
   A. Homes
      1. Location
         a. Clearing of the ground
      2. Size
      3. Furnishings
      4. Fireplace
      5. Dishes and utensils
      6. Heat and light
   B. Clothing
      1. Material
         a. Skins
         b. Textiles
      2. Style
   C. Food
      1. Kinds
         a. Animals

   b. Fish
   c. Plants
      2. Preparation
   D. Industries
   E. Travel and communication
   F. Churches
   G. Schools
   H. Amusements
   I. Government

III. *Indian Neighbors*
   A. Indian Friends
   B. Indian Enemies

IV. *Leaders in the Early Settlements*
The day of Open House the committees stationed themselves in places convenient to explain the making of the articles in our room and seemed to have a glorious time expounding their knowledge.

20. Prepared and gave a "frontier tea" in our log cabin for the parents on the afternoon of Open House. The foods served were typical of colonial days:

Raspberry Shrub, a punch made of raspberry juice.

Johnnycake, cut in small squares and served with butter and a single preserved strawberry on each.

Maple sugar

Nuts

Parched corn

These dishes used in serving were collected and checked for authenticity. The hosts and hostesses dressed in their costumes.

21. Enjoyed looking at real or copies of articles from colonial homes as: handwoven textiles, pewter dishes, a quilt and quilt patterns, a spice grinder, a sampler, a warming pan.

22. A girl brought a hand-woven bed cover which had been made by her great grandmother, who was a "covered wagon baby." Another girl brought a warming pan and a bellows which her mother uses to decorate her fireside. The teacher brought a Paul Revere handmade pewter bowl. (All enjoyed seeing on the box, "Handicraft by Revere, Revere Copper and Brass, Incorporated, Founded by Paul Revere in 1801.") A quilt and a collection of patterns was loaned by a mother for a few days. A teacher in the school delighted the children by showing her sampler to them.

23. Two of the children brought daguerreotypes and tintypes and displayed much pride in their ancestry.

24. Enjoyed some illustrations of: different types of colonial homes, different types of colonial furniture, and aspects of colonial life.

25. Read stories telling about homes and furniture, occupations and amusements of the people, and leaders and heroes of the early days.

26. Enjoyed music of the colonial and pioneer periods. Also: No. 7117 "Spinning Chorus" from The Flying Dutchman.

27. Listened to Standard School Broadcast of Pioneer Music.

28. Enjoyed single pictures with art value:

Boughton: *Pilgrim Going to Church*
Marr, Carl: *Gossip*
Jacque, Charles: *The Lost Sheep*
Mauve, Anton: *Landscape with Sheep*
Millet: *Girl Churning*
Mosler: *Birth of the Flag*
Mosler: *Ring, Ring for Liberty*

29. Examined exhibits on hides and leather, wool and vegetable dyes.

30. Enjoyed stories read by the teacher.

31. Examined a copy of the Declaration of Independence, and pictures of national heroes.

32. Read stories silently for pleasure dealing particularly with colonists and pioneers and with related subjects as Indians and animals.

Outcomes: (On a 5B Level)

A. *Understandings that:*

1. The nation, the advantages of which we enjoy, was started by people who struggled with wilderness and built self-supporting democratic communities across the continent.

2. The red man's continent was one of vast forests, wide plains, deserts and mountains—full of resources that had not been utilized by the Indians.

3. White men came to explore and settle the continent for such purposes as: to spread religious teaching; to attain riches through the discovery of precious metals; trade with the Indians or acquisition of unclaimed land; to establish homes in a land where the type of worship was not dictated; to escape from besetting problems in their old home and to build a new life; and to satisfy love of adventure and free life—in short to obtain health, happiness and good fortune.

Specific Facts That Were Learned

Colonists	Leader	Location	Time	Significant features
Jamestown	John Smith	Virginia	1607	Men searching for gold
French	Samuel de Champlain	Canada	1608	French traders and missionaries
Pilgrims	John Carver	Plymouth	1620	Homes, religious freedoms, Mayflower
	William Bradford	Plymouth		
	William Preston	Massachusetts		
Dutch	West India Co.	New York	1623	Fur trading
Puritans	John Winthrop	Salem, Mass.	1628	Homes, religious freedom
Maryland	Lord Baltimore	Maryland	1634	Homes, Catholic church
Rhode Island	Roger Williams	Rhode Island	1636	Government and church divided
Quaker	William Penn	Pennsylvania	1682	Penn paying Indians for land (show Quaker costumes)
Georgia	James Oglethorpe	Savannah, Ga.	1732	Home for imprisoned debtors
Kentucky	Daniel Boone	Kentucky	1775	Hunting ground of Indian tribes (Betterland first settlement beyond Appalachian)

4. Topography, climate, native animals and vegetation, attitude of the Indians toward the settlers, the character of the people, and the purpose of its settlement affected the manner of living and the success of the various pioneer communities.

5. The howling wilderness of the continent was fraught with many and difficult problems which the pioneer had to solve largely through his own resourcefulness and courage.

6. The early colonizers brought to America the English language and laws, European traditions and religion, and a knowledge of how to utilize the natural resources to live in a more "civilized" or advanced way than the Indians.

7. The Indians were gradually driven back and overwhelmed by the white man.

8. That such qualities as courage, self-reliance, imagination and willingness to work steadily and hard characterize the pioneer.

9. The explorers, hunters, trappers and traders preceded the settlers into the wilderness.

    From 1607 to 1890 the ways of living were much the same in every new settlement—simple, rough, and generally dangerous. The ways of living in New England between 1620 and 1700 were similar to the ways in Pennsylvania between 1720 and 1850 and to those in the northern woodlands as late as 1890. The frontier gradually moved west. Log cabins were first located at Jamestown—then Plymouth. While they were being replaced by better, larger frame buildings, migrators were building them farther out in the wilderness.

10. Pioneers always looked for rivers and valleys to give them the easiest way of traveling. Trading posts and forts, which grew into cities, were located along or at the fork of waterways.

11. While the pioneers did not settle this country with the determination to found a nation apart from the mother country, later events caused the colonies to go into war in order to gain independence and carve out their own governmental destiny.

12. The pioneers set up as a guiding governmental principle ideals of good democratic living. They are expressed in the Preamble to the Constitution.

13. The fundamental needs of all people are food, clothing and shelter.

B. *Appreciations of:*

1. Colonial and pioneer life as an example of adaptation of life to physical and social conditions.

2. The high ideals that guided the colonists in forming a new government.

3. The sterling qualities of the pioneer—his courage, hardy endurance, resourcefulness and service.

4. The influence of the pioneer on our present ways of living.

5. The quaintness and charm of such colonial heirlooms as daguerreotypes, tintypes, samplers, quilts, utensils, rugs, furniture, dishes, and so on.

6. The comforts and conveniences of today as compared with those of the pioneer.

7. Beautiful pictures, depicting colonial and pioneer life.

8. The necessity of using wisely the vast resources of our country.

C. *Attitudes:*

1. The pleasure and satisfaction derived from contributing to a social enterprise. The "satisfyingness" of tolerance, consideration, co-operation and helpfulness toward fellow workers. (If dramatic play is to be satisfying, these attitudes have to be established.)

2. Sincerity in forming good work, health reading and language habits.

3. Tenaciousness in utilizing a variety of materials in studying a problem.

4. Openmindedness in verifying opinions or statements.

D. *Specific Facts [2] and Skills:*

1. Learned names, location and significant characteristics of early settlements.
    Most of the children, through discus-

[2] An interesting and significant incident took place as the children planned the exhibit for parents. One child said, "You know how parents are! They will surely ask us if we learned any facts! We better have some ready!" Whereupon a committee went over the unit and picked out the important dates and names. The children had had five years of modern instruction and were used to taking facts for granted while concentrating on the functional outcomes.

sion, research work and continual contact with the time line had firmly fixed in their minds such subject matter as that shown in the table on page 389.

2. Learned much information concerning the life and problems of early settlers in answer to proposed questions.

3. Learned processes involved in cloth making, soap making, candle making, skin tanning, food preservation, sugar making, wood carving, quilt and rug making.

4. Practiced using reference material: books, maps, and encyclopedia. Used indices, tables of contents, card files, and dictionaries.

5. Practiced making oral reports, extemporaneous and prepared.

6. Practiced evaluating materials and in making and taking constructive criticisms.

7. Practiced English composition—improvement in punctuation, margin, indentations, and use of capitals.

8. Practiced correct forms in letter writing.

9. Practiced using tools for construction.

10. Practiced washing, carding, spinning, and weaving wool.

11. Used wall maps and made our maps.

12. Practiced using crayolas, water colors, and calcimine in expression of ideas.

13. Learned to spell words needed in written reports.

14. Practiced to improve definite handwriting skills.

15. Practiced measuring yards, feet, and inches; figuring cups, pints, quarts, and gallons; and computing.

16. Computed arithmetically the number of years between "then and now," in connection with important happenings, the ages of leaders at the time of many events such as the age of Daniel Boone when he killed his first bear.

17. Learned songs of colonial and pioneer life.

18. In addition the following songs were enjoyed:
Billy Boy—*Music Hour IV*, page 112.
The Frontiers—*Music Hour IV*, page 104.
Turkey in the Straw—*Music Hour, IV*, page 137.
Pop Goes the Weasel—*Music Hour IV*, page 147.

Daniel Boone—*Folk and Art*, page 19.
Pioneer—*Intermediate Music*, page 104.
Oh, Susanna—*Music Hour II*, page 94.

19. Learned colonial and pioneer dances.

20. Increased skill in:
   I. Reading.
      A. *For information*
         1. Using reference books efficiently.
            a. Using a table of contents and index.
            b. Skimming—learning to read just that part of the page, chapter, or book which answers the question.
         2. Organizing material read.
      B. *For pleasure*
         1. Choosing from available selection and reading a variety of materials such as stories, poetry, travel, science, biography, and history.
      C. *With an enlarged vocabulary*
   II. Carrying on a discussion.
      A. Making thoughtful contributions.
      B. Listening courteously.
      C. Evaluating the information given.
      D. Drawing conclusions.
   III. Planning and attacking new problems.
   IV. Self-expression through language, music, bodily rhythm, and manual activities.
   V. Spelling words needed in written work.
   VI. Solving arithmetical problems that arise, and computing with measurement and figures.
   VII. Using a variety of materials in solving a problem as, maps, globes, dictionary, books, visual aids, and museum pieces.

DISCUSSION QUESTIONS

The foregoing account may be discussed at any length depending upon questions raised by students.

A collection of unit plans and logs should be available for distribution to the class for analysis.

CHAPTER 16: Providing Opportunity for Creative Expression

A visitor to the Vienna School of Arts and Crafts, exclaiming over the beautiful creative work of the pupils, asked the Director, Cizek, "How do you do it?" The Director replied, "I don't do it. I take off the lid; the other art masters clap it on—that is the only difference." Contrary to common opinion, original, creative expression is a normal human reaction which wells up and emerges under favorable conditions. Among the most important conditions are opportunity, freedom, permissiveness, resulting from removal of restraint and imposition. Taking off the lid is not synonymous with unbridled freedom, as previous chapters have made clear. Other important factors are also involved, as we shall see.

1: DEFINITIONS AND EXPLANATIONS.

There has been a remarkable upsurge of interest in creativity and in creative education in this country since approximately 1950-1955, although it should not be overlooked that interest in creativity goes back many hundreds of years. Current efforts are not confined to schools and professional educators, nor to the arts. Scientists, philosophers, anthropologists, literary men, and many others are involved. Some of the best symposia on this topic have been by interdisciplinary groups.

Examination of the large and growing literature shows significant differences between schoolmen and other groups. The contrast between any of the interdisciplinary symposia and the symposia or series of articles in professional education journals is not too happy. The scientists present systematically organized summaries, obviously derived from basic concepts and provocative in impact on the reader. The educators present *general* statements which, we sadly record, are often muddled and sentimental. Specialists in art education, music education, language arts, and some other fields present statements which, in contrast, are usually well organized and useful.

The indictment of the generalists and the criticisms to be illustrated below are no carping criticisms of teachers or schoolmen generally. There are also some brilliant exceptions to the indictment. The fault lies squarely with the teacher-training institutions which have never properly organized the basic background materials necessary for educational workers.

In these articles on creativity in professional educational journals and in the discussions in teacher-training institutions, definitions are spun out of the inner consciousness of naïve enthusiasts who never thought to consult definitive sources, or even usage by competent writers. The glamor associated with the word *creative* and its overuse by educators have caused many to arrogate the word to many dubious educational procedures. Moreover, a few discussions of creativity are even internally contradictory, and their omission of historic fact in the field is tragic.

In 1950 Guilford,[1] a psychologist, pointed out that *basic research* on creativity was almost non-existent. This statement was a strong impetus, among others, to the current emphasis on research. However, *descriptive, analytic,* and *genetic* accounts of creativity have been appearing for a long time. References to it may be found in the classic literature of two thousand years ago. Ribot's *Essay on the Creative Imagination* appeared in 1900 and was translated into English in 1906. The German literature on discovery (which will be discussed later), closely related to creativity, has been appearing since 1806. On the basis of observation and critical analysis, Ribot and the German writers said many things which modern research has confirmed. In some instances the conclusions are practically identical.

Anthropologists, psychologists, and the leading theoretical scientists in mathematics, physics, biology, and other fields know this background and, hence, write with power and authority. Educators generally do not know the historical and scientific background, nor sometimes even the demands of semantics and logic, hence much of their writing either (*a*) contributes to confusion on definitions, principles, and processes or (*b*) presents unsystematic and sometimes misleading suggestions for school practice.

Again we must repeat, no faultfinding with teachers is intended by these criticisms. The responsibility lies with the teacher-training institutions. The unpleasant facts must be set down in order to improve understanding and practice.[2]

The necessity for definition. Sensible discussion is impossible without definition. A universe of discourse is impossible without it. As Dewey long ago said, "the aboriginal logical sin, from which flows most bad intellectual consequences, is failure to define." Definitions do change, however, under impact of cultural change. Enlightenment can be delayed by striving for too precise definition too early. Tumin,[3] an anthropologist, sounds a sensible warning but one which, out of context, could be easily misunderstood: ". . . one of the most senseless arguments . . . is the argument which starts with someone insisting on a definition of terms." Tumin immediately makes clear that it is the extreme form of this argument which is senseless. Further, he indicates that individuals do define and act on their definitions.

We do need definitions of terms to be sure we are talking about generally the same things. But we do not need precise definitions to start talking.

We had better be concerned with (the individual's) definitions, his orientation, what he thinks is in store for him, the goals he seeks.

He points out that definitions develop and become more precise as further discussion brings enlightenment.

Creativity: a definition. The precise and unmistakable language of Bronowski,[4] internationally known mathematician with notable achievements in other fields, is accepted here: "I have used three words to describe these far-reaching changes; *discovery, invention,* and *creation.* There are contexts in which one of these words is more appropriate than the others."

He says further that Columbus *discovered* the West Indies. They were there all the

[1] J. P. Guilford, "Creativity," *The American Psychologist,* Vol. 5 (September, 1950), pp. 444-454.
———, *Bibliography of Thinking* (Los Angeles, Univ. of Southern California, 1953).
[2] See organized bibliography at close of chapter for different classes of literature in the field. It is necessary to be vigilant and discriminatory while reading in this field.

[3] Melvin M. Tumin, "Education, Development, and the Creative Process," in *Aesthetic Form and Education,* Michael F. Andrews, ed. (Syracuse Univ. Press, 1958), pp. 28-29.
[4] J. Bronowski, "The Creative Process," *Scientific American,* Vol. 199 (September, 1958), pp. 59 ff.

time. Bell *invented* the telephone by combining a set of known facts and principles. A *creative* act finds a new unity in the variety of nature, sees a likeness among items not thought of before. Induction in science, which is always partly speculative, guesses at a new unity which the facts do not strictly imply. Creation is a vivid personal matter, the person is completely involved and identified with the process. Creativity in the arts is similar in that a single mind combines in a unique whole, elements which separately may have appeared in other productions. The elements are combined, not as in an invention but in a new presentation not heretofore known. The personal element is very apparent in these areas; the new appears because of the particular mind involved. Bronowski cites as illustrations Shakespeare's plays, Blake's poetry (on which he has written), Young's theory of light, Planck's hail of quanta, Hamilton's equations. [5] We may add the Copernican and Darwinian theories. Scientific writers refer also to theories stated by Freud, Bohr, and Pavlov.

Creativity, as used in this chapter, means the ability to or quality of producing something new, unique, original, not-before-existent. This is the original meaning, one which has been accepted for centuries.

Creativity confused with discovery. Statements appearing about 1925 held that all learning was creative. When a child learns that two and two are four, that fire will burn him, that ice is slippery, or that doing as he is told will please adults, he has indulged in a creative process. The child learns something he never knew before, he does it all by himself. This is said to be creative even if what he learns is well known to the teacher

and to the whole adult world. The idea acquired by the learner could never have been acquired by anyone else, hence it is created. It exists in the learner's experience, new, original, and created by him. This is said to be an individual or psychological interpretation and entitled to equal standing with the older view, the socioanthropological definition. This interpretation that anything a child learns for the first time is creative cannot possibly be supported by semantics or logic, let alone historical usage. It could not satisfy the requirements of an effective universe of discourse. It is not found in discussions of basic sciences, or literature, or the arts. It appears rarely in psychological materials. It appears chiefly in educational writing, but references are growing fewer.

A semiflippant illustration may help to demonstrate the limitations of this definition. Assume that a child asserts that two and two are five and refuses to budge. It is his answer, he created it all by himself. It is new, original, unique to him—and to the rest of the world as well! How do we handle this? We may give him more experiences with things and numbers, but he still holds to his idea. We then say, gently or authoritatively, that two and two are four. That is the way it is in the world, and he better learn it that way! We have referred his "creative" act to something that, like the West Indies, was always there. The fact existed long before the child set out to "create," and in a showdown the already existing fact wins. Creativity is not involved. The child's processes in arriving at known facts, however, may be of fundamental importance for education. Children should be freed to *discover* the world about them, instead of having it *imposed* upon them.

Summary of arguments in favor of distinction between discovery and creation. Whitehead [6] makes a cogent statement of the difference between these two processes:

[5] A naïve young man referred to the remarkable articles in the *Scientific American*, reported back: "These men are dealing with great, big, important things. I want to know about creativity in little children." The creative *processes* of little children and of distinguished scientists are very much alike, however much the *materials* may differ.

[6] Alfred North Whitehead, *The Aims of Education and Other Essays* (New York, Macmillan, 1929).

"The thought which science evokes is logical thought. Now logic is of two kinds: the logic of discovery and the logic of the discovered." The psychologist, Calvin Taylor's [7] statement of the same view is even more forthright: "Until shown otherwise, I believe that quite different psychological processes are involved when we learn existing knowledge and systems than when we produce new knowledge, and new systems." Taylor continues with a strong plea for the desertion of education which memorizes, repeats, and worships the past in favor of education which encourages minds which can manipulate and play with knowledge, using it as a springboard for future new ideas.

There are various other reasons why thoughtful people refuse to confuse the processes and use the word *creativity* for what is essentially *discovery. First,* the definition of creativity as given has been used for centuries by both scientific and literary men and by laymen. No significant change in usage has taken place over the centuries. *Second,* many things said to be "created" by an individual are themselves products of many individual creative contributions over, sometimes, many centuries. No one person could have created them in the first place. The number system, the alphabet, many conventions of language, of social intercourse, of law and government are excellent illustrations of complex social mechanisms slowly built up over periods of time. [8] Therefore, to say that a little child "creates" *his* number system, not *the* number system, is an infantile quibble. The number system is an intricate, difficult, and complex system created in the first place only through the cumulative efforts of many bright adults. A child cannot possibly *create* it, but he can *discover* it. Too

[7] Calvin W. Taylor, "The Creative Individual: A New Portrait in Giftedness," *Educational Leadership,* Vol. 18 (October, 1960), pp. 7-12.

[8] C. H. Judd, *The Psychology of Social Institutions* (New York, Macmillan, 1926). The authoritative volume on the creation of social institutions, mechanisms, and conventions. Excellent background reading for advanced students.

often he has it *imposed* upon him. *Third,* nearly all exponents of the erroneous view of creativity overlook the fact that the circumstances in which the child's act of "creativity" takes place are fundamentally different from those in which the original creation took place. The child who discovers (creates) the number system, or any other important learning, is surrounded by an environment which constantly forces the system upon him. Not only that, the number system is forced upon him in mature form and not as first glimpsed by the original individual who set up a part of it. The child is surrounded by a world of counting and numbering. The nursery introduces him to the adventures of the three little pigs, the three little kittens, the ten little Indians, and his five "piggy" toes. The child cannot look at pictures, billboards, movies, or television, nor can he win advertising prizes without constant contact with a systematically going concern—the number system. All the adults around him use the words and processes of this system. Not so the person into whose consciousness came for the first time the first minute awareness of the number system, nor those who first became aware of various additions to the number system. Those earlier individuals evolved, originated, devised, invented, called into being, produced, achieved, *created* the number system as we use it, not merely in their consciousness for the first time but for the first time anywhere. It may be said that the natural universe forced the number system upon them, at least, upon those intelligent enough to see it. That is, the number system was discovered. Bringing such discoveries to society for the first time has been universally accepted as creative. The circumstances in which this first and original devising or creation took place are in no way similar to that in which later learners "created" their knowledge.

Discovery is a most important learning process. The argument over discovery and creativity served a very important issue, namely, to sharpen attention to imposition of knowledge, long opposed by schoolmen and psychologists. The real question is to contrast discovery with imposition. Learning should never be the blind acceptance of imposed understandings, attitudes, or skills. Valid research shows that even in the acquisition of more or less fixed skills through functional practice, the methods and insight which the individual contributes are important in producing learning. But note that it is a socially recognized skill that is being acquired. The acquisition of ancient routines and skills and of socially approved understandings and attitudes cannot be called truly creative. The processes of discovery—but discovery with full place for individual methods, questions, suggestions, and even modifications—seem to account fully for the matter. Mearns, [9] one of the acknowledged leaders of creative education, uses the term *creative* less and less, because of the curious interpretations placed upon it. He substitutes the term *individual contribution*. The individual does and should make an individual contribution when he learns, an individual contribution to what he learns. His view preserves the value of individuality and uniqueness of learning but avoids confusion with the original meaning of *creative*.

If we set out to develop creative, independent individuals we must inevitably introduce them to, among other things, the world of nature and of men. The history of mankind and of his institutions will be studied. [10] The learner will read the long anthropological, biological, and sociological record. He will see the impersonal inevitability of human institutions and systems; he will recognize their use and value. These things will come to him neither as things to be imposed upon him, nor as things which he may

accept, reject, "create," as he pleases. The introduction to the world and to human culture, properly done, will neither stifle thought and critical analysis, nor indoctrinate, nor yet make for anarchic individualism. The learner at all levels in good learning situations, in or out of school, will *discover* facts, standards, rules, social conventions, social inventions, personality traits, relationships, and processes without number. He does not *create* them, but he will *discover how to create* others, or how to improve creatively those existing. Children and adults *discover* untold amounts of knowledge which they did not and could not *create*. In other words, the modern school is designed to introduce the learner to the world and to culture in such a way that he discovers this world and does not have it thrust upon him unready and unwilling. Hopkins says, [11] "No individual should be 'pushed out' into the culture faster than he can differentiate creative behaviors which will ensure a creative remaking of the self and personality." The individual discovers not only the organized society in which he lives but discovers how it evolved. He discovers, even more important, how each succeeding generation improved both the social structure and understanding of the physical world. He *discovers* finally the methods by which he may continue the *creative* process.

Writers on teaching have for a long time discussed methods of discovery which do not differ from the so-called "creative" methods except that they are not called creative. Herbart, [12] in the early nineteenth

[9] Hughes Mearns, "Some Notes on the Individual Contribution," *Educational Method*, Vol. 17 (January, 1938), pp. 166-169.

[10] W. H. Burton, *Introduction to Education* (New York, Appleton, 1934), pp. 22-30; 60-65; 82-93; particularly 33-36 contain brief compact summaries of this general principle of education.

[11] L. T. Hopkins, *Interaction* (Boston, Heath, 1941), p. 235. Hopkins uses *creative* in this sentence under the second definition; however, this word could be dispensed with without detracting from his excellent discussion. The individual's contribution is prominent but the culture materials are recognized as independent.

[12] It is not the purpose of this introductory volume pedantically to impose remote primary sources upon beginning students. Instructors and advanced students of method may be interested, however, in the following references which are far too little known by some of the American writers on teaching:

century, advocated methods, later sadly formalized by his followers, which are completely modern in the advocacy of discovery in contrast to imposition and memorization.

Working on these lines with the guidance of her teacher [the child] will be able gradually *to make the whole multiplication table for herself.* Anyone who has taught arithmetic thus, knows the joyfully active interest which can be aroused even in a child naturally disinclined to it, how ready she is to apply what she knows, to set problems to the teacher, and finally to *discover* rules for herself. [13]

Even though subject matter seems to be the center, this paragraph is quite acceptable to moderns. A paragraph from Dickens in an earlier chapter made the same point but through clever satire. The presentation throughout this volume supports this general view of learning.

Traditional neglect of creative expression and of discovery. The announced purpose of the formal school has been for several centuries, "the preservation and passing on of cultural heritage." Widely accepted as it is, this is nevertheless an unfortunate aim if accepted without qualification. Such acceptance has resulted in much undesirable practice, in many literate but unintelligent adults. The school has been too much concerned

with *preserving* culture, too little with *contributing* to it. Emphasis has been upon a *static, fixed* culture, rather than upon a *dynamic, growing* culture. The aim has been to *inculcate* the culture, rather than to *develop contributors* to the culture. There has been much of acquisition, impression, and intake, less of expressing, producing, and outpouring; much drilling in, little leading out. Methods have been those of teacher-dominated assignments and drill, in contrast to participatory planning, deciding, and developing. The traditional school not only neglected creative expression; it very often actively repressed it. Only a few great teachers stimulated creativity here and there in high school and college. All this is natural in an exploitive and acquisitive society. The changing emphasis which is emerging in the modern school is a part of the emerging social theory and order.

"Passing on the culture" is itself, incidentally, a misleading statement. Passing on the total culture with its contradictions and struggles might actually serve educational purposes. At present only those segments of the culture are passed on to youth which those who rule the state or church wish passed on.

Modern emphasis upon creative expression. Emphasis upon originality and creativity has been honored for long on the level of scientific research and technical education. The modern school is extending this emphasis upon and opportunity for creative expression to general education from kindergarten through college. The development of personality is desirable in and for itself. Meanings, attitudes, and appreciations are distinctly enhanced through efforts at creative expression. Creative self-expression is a normal characteristic of desirable living. The person whose response is original, inventive, and atypical is extremely important socially. Progress takes place through constructive variations from the accepted and the routine.

Provision for creative expression of many

J. F. Herbart, *Allgemeine Pädagogik aus dem Zweck der Erziehung Abgeleitet* (Gottingen, J. F. Rower, 1806).

Wilhelm Rein, *Pädagogik in Systematischer Darstellung* (Langensalza, Herman Beyer und Söhne, 1902), I, pp. 67 ff.; II, pp. 186 ff., and elsewhere.

———, *Das Erste Schuljahr* (Leipzig: H. Bredt), pp. 150-158, and elsewhere.

———, *Encyklopädisches Handbuch der Pädagogik* (Langensalza, H. Beyer und Söhne, 1895), I, pp. 594-596.

Theodor Wiget, *Die Formalen Stufen des Unterrichts. Eine Einführung in die Schriften Zillers,* Fifth edition, 1895. Pp. 42 ff.

Tuiskon Ziller, *Allgemeine Pädagogik* (Leipzig, H. Matthes, 1892), pp. 257-296.

[13] Henry M. and Emmie Felkin, *An Introduction to Herbart's Science and Practice of Education* (Boston, Heath, 1900), pp. 92-93.

kinds and for all types of children is one of the finest contributions of the modern school. The theoretical discussions began appearing many decades ago; practical efforts became prominent from approximately 1917-1925. Publication of articles on the topic reached a peak in 1931. Steady, continuing interest since then has been marked by attention to the psychological background and, since 1950-1955, to research into favoring conditions as well as to descriptions of product.

A tradition of originality, of inventiveness, of creativity in the school can be developed in place of the present dominance of passivity, acquiescence, and acceptance. Great benefits would accrue not only to the school and to the individual but to society and to civilization.

The current emphasis upon creativity is a modern revival. The principle, however, is ancient. Florence, Italy, during the thirteenth and fourteenth centuries had a pervasive tradition of creativity and produced artists out of proportion to ordinary expectancy. This is illustrated by the story that when one of Giotto's pictures was completed and to be hung in St. Mark's, the town closed down for a holiday. The picture was escorted from the studio to the church by the populace with flowers, garlands, and songs. History has recorded other examples similar to that of Florence. One of the essentials for creative production is an environment which expects and encourages it. Creative artists do in many instances, however, persist in unfavorable situations.

The great upsurge of creative thought in Greece following the Peloponnesian war, the vivid and dynamic life of the Elizabethan era toward the end of the sixteenth century, are further illustrations. The remarkable rise of mechanical inventiveness in the United States which accompanied the development of the nation during the Westward Movement is another instance. Each of these periods, it should be noted, was a period in which previous values, standards, and

processes were changing. The current emphasis on creative education is no accident.

Who is capable of creative expression? Practically everyone is able to create. The lay citizen and innumerable traditional teachers think of creative expression only in terms of special talent or genius. The individual of special talent is rare; he begins production early, as a rule, with training secondary at first; his productions are easily and immediately recognized as possessing high merit. Thinking of creative ability only in terms of special talent emphasizes its rarity. Special talent is regarded as inherited; its processes are hidden and mysterious. Ordinary pupils, it is thought, will not have it and ordinary teachers could not improve it if it did appear. The school can only give genius an opportunity to flower and to reveal itself. Naïve acceptance of common sense has again misled the citizen and teacher. Critical scrutiny of common-sense experience reveals a different picture. The ordinary child and the average citizen who clearly do not possess special talent are nevertheless continuously original and creative in little ways in everyday affairs. Adaptations of tools and machinery, ingenious repairs and temporary, makeshift, homely, labor-saving devices, special adaptations of materials, quick repartee and keen argument, and clear discriminating judgment in confused situations are all partly original and creative. They are clearly akin to the behaviors of special talent; the difference is in degree. The observer who is blinded by his conception of creativity as special talent dismisses the everyday lower-level instances with such comment as, "clever," "not bad," "mother wit," "the boy has a head on him," "he has gumption, hasn't he?" "old trigger brain," and many others. The creativity of the ordinary illustrations is obscured; but these are all cases of acumen, sagacity, penetrating insight, perspicacity, all of which involve departure from the accepted, the known, the routine.

This is true also when we turn to fields long associated with creativity—the graphic and plastic arts, prose and poetry writing, dramatization, rhythm and the dance. Genuinely creative products are secured from any and all kinds of children in the modern school. Many underprivileged children, living under most unfavorable conditions and coming from the poorest social levels, will produce acceptable results when placed in favorable learning situations. The Russian schools, after the revolution and prior to the shift to ruthless indoctrination, produced astonishing creative work both with adults who had been illiterate all their lives and with children from families with no background of education. The modern school in the United States has long since demonstrated that average children in good learning environment engage in creative activity as naturally as in spelling and arithmetic. Whole volumes of illustrations and scores of descriptive articles are immediately available. The creative productions of the ordinary individual will take no prizes and will be placed in no museums, but they do contribute measurably to the growth and development of the individual himself.

An error opposite to that of emphasizing genius, rarity, and inherent ability is to forget all standards and regard as creative anything whatever produced by a child. This is a natural outgrowth of confused definitions of creativity. Any messing of colors on paper or "any flubdub in written composition can pass as creative self-expression." Caution is necessary, however. Children's representations of their own ideas in primary grades will not meet and must not be judged by adult standards. The children can not only explain what they are doing and why, but other children are often able to recognize what their classmates are symbolizing even though the adult cannot. Form, detail, technique, and skill come with maturity and experience. Form and desirable standards are differentiated out of continuous experience under sympathetic guidance. All this

has been made clear many times in preceding chapters.

Modern psychology believes that all or nearly all children can develop recognizable levels of creative expression. Mearns believes that all could, if we but knew how to reach those who now do not respond. Research has shown, for instance, that all individuals can be taught to draw acceptably if reputable training begins early enough. School guidance of creative expression is as essential as is its guidance of how to spell, how to compute, and how to solve problems.

Characteristics of creative individuals. Eric Fromm believes [14] a creative person has the capacity to be puzzled, the ability to concentrate, a sense of self and confidence in self. He is willing to let go of all "certainties" and illusions. The latter is very similar to one of Francis Bacon's admonitions. Tuska, in his book *Inventors and Inventions,*[15] says an inventor must develop the habit of observing and of questioning what he observes. Ask questions: Why did that happen? Why did not something else happen? Who started that? What stopped it? Why can a spider walk on its own web without getting tangled? Could a spider's thread be synthesized? Daydreams with a purpose. Here we have James Harvey Robinson's [16] emphasis on the "wonderers." Rhodes [17] says that any group, including school children, has a few with off-beat ideas. The conventional "go-along-with-the-crowd" individual regards these individuals as crazy. But the real point is: How crazy? Crazy enough to be useful? Crazy enough to change a trend? Crazy enough to revolutionize an industry—or a way of life?

Lists of general characteristics are as numerous as writers on the topic. Readers

[14] From *Creativity and Its Cultivation,* a symposium, Harold H. Anderson, ed. (New York, Harper, 1959).
[15] (New York, McGraw, 1957.)
[16] *Humanizing of Knowledge* (New York, George H. Doran, 1923), Ch. 1.
[17] Mel Rhodes, "An Analysis of Creativity," *Phi Delta Kappan* (April, 1961), pp. 305-310.

may make up their own lists. A composite which includes the chief ideas from several lists is:

Flexibility, easy and spontaneous personality
Intuitiveness
Observation, curiosity, and sensitivity to problems
Free flow of ideas, novel and original ideas
Questioning attitude
Strong motivation
Ability to see similarities and differences more commonly than ordinarily
Ability to handle complexities without getting confused, to rearrange and reorganize
Ability to tolerate disorder without being confused
Strong sense of self and self-confidence

Obviously creative individuals do not endear themselves to traditional or formal teachers. And therein lies a serious difficulty with education.

Guidance of creative expression handicapped by lack of knowledge. The literature of creative education until quite recently could be said to belong to the "Eureka" school of interpretation! Archimedes, leaping from the bathtub shouting, "Eureka," has made that creative moment forever historic. This famous story, however, focuses on the outward manifestation and upon a striking, non-fundamental aspect of the creative act. Not a single clue to the process is given. The story, furthermore, is misleading in that it gives spurious corroboration to the common misconception that creation is a momentary flash, a brilliant and sudden solution. Such climactic moments are a part of the creative process, as we shall see, but are far from being the whole of it. So also with many descriptions of creativity in school. Eureka! Look what my children have written! Look at their beautiful pictures! Behold the clay modeling, the interpretive dancing, the original dramatization! But when we ask, how did the children do this? how were you able to stimulate this expression? there has been no very helpful reply.

The focus has been on the description of unusual or dramatic results. The human-interest or news-value feature has been emphasized, especially if very little children or underprivileged children were involved. Teachers are in no wise to be blamed for this situation. They do not know what happened within the child. Teachers were not always aware analytically of their own processes of guidance. Some took refuge in obscurantism and mystery. Psychologists but rarely devoted much time to creative processses. Ribot's *Essay on the Creative Imagination* stood almost alone for a long time. Our position today, happily, is much better. Modern psychologists devote considerable attention to the problem. Many other sources furnished very much valuable guidance. This material is scattered in unusually far-flung sources. A huge job of collecting, analyzing, interpreting, and making available is still to be done. An excellent start has been made and excellent summaries of guidance may be presented.

DISCUSSION QUESTIONS FOR SECTION 1

The writer has found that the majority of students understand and accept the foregoing summary without difficulty. Brief discussion may be held if the class desires.

1. List any new concepts or beliefs which have come to you from reading this section. Clarified and amplified ideas may be listed also.

2. Recall and explain any incidents from your own life or schooling (or observed incidents) which were puzzling, or even inexplicable, at the time but for which you may now have some explanation.

3. List any concepts or principles which you cannot accept at the moment, or about which you are in doubt. State explicitly what your difficulty is. This is an important exercise in that it directs students and instructors to important points of emphasis or misunderstanding. (Instructors and students must be sharply on guard here against clichés about creativity, based on folklore and general misinformation.)

4. What prevalent practices in the classroom would have to be abandoned if the facts and principles in this section were accepted.

READINGS

This section is a faithful summary of explanations and definitions as found in general volumes, in texts on teaching which mention the topic, in texts in the special subjects. Hence further readings are not listed, the important general volumes being listed at the close of Section 2. Anyone wishing to read further at this point on the explanations and definitions may turn to those lists.

2: THE MAJOR OBSERVABLE PHASES OF THE CREATIVE PROCESS.

Creative activity follows developmental stages. All growth and all learning progress through stages. A baby babbles, learns to pronounce words, uses one-word sentences, makes mistakes in forming plurals and in indicating tense, produces simple sentences, and so on up to profound prose composition. The baby first has to be fed, then feeds itself very inaccurately using soft foods, learns slowly to manipulate various utensils and different foods, learns to manifest good table manners, and may even become a gourmet. Motor activity is at first diffuse, all parts of the body being involved, with gradual differentiation of skills and habits.

Creative activity, subtle as it is, also manifests developmental stages. Unawareness of these stages and of their great significance leads many teachers into serious blunders in all teaching, but particularly in the stimulation of creativity. Teachers of music and literary composition are notorious offenders, but teachers of art probably produce the most spectacular malpractice.

The chief major error is that production of a drawing or painting, a poem, a composition, or a dramatization is taken as the criterion of creative expression. The only genuine criterion is the free expression of the child who is working to fulfill a meaningful purpose, with appropriate regard for relation of means to consequence. Free expression contributes to the growth of the person and eventually to acceptable proficiency in the given field.

The chief reasons for this major error, with reference to graphic art, are, first, that the teacher has mistaken imitation for artistic production, and second, that the teacher has imposed adult standards of "reality" on the learner—and uninformed standards at that. All this is owing to ignorance of the nature and significance of the developmental stages through which learners must grow.

The subject matter of art differs from all other subject matters in that it is the same for all ages. Arithmetic has an orderly sequence of subject matter, arranged in ever increasing levels of difficulty, through which the learner must progress. In drawing, the four-year-old child, the fourteen-year-old youth, the forty-year-old adult all use the same subject matter. Each may draw a dog, a man, a house, a train, a lion, a wave, or a rose bush, but each draws these things very differently. A given child, in fact, draws these things differently at different age levels. Lowenfeld has a cogent discussion of this point. [18]

The answer to the question, "What makes the child express one and the same thing differently at different age levels?" will be of essential importance for the understanding of the child's creative work. It also will be significant for the nature of stimulation on the part of the teacher. What makes a child of four or five years express a man by drawing only a head and two legs? Does this really represent the child's knowledge of a human being? Certainly, every four- or five-year-old child knows that we have a body, two arms, hands, and even fingers. He even knows that we have fingernails if his attention is directed towards

[18] Viktor Lowenfeld, *Creative and Mental Growth: A Textbook on Art Education*, pp. 1-2, 62. Copyright, 1952, by The Macmillan Company and used with their permission. Chapter 1 should be read by all teachers.

See also an earlier book by the same author, *The Nature of Creative Activity* (New York, Harcourt, 1939), Chs. 3, 5, 7. Pages 155-272 contain excellent illustrations of children's drawings at all levels.

them. But no child of this age would ever draw such details. *What the child draws is his subjective experience of what is important to him during the act of drawing.* Therefore, the child only draws what is *actively* in his mind. Thus in such a drawing of a "man" we get only a report of the *active knowledge* the child has of a man while he was drawing. *In other words, the drawing gives us an excellent record of the things which are of especial mental or emotional importance to the child.*

For the child, art is not the same as it is for the adult. Art for the child is merely a means of expression. Since the child's thinking is different from that of the adult's, his expression must also be different. Out of this discrepancy between the adult's "taste" and the way in which a child expresses himself arise most of the difficulties and interferences in art teaching. I have seen and heard educators, intrigued by the beauty of children's drawings and paintings, asking for the "right" proportions and "good" color schemes. The child sees the world differently from the way he draws it. Precisely from our analysis of this discrepancy between the representation and the thing represented do we gain insight into the child's real experience. Therefore it is easy to understand that *any* correction by the teacher which refers to reality and not to the child's experience interferes greatly with the child's own expression. This interference starts perhaps when children scribble and eager parents expect to see something that fits their own adult conception. How ridiculous to overpower these little children's souls!

The teacher who insists that children draw "horses that look like horses," "trees that look like trees," is taking the most direct route to the destruction of any ability or wish to draw which the child may possess. As the child grows in emotional and intellectual maturity, as his experience becomes richer and more varied, the need for standards and skills emerges naturally. Youth will then work hard to draw "horses that look like horses." Another serious blunder may enter just here: the discouragement of those individuals who depart from standard forms to produce genuinely artistic work which is not of the mirror-of-nature type.

Various writers have presented the stages of development in the graphic arts. The following statement is adapted from Lowenfeld:

1. *Scribbling stages,* two to four years. First efforts at self-expression. Free drawing of lines having no representative or decorative purpose. Toward the end of this period the child names or titles the scribbles; they represent something to his imagination.

2. *Preschematic stage,* four to six years. First efforts at representation. Sometimes called the symbolic stage. Scribbles are isolated and named by the child as *mama, daddy, house, ball, dog.* A relationship wtih reality, however obscure, has been established.

3. *Schematic stage,* seven to nine years. The achievement of a concept of form. More formalized schema are developed for *mama, daddy, dog,* and so on, and these can be recognized as such by adults. Order within a given space also emerges.

4. *Dawning realism stage,* nine to eleven years. First efforts at independence, but without complete confidence because of increasing consciousness of significance of the environment. Child is no longer the judge of what is good, beautiful, correct.

5. *Pseudo-realistic stage,* eleven to thirteen. The beginnings of reasoning about productions. The unaware creative approach is changing to the critically aware approach.

6. *Stage of decision or the crisis of adolescence.* Critical awareness toward environment and representational outcome. Subjective relationship with symbols and schema gives way to increasing tendency to replace symbols and schema with a more realistic presentation.

[In an earlier book Lowenfeld called this the *Stage of Synthesis* in which there was a coordination of the mental, motor, and emotional growth of the learner toward improvement of the schema.]

The chief errors of adults in the early stages are asking "what is it?" or "what does it mean?" and insisting that the child make it "look like something."

The chief error in the middle stages is the imposition of conventional representations, the insistence on realism, on camera-like reproductions. This results in what Lowenfeld called earlier the stage of automatism, in which the child's efforts become stereotyped. Drawing now satisfies the adult;

it becomes easy for the child because there is no need for thought, individuality, or improvement. This successfully prevents the child from ever reaching higher levels.

The chief error at all stages is laughter (even if friendly), ridicule, or indifference. The material is not only meaningful to the child, even in the early stages, but it is peculiarly personal because it is the representation of his ideas and feelings. He identifies himself with it as he rarely does with other learning.

The development of skills: the use of models in creative learning. The discussion of the major phases and of the stages of growth in creative activity has indicated several times that serious errors may be made. Skill may be stressed at the expense of expression, and less often expression may be sought without much regard for skills. Models may be set up and pupils forced into sterile imitation, or all models may be denied to the learner. Imposition and direction may be overdone, or unbridled freedom may prevail. Careful balance among these several factors is necessary, and we may now turn to that topic.

Creative expression and the skills and techniques of expression. The modern school, as has been said, is often accused of neglecting skills and the necessary drill, of neglecting form and standards. This is nowhere more often said than in the field of creative expression, one of the modern school's chief triumphs. Again the uncritical reaction is false. The creative artist cannot improve his expression unless he improves the techniques and skills pertinent to his field and media. Every competent writer stresses the necessity for knowing the well-established conventions of form, for mastering a huge background of forms, patterns, and techniques. Every competent writer deals at length with the absolute necessity of painstaking practice for the acquisition of facile skills. The new school, however, *secures ex-*

pression first and allows the learner to discover the need for better skill, to differentiate it from the original whole situation. We are here discussing a principle made familiar by the whole of this volume. Children will practice faithfully and extensively upon any skills for which they can see meaning and which serve their purposes. Older pupils engage in hours of self-imposed practice to develop athletic skills. Golf-driving ranges are supported by adults who indulge in practice for an end which is important to them. Macomber [19] has an excellent paragraph:

Long periods of drill on color charts are a relatively purposeless and ineffective activity, yet a small group of children has been known to spend hours trying out different color combinations to get the particular brick color desired for the tile roof of a Spanish mission they were building. These children were confronted with a real problem. The corrugated cardboard used for the roof was a dirty brown, and this affected the final result. The calcimine paint, when dry, was of a different shade than when wet, so applications of different mixtures had to stand for some time before their true shades were apparent. The children discovered that they must keep records of each mix if they were to produce the desired shade in the quantity needed. Not only did these children receive much practice in the mixing of colors in a practical situation, but they developed a more scientific approach to problem-solving. Several hours of formal drill on the making of color charts would have availed these pupils little, but with a direct need as the motivating force they drilled themselves for hours on the technique of mixing colors to obtain a desired effect.

Formal drill on the color chart would not only have produced no useful skill with young children but would very probably have definitely antagonized them and repressed any creative urges. Teaching "composition" illustrates the same error. The high school teacher drills endlessly on kinds of sentences, upon rules of grammar, on

[19] F. G. Macomber, *Guiding Child Development in the Elementary School* (New York, American Book, 1941), p. 224. This whole chapter is excellent.

rhetoric, on syntax, on narration, exposition, and the other forms, upon tempo, upon climax, and many others. The student is then supposed by some magic to put these together in artistic expression. Adding these formal elements together can never produce understandings, appreciations, moving compositions of beauty and feeling. Expression comes first, refinement later. Mearns [20] tells how Willa Cather once asked a group of teachers of English *why the school stressed the formal side of literature at the expense of the sole reason for the existence of literature,* its value as a portrayal of the mind and spirit of man, its value for affecting that mind and spirit. We all know the answer.

Older students may engage in deliberate, systematic study of form with profit, since they have not only seen the necessity but have had enough experience to study form and relate it to expression.

The guidance for teaching is clear, though the traditional teacher shudders. Encourage and accept any rough draft first. Permit, examine, encourage, accept as quite natural first productions which are incorrect, incomplete, perhaps not well organized. *Insistence upon perfect productions early in the process is genuinely stupid; it is asking for the final edition in advance of the preliminary trials.* Let the student get down fresh, vigorous statements in any way he wishes; let him "get it off his mind." The thought once captured and recorded, the routine of supplementing, revising, and organizing can be undertaken without danger to the wings of Pegasus. A good portion of the teacher's time may be given to discussion of these rough, original drafts. Thinking, learning, and expression in process emerge in such outlines. The need for form and skill comes to the pupil naturally. This has been explained in detail in previous chapters. Remarks concerning language apply equally to all other types of expression.

[20] Hughes Mearns, *Creative Power,* rev. ed. (Garden City, N.Y., Doubleday, 1959), p. 10.

The error opposite to the foregoing is encountered with sentimentalists or muddled thinkers. They speak much of "inspiration" and "spontaneity," as if these were sufficient. They decry as unworthy of artistic expression any tinkering with rough drafts, any revision, any painstaking effort at improvement. Analysis kills the spirit, they say. The wrong kind of analysis can, but that is another story. Most of these enthusiasts have never done any important writing and their superficial view may be disregarded as misleading.

Creative expression and the imitation of models. The original act of creation used a model: God created man in His own image. The place of models and imitation has always been controversial among teachers of fine arts. The compulsory, slavish imitation of models condemned throughout this volume is undoubtedly thoroughly detrimental to learning. Close imitation of models, even without compulsion, is probably not wise for beginners. The inspection of many models, comparison of them, efforts to reproduce more than one or parts of several seem, however, to have beneficial effects upon learning. This is a part of getting acquainted, of developing insight, of the varied preliminary practice which is so important. Familiarity with superior models and attempts to produce something similar are likely both to stimulate creative expression and to aid it. With mature learners, acquaintance with what has been done in the field is necessary not only for the development of taste but for preventing much tedious rediscovery of what is already well established. A certain well-known university always refuses its scholarships to applicants who submit their works with the comment, "I know this is original because I have carefully avoided studying what others have done." Many well-known writers testify that intentional efforts to copy the "style" of earlier great writers definitely aided their own development. The provision of many models for examination and the avoidance of slavish imitation will preserve plasticity and originality while giving motives, leads, and opportunity for achieving skills. Modern psychologists are not fearful of the proper use of models.

Children's spontaneous expression is creative and may be capitalized. Children are continuously describing things, composing narratives about their experiences, arguing, chanting, singing. Some of this is routine repetition, but it is shot through with genuinely creative material. Children make up adventures, they invent imaginary playmates and carry on coherent lives with them. They will make up poetry and draw pictures. This activity grows naturally if not ridiculed. Parents and teachers who listen will find that creative expression is natural and more widely distributed than is thought. A mother noticed that her four-year-old son sang an endless chant when in his bath. She listened and was able to get down the following fragment. The *New Yorker* published it with the comment that ". . . this is one of the handsomest literary efforts of the year, as well as another proof that children are the really pure artists, with complete access to their thoughts and no foolish reticence. We reprint it here because seldom, we think, has the vision of heart's desire been put down so explicitly." The chant was later reprinted in the *Reader's Digest* and is reproduced below by permission of the original publishers:

He will do just nothing at all,
He will just sit there in the noonday sun.
Because he does not care to.
He will stick them with spears and put them
    in the garbage.
When they tell him to eat his dinner, he will
    just laugh at them,
And he will not take his nap, because he does
    not care to.
He will just sit there in the noonday sun.
He will go away and play with the Panda.

And when they come to look for him
He will put spikes in their eyes and put them
    in the garbage,

And put the cover on.
He will not go out in the fresh air or eat his
    vegetables
Or make wee-wee for them, and he will get
    thin as a marble.
He will not do nothing at all.
He will just sit there in the noonday sun.

A little girl washing her hands at home said to her mother, "I must hurry to school. I feel a poem; it's about the soapsuds, Mummy. I must hurry to tell Miss Herrick." [21] The last few lines the teacher had to take down because the little girl could not write fast enough and "it will go away if you don't put it down."

When I wash my hands
It seems to make a white mountain.
The water up ahead fades into blue.
I feel the soap like snow flakes.
Bubbles float around the water,
Many pretty colors I can see.
When I let out the water
I see a big cloud.
It has red, blue colors.

The stories, poems, pictures, and songs produced by children will lead to more and more creative work if received as natural and as commendable. Children themselves will suggest improvements, as the illustrations later will show.

Conversation periods in lower grades a prime source. Children exchange experiences; they get acquainted during free conversation. Their ability in oral language is far above their ability to read and to write. They already have the materials and the ability for oral expression and this may be capitalized on easily. Conversation leads into all sorts of story and poem construction which the teacher puts on the board as it is orally suggested and improved by the children.

In addition to the development of creativity, all other learning outcomes are improved in astonishing degree in the con-

[21] This illustration was supplied by Miss Anita Herrick, Angier School, Newton, Mass.

versation period. There is much desirable training in oral language, in discriminating and choosing words, in good verbal expression. Children engaged in co-operative work of their own choosing do not argue (nor come to blows) as do adults. They are more interested in discovering than in maintaining views. The effect upon their attitudes, appreciations, and personality traits is unusually valuable. The child forgets himself when expressing something which is near to him and overcomes many personality difficulties.

David, a shy and silent boy, who could not take part in conversation and who was immature socially, burst forth one morning to tell of the amusing antics of his baby brother. The incident was extremely funny to him, and he told it before he thought. He was full of it; he knew enough about it to talk freely. His tale was greeted with gales of appreciative laughter. Social approval had its effect, and he was soon taking part in conversation and in co-operative construction of stories and poems. John, in the same class, had a baby sister whom he disliked, since her coming had put his nose out of joint. The approval given to David's tales about his baby brother started John telling about his baby sister. His amusing stories were also accorded approval and he came to see the baby as a source of approval for himself. His parents reported that his attitude at home became wholly different. Many parents reported that the children noted and commented upon many beautiful cloud effects, sunsets, and flowers, as a result of creative work at school. One family had to leave the supper table to see the light of the sunset on the river.

Experimentation with materials another excellent source. Ann, a reticent, immature child who could not speak well, would confide in but one chum. She did not mix, did not contribute. She liked working with paints, but her efforts were mostly color puddling of the kindergarten level. One day she happened to hit upon a new color com-

bination which was truly beautiful. Children passing exclaimed, "Gee, fall twilight." Other approving comments came. Ann was startled but very pleased with the social approval. The children were so taken with the new color that they co-operatively composed a poem to go with it. Ann began to contribute more in group work and was soon writing little poems and factual stories of her own.

Another similar incident involved Billy, who quite by accident hit upon a new stroke with his paint brush and produced a beautiful effect. Proudly he said, "Isn't this good enough to make a poem about so we can hang it on the screen?" "Good, you make us the poem to go with it." This high-strung, emotional, unorganized boy with a very short attention span worked on his poem for about twenty minutes, quite oblivious to the world. Billy decided the first attempt was not good enough to be hung at the front of the room but could go in his book to take home. The color effect which started this episode was, however, hung up for the children's examination. They did not know of Billy's efforts to write a poem but began exclaiming, "It looks like shadows," "purple shadows from mountains," "purple shadows on snow," "winter," "evening." A poem began to emerge, with the teacher writing it on the board as it was worked over by the children. When the composition was finished, they decided it should be called "Purple Shadows."

Purple shadows
On the snow,
See them glow,
Very soon the sun will go,
Night will fall,
The shadows grow longer
The day is tired.
Clouds grow darker,
The stars sparkle
The shadows fade.

One little boy, who would contribute only by whispering to the teacher said, "I think the day should be weary, not tired; it would be much more beautiful."

Everyday experiences stimulate expression. The children, while on an excursion to the firehouse, discovered a new house being built. They observed, listened, explored, asked questions. On their return they insisted upon making a poem. The children spelled out the sounds their own way. Authorities on beginning reading believe that ear training in hearing initial and end sounds aids reading. This incident illustrates the faithful reproduction when attention is good.

The New House

Thrr-brr, the steam shovel digs the foundation.
Putt-bang, putt-bang goes the cement mixer,
Down goes the cement.
Bang, bang, the sound of the hammer.
Zzz, zzz, the noise of the saw.
Bthr, bthrr, the drill does its work.
Clatter, clatter, up goes a ladder,
The carpenter works all day.
Slish, slosh, the sound of the painter's brush,
The house is ready, the work is done.

The teacher then read this group Walt Whitman's *I Hear America Singing,* whereupon a seven-year-old boy gave his approval: "Whitman is a nice guy, he writes the way we do!"

Tastes, standards, and skills develop naturally as needed. Miss Herrick's children started on their creative work at first by writing limericks. A supervisor's comments one day gave the teacher new insight and led to development over a period of years. The supervisor passed by the limericks to comment upon two lines which had been left over on the board.

The Christmas tree has many lights
The Christmas tree is very high.

"These lines are good, but you can go further. Read them more poetry so that they can see that all lines need not rhyme. If they wish to express the wind, let them feel the wind. Let them fly a kite in the wind. Let them sail a boat in the wind. Give them experiences with the wind."

The two lines on the board were taken up later with the children. They were asked to close their eyes and think of the most beautiful Christmas picture they could. Conversation resulted in the selection of Mother, Father, and a child going to church in a sleigh on Christmas night. Two excellent group poems resulted. For one of them an unassuming child with a speech difficulty supplied the line, "Dainty crocus we always notice," which earned him commendation from the children who had hitherto not regarded him highly because of his failure to contribute.

The children themselves begin to judge their own productions. They recognize difficulties and seek assistance. A line is said to be "jerky" and is worked over until it is smooth. That line does not "sing" and is reworded. Standards for other, more prosaic learnings also emerge. Because of difficulty in reading, in understanding, and because of dislike for poor appearance, this set of standards was set up by the eight-year-olds.

We will leave wide margins on each side.
We will size our letters.
We will punctuate the sentences.
We will begin each sentence with a capital.
We will write neatly.

Are there distinguishable phases in the creative process. Creative thinkers have often given very enlightening accounts of their own processes, so far as they can recognize what occurred. Autobiographical accounts have been supplemented by accounts secured under controlled conditions. After examining extensive accounts of thought processes reported by distinguished mathematicians, scientists, technicians, inventors and artists, and comparing these with his own thought processes in the social sciences, Wallas [22] believed that four distinguishable stages existed: *preparation, incubation, illumination,* and *verification.* The present writer

[22] Graham Wallas, *The Art of Thought* (New York, Harcourt, 1926).

has examined much material upon the psychology of intuition or "hunch" and some references in religion and mysticism. Religious writers see four stages in revelation: reverent contemplation, revelation, communion, and fruition. The mystics state them thus: meditation, contemplation, ecstasy, and fulfillment. Psychologists, dealing with intuition, see four phases: preparation, incubation, illumination or inspiration, and elaboration or verification. Linley,[23] in his excellent study of seven painters, seven musicians, and three poets, each of whom was renowned, found four phases for which he accepted the psychological names listed above. Wallas sees his four phases as sequential. While they doubtless are roughly so, the current view regards them as interwoven. The term *revision* is probably a better term for the fourth phase than any of those given above.

The four phases must under no circumstances be interpreted as "steps," or as a formula. They are but a convenient method of describing a complex process. Practically any learning process has the same characteristics. The phases are not either consecutive nor mutually exclusive. Students should read the brief but excellent case for and against the four phases presented by Russell.[24]

Educational implications of the major phases. The titling of the major phases may be reworded better to serve educational purposes.

1. *The phase of preparation,* of achieving familiarity, of securing experience, of becoming absorbed.
2. *The phase of effort to achieve,* or of incubation.
3. *The phase (sometimes a moment) of illumi-*

nation, of inspiration, of insight, of fulfillment.
4. *The phase of revision,* of elaboration, of polishing.

These are not separate steps; they do not constitute a formula. They are offered only as a scheme for organizing our thinking. The teacher, it is hoped, will be aided in recognizing creative expression when it appears, or in stimulating it, and in either case in aiding through guidance.

1. *The phase of preparation, achieving familiarity, securing experience.* History records one instance in which a world and its content was created out of chaos. The average individual needs more material than that, even though he seems to be able to create chaos itself with little effort or preparation: Worthwhile creative effort does not "just happen." Preparation is necessary. Preparation in *general* encompasses the total educational experiencing of the individual to date. Regarded thus, the period is long, continued, and incidental to any specific creative experience. Preparation in specific instances may be brief, crowded, deliberately exploratory. The purpose of preparation in any case is like that in any type of learning— becoming familiar with and securing background in general or specific areas. Creative expression is not a flash from the blue any more than is securing a complex understanding or developing a difficult motor skill.

The type of curriculum and method advocated throughout this volume is the best *general* preparation for creative expression. Results in modern schools demonstrate this. Creative expression is stimulated by a rich and varied experience, organized around pupil purposes, with free participation and expression, all aided by the sympathetic and insightful guidance of the teacher. Preparation in special cases would involve deliberate study of the purpose to be achieved and of illustrations of the variations of form and content suited to the pupil's urge to express.

[23] James M. Linley, *An Analytic Study of the Creative Process as Revealed by Accounts of Specific Creative Acts.* Unpublished Doctoral Dissertation, Univ. of Southern California, April, 1938.

[24] David H. Russell, *Children's Thinking* (Boston, Ginn, 1956), pp. 311-313. All of Chapter 11 should be read also.

This type of preparation is more useful as pupils become more mature.

2. *The phase of effort to achieve, or of incubation.* Effort in creative expression does not, as a rule, arise from assignment, except with mature artists. Following the urge of his own purposes, a pupil will engage in deliberate effort to produce something which satisfies him. Earlier paragraphs point out that this is a subtle matter, easily upset or easily enhanced. Delicate balance must be maintained. Physical and emotional conditions, as well as the psychological climate, are vital. Continued effort of any kind is, as the world goes, often interrupted. The necessity of attending to other tasks and responsibilities takes one away from poem-writing, painting, or problem-solving. Sometimes an interesting phenomenon occurs. After interruption, the individual picks up the creative or problem-solving task with renewed insight, new ideas, and added zest. Psychologists differ as to the explanation. One group believes that there has been "unconscious cerebration"—mental activity below the level of consciousness. The "subconscious" mind is mentioned. Another group believes that the explanation is the simple one of relaxation and rest. In any event, there is definite recognizable progress toward the goal. This phenomenon has given rise to the term *incubation*. Nothing magical is involved; the word is merely descriptive. Mature writers, artists, mathematicians, or others engaged in reflective or creative thought deliberately take advantage of a period of incubation. Problems and creative efforts are laid aside; other life activities are pursued. Except in rare instances, recognizable benefit results. *Forced interruptions* often have the opposite effect and the individual has to get "warmed up" all over again upon return to the task. Sometimes he can never get "warmed up" again, as witness the tragic interruption suffered by Coleridge as he had just started to write *Kubla Khan*. Called away for an hour on a matter of business, he was never able to recapture the vivid imagery of his vision

nor the flow of creative expression. The poem has remained forever a fragment. [25]

We may digress to note that modern life sets a pace which more and more destroys *contemplation, reflective thought, moments of meditation*. The school which is devoted to "covering" the curriculum or text, to promoting pupils a grade a year, to preparing for college instead of for living; which is overwhelmed by numbers, forty-minute periods, bells, and fixed, arbitrary standards, more and more makes of education a hurlyburly in which reflection and meditation are destroyed. Contemplation and the slow turning over of matters and motives in the mind, are, however, inescapable necessities in any scheme of decent education. The problem is actually one of the most serious facing modern education, though this is not always recognized. Learned [26] of The Carnegie Foundation for the Advancement of Teaching quotes with approval from a composition by a high school student.

I am tired of school, tired of this incessant hurrying from class to class in an attempt to obtain an education. There is not enough time for the things that matter to me—I am carried swiftly down a sea of faces that I dimly recognize to be my friends. I think that they are tired too; tired of putting down a paint brush and paper, of being told to wipe this brush and put that paper away because the all-important bell has rung. They learn very soon to mask their enthusiasms to suit the hourly bells and find it easy to lose interest in what, with leisure for thought and study, might become absorbing. For students like me and my associates, new-born ideas must be carefully tended before they can expand, or we shall forget that they ever came to us.

High school students are called superficial, with no thorough knowledge of any one subject. It is true. Mediocrity is our god. Copying

[25] C. E. Andrews and M. O. Percival, *Romantic Poetry* (Columbus, Ohio, R. G. Adams and Company, 1924), p. 78. If this book is available, students will be well rewarded to read the account of Coleridge's experience.

[26] William S. Learned, *"Credits" versus Education,* a pamphlet (New York, The Carnegie Foundation for the Advancement of Teaching, 1933), pp. 1, 2, 3.

is accepted as a matter of course among us; we slide by on whatever we can force ourselves to accomplish in an odd moment. . . .

I should like to write an essay without being disturbed, to make a book report that rings true with what I feel. If I do justice to these, the time is stolen from other classes and the hourly bells are not appeased until I have made peace with them. Of course, I can fill a paper with platitudes and hand it in to a teacher who is so used to mediocrity that she accepts it, perhaps surprised that I have written a book report at all. And I can go to my next class with the feeling that, here again, I have slipped in any standard which I may have.

Warmed-over lessons are a painful duty and I am so used to sliding over them that I will go to a movie if the opportunity offers, rather than do them in the evenings. What good will it do me to finish the poem for which I cannot now find an ending? Is this education? Can this mincemeat spread over four years of high school, give us anything but a coating of slap-bang culture?

Learned also quotes from a statement made by a foreign exchange student in one of our colleges.

So I finally learned to follow the line of least resistance and to divide my day in those tyrannical units in order to get everything done in its proper time, although now I was not at all satisfied with the results of my studying. I learned to read the assignments at top speed whether the thought was perfectly clear to me or not. I learned to shut the book promptly after two hours' work and dismiss the subject from my mind no matter whether I came across some interesting points over which, under normal conditions, I should have liked to ponder long. The pressure of the next assignment pushed me on. Speed, speed, speed was the word. Hurry up your economics chapter, or you cannot finish the Shakespeare play for tomorrow! When I had swallowed but not digested one mass of material, another mountain of facts was presented to be swallowed after it. I could manage to read forty pages for this, fifty pages for that, and a Shakespeare play for one day in addition to my class recitations; I could write a theme and make a history report and study the life and works of Cotton Mather for the next day. But I had to give up every attempt to assimilate what I had read. There was no time for "taking walks and thinking things over." It was a desperate cram-

ming of facts in a compulsory piecemeal fashion which paralyzed all the interest and satisfaction that could have come out of the same work under individual initiative and under more continuous, deliberate, and intensive study.

The length of the digression in preceding paragraphs is legitimate in view of the seriousness of the problem, not merely for creative expression but for all education. In creative expression, particularly, the teacher who hurries the pupils, who is not patient with the curious, devious ways of the producer of beauty, will effectually destroy the process.

3. *The phase (sometimes moment) of illumination, inspiration, or fulfilment.* The inner mechanism is unknown, but everyone from average citizen to expert clinical psychologist recognizes the overt manifestation. Archimedes' classic "Eureka" is matched by the homely American expression, "I've got it!" Children are truthful when they say that "the poem just seemed to write itself." Children who write music must put it on paper when it comes or lose the forming melody.

The sudden flashes of inspiration are publicized to the detriment of understanding. Archimedes' instance; the fact that "Fechner developed his psychophysical formula on a sickbed, after he had literally soaked his brain with information about the body-mind question; that Kekule hit upon the benzene ring during the writing of a chemistry chapter which resisted easy composition and while in a dozy fuzzy mental state from distaste for a boring job" [27]—often give rise to theories of mystery and mysticism concerning creative production. We must emphasize instead that creative moments are often calm and collected instead of explosive and exclamatory; they may be long and sustained instead of momentary; they are preceded by long periods of preparation. Deliberate efforts, furthermore, are often made by mature individuals to observe and guide their own productive moments. Hart-

[27] George W. Hartmann, *Educational Psychology* (New York, American Book, 1941), p. 369.

mann points out that "insights about physics usually come from physicists, musical themes from persons competent in this art, and astronomical theories from astronomers." Striking exceptions exist but prove the rule. Outsiders called in do, on occasion, supply a lead which comes from an uninhibited approach.

Illumination or fruition is unpredictable. We do know that it will not come without preparation and incubation, nor in an unfavorable social and psychological climate.

4. *The phase of revision, elaboration, or polishing.* The necessity of this phase is often overlooked by superficial enthusiasts for creative work. Writers themselves sometimes refer to "a little thing I dashed off in a spare moment." Sometimes things of importance are "dashed" off, but not commonly. Inspection of the originals of great manuscripts, both prose and poetry, supplies objective evidence of the great amount of tedious, patient, painstaking rewriting, revision, substituting, changing, erasing that goes on. Some pieces of beautifully smooth writing were produced by lengthy, detailed tinkering. Portrait painters often have to rework a canvas from two to ten times. Sculptors and modelers may construct a dozen forms before achieving a satisfactory product. Contrary to public opinion, this is a necessary aspect of creative work. Educational guidance is clear; let the creative individual produce his first copy as he will. Evidence shows that the first fruits of creative effort are rarely the best. The individual himself will engage in the necessary revision and improvement. The detailed, sensitive report in Mearns' volumes show clearly how much changing and tinkering goes into products which eventually possess real beauty.

Certain over-all characteristics of creative activity. The process of creating as a whole has certain important characteristics, knowledge of which is valuable to the teacher. Some of these are positive, some negative.

1. *Creative expression is uncertain—it comes or it does not come.* The creative person, neither mad nor turbulent, is sensitive beyond the ordinary. The outpouring of one's inner thoughts is a peculiarly personal thing. It is invited, stimulated, or destroyed by slight and subtle influences. Fortunately, other factors compensate in part for this uncertainty, as will be seen below.

2. *Creative expression is easily stimulated, repressed, or destroyed with finality in little children.* Encouragement and sympathetic understanding are necessary; without them, little will be accomplished. Ridicule or too mature analysis and criticism are fatal. Smiles and laughter must be avoided. The wholly friendly laughter of adults over a childish poem or drawings has effectually stopped a child from further production. Practically every normal child draws pictures, writes stories and makes rhymes; but these activities rarely persist into adulthood. Lack of training is one factor, but the indifference and careless criticism of parents and teachers are probably the chief influences. On the other hand, individuals of special talent or genius are not at all discouraged by indifference and criticism. Linley's study, noted above, and many biographies show that these individuals persist in creative work in defiance of ridicule, abuse, starvation, beatings, and imprisonment.

3. *Creative expression is favored as a rule by freedom from compulsion, but this is not universal.* Mearns likens the creative spirit to Poe's Imp of the Universe in that it obstinately refuses to serve those who try to command it. He tells of the girl who had produced an unusually beautiful first poem. The director of the school, curious to see what she would do, said to her as if serious, "Now I want you to write me a poem, and I shall give you the subject." He named the subject and continued, "As to its length— about so long," and he measured. "I want it done for a meeting of the junior high school pupils tomorrow afternoon. There will be no objection if it is humorous." The young poetess, somewhat bowled over at the

assignment, replied, "But, Doctor C—, poems are not written that way! They come because of the way I think and feel myself. I will try to write one for you, of course, but I don't think it will be the one you want, for I don't know even myself what it is going to be; but it must be my own, and when you tell me what to write about—that, I'm afraid will make me not want to write at all, because it wouldn't be mine, you see, but—" pathetically desirous of not offending—"but yours, if you see what I mean." Mearns also cites cases of excellent production under pressure of time limits and publication deadlines. The degree to which the compelling factor is recognized and accepted by the learner is important.

4. *Creative expression is aided by order and regularity of effort once production is under way, by a place and facilities for work.* Voluntary attention, easy access to materials, relaxation and comfort all aid any task. Creative work is no exception.

5. *Creative periods of work are marked by intense concentration and absorption, sometimes by complete dissociation.* This characteristic is commonly observed and well known. The "absent-minded" professor really has his mind completely on something else. Lawyers, physicians, engineers, architects, businessmen—all who solve difficult problems are "absent-minded" at times. It is no prerogative of the professor. The author who called downstairs to his wife's guests to "shut up" because he "was having an idea" was not rude, merely partially dissociated by concentration. Periods of absorption are marked by feelings of elation. Long hours of truly arduous labor, physical and mental, are endured without intermission. (Fatigue is not felt until afterwards during the "let down.") Interruptions at *this stage* are disheartening and often fatal to the creative spirit.

Three negative points may now be outlined briefly.

1. *Creative expression is not "imagination" in the popular meaning of that term.*

Parents and teachers constantly discuss "imagination" as if it were a separate power or function, capable of training in and for itself. This belief is a relic of the faculty psychology and is flatly contradicted by all modern psychology. The currently accepted concept is that of the integrated and integrating mind. Any mental activity is that of the total mind. Activity may be directed now to problem-solving, now to recalling a formula, now to reproducing "in the mind" scenes from faraway places, now to analyzing, now to judging, now to creative expression. Separate powers or faculties are not involved. Teachers who try to "train the imagination" are wasting time. Desirable effort will be directed rather at giving learners a rich background of experience, at utilizing learning situations which have purpose and meaning for the learner, at giving ample opportunity for free expression.

2. *Creative expression is not mere revolt.* Creativity by its very meaning necessitates a departure from the traditional, the accepted, the conventional. A literature exists which identifies creativity with revolt from and disregard for standards whether of art, or of literature, or of morals. Part of this is produced by mediocre individuals who cannot quite achieve recognition under acceptable standards of skill. Standards are ridiculed as "conventional"; conservatives are said to be blind to the merit of "new" principles and methods. Artists and writers who merely revolt against historic evolved forms and standards and who substitute no other rational basis, turn out productions which are similar to those of primitive persons, of little children, or of the mentally deranged. Distinction must be made between irrational revolt and that type of modern art which—bizarre as it may seem to the untrained observer—is actually either a bold modification of ever-changing forms or is a truly new structure based on new concepts, new interests, and new purposes.

Constructive, creative production takes place within the institutions, the traditions, and the media of one's civilization. An English boy produces typical occidental art or poetry; a Japanese boy, typical oriental art or poetry. Japanese children reared entirely in the United States produce western and not oriental drawings, prose, or poetry. Children should not be discouraged from trying different media, from persisting for some time with odd, unconventional methods and results. Standards and skills will be differentiated with maturity and experience.

3. *Creative expression is not mad, turbulent, "temperamental."* Temperament, so-called, is distributed among artists, musicians, and writers probably about as it is among engineers, lawyers, and housewives. Many well-known painters and poets of the first rank are phlegmatic, prosaic individuals, though capable of intense absorption and concentration while working. The few research studies available show inventors and original thinkers among engineers and technicians are more orderly about their work and about keeping tools and workshops well arranged than are the less original and creative. Painters and poets indulge as a matter of course in much revising, polishing, in much painstaking work on details. Sober, serious work, even drudgery in some instances, is far more typical than mad, turbulent ecstasy. A good deal of the temperamental behavior of certain prominent figures is deliberate window dressing carefully planned for publicity. With some it is nothing but the display of immature, infantile personality. Some creative artists are nervous and excitable and display "temperament" under pressure. So do policemen, bus drivers, lawyers, and bookkeepers. This is natural; it is not peculiar to creative individuals.

Two general summaries on the development of creativity. No one can set down in formal fashion the many subtle factors in the stimulation of creativity. Foregoing pages have contained many, many specific suggestions. The two practical summaries to fol-

low, while not exhaustive, will make for ready reference by teachers.

Lee and Lee [28] believe that teachers can aid children and youth to respond creatively by:

Providing an atmosphere in which each child is accepted as he is and in which he feels that he belongs, has status and the respect of both teachers and peers.

Helping each child to understand and accept himself and his own thinking.

Giving courage and confidence to each child to try, accepting the results whatever they are, encouraging him to evaluate and try again.

Providing freedom—for a purpose, not freedom from responsibility but freedom to explore, to experiment with himself, with his environment, freedom to learn.

Rewarding the inventive, the different, rather than the following of the prescribed formula to the last letter.

Always searching for alternatives, and helping the child to find "other ways," not to stick with the "obvious."

Making the questioning attitude a main goal of his teaching.

Listening to the child in order to understand *his* thinking and feeling, to see how the situation or problem looks to him.

There are some things a teacher can refrain from doing which will be equally valuable in releasing creativity.

Teachers should work toward:

Not creating situations which produce high tension and anxiety, for these stresses block mental activity, make ideas unavailable and problem-solving inefficient. Insecure people are not able to suspend judgment to hunt for better answers or explore alternatives.

Not having assignments rigid so that they must be finished in too short a time or cause the student to feel that he is merely expected to produce a certain predetermined response, a ready-made answer; for when a child finds that a certain response succeeds time after time, he is likely to respond that way whether or not it is desirable or appropriate.

Not rewarding a child for accepting someone else's opinion uncritically, or blindly following a rule.

[28] *The Child and His Curriculum*, 3rd ed. (New York, Appleton-Century-Crofts, 1960), pp. 511-512.

Not developing fears of authoritarianism and of value judgments made by either the teacher or the peer group.

Not telling children too much. Sometimes we offer them information which, if they discovered it for themselves, would give them much greater growth and satisfaction. What they really want and need are the teachers' assurances and confidence in their ability.

Zirbies [29] has presented a set of paired alternatives she believes will advance creative education. We may add that they will, if applied, advance and aid all kinds of education.

From stereotyped conformity *toward* free expression

From passive compliance *toward* active identification

From imposed direction *toward* co-operative planning

From coercive requirements *toward* voluntary commitments

From mass handling *toward* individuated guidance

From extrinsic motivation *toward* intrinsic value concerns

From submissive acquiescence *toward* wholehearted involvement

From restrictive domination *toward* responsible self-direction

From stultifying repression *toward* spontaneity

From the fixing of habits and skills *toward* cultivation of adaptive responses to life-related situation.

Systematic training of creative expression in special subjects. This chapter has been concerned with the initiation and development of creative expression with little children and as a part of general education. It is not concerned with the continued development in secondary schools, since this should be discussed in special-methods courses. Books are available on this level for interested students. This chapter is concerned also only with the ordinary expressions of

[29] Laura Zirbies, "The Contribution of Creative Education to Human Development and Fulfillment," *Aesthetic Form and Education,* Michael F. Andrews ed. (Syracuse, N. Y., Syracuse Univ. Press, 1958), p. 42.

average individuals. The principles and techniques applicable to cases of special talent are to be found elsewhere.

DISCUSSION QUESTIONS FOR SECTION 2

1. Brief summary reports may be made upon:

   a. The psychology of intuition or the "hunch."

   b. The religious or mystic revelation.

   (This exercise should be done only if the class wishes to explore these, and if time permits.)

2. A number of interested students may make individual reports on the creative processes, either self-revealed or described by biographers, for a selected man of fame in mathematics, the physical sciences, or the biological sciences; for a musician, a poet, a prose writer, or a graphic artist; for a research man in medicine or any other field which appeals.

Accounts of inventive work in industry, manufacturing, and business are now increasingly available. (See, for instance, Raymond F. Loewy, *Never Let Well Enough Alone* [New York, Simon & Schuster, 1951].)

3. The difficult processes of social invention which usually involve efforts of many people and groups over a period of time should be reviewed if there is interest.

4. Experienced teachers may relate their experiences in securing creative work in any area. Bring out particularly the conditions which stimulated or retarded; the processes of the learner; the polishing or perfecting which comes after the first flush of production.

5. Experienced teachers and students who are observing should report, without identification, cases of serious blundering, as for instance imposing adult standards, insisting on reproduction of models, demanding perfection, and particularly, disregarding or over-riding the necessary stages of development.

6. A teacher might exhibit and explain children's production, particularly in graphic art, to illustrate the stages of development. Similar exhibits should be made of poems, brief prose compositions, modeling, ceramics, and if possible, dramatic play and dances.

   (The instructor should collect a considerable exhibit for use at this point.)

7. Experienced teachers should report particularly on the creative suggestions made by children and youth during the definition and fulfillment of a unit. Creative thinking may be observed in all phases; defining the problem,

suggesting ways and means during the planning period, finding ways around difficulties either of materials or personnel or process, summarizing, and explaining or presenting results to others.

8. If there is class interest a report or two may be made on stages or levels of development in other fields. Material is available in language and mathematics, and may be in other fields also.

9. Experienced teachers may exhibit and report upon any especially original and creative processes demonstrated by children in history, geography, mathematics, science, or other subjects. The originality may be in illustrating, interpreting, or explaining to others. (This is an important aspect of creative learning.)

SPECIAL REPORTS

Reports may be made by individuals or small committees for each of the special fields represented in the class group. Reports may be based on either or both: (a) the literature available; (b) experience in the classroom. These reports may be oral if there is wide class interest, but time will be saved through written reports if only a few students are interested in the special fields.

The literature on the teaching of special subjects, particularly in the arts and literature is extensive and easily available in college libraries. Even a selective list is beyond our purpose here. One brief summary is available in Lee and Lee, *The Child and His Curriculum,* previously referred to, pages 513-551. An excellent bibliography is found on pages 552-557.

READINGS

1. Comprehensive, interdisciplinary symposia. These are new in the field and extremely valuable for basic definitions and principles.

ANDERSON, H. H., ed., *Creativity and its Cultivation* (New York, Harper, 1959.) Addresses from an interdisciplinary symposium held at Michigan State University. All should read the Preface and articles by Eyring and by Guilford. Some of the others are pretty difficult, but students may make selection. Excellent bibliography on advanced theory and principle.

ANDREWS, Michael, F., ed., *Aesthetic Form and Education* (Syracuse, N. Y., Syracuse Univ. Press, 1958). Four contributors are from one or another educational field, six are from other disciplines. Students may read with profit articles by Tumin, Andrews, and Taylor, though all discussions here are useful to average students. Excellent bibliography.

———, ed., *Creativity and Psychological Health* (Syracuse, N. Y., Syracuse Univ. Press, 1962). Excellent bibliography.

"A Symposium on Innovation in Science," *The Scientific American* (September, 1958). This is a remarkable collection of articles. All students can read with profit J. Bronowski's "The Creative Process," J. R. Pierce's "Innovation in Technology," and Frank Barron's "The Psychology of Imagination." The excellent articles by Halmos, Dyson, Wald, Eccles, on mathematics, physics, biology, and the physiology of the imagination are better for advanced students majoring in the designated fields.

2. References dealing generally with definition, explanation, and exposition of the creative process. References to special fields will be dealt with elsewhere.

It seems futile to present a *brief* listing. The 1958 Syracuse Symposium, for instance, gives eight pages to bibliography. Other references give from four to ten pages.

A few older references are omitted here though they are still valuable. They are easily available in most libraries: Bergson, Downey, Follett, Griswold, Mearns (one of Mearns' volumes published in 1930 was revised in 1958), Spearman.

BARRON, Frank, "The Disposition Toward Originality," *The Journal of Abnormal and Social Psychology,* Vol. 51 (November, 1955), pp. 478-485.

———, "Some Personality Correlates of Independence of Judgment," *Character and Personality (Journal of Personality),* Vol. 21 (March, 1953), pp. 287-297.

BUTTERFIELD, H., *The Origins of Modern Science; 1300-1800* (London, Bell, 1949).

CRAWFORD, R. E., *The Techniques of Creative Thinking* (New York, Hawthorne, 1954).

GHISELIN, Brewster, *The Creative Process: A Symposium* (Berkeley, Cal., Univ. of California Press, 1952).

GUILFORD, J. P., *Bibliography of Thinking* (Los Angeles, Univ. of Southern California, 1953).

———, "Creativity," *The American Psychologist* (September, 1950), pp. 444-454.

HADAMARD, Jacques, *An Essay on the Psychology of Invention in Mathematics* (Princeton, N. J., Princeton Univ. Press, 1945).

HARDING, Rosamund E. M., *The Anatomy of Inspiration*, 3rd ed. (Cambridge, Eng., W. Heffer & Sons, 1948).

KNOLES, George H., and SNYDER, R. K., eds., *Readings in Western Civilization* (New York, Lippincott, 1960).

LOWENFELD, Viktor, *Creative and Mental Growth*, 3rd ed. (New York, Macmillan, 1957). See also author's older volume *The Nature of Creative Activity* (New York, Harcourt, 1939). Lowenfeld was in art education, but his general discussions are among the best available. Excellent illustrations also from the art field.

PATRICK, Catherine, *What is Creative Thinking* (New York, Philosophical Library, 1955).

PUPIN, Michael, *From Immigrant to Inventor* (New York, Scribner, 1924).

REYNOLDS, Richard H., *Aspects of Creativity*, The Tenth Annual College of the Pacific Faculty Research Lecture, May 16, 1960. Available from the College, Stockton, Cal. An excellent statement, good bibliography.

RUSSELL, David H., *Children's Thinking* (Boston, Ginn, 1956). Chapter 11 is not only a summary of research on children and creativity, but also one of the best general, critical discussions.

Syracuse University symposiums, edited by Michael F. Andrews, referred to earlier. (Syracuse, N. Y., Syracuse Univ. Press, 1958 and 1960).

TAYLOR, Calvin W., *The Identification of Scientific Talent*, University of Utah national research conferences in 1956, 1958, 1959 (Salt Lake City, Univ. of Utah Press, dates as above).

BRUNER, Jerome S., "The Act of Discovery," *Harvard Educational Review* (Winter, 1961), pp. 21-32.

3. References dealing more specifically with the actual processes in given cases: originality, discovery, inspiration, intuition, imagination, and so on. Sample references only.

See Anderson, Barron, Ghiselin, Guilford, Hadamard, Lowenfeld in previous list.

CONANT, James B., ed., *Harvard Case Studies in Experimental Science*, Vols. I and II (Cambridge, Mass., Harvard Univ. Press, 1957).

GILFILLAN, S. C., *The Sociology of Invention* (Chicago, Follette, 1935).

JEWKES, John, SAWYERS, David, and STILLERMAN, Richard, *The Sources of Invention* (New York, Macmillan, 1959).

KRETSCHMER, Ernest, *The Psychology of Men of Genius* (London, Paul, Trench, Trubner, 1931).

SARTON, George, *A History of Science* (Cambridge, Mass., Harvard Univ. Press, 1959).

SCHWARTZ, George, and BISHOP, Philip W., eds., *Moments of Discovery: The Origins of Science*, Vols. I and II (New York, Basic, 1958).

Lest these references seem to deal with "great big important" things, far removed from childhood, let it be noted that a few do deal with children and that specific references to children and creativity will be given later at an appropriate location.

4. Biographies, autobiographies, and private journals of writers, artists, musicians, inventors, scientists often supply excellent insights into the specific processes of creativity.

Several volumes already listed contain materials from these sources. Two older books, Whewell's *History of the Inductive Sciences*, 2nd ed. (New York, Appleton, 1901, originally published much earlier), and D. L. Watson's *Scientists Are Human* (London, Watts, 1938) are useful. Pupin's book, noted above, is a good one also. Currently there is great interest in this type of material; references are easily available.

5. The literature of *aesthetics* may be examined by advanced students who are interested.

6. The literature of *philosophy, religion,* and *mysticism,* which treats of revelation, inspired pronouncements, or transcendental insights.

7. The literature of *artistic* and *literary criticism.* Much of this is keenly analytic and supplies excellent guidance.

8. *Observational or experimental analyses* of creative thought in process. Good sample references are Catherine Patrick, "Creative Thought in Poets," *Archives of Psychology*, No. 178 (1935), and "Creative Thought in Artists," *Journal of Psychology* (July, 1937), pp. 35-73.

9. *An illustration of unusual creativity in advertising, industrial design, and business promotion* is found in Raymond F. Loewy, *Never Let Well Enough Alone* (New York, Simon &

Schuster, 1951). This is excellent general reading for anyone quite apart from its bearing upon creativity. Very few such books are available and any found should be reported by students.

The Periodical Literature

The periodical literature, taking all fields into consideration, is literally enormous. As usual no attempt is made here to list it. Some of the references above give excellent samplings. It is far better to have a report or two by students bringing the class up to date in the special fields.

Students preparing to teach in secondary schools and who may not be securing materials in their special methods courses may read in one or more volumes on creative expression in their subject fields.

Certain city systems, San Diego, California, and Madison, Wisconsin, plus some others, give special attention to the stimulation of creative learning in various fields.

The San Diego city system has what is probably one of the best programs. An annual magazine, *Creative Writing*, presents prose, poetry, and graphic art from the elementary schools. This bulletin, now in its seventeenth year, contained 124 pages this year. The format and contents are artistic and stimulating. Another magazine, *Quest,* presents similar material from grades seven to twelve. Material from gifted children does not monopolize the space, all levels of creative ability being included. There is a teacher committee on creative learning, which issues bulletins from time to time, one useful one being on creative writing. Both teachers and consultants contributed. Outside consultants are used as participants in judging creative productions.

The superintendent's office issues these special publications and in addition a printed weekly *Superintendent's Bulletin* dealing with all school affairs. Attention is given to varied aspects of creative learning as occasion warrants. The school library and the audio-visual aids departments issue bulletins and lists from time to time. Perhaps most important of all is a quarterly printed bulletin addressed to parents and dealing wtih all curriculum matters. Achievements of various types, including creative teaching and learning, are described and explained. Keeping parents informed in advance prevents criticism and objection to many new departures.

CHAPTER 17: The Use of Instructional Resources, Aids, and Materials

The relative merits of direct and vicarious experience were presented in detail earlier, as well as the dangers of too great reliance upon vicarious experience far removed from appropriate direct experience. The avoidance of verbalism is one of the major objectives of modern teaching methods. Accordingly, the extensive use of a wide diversity of instructional aids has developed. A traditional school is often bare of anything beyond desks and blackboards, with perhaps a lithograph or two and a map. Visits in many school systems will demonstrate that these conditions are still common. The pupil in a modern school is literally surrounded by a profusion of instructional materials, ranging from textbooks and periodicals to motion pictures, radio, and perhaps television. The modern curriculum demands this profusion.

The kinds of instructional aids available. The wealth of materials now in use in good schools may be classified roughly as follows:

Printed Aids

Books (texts and supplementary), periodicals, bulletins, pamphlets, newspapers.

Audio-Visual Aids

Maps and globes; relief, product and industry, population, rainfall, and other special purposes, in addition to typical physical-political ones.
Charts, diagrams, graphs.
Cartoons.
Posters.
Stereographs.
Motion pictures, with or without sound tracks.
Lantern slides, filmstrips, television.
Photographs or other pictorial representation of persons, places, or processes; reproductions of masterpieces of art.
Radio presentations, transcriptions, wire or tape recordings.
Phonograph records.
Museum or other lesser collections; exhibits of fauna and flora, models of machinery or famous places, natural and industrial products.

Resources in the Co-Curricular Activities

Each of the following is a potential source of aids to learning as well as being a mode of learning also.

School social affairs of all kinds: dances, class parties, and so forth.
Clubs covering many types of interest and activity.
Dramatics; school programs of various types.
Athletics.

Student government.
Publications, school newspaper, literary magazine.

Each of these classifications contains from two or three to scores of subgroupings. The number of actual materials is almost limitless. Certain apparatus is required:

Motion picture projectors and screens.
Sound projectors.
Phonographs.
Radios.
Blackboards.
Bulletin boards.
Sand tables.
Museum rooms and exhibit cases.
Recorders, wire or tape.

The relation of these types of apparatus and the corresponding materials to the scale of vicarious experiences is clear.

The following summary shows the types that can be secured free or at small cost by any school:

1. *Bulletins, pamphlets, catalogs.* Many book catalogs give descriptions of books, information about authors and illustrators, and illustrations that will be interesting and stimulating for children's use. Such catalogs often give an acquaintance with books and writers which may not be acquired in any other way. Children enjoy looking over book catalogs, selecting books for Christmas gifts, or for the library order. Seed, picture, and toy catalogs may be used in the same way.

   Travel bulletins add interest to work in geography and are valuable in developing units of work having to do with industries, with different sections of the United States, and with foreign countries.

   Many bulletins published by departments of state and national government and by state universities will be found helpful in classroom work.

   It is undesirable to have every pupil write for the same material, or for each succeeding class to collect materials that can be preserved from year to year as a part of the permanent school collection of materials. Pupils may write for some of the material as it is needed, but much of the information will have to be located and often secured before the group begins the unit of work, in order to prevent too much loss of time. Requests for materials should be written on school stationery and should be approved by the teacher. Children should write for definite information or material, not make a general request for information or bulletins.

2. *Magazines, papers* (state, local, Sunday, foreign). These offer rich material for instructional use. Feature articles; accounts of special exhibits; reviews of books, plays, and movies; radio programs, and the like, may be clipped and used for the bulletin board and later for the files, as a contribution to the material under some special unit or topic used in the curriculum of the school.

3. *Posters of railroad and travel bureaus, maps, and charts.* These furnish graphic and often colorful illustrative materials. Maps are being used in many ways to show places of historic interest, sports and recreation centers, flowers and herbs grown in different localities, weather conditions, and topographic survey. Graphs may be obtained showing production and distribution of products, market analyses, and trends in economic life. These are valuable as source materials, presenting the information in a manner which is not possible in the textbook.

4. *Prints and pictures.* Copies of famous pictures, colorful prints from various foreign countries, pictures from magazines, the picture supplement of the Sunday papers, advertisements, Kodak pictures, post-card views of points of historic and geographic interest, of costumes in different lands, and of fairy tales and nursery rhymes have a very real place among instruction materials.

5. *Tapestries and wall hangings.* Prints and pictorial cretonnes, which may be bought by the yard, hemmed, and mounted, add a note of color to the classroom and furnish illustrative material for transportation and other units of work.

6. *Exhibits.* Silk, rubber, and other manufactured products; collections of minerals, stamps, pictures, books, and the like, add vividness and reality to the instructional program.

7. *Properties and costumes.* Such items used in plays and programs may go into the properties' box of the school, the materials

to be used as need arises in school programs and entertainments.

8. *Programs.* Radio, theater, lecture, exhibit, museum, garden club, and book club programs offer suggestions.

9. *Reviews* of plays, movies, and books furnish current information.

10. *Biographical sketches.* Information about the lives of authors, writers, and actors may be obtained from such material.

11. *Mimeographed units of work and teacher-and-pupil-made helps.* Such materials meet immediate needs.

12. *Annotated bibliographies of source material and of available illustrative materials.* These are materials which should be preserved for reference.

Community Resources

Community resources will be found in the geographic setting and influences, the origin and historical development, the economic life, the political processes, the social organization, and the general pattern of living.

The general categories of resources may be clarified through examination of the outline suggested by Wesley [1] for the survey some years ago of Cumberland, Wisconsin. The resources are clearly indicated, together with the sources through which they may be tapped.

I. THE AREA: the city of Cumberland (location, population, chief industries); the trade area (extent, nature accessibility to Cumberland)

II. PHYSICAL SETTING: topography; soil (original and present condition); drainage; rainfall; temperature
sources: geological survey of Wisconsin; topographical maps, weather charts, observation by students

III. HISTORY: settlement and growth; early settlers; outstanding events; outstanding individuals
sources: local newspaper file (since 1880); council, school, court, business, and church records; personal diaries, letters, etc.; interviews with old inhabitants

[1] Edgar Wesley, *Teaching the Social Studies in High School,* 3rd ed. (Boston, Heath, 1950), p. 407.

IV. POPULATION: number by age, sex, nationality; density; growth and decline (birth and death rates, movement into and from area); distribution of population as affected by nationality, location and roads, land values

V. FARMS: number and size; value; products (crops, livestock, fruit, fish, game); farm debt, tenancy, farm labor
sources: United States Census; Department of Agriculture yearbooks; county agricultural agent's records; register of deeds office; assessor's lists and maps; private farm records; questionnaires and interviews

VI. BUYING AND SELLING: stores (number and type, ownership); buying in other towns; catalogue houses; co-operatives; peddlers; summer resorts
sources: business records; records of freight; bank statements; assessor's lists; interviews

VII. MANUFACTURING: number and types of establishments; employees, distribution of products

VIII. FINANCE: bank; savings-and-loan associations; federal agencies; extent of mortgaged property; insurance (types, prevalence)

IX. TRANSPORTATION: passengers (train, bus, automobiles); freight (train, trucks); roads
sources: enumeration of passengers; train, bus, and truck records

X. COMMUNICATION: telephones; radios; telegrams; volume of mail

XI. OCCUPATION: professions, doctors, lawyers; etc.; trades, barbers, plumbers, etc.; farmers, number; laborers, number and status
sources: interviews

XII. DISTRIBUTION OF WEALTH: per capita; incomes; wages; rental values; unemployment
sources: United States Census; income tax returns; payroll records; relief records

XIII. STANDARD OF LIVING: housing (city, types and conditions; country, types and conditions; hotels); conveniences (bathrooms, electricity, telephones, radios, automobiles per capita)
sources: observations; interviews; United States Census; insurance records; questionnaire for pupils

XIV. HEALTH: prevalent diseases; doctors and nurses; health regulations; water supply; sewage disposal
sources: interviews; county and state health records; observation; school health records

XV. EDUCATION: schools (city and country, attendance, curriculum, equipment, faculty, costs, graduates); library (books available, circulation records); adult education (types of classes, attendance); lectures, etc.
sources: school records; attendance records; library files; circulation records

XVI. CHURCHES: number and kinds; membership; attendance; activities; ministers
sources: membership lists; conference records; marriage and Sunday-school records

XVII. GOVERNMENT AND POLITICS: mayor and council; town officials (number, duties, etc.); taxation (types, disbursements, indebtedness); political alignment (parties, percentage of active voters)
sources: State laws; city charter; statutes; city council proceedings; town board proceedings; court records; election returns; *Wisconsin Blue Book*

XVIII. RECREATION: public (parks, playgrounds; hunting, fishing); commercial (picture shows, pool rooms, beer rooms); recreational clubs
sources: advertisements; observations

XIX. SOCIAL IDEAS AND STANDARDS: political and social clubs; local leaders; crime; divorce; attitudes toward Sunday amusements, drinking, smoking, dancing
sources: newspaper files; court records; observations, interviews

Students and teacher may make catalogues of community resources which eventually become part of the permanent files of the school. An important resource not clearly indicated by the survey outline, but one in which the schools will be greatly interested, lies in persons. Individuals, both active and retired, are often able to bring to the school vivid and important experiences. These may range from the historical data of the old settler to information about very recently developed processes in industry, in preservation of health, in police methods, and so on.

Another important listing of similar type should contain the location and availability of any personal collections of objects from a foreign country or from early days, models of ships and machines, and similar materials. A teacher in a tiny New England village was discouraged by her superintendent from attempting a unit on Arabia during the period of newspaper publicity about the Near East. Surely no materials of any sort would be available. The children, however, discovered a family in the village with a very large number of objects brought from the Near East many years before. Enough was borrowed to fill three tables in the schoolroom.

Community resources should be widely used. Another source of information and guidance is the past experience of the pupils. This is tapped through group discussion, through written autobiographies, and through reports on special topics. The experience of other persons in the community or farther afield may be utilized as sources through letters or interviews. When interviews are used, definite preparation must be made. Conversations do not just develop as the average citizen all too often thinks they do. Many good learning opportunities have broken down because of failure to plan the interview. Many business and professional men have refused to co-operate again after an embarrassing and fruitless experience with unprepared, tongue-tied pupils. In contrast, interviews organized around definite topics and questions upon which the interviewee is well informed are valuable and enjoyable. Preparation should not be carried down to minute detail, or the procedure becomes stilted and artificial. The children in group discussion decide just what it is they wish to find out, decide upon some broad general topics or questions which will initiate the conversation and keep it going. Provision for terminating an interview is as necessary as planning its initiation. [2]

An excursion to a museum, mill, factory, farm, store, forest, mine, harbor, lake, or beach is another excellent source of materials.

The activities which will bring learner and community into interaction may be (*a*) observational, (*b*) participatory, or (*c*) contributory. The majority will doubtless be observational, though the other types are on the increase. The contributory type, the most important of all, was unknown a few years ago.

Observational contacts. The excursion, as noted above, is the chief means of observational contacts. Trips may be made, in addition to those just listed, to municipal offices, public utilities, recreation and social service centers, or any others available.

The following is a good generalized list of excursions, suitable for elementary grades together with the questions they may help resolve: [3]

[2] Annette M. Garrett, *Interviewing, Its Principles and Methods* (New York, New York Family Service, 1942). Other similar materials widely available.

[3] W. A. Weaver, "Excursions in a Metropolitan Center," *Aids to Elementary School Teaching,* Thirteenth Yearbook of the Department of Elementary School Principals (Washington, D. C., N. E. A., 1934), pp. 292-293.

Extensive directories of possible school trips within the community have been issued by San Diego and Los Angeles, Cal.; Des Moines, Iowa; Vancouver and Longview, Wash. Others are available.

Several cities have issued bulletins also on the arrangements, both physical and educational, which should be made for trips.

1. *How do people on various social and economic levels live?*
The richer residential sections of the city: Park Avenue, Fifth Avenue, Riverside Drive, and Central Park West; the poor residential section of the town: Lower East Side; the wealthy hotels; the Waldorf Astoria; the breadlines. (Today we would add to this list the new federal housing projects.)

2. *How can housing for the poor be improved?*
The Lavanbury Houses
Co-operative houses

3. *What are the racial and religious groupings of the community?*
Little Italy, Little Russia, Harlem, Chinatown and Yorkville; Temple Emmanuel, and East Side Synagogue, The Cathedral of St. John the Divine, St. Patrick's Cathedral, Riverside Church, Father Divine's Peace Mission

4. *How does the city get its power?*
A large power plant

5. *How do people make a living?*
The garment center
Wall Street
A metal manufacturing firm

6. *How and where do people get their life necessities?*
A dairy farm   A department store
A bottling plant   A freight depot
A bakery   A trucking corporation
                   A clothing factory

7. *How do people travel to places?*
Subway and buses, a bus depot
A ferry
Bridges
Automobile assembly plant

8. *How do people communicate?*
A telephone exchange
The central post office
A central telegraph office
A radio station

Univ. of Minnesota Elementary Demonstration School Faculty, *Using Community Resources* (Minneapolis, Minn., Univ. of Minnesota Press, 1948).

Edward G. Olsen, *School and Community* (New York, Prentice-Hall, 1945), Ch. 8.

9. *How are people informed about events?*
   The city room of a large newspaper

10. *How do people govern themselves?*
    A political rally
    The meeting of a legislative body

11. *How are the people protected?*
    The police department
    A magistrate's court
    A fire station
    The street-cleaning department

12. *How do people enrich their lives?*
    A recreational center
    A public library
    The theater section
    A museum
    A radio broadcasting studio

13. *How does a particular community exchange products with the outside world?*
    A railroad depot   An airport
    A steamship dock

14. *How do people work toward another social order?*
    A meeting of a party aiming at social reconstruction
    Symposia, debates, and discussions

A list in interesting contrast to the foregoing is supplied by J. D. Aikenhead, who used to be School Inspector, Claresholm, Alberta, Canada, and is now with the provincial university. The list was developed by a remote frontier school. Visits to:

Fort Macleod.
Nearby foothills to see water-shed, drainage basins, erosion.

Over the first ridge of the Rocky Mountain foothills.
Crawford-Frost herd of Hereford cattle (among the best on the continent).
Miss Annora Brown's painting at Macleod.
The Claresholm model municipal hospital.
Four airfields.
Pat Burns' Ranch.
A remote home in the foothills. (The young of the Prairie chickens and of the Hungarian partridge will come up to feed with the domestic fowl.)
Beaver in the natural state (also many visits to extensive fields of wild flowers, birds, fish, and game in natural state).
A ski-meet.
The Road Maintainer outfit (machinery, McMurray tar sands, gravel, sand, etc.).
Observe a Chinook wind and its effects.
Calf clubs, grain clubs, etc.
A cattle auction.
A grain elevator.
A small lumber mill.
A demonstration farm.
The auxiliary mental hospital (for harmless older people).
A flour mill.
A creamery.

An interesting list is presented by Burr, Harding, and Jacobs [4] showing the alignment between the location of an excursion, its purpose, and point of primary emphasis:

[4] J. B. Burr, L. W. Harding, and L. B. Jacobs, *Student Teaching in the Elementary School*, 2nd ed. (New York, Appleton-Century-Crofts, 1958), p. 347.
See also R. W. Frederick, *The Third Curriculum* (New York, Appleton-Century-Crofts, 1959). Chapter 38 has an extensive list of co-operative agencies through which learners' experiences can be extended. See also certain selected chapters for activities and instructional materials.

Destination	Specific Purpose	Primary Emphasis
Wholesale house	to answer specific questions	about how bananas are brought to wholesale houses, cared for, and distributed to retailers
Cannery	to observe the process	by which whole ears of corn become cans of corn
Dairy farm	to answer specific questions	about how cows are cared for and milked
Lumber yard	to answer specific questions	about different kinds of building materials
Stone quarry	for general exploration	of the excavation, and of how the stone is obtained

Destination	Specific Purpose	Primary Emphasis
Print shop	for general exploration	of how printing is done
Post office	to observe processes	by which letters and packages are received and prepared for distribution
Model home	for general exploration	of modern improvements made possible by technological progress
Department store	for general exploration	of various departments and workers
Radio station	to answer specific questions	about how broadcasts take place
Farm	to answer specific questions	about how baby animals are born and raised
Wharf	to answer specific questions	about freighters: from where they came; products; how unloaded
Dairy	to observe the process	by which ice cream is made
House under construction	to answer specific questions	about what various construction workers do
Supermarket	for general exploration	of products sold
Shoe factory	to observe the process	by which leather is made into shoes
Water works	to answer specific questions	about source and quantity of water, and how purified.

Modern educational leaders have inaugurated programs of visitation between city and country, between regions, and between cultural groups. City children go on excursions through farming areas; rural children spend a week or more visiting a city or cities. Several groups from New York City went to visit the tenant farmers and Negroes of the South. These programs are expensive and will always be limited unless there comes a fundamental change in methods of financing education. Excursions should be used far more than they now are. They must be definitely planned in advanced by the group. An unorganized excursion not only fails to give the pupil the desired experiences but has a detrimental effect upon conduct and upon attitudes toward school experiences. Several city systems now issue excellent bulletins summarizing the planning of excursions. The following summary is based upon study of several bulletins and upon wide experience.

Advance Planning by the Teacher for Excursions

1. The teacher should make the trip himself before he takes the class.
2. The teacher should make arrangements with all the persons whom the children are to meet, to interview, or to hear.
3. The teacher will arrange with the persons met, the routines of the visit, meeting places, exhibits, lectures, pictures, interviews. In case of long excursions, the teacher will arrange lunch and rest periods.
4. The teacher will familiarize himself with the transportation facilities and routes (or arrange for parents' cars or school buses).
5. The teacher in some school systems must secure clearance for the trip from the central office; meet certain legal requirements; arrange extra carfare, and so on. Some school systems require the carrying of first aid kits on excursions. Others require police co-operation at certain points, for example, crossing guards.

With older groups, particularly in junior and senior high school, there can be much pupil participation in the advance planning.

Direct personal contacts, confirmed subsequently by letters setting down the agreements, are best. Telephone contacts are not satisfactory at all in arranging a trip for the first time. After a routine has been developed for a given excursion through a number of repetitions, telephone discussions will save much time.

Advance Planning by the Group for Excursions

1. A list of questions to ask is prepared.
2. Responsibility for asking these questions is delegated. The questions are usually grouped around some topic or problem. Individuals or small groups will volunteer to take these lists in terms of interest. The teacher may distribute those left over.
3. A list of things to look for and examine is prepared.
4. Responsibility is delegated for making notes, making sketches, taking photographs, collecting pamphlets, posters, manufactured products given away.
5. Methods of transportation are discussed, so that there is no confusion at the last moment.
6. The conduct of all while on the trip is discussed. Standards of conduct, of courtesy, and of responsibility are set up.
7. Responsibility is distributed for keeping the group together, for leadership of subgroups, for crossing streets, for avoiding hazards.

Responsibility and detailed planning differ greatly, of course, according to the level of maturity involved. The group discussion which follows will include delegating responsibility for summarizing findings, making exhibits if desired, reporting, filing for future use, and so forth.

Participatory contacts. Pupils should take an active part in a large number of community enterprises. This not only adds meaning to their education but initiates them into the affairs they will manage as adults. During the war children participated in all manner of drives, acted as airplane spotters, and served as messengers to adults engaged in some of the more complicated auxiliary services. Many activities had grown up in peace

time: the community clean-up campaign, an early and much overworked illustration of pupil participation; the control of pests from rats to tussock moths, a program carried on by regular city agencies and greatly aided by organized groups of children; traffic control; surveys of sanitary conditions and facilities, of mosquito breeding places; compilations of a tree census; the distribution of material prepared by city health and safety agencies; the repair of toys for distribution to less fortunate children; supervision of playgrounds. These and many other activities are still found in practice.

Contributory contacts. Learning situations of the participatory sort enable the pupils not only to learn and to understand the community better, but enable them to make an actual and effective contribution of their own to the community. The traditional school is particularly barren of these learning activities. The modern school has already developed an astonishing number of illustrations. *Progressive Education* contains a list of 170 actual illustrations gathered from the United States, Puerto Rico, Mexico, and Russia. [5] These projects are briefly described and the source noted. They vary all the way from feeding birds in winter and landscaping school grounds to placing a city electric system underground at a cost of $8,000. The summary should be read by all students.

The general categories under which the experiences were catalogued were:

Category	Number of Illustrations
General Civic Improvements	39
Bettering Agriculture	23
Conserving Forests and Soil	8
Developing Co-operatives	12
Exterminating Pests	5
Handicrafts	5
Health	28
Housing	7
Recreation	21

[5] Morris R. Mitchell and others, "Youth Has a Part to Play," *Progressive Education*, Vol. 19 (February, 1942), pp. 88-109.

This sort of vivid modern education is increasingly attracting the attention of prominent lay citizens. An excellent popular account similar to the professional summary in *Progressive Education* is found in Stuart Chase's article, "Bring Our Youngsters into the Community." [6]

Interest is high in developing school-community relationships and is likely to increase. Benefits to both school and community are very great. A few key references are given:

CLAPP, Elsie R., *Community Schools in Action* (New York, Viking, 1939). A pioneer volume still valuable for its collection of case studies.

See also further developments of this idea in many American communities in several of the books listed below dealing with community schools:

CLAPP, Elsie R., *The Use of Resources in Education* (New York, Harper, 1952). A case history, telling in vivid, personalized narrative, what was actually done in two rural schools in Kentucky and West Virginia to develop the personal and community resources which children and their families use in daily living.

COLCORD, Joanna C., *Your Community: Its Provision for Health, Education, Safety, and Welfare* (New York, Russell Sage Foundation, 1949). Outlines detailed suggestions for making non-technical studies of any community.

Community Living and Elementary School, Twenty-fourth Yearbook of the Department of Elementary School Principals (Washington, D. C., N.E.A., 1945). Presents numerous descriptions of actual practice in both rural and urban situations. The underlying philosophy is stressed, as are tested procedures in utilizing community resources in the curriculum, building community understanding of the school, meeting new community needs, and adventuring in school-community co-ordination.

[6] *Reader's Digest,* Vol. 40 (January, 1942), pp. 5-8.

The Community School, Fifty-second Yearbook of the National Society for the Study of Education, Part II (Chicago, Univ. of Chicago Press, 1953). Reports, analyzes, and evaluates research findings on community school philosophy, practices, progress, and problems in the United States and abroad and in local, regional, national, and international terms.

COOK, Lloyd A., and COOK, E. F., *A Sociological Approach to Education* (New York, McGraw, 1950). Analyzes American community life as it bears upon all aspects of school practices and community relations.

Education for All American Children (Washington, D. C., Educational Policies Commission, N.E.A., 1948). Describes in detail the desirable program of the life-centered community school.

Education for All American Youth: A Further Look (Washington, D. C., Educational Policies Commission, N.E.A., 1952). Defines and illustrates needed policies for youth education in "Farmville," "American City," and "Columbia." The essential orientation is that of the community school.

FOX, Lorene K., *The Rural Community and Its School* (New York, Kings Crown, 1948). Analyzes interrelationships between rural life and education and proposes a rural school program which relates educational patterns and practices to actual life needs.

HANNA, Paul, and others, *Youth Serves the Community* (New York, Appleton, 1936). Describes several hundred varied community service projects in public safety, civic beauty, health, agricultural, and industrial improvement, civic arts, local history, surveys, and protection of resources.

IVINS, Wilson H., and RUNGE, William B., *Work Experience in High School* (New York, Ronald, 1950). Defines the nature and objectives of a work experience program, with step-by-step procedures for putting such a program into operation and suggestions on how to correlate it with the existing curriculum.

McCHAREN, William K., *Selected Community School Programs in the South* (Nashville, Tenn., George Peabody College for Teachers, 1948). Examines the community concept in education, describes 22 specific school programs, and analyzes their organization, administration and personnel in terms of the community school idea.

OGDEN, Jean, and OGDEN, Jess, *These Things We Tried* (Charlottesville, Va., Univ. of

Virginia Extension Division, 1948). Describes and evaluates a five-year experiment in community development initiated and carried out by the Extension Division of the University of Virginia.

OLSEN, Edward G., ed., *The Modern Community School* (New York, Appleton-Century-Crofts, 1953). An excellent short collection of cases with appropriate discussion.

———, ed., *School and Community Programs* (Englewood Cliffs, N. J., Prentice-Hall, 1949). Includes over 150 concrete illustrations of successful community study and service practice in many fields from art to zoology and at all levels from kindergarten through college and adult education.

———, and others, *School and Community* (Englewood Cliffs, N. J., Prentice-Hall, 1945; rev. ed. 1954). Presents the philosophy and procedures of community study and service, with detailed attention to the community school movement; community analysis; community experiences through resource people, field trips, school camping, surveys, work experiences, and community service; steps in organizing a community resources program; and ways of enlisting public support through community use of school facilities, lay participation, and community co-ordination.

Organizing the Elementary School for Living and Learning (Washington, D. C., The Association for Supervision and Curriculum Development, 1947). Chapter 3, "Toward Community Planning," discusses guides for service to the community, the elementary school as a participant in community affairs, community resources for an enriched program, school-community planning, schools as centers for community living, and the community co-ordinating council.

POSTON, Richard W., *Small Town Renaissance* (New York, Harper, 1950). Dramatic account of the famous Montana Study, showing how small communities improved their own quality of living through self-study groups which eventuated in creative community action in such areas as industry, art, recreation, and education.

SMITH, B. Othanel, STANLEY, W. O., and SHORES, J. H., *Fundamentals of Curriculum Development* (New York, Harcourt, Brace & World, 1950). Chapter 22 discusses and illustrates the three community school concepts analyzed by Muntyan: the school as a model community, community activities in the school for school purposes and for community purposes, and school activities in the community for school purposes and for community purposes.

Principles determining the use of instructional materials.

Aids to instruction were often badly misused when first introduced. Many of the errors still persist. Illustrative materials were often used because they were "interesting." Interesting for what? Motion pictures are still too often used merely for entertainment, which is but one of several purposes. Students are grouped indiscriminately in the auditorium and shown a film which is unrelated to any of their activities. No preparation is made for seeing the film understandingly and there is no follow-up. Museum exhibits and other realia are used promiscuously under the vague impression that they "make things concrete," "illustrate," or "give the children better ideas." Often instructional materials are used as substitutes for carefully planned series of activities. All this is evidence of careless thinking. All instructional aids should be used for specific and defined purposes within an on-going series of activities, whether they be assigned or initiated by the pupils.

The first and all-inclusive principle has been stated several times: instructional aids are provided to give pupils vicarious experiences useful to their purposes when the real experiences are outside the pupils' immediate environment.

1. *A given instructional aid should be chosen to serve a direct need of the learner as that need appears in the series of learning activities.*

Aids and materials are not used merely because they are "interesting," "real," or "concrete," but because they explain or clarify a needed understanding, contribute to the development of an attitude, explain a motor or machine process. The next principle is equally important.

2. *Instructional aids should be chosen in terms of the pupils' maturity and experience, and in accord with individual differences within the group.*

Is the language used within the reading and speaking vocabularies of the learners?

Is the material portrayed close enough to pupils' past experience to be readily assimilable?

Is the manner of presentation understandable to the pupils?

Is the material sufficiently comprehensive to secure varied responses, thus enabling various types of children to react on their levels and in their own way?

Is there possibility of differentiation in the follow-up?

Is there possibility to continue growth along the lines already apparent at the given level of maturity?

3. *Instructional aids should be examined for accuracy and validity as well as for appropriateness to need and maturity.*
Is the material accurate and up-to-date?
Is it of desirable quality?
Is it acceptable under aesthetic as well as utilitarian standards?
Is it easily available?

4. *The use of given instructional aids should be carefully planned.*
The teacher should preview or otherwise examine the material in order to be sure that it fits the need which has arisen or which he plans to stimulate.
Teacher and pupils together should prepare themselves to use the materials intelligently in the light of the need which it is to serve.
A list of questions may be developed.
An outline of points to observe may be developed.

5. *The use of instructional aids should include a definitely planned follow-up.*
This may be through further discussion or analysis in the light of the questions or points to observe or through an evaluation device.

6. *Preference should be given to those supplementary materials which approach most closely the comparable direct experience.*

7. *Instructional aids should be chosen within reasonable limits in terms of cost.*

Extended treatment of various instructional aids available in special volumes and in special-methods classes. A truly enormous literature now exists concerning most of the general resources and types of instructional materials. A general volume such as this cannot pretend to give more than an introduction which will be supplemented in other special courses. The following pages, therefore, present summaries for a few of the more crucial aids. The treatment illustrates what might be done with others. [7]

Proper use of printed materials. The typical and most widely used instructional material is that contained in textbooks, supplementary books, bulletins, pamphlets, periodicals, newspapers, and the like. Learning through the use of books is and will continue to be one of the most important activities in and out of school. The development of extensive and effective aids of other types should not blind us to this point. Contrary to much popular opinion, "book larnin" is extremely valuable. The ability to learn through abstractions in print is reliable evidence of mental maturity. A "book-learned fool" is not a fool because book-learned but because he was a fool in the first place. True, persons of little ability can master books and parrot the contents. Poor books are widely distributed. Many traditional teachers make vicious misuse of good books. None of these things detracts from the great importance and value of learning from and through books. Except for persons of very limited ability, and those engaged in routine activities, most of what we know is derived from printed matter. When properly handled by a competent teacher and adjusted to the experiential backgrounds of the learners, books are among the most important vehicles of learning ever discovered. An obligation rests upon teachers to understand the purpose and organization of any text or supplementary volume selected for use.

Printed materials must be carefully eval-

[7] A reference containing many lists of instructional aids, principles governing their use, and sources of materials, all in brief compact form is the one-hundred-page pamphlet by Amo De Bernardis, *The Use of Instructional Materials* (New York, Appleton-Century-Crofts, 1960).

uated. A check should be made of all printed materials, particularly textbooks. Definite standards should be available for determining accuracy and value, mode of presentation, appropriateness of vocabulary and illustrations, and adaptation to level of maturity among the learners. The standing, training, and experience of the authors, as well as the standing of the publishers, should be examined. Mechanical features of size, binding, type, placement of pictures and margins, and other details may be checked against accepted standards.

Many textbooks present the subject matter of the course in such difficult form that teachers must illustrate and explain at great length, something many teachers are unable to do. Books often contain unteachable material, that is, matter which is isolated and unrelated to typical learning activities. This material cannot be taught because it does not mean anything. Teachers often struggle through it, forcing students to memorize many useless and unrelated, if not trivial, facts.

A number of other points can be enumerated. Checklists have been developed under which texts and other books may be judged. Space will not be used to reproduce a checklist here, since students should have met and used such lists in special-methods courses. Students unfamiliar with these instruments may be given practice in their use at this point. (See Exercise No. 12, p. 432.)

The reading of newspapers and periodicals: a special case of critical evaluation. Modern schools make increasing use of daily newspapers, weekly news summaries, and journals of opinion. The general public is largely dependent upon these sources for most of its information and opinion. Propaganda techniques and their great importance in public affairs are phenomena of modern civilization with its facilities for the dissemination of information and interpretation. Modern newspapers and periodicals have rendered great service to the public in certain areas and on certain problems. In other areas, newspapers and periodicals are unfortunately unreliable and irresponsible. The advertising in these publications has greatly improved public taste in certain fields and debased it in others. It has disseminated a great amount of valuable information useful to all citizens. It has also spread much vicious misinformation, and developed unnecessary fears and taboos. It is therefore highly important that everyone develop competent critical methods and standards for reading of this type. Excellent training is now given in many departments of English, of social studies, and in the modern core curriculum. All other fields, particularly science, may contribute to this training. Students preparing to teach should demand treatment of this problem in appropriate special-methods courses.

Newspapers and periodicals can be one of the strongest forces in the furtherance of education; they can also be among the most serious obstacles. The public needs competent honest education from the elementary grades onward with direct reference to this problem.

Motion pictures, one of the most important instructional aids. The motion picture comes closer to actual experience or first-hand observation than any other teaching device. It can be adjusted to appeal to all levels from the kindergarten through college, from illiterates to research scholars. Schools and industrial establishments have been using films for instructional purposes for some time. The armed forces of the United States have made extensive use of motion pictures in training for the most diverse skills and understandings. Tremendous progress was made under the pressure of war training. The public schools are probably about to enter upon an era of enormous expansion in the use of motion pictures and all related audio-visual aids.

The general principles stated earlier in the

chapter should govern the use of pictures. Educational aims and not immediate instructional necessities should be served. Arousing "interest," "illustrating" in general, and the like are subordinated to the development or clarifying of understandings, attitudes, and appreciations and to the demonstration of skills and machine operations. Applied to the use of motion pictures, certain of the general principles suggest that the teacher should:

1. Preview the film to determine content, whether to project all or a part, whether to repeat certain parts, and so forth.
2. Evaluate the film to determine fitness and value.
   a. A film may be valuable on one level and not on another.
   b. The titles and explanatory material should be within the vocabulary of the children; should contribute to aim as does the picture content.
   c. The sequence should be natural and understandable to the viewers, be without arbitrary breaks and unnatural connections.
   d. The material should be accurate and up-to-date.
   e. The effect upon attitude as well as upon understanding should be estimated.
   f. The quality of the photography should be noted.
3. Prepare the pupils to see, to understand, and to draw inferences.
   a. A list of questions to be answered or points to be noted may be developed co-operatively in advance of showing.
   b. An outline of events may be supplied, particularly with longer or more difficult films.
4. Conduct a follow-up discussion or other exercise based upon the questions, the points to observe, or the outline.

Abstractions can be objectified with great ease. The understanding of and comparison between cultures, for instance, our own with that of Mexico, of China, or of Norway, is often difficult on the basis of reading materials alone. Motion pictures enable even primary children to achieve usable understandings on their level. Children and adults achieve understandings and develop attitudes concerning current social, economic, and political problems through viewing pictures which do not come readily through other means. The chief limitation of films also appears at this point. It is very difficult to portray quickly in simple objective manner the effect of subtle, long-time, impersonal forces which underlie social movements. Films designed to explain why we fought World War II did not explain why we fought in any real sense. They portrayed a series of incidents which make persons angry enough to fight but did not explain even remotely why we should fight. Many of the films developed since the depression, designed to explain certain economic and social problems, illustrate but cannot explain the difficulties. Well-planned films competently handled by good teachers do, however, supply a tremendous amount of material which will serve as a basis for vigorous discussion and as motivation for further exploration by direct experience or reading. Thus motion pictures serve greatly, even though indirectly, in the development of important abstract ideas.

The motion picture is certain to become one of the most extensively used instructional aids because of its nearness to reality, its flexibility, and its wide range of application. All special-methods courses should include training in the use of films. Special courses have developed rapidly in the country, though a number of them do not go beyond the mechanics of handling equipment.

Good catalogues of films are available from various sources. Several educational magazines maintain columns in which current productions are reviewed or noted. [8]

[8] Edgar Dale, *Audio-Visual Methods in Teaching*, rev. ed. (New York, Holt, Rinehart & Winston, 1954). Complete and detailed. Lists of film catalogues and film sources are included. Good analysis of use of various aids.
Mary F. Horkheimer and John W. Differ, *Educator's Guide to Free Film Strips*, 12th ed. (Randolph, Wisc., Educators Progress Service, 1960).

The radio in the schoolroom. The radio has gone through approximately the steps all new materials or methods seem to follow. First uses were desultory and fragmentary. Interest and novelty seemed to be the chief characteristics. Part of this was owing to lack of training available for teachers. The radio, like the motion picture, is becoming integrated properly into the educational program and serves definite uses.

Television in education. Interest is and has been high. Many programs are available on all levels from primary to adult education. Experimental evidence so far is meager, although critical analysis is increasing and giving good insights. Use at present should be highly selective and critically evaluated in terms of purposes to be served. Considerable progress may be expected but at present no sweeping statements should be accepted.

Extended treatment of motion pictures, radio, television, or any other specialized materials may be obtained, if students are interested, through class reports and exhibits. Visits may also be made to materials centers maintained by colleges and by city or state departments of education.

Teaching machines. Interest in programmed teaching through machines is very high at this writing. Extravagant claims for the machines are matched by equally extravagant criticisms. Research is developing apace though much of it is uncritical. Conclusions for and against are not yet fully validated. Instructors and students must keep fully abreast of the periodical and pamphlet literature.

Walter A. Wittick and Gertie H. Halsted, *Free Tapes, Scripts, Transcriptions,* 6th ed. (Randolph, Wisc., Educators Progress Service, 1960).

Mary F. Horkheimer and John W. Differ, *Free Films,* 20th ed. (Randolph, Wisc., Educators Progress Service, 1960).

The preceding three references are usually revised annually.

Note also that many colleges, city and state departments of education issue bulletins on all kinds of instructional aids.

DISCUSSION QUESTIONS

1. What bearing upon the selection of instructional materials has the current emphasis upon living in a changing democratic society?

2. The statement is made by Burr, Harding, and Jacobs that: "The elementary school which is not utilizing directly and continuously the resources of the community is not playing a major role in the education of children."

    a. What are the obstacles which in general prevent the schools from so utilizing these resources?

    b. What are the obstacles in your particular school or system?

    c. Relate any experiences in overcoming the obstacles.

3. Summarize quickly from experience, reading, or observation a few points showing:

    a. How living in slum areas affects the development of pupils as learners and as persons.

    b. How financial support affects materials of instruction. Tell how financial handicaps can be in part overcome.

    c. That teachers should or should not participate in community surveys.

4. List several of the most important material and social elements in your community that you think affect pupil learning for better or for worse.

5. Outline briefly and make critical analysis of the methods used in your system for the selection of instructional materials.

6. Make a list of some of the new kinds of instructional materials found in modern schools that were not used twenty years ago. Fifty years ago.

    a. Observe a room or rooms in any nearby co-operating elementary or secondary school and note the presence or absence of supplementary materials.

    b. Make a few suggestions for materials which are easily available for a given subject and room observed in which few or none are used.

7. Experienced teachers may describe the actual aids and materials they are now using or have used in connection with given units or assignments. Describe also specified situations where the appropriate materials were not available.

8. Describe and critically evaluate your own use of any audio-visual aids, particularly motion pictures. Students in training may report on the basis of observations. (This exercise implies a set of criteria, and these may be set

up co-operatively in class or by committee prior to reporting.)

9. Maps are among the most carelessly evaluated and used instructional aids. Develop a check list of criteria and apply to the map equipment of a given room or department.

10. Examine two textbooks in the same field, published thirty years apart (longer or shorter interval as necessary to show important contrasts) and summarize important differences and improvements.

11. What improvements have been made in textbooks during your own teaching experience? During the past two or three decades? Be specific.

12. Select from the literature a check list for textbooks in your field. Apply to one or two well-known books and report. A score card may be co-operatively developed in class or by committee if desired.

13. Describe and explain text material which you have met which is "so difficult that it is of no use unless greatly amplified by the teacher."

14. What is meant by unteachable material?

15. Report briefly on any effort you know about in high school or college directed at improvement of reading. Report the methods of diagnosis and remedial teaching. Report any illustrations of training in any one of the types of reading. Explain, if you know, how the high school or college project started, how conducted and evaluated.

16. Describe in detail any experience you may have had with a teachers' workshop designed to improve the use of or to manufacture instructional aids and materials.

17. Describe and critically evaluate the uses made by your community of the school plant.

REPORTS BY INDIVIDUALS OR COMMITTEES

1. Describe briefly any project in which you may have participated wherein the school attempted to make systematic use of community resources. (Inexperienced students may report critically on this same topic, using any published school survey as the basis.)

2. Experienced teachers may report upon any program of observational, participatory, or contributory experiences carried on in their systems. (Isolated excursions or random projects need not be reported, though if there is class interest a report could be made of the type of excursion made in a given system, with critical evaluation.)

3. Experienced teachers in committee may prepare a list of field trips for teachers, based on their own community, which would aid teachers to know the community resources for teaching. (This cannot be done from memory or "general knowledge." The committee will need to make visits, consult local authorities, use guide books and historical references.)

4. Students in training might plan and carry out an excursion which fits a unit or assignment going on in a nearby co-operating school.

5. A report could be made especially on the use of local museums, many of which make special effort to work with the schools.

6. A similar report may be made on local library facilities.

7. A report may be made on the school library, checking against the American Library Association's list of titles for children, and against other lists issued by school systems, publishers, and individuals. (A recent survey showed that some schools gave children access to 6 per cent of the desired books, others to 60 per cent.)

8. Make a study of materials necessary in the teaching of any one of the several subject fields (reading, language arts, arithmetic, and so forth), together with a statement of the adequacy of the materials supplied locally. Blanks are available for aiding such summaries in various yearbooks and special method books. (See Burton and Brueckner, *Supervision*, Chs. 13 and 17, for a sample. Sometimes the blanks will have to be devised.) (Schools using a unified instead of a subject curriculum will still be using materials under the above classifications.)

9. Reports may be made upon the use of motion pictures in the local system. (Similarly for radio and television.)

10. Reports should be made on the making and use of slides, film strips, puppets and marionettes, and many other similar devices. Experienced teachers may report on and demonstrate use of these items.

11. School camping is rapidly coming to the fore as a school experience of great value. Sections of the country vary greatly in the use of this. A report could be made based on the growing literature, plus reports from those who have had experience.

12. Outline a plan based on your community which might bring about the establishment of a community council to study local conditions with a view to providing better settings for education.

13. A report may be made on those magazines devoted to certain types of aids, chiefly

audio-visual, and including those general magazines which carry columns dealing with instructional materials. (Lists are available in several of the key references, or may be found in good libraries.)

14. A report should be made concerning the use of human resources in the community, either in general (see Burr, Harding, and Jacobs, pp. 308-313) or specifically as used by an experienced teacher in the group.

READINGS

General References Similar To This Chapter

Most of the books on general method or general principles of teaching contain chapters similar to this one, though each one usually contributes some ideas not contained in the others.

BURR, James B., HARDING, L. W., and JACOBS, L. B., *Student Teaching in the Elementary School*, 2nd ed. (New York, Appleton-Century-Crofts, 1958). Chapters 11 and 12 good supplement to this chapter. Short bibliography.

LEE, J. Murray, and LEE, Dorris M., *The Child and His Curriculum*, 3rd ed. (New York, Appleton-Century-Crofts, 1960). Chapter 8 one of the best available. Extensive bibliography.

RIVLIN, Harry N., *Teaching Adolescents in Secondary Schools*, rev. ed. (New York, Appleton-Century-Crofts, 1961). Chapter 8 very good.

Sources of Free and Inexpensive Material

DE BERNARDIS, Amo, *The Use of Instructional Materials* (New York, Appleton-Century-Crofts, 1960). Pamphlet of one hundred pages giving many summaries of principles governing use of different types of materials and at the end a selective list of sources.

Free and Inexpensive Educational Materials, Including Sources of Visual Aids, Special Report No. 17 (The Quarrie Reference Library, 35 West Wacker Drive, Chicago, constantly revised).

FOWLKES, John G., and CODY, Paul T., *Educators' Index to Free Material* (Randolph, Wisc., Educators Progress Service, annual editions). This is the most detailed and exhaustive list available. Comes in card index form. In addition to materials by subject fields, it gives extensive lists of sources, including scores of corporations and industrial firms. Includes also list of government departments from which materials can be secured.

FOWLKES, John G., and MORGAN, D. O., eds., *The Elementary Teachers' Guide to Free Curriculum Materials* (Randolph, Wisc., Educators Progress Service, revised annually). A mimeographed comprehensive list of teaching materials.

SINCLAIR, Thomas J., *Business-Sponsored Teaching Aids* (Dansville, N. Y., Owen). Contains a list of about ninety corporations or industrial associations which supply free materials.

Sources of Free and Inexpensive Teaching Aids (Bruce Miller, Box 222, Ontario, Cal., constantly supplemented).

BOTTRELL, Harold R., *Using Community Resources within the Curriculum; Using Community Resource Persons in the Classroom; Community Resources* (Gulf School Research Development Association, 3801 Cullen Blvd., Houston, Texas).

University Publications

A large number of colleges now maintain materials departments or publish bulletins dealing with free and inexpensive materials. The best known are probably the annual bulletin published by George Peabody College for Teachers, Nashville, Tenn., and periodical bulletins by Hugh B. Wood, School of Education, University of Oregon.

Instructors and teachers should check nearby colleges for such bulletins.

Government Bulletins

A large number of departments in the Federal government sell or give away many kinds of materials useful in the schoolroom. A complete list of these departments is found in the Fowlkes-Cody reference above.

Part IV

IMPROVEMENT
OF TECHNIQUES
COMMON
TO TRADITIONAL
AND MODERN
METHODS

A number of techniques and types of information are necessary whether one is using traditional or modern methods, or any variation of either. The chapters following present these materials.

CHAPTER 18: Improvement in the Use of Questions

The results of early investigations of the teacher's use of questions somewhat shocked educational leaders. Teachers were found asking regularly 150 questions per class hour. In a class of twenty-two pupils, one was questioned twice in two weeks, whereas a classmate was called on eleven times in the same period. In a small class of thirteen, one pupil was questioned four times, whereas another was called upon eighteen times.

These facts should not have shocked those who discovered them. They evidently do not shock thousands of so-called practical teachers, since the practices described are in common use. And why not? As long as the aim of education is believed to be the mastery of content, the memorization of masses of unrelated, fragmentary facts, a barrage of minute fact questions is a natural and legitimate procedure. As long as the school is not concerned with causes of failure, nor with adaptation to individual differences, accidental and uneven distribution of questions will be found.

In a recent investigation (soon to be published) 2600 tape recordings were made of class sessions in over forty rooms. In one room only, were students asked thought questions! Students were clearly trying to formulate their own conclusions and reactions, to figure out answers, to use various sources, to critically evaluate. In the other 39 rooms, impossible though it seems, the questions were all similar to: "What did the book say about this?" "What can you remember about this?" Other types of questions, or pupil response, did not appear. The criticism is again, not altogether of the teachers, but of the institutions which trained them.

When the aim of education is conceived not as memorization of fact but as the development of complex controls of conduct—understandings, attitudes, appreciations, skills, and special abilities—a wholly different technique of questioning becomes imperative. A questioning technique suitable to the older method of learning cannot develop pupil judgment, independence in study, suspension of judgment, or abilities to analyze and discriminate.

Sound conception of aim: good general education necessary for improvement of questioning. Butler calls attention sharply to the error of earlier writers on questioning. They endeavored to improve questioning by improving the wording, the form, the mechanics—that is, the technique. The *chief* weakness lies, however, not in the technique but in the teacher's conception of the purpose or aim. If his aim is pupil mastery of facts, then his rapid-fire questioning technique cannot be condemned. It is well fitted to his aim. To improve questioning, the teacher's knowledge of aims must be improved. A *secondary,* allied weakness is lack of knowledge of the mental processes of learning. A *third* important weakness is often found in the teacher's own lack of general education and intellectual interest. Teachers cannot ask questions which lead the child to develop values or appreciations if they have never achieved values or appreciations of their own. Individuals who have not read critically and endeavored to interpret a number of conflicting statements cannot ask interpretive questions. The writer recently observed a high school teacher stumble through an atrociously incompetent lesson in modern literature. Later in conversation the teacher quite casually said that she had not had time for several years to read any of the books "on the list." No wonder her questions designed to guide pupils in evaluation, in discrimination, and toward appreciations were peculiar!

Butler's blunt indictment is worth repeating: [1]

When we say that a teacher's questions are poor, we actually mean that her knowledge and thinking are poor. Why not be honest and call a spade a spade? We endeavor to do everything by techniques; on the contrary the source responsible for the weakness should be strengthened and invigorated. . . .

It is essential that beginning teachers and experienced teachers realize the importance of developing their own minds before their teaching can be improved. The person who has ideas, thoughts, different viewpoints, notions of genuine values, and real purposes and aims in mind will ask questions in keeping with profitable achievement without seeking a mechanical clue in the specific words or forms in framing questions. The purpose of the question, rather than its form or wording, is the all-important factor. A thought question is a thought question regardless of the vocabulary used. Purposes pull in words needed to give the purpose proper expression.

This is excellent. Nevertheless, considerable assistance can be given to teachers about wording and form after purposes have been clarified. To this we will turn later.

Good native ability to think and teaching experience are necessary for improvement of questioning. As was said of the socialized techniques in the section on the recitation, no one can tell another how to concoct good questions. Advice almost reduces itself to the equivalent of telling students and teachers to lift themselves by their boot straps! Expert or even passable questioning and the ability to lead discussion by means of questions is greatly affected by native ability and by experience. The actual development of the art of questioning is one of the most difficult and, oddly enough, one of the most neglected problems in teaching. It remains a constant problem for many good teachers. Good questioning requires the ability, native or acquired, to think quickly and easily while facing a class, to shift and change as thought progresses, and to phrase questions in clear and unambiguous terms.

The teacher must also be able to sense quickly the causes of misinterpretation of his questions. For every curious answer, "schoolboy howler," or simple misinterpretation, there is good reason in the mind of the pupil. The ability to direct thought by questioning is one of the most valid proofs of teaching skill known. Through it all, the teacher has to move with the thought of the group, guiding but not dominating.

These requirements puncture in some measure the pleasant fiction that the slow but efficient thinker can, in the end, do anything that the quick person can. A slow thinker, no matter how efficient and conscientious, will always have difficulty with a class of normal pupils. The quiet, retiring, scholarly young person who often goes in

[1] Frank A. Butler, *The Improvement of Teaching in Secondary Schools* (Chicago, Univ. of Chicago Press, 1939), pp. 195, 197.

for teaching so often turns out to be a misfit because he lacks these very requirements.

Planning is clearly demanded. Few persons are gifted enough to be able without some previous preparation to follow the thought of a group, to shift and turn quickly enough, to guide the lesson coherently without domineering. A preview which is not the formulation of a rigid sequence will be helpful. In fact, the writer, after some years of minimizing lesson planning, has returned to it in flexible form. Practice teachers for several years now have been unanimous in declaring that being forced to write out some questions in advance with probable answers, and to plan continuity thus, was one of the most helpful devices given them. One brilliant student who was about to fail in his practice teaching rejected this suggestion for some time. He was not required to accept it. Finally, in desperation he tried it. Within ten days he, his supervising teacher, and several members of his high school class were astonished at the change.

Learning to concoct good questions is not, however, quite so difficult as lifting oneself by the boot straps. Native knack and experience are vital, but one can profit from advice and training. Plato, probably reflecting his training under the great questioner, Socrates, wrote in the *Republic,* "Then you will enact that they (the rulers) shall have such an education as will enable them to attain the greatest skill in asking and answering questions."

The purposes to be served by questions. The aims and purposes to be served by questioning are obviously fundamental. The number would be large if all subpurposes were included. The most important are:

1. *To stimulate reflective thought.* This is, of course, a blanket term. The various elements include analysis, comparison, definition, judgment, and interpretation.

2. *To develop understanding.* Questions may direct attention to important elements basic to the understanding. The pupil's own experience can be searched, analyzed, and organized through questioning.

3. *To bring about the emergence of new concepts.* This may call for comparisons with simple known facts, for pointing out of analogies.

4. *To apply information.* Good problem questions and certain "exercises" in texts and syllabi illustrate this. Many exercises are unfortunately composed of memory questions or call for the following of recipes.

5. *To develop appreciations and attitudes.* Analytic questioning, so widely used for this purpose, is definitely detrimental. The teacher should provide opportunities for appreciation to emerge.

6. *To develop the power and habit of evaluation.*

7. *To change beliefs or attitudes.* This is a delicate matter. Beliefs acquired in emotional settings cannot be changed ordinarily by fact or logic. Hence the questions which encroach upon an emotionally held belief must be indirect and free from emotional content. In fact, education should first attempt to train persons in knowledge of mental and emotional processes before attempting to change beliefs.

8. *To focus attention on cause-and-effect relationship.* This aim, of course, overlaps with two or three others. Socratic, conversational questioning of the "if this, then that" type is valuable.

9. *To determine the informational background, interests, and maturity of individuals or class groups.* General techniques for pretesting listed in the chapter on the assignment supply guidance here. Here, if anywhere, direct fact questions might play a legitimate part along with other forms.

10. *To create interest, arouse purpose, develop mind-set.*

11. *To test directly for designated achievements.*

Illustration of contrasting purposes revealed by questions. The story told in Chapter 5 of the boy whose composition about the Washington monument was rejected illustrates the different purposes which a question may serve. The teacher aimed the question at a series of facts. The boy assumed that the question was aimed at understandings and attitudes, and answered accordingly.

Butler gives a simple and explicit illustration. [2] Two sets of questions about Lincoln's Gettysburg Address are contrasted to show how aims vary and how the variation determines the quality of the questions.

In one classroom:

1. Where did he give it?
2. When did he give it?
3. What was the occasion?
4. How many years are there in a score?
5. How many years are there in four score and seven?
6. Who is ready to recite the Address?

In another classroom:

1. What was the basic principle upon which Lincoln developed the Address? Did Lincoln think of the principle first or did others before Lincoln believe in it?
2. Did you notice any time sequence?
3. What message did Lincoln leave for his fellow-citizens?
4. What feelings would you have had if you were at the dedication and heard Lincoln?
5. Suppose you had never heard Lincoln, do you think you could tell something about his character from just reading the Address?

The second set is by no means perfect, but the difference between the two sets is too striking to need extended comment. The difference is not in the words, both vocabularies being simple; it is in the purposes served.

The following interpretive questions listed by a practice teacher are in pleasing contrast to the typical "who, what, when, how many, and what happened next" questions.

[2] Frank A. Butler, *The Improvement of Teaching in Secondary Schools* (Chicago, Univ. of Chicago Press, 1939), p. 198.

Questions To Be Used as a Basis for Discussion of Carl Sandburg's "Abraham Lincoln"

1. Through Chapter 18, page 41
   a. Why was Nancy Hanks called a pioneer sacrifice? What are the implications?
   b. Do you agree with Dennis Hanks' statement, "Exceptin' for an interest in politics and religion, they lived just like Injuns"? Why?
   c. Why does Sandburg keep repeating "the wilderness is careless"?
   d. Where and how would you say that Lincoln got his real education?
   e. Is the style of writing suitable to the subject?

2. Through Chapter 29, page 82
   a. In the various jobs that Lincoln had, what could he have learned which would later help him?
   b. Jefferson said, "Sometimes it is said that man cannot be trusted with the government of himself. Can he then be trusted with the government of others?" Apply this to Lincoln. Apply it to Andrew Jackson.
   c. Does Sandburg give the historical background of these times? Give instances.
   d. How did Lincoln's idea of God affect his actions?
   e. What did Lincoln's first election speech show of his character?
   f. Find instances of symbolism in these chapters.
   g. Could you tell from reading this book that Sandburg is a poet? How?
   h. What is the relation of this book to the school of interpretive biography?

Knowledge of purposes is then the first step in preparing good questions. Attempting to aim the wording directly at the purpose to be served will help to prevent pointless questioning.

General principles basic to good questioning. With the place or purpose clear as one important guidepost and before turning to the details of wording and form, we may set up a list of general principles. [3]

[3] The writer's original list was improved by some items and wordings adapted from other authors. Grateful acknowledgment is made to Bossing, Frederick, Ragsdale and Salisbury, and particularly to Butler.

1. *The general sequence of questions should be organized around a thread or core.* This refers to the general continuity of the lesson and not to the minutiae which are arranged as the lesson progresses. The evils of rambling discussion have already been mentioned in the section on recitation. Maintaining reasonable continuity is extremely difficult for beginning teachers. Practice teachers who are unable to make progress in developing this ability should doubtless be discouraged from continuing in the profession. The development of the particular objectives of the unit or lesson series—understanding, appreciation, or attitude—furnishes the thread.

2. *Answers, to be acceptable, should be reasonably full, rounded replies.* Short, choppy questions invite short, choppy answers. Probably as an outcome of the rapid-fire fact question, there has grown up in schools of the United States a thoroughly reprehensible practice, namely, the acceptance from pupils of fragmentary one-point answers. Our typical procedure is to secure one point from the first pupil, a second point from another, and so on until several pupils have contributed enough fragments to complete a reputable answer. This is true from elementary school through college. Genuine effort is necessary to break it up, and so far little progress has been made. The modern school, because of the different setting of questions and discussion, cares for the matter properly for the most part.

The writer had a most revealing experience while teaching in the University of Puerto Rico. After the usual preliminary days of explanation, defining of problems by the students, planning methods of procedure, and so on, the day came when the first set of the study questions was to be analyzed in class. The first student called upon glanced at some notes, laid them down, and proceeded to speak without interruption for nine minutes! There was nothing much to be said further and everyone knew it. Thinking he had by accident called upon a local

honor student, the writer studied his class to find a student who seemed to be average or poorer. He fell into the ancient error of assuming that the beautiful are dumb and assigned the next question accordingly. The young lady looked at her notes, rose, and spoke for six minutes! Again there were no corrections or additions warranted. It should not be assumed that this formal procedure was used exclusively. Many of the questions called not for summaries but for comparison of views, whereupon the discussion was fast and furious—so fast, in fact, that the Spanish-speaking students asked permission to carry on in Spanish because thinking in English slowed them down! The argument was then summarized in English for the instructor, who guided the continuing analysis. The point to be emphasized was that these Puerto Rican students had been thoroughly trained to answer in adequate, coherent summaries. In this one respect at least, these students are superior to ours.

3. *Accept any answer or part thereof which can be used.* If reasonably full responses to questions are not, for any reason, obtainable, it is well to encourage pupils by attempting to use, with proper comment, any contribution. This begets more and better volunteering. Even an answer which is not too close to the point should not be just ignored. A comment or question may aid the pupil in seeing how he missed the objective. Rarely should a teacher flatly reject an answer, possibly never reject without explanation. "That's part of it, let's see if you (or anyone else) can elaborate it." "That's on the point, but it's a minor point which supports another major idea—what might the latter be?" "Hold that a moment; we will use it later." A teacher who says that an answer is "dead wrong" or otherwise ridicules an honest effort is preventing the very thing he is there to encourage—learning activity.

4. *The questions should be within the pupil's experience and knowledge.* It is difficult for students fresh from high-grade lib-

eral arts colleges to realize that what is everyday knowledge to them is utterly and completely unknown to high school pupils. The differences in experience and knowledge between high school pupils of the same age but of different socioeconomic backgrounds are enormous. Differences in maturity and special interests also affect this matter vitally. Some specific suggestions for the improvement of questioning will be made in later pages when discussing the vocabulary of questioning. For the moment, the general principle is important.

The writer observed a high school teacher present to a class an exhibit of extensive statistical material. He repeated several times that *"no one except a trained expert* in statistics could understand these statistics and their implications." Without pausing for breath, he then assigned the tables to the class for overnight study, full explanation to be brought to class next morning! No one else saw the joke, least of all the teacher. The class naturally did not see the joke—such things are no joke to them!

5. *Allow time to think of an answer and to put it into words.* It is difficult for an eager, quick-thinking teacher to remain silent while a slow-thinking, or even a quick, pupil figures out an answer. The pressure on the teacher is increased because the answer is already in his mind, full-formed and "perfect." It is in the forefront of his consciousness, and he completely forgets that a pupil may have to recall data, try to relate them to the question, think of words or perhaps illustrations. The teacher must simply school himself to stand quietly while thinking takes place.

To insist on quick answers gives excellent training in superficial, inaccurate thinking. It encourages the practice, too common in adult life, of stating ignorant and half-formed opinions as if they were important contributions to conversation.

Time should not be wasted, however, attempting to extract from a pupil an answer which he does not know, but which the rest of the class does. Many teachers think it an index of pedagogical expertness to pursue a child with a volley of questions in an effort to secure a desired response. They say, "It makes him think; he must get it himself." Anyone who has seen a blushing, stammering child subjected to this knows that the opposite is true. The procedure clearly embarrasses and muddles the poor child so that he cannot think. If the rest of the class knows, and the question is simple, another child should supply the information immediately and let the thinking move forward. When the learning situation is complex and most of the class needs guidance in analysis, then a series of questions slowly and sympathetically given, with class participation, is valuable.

6. *The teacher's attitude during questioning should be natural, friendly, and conversational.* This is merely in keeping with the practice of both old and new schools which are trying to apply modern psychology. Its effect on pupil attitudes and upon learning has been discussed earlier in several places.

7. *Pupils should be encouraged to ask questions.* Good teachers encourage and welcome questions from the class. To secure interested, competent response is an index of high teaching skill. The best type of pupil participation is being secured. Careful distinction should be made, of course, between the interested, alert pupil who asks intelligent, legitimate questions, and the bluffer who wastes time with many foolish and irrelevant ones. Good teachers attempt to use any part of a question which will contribute to class thought. Even a pointless question should not be summarily dismissed if further conversation may bring the pupil to see wherein his question is useless. Recurring pointless questions from the same pupil call for individual assistance outside class time.

Unfortunately, some teachers dislike pupils who ask questions. They strive to discourage such activity. Teachers who consistently discourage the alert questioning child are either very lazy or completely misunderstand their functions as teachers. Teachers who will not or cannot encourage, guide, and enter into the learning processes of the pupils should be removed, if possible.

8. *Develop an attitude of pupil responsibility for answering questions from the class as well as those from the teacher.* Again this is but good modern psychology. Children are not to look to the teacher as final and unanswerable arbiter. They are to take responsibility, come to conclusions, and support them.

9. *Do not hesitate to say, "I do not know" to a pupil's question.* Many traditional teachers were as bad bluffers as some of their pupils! No one is supposed to know everything. Learning is continuous for all of us. Teachers who feel they "lose face" by not answering lose much more, if they only knew, when they pretend to answer everything. Questions for which the teacher does not have an immediate answer can be made the subject of discussion, of minor assignments to individuals or to small committees. Sometimes, the teacher alone will be able to get the answer, and he should volunteer to bring it in when available.

The wording and form of questions. With purpose-to-be-served and other major principles understood, we may turn to some of the minutiae. The following suggestions will aid in the actual construction of questions.

1. *The objective of the question should be clear and definite.* If the objective is not clear, there is no fair criterion for judging the answer. The chief errors here are the "discuss," "what about," "tell about," "what can you say" questions. These are vague and general and unfair to the student. They indicate lazy, inexact thinking or no preparation on the part of the teacher.

a. *Avoid "discuss" questions.* This type abounds in high school and college: "Discuss the reign of Nero," "Discuss the results of the Westward Movement," "Discuss the Missouri Compromise," "Discuss the novel as a literary form." The following are culled from recent examinations. "Discuss a speech on ceremony," "Discuss eavesdropping as a device in *Much Ado About Nothing* and in *Twelfth Night,*" "Discuss the arithmetic mean, the probable error, and the mean error," "Discuss the thermodynamic principles involved in the determination of the Heat of Combustion of a substance with the Bomb Calorimeter," "Discuss the Federal Reserve Act," and "Discuss:

Let music sound while he doth make his choice;
Then if he lose, he makes a swan-like end,
Fading in music."

These questions are absurd. They indicate no beginning, no end, and no organization for the answer. Some could be "discussed" for six months. Some have been "discussed" for years. There is no guidance or stimulation of any sort. Such questions are responsible for much harsh unfairness in marking pupils.

For instance a pupil might answer the question "Discuss Roosevelt's silver policy" with one sentence: "The policy was one of expediency, unjustified, and detrimental to our economy." He has fulfilled the conditions of the question. "But," says the instructor, "I meant that he was to outline the circumstances leading to the emergence of the policy, the events following its announcement, results to date, and the probable future developments. I wanted a detailed, organized discussion." The pupil cannot be a mind reader. The question neither demands nor implies anything of the type of answer concealed in the instructor's mind. It suggests no such beginning, sequence, or terminus. The pupil cannot with any honesty be held for such an answer. As the question stands any "discussion" is satisfactory: lengthy, brief, organized, or unorganized. An ancient schoolroom joke illustrates the point. A student was confronted with the question, "Discuss the reign of Caligula," and realized he knew nothing whatever about this reign.

Purely as a shot in the dark, or perhaps as a satire on his own state of mind he wrote, "The less said about the reign of Caligula the better." This is said to have been accepted.

High school teachers and college professors addicted to use of "discuss" questions follow the argument further. They claim that such questions teach pupils to organize. Not at all; they may equally teach them to make rambling incoherent presentations. If the instructor refuses to accept a poor organization, he is marking by a criterion not implied in the question and not within the knowledge of the pupil. As indicated above, the crux lies just here. Most instructors do have in mind a type of organization and treatment they wish reproduced when they ask "discuss" questions, but the type accepted varies from instructor to instructor. Students can be taught to organize by far better devices than vague, indefinite questions. In fact, there is much material available in the literature on study skills showing how to do this. Further, pupils should have been taught to organize long before test or summary questions appear.

Again, the instructor may desire a critical comparison. He may reject not only a rambling discussion but the expository organization acceptable to another professor. Again the pupil cannot be clairvoyant. If the instructor means by "discuss" a critical comparison thrown into certain form, he should ask for it.

The question stated above may be thrown into better form, "Present in organized form, the origin, development, present status, and probable future of Roosevelt's silver policy." This by no means "gives the answer away" but it implies a definite type of answer which can be marked under a criterion clear to any honest pupil. One teacher, defending the "discuss" question as a stimulus to thinking, criticized the form of the "Roosevelt silver policy" question just given by saying that all it did was call for repetition of assigned text. Certainly it does! That is exactly what the majority of secondary and college teachers want, especially when they ask "discuss" questions. Training pupils to think demands not only a change in the form of question but in the teaching. Several sources may be assigned, controversial data should be introduced, reference to related material included. The question to stimulate thinking will not be the sloppy "discuss" question, but perhaps, "Present in organized form the origin, development, present status and probable future of Roosevelt's silver policy as you derive it from the readings and class discussion. Indicate clearly why you accept certain data and views, rejecting others. Support your summary with argument at all points."

Some teachers instruct and drill their pupils in the desired type of answer to "discuss" questions. Under specific, limited conditions of this sort the question is fair, but this procedure seems a long way around a simple point. Ordinarily, this type of question is a shot in the dark, a "sloppy" device, a lazy teacher's refuge.

Stimulated evidently by the sharp criticisms made of such questions by psychologists, there have recently appeared some paragraphs in defense of "discuss" questions. Most of them are more indicative of hurt surprise that a time-honored technique should be assailed than they are of any critical analysis of the issue. Are not "discuss" questions used by the best professors, and in respectable schools, forsooth! Some of the comments are quite transparent defense mechanisms. Nothing has yet appeared which invalidates the criticisms.

b. *Avoid "what about," "what can you say about," "talk about," questions.* These are but variations of the "discuss" procedure. The same analysis applies. Such questions have no clear objective; they give the pupil no guidance whatever; the answers cannot be marked with fairness. They indicate complete failure on the part of the teacher to give attention to analysis of his objectives and to the wording of his questions.

Improvement in the Use of Questions   443

c. Avoid leading questions. The opposite of the discuss question is the question which gives too much guidance, the type condemned in courtrooms as "leading" questions. This error is so obvious and simple that it should not need mention. Teachers everywhere, however, use such questions. "Pericles was banished from Athens, was he not?" "Lincoln was right in freeing the slaves, was he not?" Pupils are constantly crowded into a desired answer by questions which contain, within them such phrases as "don't you think so?" "it is true, isn't it?" "you would have to agree, wouldn't you?" Leading questions result sometimes from poor ability to think and to phrase questions but sometimes from the teacher's insistence that a predetermined answer be forced upon the class. In the social studies, such questions are very serious blunders.

d. Avoid catch questions. Most of us have been caught by such questions as the following:

An athlete is to run around a square field. It takes him 40 seconds to run the first side which is 140 yards. It takes him 50 seconds to run the second side. How long is the second side?

A train leaves Chicago for New York traveling 50 miles an hour. At the same time a train leaves New York for Chicago going 65 miles an hour. Which will be the farthest from New York when they meet?

Following normal and sensible mathematical attitudes and precedents, many pupils will try to work such problems. The catch is then explained.

Intrigued by the trick, one tends to say, "Such problems make one think." The direct opposite is true. Such questions confuse thinking by making one "think" in ways which are not valuable in real problems. The uncritical teacher confuses "hunting for the catch" with true "analysis of a problem." Real thinking has to do with ferreting out true and logical connections, not with dis-covering odd and bizarre tricks which rarely appear in real problems. The mental attitude engendered by catch questions is inimical to analytic thinking. Looking for the catch prevents one's seeing the logical connections. These questions are good parlor entertainment and are prominent in many intellectually perverted radio programs.

2. *The question should be directed at attainable objectives.* Certain questions, although clearly stated, are confusing because they call for more or less final answers when such answers are either not available, or can only be guessed at by the pupils. They are directed at the causes or solutions of certain historical events—wars, revolutions, economic upheavals, political movements—or call for moral judgments to be passed upon such events. If the teacher accepts superficial answers, his pupils are receiving training in poor thinking. They all too often feel a smug and ignorant satisfaction when their simple answers are accepted for complex problems. The real answers to some of these problems have puzzled the best thinkers we have. Such questions are clearly permissible when it is understood that the objective is to stimulate discussion, the search for and organization of data, and the suspension of judgment. Wide difference of opinion regarding final answers should be permitted and encouraged.

3. *The wording of the question should be precise and direct.*

a. Avoid digressions and involved statements. If questions are to direct thought they must be to the point, avoiding long involved phrases, or supposedly facetious or even explanatory digressions. Many teachers believe they are engendering good feeling in the class when they interlard the question with humorous commentary. A college professor was heard to ask, "A group of bright young men such as we have here must in their previous variegated academic careers have met the Law of Parsimony—sometimes called Occam's razor—and why do you suppose it was called Occam's razor—and have some dim realization of its applications to thinking and so we will have Mr. Blank apply it to the several explanations which seem derivable from the pedagogical experiment upon the efficacy of several ways of increasing the vocabulary."

b. Avoid ambiguity. The difficulties inherent in using language carefully have been discussed earlier. The young teacher and the hurried older teacher often use words which may be interpreted quite honestly by pupils in several different ways. A teacher, developing concepts of latitude and longitude by means of street directions in a small town, asked an inattentive boy how he would get from the depot to the hotel and received the reply, "I'd walk." The teacher, desiring the reply "One block south and four blocks west," became very angry, failing to realize that the boy's interpretation of his question was honest. With more mature bright students, words must be chosen with real care.

c. Avoid asking the question two or more ways in one statement. Teachers often fall into this error in a sincere effort to aid the pupil. "What is a ballad, or can you define this type of poetry?" It is better to ask it one way and give time for recall or volunteer answers before changing the wording. It is good practice to rephrase a question in different words, since different wordings strike responses in different minds; an interval, however, should elapse.

d. Avoid calling for more than one unified reaction at a time. This is sometimes called a "double" question. "Why is alcohol not a food and why is it bad for us?" "Did the belligerent submarine have a right to enter our neutral port to exchange goods, and what should we have done about it?"

A more complicated form of the double question is one that states alternatives. "Is there great rainfall or not in Western Oregon?" "Was Pizarro a Spaniard or a Portuguese?" Questions may legitimately present alternatives when controversial issues are involved and when the question is designed to initiate a continuing comparison and evaluation of data.

4. The vocabulary should be within the comprehension of the pupil. The case is cited of a junior-high school history text which included on one page in the first chapter such words as *embryonic, vicissitudes,* and *economic stability.* The writer observed a teacher who asked a junior-high school class, "Did not the group of signers to the Declaration of Independence constitute a *felicitous galaxy* of statesmen?" Still another asked a pupil to *"embroider* on the theme." "Did the conference *culminate* in *unification?"* "What is the *thesis* of the book you are reading?" Such words as *mercenary, romanticist, mores,* have little meaning for young pupils. Many children are even confused by being asked to "Tell the *influence* of" or *"Compare* the industries of" since the words *influence* and *compare* have not ordinarily been used that way by them. One class failed to answer a question which included the word *semester* because they had never heard the word before, *term* being the usage in their school.

The question may be asked whether extension of vocabulary is not one aim of teaching. Assuredly. In all educational procedure, questioning included, the pupil's vocabulary—as well as many other achievements—is to be improved. This is done in questioning as in reading, through contextual clues and through direct study. New words which can be properly interpreted by ordinary pupils may be used freely. The criticism refers to words which have not, and cannot have, meaning for the pupil.

Mechanical features of questioning. Before we list the mechanical features of questioning, note that we are referring to the improved recitation period and not to the completely modern working period of a unit. Frederick, Ragsdale, and Salisbury poke considerable fun at certain of the advices commonly given about the actual mechanics of presenting and distributing questions. [4] Their criticisms are quite correct if we abandon the typical formal recitation. But since the recitation will be common practice for some time to come, attention is still necessary to the improvement of a practice which is not itself basically sound.

1. *Present question to class before calling upon someone to answer.* This tends to secure attention from all, and all at least start thinking about an answer.

2. *Distribute questions.* Teachers tend naturally to favor those pupils who volunteer, who contribute, and who themselves ask questions. Some device to insure distribution of opportunity to participate is necessary. Alphabetic or other fixed orders for calling upon pupils should be avoided. These are too useless even for the traditional recitation. Glancing over the roll just previous to class and noting those who have not contributed recently will help. Writing those names on a card is even better. Shuffling class cards is another recommended device.

Suggestions 1 and 2 are those chiefly ridiculed by Frederick, Ragsdale, and Salisbury as being wholly out of line with reputable learning situations and as provocative of undesirable attitudes. This is correct unless, as stated, we are already operating under a system which makes forced attention necessary.

3. *Do not repeat questions.* Questions should not be repeated habitually, because this makes for lack of attention. Care should be taken not to offend or embarrass the conscientious pupil who occasionally asks for repetition of a question which he does not understand. In the case of consistently inattentive pupils a sharp refusal to repeat is legitimate—if such an attitude is ever legitimate.

This suggestion, also, is one which would be ridiculous under modern teaching conditions.

[4] *Directing Learning* (New York, Appleton, 1938), pp. 170-171.

4. *Do not repeat answers.* This is a seriously bad habit, one easily acquired and most difficult to overcome. It arises from the teacher's natural desire to emphasize, to interpret, and to extend thinking. Teachers should be rigidly on guard against this, as it encourages fragmentary, incomplete, and poorly worded answers from pupils.

5. *With certain exceptions, secure answers in complete sentence form.* Complete answers in good English are ordinarily desirable. This is particularly true during important class discussions. Otherwise, bad habits in expression arise and misunderstandings occur. Answering in complete and coherent form should be a matter of course. In some kinds of discussion, as in real life, this type of answer would slow thinking, if not actually confuse it. Contrary to the opinions of some teachers, it is quite all right to ask "yes or no" questions. Criticism should be directed at the teacher's failure to follow up with other questions aimed to secure reasons and argument.

Adapt to individual differences. Adaptation of all procedures to individual differences has been stressed throughout this volume as a prime characteristic of modern teaching. This is particularly true of questioning. Teachers should make earnest, reasonable effort to take into consideration pupils' abilities, special interests, personal characteristics, and so forth, in distributing questions.

The distribution of difficult thought questions has caused some debate among teachers. Some hold that these should be given to the weaker pupils in order to spur them to effort and to give them practice in analyzing difficult problems. Success is said to bring satisfaction and confidence. Others maintain that the poor pupil is not able to solve difficult problems, and that instead of getting practice in thinking, he is more likely to become confused and embarrassed. Instead of confidence, he suffers the opposite and avoids participation. A waste of class time also results. It seems better to distribute difficult problems to brighter children. Their analysis is of value to slower pupils, who can often understand their fellows better than they can the teacher. Weaker pupils would then be given easier questions which they can solve with some degree of facility. Properly adjusted to levels of ability, such questions will probably afford all the opportunity for thinking these pupils can use. The flashy, superficial pupil may be given difficult questions and held firmly to results in order that he may appreciate and experience the value of good work.

Common weaknesses in pupil answers. Observation and teacher reports indicate certain typical weaknesses in answering which can be remedied.

1. Pupils begin to answer before thinking out the complete implication of the question.

   A fragmentary answer results.
   Minor points may be magnified and major points neglected.

2. Pupils seem to expect continued stimulation from the teacher.

   Fragmentary, choppy, one-point answers are given.

3. Pupils believe that they have answered a question if they give any one or two of several points which could be given.

   Inadequate, unorganized answers are given.

4. Pupils take no responsibility for organization, sequence, and coherence.

   Rambling, discursive answers result.
   Relative values are neglected.

5. Pupils seem to be seeking to discover what the teacher wants, rather than to evolve answers based on the data and implications.

   Answers are dictated by suggestibility rather than by analysis and thought.

These points overlap but are listed separately for emphasis. It is clear that the teacher's mode of questioning and the type of answer accepted will contribute to the development of good or poor habits of answering. An analysis of pupil answers and habits of answering supplies guidance toward the improvement of questioning.

DISCUSSION QUESTIONS

1. For each of the faults listed above show briefly how the teacher may unwittingly contribute to their development; how he may help eliminate them.

2. Give examples, if you can recall them from your own school experience (or watch for them now in observing), of particularly skillful guidance of class discussion by questions either prepared in advance or developed in terms of class-hour demands. (Several reports may be made on this to illustrate different points.)

3. Do the same thing for cases of particularly poor practice. Could you suggest improvements?

4. How will you probably learn to construct good questions?

5. In general, how would you handle a bright pupil who rarely studies carefully and who is a good bluffer?

6. List a number of suggestions for stimulating pupils to ask questions.

EXERCISES AND REPORTS

1. Secure a lesson plan, or lesson report, or unit plan or log, containing a fairly detailed account of the question-and-answer procedure in the class period. Accounts of traditional daily lesson plans are to be found in practically every text on general method or principles of teaching. Both traditional and modern plans appear in the periodical literature and in books on unit teaching. Instructors should have built up a large personal collection of plans and unit outlines.

Read the general questioning sequence carefully and analyze critically in the light of the principles and suggestions summarized in this chapter. Prepare an organized, detailed critique.

2. Select a typical segment of material used as the basis of a traditional recitation. Organize a general sequence of major questions based upon it but designed to get as good learning as is possible under formal conditions.

3. Do the same thing for the approach or initiation of a typical experience unit.

READINGS

A number of current books on teaching make no mention of questioning or its improvement. Several do have good chapters. Students may quickly run through a collection of recent books on principles of teaching.

One modern book which has an excellent chapter and also a very good listing of other books with similar discussions is:

RIVLIN, Harry N., *Teaching Adolescents in Secondary Schools*, 2nd ed., (New York, Appleton-Century-Crofts, 1961), Ch. 7.

Two older books of value despite early copyright are:

BUTLER, Frank A., *The Improvement of Teaching in Secondary Schools* (Chicago, Univ. of Chicago Press, 1939). Chapter 10 is one of best available.

FREDERICK, Robert W., RAGSDALE, C. E., and SALISBURY, Rachel, *Directing Learning* (New York, Appleton-Century-Crofts, 1938). Chapter 8 on the recitation contains excellent brief discussion of questioning.

CHAPTER 19: The Guidance of Drill or Practice

Drill is necessary to facilitate three general types of learning product: (a) *motor skills,* as in handwriting, pronunciation, handling tools and machinery, athletic events and games; (b) *mental skills,* as in multiplication and addition, recognition of symbols in silent reading, and many others; (c) *arbitrary associations,* such as the sequence of letters in spelling, use of symbols in map-reading, and the like. The object of practice is to develop facility in the skill and to secure automatic recall of arbitrary associations.

Controversy over drill. One of the paradoxes within the teaching field relates to drill. On one hand there is an extensive body of valid fact about drill; on the other hand, a large number of teachers who are quite unaware of the facts. (One cannot resist asking, what has been going on during the teachers' training period?) Vigorous discussion results; differences of opinion are violent; silly nonsense is widely disseminated; children are subjected to incredibly incompetent practices. Arguments arise, first, as indicated, because the facts are not known; second, because valid research is often stated in terms unfamiliar to the average teacher; and third, because the facts contradict in startling fashion many time-honored stereotypes. A paragraph is cited below, too extreme in its language to be typical, but not extreme in representing the widely distributed muddled thinking.

The Right to Drill

Of all the restraints placed on teachers in recent years, the one in opposition to drill is the most absurd. Recently there has been some back-tracking by a few education professors when they admit that "meaningful" drill is legitimate. Previous to this admission, opposition to drill as an educational technique had been run into the ground so far that the word had much the same naughty connotations as "formal discipline." Please, Mr. Education Professor, tell me where Van Cliburn, Anna Pavlova, Lily Pons, the Barrymores, Albert Einstein, and Wernher Von Braun, would have achieved their particular skills if it hadn't been for hard work and concentrated study, which is in itself drill. [1]

This paragraph is incredible! It is probably without parallel in educational literature. The sheer unawareness of facts in existence for a third of a century, the inconceivable confusion between two distinct concepts of drill staggers the reader. Here indeed is confusion doubly confounded. The paragraph could be dismissed for the nonsense it is, but because of the importance of the general issue a short analysis will be made.

1. "Restraints placed on teachers . . . in opposition to drill. . . ." No such restraints are voiced anywhere in educational literature. The writer has observed none during 49 years of teaching. Wherever such restraints appear the

[1] Bruce McDowell, "A Bill of Rights for Classroom Teachers," *Phi Delta Kappan,* Vol. XXXX (May, 1959), p. 332.

fault lies solely with an incompetent local administrator or supervisor.

2. ". . . Some backtracking by a few education professors . . . who now *admit* that *meaningful* drill is legitimate. . . ." One is tempted here to give voice to one of those rolling, thundering, crashing, mouth-filling, soul-satisfying, medieval oaths which were as much facetious as profane. Homeric laughter will have to do instead! The educational psychologists and professors did not *admit* meaningful practice to be legitimate. They *demonstrated* and *proved* its effectiveness in contrast to dreary, routine repetition. Instead of *admitting* they have been *advocating* meaningful practice for approximately a *third of a century*. Their books are full of this. (How did the teacher-training institutions fail to introduce all this to the paragraph author—or maybe they did without effect.)

3. ". . . Opposition to drill . . . has been run into the ground. . . ." Opposition to drill is voiced nowhere in competent educational literature. Opposition to stupid, routine repetition as contrasted with purposeful drill has been appearing for several decades. Local opposition is due solely to incompetent leadership . . . or perhaps the observers are hopelessly confused between the two concepts of drill.

4. "Please, Mr. Education Professor, tell me where Van Cliburn, Anna Pavlova, Lily Pons, . . . would have achieved their particular skills . . . (without drill)." The Mr. Education Professors, backed by the Mr. Educational Psychologists, reply with pleasure that these distinguished artists are doing exactly what they, the professors, recommend throughout educational literature and have been recommending for thirty years, . . . engaging in meaningful practice, under purpose, and with insight. This is in flat, direct opposition to the concept of drill supported by the paragraph writer and which he hopelessly confuses with the modern, valid concept of drill.

Comments of truly savage nature could be made concerning this hopelessly incompetent statement about drill. It is, unhappily, representative of views held by a number of teachers. Our indictment, however, should not be brought against the teachers but against the teacher-training institutions which sent out certain teachers completely innocent of the most elementary facts concerning an important phase of instruction—drill or practice. Teachers upholding outmoded concepts of drill in opposition to the modern concept fall into two classes: (*a*) honest and sincere individuals who are ignorant of the facts; (*b*) those whose reaction is an irrational defense mechanism because a personal belief or routine has been attacked.

Emphasis must be placed here on the fact that competent, well-trained teachers and the research experts are in complete accord concerning drill. Before taking up principles governing drill, let us dispose of some common criticisms of psychologists and educators. The commonest are that the experts say:

1. Drill should be eliminated from school.
2. One cannot learn by repetition.
3. One does not learn anything through drilling.

Analysis will not only clear the record but will supply some little known facts about drill. The traditional teacher stands fast upon the dictum that "drill and lots of it is the only way to learn certain things."

The elimination of drill from the classroom.
The position of modern educators and psychologists with regard to drill in the classroom can be unequivocally stated as follows:

1. The elimination of drill from the classroom has never been advocated by any competent psychologist or educator anywhere at any time. [2]
2. Typical traditional drill methods waste huge amounts of time and energy and result

[2] The excellent discussion of the development of skill in Chapter 8 of L. Thomas Hopkins, *Interaction* (Boston, Heath, 1941), is sometimes quoted as advocating the elimination of drill. The discussion is somewhat ideal but clearly provides for refinement of skills. Careful reading of the entire volume further supports this view. Hopkins' discussion is an antidote for the view which upholds excessive repetitive drill.

All texts on methods or principles of teaching contain a chapter on drill. Many texts on educational psychology contain chapters on practice and the learning of skills.

in poor learning. Detrimental results are actually produced by too much drill.

3. Modern educators and psychologists developed several material and fundamental changes in the amount and nature of drill.

The evidence and the arguments supporting these statements are extensive and clear-cut, appearing widely in journals devoted to experimental education and experimental psychology. As a matter of fact, early writers, both lay and professional, long ago recognized the facts now being demonstrated through research. The traditional teacher could have arrived at the same conclusions had he been trained to analyze his own processes and results. Lacking this training, he is honestly bewildered by criticisms of procedures he has regarded as safe and sure. Many teachers who repeat the charge that the modern school eliminates drill are ignorant of the fact that the modern school provides more and better practice than the traditional. A few teachers repeat this charge as a form of "fifth-column" sniping against educational methods which they do not understand, do not like, and are afraid to try.

Simple explanations will be attempted in the following paragraphs in the hope that misunderstandings will be clarified, that the fears of sincere traditional teachers will be removed, and that classroom procedure eventually will be improved. A good deal of the difficulty, as will be seen, turns upon definitions of words and clarifications of common-sense meanings.

"One does not learn by mere repetition."
The traditional teacher and the average parent are sure this is "theory," "high-falutin' nonsense." It seems so clearly opposed to common sense. On the contrary, however, brief attention to everyday common-sense experiences in and out of the classroom shows that mere repetition is not educative. One hesitates to repeat the ancient and be-whiskered joke about the boy kept after school to write 150 times "I have gone." Finishing the stint in the absence of the teacher, he left his paper with a note stating, "I have went home." The repetition was recent and frequent, but without meaning or purpose. It did not change his language usage. Scores of schoolboy howlers involving curious blunders in spelling and arithmetic and reading are available, showing that gross errors are made in real situations regardless of the amount of isolated repetitive drill. Ask any individual how many steps there are in the staircase in his home, how many steps up to the coach of the commuter's train he rides twice a day, or for similar information from any other situation in which he has acted repetitiously ten thousand times. Mere repetition without attention or motive will not give the answer. These are but anecdotes or stories and prove nothing. However, excellent research studies are available and in quantity. Teachers who were brought up on the connectionist S-R bond theory of learning but are not familiar with recent research by connectionist psychologists are the most sure that repetition is educative. On the contrary, Thorndike,[3] the leader of the connectionist school, has presented some of the best evidence that mere repetition will not produce desirable learning.

The discussion to follow may in part seem to some teachers like quibbling. Careful analysis and understanding are necessary, however, if drill processes are to be operated effectively. Let us then analyze and explain further the statement verified by research, that mere repetition is not educative.

First, pure, precise repetition does not

[3] E. L. Thorndike, *Human Learning* (New York, Appleton, 1931). Contains much research material and many modifications of the original statement of the laws of learning.

The majority of texts on educational psychology present in detail the problems of skill learning. Any one may be consulted by interested students. One or two reports of research studies on drill might be made if there is interest. We cite one of the best texts as representative of a large group.

Lee J. Cronbach, *Educational Psychology* (New York, Harcourt, Brace & World, 1954). Chapters 12 and 13 are excellent. Note the footnotes and other references to research background.

actually occur. One never performs an act twice in exactly the same way. Arbitrary associations, formulas, or series of symbols can, of course, be repeated precisely under dictation and correction. Experiments show that mere repetition even here may be definitely miseducative. *Second,* it is the stimulus situation, not the response, which is repeated. Each stimulus calls for a retrial of the skill. If the stimulus situation is real to the learner, it guarantees motive and attention. Retrials with insight, which in turn add insight, do promote the development of the desired skill. Retrial under sensible conditions will promote learning, whereas mere repetition will not. *Third,* the stimulus situations themselves vary, demanding exercise of the skill under differing conditions and from different positions. This in turn calls for variations in the skilled act itself. The development of effective skill is distinctly enhanced by this variation. Repetition of the traditional type, however, is precluded. Continued insistence upon mere repetition by itself will actually hamper the development and use of the desired skill. *Fourth,* many acts are performed with reasonable skill without previous repetition. A common-sense demonstration is found in the use of the left hand when the right is lost or temporarily incapacitated. Experimental evidence is also available. *Fifth,* insistence upon repetition of a fixed routine often blinds the teacher to what is actually going on within the pupil. The teacher assumes that he is repeating the number combination or the letters in the word or what not. The learner, instead, may be devising any number of ways to secure the answer. Some of these will be desirable and represent progress toward meaning and skill; others will be clumsy and detrimental. The teacher interested in enforcing faithful repetition of the model may not discover this learning process and thus will not be able to participate and give guidance to the learner. Discovering this normal variable behavior, some teachers actively repress it. The learner, however, learns what he repeats

with meaning to him, not what he verbalizes for the teacher without meaning to himself.

"One does not learn through drill." We may be sympathetic to the teacher's annoyance with this statement, even though it is largely correct. The statement is a loose one, misunderstanding being due in part to a play on words. Learning, in truth, *precedes* drill. Drill cannot enter until something has been learned to some degree. The significant statement is "to some degree." Some meaning and insight must precede drill, but meaning and insight are also extended during the progress of drill. Drills aim to polish a skill or association so that its use is facilitated, but skill itself is not a fixed and rigid thing. The inference for teaching is important and once understood will remove the teacher's annoyance: understanding or meaning in some degree must be attained before drill can be of value.

"Drill and lots of it is necessary! the only way to learn certain things." Few statements are insisted upon so vigorously by traditional teachers as is this one. We may disregard the few who so insist because they are afraid of new procedures; because they will not allow their comfortable routines to be disturbed. The majority of teachers who insist upon "drill and lots of it" are quite honest. They are ignorant of the facts and naïvely unaware that other methods are available. They are often quite unconscious of the real effects of their kind of imposed drill.

The process of acquiring skills and associations, *if these are imposed upon the learner in advance of need or understanding,* certainly does necessitate great expenditure of time and energy. It does actually demand "drill and lots of it." The traditional school, centered upon adult-determined skills and not upon the growth of the learner, cannot possibly avoid excessive drill. Traditional teachers who lack recent contact with training courses cannot help believing that drill and lots of it is natural, desirable, inevitable. A wholly different conception will emerge, however, if the total learning situation is changed. Suppose that skills are not introduced until a need is felt or stimulated; that meaning is developed through exploration and insight before practice starts. Skills to be practiced will then be derived from a functional situation and will serve a recognized need of the learner. The experimental evidence is clear-cut. The amount of time and the number of retrials necessary for the development of the desired skill are enormously cut down. The evidence shows also that the antagonistic attitudes and detrimental work habits which result from excessive routine drill are absent where modern procedures prevail. This has been mentioned frequently in previous chapters.

Even worse, the evidence shows further that insistence upon excessive drill can in given cases *actually prevent the development of the desired skill*. Moreover, disintegration of such skill as has been developed can result from excessive drill. The pupil actually gets worse in the very thing which he is being forced to repeat! Excessive drill on number facts has been shown to destroy understanding of the relationships governing the number system itself.

The belief that drill and lots of it—in the traditional sense of mere repetition—is good is flatly contradicted by the facts. Teachers, sincere and otherwise, will profit greatly, as will their pupils, by understanding modern methods of teaching which enable pupils to achieve satisfactory levels of skill rapidly and economically.

The nature of a skill. The teaching of skills in school and in industry has been handicapped for generations because of the persistence of uncritical, common-sense notions concerning the nature of a skill. A number of new conceptions based on extensive and valid research must be acquired by teachers before the guidance of skill learning will be well done.

First, teachers in school and in industry will be helped greatly if they will regard *skills as refinements of meaning and not as isolated mechanisms.* Skills are the means for making understandings operative. Skills have no meaning themselves separate from functional situations. This general conception of learning has been developed throughout this volume. The prime corollary is that skills to be learned must be met first within, and derived from, a functional or meaningful situation. The skills are then meaningful to the learner; this alone will reduce the time and energy necessary to develop facility. The second corollary is that after first meeting a skill in a functional situation, the learner must meet it again and again in meaningful situations before practice is even thought of. Learners should engage in many exploratory and experimental trials, should ask questions, study diagrams, observe skilled performers, for the purpose of developing clear perception of the movements and understanding of the use of the skill. Practice should not begin in fact until sufficient understanding has been achieved.

Second, skills are not precise, fixed routines to be achieved through unthinking repetition. Skill performance is inherently variable. It varies from person to person, from time to time with the same person, and from situation to situation. Skills must also be developed for use in varying situations and positions. This is another way of stating a point made earlier: namely, that while insight and meaning must in some degree precede practice, the very practice to attain skill enhances the insight.

Third, the acquisition of a skill has two phases: (*a*) the integrative phase in which perception of the process and meaning are developed; and (*b*) the refining or facilitating phase in which precision is developed. Many children of normal intelligence, often superior intelligence, present puzzling inability to learn to read or to compute, or to master certain simple tool skills in tradinal schools which present the skills in advance of understanding. Placed in meaningful situations with ample opportunity to develop understanding, these children learn easily and rapidly. This is true with adults in industry. The introduction of modern methods of training foremen, and in turn the workmen, has greatly improved skill learning in industrial establishments.

We may be sure of one thing: no amount of drill will produce skill which is beyond the learner's perception of, or insight into, meaning.

The nature of educative practice.   The student, by this time, is doubtless wondering if his common sense is of any value! Surely repetition must have some place. How can one achieve a skill except by repeating it, by practice? Practice is obviously necessary in the affairs of the schoolroom and life. The foregoing pages should have prepared us for the answer. The analysis was not quibbling but a necessary preliminary to stating the principles governing practice or drill. Drill is necessary in school if for no other reason than the time factor. Skills must be attained, granted they are in keeping with maturity levels, more rapidly than they ever could be by incidental and accidental practice. Modern principles in the guidance of practice, are, as has been hinted, very different from those now widely used.

A quick summary of points from preceding pages will aid in understanding the discussion of the principles of practice which follows.

1. Skills are refinements of meaning and not isolated mechanisms. Perception of the process and understanding are essential.
2. Skills are not precise fixed routines but are inherently variable.
3. The acquisition of a skill includes two phases, the integrative and the refining.
4. Trial-and-error learning usually develops when the learner does not understand the use of the skill or does not have clear perception of it.
5. Initial delay and exploration usually develop insight which facilitates practice.

6. Retrial with insight seems to be superior to trial and error. Approximation-and-correction is a better term than trial-and-error.

Several of these principles, with modification, apply to the learning of arbitrary associations as well as to skills.

Organized practice should be preceded by an exploratory stage during which the learner experiments, seeks guidance, devises several alternative ways of acting. The learner's performance should approximate a desirable method ever more closely as meaning develops. The many "crutches" devised and used by children in arithmetic since time immemorial actually represent methods devised in the light of the children's insight or level of understanding. Contrary to common belief the use of such crutches is not detrimental, [4] provided that practice is accompanied by increasing understanding. Crutches will be dropped as new meanings develop in the children. Persistence of crutches indicates that the learners are not developing understanding. This may be owing to the imposition of too complex skills, to poor teaching, or to indifference, in turn owing to some factor in the past history of the learner. The majority of evolved methods under good teaching will not be "crutches" but will be ever closer approximations of what is known to be a good procedure.

The *integrative* phase of skill learning in which meaning is developed demands *varied* practice, which means many functional contacts and exploratory activities. The *refining* phase in which precision is developed demands *repetitive* practice. Varied practice by itself yields meaning but not proficiency; repetitive practice by itself yields efficiency but not meaning. Competent varied practice in early stages will reduce greatly the amount of repetitive practice needed later.

Derivation of skill initially from functional situations with varied practice in early stages

[4] William A. Brownell, "The Place of Crutches in Instruction," *Elementary School Journal*, Vol. 34 (April, 1934), pp. 607-619.

will not enable children to pass "standard" tests whose norms are based upon repetition of the answer without meaning. Repetitive practice from the beginning will achieve this result but will not necessarily enable the child to use the given response intelligently. A poor form of response without meaning may be "frozen" by too early repetitive practice and the later development of both meaning and increased skill definitely prevented. Parents and teachers must accept lower scores in early grades as necessary and desirable. Mature learners with need established, meaning cleared, and goal understood can engage increasingly in the second type of practice, the repetitive. Analysis and added insight will still be present.

The terms *repetition, drill,* and *practice* may be used safely in the light of the foregoing pages. Intelligent, meaningful, attentive, repetitive practice will increase the usefulness of the learning which is repeated. Repetitive practice should be preceded by a period of varied practice. Due allowance must be made at all levels for variability of performance and of individuals. Repetition which is interesting, lively, and rhythmic is definitely enjoyed by children, as witness the liking for the nursery rhymes and bedtime stories in which jingling or rhythmic repetition is the feature. Adults enjoy musical and vocal roundelays and songs in which the chorus is repeated. Repetition which is dull and dreary because it is meaningless is the type which prevents learning and develops antagonistic attitudes.

General applications to classroom practice. Applications and illustrations have been included many times in previous chapters. Suffice it here to illustrate briefly for emphasis and integration. Teaching the multiplication tables and the parts of speech as direct objectives is putting learning in reverse with a vengeance. Isolated skills in naming and using parts of speech, identifying and reproducing types of sentences, in handwriting, and in spelling cannot be combined into understandings, attitudes, and values. These skills can be attained only within the total meaningful situations which they serve and from which they derive meaning. Initiating penmanship through a series of graded exercises with curves, ovals, and angle strokes practiced separately, or art and music through practice on abstracted elements, is seriously detrimental to learning. Varied practice of meaningful skills should come first, followed by more systematic practice though still of meaningful materials.

Summary concerning initial, integrative drill. The material to this point is admirably summarized in the most famous of the research studies dealing with drill. The experiment dealt with teaching number combinations through drill methods. [5]

To summarize, the data collected in this investigation seem to warrant several inferences. First, drill, as it was administered in this study, does not guarantee that children will be able immediately to recall combinations as such. The reason lies in the fact that drill as given by the teachers does not necessarily lead to repetition on the part of pupils. Second, in spite of long-continued drill, children tend to maintain the use of whatever procedures they have found to satisfy their number needs. Third, drill makes little, if any, contribution to growth

[5] William A. Brownell and Charlotte B. Chazal, "The Effects of Premature Drill in Third-Grade Arithmetic," *Journal of Educational Research,* Vol. 29 (September, 1935), p. 26. See also:
William A. Brownell, "Two Kinds of Learning in Arithmetic," *Journal of Educational Research,* Vol. 31 (May, 1938), pp. 656-665. A very good discussion for the average student.
Guy T. Buswell and Lenore John, *Diagnostic Studies in Arithmetic,* Supplementary Educational Monograph No. 30 (Chicago, Department of Education, Univ. of Chicago, 1926).
Herbert T. Olander, "Transfer of Learning in Simple Addition and Subtraction," *Elementary School Journal,* Vol. 21 (February, 1931), pp. 435-436.
T. Raymond McConnell, "Discovery vs. Authoritative Identification in the Learning of Children," *Studies in Psychology of Learning,* II, Educational Psychology Series, No. 2, University of Iowa Studies in Education, Vol. 9, No. 5 (Iowa City, Univ. of Iowa, 1934). This study presents evidence which differs from the majority of studies in the field.

in quantitative thinking by supplying maturer ways of dealing with numbers.

The statement of these conclusions in no way implies that drill has no place in arithmetic. The contrary is the fact: drill is exceedingly valuable for increasing, fixing, maintaining, and rehabilitating efficiency otherwise developed. Nevertheless, these conclusions do particularize the things which drill will *not* do. To be more effective, drill must be preceded by sound instruction. This fact, obvious enough upon second thought, should lead to a change in research interest in arithmetic. It should encourage the more vigorous study of the problems of learning and of initial instruction, even if this change in interest should lessen somewhat the extraordinary attention now given to drill. Learning, *not drill,* is the important question in arithmetic.

Brownell made the following criticism of the theory that the teaching of primary arithmetic should consist in drill on individual combinations. [6]

When the process of learning in arithmetic is conceived to be the mere acquisition of isolated, independent facts, the process of teaching becomes that of administering drill. [7] This is the second debatable theory which now dominates instruction in primary arithmetic. True, the drills may be sugar-coated as games and races, but the process—drill or repetition—remains the same. Repetition alone is regarded as sufficient to build up the specific, direct connections which are sought in the case of $8 + 4 = 12$, $7 - 5 = 2$, and the host

[6] William A. Brownell, *The Development of Children's Number Ideas in the Primary Grades,* Supplementary Educational Monograph No. 35 (Chicago, Department of Education, Univ. of Chicago, 1928), pp. 197-199.

[7] It will be noted that the term *drill* is here used as synonymous with *repetition*. Thus, when a child is "drilled" on the combination $7 + 5$, he repeats $7 + 5 = 12$ time after time, without deviation from the formula and without "thinking" about it, until a direct association has been established. It will be noted, further, that, if a child rebels against the monotony of the drill (repetition) and through curiosity endeavors to find reasons for the fact he is required to learn, he is no longer being "drilled" in the sense in which the term is here used; still further, it should be noted that, if he actually learns the number fact through his own exploration and reasoning, the credit for the learning in no way belongs to "drill." Brownell and Chazal, *loc. cit.*

of similar items of which arithmetic is held to consist. One of the new books on methods of teaching arithmetic states that the forty-five simple additive combinations are intrinsically no harder for children to learn than are the names of forty-five children in the school or in the neighborhood; in both cases the children have only to establish bonds or connections. The process of teaching the combinations is simplicity itself according to the scheme of instruction recommended by this same book: Tell the children that 7 and 5 is 12, make sure that they can give the answer 12, and then drill them. If later a child cannot give the correct answer for $7 + 5$ or if he delays unduly long in giving the answer, tell him the answer in order to prevent his counting or solving the combination for himself and drill him some more. Use flash cards and other standard forms of drill, and drill him until he at once gives the answer 12 to $7 + 5$ however and whenever it is presented. Drill him, in other words, until, as one boy said who was being instructed in arithmetic according to this plan, the answer is "drilled into" him.

Such a theory of teaching the combinations fails to give adequate consideration, first, to the nature of the material which is to be learned and, second, to the behavior of children under conditions of drill. These two weaknesses in arithmetic instruction by means of drill need further elaboration.

In the first place, drill, that is, repetition, is inadequate as the chief method of teaching arithmetic in the primary grades because it is ill adapted to the type of material which is to be taught. The child who can promptly give the answer 12 to $7 + 5$ has by no means demonstrated that he knows the combination. He does not "know" the combination until he understands something of the reason why 7 and 5 is 12, until he can demonstrate to himself and to others that 7 and 5 is 12, until he is so thoroughly convinced that 12 is the right answer for $7 + 5$ that he can give it as the answer with assurance of its correctness, and until he can use the combination in an intelligent manner—in a word, until the combination possesses meaning for him. The additive combinations are vastly harder for children to learn than are the names of other children because the children's names are concrete and tangible and already possess meaning while the combinations are abstract and intangible and at the beginning quite meaningless. Furthermore, it is futile to expect the intelligent use of combinations when intelligence plays no part in acquiring command over the verbal statements of the combinations.

In the second place, reliance on drill as the method of teaching the primary number facts neglects the behavior of children under conditions of drill. The truth is that children do not react to drill in the manner in which their teachers expect them to react. The pupils who served as subjects for the individual analyses in Grades IIA, IIIA, and IVA were taught the additive combinations, with the exception of a very few of the simpler combinations which they learned in Grade IA, very much after the fashion which has been outlined, namely, by being told the answers and by being required to repeat the formulas. Drill was the chief, if not the only, method of teaching, and roundabout procedures not only were not suggested by the teachers but were discountenanced by the teacher when they were used by the pupils. The analyses reported in chapters vi and vii reveal how these children, taught the combinations by drill, actually think of these number facts. As has been shown, some of the pupils have tried blindly to memorize the combinations. These pupils varied in their answers for given combinations, were never certain of the correctness of their answers or were always certain of them regardless of their correctness, and had no method, except perhaps counting, by means of which to secure answers for combinations which they did not know. Other pupils regularly counted the combinations without the knowledge of their teachers. Still other pupils gave evidence of having habituated certain solutions for combinations, such as $8 + 4 + 1$ for $8 + 5$, instead of habituating the combinations themselves, as their teachers expected them to do. Still other pupils had apparently habituated the combinations in spite of the conditions of classroom drill in arithmetic, that is, by first acquiring meaning for the combinations through a series of steps in their thinking about the combinations and then by "short-circuiting" these methods of thinking indirectly of the combinations in favor of direct habituation of the combinations. In short, if one may generalize from these cases, many pupils tend to build up for themselves meanings for the combinations and then, and not until then, do what their teachers think they have done from the first, namely, memorize the combinations as combinations. In view of the careful efforts of the teachers to keep the children from indirect, roundabout procedures in thinking of the combinations, they were amazed to learn what had actually been going on in the minds of the pupils during the course of the drill by which they were expected to learn the number facts.

Such considerations clearly suggest the futility of drill as the sole method of teaching number facts, for many children, even under the conditions of drill which are made to prevail in the classroom, learn arithmetic not by the repetition of formulas but by methods which emphasize for them the meaning aspect of the facts which they are required to learn.

Systematic practice following initial understanding. The foregoing discussion has been aimed chiefly at the initial stages of practice in which little children or mature learners are attacking a complex skill for the first time. The characteristics of later practice are easily summarized.

Children will often be further interested in a skill which they have met in a functional situation. The teacher may supply exercises at this point through which children gain further skill and also further understanding. Children will often propose that on-going activities be temporarily suspended while a skill is perfected. Repetitive practice ensues, but it is meaningful. Modern schools ordinarily provide practice or "skill" periods separate from the unified activity period. The common skills of reading, writing, arithmetic, spelling, of language arts, and of handling tools and materials are practiced. These practice periods grow out of, are motivated by, are given meaning by the activities of the learning unit. The materials used in these practice periods, furthermore, must themselves be meaningful.

Children themselves will derive, with maturity and experience, an extremely important understanding of and generalization about drill and practice. The experience of practicing is itself recognized as sensible and useful in achieving purposes set up by the learner. Drill is recognized as a natural accompaniment of learning. Pupils are then ready to accept and profit from considerable repetitive practice. The thing practiced must be sensible, but the relation to the goal may be more remote in time. The earlier discussion of deferred values and acceptance of remote aims explains this. This recognition of the place and usefulness of practice activity may come at any age, but its extension and drive will naturally differ with maturity level. This recognition does not emerge readily and may never emerge in traditional schools, since pupil experiences are with the wrong type of drill.

Theoretically, it might be possible to provide enough functional learning situations to produce skill without drill. More can be done in this direction, but practical, functional illustrations of rather remote connection should not be dragged in artificially or they will be almost as meaningless as some of the abstract exercises. Teachers need definite training in recognizing valuable meaningful applications, especially in arithmetic and mathematics. Illustrations in the social studies, language arts, nature study, health, and the like are recognized more easily by more teachers. Truly functional, real-life applications simply cannot be supplied in sufficient number to develop necessary skill. Furthermore, learners come eventually to recognize and accept drill as sensible. Therefore teachers, particularly on upper levels, may safely use systematic drill experiences. Obligations exist to see that meaningful teaching precedes the initiation of practice and that continuing practice utilizes sound principles. There is no inconsistency between functional teaching and practice for skill.

General principles underlying practice or drill. A number of guiding principles may be stated.

1. *Practice should be only upon materials susceptible to automatization.*
   a. Skills and arbitrary associations are perfected through practice.
   b. Meanings, attitudes, and appreciations should not be included in this procedure. (Much so-called "review" in many schools is in reality drill. This indicates a gross misunderstanding of the nature of learning.)

2. *Practice must be meaningful.*
   a. *Varied contacts* to develop meaning should precede *repetitive practice.* Allow time for meaning to develop before starting practice.
   b. The element to be made precise should be *derived from* a meaningful unit; be useful in the unit; be useful in life.
   c. The element must be *applied* soon and often in real, non-practice situations. (This is another way of saying that it should be useful in life, hence meaningful to the pupil, hence attacked willingly.)
   d. The attitude should be achieved and maintained that *practice is a normal and needed adjunct to complete learning,* not just a chore.

3. *Practice must be on the things to be acquired.*
   (This was formerly stated as, "A correct start must be guaranteed." A preferable statement today would be, "Initial learning must be carried to the point of understanding what is to be done.")

4. *Practice periods at first will have large diagnostic emphasis.*
   a. Perfect reproduction will not be asked or expected.
   b. Retrials will be scrutinized.
   c. Correct responses must be recognized as contributing to the learner's ends; incorrect responses must be recognized, explained, and consciously avoided. Feedback and self-correction are important.
   d. Self-guidance and supplementary suggestions from the teacher will be prominent. Demonstration and explanations are important.
   e. Time will be allowed for varied trials and development of meaning and control.

5. *Practice for speed should be subordinated to practice for accuracy at first, and the two progressively balanced.*

6. *Practice periods should be relatively short and distributed over a period of time.*
   a. Practice periods should taper off as mastery is achieved.
   b. Practice periods for refreshing or recall may sometimes be necessary under formal learning conditions.

c. Overlearning within reasonable limits and in relation to maturity level is desirable.

7. *Practice periods should be lively, interesting, and pleasant.*
   a. Intrinsic interest will result if the skill or association grew originally out of a meaningful situation.
   b. A variety of devices may be necessary in formal schools where drill work does not grow out of meaningful situations, or in cases where intrinsic interest cannot carry over a long period. Applications to meaningful situations are superior but may not always be available.

8. *Practice time and effort should not be wasted on accessory and nonessential processes.*

   Probably everyone remembers from school days the laborious copying of practice exercises from the board preparatory to working them. In shop work, drawing, nature study, and the like, it often took more of the period to get the materials and to put the tools in shape than was left for actual work. Long paragraphs and sentences were copied for purposes of correction. Compositions were recopied endlessly because the margins were a sixteenth of an inch too wide, or because a few words were misspelled. Traditional teachers by the hundreds use these procedures and think nothing of it. The waste of time involved borders on the stupid.

   A few young teachers fresh from training schools often possess systematic plans for the elimination of common errors in language, or for the teaching of some given motor skill. These procedures are then applied with children who never heard of the language error or who can have no use for the specific skill. This again wastes time.

   Multigraphing machines and hektographs are now readily available even in rural schools. Teacher-and-pupil-prepared material is superior, but commercially prepared materials are often wholly legitimate and fit into meaningful situations.

9. *Practice should proceed under some pressure.*

10. *Practice proceeds best under a small amount of emotion.*

11. *Progress should be apparent to the pupil.*

12. *Practice processes and requirements should be adjusted to individual differences.*
    a. Mastery of acceptable skill levels will be achieved at different times by different pupils. Some will be excused earlier than others.
    b. Individual practice is necessary in addition to the group exercises.
    c. Each pupil should make several responses during oral practice.
    d. When it is necessary to use devices, these should be suited to different levels of maturity, temperament, and ability.

13. *Practice procedures should make liberal use of material prepared by teachers and pupils, but commercially prepared materials are in many cases useful and legitimate.*

14. *Practice should eventually be individualized.*

Memorization. A few instructors using the first edition of this book and not a few students wrote in asking why rules for memorizing were omitted. Comment is especially stimulated when students read the attack in Chapter 5 on memorization as a *substitute* for learning. Widespread malpractice in the use of memorization characterized the schools of yesteryear, but the writer had believed that this had largely died out. Evidently it has not and prospective teachers brought up on older practices uncritically hold to them. All this is definitely astonishing in view of the wide dissemination of research facts (not to mention common-sense evidence) concerning memorization.

Arbitrary associations, obviously, must be memorized by rote. Forcing rote learning was a path of least resistance and incompetent teachers applied the method to subject matter for which it was quite unfitted. The effects on learning and on the learners' attitudes were tragically detrimental. One may still find, in educational slums, insistence on memorization of the capitals of all the states (in two or three places, the memorization of all county names), of the Constitution of the

United States, of long strings of dates of battles, inventions, and presidential terms, or geometric theorems. Long passages of prose and poetry are still assigned arbitrarily for memorization. The latter is said to enhance appreciation, whereas it more often develops serious hatreds and antagonisms. One must memorize vast areas of fact, it is said, before one can think. A frighteningly large number of elementary teachers still insist that "drill and memorization" are the only ways these children can learn. The foregoing claims and practices are not only nonsense; they indicate a very serious ignorance of simple facts. Principles or suggestions for this type of memory work cannot be supplied because the process is not sensible—it has no aim.

The foregoing sentence supplies one of the important clues to the proper use of memory; there must be a rational and useful purpose. Also, remembering follows instead of precedes understanding and appreciation. The effort to memorize, as with drill on skills, does not merely ensure recall; it also contributes to improvement of meaning, insight, and understanding.

Understanding of historical events should be sought first, particularly insight into the interrelationships involved. Dates are then seen in relation to understandings of the movements of events. Memorizing the dates not only reverses normal learning but usually prevents it. The historical development of ideas of freedom and human rights, the struggle to embody these ideas in the Constitution of the United States, the attacks upon the Constitution, and the necessity for defending these rights should be studied under aims which are sensible to the learners. Memorization in the traditional sense will not be necessary, the children having acquired a firm grasp of the important thing: the values and meanings written into the Constitution. Here, understanding and the derivation of facts go hand in hand, developing together. Poetry, too, is more easily memorized after appreciation has dawned.

Choice of selections to be memorized should be strictly individual, since appreciations in the field of poetry are individual.

Memory is of basic importance, otherwise there would be no sense in studying anything. Memorizing under arbitrary assignment merely to have the facts in cold storage ("it might turn out to be useful") is stupid. The general principles governing memorization are the principles governing practice. A few may be restated for emphasis.

1. The memorization or remembering must be for a *purpose or aim which is clearly sensible to the learner*. No one remembers, for long, material which is of no use to him.
2. The subject matter to be memorized must be examined, discussed, *studied for meaning first*. The meanings in any body of rational material are themselves major aids to remembering.
3. The material productive of appreciations must be so presented to and received by the learners that *appreciations appear*, are achieved by the learner. (No amount of assignment, pointing out, or pressure will ensure this; in fact, they are likely to prevent it.) Selections which are to be memorized should be selected by the learners, in fact usually are by appreciative pupils. Memorizing, here as nowhere else, must be voluntary.
4. The modified *"part-whole" method* is, on present evidence, the better procedure through which to practice repetitions.
5. The method of *correct recall* should be used. Learners deceive themselves by practicing with book or copy open before them.

Important distinction between drill and review. Traditional schools often devote the last week or two of a semester to "review." The writer, visiting high schools continually, has seen several hundred of these reviews in progress. In practically all instances nothing that could be called a review was present. The process was pure drill. The old material was gone over again just before examinations in an effort to recall much that had been studied earlier in the term. The application of repetitive drill methods to content materials grows out of a wholly erroneous conception of learning. It is a natural outgrowth of the "text-covering" point of view and can result only in verbalisms.

A drill attempts to fix certain automatic skills or other associations. A review is the *re*viewing or *re*teaching of old materials for the purpose of gaining new meanings and understandings, or attitudes, for clarifying and extending meanings derived from original learning contact. A well-selected and skillfully taught review lesson in the traditional school is an index of good teaching ability. Teachers with a good view of the course of study, and possessed of ability to see relationships which are important but not obvious, can construct such lessons. The review of the old material is often introduced so skillfully and with such seeming inevitability that the class will work well on subjects already known from one angle but now reinterpreted from another angle. They do not see themselves as working repetitiously on material previously sucked dry of interest. A teacher in intermediate grades taught the "William Tell stories" under the aim, "Let us see how William Tell became the Father of his Country." Before the series of lessons was over, the class had recalled and used nearly all they had previously known about the life and activities of George Washington. Another class, engaged in a popular campaign, "Let us see why we should swat the fly," reviewed and restated much that they had learned previously under a different aim about germ carriers. An upper-grade class working on the problem, "Should our local government institute civil service requirements for certain designated offices?" obtained a very good review of the "Spoils System" which they had studied previously in connection with Jackson's administration. The introduction to the reading of "The Man Without a Country" might well be a review lesson, bringing in previous study of Aaron Burr and Benedict Arnold. There is wide opportunity for such lessons, limited only by the teacher's ingenuity. The illustrations just cited are all taken from typical traditional teaching of the improved type. Modern units, whether subject-matter or experience, almost naturally provide for continuous lifelike review.

The workbook as a source of drill material. Commercially prepared drill material has been available for years in the form of flash cards, reading charts, printed sheets of arithmetic problems, tablets of such problems, sentences and paragraphs in which language errors are to be corrected, and many others. The most carefully prepared and organized form in which this type of material appears is the "workbook." A workbook is a paperbound volume (as a rule) approximately 8½ by 11 inches. It contains an organized series of drill exercises, together with directions for use, instructional aids, diagnostic devices, and self-testing materials. Workbooks are usually printed on soft paper for pencil and illustrated with pictures, diagrams, graphs, and the like. Many are designed to accompany a given text, others cover a field without reference to the particular texts which may have been used. Several hundred workbooks are available; thousands of school systems use them; all subjects and levels are covered, from primary to college.

A distinction needs to be made here between (*a*) "self-instruction bulletins," or "instructional booklets," or "study manuals," or individualized instruction materials such as the Winnetka organization for learning the fundamental skills, and (*b*) currently used workbooks which are chiefly concerned with supplementary drill. Instructional material is included in many of these also. The first type is essentially a textbook for self-instruction by the pupil. The latter is designed to supplement a text or texts or to supply practice materials valuable in a given field. The first type of book is admirably discussed by Umstattd. [8] He has developed and uses in his book a good score card, many points in which apply to the second

[8] J. G. Umstattd, *Secondary School Teaching* (Boston, Ginn, 1937), Ch. 8.

type of book. The second type, the drill workbook, is our concern here.

Widespread use of these books is inevitable, since they relieve the teacher of much effort and provide large amounts of drill material ready to hand. This releases time and also makes it easier to keep pupils occupied at their desks while others recite at the front. Widespread use and approval by pupils and teachers are not, however, valid evidence that the workbook is a valuable instrument. Previous pages have made clear the real dangers of isolated or non-meaningful drill, of drill ill-adapted to individual needs and differences. The workbook is in need of extremely careful appraisal. A large number of articles and a few critical analyses both pro and con have appeared in educational journals. The majority of these are distinctly naïve. Workbooks are said to be valuable because they "stimulate interest," "supply drill materials quickly," "provide for developing skill or vocabulary," "encourage pupil activity," "save time," "simplify the assignment," and "provide for home study." Workbooks could do every one of these things and still be distinctly detrimental educational devices. Workbooks are condemned because they "contain too many trivial unrelated facts," "are poorly graded," "are formal and inflexible," "are used without discrimination by teachers," and "make for mechanical learning." Workbooks could be constructed to avoid all of these except overuse by the teachers. These are not inherent weaknesses in wookbooks. Some arguments turn upon the value of the workbook for stimulating thinking, initiative, appreciation, and even creativity. Workbooks are intended to supply practice materials and if they do that well, there is little need to glamorize them as opportunities for thinking, creativity, and the like. These are better cared for elsewhere. Drill materials should provide for continued insight and increasing meaning, as made clear earlier.

A critical and discriminatory view will not attempt to set up values and weaknesses in final or absolute terms but will set up desirable characteristics or criteria to be applied to specific workbooks. Brueckner [9] has listed the steps which should be taken to improve workbooks. The following paraphases his summary. The desirable workbook will:

1. Be organized around a definite purpose which is meaningful to the learner and which is related to a socially desirable objective.
2. Make definite, adequate provision for individual differences in need, ability, and rate.
3. Make available to teachers proven methods of diagnosing strengths and weaknesses among pupils.
4. Include a considerable variety of developmental and remedial materials of demonstrated value which may be used in the light of the diagnostic analysis.

Brueckner points out that research is needed to determine more than we now know about preventing learning difficulties in the first place. Results of such research are being and will increasingly be incorporated into workbooks.

We need to be sure that drill materials contained in workbooks are actually and naturally derived from a meaningful unit, or are readily integrated with such a unit. The organization and sequence and use should be scrutinized in terms of the principles of drill given earlier. Sometimes brief explanations or brief reproductions from the original subject-matter unit are included in the workbook. Reference is made to real-life applications. The book itself should be of good construction, well printed, and properly illustrated. The use of formal materials should condemn the book. Overworked or routine-minded teachers will always make poor use of good workbooks, but this is not the fault of the book.

PRELIMINARY DISCUSSION QUESTIONS

Beginning students and untrained teachers should profit from analyses of these questions.

[9] Leo J. Brueckner. "The Improvement of Workbooks," *Curiculum Journal*, Vol. 6, pp. 41-44.

Students with some background in psychology and experienced teachers may omit this list.

1. Why are habits formed in youth much harder to break than those acquired later?

2. It is commonly believed by many parents and teachers that children "will outgrow" certain bad habits or undesirable actions.

Distinguish between situations in which this is likely to be true and those in which it is not. What is the guidance for teaching?

3. A fifth-grade teacher found her class growing poorer and poorer in spelling. She gave much practice, marked papers carefully, was generous with help to pupils after school, but improvement did not result.

What might be some of the causes of this situation?
What questions would you like to ask before advising her?
Assuming that you have answers to the questions you would ask, what advice might you give her?

4. A typical and widespread method of teaching language is to have the pupils learn rules and definitions, followed by exercises in making written applications.

Evaluate this procedure critically.

5. Many persons make excellent progress at first in learning to play golf or tennis, in learning to swim and so forth. Then comes a period in which they seem unable to improve at all.

What probable explanations can you advance? How remedy the situation?

6. Show how the careful initial study of a poem, a piano selection, or some similar item, might involve a very different study process from that used later for purposes of retention.

7. When school opens in September, many teachers complain that the pupils must have been poorly taught the previous year, since they do not know even the simple fundamental skills in arithmetic, spelling, and so forth.

What is the probable basis for this situation? (Do not answer by saying the children have forgotten the material.)

An Important Question

8. Students often state that the achievement of understandings or meanings is made through drill, i.e., repetition of the understanding until learned. They point to the development of understandings in unit teaching through repeated experiences with the understanding.

The two processes are not remotely alike. Explain clearly the difference. Explain also the probable reasons for this odd error on the part of some students, because the reasons are important.

REPORTS

1. Report from observations any skillful derivation of materials for drill from a functional situation. Note how future practice is provided for times which appear within the on-going activity of a unit.

2. Report in detail any exceptionally good management of initial practice periods for development of insight.

3. Report (without identification) any observed situations in which drill was the major activity to the exclusion of other valid procedures. Note especially those situations in which drill is exercised when other far more valuable learning activities should have been used. Make such suggestions as you can for remedy—that is, tell how you would hope to handle such learning.

4. Report any examples (all too common) of confusion between drill and review. Indicate briefly how it might have been handled.

Based on the Periodical Literature

This is one of the most valuable sources of current thinking about drill or practice. References will be found both in educational and psychological magazines and monographs.

1. Report in critical summary the gist of three or four current articles on drill methods which report classroom problems, procedures, and opinions.

2. Report similarly a number of research studies on drill (any phase) in which controls and validated results were achieved. These will usually deal with reading, writing, arithmetic, and spelling, but other areas will be found also.

Based on Special Methods Texts or Materials

1. A student or small committee may make a fairly extended report on drill devices, suggestions, and illustrations as found in texts devoted to the special methods within a given

subject. Texts are available both for elementary and secondary subjects.

2. A critical summary may be made of current articles on workbooks and their uses, strengths, and weaknesses.

3. An individual or a small committee may evaluate a given workbook or other body of instructional material for facilitating drill.

READINGS

1. *General discussions of classroom practice.* The foregoing chapter is far more extended than any other available. All standard texts in principles of teaching have similar treatments. Reading may be assigned if the instructor sees fit.

2. *Textbooks in special methods.* An extensive array of books is available, each dealing with the special methods and devices used within a given elementary or secondary subject area. These will prove to be sources of excellent concrete materials. Note reports above.

3. *The periodical literature.* This is an excellent source for both classroom procedures and research data. Note reports above.

CHAPTER 20: The Measurement and Evaluation of Learning Outcomes

A preliminary discussion based upon students' own experience with examinations should precede an analysis of the text. This is particularly valuable for beginning students and for teachers with little training. Often students possess many honest but wholly naïve ideas about examining or testing and at the same time have some real protests against the inept methods to which they were subjected. The new ideas emerging in the discussion and the size of the problem usually present a mild and challenging shock. Advanced students and well-trained teachers may omit preliminary discussion and proceed directly to problems on their own level of understanding. The following questions will be of value for the beginners' discussion:

1. Why are pupils given examinations from time to time? Make a list of several purposes.
2. Recall the pupil who passed an examination in agriculture after reading the textbook the night before. (Question 1, Section 1, Chapter 5.)
   a. What did that examination really test?
   b. What did the examination supposedly test in general? specifically?
   c. How should the functional outcomes of a course in agriculture be tested?
3. The traditional written examination in content subjects aims at everything in the hope

of hitting something. Actually we should test directly and specifically for a number of designated outcomes.
   a. What general types of outcomes may we test for?
   b. List a number of specific illustrations within the general types. Use your major subject as source for these.
4. Make as long a list as possible of the definite weaknesses of traditional written examinations. Base this directly upon your own experience in high school and college. Can you suggest some improvements even now without further study of the problem?
   Make a similar list of definite strong points you found in examinations given by careful instructors.
5. Try to state a few principles of guidance for the construction of examinations. Do not go beyond your personal experience as developed by the foregoing questions.
6. Describe any examinations you were given in high school or college which differed significantly from traditional examinations.

1: AN INTRODUCTION TO DEFINITIONS AND PRINCIPLES.

The problems involved in determining what the pupil has learned and how well he has learned it have been with us for centuries. These problems are acute currently, however, because of our rapidly increasing insight into the nature of the learning process, the nature of outcomes, and the nature of individual differences.

Learning outcomes are affected by many agencies outside the school. The learning and behavior of any pupil is determined not alone by organized learning experiences within the school but also by all other social experiences encountered since birth. Experiences within the community (particularly within the immediate neighborhood), in the home, with the church, with recreational facilities desirable and otherwise, with civil authorities, with printed materials, with business, and with many other agencies all contribute in developing the understandings and attitudes held by the learner. The efforts of many of these agencies are often undirected, very often unco-ordinated. The effects, even from home and church in given instances, are often negative, unfortunately, and may even counteract the constructive efforts of the school. An excellent program of character development in the school, to cite but one common example, may produce few desirable results because of much stronger unwholesome social and moral influences in the immediate environment. Definite investigations have shown, however, that the organized co-ordination of school and community efforts will produce highly desirable results.

The school must face the problem of evaluation courageously. Many current severe criticisms of the school, relating particularly to pupil conduct but including many of the typical school learnings, are unjustified. The school cannot possibly be held *wholly* responsible for shortcomings among children who are affected by strong influences over which the school has no control. Homes and churches must accept an important part of the blame, just as they must receive a share of the credit for desirable results. Community leaders who determine policy concerning provision of recreational facilities, of police procedure, of decent housing, and many other aspects of the child's environment, all share in blame and credit.

Educators have no wish to shirk responsibility in this complex problem. They realize clearly that the ultimate objectives of the school are those qualities, abilities, and attitudes necessary for effective, desirable living on the adult level within an evolving democratic society. They realize further, that the immediate objectives of the school are to help the child achieve progressively higher levels of these basic qualities and abilities. The work of any given group of children will be determined by immediate objectives derived on the one hand from the needs of the learners and related on the other hand to the socially desirable outcomes. The school exists to guide and stimulate desirable developments toward directional goals. The effectiveness of the school program in meeting its responsibility can be determined only by definite efforts to measure or evaluate what is going on. The final valid evaluation of the effects of schooling can come only as the pupil meets social situations in real life, particularly after leaving school. The school, however, is the formal agency of schooling; it has the children under favorable conditions for the study of progress and of results. The school must devise means for continuously evaluating pupil growth. The primary consideration is to devise instruments and techniques which as nearly as possible approach lifelike situations. *Lifelike here means like the life of immature but growing children, not the life of mature, organized society.* Unable to secure final and conclusive evaluations, the school will endeavor to gather as much presumptive and symptomatic evidence of learning as possible. The problem of evaluation and the devising of instruments is clearly one of the most prominent and dynamic educational problems of the moment.

Valid evaluation is ever more difficult. A number of factors seriously complicate the problem and procedure of evaluation.

The scope of evaluation has been greatly expanded. Early emphasis upon testing fact and skill outcomes has been supplemented by attention to testing or evaluating the newer outcomes such as understandings, appreciations, attitudes, values, special abilities, skills, and other controls of conduct or personal-social-moral traits.

The outcomes to be evaluated are complex integrations of many learnings. Pupil behavior in any situation is controlled by a constellation of understandings, attitudes, abilities, and skills. The parts cannot be tested separately, nor would the results be valid if the arbitrary separations could be made. The "whole child" cannot be measured or evaluated as such, but sufficient samplings of behavior of different types, at different times, and under different conditions must be made as a basis for judgment. Many different types of instruments are necessary.

The outcomes to be evaluated are usually general and abstract, but pupil behavior is specific and concrete. Specific and objective outcomes are legitimate goals for both teaching and evaluating on lower levels of maturity. As maturity progresses, we teach toward generalizations which will govern the child's conduct when choice is called for. The initial skills and simple understandings can be measured and evaluated with reasonable ease. Evaluation is progressively more difficult with the higher levels of learning.

We constantly speak of evaluating such abstract qualities as the pupil's initiative, dependability, resourcefulness, and co-operation. *Actually all we can do is observe specific behavior and infer that a pupil has initiative, is dependable, resourceful, and co-operative.* Checklists, rating scales, and behavior records are instruments designed to aid us in gathering data to validate our evaluational judgments.

An illustration will aid in clarifying this point. A man finds in the street a purse which contains a considerable sum of money and he returns it to its owner. We then speak of the man (evaluate him) as *honest.* We easily fall into the error, if we are not careful, of regarding honesty as an actual characteristic of the man, similar in nature to blue eyes, short stature, or short reaction time. No such actual entity exists.[1] There is no such personal characteristic as *honesty.* Honesty is a *name* given to certain types of specific behavior which can be observed. The man's *action* was honest, not the man. The man does, however, possess certain understandings, principles, attitudes, and ideals which cause him to act honestly. These can be specified, set up as objectives, and evaluated. Before analyzing them, let us note that the misuse of the word *honesty* is not serious in ordinary intercourse, since we all know what is meant. Hopeless confusion is induced, however, if we give the figurative language a literal interpretation. Honesty and all other abstract names for types of conduct (such as initiative, co-operation, dependability) are not personal attributes that can be defined, developed by teaching, and measured or evaluated as such. To teach for these or to try to test them is wholly absurd. *Each of them refers to action which results from constellations of meanings, attitudes, and values.* The latter can be defined and made objectives of teaching. Yet every once in a while a system of "character education" appears, based on the assumption that one can teach for and develop these supposed personal attributes.

With reference to honesty, the learning outcomes which can be developed and evaluated would include, among several others: (*a*) a system of ideas concerning the nature of property; (*b*) understandings that the conventions of society protect ownership and punish stealing; (*c*) appreciation of the attitudes of society toward certain types of conduct; (*d*) sufficient knowledge and maturity of judgment to distinguish between *meum*

[1] Graduate students might be interested at this point in looking at some of Jeremy Bentham's writing on "fictions" or C. K. Ogden's commentary on Bentham.

and *teum* among lost property, discarded property, and property open to seizure by anyone; (*e*) an active attitude of desiring to act in accord with the ideas of right, of meriting social approval within one's society. These learning outcomes can be tested or evaluated by observation of behavior.

The digression in the preceding paragraphs seems justified in view of common absurdities in curriculum materials, in teachers' objectives, and in efforts to evaluate in a realm where metonymic language constantly leads to confusion. Language leads us to attribute certain abstract values to persons instead of to actions, for which they are convenient classifications.

Evaluation on advanced levels of maturity is still further complicated by the fact that the generalizations, attitudes, and the like, which govern conduct are not always completely or even widely generalized. An individual acts honestly in one field but not in another. Pupils who act co-operatively with some classmates and teachers, and in certain circumstances, may remain indifferent or be actively non-co-operative with other persons and in different circumstances.

Evaluation of many important outcomes is therefore seriously complicated. *Many desirable outcomes in the form of general understandings and attitudes can be judged only in the light of specific actions within given circumstances. The evaluation is an inference, a leap beyond the observable data.*

The outcomes to be evaluated are difficult to state in unequivocal language. This has been indicated in part by the preceding discussion; outcomes are complex, often general and abstract. Careless or figurative use of words still further complicates the problem of definition. The language used must be definite enough to set up an outcome which may be tested or evaluated. A vague, indefinite outcome cannot be evaluated. This is a serious problem with the newer outcomes and with teachers of poor or ordinary training.

Modern evaluation is continuous and adjusted to the nature of the learner. Unlike traditional testing at stated periods, evaluation today must be continuous and flexible. Pupil growth and development are continuous and there are demonstrable individual differences. Goals of learning are continuous directional-process goals. Fixed standards to be met at stated times are pure absurdities in the light of modern knowledge about the nature and development of children. This complicates processes of evaluation, since it calls for a teacher attitude very different from the traditional, for a far more subtle insight into learning processes and results, and for the construction of evaluation instruments and techniques to fit given learning outcomes.

Directional-process goals must be related eventually to relatively fixed standards. Movable and flexible standards of achievement, constantly adapted to levels of maturity and to individual differences, are inevitable in the light of modern knowledge. This has been adequately explained in previous chapters. Parents and teachers are seriously confused and oppose the modern theory and practice with the statement that after all children must meet the standards set by the world. Both views are correct, but the parent and poorly trained teacher err in logic when they then apply fixed adult standards to the immature child. The standards for evaluation, which are emergent and flexible, move constantly upward as the learner matures. The learner, progressing through a series of directional-process goals and standards, will see for himself, and quite naturally, the necessity for achieving socially desirable levels. Current social standards must eventually be taken into account. They themselves, however, are not fixed and arbitrary as many adults believe but are themselves subject to change as society changes. They are not fixed, arbitrary hurdles to be passed at stated intervals but merely the final stages of directional-process goals. *Final* does not here mean complete and done with but merely the level to which a child of given ability can reach. Efforts to evaluate the learning of immature children of different abilities, interests, and rates of reaction in terms of fixed standards result in serious disturbances of the mental hygiene of the learners.

Objective measurement and subjective evaluation are both essential. An important distinction between certain types of outcome and hence between methods of determining achievement was thrown into sharp relief by a now famous incident at the Indianapolis meeting of the National Education Association in 1897. A paper was presented by Rice [2] showing the results of spelling tests administered in a score of cities. There were no standard tests in those days; hence a list of words was compiled and presented to all pupils alike. The pupils were subject to different methods of instruction from city to city, studied different books, were under very different time allotments. Regardless of wide differences in instruction and time spent, the pupils from different cities made approximately the same average group scores. This experiment *tested* precisely the pupil's mastery of a given list of spelling words, and *evaluated* in general the effect of teaching methods, texts, and time allotments. Rice's proposal to evaluate both teaching and the pupil's achievements by measuring precisely what the pupil knew or could do was greeted with ridicule verging upon abuse. (Incidentally, it is interesting to note that seventeen years later the National Education Association devoted its annual convention and proceedings to just that topic—precise measurement of outcomes.) The discussion from the floor was vigorous and emotional, straying far afield from the problem of precise measurement in spelling and other similar learnings. A sentimentalist, decrying the idea of

---

[2] J. M. Rice, "The Futility of the Spelling Grind," *The Forum*, Vol. 22 (April and May, 1897), pp. 163, 409. See also proceedings of the N. E. A.

measuring human reactions, thundered at Rice, "How would you *measure*, sir, a mother's love for her baby?" Imperturbably and without hesitation, Rice replied, "I'd *estimate* a mother's love, sir, by observing whether or not the baby was fed regularly and with good food, whether or not the baby was attended to and bathed properly, whether it was put to sleep at the proper times or kept up while the mother went to a dance." This reply contained the clue to modern evaluation as distinguished from precise measurement. Understandings, attitudes, appreciations, values, and ideals cannot be measured precisely. We can, however, observe and note behavior and then judge whether or not such action accords with given understandings or attitudes. *The observed and recorded objective acts are symptomatic and presumptive evidence of the possession of given ideals, beliefs, and standards.* Judgments based on observed behavior cannot be precise or final, but this type of evaluation is inescapable in evaluating human learning of the more advanced types. The difficulties in making this type of evaluation and the skills necessary to overcome the difficulties will be outlined in succeeding pages.

The term *measurement* usually refers to the use of objective tests or instruments of precision which yield quantitative data. These precise, quantitative data are direct measures of the pupil's achievement in fact and skill learnings or in rote mastery of subject matter.

The term *evaluation* usually refers to the use of behavior records, inventories, scales, or check lists which yield descriptive, qualitative data. These qualitative data form the basis for judgments about the pupil's acquisition of the more general, more subtle, and more important outcomes.

The distinction between measurement and evaluation is not accepted by certain statisticians but is quite acceptable to classroom teachers, supervisors, and administrators.

Measurement developed more rapidly than

evaluation. The turn of the century saw the beginnings of the movement away from traditional quizzes and essay-type examinations toward the more exact type of measurement such as the standard test, the check list, the rating scale, and the homemade objective test.

Evaluation of the more complex outcomes did not become prominent until about 1930. We are at the moment in the midst of an important, far-flung development of new methods and new instruments including inventories, interviews, problem-situation tests, anecdotal and other behavior records, diary records, analysis of creative products, and many others. The improvement of the essay-type test is a part of this movement.

Subjective evaluation necessary and respectable. The newer developments call for adequate understanding of the nature of objective and subjective evidence and judgment. The introduction of precise measurement into education brought with it, naturally, a glorification of "objective" methods and data. There was a distinct tendency to minimize and even to treat with contempt "subjective" methods and data. A common method of condemnation was to apply the word *subjective* as an epithet. Great care must be exercised just here. It is difficult to find a datum which is not both objective and subjective. All types of phenomena vary all the way from the highly but not completely objective to the highly but not completely subjective.

A further factor which influenced thinking is that the subjective judgments of the average citizen are notoriously absurd, particularly when uttered concerning technological problems, and in fields where the citizen is not at all informed. Subjective judgments made by trained and competent specialists using agreed-upon standards are very different. These judgments, though subjective, are not the capricious and personal opinions of the average citizen, but the critical judgments of experts controlled by such data as there are and by the canons of logic. These judg-

ments are based upon, guarded by, and illuminated by all the objective data which can be secured.

The respectability and real value of careful judgments made by competent teachers is acknowledged by some of the most careful objectivists we have. [3] Observers with reasonable training can collect the data of individual and group behavior with sufficient accuracy to give validity to results. The so-called objective techniques are often simply not applicable. Guidance in the improvement of observing and recording significant behavior is available from many sources.

Overemphasis upon objectivity leads to emphasis upon narrow, limited, immediately measurable types of learning outcome to the neglect of more important non-precise outcomes. Subjective evaluations made by competent specialists are necessary, inescapable, and wholly respectable.

Overemphasis upon subjectivity without proper controls usually centers upon the use of a word which should be eliminated from educational vocabularies, namely, *intangible.* Teachers using this term usually assert that the "intangibles" cannot be measured and that to try to do so is destructive of "finer" values. This is merely immature and fuzzy thinking; it is very often a rationalization and an excuse for ignorance or laziness. Inaction results in a field where action is sadly needed. The so-called intangibles are actually the vitally important non-precise outcomes stressed by modern education. To say that they cannot be *measured* is to befuddle the issue. They cannot be *measured,* but they can be readily *estimated, judged, evaluated.* There would be no sense in seeking valuable outcomes unless we could in some way determine pupil development in them.

Certain types of essay tests, scales, inven-

[3] *The Measurement of Understanding,* Forty-fifth Yearbook of the National Society for the Study of Education, Part I (Chicago, Univ. of Chicago Press, 1946).
Eugene R. Smith and Ralph W. Tyler, *Appraising and Recording Student Progress* (New York, Harper, 1942).

tories, and check lists can be used either for fairly precise measurement or as a basis for controlled subjective judgment. Care must be exercised, however, to avoid "frozen subjectivity," that is, data which seem to be clearly objective but which are fundamentally subjective. Superficial understanding of the instruments of evaluation, of the nature of data, of the canons of logic, and of statistics leads into this error.

Currently several criticisms have arisen concerning several of the standardized or objective tests. More will be said in Section 3.

2: GENERAL PROCEDURES IN MEASURING AND EVALUATING.

Determine what is to be measured or evaluated. The purpose of any test or evaluational procedure is to determine how well the pupil has learned something. The "something" must be defined clearly first or evaluation is a waste of time. For instance, we may test a learner to determine whether or not he possesses a given, defined motor skill and to determine his level of facility in the use of the skill. We may test for study skills and habits or observe behavior relating to these. We may test or observe for more complex mental skills involved in problem-solving. The various major skills can be broken down into many subsidiary skills. For instance, computational speed and accuracy in arithmetic is more specifically speed and accuracy in addition, multiplication, subtraction, and division. These, in turn, can be broken down into many necessary sub-processes. Illustrations are available in special-methods texts, in teaching manuals which accompany textbook series, and in books on diagnosis. We may test for retention of subject matter or observe behavior to judge whether certain understandings or appreciations have been derived from experience involving the subject matter. We may test or observe for any of the scores of outcomes derivable from modern courses of study and units. *A given teacher must set down in precise language the given understandings, values, appreciations, and skills which he expects the pupil to achieve before he can start to test or evaluate.* For specific illustrations, the student must turn to the local collection of courses of study and units. Space is given here to two. The first illustration shows how general objectives are broken down into more specific measurable or evaluatable objectives. The material also demonstrates admirably the fact that objectives are actually progress goals to be achieved at different rates by different pupils. Reading, as a general objective, is first broken down into five developmental stages: [4]

1. *The stage at which readiness for reading is attained.* This stage usually comprises the preschool years, the kindergarten, and often the early part of the first grade. The chief purpose of the guidance recommended is to provide the experiences and training that promote reading readiness. In addition, steps should be taken to overcome physical and emotional deficiencies that might interfere with progress.

2. *The initial stage in learning to read.* For pupils who advance normally, this stage usually occurs during the first grade. Among other attainments, pupils acquire keen interest in learning to read and a thoughtful reading attitude. They learn to engage in continuous meaningful reading, read simple, interesting material with keen interest and absorption in the content, and begin to read independently.

3. *The stage of rapid progress in fundamental reading attitudes and habits.* This stage of development occurs usually during the second and third grades. It is characterized by rapid growth in reading interests and by notable progress in accuracy of comprehension, depth of interpretation, independence in word recognition, fluency in oral reading, and increased speed of silent reading. By the end of this stage of development pupils should read silently more rapidly than orally, and should be able to read with reasonable ease, understanding, and pleasure both informational and literary materials such as are usually assigned

[4] *The Teaching of Reading,* Thirty-sixth Yearbook of the National Society for the Study of Education, Part I (Bloomington, Ill., Public School Publishing Co., 1937), pp. 76-77.

early in the fourth grade. To do this efficiently, a grade score of 4.0 in silent reading should be attained.

4. *The stage at which experience is extended rapidly and increased power, efficiency, and excellence in reading are acquired.* The fourth stage of development occurs normally during grades four, five, and six and is characterized by wide reading that extends and enriches the experiences of the reader and broadens his vision. The chief purposes of the guidance provided are to promote greater power in comprehension and interpretation, greater efficiency in rate of reading and in reading for different purposes, improvement in the quality of oral reading, the extension of the pupil's interests, the elevation of reading tastes, and greater skill in the use of books and other printed sources of information. A grade score of 7.0 in silent reading is desirable by the end of this stage of development.

5. *The stage at which reading interests, habits, and tastes are refined.* The fifth stage of development occurs as a rule during the junior high school, senior high school, and junior college periods. The chief purposes of guidance in reading during these years are to promote the further development and refinement of the attitudes and habits involved in various types of reading, to broaden interests and elevate tastes in reading, to develop increased efficiency in the use of books, libraries, and sources of information, and to secure a high level of efficiency in all study activities that involve reading.

These stages are further reduced to specific objectives which can be tested or observed in behavior. Stage 3 above is analyzed into the following: [5]

1. To provide a rich variety of reading experiences based on the world's greatest stories for children and on informational materials that challenge interest, including topics relating to various curricular fields.
2. To stimulate keen interest in reading wholesome books and selections for pleasure and to establish the habit of reading independently.
3. To secure rapid progress in the development of habits of intelligent interpretation when reading for a variety of purposes.
4. To increase the speed with which passages are read silently within the limits of ac-

[5] *Ibid.*, p. 101.

curate comprehension. (This includes rapid increase in span and rate of recognition and a corresponding decrease in number and duration of eye-fixation per line in both oral and silent reading.)
5. To provide for the development of desirable standards and habits involved in good oral reading.
6. To promote continuous development in accuracy and independence in word recognition.
7. To continue training in the skillful use of books and to familiarize pupils with the privileges and opportunities of libraries.

Some of these objectives are directly measurable through the use of standard tests; others can only be inferred from observed behavior. To help the teacher to visualize more clearly the significance of these aims Gray also describes the characteristics pupils should possess before they can be regarded as having completed the requirements of the period successfully. [6] The characteristics listed for the end of Stage 3 are as follows:

1. They have established the habit of reading independently.
2. They interpret accurately the materials related to other curricular fields.
3. They seek reading materials that relate to activities in which they are interested.
4. They read more rapidly silently than orally.
5. They are able to read at sight materials suited to their stages of development.
6. They show increasing skill in combining contextual clues with visual and auditory elements in recognizing unfamiliar words.
7. They show increased ability to make the adjustments required when reading for different purposes.
8. They exhibit rapid progress in acquiring wholesome and diversified reading interests.

This analysis recognizes the fact that the ability to read is the result of a long process of development and that at each of the five

[6] *Ibid.*, p. 107. An excellent illustration of levels of objectives to be evaluated is found in I. N. Thut and J. R. Gerberich, *Foundations of Method for Secondary Schools* (New York, McGraw, 1949), pp. 319-322. This is based on Chapters 1 and 2 of Eugene Smith, Ralph W. Tyler, and others, *Appraising and Recording Pupil Progress* (New York, Harper, 1942).

Objective 1: To Understand and Practice
Desirable Social Relationships

Definition of Objective

Since character is largely determined by the relationships of an individual to his fellows, the public school will continue to encourage the pupil's practice of the older virtues, namely, trustworthiness, reliability, obedience, kindness, courtesy, and loyalty.

More specifically, the goals to be sought in developing not only the pupil's ideals but also his conduct with his fellows are:

A. Respect for authority.

B. Leadership activities.

C. Self-initiated activities.

D. Respects for the rights and contributions of others.

E. Co-operation (team spirit).

F. An appreciation of the interdependence of all people.

G. An interest in civic functions and participation for community betterment.

Suggested Approaches to Measurement

The measurement of such specific relationships or factors as respect for others, leadership, initiative, and co-operation may be attempted by means of *observational techniques* and cumulative *observer-diary records* such as those described by J. W. Wrightstone, "Constructing an Observational Technic," *Teachers College Record*, Vol. 37 (October, 1935), pp. 1-9.

Such aims as F. and G. in the left-hand column presumably might be measured by specially devised *pencil-and-paper tests*, supplemented by *anecdotal records* of the kind suggested in J. A. Randall, "The Anecdotal Behavior Journal," *Progressive Education*, Vol. 13 (January, 1936), pp. 21-26.

Objective 5: To Gain Command of the
Common Integrating Knowledges and Skills

Definition of Objective

While the subordinate elements of this objective are classified under the general heading of "abilities," the attainment of each one assumes the development of an ideal concerning it and an appreciation of its value.

A. The ability:

1. To speak easily with freedom from gross errors.

2. To organize and present ideas clearly and consecutively in oral language.

3. To listen attentively to the oral expression of others.

4. To organize and express thoughts in written form.

5. To use good form, order, and arrangement; margins, spacing, paragraphing, capitalization, punctuation, abbreviation, syllabication.

6. To spell correctly one's vocabulary.

7. To write with ease, legibility, and speed.

8. To understand and use title page, index, table of contents, and appendix of a book.

Suggested Approaches to Measurement

Rating scales on habits and qualities of speech, constructed by a teachers' committee.

Rating of a stenographic record of several samples of the pupil's oral expression.

Records of teacher observation related to the attention of the pupil, and subsequent relevant questions or comments.

Rating samples of pupil's work by means of a qualitative scale (Hillegas, Trabue, Hudelson, etc.) [8]

Pencil-and-paper test, or rating of samples of pupil's work upon a basis of error count per 100 words.

Spelling scale (Morrison-McCall, etc.). [9]

Handwriting scale (Thorndike, etc.). [10]

Standardized achievement test, such as the Iowa Every-Pupil Tests of Basic Skills (Test B). [11]

[8] Published by the Bureau of Publications, Teachers College, Columbia Univ., New York.

[9] *Ibid.*

[10] Published by Harcourt, Brace & World, New York.

[11] Published by the Bureau of Educational Research and Service, State Univ. of Iowa, Iowa City, Ia.

levels there are definite objectives which should be adjusted to the growth process. The objectives are not stated by grade levels as is so frequently done in courses of study, but according to recognized stages of growth. It is known that pupils do not progress from stage to stage at the same rate in any field. This listing of objectives for successive levels of growth rather than by grades illustrates admirably the directional-process goals which have been referred to so often in this volume.

The second illustration is a fragment only from a method suggested by Wrightstone. [7] The relation between outcomes to be tested or evaluated and the means of evaluation is also shown. The complete statement should be examined in the original.

The *first* step then is clear definition of what is to be measured or evaluated. Numerous experimental studies cited in Chapter 5 demonstrate conclusively that attainment by the learner of one objective does not insure the achievement of any others, even those more or less related to one another. The only way to be sure of pupil achievement and growth is to test carefully and evaluate all outcomes.

Define the objectives in terms of pupil behavior.   The *second* step is the description of the learning outcome in terms of specific pupil behavior which is indicative of the possession of that outcome. The compilation of lists of behavior traits or the preparation of general descriptions of evidence which may be taken as proof of learning is one of the most valuable training devices for teachers, particularly for those accustomed to testing through requiring repetition of sub-

[7] J. Wayne Wrightstone, "Measuring the Attainment of Newer Educational Objectives," *Appraising the Elementary School Program,* Sixteenth Yearbook of the Department of Elementary School Principals (Washington, D. C., 1937), pp. 495-501.

Another excellent illustration of the relationship between outcomes and instruments of evaluation will be found in Edgar B. Wesley, *Teaching the Social Studies* (Boston, Heath, 1937), pp. 595-596.

ject matter. Many traditional teachers have no clear idea of the actual results of their teaching or of the valid evidence that the pupils have learned. More effective practices are, however, on the increase.

Confusion among teachers regarding the nature of outcomes and their evaluation is widely observable. For instance, many teachers claim they are testing appreciation of literature when actually they are testing merely the ability to retain certain facts about certain literary productions and their authors. The majority of music-appreciation tests are not tests of appreciation at all but tests of memory. Many of the facts called for in this type of test are relatively unimportant for any purpose. Learning outcomes lumped together under the blanket phrase "appreciation of literature" should be specifically defined as given understanding, appreciations, and attitudes. Typical tests with objective questions or with improved essay questions are not appropriate here. Lists of specific pupil behavior regarded as valid indications of appreciational development should be compiled. Check lists should be made up on the basis of the listed behaviors. Anecdotal and diary records should be made based on uncontrolled observations. Exhibits of pupil work may be made. The procedure outlined for appreciation holds also for other complex outcomes, particularly those in the sciences and the social studies.

Select or design an instrument: collect test problems and situations appropriate for measuring the outcome.   Clear understanding of the evidences of learning enables the teacher to choose a commercially available instrument or to set about the construction of a new one. The latter is the preferable course in modern learning situations.

The better standard tests, check lists, scales, and behavior guides are based upon and include specific pupil behaviors which are truly indicative of learning. Many carelessly constructed instruments are not valid because either they are not based on behaviors truly indicative of the learning to be tested, or they are based on behaviors indicative of other learnings instead. Many a so-called reading test turns out to be more accurately a test of general intelligence and ingenuity. Intelligence tests are often tests of reading and of certain academic skills. Arithmetic tests often contain language so difficult that the pupil never reaches the arithmetic. The pupil "fails" the arithmetic but actually failed the reading. The test did not test his arithmetic ability at all.

New instruments constructed by the teacher himself or with the co-operation of the pupils, or by the pupils with some guidance from the teacher, will be based squarely on the compiled lists of pupil behaviors. These testing devices may be of any type: homemade objective tests, improved essay tests, or one of several types of observational guides to behavior.

Test situations and problems which are found to be indicative of the development of certain generalized understandings or habits may be collected and modified for repeated use.

Whatever the outcome—memorized fact, simple or complex motor skill, any of the various complex mental skills, study habits, specific understandings, designated appreciations, any of the scores of personal-social-moral traits—the necessary *third* step is the selection or construction of an instrument based squarely upon the requirements of the specified outcome. The continuous construction of evaluational devices for given learning situations is a feature of modern instruction.

Record the results of testing or evaluating. Results have been recorded for generations in the form of teachers' marks. Properly defined and used by competent teachers, marks are useful records of achievement. [12] Marks used without adequate definition of what they represent, used carelessly by indifferent

teachers, become mere administrative stereotypes. Marks may actually have little or no relation to the learning achievements of the pupil, may even conceal them, may actually interfere with learning.

Scores from standard tests, percentile ranks, profile graphs, and the like often appear in pupil records. These too may be valuable, or they may be effective obstacles to understanding the actual facts about pupil achievement.

Modern records include, in addition to all of these, reports of observed pupil behavior either in anecdotal form or based upon a check list, scale, or other trait-rating device. The instruments themselves are often parts of the record. Exhibits of pupil work such as compositions, book reports, creative products of any type, types of questions asked, problems solved, contributions made to group work, are increasingly found in pupil records. The form of record used depends upon the nature of the behavior being evaluated. In any event the modern record is far more extensive and detailed than the meager, formal record of the traditional school. [13]

The record, whatever its form, should include accurate descriptions of all reactions which may be significant for the later evaluation. The larger the number of significant records, the more objectively and validly the behavior can be evaluated. A cumulative record of previous behavior and other information about the learner is an inescapable adjunct to good modern teaching. Extensive records are a necessity, but devices should be used to keep the time and effort expended within practical limits.

Evaluate the evidence and make a judgment concerning pupil achievement. Traditional teachers often regard the *record* as the *evaluation*. This is a natural mistake owing to weaknesses in current teacher-training. The record shows that a pupil received a mark of "B," or that he behaved in

---

[12] See Chapter 22 for discussion of principles of marking.

[13] See Chapter 10 for description of cumulative record cards and types of information included.

described manner. Now what does a "B" mean? The record shows only what the pupil did. The evaluation is a statement showing the relation of that record to the directional-process goals of education in the light of the pupil's ability and background. Evaluational judgments are necessary even with so-called objective tests. The evaluation itself should become part of the pupil's record.

Evaluations must take into account the pupil's individual characteristics, his background, and the immediate environmental factors. Evidence and argument have been presented continuously throughout this volume showing the futility of evaluating pupil growth in terms of arbitrary fixed standards. Large volumes of evidence supporting the same conclusion are not even mentioned in this volume but are available in the fields of guidance and counseling, prevention of delinquency, social work, mental hygiene, and psychiatry. Extensive data concerning the individual pupil, his background, and the community within which learning takes place are basic to evaluation. Chapters 8, 9, and 10 are devoted to these basic factors. Teachers who evaluate pupils' learning achievements or general behavior without regard for individuality and background are so dangerous to the growth and to the mental hygiene of the learners that it is doubtful if such teachers should be permitted to continue in the classroom.

Evaluation is exercised on all parts of the setting for learning. The discussion so far has stressed evaluation of learning outcomes. Modern schools, however, evaluate materials, processes, goals, discussions, suggestions, decisions, and plans.

Evaluation is continuous and participatory. Evaluation is no longer confined to "final examinations" or to periodic quizzes. Evaluation is a constant aspect of instruction and of learning, appearing every day as any part of the learning situation may come in for question, analysis, and improvement. The teacher is no longer the sole agent of evaluation. The teacher, individual students, the group, and in many instances the parents are included. Test technicians, psychologists, diagnostic experts, and others may be involved from time to time. Pupil participation not only improves evaluation but is the only way to achieve certain desirable learnings; to discriminate, to judge, to weigh evidence, to evaluate goals and methods used to achieve them. The same instruments and processes are used by teachers, individual pupils, groups of pupils, and participating laymen.

Evaluations should be followed by diagnosis of failures and by remedial procedures. The modern school does not stop with telling a pupil he has passed or failed, but attempts to find reasons for poor achievement and to aid the pupil to achieve up to the limits of his capacity. This problem is too important to discuss briefly, hence Chapter 21 is devoted to it alone.

Should examinations, quizzes, and evaluation procedures be abolished? The discussion has proceeded upon the assumption that examining and testing are necessary phases of education. Two misconceptions need to be cleared at this point.

First, the modern or progressive educator is accused of "not believing in examinations," of "doing away with standards and examinations." As usual, lack of information and misunderstanding, and sometimes defense mechanisms are responsible. The critic is thinking only of the final-exam-at-end-of-term stereotype, which is an inevitable phase of education which aims at mastery of subject matter as such. The modern educator, far from omitting examining and testing, has made it a natural, continuous, and participatory part of everyday teaching. The understanding and application of principles or meanings, the exercise of appreciations, and the demonstration of skill occur all day long under good teaching. Alert teachers compile regularly anecdotal records and inventories of participation and note finished products of constructive or creative nature. By the end of the period the teacher has an adequate knowledge of the pupil's status, progress, strength and weaknesses, and probable future needs for development. The traditional teacher uses fixed tests to determine passing and failing. The modern teacher is interested in status, rate and nature of growth, diagnosis, and future guidance. He does often omit final examinations because they could serve no useful purpose in a setting for learning which has been producing continuous evidence of achievement.

Second, another group would minimize or eliminate all examination procedures, but the reasons given are not sound, are often mere sentimentality.

Examinations, quizzes, and other evaluation procedures are inevitable phases of education, certain objections to the contrary. Examinations properly fashioned to serve genuine purposes will appear in both modern and traditional schools. The same is true for all evaluation procedures. Modern, functional examinations which utilize problem-solving, interpretation, critical analysis, and the like are highly desirable both as examinations and as teaching procedures. They may appear at any time a purpose can be served and are not confined to stated times.

One group of objectors to examinations refer to the difficulties of securing reliability and validity, to the time and effort necessary for construction, and to difficulties of marking. These are not reasons for abolishing examinations but for improving them. Time and effort must be devoted to constructing examinations carefully; results must be interpreted in some detail rather than merely marked. Examinations have been shown to be valuable instruments under given conditions. Difficult as the task is, valid and reliable examinations must be constructed and the results interpreted.

Sentimentalists object to all types of examinations and evaluations on the ground that pupils are subject to serious strain which is injurious to emotional stability and even to physical health. Definite ill effects upon health traceable to preparation for and undergoing examinations have actually been shown by research studies. The traditional memory-type examination covering an impossible amount of ground is, however, the cause. Cramming and last-minute "boning" for stupidly organized examinations is unquestionably a strain upon mind and body— not to mention the soul! The pupil himself was often at fault, though the instructor was the chief offender. Excessive use of memory examinations by the instructor and "cramming" by the pupil are evidences of incompetent teaching. The proper definition of the learning products and the organization of teaching around these outcomes with regard to the actual learning process will progressively eliminate this difficulty. Under good teaching-learning conditions, examinations appear in the process as naturally as supervised study, library work, group discussion, or what not. If the instructor knows how to teach and the pupil has really been learning as he has gone along, examinations cannot unduly upset anyone.

Granted desirable educational conditions, the statement that examinations injure health is wholly silly. Parents who allow children to stay up till all hours, allow them to eat irregularly and to violate many simple rules of hygienic living, and allow them to disturb the entire organism through injudicious emotional stress induced by radio, television, and moving pictures, are displaying genuine intellectual immaturity when they assert that a forty-five-minute written examination is dangerous to health. College and high school students who can dance until dawn, practice night after night for a class play, or go through the grueling training for athletic contests are talking pure nonsense when they claim that a two-hour examination completely exhausts them.

A related objection is raised by many students, even including scores of experienced teachers in advanced courses: "I get so flustered and excited that I wear myself out; I cannot think. I do not do nearly so well on examinations as I really can." This again can be traced to, and partly excused by, experience with the cram-type memory test. The basic point, however, is that the individual lacks the poise, balance, and control necessary to meet tests. This is a form of intellectual and emotional immaturity. The ability to meet simple tests or crises in school and out is itself a legitimate learning outcome and *any normal person can achieve it*. That an examination upsets one is a confession of definite weakness and instability and not a reason for abolishing examinations. In fact, a little excitement over an examination, if it does not become tenseness, is distinctly beneficial.

A related objection is to the effect that examinations are not typical of life. The direct opposite is true. Life constantly tests one's abilities, skills, and understandings. Hardly a day goes by, except for the routine worker, in which problems exactly comparable to tests do not arise. Furthermore, life is much harsher than the school in setting examinations. An individual may receive a severe test of his uttermost power and ability late in the afternoon of a hard day. He cannot avoid it. The demands of his chief, or of the business in which he is engaged, force him to display his ability in solving a technical problem or in handling a difficulty which has arisen. He may have been ill the day before, he may have had a severe headache all day, but if he is on the job the demand is there, and he cannot avoid the test. The school at least will excuse him if ill, or will arrange for a make-up or second trial if legitimate excuse is presented.

A fair analysis of the various objections to examinations seems to justify the conclusion that there are no fundamental arguments against them, but that there is ample ground for complaint against poorly devised tests and unorganized, inflexible examination procedures. This is readily granted.

Some objections to examinations are not honest, but are motivated by a desire for peace and harmony undisturbed by arguments with parents and pupils over failures, low marks, or non-promotions. A few individuals, perhaps, merely wish to avoid the work involved.

The uses of, reasons for, and real value in examinations are apparent to any fair-minded and competent analyst of the learning situation. Testing is as necessary in teaching as accounting in business, evidence in a court, or as proof of efficacy after medicine has been administered.

Evaluating the pupil is also an evaluation of the teacher. Pupil failure in the traditional school was blamed on the learner. He was immature, or not bright, or lazy, or antagonistic, and so forth. These are undoubted causes of poor performance but currently it is recognized that examination and tests of the pupil are often examinations of the teacher and his classroom procedures. Space prohibits extended discussion. It is suggested that interested students or instructors take any list of teacher competencies or other characteristics and attempt to relate given test results secured from student papers.

General summary on functions of examining. The uses of, reasons for, and real values in examinations are apparent to any competent and fair-minded analyst of learning situations. Testing is as necessary in teaching as is accounting in business, evidence in court; it is as much a proof of efficacy of teaching as is a health record after administration of medicine. In general, testing is useful:

1. To discover whether the pupil has learned— how much and what.
2. To discover if the teaching has been effective.

3. To diagnose pupil and group difficulties or shortcomings, so that teaching may be redirected to specific points.
4. To supply data (together with other procedures) for routine administrative purposes.
a. School records, reports to parents.
b. Grouping pupils for instruction.
(Note that we do not include as a function the determination of the student's grade! Testing may *contribute* but should not be, as it often is, the sole determinant.)

DISCUSSION QUESTIONS
FOR SECTIONS 1 AND 2

A discussion of general principles and theory may be of value here for beginning students before taking up the specific instruments and processes.

1. List any new concepts or beliefs which have come to you from Sections 1 and 2 and the supplementary reading, and which you readily accept. Ideas which are not new but which have been amplified or clarified should be included here.

2. Ask for further discussion, clarification, or illustration of any item not clear to you.

3. State any ideas long held by you and regarded as sound which now seem to be contradicted, or at least called into question, by materials in Sections 1 and 2

4. List any concepts or principles advanced by the reading which you cannot accept at the moment, or about which you are in doubt. State explicitly why you cannot accept them. This is one of the best exercises for uncovering misunderstandings or points which need greater emphasis and illustration.

5. State three or four principles or concepts of summary nature which best present the thought of the chapter.

6. What principles of education widely accepted by the rank and file, what prevalent practices in the classroom would have to be abandoned if the facts and principles presented in these sections were accepted.

READINGS

This list is selective, a total list would be impossible in a general reference such as this.

AHMANN, J. S., and GLOCK, M. D., *Evaluating Pupil Growth* (Boston, Allyn & Bacon, 1959). Comprehensive. Principles and instruments both discussed.

BARON, Denis, and BERNARD, H. W., *Evaluation Techniques for Classroom Teachers* (New York, McGraw, 1958). Written for teachers.

BRADFIELD, J. M., and MOREDOCK, H. S., *Measurement and Evaluation in Education* (New York, Macmillan, 1957). Good overall summary.

BUROS, Oscar K., Various Yearbooks on Measurements, published periodically by The Gryphon Press, Highland Park, N. J. Listing and review of all standard tests and books on measurement.

BURR, James B., HARDING, L. W., and JACOBS, L. B., *Student Teaching in the Elementary School*, 2nd ed. (New York, Appleton-Century-Crofts, 1958). Chapter 10 is an excellent supplement to this chapter. Covers items from different angles. A few specific examples.

CRONBACH, Lee J., *Essentials of Psychological Testing*, rev. ed. (New York, Harper, 1960). One of best on psychological testing.

GERBERICH, J. R., *Specimen Objective Test Items* (New York, Longmans, 1956). Very useful to teachers making own tests.

LEE, J. Murray, and LEE, Dorris M., *The Child and His Curriculum*, 3rd ed. (New York, Appleton-Century-Crofts, 1960). Chapter 15 gives excellent coverage. Bibliography for this chapter most extensive in any general text.

ODELL, C. W., *How to Improve Classroom Testing* (Dubuque, Iowa, Brown, 1953). A guide to test construction.

REMMERS, H. H., and GAGE, N. L., *Educational Measurement and Evaluation* (New York, Harper, 1955). Excellent on standardized tests. Good suggestions for constructing tests. (Watch for any other books in this field with Remmers' name.)

Review of Educational Research, a quarterly published by American Education Research Association. An issue is periodically devoted to testing. Excellent for technical materials.

THORNDIKE, R. L., and HAGEN, Elizabeth, *Measurement and Evaluation in Psychology and Education* (New York, Wiley, 1955). Unusually good in relating measurements to the purposes or objectives of the curriculum.

TORGERSON, T. L., and ADAMS, Georgia Sachs, *Measurement and Evaluation for the Elementary School Teacher* (New York, Holt, Rinehart & Winston, 1954).

"Uniform Standards for Eagles and Eels," *Essays in Educology*, Lowry W. Harding, ed. (Dubuque, Iowa, Brown, 1956). Humorous needling of some aspects of testing. Excellent reading.

WRIGHTSTONE, J. W., JUSTMAN, Joseph, and ROBBINS, Irving, *Evaluation in Modern Education* (New York, American Book, 1956).

Two older books are included here because of illustrations of certain types of instruments not too frequently given elsewhere. Considerable pioneering was done by the authors.

LEONARD, J. Paul, and EURICH, Alvin, *An Evaluation of Modern Education* (New York, Appleton, 1942).

SMITH, Eugene, TYLER, Ralph W., and others, *Appraising and Recording Pupil Progress* (New York, Harper, 1942).

Many texts dealing with *teaching of special subjects* contain discussion of theory and many illustrative instruments in the given field.

The periodical literature is extremely important. Reports may be made on current developments and controversies.

Modern texts in educational psychology are increasingly including a chapter on evaluating or judging pupil performance. One of the best is noted as a sample:

CRONBACH, Lee J., *Educational Psychology* (New York, Harcourt, Brace & World, 1954). Chapter 16 is excellent. See also Chapter 6. Use index for references to diagnosis.

3: TYPES OF INSTRUMENTS WHICH ARE AVAILABLE OR MAY BE CONSTRUCTED LOCALLY.

General texts on teaching are increasingly omitting extensive illustration of instruments of evaluation. Today students will almost universally have a course in tests and measurements. However, extensive supplementary illustrative material should be used with a textbook of this type.

1. *A large local collection of instruments should be available.* Many teacher-training institutions now maintain large files of tests, scales, check lists, inventories, interview forms, logs, diaries, autobiographies, cumulative record forms, and other data. Lacking such a collection the instructor can build his own quickly and at little expense. Students must have op-portunity to read, examine, take, and perhaps administer the various types of instruments.

2. *A collection of textbooks on tests and measurement,* diagnostic procedures, guidance, and pupil accounting, which contain illustrations of instruments, should be available. Nearly a score of books will be found in the card catalogue in any standard library. A brief list of texts specializing in tests and measurement is given below. Instructors can add those in diagnosis, guidance, and so forth.

3. *A number of catalogues are available.* The bulk of test and scale publishing is con-centrated in a few companies. The following are representative:

Bureau of Educational Research, University of Iowa, Iowa City, Iowa.

Bureau of Publications, Teachers College, Columbia University, New York 27, N. Y.

California Test Bureau, 5916 Hollywood Blvd., Los Angeles 28, Cal.

Educational Test Bureau, 720 Washington Ave., S. E., Minneapolis 14, Minn.

Educational Testing Service, Princeton, N. J.

Harcourt, Brace & World, 750 Third Ave., New York 17, N. Y.

Houghton Mifflin, 2 Park St., Boston 7, Mass.

Public School Publishing Co., 509 North East St., Bloomington, Ind.

Science Research Associates, 57 West Grand Ave., Chicago 10, Ill.

World Book Co., 313 Park Hill Ave., Yonkers 5, N. Y.

Yearbooks and lists appear constantly under the editorship of Oscar K. Buros of the School of Education, Rutgers University, New Brunswick, N. J. These are found in all libraries.

Other catalogues are available but are not listed, since they become out of date rapidly. Consult the library for those which publish regular revisions.

4. *Bulletins on evaluation issued by state and local school systems.* Many city, county, and state systems engaged in modern programs of curriculum reorganization or staff study of instruction issue from time to time mimeographed or printed bulletins. These are particularly valuable for samples of instruments constructed by teachers on the job.

5. *The Education Index.* This well-known source contains many articles dealing with all phases of evaluation.

6. *The Quarterly Review of Educational Research.* This is also a well-known reference which contains at intervals chapters on evaluation.

A list of the most frequently used instruments. The traditional types of final examinations, tests, and quizzes are not only hopelessly inadequate; they are often definitely detrimental to learning. The more recently developed standard test has definite advantages and equally definite disadvantages. A large number of wholly new instruments for testing and evaluating have been emerging. The last ten years has seen steady increase in the development of instruments for observing and recording behavior, in projective techniques, and in clinical or diagnostic methods. This is all in line with the modern effort to achieve better balance between teacher and materials on one side, and the pupil and his growth on the other.

The average teacher makes excessive use of old-type essay examinations, with vague, indefinite questions that do not adequately sample the learning, and of standard tests. Teachers are often surprised to learn at least a dozen other types of instruments are available. The competent teacher uses all that are available and develops, often with the participation of pupils and laymen, still others fitted to specific needs. The following outline gives the major general classes of instruments available or constructible by teacher and pupils.

General Types of Evaluational Instruments

1. Traditional essay-type examinations with general questions.
2. Improved essay-type examinations with definite questions designed to sample adequately the learning outcomes, and eventually refined through scrutiny of results secured through repeated use.
3. Standard tests.
   a. Intelligence tests.
   b. Achievement tests in school subject areas.
   c. Achievement tests in motor skills, coordination, mechanical ability, rhythm.
   d. Aptitude tests.
   e. Physiological measures and medical examinations.
   f. Personality and adjustment tests of several types.
4. Unstandardized (usually homemade) short-answer objective tests. There are sixteen types, with approximately thirty forms available. The commonest are:
   a. Simple recall or free response.
   b. Completion.
   c. Alternate response: true-false; agree-disagree.
   d. Multiple choice.
   e. Matching.
5. Problem-situation tests.
   a. Direct.
      (1) Experiment to be performed.
      (2) Life situation to be met (actual).
   b. Indirect.
      (1) Improved essay question.
      (2) Objective tests requiring judgment.
      (3) Life situation to be met (described).
6. Behavior records.
   a. Controlled situations.
      (1) Check lists (items to observe), rating scales, score cards, codes.
          Personality traits.
          Behavior.
          Attitudes, opinions, interests, emotional adjustment (evidence of).
      (2) Guess-who tests, self-descriptions, sociograms.
      (3) Time and frequency studies of various activities.
      (4) Cameras for still or motion pictures: recorders.
   b. Uncontrolled situations.
      (1) Diary, log, autobiography, narrative accounts, with or without guiding outline.
      (2) Anecdotal record.
      (3) Camera for still or motion pictures.
      (4) Stenographic reports.
      (5) Dictaphone and tape recordings.
7. Inventories (interests, problems, attitudes, behavior, work, play, likes, dislikes).
8. Questionnaires.
9. Interviews, conferences, personal reports, with pupil, parents, or others.
10. Analysis of creative products.
11. Samples of work: reports, exhibits, plays written, pictures or other illustrations, models or constructive productions.
12. Case studies, biograms.
13. Sociometric procedures for studying group relationships and growth in desirable attitudes and skills.
14. Evaluation of reactions using projective and expressive techniques.
    a. Psychodrama and play techniques.
    b. Free association tests.

c. Interpretation of reactions to selected pictures and drawings.

d. Interpretation of free oral and written expression.

Other methods of listing these instruments are available, the chief one being the listing of instruments under the outcomes which each evaluates or measures.

A few special recommendations and cautions. A number of cautions, controversies, and valuable new directions are appearing in the field.

Standard objective tests have been under criticism on several counts, despite their usefulness in given circumstances. Read the recent literature and make a class report.

The diagnostic use of standard tests may be more important than their use for scoring or rating individuals. In fact the diagnostic emphasis is increasing throughout the testing field.

The essay examination, long condemned, is becoming prominent again. Properly constructed it is a valuable instrument. Several immediately current articles bear on this. Interested students may report.

The problem-situation tests and the behavior records of various types are increasingly recognized as valuable. Attention is being given to construction, use, and interpretation.

Recordings of various types are increasingly used for evaluation, diagnosis, and analysis.

Projective techniques must usually be handled by trained personnel, but their usefulness is receiving ever greater attention, especially in diagnosis.

Various of the projective techniques and the sociometric procedures can be managed by good teachers and should be increasingly used.

Creative expression. The evaluation of creative activity is by all odds the most difficult of evaluation tasks. *First,* standards of taste cannot be routinized. *"De gustibus non est disputandum." Second,* confusion arises easily between judgments of content and judgments of form. *Third,* undue analysis easily kills the creative spirit, especially with young pupils and with older ones who are beginners. *Fourth,* individual differences may be as important here as standards. *Fifth,* careless negative judgments have greater detrimental effect here than in most fields. The careful evaluation of creative work must be undertaken, nevertheless, despite these and other difficulties.

The Committee on Appraising and Recording Pupil Progress of the Eight-Year Study suggests the following characteristics and levels of "creativeness and imagination."

General: Approaches whatever he does with active imagination and originality, so that he contributes something that is his own.

Specific: Makes distinctly original and significant contributions in one or more fields.

Promising: Shows a degree of creativeness that indicates the likelihood of valuable original contribution in some field, although the contributions already made have not proved to be particularly significant.

Limited: Shows the desire to contribute his own thinking and expression to situations, but his degree of imagination and originality is not in general high enough to have much influence on his accomplishments.

Imitative: Makes little or no creative contributions, yet shows sufficient imagination to see the implications in the creation of others and to make use of their ideas or accomplishments.

Unimaginative: Has given practically no evidence of originality or creativeness in imagination or action.

The pupil's creative expression may be in the graphic arts, music (singing, playing), writing prose or poetry, dramatic play, rhythm and dancing. General evaluation may be made in terms of the very general criteria above. Beyond this, specialized instruments and procedures are available in the special subjects. Note that here we are not concerned with objective measurement of productions in terms of set standards but with judgment on the creativity displayed.

QUESTIONS AND EXERCISES

The Essay Examination

Instructors should collect typical essay questions, complete quizzes and examinations with identification removed. The collection should range from the best obtainable to the truly incompetent question. Students should be encouraged to add to this collection through turning in illustrations from high school and college. All must be prepared to find questions so bad as to provoke unbridled merriment from informed students. Good questions will impress students with the ingenuity and careful thought that preceded the writing of the question.

1. Examine typical questions and examinations in the instructors' collection. Evaluate in the light of the principles given above.

2. A student may report on any recent article which deals with the analysis or improvement of essay questions.

3. Select a unit, or typical topic, or other area commonly used for teaching.

    a. Define several understandings or meanings which would be legitimate outcomes. Devise two or three valid essay questions to test for one or more of the meanings.

    b. Define one or two thought processes or problem-solving skills utilized in the selected teaching area and devise two or three essay questions designed to test these.

    (If (*b*) proves too difficult for beginners it may be delayed until the problem situation test is discussed later.)

(Question 3 has the additional merit of clarifying further for the student an earlier point: the necessity for definite statement of objectives. The student who attempts to devise testing instruments for vague, indefinite, sloppily worded objectives will see the necessity for restating the objectives.)

Beginning students without background can do little more than is indicated above. Advanced students may, if time permits, read the references below and then answer Question 3 in the light of the advanced discussion. Students may divide up in terms of subject area and report for the benefit of the group their own questions.

The Measurement of Understanding, Forty-fifth Yearbook of the National Society for the Study of Education, Part I, (Chicago, Univ. of Chicago Press, 1946). (Ch. 4 good also on general theory.) A few illustrations, pp. 17-21, and then by subject area in Chs. 5-16.

Another valuable reference at this point is: WOODWORTH, Hugh, *The Nature and Technique of Understanding: Some Fundamentals of Semantics.* (Vancouver, B.C., Wrigley Printing Co., 1949).

The periodical literature should be consulted regularly.

Standard Tests and Informal Objective Tests

Students who have had or are about to have a reputable course in tests and measurements may omit the following paragraphs.

The writer has no suggestions of any value for students with no background in this area. The amount of material is so vast, the details of constructing, administering, scoring, and interpreting results are so extensive that it seems hopeless to make any systematic attack. About all that can be done is to acquaint the students with the fact that such tests are available commercially.

1. Students may examine the local collection of tests, measures, scales, cards, and so forth, and ask such questions as may occur.

2. The instructor or an experienced student in the group may administer one or more tests to the group.

3. Experienced students in the group, if any, may divide into committees by subject interests and make brief presentations to the class showing types of tests available and such explanations as may be of interest.

Instructions for making informal tests are available widely in the literature.

4. Students may attempt the construction of some informal tests to fit materials in units they may be preparing or for any other typical teaching materials. (This is somewhat risky, however, since construction of these tests without extended study may lead to very superficial and inaccurate instruments.)

The Problem-Situation Test

The problem-situation test is inadequately treated in the texts on measurement; hence, time should be taken, if at all possible, for further study. At best, discussion will be inadequate.

Students may engage in any one of three following projects.

1. Read Chapter 2 in Smith and Tyler. Note the great variety of outcomes and instruments of evaluation. In view of the length and complexity of the chapter it will be economical for students to form committees based on chosen interests in type of outcome, type of instrument, or subject area.

Each committee would then (a) report briefly to the class on any additional items of general theory which might be found and (b) construct one or more problem-situation tests in the chosen area. The test should be preferably for some unit, topic, or other teaching organization which the student is developing but can be devised for any probable situation.

In this way the whole class group will have a more detailed introduction to the materials than a hasty reading by all would give.

2. Chapter 3 in Smith and Tyler may be chosen by some students in place of Chapter 2 and treated as above.

3. A third choice may also be offered, students choosing a chapter from Chapters 5-16 in the Forty-fifth Yearbook, Part I. (Other instruments are illustrated also in these chapters, but for the moment we will consider only problem-situation tests.)

(Chapter 2 in Smith and Tyler is on "Aspects of Thinking"; Chapter 3 on "Social Sensitivity"; the chapters in the yearbook are by subject areas.)

The writer has found it economical, following the initial discussion, to proceed to other matters, allowing sufficient time for the class committees to complete reading and the development of these tests. The work cannot be done on overnight assignment.

Still other materials will be found in the three volumes by Wrightstone and in current periodical literature. A summary report on the latter may be made by a student or committee for the benefit of the class.

Recall also the volume by Woodworth on the nature of understanding listed earlier.

Behavior Records: Inventories, Conduct Adjustment, Lists, Diaries, Logs, Projective Techniques, Sociometric Analyses

Behavior records are treated with reasonable adequacy in the texts on measurement and very well in special references devoted to given types of record.

A large exhibit should be in the possession of the instructor so that instruments are easily available to students.

Anecdotal records are very well presented in special references. A large collection of illustrations should be available.

Diaries, logs, and other narrative records are available in only a few texts. A collection should be developed.

1. How could we tell by observing the ordinary activities of a high school girl that:
   a. She *understood and desired to apply* dietetic principles presented in home-economics courses? Or did not understand?
   b. She understood and desired to apply principles involved in design or in household decoration?
   c. She *understood and desired to apply* the advice of a counselor regarding the importance and significance of choosing a life work and preparing for it?

2. Why is the foregoing question asked?

3. A student or series of small committees may compile a brief bibliography of recent articles which present any type of behavior record, their construction and use. Several committees should doubtless divide the field, since so many types of outcome with corresponding types of instruments are available. Report orally with illustrations. *Pay particular attention to instruments designed to evaluate pupil activity within units; participation in defining problems, in developing the plans, in making suggestions, in choosing appropriate activities, doing research, making reports, working in groups, exercising leadership, etc.*

4. Critically evaluate a sampling of instruments from the local collection or as found in the texts and periodical literature.

5. We wish to determine whether a pupil has acquired a good understanding of the principle of evolution—not merely the evolution of man but the principle as a basic method of viewing the world and affairs. Forget the traditional school test of information. Give some of the everyday responses in the language or overt behavior of the individual which would indicate that he understood the evolutionary or developmental point of view. Use possibilities of everyday life; do not use typical school situations.

6. A student committee may choose to construct one of these: a check list for any type of behavior; a personality trait inventory; a conduct adjustment list; an interest or problem

inventory; or any other instrument of evaluation.

7. Examine and critically evaluate a log, diary, or other narrative account in the local collection.

8. Students doing practice teaching or teachers in service should keep a log for a short period of time, discussing it in class as it develops.

9. Search units and logs of units in the local collection for anecdotal records; do the same for the periodical literature. Critically evaluate and report.

10. Construct anecdotal material based on your classroom observations or on your current teaching.

Creative Expression

If time permits and the group is interested, students majoring in the special fields may present quickly the specialized discussions of creativity found in the specialized literature. Ordinarily this may be left to the special-methods courses.

Films, Wire or Tape Recorders

Wire and tape recorders are being used increasingly and with excellent effect both for teaching and for evaluating. Records are made of tone of voice, of enunciation, of a dialogue or other dramatic event.

1. Show a film, if available, of a unit or sequence of lessons, or of any specified type of pupil behavior. Still pictures are usually available in considerable quantity.

2. Demonstrate the use of the recorder in class, working on different types of voice, enunciation, sustained discourse.

3. Where facilities permit, a student or small committee may make a motion picture record of a classroom event or other learning experience.

4. Where facilities are available, students should be given the experience of observing children through a one-way screen, followed by analysis of the observation.

GENERAL PROBLEMS FOR FINAL DISCUSSION

1. Go over the discussion questions and exercises at the close of the chapters in this volume. Select one which in your judgment is a very good test of the understandings presented in the chapter; one which is fair; and one which tests poorly or not at all the learnings involved. Support your choice in each case with argument.

2. Select any major understanding, attitude, or ability which might be a legitimate outcome from this course. Make up a check list of observable evidences which might indicate possession or non-possession of the specified outcome.

CHAPTER 21: The Diagnosis of Learning Difficulties

Diagnosis is called for when there is a case of learning difficulty or a failure. Who fails? It is always the pupil. We never hear of failure by the teacher, by the school, by the curriculum, by the community. Looking further in this matter may be rewarding.

The traditional teacher diagnoses the causes of failure to learn very glibly. A pupil who does not learn is "dumb," that is, he lacks the requisite mental ability, or it may be that "he could learn but he just won't work." The weakness in these diagnoses is that they have little relation, in most cases no relation, to the facts. These diagnoses may dull the conscience of the teacher and bring him peace of mind, but they do not improve the teaching-learning situation.

Pupil failure is a serious matter for all concerned—pupil, teacher, and society. Simple, superficial answers as to the cause are more dangerous than no answers at all. The causes of pupil failure are actually very complex and numerous. A combination of causes, moreover, is usually found in any given case. Secondary causes are often treated as if they were primary. Symptoms of failure are often confused with causes. A given factor may be either a symptom or a cause.

1: THE CAUSES OF FAILURE.

Current discussions of failure thoroughly confused. The majority of monographs, articles, and discussions concerning pupil failure are shockingly superficial. Current lay criticism is even worse. Definitions of failure are often not included, or if they are, there is usually complete neglect of the fundamental difference between general and special education. Many discussions are therefore pointless, even sharply contradictory. The literature reveals that failure may be defined variously, depending upon (a) the theory of education and of learning accepted, and (b) whether we are referring to general or special education.

The first necessity is to distinguish between general and special education. Much discussion of failure by teachers, administrators, and the lay public is thoroughly nonsensical because a clear distinction between general and special education is not made.

General education, as has been pointed out repeatedly, includes the materials and experiences necessary for the common-life activities of all citizens as citizens. We are not here concerned with training for specialized vocational pursuits. The only possible standard for success or failure with normal pupils within the area of general education is growth in terms of individual capacities toward socially desirable ends. Continuous progress goals need to be substituted for grade standards. A pupil who cannot progress under favorable learning conditions, who cannot achieve results necessary for his own maintenance in society, is subnormal and should be placed in a special class or school.

The situation changes fundamentally when the pupil enters the level of exploratory courses and specialized subjects leading to eventual vocational or professional training. Here the standard of success or failure lies clearly outside the pupil. The standard is now the achievement of certain knowledges, attitudes, and skills which are demonstrably necessary for success in given vocations or professions. Levels may now be set for the mature pupil to pass or fail. *Much of the confusion in schools today results from applying this standard, which is wholly sensible in special education, to general education where it is senseless.*

The discussion here is concerned solely with *general education.* Unlimited confusion will result from failure to keep this in mind.

The second necessity is to make clear the theory of education and of learning under which we operate. Education for some consists in the mastery of the cultural heritage, and the process of learning is largely memorizing. Education under this theory is intellectual. Another view is that education consists not only in the derivation of necessary meanings from the cultural heritage but also the development of a great number of personal, social, moral traits. The process of learning here is active experiencing, rather than passive absorption.

Failure must be defined. We may sort out various definitions, correct and incorrect, which are in current use.

Failure in general education is defined as:

1. Failure of the pupil to achieve within a given time limit a level of subject-matter mastery or skill arbitrarily designated by adults. Such standards are usually set without regard for, often in defiance of, the known facts about the learner and his learning processes, the known facts about individual differences.

2. Failure of the pupil to do as well as he can do in subject-matter mastery or skill development. The standard is still adult-set levels of subject matter or skills, but there is some attempt to relate the standard to individual abilities, to interests, and to differences among learners.

3. Failure of the pupil to develop and grow in terms of his own organismic pattern—that is, in terms of his own native ability and rate of growth—toward socially desirable goals.

Failure in special education is defined as:

4. Failure of the pupil to achieve within a given time a level of subject-matter mastery or skill which is demonstrably necessary for continued progress in the special field. The standard is set by the nature of the field and the accepted social goals for the field.

The first and third definitions indicate fundamentally different conceptions of the aims of education, of teaching and learning, of the curriculum, and of school administration. The second is an effort toward compromise. Attempts to utilize within a given school system features from the two different types of education are doomed to failure, as we shall see in the following pages.

The difference between the first basis for failure, which we may call the "grade-standard-basis," and the third, which we may call the "continuous-progress-system," has been set forth consistently throughout this volume and will not be repeated here. Incidentally, we may note that many pupils who do *not* fail under the first standard do often completely fail to grow in emotional stability and in personal-social-moral traits. The first standard and the conception of education on which it is based are limited. [1]

[1] The immediately following pages will set forth in summary fashion many important implications of the two conceptions of failure, with many specific suggestions for diagnosis of cause and for remedial procedure. The detailed facts and figures and other research materials (which are extensive) serving as background are admirably set forth in an excellent reference:
Leo J. Brueckner and Guy L. Bond, *The Diagnosis and Treatment of Learning Difficulties* (New York, Appleton-Century-Crofts, 1955). See at this

Failure in the traditional elementary school. All failures in the traditional school come under the first definition. The traditional school is obligated to answer two serious questions.

First, we may ask, is this truly failure by the pupil? Can a pupil be said to have failed if he works to the very best of his ability, works conscientiously and continuously, and still does not reach a standard set without regard to his native ability? Failed in what? *The pupil has here clearly failed to "pass" a standard which he could never pass under any known circumstances.* The objection may be raised at this point that in some cases the standard may not be wholly arbitrary but determined by the *average* performance of large numbers of pupils of given ages and grade levels. This alleviates but does not cure the difficulty. If a pupil works to the *best of his ability,* expends his best efforts consistently, and still does not come up to the *average for his age and grade,* has he failed? Obviously not. Failing a pupil under this standard is as absurd as to tell a child on his ninth birthday that he cannot be nine because he has not grown so tall or so heavy as the other children in the neighborhood. No one would think of making a child "repeat" his ninth year of life, but schools constantly require pupils to "repeat" a grade in which the pupil has *already done as well as his ability and strength permit him to do.* The pupil needs, not repetition of the same experiences, but more experiences of similar nature and more time in which to grow.

The majority of pupil "failures" in the traditional school are not truly pupil failures at all but failure of the school, or of the home, or of some other factor. Failure of the school is clearly seen when it "fails" to adjust to the known and inescapable facts concerning the nature of the learner, his needs and purposes, and his learning process. Changes need to be made in the philosophy and aims of those in charge of the system, in the curriculum, in the methods of teaching, in guidance and counseling. Sometimes the fault lies not with the school but with the home, which fails to supply favorable study conditions, to maintain an attitude favorable to education, to insist on study habits, hygienic living, and proper nutrition. The fault may lie with the general economic status which necessitates work during out-of-school hours, or which makes malnutrition inescapable. Other community factors contribute.

Second, we may ask why the school bases failing or passing on the "academic" learnings only, to the neglect of growth in personal-social-moral traits. Stress upon immediate specific subject-matter learning has in many instances obscured the importance of social learning. Comparisons of the worth of the two types of outcomes are invidious and useless. Each is important, and in desirable settings for learning, the two are interrelated. This point has been well established elsewhere. Two incidents will be used here merely to illustrate the accepted principles.

A newspaper cartoon shows a severe-looking teacher who has brought a fifth-grade boy to the principal's office. The boy stands with hanging head as the teacher speaks:

I just don't know what to do with Jimmie. He is failing in spelling and geography. We cannot promote him. He is the best traffic policeman we have; adult motorists like to follow his signals. He sold more Red Cross seals than anyone. He got that crotchety old Mrs. X to allow the children to see the Oriental curios in her home. He keeps committees of boys and girls working together. He collects the milk money better than anyone else, and helps the kindergarten children with the bottles—but he just won't learn. We cannot promote him if he fails spelling, geography, and perhaps arithmetic.

Failing spelling and arithmetic—so we keep him back a year! But what was he

point Chapter 3, excellent summary. Note also footnotes and Bibliography leading to extensive supporting background. Special chapters deal with reading, arithmetic, language, spelling, and handwriting. Books specializing in one subject or another will be found in some of the chapter bibliographies.

passing in? He is developing leadership and self-reliance. He can manage people—adults, peers, and younger children. He is evidently well advanced in his grasp and management of human relations. He can plan and organize. He demonstrates excellent growth toward intellectual and emotional maturity. The necessity of learning to spell and to compute must not be minimized, but of equal importance is the development of personal-social-moral traits. Perhaps the school is failing to teach spelling and arithmetic properly.

The writer observed a striking, contrasting instance in which a sixth-grade pupil was chosen chairman of a committee by a class trying group work for the first time. The boy was clearly the best student in the room academically, receiving "A" or "100" in nearly everything. His prestige caused the children to turn naturally to him. The boy turned out to be a spectacular failure. He criticized, sneered, deprecated the efforts and suggestions of everyone. He would let no one suggest or carry through anything, nor would he do it himself. His whole manner was contemptuous, condescending, and antagonistic. At the same time he berated his committee for "not getting anything done." The committee disintegrated quickly and completely. One of these striking coincidences occurred when the boy of least academic ability arose as leader, spontaneously chosen by the children. This boy, a happy, cheerful one, was so poor in his subjects that he had been passed several times just to let him move up. He manifested, in remarkable degree, socially useful abilities in showing children how to make and repair things used in the project, how to secure materials, and how to work together on construction projects. Everyone recognized his leadership and his ability to give security, to give recognition, and to beget success without conscious analysis or attention to what was going on. Incidentally, the teacher arrived early one day and found this boy making two of the brighter children help him with his arithmetic. The prestige he had achieved made him desirous of keeping up in these other fields. The school had tried by drill methods to get this boy to learn. The first trial of purposeful learning achieved what years of imposed learning failed to do.

The boy in the first story was *failed* by the school; the first boy mentioned in the second story *passed*. Obviously the failed boy was passing with high success some important learnings; the passing boy was a serious failure in these same learnings. Neither boy was completely "educated"; neither is achieving a balanced development; the school is seriously at fault with its arbitrary standards of failure and passing. The school and the pupils should be judged on the achievement of both kinds of learning.

Failure in the modern elementary school. The modern school, in contrast, aims to give learners opportunity to achieve both kinds of learning. Failure is applied only to pupils who, so far as we can tell, are not learning as well as native ability and rate of growth permit. The modern school attempts to arrange all learning conditions, from the philosophy and aims of the staff down to routine physical conditions, so that all pupils who will may learn. Curriculums, methods of teaching, standards, and all other instructional factors are arranged in the light of the known facts about the learner. Effort is made to correct or to alleviate some of the factors wholly outside the school which affect the learning and growth of pupils. Hence the problems of imposed failure and of retardation and repetition, the stigmas of "being kept back" and "not promoted" are avoided. Progress toward this desirable goal is of necessity slow.

Pupils on all levels already possess many beliefs, attitudes, and habits inimical to learning. They do not come to any given teacher unscathed by previous experiences. There will be failures, therefore, even in good modern schools: pupils who do not achieve to the best of their ability.

The so-called no-failure program, or continuous-progress system: *Application to the modern school.* The effort to organize the modern elementary school so that continuous progress in terms of capacity would result brought into being the term *no-failure program.* Misunderstandings of far-reaching import arose, as will be seen a few lines below. The term *no-failure* should be eliminated from the educational vocabulary, to be replaced by *continuous-progress system.*

The development of a true continuous-progress system is a long, slow process. Philosophies, curriculums, methods of teaching, and administration must be slowly reorganized. Teachers must be retrained and the public kept abreast of developments. The modern school makes every effort to discover the real, often deeply hidden, cause of failure, to adjust to pupil sympathetically, so that he is able to profit from the learning experiences provided which are well adjusted to his level and maturity. Flexible grouping on the basis of social maturity is provided, with passage from group to group coincident with growth. Directional-process goals replace arbitrary grade standards. Remedial work is prominent. Under ideal conditions failure could theoretically be eliminated. In any event it can be materially reduced.

Application to the traditional school. The traditional school uses diagnosis and remedial work also, but the criterion of success or failure is still an arbitrary standard outside the pupil and perhaps beyond his capacity. Hence, there will be in this school a varying number of "failures" who cannot possibly be saved no matter what remedial measures are applied. Failure is imposed on certain pupils by the school itself. The traditional school cannot truly ever avoid a certain residual percentage of failures.

Many traditional school systems have recently attempted to meet their problem of failure by the wholly uncritical adoption of a "no-failure" program. The usual procedure in this program is to promote every pupil at each promotion period regardless of the pupil's efforts, attitudes, or achievement. This is often called "100 per cent promotion." This can only result in chaotic confusion. Everyone is relieved of responsibility for results, for diagnosis of learning difficulties, for adaptation to individual differences, for guidance, and for remedial effort. This uncritical use of the no-failure concept in traditional schools is clear-cut evidence of ignorance on the part of the leadership. The whole structure of learning, particularly the difference between traditional and modern teaching, is apparently quite unknown. The elimination of non-educative failure cannot be achieved through the unintelligent borrowing of a procedure from a fundamentally different scheme of education; it can be achieved only through a genuine reorganization of the whole system. *A true no-failure, or continuous-progress, or 100-per-cent-promotion, procedure is impossible in an unreconstructed traditional school.* The question in the traditional school is not failure versus non-failure: it is, rather, what to do with the failures? Should failing pupils be promoted to "get what they can" from the next grade, or should they be made to "repeat the grade"?

Wholesale promotion versus repeating grades. The dilemma, promotion or retardation for failures and borderline cases, has always existed in the traditional school. The uncritical interpretation of "no failure" has merely made it more complicated and chaotic. Practical teachers are genuinely disturbed and constantly ask for advice: shall failing pupils be promoted or made to repeat? There is no one right answer; it is strictly a matter of local policy, which in turn rests upon several factors.

First, we know that repetition of what has once been covered is a distinctly detrimental procedure. The evidence is clear-cut and voluminous to show that repeating a grade is rarely beneficial; it is often accompanied by actual lowering of achievement. In too many cases it is destructive of mental hygiene. The more docile pupils may not show this through overt disorder, but they do build up antagonistic attitudes, defense mechanisms, and in some cases serious personality maladjustments. Teachers in the past have been completely uninformed concerning causes and symptoms of bad mental hygiene, but fortunately there is an increasing amount of excellent practical material being disseminated among teachers. The more aggressive pupils develop active antagonism and engage in open disturbance, play truant, and sometimes openly revolt. Repeating a grade is, then, definitely undesirable and to be avoided if possible. Repeating a grade, however, seems forced upon us sometimes by the limited facilities and possibilities of a given system.

Second, the local background, spiritual and material, must be considered in developing a policy. The traditional school system has several choices, depending upon size, money, facilities, and leadership and training of the staff. A school or system large enough to have several sections of the same grade will do well not to fail pupils but to transfer them to other sections at promotion periods. The pupil does not repeat but does get further experiences on a level which will promote his growth. The very change of teachers, classmates, and learning experiences is often beneficial. In any event, certain stigmas and antagonistic attitudes are avoided.

A school system too small to permit this sort of transfer is forced to choose between evils: the promotion of insufficiently prepared pupils or repetition of the previous grade. Teachers favor the one or the other in given circumstances purely because of prejudice, self-interest, or honest but mistaken reasons based on experience. Arguments go on endlessly, but there is no real answer. Superintendents and teachers may choose freely; one of the solutions is as bad as the other. The only alleviation possible in small systems is to provide as much diagnosis and remedial work, as much individual assistance, as much counseling and guidance as is possible with limited staff and money.

The lazy, the uninterested, the antagonistic pupil and failure. Many teachers will agree to the foregoing as good theory applicable to ideal conditions but will object that it will not work "practically." "For," say these teachers, "we have many stupid, lazy, indifferent, or actively antagonistic pupils who cannot or will not learn. Are not such pupils to be failed and made to feel the weight of failure regardless of the type of school?" Complete sympathy may be extended to these teachers but not complete agreement. The question is not so simple. Further analysis will develop a sounder policy.

First, we must avoid the error of confusing a symptom with a cause, of confusing a secondary with a primary cause of failure. No normal child is inherently lazy, or indifferent to new experiences, or antagonistic to situations and persons: he becomes so because of his life experiences. Many pupils are said to be lazy, indifferent, or antagonistic because in reality the curriculum is not worth any attention, is not relevant to the lives of the pupils. Teaching methods which are uninteresting and repressive are the causes of indifference or antagonism. Sarcasm, punishment, and pressures build up indifference and antagonism. Unsympathetic teacher personalities have the same effect. Home conditions, parental attitudes, and poor discipline may be the primary causes of "laziness, indifference, and antagonism." Again, malnutrition or fatigue may be the real causes. This kind of analysis could be continued indefinitely, as will be seen from the listing of primary and secondary causes of failure later in this chapter. Failing the pupil for the symptoms will not cure the cause. The real cause is not touched, often not even recognized. Failing or punishing the pupil only aggravates the condition it is to cure. Should these pupils be failed? Certainly not. The whole scheme of their education should be changed.

The practical teacher will object further, saying that this is all very nice but that she cannot change the scheme of education; cannot change the curriculum, the superintendent's policy, the home conditions, or the economic status; cannot change the neighborhood influences, or what not. She has pupils on her hands who must be taken as they are now. What to do? She is quite right, but her common and immediate solution of this problem—indiscriminate "flunking"—is not the only answer. First, the fundamental principle of all teaching still stands. Sincere efforts must be made to secure the interest of the indifferent, the confidence of the antagonistic. This is a long, slow process of re-establishing confidence in the school and in the teacher. Many individual teachers have taken this hard way and have helped scores of pupils, redirecting them on the way to useful citizenship. Second, firm pressure sympathetically applied is quite legitimate, as outlined in Chapters 3 and 4. Third, a teacher overwhelmed with numbers, overworked, and undertrained cannot avoid failing the worst cases. It is quite true that a certain proportion of pupils arrive at a given level possessed of attitudes and habits so antagonistic that they cannot be overcome quickly and in ordinary ways. The practical teacher is then correct in failing some of these pupils. However, such a teacher and the administrator must recognize that this is an ultimate resort, and that the fundamental cause of the difficulty is not being touched. These pupils should be directed into long-time programs of rehabilitation which only large systems can provide.

Pupils who are actually too retarded mentally to learn at anything like a normal rate do not belong in an ordinary class. The real solution is the special class or school. Small systems who must keep these children in regular classes may promote or retard as they wish; there is no right answer.

Pupil responsibility for avoidance of failure. The poor, harassed teacher probably asks at this point whether the pupil has any responsibility in the cure of failure. Most assuredly he has. The foregoing discussion, which seemingly assesses responsibility to everything and everyone except the pupil, has been necessary to correct erroneous beliefs which are widely held and firmly entrenched. Before defining pupil responsibility it is important to know, for instance, that the causes of failure are far more often outside the pupil than within him; that many causes of failure are wholly beyond the control of the pupil; that many causes are complex and hidden; that the practical classroom teacher is often seriously misled in diagnosing failure. It is important to know that attacking symptoms, which is what most teachers do, will not cure the disease; to know that any cure is a long-time process is likewise important. Some conditions making for failure are, however, within the understanding and control of the pupil. Responsibility is clear, but this responsibility will not necessarily be assumed automatically by all pupils. Methods of developing this responsibility are delicate and complex; inept methods often lead to refusal of the responsibility.

Pupils in early primary grades cannot be expected to take much responsibility for avoidance of failure. The whole scheme of their education should be such that failure does not enter the picture. These children are getting varieties of necessary experience, building understandings, attitudes, and habits. Understandings and attitudes about and toward education, about and toward the nature of society, and of the abilities required for success within society are among the most important that will develop. With increasing maturity and insight, older pupils may be expected to apply these learnings to their own conduct; to assume responsibility for their results.

Even in good schools the pupil meets many situations in which he may take one of two paths. Unfortunately, little social criticism attaches if he takes the easier. Pupils may do "fairly well," or they may do their very best; they may "get by" or turn in a finished product. But learning itself clearly includes recognition of socially desirable procedures, realization of the effects upon the individual and on society of different types of effort, different levels of conscientiousness. Organizing education around pupil purpose should eventually make purposeful work habitual. Ability and willingness to carry tasks to completion, to fulfill undertakings, are desirable learning outcomes. Certainly pupils are to take responsibility for learning and avoidance of failure in so far as they can control the factors. They will do this readily in a desirable learning environment.

Young persons, being young, are discovering the world. A multitude of interests and activities beckon. Adults forget that children do not (and should not) think like adults. Pupils must sometimes be reminded of responsibilities and desirable procedures. Herein often lies one of the tragedies of the school. Being told that they should study because "schools cost the community a lot of money," because "your parents sacrifice to send you," because "it is your duty," simply leaves the average pupil indifferent. These are verbalisms and mean nothing to him. Bullying, threatening with failure, sarcasm, and ridicule beget active antagonism to the school and defiant refusal to study. Keen judgment and social sensitivity on the part of the instructor will lead to positive methods adapted to individual differences. One of the best devices is a sympathetic, informal inquiry into the difficulties and obstacles, the real problems of the young person. He may be in desperate need of aid, of security, of someone he can trust not to laugh at him. A few simple hints on study or upon the control of outside factors have saved many a failure. More direct counsel and guidance on specific problems will aid in other cases. Casual comments, joking but encouraging remarks about potential abilities will suffice with many pupils. Direct criticism and pressure may be necessary in given cases but must always be courteous, sympathetic,

and forward-looking. Sarcastic reference to past blunders and a probably unfavorable destiny may be omitted!

Failure as indicative of "high standards." A certain variety of private school and many traditional high schools point with pride to their high percentage of pupil failure. These schools assign "hard lessons," tolerate "no nonsense," and ruthlessly fail pupils who do not reach the standard. No inquiry of any sort is made into the cause of failure, the school glibly reporting that failing pupils are dull, lazy, or otherwise unfit for academic work. They are "not our caliber." Since many of these pupils are eminently successful in out-of-school activities at the moment, since many succeed later in life, the reasons given by the school are patently absurd. Despite this curious blunder in logic, many older schools have advanced the slogan that a high percentage of failure is proof of the "high standards" of the institution! Many public high schools, whose sole purpose and reason for existence is to educate persons, unblushingly state that the more they fail the better job they are doing! High pupil-failure rate, far from being indicative of high standards, is direct, first-hand evidence of gross incompetence on the part of the school and of its teachers. It indicates the very lowest standards of teaching efficiency. The modern democratic school realizes that high pupil-failure is a criticism of the school and eventually a danger to democratic life. Diagnosis of failure, remedial work, and eventually—it is hoped—the elimination of failure are the true indications of "high standards." The extensive current studies of "drop-outs" are throwing new light on this.

A medical, engineering, or other vocational or professional school might be able to achieve truly higher standards by failing large numbers of mediocre candidates, but not a school devoted to general education. Even in the professional school, care would have to be exercised to see that failure was not connected merely with poor teaching.

The educative effect of failure. Is there, then, to be no failure at all in schools? Will not this make the pupil soft and unable to face disappointment, unable to meet standards? Surely, the critics say, pupils will meet with failure in real life and a soft policy in school will leave them unprepared for the harsh demands outside of school. This problem was adequately discussed twice in earlier chapters. Details will be omitted here, only two summary statements being repeated. First, failure imposed arbitrarily upon individuals and by circumstances beyond the control of those individuals is definitely destructive of personality values and of mental hygiene and conducive to the most undesirable attitudes and practices. Second, failure resulting from the individual's own immature judgment, hasty or ill-considered reactions, or emotional interferences, and definitely recognized as such, is definitely educative. The modern school provides ample opportunity for the latter type of experience. Failure in the area of specialization will be based on inability to meet the necessary standards.

Complexity of problem indicated by difficulty of constructing a logical outline of causes of failure. The genuine difficulty of the problem of failure becomes apparent when one attempts to construct a coherent, logical summary of the causes of failure. The amount of cross-reference and interrelationship necessary would result in an outline so detailed, voluminous, and cumbersome as to defeat its own purpose. For instance, any given, specified case of failure may be owing to (*a*) any one of several different primary causes or (*b*) any combination of several primary causes. Complexity is increased by the fact that (*c*) any one primary cause may produce a dozen different types of secondary causes and different sets of symptoms in as many different pupils.

A teacher may report a boy failing because he will not work. The primary cause in one case may actually be malnutrition resulting from poverty; in another case, malnutrition resulting from an unbalanced diet in a home well able to supply adequate meals; in another, malnutrition owing to unsupervised eating habits even where good meals are provided. In still another case, the real cause may be fatigue resulting from overwork outside school which in turn is due to poor economic status; in another, owing to earlier illness; in still another, to antagonistic home attitudes; in others, to poor teaching in earlier grades, to a poor curriculum, to worry over family matters, to emotional insecurity, which in turn may be owing to any of a score of causes. Any one of these primary causes can in turn be broken down into numerous details ranging all the way from incorrect educational aims on the part of the school to the minutiae of poorly made assignments, inadequately initiated units, or poorly worded questions. This type of analysis can go on and on indefinitely testifying to the complexity of the problem. A boy reported failing because he will not work may actually be failing for any one of a dozen different reasons or combinations of reasons. The difficulty faced by "practical" teachers is seen in the fact that in given cases of failure six teachers often turn in six wholly unrelated reasons for the failure. Three different reasons for a given failure is a commonplace in ordinary practice.

An illustrative listing of the causes of failure. A complete outline of specific causes of failure would necessitate repeating every detail included in any volume on the principles of education and of teaching. A logical outline is likewise impossible for the reasons set forth just above. The guidance derived from the following analysis will not be, therefore, in terms of detailed answers for all specific cases encountered by the teacher; it will be found instead in a set of principles based upon the outline.

The Primary Causes of Failure

I. *Resident in the Pupil*

 A. *Physical shortcomings* (congenital or acquired deficiency or deformity) not curable by individual effort or by education.

  1. A central nervous system inadequately developed, injured, or diseased, thus making mental or emotional normality difficult or impossible.

  2. A peripheral nervous system, sense organs (eye, ear, vocal apparatus, etc.) inadequately developed, injured, or diseased, thus making normal interactive experience with the environment difficult or impossible.

  3. Glandular imbalance.

  4. A physical deformity making for mental or emotional instability.

  5. Incurable illness.

 B. *Mental shortcomings* (congenital or acquired deficiency or disability) not curable by individual effort or by education. Insufficient mental ability is listed here as a primary cause, but it may be in fact a secondary cause based upon a defective nervous system, glandular imbalance, or the like.

  Furthermore, sharp distinction must be made between definite mental inadequacy and seeming or deceptive lack of mental ability. Lack of mental ability, so-called in many cases, actually turns out to be lack of interest in poor curriculums and the result of poor teaching; lack of interest or active antagonism due to unfavorable teacher personality, unfavorable home attitudes toward school; lack of energy owing to malnutrition or overwork outside school; lack of interest owing to continued failure, which in turn may be owing to poor study habits, in turn to poor teaching, or poor home environment not conducive to study, and so on.

  Finally, it must be remembered that intelligence, defined as ability to do school work, manifests itself very differently in different situations. Previous experience, guidance, success or failure, the total educational situation—all affect this. The motives and ambitions of the pupil also definitely affect the results obtained as well as the level of mental ability.

II. *Resident in the Social Order*

 A. *Inequitable distribution of resources,* resulting in inadequate financing of schools and poor economic status of many homes.

  1. Inadequate educational situation:

   a. Poorly constructed, unattractive buildings with poor facilities; inadequate play space and other special items.

   b. Inadequate curriculum; poor or non-existent instructional materials; large overcrowded classes; inadequate pupil experiences; heavy teaching load.

   c. Poorly selected, poorly trained, poorly paid teachers.

  2. Undesirable housing, neighborhoods; inadequate recreational facilities.

  3. Low economic status of many homes:

   a. Lack of education resulting in parental antagonism toward school and in lack of co-operation, resulting in truancy and absence.

   b. Necessity to supplement family income involving work after school, resulting in fatigue and other contributing causes.

   c. Stress and strain within family group owing to economic insecurity.

   d. Absence of books and magazines, library cards, travel experiences, and other cultural items.

   e. Malnutrition. (This is found also in homes of good economic status, but for different reasons.)

   f. Frequent moves in search of employment resulting in changes in schools and in gaps of schooling.

   g. Lack of protection from disease, failure to have adenoids removed or other necessary care; lack of glasses or other physical aids.

   h. Lack of quiet place to study.

 B. *Control of school by conservative elements* in present adult generation who received their education in the past; *by untrained, inert, and often cowardly educational leaders.*

  1. Aims of education out of date; an undemocratic philosophy of education.

  2. Lack of modern scientific approach.

  3. Undemocratic administration and supervision.

  4. A curriculum poorly or not at all adapted to the needs, interests, and

abilities of the pupils, or to the needs of the community.

5. Traditional teaching methods based upon an erroneous conception of the learner and of learning.
6. Traditional grade organization, arbitrary standards for promotion, wholly theoretical grade-a-year progress.
7. Adult standards of success set up without regard for the nature of learner, of learning, of individual differences.
8. Lack of an adequate program of professional improvement for the staff.
9. Failure of the professional leaders to inform and educate the public.
10. Inadequate local financing of school program in all its details with concomitants already listed.
11. Inevitable direct contact with racial, national, religious, and political prejudices.

C. *Low regard for education,* for teaching, and for teachers on part of substantial numbers of lay public.
  1. Poor financing, equipment, and program as already listed.
  2. Poor standards for teacher selection and training, low required levels of:
    a. Professional equipment: meager training and experience; poor methods; ignorance of modern concepts of learning, of teaching, of results, of evaluation.
    b. Physical equipment: ordinary appearance, average or less than average good health, lack of energy.
    c. Personal equipment: ordinary appearance; lack of poise, enthusiasm, good judgment, open-mindedness, and many other traits; lack of ambition.
    d. Social equipment: lack of ability and willingness to co-operate, to adapt oneself, to be considerate, and many other items.
    e. Intellectual equipment: ordinary or less native ability, poor cultural background, narrow interests, poor general information, lack of interest in world affairs.

D. *Inadequate understanding by parents* (on all economic levels) of principles of child care and rearing, of human motivations, and of controls of behavior.

1. Harsh, imposed, authoritarian discipline.
2. Overprotection and coddling.
3. Failure to participate in and guide children's leisure-time activities, reading, radio-listening, TV, movie-going, choice of companions.
4. Failure to give security through the above-mentioned factors plus inconsistent discipline and guidance, indulgence; through lack of protection from adult tensions, problems, quarrels.
5. Failure in broken homes to protect children from the particular emotional strains involved in this situation.
6. Exposure to racial, national, religious, and political prejudices.

E. *Presence in our society of large immigrant populations.*
  1. Bilingualism in many homes.
  2. Double load on pupil if required to attend native language or religious school in addition to public.

The implications of the primary causes of failure. The foregoing list of primary general causes could be broken down into literally hundreds of implications, more immediate causes, and symptoms. The general causes and their implications could be still further supplemented through listing of hundreds of causes of failure which are relevant to learning within special subjects or areas. A complete listing of specific causes of failure would fill a small volume.

Before passing to an examination of the types of pupil attitudes and behavior which teachers commonly regard as causes of failure, we may examine further implications of the primary causes with a view to clarifying the relation between these causes and the pupil's attitudes and symptoms. The following paragraph, still on the level of generalization, points directly at the immediate causes of failure and at symptoms of failure.

The various primary causes in the learner, in the school, in the home, and in the community, operating in conjunction, place pupils often in physical settings for learning which are uninviting and uninspiring. These in turn produce attitudes of indifference to, lack of respect for, and even antagonism to, education and its aims. Interest and energy are affected by unfavorable light, heat, and ventilation. The curriculums and text materials are often dull and uninteresting, irrelevant to the life interests and activities of the learners, and unsuited to the needs of the community. Individual differences are often not recognized, are even disregarded; materials are not adapted to the levels of maturity within a given group; unattainable standards are combined with lack of recognition for effort—all combine to discourage and antagonize the learner. An undemocratic administration aimed at business "efficiency" instead of at the development of the learners inevitably produces conditions inimical to learning and is thus productive of failure. Traditional teaching methods based on erroneous conceptions produce thousands of specific errors in technique which are actual causes of failure—numberless errors of motivation, questioning, assigning, initiating units, developing study habits, evaluating, diagnosing, disciplining, giving marks and rewards, promoting, and so through the entire area covered by this volume and by many volumes on the psychology of learning. Many traditional teachers and many parents are but "babes in the woods" in regard to their knowledge of human motivation and of methods of controlling conduct. These things are the actual causes of failure, since they produce the pupil attitudes and behaviors which are usually listed as causes. Again, scores of immediate causes and symptoms of failure can be traced to undesirable teacher personality and manner. Unsympathetic attitudes, lack of understanding and of interest in pupil problems, harsh, unyielding insistence on certain rigmaroles and prerogatives, upon "respect" and order; sarcasm, ridicule, bullying, and threatening all appear here. The seriously frustrated personality actually engages in punishments and requirements so unreasonable as to border on the sadistic.

The sharp focus on the school and the learning situation does not mean that the school and the teachers are solely to blame. Many and various primary causes contribute. All the unfavorable conditions and attitudes within home and neighborhood, together with the more basic conditions within the total community, contribute mightily.

The secondary causes and symptoms of failure. Teachers and parents naturally see the more immediate cause, sometimes to the neglect of the remote and more important aspects. To attack a case of failure as if it had no background will not only not cure failure; it will very likely aggravate it by enhancing the cumulative effect of the neglected primary cause. First steps, however, must be taken within a given, immediate, and specific situation. Therefore, it is important to know and to identify the factors which teachers regard as important. The problem then becomes the training of teachers to remedy these immediate causes with due regard for the underlying, more fundamental factors.

The Causes of Failure as Commonly Recognized and Listed by Teachers

(Causes given by teachers are sometimes the real causes, sometimes secondary causes, but very often are only symptoms mistaken for causes).

I. *Resident in the Pupil*
   A. *Mental inadequacies;* obstacles to mental functioning.
      1. Genuine lack of mental ability.
      2. Seeming lack of mental ability; more truly, lack of interest, indifference, lack of effort, active antagonism, lack of energy owing to malnutrition or overwork; lack of mastery of fundamentals and study habits.
      3. Immaturity or unreadiness (to be clearly distinguished from the two listed above).
   B. *Physical inadequacies.*
      1. Limited functioning of sense organs, vocal apparatus, and so forth.
      2. Ill health.

C. *Emotional inadequacies.*
1. Insecurity.
2. Maladjustments to persons, situations, requirements.
3. Complexes, phobias, presence of escape mechanisms.
4. Immaturity.
D. *Detrimental general attitudes and habits* (fragmentary and illustrative listing only).
1. Indifference to and lack of interest in school work.
2. Active antagonism to school work; refusal to study and learn.
3. Discouragement and failure to persist.
4. Non-co-operation, avoidance of responsibility.
5. Laziness, so-called.
6. Truancy, irregular attendance.
7. "Nervousness" (variously interpreted).
E. *Non-possession of elementary skills.*
1. Inability to read, to compute; lack of background in subjects which are of necessity sequential; inability to speak English.
2. Ignorance of study skills and work habits.

II. *Resident in the Educational Situation and Community.*

Teachers ordinarily see the chief causes of failure as lying in the pupil's abilities, attitudes, and habits. Many of them, however, look beyond this and can see some of the more remote causes and clearly attribute failure to them.
A. Uniform curriculums, texts and materials unsuited to levels of maturity and to individual differences.
B. Inappropriate administrative standards and practices.
C. Unduly heavy teaching load, too large classes, outside duties, etc.
D. Too frequent transfers, double promotions, etc.
E. Poor teaching in the previous grades.
F. Poor home conditions.
G. Overwork outside school hours or too many extracurricular activities.
H. Malnutrition.

A Few General Principles of Guidance

I. The cause of failure to learn in the case of any given pupil is far from simple. A complex tangle of causes lies behind the immediate causes and symptoms.
II. Immediate causes and symptoms are often seriously misleading. Treatment of the pupil based on the naïve interpretation of immediate data may be seriously disastrous.
III. Many of the primary causes of failure are beyond the teachers' control. This does not mean that nothing can be done, but that the cure of these necessitates a long-time program aimed at changing public opinion and the system of education.
IV. Detailed programs of diagnosis and remedial procedure are a necessary and normal part of all teaching situations as at present constituted.
V. Programs designed to cure immediate causes and symptoms will be valuable only in so far as they take into account the hidden primary causes.

DISCUSSION QUESTIONS FOR SECTION 1

1. What do you think is meant by the expression applied to some pupils, "school dull and life bright"? How do you account for the situation indicated?
2. Teachers rarely list as causes of failure:
   a. Material in textbook beyond understanding of pupil.
   b. Vocabulary of book or teacher too difficult for pupil.
   c. Teacher was unable to arouse interest of pupil in valuable and desirable learning materials.
   d. Teacher had insufficient knowledge of nature of mental processes of learners.
Explain why this is so, but do not stop with the obvious first answer.
3. Describe the general features of the policy of promotion operative in the system where you teach, in schools you attended if you are not teaching. *Differentiate clearly between elementary and secondary schools.* Explain as well as you can the probable assumptions behind the system.
4. Describe briefly the operation of any continuous-progress system with which you may have had contact.

REPORTS

Individuals or Small Committees

1. Marshal a series of arguments for and against the continuous-progress policy. Differentiate sharply between basic reasons for and against and mere obstacles or difficulties in

operation. Supplement the brief summary in this chapter through recent periodical articles.

2. Summarize the studies on repetition which results from retardation or non-promotion. (Experienced teachers and students generally accept without question the statement that repetition of a grade is measurably detrimental, and when this is so the exercise may be omitted. Teachers and students who are doubtful may be asked to make this report.)

3. Report briefly upon any specific case which you have observed or experienced, in which it seemed clear to you that a given remote primary cause was at the root of the difficulty, whether or not recognized by the teacher.

4. Secure from teachers in co-operating schools an analysis of causes of failure in two or three specific cases. (The instructor may build up a file of such material.) Analyze the statement in the light of this chapter, seeking further facts if necessary.

5. One or more reports may be made on the following topics or similar ones, based on current periodical literature.

    a. Why teachers say pupils fail.

    b. Why pupils say they fail.

    c. The relation between failure or success and the general growth and behavior of the learner between failure and success and truancy, personality maladjustment, delinquency.

(Any others which appeal to instructor or students.)

READINGS

General textbooks do not treat the matter of failure, pupil progress through the school, and related problems very well. The following reference, already noted in footnotes, handles the matter adequately and may be used, if desired, for supplementary reading.

BRUECKNER, Leo J., and BOND, Guy L., *The Diagnosis and Treatment of Learning Difficulties* (New York, Appleton-Century-Crofts, 1955).

A selected list of books dealing with diagnosis in given subject areas will be given later. Most of them appear in the chapter bibliographies for the volume here noted.

2: THE TECHNIQUES OF DIAGNOSIS.

PRELIMINARY DISCUSSION QUESTIONS

These questions are designed for students with little or no background in this area. Experi-

enced teachers may omit them and proceed to study of the text.

1. Have you ever failed a subject and later passed it with reasonable ease? If so, were you at the time aware of the factors which caused the failure and success? Or did you later become aware? Describe as explicitly as possible.

2. Recall specifically some difficulties with learning which you had in elementary or secondary school or college. If your teachers noted and diagnosed your difficulty, describe what was done. If you had to solve the difficulty yourself, describe what you did and why. Estimate the proportion of times that teachers did and did not diagnose.

3. Can you describe actual cases from your own observation in which, as far as you could see, the learner was materially aided or seriously handicapped by the home environment? By a given personal trait? By any other factor extraneous to the school?

4. It is commonly believed that an "only child" differs significantly from other children in certain important characteristics. Disregarding for the moment the validity of this belief, explain why it is held by many persons. What has this to do with our problem here?

5. Certain educational authorities say that the failure of a pupil is actually the failure of the school. Is this partially, wholly, or not at all true?

The influx into the school of "all the children of all the people" profoundly changed the attitude of the school toward the pupil. Each child in a democracy is entitled to the opportunity to develop to the limit of his capacities. The effects of failure to grow or to learn are disastrous for both individual and society.

The discovery that many influences seemingly far removed in both time and space from the immediate classroom situation to definitely affect learning for good or ill also contributed to the changing educational process. Finally, it was discovered that thousands of pupils had no clear understanding of how to study, how to learn, or how to develop work habits. Thousands of teachers knew no more about these things than did the pupils, hence could be of little help. One result has been the increasing attention to diagnosis of the causes of failure and to remedial measures.

General levels of diagnosis. Analysis usually begins with a survey to determine the general status of a class group. Specialized techniques are then used to determine the specific difficulties of individual pupils or of small sections within the total group. One acceptable outline of procedures would be:

1. *General diagnosis*
   The instruments are standard tests and practically all of the techniques listed in the chapter on evaluation.

2. *Analytic diagnosis*
   The instruments are diagnostic tests prepared for this purpose.

3. *Psychological diagnosis through*
   a. Controlled observation as outlined in the chapter on evaluation.
   b. Analysis of written work.
   c. Analysis of oral responses and accounts of procedures.
   d. Analysis of objective records of various types.
   e. Interviews.
   f. Laboratory and clinical methods.
   g. Case studies.

The instruments used in diagnosis. A sampling of instruments would cover many pages and is impossible in a general text. Discussion will be confined to general principles and processes as it was in the chapter on evaluation. Scores of specific techniques are available in books devoted to diagnosis, particularly in those dealing with special subject areas. (See bibliography later.)

General diagnosis. Typical standard tests or test batteries are the chief instruments used. Check lists, rating scales, and observational records are often utilized. A survey or overview is made in order to secure a general picture of class status. Specific factors may then receive detailed study.

Survey testing reveals the status of a given class in relation to certain norms, usually the medians and averages for standard tests. The average score for the group and the distribution of scores within the group are both important. A given class may exhibit any of several combinations of these factors. The score of the class in arithmetic, for instance, may be below standard for rate but up to or above standard for accuracy. The individual scores may be scattered widely or grouped closely about the norms. Scores in reading may show any number of variations from class to class as among word meaning, sentence meaning, paragraph meaning (all aspects of comprehension), and rate of reading. Organization and critical analysis of what is read enter into advanced tests and add other possible variations.

For all common difficulties revealed, general causes and cures can be suggested. All types of good and poor teaching, and all combinations of other primary causes as outlined in Section I may be involved. Analysis of all pertinent facts is necessary. The procedure is part of the course on tests and measurements and is not included here.

The differing levels of achievement from grade to grade within a school and from school to school can be shown by combining the scores from various rooms and buildings into graphs. For instance, scores on speed and quality in handwriting, or on speed and comprehension in reading, gathered from half a dozen sixth grades, or for all grades, in schools serving similar socioeconomic groups may be graphed. In some rooms or schools speed and comprehension will proceed in close relationship to each other. Other cases will show wide discrepancies in growth of the two, sometimes one will even regress while the other goes ahead. Great differences in factors affecting learning are indicated. Students may advance tentative explanations of the general variations hinted at above or, preferably, may secure actual graphs from co-operating schools. Graphs from books on diagnosis may also be used.

General diagnosis may also point very directly at a poorly arranged course of study or to poor teaching methods. In one city, for instance, graphs showed that failures in reading steadily decreased until they were negligible in seventh and eighth grades. Arithmetic failures for the same children and the same teachers, however, showed a very steep rate of growth, out of all proportion to expectancy, up through the fifth grade, with failures dropping after that but still high. Suspicion may be directed at the nature and arrangement of arithmetic materials in the primary grades. Scrutiny of teaching methods is also indicated.

One particular high school showed steadily decreasing failure rate for French, Latin, and German, but an extremely erratic graph for failures in English. The foreign language curriculum and teaching procedure are evidently adjusted to pupil interest and maturity. We must note, however, that early failures in foreign language tend to drop out, hence reducing the number of failures as the years progress. The graph in mathematics for this school showed a high rate of failure through the first three years and a sharp decline thereafter. What factors other than drop-outs of failing students in early years might account for this? The failure rate for the first three years was quite uniform perhaps indicating factors other than dropouts.

Analytic diagnosis. The elementary processes in arithmetic, reading, and handwriting, which seem simple, are in reality fairly complex. Adding a column of two or three figures is not the same process as adding one of eight or ten figures. From three to ten different processes may appear in simple addition, subtraction, multiplication, and division. One hundred fourteen different kinds of errors may appear in working decimals. Many a pupil has been failed in "arithmetic" when actually he failed only in subtraction. Failure in subtraction may be due in turn to difficulty with only a few number combinations. Each person has his idiosyncrasies

in the manner of handling number combinations. One child sent to a clinic for diagnosis was said to be unable to do arithmetic, making many mistakes in each paper. One paper, on which the teacher had marked thirty-two mistakes, turned out to have only five different mistakes, each one made approximately six times. The child's trouble was not "arithmetic" but weakness in a few specific number combinations.

The differentiation between oral and silent reading was made in comparatively recent times. Many teachers are still unaware of the differences between them and that several different processes are used in silent reading alone. Handwriting has been analyzed by a number of scholars into its elements, showing that the composite, a written word, involves a number of skills on the part of the pupil.

The second phase of diagnosis then is to select those pupils who have special weaknesses and to apply remedial measures. Many tests are now available specifically for diagnosis in the typical subjects of the curriculum: arithmetic, reading, writing, language, science, social studies, algebra, and so forth. Many of the modern instructional materials, texts, and workbooks include tests for diagnostic purposes. Complete lists of these tests may be found in professional or commercial catalogues and in texts on measurements.

The same sort of diagnosis can be made for the far more important learnings in the form of attitudes, understandings, and values by use of the check lists and behavior records discussed in the previous chapters. Some authorities recommend securing the emotional reactions and observing the behavior of all pupils subjected to a diagnostic test. The foregoing emphasis upon the diagnosis of learnings closely connected with formal subject matter should not overshadow these other learning outcomes. Diagnosing the difficulties with the latter is far more complex than diagnosing weakness in skill learnings.

Psychological diagnosis. The diagnostic tests will reveal the typical classes and number of errors made by the pupil. The next step is to determine very specifically the exact nature and causes of these weaknesses. The method is the close observation and detailed analysis of the pupil's behavior or learning processes. The instruments and techniques are not as precise as the tests heretofore discussed, but they often yield more important data. This is particularly true if the teacher knows the relationship between certain kinds of behavior and certain causes of failure and knows how to arrange situations in which situation and reaction can be studied together.

1. *Controlled observation.* The previous chapter on evaluation made clear that many important learning outcomes cannot be measured by typical tests. Evidence must be gathered by observation of behavior. This is as true for processes of learning as for products. The causes of failure can be inferred safely from the accurate and detailed behavior records mentioned previously. The numerous check lists, rating scales, observation records, and anecdotal records are all useful in this connection.

Several lists of incorrect procedures, faulty study habits, and the like have been compiled to help the teacher in watching for causes of failure. These are available on elementary, secondary, and college level. Vocalization and lip movement in reading, counting (beyond the level where crutches are legitimate) in arithmetic, incorrect use of materials and apparatus are easily observed. The number and kind of contributions made by pupils to the on-going class activity are easily observed and when analyzed may lead to important causes of poor learning. This type of observation can be applied, as indicated previously, to the playground and community activities of the children. Lists of common errors in reading, especially oral reading, in arithmetic, and in language usage are available. Diagnostic tests are many of them of this nature.

2. *Analysis of written work.* The analysis of errors revealed in general by diagnostic tests is aided by the use of lists of common and continuing errors. Errors listed may vary from those of minor consequence to those indicative of basic weakness of some sort. Random, unintelligent misspellings are a much more serious symptom of disability than mere phonetic misspellings. For instance, one boy misspelled *lieutenant* five times and in four different ways, with the correct spelling in front of him all the time!

3. *Analysis of oral responses.* A very important technique is to sit down with a pupil and ask him to work aloud. The teacher tabulates what happens while the pupil repeats aloud his mental processes, reads aloud, or describes how he thinks as he does the work. Faulty, round-about, or definitely incorrect processes come to light which cannot be discovered in any other way. Extensive applications of this technique by Buswell, [2] Brueckner, [3] and others have revealed a literally astonishing amount of curious mental procedure in the workings of examples in arithmetic. The table on page 504 lists just those found in the subtraction of whole numbers.

A good illustration of oral analysis is given by Lee and Lee: [4]

T.S. had the first eleven problems of the Modern School Achievement Test-Arithmetic Computation correct. These consisted of addition, subtraction, and multiplication problems. Problems 12, 16, and 20, which were long column addition problems, were missed. An inspection of the work did not reveal where the girl was having difficulty, but on consultation it was found that she was trying to carry from the previous column until she reached the top of the column. This procedure resulted

[2] Guy T. Buswell, with the co-operation of Lenore John, *Diagnostic Studies in Arithmetic,* Supplementary Educational Monograph No. 30 (Chicago, Univ. of Chicago Press, 1926).

[3] Leo J. Brueckner, *Diagnostic and Remedial Teaching in Arithmetic* (Philadelphia, Winston, 1930).

[4] J. Murray Lee and Dorris M. Lee, *The Child and His Curriculum,* 3rd ed. (New York, Appleton-Century-Crofts, 1960), pp. 396-397.

in forgetting and many mistakes. Problem 13, which was ⅛ of 576 ? was omitted. She stated that she did not know what "of" meant, which difficulty was immediately corrected. Problems 14 and 15, short division and multiplication problems, were missed through carelessness. Problem 17, addition with only one fraction, was correct. Problem 18, subtraction with mixed numbers, was wrong. She did not know how to subtract fractions. An analysis of problems 19, 22, and 23 in division showed lack of ability to place the answer and to handle zeros in the answers. Errors in problems 26 and 31 indicated that T.S. did not know how to handle the fraction in multiplication when the problem was as

$$\begin{array}{r} 452 \\ \times \ 2\frac{1}{2} \end{array}$$

She did not place the decimal points correctly in multiplication of decimals.

4. *Analysis of objective records.* The cumulative records mentioned several times and described in Chapter 10 supply several types of data which may be scrutinized. The chief record will be the age-grade-progress of the pupil, together with the reasons noted for retardations, accelerations, and so on. Records of attendance and of changing residence are important. The health history is often very revealing. Notations of extracurricular achievements, of employment, or of general outside activities are useful. The socioeconomic ratings of home and community should be included here. Sociometric studies of the class group are also valuable.

Attention studies and time distribution studies may be made specially at given times to supplement the permanent record, though such studies of course, overlap with the controlled observation technique. Pupils may be asked to produce a record of their study programs or analyses of distribution of total time, which then constitute good objective records for analysis.

5. *The interview as a diagnostic technique.* Interviews may be necessary in some cases to supplement the techniques just described. The examiner may be uncertain concerning the full or the exact implications of the data

so far secured and wish to secure even more details and intimate information. The most important interviewee is the pupil himself. Interviews may be held also with parents and other members of the family, teachers, and other adults, and playmates.

The general purposes of interviews with the pupil are to discover (a) his beliefs and attitudes toward other persons with whom he must deal: parents and teachers, brothers, sisters, and playmates; (b) his interests, likes and dislikes, abilities and disabilities; (c) his individual methods of thinking, feeling, and acting. Interviewing parents and other adults is chiefly for the purpose of (a) learning about the kinds of adults who are influencing the child; (b) discovering parental attitudes toward the child, his behavior, and his talents or disabilities, and discovering, if possible, the pupil's attitudes toward these adults; (c) learning some of the general environmental influences which play upon the child; (d) discovering the parent's attitudes toward teachers and other children with whom the child lives and works, toward the conventions and situations within which he must work. Anything from the child's past history may be probed by means of the interview. Interviews with teachers are for the purpose of finding out (a) the teacher's estimates of the pupil's abilities, attitudes, and conduct; (b) the teacher's attitudes toward this individual pupil; (c) the teacher's attitudes toward racial, national, social, or economic groups and levels; (d) anything about the pupil's school record and present status which might be enlightening.

The average individual believes that interviewing is simple and that anyone can do it. "It is just conversation." On the contrary, interviewing either adults or children, particularly on personal matters, is a genuinely difficult task. Random discussion not only fails to produce positive data; it may very likely produce highly unreliable data. Careful preparation is necessary. A volume or two and many separate chapters in other texts are available, devoted to the details of

Errors	III	IV	V	VI	Total
	Grades				
1. Errors in combinations	62	75	69	40	246
2. Borrowing					
a. Did not allow for having borrowed	19	50	57	36	162
b. Errors due to zero in minuend	25	39	26	15	105
c. Subtracted minuend from subtrahend	47	33	12	4	96
d. Failed to borrow; gave zero as answer	21	20	14	4	59
e. Deducted in minuend when no borrowing was necessary	2	8	10	5	25
f. Deducted two from minuend after borrowing	1	5	8	6	20
g. Increased minuend digit after borrowing	2	2	6	2	12
h. Deducted all borrowed numbers from lefthand digit	1	0	1	0	2
3. Counting	43	44	39	10	136
4. Faulty procedures					
a. Said example backward	21	38	29	12	100
b. Added instead of subtracted	18	9	19	1	47
c. Used same digit in two columns	18	15	3	4	40
d. Omitted a column	9	13	8	5	35
e. Split numbers	7	5	10	2	24
f. Ignored a digit	12	6	2	3	23
g. Used minuend or subtrahend as remainder	10	6	2	0	18
h. Began at left column	2	0	1	0	3
5. Lapses, etc.					
a. Derived unknown from known	12	9	13	3	37
b. Error in reading	14	5	13	10	42
c. Error due to numbers in minuend and subtrahend being the same	1	5	10	3	19
d. Reversed digits in remainder	4	7	2	4	17
e. Confused process with division or multiplication	5	6	3	2	16
f. Skipped one or more decades	3	4	7	0	14
g. Based subtraction on multiplication combination	1	2	3	0	6
h. Error in writing answers	2	1	0	1	4
Total cases	84	109	109	70	372

* Adapted from Buswell and John, *Diagnostic Studies in Arithmetic,* Supplementary Monograph No. 30 (Chicago, Univ. of Chicago Press, 1926).

interviewing. An interviewer may well prepare in advance by:

1. Listing the specific information he desires to secure.
2. Preparing a number of leading or pivotal questions around which to organize the sequence of the interview.
3. Arranging these questions in as natural an order as he can determine in advance. Judgment will be refined by experience.
4. Preparing necessary instructions, directions, or other guidance to be supplied to the person interviewed.

The use of a formal interview blank makes it far less likely that important items will be overlooked than if a casual, conversational form be followed. However, the use of the formal blank should be through easy conversation in so far as possible. The purpose of an interview is to secure information specific and peculiar to a given person; hence the examiner, whenever his judgment indicates, should depart from or supplement any formal outline he uses. The homemade, specially prepared outline is preferable. A number of useful general and inclusive blanks for preliminary interviewing are available in the literature.

General blanks will be supplemented with more specific inquiries, directed at further details on any aspect of the pupil's background, interests, leisure-time activities, likes and dislikes, or neighborhood activities which might be enlightening.

The inventory may be used both in evaluation and in diagnosis. Inventories taken at different times and after additional learning experiences will supply evidence from which to evaluate changes in interests, attitudes, or problems. As a diagnostic instrument, the inventory may reveal any of several factors which may be blocking learning, and may also reveal interests and abilities which can be utilized.

6. *Laboratory and clinical methods.* Laboratory tests and instruments are available in university clinics and at the central office of large city systems for the purpose of extremely detailed inquiry. Many significant factors and causes of poor learning are unearthed by the clinic which cannot be detected by the teacher or parent. Ordinarily, pupils needing this type of analysis will be referred to clinics by the teacher. Details of procedure are omitted.

7. *Case studies.* An exhaustive study may be made of all factors involved in any one personality. Outlines for such detailed studies are found in specialized texts on diagnosis, on social work, and the like. Details of procedure are omitted, since teachers will not ordinarily be making extensive studies of this type.

Specialists available for diagnosis. Many cases need more detailed and more technical diagnosis than any teacher can give. Larger city systems provide the services of bureaus of research, of psychological and guidance clinics, and of child centers. A few state departments provide traveling clinics to serve the small communities and rural areas.

Teachers should be informed of all services available and call upon them freely.

Remedial programs. Remedial programs are extensive and specific to subjects or types of conduct. General principles are those of good teaching applied to special circumstances. Details of organization and technique are to be found in the special literature on remedial teaching within the special subject areas.

DISCUSSION QUESTIONS FOR SECTION 2

Beginning students without background may answer the four questions below. Experienced teachers may omit them and proceed to reports and exercises.

1. What are some tentative diagnoses you might make for certain cases of failure by examining scholastic records (marks) in the light of intelligence scores? Use available school records or make up hypothetical cases. For instance, a student has

   a. A high I.Q. and low grades in all subjects.

   b. A high I.Q. and low grades in one or two subjects only.

2. Interpretations based upon marks and I.Q. scores alone can be only general and very tentative. Other information is essential.

   a. What other factors could influence the two cases advanced?

   b. How would you go about getting specified data necessary?

3. The instructor may administer a diagnostic test or parts from two or three as a demonstration and basis for discussion.

If possible, several students may administer a test in one of the co-operating schools, results to be analyzed in class.

REPORT

1. Individuals or small committees may report upon diagnostic tests by subject or by type of behavior being observed. Describe and show some tests; method of giving, scoring, and interpretation; aid given by manuals.

The best sources next to publishers' catalogues will be the standard texts on testing and on diagnosis, and some of the texts on guidance. The periodical literature is also rich in material.

EXERCISES

1. Secure tables or graphs showing class results or individual profiles from the local training school or from any nearby co-operating schools. Make tentative general interpretations based on these data without consideration, for the moment, of other factors.

2. Observe a teacher using any of the techniques of psychological diagnosis, particularly analysis of written work, oral responses, or the interview. Summarize the procedure and results together with teacher comments, and report to the class.

3. Wherever possible in local schools extend the observation in Exercise 2 to participation and assistance to the teacher. Summarize and report experiences.

4. Where possible in local schools, make an independent effort at psychological diagnosis of a case. Check your procedure and results with the regular teacher and report experiences to the class.

5. Experienced teachers may report any experiences with diagnostic procedures used in their regular work.

6. Individuals may report on the special services available in their own school systems.

7. Case-study accounts from local records or in the literature may be reported upon by individuals or small committees.

ADVANCED EXERCISES

1. Lists of specific errors in written work, such as for spelling errors, oral reading, language sense, are available in most of the skill or fact subjects. Find two or more in the literature.
   a. Make a critical summary report if two or more can be found in the same subject.
   b. Construct one for your major subject, or for any area, if no good ones can be found.

2. Lists of specific symptoms of non-learning in given fields are available in the periodical literature, in texts on special methods, and in various yearbooks on learning or on special teaching. An excellent illustration is found on pages 281-283 of the Thirty-fourth Yearbook of the National Society for the Study of Education, *Educational Diagnosis*.
   a. Search the literature for others in various subjects and report.
   b. Construct a similar list for your major subject. (Note that if a skill subject is

used, the categories will be similar to the illustrations in the *Yearbook* but the details within the categories will need to be evolved. In content subjects, both categories and explanatory material will differ from those used in skill subjects.)

3. If permission can be secured, select a pupil who needs attention and help. Some teachers will gladly assign one to you. Make a brief study of this pupil covering such time as is necessary to
   a. Observe classroom performance in the light of a selected check list.
   b. Secure a few valuable anecdotal items.
   c. Analyze personality in terms of a selected check list.
   d. Interview the pupil.
   e. Analyze some of his school work with him.

READINGS

The instructor will have to decide, as with the chapter on evaluation, how much supplementation this chapter needs for his students; how much time will permit. Ordinarily a brief treatment here is sufficient, since extended treatment is usually given in special-methods courses.

The futility of attempting to make a bibliography for this chapter is indicated by the listing in Bond and Tinker, eight pages and 191 general titles, with 16 pages of specialized references. Brueckner and Bond give no general bibliography but each chapter has from four to ten references.

Older References of Value

Educational Diagnosis, Thirty-fourth Yearbook of the National Society for the Study of Education (Bloomington, Ill., Public School Publishing Co., 1933). This is the older classic in the field and, despite the date, is valuable for general principles and types. Developments in the field since 1933 have been largely in the instruments themselves, and these will be found in recent texts in measurement, in guidance, and in diagnostic and remedial teaching and in the periodical literature.

BRUECKNER, L. J., and MELBY, E. O., *Diagnostic and Remedial Teaching* (Boston, Houghton, 1931).

FERNALD, Grace, *Remedial Techniques in Basic Skill Subjects* (New York, McGraw, 1943).

TORGERSON, T. L., *Studying Children: Diagnostic and Remedial Procedures in Teaching* (New York, Holt, Rinehart & Winston, 1947).

The Major Current References

BRUECKNER, L. J., and BOND, Guy L., *The Diagnosis and Treatment of Learning Difficulties* (New York, Appleton-Century-Crofts, 1955). After presenting general principles and procedures, devotes attention to reading, arithmetic, language, spelling, and handwriting.

BLAIR, G. M., *Diagnostic and Remedial Teaching*, rev. ed. (New York, Macmillan, 1956).

The Specialized References

BOND, Guy L., and TINKER, Miles, *Reading Difficulties: Their Diagnosis and Correction* (New York, Appleton-Century-Crofts, 1957). This book stands almost alone, although there are similar, but more specialized, books in other fields.

See Brueckner and Bond chapter bibliographies for the books there are. Note also here and elsewhere the extensive periodical literature, which is very valuable.

Books on the teaching of various subjects, as noted earlier, will have a chapter or section on diagnostic procedures and principles. See any standard text in the specialized fields.

CHAPTER 22: Marking and Reporting Progress

PRELIMINARY DISCUSSION QUESTIONS

1. What are the purposes of a marking system? List at least five or six as you see them now. What is probably the one chief purpose of marking?

2. If you had your choice, what system of marks would you prefer to be rated under: a percentage scale from 0-100 with passing at about 75? a series of letter grades, *A, B, C,* etc.? descriptive terms, *excellent, good, poor,* etc.?

   a. Support with arguments your choice of a system.

   b. Would you suggest some system not mentioned above?

3. State specifically and unequivocally what a mark of *B* or of 83 means in French. In Algebra. In Constitutional Law.

4. You have doubtless noted that marks vary from teacher to teacher and even sometimes with the same teacher.

   a. Can you explain why this is so?

   b. What suggestions might you make, without further study, for the reduction of these variations?

5. What are the merits and weaknesses of what students commonly call "stiff" marking and "easy" marking?

6. What seems to you, on the basis of your experience only, to be the chief weakness of any and all marking systems? (This question should not be answered quickly or superficially. Attention is directed to a fundamental educational issue amply discussed in previous chapters.)

An educational speaker is said to have remarked, "The school, with its formal lifeless curriculum and its poor teaching methods, has gotten into such a fix that a marking system had to be invented to make pupils work." This may have been an attempt at humor but it is not entirely humorous; it is too close to partial truth for comfort. Whatever their exact origin, marks are too commonly used as extraneous motivations, either as rewards or as punishments. Threats based on marks are too common in many schools.

The problem of determining the pupil's mark or index of achievement brings into sharp relief again the two theories of education and of learning which have been contrasted throughout this volume. One theory sees education as the mastery of designated segments of subject matter. The segments are arranged in a series of grade levels. Marks are assigned largely on the basis of teacher judgment as to how well the materials have been retained. The other theory sees education as the progressive development of the personal-social-moral traits, understandings, abilities, attitudes, and appreciations of the learner. Marks, if given at all, are usually accompanied by descriptions of the pupil's actual achievement of functional learning outcomes. The logical outcome of this theory is to abandon marks and to substitute for them descriptions of actual learning products and progress. Earlier chapters have discussed in some detail the serious detriment to education and to learning which results from substitution of a mark or symbol for true learning. Marks will be used, however, for a long time yet in traditional schools. Teachers need to know how to use a fundamentally unsound device as sensibly as possible; the first section of the chapter will, therefore, present principles designed to improve the validity and reliability of marks. The second section will develop the newer practice of descriptive evaluations in terms of the new-type report card.

1: PRINCIPLES OF MARKING.

Purposes of marking systems. Traditional schools use marking systems for various definite reasons:

1. To inform parents and pupils of the quality of work being done and of progress being made.
2. To enable home and school to work together more effectively on the common problem of encouraging learning.
3. To motivate or stimulate the pupil to continued or to greater effort.
4. To furnish a simple system of administrative shorthand for such routine purposes as classification, promotion, transfer, and certification to higher institutions.
5. To supply data upon the basis of which analyses of local marking practices, comparative studies between teachers and schools, and so forth, can be made.

The first two are the important purposes. The third should be eliminated. Marks, prizes, and other symbols do unquestionably stimulate effort, but they tend to become ends. Detrimental learning products and processes do result, as set forth in detail in earlier chapters. The traditional school recognizes this in many instances and has attempted to set up descriptions of marks in terms of evidences of learning. Later pages illustrate the effort to describe learning and the symbol—each in terms of the other. This, however, is not simple.

The fourth purpose of marking is losing some of its erstwhile prominence because of the growing tendency of colleges to accept students not on the basis of marks but on the basis of recommendations from the principal, or composite recommendations from a school staff. The fifth purpose is administrative and will not concern the student until he has occasion to participate in a study of marks in a given situation.

Typical marking systems. The three most widely used marking systems are (1) numerical, (2) letter, and (3) descriptive.

Numerical systems. These have been compactly summarized by Taylor, McMahill, and Taylor: [1]

The Percentage Marking System

This system has been long in use and is popular with parents. It is flexible enough so that percentages may be adjusted somewhat to the difficulty of the tests.

A theoretically perfect paper is given the mark of 100. The marks are based upon an absolute standard and not upon growth or achievement. It is employed with the essay-type examination where it is assumed that a student can write a perfect paper.

The Percentile Rank System of Marking

This system of marking is an innovation of recent years. It is easily explained. The percentile rank score does not reveal what the person earning the score can do.

A percentile rank mark indicates the percentage of the class excelled by any one student: thus, if there are 98 students in a class, the fiftieth percentile is the point below which 49 of the students will fall. It does show an individual's standing within a specified group.

The Rank Order System of Marking

This system is employed by such schools as the U. S. Military Academy at West Point. Since classes in our American high schools vary greatly in size, this system is not a popular one in our high schools.

Students are ranked in the order of achievement: thus, in a class of 30 students, the stu-

[1] *The American Secondary School* (New York, Appleton-Century-Crofts, 1960), p. 274.

dent with highest achievement earns a rank of "1," while the one with the lowest achievement earns a rank of "30."

The Standard Scores System of Marking

In general the standard scores system of marking tends to correct the defects found in all other systems; it is probably the most reliable of all. If the class distribution is approximately normal, standard scores are easy to interpret. Otherwise, a mastery of phases of statistics is necessary.

Each mark is determined by its position in standard steps or deviations from the class average. One practice is to establish the mark of "50" as the mean or average grade with three standard deviations of ten above and below the mean. Thus, the range of marks in a large class would be as follows: 20, 30, 40, 50 (average), 60, 70, 80. The mark of any one student could fall at any point between 20 and 80.

The traditional percentage system still widely used is probably the poorest known method of marking. A petition presented in Boston demanding the return of the percentage system in a given high school bore five thousand signatures. The arguments were that the perecentage system represented actual degrees of learning and gave pupils and parents definite information. Despite the naïve faith of these petitioners—shared by many teachers—the percentage is the least exact, least objective, and least meaningful of all known systems. Parents and teachers are completely deceived.

Parents and teachers are deceived, first, by the seeming precision inherent in the use of numbers. The fundamental nature of a true percentage system is completely overlooked by most persons advocating it for school use. Percentage can be used legitimately only when based upon an actual known quantity. This is an obvious impossibility in marking the growth and development, or even the limited learning responses of the pupil. What does 83 or 79 mean in arithmetic? Does it mean that the pupil has solved (a) 83 or 79 per cent of all possible life problems in arithmetic, (b) 83 or 79 per cent of the problems included in a particular textbook, (c) 83 or 79 per cent of the limited and specific lists of problems handed out by the teacher and themselves fragments of larger lists? A percentage mark cannot withstand critical inquiry; that it means just nothing at all in terms of learning can be shown with ease. A percentage mark, however, when set down attains stability and a finality in the minds of uncritical individuals.

The teacher falls naturally and inevitably into another error based upon failure to understand the nature of percentage. He may average marks given on different learning outcomes into a total grade for a diverse and complex learning situation. We saw in earlier pages how a pupil might secure a mark of 90 per cent on one phase of grammar, 50 per cent on another, and receive a final passing grade of 70 per cent for the whole subject. A good grade on one phase of the subject here compensates for clear-cut serious failure on another phase. This is a pure absurdity. Passing marks are attained by many pupils regularly in subjects and for learnings of which the pupil may be in part completely ignorant. Averaging percentages for different parts of a subject or for different types of learning makes this inevitable.

The second element of deception is hinted in the preceding sentences. Desirable learning outcomes cannot be marked by percentages or numbers of any kind, since they are not mathematical quantities. Understandings, attitudes, appreciations, and many pupil abilities cannot possibly be indicated except through descriptions of appropriate behavior. An exaggerated illustration has been based upon one of the Beatitudes: Blessed be the pure in heart for they shall see God. Purity of heart is clearly a desirable attitude, appreciation, or value to be developed in or out of school. How shall we grade pupil progress? Is he 90 per cent pure in heart? If he is 90 per cent pure, is that pure at all? How pure must he be to pass? Will 99 and 44/100 be demanded or will 70 per cent purity do? The trivial, factual, measurable outcomes of education alone can be measured, and even there the measurement is a false one. Stress on percentage marks does actually prevent the development of the more important aspects of pupil growth and development. This fact has long been recognized by alert traditional educators and effort has been made to develop descriptive standards to go with the percentages (or other symbols) which will bridge the gap between symbol and true learning.

Educators who are heard to agonize over choosing a valedictorian or a scholarship candidate from among pupils who average 97.6, 97.5, and 97.55 supply evidence of their complete lack of understanding of the nature of learning, both process and product.

The other numerical systems all have shortcomings of one type of another though they are widely used.

Letter systems. The use of letter or word symbols, *A, B, C, excellent, good,* emerged partly to alleviate the evils of the percentage system but cannot wholly succeed, since again the symbol is not inherently related to true learning outcomes. In changing to letter marks, certain die-hard administrators required the teachers to base them upon percentage grades for recitations, examinations, papers, and the like! Certain other systems have appeared in the country, *H, S, M, U,* for honor, superior, medium, and unsatisfactory; I, II, III, IV, and V; Pass and Fail; Satisfactory and Unsatisfactory. It is generally agreed that such symbols as average deviations or sigmas, percentiles, deciles, and the like are of little use with parents and average teachers. These are better used in research and in detailed diagnosis by specialists.

The letter system is better liked because it is familiar, but it has no more meaning than any other abstract system. Wrinkle [2] has a forthright and devastating criticism of this system, which should be read. Strang [3] also summarizes arguments on this point. These authors show also considerable decrease in the use of percentage grades and considerable criticism by parents of the *U* (unsatisfactory) and *S* (satisfactory) scheme. The latter at the moment is, oddly enough, increasing slightly in use. Strang and Wrinkle particularly stress the necessity for descriptive statements to accompany marks, with perhaps eventually the substitution of letter form reports and conferences.

Administrators, teachers, and parents operating under any marking system with *undescribed symbols* need give no thought to the differences in efficiency between systems, nor to the possibility of changing systems. All such systems are about equally useless for educational purposes even though they may be falsely meaningful to all concerned. But as stated earlier, marks must be used in many schools for some time to come. Can the use of marks be improved? Undoubtedly. Serious obstacles exist in the form of stereotyped thinking about learning and marks, traditional mechanisms, administrative demands, and modes of thought based thereon. Better traditional schools, however, have been making progress for some time.

Any system of symbols can be defined clearly enough to improve marking. The letter or word system, however, even when defined, is likely to lead teachers eventually back to the errors of the traditional percentage system. Various attempts have been made to substitute new symbols which are free from traditional associations and which are selected to have some relation, however attenuated, with the learning. Some high schools for instance use *R,* meaning "recommended for college or equivalent"; *S,* Satisfactory or acceptable for a Diploma of Graduation; *Cc,* meaning a Certificate of Completion will be issued; *N,* for needs to

[2] William L. Wrinkle, *Improving Marking and Reporting Practices* (New York, Rinehart, 1947), Chs. 6 and 7.

[3] Ruth Strang, *Reporting to Parents* (New York, Teachers College, Bureau of Publications, Columbia Univ., 1947), pp. 10-11.

improve, no credit granted. The symbol and its significance are clearer, but no progress toward relating the symbol to varied desirable learnings has been made. The University of Chicago high school, operating under the Morrison "mastery" concept, gave a grade of *M* for mastery of designated learning products; an *N* was added giving *MN* if sustained interest was indicated; an *R* was added for resourcefulness or ability to carry on self-dependently. Learning outcomes in this school were defined in terms of desirable understandings, attitudes, and so on, so that symbol and learning approached each other.

Descriptive systems. Statements describing the learner's achievement or his personal-social-moral traits are given on the card, or are to be filled in by teachers. Brief illustration is given just below and again in Section 2 of this chapter.

The writer has found that most class groups are interested in developing a descriptive marking scale for use in this course, principles of teaching. The students know that the desired outcomes are certain understandings or principles, certain attitudes toward teaching, and certain mental skills. They know also that certain behaviors are reasonably valid evidences of learning, and that these behaviors cannot be simulated or faked. The students may organize the scale in any form they wish, selecting symptoms and evidences of learning on their own judgment. A compromise is all that can be achieved between an ideal but voluminous scheme, and the necessities which demand a compact, defensible, and usable scale. There will also always be difficulty over interpretation of terms. Nevertheless, fair-minded students can achieve not only working agreement on a scale but astonishing agreement in determining marks. The project can be undertaken by a committee of interested students or co-operatively by the class as a whole.

Scales of this type are being more widely used, as the periodical literature shows. The

following illustrative paragraphs are from a general scale in use in a junior high school:

"A" Pupil (95-100 Per Cent, Superior Work)

One (1) whose work consistently shows an intelligent comprehension of the subject matter through his ability to retain facts and principles learned; (2) who is able to apply subject matter learned to new problems; (3) who organizes his work well; (4) who speaks clearly and forcibly in discussions; (5) who presents neat, well-arranged, accurate, complete work on time; (6) who performs required skills with a high degree of techniques; (7) who completes both the average and the enriched assignment; (8) who has good study habits; (9) who has the power of analyzing his own work to discover his strong and weak points; (10) who shows marked initiative, industry, and attention.

"E" Pupil (0-64 Per Cent, Failure)

One (1) who is incapable of doing the work of his grade or who is not interested and makes little effort; (2) who takes little part in oral discussion; (3) whose work is careless, untidy, inaccurate, or incomplete; (4) whose vocabulary is very limited; (5) whose span of attention is short; (6) who may have much absence; (7) who has poor study habits.

The paragraphs on page 514 are from a general scale used on the high school level.

Note that both the foregoing samples, while descriptive of pupil behavior, are not only very general but are translated into letter marks. This is often a first step in attempting to get away from formal systems to the truly descriptive. Illustrations from elementary schools given in later pages are descriptive of behavior with no thought of translating into letter or number grades. The descriptive ratings themselves are the key to achievement, diagnosis, and guidance.

Shortcomings of traditional systems. The chief objections to marks are (*a*) that they tend to become ends in themselves, and much worse, (*b*) that, in most instances, they are not indicative of learning at all. The key to improvement lies in (*a*) setting up descriptive standards to accompany each mark or symbol and in (*b*) training teachers in the use of these standards. The logical outcome of increasingly accurate descriptions in terms of learning is the abandonment of marks in favor of the descriptions themselves.

Essentials of a sound marking system. The *chief* essential in a good marking system has already been indicated: *the symbol must be clearly defined in terms of evidences of the learning product being marked.* The *second* essential is that provision must be made for compiling and using extensive, detailed data which are, as far as human judgment can determine, reliable evidences of possession or lack of the learning product under consideration. A *third* essential is that misleading, extraneous factors be excluded from the determination of that mark.

Defining the symbols. This has been presented in foregoing pages dealing with letter and descriptive systems.

Gathering and compiling data as a basis for the mark. A mark should rest upon an extensive body of data gather by the instructor from many varied sources and over a period of time. Teachers have always marked daily recitations, papers, and examinations and averaged these data for a final mark. The whole theory of learning presented in this volume indicates the inadequacy of this procedure. Far more data, far more varied data, far more valid data, and data from many more sources are necessary. The descriptive marking schemes outlined in the preceding pages are but one simple step. The whole range of instruments described in Chapters 20 and 21 on evaluation and on diagnosis are at the disposal of the teacher. Evaluation, diagnosis, and marking are each inseparable elements in a functioning whole-life situation.

Excluding extraneous factors. Many research studies show that a very large number of factors quite unrelated to pupil growth or achievement may and do enter into the determination of a mark. Teachers themselves have listed a total of seventy-five or more factors which influence their marking. Effort, attitude, conduct in class, neatness, courtesy, co-operation, attendance, avoidance of tardiness, good attitude in class, standing or sitting erect while reciting, and clear enunciation are all mentioned as factors in marking. None is legitimate. A pupil could manifest all of these and still fail to learn.

Courtis long ago presented evidence that boys must do approximately 14 per cent better than girls to get the same mark with average teachers. [4] Girls manifest certain qualities which cause teachers to mark them more favorably than boys. Docility, willingness to do assigned tasks, absence of disorder, and many other factors are involved. Many other studies show that certain instructors, particularly in high school and college, are greatly influenced by personality, economic status, race or nationality, and other factors. Analysis of marks given over a period of years in one teacher college revealed that one woman instructor had never given an *A* rating to any girl who was notably nice looking or socially popular. A male instructor was found to give a preponderance of *A* marks to the very group of girls who could not receive an *A* from the woman instructor.

The relationship of English usage (grammar, punctuation, spelling) to marking in other subjects has long been a bone of contention among teachers. Should a chemistry paper or essay in history be marked lower because of poor writing, spelling, grammar? Probably not, unless the poor English actually obscures the meaning and indicates confused thinking. The better traditional schools are slowly moving toward the requirement of a school mark in English usage to which all teachers in the school contribute. Proficiency in English usage on any and all occasions should be required of all pupils.

[4] S. A. Courtis, *Why Children Succeed* (Ann Arbor, Mich., Univ. of Michigan, 1926).

"A" grade indicates	"B" grade indicates	"C" grade indicates	"D" grade indicates	"E" grade indicates
The student attacked new tasks and got them done with a minimum of help.	The student was less dependent than the average upon teacher or others in getting assigned work done.	The student is frequently unable to proceed promptly with an assigned task and is often dependent upon others for help.	The student required special work constantly but has shown some improvement in study habits during the semester.	The student's study habits were poor and ineffective and showed no improvement while taking the course.
The student made the subject a part of his own knowledge and used it in creative thinking. He showed a high degree of real mastery.	The student was better than the average in attaining mastery, although the knowledge gained might have been used in a more creative way.	The student rarely applied principles creatively; he showed only a degree of mastery and depended more upon memory than understanding.	The student has shown sufficient mastery of fundamental work to warrant the opinion that he will grow more through advancement than through repetition of the subject.	The student got no comprehension of the subject, made the same errors over and over, and expressed himself as a matter of memorized knowledge rather than with any understanding.
The student consistently passed tests with a high average	The student generally passed tests with "above average" grade.	The student seldom got high grades on tests; generally got "average" or "below average" grades but rarely failed.	The student rather consistently passed tests in lower quartile and frequently failed.	The student rarely passed a test.
The student showed independence of thought and action and used this independence for the good of the class group.	The student generally depended upon himself for his work and always conducted himself in a way which was for the good of the class group.	The student was inclined to get help from others and generally let the good of the class group guide his conduct.	The student was dependent upon others but his class conduct was generally loyal, dependable, and helpful to the class as a whole.	The student did not control his class conduct for the good of the class.

514

Instances of serious deficiency should be referred to a remedial teacher. Graduation should be refused to pupils lacking mastery of good language habits regardless of marks which may have been earned in other specialized subjects. This whole problem disappears in the modern school which attempts either to mark actual learning or substitute for marks a description of learning achievement or growth.

Credit for effort, co-operation, persistence, and other desirable traits.

Marks must be determined as closely as possible on the basis of actual learning achievement. Extraneous factors are to be excluded. Is the pupil then to receive no credit for effort; no reward for attention, persistence, co-operation or other desirable traits and attitudes? Certainly— but *not* as part of the mark for achievement of mathematical skills, of historical understandings, of appreciations in literature. Ability to solve quadratics is one thing; the effort to learn how to solve quadratics another. The fallacy in considering effort as a factor when determining marks is easily seen in any phase of mathematics. A pupil can progress in arithmetic only as he acquires in sequence the necessary understandings and skills. To give him a passing mark because he "tried so hard," "was so earnest," "was so determined to succeed" is to put the pupil in an impossible learning situation which will retard if not prevent his further learning.

The solution lies in the development in both traditional and modern schools of the rating cards, check lists, codes, and other instruments presented in preceding chapters. The many desirable personality traits and attitudes, the many appreciations and values are all legitimate learning outcomes in their own right. The pupil is to be evaluated in terms of these as well as the formal subject learnings of the traditional school. The old marking systems reported only upon the limited, formal, and often trivial outcomes of learning. The newer systems attempt to evaluate and rate more numerous and more important outcomes.

Reliability and validity of teachers' marks can be increased greatly.

One of the oft-quoted studies in education is that in which a number of teachers were asked to mark independently the same examination paper. One first-year high school English paper was marked by 142 teachers in as many high schools, a geometry paper by 118 mathematics teachers, and an American history paper by 70 teachers. The differences among marks assigned to one and the same paper by different teachers were almost unbelievable. The marks for any one paper covered practically the entire range of the percentage scale. The English paper received marks varying from 50 to 98; the history paper, from 43 to 90; and the geometry paper— dealing with supposedly mathematically precise material—actually received the most diverse grades, the range being from 28 to 92! [5]

A fact even more startling was revealed by another experiment. One teacher constructed a model answer paper to aid him in marking a series of papers which were being evaluated by a number of teachers. This paper was accidentally mixed in with the others and as it made the rounds of the other teachers received marks varying from 40 to 90! Such data as these are made the bases for criticisms of marking and complaints about the unreliability of teachers' marks. These data attract attention because they are odd and startling. They have had far too much currency among teachers. Far less well known is the fact that similar experiments show not only a high percentage of agreement among teachers' marking but also very great reduction in variation when standards are developed and training in marking is given. Coincident with these early studies, others, less spectacular, developed

[5] Daniel Starch and E. C. Elliott, "Reliability of Grading High School Work in Mathematics," *School Review*, Vol. 21, 1913, pp. 254-259.

showing that the question was not simple and that early opinions were subject to revision. [6]

Wood, [7] in a later study, had 413 algebra and 396 English papers marked twice by a number of readers, all of whom had received instruction in the technique of marking. Correlations between the two marks was so high that criticism of variability was a waste of time. Ashbaugh had a set of arithmetic papers marked three times at four-week intervals by 49 readers. [8] Variability showed a range of 51 points, 50 and 39 on the first three markings. Extensive discussion was then inaugurated and the readers set up standards of marking and relative values for subpoints. The range was reduced to 18 points. A study by Hudelson [9] showed the most astonishing reduction of variability in the difficult marking of written compositions.

The increase in reliability may or may not be an increase in validity. Reduction of the range might mean merely that teachers had agreed upon what to mark and had attained skill in marking the agreed-upon outcomes. The standards set up for marking must naturally be concerned with evidences of desirable learning in order to increase validity along with reliability.

A number of writers still believe that

[6] For opposing studies of approximately the same dates see C. T. Gray's on judging handwriting papers; Shriner's on marking papers for a whole class instead of but one paper, and others.

[7] Ben D. Wood, "Measurement of College Work," *Educational Administration and Supervision,* Vol. 7 (September, 1921), pp. 301-334.

[8] E. J. Ashbaugh, "Reducing the Variability in Teachers' Marks," *Journal of Educational Research,* Vol. 9 (March, 1924), pp. 185-198.

[9] Earl Hudelson, "Effect of Objective Standards upon Composition Teachers' Judgment," *Journal of Educational Research,* Vol. 13 (1925), pp. 329-340.

————, *English Composition: Its Aims, Methods and Measurement,* Twenty-second Yearbook of the National Society for the Study of Education, Part I (Bloomington, Ill., Public School Publishing Co., 1923).

Check periodical literature for recent studies on this topic, which appear with reasonable frequency. Note also the literature on descriptive summaries designed to replace marking.

teachers' marks are highly unreliable, but a larger number believe them to be more reliable than formerly thought; and a large number show that variability can be sharply reduced by (a) the co-operative establishment of valid standards, and (b) definite training in using these standards in determining marks.

Marking is complicated by various forms of homogeneous grouping. Grouping pupils in terms of ability, achievement, information, or other formal basis immediately raises the question of assigning marks to the various levels. Many schools and rooms within schools operate three groups, bright, average, and slow. Shall all levels of marks, whether percentages or letters, be given within each group or should the high marks go to the bright group alone and the lower marks to the slow group? Considerable argument has resulted but few constructive suggestions. The commonest procedure is either to give all marks in all groups and meet arguments over promotion, college entrance, and the like, as they arise, or to assign marks with an exponent: A^1, B^3, or C^2 and the like. This seems fair in that it judges the pupil in terms of the requirements set for his group. Any such system, however, has many administrative and popular repercussions. Local administrators will need to devise such systems as they can make work and can use with their constituents. The crux lies in the fact that the whole scheme being discussed is based on an erroneous conception of learning. Grouping pupils on the basis of social maturity, providing for continuous progress and easy passage from group to group, and *using modern descriptive ratings of actual learning achievement eliminate the problem of marking by levels or groups.*

The passing mark. Modern knowledge of the nature of learning processes and products makes the concept of the passing mark an absurdity in general education. There cannot possibly be a specific passing point, dividing the successful from the failing, if learning outcomes are properly defined, and if pupils are learning steadily in terms of their capacities. This has all been adequately explained several times in preceding chapters. Traditional administrators and teachers who believe in the myth of a passing mark in elementary schools or in secondary core curriculums do so only because they do not understand the nature of learning. There is a difference between the determination of failure in general education and in special subjects, as was explained in the chapter on evaluation.

Traditional schools will, however, use passing marks for a long time to come. Desirable procedures should then be understood. The least detrimental method is a compromise in which actual learning is determined as accurately as possible under traditional conditions and by various means previously described. Differentiation of marks above passing may then be in terms of levels of insight, interest, and skill. This, of course, carries us far toward the abolition of marks.

The determination of the passing mark in strictly traditional schools is easy. The repetition of text material, the working of exercises, and the repetition of formulas are usually the basis for any mark. Such work can be easily marked by percentages or letters because meaning for the marks can be disregarded. Passing level may be placed at any arbitrary given point, since it does not really matter—except to the slow pupil who should not be allowed to interfere with administrative efficiency! Passing marks are, in fact, usually determined by local public opinion, depending upon the demands of the local board, the parents, the superintendent, or some neighboring university. Passing marks vary in this country from 60 to 75 for no logical reason.

The distribution of marks. Regardless of where the passing mark is set, the question then arises: how many marks above and be-

low passing should be given? How many pupils should receive marks of *A,* or above 90; of *C,* or just barely passing? The modern school has no such problem if it provides each pupil with a descriptive rating of status and progress. The better traditional schools attempt to determine levels of actual learning by securing evidences of insight or of skill—or of any desirable learning outcome—without regard for any arbitrary formula for distribution.

The formal traditional school, which marks subject-matter learning and in which few teachers have made any study of marking, needs some formal device to aid in securing a sensible distribution and to ensure fairness to the pupil. The normal curve of distribution was once widely used and still appears in many places. The statistical derivation and meaning of the curve are now reasonably well known to teachers. Statisticians differ somewhat in details when applying the curve to school marking but in general agree upon some such distribution of marks as the following:

Grade	%	or	%	or	%
A	3		7		10
B	22		24		20
C	50		38		40
D	22		24		20
F	3		7		10
	100		100		100

The normal curve as an aid to distributing marks is largely a snare and a delusion. It was derived originally from and is based upon the assumption of infinite populations of unselected individuals. The curve actually fits only such a condition. No group of pupils beyond the primary is unselected. Even there, many at the lower end of the distribution have been eliminated. Any curve based upon marks actually earned by large numbers of pupils in many courses and over a period of time, regardless of the basis for marking, will always be skewed toward the upper end, unless the group is definitely retarded, in which case the skew will be the other way. The cue to proper use of curves as aids to distribution lies in the preceding sentence. Master curves should be made up based upon local data covering a period of years. This ensures a guidance device which has taken into account any local conditions of any weight. The type of pupil, efficiency of teaching, theory of education, and materials available in the given situation—all affect the local curve. The idiosyncrasies of individual instructors who mark too leniently or too severely are canceled out. Many school systems and universities make up such curves from cumulative data in their own offices. For instance, the actual distribution of marks over many years and with all types of instructors at a certain university produces the following percentages:

Grade	Percentage
A	13
B	35
C	36
D	8
F	3
No Grade Given	1
Provisional Grade	4
	100

Devices are intended not to determine marks but to aid instructors. The use of these curves has resulted in some serious errors and injustices in some circumstances. Instructors have distributed marks in terms of the curves regardless of the achievements of individual pupils. One registrar actually attempted to force an instructor to give one *A,* one *B,* one *C,* and one *D* in an advanced technical course for which four *A* marks had been turned in. This is plain stupidity. The assignment of an arbitrary number of failing marks because the curves indicate that number, when actually no student failed, is a serious injustice. Extreme cases are known in which dummies were employed to register for courses, do nothing, and absorb the arbitrary percentage of failing marks, thus ensuring that the bona fide (?) student would pass!

Devices for distributing marks are solely for the purpose of aiding instructors to understand more clearly the nature of marking. The distribution of an instructor's marks in courses of general interest over a period of years should approximate the general curve for the local practice. The distribution for given classes, especially small advanced groups, may vary widely from the curve. Serious variations from the general tendency within a local system cannot be dismissed with a shrug. Instructors are under obligation to account for such variations. Sometimes variations will be found to be legitimate; sometimes, purely capricious. The value of this general check is easily seen in the case of the unduly severe or unduly lenient marker. The teacher with a high percentage of failures ridicules the curve and hides behind the traditional smoke screen of "high standards." The too lenient individual minimizes specific attainments and evidences of learning and states that he is interested in developing "point of view," "attitude," "general interest in the field." Each type of instructor is given pause when confronted with continuous factual evidence that he is out of step. The distribution formulas and curves are in no sense intended to determine the actual marks or distributions but are to be used as general guides to thinking about marking in given schools.

Relative ranking and competitive marking. Marking pupils on the basis of rank-in-class is widespread among "practical" teachers and is accepted if not in fact desired by many parents. The procedure is severely condemned by all competent educational authorities. Psychologists, psychiatrists, and physicians join in this condemnation. Because of this sharp cleavage between some teachers and those who have the facts and because arguments over competitive marking constantly crop up, treatment here is somewhat more extended than the point warrants.

The time-honored technique is to determine which pupil answers the most questions, does the most exercises, and makes the fewest errors; then the next best pupil, and the next, and so on through the group. Compositions are grouped in terms of relative excellence as judged by the reader, those in the first group receiving an *A,* or a *B* if not up to the arbitrary standard set by the instructor, and so on through five or so groupings of papers.

Immediate and specific weaknesses in and objections to competitive marking. The *first* immediate and obvious blunder underlying this practice is the defiance of known facts about individual differences in ability, in rate of learning, in interests, and in background; the defiance of facts about the learning process and its motivation. Previous chapters have made clear that children of different organismic patterns learn different things in different ways and at different rates. Relative or competitive marking insists that all types of pupils learn the same things in the same way and at the same rate. Competitive marking is not only a flat defiance of known facts; it is a vicious policy, working severe and measurable hardships upon learners. A child working to the very limit of his ability, energy, and interest should not be given a mark of *C* because another child did more work within the same time limit. What other pupils have accomplished cannot possibly have any bearing upon what one given pupil has done. Herein we see again the fallacy of the whole concept of marking. Each child is entitled to a statement that he is learning satisfactorily, or not learning, in terms of his capacity, insight, and reaction time. Evidence should be gathered continuously showing explicitly, not whether one pupil is better than another, but whether the given pupil has learned or not. The compromise between modern descriptive ratings fitted to individuals and competitive marking lies in the marking devices described earlier in this chapter.

The *second* important weakness of competitive marking is that it distracts attention from desirable learning outcomes and inter-

feres directly with sound teaching procedures. Teachers and pupils both center upon the subsidiary and non-important evidences of subject matter memorized, exercises worked, formulas repeated—all of which can be marked easily. The more important outcomes which cannot be evaluated so superficially are neglected. Pupils can be bullied by threats of poor grades, or wheedled with promise of good ones into engaging in the most non-educative and miseducative activities. Lists of wholly useless drill exercises, bodies of subject matter quite unrelated to life, and deadly dull assignments will be completed by pupils under threat of not doing so well as the others.

One aspect of this is important enough for separate comment. One major objective of education is to develop social adjustments, co-operative abilities, participation in group discussion and decision, working together for common goals, and many similar outcomes. Competitive marking is contrary to the needs of society as well as to the needs of individuals. Pitting pupils against one another inevitably breeds discord and unwillingness to contribute toward common enterprises.

A *third* objection is that competitive marking is productive of seriously bad mental hygiene. The slow, earnest pupil is discouraged and antagonized, and eventually engages in dishonest practices. Cheating, copying, lying, and other defense mechanisms are natural results of forcing competition upon children of unequal ability. The quick pupil often acquires a false outlook on life and a false sense of values. Envy, jealousy, and antagonisms between pupil and pupil, between pupil and teacher, and between parent and school cannot be avoided if competitive marking is employed. These points have been elaborated previously in this volume.

Remote, general, and fundamental arguments against competitive marking. Parents and teachers often approach competitive marking from the angle of basic social and psychological theory. Individuals proceeding thus are usually wholly honest but uninformed and uncritical. Their general argument is that competition is the rule of life, that competition is a dominant characteristic of life outside the school, and that therefore pupils had better learn to compete.

So competition is the rule of life and is characteristic of society outside school; hence there should be competitive marking among the children in a typical classroom! Let us see. *First,* this argument rests upon a naïve but serious logical error: namely, applying a remote, general, social *theory* to an immediate, limited, and specific *situation* without regard for the detailed phenomena of the latter. Theory and situation must always be fitted to each other through analysis of circumstances. The limited classroom situation including immature children of differing abilities, interests, and rates of learning cannot possibly be regulated under a general social theory based on different circumstances. Competition in life is within reasonably homogeneous groups. In any event, unskilled laborers are not asked to compete with engineers, accountants with novelists.

Second, it is philosophically and logically naïve to believe that since competition is a characteristic of life and of society, it is therefore either necessary or desirable. Competition in life was produced by certain known factors. Some of these factors are disappearing or are being minimized as time passes. Competition unquestionably produced certain specifiable benefits. Competition with equal certainty is responsible for certain specifiable and serious evils, particularly in economic life and in the field of mental hygiene. Many of these evils in real life are counterparts of the evils produced by competitive marking among children. Distinguished thinkers have been insisting for some time that we can never have either a democratic or a Christian civilization if we retain uncontrolled competition. This leads directly to the third point.

Third, history reveals a steady and increasing trend toward the proper control of detrimental types of competition, toward a world in which competitive and co-operative forces and processes are each given a rightful place. There will always be competition in the world, but the peoples of the world are increasingly refusing to accept those forms of competition which involve exploitation of persons or of common natural resources. The destruction of personality values and the miseries resulting from robbing society of its resources are too high a price to pay. Competitive marking in school is an excellent illustration of a process seriously destructive of personality values. It is out of step with the developing trends in society.

There are no fundamental philosophical, psychological, or sociological arguments to support competitive marking in school classrooms.

Competitive marking is legitimate in specialized subjects in technological or professional training. The basic difference between general and special education has been pointed out several times in previous chapters. The application here is obvious.

Recognition of individual limitations; acceptance of different types of contribution. It is increasingly important that individuals come to recognize and to accept cheerfully their own individual limitations; to recognize that the complex group life of modern civilization necessitates varying types of contribution; to recognize that the democratic ideal holds the various types and levels of contribution to be worthy of respect. Many honest but superficial observers believe that competitive marking will achieve this end. The preceding paragraphs indicate the futility of this hope. The development of a truly democratic philosophy in the operation of a modern curriculum and teaching method centering upon democracy and upon personality integration is the route to the desired end.

General programs for improving marking. A pupil's mark should be (*a*) based upon valid evidence of genuine acquisition of desirable learning outcomes, (b) gathered from the daily activities of the pupil in any and all kinds of situations. The following statements summarize some of the major features of an improvement program.

1. Standards for marking should be cooperatively determined by the staff. Departmental committees or the staff in small schools will define in detailed descriptive statements the evidences of learning and the distinctions between levels in the marking scale.

2. Programs of training in marking should be used wherever there is need. The staff will study the research investigations, the development of descriptive standards, the explanations of extreme variability, the use of local curves, and so forth.

3. The distribution of teachers' marks, individually and by departments, should be published in an open bulletin.

4. Discussion of these bulletins should take place in teachers' meetings as need arises.

5. Teachers or departments whose marks depart in sharp degree from the typical, overall, long-time distribution within a given school may present data to justify their departure or may engage in study to reduce it.

Marks eventually should be replaced by personalized statements. The ultimate outcome desired is the substitution for marks of statements about the individual pupil, showing how he is progressing and in what areas, what strengths and possibilities and what shortcomings he possesses, what obstacles or difficulties he may be encountering. Considerable progress has been made toward this goal. The next section on report cards will describe and illustrate this further.

Under present conditions, many school systems are maintaining two systems of marks. A system of letters or numbers is maintained for administrative purposes but ordinarily is not given to pupils or parents. A system of reporting which does go to the pupils and parents will consist of descriptive statements, lists of points to check, and so forth, as will be seen in the following section of his chapter.

EXHIBITS

The instructor should build up a collection of (a) descriptive marking systems, and (b) bulletins issued by school systems in which the marks given by individual teachers and by departments are summarized and compared. Students may contribute to this collection.

EXERCISES FOR SECTION 1

1. The class or a committee may, if interested, undertake the construction of a descriptive marking scheme for this course.

2. After class discussion and analysis each student may attempt to determine his own class mark. (Instructors can make comparative summary with their own marks, without names, for the interest of the class.)

3. A class committee may search the literature for a number of descriptive schemes, presenting an account and critical evaluation to the class.

4. Individuals or small committees may construct for their own major subject a descriptive scheme which they might expect to use in teaching.

Note. In determining one's own mark in Exercise 2, or in making up original schemes as in 2 or 5, students should keep in mind that

a. Marks should be given only on the basis of clear and unmistakable evidence showing acquisition of given understandings, attitudes, intellectual skills, or other desirable outcomes.

b. Marks should not be given for mere reproduction of the facts but for the derivation and use of principles embodying the facts.

c. Marks should not be given for the successful solution of study questions or the working of learning exercises but for the interpretation of the answers into controlling understandings and attitudes.

d. Marks may be differentiated (a compromise between the ideal and the practical) on the basis of frequency of appearance and insight in the use of the understandings and attitudes; of such intellectual skills as clarity in defining problems, resourcefulness in discovering solutions, ingenuity in analysis, discrimination in selecting or rejecting solutions or data, ability to formulate hypotheses, ability to use these skills in varied situations, and many others.

5. Experienced teachers may report upon
   a. Marking systems they have used or worked with which are significantly different from those suggested in this chapter.
   b. School bulletins used in their own systems to summarize and compare marks.

6. Individuals or small committees may report on a collection of current articles on the problems of marking. (Several phases may be considered.)

READINGS

The general texts in principles of teaching do not contain extensive discussions of marking, but may be consulted as desired.

The periodical literature is an excellent source for all types of discussion, from theories of marking through actual marking systems to parents' reactions to various systems. Several class reports should be made.

2: THE REPORT CARD.

The report card is the chief means used to carry out the main purposes of the marking system, namely, to inform pupils and parents about the learner's progress. The report card reflects the many far-reaching changes which are taking place in education, and is rapidly changing in form and content.

Traditional report card developed during period of subject-matter dominance. The report card with which most adults are familiar developed during the nineties and reflects the educational philosophy and practice of the day. Subjects were listed and marked with percentages or letters or some other symbol, but chiefly in percentages. Practically the only other factors mentioned were absence, tardiness, and deportment. The characteristics and the weaknesses of these cards can be summarized briefly.

1. Emphasis was entirely upon the subject, not upon the learner. The traditional items, absence, tardiness, and deportment appear also but little else.

2. Marks were most commonly in the form of percentages. Letters and word ratings appeared later.

3. No description or interpretation of marks accompanied the card. Thus the traditional cards were not very informative to either pupils or parents, though false meanings grew up and are today one of the chief obstacles to intelligent thinking about reports.

4. The real purposes of education and outcomes of learning were concealed and eventually neglected.

5. Wrong attitudes and ends were engendered among the children. Attention was focused not on real outcomes but on the mark. Pupils worked for the mark and to "get by." Detrimental attitudes of superiority or inferiority, envy, and jealousy were engendered. Cheating and cramming were natural.

The new-type report card a natural development as educational thinking changed. The breakdown of traditional formal education and of the assign-study-recite stereotype, the development of huge bodies of information about the nature of the learner and of learning, and clearer conceptions of the ends of education within a democracy have all been discussed in previous chapters. Reports to parents and pupils inevitably had to change to reflect the new emphasis and ends. The bare listing of subjects has given way to descriptive statements of major learnings within these subjects, degrees of skill, and the like. All phases of growth are included, so that the many attitudes, interests, habits, personal-social-moral traits receive a mark or a check in terms of a rating scale. Great progress has been made, particularly within the past ten years. Thousands of new-type cards are in use and available for inspection. Nevertheless many school systems have never heard of improved reports and literally thousands of practical teachers are wholly unaware of them.

The general characteristics of newer report cards. The features of the developing report cards may be contrasted directly with the characteristics of the traditional card listed above. The detailed characteristics will be listed immediately following this general list.

1. The school philosophy and curriculum objectives are increasingly given a page in the report card, or are included in an explanatory booklet.

2. Emphasis is upon the learner rather than upon the subject. Report shows what learner is doing and how he is progressing within given subject areas, and not how much subject matter has been mastered or "covered."

3. Adequate description and interpretation accompany the new cards, sometimes embodied in the card itself, sometimes in a separate booklet or bulletin of some size. Pupils and parents are definitely informed as to ends and progress, and in understandable terms.

4. The real purposes of education and the real learning outcomes are clearly indicated and often included in the descriptive ratings. (This greatly reduces detrimental attitudes and habits among the children.)

5. The reasons for difficulty in learning are increasingly explained.

6. Greater participation by parents and pupils is encouraged.

7. A great increase in the items subordinate to subject headings or personality trait headings is noted; also with health and physical development.

8. The space for comments by teachers and parents is increasing.

9. A swing toward briefer cards may be noted, with explanations and interpretations of school policy placed in a separate booklet.

Three direct implications are clearly discernible which may guide those groups developing new cards:

1. If the subjects are retained as categories, the learnings within them must be specifically described for both pupil and parent. Ratings within learning to be derived from subjects must be in terms of pupil growth and characteristics. Status in a "subject" cannot be lumped off under a meaningless figure or letter mark.

2. All phases of pupil growth must be included—physical, social, and emotional, as well as intellectual. This means the addition to the report card of definite places for these newer outcomes.

3. Reports will increasingly be in terms of pupil's own capacity and growth and not in terms of rank in class or competition. This means that as far as possible three factors will be recognized and kept distinct.
a. The native ability of the pupil.
b. The present achievement of the pupil.
c. The growth of the pupil in achievement and his rate of progress. (Cards should show clearly that judgments are in terms of the ability of the pupil, or the average of the group, or the previous record of the pupil, or some other standard.)

The writer has gathered several hundred new-type report cards during the past few years and finds the following specific developments:

1. *Conspicuous changes appear in markings by subjects.*
   a. Traditional, unexplained, single marks by subjects are steadily decreasing.
   b. Subjects are increasingly grouped under major broad fields.
   c. Important objectives to be gained from individual subjects are listed increasingly.
   d. Definitions for marks, where retained, are increasing.
   e. Scores on standard tests in fact and skill knowledge are increasingly included; relation of the individual to the norm and to class average is indicated.
   f. Several cards show marks in relation to ability groups.
   g. Mention of improvement or of reasons for poor progress is increasing rapidly.
   h. Profiles for individual pupils appear often.

2. *Social and emotional growth, special interests, attitudes, and habits are increasingly included.*
   a. Subjects are marked separately for effort, or for general attitude manifested, as well as for achievement.
   b. Special interests, abilities, and extra-curricular activities are increasingly listed.
   c. Profile charts for citizenship habits and attitudes often appear.
   d. Social and emotional traits and attitudes are included in nearly all recent cards.
      (1) Described in terms of general words for character traits
      (2) Described in terms of specific behavior

(These factors, however described, may appear as an unclassified list or may be grouped under various categories.)

3. *Physical growth and well-being, health knowledge and habits are increasingly included.*
4. *Increased opportunity for co-operation with parents is indicated.*
   a. The philosophy and aims of the school may be briefly stated on the card or included in a pamphlet to parents.
   b. The purpose and organization of the school report itself are increasingly explained, either briefly on the card or in a separate booklet.
   c. Advice for the assistance of pupils who are not progressing satisfactorily is increasingly included.
   d. Special interests, abilities, or aptitudes are called to parents' attention.
   e. Written comments by parents are increasingly invited.
   f. Opportunity for the parent to make a written report to the school on certain definite pupil characteristics is beginning to appear.
   g. Parents are increasingly invited to visit school and confer.
5. *Comparative or competitive marking is disappearing with reasonable rapidity.*
6. *Individual, personalized, letter-form reports from teacher to parent are increasing slowly.*
7. *Conferences between parent and teacher appear both as supplements to report cards and as substitutes.*
8. *Special notices of failure sometimes supplement the report card.*
9. *New-type report cards are increasingly printed in large type, decorated, or otherwise given a pleasing appearance.*
10. *A very marked tendency is apparent so to organize and word all items that the report is easily and immediately understood by any pupil or parent.*
11. *Separate cards for various levels (kindergarten, primary, upper grades, high school) and for single subjects in high school are increasing.*

Classes of new-type report cards. The writer has attempted to classify report cards in terms of their departure from the traditional form. The differences which appear are in the degree to which new categories of learning outcomes are included and in the amount of detail included in the descriptive ratings. Other analysts might wish to use very different classifications.

1. Separate subjects marked without analysis or explanation.
2. Subjects marked traditionally; plus very brief list of traits or attitudes or both, designated by general trait names only and to be checked; no explanations.
3. Subjects marked traditionally, but brief explanations of the marks included on the card or in separate bulletins.
4. Subjects and skills scored by tests. Attitudes or traits distinguished by levels and checked. Profiles or bar graphs may or may not appear for test scores here.
5. Subjects and skills checked in terms of described desirable levels of achievement; brief list of attitudes, traits, and so forth, checked in terms of levels of growth.
6. Subjects and skills checked in terms of described desirable levels of achievement; attitudes and traits checked in terms of growth; space provided for comment by the teacher.
7. Subjects and skills checked in terms of described desirable levels of achievement; extended list of attitudes and traits described on several levels to be checked.
   a. Attitudes and traits described in paragraph descriptions instead of very brief sentence statements of levels.
   b. Descriptions of attitudes and traits written out by teacher for each pupil.
8. A very brief card embodying best features so far developed but containing in itself a mere record; detailed explanations to pupils, parents, and teachers in separate booklet or bulletin.
9. Letter form report substituted for all subject or attitude lists.
10. Report card from parent to school.

The progress is from a simple formal report of status in subject-matter mastery to a detailed, specific report of growth in many aspects of personality development. Many variations within and between the types listed appear in practice. Goal cards and provisions for lists of units completed or voluntary projects originated appear on some cards.

New-type cards do necessitate considerable work upon the part of teachers at first. The early ones gave little help to the teacher in guiding his ratings. The development of the descriptive explanation of marks, of described levels of behavior, and of described illustrations of traits has been in an attempt to give the teacher a guide which would cut down the amount of work and still avoid stereotyping. The letter-form cards naturally cannot be formalized and will always require definite attention and effort from the teacher. Teachers find that as familiarity and skill develop, the amount of work decreases. In any event, the results achieved far more than compensate for the effort. Teachers with large numbers of pupils should develop some form of descriptive report card which can be marked rapidly but without undue sacrifice of individuality.

Sample cards at different levels of development. The sample card just below represents a very simple step forward from the traditional. A very small list of general citizenship traits is to be checked; subjects are written in by teachers.

First Report

Date....................

CITIZENSHIP

Works well with others ....Ex ( )   Av ( )   Poor ( )

Initiative ....Ex ( )   Av ( )   Poor ( )

Self-control ....Ex ( )   Av ( )   Poor ( )

Depends upon himself ....Ex ( )   Av ( )   Poor ( )

Health {Cleanliness ....Satisfactory ( )   Unsatisfactory ( )
Habits {Posture ....Satisfactory ( )   Unsatisfactory ( )

Work   {Thorough ....Ex ( )   Av ( )   Poor ( )
Habits {Prompt ....Ex ( )   Av ( )   Poor ( )

Effort ....Ex ( )   Av ( )   Poor ( )

SCHOOL STUDIES

Does satisfactory work in...

....

....

....

....

....

....

Does strong work in ....

Does weak work in ....

Effort ....Ex ( )   Av ( )   Poor ( )

Days Present ....Days Absent ....Times Tardy ....

Teacher ....

Remarks ....

Another type of card carries the detailed listing of items and evidences much further along. Space is often allowed for listing units or projects completed and for teacher or parent comment. The general traits in many of these scales are broken down into sub-points and into levels. This makes for readier recognition by teachers and parents and for reduction of labor in making out reports.

Co-operativeness

A. *Takes part in group activities.*
1. Sacrifices own interests to carry out group decisions.
2. Works actively toward carrying out group decisions.
3. Sometimes leads and sometimes follows. Abides by group decisions.
4. Follows directions in the group but avoids leadership.
5. Works and plays alone or with one other.

B. *Helps others.*
1. Sacrifices own interest to help others when necessary.
2. Helps others when his own work is finished.
3. Lays aside own work to help others when asked.
4. Helps others when not necessary.
5. Gives no help.

C. *Takes turns: shares with others.*
1. Sacrifices own share or turn for the good of the group.
2. Voluntarily shares materials, turns, etc.
3. Shares materials, turns, etc, when suggested by leader.
4. Seldom shares, takes turns, etc.
5. Shares when urged.

A variation of such cards includes selected general categories of habits and divisions for the special subjects in the high school curriculum. The illustration below provides for a report on the core curriculum or "Social Living" course in a junior high school.

Progress Report

1941-1942
First Quarter

Pupil ....Subject: SOCIAL LIVING........Grade........

	Consistently	Usually	Occasionally
I. SOCIAL HABITS			
A. Shows desirable initiative	____	____	____
B. Respects general school regulations	____	____	____
C. Shows self-control	____	____	____
D. Is courteous	____	____	____
E. Accepts criticism well	____	____	____
F. Co-operates in group activity	____	____	____
II. WORK HABITS			
A. Is prompt in beginning work	____	____	____
B. Is prompt in completing work	____	____	____
C. Gives thoughtful attention	____	____	____
D. Follows directions accurately	____	____	____
E. Does neat and orderly work	____	____	____
F. Works independently	____	____	____

	Above Grade Level	Below Grade Level	At Grade Level
III. ACHIEVEMENT IN SOCIAL LIVING			
A. Understands the problems studied in the unit of work and takes part in the discussion of them	____	____	____
B. Organizes material and presents it clearly (Includes using references, outlining, clear thinking, giving reports, etc.)	____	____	____
C. Shows a growing interest in, and understanding of, reading materials	____	____	____
D. Uses necessary skills in written expression (includes spelling, handwriting, grammar, punctuation, capitalization, etc.)	____	____	____

E. Expresses self well orally (includes pronunciation, choice of words, grammatical correctness, etc.) _____ _____ _____

IV. Remarks

V. Attendance

Number of absences.......... Number of tardiness..........

....
Teacher

The first illustration below shows a simple breakdown of the subjects into types of learning included within the subject, plus the beginnings of a list of work habits and skills.

Progress Report for the First Quarter

Progress in Essential Skills	Exceptionally Well	Satisfactorily	See Teacher's Comments
Mathematics			
1. Uses fundamental processes	_____	_____	_____
2. Solves problems	_____	_____	_____
Language Arts			
1. Uses correct forms of speech	_____	_____	_____
2. Expresses ideas in writing	_____	_____	_____
3. Expresses ideas orally	_____	_____	_____
4. Enunciates words	_____	_____	_____
5. Uses and spells needed words	_____	_____	_____
6. Writes with speed and legibility	_____	_____	_____
7. Reads with speed	_____	_____	_____
8. Reads with comprehension	_____	_____	_____
Social Studies			
1. Finds and uses information	_____	_____	_____
2. Acquires understandings of people and environment	_____	_____	_____
Art			
1. Uses art materials	_____	_____	_____
2. Expresses ideas through art	_____	_____	_____
Music			
1. Acquires a sense of tonal memory	_____	_____	_____
2. Acquires the technique of note-reading	_____	_____	_____

Progress in Work Habits	Consistently	Usually	See Teacher's Comments
Plans work well	_____	_____	_____
Works well independently	_____	_____	_____
Works well with others	_____	_____	_____
Concentrates while working	_____	_____	_____
Follows directions carefully	_____	_____	_____
Works in an orderly manner	_____	_____	_____
Is careful and neat in his work	_____	_____	_____
Prepares work on time	_____	_____	_____

The second illustration gives two pages from a card which carries the breakdown within subjects and within social development and work habits into considerable detail.

	First Semester						Second Semester					
Below are listed some of the major learnings as related to subject matter. These will apply to the work to be undertaken by the child according to his growth and abilities. A check mark (√) will be used to indicate the child's progress in any one of the subjects listed below.	First Report			Second Report			First Report			Second Report		
	Needs much improvement	Shows marked development	Shows satisfactory growth	Needs much improvement	Shows marked development	Shows satisfactory growth	Needs much improvement	Shows marked development	Shows satisfactory growth	Needs much improvement	Shows marked development	Shows satisfactory growth
Reading:												
Understands what he reads............												
Reads independently.................												
Reads well to others................												
Enjoys reading good books...........												
Shows growth in the use of new words..												
English:												
Expresses ideas well orally...........												
Speaks clearly and distinctly..........												
Expresses ideas well in writing........												
Shows originality...................												
Uses correct forms in writing.........												
Spells correctly....................												
Social Studies: History, Geography, and Science.												
Contributes intelligently to group discussions												
Uses reference material wisely........												
Has fund of accurate information......												
Bases conclusions on facts...........												
Arithmetic:												
Knows number facts................												
Shows reasoning ability..............												
Works accurately...................												
Handwriting:												
Writes legibly and with ease..........												
Strives to write well at all times.......												
Industrial Arts:												
Shows originality...................												
Does careful work..................												

These aspects of development are very important but are difficult to estimate in terms of grade level. We have used the words in the columns at the right to indicate this development.	Almost Always				At Times				Seldom			
	Quarter				Quarter				Quarter			
	1	2	3	4	1	2	3	4	1	2	3	4
Music:												
Enjoys group singing......................												
Enjoys listening and shows appreciation for music...												
Shows creative ability in music.................												
Art:												
Shows originality in creative expression...........												
Is able to express ideas clearly.................												
Is able to handle art mediums.................												
Health and Physical Development:												
Is active and full of energy....................												
Has good muscular coordination................												
Enjoys active games........................												
Is alert and wide-awake in class.................												
Practices good health habits...................												
Social Development:												
Is courteous to others.......................												
Cooperates well in a group....................												
Shows good sportsmanship....................												
Is willing to accept responsibility...............												
Accepts criticism well.......................												
Demonstrates self-control....................												
Abides by group decisions....................												
Respects the property of others.................												
Is tolerant of the beliefs and opinions of others....												
Work Habits:												
Begins work promptly.......................												
Is able to follow directions...................												
Completes work on time.....................												
Uses own initiative in planning.................												
Is able to concentrate.......................												
Budgets time efficiently.....................												

Teacher's Signature: **Parent's Signature:**

1st
Quar._____   _____

2nd
Quar._____   _____

3rd
Quar._____   _____

4th
Quar._____   _____

The letter-form report is steadily gaining in popularity and has led to the teacher-parent conference method of handling pupil progress reports. Letter-form reports vary from brief paragraphs to full-page letters.

Many school systems issue bulletins giving teachers definite guidance in preparing letter-type reports. The sample below illustrates two forms of letter report.

December 1, 1938

BETTY BLANK   GRADE II

ATTITUDE TOWARDS:

Work—Betty has a spasmodic interest in work. She does not always complete assigned work on time and concentrates with difficulty. I have noticed that Betty has improved slightly since the beginning of the year.

Play—Does not mingle with many children. Likes to tell tales on others.

Teacher—Does not always obey promptly and frequently interrupts. Demands a great deal of attention.

SPECIAL ABILITY: Betty shows a special interest in writing and frequently practices by herself.

SPECIAL DISABILITY: Phonics. Betty requires individual help in applying sounds and building new words.

READING: Betty reads fairly well orally, but does not comprehend very well silently. We have noticed progress in her reading and much more interest in supplementary books.

WRITING: Good.

SPELLING. Fair.

ARITHMETIC: Shows an interest in numbers, but is not very accurate.

ABSENT: 0 Sessions

TARDY: 0 Sessions

NOTE TO PARENTS: Your comments on this report and suggestions to me for your child's welfare are invited. If you wish, you may use the back of this sheet.

Please sign and return. ....

Mary is overcoming her early shyness and is beginning to adjust herself to other members of the group. She seems to know more than she is able to express and we are arranging situations which will give her opportunity to grow here. She is overly conscientious to the extent that she often carries tales concerning the misbehavior of other pupils, but we are helping her to overcome this.

She plans her work carefully and works industriously, though individually. She is making progress in reading, but we believe she can grow more rapidly. The additional help she receives in the afternoon session is showing results.

Her writing, spelling, and language are showing growth. She seems interested in social studies and contributes more and more to the discussion and planning. She is beginning to show signs of leadership within small groups and works hard to achieve the thing her group plans to do.

Parent-teacher conferences in reporting progress. This procedure is steadily gaining in use. There are both difficulties and advantages. Difficulties stem largely from lack of training in conducting interviews. Personality clashes may arise. Failure of either party to communicate results in an inconclusive meeting. Teachers need definite training in conducting conferences. Some parents cannot attend, some will not, for various reasons, both good and bad. Fathers have less chance to attend than mothers.

The advantages can be great as parents and teachers learn how to operate a conference. When successful, the conference brings to parents greater insight into and appreciation of the school's objectives, efforts, and obstacles to its success. The teacher gains understanding of some out-of-school conditions affecting her pupils. Co-operation between school and home can be greatly enhanced, as can co-operation between school and community.

Reports and co-operation from parents. Parent reports to the school are definitely on the increase as well as efforts at co-operation between home and school for the attainment of the general aims of education. Report cards are as yet simple and elementary.

One School Indicates on the Card Why Parents Should Visit Schools

---

REASONS PARENTS SHOULD VISIT SCHOOLS

1. To keep in touch with the work of their children.
2. To encourage the teachers.
3. To get first hand information about the work of the schools.
4. To become acquainted personally with the teacher and principal.
5. To learn at first hand the conditions under which their children work.
6. To learn the problems the children must meet.
7. To make it possible for the school officials to interpret to parents the policies under which the school operates.
8. To aid in developing real school spirit in the community.

WHAT TO OBSERVE

1. Sanitary condition of the school buildings.
2. The general discipline and management of the school.
3. The attitude of the teacher toward the children.
4. The attitude of the children toward the teacher.
5. The size of the classes.
6. The physical conditions under which the teacher and pupils work.
7. Facilities offered for the development of health.
8. To what extent their own children participate in the school's activities.
9. The equipment of the school, especially as to libraries, musical equipment, and playgrounds.

A Sample From Another Card Shows the Type of General Habits Being Checked and the Technique

---

Section II

HEALTH AND HOME REPORT

All facts asked for in this section will be helpful to the school. It is to be hoped that parents will fill this out as completely as possible. This part need not be marked the second semester unless there is some change.

	First Semester	*Second Semester*
1. At what time does he arise in the morning?	_____	_____
2. At what time does he go to bed?	_____	_____
3. Does he eat his breakfast?	_____	_____
4. Does he drink coffee or tea?	_____	_____

5. Does he sleep with his window open?
6. Is he regular in habits of intestinal elimination?
7. Are there any physical defects that would retard his progress, such as headache, toothache, earache, etc.?
8. Does he seem to enjoy school?
9. Does he worry over school?
10. What subjects seem most difficult?

Some schools have a definite report card especially for the parents. It is as yet confined to a score of very general traits and habits plus space for extended comment.

Parent's Report to Teacher

Name of Child .... *Date*....................

Dear Parent or Guardian:

Parents and teachers are partners in educating children. In order to meet this responsibility they need to work together; hence a report from home to school, as well as from school to home, is desirable. Since the school sees only a part of your child's life, information of the kind indicated below will help us in understanding your child and in better meeting his or her needs. Therefore, if you are willing to do so, we shall appreciate your commenting upon any or all of the items listed below. Additional information may be written in the space provided for comments. Whether or not you share this information with us, we are asking you to sign and return this form so that we may know you have received it.

Sincerely,

_____, Teacher

1. Does your child play actively in the fresh air and sunshine?
2. Does he sleep from 10 to 12 hours daily?
3. Does he eat his meals regularly?
4. Does he drink milk daily?
5. Does he seem tired after a day at school?
6. Does he have certain home responsibilities?
7. Does he come home at the time you expect him?
8. Does he enjoy his school life?
9. Does he talk about his school interests at home?
10. Does he read at home?
11. Does he pick up his things without being told?
12. Does he obey willingly?
13. Does your child have companions of his own age?
14. Does he play happily with his friends?
15. Does he go on short trips with the family? (As harbor, airport)
16. Does he take care of a pet or garden?
17. Does he belong to a club? (As Cub Scouts, Brownies, Y.M.C.A.)
18. Does he take private lessons? (As music, dancing, art, speech)
19. How much time does he spend in daily practice?
20. What is his favorite radio program?

COMMENTS

Date .... *Parent's Signature* ....

	First Report			Second Report			Third Report			Fourth Report		
We cannot teach children separate and apart from the home. It is possible to accomplish more if we work together. Will you help us to make our program more vital and meaningful by checking these questions in the column to the right. We welcome further comments and invite you to come for a personal conference at any time. Our Child:	Yes	No	Does not know	Yes	No	Does not know	Yes	No	Does not know	Yes	No	Does not know
Is happy at school..................												
Regards work as worthwhile..........												
School interests are reflected in his home reading and discussion...........												
Shares his materials and knowledge with others												
Has pride in his health and appearance...												
Gets ready for school without being told repeatedly												
Reflects his school training for citizenship at home and on the street......												
Practices safety at home..............												
Takes part happily in activities of the family												

An interesting and well-arranged card has been devised and copyrighted by Helen R. Priske, a first-grade teacher in Pelham, N. H. The whole effect of the card stresses pupil-teacher co-operation, introduces the pupil even in the first grade to careful scrutiny of his own work, and finally provides for a parent's report back to the school. The latter is still an uncommon feature. The cover of the four-page leaflet contains blanks for identification data, with the heading: "Working My Way Through the First Grade: A Child's Report to the Parent." The text of two inside pages and the back cover is reproduced herewith.

A Child's Report to the Parent

MY PROGRESS

I have been in school .... month

MY TEACHER AND I THINK:

My adjustment has been:
    Excellent: Good: Fair.

I have cooperated: Very well: Fairly well.

My attendance was: Perfect: Not perfect.

My absence was due to:
    Weather: Sickness: Family Business.

I was present .... half days.

My record for the year; so far:
Present: Absent:

Reading: I find: Easy: A little difficult: Difficult.

I read from: Pre Primer: Primer: Book One.

Arithmetic is:
Satisfactory: Uncertain: Unsatisfactory.

Art: I like: Use it in many ways.

Music is fun: We sing: Play: and Dance.

My corridor behavior is: Good: Fair.

I obey Teachers; Monitors; and Patrols:
Very well: Fairly well.

On the School Bus, and on the Playground, I get along with other children:
Very well: Fairly well: Find it difficult.

My desk is: Very neat: Fair: Bit untidy.

My Glamour report: (Hands: Hair: Face, etc.) is:
Excellent: Good: Fair.

My wide-awakeness in the mornings is:
High: Medium: Low.

My general improvement is:
Normal: Slow, but sure: Too slow to be sure.

That which I like best at school is:

This is how I write my name now:

Mine: ....

Yours: ....

Note: The Parent signs as indicated above. The Progress Sheet is then returned to the school. At the end of the school year all Progress Sheets will be returned to the Parent.

If parents wish to score the child's behavior and social development as observed in the home, the following could be used as a guide, and this information would be very helpful to the teacher in her understanding of the pupil.

Does the child have a good appetite for breakfast?
Yes: No: Variable.

Does the child have sufficient sleep?
Yes: No: Variable.

With his or her personal properties is the child:
Very careful: Reasonably careful: Destructive.

Is the child's attitude toward the school, as expressed at home:
Enthusiastic: Indifferent: Hostile.

Does the child enjoy books and stories?
Yes: No.

Remarks:

Important new departures in making systems and in report cards must have support of parents and laymen. Great progress has been made in developing new-type report cards. Many hundreds, perhaps thousands, are in use. This is particularly true in the elementary school. The marking system usually reflects the emphasis of the new cards. The situation in the secondary school is not as favorable.

A number of promising efforts on the part of the professional staff have been delayed, and often destroyed, by public criticism and disapproval. Changes in marking and reporting should never be made without adequate, detailed interpretations to the school patrons. This may take a school year. The very best solution to the problem here is to invite complete lay participation in the study and development of the new procedures. The widest possible lay participation in all aspects of school administration has been advocated for a long time.

EXHIBIT

The school library or the instructor should develop an extensive collection of new-type report cards for examination: Failing this, there are a number of good sources for ready reference.

EXERCISES FOR SECTION 2

Individuals or small committees may report on current periodical literature dealing with new-type report cards.

READINGS

1. *The Education Index.* Articles discussing and illustrating new-type report cards appear from time to time.
2. *The U. S. Office of Education.* Various state and city departments of education publish from time to time bulletins including illustrations.

D'EVELYN, Katherine E., *Individual Parent-Teacher Conferences: A Manual for Teachers of Young Children* (New York, Bureau of Publications, Teachers College, Columbia Univ., 1952).

Evaluating Pupil Progress, Vol. 21, No. 6 (Sacramento, Cal., State Department of Education, April, 1952).

IMHOFF, Myrtle M., *Early Elementary Education* (New York, Appleton-Century-Crofts, 1959). Good brief statement, pages 234-245.

LEWIS, G. L., *Reporting Pupil Progress to Parents,* Brief No. 24, U. S. Office of Education (Washington, D. C., 1957).

ROTHNEY, J. W. M., *Evaluating and Reporting Pupil Progress, What Research Says to the Teacher,* Series No. 7 (Washington, D. C., N. E. A., 1955).

STRANG, Ruth, *Reporting to Parents* (New York, Bureau of Publications, Teachers College, Columbia Univ., 1947).

TAYLOR, L. O., McMAHILL, D. R., and TAYLOR, B. L., *The American Secondary School* (New York, Appleton-Century-Crofts, 1960), Ch. 12.

WRINKLE, W. L., *Improving Marking and Reporting Practices* (New York, Rinehart, 1947). An older reference, much quoted, good materials.

CHAPTER 23: Classroom Management and Control

The importance of the total teaching-learning situation has been emphasized throughout this volume. The details of the same situation must not be overlooked. The supposedly simple elements of classroom management and housekeeping may make or break a learning situation. The truly competent teacher has reduced many of these details to routine without undue mechanization. Routine details have been neglected in some quarters; discussion of them has been omitted in many texts because of a mistaken idea of freedom. Research studies in a number of areas have shown that the most imaginative and creative individuals are also the ones who have reduced the necessary routine activities to automatisms. The popular superstition that an imaginative person is also careless of detail is unfounded. The consensus of practice teachers, beginners, and even many experienced teachers is that routine factors should be discussed. The treatment is presented here with the hope of avoiding the extremes of deadening routinization and confusing lack of necessary organization.

Factors of management and discipline are treated as integral parts of the total teaching-learning situation and not as separate, discrete elements. Previous chapters have developed in very great detail the necessary background of general principles, research findings, and illustrations. This chapter will therefore summarize specific suggestions without repetition of supporting material.

1: CLASSROOM ORGANIZATION AND MANAGEMENT.

The degree to which elements of management should be made habitual differs. Some will be made completely automatic; others will remain highly flexible even though well organized. Learning is facilitated, disorder prevented, and time saved for more valuable activities through the reasonable mechanizing of certain elements.

The policy of the school system in which the teacher works will determine many procedures for him. An outline of policy, standards, and procedures is furnished by the better systems. All suggestions are therefore subject to interpretation in the light of the local policy. Free passing of pupils from class to class cannot be introduced by one teacher into a building where marching silently in line has been the custom for years. Routinized marching cannot be introduced by one teacher into a school which for years has developed pupil responsibility for informal passing.

The elements of management usually subject to more or less routinization are:

1. The physical conditions within the classroom: heating, lighting, ventilation, equipment, and general appearance.
2. The seating of pupils and passing from room to room.
3. The storing, distribution, and collection of supplementary books, and materials.
4. The distribution or collection of class papers.
5. The daily program.
6. The keeping of necessary reports, records, and requisitions.
7. Preparation for the first day of school.

The physical conditions within the classroom. It is very easy for the teacher to neglect certain physical factors when he is interested in the more important teaching procedures. Furthermore, he becomes conditioned to the surroundings.

Heating. A temperature of 68 degrees is considered satisfactory, though a variation of a few degrees does not matter. Investigations show, however, that a variation of more than five degrees either way is likely to increase respiratory illness and to reduce measurably the amount and quality of work. Teachers should familiarize themselves with the type of heating system in the building, with its controls, and with supplementary devices. A thermometer should be consulted regularly. Windows, window boards, registers or radiators, and doors may all be manipulated. (A few schools prohibit the opening of windows since it adversely affects the heating system throughout the building.) The principal and janitor should be consulted if any room gives special difficulty. In any event, the teacher should give constant attention to the room temperature, since its effect upon work is considerable.

Humidity. Consensus among the authorities gives 50 as the desirable level. Considerably lower humidities have little effect but a small rise brings discomfort with attendant

reduction of effort and achievement. Humidity is easily measured by any of several devices but is much more difficult to control. Excess humidity can be controlled probably only through the installation of air conditioning systems in school buildings. Insufficient moisture can be supplemented through evaporation, but it is difficult to secure enough. The old device of a pan of water on the radiator is now said to be inadequate; large amounts of water must be evaporated from large containers. Towels or desk blotters may be used as wicks.

Ventilation. The dullness resulting from poor ventilation was for years attributed to excess carbon dioxide in the air. Recent research suggests that excessive humidity and interference with normal processes for reducing body temperature—evaporation of perspiration, for instance—and lack of air movement are the important factors. Air in movement is the remedy. Some experiments show that the use of window boards to give air movement without drafts upon the pupils is about as satisfactory as the more expensive circulating systems. In any event the teacher will secure more effective learning situations through careful attention to the temperature and humidity of the room.

Lighting. Earlier standards were to the effect that lighting should be unilateral and that window space be approximately one quarter of the floor space. Such standards are only vague general guides. The size of the room, particularly its width, the color of floors and walls, the type of work being carried on, and the development of modern illumination all affect the formula. The best procedure is to measure the light in various parts of the room with a meter and under varied weather conditions. The desirable amount of light to be delivered to the pupil's desk is known. Its provision is partially beyond the teacher's control, but every advantage should be taken of facilities available. Much use is now made of artificial illumination. Modern devices make possible the rather accurate distribution of this light so that part of the room can be brought up to par without disturbing the rest of the room. Modern activity programs and movable furniture make unilateral lighting less necessary.

The teacher may rearrange desks, ask for adequate electric lighting equipment, or manipulate shades and reflectors. Painting of walls a light color and the lightening of dark floors may be suggested to the proper administrative authorities. Care should be taken to see that the additional light supplied does not produce glare from page or blackboard, or elsewhere. Pupils with defective eyesight should be seated so as to secure for them the best lighting. Left-handed pupils may be seated to avoid shadowing what they are reading or writing.

Teachers should avoid standing in front of a window or leaning upon a window sill while conducting a class period, because this forces the pupils to look squarely into the light. This is done unthinkingly by many teachers who are otherwise thoughtful of pupil comfort.

Noise. This factor is usually beyond the teacher's control, particularly if the building has been poorly placed in relation to fire stations, railroads, and other outside sources of noise. All noise within the control of the group should be minimized wherever possible. Research studies from the sound laboratories in both universities and commercial concerns show an astonishing decrease in errors and in fatigue when noise is reduced. Eventually it is hoped that sound-proof wall covering will be within the budget of school systems. The caution expressed here does not apply to the subdued hum or murmur accompanying group work but to noise in the usual sense. The use of music to accompany rhythmic activities such as learning to type and the use of certain kinds of music to accompany study are also not cases in point.

Equipment. Any and all types of standard equipment necessary in ordinary classrooms should be immediately available and in working order. Much time is wasted and

disorder precipitated when apparatus is not ready in working order when needed. By the time a defective electric connection for the motion picture projector or lantern is mended, the class has lost interest in the lesson and is out of hand.

Ingenious teachers manage to proceed with very little equipment, but no one should underestimate the assistance and increased efficiency resulting from even a minimum of equipment. Teachers should make sure that the supply of chalk, erasers, blackboards, pencil sharpeners, and wastebaskets is sufficient and in order. Every teacher should learn to use a simple hektograph unless the school furnishes adequate mimeograph service. Bookcases or shelves, tables for reading or construction work, tool benches and tools, electric connections, and other objects are necessary. These are all useful in the elementary school and in many high school rooms. The special equipment necessary for science, athletics, or other subjects is usually listed and analyzed in special texts on the teaching of those subjects.

Teachers and pupils can construct many necessary pieces of equipment. Money may be raised for the purchase of manufactured articles. In any event the teacher should constantly add to room equipment and see that it is properly stored and kept in order. Apparatus should be set up in advance of use whenever possible so that class time is not lost.

Appearance and decoration of the room. The difference in general appearance between rooms within the same building is astounding. One room may be neat and tastefully decorated; the next one, untidy and unattractive; a third, clean and neat but wholly devoid of any decorations. The general effect upon the attitude and work habits of the pupils may be very good or very bad. Older buildings with dark woodwork, badly scarred desks, bolted to the floor, and poor lighting equipment present some elements beyond the teacher's control. It is possible, however, to keep desks, shelves, and tables neat, paper picked up, and window shades uniformly raised. Even in older buildings teachers and pupils may brighten the room with pictures, plants or flowers, exhibits of book covers, current posters, and the like. Permission. may be sought to paint the woodwork or parts of it. Window boxes and curtains may be provided in elementary rooms. The art work and construction projects of the pupils are often used for decorative purposes. These should be replaced frequently by new up-to-date exhibits.

Modern buildings are harmonious in color and tone; teachers are encouraged to suggest pictures and other decorations. Yet, in spite of this, pupils may be promoted from a room tastefully decorated with pictures appropriate to their maturity level and activities, to a room decorated with smudged postcards, shoddy crêpe-paper streamers, and pictures which have been in place for years. The writer recently visited a room in which there were pictures on the wall placed there, the principal proudly said, nearly seventy years before; no changes were permitted!

The teaching of Shakespeare's plays, of problems of American democracy, or of journalism in rooms bare of a single exhibit, poster, model, picture, or any supplementary materials is difficult.

A certain amount of displacement of materials and of seeming untidiness is inevitable in a good working situation and is indicative of wholesome activity. This condition will not be confused with lack of system. There is no reason why books, pamphlets, and magazines should overflow tables and chairs, or why pictures, posters, and pupil work should be jammed together on walls or bulletin board. Children soon acquire the attitudes and habits of their teachers, and will either aid in keeping a room neat and workmanlike or will become indifferent to confusion and disorder. The use of pupil assistants plus a minimum of planning will enable teachers to maintain rooms which are places for work and at the same time are pleasing and attractive in appearance.

The seating and passing of pupils. The mechanical aspects of seating are easily cared for. Pupils should be given seats, desks, and tables suited to their size and to the type of activity. Modern schools have adjustable seats and desks. Elementary schools increasingly use movable furniture and high schools increasingly use chairs with writing arms or movable desks with convenient book storage space. Special attention should be given to the placing of children who have difficulty with vision or hearing. Smaller children should be seated in front of the tall ones.

The psychological aspects also need consideration, since the grouping of pupils noticeably affects work habits and results. One set of children will work together; another notoriously will not. One individual may weld a group together; another will be a certain source of disorder when placed with some pupils but may be controlled when placed with another group. Flexible seating arrangements are more easily manipulated than fixed arrangements. Alphabetic or other mechanical schemes serve no very important purpose and are harder to change. It is probably wise to let pupils seat themselves at first except for necessary mechanical features. As the term progresses, changes may be made when the need arises. During the first day or two a seating chart should be made which facilitates the learning of names, taking the roll, and calling upon pupils without confusion. Seating plans with small pockets for individual cards bearing the name of the pupil can be purchased or made. They present several advantages over the single sheet of paper used in many school systems. Changes in the seating order may be made with no added clerical work. The individual cards may be used for the recording of grades and standard test scores, the noting of book numbers, and many other clerical items in the daily business of the classroom. The cards may be marked so that a substitute replacing the absent teacher will know at a glance the names of pupil assistants and the jobs assigned to them.

The general movement of traffic in the halls is usually regulated by school policy. Traffic control methods have been worked out in most buildings. Within the room the individual teacher may work out with the pupils regulations for passing into and out of the room, for using various pieces of equipment, for moving furniture and apparatus, and for separating into groups. This procedure should be definite and well understood with a minimum of signalling and bell ringing. Teachers should train themselves scrupulously to gauge their teaching so that a natural break coincides with the signal for the end of the period. In this way the teacher will not have to shout his parting words to a retreating class. The teacher who "teaches down to the ringing of the bell" without giving the class time to put away equipment is not zealously professional. What he does is not commendable; he is inconsiderate of the pupils who are forced to hurry to their next class and inconsiderate of the next teacher who must wait for the tardy ones to arrive. This adaptation to an arbitrary time limit is an unfortunate but necessary adjustment to administrative factors. The elementary school with its unified program does not present this difficulty.

The storing, distribution, and collection of supplementary books and materials. Books, materials, and tools should be kept in orderly supply closets and lockers. Materials necessary for a given work period or recitation should be ready for use before class time. Securing and distributing song books often takes more time than is given to singing. This waste of time in handling equipment is true of band practice, reading, art, and construction activities. There is no known excuse for using class time for finding, arranging, and distributing instructional materials. Teachers often fail at a crucial moment in a lesson because no chalk is available for a quick summary or diagram. Competent teachers distribute materials for use in a manner that in some cases ap-

proaches the magical. The assistance of pupils should be utilized freely.

A related error here is the dictating in class of long assignments, summaries, or references. This is a stupid waste of time which may be avoided through use of the school mimeograph or one's own hektograph. All uniform material should be prepared in advance and distributed without loss of class time.

The guiding principle is to avoid waste of time on accessory processes. Teachers alert to the problem can work out any number of time-saving devices and routines, and many have done so.

The distribution and collection of class papers. The problem is similar to the preceding one. Much time is wasted in many classrooms by passing out papers one at a time to pupils distributed over the room, or by collecting work in the same manner.

Papers may be laid in alphabetic piles on a desk near the door. They may be sorted by the teacher by rows and in pupil order within the row and passed rapidly back. A few high schools have pigeonholes or paper racks in the hall for the return of papers. In isolated instances this detail is cared for through the homeroom.

The daily program. The high school teacher will usually find that his daily program is arranged as a part of the total program of the building. Principles are presented in courses on high school administration. The elementary teacher has considerable freedom in organizing the program within his room. [1]

Early research studies indicated that the time of occurrence of subjects in the program could be related to fatigue curves. A warm-up period and an easy subject came first, followed by a "hard" one, then by recess or other relaxation. Construction work was placed in late afternoon. This, however,

[1] Excellent sample programs with detailed discussion will be found in various standard textbooks on administration or management.

was based upon the subject curriculum, upon overgeneralizing the research data. The emergence of modern teaching methods and the greater knowledge of the nature of childhood have changed all this. The great variety of learning activities within the working period of a unit necessitates a new conception of the relation of fatigue to the classroom, of change of pace, of time allotment and placement. The development of units prohibits fixed daily time allotments of subjects. Modern emphasis is upon pupil growth in certain understandings and traits, not upon subject coverage. Where subject organization must be retained, teachers are increasingly aiming at weekly time allotments to be adjusted as necessity indicates, increasingly grouping related subject matters to secure more lifelike learning situations. Even within the unit plan there must be a balancing of activities to ensure rounded development. Flexibility is the important factor in both old and new school. It can be secured without going to the extreme of no program at all.

Modern principles of program-making in the elementary school include:

1. Provisions for some time-blocks of one, two, or even more hours. This provides for planning, for the developmental working period of the unit, and also for the development of those social skills and attitudes which come from group work.

2. Provision within or outside the working period for certain individual activities of study, of pursuit of individual problems or interests, of organization of data, and so forth.

3. Provision of adequate practice periods for the so-called fundamental skills of reading, writing, computation, spelling, and the use of oral and written language.

4. Provision for both enjoyment and development of skill in the arts: music, drawing, modeling, constructing, dancing, dramatizing, and others.

5. Provision for creative expression of all types, depending upon individual interest. This may be within the unit, or later in separate periods.

6. Provision for the necessary daily routines demanded by school administration: pupil accounting, reporting, health examinations, and so forth.

7. Provision for necessary play, recreation, relaxation, rest periods.

Common practice in many modern elementary schools is to use all or nearly all the morning for the working period of the unit with its many diverse activities. Morning programs cannot be alike from day to day, since a planning conference may open one day, an evaluational activity another, individual reports another. Different groups within the class will be carrying on different activities at different times. All programs will be orderly in that the working plan for the unit is the controlling factor. Afternoons may be divided among practice periods for basic skills, expressive activities, or even for an extension of the working period. Skill periods grow out of and are made meaningful by the unit. A few schools claim to develop skills without giving them special attention, but the accuracy of this assertion has not been demonstrated.

The keeping of records and reports. School-keeping necessitates just so much "paper work." Rolls must be kept, absence and tardiness reported, health reports made. Pupils must be admitted, transferred, given permission to work in library or shop. Many modern high schools with huge student bodies must maintain complicated systems of pupil accounting with many reports to be filed. In addition there are various requisitions to be made, receipts signed, materials and apparatus to be checked in and out. This necessary but uninteresting work can so monopolize a teacher's time and effort that teaching and learning actually suffer major losses. A few formal-minded, unimaginative individuals so love this routine that the paper work clearly dominates their lives. Maintaining the routine in explicit and painful detail becomes far more important than the learning situation the routine is designed to serve. A few carefree individuals ignore records and routine to the extent of interfering with the orderly management of the entire school. The competent teacher will devise means to care for this aspect of his work on time and with a minimum of effort.

Teacher complaints that these many routine demands interfere with the business of education are loud and long. In some schools this work must be done by teachers, and the only solution is to work out time-saving devices. In larger schools, however, clerical assistance and various types of teacher helpers are beginning to appear. This is a highly desirable development wherever it can be afforded.

Formal calling of the roll is a relic of antiquity which always strikes a well-trained teacher as completely absurd whenever she observes it. A quick glance at an accurately kept seating chart is all that is necessary in the opening weeks of school. After this "getting-acquainted" period is over, the personalities of the students in his classes should be so well known to the teacher that he does not need a seating plan to tell him that a pupil is absent. The necessary period report blanks called for by office monitors should be checked and ready so that class work is not interrupted when they are called for. School registers, where required, should be filled in daily, as should all other recurring reports, so that time may be saved and confusion avoided. Co-operation with all colleagues and school officers is necessary. The competent teacher will arrange time and devices, use pupil help, and otherwise see to it that caring for records and reports is routinized. A little time taken at the beginning of the school year to organize the teacher's desk will pay dividends as the year progresses. A homemade filing system constructed of cardboard guides with legible gummed labels will serve to keep the right-hand top drawer usable: office forms, reports, blanks, and book receipts can be kept clean and immediately available. Notes for absence and tardiness, program cards, vaccination certificates, warning notices, and other data can be kept in orderly fashion and referred to at a moment's notice in an alphabetically arranged pupil file (also kept in the right-hand top drawer) made of inexpensive manila envelopes, lettersize, one for each pupil, with his name typed in the "stamp" corner. Large schools will usually supply the teacher with a manual and a set of blanks covering local policy and procedure.

Preparation for the first day of school. The first day may set the tone for the year both for the institution and for the individual teacher. The waste of time and simple stupidity of administration in many schools is unbelievable unless witnessed. The impression upon the children can be seriously detrimental. Tedious unnecessary details of registration take hours, even days. Some schools take one week to get started. Supplies are distributed upon individual request, necessitating much waste motion. Pupils stand around or add to the confusion by aimless movement. Persons are not on hand when needed. The abuse has grown so bad in a few places that school boards date contracts ahead of the opening of school and require the teacher's presence in advance. Teacher's meetings are held several days in advance of the opening. The same procedures appear in many schools, not as the result of compulsion by the board but as aspects of intelligent administration by the superintendent and principal. Many schools, in contrast, make the first day friendly, cheerful, thoroughly well organized, and a businesslike introduction to the year's work. Registration has been cared for during the previous semester except for newcomers, who are quickly assigned to classes by an efficient staff designated for just that purpose. Supplies have been in place for several days; traffic control is in the hands of experienced pupils; machinery is ready for any emergencies, odd registrations, or interruptions. Classes start at once, and by the end of the first day the school is in full swing. There is no known reason why the first day should not be a regular school day in most schools.

A class of inexperienced students working with the writer set up as a minor unit growing out of their own thinking, "What Preparation Should I Make for the Opening Day of School?" Reading, discussion, and contemplation resulted in a list of seventy-nine specific questions relating to major or minor aspects of the first day. A committee classified these under seven headings:

1. What must I know about the community and how shall I get the information?
2. What should I know about the school building itself and how shall I get the information?
3. What should I know about the school regulations, routines, records, and blanks, etc.?
4. How may I ensure a sufficient supply of materials, books, apparatus, etc., for the first day?
5. How may I secure some preliminary information about my prospective students?
6. What preparation shall I make for the actual first contact in the recitation room?
7. How may I create a good impression on the pupils?

The group, individually and by committees, read texts and current articles, consulted experienced teachers, gathered bulletins issued by school systems on the orientation of new teachers, and interviewed a number of superintendents and principals. A composite class report resulted, the bulk of which is reproduced below. Space is given to this, since students are much interested in these crucial first contacts and because the report emphasizes again a number of important routine points. The wording is that of the students.

Class Report on Preparation for First Day of School

I. *Getting acquainted with the community.*

Teachers should arrive in the city where they are to teach several days before the opening of school, whether the contract demands this or not. They should take their time in finding a place to live. Except in the smaller cities, it is possible to secure a rooming place and to eat elsewhere. This is probably desirable.

One should walk about, particularly in the school neighborhood, noting the type of homes, the dress of the people, the manners of the children, the appearance of the older members of the community, the care given to streets, alleys, parkways and yards. Much can be inferred from these observations regarding the social and economic class from which the pupils will come.

These first impressions may be supplemented by direct inquiry of the principal, former teachers, or acquaintances made during the first week.

Note. The class had previously made a community survey of the type indicated in Chapter 16 for major curricular purposes. The summary here was of simple immediate items.

II. *Getting acquainted with the school building; one's own classroom.*

It is well to visit the building before school opens, familiarizing oneself with the entrances, exits, hallways, supply rooms, study halls, the heating and ventilating devices, etc. This will save confusion on the first day.

III. *Securing information about school policies, regulations, routine.*

One may expect in progressive school systems that there will be faculty meeting on the Saturday prior to the opening of school. If this is not the case, the new teacher should seek out the principal and ask such questions as are necessary to get the information required. It is well for a teacher in cases like this to have prepared a list of definite questions which will save the time of both himself and the principal.

IV. *Insuring a sufficient supply of materials, books, apparatus.*

It is essential that the room be supplied with chalk and erasers; with paper, pencils, and textbooks if possible. Ordinarily the common classroom supplies will be placed by the janitor. The teacher should see, however, that they are there and ready. This enables one to conduct a somewhat organized class period at once and aids greatly in preventing confusion.

V. *Securing preliminary information about prospective pupils.*

This may be done by inspecting the registers or cumulative records in the office. It may also be done by speaking to older teachers. Information of this nature may be very valuable, but one must guard against prejudice formed by the reports of previous teachers.

VI. *Preparing for the actual first contacts in the recitation room.*

It is essential that the teacher have thought out in minute detail the possibilities of the first class hours. Things should not be left to chance, but a definite procedure should be outlined and ready. If this has to be changed it will be much less confusing than having to construct a procedure on the spur of the moment.

The teacher should know exactly how he will receive and greet the incoming classes, have decided in his own mind how to seat them, how to get a class roll, what remarks and announcements to make.

Depending upon the subject matter to be taught and the amount of time allowed in first day periods, he should have planned an actual class exercise. This may be in the nature of an informal discussion of previous work; it may be a provocative discussion stimulated by the teacher; it may be written or oral.

As a rule, it is probably not wise to outline the course in traditional manner. It is probably not wise to make a general talk on "what I am going to expect from the class." Strive to make a pleasing and interesting introduction and let the other matters come up later.

A point of view concerning the probable types of first-day misbehavior should be formulated. This will be probably one of the most difficult problems.

VII. *How to create a good impression on the pupils.*

A good impression will be materially aided by the self-confidence and assurance which the teacher manifests the first few minutes. This in turn will be aided by the definite preparation made by the teacher as indicated above. The teacher should know what he is going to do and do it. A quiet assurance is a marked asset.

The teacher must strive for self-control and poise and know how to maintain it in the face of rather trying difficulties.

Above all, one should remember not to make any decision too quickly, particularly in relation to any disturbance.

Manifesting a genuine enthusiasm is likely to beget the same type of response from the class.

The teacher should show by his attitude, remarks, and facial expression, and replies to questions that he is friendly and approachable. Let the students feel that they may ask questions and get information.

A sense of humor is important. One should probably not tell jokes the first day or so which would result in boisterous laughter, thus loosening control over the class. One should, however, manifest an appreciation of any odd incident which happens and not attempt to "high hat" such a situation. The telling of interesting and humorous anecdotes for illustrations may constitute a perfectly natural and normal introduction to the work and is permissible.

It is probably well to maintain something of reserve, however pleasant, at the same time answering the students' questions kindly and sympathetically.

Because one's general appearance will be noted by the class, care should be taken that this is neat and attractive.

The instructor will, by his attitude, create the general impression that everyone is there for business. He will not threaten or lecture or lay down the law, for threats are challenges to pupils.

Many things may happen the first day which will interrupt the best-laid plans. Some occurrences are beyond the control of the individual teacher. But barring accidents and granted reasonably well-trained administrators, the first day of school should be an orderly and interesting day of regular work.

EXERCISES AND REPORTS FOR SECTION 1

1. On the basis of a series of observations, report with evaluational comment of your own:
   a. Methods used to care for light, heat, ventilation with a minimum of interruption. Report also situations in which the available mechanisms were poorly used or ignored.
   b. The traffic controls, or lack of them, within the building; the teacher's management within his room.
   c. The devices used to make available books, instruments, apparatus, tools, or other materials. Report in detail any wasteful procedures observed and suggest corrections.

d. The methods used to distribute and collect class papers and construction materials.

e. Time wasted on any accessory and incidental elements which should have been routinized.

2. Report in some detail on attractive room decorations or the opposite as observed. Make suggestions for rooms without decorations or exhibits of any sort, in terms of the subject or activity housed.

3. Interview a number of elementary teachers about the construction and operation of their daily programs. Report any ingenious arrangements.

4. Examine an exhibit (in library or in instructor's possession) of the blanks necessary for the administration of a large high school. Make comparisons between systems.

5. Write out fifteen or twenty questions concerning problems which you believe will confront you in preparing for the first day of school. Class discussion may be based on these.

6. How can you justify the necessity for routinization in the light of the general theory of democratic choice and freedom advocated for the schools?

THE PERIODICAL LITERATURE

The list of readings indicates that major texts in this field have not been appearing for some time. Those in existence cover the area satisfactorily. The general texts on principles or methods of teaching usually include a good chapter. The periodical literature continues, however, in good volume. All aspects of classroom management get attention from time to time. Good practical material is available for both beginning and experienced teachers.

1. A report may be made to advanced groups summarizing quickly the type and range of materials available currently.

2. A series of reports may be made with beginning groups summarizing the practical materials on each of many specific problems in the field. A glance at the listings in the *Education Index* will supply report topics.

2: DISCIPLINE AS SELF-CONTROL FOR INDIVIDUAL AND GROUP.

Public criticism and complaint about "discipline" in the schools is widespread and vigorous. There is considerable pressure to "get tough" with the children. As with all modern criticisms of the schools, there is reference to the superior conditions in "the good old days." On this point the public is, as usual, grossly misinformed. Horace Mann's Sixth Report to the Massachusetts Board of Education in 1843 contains on page 38 this startling statement:

Five years ago, not less than between three and four hundred of our Public Schools were annually brought to a violent termination, either by the triumph of a rebellious spirit on the part of the scholars, or by gross incompetence on the part of the teachers .... Last year, according to the committee's reports, only about forty schools were broken up from both the causes of the insubordination of the scholars, and incompetency of teachers.

Things were, of course, far better than this in the "good old days" which are closer to us than 1843. Today there is a resurgence of disciplinary problems in particular urban areas and with particular pupil populations. The situation is not representative of public schools generally. Those who present simple diagnoses and simple remedies are sure to be mistaken, the situation is far too complex for simple solution. Many parents and lay critics have a remarkable collection of old wives' tales concerning proper methods of disciplining children. In the general run of schools, disciplinary problems are not too frequent and are of far less violence than in the "good old days" or as portrayed in modern stories about the "blackboard jungle." Both levels of disorder need attention. A beginning text such as this cannot attempt the difficult analysis of the serious violence to be found in some schools. This is a matter for the combined efforts, of psychologists, psychiatrists, social workers, and others. Our discussion is confined to discipline as an everyday aspect of everyday schools.

The teacher in training probably worries more over questions of discipline than over any other aspect of his prospective teaching. Experienced teachers, with many notable exceptions, probably know less about the principles of desirable discipline than they know about any other problem, possibly excepting drill. Parents and teachers do not improve their methods of disciplining with experience as easily as they improve many other skills. Methods used by experienced teachers, headmasters, and principals are not significantly different as a rule from those used by untrained beginners. The techniques most commonly used to curb disorder, to restrain certain personalities, to bring children into accord with conventional behavior actually aggravate and encourage the very maladjustments they are to cure.

The picture is not so dark as the foregoing statements indicate. The long, slow, patient research work of child psychologists and of psychiatrists, together with the clinical findings of students of juvenile delinquency, are having their effect. Certain teachers and principals in given schools are famous locally for their ability to manage children. Whole schools have made studies of the intricacies of behavior control and are far on the way to developing the most desirable type of democratic order through self-discipline. The maintenance of order is by no means a simple thing. It cannot be learned by uncontrolled and unanalyzed "experience," since many of the fundamental factors cannot be observed or understood without knowledge of the clinical findings mentioned above.

Definitions of discipline differ materially. Parents and conservative teachers are often very aggressive in their insistence on "discipline," "order," "obedience," and "respect for authority." School boards and superintendents demand teachers who can discipline the children. They assert with vigor that they believe firmly in discipline and order. Well, of course! Who is there who does not believe in discipline and order? Modern or "progressive" educators are sometimes accused of neglecting discipline, even of openly encouraging lack of respect for authority. The criti-

cism is nonsensical and based upon the observation of or hearsay about chaos and uproar in certain schoolrooms where insufficiently trained teachers were attempting to use the difficult processes of modern teaching. The fact that many traditional classrooms present exactly similar scenes of noisy anarchy is conveniently forgotten. The traditional school, in fact, despite its rigid rules and harsh punishments, has presented in the past scenes of physical violence to persons and destruction of property, scenes which very probably cannot be duplicated in the modern school. A second reason for the criticism of modern schools stems from fundamentally different conceptions of discipline and order. Many conservative teachers and parents are shocked when they find children speaking freely to each other, conferring in groups, walking about the room, and engaging in different activities. Such classrooms, regarded by some as disorderly and lacking in discipline, may in fact represent the very highest and most desirable type of orderly organization and discipline. The sepulchral calm of many traditional classrooms may not represent order and discipline at all but be in truth a situation seething with revolt, productive of seriously detrimental attitudes of antagonism and contempt toward authority. Extremes are admittedly being contrasted here. The great majority of ordinary classroom situations fall between these antithetical extremes.

Real problem is in determining aim and method of discipline. All sane persons, conservatives and progressives alike, believe in order and discipline. Order and discipline are characteristics of all sensible social situations; they are necessary in order to get anything done. The argument is not whether to have discipline. The real clash comes over what is meant by discipline, and over methods of securing order.

Many parents and conservative teachers mean by order a situation free from annoyance to themselves. They place great faith in rules and regulations, in punishments, in demanding respect for authority. They believe that children must be taught to obey authority without question. They will have order or know the reason why. Children must do as they are told. Coercion is regarded as legitimate to secure obedience, respect, order, discipline. Children must conform—or else. The general attitude is summed up in the old saying, "Spare the rod and spoil the child." Persons holding these beliefs fall into two groups. First, there are those who are completely honest and sincere, but who are wholly unaware of the effects of coercion. Second, there are those who are intellectually or emotionally unstable and insecure. These individuals insist on obedience, arbitrarily demand respect, are constantly demanding apologies from other persons, are unhappy unless dominating other persons, ordering them about, and otherwise manifesting superiority. These persons range from the mildly unstable to the seriously neurotic. Many in the first group can be won over through competent, sympathetic supervision and education. The second group needs the most gentle and sympathetic introduction to the nature of personality disorders followed by sympathetic guidance in personality improvement.

An increasing proportion of parents and most modern teachers are concerned with developing the much more valid and reliable controls of self-discipline. They know that children are developing organisms and will therefore manifest behavior tendencies which from time to time are inconsistent. They also know that many things done by children which are annoying to adults are perfectly normal and to be expected from children. Certainly little children must be trained, and occasionally punished, but the aim is not perpetual control by rule and regulation, by fear, and by punishment. As explained in Chapter 3 even imposed control must be used with an eye to the effect. The individual so controlled must eventually be able to agree with the imposition. The aim is to produce a poised, self-reliant personality able to live in a democratic group. This is not only in accord with all modern research in child study, psychology, psychiatry, and juvenile delinquency; it is necessary if we are ever to realize democracy. The home and the school should foster the development of the individual through giving ever-increasing responsibility in keeping with developing levels of social maturity.

Public interest high, information low. Aims and methods of discipline are still matters of public controversy particularly with regard to home and school training. Articles constantly appear in the daily press, as well as in serious and humorous magazines. An interesting sample of public discussion is contained in the symposium carried in the *Atlantic Monthly* for June, August, and September, 1943, under the title, "Children Out of Hand." A number of teachers related their own personal experiences with unruly children and advocated frequent and thorough thrashings as the cure. One school "counselor" indicated that "knocking boys down might help." These individuals are not merely ignorant of huge areas of modern research, they seem to be unaware that their own accounts of school experiences, their diagnosis and prescriptions show them to be suffering from some of the very personality frustrations, from aggressions due to suppression or frustration similar to those from which the unfortunate children are suffering. No suggestion of diagnosis is given, no discrimination between types of children or between types of misbehavior is made. Thrash them all and do it thoroughly, is the safe and sure answer. In striking contrast are articles by physicians, trained social workers, psychiatrists and psychologists. Careful, cautious analysis is substituted for angry temperamental reaction. The facts and principles derived from long, careful research are substituted for the opinions derived from fragmentary, insufficient, and incorrectly analyzed personal experience. The popular literature on discipline is extensive but sadly uninformed.

Conflicting aims and methods natural result of historical development.

Conceptions of order, of discipline, and of punishment or other means of securing order have changed through the centuries as have all other social institutions and conceptions. The confusion in parental and educational thinking is a quite normal result and is duplicated in public thinking on practically all social, economic, political, or religious problems which involve control. Religious theory and changes within it have been particularly associated with theories of discipline and punishment; likewise with changing conceptions of the state, of government, and of their place in the regulation of human affairs. Teachers increasingly realize that discipline is not a simple classroom affair but is, in the long run, bound up with the dominant social and religious theories of the day.

The first conception under which unconventional behavior was treated was purely *vindictive*. Actually there was little or no thought of reforming the individual or of aiding him toward more socially acceptable behavior. Vengeance was the goal. The religious and social theories of the most primitive people made this disciplinary theory inevitable. Animism attributed motives to inanimate objects which should be, and were, punished for injury to persons. Such gods as there were, were capricious, despotic, and vengeful. If the deities could exact vengeance, why not the faithful followers and believers? The vindictive attitude persists in human thought. The meaningless repetition of many religious verbalisms which long ago lost their original sense aids in this unfortunate survival. More important, the general public is not even slightly informed about modern research into the nature of human personality and human motive, the effects of punishments and satisfactions, the curious perversions of personality set up by persons under pressure. The teacher who takes pupil mischief and disturbance personally, who gives way to strong emotion, who inflicts severe punishments, who punishes indiscriminately, who adopts the "I'll-show-them-who's-boss" attitude, is acting on this simple, barbaric level. There is no social or educative factor here. The individual is not to be educated or saved. He is to be made to suffer.

The next conception was that of *retributive* punishment and discipline. If one does evil, then let him suffer the consequences. This is a step beyond vengeance.

A basis for this conception could be found in natural law, though it doubtless emerged long before natural laws were well understood. The origin is likely found in the emergence of better ethical and religious conceptions, primitive as they still were. Capricious dieties gave way to gods or a God who would give us rules by which to live. The codes of Hammurabi and of Moses, the latter attributed directly to God, embody this conception and have had tremendous influence in shaping human thinking. The theory is inadequate in the light of modern knowledge about human conduct, its motives, its manifestations, and its perversions. Further, it very easily becomes focused on the retribution and not on the purposes of retribution. However, the theory that natural punishments should follow misbehavior is sound. Adults will protect the immature from the dangerous or fatal results but will use every ordinary care to the end that children increasingly see that discomfort and unhappiness to themselves follow from certain acts. The emphasis is not to be upon the retribution but on the development of understandings and attitudes making for desirable conduct. Untold numbers of children reared by competent parents, and teachers have learned through many simple, painful, but non-dangerous natural punishments that it is sensible to anticipate consequences and to attempt forecast of results of their behavior.

The *deterrent* theory is self-explanatory. Fear is the basis even more clearly and openly than in the earlier theories. The religious doctrines and methods are too well known to need repetition. Social and political instruments of this theory are the public whippings in the village square, the stocks, and the public hangings or executions of other sorts. Many other forms of humiliation were used by church and state. The school using this theory makes children "stand in the corner," puts dunce caps on them, holds them up to ridicule. Many of the techniques of vengeance appear here, but now for their deterrent effect.

Educators are not quite, but almost, unanimous in condemning fear as a motive. They believe rather that a far more ethical and desirable citizen will result if individuals are taught to do the right thing not because they *must,* not even because they *ought,* but because they *recognize that they ought.* The use of fear in the control of little children is one of the ugly chapters in the history of education.

The *remedial* theory is comparatively recent in origin and is based upon our very greatly increased knowledge resulting from wide research into the nature of personality and its controls. Research into the nature of society and into the results of interaction between individuals and the social and physical environment has also supplied vital data. The weakening of the religious conception that persons are inherently evil because of original sin aids the developing social concept. Scientific facts concerning heredity have rendered untenable certain earlier conceptions of causation and guilt. Blame for misbehavior cannot always be placed wholly upon the individual. Sometimes even the individual is less to blame than certain other persons and factors in his environment. Individuals are not excused from responsibility, but misbehavior is now regarded as an outgrowth of the total life history of an individual. Diagnosis and cure are the desired processes. The aim is to save or remake the individual: to restore him to socially acceptable status. Punishment and reform-school

methods are giving way slowly to careful scientific diagnosis followed by sympathetic re-education. Some individuals are not receptive to this treatment, but this is no reason to revert to more primitive methods for all. The place of punishment and of definite methods of imposed control for certain cases will be discussed in later paragraphs.

The *preventive* theory is the natural outgrowth of the social thinking and research of the modern era. Its aim is to prevent from arising at all the situations which call for remedial measures. An enormous amount of antisocial behavior would never arise if we could remove its causes and provide a desirable environment within which children could grow. The religious concept of inherent evil resulting from original sin is being replaced by the concept that man is neither good nor bad by nature and that he can aspire to and achieve the highest moral and ethical values. Modern research and enlightened thinking in religion are here in accord. *The school which accepts this theory believes that discipline and order are natural accompaniments of a desirable learning situation.* A modern curriculum adapted to individual differences, well-trained teachers, adequate materials, and desirable physical facilities are regarded as the prime essentials in securing valid discipline and order. The aim of the school is to produce, through its well-integrated system of education, an individual possessed of a social conscience, who sees the good sense in acceptable behavior. A democratic society is not possible otherwise.

Definitions. The following are suggested for consideration. Instructors and students may wish to use wording which satisfies them.

Order is an imposed state of affairs ordinarily. Order is imposed by any superior power, parent, teacher, the police. Immediate obedience to commands is indicated. This is quite satisfactory in the case of emergencies or accidents, in fire drills, and the like.

Discipline means, or should mean, self-control and self-direction. It is based on understanding social relationships, the limits of one's freedom of action in relation to others, on acceptance of responsibility and understanding the reasons therefor.

Discipline of the democratic type requires a certain degree of maturity, a developed social viewpoint. It is an achievement or goal. It cannot be imposed as can order or obedience. An English scholar long ago said that one measure of a civilization was the extent of obedience to the unenforceable.

Some authorities hold that order must be imposed first, out of which discipline may grow. Other writers do not accept this.

A group of prospective teachers think the problem through. The problem of discipline is always raised early in courses for teachers. Students in one of the writer's courses in principles of teaching set up as one of the early units, "How may I exercise disciplinary control over my pupils?" The wording was accepted by the instructor without comment. During the planning period, the group decided that one committee would bring in as many specific illustrations of classroom disturbance as they could gather from their own thinking, from preliminary reading, and from interviewing many teachers. These were to be grouped under major categories or types of misbehavior. Another committee was to compile a number of principles of discipline of which they knew or which they could secure from experienced teachers and principals.

Vigorous class discussions showed that several different types of classifications were possible. Class question: Could we construct one system which would be better than the others? Meanwhile, the discussion naturally included application of principle and possible solutions for various specific incidents. Within a short time, two or three students volunteered the suggestion that a fundamental difference in cases could be seen which would enable us to divide all of them into two major categories: (1) serious breaches of discipline calling for rather serious corrective measures and (2) innocent, incidental matters easily and quickly corrected. This immediately drew from the class the suggestion that careful diagnosis was necessary to determine causes and responsibilities, especially in the serious cases.

The class manifested increasing reluctance to use the terms *disciplinary control, discipline, correction,* and after a time revised the original question to read:

How may I exercise due authority over my pupils?
 a. By setting a good example, by providing proper conditions for right actions, by honest explanations, and through simple correction.
 b. By punitive and corrective means.

As this was being written on the board, one student made the suggestion out of a clear sky that the whole discussion so far was wrong end to! He said the whole purpose is not to discipline or to exercise control; the reference should not be to the teacher. The purpose is to train the pupil to behave properly on his own initiative! This precipitated a vigorous argument, the conservative students being particularly articulate. A majority eventually agreed to the following question:

How may I train students in right habits of action, good conduct?
 a. As above.
 b. As above.

The class remained divided upon the validity of this later conception, though nearly all were convinced as the course developed. Attention was now given for some days to constructing classified lists of typical incidents calling for teacher action and lists of acceptable principles to govern action. The classifications and lists given below are based partly on the class efforts and partly upon other sources.

Titles on chapters in modern books and on pamphlets in this field are significant: Discipline, an Aspect of School Morale and Character Building; Making Discipline Educative; Understanding the Behavior of Boys and Girls.

Typical classes of misbehavior with illustrations. The following list is by no means exhaustive. The classifications are not mutually exclusive. The categories are deliberately worded so as to prepare for the emphasis upon diagnosis and certain other principles which are to come. The listing also brings the problem down to earth instead of leaving it on the level of generalities and vague principles. [2]

1. *Incidents due to surplus energy.* These are natural to childhood and can best be cured by substituting more worthwhile activities resulting from a good curriculum and teaching method. Simple explanations are also effective. Properly handled these are easily eliminated.
   a. Whispering.
   b. Throwing "spit balls," paper wads, darts.
   c. Throwing chalk or erasers.
   d. Writing notes.
   e. Cutting initials on desk.
   f. Chewing gum.
   g. Making faces, "acting up."
   h. Humming in an undertone.
   i. Scribbling on blackboard.
   j. Teasing others.
   k. Drawing funny pictures.
   l. Minor horseplay during passing of classes.
   m. Accidentally dropping things, knocking books off desks.
   n. Pinning labels on backs of companions (sometimes under 3).

2. *Incidents due to physical discomfort.* Usually these cannot be helped by the children. Punishing them for things beyond their control is not merely stupid; it breeds antagonism and distrust.

[2] Margaret L. Hayes, *A Study of the Classroom Disturbances of Eighth Grade Boys and Girls* (New York, Teachers College, Bureau of Publications, Columbia Univ., 1943). An interesting and extensive study of the first class of misbehavior. Chapter 7 good reading for students.

   a. Restlessness due to poor ventilation; wriggling, fidgeting.
   b. Excessive yawning, sleepiness due to poor ventilation or excessive temperature.
   c. General inattention.
   d. Giggling can often be traced to physical discomfort.
   e. Eating due to hunger; excessive water drinking due to dryness of the air.
   f. Coughing; may start in minor way and through mass imitation become a major disturbance with no thought on pupils' part; may stem from any of several physical causes.
   g. Noise outside room distracts attention, causes movement, etc.
   h. Carelessness with own waste paper, pencil sharpenings, lunch refuse if room is generally untidy.

3. *Incidents due to poor curriculum and methods, poor classroom management.*
   a. General inattention plus any and all of the items under 1 and 2 may appear due to this cause.
   b. Inattention, noise, and movement because of frequent interruption of regular work; pupil becomes unconsciously convinced that attention doesn't matter.
   c. Minor disorders caused by poor arrangements of boards, cloakrooms, supply closets, etc.
   d. Disorders caused by or starting during distribution of supplies.
   e. Turning in late papers, carelessly prepared papers.
   f. Failure to have material ready on time.
   g. Frequent absences without any good reason.
   h. Frequent tardiness without good reason.
   i. Loitering in halls and washrooms.

4. *Incidents due to simple, uncomplicated desire to be noticed, to attract attention.* Part of this, particularly at certain ages, is a natural accompaniment of a developing personality, and of increasing self-consciousness. Small boys (grown ones as well!) do it to attract the opposite sex. Great care must be exercised, however, to distinguish between this type and that which is due to serious and usually hidden personality disturbances and frustrations. Certain symptomatic behaviors which are similar may indicate either type. Diagnosis and case history are called for.

a. Making unnecessary trips to teacher's desk, wastebasket, etc.
b. Drawing caricatures of teacher, or of less prominent children.
c. Playing practical jokes on the teacher (mouse in the desk, alarm clocks in study period, limburger cheese in teacher's desk, etc.).
d. Officiously bearing tales to teacher.
e. Making impertinent remarks for benefit of classmates; sometimes these are carefully just out of earshot, sometimes openly made.
f. Telling highly imaginative stories as true. (In little children this is a natural result until distinction has been built up between the real and the imagined.)
g. Showing off in various ways.
h. Bragging.
i. Trying to make a fool of the teacher.
j. Scaring girls with mice, toads, snakes, etc.
k. Passing out candy or food under cover of desks or books.
l. Impudent recitations.

5. *Incidents which may be due to subtle and hidden causes.* Causes here are usually only to be found through an examination of the pupil's life history. Personality disturbances, particularly frustrations, bring all manner of peculiar manifestations. The assistance of school psychologists and psychiatrists is necessary. These are the cases with which the "practical" teacher does the serious damage with her uncritical diagnosis and harsh punishments. Parents and teachers often attribute these to bad heredity, perverted ideals, bad morals. These are verbalisms and the last named one actually begs the question.
a. Aggressive and domineering behavior constantly indulged in seemingly without reason and unresponsive to punishment.
   (1) Physical bullying and inflicting pain.
   (2) Argumentative insistence upon own opinions.
   (3) Insistence upon position of leadership in the face of demonstrated incompetence.
b. Lying; fighting.
c. Cheating; gambling.
d. Stealing.
e. Stubborn refusal to obey rules, deliberate and serious impertinence or impudence; inciting others to revolt.

f. Absolute indifference to school assignments, study requirements, etc.
g. Destruction of school property maliciously.
h. Playing tricks on teacher or classmates which may have painful and genuinely dangerous results.
i. Drinking and smoking.
j. Profane language used ostentatiously; "hard boiled" attitude.
k. Formation of cliques.
l. Indecent acts; use of sex symbols and language which is taboo.
m. Playing hookey.
n. Undue retirement from activity, shyness and timidity, crying, and even hysteria.

Diagnosis the important factor. Casual inspection of the foregoing listing shows clearly that the cause and cure of school disorders are not simple problems. Misbehavior must be carefully defined and classified. The same incidents appear in a very different light when classified according to overt manifestation, or according to cause, or according to adult reaction. Incidents must be carefully diagnosed before decision and action. The similarity between diagnosing causes of failure to learn and failure to behave in a socially acceptable manner is clear. The two are often intimately related in causation. Practically everything in Chapter 21, particularly in Section II, is applicable and will not be repeated here.

Personality disturbances difficult to diagnose. It is clear that many common and recurrent classroom disturbances are simple and easily handled. The instances owing to hidden personality difficulties are complex and subtle. Teachers in the past have had no training whatever in recognizing and dealing with these cases. The current emphasis upon mental hygiene and upon simple preliminary understandings derived from psychiatry is highly significant for teacher training.

A study in this field which has become famous and which should be known to every teacher is the astonishing and illuminating analysis made by Wickman. [3] He undertook to discover the types of behavior which were regarded by teachers as evidences of present social or emotional maladjustment; the types of behavior which were regarded by teachers as possibly foreshadowing more serious maladjustments later in life. The teacher judgments were then compared with the facts as obtained by competent psychiatrists and mental hygienists in the actual study and care of maladjustment. The most astounding differences in insight and judgment appear.

Teachers consider:	Mental hygienists consider:
Immoralities	Withdrawing recessive
Dishonesties	personality and
Transgressions against authority	behavior traits

More serious than:

Violations of:	
Orderliness in classroom	Dishonesties Cruelty
Application to schoolwork	Temper tantrums Truancy

More serious than:

Extravagant, aggressive personality and behavior traits	Immoralities Violations of school work requirements

More serious than:

Withdrawing, recessive personality and behavior traits	Transgressions against authority Violations of orderliness in class

The teachers' judgments of the importance of certain pupil activities are almost directly reversed by judgments made by competent specialists in behavior problems. Teachers stress actions which disturb the peace of the room but which are actually of little or no

[3] E. K. Wickman, *Children's Behavior and Teachers' Attitudes* (New York, The Commonwealth Fund, 1928).

importance as symptoms of personality difficulty. Disorderly lines in passing, whispering, standing on wrong side of desk to recite, failing to put pencil down immediately, are noted as serious by many teachers. Furthermore, differences in judgment are very great, some teachers reporting that disorderliness in the room appears in 100 per cent of their pupils, whereas others report it for less than 15 per cent. One teacher reports that over 90 per cent of his pupils are habitually dishonest, whereas another observes no evidences whatever of untruthfulness in his pupils. In given instances, these differences might actually be true to the facts, but over a period of time and with many classes, they could not be accurate.

Many, if not most, of the behaviors regarded by teachers as evidence of maladjustment are the natural and inevitable reactions of healthy, active children under the artificial restraints of the traditional type of classroom situation. On the other hand, many teachers completely fail to recognize the importance of certain serious evidences of maladjustment which are covered up under recessive, timid, or bashful conduct. These latter do not disturb the peace and so do not come to the attention of the teacher.

All this is of tremendous importance when we consider that many classroom incidents involving pupil behavior are handled on the basis of the immediate, often emotional, almost certainly uninformed judgment of the teacher. Honest and sincere as the teacher may be in diagnosing a behavior, he is sure to do damage to learning and to personality if uninformed on technical factors affecting the teaching-learning situation. Clearly the attitude of the teacher toward pupil behavior and personality traits will have definite effects upon his teaching procedures and upon his reaction to classroom incidents. In addition, there are important repercussions on the mental hygiene of the pupil which in turn affects learning. There will even be very important effects upon the teacher's own mental hygiene.

The teacher who emphasizes "order" or discipline in a room, placing a premium on quietness, docility, and obedience, is certain to antagonize those pupils who are naturally curious, spontaneous, and creative. Definite inhibitions to learning and disturbances to personality will result from the failure to understand. The same pupils, placed with a teacher who values these personality traits, who understands that some irregularity will attend spontaneous expression, will grow and learn as they cannot in the first room. This discussion must not be interpreted as reason for doing away with reasonable order and regularity in school affairs. The place and basis of order and discipline will be analyzed later in the chapter.

The cheerful side of this problem is found in a number of follow-up studies made by other students. [4] It has been clearly shown that if definite attention is given to training teachers in the recognition of significant behavior patterns no matter how subtle, the teachers so trained can meet the problem satisfactorily.

The adjustment of individuals is evidently furthered through the satisfaction of certain basic needs, desires, urges. There is not as yet complete agreement on a listing of these needs, nor upon pupil behaviors which satisfy them. Many of the behaviors which disturb teachers are clearly normal, whereas others which attract little attention are often evidences of maladjustment. An extensive analysis of the school's responsibility for meeting these needs and for attention to personality adjustments and disturbances is found in Prescott's stimulating book, *Emotion and the Educative Process*. [5]

The effect of social-class origins on behavior. Many actions by pupils which annoy teachers and are regarded as misbehav-

[4] J. Murray Lee and Dorris M. Lee, *The Child and His Curriculum*, 3rd ed. (New York, Appleton-Century-Crofts, 1960), pp. 121-123.

[5] Daniel A. Prescott, *Emotion and the Educative Process* (Washington, D. C., American Council on Education, 1938).

ior are actually behaviors which are fully approved by the peer group. Parents generally in a given social class may approve conduct which is not approved in another class. The middle-class teacher, particularly, is dismayed by pupil behavior which is quite acceptable to children and parents in the lower social class. The facts were set forth in Chapter 8 and will not be repeated here. The point emphasized here is that the teacher needs to understand and deal sympathetically with children whose standards differ widely from those of the school.

Pupil responsibility for good behavior. The foregoing analysis of conduct seems to assess responsibility to everyone and anything except the pupil himself. But, just as in the case of failure to learn, definite responsibility rests upon the pupil. He will achieve that responsibility, however, just as he does all other responsibilities—by educative experiences that are sensible to him and which develop within him the proper understandings and attitudes, with accompanying habits and skills. Pupils do not learn responsibility for conduct by undergoing bullying, through enduring sarcasm, by suffering harsh punishment, by the inflexible enforcement of rules and regulations. They learn responsibility for conduct through being shown the reasons for good conduct, through being treated as honest, sincere individuals who will co-operate if given a chance, and through being given increasing opportunity for exercising decision and self-control.

Pupils with developed antagonisms and antisocial attitudes, with habitual misbehavior patterns, need special treatment. Many pupils will not respond to constructive control. It is quite true that many pupils arrive at a given grade with defiant attitudes and habits of misconduct which are highly undesirable. A long history lies back of each such case. These will not respond to the ordinary procedures of positive, remedial, or preventive discipline. These are the cases

**A Partial List of Behavior Problems with Ratings by
Mental Hygienists and Two Groups of Teachers***

Behavior	Mental Hygienists	Denver Teachers	Wickman's Teachers
Unsocial, withdrawing	1	8	40
Suspicious	2	32	37
Unhappy, depressed	3	7	22
Resentfulness	4	17	29
Fearfulness	5	24	36
Cruelty, bullying	6	5	8
Easily discouraged	7	14	23
Suggestible	8	10	28
Overcritical of others	9	29	45
Sensitiveness	10	26	48
Stealing	13	1	2
Unreliableness	21	3	12
Truancy	22	27	6
Untruthfulness	23	4	5
Cheating	24	6	9
Heterosexual activity	25	2	1
Obscene notes, talks, pictures	28	12	4
Impertinence, defiance	37	16	7
Masturbation	41	9	3
Destroying school materials	45	13	10

* D. B. Ellis, and L. W. Miller, "Teachers Attitudes and Child Behavior Problems," *Journal of Educational Psychology*, Vol. 27 (October, 1936), pp. 501-511.

which cause the "practical" teacher to reject all sound theory and to handle all cases by the harsh method of corrective discipline. Principles for dealing with these cases are included in later pages.

General inclusive principles. We may move now toward general principles and specific activities for governing behavior. The broad, general principles should include the following:

1. *The teacher's general aim in the maintenance of order with special reference to the group should be the development within the group of a social conscience and group co-operation.*

Discipline is not a matter between the teacher and a pupil but between the pupil and his social group. An interested group resents interruption and disorder and will usually control a trouble-maker through so-cial disapproval, open criticism, and sometimes through overt action.

2. *The teacher's general aim in the maintenance of order with special reference to the individual should be the achievement by the individual of social ideas, attitudes, and habits which make possible self-control and responsibility.*

3. *Public opinion within the group is, in the last analysis, the determiner of the level of behavior.*

4. *Group and individual standards are far more effective than imposed rules and regulations.*

5. *The development of group and individual standards should be recognized as a long slow process of social growth.*

6. *The standards already operative in the group must be recognized and taken into account.*

Growth will begin with intelligent self-criticism by the group, rather than with the imposition of rules and patterns of conduct. The long slow process of developing new standards is preferable to peremptory demands that existing standards be forgotten. Home and community standards which are low, with resultant effect upon school life, can be improved only through a patient and tactful long-range program.

7. *The personality of the pupil must be respected, whether the situation is a simple one of redirecting activity or a serious one of formal punishment.*

This does not mean, as superficial critics sometimes claim, that the pupil is to run wild, to express himself in disregard of group standards. It does mean that the pupil is not ever to be disciplined for the sake of comfort and quiet for adults. It does mean that correction is to be directed at the underlying cause and not at the embarrassment of, or revenge upon, the individual. It implies that the initial means used will be frank and honest requests for explanation from the pupil, equally honest explanations of reasons for changed behavior. Authority and punishment should not be used until the pupil has demonstrated that he is not entitled to respect and to the more rational means that accompany respect.

8. *The personality of the teacher is an important factor which must be used with care.*

Teachers with certain personality traits can maintain order with ease by taking advantage of youthful hero-worship and loyalty. This is legitimate if desirable attitudes and habits result. It is highly undesirable if the control is so highly personalized that no lasting results are achieved.

Teachers often ask if they too are not to be respected; if only the pupil personality is always to be respected. Certainly, but there is a significant difference. The child is immature and helpless in the control of the adult. The adult must be sure that develop-

ing personalities are not repressed or frustrated. The public makes much fun of "personality development," "repressed," and the like. "Spank it out of them," says the public. The psychologist does not make fun of this because he knows misbehavior is not spanked out but spanked in. Controls must be exercised, to be sure, as has been explained in several previous chapters, but in such manner as to beget growth. The adult, on the other hand, will endeavor to secure the respect and confidence of pupils through excellent teaching, cheerful assistance with difficulties, and impartial management of behavior incidents. One of the most tragic misfits in the profession is the teacher who constantly demands of the principal or superintendent that, "You must make (force) the children (to) respect me. I cannot teach them until they do." Pupils quickly and accurately recognize the teacher personalities which are entitled to respect and give this respect freely.

9. *The clinical view should dominate at all times.*

The cause of practically all types of behavior are determinable by diagnosis, given time, technical knowledge, and skill. Specialists may have to be called in on difficult cases. Details were presented in Chapter 21. The whipping boys of "bad heredity," or "evil nature," should be eliminated from teachers' thinking. Children are not born with evil tendencies but develop them through contact with certain types of adults and in certain environments. Teachers will also progressively abandon the view that disciplinary incidents are personal affronts, perpetrated for their annoyance only. The teacher will be as impartial and objective as humanly possible.

Causes of misbehavior are sometimes beyond the control of the pupil. It is worse than useless to reprimand and punish for behavior the cause of which is beyond the control of the individual.

10. *Punishment and authoritarian control will be necessary in a limited number of cases.*

In all rooms (including the primary, but more seriously in upper levels) pupils will appear who have developed definite attitudes of antagonism and non-co-operation. Their conduct is openly and regularly antisocial. They are defiant of controls and punishments. These attitudes are of long standing and have been built up through home, and neighborhood, and, often, school experiences. A life history of unhappy home life will usually be found, hostility within the home and neighborhood, violence toward the child, resulting in anxieties which in turn produce aggressions.

11. *The final outcome desired is always understanding and responsibility resulting in changed behavior. The desired outcome is not outward conformity with and control by rules.*

General procedures in the development of self-control. Many of the incidents catalogued a few pages earlier are easily controlled by simple common-sense management of the total school situation, by the exercise of ordinary good judgment, by the manifestation of certain desirable personality traits.

Discipline is not a separate item or aspect of school, it is a natural accompaniment of good teaching. Circumstances and cases call for separate and specific attention to discipline, correction, and even punishment at times. Stress should be, however, on maintaining a good teaching-learning situation. Many city systems issue a bulletin on the general principles and procedures relating to teaching and discipline. A collection of these should be available since they can be read by all students with profit.

1. Provide a desirable learning situation which is adapted to the pupil needs and maturity.
   a. Provide a good modern curriculum and teaching method which invite the pupil into many diverse learning activities.
   b. Provide an attractive physical setting for learning.
   c. Adjust all details of materials and activities to the individual differences in need, ability, and social maturity. Pupils cannot learn what they cannot learn and will turn to other activities if school activities are not sensible to them.
   d. Provide challenge, however, within this adjustment to ability and experience. Too easy tasks antagonize as do too difficult ones. Challenging ones invite vigorous effort which precludes opportunity for disorder. (This was discussed in detail in Chapter 4.)
   e. Provide for recognition for success in these challenging tasks. Invite pupil participation in evaluating.
   f. Utilize a wide variety of teaching techniques and devices.
   g. Invite pupil participation in planning the development of learning situations. (A dozen specific points were listed in Chapter 11.)
   h. Provide, wherever possible, new-type furniture especially in the lower grades.

The formal, meaningless curriculum of the traditional school is an invitation to inattention and incipient disorder. The dull, drab rooms and buildings do not invite interest, attention, or feeling of loyalty. The routine recitation of meaningless materials is recognized as silly by bright pupils who do not dare say so but whose energies are inevitably directed elsewhere and eventually into mischief. The pupil is then blamed for disorder, for poor discipline, even for serious misdemeanor when the fault lies squarely with the poor curriculum and teaching method, with a school atmosphere which does not invite co-operation. The wonder really is that more serious revolts do not occur. The high school pupil, sadly enough, has learned excellent techniques of sitting idly by and keeping reasonably quiet while the meaningless mumbo-jumbo of poor teaching goes on. The vigorous hair-trigger attention and participation in well-taught classes are in happy contrast.

Traditional teachers often say, mistakenly, that pupils should be forced to pay attention, forced to maintain order while being taught. These same adults themselves refuse to pay any attention to materials and activities in life which do not concern them.

2. Provide supplementary activities and materials, particularly reading materials and construction projects related to the assignment or unit. Take advantage of all related extracurricular activities.
3. Mechanize all routine factors which are susceptible to mechanization.
4. Invite the co-operative participation of pupils in all phases of the learning situation, including the maintenance of order.
5. Maintain a friendly, informal, approachable, but organized, businesslike manner at all times.
6. Maintain a positive and constructive attitude. Use "do" in place of "don't." Give the pupil experience with and practice in the desirable conduct patterns.

The teacher who is organized and knows what he is doing and acts as if he did makes a favorable impression which invites attention and co-operation; he secures pupil participation easily.

7. Develop criteria for determining which incidents may be safely ignored, which may be corrected informally and in a moment, which show a need for more organized guidance, and which mean that the pupil needs to be segregated for punishment.

The old-fashioned "practical" teacher creates much of the disorder in his room by his hard-boiled comments upon and punishments for anything and everything which happens in the room. Children full of energy are not going to sit still and refrain from communication, no matter what the punishments. Good teaching and routines will eliminate all but a minimum of disorder. Whispering, minor horseplay, dropping of books, and the like will go on under the best conditions. Parents and teachers who believe that children can be forced to be otherwise should note that no one has ever accom-

plished it in several thousand years. The harsh and brutal schools of yesteryear completely failed. The modern school with a meaningful program accepts and utilizes this surplus energy. The school must accept childhood and youth as it is and progressively develop controls and responsibility in keeping with developing maturity.

Judgment will come only through analyzed experience. Little help can be given the beginning teacher other than summaries and cautions such as those found throughout this book and others like it. The overt actions are but symptoms. Treating these will not help the pupil, nor materially better the classroom. Many innocent incidents may pass without comment. Teachers are often advised to let nothing pass for fear minor incidents will grow into major difficulties later. The teacher must learn to use judgment in determining which incidents are to be ignored and which show a need for guidance. Many minor incidents can be settled with a nod, a quiet word, an inquiring look. Courteous and sympathetically given explanations will correct many harmless misdemeanors. Sometimes a calm but firm statement from the teacher may be necessary. Public reprimands are practically never effective, whereas individual conferences can be very effective. Open class discussion will care for still other problems. Methods should attempt to utilize class opinion, not antagonize it. In any event, sarcasm, ill-bred personal criticisms, displays of temper or annoyance are to be avoided. Loss of personal control by the teacher is fatal to his control of the pupils in the future.

8. Corrective discipline is necessary to supplement constructive guidance.
   a. Establish guilt beyond doubt before deciding that a pupil needs formal punishment.
   b. Determine the cause or causes as clearly as can be determined.
   c. Consider attendant circumstances and the total situation within which the misdemeanor occurred. Punishment must be adjusted to the individual and to the

given situation. Fixed schedules of punishment are undesirable.

d. Try to make the punishment a natural result of the misdemeanor.

e. Select punishment for its effect upon the cause and upon the development of desirable attitudes and habits and not for vindictive reasons. Punishments should not humiliate or cause suffering unrelated to the natural consequences of the act.

f. Give the offender every opportunity to see the reasonableness of the action taken. Let him "meditate" or think things over before any discussion is held.

g. Avoid perversions of typical school work as punishments, for example, copying poetry, doing extra arithmetic problems, writing sentences over and over, and the like. This attaches dislike to material which pupils should learn to like as aids to normal learning. Suspension and expulsion are administrative devices and should be used only in extreme cases, since they curtail educational opportunity.

h. Isolate the offender from normal contacts and take away privileges until case is settled.

i. Determine punishment unhurriedly but close enough to the event to be effective. This provides for calm analysis, allows tempers to cool but ensures connection in the pupil's mind between offense and inevitable result.

j. Be frank and sympathetic but firm and businesslike.

k. Do not force apologies. Apologies under duress are worse than useless, since the pupil's inner attitude of antagonism and revolt is strengthened. Apologies may be regarded as an easy out and given with glib insincerity. Even worse, forcing apologies indicates that the teacher is making it personal and is displaying some immaturity. Voluntary apologies to the social group are effective.

l. Do not publicize any aspect of the case. When it is over, forget it.

m. Judge punishments solely by the effect upon the convictions, attitudes, and behavior of the pupil, never by the satisfaction or comfort of the teacher.

Corrective discipline should be applied only to cases which are persistently defiant, truly disruptive of the orderly work of the group, and indicative of genuinely wrong attitudes and habits on the part of the offender. Do not make mountains out of molehills. Teachers would do better to lean backwards and give the benefit of the doubt even at the expense of minor discomfort than to apply authoritarian methods too soon. Once the necessity for corrective control and punishment is clear, however, no one should hesitate to act. Parents and teachers should never under any circumstances say that punishment is going to be applied and then fail to apply it. Once committed to action, they must make that action follow without fail. Firmness and consistency are essential to the success of corrective discipline. This is especially true with little children.

The educative effect of punishment. The general public and the untrained teacher do not as yet agree with psychologists, psychiatrists, anthropologists, and historians about the effectiveness of punishment. This is merely one of the "growing pains of democracy." Public opinion on technological matters is usually far behind the facts. The legitimate uses of punishment have been set forth, even if too briefly. Since punishment is widely regarded as effective in any and all disciplinary situations, the following brief summary is presented. Ample reading materials are available to give it validity.

1. *Punishment has a history of ineffectiveness and futility covering several thousand years.*

The reading on this is extremely interesting. A semipopular volume of interest to any lay citizen is Barnes' *The Story of Punishment.* [6] A specialized monograph is Falk's *Corporal Punishment: A Social Interpretation of Its Theory and Practice in the Schools of the United States.* [7] Books on modern criminology usually have a chapter on discipline

[6] Boston, Stratford, 1930.
[7] New York, Teachers College, Bureau of Publications, Columbia Univ., 1941.

and punishment: for instance, Sutherland's *Principles of Criminology*. [8] These three are but illustrative samples from a large literature. Nothing that is said negates the value of punishment properly applied under conditions necessitating it.

There has been considerable interest in the question of punishment recently, largely as part of the current lay criticism of the schools. It is suggested that selected studies from this list be read and then supplemented by current references. Some interesting contrasts and contradictions will be revealed.

BROWN, W., "Punishment Does Work: A Note on a Paper by Tolman and Honzik," *Journal of Comparative Psychology*, Vol. 24 (1937), pp. 145-146.

ESTES, W. K., *An Experimental Study of Punishment*, Psychological Monographs, No. 3, Whole No. 263 (1944).

HILGARD, E. R., and MARQUIS, D. G., *Conditioning and Learning* (New York, Appleton-Century-Crofts, 1940).

HORNEY, Karen, *The Neurotic Personality of Our Times* (New York, Norton, 1937).

SNYGG, Donald, and COMBS, A. W., *Individual Behavior* (New York, Harper, 1949).

HOHMAN, L. B., "Directive versus Permissive Techniques in Counseling Children," *Marriage and Family Living*, Vol. 11 (Spring, 1949), pp. 66-67.

2. *Punishment, with the exceptions noted throughout this chapter and volume, is detrimental to the development of democratic views and truly democratic discipline.*

3. *The dominating tendencies and the aggression manifested by many persons in applying punishment indicate that these persons are slightly or considerably neurotic.*

These persons are suffering from insecurities, anxieties, and fears which drive them to aggressive behavior, to acts which feed their ego. This is clear to trained observers; and the brighter children even recognize that something is wrong with the teacher's per-

[8] Philadelphia, Lippincott, 1939.

sonality. The literature on this is so large that sampling would be a waste of time. Volumes are available on various phases of psychotherapy and counseling, on psychiatric diagnosis and case work, on clinical psychology, on mental hygiene, on delinquency and crime.

4. *The methods of authority, of dominance and aggression, of hostility, and of violence are rapidly learned by children on whom they are exercised.*

This is one of the real tragedies of the mistaken views of punishment. Children who know nothing but violence and pain as methods of control turn unhesitatingly to these same methods when they want to control a situation. Children from homes in which there is hostility between parents and between parents and children, where authority is arbitrary and punishment frequent and severe, are notoriously neurotic, hostile, and arbitrary themselves. Hostility to unkind parents is transferred by primary children to their first teachers. The teacher is another adult and can be expected to act as the adults the child knows—so the child's reasoning will run. [9]

Modern educators are often laughed at—erroneously, as it happens—for supposed opposition to any and all spanking. Parents often ask indignantly, "Is a child *never* to be spanked?" Certainly children will occasionally need to be spanked—but far more infrequently than adults think and not for the reasons adults give. A very simple principle is involved: a child may be spanked when he himself thoroughly well knows he ought to be spanked. And make no mistake, children know! Children who commit misdemeanors which they well know are forbidden after they have been given sensible reasons for the prohibition, who persist in behavior which they well know is detri-

[9] A small number of very enlightening research studies are now available on point 4. Class reports will be very worthwhile.

mental and disapproved by their own age group, who for no good reason do things which they and everyone else has agreed are not to be done, may sometimes need spanking. Honest diagnosis should precede any action. Spanking children who do not know why they are punished, or who do not know that the given behavior is punishable, or who do not see that the misdemeanor merits the punishment, is definitely and demonstrably detrimental in several ways. Spanking babies and very little children, jerking them around, slapping them for acts which are wholly natural to the children but annoying to adults, is genuinely stupid. Most spankings are administered by angry or annoyed adults, or by honest but uninformed adults. The adults are greatly benefited but not the children. Fortunately, many competent parents everywhere are rearing thoroughly well-behaved children without resort to spanking or to harshly repressive measures. This can be done by anyone of mental maturity who will inform himself of the means. Mastery of the principles of child-rearing takes somewhat longer than mastery of the principles of bidding in bridge, but the results are worth it. In any event, whatever procedures are used, reasonableness and consistency are the keywords.

5. *Reliance on punishment and upon strong-arm methods is wasteful and truly stupid when methods are available which are demonstrably more effective.*

The more effective methods do not include "coddling the criminal," "soft discipline," "letting Willie express himself." The effective methods are patient, careful diagnosis, honest search for subtle causes, pressures and other motivations, honest effort to make punishment fit the individual and the circumstance, patient and continuous effort to develop understandings, attitudes, habits, and growth toward intelligent self-control. It is much easier to "give them a thrashing" than to find out why shy children manifest stubborn impertinence upon occasions. "Slapping them down" is much easier than patiently untangling frightened, near-neurotic children and nursing them back to normality.

The reasons for the backwardness in human thinking about punishment are clear to any student of human evolution, to anyone who reads the history of civilization, to anyone who knows the history of control by church and state. Many relics of bygone views still remain. Convictions based upon gossip and repetition of clichés persist despite voluminous data to the contrary. Most important of all, the naïve individual does not distinguish between the effect of punishment on the child and the effect on the adult administering it. Tensions are relieved within the adult; irritations and annoyances are reduced. The adult complacently feels that "it is for the child's good"; "This hurts me worse than it does you." The neighbors agree. The proper thing has been done. The effects on adults of punishing children are often excellent! The effects upon the child are often completely unknown. Fortunately, human thinking is slowly moving away from the harsh conceptions of punishment toward those which are based on the valid results of careful research, upon better religious views, upon better understandings of personality. Character education and educating for democracy are more important than enforcing conformance to external controls.

The mistakes made by parents and teachers in disciplining children, and by employers in managing employees, grow out of a natural blunder in logic. *Control* is confused with *knowledge.* [10] Parents think they *know* how to rear children because they can *control* children, can reward or punish them, can "discipline" them. Teachers think they *understand* human behavior merely because they can *control* it, can pass or fail, reward or punish pupils. Employers believe they *"know* how to handle labor" merely because

[10] F. Alexander Magoun, *Balanced Personality* (New York, Harper, 1943). Contains interesting elaboration of this idea.

they have *power* to hire and fire, that is, control, labor. Many Southerners say of the Negro, "We know how to handle them," failing to see that all they have is control. Parents, teachers, and others in authority over persons admit freely that they are ignorant of physics and chemistry but do not see that this admission is because they cannot control the behavior of the molecules or of physical forces.

School authorities are helpless for the moment if public opinion is against modern methods. School authorities have a responsibility for leadership, however. At present, they must operate within the standards of the community, but long-range programs of competent education of the public should be undertaken.

EXERCISES AND REPORTS FOR SECTION 2

1. Report with critical analysis incidents from home or school showing:
    a. Skillful diagnosis and treatment of a disciplinary situation.
    b. Ignorant and bungling handling of a situation.
2. Report research studies on any phase, particularly those subtle phases of personality maladjustment.
3. Report with critical analysis any popular discussions appearing in the general periodicals.
4. Report with critical analysis one or several articles dealing with school discipline procedures appearing in educational magazines.
5. If available, study Exercises 1-12, pages 108-113 in Schorling's *Student Teaching*. Be prepared to present answers for class analysis.
6. A student could make a quick summary of Horace Mann's paragraphs on discipline as given in his annual reports. This is of interest in view of the current errors in regard to modern discipline.

READINGS

Specialized references upon punishment, aggression and frustration, psychotherapy, and so forth, are omitted because the volume of material available is growing so rapidly that samplings are futile.

General texts on principles of teaching practically all carry a chapter on this topic. These are not listed here.

References Dealing Primarily with Discipline

BARUCH, Dorothy, *New Ways in Discipline* (New York, McGraw, 1949).

BOND, Jesse A., "Analysis of Observed Traits of Teachers Who Were Rated Superior in School Discipline," *Journal of Educational Research* (March, 1952), pp. 507-516.

BUHLER, C., SMOTTER, F., and RICHARDSON, S., *Childhood Problems and the Teacher* (New York, Holt, Rinehart & Winston, 1952).

CELLER, S. S., "Practices Associated with Effective Discipline," *Journal of Experimental Education*, Vol. 19 (June, 1951), pp. 333-358.

COHLER, Milton J., "A New Look at the Old Problem of Discipline," *School Review*, Vol. 56 (October, 1948), pp. 468-475.

COLIDARCI, Arthur P., "The Class as a Group," *Educational Psychology: A Book of Readings* (New York, Holt, Rinehart & Winston, 1955), Ch. 4.

CUNNINGHAM, Ruth, and associates, *Understanding Group Behavior of Boys and Girls* (New York, Bureau of Publications, Teachers College, Columbia Univ., 1950).

CUTTS, Norma E., and MOSELEY, N., *Practical School Discipline and Mental Hygiene* (Boston, Houghton, 1941).

Discipline, An Interpretation (Washington, D. C., Association for Childhood Education, 1944). Excellent summaries of seven articles.

Discipline for Freedom (Washington, D. C., Association for Childhood Education, 1951).

DUNSMOOR, C. C., and MILLER, L. M., *Principles and Methods of Guidance Teachers* (Scranton, Pa., International Textbook Co., 1949).

Fostering Mental Health in Our Schools, 1950 Yearbook of the Association for Supervision and Curriculum Development (Washington, D. C., N. E. A., 1950).

Growing Up in an Anxious Age (Washington, D. C., Association for Supervision and Curriculum Development, N. E. A., 1952).

HYMES, James L., Jr., *Behavior and Misbehavior* (Englewood Cliffs, N. J., Prentice-Hall, 1955).

———, *Discipline* (New York, Teachers College, Bureau of Publications, Columbia Univ., 1949).

———, *A Child Development Point of View* (Englewood Cliffs, N. J., Prentice-Hall, 1955.)

REDL, Fritz, *Understanding Children's Behavior* (New York, Teachers College, Bureau of Publications, Columbia Univ., 1949).

————, and WATTENBERG, W., *Mental Hygiene in Teaching* (New York, Harcourt, Brace & World, 1951).

————, and WINEMAN, David, *Controls from Within* (Chicago, The Free Press of Glencoe Illinois, 1952).

SHEVIAKOW, George V., and REDL, Fritz, *Discipline for Today's Children and Youth*, rev. ed. (Washington, D. C., Association for Supervision and Curriculum Development, N. E. A., 1956).

Texts in Educational Psychology

Many current books in this field have excellent treatments of discipline and punishment. The best one so far found by the writer is cited here as an illustration:

CRONBACH, Lee J., *Educational Psychology* (New York, Harcourt, Brace & World, 1954). Chapters 15, 17, 18, and 19 are enlightening and provocative. Excellent selected

references at end of each. Footnotes within chapters lead to many research studies.

Problem Cases and Mental Hygiene

An extensive literature is available. A general course such as this will not give special treatment beyond that already contained in previous chapters. Instructors may organize special reports here if desired. Separate courses are available in many institutions.

Periodical Literature

The periodical literature is especially rich in articles on discipline, punishment, and control. These vary all the way from the purely nonsensical to the carefully validated research studies. Special reports may be made.

Childhood Education devoted its issues for 1943-1944 to the general topic, "Discipline." Broadly interpreted and contains many valuable articles.

Appendix

Vivid, purposeful learning is possible in school. A beginning student may doubt that in-school learning situations can be as natural, as interesting, and as vivid as out-of-school experiences. It may be said that any boy would work hard to get on the team because he is interested and regards the achievement as valuable to him. But what does he care about studying the War of 1812? Of course he will persist through difficulty and unpleasantness in learning to bat because the end-in-view is worth it; but he will not persist in learning correct language usage or attitudes of co-operation or skill in solving quadratic equations unless he is forced to it. Let us not be too sure! It is to be granted, of course, that all of school life cannot be maintained at a high level of interest and enthusiasm, but it has been demonstrated that competent teachers can keep so much of it at desirable levels that the whole is thereby vitally affected.

The specific illustrations cited below include some drawn solely from subject fields; others are drawn from several fields. The tendency to set up lifelike situations without regard to subject lines is well established in the modern elementary school and is spreading with reasonable speed. The technique is paralleled in some of the new core curriculums in the secondary school, where the majority of learning situations develop out of the natural activities and needs of children. Subject matter of many kinds and learning activities are organized by pupils and teacher as need and insight develop. Even within the limits of the independent special subjects on the secondary level, the materials are now being organized into functional units more closely related to life needs, purposes, and natural learning processes. Systematically organized subject-matter sequences are introduced when maturity warrants. Such procedure represents the most skillful type of teaching now known. Many modern courses of study are definitely designed to fit this type of teaching.

Many elementary schools still use a prescribed, formal course of study which is poorly, or not at all, related to pupils' interests, needs, abilities, and learning processes. Many secondary schools retain a formal, logically organized curriculum. The average teachers assign segments of this material and achieve such learning as they can. Better teachers, however, are not so docile. Forced to use a formal curriculum, they make every effort to connect it with the life interests, needs, and activities of the pupils; they try to make it meaningful and useful, hence learnable. When successfully used, this method represents the highest type of formal teaching.

Illustrations of desirable in-school learnings. The following illustrations are taken from ordinary, average classroom situations in distinctly typical public schools. Not one represents a "show" situation. All were regular "next-lesson" types and were not specially prepared for demonstration or written up for publication. Four cases actually arose spontaneously during the natural conversations and activities of the pupils. In the first and fourth cases described below, the unit was not merely initiated through the children's activities, but was organized and developed that way as it progressed. Good course-of-study material was available for the second and third units, which was readily adapted to pupil inquiries and purposes cooperatively by pupils and teacher. This illustrates the use of systematically organized subject matter which the modern school is erroneously accused of neglecting. The history lesson on the Reconstruction Period used in Chapter 1, illustrates skillful connection made by the teacher between arbitrary, required, and by itself useless subject matter and the life needs of the learners. Contrary to the belief of many experienced teachers, thousands of such lessons are taught every day.

Unit Based on Spontaneous Interest and Natural Activities, and Not Bound by Subject Fields. No Formal Subject Matter Available. Unit Developed As It Went Along.[1]

People who help us in school. *A first grade is introduced to interdependence and co-operation.* An insistent plea of modern education is that children be introduced to the nature of the political, economic, and social world in which they live. The traditional school does this through formal description, verbalisms, and the memorization of formulas and relationships. The new school attempts to do this through first-hand experience with such aspects of community life as directly affect the lives of the children. Kindergarten and first grade are not too early to

[1] First grade, Tufts School, Medford, Mass. Theresa Mack, teacher.

begin integrating learning with the actual environment.

A first grade, returning after a holiday, found that water had been spilled recently The plants, which were a group project, had, on the racks where some potted plants stood, in the absence of the class, burst into bloom. How could this have happened when no one was there to water and care for them? Closer inspection revealed that all the plants had been watered, so well, in fact, that water had been spilled on tables, window seats, and floor. The little boy who usually served as "plant waterer" said he had not been in the building during the holiday. Questioned next, the teacher said she had been far away. A child volunteered that she had seen the janitor shoveling snow and entering the building during the holiday. A committee was sent to ask if the janitor had cared for their plants and, if so, to thank him. The children ascertained that the janitor was busy shoveling snow and then had next to tend the fires before being interviewed. Said one boy, "The janitor has to do about everything around here, doesn't he?" As is natural with small children, all began telling things they had noted the janitor doing. Shortly someone named another person, the teacher, who helped the children; they mentioned the school nurse, the special art teacher, and others. The teacher led the children in making a list of "people who help us in school." In the weeks that followed, the children were amazed to find that twenty-three different persons did things for them. They formulated questions and found the answers. They had recourse to excursions and interviews. They wrote stories based on the experiences and used them for reading material. In booklets they found pictures of many helpers, and drew with crayola those that were missing. Eventually the children decided to reciprocate; they made gifts and delivered them to some of their helpers, and others they thanked in different ways. Even with children as little as first graders, some very simple understandings and appreciations of community organization were gained. These learnings can be matured and expanded in succeeding grades by further contacts with the environment as it functions in their lives.

Unit Based on Spontaneous Interest and Natural Activity, Not Bound by Subject Fields. Organized Study Material Available but Readily Adaptable to Pupil Purposes.[2]

How Merced protects our health and safety. *A fifth grade studies the health and safety services of its own community.* Elementary school children continually comment upon all aspects of their environment. They ask questions about the street-cleaning apparatus. They investigate where gangs are putting in water mains or sewers. They ask why milk is served in the schools. They note how the doctor protects them from having diphtheria or scarlet fever by scratching their arms. They talk about how the policeman stops traffic so they can cross the street safely. The teacher one day gathered a number of these comments, developed the reasons for these well-known facts, and moved on to a discussion of costs. It was soon apparent that a large number of things were done continually to keep the public healthy and safe. The children were vaguely aware that the city did all this and that taxes paid for it. A problem was soon set up: "How Does Merced Protect My Health and Safety?" From this simple beginning the whole structure of local government dealing with health, sanitation, and safety was studied. Since the point of reference was the effect upon the child's own actual life, the problem, the organized subject matter, the readings, interviews, letter-writing, committee work, and making of exhibits were all attacked with vigor. This procedure is quite different from memorizing the names of the city departments and lists of their services and costs.

[2] Elementary school, Merced, Cal. June Graham, teacher.

Unit Based on Spontaneous Interest and Pupil Purposes, but Within a Subject Field and Correlated with Various Other Subjects. Course-of-Study Material Available.[3]

Designing stage settings, costumes, etc. for a student-written musical comedy. *A twelfth-grade class plans and makes settings, costumes, etc., for a student play.* A regular high school class in Art III was just undertaking a study of stage designing. It became known that one ambitious student had been writing a musical comedy and was planning to produce it himself. A class member casually asked if the group could work upon the actual scenery and settings for this play. A girl immediately said that she would like to design the costumes. Sensing the possibilities, the teacher encouraged the discussion. Eventually the class members embarked upon what turned out to be a complex series of activities. Students enthusiastically organized and carried out detailed plans for the whole project. Individual and group research went far afield for the necessary information and materials. Committees were formed to study scenery, characters, costumes, direction, and stage business. This led into research on the authenticity of scenery and costumes, the problems of casting, the techniques of make-up, music, lighting, and so forth. Attempting to produce the play led into financing and publicity, and this in turn into poster work. The sewing classes participated in choosing, evaluating, and making up costumes. Other school departments and officers were drawn in; one department only did not co-operate. A boy in another course asked permission to make a complete photographic record of the procedure from formation of the committees to production of the play. In addition to technical knowledges and abilities (the original desired outcomes of the course), the class learned many gen-

[3] Senior high school, Belmont, Mass. Norman Brule, art teacher; M. Donald Plummer, supervisor.

eral principles and attitudes of use in all democratic, co-operative enterprises. The students actually dealt more adequately with the "required" material of the course than if they had studied it under typical assigned lessons. Details are omitted in this account, since we are concerned for the moment with but one point, the effort to connect school learning experiences with real-life purposes.

Unit Based on Spontaneous Interest and Natural Activities, not Bound by Subject Fields. No Formal Subject Matter Available. Unit Developed As It Went Along.[4]

The American flag speaks to a special class. *A group of retarded children studies patriotism, loyalty to the flag, citizenship.* The age range in this special class was from eight years to nearly fourteen; the grade level range, from preprimary to fourth grade. The highest I.Q. was 80, ranging down to unbelievable lows. The children noted that one month after our entry into World War II every magazine on the newsstand carried an American flag on the front cover. "Why is this?" "Is it the same flag we salute every morning?" A barrage of questions and earnest but wild answers showed the teacher that the children had no conception of what a national flag stands for, had no meanings at all for the flag salute they dutifully recited by rote every day. She read them a little story, "What Is the Flag?", carefully adapting it to their understanding. Her gentle and understanding questions and comments fired this little group with an enthusiastic desire to do things for flag and country. They proposed to make a scrapbook (an activity with which they were familiar) about the flag. Consideration of several titles for the book led to acceptance of the one given above. The "book" grew into an astounding study of history and ritual surrounding the flag; all, of course, skillfully adjusted to the children's level of understanding. The children themselves suggested that the spelling, reading, arithmetic, and handwork be based on study of the flag. Display stands for flags were made, as were book ends and other articles. Genuine creative work in poetry, prose, dramatics, and arts and crafts appeared—something which many say is impossible with backward children. The most retarded child in the group, who ordinarily learned very little and that with difficulty, came up with a completely original idea for decorating his scrap book. These children made very great progress in the so-called fundamental subject matters. They also manifested a keen and continuing interest in participating in all war-effort activities. The teacher kept detailed records showing great gains in social attitudes and behavior patterns. The citizenship and patriotic behavior of this class was deeply affected, as it never had been by enforced daily repetition of the flag salute containing many words they could not understand. The learning experience deserves far more space than is available here, since it was a brilliant example of what can be done with defective children by a teacher who takes time to adjust his teaching to meager backgrounds and slow learning processes.

The following units are from the public schools of Corvallis, Oregon, and were collected for use here by Mrs. Blanche McBee, Elementary Supervisor.

Unit Based on Spontaneous Interest and Natural Activities, Keeping Reasonably Within One Subject Field, Science, and Drawing Materials From A Variety of Sources.[5]

The weather. *A second grade discovers many things about the weather: causes, prediction, effects on life.* Weather always

---

[4] Special class, Martin School, Boston, Mass. Miss Gerardine Haggerty, teacher.

[5] Second grade, Lincoln School, Corvallis, Oregon. Mrs. Shirley Carstenson, teacher.

stimulates conversation among primary children. A windy rainy day usually results in clothing to dry. Weather determines in part what kinds of clothing must be worn. Planned activities are interrupted by weather: fog prevents a trip; rain, an outdoor game.

In this particular second grade, many questions were asked about the weather, but one caught the fancy of all: Is there any way we can tell what the weather will be like tomorrow and other days so we can be ready for it? A few children knew of forecasts appearing in newspapers and on television. But, said others, how do they know what to print or say? A few others had vague ideas about a "weather bureau," and about "instruments" used there, about the relation of wind to weather. All this stimulated other questions. The teacher listed these as they appeared, and a unit on weather was under way.

Certain materials and activities introduced by the teacher both carried the class further into a more organized inquiry and increased motivation. These were the children's telling of incidents that actually happened to certain individuals because of weather; discussion of forecasts seen on television and read in the newspapers; the teacher's reading of a story related to weather; a bulletin-board display of pictures characteristic of the seasons; the placing of many supplementary storybooks dealing with weather on the browsing table.

Later, instruments used by weathermen were brought in and demonstrated. (A trip to the Weather Bureau could have been made in an area where one was available.) The children learned the importance of temperature by using the thermometer and making a clothing chart relating kinds of clothing to varying temperatures. This led to consideration of seasons and their characteristics. Special attention was given to such things as trees, plants, flowers, and other growing things. The hibernation habits of certain animals was mentioned briefly.

Films were shown, books and stories read, a mural painted, dolls were dressed in keeping with seasonal changes. The evaporation of water, subsequent formation of clouds, and eventual rain was talked about and in part demonstrated through evaporating a pan of water on a radiator. The class made some trips as well.

Inevitably the effect of weather on crops, on prices, on recreation and health, upon industry, and transportation appeared in brief form. All this is somewhat advanced but was introduced whenever children asked questions relating to it.

The foregoing is but a sampling of the extensive materials and activities used. Many simple understandings and attitudes were achieved by the children. These will be amplified into more mature principles in later units. The beginnings of observation, of collecting facts, of working with other people, and of an understanding of the weather service in relation to the community appeared.

Unit Based on Current Interest, but Within a Subject Field, Elementary Science. Some Formal Subject Matter Available but Not Sufficient, Hence Some Was Developed.[6]

The earth we live on and the universe of which it is a part. *A second grade learns many things about our universe.* This was an extensive and diverse unit but interest was maintained. Children's conversation reflected discussions heard at home or viewed on television concerning spaceships, the possibility of a moon shot. They read "You Will Go to the Moon," a small booklet with excellent illustrations. Children duplicated some of the illustrations, made a spaceship, rockets, stars, wrote stories, brought materials for the bulletin board, and cut items and pictures from newspapers and magazines.

[6] Second grade, Washington School, Corvallis, Oregon. Mrs. Florence Weston, teacher.

Science booklets were a bit difficult to read on this grade level, but excellent pictures were available.

Eventually the question arose: How will these spaceships and explorations affect our lives? The teacher capitalized on this to introduce a Unit on "The Earth and the Universe." She skillfully developed with the children a series of activities and readings which were organized around ten concepts she wished the children to achieve. The children's objectives were much more simple and direct.

A few samples will indicate the general organization of the unit. These are given in terms of the teacher's outcomes.

Concept 1. *Our sun is a star and is the nearest one to us.*

The old familiar questions arose among the children: If the sun rises and sets it must move around the earth. Why is the sun so hot sometimes and not others? How can you tell how far away it is? What makes it so hot and so bright? Why does the sun not burn up the clouds? Many others appeared also.

The typical methods of demonstrating movement of earth around the sun were used. A magnifying glass was used to burn paper, showing what concentration of the rays will do. Light from moon and stars was shown to be reflected light. Many specific facts appeared incidentally: size of sun, relation of size to that of earth and moon, speed of light, relation of sun to plant and animal life, and many others.

Concept 5. *The sun appears to rise and set at different times each day.*

Children's questions about this initiated a series of activities. Each day for two weeks, the blackboard was marked where the sun first touched it. A stick was placed on a large piece of cardboard and the shadow marked every hour for some days. This led to demonstrations and explanations, as well as pictures showing facts about rotation and change by seasons. Similar work was done to show why the moon appears to change shape.

For the whole unit children made a vocabulary list of new terms. Many facts were listed. Materials were scarce, but the teacher managed to find seventeen good references for reading by the children. Seven or eight good ones for teacher information were available. A few films were used.

An Organized Unit Within a Subject Area and Within a Series of Related Units.[7]

Pioneers. *A third grade studies the pioneers with special reference to Oregon.* The general sequence began with a physical geography unit on maps. Many questions were asked as to how the Indians adjusted to the geographic features in which they found themselves. This in turn led to questions about early white settlers, and the word *pioneer* entered. Several of the children were descendants of local pioneers. Kinds of pioneers were mentioned: explorers, trappers, traders, and settlers. Missionaries were also included. The teacher told stories about early Spanish explorers in the Southwest. Incidents were dramatized. Children began asking a volley of questions about Oregon pioneers: How did they get here? How did they live? What did they do? Where did they get their food and clothing? An outline developed quite naturally, under main heads as listed. Details are abbreviated or omitted.

1. *What is a pioneer?* Books were read about the different types of early arrivals.

2. *How did they get here?* The students did extensive reading about those who arrived by sea, by overland trail. Maps were used and routes traced; the Oregon Trail was studied particularly.

3. *What did they travel in?* The class concentrated on overland travel, covered wagons, clothing, utensils, weapons, furniture.

4. *What were pioneer houses like?* Different types were studied through reading and pictures. Models were constructed.

[7] Third grade, Roosevelt School, Corvallis, Oregon. Mrs. Marilyn Holmes, teacher.

5. *How did the pioneers get food and what was it like?* Much reading was done.

6. *Where did pioneers get clothing? What was it like? How made?*

7. *What crafts were necessary?* Candles were made by pioneer methods.

8. Entertainment, songs, dances, community affairs, etc.

9. The circuit rider and religion.

10. Peddlers.

11. The Gold Rush.

12. Pioneer education and schools.

13. Pioneer medicine.

14. Detailed study of prominent Oregon pioneers.

The account will be abbreviated at this point. The motivation and organization here were original, as were the activities and readings; the details, however, are similar in many respects to those presented in Chapter 15, where a unit on pioneers was also analyzed.

A Typical Unit as Listed in a Course of Study For Geography or Social Studies. Organized Subject Matter Available but Greatly Supplemented by Current Materials.[8]

Hawaii. *A fifth grade learns about life and work there.* The course of study lists Hawaii as a possible unit. A few of the children had been there and could describe the beaches and the volcano, the profusion of flowers, and other characteristics. The efforts to make Hawaii a state were under way at the time and were mentioned. Children began to bring in exhibits. A film was shown. All this precipitated a long list of questions. Was the volcano dangerous? How do pineapples grow? What else do Hawaiians grow? Were the Hawaiians like our Indians? Are there many kinds of people there now, as we often hear? What do they all do for a living? Is our naval base still there, and how is it protected? All questions were written down and divided into groups.

[8] Fifth grade, Harding School, Corvallis, Oregon. Miss Ruth Seitz, teacher.

Many learning activities resulted. Exhibits were made—several types. Many books were read, some from the city library. A study was made of tropical fish, of the pineapple industry, of the tourist industry, of native music and dances, of musical instruments, of shells from the beaches, of various traditions. A college student from Hawaii visited and spoke to them in the native language and then translated, explaining briefly the original language. Correspondence was initiated between Corvallis children and some in Hawaii. Scrapbooks were made by each group and exchanged. A study was made of the origins of the various racial strains now in Hawaii. Contrasts were made between Hawaii and Alaska, both working for statehood at the time. Why did Hawaii want to be a state? What is the importance of Hawaii to us, and our country to them.

The unit culminated in a program and exhibit. Parts of the exhibit were kept for a time on the bulletin board and in the hallway showcase.

Unit in the Field of General Science, Introduced by Comments and Questions by Children. Some Formal Subject Matter Available, Supplemented by Much Current Material.[9]

Rocks. *A fifth grade develops a random interest into a unit in elementary geology, leading to further simple scientific units.* Two boys brought in two pieces of rock which interested them and asked for identification and facts about such rocks. Conversation before school stimulated others to bring in still other kinds of rocks. A small exhibit emerged of volcanic rock, lava, pumice, and others. In answer to some questions the teacher put acid on some rocks to show what would happen. Others could hardly be

[9] Fifth grade, Franklin School, Corvallis, Oregon. Mrs. Mary Healy, teacher.

scratched with steel tools. The teacher answered questions and gave out a small scientific booklet on rocks.

Questions increased. What makes holes in this kind of rock? Why are these smooth? What makes these funny colors through the rock? Could there be gold in any of these? (The pupils had studied about Sutter's Mill and gold in Oregon in a social studies class.) What type of soil would have this or that type of rock? Would there be any effect on crops raised in this or that type of soil? A long list was made.

Wide reading resulted. Simple experiments were made with crystals, sedimentary rocks, and so on. Fluorescent rocks were explained. A professor of geology from the local college spoke to the class about the many kinds of rocks. A film was used (and could have been used in three different ways: at the beginning to initiate the unit; during the unit to renew or redirect interest; at the end as a summary). Several large collections of rocks resulted, made by boys in the class.

A summary was made. The unit led directly into another unit in elementary chemistry.

A Unit as Listed in the Course of Study For Geography or Social Studies. Organized Subject Matter Available in Quantity, Supplemented by Current Materials.[10]

The Approach

The Room Atmosphere
1. Library table has as many books on Mexico as possible to secure. A globe is on the table.

[10] Sixth Grade, Harding School, Corvallis, Oregon. Mrs. Dorothy Cruickshank, teacher. This unit account, while abbreviated, is in somewhat greater detail than most of the others. The teacher was deliberately seeking two sets of objectives: first, facts and concepts about Mexico, and attitudes toward the country and its people; second, skills in thinking, such as defining the problem, getting facts, determining the validity of facts, setting up hypotheses, and drawing conclusions.

2. There is a place for two flags, so I will have one Mexican flag and one U. S. flag.

3. Use one bulletin board for a map of Mexico.

4. One bulletin board for bullfight poster and the bulletin board next to it with scenes of Mexico including people.

5. Front bulletin board for current material, also table for magazines (I plan to subscribe to "Life" in Spanish.)

6. Phonograph on table and many records of Mexican and Spanish music; also I have records teaching Spanish which they are free to listen to and use the book to translate if they so desire.

7. Display area on top of bookshelves for Mexican shawl, Mexican heavy handwoven skirt, castanets, and dolls dressed in dance costume. There will be many things they will add to the display from their Mexican visits or their friends and relatives.

8. The desks will be grouped together in respect to their projects.

9. The date on the board each morning in Spanish (continued [spoken] through Central and South America except Brazil). Let them write the date after the first few times.

Comments which may come from the atmosphere in the room, before school starts or during the course of the day and the week.
1. I think it's cruel to kill bulls.
2. Does the fighter ever get killed? etc.
3. This skirt certainly is heavy; feel how scratchy it is.
4. The skirt certainly has bright colors in it.
5. What are these gadgets for (castanets)?
6. Those are castanets and they are clapped together in a dance.
7. I wonder what flag that is?
8. There are flags in the encyclopædias. Let's look.
9. Sounds like guitar music, doesn't it?
10. Look here; an article about a volcano erupting in Mexico.
11. I saw that on TV this summer.
12. Look at this social studies book; it was printed before I was born.
13. *Teachers.* Do we have the real facts about Mexico in our social studies book. Let's take a look.
14. *Students.* All of the pictures in this part on Mexico give you the idea that they are all pretty poor.

Students' Objectives

Through discussion, they have decided how to find out why the people in Mexico are different and what similarities there are to U. S. citizens. The following things, they have decided, may make them different or alike.

1. What they look like; what they wear.
2. What they eat.
3. What kind of education.
4. What kind of jobs.
5. How do they live?
6. What is their history?
7. What is the land like?
8. What about their language?
9. What is the government like ?
10. What is the climate like?
11. Family life.

Hence they decide their system for working. They can decide to divide into groups and find the information about Mexico and report, or we can all take each item and bring back our information for discussion. There may be other suggestions which they will consider.

Projects

Projects which will help them understand, explain, and feel like they are becoming familiar with Mexico.

1. Write to Mexican School. We will write
2. Write to Mexico's Tourist early and send Department. air mail in or-
3. Write to Washington, der to receive D. C. to the Pan Ameri- word quickly. can Union Building.
4. Many other addresses are available in magazines and papers.
5. Learn some Spanish. (I have two years of Spanish and spent two weeks in Spain and got some practice.)
   a. Take Spanish names.
   b. Write date in Spanish.
   c. Spend a short time speaking in Spanish each day.
   d. Use Spanish records.
6. Plan a Mexican lunch.
7. Films on Mexico. Social Studies films are *not dated* and most of them are ancient. This can make an interesting problem figuring the date it was filmed. What determines the reason for their idea of the date? How can we find out.

8. Dramatize the conquering of Mexico by Cortes (relate it to our relation with the Indians in U. S.).
9. Illustrate some phase of Maya or Aztec Indian life based on some facts they have found.
10. Act out a bullfight (music and costumes) based on information found on bullfighting. (I have many slides of a bullfight plus a program and explanations.)
11. Sing songs in Spanish. (I am familiar with three.)
12. Mexican dances.
13. Make maracas for dancing.
14. Make Piñata for a party in ending unit.

A Student's comment: I heard that Mexicans were dirty and had greasy black hair.
A Student's comment: I've seen a Mexican and he did look dirty and had greasy black hair. He was picking beans where I picked this summer.
A Student's comment: I've seen dirty Americans with greasy hair that were working in the bean yards and a lot of other places too.
A Student's comment: We aren't all the same; I doubt if they are. (Discussion continues and they decide to find out about the people of Mexico.)

How are you going to find the facts? (Class suggestions)
Student: Ask someone who knows.
Teacher: What shall we call someone who knows?
Student: An authority.
Teacher: On what terms would someone be an authority?
Student: Maybe they have been there and read about it.
Teacher: Has anyone here been to Mexico?
Student: Yes, I've been over the border.
Teacher: Have you read about Mexico?
Student: Yes, I studied Mexico last year in the fifth grade, in Arizona.
Teacher: Do you think we could add some more, so that we can identify an authority?
Student: I found *authority* in the dictionary and the last part sounds right to me—"a person with much knowledge or experience in some field, whose opinion is hence reliable."
Teacher: Do any of you know some authorities in certain fields?
Student: (Many references are given.)
Teacher: What other ways do we have for finding information on Mexico?

Student: Look in the encyclopædia.

Teacher: That is one place to look, let us see how many pages are written on Mexico.

Student: There are ten pages in this encyclopædia.

Teacher: Can we expect to find everything we are looking for in the encyclopædia and also find it right up to date?

Student: Some things change, I suppose, and we could send to Mexico for recent information.

Student: The library downtown is full of books.

Student: I've seen some in our school library.

Student: There is a whole bunch on that table.

Student: Couldn't we take a visit to Mexico?

Teacher: I am afraid the expense is too much, but you can find out about it, if you like.

Teacher: If you read one book about the people, would this be adequate information?

Student: If it was the social studies book, it wouldn't.

Teacher: What does *cross reference* mean?

Student: To check it with another book or to find more facts.

Teacher: Why do we cross reference?

Student: It helps us to get the more reliable information.

After the children have found information, they begin comparing with facts about U. S., which they derived last year or have looked up.

Hypotheses are set up on reasons; *why* we have differences and similarities when they have become aware of the differences and similarities.

Evaluation Techniques

Observation
Discussion
Essay test (writing two or more reasons why Mexico is different from or similar to U. S.)

The purpose of my evaluations is to determine how effective I am as a teacher and to see what understandings and skills were acquired during our course of study with this unit on Mexico.

Bibliography

BURTON, William H., KIMBALL, Roland B., and WING, Richard L., *Education for Effective Thinking* (New York, Appleton-Century-Crofts, 1960).

"Mexico," *Britannica Junior* (1947).

MEYER, J. G., and others, *Our American Neighbors* (Chicago, Follett, 1949).

NYSTROM, J. W., and others, *Beyond Our Borders* (Skokie, Ill., Rand McNally, 1954).

POWERS, L. L., and BOWEN, G. M., *Living in Latin America* (New York, Holt, Rinehart & Winston, 1952).

Other Material for Teachers

Description and travel

BENITEZ, Fernando, *In the Footsteps of Cortez* (New York, Pantheon, 1952).

CROW, John A., *Mexico Today* (New York, Harper, 1957).

DEL VILLAR, Mary and Fred, *Where the Strange Roads Go Down* (New York, Macmillan, 1953).

HORGAN, Paul, *Great River: The Rio Grande in North America* (New York, Holt, Rinehart & Winston, 1954).

LARRALDE, Elsa, *The Land and People of Mexico* (New York, Longmans, 1950).

MELVIN, Arthur G., *Mexican Travel Guide* (Baltimore, Ottenheimer, 1956).

Mexico: A Sunset Discovery Book (Menlo Park, Cal., Lane Magazine, 1959).

RODMAN, Selden, *Mexican Journal, The Conquerors Conquered* (New York, Devin-Adair, 1958).

History

DIAZ DEL CASTILLO, Bernal, *Bernal Diaz Chronicles* (Garden City, N. Y., Doubleday, 1956).

VANCE, Marguerite, *Ashes of Empire* (New York, Dutton, 1959).

Social life and customs

BEDFORD, Sybille, *The Sudden View* (New York, Harper, 1953).

CROW, John A., *Mexico Today* (New York, Harper, 1959).

SMART, Charles A., *At Home in Mexico* (Garden City, N. Y., Doubleday, 1957).

Material for Students

Description and travel

EPSTEIN, Samuel, and WILLIAMS, B., *First Book of Mexico* (New York, Watts, 1955).

GOETZ, Delia, *Neighbors to the South* (New York, Harcourt, 1941).

LARRALDE, Elsa, *The Land and People of Mexico* (New York, Longmans, 1950).

History

CHAMBERS, Maria C., *Boy Heroes of Chapultepec* (New York, Holt, Rinehart & Winston, 1953).

LOBDELL, Helen, *Golden Conquest* (Boston, Houghton, 1953).

LOVELACE, Maud, *What Cabrillo Found* (New York, Crowell-Collier, 1958).

MCNEER, May Y., *The Mexican Story* (New York, Farrar, Straus, 1953).

Social life and customs

MAY, Stella B., *Let's Read About Mexico* (Grand Rapids, Mich., Fideler, 1949).

ROSS, Patricia F., *Made in Mexico* (New York, Knopf, 1952).

Stories

BANNON, Laura M., *Hat for a Hero* (Racine, Wisc., Whitman, 1954).

CARR, Harriett H., *The Mystery of the Aztec Idol* (New York, Macmillan, 1959).

COLLIN-SMITH, Joyce, *Jeremy Craven* (New York, Hodder, 1958).

GOOD, Loren D., *Panchito* (New York, Coward-McCann, 1955).

LAY, Marion, *Wooden Saddles* (New York, Morrow, 1939).

MEANS, Florence C., *Alicia* (Boston, Houghton, 1953).

PHILLIPS, Eula M., *Chucho, the Boy with a Good Name* (Chicago, Follett, 1957).

WILTON, Dorothy, *Crossroads for Chela* (New York, Messner, 1956).

Indexes

Indexes

Subject Index

Ability, defined and illustrated, 98
Absolutes, 33, 36
Activities, learning, defined and illustrated, 99; illustrative lists of, 6-7, 12; in unit, 364-365
Appreciations, defined and illustrated, 97
Assignment, characteristics of good, 295-296; differentiated, 292; difficulties and problems in, 294; low level persists, 289-291; pretest and, 291; pupil participation in, 293-294
Attitude, defined and illustrated, 98

Behavior pattern, brief description, 97
Buzz group, 204-205

Classroom management, Ch. 23; daily program, 540-541; distribution and collection of supplementary materials, papers, etc., 540-541; physical conditions, 537-539; records and reports, 541-542; seating and passing of pupils, 539-540
College teachers, preparation of, 261-265
Community, excursions in, 422-425; resources, 420-427
Competition as motive, 59
Connectionist, mental life and laws of learning, 153-155
Continuity, efforts to provide, 76-79; violations of, 73-76
Continuous progress system, 78, 490-491
Co-operation as motive, 59
Creative learning, characteristics of, 411-413; definitions, 392-394; discovery confused with creation, 394-397; developmental stages in, 401-403, 407-411; factors favoring, 413-415; models, use of, 404; skills in, 403-404; who is creative, 398-400
Cultural impositions, 169-175
Cumulative records, 217-219

Developmental method, 318
Developmental tasks, 131-132
Diagnosis of learning difficulties, Ch. 21; general techniques, 499-505
Difficulty and learning, 68-69, 74
Direct experience, 37-42

Disagreeable tasks, learning to do, 63-69
Discipline, aim and method, 546-547; conflicting aims and methods, 548-549; definitions of, 546, 549-550; diagnosis in, 552-555; mental hygiene and, 554-555; misbehavior, classes of, 551-552; principles of, 555-559; public interest high, information low, 547; punishment, 559-562; social class origins and, 554 ff
Discovery, in learning, 394-397
Disintegrative behavior, characteristics of, 82-84
Drill, see Practice

English, fantastic methods of teaching, 74
Environment and learning, 142-151
Equilibrium and learning, 54-56
Evaluation, Ch. 20; definitions and principles, 465-471; general procedures, 471-479; objective and subjective, 469-471; types of instruments, 480-482
Examinations, objections to, 476-479; values of, 477-479
Excursions, as activity, 422-425
Experience, characteristics of educative, Ch. 4; continuous, 70-71; direct and vicarious, balance between, 37-42; interactive, 71-72

Fact, brief definition, 99; relation to meaning, 90-93; relation to thinking, 106-112
Failure, definitions of, 486-492; educative and miseducative, 494; general and special education, failure differs with, 486-487; high standards and, 493-494; primary causes of, 495-498; pupil responsibility for, 492-493
Field theory, mental life and laws of learning, 155-161
First day of school, preparation for, 542-545
Flow chart, observers, 209
Functional learning, 47-51, 97

General education, principles of learning differ from those of special education, 22-23
Gestalt psychology, 154
Goals, Ch. 6; caution on felt needs as goals, 164-165; confusion between levels, 128-130; direc-

tional progress goals, 130-131; developmental tasks as goals, 131-132; learners and social, 164-165; levels of, 125-128; relation to process, 128; teachers, 126; in units, 348-351; pupils, 127, in units, 356

Gradients, 137

Grammar, teaching of, 88-90

Group process, buzz groups, 204-205; consensus and majority vote in, 200-204; dangers in misuses, 206; definition of, 191; democracy and, 186-187; in classroom, 194-196; logic of, 199-200; major roles in, 206-210; major types of, 193; not always satisfactory, 205; on a problem, 193-194; psychotherapy, 211-212; role playing in, 210; sociodrama, 210-211

Growth, periods in, 151-152; principles of, 150-151

Heredity and learning, 142-151

Home study, 313

Human nature and change, 143

Individual differences, 233-243; administrative provisions for, 240-241; between bright and dull, 234-235; individual projects for, 242-243; teachers' adjustment to, 239

Indoctrination, 43-47, 395-397

Instructional materials, supplementary, Ch. 17; community resources, 420-427; free and inexpensive, 419-420; kinds of, 418-420; motion pictures, 429-430; newspapers and periodicals, 429; principles governing use, 427-428; printed materials, 428-429; radio and television, brief note, 431; teaching machines, brief note, 431

Integration, introductory description, 11-12; explanation and description, 79-84

Integrative behavior, characteristics of, 82-84

Interaction, efforts to provide, 76-79; violations of, 73-76

Inventories and questionnaires about the learner, 221-222

Knowledge, origin of, 26-29, 32-33; imposition of, 42-47

Latin, fantastic methods of teaching in, 74; original use in secondary curriculum, 91

Learner, affected by many cultural factors, Ch. 8; cultural impositions, 169-175; group and, Ch. 9; gradients, 137-138; individual differences, 233-243; information about, Ch. 10; learning situation and, 166-167; maturation, 141-151; mental life, 152-163; organismic concept, 136-140; peer society, 181-182; pupil perception of, 11-13; purpose and, 54-56; social class structure and, 170-180

Learning, activities in, 6-7, 12; complex, not simple, 113-116; connection with life, 14-15; continuity in, 11-12; definition of, 12-13; experience and, Ch. 3; functional, 47-48, 48-51; goals of, Ch. 6; heredity and environment, 142-151; illustrations

of, 4-6, 10-11, appendix; integration in, 11-12; knowledge and, 26-29, 32-33; imposition and, 42-47; learners' perception of, 11-13; meaning and, 30-32; misconceptions of, Ch. 5; verbalisms in, 93-100; symbols confused with, 117-121; theories of, 17-18; principles of, 18-21

Lecture method, indictment of, 264, 286

Lesson plans, 322-324

Life and learning, 14-15

Marks, competitive, 518-520; credit for effort, 515; distribution of, 517-518; homogenous grouping and, 516; marking systems, 509-514; improvement of, 520-522; passing, 516; principles of, 509; reliability of teachers, 515-516

Maturation, 141-151; heredity and environment and, 142-151

Maturity, social and mental, 149-150

Meaning, learning of, 30-32

Measurement, see Evaluation

Memorization and learning, 90-96, 459-460

Methods, criticisms of modern, 285; developmental, 318; general, 275-281; modern, 279-282; modern to be introduced cautiously, 284; traditional and modern, summary contrast between, 279-282

Misconceptions of learning, Ch. 5

Motivation, general principles, 58-63; intrinsic and extrinsic, 58; marks, rewards, punishments, rivalry, sarcasm, ridicule, 59; purpose and, 57-63

No-failure program, see Continuous progress system

Non-graded school, 78

Objectives, see Goals

Organismic concept, 136-140; behavior and, 139-140

Outcomes of learning, confusion over power of, 104-112; illustrative lists of, 7-9, 96-99; numerous and varied, not single and simple, 113-116

Peer society, 181-182

Perception, effect of pupil's, 11-13

Practice, Ch. 19; controversies over, 449-453; educative practice, 454-459; memorization, 459-460; workbooks, 461-462

Products of learning, illustrative list of, 7-9

Projective techniques, 219-221

Psychotherapy and group process, 211-212

Punishment, educative effect of, 59, 559-562

Purpose, elements in, 56-57; difficult, disagreeable tasks and, 63-69; learner and, 54-69; "out in the world," 64-69

Questioning, basic principles, 439-447; improvement of, Ch. 17; purposes of, 438-439; purposes of, 438-439

Readiness, 160-161

Recitation, improvements in, 317-321; traditional, 316-317

Report cards, characteristics of new type, 522-524; classes of new type, 524; from parents, 530-534; illustrations of new type, 524-530

Role-playing, 206-211

Sarcasm and motivation, 59

Skill, definition brief, 99; experience in learning, 29-30

Social-class structure, 170-180; school achievement and, 175-176; intelligence-test score and, 176-178

Social distance scale, 228

Social group, birth and growth of, 192; definitions of, 191; effect on individual pupil, Ch. 8

Sociodrama, 210-211

Sociogram, 223-238

Special education, principles of learning differ from those of general education, 22-23

Study, course in, 311-313; development of independent habits, 300-313; guides in, 292-293; home, 313; programs in initiation of, 313-314; supervised, 300-401

Subject matter, in units, 337-342; knowledge of does not guarantee use of, 106-112; logical and psychological organization of, 340-342

Symbols, confused with learning, 117-121; confusion common in real life, 121

Teacher, attitude, general, 257; college, 261-265; differences in ability, 259-261; domination versus pupil freedom, 265-267; group member, Ch. 11; individual differences, adjustment to, 239; knowledges and skills necessary, 246-253; mental hygiene of, 258; methods, choice of, 281-284; personal characteristics, 253-256

Teaching, characteristics of, Ch. 10; domination vesus pupil freedom, 265-267; inventive and creative, 267-269; methods, basic, 275-281; necessary knowledges, 246-253; team teaching, 285-287

Team teaching, 285-287

Transfer of training, 106-112

Trial and error, 161-162

Understanding, definition and illustration, 97

Unit, activities in, 364-365; approaches, 353-356; assignment, contrast with, 338-339; characteristics and values, 320; choosing, 346-347; course of study, relation to, 342; controversial problems, 334-346; culminating activities, 368; differing emphases within, 330-334, 326; criteria for, 375-376; discipline in, 368; drill, relation to, 368-369; evaluation in, 367; informational projects, 334; illustrative unit, Ch. 15; outcomes, not fixed, 337; overview, 348; participatory processes in, 371; planning, 371-373; planning period, 357-363; preparing units, 347-348; source, 343-344; subject matter in, 337-342; working period, 363-367

Value, brief definition, 97

Verbalism, 93-94; defined, 94; methods of avoiding, 94-100; substituted for action, 104-106

Name Index

Anderson, H. H., and Andersen, Gladys L., projective techniques, 220-221

Andersen, Robert H., bibliography on team teaching, 285

Barnes, Elmer, on punishment, 559

Bassone, R. M., grammar teaching, 89

Beauchamp, Wilbur L., study skills, 310; early science courses and the unit, 342

Bentham, Jeremy, fictions, 467

Bestor, Arthur, on subject-matter learning, 108

Biddick, Mildred, preparation of source units, 344

Billett, Roy, assignment, 292, 297; experience and education, 85; individual differences, provision for, 241

Blair, A. W., and Burton, W. H., preadolescent in the culture, 171ff, 182

Bogardus, E. S., Social Distance Scale, 228

Breuckner, L. J., diagnosis and remedial teaching, 506; diagnostic techniques, 487; workbooks, 462

Brink, William G., study activities, 303

Bronowski, J., definition of creativity, 393

Brownell, William A., drill, 454-457; supervised study, 299

Browning, Robert, poem on experience and learning, 38

Buros, O. K., measurement yearbooks, 231

Burr, James B., Harding, L. W., and Jacobs, L. B., individual differences, provisions for, 242; individual and group, 194-196; community excursions, 423-424

Burton, W. H., children's civic information, 27, 183; meaning, 103; study skills (with McKinnon), 310

Burton, W. H., Kimball, R. H., and Wing, R. L., experience and knowledge, 39; difficulty and learning, 67; facts and learning, 8; meaning, 103; problem-solving, 193; study and thinking, 308; thought-in-process, logic, of, 199

Buswell, Guy, and John, Lenore, diagnosis in arithmetic, 502-504

Butler, Frank A., questioning, 437, 439

Cameron, Norman, verbal versus real learning, 88

Cartwright, D., and Zander, A., critical analysis of group process, 205

Caswell, H. L., and Campbell, D. S., criteria for unit, 375-376

Child, C. M., organismic concept, 136-137, 139

Combs, Arthur W., learning and teaching, 25; principles of learning, 20; phenomenological field, 153

Corvallis, Ore., schools, sample teaching units from, 562-573

Cronbach, Lee J., behavior patterns, 139, 141; discipline, 563; drill, 451; measurements, 480; motivation and principles of learning, 60; principles of learning, 20

Cronkhite, Bernice, ed., handbook on college teaching, 262-263

Cunningham, Ruth, and others, children's preference for certain activities, 365; individual and group, 187-189; instruments for social analysis, 229

Darwin, Charles, controversy over views, 61-62

Davis, Allison, social class and intelligence-test scores, 177; youth and the culture, 171, 173

Dickens, Charles, as educator and social reformer, 67

Diederick, Paul B., cumulative records, 217; learning activities, 99

Dewey, John, experience and learning, 71, 72; learning outcomes, 117; teaching methods, 266

Dobbins, Chas. G., college teaching, 263

Educational Policies Commission, aims of education, 126

Ellis, D. B., and Miller, L. W., teacher attitude and child behavior (a follow-up of Wickman Study), 555

English, H. B., and Raimy, V., social development analysis, 222-223

Frederick, R. W., Ragsdale, C. E., and Salisbury, Rachel, motivation challenge to teacher, 63; "ridiculous imperative," 93, 295; questioning, 445-446

Fromm, Erich, creative persons, 399

Goode, Delmer, college teaching methods, 262
Goodlad, J. I., and Andersen, Robert H., non-graded elementary school, 78
Goodson, Max, individual and group, 191
Guilford, J. P., creativity, research on, 393

Hall, G. Stanley, adolescent growth, 147; children's information, 27, 183
Hanna, Lavonne, Potter, Gladys, and Hagaman, Neva, unit definition and discussion, 329-330
Hanna, Paul, learning procedure, outline of, 282
Hanson, Earl H., reply to Rafferty's Grim Fairy Tales, 88
Hart, Frank W., teacher, characteristics of, 254-255
Havighurst, Robert J., culture and youth, 171, 185; developmental tasks, 131-132
Hayes, Margaret L., misbehavior, classroom, types of, 551-552
Herbart, J. F., discovery and creativity, 396
Highet, Gilbert, college teaching, 264
Hilgard, Ernest R., field theory, 152-153; learning theories, 17, 18; motivation, experimental evidence on, 58
Hook, Sydney, on rude and contemptuous critics, 88
Hopkins, L. T., creativity and the individual, 396; directional-process goals, 130-131, 337; drill, 450; experience and learning, 71; integration, 81, 82-85; learning outcomes, 117; planning in advance, 45; teachers' reading, 249; unit outcomes, 371; traits and heredity, 144
Huse, H. R., verbalisms, 93
Huxley, Aldous, satire on learning, 80
Huxley, T. H., Darwin's theory, arguments over, 61-62; subject matter, 107

Jenkins, David H., group discussion, observation of, 208-209
Judd, C. H., and Buswell, Guy, correlation among outcomes, 110; reading of Latin, 74

Lashley, K. S., nervous system, primary unity in, 138
Lane, Howard, and Beauchamp, Mary, human relations in teaching, 196
Learned, W. S., credits, satire on, 120
Lee, J. Murray, and Lee, Doris M., competencies of teachers, 250; creativity, stimulation of, 413; diagnosis in arithmetic, 502-503; motivation, principles of, 60; principles of learning, 20; social goals, 128; sociogram, analysis of, 227-228
Leonard, J. Paul, and Eurich, Alvin, modern teaching methods, 261
Lewin, Kurt, and others, re-education, principles of, 21
Lewin, Kurt, Lippitt, Ronald, and White, R. R., experiment on social climates, 67, 189-190, 257
Lowenfeld, Viktor, creativity, 401-402

McConnell, T. R., learning theory, 17; motivation, experimental evidence on, 58
McDowell, Bruce, Bill of Rights for Teachers, 88; drill, 449-450
McMurry, Charles, recitation, 316; satire on useless learning, 95; study methods, 340
Macomber, F. G., drill and creativity, 403
Magoun, F. Alexander, discipline, 561
Maslow, A. H., and Mittelman, B., motivation, 67, 164
Mead, Margaret, co-operation and competition, 62; primitive cultures and the child, 169
Mearns, Hughes, creativity, 396; quote from Willa Cather on form and content in creativity, 404
Miel, Alice, group consensus, 201; learning and teaching, 25
Miller, N. E., and Dollard, John, social class and school achievement, 176
Moreno, I. L., sociogram, analysis of, 226
Montagu, Ashley, competition and co-operation, 62
Mowrer, O. Hobart, learning theory, 17; motivation, experimental evidence on, 58
Morrison, H. C., lesson learners, 111; marking confusion over, 119; pretest, 291; subject matter, 108; unit, definition of, 326; useless learning, satire on, 95
Mossman, Lois C., activities, learning, 99; lesson planning, development of, 322
Mursell, James L., subject matter, use of, 43
Murphy, Gardner, youth and the culture, 170-171

O'Brien, Father Thomas C., lecture method, indictment of, 264, 286
Olsen, Edward G., community, study of, 422
Ortega y Gassett, subject matter and learning, 108
Otto, Henry J., sociograms, 224-225

Parker, J. Cecil, group discussion, principles of, 202-203
Penn, William, satire on useless learning, 95
Peter of Blois, satire on useless learning, 95
Piaget, Jean, children's concepts, 28
Pooley, Robert, grammar teaching, 89
Pressey, S. L., transfer, experimental evidence on, 110

Rafferty, Max, The Seven Grim Fairy Tales, 88
Redl, Fritz, discipline, 256, 562-563
Rhodes, Mel, creativity, 399
Rice, J. M., evaluation and measurement, 469
Robinson, James Harvey, on the wonderers, 399
Roethlisberger, F. I., motivation of workers, 65
Rogers, J. F., health record blanks, 218-219
Rugg, Harold, and Shumaker, Ann, child-centered school, 72
Russell, David H., concept development in children, 26, 73; creativity, critical analysis of

phases, 408; difficulty and learning, 67; principles of learning, 20

Russell, Clyde, subject matter and learning, 109

St. Augustine, on motivation, 69, 74

Sayers, E. V., and Madden, Ward, competition and co-operation as motive, 62

Schorling, Raleigh, interest questionnaire, 221-222

Smith, B. Othanel, process units, 327

Smith, Eugene R., and Tyler, Ralph W., evaluation, 470

Snygg, Donald, phenomenological field, 153; principles of learning, 153

Spencer, Herbert, aims of education, 125

Stephens, J. M., behavior pattern, 141; learning theory, 17; motivation, principles of, 60; principles of learning, 18

Strang, Ruth, report cards, 511

Sumner, S. C., confusion in mathematics teaching, 91

Taylor, Calvin W., creativity and discovery, 395

Taylor, L. O., McMahill, D., and Taylor, B. L., marking systems, 509

Tead, Ordway, subject matter and learning, 109

Thayer, V. T., recitation, 316

Thompson, George, Gardner, Eric R., and Di Vesta, F. J., behavior pattern development, 139, 141; motivation, principles of, 60; principles of learning, 20

Thorndike, E. L., drill, 451; laws of learning, 154; S-R bonds vesus organismic view, 138

Thorpe, Louis P., learning theory, 17; motivation, experimental evidence on, 58

Tumin, M. M., creativity, definitions, 393

Tyler, Ralph W., correlation between outcomes, 110

Ulich, Robert, college teaching, 264; education and life, 3

Umstattd, J. G., on workbooks, 461

U. S. Office of Education, *Cardinal Principles of Education,* 125

Walcott, F. G., grammar teaching, 89

Wallas, Graham, creative activity, phases of, 407

Warner, M. L., and others, youth and the culture, 171-172

Watson, Goodwin, motivation and morale, 65

Wells, H. G., *The Undying Fire,* 247

Wesley, Edgar, community study, outline for, 420; outcomes and measurement, 474

Wheeler, R. H., and Perkins, F. T., gradients, 139; field theory, 155; work experience, 78

Whipple, Gertrude, activities in a unit, 364

Whitehead, Alfred N., discovery and the discovered, 395

Wickman, E. K., children's behavior and teacher attitudes, 553

Witty, Paul, characteristics of teachers, 255-256

Wolfe, Thomas, experience and learning, 29

Woodring, Paul, subject matter and learning, 109

Wrightstone, J. Wayne, teaching, traditional and modern, summary on, 277; varied measurements, 473-474

Wrinkle, William L., marking, reporting, improvement of, 511

Wynne, John P., experience and learning, 55

Yoakam, Gerald H., assignments, 283, 296-297

Zirbies, creativity, factors in, 414